encyclopedia of
african and
african-american
religions

ROUTLEDGE ENCYCLOPEDIAS OF RELIGION AND SOCIETY

David Levinson, *Series Editor*

The Encyclopedia of Millennialism and Millennial Movements

Richard A. Landes, *Editor*

The Encyclopedia of African and African-American Religions

Stephen D. Glazier, *Editor*

The Encyclopedia of Fundamentalism

Brenda E. Brasher, *Editor*

encyclopedia of
african and
african-american
religions

Stephen D. Glazier, Editor

Religion & Society
A Berkshire Reference Work

ROUTLEDGE
New York London

Published in 2001 by

Routledge
29 West 35th Street
New York, NY 10001

A Berkshire Reference Work
Copyright © 2001 by Berkshire

Printed in the United States of America on acid-free paper.

10 9 8 7 6 5 4 3 2 1

Library of Congress Cataloging-in-Publication Data

The encyclopedia of African and African-American religions / Stephen D. Glazier, editor.

    p. cm.

    "A Berkshire Reference work."

    Includes bibliographical references and index.

    ISBN 0-415-92245-3

    1. Africa, Sub-Saharan—Religion—Encyclopedias.   2. Afro-Americans—Religion—Encyclopedias.   3. Blacks—America—Religion—Encyclopedias.   4 America—Religion—Encyclopedias. I. Glazier, Stephen D.

BL2462.5 .E53 2000

299'.6'03—dc21

125.00   00-059136

Contents

Editorial Advisory Board   *vii*

List of Entries   *ix*

Series Editor's Preface   *xi*

Introduction   *xv*

Entries A to Z   *1*

Appendix A. The Anthropology of Religions in Africa   *405*

Appendix B. Select Bibliography   *415*

List of Contributors   *421*

Index   *425*

List of Entries

Abyssinian Baptist Church *1*
African Charismatics *2*
African Geomancy *6*
African Methodist Episcopal Church *8*
African Methodist Episcopal Zion Church *13*
African Orthodox Church *15*
African Pentecostalism in the Netherlands *17*
African Zoar United Methodist Church *20*
African-Derived Religions *21*
Ahmadiyya Movement *22*
AIC *26*
Akan Religion *26*
Aladura *32*
amaNazaretha *34*
Apostolic Church of Johane Masowe *37*
Apostolic Church of John Maranke *38*
Azusa Street Revival *40*
Barbados, African-Derived Religions in *41*
Batuque *43*
Big Drum Dance of Carriacou *44*
Black Catholics in the United States *47*
Black Jewish Movements *52*
Black Muslims *55*
Black Spiritual Churches *59*
Black Theology *62*
Brazil, African-Derived Religions in *66*
Bushman Religion *72*
Candomblé *75*
Caribbean, African-Derived Religions in *77*
Cherubim and Seraphim Society *82*
Christ Apostolic Church *84*
Christian Evangelism in Africa *86*
Christian Missionaries in Africa *92*
Church of Christ Holiness *97*

Church of God and Saints of Christ *97*
Church of God in Christ *98*
Church of the Twelve Apostles *99*
Convince *101*
Costa Chica, Mexico *102*
Cuba, African-Derived Religions in *107*
Cyberspace, African and African-Derived Religions in *111*
Diabolism *114*
Dinka Religion *115*
Diola Prophets *116*
Divination *118*
Elder Solomon Michaux's Church of God *122*
Ethiopian Orthodox Church *123*
Faith Tabernacle Church *125*
Fire Baptized Holiness Church of God *126*
Gaga *127*
Grenada, African-Derived Religions in *128*
Guadeloupe and Martinique, African-Derived Religions in *130*
Harrist Movement *131*
Healing in African and African-Derived Religions *132*
Healing in Sub-Saharan Africa *139*
Holiness-Pentecostal (Sanctified) Movement *144*
Ifá *149*
Islam, East Africa in *151*
Islam, West Africa in *156*
Jamaa *162*
Jamaica, African-Derived Religions in *165*
Kardecism (Kardecismo) *169*
Kongo Religion *172*
Kumina (Cuminia) *174*
Lumpa Church *175*
Macumba *176*
Maitatsine Sect *177*

Manjako of Guinea-Bissau *179*
Media Evangelism *180*
Metropolitan Spiritual Churches of Christ *184*
Mexico, African-Derived Religions in *185*
Mission Schools in Africa *188*
Moorish Science Temple *191*
Mother Earth and Earth People *193*
Mt. Zion Spiritual Temple *196*
Mouride Brotherhood *197*
Movement for the Restoration of the Ten Commandments
    of God *198*
Music, Black Hymnody *199*
Music, Spiritual Baptists *205*
National Baptist Convention of America *208*
National Baptist Convention, USA *210*
National Conference of Black Christians *212*
Ndembu Religion *214*
Nuer Religion *215*
Obeah in the West Indies *216*
Ogun *217*
Orisha (Shango) Movement in Trinidad *221*
Oromo Religion *223*
Oshun *225*
Pagelança and Catimbo *226*
Pastoralist Cosmologies *228*
Peace Mission *231*
Pentecostalism in Africa *235*
Peoples Temple *240*
Pilgrimages *243*
Primitive Baptists *247*
Progressive National Baptist Convention *248*
Puerto Rico, African-Derived Religions in *250*
Pygmy Religion *253*
Rainbow Coalition *255*
Rastafari *256*
Rastafari in Global Context *266*
Rastafari in the U.S. *272*
Rastafari in West Africa *274*
Religious Skepticism in Africa *280*
Revival *282*
Santeria *285*

Santeria, Material Culture *290*
Santeria, United States *295*
Secret Societies *297*
Seventh-Day Adventist Church *300*
Shrine of the Black Madonna, Detroit *301*
Slave Religion *302*
Social Activism *309*
Southern Christian Leadership Conference *314*
Spiritual Baptists *315*
Spiritualism *319*
St. Kitts and Nevis, African-Derived Religions in *321*
St. Lucia, African-Derived Religions in *323*
Storefront Churches *325*
Sudanese Brotherhoods *330*
Suriname, African-Derived Religions in *334*
Tambor de Mina (Maranhao) *337*
Trinidad, African-Derived Religions in *338*
Unification Church *343*
United Church and Science of Living Institute *345*
United House of Prayer for All People *346*
United States, African-Derived Religions in *347*
Universal Hagar's Spiritual Church *353*
Universal Negro Improvement Association *354*
Venezuelan Cult of Maria Lionza *357*
Vodou *361*
Vodou, Material Culture *364*
Watchtower *369*
West African Religions *369*
Women and Religious Movements in Sub-Saharan
    Africa *375*
World Vision International *381*
Xango (Pernambuco) *382*
Yoruba Religion *384*
Zande *387*
Zar *392*
Zimbabwe Assemblies of God *397*
Zionist Churches *398*
Zulu Religion *403*
Appendix A. Anthropology of Religion in Africa: A Critique
    and Model *405*
Appendix B. Select Bibliography *421*

Series Editor's Preface

The volumes in this series all deal with the complex and often-changing relationship between religion and other structures and processes in "society" and in societies around the world. The first volume on millennialism and millennial movements covered the use and role of religion in rapid social transformations throughout history and across cultures and religious traditions. This second volume is about African and African-American Religions, and I can think of no other general topic within the religion rubric for which the religion-society link is so profound and complex. As articles throughout this volume show again and again, the history and culture of African and African-American religion is both informed by and informs our understanding of such salient political, social, and economic processes as colonialism, immigration, nationalism, pan-Africanism, civil rights, religious freedom, missionization and conversion, and assimilation.

It is fitting, and somewhat ironic, that this encyclopedia was conceived and compiled within a few blocks of the birthplace and boyhood homes of African-American scholar and activist W. E. B. Du Bois, in the small western New England town of Great Barrington, Massachusetts. It is fitting because Du Bois was a towering figure in the African-American fight for equality and is now regarded as one of the leading architects of the civil rights movement. The irony is that Du Bois had an ambivalent view of religion and its role in African-American life. His biographer, David Levering Lewis, suggests that Du Bois downplayed the extent of his involvement in churches in Great Barrington during his youth. Later in his life, Du Bois, while continuing to value the unique contributions of African-American religion, took a negative view of the role religion could play in the fight for equality. Many scholars today take the opposing view and

see religion as a powerful source for political and social change in African-American communities and in Africa. Berkshire Reference Works is located on Main Street, across the street from where Du Bois attended high school and two blocks from his birthplace and the two churches (Congregational and A.M.E. Zion) he attended as a boy. It seems appropriate given the topic of this volume and the spirit of the Religion and Society series to open this volume by providing a brief and impressionistic ethnographic profile of the African-American community and religion in Great Barrington in 2000 and comparing it to the situation during Du Bois's boyhood (1868–1885).

With some 7,500 residents, Great Barrington has added more than 3,000 people since 1880. But, the African-American population remains small (208 according to the 1990 census as compared to 107 in 1885), and at 2.7 percent it is about the same percentage of the population that it was during Du Bois's youth. And, now as then, the African-American community remains in some ways apart from town life. There are no African-Americans town officials, police officers, volunteer firemen, teachers, lawyers, or physicians. And, African-Americans live largely outside the tourist-based economy just as in the nineteenth century they lived outside the mill-based economy. In the past, there were one or two African-American-owned businesses that thrived for at least awhile, and that is true today as well. The most visible recent manifestation of this was Hickory Bill's Barbeque, which relocated to Pownal, Vermont, in 1998. About the same time, the Dos Amigos Mexican restaurant was taken over by an African-American owner.

Great Barrington is still almost entirely white. Several African-American families live in Du Bois's old neighborhood running east of Main Street down to the Housatonic

River. That neighborhood is still defined by whites as African-American, although there are more white families there than African-American ones. A friend who lives in the neighborhood jokes that he lives in "the ghetto," while noting that there is only one African-American family on his street. Du Bois's birthplace (the house is long gone) is marked by a plaque (erected in 1994) as are his first wife and son's graves in Mahaiwe Cemetery. The placement of these markers was one of the first public acknowledgments of the presence and role of the African-American community in Great Barrington. Other recognition came with the 1999 publication of Bernard A. Drew's *Great Barrington: Great Town, Great History* by the Great Barrington Historical Society, which gave much attention to the African-American community, past and present. African-Americans had been ignored entirely in Charles Taylor's 1882 history (later updated), even though Taylor had personally supported and encouraged Du Bois's education.

While it remains small, the African-American population is perhaps now more widely dispersed. Several families live across Main Street on and near Rosseter Street and Elm Court in another small cluster of houses also defined as "a ghetto." The two black churches in town, Clinton A.M.E. Zion and Macedonia Baptist, are located in the Rosseter neighborhood. A few families also live up on Castle Hill (now a national historic district) where Du Bois sledded in winter and visited his friend Louis Russell in apartments on Main and Railroad streets, and in the village of Housatonic at the north end of town. The Russell house still stands, although it was moved several hundred yards to the west in 1997 to make way for an upscale condo development on the abandoned and derelict Russell estate.

In some ways, the Great Barrington social order in 2000 continues to resemble the old New England social order of the 1880s described by Du Bois in his autobiography. For example, wealthy local people continue to live modest lifestyles (in contrast to wealthy newcomers) with little visible display of their wealth, and people are polite but conservative in their social greetings. The most dramatic change in the social order affecting the black community has been the arrival of other ethnic minority groups, which means that African-Americans are no longer the only ethnic minority and not even the largest "visible" minority. The 1990 census lists 62 Asians and 134 Latinos. The latter group expanded through the 1990s, and Latinos, with many being Latinas from the west coast nations of South America, are now the largest visible minority. Many Latinas work in factories, the food-service industry, and as domestics. There is also now a large Jewish population and two synagogues in town.

The arrival of immigrants and their employment in the tourist sector of the economy (tourism is now the largest economic sector) are typical of a pattern that has existed over the last 150 years as the local economy has developed and changed. Whenever there has been a local demand for labor it has typically been new immigrants—Irish (before and in Du Bois's time), Italians, Poles, and most recently Latinos—who have arrived to take the jobs in the mills and now in the tourist industry. As in Du Bois's youth, when African-American citizens of Great Barrington remained outside the mill-based economy, they are today outside the tourist economy. Employment is found mainly in factories, health care facilities, shops, and town government departments.

As with the community in general, African-American religion in Great Barrington remains alive and also separate, perhaps even more separate than in Du Bois's time when he and his mother often attended the white Congregational Church on Main Street and white ministers supported his education. The first Black church, the Clinton A.M.E. Zion Church, was founded in the 1880s by recent settlers in Great Barrington. Evidently, most of its early members were women who worked as domestics for wealthy white families with summer homes in the Berkshires. It took some time before it gained the support of the local African-American community (many of whom continued to attend white churches or both churches), and it was the only black church for more than eighty years.

In 2000, African-American religious life is centered on the two black churches in town. Unlike in the past, when wealthier African-Americans attended white churches, there seem to be few such members today. Du Bois attended the A.M.E. Zion Church at times and was involved in several church groups, and he returned to speak at the church in 1894 about his experiences in Europe. It remains a small though active congregation. In June 2000, it gained some attention in the local press when a woman, the Rev. Esther Dozier, was appointed pastor. The original wood-frame church, built in the early 1880s, still stands on Elm Court, although it is now larger as a parsonage was added to the rear in 1937 and a front porch more recently.

A second African-American church, the Macedonia Baptist Church was founded in 1944 by a group who broke away from A.M.E. Zion Church and has been in its Rosseter Street building since 1957, located around the corner from the A.M.E. Zion Church, with Joseph Forte as pastor. Another attempt to found an African-American church—a Moorish Science Temple—also began in 1944 with the purchase of property on South Main Street. However, a dispute over taxes soon developed and the land and building were foreclosed in 1948. There is cooperation between the two

African-American churches: Rev. Dozier's sister is associate pastor of the Macedonia Church, each pastor leads services in the other church once each year, and the churches jointly celebrate Martin Luther King Jr. Day. Du Bois would likely be pleased to know that in the 1960s when there were several race-based incidents in town and race relations became an issue, the pastor of the A.M.E. Zion Church took the lead in speaking out for the African-American community, and also served on a town committee to deal with racial issues. In 2000, there is little contact between the black churches and white churches and synagogues, although ecumenicism and interfaith initiatives are common in town and there is considerable contact among the white churches and between several churches and the synagogues. One's impression is that the African-American churches are culturally distinct and exist alongside but apart from other religious institutions. The separateness of the two African-American churches is indicated most clearly by their location. They are both on side streets off Main Street. One would not know that they are there unless one walked down Rosseter Street and Elm Court. All other churches and synagogues are located either on Main Street or on major roads on the edge of the downtown. This location is probably a product of the past and the relative poverty of the black churches, which would have made it impossible to build on Main Street.

Perhaps the greatest compliment I can pay Steve Glazier and the editors and contributors to this volume is to tell them that their work has stimulated me to begin studying the Clinton A.M.E. Zion Church, which will celebrate its 120th anniversary next year in its original building. Much waits to be done to document the history of the church, its culture, and its role in Great Barrington in the past and today.

David Levinson

Introduction: "All These Things and Others Like to Them"

Religion and Society in Africa and African America

> How the fine sweet spirit of black folk, despite superstition and passion has breathed the soul of humility and forgiveness into the formalism and cant of American religion.

In what were perhaps his most conciliatory remarks concerning African-American religion, scholar and activist W. E. B. Du Bois suggested in *The Gift of Black Folk* (1924: 54–55) that "above and beyond all that we have mentioned, perhaps least tangible, but just as true, is the peculiar spiritual quality which the Negro has injected into American life and civilization. It is hard to define and characterize it—a certain spiritual joyousness, a sensuous, tropical love of life, in vivid contrast to the cool and cautious New England reason; a slow and dreamful conception of the universe, a drawling and slurring of speech, an intense sensitiveness to spiritual values—all of these things and others like to them, tell of the imprint of Africa on Europe in America. There is no gainsaying or explaining away this tremendous influence of the contact of the north and south, of black and white, of Anglo-Saxon and Negro."

As might be expected over such a long and varied career, Du Bois changed his mind about religion many times. He was especially ambivalent about the role of religion in pro-

moting social change, and by the middle of the twentieth century saw religion as an overwhelmingly conservative force. But he was always willing to reconsider his position. His biographer David Levering Lewis notes that in 1955 Du Bois—at that time thoroughly agnostic and anticlerical—said of Martin Luther King and the Montgomery Bus boycotts that he had "expected to live to see many things, but never a militant Baptist preacher" (Lewis 1995: 11). Du Bois's most ambitious project, his *Encyclopedia Africana*, was intended as a compendium of knowledge and a celebration of the Pan-African spirit. The encyclopedia was to encompass all knowledge concerning the history, cultures, and social institutions of people of African descent. Du Bois argued passionately for his proposed encyclopedia claiming that it could be useful as a weapon in the war against racism and would inform future discussions of issues pertaining to the black race. He made a strong case, but was never able to secure adequate funding to complete the project.

It is unclear how many entries in Du Bois's projected encyclopedia would have dealt explicitly with African and African-American religions. He envisioned a multivolume work, but none of the various proposals he submitted over a fifty-year period included a separate volume—or even a separate section—devoted to the religions of African and African-American peoples.

The present volume, the *Encyclopedia of African and African-American Religions*, focuses exclusively on religion, its place in African and African-American societies, and its impact on society in general. As such, it is intended to fill a gap in the growing reference literature on Africa and African America. The 1990s have seen an explosion in the quantity of reference publications on Africa and African America. Included in this long and growing list of reference works are the *Encyclopedia of African-American Culture and History* (Macmillan Library Reference USA, 1996), the *African-American Encyclopedia* (Marshall Cavendish, 1997), the *Encyclopedia of African-American Religions* (Garland, 1993), *Contemporary Black Biography* (Gale Research, 1992), *African-American Women: A Biographical Dictionary* (Garland, 1993), *Black Women in America: An Historical Encyclopedia* (Carlson Publishing Inc., 1993), *Africana: The Encyclopedia of the African and African-American Experience* (Basic Civitas Books, 1999), and the *Encyclopedia of Africa South of the Sahara* (Scribners, 1997). These works taken as a whole provide much information on Africa and African America, but they do not cover many of the religions, movements, and topics covered in this volume. The primary purpose of this encyclopedia is to provide an up-to-date and authoritative guide to the religions of African and African-American peoples with special attention given to religious movements in Africa and the religions of the African diaspora in North America, South America, Central America, and the Caribbean. Many of these religions such as Santeria and Vodou are products of contact between major world religions (such as Christianity) and indigenous African traditions whose influence has now spread to Europe, Asia, and the South Pacific.

The Broad Spectrum of African and African-American Religions

This volume contains 145 articles written by 72 scholars from thirteen nations including Jamaica, Mexico, Venezuela, Nigeria, Ghana, Senegal, Austria, the Netherlands, and Canada. African and African-American religion is a topic that has drawn the attention of scholars from a wide range of disciplines and the contributors to this volume include experts trained in anthropology, geography, history, sociology, psychology, religious studies, theology, education, psychiatry, medicine, political science, music, and art. Nearly half the contributors (including the editor) were trained in anthropology. A unique feature of this encyclopedia is that most of the contributors have conducted ethnographic research among the followers of these religions. Many entries, such as Costa Chica, Mexico; Ifá; Rastafari; Santeria, Material Culture; Spiritual Baptists; and Storefront Churches, are enriched and provide a human dimension by the contributors' inclusion of information about their personal experiences with believers. Many of these arti-

cles also benefit from the inclusion of photographs supplied by the contributors. In accord with the ethnographic "ethos" of the volume, we have allowed contributors some editorial freedom in the spelling of terms specific to African and African-American religions and have not insisted on the use of one arbitrary though standard form. Thus, readers will occasionally find alternative (but close) spellings for concepts such as *orisha* (*oricha*), *shango* (*xango*), Santeria (Santería), and Vodou (Vodun, Voodoo).

Ninety-two of the articles cover religions, religious movements, churches, and organizations and document literally hundreds of movements, many associated with African traditional religions, many associated with the African diaspora, and many more that are the products of a combination of African and other world religions. A useful feature is our attention to lesser-known and emerging religious movements in both Africa and the Americas. Full entries are devoted to Big Drum, Convince, Mother Earth, the Spiritual Baptists, Jaama, the Apostolic Church of John Maranke, the Ahmadiyya movement, amaNazaretha, Zar, Batuque, Kumina, the Fire Baptized Holiness Church of God, the Church of the Twelve Apostles, Shango, the Venezuelan cult of Maria Lionza, and the religion of Costa Chica, Mexico. Many of these smaller groups or movements have themselves spawned other, more prominent religions. The influence of small religions always exceeds their relatively small memberships.

Exact genealogies of African and African-American religions are often difficult to discern. Sometimes, it is impossible to establish precise boundaries. Mother Earth, for example, was a Spiritual Baptist who established a nudist commune in the north of Trinidad. Since her death many of her followers have joined Rastafarian communities, while others have become active in the Spiritual Baptist religion. Although Mother Earth never attracted more than twenty followers (including the members of her immediate family), it is difficult to know where Mother Earth's influence will end. The same might well be said for Diola Prophets and some Rastafarian sects like Twelve Tribes. Inclusion of these and other groups gives readers a sense of the tremendous diversity, and perhaps unity, to be found within African and African-American religions. Entries on African and African-derived Religions in Cyberspace and on Media Evangelism show how modern means of communication erode—or expand—boundaries.

Some religions considered in this volume could best be described following Werbner (1977: ix) as regional cults: "They are cults of the middle range—more far reaching than any parochial cult of the little community—yet less inclusive in belief and membership than a world religion in its most universal form." Regional cults, as Werbner conceived them, cross political, economic, and ethnic boundaries; and they do not replicate social divisions existing apart from their ritual relations. They draw attention to the historical transformation of cults as well as to broader changes in transcultural religious symbolism. The Harrist Movement, the Apostolic Church of Johanne Masowe, and the Apostolic Church of John Maranke are prime African examples of regional cults, while Santeria, Rastafari, Vodou, and Umbanda in Brazil serve as prime examples in the New World.

Some New World religions like Rastafari, Vodou, and Santeria are covered in multiple entries written by different authors. Again, this gives a sense of religious diversity as well as illustrating their widespread importance. Moreover, multiple entries underscore the diversity of theoretical and methodological approaches that have been utilized successfully in the study of African and African-American religions. Rasta, Vodou, and Santeria are expanding in North America, attracting both black and white converts. They are no longer confined to the Caribbean. A Rasta beat can be discerned in J'waiian music, Hopi chants, among recent Maori converts in New Zealand, and in the popular music of South Africa (see Rastafari in Global Context and Rastafari in West Africa).

Thirty articles cover concepts and theories central to our understanding of African and African-American religions including widespread religious practices (Divination, Secret Societies), social activism, politics, theology, the role and status of women, art, music, and material culture. In addition, twenty-three articles provide surveys of African or African-American religions in nations or regions.

Some topics covered here might at first appear outside the domain of African and African-American religions (e.g., Religious Skepticism, African Pentecostalism in the Netherlands, World Vision International, Watchtower, and Unification Church). But these intellectual and religious movements have had a tremendous impact on Africa and African America. Pentecostalism is one of the fastest growing religions among European blacks and among blacks in South Africa; and World Vision, Seventh-Day Adventists, and the Unification Church are expanding their operations in Africa and throughout the Caribbean and Latin America. All of these groups have had a profound influence on African education (see Mission Schools).

Although we categorize the articles in this way, we recognize that African and African-American religion is much more than the sum of its parts. We have focused on what W. E. B. Du Bois in *The Souls of Black Folk* (1969 [1903]: 211) posited as the key elements in black religion—"the preacher, the music, and the frenzy"—while at the same time paying close attention to those "peculiar spiritual qualities" Du Bois (1924: 54) saw as the greatest gift of African and African-American peoples to world civilizations (see also Paris, 1995: 27–49).

Bibliographies at the end of each article emphasize generally available books on the topic and Appendix B provides a bibliography of major books—classic and contemporary—on African and African-American religions. Articles are extensively cross-referenced and blind entries are provided for several general topics such as Black Churches in the United States.

Readers seeking information on a specific topic, religion, movement, or nation can go directly to those articles. Readers seeking an introduction to religion in Sub-Saharan Africa would do well to begin with the articles on Christian Missionaries in Africa; Healing in Sub-Saharan Africa; Islam, East Africa; Islam, West Africa; Pentecostalism in Africa; Secret Societies; Yoruba Religion; and West African Religion. Readers seeking an introduction to African-derived religion in the Caribbean and Central and South America would do well to begin with the articles on African-derived religions in Brazil, the Caribbean, and Jamaica; and also entries on Healing in African and African-Derived Religions; on Ogun; and on Spirtualism. Readers seeking an introduction to African-American religion in the United States might best begin with the articles on Black Muslims; Black Theology; Holiness–Pentecostal Sanctified Movement; Music, Black Hymnody; Slave Religion; Social Activism; and United States, African Religions in.

The Social and Political Context

Scholars have typically seen African and African-American religions as agents of social change, but—as is apparent in the article on Social Activism—the relationship between religion and political consciousness is paradoxical and sometimes contradictory. A great deal of the literature on African-American religions questions whether African-American churches have been accommodative to white-dominated society or emancipatory for blacks. By posing the question in this manner, there is great risk of oversimplifying the situation and downplaying the tremendous diversity to be found among African-American churches. Nevertheless, as Baer and Singer (1992: 3) note, the need to respond to racism and economic oppression "is of such compelling urgency that its effect has closely shaped the very heart and soul of African-American religion in all of its complexity." Gayraud S. Wilmore (1998: ix) emphasizes that "there has always been and continues to be a significant difference between black religion and white religion in their approaches to social reality and social change." In the case of African religions, differences between black and white approaches to social change are illustrated by studies like Karen E. Fields's (1995) *Revival and Rebellion in Colonial Africa* and Jean Comaroff's *Body of Power, Spirit of Resistance* (1985).

Moreover, religious institutions provide considerable insight into the inner workings of African and African-American societies and cultures. In contrast to growing secularism in Europe and North America, African and African-American peoples do not conceptualize religion as separate from the rest of their culture. Art, dance, and literature are understood as integral to the religious experience. This is aptly illustrated by musician B. B. King's comment that he feels closest to God when he is singing the blues (see also Jon M. Spencer's 1993 *Blues and Evil*). Moreover, it is appropriate for social scientists to devote their attentions to religion because, as C. Eric Lincoln and Lawrence Mamiya so effectively argue in *The Black Church in the African-American Experience* (1990: xi), "religion, seriously considered, is perhaps the best prism to cultural understanding, not as a comparative index, but as a refractive element through which one social cosmos may look meaningfully at another and adjust its presuppositions accordingly."

Two erroneous assumptions have informed past studies of African and African-American religions. The first erroneous assumption is that the black experience of religion simply replicates white religious experience. The second is that the black experience of religion is totally dissimilar to white religious experience. Neither assumption is true because neither assumption takes into account the complex interactions between African-based religions and other world religions. Correctly viewed, African-American religious experience cannot be separated from North American religion. It is one fabric. African religious experience is part and parcel of North American religious experience, just as Christianity and Islam are now part and parcel of African religious experience.

The goal is finding the right mix. In *A Fire in the Bones*, Albert J. Raboteau cites a passage from Ralph Ellison's *The Invisible Man*. The novel's unnamed protagonist finds a job working in a factory for Liberty Paints, a company that makes a product called "Optic White" used as a whitewash on government buildings, churches, and national monuments. The secret formula for mixing the paint is known by only one person in the factory, a black janitor. His job is to add exactly ten drops of black pigment to the paint base. If the right amount of black pigment is not added, the paint will turn brown or gray—not "Optic White." The study of African and African-American religions, Raboteau contends, changes our views of history and changes our views of our-

selves. "It is not simply to furnish the additional drops necessary to continue the whitewash of our national experience" (Raboteau 1995: 6–7).

Recent years have seen the development of new approaches in the study of African and African-American religions. Most notable among these is Afrocentrism championed by Cheikh Anta Diop (1974) and Molefe Asante (1998). These new perspectives—devoted to overturning colonial and racist misinterpretations of the nineteenth century—have provided a valuable corrective to Eurocentrism. Diop and Asante take their places alongside other critical traditions exemplified in the scholarship of Alexander Crummel, Arturo Alfonso Schomburg, Casley Hayford, John Hope Franklin, Carter G. Woodson, Mark Miles Fisher, W. E. B. Du Bois, Edward Blyden, and C. L. R. James. All contributed dramatically to the death of European cultural hegemony. But as Joseph M. Murphy contends in *Working the Spirit*, it was a very slow death. Even today, outmoded models and old interpretations abound in popular media treatments of African and African-American religions. Murphy points out that one of the greatest barriers to overcome in interpreting African diaspora traditions to outsiders is the deep-seated popular image of them as a form of malign (black) magic. He correctly traces many of these images and ideas to the French colonial reaction to Haitian slave revolts. These images, he believes, may reflect "the horror felt by whites at the prospect of independent black power in the Americas" (Murphy 1994: x).

African and African-American religions have always been at the center of debate concerning African retentions in the New World. A number of prominent theorists, most notably E. Franklin Frazier, suggested that New World slavery was so disruptive that few African traits survived. Other scholars, most notably Melville J. Herskovits (1941), argued effectively for the survival of African traits in New World societies. Herskovits's view has predominated, but the issue remains complex (see Mintz and Price, 1992). The relationships between religions in Africa and African religions in the New World are replete with examples of what Pierre Verger (1968: 31) termed "flux and reflux." Building on a lifetime of fieldwork and archival research, Verger documented extensive and continuous contact between religious specialists in Africa and religious organizations in the New World. He painstakingly demonstrated that the slave trade was not only "of" Africans (i.e., the trade itself), but "by" Africans as well. Africans and African-Americans were producers and traders as well as laborers in the plantation system, and they played an active role—not just a passive one—in the ongoing drama of slavery.

The quest for Africa in the New World continues, but with new and refined sensibilities. The question is no longer whether it is there, but, rather, how much and of what nature? As Stuart Hall (1990: 228)—commenting on the *Presence Africaine* in his native Jamaica—noted "Africa was, in fact, present everywhere, in the everyday life and customs of the slave quarters, in the language and patois of the plantations, in names and words; often disconnected from their taxonomies, in the secret syntactical structure through which other languages were spoken, in the stories and tales told to children, in religious practices and belief in the spiritual life, the arts, crafts, music and rhythms of slave and post-emancipation society.... Africa remained and remains the unspoken, unspeakable 'presence' in Caribbean culture. It is 'hiding' behind every verbal inflection, every narrative twist of Caribbean cultural life."

Few scholars have embraced these new sensibilities as effectively as Leslie G. Desmangles. Desmangles's work identifying patterns of symbiosis and juxtaposition in Haitian Vodou, contrasts markedly with the earlier scholarship of Roger Bastide, and Melville J. Herskovits. What makes Desmangles's research unique is his careful attention to the tremendous variety of religious forms and influences within African and African-American religions. Drawing on firsthand research in Haiti and the People's Republic of Benin, he underscores Vodou's continuities and discontinuities with its African past.

Decidedly, some theoretical concepts in the study of African and African-American religions have proven to be more fruitful than others. John Mbuti (1969: 289), in *African Religion and Philosophy*, has expressed his dissatisfaction with Western interpretations and misinterpretations of African religions thus: "Western missionaries, anthropologists, journalists, and scholars who keep harping about 'ancestor worship' should look at and consider cemeteries in their home countries and see how many flowers, candles and even photographs of the dead, are put on the graves of relatives and friends. This is often more extreme than anything we find in Africa.... These and other previous terms show how little the outside world has understood African religion." Johannes Fabian's latest book, *Out of Our Minds: Reason and Madness in the Exploration of Central Africa*, provides considerable insight as to how these strange categories and misinterpretations of African religions may have come into being.

Keeping both Mbuti's and Fabian's criticisms in mind, Appendix A sounds a valuable cautionary note. Wyatt MacGaffey's *Anthropology of Religion in Africa: A Critique and Model* offers an analysis of erroneous categories and assumptions that have plagued the study of African and African-American religions since the nineteenth century. MacGaffey argues that opposing terms like "witchcraft" and "sorcery," "spirit mediumship" and "spirit possession," and "ancestors" and "shades" represent an imposition from out-

side and are, as John Mbuti (1969: 222) and others have suggested, a result of mistaking local phenomena for universal ideas. MacGaffey's proposed solution to this problem is to develop analytical concepts that start at the local level and assume a "Social Action" perspective. His approach represents a significant advance over earlier approaches and is a fitting conclusion for a volume such as this focused on the interaction of religion and society.

Acknowledgments

There are many people to thank for their contributions to this encyclopedia. The current volume—indeed the entire *Religion and Society* series—was conceived and initiated by David Levinson and Karen Christensen of Berkshire Publishing Group. Special thanks are due to staff members at Berkshire Publishing Group who helped bring this volume to completion; especially Ben Manning and Debbie Dillon who coordinated the project and Maarten Reilingh who did the copyediting. Their collective efforts make this a stronger volume than it might otherwise have been.

My contributors, of course, deserve commendation. Contributions to this volume were both volunteered and solicited. To ensure wide coverage, I sought out contributors at various professional societies; most notably the Society for the Anthropology of Religion Section of the American Anthropological Association, the Society for the Scientific Study of Religion, the Caribbean Studies Association, the American Ethnological Society, the American Folklore Society, the African Studies Association, the Latin American Studies Association, the American Folklore Society, the Society for the Anthropology of Consciousness, and the Rastafari Seminar of the American Academy of Religion.

I want to acknowledge indebtedness to my Associate Editors—Hans Baer, Leslie G. Desmangles, Frances Kostarelos, and Richard P. Werbner—for their invaluable help in reviewing articles and suggesting possible topics and likely contributors. It is an honor to have worked with such outstanding scholars. Each has made important contributions to the contemporary study of African and African-American religions. Their major publications include Baer's *The Black Spiritual Movement* (University of Tennessee Press, 1985) and (with Merrill Singer) *African-American Religion in the Twentieth Century* (University of Tennessee Press, 1992); Desmangles's *The Faces of the Gods: Voudou and Roman Catholicism in Haiti* (University of North Carolina Press, 1992); Kostarelos's *Feeling the Spirit: Faith and Hope in an Evangelical Storefront Church* (University of South Carolina Press, 1995); and Werbner's *Memory and Postcolony: African Anthropology and the Critique of Power* (St. Martin's Press, 1998). I also want to acknowledge the advice provided by C. Eric Lincoln in the early planning for the *Religion and Society* series. Unfortunately, his declining health and death in 2000 prevented his participation in this project, although his contributions to the study of African-American religion are noted in a number of articles.

My knowledge of African and African-American religions was greatly enhanced by having studied under Leslie G. Desmangles, Seth Leacock, Ben Ray, the late Peter Rigby, Al Raboteau, Mary Douglas, Angelina Pollak-Eltz, and Jim Fernandez. Research on this volume was facilitated by my appointment as a Visiting Scholar at the Harry Ransom Center of the University of Texas at Austin. While in Austin, W. Roger Louis and members of the NEH summer seminar "Decolonizing the British Empire" provided an invaluable opportunity to gain a better perspective on African religions in the postcolonial era. I also want to thank the librarians at the West Indian Collections of the University of the West Indies (Mona and St. Augustine) and librarians at the Benson Collection of the University of Texas for their help in compiling the Select Bibliography.

My wife, Rosemary, and daughter, Katie, have been patient and understanding while I was busy performing the various editorial duties associated with this volume. As always, I thank them for their love, encouragement, and support.

Stephen D. Glazier

Bibliography

Appiah, Kwame Anthony, and Louis Henry Gates, Jr. (1999) *Africana: The Encyclopedia of the African and African-American Experience.* New York: Basic Civitas Books.

Asante, Molefe Kete. (1998) *The Afrocentric Idea.* Revised and Expanded Edition. Philadelphia: Temple University Press.

Baer, Hans A., and Merrill Singer. (1992) *African-American Religion in the Twentieth Century: A Religious Response to Racism.* Knoxville: University of Tennessee Press.

Comaroff, Jean. (1985) *Body of Power, Spirit of Resistance.* Chicago: University of Chicago Press.

Diop, Cheikh Anta. (1994) *The African Origin of Civilization: Myth or Reality?* New York: L. Hill.

Desmangles, Leslie G. (1992) *The Faces of the Gods: Vodou and Roman Catholicism in Haiti.* Chapel Hill: University of North Carolina Press.

Du Bois, W. E. B. (1969 [1903]) *The Souls of Black Folk.* New York: New American Library.

———. (1975 [1924]) *The Gift of Black Folk: The Negroes in the Making of America.* Millwood, NY: Kraus-Thompson.

Drake, St. Clair, and Horace Clayton. (1945) *Black Metropolis.* New York: Harcourt Brace.

Fabian, Johannes. (2000) *Out of Our Minds: Reason and Madness in the Exploration of Central Africa.* Berkeley and Los Angeles: University of California Press.

Fields, Karen E. (1985) *Revival and Rebellion in Colonial Central Africa.* Princeton, NJ: Princeton University Press.

Frazier, E. Franklin. (1964) *The Negro Church in America.* New York: Shocken Books.

Hall, Stuart. (1990) *"Cultural Identity and Diaspora Identity": Community, Culture, Difference,* edited by James Rutherford. London: Lawrence and Wishart.

Herskovits, Melville J. (1941) *The Myth of the Negro Past.* New York: Harper and Brothers.

Kostarelos, Frances. (1995) *Feeling the Spirit: Faith and Hope in an Evangelical Storefront Church.* Columbia: University of South Carolina Press.

Lewis, David Levering, ed. (1995) *W. E. B. Du Bois: A Reader.* New York: Henry Holt.

Lincoln, C. Eric, and Lawrence Mamiya. (1990) *The Black Church in the African-American Experience.* Durham, NC: Duke University Press.

Mbuti, John. (1969) *African Religion and Philosophy.* London: Heinemann.

Murphy, Joseph M. (1994) *Working the Spirit: Ceremonies of the African Diaspora.* Boston: Beacon Press.

Murphy, Larry, J. Gordon Melton, and Gary I. Ward. eds. *Encyclopedia of African-American Religions.* New York: Garland.

Mintz, Sidney, and Richard Price. (1992) *An Anthropological Approach to the Afro-American Past: The Birth of African-American Culture: An Anthropological Perspective.* Boston: Beacon Press.

Paris, Peter J. (1995) *The Spirituality of African People: The Search for a Common Moral Discourse.* Minneapolis: Fortress Press.

Raboteau, Albert J. (1995) *A Fire in the Bones: Reflections on African-American Religious History.* Boston, MA: Beacon Press.

Spencer, Jon Michael. (1993) *Blues and Evil.* Knoxville: University of Tennessee Press.

Verger, Pierre. (1968) *Flux et Reflux de la Traite des Negres entre le Golfe de Benin et Bahia de Todos los Santos, du XVIIe au XIXe Siecle.* The Hague: Mouton.

Washington, Joseph R., Jr. (1972) *Black Sects and Cults.* New York: Doubleday and Company.

Werbner, Richard P., ed. (1977) *Regional Cults.* New York: Academic Press.

Wilmore, Gayraud S. (1998) *Black Religion and Black Radicalism.* 3d ed. Maryknoll, NY: Orbis Books.

Abyssinian Baptist Church

Founded in 1808, the Abyssinian Baptist Church is the oldest black Baptist church in the state of New York and one of the most prominent and politically active congregations in the United States. Located in central Harlem, the church was started by a group of African-Americans who, protesting the practice of racially segregated seating, separated themselves from the First Baptist Church of Gold Street. Organizing themselves together in a building on Anthony Street (later Worth Street) in lower Manhattan, they established their own congregation. Having among them a group of Ethiopian immigrants, they named the new Christian fellowship, "Abyssinian," after the nation of Ethiopia, "Abyssinia."

The group was soon aided in its organizational efforts by the Rev. Thomas Paul, a white liberal minister from Boston who would later become a missionary to Haiti. The early history is sketchy and a bit difficult to corroborate. However, as far as can be gathered, the struggling little church needed, after several years, a new building and hence sold the Worth Street property for $3,000. Over the next forty-eight years, they held services in the Broadway Tabernacle and in various other houses and halls in lower Manhattan while they sought a permanent place for worship.

During this period until 1856, the church apparently changed pastors twelve times. The pastors were the Reverends Josiah Bishop, Van Vessler, Sigle, James Hayborn, Thompson, Loomis, Sampson White, Moore, John T. Raymond (served twice), Thomas Henderson, and Dutton. On 18 May 1847, the Reverend Sampson White went to Brooklyn, with six members of the Abyssinian Church who were living there, to organize the now-historic Concord Baptist Church.

In 1856, Father William Spellman (as he was called) assumed the pastorate of the church. Under his leadership, Abyssinian acquired its first permanent edifice, located at Waverly Place in New York's Greenwich Village. It was also during his tenure that Abyssinian increased in membership to sixteen hundred, becoming the leading Black church in New York City.

William Spellman was succeeded in 1885 by the Rev. Robert D. Wynn, who became the first of three consecutive pastors to point the congregation in the direction of upper Manhattan. He dreamed one night that the church was going to move to Harlem. When he relayed his dream to the congregation, the people pronounced it a nightmare. Nevertheless, Wynn was so convinced that his dream was a vision from God he resigned, ending an effective pastorate of sixteen years. In May 1902, Dr. Charles Satchell Morris became Abyssinian's next pastor. Following Wynn, he began to argue the case for a Harlem church to accommodate the "Great Migration" of African Americans from the South to the North—those in New York settling mostly in Harlem. Though his powerful and persuasive eloquence could not convince the congregation to move to Harlem, the congregation did move further north to Fortieth Street. Due to illness and some doctrinal and administrative disagreements, Morris was forced to relinquish the pastorate of the church after just six years, a relatively short tenure for a Baptist minister.

In December of 1908, on the threshold of the first significant wave of black immigrants to northern cities and one hundred years after the church was founded, Adam Clayton Powell, Sr. became the church's new pastor. Powell embraced the Social Gospel model of an "Institutional Church." It was his dream to move the congregation from Fortieth Street to Harlem and build a model institution that would respond effectively to the spiritual and social needs of the thousands of African Americans who were migrating from the South. Racial demographics in the city were shifting; as Jews and other ethnic groups who had lived there earlier left, blacks were settling in Harlem. Thus, Harlem became the focus of Powell's dream. He believed that "the Church should be the social center of the community in which it is located" (Powell 1923).

In 1923, the Abyssinian Church and Community House, a Gothic and Tudor structure, was erected at a cost of $400,000 and was paid for in full in 1928, just four and a half years later. The Abyssinian Church was thus well positioned to respond to the vast needs of the poor, following the crash of the stock market in 1929 and the onset of the Great Depression. Following Powell, Sr.'s sermonic vision of "A Hungry God," preached in December 1930 at the peak of the Depression, the church greatly increased its social relief efforts. The church's Home Relief Bureau, which offered much-needed jobs to the unemployed, expanded its service along with the old-age pension program, developed in the 1920's. A free nursery was made available to provide care and nourishment for children; a school of adult education provided jobs and training; and the church's kitchen provided two meals per day for the hungry.

In 1937, Powell was succeeded by his son, Adam Clayton Powell, Jr. His passion for justice and concern for the oppressed pushed the younger Powell and his congregation beyond providing social relief to addressing social policy. Powell, Jr. combined his career in the pastorate with the holding of political office, serving first in the City Council, and subsequently for fourteen terms in the U.S. Congress. There he became the chairman of the House Committee on

Education and Labor. A street activist, he led the kind of protests against segregation in the 1950s that would become more popular with the civil rights leadership that would emerge only later in that decade and mature in the 1960s. During his pastorate, the Abyssinian Baptist Church grew to boast a membership of 18,000, making it at the time the largest protestant church in the world.

Following Powell's death in 1971, Dr. Samuel Proctor, former president of Virginia Union University and North Carolina Agricultural and Technical University, became the pastor of the church in 1972. During Proctor's tenure, the church expanded its ministry to include several major housing and development initiatives, including senior citizens housing and housing for the homeless and middle-income families. Proctor, who died in 1997, was nationally recognized as a world-class preacher, author, and academic. He also held a chair as the Martin Luther King, Jr. Professor at Rutgers University while serving as pastor of Abyssinian and as a mentor to hundreds of ministers, including Jesse Jackson.

Under the leadership of the church's current pastor, Dr. Calvin O. Butts, III, the church continues as an important center for conversation about social policy and public discourse about issues as diverse as police brutality, tobacco and alcohol billboard advertising targeted to minorities, and the privatization and closing of municipal hospitals that serve largely indigent populations. Under the auspices of the Abyssinian Development Corporation, nearly fifteen-hundred units of housing have been renovated in Central Harlem, a high school called the Thurgood Marshall Academy for Learning and Social Change provides an alternative public education for Harlem youth, and Harlem's first full-service supermarket was built. Thousands of tourists visit the world-renowned church each year.

Raphael G. Warnock

Bibliography

Hamilton, Charles V. (1991) *Adam Clayton Powell, Jr.: The Political Biography of an American Dilemma*. New York: Atheneum.

Haygood, Wil. (1994) *King of the Cats*. New York: Houghton Mifflin.

Kinney, John William. (1979) "Adam Clayton Powell, Sr. and Adam Clayton Powell, Jr.: A Historical Exposition and Theological Analysis." Ph.D. diss., Columbia University.

Powell, Adam Clayton, Sr. (1923) A speech reprinted in *Opportunity*, National Urban League, January, p. 15.

———. (1938) *Against the Tide: An Autobiography*. New York: Richard R. Smith.

Powell, Adam Clayton, Jr. (1994) *Adam by Adam: The Autobiography of Adam Clayton Powell, Jr.* New York: Carol Publishing Group.

Freedman, Samuel G. (1994) *Upon this Rock: the Miracles of a Black Church*. New York: HarperCollins.

Proctor, Samuel Dewitt. (1994) *The Certain Sound of the Trumpet: Crafting a Sermon of Authority*. Valley Forge, PA: Judson Press.

———. (1994) *My Moral Odyssey*. Valley Forge, PA: Judson Press.

———. (1995) *Substance of Things Hoped for: A Memoir of African-American Faith*. New York: Putnam.

Sullivan, Frank. (1930) *Watchman-Examiner*, 25 December.

African Charismatics

Charismatic movements in Africa are a phenomenon of major scope and persistence. They continue to spread because they are responding to the existential needs of Africans within contemporary situations of sociopolitical disequilibrium. These movements are engendering fundamental transformations of religious and social values. Their pragmatic approaches, capacity for innovation, and adaptability to situations are bringing renewal to the continent.

Beginnings and Growth

Beginning in the 1970s, a new wave of Christian awakening started sweeping across many African countries. By the 1980s, this awakening had assumed social prominence due partly to increased media attention and also to the proliferation of new churches, "ministries," and "fellowships." Unlike previous renewal movements that were primarily regional, the present one is continentwide, and there is some degree of networking among the leaders of the movements. The revival had an evangelical background, but its present form greatly manifests Pentecostalism mixed with African participatory and vibrant ethos.

The charismatic movements in Nigeria were the first to be articulated. In January 1970, a revival among existing evangelical students groups at the University of Ibadan (Nigeria), including Student Christian Movement, Scripture Union, and Christian Union, transformed the existing evangelical Christianity into a Pentecostal one when baptism of the Holy Spirit, speaking in tongues, and manifestation of the fruits of the Spirit were accepted as new doctrinal emphases. Despite opposition from other evangelicals, the revival spread to other universities and colleges largely through evangelistic activities. By 1975, the renewal had stabilized with the emergence of charismatic organizations established by graduates who had participated in the revival on the campuses.

In East Africa, the Fellowship of Christian Unions (FOCUS), which linked several national Christian Unions, facilitated the spread of the charismatic renewal across borders. A training course with emphases on evangelism and Bible study, held in Kenya in June 1974 and attended by many students from other countries, created the right setting for the emergence of the new religious expression. By the late 1970s, the campuses of Kenyan higher institutions had witnessed the renewal. In Tanzania, high school students first had the Pentecostal experience. Then it spread to higher institutions, where it caused divisions in the Christian Union groups. However, by 1982 the gap between the charismatics and evangelicals had narrowed. In Uganda and Ethiopia, political instability and the harassment of students in higher institutions partly delayed the emergence of the renewal in these countries until the early 1980s. Southern African countries like Zimbabwe, Malawi, and Zambia, experienced the renewal from the early 1980s through evangelistic visits and distribution of literature by charismatics from other countries.

French-speaking Africa witnessed the charismatic renewal only from the mid-1980s. The delay in the formation of national student Christian organizations partly contributed to this. The beginnings could be traced to the activities of some Nigerian charismatics who did their one-year language study in Benin Republic, Ivory Coast, Guinea, and other Francophone countries. By the mid-1980s, Nigerians had facilitated the growth of the charismatic renewal across Africa, as they interacted with other Africans in some of the regional and international activities of evangelical groups.

The revival progressed initially as an indigenous initiative. The foreign influence, mostly from American tele-evangelists came later in the forms of evangelistic visits, literature, and networking. In fact, American Christian tracts provided the first corpus of literature for African charismatics. Moreover, the crusades held by Westerners introduced new evangelistic methods and partly gave impetus to some persons outside the colleges and universities to set up their own evangelistic and charismatic organizations. Nonetheless, the charismatic movements were clearly indigenous, and they developed new traditions of Christianity contextually relevant to the contemporary African situation.

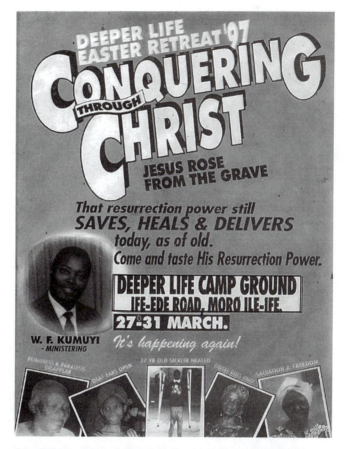

A handbill announcing a charismatic healing service held in More Ile-Ile, Nigeria.

Dynamics of Charismatic Movements

Charismatic movements are proliferating in Africa and are everywhere in evidence in a wide range of types and sizes. The total number of African charismatics by the end of the twentieth century was about ten million, with about five million in Nigeria alone. Though small in comparison to the mainline Protestant and Catholic organizations, charismatic movements are marked by vigorous activity, committed membership, and rapid growth.

The leadership and a substantial percentage of membership are the educated elite and youths—university and college students, dropouts, and graduates. This class of people, though small in number, has immeasurable influence in African society. Women constitute a slight majority in this group, but they exercise less authority compared to their male counterparts. The domestication of the messages gives much appeal to women, as does the charismatic emphasis on spiritual equality, which, for women, is opening new roads for self-determination and self-actualization. Uniquely modern, market-oriented, and success-directed, charismatic style helps the movements to propagate their doctrines to the mobile, educated middle class who live in urban areas.

Charismatic literature, songs, choruses, sermons, and values are usually conveyed in the English language. The liturgy is simple, but the services are full of warmth with clapping and dancing to Western-styled gospel music or indigenous choruses with accompaniment by electronic keyboards and band sets. Members derive their dynamism and commitment from the conviction that they are revitalizing the Christian faith in preparation for the "endtime."

The urban communities are important generative centers for the charismatic movements, and they proliferate more and are clearly visible in the urban areas. Charismatic emphases seem to gain wide acceptance in geographical areas that have witnessed great social change, and that is partly why charismatic organizations address their messages to the contemporary urban problems such as unemployment, loneliness, inadequate health care, and poor social services. The decay in urban areas calls for more intense religious expression to compensate for the depersonalization of urban life. Moreover, urban areas provide much of the economic resources needed to run massive organizational structures. The multiethnic nature of urban areas facilitates the formation of new religious and social ties that replace traditional ones. Certainly, rapid social change, which disrupted existing traditional religious structures, created conditions conducive to the acceptance of a new spirituality and its rapid spread.

Pentecostalism has been a purveyor of modern culture. From the use of modern musical instruments, charismatics have continued to appropriate sophisticated media technologies such as video, satellite broadcasting, and the Internet. Indeed, global communication has greatly aided the internationalization of charismatic renewal all over the world. African charismatic movements have become transnational as they continue to forge links across the continent and with similar charismatic organizations in North America and Europe for generating material and financial resources. Increasing migration from the mid-1980s has facilitated constant networking with charismatic groups of the African Diaspora in the West. African charismatic groups in the West have shown that they can transcend their African origins and enter into new cultural milieus.

Typology of African Charismatics

A paradigm of piety and power could be used as the conceptual basis of a typology of African Charismatic movements into six groups. Piety refers to the goal of the organizations to deepen the religious experience of their members. The other major focus of the Charismatic organizations is the articulation and appropriation of religious power in very pragmatic terms to mediate and address the contemporary needs of members. This new form of power is usually domesticated and portrayed in terms of material wealth, large membership, miracles, healing, and so on. Therefore, the crucial question underlying this typology is "what methods do various Charismatic organizations assume that power would accrue to their members in order to help them address their felt needs?"

Using the paradigm of power and piety, African charismatics can be classified into six groups.

First, are the faith-seekers who insist that the means of acquiring power is for the individual to establish a relationship with God, through conversion. Conversion is the renunciation of past identities and efforts. Faith-seekers organize regular evangelistic activities such as door-to-door witnessing, retreats, and camp meetings. Their testimonies are usually of deliverance and of changed situations brought about by intimacy with Jesus Christ.

Second, are the faith-builders who emphasize the realization of human potential in individuals to overcome contemporary difficulties of life or to achieve rapid social mobility through the acquisition of material comfort or societal recognition. Most of these groups tend to prosper in the urban areas and among the educated middle class. These groups emphasize prosperity and productive faith. They frequently organize "breakthrough" and success seminars, arrange banquets, and "sow seed money." Their testimonies are usually of successes and achievements.

Third, faith-transformers are charismatic organizations that seek to alter the sociocultural and religious milieu of large groups of people, frequently along ethnic or national lines. These groups are aggressive in locating ethnic groups and establishing contacts with them through educational, medical, social, agricultural, and industrial missions. A subgroup are those charismatics who see whatever is happening within any nation as the result of spiritual exercises. Both look at the redemption of the nation or the ethnic group as a means of empowering the people. Most of the indigenous mission-sending agencies fall into this group.

Fourth are those who seek to rekindle revival and renewal within existing non-Pentecostal denominations. Known as Reformists, they are literalists, educated middle class, and students, who see their denominations as a religious inheritance that must be nurtured and developed. They participate in the activities of the other charismatic groups, yet they are keenly attached to their non-Pentecostal denominations.

Fifth are the Modernists, who are mostly those independent African churches like the Zionists and Aladuras who have adopted or are trying to adopt the religious style of the charismatics and Pentecostals. Their preoccupation is how to present the "old" Zionist or Aladura religion to a modern world of the educated. They usually start from the premise of imitation, and may later adopt certain religious emphases of the charismatics.

Sixth are the Deliverance Churches, which are preoccupied with liberating or extricating Christians from their traditional pasts, which they consider stumbling blocks to a fulfilling life in the contemporary world. They specialize in casting out the demonic past, the ancestral curses, and the traditional gods. They operate as clinics. Their clients come for consultations at appointed times and are given "prescriptions" of certain spiritual exercise to break the past. Some of these "religious clinics" find it difficult to retain patient-members once they are healed.

Doctrinal Emphases and Practices

Divine healing is a major doctrinal emphasis among African charismatics. There are four major areas of application of healing. First, is physical healing; second, is healing of demonic attacks and satanic oppression, which is termed "Deliverance." Third, there is healing of all forms of failures in life, which is termed "Success and Prosperity," and, fourth, there is healing of the socioeconomic and political problems of a country. All the four components are organically linked, but the emphasis varies from one charismatic organization to the other. Charismatics' application of healing is very dynamic and extensive, and it covers every possible area of life—business, personal aspirations, education, family life, and national issues. Charismatics therefore address themselves to prevalent conditions and have attempted with much success to touch those concerns that are important to the individual's present life.

Evangelism is another major preoccupation. Charismatics regard evangelism as the most important work for Christians. There is a threefold consensus among charismatic organizations about the goals of evangelism. Primarily, when the biblical aspect is stressed, evangelism is directed at conversion. Second, it is a work of redemption to loosen and free humans from the grip of evil spirits, witches, forces of darkness, principalities, enemies, bad luck, and repeated failures, which are prevalent phenomena in the African worldview. This cultural dimension of evangelism is largely why the healing sessions, which are integral to evangelistic activities, attract large attendance. Third, through evangelism, charismatics hope that the economic, social, and political situation of Africa will be transformed. They believe that the present adverse predicament in the continent is due to collective and individual sin. Thus, the doctrinal emphases and religious practices of the charismatic movements can be seen as a sharply focused reflection of the political and socioeconomic situation of contemporary Africa.

Charismatics' concern for power is further reflected in their publicity materials that often depict the grandiose: miracle, success, health, and wealth. This quest for power manifests continuity with the African worldview of power, means of acquisition, and its various uses. Charismatics believe that power can be harnessed through a religious platform, and that the power obtained through the Holy Spirit is a power greater than any other power. In terms of its social significance, it depicts charismatics' capacity to accomplish things, to change lives, characters, and situations. Such operation of power is a way of bringing theology to bear on the contemporary scene and thus reorder the religious basis of the society.

Charismatics focus essentially on power, and charismatics have evolved a unique militarization of popular speech. The images of invasion, conquest, destruction, "prayer missiles," "fire power," wind, and the like are mixed with the worn-out but still popular images of the grandiose: miracle, success, health, and wealth. Africans who are politically disenfranchised and are socially or economically marginalized have embraced this imagery because religion has continued to give them a feeling of socioeconomic and political empowerment.

Sociopolitical Relevance of African Charismatics

The political upheaval in many African countries and the democratization processes in the 1990s had some bearing on the charismatic movements. Various political founders and leaders made appeals to the religious beliefs of their countrymen and utilized the political and economic power of charismatic organizations, which, in turn, were able to expand their own influence. For example, President Frederick Chiluba's declaration of Zambia as a Christian nation on 29 December 1991, only two months after his election, provided charismatics and Pentecostals a moral platform to further penetrate the country's political sphere and become a relevant social force. However, this Pentecostal identity has not prevented corruption, attitudes intolerant to political opposition movements, or the opposition of the mainline churches to this identification of the national ethos with Christianity. It would appear that Chiluba only exploited the support of the Pentecostals and charismatics for selfish ends.

In Ghana, the charismatic churches have moved close to the government of President Jerry Rawlings and have provided the regime a religious and moral legitimacy, which it was not able to get from the Protestant and the Catholic Churches. This relationship with the president has established the charismatic churches as a new powerful force and an alternative religious model to the existing mainstream churches.

From the late 1970s, Nigerian charismatics used prophecies to stir up Christians to sociopolitical actions through a theology affirming that whatever happens in the spiritual realm has implications for the socioeconomic and political developments of any nation. They soon constructed their own moral political sphere where forces of good always triumph over satanic agents that caused socioeconomic and political crises. Later, these charismatics developed religious and political influence extending beyond Nigeria to include other African nations. Evangelism supplied the locomotion for this belief, and evangelistic thrusts into other African nations carried Nigeria's image as the "big brother" of Africa. The missions also benefited from the bold thrust in Nigeria's external relations and influence, which had come from the oil boom of the 1970s. To conclude, African charismatics constitute a social force, and they continue to generate remarkable sociocultural and political changes in the continent.

Matthews A. Ojo

See also Aladura; Christian Evangelism in Africa; Pentecostalism in Africa; Religion and Healing in Sub-Saharan Africa; Zionist Churches

Bibliography

Bediako, Kwame. (1995) *Christianity in Africa: The Renewal of a Non-Western Religion.* Edinburgh: Edinburgh University Press & New York: Orbis Books.

Gifford, Paul. (1998) *African Christianity: Its Public Role.* Bloomington: Indiana University Press.

———. (1994) "Ghana's Charismatic Churches." *Journal of Religion in Africa* 3, 24: 241–265.

Gifford, Paul, ed. (1992) *New Dimensions in African Christianity.* Nairobi: All African Conference of Churches.

Hackett, Rosalind I. J. (1998). "Charismatic/Pentecostal Appropriation of Media Technologies in Nigeria and Ghana." *Journal of Religion in Africa* 3, 28: 258–277.

———. (1993) "From Exclusion to Inclusion: Women and Bible Use in Southern Nigeria." In *The Sociology of Sacred Texts,* edited by Jon Davies and Isabel Woilaston. Sheffield: Sheffield Academic Press, 142–155.

Marshall, Ruth. (1991) "Power in the Name of Jesus." *Review of African Political Economy* 52: 21–38.

Marshall-Fratani, R. (1998) "Mediating The Global and Local in Nigerian Pentecostalism." *Journal of Religion in Africa* 3, 28.

Meyer, Birgit. (1992) "'If you are a Devil you are a Witch and if you are a Witch you are a Devil': The Integration of 'Pagan' Ideas into the Conceptual Universe of Ewe Christians in South-eastern Ghana." *Journal of Religion in Africa* 2, 22: 98–132.

Ojo, Matthews A. (1997) "Sexuality, Marriage, and Piety Among Charismatics in Nigeria." *Religion* 27: 65–79.

———. (1996) "Charismatic Movements in Africa." In *Christianity in Africa in the 1990s,* by A. F. Walls and Christopher Fyfe. Centre of African Studies, University of Edinburgh, Edinburgh, Scotland, 92–110.

———. (1996) "The Place of Evangelism in the Conception of Work Among Charismatics in Nigeria." *Asia Journal of Theology* 1, 10: 49–62.

———. (1995) "The Charismatic Movements in Nigeria Today." *International Bulletin of Missionary Research* 3, 19: 114–118.

———. (1992) "Deeper Life Bible Church in Nigeria." In *New Dimensions in African Christianity,* edited by Paul Gifford. Nairobi: All African Conference of Churches, 135–156.

———. "The Contextual Significance of the Charismatic Movements in Independent Nigeria." *Africa: Journal of the International African Institute* 2, 58: 175–192.

Ter Haar, Gerrie. (1995) "Strangers in the Promised Land: African Christians in Europe." *Exchange* 1, 24: 1–33.

van Dijk, Richard. (1997) "From Camp to Encompassment: Discourses of Transsubjectivity in the Ghanaian Pentecostal Diaspora." *Journal of Religion in Africa* 27, 2: 135–160.

———. (1992) "Young Puritan Preachers in Post-Independence Malawi." *Africa* 2, 62: 159–181.

African Geomancy

African geomancy is a method of divination based on the interpretation of figures or patterns drawn on the ground or other flat surface with grains of sand or similar granular materials. This oracular system with the widest distribution in Africa and the Americas must be distinguished from other forms of locational geomancy such as *feng shui* as practiced in China and other parts of Asia and in various westernized forms in North America and Europe. The most coherent and fully developed system of geomancy was developed by the

Arabs of North Africa. Arab geomancy is known as *Raml*, from *'ilm al-raml* (the science of sand), and this is the form of geomancy found today all around the world. From North Africa, geomancy was carried south with the expansion of Islam from the eighth century CE onward, so that it eventually took root in both West Africa and in East Africa, including Madagascar.

There are several distinct regions of geomantic practice in sub-Saharan Africa and the Americas. The first is Madagascar where Arab colonies existed in the ninth century. Through these outposts of Arab and Muslim culture, *Raml* entered Malagasy culture (the Malagasy being one of the native peoples of the island) and was known as *Sikidy*. Later, it was synthesized with the Malay magico-religious tradition of *Bintana* and the Chinese system of *feng shui* to form a distinctly Malagasy system called *Vintana*.

The second region of sub-Saharan geomancy is in West Africa, which *Raml* reached overland via the Sahara. Among the Mande-speaking peoples of Mali, and especially among the Bamana, it became known as *Cèn, Tiyen* or, *Tyen'* (meaning sand, time, and truth, respectively). Among the Dogon, geomancy is practiced in the mythological context of *Yurugu* (the Pale Fox). And in the nations on the Gulf of Guinea, it was completely reinvented and blended with other local divination systems to form what is called *Fa* and *Ifá*.

In the Americas, *Ifá* is the primary form as it was brought by the Yoruba of Nigeria who were imported to the Americas as slaves by the European nations which colonized the region. In the twenty-first century, it remains a central part of African-derived cultural traditions in Cuba, Puerto Rico, Haiti, Trinidad, Brazil, and the United States.

African geomancy, practiced by traditional healers and scholars alike, became a rich and complex divinatory art, which is used for guidance in making political and strategical decisions, answering mundane questions of everyday life, as well as answering more important and general questions about existence. The geomantic theme is a "mirror" in which an individual may discover more of oneself—reflections of one's personality and of its hidden aspects and influences, including events and forces in the past, the present, and the future. The fundamental common feature of African geomancy is a pattern of binary oppositions of markings grouped into sixteen combinations of four positions—that is, there are sixteen possible geomantic figures (tetragrams), each composed of dots or lines (see sidebar photo and illustration). Each geomantic figure has a name and a corresponding meaning, and may be interpreted either alone or in combination with the other figures. Each ethnic group has its own names for the geomantic figures,

but, wherever they are used, the meaning for each figure is the same.

From the formal point of view, African geomancy, as the most universal of all divinatory systems based on the binary code, is frequently regarded by African-American authors such as Ron Eglash as the cultural origin of digital computing: "In other words, all those ones and zeros, running around in every digital circuit from alarm clocks to supercomputers, originate in African divination."

Manfred Kremser

See also Divination; Ifá

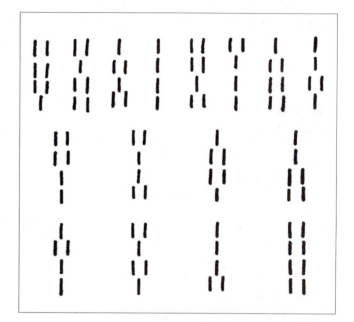

The sixteen figures of the geomantic table of the Bambara geomancer Tiéfing Boare, Sonongo, Mali. The figures are read as follows:

8	7	6	5	4	3	2	1
	12	11	10	9			
	14	15	13	16			

1 Seydou	9 Alah
2 Adam	10 Salomon
3 Mahomed	11 Badara Aliou
4 Idris	12 Noah
5 Abraham	13 Lansseyni
6 Jesus Christus	14 Ton Tigui
7 Omar	15 Ismael
8 Youba	16 Moses

The first 12 figures of a geomantic theme drawn in the sand by a Bambara geomancer in Mali. The figures are read from top right to bottom left. PHOTO COURTESY OF MANFRED KREMSER.

Bibliography

Eglash, Ron. (not dated) *African Fractals*. Online edition of book by same title, Rutgers University Press (1999). www.rpi.edu/~eglash/eglash.dir/afbook.htm.

Jaulin, Robert. (1966) *La Géomancie: Analyse formelle*. Paris: Mouton.

Maupoil, Bernard. (1943) "La Géomancie à l'ancienne Côte des Esclaves." *Travaux et memoires de l'Institut d'Ethnologie* [Paris] 42.

Pennick, Nigel. (1975) *Madagascar Divination*. Cambridge: Fenris-Wolf.

Savage-Smith, Emilie, and Marion B. Smith. (1980) *Islamic Geomancy and a Thirteenth-Century Divinatory Device*. Malibu, CA: Undena Publications.

Skinner, Stephen. (1980) *Terrestrial Astrology: Divination by Geomancy*. London: Routledge and Kegan Paul.

Van Binsbergen, Wim. (1999) *Board-games and divination in global cultural history: a theoretical, comparative and historical perspective on mankala and geomancy in Africa and Asia*. www.geocities.com/Athens/Atrium/2327/gen3/mankala/mankala1.html.

African Methodist Episcopal Church

The African Methodist Episcopal Church is the largest of several predominantly African-American Methodist churches founded in North America. It is commonly referred to as either the A.M.E. or AME church. Its organization and polity are very similar to that of the majority white Methodist denomination (then called the Methodist Episcopal Church, but now the United Methodist Church) from which it formally separated in 1816. Like the United Methodist Church, for example, the supreme governing body of the A.M.E. church is its General Conference, which meets quadrennially. The General Conference selects the bishops. In further similarity to the United Methodists, the A.M.E. Church is divided into episcopal districts (it now has twenty-one), and a bishop elected by the General Conference supervises each district. The discipline of the A.M.E. Church and the United Methodist Church are almost identical. To locate the reasons for the separation of the A.M.E. Churches from other Methodists, one must delve into its historical and sociological background. In brief, the A.M.E. Church arose as the result of an early and forceful protest against racial discrimination within white-dominated churches, and secondarily from the desire to develop and nurture African-American culture and community, both religious and nonreligious.

Establishment of Characteristic Religious and Social Principles

The African Methodist Episcopal Church has its roots in the African-American community of Philadelphia and in the life and work of a remarkable African-American preacher, Richard Allen. Allen, born a slave in Philadelphia in 1760 but sold to a Delaware farmer at age six, moved to Philadelphia in 1785 after buying his freedom and undertaking a brief career as an itinerant Methodist preacher. He became the chief spiritual leader of African-American Methodists in Philadelphia, then meeting in St. George's Methodist Church.

Allen, in 1787, helped to form the Free African Society, an organization of African-Americans of varying religious persuasions that sought to build up the infrastructure for the black community in Philadelphia. When it became evident that the church planned by the Free African Society would affiliate with the Episcopal Church, not the Methodists, Allen left the society, stating that "the plain and simple gospel" of the Methodists was most suitable for African-Americans.

But all was not well with the black Methodist relationship with white Methodists in Philadelphia. After the St. George's Church was renovated in the early 1790s to include a gallery, Allen and a group of black worshippers were disturbed during prayer by a white Methodist deacon who told them that they were sitting in seats reserved for whites. After the prayer, Allen and his friends left the St.

RICHARD ALLEN RECOUNTS THE EVENTS LEADING TO THE ESTABLISHMENT OF THE AFRICAN METHODIST EPISCOPAL CHURCH

A number of us usually attended St. George's church in Fourth street; and when the colored people began to get numerous in attending the church, they moved us from the seats we usually sat on, and placed us around the wall, and on Sabbath morning we went to church and the sexton stood at the door, and told us to go in the gallery. He told us to go, and we would see where to sit. We expected to take the seats over the ones we formerly occupied below, not knowing any better.... Just as we got to the seats, the elder said, "Let us pray." We had not been long upon our knees before I heard considerable scuffling and low talking. I raised my head up and saw one of the trustees, H – M –, having hold of the Rev. Absalom Jones, pulling him up off of his knees, and saying, "You must get up – you must not kneel here." Mr. Jones replied, "Wait until prayer is over." Mr. H – M– said, "No, you must get up now, or I will call for aid and force you away." Mr. Jones said, "Wait until prayer is over, and I will get up and trouble you no more." With that he beckoned to one of the other trustees, Mr. L – S –, to come to his assistance. He came, and went to William White to pull him up. By this time prayer was over, and we went out of the church in a body, and they were no more plagued with us in the church. This raised a great excitement and inquiry among the citizens, in so much that I believe they were ashamed of their conduct.

But my dear Lord was with us, and we were filled with fresh vigor to get a house erected to worship God in.... We got subscription papers out to raise money to build the house of the Lord.... But the elder of the Methodist Church still pursued us. Mr. John McClaskey called upon us and told us if we did not erase our names from the subscription paper, and give up the paper, we would be publicly turned out of meeting.... We told him we had no place of worship; and we did not mean to go to St. George's church any more, as we were so scandalously treated in the presence of all the congregation present; "and if you deny us your name, you cannot seal up the scriptures from us, and deny us a name in heaven. We believe heaven is free for all who worship in spirit and truth." And he said, "So you are determined to go on." We told him, "Yes, God being our helper." He then replied, "We will disown you all from the Methodist connection." We believed if we put our trust in the Lord, he would stand by us.... Notwithstanding we had been so violently persecuted by the elder, we were in favor of being attached to the Methodist connection; for I was confident that there was no religious sect or denomination would suit the capacity of the colored people as well as the Methodist; for the plain and simple gospel suits best for any people; for the unlearned can understand, and the learned are sure to understand; and the reason that the Methodist is so successful in the awakening and conversion of the colored people, the plain doctrine and having a good discipline. But in many cases the preachers would act to please their own fancy, without discipline, till some of them became such tyrants, and more especially to the colored people. They would turn them out of society, giving them no trial, for the smallest offense, perhaps only hearsay. They would frequently, in meeting the class, impeach some of the members of whom they had heard an ill report, and turn them out, ... notwithstanding in the first rise and progress in Delaware state, and elsewhere, the colored people were their greatest support; for there were but few of us free; but the slaves would toil in their little patches many a night until midnight to raise their little truck and sell to get something to support them more than what their masters gave them, and we used often to divide our little support among the white preachers of the Gospel....

I feel thankful that ever I heard a Methodist preach. We are beholden to the Methodists, under God, for the light of the Gospel we enjoy; for all other denominations preached so high-flown that we were not able to comprehend their doctrine.... It is to be awfully feared that the simplicity of the Gospel that was among them fifty years ago, and that they conform more to the world and the fashions thereof, they would fare very little better than the people of the world. The discipline is altered considerably from what it was. We would ask for the good old way, and desire to walk therein.

Source: *The Life Experience and Gospel Labors of the Rt. Rev. Richard Allen.* (1983) Philadelphia, PA: Martin and Boston.

George's Church, never to return. Still, Allen retained some ties with white Methodists. He arranged for the white Methodist bishop, Francis Asbury, to help him consecrate the Bethel African Methodist Church in 1794, and it was Asbury who ordained Allen as a minister five years later in 1799. However, a protracted battle over the ownership and control of the Bethel Church ensued in the early nineteenth century, with the white Methodist ministers of the St. George's Church claiming the right to administer sacraments and to draw a salary of Bethel. Allen and his congregation resisted these encroachments, even taking the white Methodists to court. In April 1816, three months after the Pennsylvania Supreme Court ruled in Allen's favor, Allen called a conference of black Methodists to convene in Philadelphia. Black Methodists from four states—Pennsylvania, Maryland, Delaware, and New Jersey—assembled at Bethel Church in response to Allen's call, and thus inaugurated the African Methodist Episcopal (A.M.E.) Church as a denomination.

Allen was eventually elected and consecrated the first bishop of the fledgling A.M.E. Church, although not until another powerful African-American leader, Daniel Coker, pastor of a black Methodist Church in Baltimore, was first elected to the post, only to decline election, for reasons that are unclear. In succeeding years, Coker would leave the United States in 1820 to serve as a missionary in Liberia, setting up a Methodist church there. From the beginning, the A.M.E. Church was oriented toward expansion. One stronghold of African-American Methodism was Charleston, South Carolina, and Morris Brown, the leader of the black Methodist church there, sent two men to Allen to be ordained. In 1822, many members of the Charleston A.M.E. Church, mercilessly hounded by the South Carolina authorities, were implicated in the revolt against slavery led by Denmark Vesey, a lay leader in Brown's church. Brown himself was forced into exile by the South Carolinian authorities, and he chose to come to Philadelphia, where he was welcomed by Allen. Morris Brown later became the second bishop of the A.M.E. Church. The A.M.E. Church would not return to Charleston until 1865, after Emancipation, although in pre-war decades it developed roots in other southern or border state cities, such as Washington, D.C., Louisville, St. Louis, and New Orleans.

The A.M.E. Church also expanded rapidly to the West in the early decades of the nineteenth centuries. Two of the more energetic missionaries were William Paul Quinn, a native of India who later became the fourth bishop of the A.M.E. Church, and Jarena Lee. Lee, a New Jersey native and the widow of an A.M.E. minister, suc-ceeded after several efforts in gaining Richard Allen's informal blessing for her ministry in 1818, and she established a soon well-accepted pattern in itinerant evangelism by eloquent, Spirit-filled A.M.E. women. When Lee, at the 1840 and 1844 General Conferences, attempted to gain formal ordination, she encountered very strong resistance from male ministers. The first woman to be ordained a minister in the A.M.E. Church was Sarah Ann Hughes of North Carolina in 1885, but Hughes's ordination was removed two years later. The first woman to receive an uncontested ordination to the A.M.E. Church was Rebecca Glover in 1948. More than six hundred women in the A.M.E Church are ordained ministers today.

National and International Expansion and Evangelism

The mid- and late nineteenth centuries saw the fruition of many of these evangelistic efforts. A British Methodist Church was formed among fugitive slaves in Canada, but the B.M.E. Church was reunited with the A.M.E. Church in 1884. In the aftermath of the California Gold Rush, Thomas M. D. Ward was sent as a missionary to the West Coast. A California Conference was formed in 1865. But the A.M.E. Church expanded most rapidly in the southern states after the Civil War. Due to the tireless efforts of such missionaries as Henry McNeal Turner and Richard Cain, both of whom were later elected bishops, by 1890 three-quarters of the membership of the A.M.E. Church was to be found in the eleven states which had formerly constituted the Confederate States of America.

The late nineteenth century saw numerous attempts to establish A.M.E. missions outside North America. Haiti was a country that the church often targeted for its missions. Examples include the work of Scipio Bean and Richard Robinson in the 1820s, and Charles W. Mossell in the 1880s. But the work of missionaries from this fervently Protestant denomination came to little, not making much of an impression on people who had been shaped by a culture steeped in Catholic and vodou religions. Perhaps the most significant contemporary aspect of the A.M.E. Church's Haitian work was its medical missions carried forward by its Service and Development Agency, Inc. (SADA). SADA's Child Survival Project has brought about a reduction of infant mortality in the regions that it serves.

The A.M.E. Church made persistent efforts to gain converts in Liberia and Sierra Leone, founding church conferences there in 1891. Besides a small group of devoted settlers from the United States and Great Britain, it made the most progress in attracting converts from indigenous ranks. Later, A.M.E. churches were established in the neighboring countries of Nigeria, Ghana, and the Ivory Coast. Recent civil warfare in Liberia and Sierra Leone has drastically affected the church's work in West Africa, making visitation of nearly half the churches in Liberia by its bishop impossible in 1997. The church's most successful missionary efforts have come in southern Africa. There, an independent Methodist church founded by M. M. Mokone and led by indigenous Africans applied to join the A.M.E. Church in 1895 was accepted by the General Conference of the following year. By some estimates, of the 3.5 million members claimed by the A.M.E. Church worldwide, as many as one million may be located in Africa and the Caribbean, the bulk of these overseas members in southern Africa.

Social and Cultural Activism

The A.M.E. Church was also noted for its efforts on behalf of education. The chief promoter of education within the denomination was Daniel A. Payne, an 1835 graduate of Gettysburg Theological Seminary and a convert to the A.M.E. Church from Lutheranism. Payne convinced the 1844 General Conference to prescribe a minimum level of studies for A.M.E. pastors, to be achieved either through a school education or through self-study. Payne was elected a bishop in 1852. He was instrumental in the foundation near Xenia, Ohio, of the A.M.E. Church's leading educational institution, Wilberforce University, in 1863, when the Methodist Episcopal Church withdrew its support for a school for African-Americans in the same location that had been established in 1856, seven years earlier. Wilberforce University received funds from both its denomination and the state of Ohio, an arrangement that ceased in 1946 when the state insisted on the separation of its funding from that of the church, and founded Central State University next door to Wilberforce. Numerous other A.M.E. schools were founded after the Civil War. Those that survive today include Morris Brown College in Atlanta, Georgia; Paul Quinn College in Waco, Texas; Allen College in Columbia, South Carolina; Shorter Junior College in North Little Rock, Arkansas; and Edward Waters College in Jacksonville, Florida. In addition, the church sponsors two theological seminaries, Payne, which is affiliated with and located at Wilberforce, and Turner, affiliated with the Interdenominational Theological Center in Atlanta. The Interdenominational Center is a consortium of six seminaries of various theological persuasions (Methodist, Baptist, Pentecostal) that have joined together to pool their course offerings without an actual merger.

The African Methodist Episcopal Church was a major political, social, and cultural force for African-Americans

An advertisement for Wilberforce University that appeared in the December 1911 issue of *The Crisis: A Record of the Darker Races*, published by the NAACP in New York City.

during the late nineteenth and early twentieth centuries. The African-American historian George Washington Williams scarcely exaggerated when he stated that the A.M.E. Church "exerted a wider and better influence among the Negro race than any other organization created and managed by Negroes." Sometimes the A.M.E. Church was referred to as "a nation within a nation." From the Reconstruction forward, many A.M.E. Church ministers and bishops were politically influential. Virtually all of the important debates within the African-American community were conducted at least in part within the A.M.E. denominational framework, especially the pages of the church's influential quarterly journal, the A.M.E. *Church Review* (founded in 1884) and its weekly newspaper, the *Christian Recorder*. Bishop Daniel Payne was renowned for his Puritanism, ecumenism, and insistence on education. Henry McNeal Turner, elected bishop in 1880, was well known for his advocacy of black emigration to Africa and black nationalism.

The large-scale migration of African-Americans from the South to the North, beginning about 1915, increased the opportunities for A.M.E. political and social involvement. Reverdy Ransom, elected to the bishopric in 1924, was an influential advocate of the social gospel. Even such secularly minded men as Booker T. Washington and W. E. B. Du Bois did not neglect to bring their perspectives to A.M.E. periodicals and church conferences. During the height of the civil rights movement, the A.M.E. Church counted among its members such activists as Oliver Brown, chief plaintiff of the Brown *v.* Board of Education lawsuit, which resulted in the 1954 Supreme Court's landmark decision in favor of school desegregation; Daisy Bates, leader of the 1956 effort to desegregate schools in Little Rock, Arkansas; and Roy Wilkins, long-time executive director of the NAACP. Brown Chapel A.M.E. Church was an important movement base during the voting-rights campaign in Selma, Alabama, in 1965. Some A.M.E. churches in the South, such as Mount Zion A.M.E. Church in Longdale, Mississippi were bombed; J. A. Delaine, a minister in South Carolina, suffered the loss of his church and his home to fire after taking an active stance in favor of school desegregation in 1951. This denominational orientation toward political activism continues until the present day. Former U.S. Representative Floyd Flake of the Allen A.M.E. Church in Queens, New York, is perhaps the most notable of many A.M.E. ministers who possess a large political influence.

The A.M.E. Church has also possessed a great deal of influence in the Black Theology movement of the late 1960s and beyond. Bishop John D. Bright and three other A.M.E. ministers were signatories to a widely noticed statement by the National Committee of Negro Churchmen (later known as the National Council of Black Churchmen), that spoke forcefully on behalf of the "Black Power" movement. Perhaps the most influential advocate of Black Theology, Professor James Cone of Union Theological Seminary, author of numerous works including *Martin and Malcolm and America: A Dream or a Nightmare*, grew up in an A.M.E. Church in Bearden, Arkansas, and remains a member today.

Stephen W. Angell

See also African Methodist Episcopal Zion Church; Black Theology; Music, Black Hymnody; Social Activism; United States, African Religions in

Bibliography

Angell, Stephen W. (1992) *Bishop Henry McNeal Turner and African-American Religion in the South.* Knoxville: University of Tennessee Press.

Angell, Stephen W., and Anthony Pinn, eds. (2000) *Social Protest Thought in the African Methodist Episcopal Church, 1862–1939.* Knoxville: University of Tennessee Press.

Campbell, James T. (1995) *Songs of Zion: The African Methodist Episcopal Church in the United States and South Africa.* New York: Oxford University Press.

Dickerson, Dennis C. (1995) *Research Notes on A.M.E. Church History.* Nashville: AMEC Sunday School Union.

Gravely, Will B. (1997) "The Rise of African Churches in America (1786–1822): Re-examining the Contexts." In *African-American Religion: Interpretive Essays in History and Culture*, edited by Timothy Fulop and Albert Raboteau. New York: Routledge, 133–152.

Gregg, Howard D. (1980) *History of the African Methodist Episcopal Church (The Black Church in Action).* Nashville, TN: The AMEC Sunday School Union.

Gregg, Robert. (1993) *Sparks from the Anvil of Oppression: Philadelphia's African Methodists and Southern Migrants, 1890–1940.* Philadelphia: Temple University Press.

Sernett, Milton, ed. (1985) *Afro-American Religious History: A Documentary Witness.* Durham: Duke University Press.

Wright, Richard R., Jr. (1963) *The Bishops of the African Methodist Episcopal Church.* Philadelphia: AMEC Sunday School Union.

The African Methodist Episcopal Zion Church

The African Methodist Episcopal Zion Church is one of the seven major independent black denominations in the United States. It arose in the context of evangelical Christianity, Methodism, and the growing sense of African-American Christians, particularly in northern states, that they should pursue separate denominational paths from whites. These independent-minded African-American Christians sought nonracist treatment in church worship and governance, freedom to practice ministry, better efforts at evangelizing their unchurched racial siblings, and stronger stands against slavery.

The AME Zion's origins date to the mid-1790s, when a number of African-American Methodists under the leadership of William Miller and others became dissatisfied with the discriminatory treatment received in a predominantly white Methodist Episcopal Church congregation in New York City and withdrew for separate worship. For a while this independent black congregation continued its affiliation with the mother denomination. It became an independent congregation in the 1820s, originally calling itself the African Methodist Episcopal Church. ("Zion" was added to the name in 1848 to avoid confusion with another black Methodist body.) Also during the early 1820s, a number of congregations from several states of the Northeast united and declared themselves an independent Methodist connection, naming James Varick as their first superintendent.

The AME Zion Church grew steadily but slowly in numbers prior to the Civil War. During the 1850s there was a severe schism among Zionites involving questions of episcopal equality and governance structure. By the early 1860s, however, this rift was healed and the AME Zion joined the AME, various black Baptist associations and conventions, and some white denominations in journeying south to missionize and organize churches, incorporating great numbers of members into its organization. This extension southward had a dramatic impact on the denomination. The AME Zion grew from approximately 5,000 members at the eve of the Civil War to approximately 700,000 by 1916. Like other

Pastor Esther Dozier and some members of the congregation on the steps of the A.M.E. Zion Church in Great Barrington, Massachusetts, in July 2000. The cornerstone of the church was laid in 1882 and African-American scholar and activist W. E. B. Du Bois attended the church as a teenager. PHOTO COURTESY OF KAREN CHRISTENSEN.

THE AFRICAN METHODIST EPISCOPAL ZION CHURCH AND ANTISLAVERY

Many early Black churches in the United States and their pastors were involved in the antislavery movement in the years before the Civil War. The following account was provided by Thomas James, the pastor of the African Methodist Episcopal Zion Church in New Bedford, Massachusetts. It details his and church member's efforts to win freedom for a black slave woman brought north on vacation by her owner.

We took the girl to a chamber on the upper floor of the residence of the Rev. Joel Knight, and that evening we prepared to lie down before the door. Lucy displayed the handkerchief as she had promised, and when we questioned her about it, answered, "Master told me to do it; he is coming to take me home." At this we quietly called together twenty men from the colored district of the place, and they took seats in the church close at hand, ready for any emergency. At one o'clock in the morning, Ludlam appeared on the scene, with the backing of a dozen men, carrying a ladder, to effect the rescue. The sheriff hailed them but they gave no answer, whereat our party of colored men sallied forth, and the rescuers fled in all directions. The entire town was now agog over the affair.

By the intervention of the local police the girl was finally escorted to Boston, where she appeared in court, asked for her freedom and received it the next day, despite another attempt by her owner to "rescue" her by intercepting the sheriff's posse. She later married, had children, and continued to live unmolested in the North.

Source: Bradley, David H., Jr. (1956) *A History of the African Methodist Episcopal Zion Church.* Nashville, TN: Parthenon Press, 113–115.

black denominations, Zion during the nineteenth century also moved west with the historical expansion of the nation. By the mid-1880s there were Zion congregations in Missouri, Wyoming, Oregon, California, and Nevada.

Partially because of criticisms from other Methodist connections regarding the validity of its episcopacy, Zion ceased to elect or reelect its chief officers every four years, instead electing them for life since 1880 and completely substituting the term "bishop" for "superintendent" in ordinary and official usage. Zion has always allowed more lay participation than its major Methodist counterparts. Indeed, the choice of the title "superintendent" rather than "bishop" (or at least the interchangeable use of these titles) during the early decades, and the requirement that they stand for reelection every four years represent attempts to curtail possible abuses of episcopal governance.

Since the mid-1860s the Zion denomination has seriously engaged in merger attempts or conversations at one time or another with each of the following: the AME, the Christian Methodist Episcopal Church (another black group formed in 1870), and the Methodist Episcopal Church. As recently as the 1990s there were serious discussions involving Zion, the two other black groups, and the mainly white but racially diverse United Methodist Church.

Since antebellum years Zion has carried the nickname, "the Freedom Church," because so many abolitionist, antislavery, and civil rights luminaries were affiliated or associated with that denomination at some point. Among these were Sojourner Truth, Harriet Tubman, Frederick Douglass, Jermain Loguen, James W. Hood, and Alexander Walters. Harriet Tubman helped to develop the Underground Railroad as a secret network of persons, activities, and locations aiding refugees from slavery to find freedom in the North and Canada. James Walker Hood, later bishop, not only missionized very successfully in the Civil War and postwar South, he also played a great role in Reconstruction and other political activities in North Carolina during the late 1860s and early 1870s. Alexander Walters, also a bishop, was a major force behind the formation of the Afro-American Council and the National Association for the Advancement of Colored People during the early 1900s.

The AME Zion Church achieved the distinction of being among the very first American denominations to ordain women as elders (full ordination to the pulpit ministry) when Bishop Charles Calvin Pettey, with the approval of the Baltimore and Philadelphia Annual Conference, ordained Mrs. Mary Small in 1898. Unlike a few other groups that preceded Zion in ordaining women, Mrs. Small's appointment as elder was officially recognized in

1900 throughout the church and paved the way for other Zion women pulpit ministers, including Julia Foote and Florence Randolph. Indeed, during the 1890s there were a number of women activists in Zion, such as Sarah Pettey, an early feminist who supported women's equality in church and society.

In the late nineteenth and early twentieth centuries those persons actively involved in the Holiness movement, committed to the traditional Methodist belief that it was possible to be so filled with God's love that one could live free of all known sin, found a welcome home in Zion, with many of its most prominent bishops at the time acting as major proponents of the movement.

The AME Zion Church has often been and continues to be confused with its larger rival, the AME Church, even in academic circles. This confusion is understandable because of their common derivation from Methodism at about the same time, the similarity in names, and commonalities in church structure, and governance from the Methodist Episcopal Church.

Today the AMEZ flourishes with 2.2 million members, making it the second largest black Methodist denomination. Its schools are Livingstone College and Hood Theological Seminary in Salisbury, North Carolina; Clinton Junior College in Rock Hill, South Carolina; and Lomax-Hannon Junior College in Greenville, Alabama. Overseas schools are AME Zion Community College University in Monrovia, Liberia, and Hood-Speaks Theological Seminary in Nigeria. Much of its operational activities, including its publishing house, are headquartered in Charlotte, North Carolina. Zion has twelve active and five retired bishops. It publications include the newspaper, *The Star of Zion*, and the journal, *AME Zion Quarterly Review*.

Sandy Dwayne Martin

See also African Methodist Episcopal Church

Bibliography

Martin, Sandy Dwayne. (1999) *For God and Race: The Religious and Political Leadership of AMEZ Bishop James Walker Hood*. Columbia, SC: University of South Carolina Press.

McMurray, George W., and Ndugu G. B. T'Ofori-Atta. (1993) *Mother Zion African Methodist Episcopal Zion Church: 200 Years of Evangelism and Liberation*. Charlotte, NC: AME Zion Publishing House.

Walls, William J. (1974) *The African Methodist Episcopal Zion Church: Reality of the Black Church*. Charlotte, NC: AME Zion Publishing House.

African Orthodox Church

The African Orthodox Church is an independent African-American church that emerged in part because of segregation and discrimination in white American churches, which prevented African-American clergy from rising to the highest positions in the church. Despite the name, the church is not affiliated with the (Eastern) Orthodox Church. Instead, its theology and practices are closest to those of Roman Catholicism, with an emphasis on programs that benefit the African-American community and on the uses of images of a Black Madonna and a Black Christ.

The church was founded by George Alexander McGuire. McGuire was born on the island of Antigua in the Caribbean in 1866, attended school there, and was ordained a Moravian pastor in 1893. He moved to the United States

George Alexander McGuire, founder of the African Orthodox Church and Chaplain-General of the United Negro Improvement Association. PHOTO COURTESY OF RANDALL BURKETT.

CHURCH OF ST. JOHN COLTRANE

The best-known African Orthodox Church is the St. John's African Orthodox Church, a small, storefront church in San Francisco. Better known as the Church of St. John Coltrane, it is named for legendary jazz saxophonist John Coltrane, who died at the age of 40 in 1967. Coltrane's life was marred by addictions to heroin and alcohol and a compulsive eating problem. In 1957 he experienced a "spiritual awakening," and his music during the last ten years of life was imbued with a deep spirituality. Members of the church consider Coltrane a saint and worship centers on performances of his music and dancing. The church was founded by Bishop Franzo King, a former hairdresser, who was drawn to Coltrane's music in 1965 and began playing the saxophone himself. In 1971 King founded the One Mind Temple Evolutionary Transitional Body of Christ which in 1982 joined the African Orthodox Church. The church draws a mixed-race membership, provides food to the poor, and promotes Coltrane's music.

in 1894, joined the Episcopal Church in 1895, and was ordained in 1897. Following a series of pastoral assignments, in 1905 he was appointed archdeacon for the African-American community in Arkansas, the highest position in the church available to an African-American. He was successful in attracting new members in Arkansas and, in 1911, was made field secretary of the American Church Institute for Negroes, making him the most prominent African-American official in the Episcopal Church. In 1913, he returned to Antigua and spent the next five years in the Caribbean, where he was attracted to the work of Marcus Garvey and his Universal Negro Improvement Association (UNIA). After returning to the United States in 1919, McGuire left the Episcopal Church and founded the Good Shephard Independent Episcopal Church in New York, and several other churches in his travels as he worked for the UNIA. But Garvey rejected his dream of a single black church linked to the UNIA, and McGuire was expelled from the organization.

On 21 September 1921, McGuire founded the African Orthodox Church with the support of other immigrants from the Caribbean islands. He was elected the first bishop. McGuire sought but failed to receive consecration from the Roman Catholic and Russian Orthodox Churches but later in the month, received consecration from Archbishop Rene Vilatte of the American Catholic Church, which Vilatte had founded in 1915.

Employing the same skills and devotion he had used while serving the Episcopal Church, McGuire led the new church through a period of rapid growth and expansion. In the years up to his death in 1934, the church added parishes in Brooklyn, Pittsburgh, New Haven, Nova Scotia, Cuba, Santo Domingo, Philadelphia, the Bahamas, Florida, Boston, and South Africa. The church also established an order of deaconesses, opened the Endich Theological Seminary, and expanded the leadership to four bishops. At the time of McGuire's death, the church had about 30,000 members.

Following his death, the church was divided by factionalism, the seminary could not maintain a regular schedule, and disillusioned members left the church for others. Two dissident churches, the African Orthodox Church of New York and Massachusetts and the Holy African Church incorporated in Florida, were founded and some other dissidents affiliated with the North American Old Roman Catholic Church. A series of lawsuits over the use of the church's name added to the rifts. Some order was restored in 1945 when the church and the North American Old Roman Catholic Church agreed to intercommunion and in 1964 when the church and the Holy African Church reunited. In the 1980s, the church had seventeen parishes and about 5,000 members and was divided into the African Orthodox Church and the African Orthodox Church of the West, which was founded in 1984.

David Levinson

See also Black Theology

Bibliography

Murphy, Larry G., J. Gordon Melton, and Gary L. Ward, eds. (1993) *Encyclopedia of African American Religions.* New York: Garland.

Terry-Thompson, A. C. (1956) *The History of the African Orthodox Church.* N.p.

African Pentecostalism in the Netherlands

In several of the larger cities of the Netherlands, sizable communities of migrants originating from Ghana can be found. These communities are characterized by a remarkable and vibrant interest for Pentecostal churches that have been founded in their midst under Ghanaian leadership. Since the mid-1980s, between twenty to thirty Ghanaian Pentecostal churches have been established. Due to both a process of fission within these churches and continued immigration of Ghanaians, this number is still growing. Similar developments have been reported from other Western countries, such as the United Kingdom, United States, Germany, and some Scandinavian countries. Moreover, the rise of migration from Africa in conjunction with the spread of African Pentecostal churches to other parts of the world has not only been noticed from Ghana but also from other countries, such as Nigeria and the former Zaire.

This phenomenon is part of what can be regarded the globalization of charismatic Christianity, a process whereby a variety of faith gospel and Pentecostal churches from different parts of the world have begun to link up and create global networks of exchange and mutual support (see Poewe 1994; Brouwer et al. 1996; Coleman, forthcoming). The cultural specificity of this globalizing process and the manner in which it is received locally, that is, in Africa, has, however, been little studied (see however Van Dijk 1997, 1999, forthcoming).

Ghanaian Pentecostal Churches in the Netherlands

The rise of Ghanaian Pentecostalism in the Netherlands, specifically its prominence outstripping that of any other denominational affiliation in this migrant community, corresponded closely to the growth of the entire Ghanaian population in Dutch society. Since the late 1970s the Netherlands experienced the emergence of a number of immigrant groups from sub-Saharan African countries, Ghanaians being one of them. Whereas the large minority groups mainly consist of people from Morocco, Turkey, or Surinam (each with several of hundred-thousands), within the entire African population in Dutch society of tens of thousands, the Ghanaian community became one of the largest, sharing that position with Somalians, Ethiopians, Zairians, Sudanese, and, most recently, Nigerians. The official number of Ghanaians residing in the Netherlands stands at approximately fifteen thousand, but unrecorded and illegal immigration has led to an estimated doubling of that number.

Most Ghanaians have settled in Amsterdam and in the Hague. Like the migrants themselves the Ghanaian Pentecostal churches have largely been established in the low-cost housing areas of these two cities: in Amsterdam particularly in an area called "de Bijlmer," in The Hague in and around an area known as the "Schilderswijk." Influential churches among them are the Church of Pentecost, the Resurrection Power Evangelical Ministries, Bethel Prayer Ministries, International Central Gospel Church, and Acts Revival Church. Some of these and other churches are "branches" from churches in Ghana, others have, however, been founded in the Netherlands and are establishing congregations "back home" in Ghana.

Membership of these Pentecostal churches varies between 100 to 500 adults and often comprises, in addition to Ghanaians, other English-speaking sub-Saharan African nationals. It is for that reason that although major parts of the sermons are conducted in one of Ghana's most popular languages, that of Twi, simultaneous translation into English takes place. Other churches have decided to switch to English entirely. At these churches occasionally translation back into Twi takes place specifically for those Ghanaians (a minority) who haven't mastered English before they migrated to Europe. Dutch membership is not very common (the language barrier is an important factor) nor are relations with Dutch churches well developed, not even with those Dutch churches that could also be characterized as Pentecostal. Nor are there extensive contacts with Pentecostal groups of other migrant communities, such as those of the French-speaking, mostly Zairian/Congolese groups known as "Combats Spirituelles." There is a slight predominance of young adult males over women in these churches, which reflects the overall composition of the Ghanaian and wider West African migrant population.

The popularity of Ghanaian Pentecostal churches in these migrant communities can be explained by pointing at a range of factors. One set of reasons for that popularity relates to the many social and religious functions these churches and their leaders fulfill in view of the migrant's position in Dutch (Western) society. Another dimension is associated with some particular features and symbolic meanings of its ideology and ritual practice, which bear specific reference to elements of the African cosmology. A third aspect of its popularity relates to the historical development of Pentecostalism in Ghana and West Africa, and its current significance in the public domain. In this contemporary setting its salient transnational dimensions coincide with a widely shared fascination in Ghana with the West, and with an eagerness to travel abroad in search of fortune.

Pentecostalism in Ghana

To begin with this last-mentioned dimension, mission Pentecostalism was introduced on the West African coast by missionaries from Full Gospel and Faith Gospel churches from England and the United States in the first decades of this century. Marked by episodes of mass revivalism, this mission-based form of Pentecostalism expanded and gained denominational features through the 1940s. Churches such as the Assemblies of God were able to open branches both in rural and urban places. Mainly because of their emphasis on possession by the Holy Spirit, glossolalia, and faith and prayer healing, they maintained their distinguishable features from countless other churches that originated on the basis of a syncretism between Christianity and African forms of healing, possession, and worship. These last-mentioned African Christian churches were usually inspired by the charismatic powers of a healing prophet who combined African divination systems, medicines, and the like with elements of Western Christianity. Pentecostalism, however, though beginning to Africanize its leadership and liturgy from the early 1950s onward, remained vehemently opposed to that form of syncretism. Toward the end of the 1950s, the very first Ghanaian denominational Pentecostal church was established as an off-shoot from an earlier mission-based predecessor. This church, the Church of Pentecost, to date is the largest and most influential of this type of denominational Pentecostalism in Ghana. It has actively supported the establishment of the Ghana Pentecostal Council, which has been joined by approximately 130 congregations in recent years.

Toward the end of the 1970s, a new, largely charismatic type of Pentecostal church emerged. The first to appear was Bishop Duncan Williams's Action Faith Ministries, later followed by the highly influential International Central Gospel Church of Dr. Mensa Otabil. Within a couple of years these churches were able to attract a massive following of mainly young people and those belonging to the emergent middle classes within Ghana's rapidly expanding urban areas (in particular the cities of Accra and Kumasi). This success of charismatic Pentecostalism in Africa's cities and among its young urbanites has been reported from other countries as well (see Van Dijk [on Malawi] 1998; Marshall [on Nigeria] 1998; Maxwell [on Zimbabwe] 1998). These energetic churches are predominantly characterized by strong, personal leadership of its founder; by an entrepreneurial style of operation; by their highly efficient use of all forms of public media, including new technologies of communication, printing, music, and video recording; and by an ideological emphasis on personal success, prosperity, and salvation. Becoming "born-again" is stressed, not only as a trajectory for full-fledged membership, but moreover as a way of disentangling oneself from old ties and obligations in seeking success, fortune, and prestige in a new life and (religious) environment. Virtues are emphasized, smoking and drinking are abhorred, and all sorts of moral commitments are usually put in place for the confirmed believer. Particularly among secondary, college, and university students, the new Pentecostal movements took root and these groups are still important sources for positions of leadership within the churches' organizational structures. Many of the higher educated perceive the rise of Pentecostalism as a sign of revival and moral rejuvenation of society.

The popularity of these churches was further enhanced by the fact that many of them began linking up with global networks of exchange and claimed an international outlook and level of ambition and aspiration. Many churches began placing terms like "international," "world," and "global" in their names and actively ventured to establish branches outside Ghana, particularly in the West. In Ghana this created an appealing image of international prestige, success, and promise of "greener pastures" elsewhere, in a society facing a retrenching economy, an increasing marginalization of its international position, and decreasing possibilities of migration to the West resulting from a tightening of Western immigration laws. By putting up flags at the pulpit of the countries to which a church has been able to branch out to successfully, this image of international prestige is usually visualized.

African Cosmology and the Appeal of Deliverance

In addition to these modern international features the ideological claims of these churches contributed greatly to their popular appeal. Their ideology stresses the creation of a modern personhood and a modern society by bringing the past and its traditions under moral supervision. In deliverance rituals, which are considered vital for every believer, a close inspection of the individual's personal past, the traditional rituals one may have been exposed to, or the influence of the ancestors, may determine that person's present state of affairs. Whereas the mainline Christian churches deny the existence and efficacy of occult forces in society, these Pentecostal churches rather take their influence seriously and perceive them to be part of the powers that are embedded in ancestry and kinship relations. Pentecostalism thereby offers for many a powerful ideology and ritual practice to bring circumstances and one's personal fortune under some form of moral control. Among Pentecostal groups the general feeling is that an individual cannot achieve progress unless ties with the family are inspected and delivered from its circumspect ancestral roots. In view of the worsening socioeconomic conditions of Ghanaian society, many tend to consider this ritual deliverance from those powers that block progress and prosperity as highly valuable.

Pentecostal's demonology rests on an implied and rigid diabolization of the realm of ancestral powers, spirits, and traditional healing systems that are part of the local African cosmology. It is in that sense that anthropological studies interpret the popular success of their (deliverance) ritual practice as a form of religious modernity: a discourse that creates sharp distinctions between the past and the present in terms of the inferior against the superior (see for extensive discussions Van Dijk 1998; Marshall 1998; Meyer 1998).

The Social Role of Pentecostal Churches in the Diaspora

Many of these ideological and ritual elements are brought forward by the Pentecostal churches in the Diaspora. In the migrant communities, the churches fulfill many important social functions, which on the one hand deal with the conditions that are encountered by living as a stranger in a host society, but on the other hand also deal with the obligations toward the family in Ghana. Although kinship relations are an essential part of cultural identity, these churches, because of their ideological orientation, do not regard themselves as custodians of that cultural heritage in the Diaspora. Instead, kinship obligations and the authority of the family in important aspects of life, such as birth, marriage, and death are critically examined. The churches can be seen to create "Christianized" versions of the rituals that usually accompany such occasions.

With regard to the Dutch host society, the churches are marked by preserving a critical distance. Church leaders are often consulted by members in times of difficulties with Dutch authorities and institutions, for seeking help in finding jobs, housing, or schooling and for sorting out personal perspectives for settling successfully in society. In addition to these support systems, Pentecostal churches convey the sense that Western society is embroiled in much immoral conduct. True believers therefore should focus on those domains of social interaction that are fully determined neither by such Western influences, nor by certain cultural traditions in Ghana. Becoming part of globalized charismatic Christian networks, as many of these churches in the Netherlands have done, appears to provide the kind of ideological ground from which this two-pronged ideological distance has been developed.

Rijk van Dijk

See also African Charismatics; Pentecostalism in Africa

Bibliography

Brouwer, Steve, Paul Gifford, and Susan Rose. (1996) *Exporting the American Gospel: Global Christian Fundamentalism.* London: Routledge.

Coleman, Simon. (forthcoming) *The Globalisation of Charismatic Christianity: Spreading the Gospel of Prosperity.* Cambridge: Cambridge University Press.

Marshall, Ruth. (1998) "Mediating the Global and the Local in Nigerian Pentecostalism." *Journal of Religion in Africa* 28, 3: 278–315.

Maxwell, David. (1998) "'Delivered from the spirit of poverty?': Pentecostalism, Prosperity and Modernity in Zimbabwe." *Journal of Religion in Africa* 28, 3: 350–373.

Meyer, Brigit. (1998) "'Make a Complete Break with the Past.' Memory and Postcolonial Modernity in Ghanaian Pentecostalist Discourse." In *Memory and the Postcolony,* edited by R. P. Werbner. London: Zed Books, Postcolonial Identities Series, 182–208.

Poewe, Karla, ed. (1994) *Charismatic Christianity as a Global Culture.* Columbia, SC: University of South Carolina Press.

Van Dijk, Rijk. (1997) "From Camp to Encompassment: Discourses of Transsubjectivity in the Ghanaian Pentecostal Diaspora." *Journal of Religion in Africa* 27, 2: 135–169.

———. (1998) "Pentecostalism, Cultural Memory and the State: Contested Representations of Time in Postcolonial Malawi." In *Memory and the Postcolony,* edited by R. P. Werbner. London: Zed Books, Postcolonial Identities Series, 155–181.

———. (1999) "The Pentecostal Gift. Ghanaian Charismatic Churches and the Moral Innocence of the Global Economy." In *Modernity on a Shoestring,* edited by R. Fardon, W. van Binsbergen, and R. van Dijk. Leiden and London: Eidos, 71–90.

———. (forthcoming) "Time and Transcultural Technologies of the Self in the Ghanaian Pentecostal Diaspora." In *Pentecostalism and Transnationalism,* edited by Andre Corten and Ruth Marshall. London: Hurst Publishers.

African Traditional Religion
See African Geomancy; Akan Religion; Bushman Religion; Diabolism; Dinka Religion; Diola Prophets; Divination, African; Healing in Sub-Saharan Africa; Kongo Religion; Ndembu Religion; Nuer Religion; Ogun; Oromo Religion; Oshun; Pastoralist Cosmologies; Pilgrimage; Pygmy Religion; Religions Skepticism; Secret Societies; West African Religions; Yoruba Religion; Zande Religion; Zar; Zulu Religion

African Zoar United Methodist Church

In 1787, not all African-Americans who worshipped at St. George's Methodist Church in Philadelphia left with Richard Allen (the founder of the Bethel African Methodist Episcopal Church in Philadelphia) and Absalom Jones (the founder of the African Episcopal Church of St. Thomas). Another group left in 1794 and temporarily met in their homes in Northern Liberties, a district outside the city. Subsequently the small group worshipped at a building at Fourth and Brown Streets and chose the name of Zoar for their church. More than one hundred years later, W. E. B. Du Bois (1899: 22) noted that the church was organized in Northern Liberties because "the Methodists of St. George's viewing with some chagrin the widespread withdrawal of Negroes from their body, established a mission at Camperdown . . . which eventually became the present Zoar Church."

As St. George's mission, Zoar served several purposes for the Incorporated Methodist Church: its presence removed more blacks physically from St. George's, but did not totally eliminate them from Methodism, and it stemmed the tide of blacks who were seeking autonomy from the denomination. The church was dedicated in 1796. In the 1880s, one of its pastors would write in the Minutes of the Zoar Church that "the organization of [Zoar] and the construction of the little church building followed the difficulties which is seen in the race question which grew more out of suspicious frictions than it did out of fact on the part of Zoar M.E. Church."

The lot at Fourth and Brown was purchased by its congregants in 1804 for $570.00 according to the rules and discipline of the Incorporated Methodist Episcopal Church, which stipulated that the members of the African Zoar Church would permit those authorized by the General Conference to preach there. For the next thirty-one years, those who preached at African Zoar were always white. All the early black Methodists continued the practice of separate seating by gender, contributed financially to the Incorporated Methodist Church, and had little autonomy in their own churches. Several years after purchasing the property, eighteen members left Zoar and established Union Mission less than two blocks away.

Racial conflict erupted in Northern Liberties in 1813 and Zoar was destroyed. It was rebuilt, but uneasiness persisted. Although many black Methodists severed relations with the Incorporated Methodist Episcopal Church in Philadelphia and formed separate denominations, Zoar's congregation remained at Fourth and Brown Streets and under the control of St. George's. Never averaging more than fifty-six members through the 1830s, Zoar maintained a presence in Northern Liberties in spite of conflict within and without.

More members left in 1837 because of "tension between the members who lived in the Northern part of the city and those who resided in the Southern section" (Dickerson, March 1886: 2–3). However, despite "incursions in its membership," Zoar continued to expand, although not always numerically.

In 1835, Zoar, along with other churches under St. George's charge, became autonomous. Perry Tilghman, a porter, was the first black pastor assigned to Zoar. The congregation began renovating the small building. Remaining within the Methodist Episcopal denomination, in 1837, Zoar received its charter from the Commonwealth of Pennsylvania.

Members of African Zoar were dedicated to their race, the Methodist church, and their community. African Zoar was a stop on the Underground Railroad, and, in 1838 a public meeting was held at the church to raise funds for the Vigilant (Fugitive Aid) Association and Committee (Blockson 1981). Evidence of the influence that Zoar began to exercise is apparent when, in 1846, a joint resolution from Zoar Church and John Wesley Chapel, another black Methodist church, requested that black preachers, appointed to take charge of the black churches, "be authorized to travel within and without the bounds of the Conference to receive collections for their aid" (Dickerson, March 1886: 3). Later in 1852, the first Convention of Colored Local Preachers and Laymen met at Zoar. This meeting was the beginning of the formation of the Delaware Conference, to which, beginning in 1864, all black Methodist churches belonged. (The Delaware Conference was dissolved one hundred years later.)

Because Zoar's members were leaving Northern Liberties and the neighborhood was in decline, Zoar followed its members to its present location at Twelfth and Melon Streets in 1883. The church was rebuilt in 1897. As the new century dawned, Zoar was ministering to new and old members and becoming part of and establishing a new community. Always attentive to the needs of African-Americans, Zoar has been socially and politically active in North Philadelphia. In 1970, more land was purchased in order to construct the Licorish Educational Building, which was completed in 1985.

The term "Mother" is used to refer to African Zoar because it is the oldest African-American congregation in the United Methodist Church and from it has sprung a number of other congregations. Always serving the working class, Zoar has met the needs not only of its neighbors, but also of its parishioners. It has established innumerable social service programs to help all who need them. It continues to be politically active. In the new millennium, Mother African Zoar United Methodist Church stands in the midst of neighborhood and social change and remains a constant reminder of the needs, struggles, and accomplishments of African-Americans.

Janet Harrison Shannon

See also African Methodist Episcopal Church; African Methodist Episcopal Zion Church

Bibliography

Blockson, Charles. (1981) *The Underground Railroad in Pennsylvania*. North Carolina: Flame International.

Catto, William W. (1857) "A Semi-Centenary Discourse Delivered in the First African Presbyterian Church, Philadelphia, on the Fourth Sabbath of May 1857." Philadelphia: Joseph M. Wilson.

Dickerson, Willis C. Minutes of Zoar Church, 1876 to 1878. Archived at the Zoar Church, Philadelphia, Pennsylvania.

Du Bois, W. E. B. (1899; 1971) *The Philadelphia Negro*. New York: Schocken Books.

Shannon, Janet Harrison (1991) "Community Formation: Blacks in Northern Liberties, 1790–1850." Ph.D. dissertation, Temple University.

Tees, Francis H. (1951) *The Ancient Landmark of American Methodism or Historic Old St. George's*. Philadelphia: Message Publishing Company.

African-Derived Religions

African-derived religions have been practiced throughout many areas of the Caribbean, North, Central, and South America, and Europe. Scholars use this general classification to describe religious traditions that were established in the New World by the resettlement of Africans in the Western Hemisphere. During the fifteenth to nineteenth centuries, millions of Africans were captured and transported to work as slaves and indentured laborers in British, French, Portuguese, Dutch, and Spanish territories across the Caribbean and Americas. A significant percentage of the Africans were reportedly from the west and central regions of the continent.

African-derived religions of Haiti (Vodou), Cuba (Lucumi and Santeria), Brazil (Candomblé), Jamaica (Kumina), and Suriname (Winti) are easily traceable to parent traditions among the Fon of the Republic of Benin, the Yoruba of Nigeria, the Bakongo of Central Africa, and the Asante (Ashanti) of Ghana. They have also been influenced

by Western Christianity, especially Catholicism. However, African-derived religions exhibit six major features that have distinguished them from Western Christianity: 1) a notion of the divine as a community (communotheism), 2) ancestral veneration, 3) divination and herbalism, 4) ritual food offerings and animal sacrifice, 5) possession trance as essential in worship, and 6) a belief in neutral mystical power which can be accessed by humans. These characteristics can be observed in systematic and unsystematic configurations within African-Caribbean and African-American cultural and religious life.

During the period of African enslavement in the Caribbean and the Americas, African-derived religions and practices often inspired and reinforced slave uprisings against colonial slaveholding regimes. The most noted revolt was the Haitian Revolution of 1791, which eventually led to the expulsion of French settlers from the island and the establishment of the first independent black republic in the Western Hemisphere in 1804. Due to its potential to unify and organize Africans in their protests against the slaveholding class, African-derived religions were outlawed across the New World. Legal codes against African religious practices were abundant throughout the seventeenth, eighteenth, and nineteenth centuries. For example, in Jamaica, acts against African gatherings, drumming, music of all kinds, and Obeah (an African-derived religious practice) were passed in 1781 and 1784. In 1788, prohibitions against Obeah were restated with the specification "In order to affect the health of lives of others, or promote the purposes of rebellion" (Williams 1932, 164). In 1808 and 1816, acts were passed to ensure better material provisions for enslaved Africans. The 1816 Act allowed for "amusements on the properties 'so as they do not make use of military drums, horns and shells . . . [and] are put an end to by ten o'clock at night' (Williams 1932: 165–166). This same Act includes prohibitions against 'poisoning,' and possession of poisons, pounded glass, and other paraphernalia associated with Obeah practices. In 1826 and 1827 additional legislation was passed banning Africans from teaching and preaching to one another and from holding private meetings.

During this time, African-derived religions were also incriminated and disparaged by European Christian missionaries as they endeavored to convert Africans to the Christian faith. Missionary documents from the seventeenth to the nineteenth centuries are replete with passages repudiating the practice of African-derived religions among enslaved Africans. To be sure, the missionaries did not consider them religions, but rather demonic practices of fetishism and heathenism, and worked tirelessly to eradicate them from the cultural and social life of their converts. Censored and condemned, practitioners of African-derived

POSSESSION AMONG THE GANDA OF UGANDA

A Medium (Mandwa) has only one duty to perform, that of being the mouthpiece of the god whom he represented. It was always the god who chose his representative; in some cases women might be chosen as mediums, in others only men. In each case the choice was indicated in some such manner as the following: the person was suddenly possessed by the god, and began to utter secrets or to predict future events which, apart from the divine influence, it would have been impossibly for him to do. The bystanders thus knew that a god had selected the man to be his medium, and he was at once taken to the temple. Possession was called "being married to the god" (kuwasa), at a time when a person first became possessed; whilst subsequent possessions were called "being seized by the head" (kukwata ku mutwe). . . . When a medium wished to be possessed in order to give the oracle, he would smoke a sacred pipe, using in most instances the ordinary tobacco of the country. . . . He sat in the temple, near the fire, and after smoking the pipe, remained perfectly silent, gazing steadily into the fire or upon the ground, until the spirit came upon him. During the time that a medium was under the influence of the god he was in a frenzied state, and his utterances were often unintelligible to anyone except the priest, who was the interpreter. A priest often had to tell the medium afterwards what he had been talking about. As soon as the spirit of the god had left the medium, he became prostrated, and was allowed to sleep off the effects. When a woman was chosen to be the medium, she was separated from men, had to observe the laws of chastity for the rest of her life, and was looked upon as the wife of the god.

Source: Roscoe, John. (1911) *The Baganda: An Account of the Their Native Customs and Beliefs.* London: Macmillan, 274–275.

---

religions were compelled to practice their religions clandestinely. Even today, practitioners struggle to preserve their traditions in societies that still view African religions as pathological and antisocial. Nonetheless, where practiced, African-derived religions have been well integrated into the fabric of the personal and social life of adherents. For practitioners, they are life-sustaining traditions that maintain health, well-being, and productivity in all areas of their lives.

Dianne M. Stewart

Bibliography

Bastide, Roger. (1971) *African Civilisations in the New World.* New York: Harper & Row.

Deren, Maya. (1953) *Divine Horsemen: The Living Gods of Haiti.* London: Thames & Hudson.

Herskovits, Melville. (1945) "The Problem of Method and Theory in Afroamerican Studies." *Afroamérica* 1: 5–24.

——. (1990) *The Myth of the Negro Past.* Boston: Beacon Press.

Lewis, Gordon. (1983) *Main Currents in Caribbean Thought: The Historical Evolution of Caribbean Society in its Ideological Aspects, 1492–1900.* Baltimore, MD: John Hopkins University Press.

Mbiti, John S. (1969) *African Religions and Philosophy.* London: Heinemann.

Mintz, Sidney W. (1960) *Papers in Caribbean Anthropology.* New Haven, CT: Yale University Publications in Anthropology 57.

——. (1989) *Caribbean Transformations.* New York: Columbia University Press.

Mintz, Sidney W., and Richard Price. (1976) *An Anthropological Approach to the Afro-American Past: A Caribbean Perspective.* Philadelphia: Institute for the Study of Human Issues.

Murphy, Joseph. (1994) *Working the Spirit: Ceremonies of the African Diaspora.* Boston: Beacon Press.

Simpson, George. (1978) *Black Religions in the New World.* New York: Columbia University Press.

The Ahmadiyya Movement

Founded in 1889 in Qadian, then in India and now part of Pakistan, by Mirza Ghulam Ahmad (1835–1908), the reformist and modernizing Ahmadiyya movement emerged as one of several types of South Asian Muslim response to the challenge of Christianity and, more generally, of Westernization in the late nineteenth century. It was also a response to reform movements within the Hindu community including the Brahma Samaj, which was founded in 1828 and labeled the "first church of Hinduism" for its attacks on polytheism and the veneration of idols, attacks that resembled those of the Christian missionaries. This movement was having a considerable impact on the Punjab at the time of the advent of the Ahmadiyya, as was the less tolerant Arya Samaj founded by Dayanand Sarasvati (1824–1883).

Origins, Beliefs, and Claims

As is customary with founders of new religious movements in the subcontinent and elsewhere, Ghulam Ahmad reportedly began to experience revelations in 1879 and soon became convinced that he had been chosen to spread these throughout the world. By the 1880s he had established himself as an exegete and commentator on the Qur'an with the publication of a four-volume work known as *Barahin-i Ahmadiyyah* (Proofs of Ahmadiyya), which addressed criticisms of Islam allegedly levied by Christian missionaries and Hindu movements including the previously mentioned Brahma Samaj and Arya Samaj movements.

The history of the Ahmadiyya has been marked with controversy on account of its "separatism"—it is a tightly knit, self-sufficient community with an avant-garde approach to Western education. Also controversial are the claims made by Ghulam Ahmad: he himself was the *Mahdi*, or God-guided one, whose mission was to wage peaceful *jihad*, or holy war, for the purpose of ensuring the triumph of Islam. Further, he claimed to be the promised messiah of the Christians, a *nabi*, or prophet of God, and the expected tenth incarnation of the Hindu God Vishnu.

Other important Ahmadiyya beliefs include the conviction that Jesus did not actually die on the cross, but through divine intervention escaped that cruel fate and, rather than ascending into heaven as Christians believe, set out on a mission to the Lost Tribes of Israel located in Afghanistan and Kashmir, where he died and is buried still in a tomb in Srinagar. This interpretation of the last period of Jesus' life was important for an understanding of Ghulam Ahmad's role as the messiah of the Christians: by affirming that Jesus was mortal like other prophets, it allowed for the possibility of the advent, not of Jesus in person, but of someone such as Ghulam Ahmad who possessed Jesus' spirit and power.

While Ahmadis maintain that these beliefs are inherently qur'anic, Sunni, or orthodox Islam strongly disagrees, especially with Ghulam Ahmad's claim to prophecy, although it should be noted that he did regard the Prophet Muhammad as the last law-giving prophet. By contrast Sunni holds as a fundamental article of faith the finality in every respect of the prophethood of the Prophet Muhammad. Claims to prophecy of any kind after Muhammad are therefore deemed heretical. Sunni Islam also differs from the Ahmadi

position on Jesus, claiming that he was miraculously rescued from the cross before dying and entered heaven alive. Other differences include the respective doctrinal positions between orthodox Islam and Ahmadis on *jihad* or holy war, the former accepting the notion of active, militant holy war, while the latter insists that *jihad* is to be carried on by peaceful means only.

From the outset there was agitation against the Ahmadis, also known as Qadianis or Mirzais. Various representatives of Sunni Islam and of orthodox Muslim organizations have frequently declared the Ahmadiyya non-Muslim. As early as 1891 Sunni Muslims in the subcontinent issued a *fatwa*, or declaration, pronouncing Ghulam Ahmad's teachings unorthodox, and in the 1930s the Ahrars (a party of nationalist Muslims opposed to the division of India) proposed that the Ahmadiyya movement be excluded from Islam. Developments in Pakistan in the early 1970s were to have serious repercussions on the future of the Ahmadiyya movement as a Muslim organization. Of particular importance was the adoption in 1973 by the Pakistan government of the "Islamic Provisions" in the new, permanent constitution. These specified that the president and prime minister must pledge their belief in the prophethood of the Prophet Muhammad and regard him as the last of the prophets. In 1974 the World Muslim League declared the movement heretical and refused to recognize its Muslim status. This decision was followed in 1984 by a judgment of the military government of Pakistan that deprived the Ahmadiyya movement of its the right to practice and teach Islam.

Missionary Outreach

Throughout its history, the Ahmadiyya movement has been concerned not only with defending Islam against misinterpretations and false charges but also with its *dawa*, or mission, to proclaim the Islamic faith throughout the world and display it as a modern, forward-looking faith with all the respect and enthusiasm for education and science of Christianity. Though a Muslim missionary movement competing with Christian missionary organizations, it did not hesitate to adopt the tactics of its main rival, using schools, hospitals, publishing houses, translations of the Qur'an, and various forms of religious literature as its principal means of proselytizing. In order to retain, regain, or attract the allegiance of those impressed by Western trends in dress and manners, and those who found Islam too traditional in these and related matters, the movement introduced ceremonies that including a form of wedding ceremony that resembled in ethos, structure, and rubric the Christian church.

The movement's active approach to the dissemination of Islam is the essence of what it means by peaceful *jihad* in the subcontinent, but it has been not successful as a method of proselytizing in the West. The first Ahmadiyya centers in the West were established in England and the United States during the first two decades of the twentieth century. By 1912 the Ahmadiyya movement had opened its mosque in Woking, Surrey, England. This attracted mainly students and professional people who had had some contact with the Asian subcontinent. From England, the Ahmadiyya movement spread to the United States where initially its plans to construct a mosque met with serious obstacles despite the care with which preparations were made before the United States mission was undertaken. This preparation included the publication in 1916 of installments of a translation of the Qur'an in English.

In 1920 Muhammad Sadiq, a missionary from the Woking mosque, left England for the United States. After overcoming initial residence difficulties, he set about to disabuse Americans of what he believed to be the distorted picture of Islam created by the press and media in that country. His answer was *The Moslem Sunrise*, a journal that aimed at presenting to the American public what Ahmadis believed to be the true image of Islam: a peaceful, progressive, modernizing faith. By 1922 the American headquarters of what became known as the Ahmadiyya Movement in Islam had been established in Chicago. The bulk of the early converts were African-Americans, some of whom became active missionaries. Today there are some thirty-five Ahmadi missions in the United States, and the headquarters have moved to Washington D.C. African-Americans make up some 60 percent of the membership of around 10,000 in the United States, with most of the remaining 40 percent coming from Pakistan, India, and Africa.

One of the more successful challenges mounted by the Ahmadiyya to Christian missionary expansion took place in West Africa where many of its early converts joined by mail during the First World War. Missionaries arrived there from India in 1921 and began to establish the movement in a number of urban centers in southern Nigeria, including Lagos and Ijebu Ode, and in southern Ghana and Sierra Leone. Though it suffered from frequent bouts of internal strife and from separatism, the Ahmadiyya movement became, nevertheless, the most effective institution in the development of a viable system of Muslim-Western education in West Africa, and also in East Africa. In Nigeria its emphasis on the introduction of a system of Muslim-Western education contributed to the foundation of a number of orthodox Muslim associations for this purpose, and also greatly influenced the thinking of the founders of those associations. A case in point in West Africa is the Nigerian Ansar-ud-din (community of believers), which came into being in 1923 to "modernize" Islam in order to prevent it

from hemorrhaging further as increasing numbers of its adolescents abandoned their faith for the more modern approach to learning and life offered by Christianity through its schools and associations.

In many parts of the colonial world where there was a Muslim presence there was need of a more flexible response by the Muslim authorities not only to Western education provided largely by Christian missionaries. Ahmadiyya also provided a moderated approach to those ceremonial and ritual occasions of Islam that gave it an image as a backward, antimodern religion. This image had been gaining ground among Islam's somewhat embarrassed youth, some of whom were ambitious enough to want to exercise serious influence over the major institutions—administrative, judicial, and political—put in place by colonialism.

Such young, able Muslims, though reluctant to attend Western schools for fear of losing their faith, were greatly assisted by the Ahmadiyya movement and those Muslim organizations that modeled themselves on it and pursued its goals without adopting its central tenets. What the Ansar-ud-din association offered, following Ahmadiyya initiatives, was a Muslim-Western system of education and rites of passage—naming, wedding, and burial services—that, while enabling Muslims to be identified as modern, at the same time screened out those elements of Western culture likely to prove detrimental to Muslim ethos and identity.

The Succession Dispute and the Emergence of the Lahoris

Charismatic movements whose early success is inextricably linked with the personal style of leadership of the founder frequently experience serious difficulties in maintaining unity at the time of succession. One method, by no means infallible, of preventing splintering at this time is by the founder appointing a successor from among his descendants, a principle followed by, among others, the Ismaili Khojas who are led by the Aga Khan. Ghulam Ahmad appointed a successor before his death in 1908 in the person of Hakim Nur-ud-Din, as Kalifat al-Masih (literally vicegerent or deputy of the messiah; he served 1908–1914). However, the next three caliphs of the movement were chosen from among his descendants. Thus was introduced, informally for a time, the dynastic principle as the basis of succession, a principle that was to split the movement.

Discontent within the movement was deep-seated and went beyond the question of leadership. While the selection of a leader by merit was later introduced—the task was handed over to an electoral college charged with appointing the most qualified person regardless of family connections—the continued appointment of members of Ghulam Ahmad's own family as caliphs created the context for dissident groups to express their opposition, not only to the way the leader was chosen but also to the structure and running of the organization in general. One such group claimed that Ghulam Ahmad's intention was to hand on his authority to a body known as the Sadr Anujman-i Ahmadiyya (Ahmadiyya central association), and, to be able to remain faithful to his intentions, decided to establish a separate branch of the movement with its headquarters in Lahore in Pakistan—hence the name, Lahoris. This new branch was led by two prominent members of the movement, Muhammad Ali, translator of the Qur'an into English and editor of the journal, *Review of Religions*, and Kamal ud-Din, a missionary at the Woking mosque in England.

Among the most important changes introduced into the teaching by the Lahoris was one that made it doctrinally more compatible with orthodox Islam. The Lahoris recognized Ghulam Ahmad not as prophet in the manner of the Prophet Muhammad, but as a *mujjahid*—renewer or reformer—an old and widely accepted belief in Sunni or orthodox Islam. The changes introduced by the Lahoris demonstrated an eagerness on the part of its members to move away from traditional approaches to leadership and organization in favor of a more modern outlook characteristic of those Hindu reform movements that arose in various parts of the Asian subcontinent in response to the impact of Christianity and Westernization in the nineteenth and early twentieth centuries, some of which have been mentioned above.

Despite its more orthodox Islamic position, the Lahori branch was slow to take off. The first Lahori center in the United States was established in 1948 only to close in 1956 because of lack of personnel. In the year 2000 there are approximately one hundred Lahoris, mostly of Indian and Pakistani origin, active in the United States. Though their official name is the Ahmadiyya Association for the Propagation of Islam (Ahmadiyya Anjuman Ishaat Islam, Lahore), there is little by way of a planned, coordinated missionary strategy, apart from the distribution of the magazine, *Islamic Review*.

The history of the Qadian branch prior to World War II was marked by overseas missionary activity and a process of institutional differentiation that transformed the movement into a complex organization with its own judicial system and its own departments of medicine, training, education, publicity, and external affairs, among others. Each December an annual meeting, or *Jalsal*, chaired by the caliph is held at Rabwah in Pakistan to audit the activities of the various departments. The movement was obliged to move from its base in India at Qadian to Pakistan by the partition of the subcontinent in 1947.

Conclusion

While subjected throughout its history to verbal and physical attacks—some of the latter took the form of riots—orchestrated in the main by Muslims claiming to defend Islamic orthodoxy, the worst blows dealt to the movement came in the form of their exclusion from Islam by the Muslim World League in 1974, followed in 1984 by the Pakistani pronouncement that the Ahmadiyya was a non-Muslim movement. The declaration prohibited the movement from using the content of the Qur'an as the basis of its teaching and worship and barred Ahmadis from fulfilling the obligation incumbent on all Muslims who have the means and the health to perform it once in a lifetime, the *hajj*, or pilgrimage to Mecca.

Though the impact of the decree has been felt mostly in Pakistan, those Ahmadiyya missions elsewhere—while benefiting from laws safeguarding freedom of worship and belief—have nonetheless been preoccupied with defending its teachings and practices from the criticisms of orthodox Muslim representatives and scholars. Interviews, which do not constitute a representative sample, still suggest that increasing numbers of Ahmadis of all persuasions are coming to regard Ghulam Ahmad more as a reformer than as a prophet. If this trend gains momentum, it will greatly influence the course of Ahmadiyya's relations with Sunni Islam.

Peter B. Clarke

See also Black Muslims; Islam, East Africa; Islam, West Africa

Bibliography

Ahmad, Mirza Bashir-Ud-Din. (1980) *Invitation to Ahmadiyya.* London & Boston: Routledge and Kegan Paul.

Ahmed, Munir D. (1982) "Pakistan: The Dream of an Islamic State." In *Religion and Societies: Asia and the Middle East*, edited by Carlo Caldarola. The Hague: Mouton, 261–288.

Brush, Stanley E. (1955) "Ahmadiyya in Pakistan." *Muslim World* 45: 145–171.

Clarke, Peter. (1997) *Mahdism in West Africa. The Ijebu Mahdiyyat Movement.* London: Luzac Oriental.

Fisher, Humphrey J. (1963) *The Ahmadiyyah: A Study in Contemporary Islam on the West African Coast.* London: Oxford University Press.

Turner, Richard B. (1985) "The Ahmadiyya Movement." *Religion Today* (since 1995 the *Journal of Contemporary Religion*) 5, 3: 9–11.

Williams, Raymond B. (1988) *Religions of Immigrants from India and Pakistan. New Threads in the American Tapestry.* Cambridge, U.K.: Cambridge University Press.

AIC

AIC is an acronym used in reference to African forms of Christian churches. At various times it has meant African Independent Churches (perhaps the most common usage), African Instituted Churches, and African Initiated Churches. The commonality is that all churches and movements in Africa placed under the label AIC are expressions of Christian faith unique to Africa. That is, the churches were founded and developed in Africa usually by African Christians seeking an "African" expression of Christianity. Estimates suggest that about 15 percent of African Christians (about 60 million people) belong to AIC churches.

Compared to Western Christian churches, AIC churches as a group are characterized by a more prominent use of traditional African beliefs, symbols, and practices; ties to the local or regional community; liberal interpretation of the Bible in accord with traditional beliefs; and a focus on the Holy Spirit and Jesus Christ.

Although there are hundreds of churches across sub-Saharan Africa that are lumped in the AIC category, they hardly display much unity in belief or practice. Many emerged in the twentieth century in reaction to localized Christian missionary efforts, colonial oppression, or the economic and political disorder that accompanied independence in some nations in the 1960s. Some churches began as millennial movements, led by charismatic figures who sought to lead their followers to a better world. Related to these were prophetic movements and churches, again led by charismatic figures who also sought a better world. Other churches emphasized the eradication of some traditional practices such as witchcraft. And still others were founded as African alternatives to mainstream Christian churches. To some extent, all AIC churches are syncretic, because they combine elements drawn from African religions and Christianity.

As with beliefs and practices, the relationship of AIC churches to mainstream Christian churches also varies widely with some in open competition and others working together to alleviate local economic and social problems. In general, however, AIC churches have functioned outside the framework of Western Christian church organizations. Barriers to cooperation include the differences in belief and practice and limited participation by AIC church leaders in ecumenical associations. Only two AIC churches, the Church of Lord in Nigeria with about one million members and the Church of Christ on Earth by the Prophet Simon Kimbangu with about five million members, are members of the World Council of Churches, which promotes Christian ecumenicism. Various churches and movements in Africa that fall within the AIC rubric are profiled in this volume, both in entries on specific churches and general survey entries.

David Levinson

Bibliography

Pobee, John S. (1991) "African Instituted Churches." In *Dictionary of the Ecumenical Movement*, edited by Nicholas Lossky et al. Grand Rapids, MI: William B. Eerdmans.

Turner, Harold W. (1962) *African Independent Church*. 2 vols. Oxford: Oxford University Press.

Akan Religion

The Akan-speaking peoples of West Africa occupy the southern half of Ghana, excluding the southeastern corner, and the southeastern corner of the Ivory Coast. Those in Ghana inhabit more than half of the land area stretching from the upper course of the Volta River to the seacoast. They form about 46.1 percent of the total population of Ghana. The traditional occupations of Akans were farming (for those inland), fishing (for those on the coast), and trading, particularly by the women.

Akans speak a number of mutually intelligible dialects of Akan. They are culturally homogenous. Generally, they show a common pattern of political, economic, social, and religious structure, including a matrilineal descent system. The various Akan groups include the Brong, Akyem, Akuapim, Kwahu, Assen-Twifo, Wasa, Fante-Agona, Nzima-Evalue, Ahanta, and Ashanti. The Ashanti and Fanti are the most numerous and most well known. This article presents an overview of Akan religion in the late nineteenth and early twentieth centuries, much of which is still valid.

Religious Beliefs in the Life of Akans

Traditional Akan life and culture was so permeated by religion that it is believed that the knowledge of God among the Akan people was intuitive, immediate, and basic to their view of the cosmology, sociology, anthropology, and ecology. Akan religion is undergirded by fundamental indigenous Akan value systems. It has its own pattern, historical inheritance, and tradition. However, as a community religion, it cannot be traced to any specific point in history. Neither can it be traced to any particular founder or founders. Nevertheless, it can be said that the Akan, like all human beings, evolved ways of fulfilling the fundamental and universal need of humankind to seek a harmonious relationship with unseen powers and thereby bind them together with their fellow humans. Akan religion is also a contemporary reality that colors their beings, hopes, and aspirations.

Akan religion, as religions elsewhere, consists of a set of beliefs, practices, institutions, religious experiences, emotions, norms, and values. These were not documented in a written scripture, but are passed down by means of oral tradition and through various symbols and practices. The Akan world of reality consists of beings and objects imbued with varying degrees or qualities of supernatural power.

Belief about God

A firm belief in the Supreme Being (Onyame) who created and sustains and owns the entire universe is fundamental to the Akan religious system. Myths tell the origin of the universe through the work of God. He is considered the powerful one, the eternal one, the wise one, and the final authority in all matters. He is venerated high above all other deities, who all derive their being, existence, and power from him.

God is essentially a spirit, a being invisible to humankind; his invisibility is expressed in concrete terms. For instance, he has been likened to the wind, which is also invisible and everywhere. This belief is expressed in the saying "If you want to speak to God tell it to the wind." In the same vein, God among the Akan is also said to be personal. This is attested to by the personal name he is referred to (Kwame) which is the name given to every male born on Saturday. It is said that God is called Kwame because he is worshipped on Saturday.

The Akan developed a stock of traditional names, attributes, myths, symbols, proverbs, greetings, and idioms that together express God's omnipotence, omniscience, goodness, dependability, immortality, and other beliefs in him. He himself is not generally worshipped directly, though his help is invoked in times of crisis. Thus there are very few direct approaches to God; consequently there are no regular and formal cults to God. He is viewed as transcendent and thus requires intermediaries to execute his purposes. Therefore, to approach Him humans have to go to their ancestors and deities. One exception is the Nyamedua. The belief is that God dwells in a vessel placed in a fork on top of this special tree in some traditional homes.

Belief in Ancestral Spirits

Perhaps the most significant aspect of Akan religion is the belief in the spirits of ancestors. Called Nananom Nsamanfo, they are the dead relatives who are alive yet not seen (except through occasional self-disclosure to individuals in dreams). Each family, clan, lineage, and state has its own ancestors. Ancestors are believed to be capable of intervening in human affairs, either to reward or to punish the living according to the way their descendants treated them. Thus the ancestors are always treated with reverence and held in awe. Proper reverence and attention is believed to ensure prosperity and blessing, but their neglect often is believed to lead to disaster. However, not all dead persons are acknowledged as ancestors. An ancestor had to have lived an exemplary life, to have had offspring, to have died a natural death at a good, ripe age, and must have been given proper burial and funeral rites. Furthermore, depending on one's impact on society during one's lifetime, one might be entirely forgotten or be long remembered, cherished, and held in honor by posterity.

There is an ongoing debate among scholars as to whether the ancestors are worshipped or simply venerated. Admittedly, this difficult issue does not lend itself to a straightforward answer. Nevertheless, insofar as Akan revere the ancestors and approach them with filial piety it suggests something more than veneration. One must quickly add, however, that the authority of the ancestors is derived from God. (For further discussion on the subject, see Sarpong 1974: 42–43; and Fink 1990: 146.)

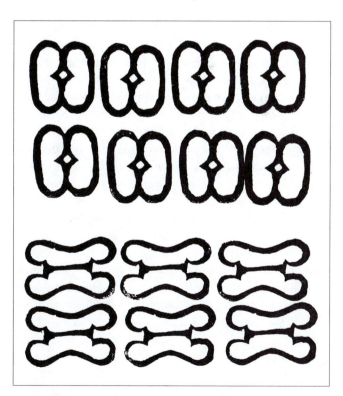

Two Ashanti "Adinkira" printing stamp patterns from Ghana. Both are stylings of the symbol of hope.

There is also a belief in evil ghosts called *samantwen-twen*. This is the spirit of one who died a kind of "evil death" such as suicide, dying at childbirth, and accidental deaths like being trapped by a falling tree, getting drowned, or being accidentally shot. It is believed such spirits are denied entry into the world of the dead (*asamando*) because their destined time in the world was wrongly cut short.

Belief in Divinities (Deities)

Akan recognize the existence of divinities or deities (*abosom*) who are intermediaries between God and human beings and derive their powers essentially from God. They are spirits but they dwell in rivers, rocks, and other objects. The Earth (Asaase Yaa) is not strictly regarded as a deity in Akan thought. Rather, "she" is conceived of as an animating principle of fertility, and should therefore not be polluted with forbidden practices such as sexual relations in it for fear of catastrophic consequences on society.

The *abosom* may be classified as deities of an entire state; deities of towns, localities, and traditional areas; deities of clan, lineage, or family. Special places of worship called shrines are set up for the *abosom* and priests and priestesses (*akomfo*) who were assisted by other shrine devotees serving them. It was believed that the deities could and did express themselves through the *akomfo* who were devoted to their service. Unlike God and ancestors, deities are treated with respect so long as they provide material and spiritual prosperity. When they fail to meet the specific needs of groups or individuals, they might be held in contempt and eventually abandoned.

One major subject of debate among students of Akan religion is whether or not *abosom* are worship objects in themselves or means of worshipping God. It has been demonstrated that while *abosom* are regarded as dependent on God in practice, they are often normally conceived as powerful in themselves, to possess powers to reward or to punish their devotees, and to demand from their devotees that they properly maintain their relationship with them.

Belief in Lower Spirit Powers

Households or individuals can own certain minor spirit agencies (*asuman*), which take various forms such as amulets and talismans or beads, which might be worn around the waist, the wrist, or the neck, or hung at the entrance to a house or room. They might also be contained in a brass pan or in a gourd and put in the corner of a room or placed under the bed.

The power of *asuman* is believed to be derived from dwarfs (*mmoatia*) or the "soul" of plants and trees or other supernatural beings. They are sometimes considered mystical objects charged with impersonal forces that can be manipulated by secret formulae. *Asuman* are used for protection and for bringing success and good health to the user. It is also believed that they are secretly used for offensive purposes. The observance of taboos associated with the *asuman* is believed to determine how effective they were.

There are other spirit powers believed to be evil and thus to adversely influence individual lives. A typical example is *sasabonsam*, a mystical forest monster known for its mischievous activities. *Sasabonsam* is believed to aid witches and wizards in the destruction of life and property.

Religious Practices in the Life of Akans

The Akan, like most Africans, define life in terms of the community, which in their religious thought includes the living, the dead, and the yet-to-be-born. These constituent parts of the Akan community are perceived as ontologically bound to each other in a harmonious relationship. The community has the extended family as its unit, i.e., grandparents, blood relatives, in-laws, who work in concert to ensure the socialization of children and security and comfort of all members in all aspects of life. The religious beliefs of the community manifest themselves in various communal and individual practices.

There is an institution of formal priesthood among Akans. The priest (*Okomfo*) assists society by communicating with supernatural beings on behalf of others for purposes of sacral mediation, prophecy, healing, exorcism, diagnosis and the restoration to wholeness of ill and disturbed persons, and general pastoral care.

The Akan idea of causality leans heavily on the spiritual. Besides purely organic causation of sicknesses, no interpretation of causality that does not include such elements as preordained destiny, punishment by angered ancestors, or witchcraft and sorcery can be fully acceptable. Thus, much medical treatment is of a religious nature. The role of the priest, who possessed knowledge of herbs and charms providing protection against witchcraft and who attended to the gods, is crucial.

The Akan have many festivals and their foundations and functions are almost invariably found in the traditional religions. Some of the festivals, such as Apoo and Odwira, are celebrated yearly. Many others, such as Adae, follow a forty-day cycle. Generally the functions of the festivals include remembrance of the dead, thanksgiving for harvest, purification, psychological release, enforcement of sanctions, and social solidarity.

The Human Person

The Akan conceive of the human person as a complex of physical and spiritual elements received from father, mother, and God; and bonded together. Apart from the body the person is thought to have three major components.

First is the soul from God (*okra*). This is thought to be the immaterial divine spark from God that is immortal and so vital that life cannot be sustained without it. The *okra* is believed to return to God when one dies. The *okra* is thought to have moods, and, depending on how one treated it, a person might be in either good or bad mood. The *okra* is believed to be highly impressionable. If a person is faced with intense disgrace or attacks by evil, the *okra* is believed to react by temporarily leaving the person, who in turn becomes ill or is exposed to other negative effects. In such a situation certain rituals are required in order to restore the okra to its normal condition. This ritual is known as "washing the soul" (*okraguare*). "Washing of the soul" can also take place for the purpose of thanksgiving for success.

The soul is associated with the seven days of the week, and names are accorded to male and females (soul names) dependent on the day a person was born; each soul name is thought to possess its own peculiar temperament. For example, those born on Monday are expected to be calm (*dwo*). Tuesday-born people were believed to be hot-tempered and warlike. Those born on Wednesday were said to be cruel, yet intelligent and wise. Those born on Thursday were believed to be courageous. Friday-born people are said to be wanderers and troublesome and yet loving and full of vigor. People born on Saturday are believed to be experienced people but also extroverts. Those born on Sunday are pure, generous, and natural leaders. There are taboos that relate to days of the week. For example, the dog is taboo to those born on Tuesday.

One concept related to the *okra* is *nkrabea*, which may be loosely translated as destiny. It is believed that before the *okra* obtained permission from God to set out for the world, it obtained from God a "commission it had to fulfill in life."

Second is the "personality soul" (*sunsum*). This is believed to be a spiritual entity that is transmitted to a person by his or her father. It is believed to link one to the patrilineal clan (*ntoro*), which is under the care of the principal gods of the Akans. This "soul" is seen as the seat of one's character, disposition, intelligence, and knowledge. The various clans are associated with certain characteristics. Bosompra (a clan name), for instance, are believed to be very tough. The several *ntoro* groups also have peculiar forms of greetings and corresponding responses.

It is believed that the personality soul possesses varying degrees of ability to withstand "spiritual" attacks on a person. It is also believed that one's *sunsum* is heavy if one was brave; by contrast, it is light when one is unable to withstand attacks of the evil powers. The *sunsum* could be altered for good or for ill and is seen as a key factor in the determination of how one fares in life. It therefore requires purity and must be protected against pollution. Hence a number of taboos have to be observed by members of a *ntoro* group. It is also held among the Akans that the *sunsum* is the aspect of a person's spiritual being that is involved in dreams.

Third is blood (*mogya*). It is believed that this "soul" is inherited from the mother and, as such, determines a person's matrilineal status in Akan society and membership in family and clan. It signifies the kinship relationship that forms the basis of Akan social structure and organization. The clan, based on a matrilineal organization known as *abusua*, is traced back over ten to twelve generations to a common ancestress who served as the focus of ancestral rituals for the group. Every Akan person belongs to one of seven clans. Membership in a family and clan determines inheritance, succession, and political leadership, as well as privileges and responsibilities within the society. It determines also whom one could marry, because it is taboo for members of the same clan to marry. Each clan is linked to a totem and is believed to have certain characteristic features of the totem in common. For example, members of the Agona clan, whose totem is a parrot, are believed to be eloquent.

Life Cycle

As mentioned above, Akan view their society as consisting of the living, the ancestors, and the yet-unborn. Life is thus conceived as a continuous cycle involving the stages of conception, birth, puberty, marriage, death, and regeneration. There are consequently various rites at various points in the life of a person that are meant to ask for blessing or to avert any conceivable spiritual or physical danger. The relevance of these rites lies in the belief that failure to perform the rite for one member of the community puts the whole society at the risk of incurring the displeasure of the ancestors.

Let us begin with the cycle at birth. For the Akan, childlessness ranks highest of all personal tragedies and is the most humiliating of all conceivable curses. In fact, fertility is the most sought-after blessing. There is thus a positive correlation between one's ability to bear children and one's honor in society. Libation prayers invariably include the request for numerous children.

AKAN PRAYER OF INVOCATION
TO COMMENCE WORK

Knocking! knocking! knocking! knocking!

Oh heaven drink, earth drink,

"Otwereduampon Kwame," Friday Earth, receive drink

River Densu drink, River Kofi drink

River Nyanno drink, Nsakye drink

Akrame drink, god Dade drink

Awenade drink Abew come and drink

Kyigyinafo come and drink, River Volta drink

Grand mother Akonadi of Tuesday, you all drink,

Grand father Bediako, receive drink, Odom Mante, drink

Kyigyinafo I call you apeafo

River Odum of Saturday! River Odum of Saturday! River Odum of Saturday!

Come and drink, Owurudu get this drink.

Female Ntoa, Male Ntoa, when we call one we call all.

The issue is this (Kwadwo Anti) says he is coming to learn your custom

And he came with his bottle of gin.

And before we begin, we should give you drink.

You all come and drink, deity Ntoa, you all drink.

With due respect, I am going to teach him,

And teach him the custom about you Ntoa, come and drink.

Source: Anti, K. K. Amos. (2000) *Libation in the Old Testament and Akan Life and Thought: A Critique.* www.u/cehd/faculty/ntodd/GhanaIUDLP/kkAnti.

Pregnancy is a clear indication that a new member of the living society is expected. Thus special medicine is administered to the woman for her safety and that of the foetus. Since the yet-unborn is considered a full human being and part of the society, abortion, whether induced or spontaneous, is abhorred among Akan.

There is a vague belief in reincarnation among Akan. It is believed that at birth a "ghost-mother" mourn the loss of her "ghost-child." Thus for seven days no one treats the child as a full member of the living society, in fact it is treated as a visitor. If the child survives the one-week period, there is a social and religious ceremony to formally welcome it into the living society. Libation prayers are said for the ancestors to bless the child.

Akan do not have formal initiation schools. Traditionally, neither circumcision (for boys) nor clitoridectomy (for girls) was practiced. The only puberty rites normally performed in rural areas are for girls who had begun to menstruate. The central aspect of the rite is a special meal (mashed yam and boiled eggs) for the initiate. The egg, swallowed whole, is an appeal to the ancestral spirits that her future labors would turn out to be smooth and easy as that of the hen when it lays an egg. After the rites, a girl is considered ready for marriage. It is a severe offense for girls to become pregnant without first going through the puberty rites.

Marriage among the Akan is a group union between two matrilineages, rather than an individual bond. Usually the family of the man pays a certain amount of money (*tirinsa*) and presents some gifts to the bride and her near matrilineal kin and her father. One high point of the marriage rite is the offering, in the presence of marriage witnesses, of a libation prayer to the ancestors asking for their presence, their participation in this formal meeting, and, most importantly, their blessings.

At death the *okra* soul is believed to return to God to give account of its earthly life. The personality soul (*sunsum*) is thought to become a ghost or an ancestor (when it qualified), and the flesh (*mogya*) is taken care of by the relatives of the deceased by giving it a fitting burial. The Akan believe in reincarnation. The dead who are believed to have been refused entry into their permanent place of rest (*asamando*) might perhaps be reborn in order to satisfy the requirements of their unfulfilled earlier "destiny" (*nkrabea*). According to this belief, ancestors might also decide to come back to complete a task they had not been able to accomplish before dying.

In Akan perception, death does not break the fellowship between the living and the dead. The funeral celebration, particularly a ritual prayer said on the night of the actual death, is regarded as a means of announcing to the ancestors that one was coming to join them. The various libation prayers make this clear.

Ancestors are believed to be in a better position to influence what goes on in society either for good or ill. Consequently, special avenues are employed to make the ancestors accessible to the living. Hence the rites of ancestors have a central place in Akan religion.

Morality

Morality here concerns what a man does, not just what he is. In fact, he does what he does because of what he is. Akans have a moral code that consists of laws, taboos, customs, and set forms of behavior that are to some extent undergirded by religious considerations. (Kudadjie 1973 presents a counterargument to this prevailing view.) An Akan person who wishes to live long keeps the various regulations in the rules that religion imposes upon him. This is mainly because death, disease, and misfortune are believed to be punishment by God or ancestors or the lesser gods because of one's misdeeds. In the same way, God and the ancestors are believed to reward those who upheld the rules. It must be quickly added that the Akan recognize the role conscience (*tiboa* or *ahonim*) plays in forming and shaping one's moral values. In fact, conscience was regarded as the ultimate norm of morality of a person. Akan morality seeks to promote harmonious and good relationship among members of the society in order to bring about peace, progress, and prosperity.

All members of the society are involved in making sure that others are morally upright, because the consequence of one person's misconduct is believed to adversely affect the larger society. Moral values are found in Akan proverbs and everyday sayings, which are expressed in such ceremonies as naming and puberty rites, as well as on their drums, through their horns, or through the linguistic staff. The linguist is the spokesman of the king or traditional ruler. Whenever the linguist is sent to deliver a message on behalf of a king or whenever the linguist performs functions, he holds a gold-plated stick, which is a symbol of the king's/traditional ruler's authority; this is the linguistic staff. Each staff has a symbol on top of it (which varies from ruler to ruler) that carries a specific message.

Salvation

Religion for the Akan serves existential needs. Religion should make life worth living and maintain and protect it against illness, mishap, enemies, and death. The universe is perceived as an arena of both benevolent and malicious spirits that influence the course of human life for good or ill, respectively. The preoccupation of the Akan is to seek a harmonious relationship with the mystical powers that control and bestow life with vitality. This, it is believed, was achieved through various sacrificial rites for propitiatory, expiatory, and reconciliatory purposes. Thus salvation in Akan thought involves whatever contributes to the reinforcement of life in the here-and-now. This includes good health, ability to ward off evil, prosperity, human and animal fertility, good human relations, and success in one's occupation.

Akan Religion in the Present Day

Akan religion is not static. Christianity, Islam, and modern world trends have significantly impinged upon it. In its turn, Akan religion has also largely influenced these two religions. And it indisputably exerts a strong influence on the Akan even now. It has survived from precolonial times, through the period of European colonial domination, and up to now because of its abiding values that provide answers to the existential questions the Akan are asking. Consequently, "immigrant" religions, particularly Christianity, are making attempts at integrating Akan worldviews and religious beliefs into them in order to be relevant and meaningful to their adherents.

Cephas N. Omenyo

See also West African Religions

Bibliography

Appiah-Kubi, K. (1981) *Man Cures God Heals: Religion and Medical Practice Among the Akans of Ghana*. New York: Osmun & Co.

Busia, K. A. (1968) *The Position of the Chief in the Modern Political System of Ashanti: A Study of the Influence of Contemporary Social Changes on Ashanti Political Institution*. London: Cass.

Danquah, J. B. (1968) *The Akan Doctrine of God*. London: Cass.

Fink, H. E. (1990) *Religion, Disease and Healing in Ghana: A Case Study of Traditional Dormaa Medicine*. Munich: Trickster Wissenschaft.

Kudadjie, J. N. (1973) "Does Religion Determine Morality in African Societies? — A View Point." *The Ghana Bulletin of Theology* 4, 5 (December): 30–49.

Opoku, K. A. (1978) *West African Traditional Religion*. Singapore: F.E.P. International.

Platvoet, J. G. (1979) "The Akan Believer and his Religions." In *Official and Popular Religion: Analysis of a Theme for Religious Studies*, edited by Pieter H. Vrijhof and Jacques Waardenburg. The Hague: Mouton Publishers, 543–606.

———. (1991) "'Renewal' By Retrospection: The Asante Anokye Traditions." In *Religion Tradition and Renewal*, edited by Armin W. Geertz and Jeppe S. Jensen. Aarhus: Aarhus University Press, 149–184.

Pobee, J. S. (1979) *Toward an African Theology*. Nashville, TN: Abingdon.

Rattray, R. S. (1969) *Ashanti*. Oxford: Clarendon Press.

———. (1979) *Religion and Art in Ashanti*. New York: AMS Press.

Sarpong, P. (1974) *Ghana in Retrospect: Some Aspects of Ghanaian Culture*. Tema, Ghana: Ghana Publishing Corporation.

Williamson, S. G. (1965) *Akan Religion and the Christian Faith*. Accra: Ghana Universities Press.

Aladura

Aladura (owners of prayer) is an indigenous religious movement that developed among the Yoruba during the 1920s. This was one of several indigenous Christian religious movements that emerged around the African continent within the first three decades of the twentieth century.

Emergence of the Movement

Between 1890 and 1920 a separatist church movement gained momentum in various pockets around the African continent. Among the Yoruba in Nigeria the African Church Movement, as it was called, was particularly strong. Christian denominations established themselves independently of their European and American mission churches. Some of the African Church denominations included the Native Baptist Church, the United Native African Church, Bethel African Church, and Jehovah Shalom, to name a few. By 1917, fourteen African churches had sprung up throughout southern Nigeria, most of them in or around Lagos, the capital city. Although these churches sought to incorporate varying degrees of indigenous cultural expressions, such as dance, poetry, art, and music, as a primary objective in their formation, they remained doctrinally similar in content to the parent church. By the end of World War I, many of the African churches had grown conservative and elitist, attracting an educated African membership. Even though there were doctrinal differences among the African churches (typically over how much Africanity was permissible in Christian worship), they were forced to unite in face of a threat from within when the Aladura religious movement threatened to overwhelm the African Church Movement.

The forerunner of the Aladura movement in the mid-1920s can be traced to the World War I era in Lagos and its surrounding interior. The economic hardship imposed by the war period brought a large number of Yorubas from the interior to Lagos seeking employment. These economic conditions also resulted in an increased number of self-styled wandering evangelists who made street corners, markets, and other public places their pulpits. Their hellfire and damnation styles were punctuated with dramatic apocalyptic prophesies. Major outbreaks of diseases between 1918 and 1919 throughout southern Nigeria prompted the British colonial administration to close a number of the African churches on the pretext of controlling these diseases. But there was apparently some punitive design in the church closings, and these actions gave the itinerant evangelists, who claimed to be able to cure and protect the faithful, an even greater audience to which to preach.

A few of the preaching evangelists established prayer groups within some of the African churches. These prayer groups, or praying bands as they were also called, gained popularity within the African churches, but one of the earliest to gain independent status was the Cherubim and Seraphim Society formed in 1925. The mystical events surrounding its formation highlights the preeminence of prayer within the Aladura movement.

In June 1925, Christianah Abiodun Akinsowon (1907–198?) (later known as Captain Mrs. Abiodun Emanuel), a teenage girl living in Lagos, began having angelic visitations during her sleep. According to her account, the angel took her on distant trips to celestial places that she had never imagined. She would always be returned by the angel by the following morning. The frequency of these trips were such that she became friends with the angelic visitor. On a certain occasion, Abiodun was taken on one of her nocturnal visits, but on this particular trip was led by another angel with whom she was not familiar. The new angel took her on a trip that was much longer than the usual overnight sojourn and apparently lasted for several days. This new angel took Abiodun to a council of other angels, and she was informed that she would have to undergo a test consisting of several biblical questions. Only after successfully answering those questions would she be allowed to return to her normal consciousness. Unbeknown to the council of angels, Abiodun was being assisted in this task by her friendly angel who stood behind her and gave her the correct answers to the series of questions.

To the outside world, however, Abiodun appeared to be in a trance that lasted several days. Her relatives in Lagos became alarmed at her comatose state and sent for one of the itinerant preachers in the area, Moses Orimolade Tunolashe (1941?–1979). It was Tunolashe (in the form of her friendly angel) who was supplying Abiodun with the correct answers to the complex biblical questions posed by the angelic council. When this story was reported, it was seen as a miraculous event because Moses Orimolade Tunolashe, as an itinerant preacher, could neither read nor write!

After coming out of the trance, Abiodun was told what had happened and how Tunolashe had helped her. She sought him out and together they formed a prayer group called the Seraphim Society (later renamed the Cherubim and Seraphim Society).

Within a few years of the society's formation, other denominations within the Aladura tradition emerged under similar mystical circumstances. For example, Church of the Lord (Aladura), inaugurated in 1930, began under similarly spectacular circumstances. Its founder, Josiah Oshitelu (1902 -?), also had begun to experience visions and celestial calls to preach as early as the late 1920s. Although he was formally a member of the Christian Missionary Society (CMS) at the time, Oshitelu eventually broke from the denomination to found the Church of the Lord (Aladura). Another charismatic figure was Joseph Babalola (1904-?) who was the principal prophet of the Christ Apostolic Church (formerly known as Faith Tabernacle). After hearing a celestial voice call his name three times while he was working on his steamroller, he discovered three palm leaves on the machine. One was completely dry, one was turning dry, and the third was completely green. He interpreted the third leaf as his rejuvenated life and, along with his name having been called three times, as a sign that he should abandon his job as a worker and preach the gospel. He was baptized into the CAC in the 1930s and became its leading evangelist. His activist religious work caused the church's membership to swell. He would become popularly known as "Baba Aladura."

By the late 1930s, there were several denominations within the Aladura tradition, including the Celestial Church of Christ (also known as "Cele," or CCC), the Apostolic Church, and the Church of Christ's People. There are close to fifteen different denominations. In their effort to Africanize Christianity, the Aladura churches allowed plural marriage (a man having more than one wife at a time), which was a Yoruba cultural expression of a man's wealth. Although the church did not practice negative magical forces, it acknowledged the presence of them and had prophylactic measures in place to counter such forces on its members. There was also the belief in visions and other worldly visitations such as those experienced by Abiodun, Oshitelu, and Babalola, but above all, the primacy of prayer and its healing power was at the base of the Aladura church movement.

The various churches also developed musical traditions. They allowed the use of drums and bells to accompany singing, and in later years other Western instruments such as trumpets, electronic guitars, and flutes were included in the worship services. Some denominations did not subscribe to the use of drums to the same degree, because traditional percussion instruments like the *bata* drum were associated with the Yoruba deity, Shango, which was seen as a negative influence.

There has also been a strong hymnal tradition to come out of the church. The Church of the Lord (Aladura), for example, produced several hymnals in both Yoruba and English. An example of a hymnal produced by the Cherabum and Seraphim Society was *Olorun Eleda to d'Egve Serafu* (God the creator who created Seraphim). There are generally three practices by which religious songs come into the church repertory. There are those songs that are borrowed and adapted from Western hymnals, those which are newly composed by members of the churches, and those channeled or revealed (as through spiritual means).

An element found throughout the hymnal repertory and the church in general is the use of holy words. An apparent form of glossolalia, the holy words within the Aladura context are words or phrases revealed or channeled to church leaders (or in some cases individual members) through divine visions. Although words and/or phrases such as *beraca berad, korrabbannon, sajj, jheje, allollol, ayybburrra,* and *sahhojjallal* appear phonetically well formed and are usually understood and explained by the individual who receives them in a vision, they are not necessarily intelligible to other indigenous Yoruba speakers. Leaders within various Aladura denominations were also given holy names. The Church of the Lord (Aladura) founder, Josiah Oshitelu, had the holy name Arrabablah-hubab, meaning "the first master and teacher." Not all Aladura denominations, however, subscribe to the power of these holy words to the same degree.

Spread of the Aladura Movement

By the mid-1940s, the movement had begun to spread outside of the Yoruba-speaking area in Nigeria and eventually spread to other English-speaking countries. The Church of the Lord (Aladura) seems to have been the most successful in its missionization: after establishing a mission in Sierra Leone in 1946, it spread to Ghana, Gambia, Liberia, Ivory Coast, and by the early 1960s, had established branches in and around London.

By the 1970s, Aladura branches were established in the United States. They were also attracting significant numbers among college students in Nigeria, mostly through musical concerts that featured electronically enhanced instruments. These musical events were also attracting Muslim students who were not Christian. This resulted in a Muslim countermovement, which began producing its own popular music concerts and appealing to its students to return to Islam and to "not dance Jesus' dance, but that of Allah."

By the 1980s, Captain Mrs. Abiodun had become a unifying presence in the Cherubim and Seraphim churches. She was making efforts at the time of her death to unify several Aladura denominations. This religious phenomenon continues to stand as an independent religious movement and as an example of an indigenous African church that was successful in interpreting Christianity in a way that made it more relevant to African cultural expression.

Christopher Brooks

See also Cherubim and Seraphim Society; Christ Apostolic Church; Yoruba Religion

Bibliography

Brooks, Christopher. (1994) "In Search of an Indigenous African Hymnody: The Aladura Churches Among the Yoruba." *Black Sacred Music* 8: 2.

Crumbley, Deidre. (forthcoming) *Spirit and Structure: Indigenous Institution Building and Gender Role Reproduction in Three African Churches.*

Peel, J. D. Y. (1968) *Aladura: A Religious Movement Among the Yoruba.* London: Oxford University Press.

Webster, J. B. (1964) *The African Churches Among the Yoruba: 1823–1922.* Oxford: Clarendon.

The amaNazaretha

The Nazareth Baptist Church, the amaNazaretha, is the oldest continually existing African-initiated religious movement in South Africa and, after the Zion Christian Church, the second largest with more than one million followers, most of whom are Zulu. Founded by Isaiah Shembe (1867–1935), the Nazarites are possibly unique in Africa as a result of the large collection of sacred texts they possess, which were recently translated into English, and the serious theological speculation and argument that the movement has generated.

Shembe and his Church

Isaiah Mdliwamafa Shembe was born at Ntabamhlophe near Estcourt, Natal, South Africa, of Zulu parents. He died at Mkhaideni in northern Natal from exhaustion resulting from continual preaching and long hours spent baptizing converts in rivers and pools. Little is known about his early life or the religious experiences that clearly influenced him. He was involved for a while with the Wesleyans before associating with Baptists, who baptized him on 22 July 1906. Thereafter, he appears to have been an itinerant evangelist until he met a former Lutheran, Nkabinde (?), whom he came to regard as a "prophet." Through this man Shembe developed a healing and prophetic ministry in 1910. Either late that year or early in 1912, he founded the iBandla amaNazaretha or Nazareth Baptist Church, an African independent/indigenous church rooted in Zulu life and tradition. A few years later he acquired the farm that became his holy city of Ekuphakameni. Around the same time he established an annual pilgrimage to the Holy Mountain of Nhlangakazi.

The oral histories show that Shembe was loved for his vivid parables, dramatic healings, and uncanny insights into people's thoughts. He either wrote or dictated many moving Zulu hymns for which he composed the music and developed sacred dances to express the devotion of the believer to God. Like many African religious leaders Shembe developed his own health and dietary rules, including a prohibition of the eating of chicken. He created a new liturgical calendar that omitted the celebration of Christmas and provided his followers with elaborate sacred costumes based on traditional Zulu dress and, as with his use of the Scottish kilt, items borrowed from Europeans, which came to him in vivid dreams. In 1930 he was involved in a serious dispute with the government over his refusal to allow his followers to be vaccinated, which was eventually resolved in Shembe's favor.

After Isaiah Shembe's death on 2 May 1935 a period of uncertainty gripped the church because he had not clearly designated his successor. This time of troubles was eventually ended when one of his sons, Johannes Galilee Shembe (1904–1976), gained general recognition as the new leader. Under the wise leadership of J. G. Shembe, the church flourished and was consolidated. An exceptionally well-educated man with a university degree during a time when university education was rare, J. G. Shembe reached out to other religious communities and established particularly close ties with the Methodist leader, scholar, and politician the great John Dube (1871–1946), as well as the Lutheran missionaries Bengt Sundkler (1909–1995) and Hans-Jürgen Becken (b. 1926). He also participated in the BBC film *Zulu Zion* that was part of Ninian Smart's *Long Search Series* shortly before his death on 17 December 1976.

In 1949, he appointed Petros Musawenkosi Dhlomo to travel around South Africa gathering and recording personal testimonies from people who had encountered and remembered the words and deeds of his father. Mr. Dhlomo (d. 1997) set about this task with great diligence, amassing hundreds of testimonies that he carefully transcribed and typed out. Not content with this innovative gesture, Bishop Shembe approached Hans-Jürgen Becken in the late 1960s, encouraging him to make his own collection of testimonies and translate the Dhlomo collection. Unfortunately, largely due to overwork and his wife's illness, Dr. Becken had to return to Germany in 1974, and the task remained incomplete. After his retirement in 1989, Becken returned to South Africa where, encouraged by Bishop Amos Shembe, he resumed his work of translation. The first volume of which appeared as *The Story of Isaiah Shembe* in 1996. Since resuming his work Becken has translated all of the oral histories (in three volumes), the hymnbook of the Nazarites, and the earliest biography of Isaiah Shembe, *Ushembe*, published in 1936 by John Dube.

Theological and Leadership Arguments in the Late Twentieth Century

Following J. G. Shembe's death the church entered one of the darkest periods of its history with open warfare between the supporters of Bishop Amos Shembe and Londaukosi Insikayakho Shembe, known as the Rt. Rev. Londa Shembe (1944–1989). Bishop Amos Shembe (1907–1996), a well-educated schoolteacher, claimed the right of succession in terms of seniority based on Zulu custom, church practice, the wishes of the majority of church members, and that he was J. G. Shembe's younger brother and a son of Isaiah Shembe. The Rt. Rev. Londa Shembe, a practicing lawyer,

claimed that his father had appeared to him in a dream telling him to forsake his legal practice and lead the Nazarites. He also argued that in addition to his charismatic calling he had a right to leadership based on the fact that he was the son of J. G. Shembe.

Eventually after a long legal battle church properties were divided between the two rival groups with Londa Shembe's followers gaining the sacred city of Ekuphaka-meni, while Amos Shembe was granted a large farm 10 kilometers from Ekuphakameni where he established the new holy city of Ebuhleni. During the disturbances that marked the beginning of these disputes a number of buildings in Ekuphakameni were burned and a large part of the Dhlomo original collection was destroyed. Fortunately, Becken had photocopies of many of the documents and the diligent archivist was able to restore almost the entire collection.

Londa Shembe was a creative leader who translated parts of his grandfather's works into English, composed his own hymns, and as a result of his dreams and visions invented new dances and church clothing. Avidly interested in theology and religion, he declared that he was "the Third

An amaNazarite dancer c. 1981. PHOTO COURTESY OF IRVING HEXHAM.

An amaNazarite church group marching in Nairobi, Kenya, c. 1963. PHOTO BY FRED WELBOURN COURTESY OF IRVING HEXHAM.

Shembe" and that after his death the line of prophetic leadership would come to an end. Strangely, he also expressed doubts about the true nature of his church and increasingly leaned toward the view that the Nazarites were an entirely new religion with either Jewish, or perhaps even Hindu, roots. He was brutally assassinated by unknown gunmen while studying Hebrew at his home on 7 April 1989. The leadership of his branch of the church, based in Ekuphakameni and numbering about seventy-thousand people, has been in flux since his death.

Bishop Amos Shembe was less innovative theologically and more conservative socially, preferring to continue his brother's work of consolidation and bring the Nazarites closer to the historic Christian tradition, rather than seeking to create an entirely new religion. Consequently, he placed greater emphasis on Bible reading and the role of Jesus in the church's theology. Under his successful leadership the church grew to approximately one million members. After his death in 1986, a fairly smooth transition occurred to the Rev. Vimbembi Shembe (1943–) who now leads the church that is prospering under his guidance.

Controversies Understanding the True Nature of Nazaretha Theology

Apart from their written scriptures the amaNazaretha are remarkable because of the fierce academic debate that was generated by G. C. Oosthuizen (b. 1922) through the publication of his *The Theology of a South African Messiah* (1967). G. C. Oosthuizen argued that the movement must be seen "in the context of the Zulu religion" and that, correctly understood, they are a new religion that sees Isaiah Shembe as "the manifestation of God." This argument was strongly attacked by Bengt Sundkler (d. 1995) in his book *Zulu Zion and Some Swazi Zionists* (1976). In Sundkler's view African religious movements "should be understood, *not* from the outside, from a Western standpoint, measuring its contents according to the standards and ideas of a European catechism, but rather from its own presuppositions." Suggesting that Oosthuizen *really* did not understand Zulu, Sundkler stridently dismissed his views. Ten years later the New York-based Zulu anthropologist, Absolom Vilakazi (d. 1993), renewed the attack on Oosthuizen's work in *Shembe: The Revitalization of African Society* (1986). He claimed that Oosthuizen did not understand the Zulu language or idiom, suggesting that he was an ethnocentric Afrikaner. Rejecting Oosthuizen's thesis, both Sundkler and Vilakazi urge their readers to accept that "Shembe's Church is deliberately and unapologetically Zulu" while at the same time entirely Christian.

Readers will be surprised to learn that both Bishop Amos Shembe and the Rt. Reverend Londa Shembe preferred Oosthuizen's interpretation of their beliefs to that of his critics and that Amos Shembe sought a court injunction to prevent the publication of what he called "Vilakazi's blasphemous book" that he believed completely distorted the life and teachings of Isaiah Shembe. Londa Shembe was equally strong in his rejection writing "About Prof. A. Vilakazi's book ... I leafed through the pages and there was nothing that I could find in it that gave joy to my heart," and "I have it in my mind to write a short work on the work life of Baba inKhulu Isaiah Shembe to counter the poison-pen of Vilakazi's." Although they disagreed with each other, both Amos and Londa Shembe agreed that Vilakazi's work was unacceptable. Amos Shembe believed Isaiah Shembe created an entirely new form of authentic African Christianity. Londa Shembe believed his grandfather founded a new religion. Both said that Oosthuizen, not Vilakazi or Sundkler, was the person who really understood their faith.

In retrospect it seems that the mistake Oosthuizen made when he published *The Theology of a South African Messiah* was that as a theologian he followed the norms of literary scholarship, not anthropological writing. Consequently, he bases his published text on the texts of the Nazarite hymns without reference to his knowledge of their oral culture and his extensive fieldwork. Therefore, he exposed himself to the charge that he imposed a Western theological framework on the texts. Actually Oosthuizen based his conclusions on the results of several years of fieldwork involving participant observation and numerous interviews with many amaNazarites. When they attacked Oosthuizen both Sundkler and Vilakazi based their arguments on primary research they did in the 1940s and 1950s that they updated only slightly from published sources and a few conversations with church leaders. Oosthuizen did his research in the mid-1960s among ordinary church members. Thus the differences between these writers may well be due to the development of doctrine within the Nazarite movement itself and the people interviewed at a given time.

Among the Nazarites spiritual experiences play a key role in the formation of their beliefs and practices. This fact allows for a development of doctrine in local congregations that eventually filters upward to the leadership. Therefore, the leaders always have to maintain a balance between educated explanations of theology and what the people actually think and feel. Recognizing this dynamic, it is possible to see why Oosthuizen and his critics could disagree so sharply about Nazarite beliefs while remaining true to their own data. Appeals by Sundkler and Vilakazi to written or published texts to establish the correct interpretation of those same texts do not work. Nazarite texts may be subject to theological exegesis in the future. But at present they can only be understood within the context of the life of the community where there is a dynamic interaction between spiritual experiences and the developing theology of the church.

Conclusion

Who was Isaiah Shembe? Are the Nazaretha authentic African Christians? Or are they a new religious movement? In the last analysis neither Amos Shembe nor Londa Shembe really knew. Both acknowledged a historic debt to Christianity, and Amos Shembe encouraged his followers to read the Bible because he saw the future of the Nazarites within the Christian community. Londa Shembe, however, was trying to find religious roots outside of the Christian fold, and both men acknowledged a wide spectrum of belief among their respective followers.

There is no easy answer to the questions raised by Oosthuizen's book. The Nazarite movement is yet in the process of formation. Whether they become an entirely new

religion, or develop into a form of genuine Zulu Christianity remains to be seen. All we can do at this time is plot their progress and continue to learn from this and similar dynamic religious movements.

Irving Hexham

See also Zulu Religion

Bibliography

Hexham, Irving, ed. (1994) *The Scriptures of the amaNazaretha of Ekuphakameni.* Translated by Londa Shembe and Hans-Jürgen Becken, with an introduction by G. C. Oosthuizen. Calgary: Calgary University Press.

Hexham, Irving, and G. C. Oosthuizen. (1996) *The Story of Isaiah Shembe.* Vol. 1. Translated by Hans-Jürgen Becken. Lewiston, NY: Edwin Mellen Press.

Hexham, Irving, and G. C. Oosthuizen. (1999) *The Story of Isaiah Shembe.* Vol. 2. Translated by Hans-Jürgen Becken. Lewiston, NY: Edwin Mellen Press.

Oosthuizen, G. C. (1967) *The Theology of a South African Messiah: An Analysis of the Hymnal of "the Church of the Nazarites."* Leiden: E.J. Brill.

———. (1981) *Succession Conflict Within the Church of the Nazarites.* Durban: University of Durban-Westville.

Sundkler, Bengt. (1965) *Bantu Prophets in South Africa.* 2d ed. London: Oxford University Press.

———. (1976) *Zulu Zion and Some Swazi Zionists.* London: Oxford University Press, 190–197.

Vilakazi, Absolom, with Bongani Mthethwa and Mthembeni Mpanza. (1986) *Shembe: The Revitalization of African Society.* Braamfontein: Skotaville.

The Apostolic Church of Johane Masowe

Africa has been the birthplace of many exciting and innovative religious movements. The motley of Christian churches that has emerged in sub-Saharan Africa has endeavored to incorporate many aspects of African culture and worldviews into their mission and theology. Many of the religious movements that emerged in Africa in the twentieth century were symptomatic of the spiritual yearnings of African Christians. There was a real need to fully incorporate African norms and culture into Christianity. This imperative led to the emergence of many charismatic prophets and a plethora of African independent churches.

One of the religious movements with a millennial tendency was established by Johane Masowe, formerly Peter

Shoniwa (1915–1973), in October 1932. He was a Shona. He became "John of the wilderness" after surviving a near-death experience. He emerged from this encounter with a new religious identity. Resplendent in a long white garment with a staff and a Bible, he proclaimed himself as John the Baptist sent as a messenger to Africans and the whole inhabited world. Masowe's religious movement started in the Hartley region of Southern Rhodesia (Zimbabwe). He moved from village to village, baptizing people who accepted his message of healing and a new golden age. The golden age embodies a time of political, economic, and spiritual liberation for the peoples of Africa. He ordered his followers to desist from wage labor for the colonial authorities and to resist colonial religious and political structures. He also promised a glorious new period of freedom, justice, and self-sufficiency. Masowe preached about the year of jubilee for African Christians. He implored the language of "release," which entails the proclamation of good news to the poor and the reign of God. He rejected all Christian sacraments except baptism. As the leader of this religious movement, he was mainly responsible for baptizing new converts. His followers believed in Jehovah, observed Old Testament dietary laws, kept the Sabbath, and practiced polygamy. Johane was often referred to as the "Word," "Spirit," or "Star of God."

The Apostolic Church of Johane Masowe was a pilgrim church that worshipped in open areas. Members claimed that Masowe had the spiritual power to fight evil forces and sickness. The poor and downtrodden were attracted to his message of holistic spirituality. The movement also included celibate religious women, who were perceived as a "Collective Ark." Masowe's followers, known as the *vahosanna* (the hosannas) or as "basketmakers" lived in their own separate communities. They made baskets, installed their own electric generator, and made furniture and metalware of different types for sale. The industrial initiatives of the *vahosanna* can be compared to those of the community of the Holy Apostles at Ayetoro in Southwestern Nigeria. Women wore white gowns and turbans, while men went around with long beards and shaved heads. Under political persecution in southern Rhodesia, the Apostolic Church of Johane Masowe immigrated to the Korsten suburb of Port Elizabeth, South Africa, in 1943. After the migration to South Africa, Masowe was called the "secret messiah" because his precise whereabouts were shrouded in mystery. After the late 1940s, he only made sporadic appearances to baptize new converts. Many interesting stories developed around him; the most enduring one was that he had died but later resurrected back to life. In 1960, his church was abolished in South Africa. Members of the Apostolic Church of Johane Masowe were considered renegades that

must be eradicated. With this development in South Africa, Masowe's followers moved to Lusaka in Namibia and Nairobi in Kenya. Masowe died in Tanzania in 1973, leaving behind a legacy of millennial promise of freedom and a golden age.

Johane Masowe was a spiritual maverick. He moved from one country to another creating a messianic aura around himself and for much of his life he could not be located. Even after his demise, his millennial idea was still sustained by his followers. His popular acceptance was rooted in the message of hope, deliverance, healing, and abundant life he offered his followers.

I believe that the activity of an African prophet like Johane Masowe is a telling testimony to the importance of African agency in the transmission of the Christian faith. It is also a confirmation that Africans were not dormant recipients of Christianity. They were able to mold and reshape it to fit their cultural worldview. The paternalistic assumption that Africans passively received Christianity belongs to a moribund intellectual tradition and must be jettisoned.

Akintunde E. Akinade

See also African Charismatics; Apostolic Church of John Maranke

Bibliography

Hastings, Adrian. (1994) *The Church in Africa 1450–1950.* Oxford: Clarendon Press.

Isichei, Elizabeth. (1995) *A History of Christianity in Africa.* Grand Rapids, MI: Wm. B. Eerdmans Publishing Co.

The Apostolic Church of John Maranke (Vapostori or Bapostolo)

Founded in 1932 by Shona prophet John Maranke (1912–1963), the Apostolic Church is one of Africa's many thriving new religions. Born Muchabaya Momberume in the Bondwe Mountain area of the Maranke Tribal Trustland of Zimbabwe (then southern Rhodesia), John (or Johane) received a spiritual calling to found the church after a near-death experience in 1932. Although records indicate that Maranke frequented the local Methodist mission as a youth and was baptized under the name of Roston, his group developed outside of mission control.

Inspired by his visions, Maranke established the church with the conversions of his elder brothers Conorio (Cornelius) and Anrod, and his uncle, Peter Mupako. The

John Maranke (center) with church leaders Robert (second from right) and Kangwa William (right) at the annual Passover ceremony in Lusaka, Zambia, 1958. FROM THE COLLECTION OF BENNETTA JULES-ROSETTE, COURTESY OF KANGWA WILLIAM.

first Apostolic ceremony was held on 20 July 1932, near the Murozi River in the Maranke Tribal Trustland, at which time approximately 150 converts joined. Maranke recorded his visionary experiences in the *Humbowo Hutswa we Vapostori* (New Witness of the Apostles), used by church members as a moral and spiritual guide. By 1934, he had firmly established the religious and social organization of the church and its major ritual practices, including a Saturday Sabbath ceremony (*kerek*), a Eucharist or Passover celebration (Paseka or Pendi), mountain prayer retreats, and healing rituals. John retained control over the group by ordaining leaders at the annual Passover ceremony until his death in 1963.

The church consists of a leadership hierarchy of twelve members based in Zimbabwe and more than 500,000 members, called Apostles (Bapostolo or Vapostori), across several African nations. The largest congregations are located in the Shona areas of eastern Zimbabwe, in southwestern Congo

(RDC), and in Angola, Botswana, Malawi, Mozambique, and Zambia. Apostles are ordained with the spiritual gifts of healing, evangelism, prophecy, and baptism. Maranke designated three ranks within each gift. The rank-holders are known as Lieb-Umahs (meaning rabbis of the congregation). All rank-holders in a congregation constitute its Committee of Twelve Elders, responsible for church governance. Although they are not political leaders, women hold the positions of healers, prophetesses, and ceremonial song leaders.

During the 1940s, the Apostolic movement spread throughout Zimbabwe. Proselytizing along the rail lines, Apostles converted new members in Zambia (then northern Rhodesia) and Malawi (then Nyasaland) as early as 1948. The first Congolese member of Lunda origin, Nawezi Petro, joined the church in southern Rhodesia in 1952. By 1956, the church had spread to the Kasai provinces of the Congo and as far north as the capital, Kinshasa (then Léopoldville).

Minor schisms eventually developed in the Congolese branch of the Apostolic movement. A similar pattern of growth and schism took place in Angola and Mozambique, where the Apostolic Church grew rapidly during the 1970s and early 1980s.

All congregations observe Saturday Sabbath ceremonies consisting of hymns in Shona, intermixed with songs in local dialects. Ceremonies outside of Zimbabwe are held in multiple languages and vary from one congregation to another, while retaining a basic format and order of worship established by John Maranke. The various branches of the church recognize Maranke as a prophet and founder. The movement, however, is not messianic, and Maranke does not occupy a divine status. Apostolic doctrine and beliefs combine elements of local traditional customs, in particular, marriage and healing patterns derived from the Shona, with Christian doctrines. The charismatic appeal of the church centers around its faith-healing activities and challenges to traditional medicine.

After Maranke's death, church leadership passed to his two eldest sons, Abel and Makebo, who continued the pattern of centralized control. Makebo died in the mid-1980s, and Abel continued to head the church until his death in 1992. A fairly smooth succession took place within the church hierarchy in Zimbabwe with consensual decisions for leadership transfer including, but not limited to, members of the Maranke family.

Within the framework of its established doctrines, the Apostolic Church adapts itself to changing conditions of the wider society. During the 1980s, some members of the group were involved in the *chimurenga* (Zimbabwean liberation struggle). Although, as pacifists, they could not bear arms, they nevertheless supported various sectors of the liberation movement. More recently, Zimbabwean Apostles have become involved in the ecology ("Green") movement in Zimbabwe, viewing the replanting of trees as a holy act. Since the 1970s, the Apostles of the Congo (RDC) have undergone persecution. Their civil status was removed in 1971, although they continued to worship clandestinely. In the other nations to which the church has spread, membership is on the rise, with an amalgam of rural, urban, proletarian, and elite members, and outreach efforts to Europe and the United States. The Apostolic Church is an example of doctrinal and ritual renewal in African Christianity. Its cultural and political innovations reflect the changing theological and organizational trends of Africa's new religions.

Bennetta Jules-Rosette

See also African Charismatics; Apostolic Church of Johane Masowe

Bibliography

Aquina, Mary, O.P. (1967) "The People of the Spirit: An Independent Church in Rhodesia." *Africa* 37: 203–219.

Daneel, M. L. (1971) *Old and New in Southern Shona Independent Churches*, vol. 1: *Background and Rise of the Major Movements*. The Hague: Mouton.

Jules-Rosette, Bennetta. (1975) *African Apostles: Ritual and Conversion in the Church of John Maranke*. Ithaca, NY: Cornell University Press.

——, ed. (1979) *The New Religions of Africa*. Norwood, NJ: Ablex Publishing Corporation.

Maranke, John. (1953) *The New Witness of the Apostles*. Translated by J. S. Kusotera. Bocha, Zimbabwe. Apostles of John Maranke: Unpublished booklet.

Murphree, Marshall W. (1969) *Christianity and the Shona*. New York: Humanities Press.

Azusa Street Revival

Regarded by many religious historians as the beginning of the modern Pentecostal movement, the Azusa Street Revival resulted from the efforts of William Joseph Seymour, an African American preacher who had briefly attended Charles F. Parham's Bible School in Houston, Texas. Parham stressed the idea that glossolalia was the necessary outward expression of the baptism of the Holy Spirit, a third stage—following conversion (or regeneration) and sanctification—in the process of Christian maturation. Seymour accepted a call to pastor a Nazarene church in Los Angeles and took Parham's theory with him.

His insistence that those who had not spoken in tongues had not actually received the baptism of the Holy Spirit offended many church members, some of whom had claimed that experience for most of their lives. Seymour argued that they had only experienced sanctification and that another spiritual experience awaited them. When the church expelled Seymour, he began to conduct meetings in the homes of sympathetic individuals, and on 9 April 1906, an eight-year-old boy was apparently the first among his audience to experience the baptism of the Holy Spirit evidenced by glossolalia. Seymour, who was joined by two other students from Parham's school, Lucy Farrow and J. A. Warren, then engaged an abandoned Methodist church at 312 Azusa Street in Los Angeles and began a three-year series of meetings characterized by a variety of ecstatic, charismatic expressions, including both speaking and singing in tongues as well as prophecy.

The success of Seymour's revival in terms of numbers was phenomenal. Fueled in part by sensationalistic newspaper accounts, crowds of people began to flock to the Azusa Street Mission. By late summer an estimated twelve hundred people might be found attending a prayer meeting at the site. The San Francisco earthquake, which occurred in late April 1906, also contributed to the revival's success. Frank Bartleman, a local Holiness evangelist who had participated in Seymour's prayer meetings even before he moved to Azusa Street, publicized the idea that the devastating quake signaled the imminence of the apocalypse and encouraged readers of his tracts to join the revival while there was still time.

By the end of the revival's first year (1906), some nine Pentecostal congregations, including one led by Bartleman, were established in Los Angeles. Though the movement had begun under the instigation of an African American preacher whose original West Coast congregation had been an African American Holiness church, the Pentecostal movement in southern California was interracial from its inception. Seymour's colleagues from Texas, Farrow and Warren, were black, but Bartleman was white, as were many of those who attended meetings at the Azusa Street church during the spring and summer of 1906.

Seymour's official position was within the Apostolic Faith movement, begun by his mentor Charles F. Parham in Baxter Springs, Kansas. Parham, though, did not immediately capitalize upon the successes in Los Angeles, preferring apparently to focus his attentions on spreading his message in the Midwest. He finally made a trip to the West Coast in October 1906 and was disturbed by two features of the Azusa Revival. Though he had shown some sensitivity to African American spiritual needs during his career, Parham could not accept the racial intermixing and equality that characterized the Azusa Street activities. His advocacy of the British Israel theory (that the ten tribes of Israel that disappeared from the Old Testament historical record during the Assyrian captivity were the forebears of the Anglo-Saxons) contributed to a clear sense of white superiority. Moreover, Parham did not believe that some of the glossolalia among participants in the Los Angeles revival was legitimate. He believed that after the initial speaking in tongues that evidenced the baptism of the Holy Spirit, Pentecostal believers would be spreading their message through xenoglossia (using earthly languages they spoke through divine intervention). He dismissed much of the Azusa Street glossolalia as mere babbling. When he unsuccessfully tried to assert his influence in the Azusa movement, Parham opened the door to the development of Pentecostal organizations to rival his Apostolic Faith organ-ization. Rather than being offshoots of established white denominations as has been the case with African American Baptist and Methodist churches, the Pentecostal movement among African Americans, which has produced such organizations as the Church of God in Christ, the Apostolic Overcoming Holy Church of God, and Triumph the Church and Kingdom of God in Christ, derives directly from the revival on Azusa Street in Los Angeles, which Seymour, an African American preacher, began in 1906. That revival also contributed to the emergence of many white-oriented Pentecostal churches, including the Assemblies of God and the United Pentecostal Church.

William M. Clements

See also Holiness–Pentecostal (Sanctified) Movement; Pentecostalism in Africa

Bibliography

Goff, James R., Jr. (1988) *Fields White Unto Harvest: Charles F. Parham and the Missionary Origins of Pentecostalism.* Fayetteville: University of Arkansas Press.

Hollenweger, W. J. (1972) *The Pentecostals: The Charismatic Movement in the Churches.* Minneapolis, MN: Augsburg.

Lincoln, C. Eric, and Lawrence H. Mamiya. (1990) *The Black Church in the African American Experience.* Durham, NC: Duke University Press.

Baptists *See* Music, Spiritual Baptists; National Baptist Convention of America; National Baptist Convention, USA; Primitive Baptists; Progressive National Baptist Convention; Spiritual Baptists; United States, African Religion in

Barbados, African-Derived Religions in

Among the 260,000 people living on this small Caribbean island of some 443 square kilometers, more than 80 percent are associated with one or another Christian denomination. Most belong to the Anglican Church and attend appropriate parish churches; Methodists, Roman Catholics, Jehovah's Witnesses, and Seventh Day Adventists constitute most of the remainder.

Zion Apostolic Temple at Richmond Gap, Barbados, during Black Civilization Week, 1994. PHOTO COURTESY OF MANFRED KREMSER.

Barbados today hosts more than 140 different sects and denominations, often similar in doctrine though different in name. Many storefront churches took root in impoverished rural areas. The intensely emotional religious experience they encourage and their joyous, hand-clapping gospel music are nearer to black African rhythms than the English hymns of the established churches.

The return of Pastor Granville Williams to Barbados in 1957, after living sixteen years in Trinidad, heralded the awakening period for many Afro-Barbadians to the realization of an African perspective to Christianity. In 1957, he founded the Sons of God Apostolic Spiritual Baptist Church, fashioned after other West Indian revivalist religions.

This Spiritual Baptist Church presently has a following of some 7,000 people, approximately 60 percent female and 40 percent male. It is one of the few churches in Barbados that espouses the teaching of the Black Divinity. One could state that they worship through the spectacles of the African persona who is fully aware of oneself as an important historical religious figure. The members are uncompromisingly Pan-African in perspective.

Since 1957, the church has connected with the Afro-Barbadian working class, many of whom broke away from the established churches to become Tie-Heads, as the Spiritual Baptists' members are called. Their message has also appealed to members of the middle class. Among its tangible achievements are two unique church buildings: the Zion Apostolic Temple at Richmond Gap, St. Michael; and the Jerusalem Apostolic Cathedral at Ealing Grove, Christ Church.

A major differentiating factor of this Afro-Barbadian church is its mysticism: the form of worship and the symbols used. Members wear colorful gowns, each color symbolic of a particular quality: white stands for purity, cream for spirituality, blue for holiness, gold for royalty, green for strength, brown for happiness, silver-gray for overcoming, and pink for success. Red stands for strength, as well as for the blood of Christ. But mostly they dress in white robes and tie their waists with colored cords, which represent their respective "spiritual degrees." Some wear sashes. Both men and women wrap their heads in cloth during services, hence the name, Tie-Heads.

As probably the only truly indigenous Barbadian faith, the church is closely tied to African religious traditions and rites. Members do not enter the *courts* (temple) wearing shoes. They worship with their whole bodies—they bow, spin, and whirl before the altar. Lively music is often accompanied by much hand-clapping, foot-stomping, and dancing. Prayers are often said in singsong, wailing, and weeping form. Sometimes the whole church "go down in Pentecostal prayers" (prays aloud together).

From the front entrance to the sanctuary, from the beginning of the service to the end, white candles are burned at various sections of the church, particularly at the altar. Sweet meditative incense burns throughout the service as well. At given points in the worship, bells are taken from the altar and rung fervidly several times, a conch shell is blown, and a gong is banged. Members "go off in the spirit," stamp their feet, make strong guttural sounds, or *adoptions*, and talk in other languages. The four corners of the church are specially marked and decorated by a member or members with the *lota* (a brass vase with flowers, water, and a lit candle in the center).

The Tie-Heads are also known for their "Mourning Ground" rituals. After accepting the faith, the members are baptized in "living water" and given instruction in the doctrine. The born-again then mourns "a godly sorrow which calls one away from the busy walks of life." The Mourning Ground is a sacred section of the church set aside for this purpose and tended by chosen members. Here, in isolation, the mind is cleansed by prayer and purification for a period of seven to ten days.

The Spiritual Baptists have worked their way into the Barbadian social mainstream in more than one way, participating widely in cultural festivals and other forums. Perhaps it is through these festivals that the Spiritual Baptists have manifested themselves more as a community-based organization than the other evangelical or established churches. The increasing demand for appearances of the Spiritual Baptists led to the formation of its folk group. Consistent with the church's outlook, the group sings Afro-Caribbean and African songs. Significantly, the church's biggest breakthrough on the cultural front was in 1981, when it formed part of the official program at the opening of the Caribbean Festival of Creative Arts (CARIFESTA) at the National Stadium.

The outward showing of the Sons of God Apostolic Spiritual Baptist Church continues in the way the pietistic rituals are observed: the baptisms, Palm Sunday, and Good Friday processions, which draw large crowds in the streets. Spiritual Baptist members are well informed about themselves, the Bible, and their social responsibility. Their solidarity with African ancestral links is noted in their conversa-tions, African attire—*dashiki* and *alpargatas*—hairstyles, and handicrafts. *Alpargatas*, also known as *alfagats* in Barbados and Guyana; poor donkeys and *saphets* in Barbados; *sampats*, *sapats*, and *zapats* in Caribbean Creole; and *shampata* in Jamaica, are a type of sandal of plaited rope or rubber cut from an automobile tire or a piece of wood. An expression of themselves is also found in their culinary arts, which are shared with Barbadians and visitors at the national Crop-Over Festival.

Manfred Kremser

See also Spiritual Baptists; Storefront Churches

Bibliography

Daniel, Mya D. (1997) "The Church as Theatre: A Dramaturgical Perspective of the Rituals of the Bajan Spiritual Baptist Church." Unpublished paper, University of the West Indies, Cave Hill, Barbados.

Elson, Omowale, ed. (1987) "The Revelations of the Spiritual Baptists in Barbados" *Thirtieth Anniversary Magazine.* December. Bridgetown.

Fields, Shonia R. (1997) "A History of the Spiritual Baptist Church of Barbados." Unpublished paper, University of the West Indies, Cave Hill, Barbados.

Guglin, Tamara. (1974) "The Spiritual Baptist Church of Barbados: A Description of an Afro-Christian Religion." Unpublished paper, Colgate University, Hamilton, New York.

Inniss, Lirlene. (1985) "Vestiges of an African Past in Barbadian Culture." Unpublished paper, University of the West Indies, Cave Hill, Barbados.

Batuque

The term "batuque" in Brazil generally refers to a public religious ceremony although, as a proper noun, "Batuque" is also used to refer to one of many Brazilian religious groups that combines certain beliefs and practices derived from a number of cultural traditions including European, African, and Native American. Although such religions have traditionally been categorized under the rubric "Afro-Brazilian," such a label is perhaps misleading in the case of Batuque, given the relative unimportance of African traits and the lack of a strong African slave heritage in and around Belem, the northeastern Brazilian city in the Amazon basin where Batuque is practiced. Other Afro-Brazilian religions, for example, Candomblé and Xango, with their salient emphasis on African heritage, are considered to be much more conservative in this regard than Batuque.

As is generally the case with religions of this type, the origins of Batuque in Belem cannot be determined with any certainty. It seems clear, however, that this practice was growing in popularity during the first few decades of the twentieth century after *terreiros* (compounds where ritual activities take place) were established in Belem by individuals who had migrated from areas south of the city. Batuque involves primarily individuals from the lower-socioeconomic classes of Brazilian society who participate in possession-trance rituals. Worshipers have a pragmatic theology that emphasizes a kind of reciprocity between humans and spirits in which the spirits agree to provide a variety of services for those individuals who act as mediums for possession and generally support the ceremonies given in honor of the spirits. This pragmatism is reflected in the fact that Batuque is not as formalized and as group-oriented as other religions of this general type in Brazil and, thus, allows the worshiper easier access to the spirit world in terms that are meaningful to the individual. Heterodoxy, a characteristic generally associated only with the fringe elements of most religions, is the norm in this case.

The vast and highly eclectic pantheon of Batuque includes spirits and other supernatural beings from Catholicism, African religions, Native American religions, as well as from legendary and mythical figures that are part of Brazilian lore. Most of these spirits, however, have Brazilian names, illustrating the local, strictly Brazilian-born, flavor of Batuque. The pantheon is generally divided into two broad categories, the Catholic saints and the *encantado*. The saints are thought to hold higher spiritual status, because it is believed that they reside on the highest spiritual plane with God and the angels and, thus, do not venture down to earth, a fact that precludes their involvement in Batuque as possessing agents. The *encantado* are spirits who inhabit the tangible regions of human existence, the sky, the air, the surface of the earth, and regions underground as well. Many *encantado*, especially those who inhabit the earth, are conceived of in highly anthropomorphic terms as demonstrated by their consumption of smoke and drink and their human-like behavior during their manifestations.

Not unlike the ceremonies of many other Brazilian and Caribbean religions of this general type, the Catholic saints are honored and prayed to at the beginning of the ritual after which attention is turned to the *encantado*. This stage of the ceremony involves an extended period of drumming and singing for the *encantado* and their manifestation in the bodies of the mediums. This interaction between the *encantado* and the worshipers is the highlight of the evening and the most important aspect of Batuque worship. The general public is welcome at these ceremonies and allowed to watch the drumming, singing, and possessions that occur in an open-sided structure that is the focal point of a *terreiro*. The sacrifice of animals, however, is done in secret, and only initiates are allowed to observe or take part.

Given the lack of standardized ritual, the eclectic ideological tradition, and the ethnically diverse population of Belem (and Brazil generally), Batuque will no doubt continue to be a dynamic religious practice as the relative strengths of this or that tradition change through time. In fact, the recent influx of beliefs and practices associated with Umbanda, Candomblé, and spiritualism (Kardecismo) has brought about yet further changes in the religion as worshipers seek to maintain a beneficial relationship with the spirit world.

James Houk

See also Brazil, African-Derived Religions in; Candomblé; Caribbean, African-Derived Religions in; Kardecism

Bibliography

Bastide, Roger. (1978) *The African Religions of Brazil: Toward a Sociology of the Interpenetration of Civilizations.* Translated by Helen Sebba. Baltimore, MD: Johns Hopkins University Press.

Leacock, Seth, and Ruth Leacock. (1972) *Spirits of the Deep: A Study of an Afro-Brazilian Cult.* Garden City, NY: Doubleday Natural History Press.

Rodrigues, José H. (1965) *Brazil and Africa.* Translated by Richard A. Mazzara and Sam Hileman. Berkeley and Los Angeles: California University Press.

Hutchinson, Harry W. (1957) *Village and Plantation Life in Northeastern Brazil.* Seattle: University of Washington Press.

Valente, Waldemar. (1976) *Sincretismo Religioso Afro-Brasileiro.* São Paulo: Nacional.

Big Drum Dance of Carriacou

The Big Drum is an age-old and enduring danced religion celebrated by the people of Carriacou, Grenada. Also called the Nation Dance, the Big Drum invokes ancestors to feed and entertain them with the playing of drums, singing of songs, dancing, and libating of rum. Conjectural studies place its inception during the era of slavery that ended on British islands in 1838. The Big Drum has preserved, in historical voices, an internal, conceptual side of Caribbean history. The songs, sung in Patois, contain a

A performance by the younger dance ensemble of the Carriacou Cultural Organization (C.C.O.). PHOTO COURTESY OF LORNA MCDANIEL.

Nation	Creole	Frivolous
Cromanti	Old Bongo	Chattam
Arada	Hallecord	Lora
Chamba	Bele Kawe	Cariso
Manding	Gwa Bele	Chirrup
Congo	Old Kalenda	Pike
Banda	Juba	Chiffone
Ibo		Man Bongo
Jig Ibo		Trinidad Kalenda
Scotch Ibo		
Temne		
Moko Yegeyege		
Moko Bange		

(PEARSE 1956: 2)

huge volume of information, and we gain insight into the sensibility of the enslaved, a view of a composite religion, a sense of the intense homeland longing, and the modes of social accommodation.

Song/Dance Classification

At a dream request from a deceased family member, it is customary for the family to give a Big Drum. Neighbors and community members attend without invitation. The ceremony may be also mounted to celebrate a marriage, memorialize a death, celebrate a new house or boat, or politicize a cultural event. A troop of six to twelve dancers and three drummers are hired. The female dancers wear brightly colored split skirts in imitation of the nineteenth-century French *douette*, which concealed a luxuriant lacey slip. The music is structured in call-and-response form, and the dance performed singly except for the Creole that may be choreographed for two dancers (*bele kawe, juba*) or for four dancers (*gwa bele*).

The classification of twenty-six Carriacou dances made by Andrew Pearse identifies Nation Dances, Creole Dances, and Frivolous Dances.

The one hundred twenty-nine songs of the Big Drum appear to come from three different eras due to the themes and poetic lengths that seem to unify them. The Nation Songs, the oldest, are set aside by the use of invocations and are often composed solely on the names of ancestors. The dances, too, which accompany the Cromanti, Igbo, and Manding Songs, are in contrast to other dances in that the dancer bends to the earth at a low angle. These dances represent a deep mood of petition and longing. The variety of themes in Creole songs are framed by social concerns elucidated by extended poetic forms. Creole songs are accompanied by syncretic secular dances such as the *bele* and *hallecord*, which exhibit European dance qualities such as an uplifted stance and ballroom footwork. The Frivolous Songs were borrowed from the neighboring islands of Grenada, Trinidad, Union Island, and Antigua (Pearse 1978–1979: 638), and as the classification suggests, the dance may incorporate fun-loving dance movements, one of which is called "winding" (of hips). From the structure and quality in the songs and dances it is suggested that the Cromanti, Igbo, and Manding songs constitute the core of the earliest ceremony that implored the spirits that were the focus of the entire multinational congregation.

The Big Drum is unlike any African rituals on neighboring islands for it does not include trance or possession and is imbued with a pattern of patrilineal lineage unusual in the Caribbean. Possession was at one time a part of the Big Drum within the Coupe Cou, a moribund ritual held at midnight. It was a dance mime, a stick fight between the moral forces of good and evil. Some of the songs, called Beg Pardon songs still survive, though the Coupe Cou, which was danced on the knees, does not.

History and Language

Carriacou, along with Grenada, its governing state, was owned by France from 1650 to 1763, when it was taken by the British. It was restored to France in 1779 and held to 1783 when it was again acquired by Britain. In spite of the many colonial exchanges, independence in 1974, the New Jewel Revolution in 1979, and the Marxist struggles ending in an American invasion (1983); the people's language (Patois) has retained its value. The English-speaking population holds the Big Drum and its language as a prize cultural product which preserves two-hundred-year-old historical texts. The meanings and memory of today's generation, however, differ from that understood and recalled by the people's forefathers and foremothers. They no longer recall specific ancestors, but instead relate a rich, tenacious legacy of a collective African past.

The names that permeate the Beg Pardon songs may be interpreted as names of ancestors or spirits. A connection is drawn between the Fanti spirit Amba and the name found in the Nation Song, *Amba dabia*, the most recondite of the Cromanti songs. The song cannot be fully translated, though "le me gunde" means "the sea scolds."

Amba dabia-e
Amba dabia-e
Amba dabia-e
Amba dabia-e
wea gunde
la me gunde
wea dende, wai-o
amba dabia-o

Though Yoruba people are not included in the early population of Carriacou there is a Yoruba spirit among the song names. It is a spirit borrowed from Trinidad. Carriacouans worked in Trinidad in large numbers after emancipation and upon their return the agricultural goddess Oko entered the Carriacou pantheon. A history of borrowing may be seen in the song words. The phrase "Iama Igbo Lele," heard in the Igbo Nation Song is the name of a mighty Vodun god. This appropriation appears reasonable due to the language relationship and slave exchange between Haiti and Carriacou. One of the earliest songs, a bongo, speaks of Haiti and the slave trade:

Plewe Mwe Lidé bongo
Pléwé mwe Lidé, Pléwé Maiwaz, oh
Hélé mwe, Lidé, hélé oh, Maiwaz
Hélé pu nu alé

Dimash pwoshi batma-la-vol-a Haishi
Vadi ya batma-la-vol-a kité, oh, Maiwaz
Sa ki kota mwe, kosolé yish mwe ba mwe
Sa ki kota mwe, kosolé Zabette ba mwe
Sa ki émè mwe, kosole Walter ba mwe.
Translation:
Weep for me, Lydia, weep, Mary Rose
Lament for me, Lydia, lament Mary Rose
Lament for us all
Sunday next, the schooner sails for Haiti
Friday the schooner leaves Haiti
Whoever loves me, console my children for me
Whoever loves me, console Zabette for me
Whoever loves me, console Walter for me.

(PEARSE, 1956: 4)

The institution of the Big Drum does not separate the spiritual focus and human interaction from politico-national organization in worship. They merge. The people themselves see the Big Drum as "an African institution" and celebrate their African origins as Cromanti (Akan), Igbo, Manding, Chamba, Kongo, Arada, Temne, Moko, and Banda. We see a humanity in the nine ethnic groups that gave rise to nine repertoires of dance and song, and nine rhythms that encode the legacy of the oppressed.

Lorna McDaniel

See also Caribbean, African-Derived Religions in; Grenada, African-Derived Religions in; Trinidad, African-Derived Religions in; Vodou; Yoruba Religion

Bibliography

Hill, Donald. (1972) "England I Want to Go: The Impact of Migration on a Caribbean Community." Ph.D. diss., Indiana University.

——. (1977) "The Impact of Migration on the Metropoliton and Folk Society of Carriacou, Grenada." *Anthropological Papers of the American Museum of Natural History* 54, part 2.

Lomax, Alan. (1999) *Carriacou Calaloo* [Recording]. Rounder Records 11661-1722.

McDaniel, Lorna. (1990) "The Flying Africans: Extent and Strength of the Myth in the Americas." *Nieuwe West-Indische Gids* 64 (1&2): 28–40. Utrecht: Johns Hopkins University.

——. (1993) "The Concept of Nation in the Big Drum of Carriacou, Grenada." In *Musical Repercussions of the 1492 Encounter*, edited by Carol Robertson. Washington, D.C.: Smithsonian Institution, 395–411.

——. (1998) *The Big Drum Ritual of Carriacou: Praisesongs in Rememory of Flight.* Gainesville: University Press of Florida.

Pearse, Andrew. (1956) *The Big Drum Dance of Carriacou* [Recording insert]. Ethnic Folkways Library FE4011.

——. (1978-1979) "Music in Caribbean Popular Culture." *Revista I Interamericana* 8 (4): 629–639.

Smith, M. G. (1963) *Kinship and Community in Carriacou.* New Haven, CT: Yale University Press.

Black Catholics in the United States

There are approximately 2.5 million African-American Catholics in the United States, with fourteen bishops, including five diocesan bishops; five hundred vowed religious sisters, five hundred priests, four hundred permanent deacons; one university, Xavier University of New Orleans; the Knights of Peter Claver, a fraternal and benevolent organization; and official presence within the national administrative structure of the U.S. Catholic Church.

Compared to other aspects of African-American religion, African-American Catholicism has drawn little scholarly attention and social scientists and historians need to conduct much more ethnohistorical and ethnographic research on the topic. The prevailing social and historiographic treatment of African-American Catholics has been leveraged on two basic misconceptions: (1) that they do not exist and (2) that they are a twentieth-century phenomenon. However, for the former, critical treatment of historical sources suggests the contrary. And, for the latter, there are vibrant African-American Catholic communities in Savannah, Baltimore, New Orleans, New York, Chicago, St. Louis, and many other places. Despite their numbers, African-American Catholics generally continue to receive cursory treatment in the scholarly study of African-American religion.

History

From 1563 until 1763, black Catholic Spanish-speaking slaves had an active devotional and sacramental life in St. Augustine in Florida. In 1738, the Spanish governor of St. Augustine erected Gracia Real de Santa Teresa de Mose as a town of freed Catholic slaves. And in 1739 South Carolina English-speaking slaves, BaKongo in culture, Catholic in faith, led the Stono rebellion, one of the fiercest uprising against enslavement in the United States.

In the West, Los Angeles was initially inhabited by people of black and Indian ancestry and Spanish California was largely "Afro-Catholic in its racial heritage, Hispanic in its culture, and Catholic in its faith" (Davis 1993: 33). In the original thirteen American colonies, black Catholics date back to the early years of Roman Catholicism in Maryland. Blacks constituted approximately twenty out of every one hundred Catholics in colonial Maryland (Davis 1993: 35).

The roots of the contemporary African-American Catholic movement lie in the nineteenth century. Fear and custom on the part of the white hierarchy deprived African-Americans Catholics of their own clergy, but laity—men and women—assumed responsibility and leadership. From 1789 until 1894, African-American Catholic laity initiated and sustained a national intellectual and social movement to importune their church to address their spiritual and temporal needs. In keeping with the African-American proclivity for mutual aid societies, black Catholics formed the Society of the Holy Family in 1843. African-American Catholic mutual aid societies existed in Baltimore and New Orleans. At the same time, this movement was not narrowly sectarian, but national and international in its assessment of social and economic issues.

The estimated 100,000 black Catholics in the South in 1860 were primarily concentrated in five regions: (1) Maryland, with some spill-over into Virginia; (2) western Kentucky, in the vicinity of Bardstown; (3) the low country of South Carolina, especially around Charleston; (4) Florida; and (5) the Gulf Coast, particularly in the vicinity of New Orleans (Miller 1980: 38). Washington, D.C., contained many African-Americans because of its proximity to black Catholic populations in Maryland in Maryland (Davis 1993: 90). The first order of black nuns was established in Baltimore in 1829. The second order of black nuns emerged in New Orleans. Southern Catholic bishops generally supported slavery. Bishop John England of Charleston, South Carolina, defended slavery in a series of eighteen letters published between 1840 and 1841, despite the fact that Pope Gregory XVI had condemned the slave trade in 1839. England contended the Bible, church councils, or canon law had never proscribed slavery. In contrast to American Catholics, European Catholics exhibited a greater tendency to condemn slavery.

After the Civil War, many black Catholics rejected their slavemasters' religion or could not practice it because of a lack of facilities or access to priests (Feagin 1968: 247). Unlike various Protestant churches, including white-controlled ones, the American Catholic Church did not make a concerted effort to evangelize freed people to its ranks. The European-based Mill Hill Fathers (or Josephites in the

The Vierge Noire (Black Virgin) on display at La Cathedral de Puy in France. The figure shows a black Virgin holding a black infant Jesus. The original, which was destroyed in 1794, reportedly dated to the thirteenth century. The figure was of much significance to Black Catholics in the early twentieth century and attracted many pilgrims from the United States. One wrote to the *Crisis* in 1916 that: "Can you believe that there are people in this world worshipping a Black Virgin who holds a Black Child?" SOURCE: *THE CRISIS: A RECORD OF THE DARKER RACES* 11 (APRIL 1916): 318. NEW YORK: NAACP.

American context) arrived in Baltimore in 1871 in order to proselytize African-Americans. Some African-American Catholics attempted to maintain some semblance of congregational life without the assistance of priests and nuns. Perhaps in response to this decline in the number of black Catholics, in 1875 the church appointed James Augustine Healy, the first black Catholic bishop in America and the second bishop of Portland, Maine (Davis 1993: 149–150). Indeed, the three Healy brothers were the first African-American Catholic priests in the United States. Patrick Healy became the president of Georgetown University in 1874.

David Rudd, a former slave, edited an African-American newspaper (*The American Catholic Tribune*) and organized a series of Black Catholic Lay Congresses that were held between 1889 and 1894. The first congress met in 1889 with nearly 100 black delegates from thirteen states, the District of Columbia, and South America, along with invited and sympathetic members of the clergy and the hierarchy. According to Davis:

> The first such congress was a celebration of unity and solidarity with greetings from Pope Leo XIII and a visit with President Grover Cleveland.... There was also a stirring address in which the delegates called for an end to racial injustice.... In this address, the delegates called for more Catholic schools; called for literary societies among their young; ... demanded the admission of African American men into the labor unions and urged the full employment of African American men and women; turned again to the question of education by urging the establishment of industrial schools for the vocational training of African American youth; called for orphanages, hospitals, and asylums for the care of African American children and sick and indigent; and deplored housing conditions for African Americans in the cities and discrimination against African Americans seeking to buy real estate. (Davis 1991: 259)

Four congresses followed this first, convening in 1890, 1892, 1893, and 1894. Women were not among delegates to the first congress, and it is not clear if they attended others, but a photograph of some participants attending the 1892 congress reveals the faces of at least four laywomen and one religious sister. At the conclusion of each congress, participants prepared and issued a statement to the whole Catholic community. The 1893 address of the Fourth Congress, written by laymen without formal theological preparation, but trained and educated in their various professions, has few, if any, parallels in American Catholic history. This document is a theological response to the social discrimination of peoples of African descent. It is distinguished by critical self-consciousness of racial, cultural, and religious identity along with a grasp of spiritual foundations for ministry that went beyond lay activism. The 1893 congress met along with other Catholics at the World Parliament of Religions in Chicago. The congress movement appears to have collapsed due to opposition on the part of the Catholic hierarchy, which viewed it as a threat to its authority.

Twentieth Century

Lincoln C. Valle, one of the participants in the congress movement, began to preach, along with his wife, in 1908 in

THE CHURCH

There are now five Negro priests in the Catholic Church in the United States; three are in the Order of St. Joseph, one is a member of the Holy Ghost Order, and the fifth is attached to Archbishop Ireland's diocese in St. Paul, Minnesota.

On Sunday afternoon, October 30, the societies of the Holy Name of the Roman Catholic Church made a big demonstration in Washington, D.C. One feature of it was the parade, with several thousand in line, including delegations from Baltimore and other nearby places. There were any colored men in line, but there was no semblance of "jim crowing." Each marched with his own parish members of whatever color. There was a full share of colored mounted marshals, and two of the six bands were colored, but the colored bands were not leading colored contingents.

This was in striking contrast to the action of the local committee of the World's Sunday School Congress here last May, which barred the few colored delegates from the parade altogether, while in other places they were segregated as far as possible.

Source: *The Crisis: A Record of the Darker Races*, vol. 1 (November 1910): 8. New York: NAACP.

Milwaukee's African-American community and facilitated the establishment of the first African-American church in the city. Following in the spirit of the congress movement, Thomas Wyatt Turner, a professor of biology at Howard University, also played a pivotal role in the creation of the Committee for the Advancement of Colored Catholics in 1916 (Davis 1993: 218) and the beginning of the first renewal among lay Catholics in the twentieth century. The committee was reorganized as the Federated Colored Catholics in 1924. This group functioned as an early Catholic civil rights organization, meeting in 1925 in Washington, D.C., in 1927 in New York, in 1928 in Cincinnati, in 1929 in Baltimore, in 1930 in Detroit, and in 1931 in St. Louis. The Federated Colored Catholics collapsed due to internal factionalism.

Catholicism in the South essentially functioned as a "Jim Crow church, with parishes, schools, church societies, seminaries, and even Catholic universities usually segregated" (McGreevy 1996: 8). Indeed, as McDonough (1993: 80) so poignantly observes, "Southern Catholicism has both accommodated to and rejected various forms of Protestant organization and thought." Only a few southern bishops permitted black priests or nuns to cater to African-Americans in the region. The Divine Word Fathers established the first seminary for African-American priests in 1920 in Mississippi. Katherine Drexel, the founder of the Sisters of the Blessed Sacrament, which had a mission to proselytize among Native Americans and African-Americans, established the first black Catholic university, Xavier University in New Orleans, in 1931. West Indian immigrants came to constitute a significant portion of African-American

Catholics in northern cities such as New York and Boston (McGreevy 1996: 29).

In 1909, more than thirty African-American men created the Knights of Peter Claver. According to Davis, the Knights of Peter Claver spread throughout much of the South in the first twenty-five years of its existence, and it became an important element in the religious life of black Catholics. It was for a long time their main social organization. The spread northward was more gradual. The first national convention outside of the old Confederacy was in 1930 in Okmulgee, Oklahoma; in 1940 it was held in Louisville, Kentucky, and in 1946 in Chicago (Davis 1990: 236).

The Vatican was bothered by the paucity of African-American clergy and the reports of racial discrimination in the Catholic Church, but did little to counter these patterns until the advent of the civil rights movement. John LaFarge and William Markoe, both white Jesuit priests, came to challenge Catholic racial practices in the United States (McGreevy 1996: 38–47). LaFarge established the Cardinal Gibbons Institute, a Catholic vocation school, in southern Maryland and later established the New York Interracial Council. Markoe published several articles on racial relations in *America*, a Jesuit weekly, and established an African-American congregation in the neighborhood surrounding St. Louis University. In contrast, Catholic bishops tended to be skeptical of such activities. Nevertheless, some liberal Catholics began to define segregation as a sin and formed in 1958 the National Catholic Conference for Interracial Justice, an organization that included thirty-six Catholic Interracial Councils (McGreevy 1996: 71). Some Catholics participated in the civil rights movement, including the march on Selma, Alabama, in March 1965 (McGreevy 1996: 155). In contrast to such efforts, many working-class Catholics, including firemen and policemen, exhibited strongly racist beliefs and practices (McGreevy 1996: 182).

The second renewal of lay movement was catalyzed by several converging events including the contemporary civil rights movement, which challenged the ethos and pattern of accommodation to segregation; the Second Vatican Council, which questioned the insularity of the Catholic Church; and the renaissance of black nationalism, which disputed the dominant cultural aesthetic. Fourteen days after the 1968 assassination of the Rev. Dr. Martin Luther King, Jr., a group of black priests, meeting in Detroit, charged that the Catholic Church in the United States was primarily a white racist institution, addressed primarily to and enmeshed in white society. The priests urged the church to make the eradication of racial discrimination and the development of black Catholic pastoral leadership priorities. From this environment, national organizations emerged: the National Black Catholic Clergy Caucus (NBCCC), the National Black Sisters' Conference (NBSC), the National Office for Black Catholic (NOBC), National Black Catholic Seminarians Association (NBCSA) and the National Black Lay Catholic Caucus (NBLCC).

In the past two decades, the concerns of African-American Catholics in the United States have been pressed forward by two offices: the Secretariat for African American Catholics, which functions as the chief advisor to the National Conference of Catholic Bishops and the United States Catholic Conference in fulfilling its mission among African-American Catholics; and the National Black Catholic Congress, an umbrella for the collaborative work of various black Catholic groups in developing an agenda for the improvement of the spiritual, mental, and social conditions of African-Americans in the context of evangelization.

Contemporary Black Catholics and Black Catholic Institutions

African-Americans, particularly upwardly mobile ones, began to join the Catholic Church in growing numbers after World War II. Lincoln and Mamiya (1990: 159) report that "[s]ince 1985 black Roman Catholics have grown from 880,000 to close to 2 million members, with the gains coming largely from Caribbean immigrants and upwardly mobile African-Americans seeking parochial educational alternatives to urban public school systems."

While black Catholics overall probably do not exhibit a higher socioeconomic status than black Episcopalians, Presbyterians, and Congregationalists, various studies indicate that they do exhibit a higher socioeconomic status than blacks belonging to black mainstream denominations.

Catholicism appears to have played a more accommodative role in African-American history than has black Protestantism. According to Hunt and Hunt, in sum, the impression of a new level of militancy on the part of Black Catholics rests on their sophistication regarding racism, an aspect of secular orientation related primarily, it would seem, to high status and assimilation. In contrast with those dimensions of militancy that are more clearly associated with the civil rights movement—black pride and collective protest—black Catholics remain "nonmilitant" and differentiated from other blacks (Hunt and Hunt 1977: 832). Indeed, relatively few African-American Catholics assumed leadership positions in the civil rights movement (McGreevy 1996: 162).

Anthropologist Gary Wray McDonough (1993) conducted an elaborate ethnohistorical and ethnographic study of African-American Catholics in Savannah. The city has three black parishes, St. Benedict the Moor, St. Anthony's, and the Most Pure Heart of Mary. The earliest of these parishes is St. Benedict the Moor Church, which was dedicated in 1889. The Franciscan Sisters arrived in Savannah in 1898–1899, and the Society of African Mission Fathers in 1907. Together they were instrumental in the establishment of a complex consisting of convent, orphanage, church, and school in the city. Savannah's black parishes constitute separate units from other diocesan ones and are much smaller than other urban parishes, although all downtown parishes have faced demographic decline. The actual geographic territories of these white and black downtown parishes overlap. Finally, the black parishes are linked by social organizations that set them apart within the city, the diocese, and the nation (McDonough 1993: 179).

Whereas St. Benedict's tends to cater to primarily middle-class black Catholics, St. Mary's draws upon its parishioners from different neighborhoods and social classes. The diocese established a black Catholic high school in 1952. The priests and nuns that have served the city's black parishes and schools have been almost exclusively white. Although a black Savannan was ordained a priest in May 1988, he was assigned to a parish in Augusta, Georgia. McDonough (1993: 202) characterizes the white priest/black congregation relationship characteristic of the city's black Catholic churches as an ambivalent one.

The Catholic hierarchy closed the black parish schools between 1968 and 1977 in its effort to conform to the spirit of racial integration promoted by the civil rights movement. According to McDonough, after the closure of all-black schools, inner-city interparochial schools were set up to reproduce an integrated *Catholic* community, rather than an ecumenical *black* one. In practice, these schools have become as much as 70 percent black, including Protestants seeking what they perceive to be a better, more disciplined education for their children (McDonough 1993: 98). Lay catechists have come to assume a pivotal role in the formation of a Catholic identity since the closing of the black parish schools. Despite the hierarchy's efforts to facilitate racial integration, Savannah's black Catholic parishes have incorporated various African-American religious practices, including gospel music, walking to the altar in order to deposit the offering in a basket, and holding of hands during recitation of the Our Father (McDonough 1993: 316–318).

In contrast to black Protestants who severed their ties with their white-controlled denominations, black Catholics have not been prone to schismatic tendencies. An exception, however, is George Augustus Stallings, Jr., the founder of the African-American Congregation. He made a request to Cardinal James Hickey of Washington, D.C. that he be permitted to establish an African-American rite that would have an independent liturgy and socioreligious structure comparable to Eastern Rite Catholics. Upon denial of this request, Stallings went on to establish a new congregation called the Imani Temple. He was consecrated a bishop on 12 May 1990, by the prelate of the American Independent Orthodox Church. Bruce Greening, one of Stalling's colleagues, went on to form the Independent African-American Catholic Rite.

Through the establishment and staffing of national offices, along with the emergence of a small, yet active, cadre of scholars in the ecclesiastical disciplines, African-American Catholics have begun to realize a distinctive religious practice shaped by the appropriation of African culture, African-American history, black Catholic theology, leadership of the laity, attention to spiritual formation and renewal, and commitment to combating racism in church and society. In 1979, at the prompting of their African-American members, the U. S. Catholic bishops circulated a pastoral letter on racism, "Brothers and Sisters to Us"; 1984 witnessed the publication of a pastoral letter on evangelization, "What We Have Seen and Heard," by the African-American bishops; and 1987 witnessed the publication of *Lead Me, Guide Me: The African American Catholic Hymnal*. On August 30, 1997, more than four hundred years after the arrival of black Catholics to these shores, the descendants of slaves dedicated a chapel in the Basilica of the National Shrine of the Immaculate Conception in Washington, D.C. to Our Mother of Africa as an expression of honor and love for Mary, the Mother of God.

Hans A. Baer (Twentieth Century section by M. Shawn Copeland)

Bibliography

Davis, Cyprian. (1991) "History of the African American Catholic Church in the United States: Evangelization and Indigenization." In *Directory of African American Religious Bodies*, edited by Wardell J. Payne. Washington, D.C.: Howard University Press, 257–263.

——. (1993) *The History of Black Catholics in the United States*. New York: Crossroads.

Feagin, Joe R. (1968) "Black Catholics in the United States: An Exploratory Analysis." *Sociological Analysis* 29: 186–192.

Hunt, Larry L., and Janet G. Hunt. (1977) "Religious Affiliation and Militancy Among Urban Blacks: Some Catholic/Protestant Comparisons." *Social Science Quarterly* 57: 821–834.

Lincoln, C. Eric, and Lawrence H. Mamiya. (1990) *The Black Church in the African American Experience*. Durham, NC: Duke University Press.

McDonough, Gary Wray. (1993) *Black and Catholic in Savannah, Georgia*. Knoxville: University of Tennessee Press.

McGreevey, John T. (1996) *Parish Boundaries: The Catholic Encounter with Race in the Twentieth-Century Urban North*. Chicago: University of Chicago Press.

Miller, Jon L. (1980) "The Failed Mission: The Catholic Church and Black Catholics in the Old South." In *The Southern Common People: Studies in Nineteenth-Century Social History*, edited by Edward Magdol and Jon L. Wakelyn. Westport, CT: Greenwood, 37–54.

Black Churches in the United States

See Abyssinian Baptist Church; African Methodist Episcopal Church; African Methodist Episcopal Zion Church; African Orthodox Church; Azusa Street Revival; Black Spiritual Churches; Church of Christ Holiness; Church of God and Saints in Christ; Church of God in Christ; Elder Solomon Michaux's Church of God; Fire Baptized Holiness Church of God; Metropolitan Spiritual Churches of Christ; Moorish Science Temple; Mount Zion Spiritual Temple; National Baptist Convention of America; National Baptist Convention USA; Peace Mission; Primitive Baptists; Progressive National Baptist Convention; Shrine of the Black Madonna; Storefront Churches; United Church and Science of Living Institute; United House of Prayer for All People; Universal Hagar's Spiritual Church

Black Holiness Churches

See Holiness—Pentecostal (Sanctified) Movement

Black Jewish Movements

Black Jewish movements have been a visible component of African-American religious diversity for at least 100 years, dating to the period after the Civil War and prior to the Great Migration.

Generally, Black Judaism has been characterized by a continual sectarian process of group emergence, development, splintering, and reorganization, although some groups have sustained their organizational names and structures for several decades. As a whole, Black Jewish groups are exemplary of a religious type that has been called *messianic nationalism* (Baer and Singer 1981; Baer 1984), which is characterized by the unification of messianic faith with the objective of winning cultural or even political independence. Messianic-nationalist movements, including those that embrace a Jewish or Hebraic identity, have at least some of the following features: (1) belief in a glorious African history and subsequent "fall" from divine grace; (2) rituals and symbols drawn from established millenarian religious traditions; (3) intense anticipation of divine chastisement of external oppressors; (4) assertion of black sovereignty through the development of nationalist symbols and

interest in territorial separation or emigration; and (5) explicit rejection of certain social patterns (such as dietary patterns) found in the wider African-American community.

Despite these common themes, messianic-nationalist sects differ in the source of their particular expression of politico-religious identity and ritual. Contemporary Jewish practice and biblical accounts of the ancient Hebrews provide the origin for many of the symbols, rituals, and beliefs found in the various and varied strands of Black Judaism. Often, Black Jewish groups are highly syncretic, adopting their ideas and practices from diverse sources, including Christianity and Islam. Indeed, it is possible to organize Black Jewish entities along a continuum, with contemporary Jewish practice serving as one pole and ideas and rituals that have their source outside of Judaism as the other. Consequently, a visit to some Black Jewish congregations would be fairly similar to experiences gained in a mainstream Jewish synagogue, while encounters with other groups would reveal only limited parallels to conventional Jewish practice. At the same time, some Black Jewish individuals and groups identify closely with mainstream Judaism while others see Caucasian Jews as impostors who have usurped their cultural and religious traditions (Chireau and Deutsch 1999).

The Roots of Black Judaism in the American Slave Experience

It is generally believed that the deepest roots of Black Judaism lie in the identification of African-American slaves with the Egyptian servitude and liberation of the biblical Hebrews (Brotz 1970; Shapiro 1970; Singer 1979). As Jones (1963) indicates, the religious imagery of African-American religion generally is replete with references to the immense suffering and heartfelt hopes of the biblical Children of Israel. This natural empathy found its earliest expression in the spiritual music of the slaves (Singer 1985). As Raboteau (1978) points out, African slaves both found and gave voice to their close identification with the ancient Hebrews through spiritual music. At the same time, folk preachers among the slaves were conversant with biblical stories and incorporated them regularly into their sermons. Genovese (1974), for example, records the case of John Jasper, a popular African-American preacher from Virginia who gave sermons on Joshua to both slaves and white audiences. Indeed, as Courlander (1966) stresses, the Old Testament, including prophetic and heroic figures like Moses and Joshua, probably had a much more personal and immediate meaning for African slaves than they did for their white masters.

For some slaves, biblical stories of salvation held a discernible political message, in addition to the spiritual comfort they offered. Uya (1971) argues that some slaves came to

Rabbi Arnold J. Ford of Beth B'nai Abraham congregation and choirmaster of the Universal Negro Improvement Association. PHOTO COURTESY OF RANDALL BURKETT.

see the Mosaic tradition as an invitation to dress themselves in messianic garments and seek freedom from their oppressors. Some of these individuals came to believe that the abolitionists and Union troops were mortal agents of Moses sent to do God's will and free the slaves (Marable 1981). Herein lay the potential of Hebraic identity to furnish a messianic-nationalist response to white oppression. It is noteworthy that important slave rebellion leaders like Gabriel Prosser, Denmark Vesey, and Nat Turner all took their inspiration from the Bible.

The specific transformation of metaphoric, symbolic, and even politically coded use of Old Testament elements to express the harsh conditions experienced by the slaves and their yearning for liberation to an actual adoption of Hebraic identity and the emergence of distinct Black Jewish movements is historically unclear. However, it is certain that by the turn of the twentieth century there were a number of African-American itinerant preachers in the Carolinas who were asserting that Blacks were the lost sheep of the House of Israel (Brotz 1970; Singer 1992). While some researchers have suggested that the origin of the earliest Black Jewish groups might be traced either to the slaves of Jewish slave owners or to individual African-American converts to Judaism, the earliest Black Jewish sects were organized by working-class men who lacked any known involvement with white Jewish congregations.

Early Black Jewish Congregations

The oldest known Black Jewish sect was called the Church of the Living God, the Pillar Ground of Truth for All Nations. Organized by a widely traveled African-American seaman and railroad worker named F. S. Cherry, the sect was founded in Chattanooga, Tennessee, in 1886, although little information exists about the emergence of the church (Shapiro 1970). Cherry's group later moved to Philadelphia, where it was studied by Fauset in the early 1940s. Fauset (1971) described Cherry as a self-educated man, conversant with Yiddish and Hebrew, who taught his followers that in a vision God called him to establish a church and to bring to the world the message that the true descendants of the Biblical Hebrews are African-Americans. Moreover, he insisted that both God and Jesus, as well as Adam and Eve, were black. White people, in his interpretation, were the offspring of the servant Gehazi, who was cursed by the prophet Elisha with skin "as white as snow" (II Kings 5:27). Additionally, Cherry preached that white Jews were interlopers and frauds (Fauset 1971). During slavery, he claimed, African-Americans were systematically stripped of all vestiges of their Hebraic heritage, but in the year 2000 they will once more assume their true identity. Ritually, Cherry's

group had many features of a holiness sect, including rigid rules against drunkenness, secular dancing, exhibiting photographs of oneself, watching television, smoking, swearing, and divorce, although speaking in tongues and emotional displays, common features of holiness groups, also were banned. The group's Sabbath ritual consisted of hymns, discussion of a Bible passage, and a sermon by Cherry, often about the usurpation of Israelite identity by white Jews. Neither Christmas nor Easter was celebrated by the group, but baptism was performed.

Perhaps the second oldest Black Jewish group was called the Church of God and Saints of Christ. William S. Crowdy, a cook on the Santa Fe Railroad, was the founder of this group. Crowdy proclaimed that he was called by God to lead his people back to their historic religion and identity. In 1896, he established his church in Lawrence, Kansas, among former slaves who had fled westward in search of land and freedom from the rising wave of white violence. Following Cherry's example, Crowdy moved his church to Philadelphia in 1900, but led it in 1905 to Belleville, Virginia, where the group prospered. Branches of the church were established in a number of cities in the U.S. and overseas as well.

In Crowdy's formulation, African-Americans were described as heirs of the ten lost tribes of Israel, while white Jews were seen as the offspring of miscegenation with white Christians. Various Jewish ritual symbols, such as the performance of circumcision, use of the Jewish calendar, wearing of skullcaps, observance of Saturday as the Sabbath, and celebration of Passover, were adopted by Crowdy. These were blended with Christian practices, including baptism, consecration of bread and water as the body and blood of Christ, and foot washing, to form a unique ritual synthesis. Efforts by Shapiro (1970) to update knowledge of current practices in the church were ignored by group leaders in Belleville who appear to prefer isolation from the wider world. Efforts by Jewish community leaders to convince the group to drop Christian practices and undergo formal conversion to Judaism also were rebuffed (Berger 1978).

Another early Black Jewish group of note is the Church of God in David. This sect was established in the 1920s in Alabama. The founder was a man named Bishop Derks Field. Possibly because of local white hostility, Field moved his church to Detroit. When Field died, a power struggle between two of his brothers and his close associate, W. D. Dickson, splintered the church. Dickson assumed the title of Bishop over his portion of the flock and renamed the group the Spiritual Israel Church and its Army. Baer (1984) reports that members of Spiritual Israel Church see themselves as the spiritual descendants of the ancient Israelites and their church as a restoration of the biblical Hebraic tradition. In the ideology of the group, Adam, who they believe

ישראלי רבני מועצה

INTL. I. B. of R. INC.

The web page of the International Israelite Board of Rabbis, Inc.

was created from the "black soil of Africa," was black, as were all of the biblical Israelite patriarchs and prophets. As for white Jews, the Spiritual Israelites believe most are the descendants of non-Jews who intermarried with the Israelites. Although Baer (1985) notes the continued use of the Star of David to adorn church buildings and costumes, the group does not appear to have adhered to any specific Jewish rituals or dietary prohibitions. For the most part, this group adopted beliefs and practices common among syncretic spiritual churches, except that it retained a nationalist tone atypical of most spiritual groups (except for the Universal Hagar's Spiritual Church, which also incorporated a number of Black Jewish elements) (Baer 1984).

As this account reveals, all three of the earliest Black Jewish groups shared several central traits: (1) formation in the South or early relocation there; (2) highly syncretic group beliefs and rituals; (3) strong identification with the biblical Israelites, including belief in lineal or spiritual descent from the Patriarchs; (4) inclusion of numerous non-Jewish practices, including acceptance of Jesus as a messiah figure; (5) messianic nationalism ideology, although limited—if any—public involvement in the civil rights movement or other public opposition to discrimination; and (6) founding by a charismatic prophet figure, who claimed to hear a calling from God.

Major Black Jewish Groups in the Later 1900s

Both directly and indirectly, through splintering and by way of ideological diffusion, the earliest Black Jewish groups became the source of a rich tapestry of Black Jewish congregations, federations, and ephemeral storefront collectivities throughout the twentieth century (Baer and Singer 1992). New York City has been one of the important centers of Black Judaism during much of this period. By the end of First World War, there were at least eight Black Jewish groups active there. Arnold Joshua Ford, A West Indian follower of Marcus Garvey, was a key figure on the New York Black Jewish scene early in the century. Ford attempted, unsuccessfully, to have Judaism recognized as the official religion of Garvey's Universal Negro Improvement Association. He was successful, however, in establishing the Beth B'nai Abraham congregation in Harlem. Three elements were central to Ford's ideology: (1) repudiation of Christian practices common among many black Jewish groups; (2) embrace of the label Ethiopian Hebrew and rejection of the term Black Judaism; and (3) strong emphasis on participation in the Return to Africa movement.

Ford ultimately migrated to Ethiopia, and with his departure leadership of New York Black Judaism was transferred to Wentworth Arthur Matthew, the founder of the

Commandment Keepers, Holy Church of the Living God, Pillar and Ground of the Truth. By the end of the 1920s, Matthew claimed over two thousand followers and by 1968, estimated that his group had grown to over four thousand members (Berger 1978) with branches in Brooklyn, Philadelphia, Cincinnati, Youngstown, Jersey City, and Chicago. Although many Black Jewish groups never accepted his leadership, his followers proclaimed that prior to his death in 1973, Matthew was the chief rabbi of all black Jews in the U.S.

Another center of Black Judaism is Chicago (Landing 1974). Unlike New York, Chicago groups have never developed publicly prominent leaders on par with Ford or Matthew. Rather, rivalry, fragmentation, and ephemeral organization have been the norm. Important Chicago Black Jewish congregations include the B'nai Zaken, the Congregation of the Aethiopian Hebrews, and the Royal Order of the Essenes. One Chicago group of particular note began as the Abeta Hebrew Cultural Center in the mid-1960s. Ultimately, this group, under the leadership of a foundry worker named Ben Carter—later called Ben Ami—migrated first to Liberia in 1968, and then to Israel several years later. Now called the Black Hebrew Israelite Nation (Singer 1982, 1988, 1999), the group has several thousand members living in Israel, as well as other followers in the U.S.

Merrill Singer

See also Church of God and Saints of Christ

Bibliography

Baer, Hans. (1984) *The Black Spiritual Movement.* Knoxville: University of Tennessee Press.

Baer, Hans. (1985) "Spiritual Israelites in a Small Southern City: Elements of Protest and Accommodation in Belief and Oratory." *Southern Quarterly* 23: 103–124.

Baer, Hans and Merrill Singer. (1981) "Toward a Typology of Black Sectarianism as a Response to Racial Stratification." *Anthropological Quarterly* 54: 1–14.

Baer, Hans, and Merrill Singer. (1992) *African-American Religion in the Twentieth Century: Varieties of Protest and Accommodation.* Knoxville: The University of Tennessee Press.

Berger, Graenum. (1978) *Black Jews in America.* New York: Commission on Synagogue Relations.

Brotz, Howard. (1970) *The Black Jews of Harlem.* New York: Schoken.

Chireau, Yvonne, and Nathaniel Deutsch, eds. (1999) *Black Zion: African American Religious Encounters with Judaism.* New York and London: Oxford University Press.

Courlander, Harold. (1966) *Negro Folk Music, U.S.A.* London: Jazz Book Club.

Fauset, Arthur H. (1971) *Black Gods of the Metropolis.* Philadelphia: University of Pennsylvania Press.

Genovese, Eugene. (1974) *Roll Jordan Roll.* New York: Vintage Books.

Jones, Le Roi. (1963) *Blues People: Negro Music in White America.* Westport, CT: Greenwood Press.

Landing, James. (1974) "The Spatial Expression of Cultural Revitalization in Chicago." *Proceedings of the Association of American Geographers* 6: 50–53.

Marable, Manning. (1981) *Blackwater: Historical Studies in Race, Class Consciousness and Revolution.* Dayton, OH: Black Praxis Press.

Raboteau, Albert. (1978) *Slave Religion.* Oxford: Oxford University Press.

Shapiro, Deanne Ruth. (1970) "Double Damnation, Double Salvation." M.A. thesis, Columbia University.

Singer, Merrill. (1979) "Saints of the Kingdom: Group Emergence, Individual Affiliation, and Social Change among the Black Hebrews of Israel." Ph.D. dissertation, University of Utah.

———. (1982) "Life in a Defensive Society: The Black Hebrew Israelites." In *Sex Roles in Contemporary American Communes,* edited by Jon Wagner. Bloomfield: Indiana University Press, 45–81.

———. (1985) "'Now I Know What the Songs Mean!': Traditional Black Music in a Contemporary Black Sect." *Southern Quarterly* 23: 125–140.

———. (1988) "The Social Context of Conversion to a Black Religious Sect." *Review of Religious Research* 30: 177–192.

———. (1992) "The Southern Origin of Black Judaism." In *African Americans in the South: Issues of Race, Class and Gender,* edited by Hans Baer and Yvonne Jones. Athens, GA: The University of Georgia Press, 139–153.

———. (1999) "Symbolic Identity Formation in an African American Religious Sect:: The Black Hebrew Israelites." In *Black Zion: The African American Religious Encounters with Judaism,* edited by Yvonne Chireau and Nathaniel Deutsch. Oxford University Press, 55–72.

Uya, Okon Edet. (1971) "Life in a slave Community." *Afro-American Studies* 1: 281–290.

The Black Muslims

"Black Muslims," a name coined by Charles Eric Lincoln in his study *The Black Muslims in America* (1960), are members of an American religious movement called the

Nation of Islam. From 1930 until 1975, the Nation of Islam only accepted blacks as members. They also considered whites as "devils" and supported the separation of black and white races. The Nation was a "proto-Islamic" movement, using some of the trappings of Islam mixed with an ideology of black nationalism. Although the name "Black Muslims" is often used for members of this movement, the members themselves reject this name. Throughout its history, the charismatic personalities of its leaders have been important to the survival, influence, and spread of the Nation of Islam in black communities.

During the largest black migrations from the rural South to the urban North after World War I, the industrial cities of Detroit and Chicago not only attracted large numbers of migrants but they also provided the background for the development of one of the most militant and separatist black religious movements in America, the Nation of Islam. Although it is not a part of orthodox Sunni Islam, the Nation can be considered as a stage in the development toward orthodoxy of Islamic belief and practices among African-Americans.

Master Fard

In the midsummer of 1930, a friendly but mysterious peddler appeared among the poor rural southern migrants in the black ghetto of Detroit called "Paradise Valley." He was selling raincoats and silks and other sundries, but he also began to give advice to the poor residents about their health and spiritual development. He told them about their "true religion," not Christianity but the "religion of the Black Men" of Asia and Africa. Using both the Bible and the Qur'an in his messages, he taught at first in the private homes of his followers, then later rented a hall that was called the Temple of Islam. This mysterious stranger often referred to himself as Mr. Farrad Mohammed, or sometimes as Mr. Wali Farrad, W. D. Fard, or Professor Ford. Fard came to be recognized in 1931 as "the Great Mahdi," or "Saviour," who had come to bring a special message to the suffering African-Americans in the teeming ghettos of America.

Master Fard, as he was called, taught his followers about a period of temporary domination and persecution by white "blue-eyed devils," who had achieved their power by brutality, murder, and trickery. But as a prerequisite for black liberation, he stressed the importance of attaining "knowledge of self." He told his followers that they were not Americans and therefore owed no allegiance to the American flag. He wrote two manuals for the movement, *The Secret Ritual of the Nation of Islam*, which is transmitted orally to members, and *Teaching for the Lost-Found Nation of Islam in a Mathematical Way*, which is written in symbolic language and requires special interpretation. Within three years, Fard had established several organizations: the temple, with its own worship style and rituals; the University of Islam, to propagate his teachings; the Muslim Girls Training, to teach home economics and proper Muslim womanhood to female members; and the Fruit of Islam, a cadre of selected male members who provided security for Muslim leaders and enforced disciplinary rules.

Elijah Muhammad

One of the earliest officers of the movement and Fard's most trusted lieutenant was Robert Poole (1897–1975), alias Elijah Poole, who was given the Muslim name Elijah Muhammad (Perry 1991: 143). The son of a rural Baptist minister and sharecropper from Sandersville, Georgia, Poole had migrated with his family to Detroit in 1923. He and several of his brothers joined the Nation of Islam in 1931. Although he only had a third-grade education, Elijah Muhammad's shrewd native intelligence and hard work enabled him to rise through the ranks rapidly and he was chosen by Fard as the chief minister of Islam to preside over the daily affairs of the organization.

Fard's mysterious disappearance in 1934 led to an internal struggle for the leadership of the Nation of Islam among several contending factions. As a result of this severe strife, Elijah Muhammad eventually moved his family and close followers several times before settling on the south side of Chicago in 1936, where they established Temple of Islam No. 2, which eventually became the national headquarters of the movement. Throughout the decade of the 1940s Elijah Muhammad reshaped the Nation and gave it his own imprimatur. He firmly established the doctrine that Master Fard was "Allah," and thus God is a black man; and that he, the "Honourable" Elijah Muhammad knew Allah personally and was anointed the "Messenger" of Allah. Muhammad continued the teachings of Fard but he also infused the lessons with a strong dose of black nationalism, which came from the earlier movements of Marcus Garvey's Universal Negro Improvement Association and Noble Drew Ali's Moorish Science Temple.

Under Muhammad's guidance, the Nation developed a two-pronged attack on the problems of the black masses: a stress upon the development of economic independence and an emphasis upon the recovery of an acceptable identity. "Do for Self" became the rallying cry of the movement, which encouraged economic self-reliance for black individuals and the black community. The economic ethic of the Black Muslims was a kind of "Black Puritanism"—hard work, frugality and the avoidance of debt, self-improvement, and a conservative lifestyle. This formula soon made the

Black Muslims conspicuously different from most of their fellows in the same socioeconomic class in the black ghetto. Their reputation for discipline and dependableness helped many of them to obtain jobs or to start their own small businesses. During the forty-one-year period of his leadership, Muhammad and his followers established more than 100 temples nationwide, innumerable grocery stores, restaurants, bakeries, and other small businesses. The Nation of Islam also became known for its famous bean pies and whiting fish, which were peddled in black communities to improve the nutrition and physical health of African-Americans. It strictly forbade alcohol, drugs, pork, and an unhealthy diet. Elijah Muhammad was prescient in his advice to his followers on nutrition: "You are what you eat," he wrote in one of his books, *How to Eat to Live* (1972).

Muhammad's ministers of Islam found the prisons and streets of the ghetto a fertile recruiting ground. His message of self-reclamation and black manifest destiny struck a responsive chord in the thousands of black men and women whose hope and self-respect had been all but defeated by racial abuse and denigration. As a consequence of where they recruited and the militancy of their beliefs, the Black Muslim movement has attracted many more young black males than any of the other black movements or institutions, including black churches.

In his *Message to the Black Man* (1965), Muhammad diagnosed the vulnerabilities of the black psyche as stemming from a confusion of identity and self-hatred caused by white racism. The cure he prescribed was radical surgery through the formation of a separate black nation. Muhammad's 120 "degrees," or lessons, and the major doctrines and beliefs of the Nation of Islam elaborated on aspects of this central message. The white man is a "devil by nature," unable to respect anyone who is not white and he is the historic and persistent source of harm and injury to black people. The central theological myth of the Nation tells of Yakub, a black mad scientist who rebelled against Allah by creating the white race, a weak hybrid people who were permitted temporary dominance of the world. But according to the apocalyptic beliefs of the Black Muslims, there will be a clash between the forces of good (blacks) and the forces of evil (whites) in the not too distant future, a Battle of Armageddon from which black people will emerge victorious and recreate their original hegemony under Allah throughout the world.

Malcolm X

All of these myths and doctrines have functioned as a theodicy for the Black Muslims, as an explanation and rationalization for the pain and suffering inflicted upon black people in America. For example, Malcolm Little (1925–1965) described the powerful, jarring impact that the revelation of religious truth had upon him in the Norfolk state prison in Massachusetts after his brother Reginald told him, "The white man is the Devil." The doctrines of the Nation deeply affected his thinking; the chaos of the world behind prison bars became a cosmos, an ordered reality. Malcolm finally had an explanation for the extreme poverty and tragedies his family suffered and for all of the years he spent hustling and pimping on the streets of Roxbury and Harlem as "Detroit Red." The conversion and total transformation of Malcolm Little into Malcolm X in prison in 1947 is a story of the effectiveness of Elijah Muhammad's message, which has

---

CHRISTIANITY AND THE HORRORS OF SLAVERY

MALCOLM X

My brothers and sisters, our white slavemaster's Christian religion has taught us black people here in the wilderness of North America that we will sprout wings when we die and fly up into the sky where God will have for us a special place called heaven. This is white man's Christian religion used to *brainwash* us black people! We have *accepted* it! We have *believed* it! We have *practiced* it! And while we were doing all of that, for himself, this blue-eyed devil has *twisted* his Christianity, to keep his *foot* on our backs ... to keep our eyes fixed on the pie in the sky and heaven in the hereafter ... while *he* enjoys *his* heaven right *here* ... on *this* earth ... in *this* life.

Source: Malcolm X. (1964) *The Autobiography of Malcolm X.* New York: Grove Press, 200.

A Black Muslim speaker draws a crowd at Speakers' Corner, Hyde Park, London, **May 1998.** PHOTO COURTESY OF KAREN CHRISTENSEN.

Harlem, the largest and most prestigious temple in the Nation of Islam after the Chicago headquarters. The Honourable Elijah Muhammad recognized his organizational talents and his enormous charismatic appeal and forensic abilities by naming Malcolm his national representative of the Nation of Islam, second in rank to the Messenger himself. Under his lieutenancy, the Nation of Islam achieved a membership estimated at 500,000. But like the other movements of this kind, the numbers involved were quite fluid and the influence of the Nation of Islam refracted through the public charisma of Malcolm X greatly exceeded its actual numbers.

Malcolm's keen intellect, incisive wit, and ardent radicalism made him a formidable critic of American society, including the civil rights movement. As a favorite media personality, he challenged Dr. Martin Luther King's central notions of "integration" and "nonviolence." Malcolm felt that what was at stake at a deeper level than the civil right to sit in a restaurant or even to vote was the integrity of black selfhood and its independence. His biting critique of the "so-called Negro" and his emphasis upon the recovery of black self-identity and independence provided the intellectual foundations for the "Black Power" and black consciousness movements of the late 1960s and 1970s in American society. In contrast to King's nonviolence, Malcolm urged his followers to defend themselves "by any means possible." He also articulated the pent-up anger, the frustration, the bitterness, and the rage felt by the dispossessed black masses, the "grass roots."

As a result of an internal dispute on political philosophy and morality with Elijah Muhammad, Malcolm left the Nation of Islam in March 1964 in order to form his own organizations, the Muslim Mosque, Inc. and the Organization for Afro-American Unity. He took the Muslim name "el-Hajj Malik el-Shabazz" after converting to orthodox Sunni Islam and participating in the Hajj, the annual pilgrimage to Mecca. Malcolm was assassinated on 21 February 1965 while he was delivering a lecture at the Audubon Ballroom in Harlem.

Louis Farrakhan and Warith Deen Mohammed

From 1965 until Elijah Muhammad's death in February 1975, the Nation of Islam prospered economically but its membership never surged again. Minister Louis X of Boston, also called Louis Abdul Haleem Farrakhan, replaced Malcolm as the national representative and the head minister of Temple No. 7 in New York. During this period the Nation acquired an ultramodern printing press, cattle farms in Georgia and Alabama, and a bank in Chicago.

been repeated many thousands of times over during the forty-one year history of the Nation of Islam under Mr. Muhammad's leadership. Dropping one's surname and taking on an X, standard practice in the movement, was an outward symbol of inward changes: it meant ex-Christian, ex-Negro, ex-slave.

The years between Malcolm's release from prison and his assassination, 1952 to 1965, mark the period of the greatest growth and influence of the Nation of Islam. After meeting Elijah Muhammad in 1952, he began organizing Muslim temples in New York, Philadelphia, and Boston in the Northeast, and in the South and on the West Coast as well. Malcolm founded the Nation's newspaper, *Muhammad Speaks*, in the basement of his home and initiated the practice of requiring every male Muslim to sell an assigned quota of newspapers on the street as a recruiting and fund-raising device. He rose rapidly through the ranks to become minister of Boston Temple No. 11 and was later rewarded with the post of minister of Temple No. 7 in

After a bout of illness, Mr. Muhammad died in Chicago and one of his six sons, Wallace Deen Muhammad (later Imam Warith Deen Mohammed), was named supreme minister of the Nation of Islam. However, two months later Wallace shocked his Black Muslim followers and the world by declaring that whites were no longer viewed as devils and they could join the movement. He began to make radical changes in the doctrines and the structure of the Nation of Islam and moved it in the direction of orthodox Sunni Islam.

The changes introduced by Imam Warith Deen Mohammed led to a splintering of the movement, especially among the hardcore black nationalist followers. In 1978, Minister Louis Farrakhan led a schismatic group that succeeded in resurrecting the old Nation of Islam. Farrakhan's Nation, which is also based in Chicago, retains the black nationalist and separatist beliefs and doctrines that were central to the teachings of Elijah Muhammad. Minister Farrakhan displays much of the charisma and forensic candor of Malcolm X and his message of black nationalism is again directed to those mired in the underclass, as well as to disillusioned intellectuals via the Nation's *Final Call* newspaper and popular musical rap groups like Public Enemy. In October 1995 Farrakhan's Nation of Islam was able to mobilize about one million black men in the Million Man March in Washington, D.C., making it one of the largest protest marches, surpassing the March on Washington led by Dr. Martin Luther King, Jr. in August 1963.

In existence for or more than seventy years, the Nation of Islam in its various forms has become the longest-lasting and most enduring of the black militant and separatist movements that have occasionally appeared in the history of black people in the United States. Besides its crucial role in the development of the black consciousness movement, the Nation is important for having introduced Islam as a fourth major alternative religious tradition in American society, alongside Protestantism, Catholicism, and Judaism.

Lawrence H. Mamiya

See also Moorish Science Temple; Universal Negro Improvement Association

Bibliography

Breitman, George, ed. (1965) *Malcolm X Speaks.* New York: Grove Press.

Essien-Udom, E. U. (1962) *Black Nationalism: A Search for Identity in America.* Chicago, IL: University of Chicago Press.

Farrakhan, Louis. (1974) *Seven Speeches.* Chicago: Temple No. 2 Press.

Gardell, Mattias. (1996) *In the Name of Elijah Muhammad: Louis Farrakhan and the Nation of Islam.* Durham, NC: Duke University Press.

Lincoln, Charles Eric. (1960) *The Black Muslims in America.* Boston: Beacon Press.

Malcolm X, and Alex Haley. (1965) *The Autobiography of Malcolm X.* New York: Grove Press.

Mamiya, Lawrence. (1982) "From Black Muslim to Bilalian: The Evolution of A Movement." *Journal for the Scientific Study of Religion* 21, 2 (June): 138–152.

———. (1983) "Minister Louis Farrakhan and the Final Call: Schism in the Muslim Movement." In *The Muslim Community in North America*, edited by Earle Waugh, Baha Abu-Laban, and Regula Qureshi. Edmonton, Canada: University of Alberta Press, 234–255.

Muhammad, Elijah. (1965) *Message to the Black Man in America.* Chicago: Temple No. 2 Press.

Muhammad, Warith Deen. (1980) *As the Light Shineth From the East.* Chicago: WDM Publications.

Perry, Bruce. (1991) *Malcolm: The Life of A Man Who Changed Black America.* Barrytown, NY: Station Hill.

Black Nationalism

Black Nationalism *See* Black Muslims; Black Theology; Jamaica, African Derived Religions in; Moorish Science Temple; Rastafari; Rastafari in Global Context; Rastafari in the United States; United States, African Religions in; Universal Negro Improvement Association

Black Spiritual Churches

Among religions in the United States, the Spiritual churches are unique. They differ from other places of worship by their combination of elaborate rituals, highly aesthetic sanctuaries, intensely emotional services of worship, flexible organization, and openness to women ministers. More than anything, however, what sets the Spiritual churches apart from other mainland North American religions is their eclectic belief system that draws on Roman Catholicism, Pentecostalism, nineteenth century Spiritualism, and African religious concepts that were incorporated into what is known as voodoo or hoodoo in the United States. In places, this eclecticism is even more extensive and includes New Thought, New Age, astrology, Christian Science, Hinduism, Islam, and Judaism. The resulting syncretism, or mixing of elements of different cultures, makes the Spiritual churches similar to religions found in the Caribbean and Latin American: Vodou in Haiti; Santeríia in Cuba; Candomblé, Macumba, and Umbanda in Brazil; Revivalist, Kumina and Convince in Jamaica; and Shango and Spiritual Baptist in Trinidad. Although all religions, including major world religions, exhibit degrees of syncretism, the term is almost exclusively reserved to describe groups such as those above, including the Spiritual churches. Critics of the concept of syncretism stress its pejorative connotation, since the belief systems formed from such mixtures often appear inconsistent or chaotic, and the groups associated with them are highly stigmatized by more powerful and elite sectors of the society. The concept's supporters, however, claim that syncretism is a dynamic and creative process in situations where people with different cultures come into contact.

Development of Spiritual Churches in the United States

The origins of the Spiritual churches are far from clear. As a movement with organized congregations and associations, the religion can be traced back to the second decade of the twentieth century. Although these early congregations were all known as Spiritualist, by the 1940s they had almost everywhere shortened the name to Spiritual. By doing so, members of these largely African-American churches distanced themselves from white Spiritualists who had begun to institute racist policies that excluded blacks from their principal organization. In addition, this strengthened leaders' efforts to legitimize the churches in the eyes of the larger religious community. According to one version of events, the earliest Spiritual churches were founded in New Orleans and from there spread elsewhere. The other version maintains that the churches first appeared in Chicago. Those who favor New Orleans see the religion as a continuation of the syncretism between African and Catholic beliefs and rituals that gave rise to voodoo in the region. While this is indeed a possibility, solid proof is lacking.

There is, however, evidence that organized congregations of Spiritual people appeared in Chicago before they did in New Orleans. Furthermore, this version of events fits with oral histories from Louisiana stating that the founder of the religion was a woman named Leafy Anderson who arrived in New Orleans between 1918 and 1920 from Chicago where she originally organized a church in 1913. Whether or not Leafy Anderson established the first Spiritual church is not certain, but there is no doubt about her importance in the early days of the movement. By the time Leafy Anderson died in 1927, she had set up congregations not only in Chicago and New Orleans, but in Little Rock, Memphis, Pensacola, Biloxi, and Houston. Together these congregations formed an organization known as the Eternal Life Spiritualist Association.

Despite the fact that members of mainstream Christianity usually have only superficial knowledge of the Spiritual churches, some Spiritual leaders and congregations have managed to become fairly well-known locally and nationally. Among them have been the Reverend Clarence Cobbs (1908–1979) of Chicago's First Church of Deliverance, Mother Catherine Seals (1887–1930) of New Orleans' Temple of the Innocent Blood, and King Louis H. Narcisse (1921–1989) of Oakland's Mt. Zion Spiritual Temple with branches in Detroit and elsewhere. From the 1920s to the 1950s, the movement's charismatic leaders and the religion's appeal generated a large number of congregations, made up of working-class and some middle-income blacks. On Chicago's Southside from 1928 to 1938, Spiritual churches increased from 17 to 51. In New Orleans, the number grew from 23 in the 1930s to almost 100 in the 1940s. Similarly, the churches were numerous in Harlem in the 1920s, constituting 15 percent of that area's congregations. During the 1920s and 1930s, Spiritual churches were also established in Houston, Detroit, Baltimore, Philadelphia, Saint Louis, Kansas City, and later on in Africa. Although the religion still remains widespread, its expansion has slowed. Actual strength, however, is difficult to measure. Spiritual churches are not affiliated with local councils of churches; only a few are listed in telephone directories; there are no complete membership records; some congregations are not integrated into any association of Spiritual churches; and others hesitate to include Spiritual in their name because of the stigma attached to the group, preferring instead to be known as non-denominational or Holiness.

Beliefs and Practices of Spiritual Churches

In many instances, Spiritual churches outwardly resemble Catholic places of worship. There is considerable emphasis on elaborate altars, holy water, incense, and statues of saints. Some people may genuflect in front of the main altar, make the sign of the cross, and light votive candles. Members turn to saints to ask for assistance by holding novenas and pay homage to them by constructing special altars on holy days. As among many traditional Roman Catholics, St. Joseph may help someone acquire a spouse or resolve marital conflict; St. Lucy cures eye ailments; and St. Jude works on "impossible cases."

Along with features of Catholic belief and ritual, the Spiritual churches have adopted aspects of Pentecostalism. Most important are the individual's conversion and subsequent personal religious experience, a process that leads one to love and accept Jesus as a personal savior and source of blessings, especially the Holy Spirit. In many of the churches, the song "Jesus is the Light of the World" is sung at the beginning of each service and the phrase is prominently displayed at the front of the sanctuary. As in Pentecostal churches, worship services are loosely structured to give participants as many opportunities as possible to feel the Holy Spirit by testifying, shouting, speaking in tongues, and praying extemporaneously.

While most members of the churches strongly deny any links to Spiritualism and voodoo, or hoodoo, these systems of belief and ritual have contributed to the Spiritual religion. Unlike Haitian Vodou, there is little evidence of syncretism of African deities and Christian saints, despite the role of saints in the churches' beliefs and rituals. Spiritual ministers do regularly use paraphernalia such as candles, oils, incense, and books that are sold in "candle shops" that have come to be associated with occult practices. Moreover, Spiritual ministers in the past have even openly proclaimed that certain nights were "hoodoo nights" in their churches, that they performed hoodoo in private, or that it was possible to hoodoo someone by reading certain passages from the Bible at noon or midnight. The Spiritual churches' link to Spiritualism is especially seen in the emphasis that both groups place on healing and prophecy. Similar to Spiritualist mediums, Spiritual ministers use their powers to contact spirits and convey "messages" to believers. These utterances vary in content, but often include practical advice regarding diet, regimen, and interpersonal relationships.

Worship in Spiritual churches usually reflects all four of these traditions and is shaped by the needs of the people who are gathered at a particular time, or, as members explain, by the way they are "led by the spirit." For the most part, a service is composed of the same elements of worship that are found in any church: prayers, testimonies, musical selections, scripture readings, preaching, congregational singing, announcements, reports, and collections. In addition, the services almost always include one or more special rituals. These range from traditional Christian rites, such as Holy Communion, baptism, and ordination, to observances that are unique, such as helping hand services, bless services, candle drills, and feasts to honor saints. In order to perform these rituals, ministers use typical church paraphernalia such as candles, incense, oils, and water; however, they can distribute an unlimited number of more common articles, including plants, handkerchiefs, nails, and kitchen matches, for blessings or good luck.

The most important ceremonies, and markers of this faith, are healing and prophecy. According to church members, the Spiritual religion was built on these two "gifts of the spirit." They may occur either in public worship or during private therapeutic sessions led by ministers who are spiritual advisors to "clients" suffering from a variety of "conditions." These include physical ills, psychological conflicts, and social tensions. The providers of healing and prophecy include prophets who "read" or "give messages" to people, divine healers who handle assorted illnesses, and spiritual advisors who provide counseling on a wide range of matters.

During worship, a complex form of spirit possession often occurs. Members may be filled by the Holy Spirit, as in Pentecostal churches, or "entertain" spirits or spirit guides, as in voodoo and Spiritualism. According to the churches' teachings, each person has a spirit guide who may be a deceased relative, biblical figure, Christian saint, or another important individual in the group's belief system. Whether one's guide is unknown or has been revealed after a period of prayer and fasting, the relationship to the believer is crucial. A guide can work for one's benefit through association with good spiritual forces in the universe, or if overcome by evil spirits can leave the person to suffer. Because these two possibilities are ever-present, Spiritual people often quote scripture that one must "try the spirit by the spirit." That is, an individual must use his or her spirit guide to determine if a spirit that is either independent or associated with another person is good or evil.

The relationship that Spiritual churches and people have to each other is complex. Fissioning has produced numerous local congregations with considerable autonomy and a large number of associations that link Spiritual churches in one city or state to those elsewhere. Among the most important associations and their headquarters are the Metropolitan Spiritual Churches of Christ (Indianapolis), Israel Universal Spiritual Churches of Christ (New Orleans), Spiritual Israel and its Army (Detroit), and Universal Hagar's Spiritual Church (Detroit). Despite the bureaucratic formal organization and hierarchy of bishops and ministers in many associations, interaction on all levels tends to be informal and kin-like in character.

Women have played an especially important role in the Spiritual churches. Barred until recently from ordination and major leadership roles in mainstream Protestantism, women turned to the Spiritual churches. A chronology of church leaders in the 1920s shows that the religion was in many places a women's movement. This pattern continued until the mid-1930s, when in cities such as New Orleans men assumed and still maintain the most important positions of leadership.

Critics of the Spiritual churches and their leaders find them flawed when compared to the black Muslims' concentration on economic and political strength, Daddy Grace's emphasis on material goods, Father Divine's stress on social equality, the black Jews' call for a return to a moral community, or the Shrine of the Black Madonna's call to build a nation within a nation. They maintain that while the worship is African-American in style, the Spiritual churches have failed to establish programs to help meet the social, economic, and political needs of blacks who continue to face poverty, disease, and racism. Additional criticism is that the Spiritual religion is ultimately maladaptive for African-Americans because it focuses on the individual, as in psychotherapy, and tends to deny the social, economic, and political dimensions of problems in America. From this perspective, a Spiritual church leader merely instructs adherents to perform a series of rituals and to change to a more positive mode of thinking.

Spiritual people have not been totally disinterested socially and politically, however. Early church leaders in New Orleans provide several examples of attempts to solve community problems. Mother Catherine Seals originally proposed that her church become a shelter for unmarried pregnant women and a home to rear their children. Mother Maud 'Shannon gave away toys, money, and food at Christmas. Other leaders during the 1930s saw the need to establish an elementary school, a home for the elderly, and an orphanage, even though they were unable to realize these plans. In Chicago, the church led by Reverend Clarence Cobbs constructed a community and convalescent facility. More typically, however, Spiritual people tend to be involved with other African-Americans through informal networks of family and friends and participation in a variety of voluntary associations, such as the Masons, Eastern Star, NAACP, local political groups, and social clubs.

While still a presence in African-American communities, the future of the Spiritual churches is uncertain as religion in general continues to evolve in the United States. Nevertheless, the Spiritual churches may well persist for some time to come, even with declining numbers of adherents, given the extensive syncretism that they can accommodate in belief and ritual.

Claude F. Jacobs

See also Candomblé; Mount Zion Spiritual Temple; Metropolitan Spiritual Churches of Christ; Santeria; Spiritualism; Universal Hagar's Spiritual Church; Vodouun; Yoruba Religion

Bibliography

Baer, Hans. (1984) *The Black Spiritual Movement: A Religious Response to Racism.* Knoxville: The University of Tennessee Press.

Baer, Hans, and Merrill Singer. (1992) *African-American Religion in the Twentieth Century: Varieties of Protest and Accommodation.* Knoxville: The University of Tennessee Press.

Jacobs Claude F., and Andrew J. Kaslow. (1991) *The Spiritual Churches of New Orleans: Origins, Beliefs, and Rituals of an African-American Religion.* Knoxville: The University of Tennessee Press.

Black Theology

More than any other issue in the history of African-American religious thought, the meaning of Christianity and its relation to black oppression has generated ongoing controversy and debate. In fact, no interpretation of black life in America can ignore the manner in which the debate concerning Christianity impacted the social, political, and religious dimensions of the African-American freedom struggle, particularly the civil rights and Black Power movements of the late 1940s, 50s, and 60s.

This article examines the emergence of black theology in the late 1960s, paying special attention to the role of the National Conference of Black Churchmen and the work of James H. Cone. The article addresses the central theological question African-Americans have asked throughout their sojourn in America: Is Christianity a liberating reality in African-American life, or is it an oppressive force that hinders black liberation? It is no accident that this question concerning the efficacy of Christianity intensified during the civil rights and Black Power movements. As black people's hope concerning integration soared in the post-World War II years, so did their belief that Christianity was the force that would help them to realize the beloved community envisioned by Martin Luther King, Jr. But the optimism of the 1950s and early 1960s turned to hopelessness and despair as blacks in the urban North discovered that the passage of civil rights legislation had no bearing on their economic plight. As the gap between the promise of democracy and the reality of poverty widened, so did the perception that Christianity provided the solution to black oppression. Increasingly alienated from the structures of white power, young blacks began to feel that violence was the only way to make their voices heard. Significantly, this mounting disillusionment was accompanied by harsh critiques of Christianity leveled by the Nation of Islam, Black Power militants, and radical black clergy who were sensitive to the cries of the masses.

Christianity, Black Power, and Black Theology

Black Power made a dramatic impact upon African-American churches. The urban rebellions that swept across the country between 1963 and 1968 reflected the mounting frustration of black youth alienated from the mainstream of American life. During these turbulent years young African-Americans, especially those in the ghettos of the urban North, quickly turned away from the ideologies of integration and nonviolence to embrace the philosophies of Black Nationalism and self-defense. Also important for understanding the emergence of Black Power, however, is the frustration of African-American youth directed toward the black church, an institution they considered unresponsive to their radical, nationalist consciousness. The nationalist teachings of Elijah Muhammad and Malcolm X had a profound impact on the younger, more militant leaders of the civil rights movement. Elijah Muhammad's claim that "Christianity is the white man's religion" influenced many African-Americans' perception of Christianity and the black church. Indeed, the relentless critique of the Nation of Islam and the ascendancy of Black Power caused "the credibility of the Christian faith to be severely tested" in black ghettos across the nation (Wilmore 1973: 83). Increasingly, young African-Americans began to view the black church as an "Uncle Tom" institution that was irrelevant to the concerns of youth during a new age of Black Power and black pride. Christianity was on trial in the African-American community. If it was to be acquitted of the charges, then black preachers and theologians would have to reinterpret the gospel so that it spoke to the specific needs of young people who were tired of the "love your enemy," nonviolent Christian ethics of older black religious leaders. More of the young civil rights activists who embraced Black Power also began to question the assumption that nonviolence was the only Christian means of struggle. Could one lay claim to the Christian faith and also reject nonviolence? Indeed, the rhetoric of some young Black Power militants called for a road to freedom that involved "*preying* not praying," and "*swinging* not singing." Many of them labeled Martin L. King, Jr. and other ministers as "Rev. Sambos," while others repudiated Christianity altogether as "the white man's religion." The rhetoric of violence replaced the traditional Christian emphasis on patience and redemptive suffering. It was in this context that a small group of clergymen from across the nation rallied to the defense of the Christian faith by seeking to reinterpret it in light of Black Power. This group came to be known as the National Conference of Black Churchmen (NCBC), and they served as the catalyst for a new black theology that would soon emerge.

Not many weeks after the cry of Black Power was raised in Mississippi, an ad hoc group of black ministers met in New York City and issued a statement in support of the new controversial slogan. The "Black Power" statement that appeared in the 31 July 1966 edition of the *New York Times* marked a major turning point in the history of the civil rights movement and the black church. By endorsing the call for Black Power, the NCBC moved away from the primary emphasis on interracial reconciliation as defined by pre-Black Power religious thinkers such as Benjamin Mays, Howard Thurman, and Martin Luther King, Jr., and toward a new interpretation of Christianity that focused on blackness and power. By pointing out the limitations of the integration-oriented civil rights movement and articulating a theological justification for Black Power, the NCBC laid the foundation for contemporary black theology.

The NCBC argued that the acquisition of black social, political, and economic power was a precondition for any meaningful reconciliation between blacks and whites. Although some pre-Black Power religious thinkers identified the issue of power relationships (as opposed to race prejudice) as the major source of tension in the 1940s, the dominant ideology that shaped the civil rights movement was integration, not the celebration of blackness and the attainment of group power. By underscoring power instead of Christian love and interracial harmony the NCBC initiated an important shift in African-American religious thought.

In subsequent NCBC public statements, a new black theology began to emerge. One of its early themes was prophetic self-criticism of the black church. Progressive black ministers and theologians acknowledged that there was a measure of truth in the nationalist claim that "Christianity is the white man's religion." They confessed that the contemporary black church failed to "celebrate, preserve and enhance the integrity of Blackness under the Lordship of Christ" in the tradition of the historic black church (Wilmore and Cone 1979: 46). Instead of dismissing Elijah Muhammad's nationalist critique forthwith, these African-American clergy openly confessed their own apostasy and admitted complicity in the oppression of their own people.

The NCBC simply expressed what many in the black urban communities already knew. But the dynamism of the Black Power movement provided the clergy with a sense of urgency as they sought to preserve the credibility of the Christian faith in the wake of the revolution. Just as the early Christians rejoiced in the assurance that God forgives penitent sinners, the NCBC preachers gladly interpreted Black Power as the means by which God would restore the black church to integrity and obedience. In 1967 a group of black ministers captured this sentiment in this way:

We rejoice in the Black Power Movement, which is not only the renewed hope for Black people, but gives the Black Church once again, its reason for existing. We call upon Black churchmen everywhere to divest themselves of the traditional churchly function and goals which do not respond to the needs of a downtrodden, oppressed and alienated people. (Wilmore and Cone 1979: 46)

With the assistance of religious scholars and theologians such as James Cone, Gayraud Wilmore, J. Deotis Roberts, and Henry Mitchell, NCBC began to confront the charge that they were representatives of white Christianity. While there were many voices that contributed to this response, no theologian had a greater impact on the development of black theology than James Cone.

The Black Liberation Theology of James Cone

Like other early responses to Black Power, Cone's conviction that black theologians must begin relating the gospel to black oppression was a direct response to Elijah Muhammad's nationalist critique of Christianity as a white religion incapable of meeting the spiritual and political needs of the African-American community. While pre-Black Power emphasized *universality* as the essence of the gospel, James Cone accentuated *liberation* as the basic thrust of the Christian message. Just as the NCBC clergy underscored the need for the black church and community to shift its emphasis from love (as defined by Martin Luther King, Jr., and the civil rights movement) to power (as defined by Stokely Carmichael and the Black Power movement), James Cone stressed the importance of shifting the emphasis in African-American theological discourse from universality to liberation. While Cone insisted that black theology was Christian theology, and therefore consistent with the universality of the gospel, the ideal of universality was not the theological norm that guided his work. On the contrary, Cone wrote during the height of the black revolution, and he knew that black youth would discard Christianity altogether if theologians did not begin to relate the gospel to "the pain of being black in a white racist society." Therefore, he contended that universality was an unacceptable norm for a radical black theology: if Christianity was to be a source of liberation and not enslavement, Cone argued, it needed "remaking in the light of black oppression" (Cone 1969: 117).

Apart from the civil rights and Black Power movements two foundational experiences shaped Cone's perspective on the relation between Christianity and racial justice: his upbringing in Bearden, Arkansas, and six years of graduate theological education at Garrett Seminary-Northwestern

University in Evanston, Illinois. Cone's introduction to Christianity at the Macedonia African Methodist Episcopal Church and his encounter with southern white racism were the first building blocks in his theological development. The fact that Cone first reflected on the meaning of the gospel in the context of racial segregation had a profound impact on his theological consciousness. Similarly, Cone's encounter with the racism of white professors at a Christian seminary in the North sharpened his awareness of the need for an interpretation of the gospel that took black oppression as its point of departure.

The assassination of Martin Luther King Jr., in 1968, intensified Cone's commitment to reinterpret Christian faith in light of Black Power. The tragic irony that the great prophet of nonviolence was killed by white violence pushed many young blacks further in the direction of Black Power. As young blacks expressed their rage and grief in the form of protests and uprisings in the streets of urban America, Cone expressed his anger by writing a book that would have a decisive impact on the American theological community.

Whereas pre-Black Power theologians tended to write in a calm, objective style, Cone wrote with a passion and rage unprecedented in twentieth-century African-American Christian thought. If Jesus and the prophets got angry, Cone reasoned, "is it not time for theologians to get upset?" In light of his rearing in the segregated South, the racism he encountered at Garrett-Northwestern, the recent murder of Martin Luther King, and the response of white preachers to the "riots" that followed; it was not possible for Cone to conceal his impatience for traditional appeals to nonviolence and reconciliation. As he saw it, there was no time to engage in scholarly debates about the fine points of classical theology. The rise of Black Power demanded that African-American theologians demonstrate their uncompromising commitment to black liberation by reinterpreting Christian faith in the light of black suffering. Thus, when Cone sat down to write his first book, *Black Theology and Black Power*, in the summer of 1968, he was guided by this commitment:

This work, then, is written with a definite attitude, the attitude of an angry black man, disgusted with the oppression of black people in America and with the scholarly demand to be "objective" about it. Too many people have died, and too many are on the edge of death. (Cone 1969: 2)

More than any other black theologian, Cone took the themes of blackness and liberation and made them essential ingredients of Christian theology in America. Indeed, his theological interpretation of these two concepts distinguished his thought from that of his predecessors, as well as some of his colleagues in the black theology movement. Regarding black theology's doctrine of God, Cone's argument was persuasive. Since black people are degraded *because* of their blackness, and the biblical record consistently demonstrates God's intention to liberate the oppressed, is it not theologically appropriate, even necessary, to speak of God's blackness when describing divine activity in America? For Cone, the answer was a resounding "yes." In his second book, *A Black Theology of Liberation* (originally published in 1970), he explained:

> The blackness of God means that God has made the oppressed condition God's own condition. This is the essence of the biblical revelation.... There is no place in black theology for a colorless God in a society where human beings suffer precisely because of their color.... Either God is identified with the oppressed to the point that their experience becomes God's experience, or God is a God of racism (Cone 1990: 63).

Likewise, in his understanding of Jesus Christ, Cone combined the themes of blackness and liberation in a style that was uniquely his own. In a society that despises dark skin, he argued, Christ "takes on blackness" as a sign of God's identification with the victims of society. Since the historical Jesus was a poor Jew in active solidarity with the downtrodden of his day, the risen Christ is present in the ghetto where people are oppressed because of their blackness. Thus, for Cone, not only was Jesus of Nazareth literally nonwhite, but his earthly ministry in first-century Palestine and his present activity in contemporary America confirm the divine intention to liberate the black oppressed. Therefore, Christ cannot be white with blond hair and blue eyes; on the contrary, Christ meets oppressed blacks where they are and becomes one of them. As Cone viewed it, to deny Christ's blackness in the twentieth century is equivalent to denying his Jewishness in the first century. Theological assertions about the blackness of God and Jesus Christ, therefore, were not merely attempts to rehabilitate the psyche of black people, as some maintained. For Cone, they were affirmations of profound theological truth that revealed the essence of the Christian faith.

Black Theology at the Turn of the Century

The Black Power movement had a tremendous impact on African-American religious thought, as did the radical theology that emerged in the late 1960s and the 1970s. With the publication of James Cone's *Black Theology and Black Power*, a steady stream of books and articles sought to recon-

struct Christian faith for a generation of young blacks who were prepared to abandon it.

For pre- and post-Black Power male theologians, racism was the greatest evil corrupting the spiritual and political life of American society. Their work was governed by the underlying premise that black liberation would be achieved once segregation and racism were eradicated from the church and society. Although black male religious scholars knew that racial oppression was compounded by economic injustice, their primary focus was on the problem of racism and its impact on the black community. However, the most glaring limitation of pre- and post-Black Power male theologians was their failure to identify sexism as a serious social and theological problem. Consequently, in the mid-1970s African-American women began to challenge black male theologians and church leaders on their interpretation and practice of the Christian faith. Scholars such as Jacquelyn Grant and Delores Williams laid the foundation for the development of Womanist theology during their student days at Union Theological Seminary in New York. With the dramatic increase in the number of black women in seminaries and graduate programs of religion across the nation in the 1980s and 1990s, a vibrant and prophetic Womanist theological movement changed the nature of black theological discourse in America. Womanist theologians have argued that an understanding of the interlocking dynamics of race, gender, class, and sexuality is needed to fully grasp the nature of black oppression. Fortunately, there are now a significant number of black female scholars in scripture, systematic theology, ethics, history, and sociology to guide the church in its efforts to be true to the gospel of Jesus.

Mark L. Chapman

See also Black Muslims; National Conference of Black Churchmen

Bibliography

Chapman, Mark L. (1996) *Christianity on Trial: African-American Religious Thought Before and After Black Power.* Maryknoll, NY: Orbis Books.

Cone, James H. (1969) *Black Theology and Black Power.* Minneapolis: Seabury Press.

———. (1990) *A Black Theology of Liberation.* Maryknoll, NY: Orbis Books.

Williams, Delores. (1993) *Sisters in the Wilderness: The Challenge of Womanist God-Talk.* Maryknoll, NY: Orbis Books.

Wilmore, Gayraud S. (1973) "NCBC Theological CommissionReprort, Fall 1968." In *Christian Faith in Black and White,* edited by Warner Traynham. Wakefield, MA: Parameter Press, p. 83.

Wilmore, Gayraud S., and James H. Cone. (1979). *Black Theology: A Documentary History, 1966–1979.* Maryknoll, NY: Orbis Books.

Brazil, African-Derived Religions in

The religions of African origin discussed here are Candomblé, generally thought to be a term of Bantu origin and to refer to a musical instrument of African provenance but the precise meaning of which is unknown, and Umbanda, a more recent, more European version of African-Brazilian religion. Other names also used for African-derived religions in Brazil include Batuque, in Belem in the northern state of Para; Shango, in Pernambuco in the northeast; and Tambor de Mina, or Nago, meaning Yoruba, in Maranhao, again in the northeast.

The presence of African religions in Brazil, as elsewhere in the Americas and Europe, is a consequence of trade and principally of the trans-Atlantic slave trade along Africa's coasts between roughly present-day Senegal and Angola in the West of the continent, and between Mozambique and Madagascar in the East. While the main focus of this article is on the African-derived religions of Brazil, it is worth making the general point that wherever African peoples settled or were forced to settle, they devised ways, often in situations of extreme prejudice or even persecution, of keeping alive their religious way of life. This religious life is not always easily distinguished from other aspects of their culture, including their art and sculpture, cosmology, music, dance, diet, and methods of diagnosing and healing sickness. A more defiant, determined response to discrimination and persecution was the establishment of *quilombos*, secret African settlements of escaped slaves.

At first the majority of the African slaves to enter Brazil originated in the region of Angola. Later they would come in much greater numbers from the coastal area of West Africa and in particular those parts inhabited by the Jeje, Yorubas from Dahomey, today the Republic of Benin, and their kinsfolk the Nigerian Yoruba, or Nago, as the Fon of Benin refer to them. The development and expansion of the tobacco industry in particular gave rise to the greater numbers of Yoruba slaves arriving in Pernambuco and Bahia in northeastern Brazil.

The Yoruba slaves from Benin and Nigeria were to have the greatest influence on the formation of African-Brazilian religion in Salvador, Bahia, northeast Brazil, which researchers have come to discover is home to the most authentic centers of worship outside Africa for the gods of Africa, and not only Yoruba gods or *orixas* (Portuguese for the Yoruba *orisha* and the term used in this article), as they are known in Brazil, but also for the gods or *inkissi* (Portuguese: *inkice*) of the Congo, Angola, and the other regions of Bantu Africa. Though much more attention has been paid to Candomblé in Bahia and Pernambuco, it is worth pointing out that the oldest center of Candomblé in Brazil may well be in St. Luiz, the capital of the more northerly state of Maranhao.

Once they were sold to merchants, slaves were organized into nations—Nago, Jeje, Angolan, Congo, and so on—to prevent the possibility of a unified rebellion. Not all the members of a nation were of the same ethnic origin. This attempt to divide and rule notwithstanding, resistance came not only in the form of the *quilombo*, but also in the form of revolts. Two of the best-documented revolts are those of the Males or Muslims in Bahia in 1808 and 1835. They were influenced by the Muslim reformers of West Africa and in particular by the Sokoto *jihad*, or holy war, in northern Nigeria, which began in the late eighteenth century and continued on in piecemeal fashion for the first four decades of the nineteenth century (Reis 1986).

In addition to the fictive nations, Africans were further divided and distinguished ethnically, religiously, socially, and politically by their membership in different brotherhoods or confraternities formed under the authority of the Catholic church. Thus, those of Angolan descent tended to join the brotherhood of the Venerable Third Order of the Rosary of Our Lady of the Doors of Carmel, founded in the church of Nossa Senhora do Rosario, situated in the Pelourinho district of Salvador, Bahia. The Jeje, or Dahomeans, generally met for worship as a group in the confraternity of Our Lord of the Good Jesus of the Necessities and Redemption of Black Men in the Corpo Santo Chapel of the Lower City. The Nago, or Yoruba, formed two lay orders: one for women called Our Lady of the Good Death and another, Our Lord of the Martyrdoms, reserved for men.

Candomblé Terreiros in Bahia

Women have played a crucial role in the history and expansion of Candomblé in Bahia and elsewhere in Brazil. Today women are responsible for a majority of the over 2,000 Candomblé *terreiros*, or centers, in Bahia, where the orixa, or gods, and the ancestors are housed, and where the ceremonies in their honor and memory are performed. The initiative to establish the first of these was taken by women from the Sisterhood of Our Lady of the Good Death of the Barroquinha church. The probable founders were Iyalusso Danadana and Iyanasso Akala, both of Yoruba origin.

SOUTH AMERICA

VENEZUELA

COLOMBIA

GUYANA

FRENCH
SURINAME GUIANA

ECUADOR

PERU

BRAZIL

BOLIVIA

CHILE

PARAGUAY

ARGENTINA

URUGUAY

PACIFIC
OCEAN

ATLANTIC
OCEAN

SOUTH
ATLANTIC
OCEAN

FALKLAND ISLANDS

From *Ethnic Groups Worldwide: A Ready Reference Handbook,* by David Levinson, published by the Oryx Press, 1998. Used by permission.

Umbanda priestess in São Paulo, Brazil, inhaling the "healing" smoke of the cigar. PHOTO COURTESY OF PETER B. CLARKE.

Disputes over the succession to the leadership of the Casa Branca ensured that two new *terreiros* would come into being. The first was the Iya Omi Ashe Iyanasse in the Upper Gantois district of Salvador, capital of Bahia, founded by Julia Maria Conceicao Nazare. Here, the fourth Mae de Santo, Mother of the Saint and high priestess, was the above-mentioned Escolastica Maria da Conceicao Nazare, popularly known as Menininha. The second new *terreiro*—Opo Afonja, or the Center of the Holy Cross of Opo Afonja—was created in the Camarao region of the Rio Vermelho district of Salvador in 1910. It was soon moved to Sao Goncalo do Retiro by Eugenia Ana Santos, or Aninha Obabiyi, whose spiritual daughter was the very impressive and widely revered Mae, or Mother, Senhora Oshunmi, who in 1952 received the honorific title of Iyanasso from the Alafin of Oyo and reportedly on receiving it exclaimed "Now I am my ancestor." She thus revealed one of the fundamental purposes of Candomblé: to enable adherents to discover their African identity and culture. The present high priestess of Opo Afonja is Maria Estella de Azevedo Santos, Ode Kayode.

The Nature and Purpose of the Orixas

The orixa are, in principle, deified ancestors who established, when alive, control over certain forces of nature—thunder, the wind, fresh or salt waters—and over specific activities such as hunting and metalworking, and over the knowledge and uses of plants. After the death of the orixa-ancestor his or her power or *axe* (Yoruba: *ase*) could be transmitted momentarily to one of his/her descendents during possession.

In Africa an orixa was connected either to a city or a nation and was worshipped by regional or national religions—Shango in Oyo, Yemanja in the Egba nation, Ogun in the Ekiti and Ondo nations, Oshun among the Ijeshas and Ijebus, Oshala-Obatala in Ife. Orixa traveled with their followers and in this way the devotion to them spread. The religion was maintained by orixa priests.

Where a person established himself alone or with his immediate family the orixa would take on the characteristics of a personal divinity. When that person was shipped as a slave to Brazil and was separated from family, the relationship with one's orixa became much more individualistic and personal. While in Africa, ceremonies were held by priests ordained for the purpose, and the only task left to the rest of the family was to provide the materials for the offerings and respect taboos regarding certain foods and other aspects of the worship of each orixa. In Brazil each individual became personally responsible for the cult of her/his orixa.

Eventually, after moving several times, this first *terreiro* was established permanently in Engenho Velho, Avenido Vasco da Gama, with the name Ille Iyanasso, or house of Iyanasso, more popularly known as the Casa Branca. Iyanasso is an honorific title granted by the Alafin, or King, of the town of Oyo, center of Shango (Portuguese: Xango) worship in western Nigeria.

When Candomblé was founded in the first half of the nineteenth century, Catholicism was the only authorized religion, Protestantism was tolerated only for foreigners, and Islam was outlawed and persecuted because of the 1835 revolt mentioned previously. The worship of African gods was dismissed as a superstition, and it is known that by 1855 meetings of Candomblé were raided and broken up by the police. One of those apprehended was Escolastica Maria da Conceicao, a free Creole who was more than likely the grandmother or mother of the famous priestess of Bahaian Candomblé, Mae Menininha of Gantois.

Correspondences between African Gods and Catholic Saints

African gods, or orixa, have been made to correspond with Catholic saints in the African religions of Brazil as in Haitian Vodun and Cuban Santeria. It is not known when these correspondences began to be created or exactly why. They are often explained as a smokescreen used by the slaves to enable them to worship their own gods, which would otherwise have been forbidden. Many of the correspondences seem far-fetched or based on far-fetched similarities between the African god and the Catholic saint in question. One pairing difficult to understand is that of the violent and virile Yoruba god of thunder Shango with the quiet, studious, pensive, balding, elderly St. Jerome. The link is possibly in the images of St. Jerome that show him with a lion sitting tamely at his feet. Among the Yoruba the lion is a symbol of royalty and Shango was, according to legend, the third king of the ancient Yoruba kingdom of Oyo.

There seems to be no explanation for the pairing of the crucified Christ with Oxala, principal of the lesser gods in the Yoruba and African-Brazilian religious pantheon. It may be the case here and in other instances that the similarities are based on attributes and virtues deemed to be common to both the African god and the Catholic saint. One can only guess in the case of Oxala and Jesus that the reason lay in the fact that both inspired great veneration, affection, faith, and devotion. Yemanja, (Yoruba: *Yemoja*, meaning mother whose sons are fish), the mother of several orixa, was made to correspond with Our Lady of the Conception; and Nanan Buruku, the oldest of the water divinities, with St. Ann, mother of Mary Oya. Yansan, the first wife of Shango and divinity of wind and lightning, was identified with St. Barbara. According to legend, the latter's father was immediately hit by lightning and reduced to cinders after he killed her because she converted to Christianity.

The connection between Ogum, god of iron, hunters, blacksmiths, taxi drivers, and soldiers, and St. Anthony is a surprising one as the latter is usually depicted as being of a gentle disposition with the child Jesus in his arms. However, legend claims that a statue of the saint hidden among the spoils pillaged by French Lutherans who sacked the Portuguese island of Argoim off the west coast of Africa while on their way to conquer Bahia, prevented this invasion by producing violent storms and plagues that sunk their ships and decimated their fighting force by inflicting it with deadly diseases. In recompense for this service St. Antony was enlisted as a soldier in the fort at the bay entrance to Salvador, which bears his name. In Brazil, the trickster god Eshu, the messenger of the gods with many contradictory aspects to his character, and without whose help nothing can be completed successfully, has been equated with the Devil. He is not, however, greatly feared; he will protect and defend those who treat him properly and harm their enemies on their behalf.

The Orixa as Archetype

There has been a further evolution in the conception and definition of orixa in the New World on account of the number of non-African members of Candomblé who cannot meaningfully be said to be possessed by the African god-ancestor who momentarily returns to earth to incorporate in a descendent. A non-African devotee, while unable to claim blood ties with a god or ancestor of African origin, may possess certain personality traits and temperaments in common with such a god or ancestor. Developing this line of argument, Verger (1993) suggests that the orixa can be interpreted in such cases as archetypes of the personality manifesting in their behavior the fulfillment of those latent tendencies and the resolution of unresolved personal conflicts arising from "unnatural" rules of socially accepted behavior. If the person in question is chosen to be the child of an orixa who archetypically reveals these tendencies then initiation will come as a form of liberation. The archetypal Ogum is violent, quarrelsome, impulsive, and incapable of forgiving offences. He is tenacious and persevering, and triumphs over adversity. He displays frequent mood swings, ranging from violent outbursts to a very calm disposition. He is an impetuous, arrogant individual who wounds others due to lack of discretion when people perform a service for him. But due to his absolute honesty he is not easily disliked. Seen from this angle Candomblé assumes the function of a social psychology.

Beliefs and Practices

African-Brazilian religions, while essentially relational with respect to both the living and the dead and nature, are preoccupied with harnessing ase (Portuguese: axe) a mystical force by means of which destiny can be lived out in the prescribed manner, the appropriate balance of good and evil maintained, good fortune sustained, and misfortune put right. The Supreme Being is the ultimate source of this force which is personified in the *orixa* and the ancestors or living dead.

While present in Brazil, (there is, for example, an elaborate version of the Yoruba-derived Egungun cult performed on the island of Itaparica situated off the coast of Salvador, Bahia) ancestor veneration is not as widely practiced in Brazil as in Africa. In Brazil, possession by the orixa is at the center of the main religious festivals and the important ritual is that of initiation as a *filha* or *filho de santo* (daughter or son of the holy one or divinity). Also in Brazil, divination, using *buzios*, or cowrie shells, has largely replaced the much more elaborate *Ifa* divining system.

Initiation

In Brazil, when a person is to become a child of the orixa, the *iyalorixa*—or *mae*, *babalorixa*, or *pae de santo* (high priestess or high priest)—will have the tasks of preparing her/him for initiation, and preparing a shrine for his individual orixa and the jar that contains his *otas*, or sacred stones, the receptacles of the orixa's power. Initiation traditionally consisted of the classic tripartite structure of a rite of passage and could last for several months depending on the rules and customs of the *terreiro* in question. The first stage is seclusion of the one called to serve the orixa. An orixa can make known her/his intentions in a number of ways including in a dream or through the symptoms of illness, a series of setbacks, or the discovery of a strange object. Ideally, the new novices are removed for a time from everyday affairs and entrusted to the care of the high priestess or high priest who acts as their godmother or godfather.

The second stage is a stage of liminal in which the *abia*, or novice, acquires the behavior attributed to her/his god. Novices also learn the *atabaques* (drum) rhythms of her/his god. These will act as stimuli for the conditioned reflex of falling into trance and succumbing to the call of the god, the most fundamental and spiritually and emotionally uplifting part of the Candomblé ceremony. The drums—*rum*, *rumpi*, and *le*—which begin the ceremony accompanied by *agogo*, or cowshells, are conical in shape with their heads made of a single piece of hide set in place and stretched by a system of tuning pegs in Nago or Yoruba Candomblé, and by wooden wedges for the Ngoma drums of the Congo and Angolan rites.

The drums are sacred. They are baptized and their *axe* (sacred power) maintained through sacrifices and offerings. Their dual role consists of invoking the orixa at the beginning of the ceremony when they are beaten without accompaniment for the purpose of maintaining the purity of rhythm associated with each orixa, and of transmitting their messages when they incarnate. Only those who have been initiated can touch them. On festive days the drums are wrapped with strips of cloth in the colors of the god being worshipped, and they salute the most important members of the *terreiro* as they enter, who in turn bow and touch the ground before the orchestra and then salute the high priestess. The ceremony is broken for several minutes for a song of contrition if a drum is knocked over. The use of the *bata* drum played for Shango in Africa has been lost in Brazil but continues in Cuba.

The third and final stage of initiation consists of the reintegration of the new *filha/filho de santo* into the community of adherents and the ceremonial manifestation of the same to the wider public. On the seventeenth day, or Naming Day, the final ceremony of the initiation takes place during which those about to be initiated reveal their new name. They make three successive appearances: the first dressed in white, the second in colorful clothing, and the third attired in the vestments of their own orixa and carrying their accoutrements and insignias—the double-headed axe of Xango, the sword of Ogum, the bow and arrow of Oxossi, the fan of Oxun, the *shashara* or broom of Obaluaye.

After the dancing the *mae de santo* requests a well-known visitor, carrying an *adja*, or bell, which she rings continuously, to lead the *adoshu*, or newly initiated devotee, now in a state of trance, to reveal her name. The *adoshu* is led from one side of the room to another until she responds twice to the question, "What is your name?" The third time the visitor shouts: "Come on try harder, and tell us loud and clear what your name is. May everyone in the city and market hear you clearly." Spinning around and jumping, the *adoshu* shouts out her new name and the announcement is greeted with applause. The drums beat loudly and other priestesses in attendance go into trances to welcome the new priestess who will henceforth be known in Candomblé by that new name.

Possession

Possession has already been spoken of as the climax of Candomblé ceremony, as it is of Umbanda and other forms of African-Brazilian religions. In Candomblé, spirit possession is as much a cultural construct as a psychological one and is as much a sociological process as an individual, personal accomplishment and experience. It consists essentially of the incorporation of a spirit in her/his devotee, an event which may but need not result in any altering of the latter's state of consciousness.

The words most frequently employed by mediums to describe the experience of being mounted by a deity are *incorporar* (to incorporate), *manifestar* (to manifest), and the more popular term *pegar* (to seize, grab, or catch), which at times seems to suggest pursuit by a god with an insatiable sexual desire for his devotee. One who describes the experience and effects of possession is likely to say something like "*eu nao ouco nada, eu nao vejo nada; so, me sinto mais leve*" (I don't hear or see anything; only, I feel much lighter). Something of the intensity of the experience can be gleaned from the "warming down" process in the form of the *ere* (childlike spirit) trance, which takes place some time after the main trance. As the gods depart from their devotees they are replaced by playful *eres*, who party and play as if they were children in a kindergarten. Their language is that of a young child aged between two and three years, and use is made of dummies and of the playthings of children. Other adults, whom they address as daddy or mummy, are approached for money.

Though exhausting, possession is rarely if ever seen as a hardship or a trial, nor is it shunned as in other societies such as the Shona of Zimbabwe or the Dinka of the Sudan. The reasons why a god should wish to possess a human being are more easily understood if considered in a wider context of beliefs about the relationship between the human and the divine, the sacred and the profane, and the nature of the person. When considered in the context of Candomblé cosmology, trance appears a quite natural phenomenon. This cosmology is derived from a variety of western African traditional religions and shaped and molded by the realities of slave culture in colonial Brazil and by economic and political marginalization since.

Umbanda

Candomblé has been compared and contrasted with Umbanda and found to be different even in central areas such as the ritual of possession (Ortiz 1988: 70). While Candomblé retains a precise model of possession derived from African sources and myths and one that is both collective and individual in character, in Umbanda the form of

Women in São Paulo, Brazil inhaling the "healing" smoke of the cigar. PHOTO COURTESY OF PETER B. CLARKE.

possession is both more indeterminate and exclusively centered on individuals. In Umbanda, possession has shed all its links with the myths recalling the exploits and adventures of the possessing spirits, the orixa or African deities. It is Ortiz's view that while Candomblé is essentially about the conservation of the African collective memory in Brazil, Umbanda is essentially about the integration of African-Brazilian practices into the modern world (71).

Umbanda is a product of industrialization and urban growth. It began in Rio de Janeiro in the 1920s and began to gain vast popularity in Sao Paulo, the industrial capital of Brazil, in the 1950s. Often presented as a religion of the marginalized and deprived because of its African elements, Umbanda started as a mainly middle-class phenomenon and today attracts members of all classes. Umbanda centers are smaller in size than Candomblé *terreiros* and typically consist of a *pai-de-santo* or a *mae-de-santo* and around twenty *filhas* and *filhos de santo* who serve as mediums and assistants during the ritual. The principal goals pursued by clients display a greater emphasis on the instrumental and utilitarian dimensions of life than is the case in Candomblé, and are more related to individual progress and upward social mobility than to questions of self and group identity.

As in Candomblé, a number of religious traditions are juxtaposed in Umbanda. However, while Catholicism and Amerindian influences are equally prominent in both, the African ritual and doctrinal base of Umbanda is narrower than that of Candomblé. Moreover, the spiritism of Allan Kardec which developed in France in the 1850s and soon spread to Brazil is much more influential in Umbanda than in Candomblé.

Conclusions: Towards Greater Convergence and Privatization

With improvement in communications between the regions of Brazil, modernization and urbanization is an almost universal experience. As opportunities for sharing views and opinions and interacting with each other increase, these different versions of African-Brazilian religion are coming to resemble each other ever more closely. Moreover, the desire to experience and experiment shown by devotees and sympathizers makes the attempt to preserve tradition and authenticity in the areas of African belief and practice risk-laden in terms of growth and support. What were once community-based religious and cultural temple complexes that provided the fragmented and dispossessed with their social cement are, with rapidly advancing industrialization, urbanization, and modernization, tending to respond more to the demands on the indi-

vidual to survive in terms of their personal relationships and their emotional and material needs in such a rapidly changing world.

Peter B. Clarke

See also Batuque; Candomblé; Kardecism; Ogun; Oshun; Tambor de Mina; Xango; Yoruba Religion

Bibliography

Bastide, Roger. (1978) *The African Religions of Brazil: Towards a Sociology of the Interpenetration of Cultures.* Baltimore, MD: Johns Hopkins University Press.

Carneiro, Edison. (1961) *Candombles da Bahia.* Sao Paulo: Editora Technoprint LTDA.

Clarke, Peter B. (1993) "Why Women are the Priests and Teachers in Bahian Candomble." In *Women as Teachers and Guides in Traditional and New Religions*, edited by Elizabeth M. Puttick and Peter B. Clarke. Lewiston/Queenston/Lampeter: Edwin Mellen Press, 97–115.

——. (1993) "The Dilemmas of a Popular Religion: the Case of Candomble." In *The Popular Use of Popular Religion in Latin America*, edited by S. Rostas and A. Droogers. Amsterdam: CEDLA, 95–109.

——. (1998) "Accounting for Recent Anti-Syncretist Trends in Candomble-Catholic Relations." In *New Trends and Developments in African Religions*, edited by Peter B. Clarke. Westport, CT: Greenwood Press, 17–37.

Ortiz, Rene. (1988) *A Morte Branca do Feiticeiro Negro: Umbanda e Sociedade Brasileira.* Sao Paulo: Editora Brasiliense.

Reis, Joao J. (1986) *Rebeliao Escrava No Brasil.* Sao Paulo: Editora Brasiliense.

Rostas, Susanna, and Andre Droogers, eds. *The Popular Use of Popular Religion in Latin America.* Amsterdam: CEDLA

Verger, Pierre Fatumbi. (1976) *Trade Relations between the Bight of Benin and Bahia from the Seventeenth to the Nineteenth Century.* Ibadan: Ibadan University Press.

——. (1993) "The Orishas of Bahia." In *Os Deuses Africanos No Candomble Da Bahia* (African gods in the Candomblé of Bahia), edited by Carybe. Salvador (Bahia): Editora Bigraf, 235–261.

Bushman Religion

The Bushmen (or San) have until recently been foragers, who, as small, loosely organized, nomadic bands, hunted

BUSHMAN PRAYER FOR HELP WITH THE HUNT

Gauwa must help us that we kill an animal.
Gauwa, help us. We are dying of hunger.
Gauwa does not give us help.
He is cheating. He is bluffing.
Gauwa will bring something for us to kill next day
After he himself hunts and has eaten meat,
When he is full and feeling well.

Source: Marshall, Lorna. (1962) "!Kung Bushman Religious Beliefs." *Africa* 32: 247.

antelope and other game animals and gathered the wild plants of a desert-like environment in the Kalahari desert of Namibia and Botswana. This is the home of most of the approximately 100,000 Bushmen today, although some are also, and were in the past, found in other regions and countries of southern Africa. Like all hunting-gathering peoples, the Bushmen are closely attuned to their natural and social worlds, enabling them to survive and even thrive in their risk-prone environment. Their religion has its roots within these two activities, as evident in its two basic themes: the abiding presence of nature, especially animals, within myth and ritual, and the egalitarian quality of human relationships, especially between men and women. Bushman myth and ritual express these two themes in multiple ways. Animals, for example, are the prominent figures in Bushman mythology and rock art, which is religiously inspired "shamanic art" reminiscent in style and content of European, Upper Paleolithic cave paintings. Animals are also a source for shamanic healing power. The key value of Bushman ethos, equality, along with the kindred values of sharing and reciprocity, which altogether constitute the moral pillars of Bushman society, are reflected in such features of Bushman religion as the complementarity of men and women in the trance curing dance, the intensely collective and sharing nature of ritual, the lack of ritual specialization, and the openness to the beliefs and ritual practices of other bands or of non-Bushman neighboring tribal groups.

The religion of this rather remote African people has long been a subject of great interest to Western scholars who

began to study Bushman notions of divinity, mythology, and rock art as early as the nineteenth century. Its uniqueness and difference from the religious traditions of Bantu-speaking peoples of southern Africa, its evident antiquity, its striking fluidity, diversity, and elusiveness as a religious system, are all characteristics that continue to make Bushman religion a challenging subject.

It is difficult to summarize Bushman religion, given its regional and interregional variability, and the ethnic heterogeneity of the Bushmen, who consist of three distinctive linguistic groups and about two dozen tribal groups (of whom the !Kung, the Nharo (Naro), the G/wi, and the extinct /Xam of the Cape are the best known). Another difficulty are the accretion of this or that feature from Bantu-speaking and European neighbors, for instance, circumcision and witchcraft practices, or the figures of "Addam" and "Effa" and "Jessu Kriste," the latter wildly syncretized, in a trickster idiom. Mythology, in this oral culture, is elaborate. Its prominent elements are creation myths that bring into being the new world and time from an earlier mythic past; and tales about that past's many and varied inhabitants, the "First People" and animals, and hybrid animal-humans. Preeminent is the quixotic, ever-present trickster, who has many names (/Kaggen, =Gao!na //Gauwa, Pate, Piisi/koagu, Jakkals) and whose guise may be human, or partially human, or animal (Mantis, Jackal, Woodpecker, Hare). This figure, in Bushman supernaturalism, overshadows the somewhat dim and remote figure of the creator god. In fact, the trickster may also himself be a divinity and as such step outside his role as droll or outrageous protagonist of the world of stories and myth to become a numinous presence at ritual events.

There are of two main types of ritual in Bushman religion: puberty initiation rites and the trance curing dance. Unlike their tribal neighbors, the Bushmen do not pay much ritual or ceremonial attention to birth, marriage, and death, nor is there any trace of any "ancestor cult." Girls' initiation rites, held for each girl individually at the onset of menarche, are more elaborate than boys' rites. The girl spends about a week in a small, secluded door-less grass hut, attended by one or two old kinswomen. For the boys the rite basically consist of an introduction, by elders, of the young hunters to the practical and magical aspects of the hunt, culminating in a "First Buck" ceremony. Antelopes are a ritual and symbolic element also of female initiation, manifested in the spiritual identification of the girl with an eland antelope and the mimetic performance, by elderly men and women, of the eland courtship dance. The "eland dance" constitutes the ritual climax of the female rite. It is followed by the girl's emergence from the menstrual hut, to be introduced back to her community as a woman—rather than the girl she had been—who is ready for marriage.

The trance curing dance, too, is informed with the mystical presence of animals. Upon trance *(!kia)*, the male dancer may undergo transformation into an antelope or a lion gaining thereby access to *n/om* (or "healing potency"). The women provide the trance-inducing song to the dancers throughout this night-long, intensely dramatic and "synergetic" ritual. Even though it may be held for only one or two sick individuals, the dance involves the entire community, which, during periods of multi-band aggregations in the drought season of the year, may number close to a hundred people, resulting in the performance of a charged rite of solidarity.

The trance dance and dancer have become rallying points for religious and cultural revitalization amongst some of those Bushman groups subjected to oppressive pastoral settler contacts and a consequent loss of land and resources, independence, and cultural integrity. Examples are in the southern Drakensberg in South Africa during colonial times and the Ghanzi and Cae Cae regions of Botswana in the 1960s and 1980s, respectively. While never resulting in anything like a full-fledged religious movement, these developments led to a markedly increased incidence in the rite's performance and attendance and in the rising prestige and professionalization of the trance dancer, as well as to a heightened, politically assertive sense of ethnic identity among the Bushman participants and attendants.

Mathias Guenther

Bibliography

Barnard, Alan. (1988) "Structure and Fluidity in Khoisan Religious Belief." *Journal of Religion in Africa* 18: 216–236.

Biesele, Megan. (1993) *Women Like Meat: The Folklore and Foraging Ideology of the Kalahari Ju/'hoansi*. Bloomington: Indiana University Press.

Bleek, Dorothea. (1923) *The Mantis and his Friends*. Cape Town: T. Maskew Miller.

Bleek, Wilhelm H. I., and Lucy Lloyd. (1911) *Specimens of Bushman Folklore*. London: George Allen & Co. Ltd.

Dowson, Thomas. (1994) "Reading Art, Writing History: Rock Art and Social Change in Southern Africa." *World Archaeology* 25: 332–344.

Guenther, Mathias. (1976) "The San Trance Dance: Ritual and Revitalization among the Farm Bushmen of the Ghanzi District, Republic of Botswana." *Journal of the South West African Scientific Society* 30: 45–55.

———. (1997) "Jesus Christ as Trickster in the Religion of the Contemporary Bushmen." In *The Games of Gods and Men: Essays in Play and Performance*, edited by K. Koepping. Hamburg: LitVerlag, 203–230.

———. (1999) *Tricksters and Trancers: Bushman Religion and Society*. Bloomington: Indiana University Press.

Katz, Richard. (1982) *Boiling Energy*. Cambridge, MA: Harvard University Press.

Katz, Richard, Megan Biesele, and Verna St. Denis. (1997) *Healing Makes our Hearts Happy: Spirituality and Transformation among the Kalahari Ju/'hoansi*. Rochester, VT: Inner Traditions.

Lewis-Williams, David. (1981) *Believing and Seeing: Symbolic Meanings in Southern San Rock Paintings*. New York: Academic Press.

Lewis-Williams, David, and Megan Biesele. (1978) "Eland Hunting Rituals among the Northern and Southern San Groups: Striking Similarities." *Africa* 48: 117–134.

Lewis-Williams, David, and Thomas Dowson. (1988) "Signs of all Times: Entoptic Phenomena in Upper Palaeolithic Art." *Current Anthropology* 29, 2: 201–245.

———. (1989) *Images of Power: Understanding Bushman Rock Art*. Johannesburg: Southern Book Publishers.

Marshall, Lorna. (1962) "!Kung Bushman Religious Beliefs." *Africa* 32: 221–252.

———. (1969) "The Medicine Dance of the !Kung Bushmen." *Africa* 39: 347–381.

———. (1999) *Nyae Nyae !Kung Beliefs and Rites*. Boston: The Peabody Museum Press.

Candomblé

Candomblé is an African-derived religion found in Brazil, primarily in the northeastern state of Bahia. It is one of a family of religions which also includes Vodun, Santeria, and Orisha among others that are found in the Caribbean, Brazil, and large urban areas of North America. These religions are generally characterized by a blending of African religious traditions and Catholicism, although certain beliefs and practices drawn from Native American religions, Protestantism, Spiritualism, and other traditions are often included as well. In Brazil, a number of such religions can be found including, Umbanda, Xango, Tambor de Mina, Catimbo, Batuque, and Macumba. Candomblé, however, is the most authentically African religious practice in Brazil and probably predates the aforementioned groups.

The origin and subsequent development of the Candomblé religion in Brazil is inextricably linked to the slave trade. The principal areas in Africa from which slaves were obtained were extreme western Africa, south-central Africa (which included Kongolese and Bantu peoples), and the easternmost areas of sub-Saharan west Africa (which

included the Yoruba and Dahomeans of Nigeria and neighboring Benin). The latter region is significant as the culture of the Yoruba eventually became the dominant African cultural tradition in Brazil.

Historical documents and court records seem to imply that Candomblé began sometime during the eighteenth century. In the early part of the nineteenth century, however, the first three Candomblé *terreiros* (compounds where Candomblé worship take place) were certainly established in Bahia and have, through time, served as the prototype for the many *terreiros* that would follow.

Perhaps the defining characteristic of Candomblé, the fusion or juxtaposition of African orisha (the Yoruba term for gods) and Catholic saints, was a development that reflects the sociopolitical context of the slave period. It is not known exactly why or how the blending of orisha and saints occurred, although a few tenable theories have been put forth. Many Africans had been exposed to Catholicism prior to their shipment to the New World, so many were no doubt already familiar, and perhaps quite comfortable, with a "pantheon" that clearly resembled their own in many ways. While the practice of African or African-derived religion

Candomblé *terreiro* at Casa do Ganrois, Salvador, Bahia, Brazil. PHOTO COURTESY OF PETER B. CLARKE.

A CANDOMBLE INVOCATION

Egbêji mori ô ri, okorin-kam

Orolu mori ô ri, okorin-kam

(Powerful One, I know thee as the first man)

Ôkum-kum biri-biri

Ajá lê mori ô korin-kam

(Even in the dark I can see thou art powerful)

A orêrê aiê, orixá loman,

Iá, ochê Egbêji orêrê, aiê

(In the whole world, nothing is hidden from the Great-One)

Source: Pierson, Donald (1942) *Negroes in Brazil.* Chicago: University of Chicago Press, 291

was, of course, not overtly encouraged by the colonists in Brazil, many of them tended to overlook the occasional gathering of slaves to sing and dance as per their native customs since they reasoned that the disparate practices of the many tribal strains present in Brazil would temper any attempts on the part of the slaves to organize in a general fashion. Be that as it may, whether the blending of the orisha and saints could be attributed to a deceptive camouflaging of African gods behind a facade of Catholicism or to reasoned analogy, it did occur and to this day remains one of the most salient characteristics of Candomblé as well as many other African-derived religions in the New World.

The *terreiro* is the focal point of Candomblé activity. These compounds range from the very small and simply adorned to the very large and elaborately decorated. A *terreiro* may be collectively owned by a group of individuals or a community or it may simply be a room or two in an individual's home. While the entire area is considered to be a sacred space, there are sanctuaries (*quartos de santo*) that are open only to initiates. The general public is, however, welcome in the open areas (*barracão*) where the drumming, singing, and many of the possessions take place.

Each *terreiro* is directed by a *pai de santo* or a *mãe de santo*, literally the "father" or "mother" of the saints. Under them there are the *filhos de santo* and the *filhas de santo*, the "sons" and "daughters" of the saints. These individuals have been initiated or are in the process of completing the many stages of initiation, and they are responsible for many of the mundane tasks associated with Candomblé worship in a *terreiro*. More importantly, they serve as mediums for possession by the orisha. Finally, the *ogã* are male benefactors that

have no explicit spiritual role but do contribute funds, goods, or services to the *terreiro*. Often their superior social position lends considerable prestige to their specific *terreiro* as well as to Candomblé worship in general. Those individuals that are not initiates do nevertheless affiliate themselves with the religion and a specific *terreiro* by attending the various religious functions and serving as clients for spiritual work carried out by the *pai* and *mãe de santo*.

In the past twenty or so years, the focus on African-nation affiliation has waned with the result being that the boundaries (linguistic, ethnic, etc.) between the different divisions of Candomblé are slowly disappearing. At the same time, students, writers, and other members of the Brazilian intelligentsia began to turn to Candomblé in a effort to find the roots of Brazilian culture. Once the religion of Africans only, Candomblé is now embraced by the many peoples and cultures of Brazil.

James Houk

See also Batuque; Brazil, African-Derived Religions in; Caribbean, African Derived Religions in; Pagelança and Catimbo; Macumba; Tambor de Mina; Yoruba Religion

Bibliography

Bastide, Roger. (1978) *The African Religions of Brazil: Toward a Sociology of the Interpenetration of Civilizations,* translated by Helen Sebba. Baltimore: Johns Hopkins University Press.

Omari, M. S. (1984) *From the Inside to the Outside: The Art and Ritual of Bahian Candomblé.* Museum of Cultural History

Monograph no. 24. Los Angeles: University of California at Los Angeles.

Ribeiro, José. (1974) *Cerimônias da Umbanda e do Candomblé.* Rio de Janeiro: Editora Eco.

Souza, Gérson Ignez de, and Tancredo da Silva Pinto. (1976) *Negro e Branco na Cultura Relgiosa Afro-Brasileira: Os Egbás.* Rio de Janeiro: Gráfica Editora Aurora, Ltda.

Voeks, Robert A. (1997) *Sacred Leaves of Candomblé: African Magic, Medicine, and Religion in Brazil.* Austin: University of Texas Press.

Wafer, Jim. (1991) *The Taste of Blood: Spirit Possession in Brazilian Candomblé.* Philadelphia: University of Pennsylvania Press.

Caribbean, African-Derived Religion in

Voodoo, Santería, Candomblé, and Shango are names that engender images of mysterious religious beliefs and practices related to harmful supernatural forces that loom in the "dark side" of nature. Thanks to Hollywood, the film industry, and tourists' travel logs, these words also conjure up images of cannibalism, witchcraft, sorcery, or whatever is evil, irrational, and destructive. A serious examination of these religions shows that none of these depictions of them are correct. These religions are practiced by millions of devotees' whose lives are shaped by their teachings and, like other religions of the world, their complex myths and symbols give meaning to life, uplift the spirits of the downtrodden, and instill in their devotees a need for self-reflection, spiritual transformation, and personal assurance. They also relate humans to powerful mythological divine beings (or spirits) who are believed to govern the universe as well as their devotees' lives.

Caribbean religions are more than belief; they are a way of life and an intrinsic part of people's lives. They include elaborate systems of folk medical practices, and systems of ethics transmitted across generations by means of proverbs, stories, songs, dances, and other artistic forms of expressions. They are also practiced primarily at home, where an altar may be kept in honor of the spirits, and a religious calendar is maintained with feast days that require devotees to attend special ceremonies in the temples, at pilgrimages, or in other sacred places. These ceremonies are officiated by prominent priests and priestesses who constitute loosely organized but powerful local hierarchies. Because these religions maintain neither theological nor ecumenical centers, their specialists are trained by other practitioners, either through inheritance or through social contacts, and their

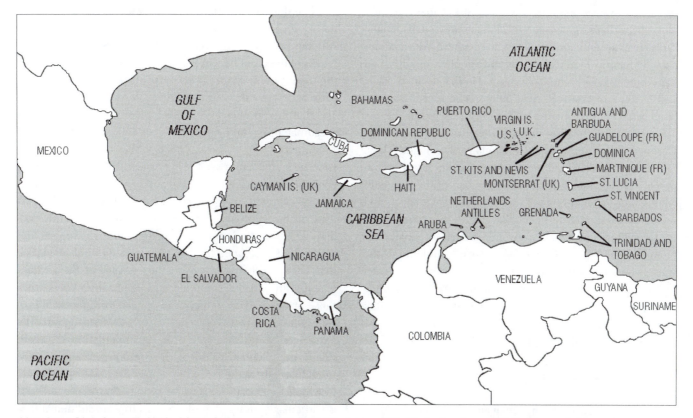

Adapted from *Ethnic Groups Worldwide: A Ready Reference Handbook,* by David Levinson, published by the Oryx Press, 1988. Used by permission.

teachings vary regionally from one temple to another. In short, Caribbean religions offer a unique dimension of experience that motivates believers to interpret their whole lives by such experiences.

By and large, the study of Caribbean religions includes the religions of the Brazilian state of Bahia as well as those of the countries found on the northern coast of South America because these countries' share a similar history of slavery and resistance to slavery, their modes of production derive from slave labor, and their socioeconomic developments were caused by relatively long periods of colonial rule. For theoretical purposes, Caribbean religions may also be classified into five major categories (Simpson, 1978: 14). First, the Neo-African religions that developed historically within the context of slavery, and have preserved a fairly considerable amount of African religious traditions that have been combined with Roman Catholic beliefs and practices. these include Vodun in Haiti; Santeria in Cuba, the Dominican Republic, and Puerto Rico; and Shango in Trinidad and Grenada. In the second category belong the ancestral religions that have preserved fewer African traditions and derive from various forms of Protestantism imported to the Caribbean by Christian missionaries during the nineteenth century. These include the Cumina and Convince in Jamaica, the Big Drum in Grenada, and Carriacou and Kele in St. Lucia. The third category includes the revivalist religions that are twentieth century phenomena and are related to Pentecostal or charismatic Protestant movements from the United States. They encompass the Revival Zion in Jamaica, the Shouters and Spiritual Baptists in Trinidad, the Cohortes in Haiti, and the Shakers and Streams of Power in St. Vincent. The fourth category emphasizes divination (the reading of one's future into an object) and folk healing through mediumship; it includes Espiritismo in Puerto Rico, Umbanda in Brazil, and Maria Lionza in Venezuela. Finally, the religio-political movements that developed during the early part of the twentieth century address many issues related to neocolonialism and social and economic justice; belonging to this category are the Rastafari and Dread movements that originated in Jamaica, but have become widespread throughout the Caribbean. The divisions that exist between these categories, however, are merely theoretical, for in reality these religions are not mutually exclusive but take diverse local of forms in which the theology of some in one category may be included in the beliefs and practices of another.

Working the Amalgam

Caribbean religions are an amalgam of various religious traditions that originated in three continents: America, Africa, and Europe. That amalgam began with Christopher Columbus' arrival to the New World in 1492 and the establishment of the first European settlement on Hispaniola in December 1492. The new settlers encountered a native population of Amerindians who derived originally from the Taino of South America. The Europeans' presence in the region in the years immediately following the encounter of the two groups had profound effects on this native population. Consumed by their determination to discover the gold reputed to exist on these islands, the Spanish conquistadors subjected the Indians to hard labor, forcing them to find the precious yellow metal or to work on their gardens. The Europeans' tyranny was so severe that merely fifteen years after their arrival in the New World, nearly four-fifths of the Amerindian population had perished. Various diseases imported from Europe, against which the Indians were not immune, also took their toll. Estimates are that by the end of the seventeenth century, the number of Amerindians in the region had been reduced from about half a million to sixty thousand. Hence, Amerindian cultures throughout the Caribbean were destroyed, but many of their religious traditions managed to survive to the present day. Some Carib, Ciboney, and Arawak myths and names of Indian "protector" spirits are included in the theologies of Cuban Santeria, Brazilian Umbanda, and Puerto Rican Espiritismo.

The drastic reduction of the number of Indians caused the Europeans to look for another source of labor, with Africans brought to the New World as slaves. While no one is sure of the exact date of the beginning of the slave trade in the New World, historical records indicate that it began as early as 1512, a mere twenty years after Columbus' arrival, and that the number of Africans brought to the New World is estimated to total nearly twelve million.

Africans who came to the Caribbean derived from a wide geographical area of West Africa, from the northwest coast of sub-Sahara to the Bakongo regions, for the slave traders captured their slaves wherever they could. These Africans brought with them their cultural and religious traditions, which they poured into the fabric of the islands' cultural and religious life—fashioning a cultural amalgam that left an indelible mark on the cultures of the region, and resulting in the continuity of Caribbean cultures with those of Africa. The influence of African cultural traditions varied in intensity from place to place and depended on the particular ethnic mix of the African population on each island, the peculiar historical circumstances of each country, the length of the period of colonialism, and the degree to which Europeans exercised a strong cultural presence in a particular country. A prolonged European cultural influence on a country tended to decrease that country's ability to maintain many African traditions. For instance, in Haiti, where European colonial domination and cultural contact ended early with the slave revolution and independent statehood in 1804, many more African cultural and religious traditions were maintained than in most of the other nations in the Caribbean, whose colonial status lasted well into the twentieth century. These nations' continuous cultural contact with Europe gradually tended to abrade the African religious traditions.

But if African religious traditions survived in the Caribbean, it was largely due to *maronnage*. The word *maroon* derives from the Spanish *cimarron*, a term used to designate a domesticated animal that has reverted to a wild state. The term soon came to be applied to the slaves who ran away from the plantations and gathered in the interior of the colonies to form secret societies known as *maroon republics* (Bastide 1971). The Africans who joined these republics probably congregated along ethnic lines and hence, the religious traditions in each republic depended upon the particular ethnic mix in each of these republics. These republics' theological diversity helps to explain the local divergences in beliefs and practices that exist in Caribbean religions today. Depending on the geographical area, some emphasized particular African ethnic traditions and not others. Despite these ethnic divergences however, the demographic distribution of Africans who came to each country in the Caribbean derived overwhelmingly from specific regions of Africa, and consequently, the religious traditions of the more prominent ethnic groups prevailed over others. Hence, Santeria in Cuba and Candomblé in Brazil derive primarily from Nigerian Yoruba beliefs and practices, while in Haiti, a large number of slaves came from Dahomey (Benin) and Kongo, and hence, Vodun's theology derives from the religious traditions of these areas.

Despite their similarities with African religions, Caribbean religions do not replicate their counterparts in West Africa. Environmental conditions, the different historical context in the region, and the different admixture of African religious ethnic traditions in various parts of the Caribbean transformed African beliefs and practices permanently and made them different from those of the motherland. Hence, Caribbean religions cannot be characterized as African religions, but as African-derived religions whose beliefs and practices originated largely in West Africa.

Another common element in Caribbean religions is the way in which they incorporated Christian traditions in their theology. The degree to which Christianity was included within the theology of these religions differed characteristically in Catholic and Protestant colonies. By and large, the territories under British rule tended to be less syncretic than the Catholic-dominated ones such as the French and the Spanish, and the period in which the systematic evangelization of Africans was undertaken by Protestants was much later, and consequently shorter than in the Catholic areas. Unlike the Catholic areas where there were significant missionary efforts to convert the slaves to Christianity, the British thought that Christianity was too sophisticated for Africans, and therefore considered their slaves unfit for it. In Jamaica for instance, the Church of England did not evangelize the slaves in any systematic way until the 1820s, shortly after the arrival of Moravian and Methodist missionaries from the United States. By contrast, the French made a massive effort to convert the slaves to Christianity as early as 1685, the date of a ruling known as the Code Noir which required all masters to have their slaves baptized by the local priests within eight days after their arrival in the colonies.

This ruling, which regulated religion in all the French colonies including Nouvelle France (Louisiana), lengthened the period of contact between Catholic missionaries and the slave communities, but did not cause the slaves to abandon their African religious traditions. Indeed, the emphasis on hagiology and sacred iconography in Catholicism corresponded to the African pantheon and fitted readily within the context of African myths and symbols. This blending of African and Catholic traditions in these religions can be seen in the use of Catholic prayers and symbols in Vodun rituals and in the correspondences between the African gods and the Roman Catholic saints. These correspondences consisted of a system of reinterpretations by which symbols associated with the African spirits were made to correspond to similar symbols associated with the saints in Catholic hagiology. Thus, in Haitian Vodun for example, the Dahomean snake spirit Damballah was made to correspond with Saint Patrick because of the Catholic legend about Saint Patrick and the snakes of Ireland. Similarly in Santeria, St. James (or Santiago), a heroic fighter who fought the Moors in Spain, becomes Ogun, the powerful Nigerian and Beninese warrior spirit who is also the perceived Lord of ironsmiths and all objects made of metal.

The Spirit World

Given the nature of Caribbean religions, it is not surprising that there are hundreds of invisible supernatural beings who exercise absolute power over the universe and over their devotees' lives. These spirits are inherent in all persons and substances, and ensure the proper physical operation of the universe. Hence the seasonal changes and the rotation of days, as well as the growth and decay of all substances, fall within the province of these spirits.

At first glance, the supernatural world of these religions is so varied that, to the non-believer, it would seem to

Women in the La Rose Procession in La Ressource, St. Lucia. PHOTO COURTESY OF MANFRED KREMSER.

theons do not limit themselves to Africa. In Cuban Santeria and in Brazilian Umbanda many Amerindian spirits exist in a pantheon that derives from the New World and has been incorporated in the theology of these religions.

These spirits are believed to live in a sacred world and can be invoked in the context of religious ceremonies. To invoke the spirits, devotees use every auditory and visual means possible. Drumming, singing, dancing, and the use of bright symbolic colors are used to call the attention of the spirits to the needs of their devotees, and to open the invisible "portals" that allow these spirits to manifest themselves in the body of their devotees though spirit possession. Spirit possession is an altered state of consciousness during which a person is believed to be "mounted" like a horse by a spirit. This invasion of one's body by a spirit is thought to displace temporarily the personality of the possessed, substituting the envisaged mythological persona of the spirit. Possession is considered to be the most profound spiritual achievement in these religions for several reasons: first, because it allows a devotee to harbor powerful spirits that use their devotees' bodies as vehicles through which they manifest themselves to the human community; and second, because it represent an individual's direct engagement with the spirit world, which is perceived by the religious community as a public commitment to the religion. Such a commitment heightens one's exercise of religious authority in the community. For these reasons, devotees wish to be possessed many times in their lives. Depending on its pantheon, every spirit has its own songs, dances, and drum rhythms, as well as its own symbols.

The Rastafari and Dread

The Rastafari and Dread are twentieth-century religio-political movements that address issues related to social and economic justice. Both derive from the teachings of Marcus Garvey, a Jamaican who preached a message of black liberation in St. Ann's Bay and in Kingston in 1914, and immigrated to New York City in 1916. A persuasive and eloquent orator, Garvey preached that blacks were the chosen people of God and that they had been forced to live in the "diaspora" against their will when their ancestors were brought to the New World as slaves. For more than three hundred years, they have been subjected to white racism, social oppression, abject poverty, and economic exploitation. Black people's devils were therefore the whites who set their course for the future with the creation of corrupt civilizations that would eventually meet their own demise. Blacks in the New World should therefore look to Africa where a king would rise; he would be a long-awaited messiah who would liberate them from oppression. To Garvey, the king-

manifest boundless confusion. Given the lack of uniform beliefs in each of these religions, many of the spirits are merely known locally, though they have been revered regularly for well over 300 years. Others are new spirits who are introduced to replace those who are forgotten. An inquiry into the theological world of these religions reveals that the spirits are organized into "families" or pantheons, each of which maintains its own characteristic ethos that requires of the devotees corresponding attitudes. Some pantheons are known for their power of healing and manifest their powers through various medicinal plants or other ritual paraphernalia prescribed to believers by folk healers. Others specialize in the physical operation of the universe and ensure the passing of seasons, the growth and regeneration of the vegetation, the passing of days and nights, and the rotation of the astral bodies. In general, these pantheons include African spirits, and the names of these pantheons derive from the names of the geographical regions or the names of the ethnic nations from which these spirits are said to have originated. But the pan-dom of heaven was to occur on earth and would entail the repatriation of all New World blacks to Africa. Although Garvey did not actively undertake blacks' return to Africa, his writings and speeches published in the *Negro World*, the official newspaper of his organization known as the United Negro Improvement Association (UNIA), inspired significant numbers of them to return there.

The Rastafari movement began in Jamaica shortly after 1930, the year that Haile Selassie became emperor of Ethiopia. His enthronement was an event that was covered widely by the international press, not only because of the ostensive opulence that surrounded it, but also because of the new monarch's flamboyant titles. He was to be known as Ras Tafari, the "king of kings and lord of lords, the conquering lion of the tribe of Judah." He also claimed to be the 225th descendent—through an unbroken succession—of king David and the queen of Sheba. The emperor's celebrated enthronement caused many poor Jamaicans to remember Garvey's words and attribute metaphorical meanings to many biblical passages. Ethiopia became the "land of the blacks," the long-awaited promised land and the emperor himself, the long-awaited messiah. According to the Rastafari, all blacks in the New World were the reincarnation of the ancient Israelites, and could also be likened to the dispersed Jews in the diaspora. The Rastafari believe that they have been forced to live in a white world that they regard as abysmally corrupt; like the ancient biblical city of Babylon, it will eventually be destroyed. That destruction will open the way for God to enact his covenant with his people and ensure their safe and final entrance into the promised land. They believe that the invincible emperor who was the divine messenger of God will ensure their repatriation, and is working out the details with the leaders of the nations in the New World.

The Rastafari today can be called a religio-political movement primarily because it equates spiritual transformation with the social and political liberation of the black community. Its members denounce the established clergy for its lack of moral integrity in its "service to two masters," and Rastafari elders quote biblical passages readily in their theological discussions, known as "reasonings," to substantiate their position concerning the relations between their beliefs and the world's current state of affairs. The Rastafari live in close knit religious communities that simulate the organizational structures of traditional African compounds. A derivative of the Rastafari movement, the Dread emphasizes the suffering of the "people of God" in a "strange land." Dreads wear dreadlocks, natural hair curls symbolizing their sorrow in having to live in a morally depraved white civilization that they did not create.

Caribbean Religions in the Caribbean Diaspora

Since the 1970s, a substantial number of Caribbean people have migrated to many parts of the world, notably the United States, Canada, and the United Kingdom. Living in this Caribbean diaspora, they inhabit many of the world's largest cities (including New York, Chicago, San Francisco, Miami, Quebec, Montreal, Paris, and London). Despite the stresses of urban life and the lingering suspicions of outsiders of these religions as mere superstition and devil worship, Caribbean peoples have managed to maintain their religious beliefs and practices abroad.

Forced to adapt themselves to new cultures, they have brought many changes to these religions. One significant change is that they have become for the most part urban phenomena in the diaspora. Except for Santeria and Candomblé, which have historically developed in the city, Caribbean religions are largely rural phenomena. But they have adapted well to the city. Their rituals have attracted members of other cultural and ethnic groups, and the abundance of goods in these cities makes it possible for devotees to find most of the paraphernalia needed for the rituals. Even pilgrimages are reproduced. For instance, All Souls' Day in the Christian liturgical calendar (1 November) corresponds to Halloween in North America, the day consecrated to the souls of the dead in the Catholic liturgical calendar. Similarly 16 July, the day devoted to the Virgin Mary in the Catholic liturgical calendar, is reserved for the spirit of love who is Ezili among Vodunists and Oshun among Santeria devotees. On that day, many devotees in Eastern Canada make a pilgrimage to Saint Anne de Beaupré near the city of Quebec.

Leslie G. Desmangles

See also Candomblé; Convince; Healing in African and African-Derived Religions; Ifá; Kardecism; Music; Spiritual Baptists; Obeah in the West Indies; Ogun; Orisha (Shango) Movement in Trinidad; Rastafari; Revival; Santeria; Santeria Material Culture; Vodou; Vodou Material Culture; Spiritual Baptists; Spirtualism; Yoruba Religion; and articles on African-Derived Religion in specific Caribbean nations.

Bibliography

Barrett, Leonard. (1988) *The Rastafarians*. Boston: Beacon Press.

Bastide, Roger. (1971) *African Civilisations in the New World*. New York: Harper Torchbooks.

Bourguignon, Erika. (1976) *Possession*. Columbus: Ohio State University Press.

Brown, Karen McCarthy. (1991) *Mama Lola: A Vodou Priestess in Brooklyn.* Berkeley: University of California Press.

Deren, Maya. (1972) *Divine Horsemen: The Living Gods of Haiti.* New York: Delta Publishing Company.

Desmangles, Leslie G. (1993) *The Faces of the Gods: Vodou and Roman Catholicism in Haiti.* Chapel Hill: the University of North Carolina Press.

Glazier, Stephen. (1991) *Marchin' the Pilgrims Home: A Study of the Spiritual Baptists in Trinidad.* New York: Sheffield Publishing Company.

Kramer, Karen. (1985) *The Legacy of the Spirits* [film]. Produced and narrated by Karen Kramer, available from Documentary Educational Resources, Watertown, MA.

Métraux, Alfred. (1978) *Voodoo in Haiti.* New York: Shocken Press.

Murphy, Joseph. (1993) *Santería: Cuban Spirits in America.* Boston: Beacon Press.

Rey, Terry. (1999) *Our Lady of Class Struggle: The Virgin Mary in Haiti.* Trenton, NJ: Africa Press.

Simpson, George Eaton. (1978) *Black Religions in the New World.* New York: Columbia University Press.

Cherubim and Seraphim Movement

Cherubim and Seraphim is the name of a group of African indigenous churches that trace their origin to the indigenous Aladura movement revival, started by Moses Orimolade and Christianah Abiodun Emmanuel in Southwestern Nigeria in the 1920s. Though the early congregations were made up of Yoruba people, by the 1950s the church had spread to other West African countries, and in the 1970s to the Western world. By the late 1960s it had about 1,5000 congregations in Nigeria, with an estimated membership of over 100,000.

Growth and Development

Moses Orimolade Tunolase, who was the first founder, is considered a saint, and prayers are often said to the "God of Moses Orimolade." In his home town of Ikare in Eastern Yorubaland, he was an itinerant preacher for about eight years before he arrived in Lagos in July 1924. Within a short time, he started to preach and pray for people. Christianah Abiodun Akinsowon (later known as "Captain" Abiodun Emmanuel), as a teenager in 1925 had visions of angels visiting her and taking her to heaven a number of times. In June 1925, she was in a trance for about seven days, and her worried guardians sent for Baba Aladura (the praying man),

as Moses Orimolade was called. When Orimolade prayed for her, the young woman regained consciousness. Afterwards, Christianah told the story of her strange experiences in the heavenly city. Within a short time, crowds of people began trooping to her residence to hear her story. Later Abiodun was taken to Orimolade's residence, where both Orimolade and Abiodun held prayer meetings for inquisitive visitors. The prayer meetings became regular, and were organized into an interdenominational prayer society, named Egbe Serafu (Seraphim society) in September 1925, following a period of fasting and prayers. Soon after another vision, the society was renamed Cherubim and Seraphim.

Orimolade then organized the Praying Band, made up of trusted followers and top-ranking members of the society, to assist him in praying for those requesting prayers as he could not manage the numerous requests on his own. Members of the Band were also sent out in threesomes to pray for people, and were forbidden to charge any fee or receive gifts. By 1926, when the Cherubim and Seraphim celebrated its first anniversary, white robes or cassocks had become the official uniform for its members. Though backed by scriptural justification (Rev. 3:4; 4:4; Exodus 28:39), this was initially in imitation of Orimolade who always wore a white praying gown. The white cassock worn at every worship service remains a prominent distinguishing feature of Cherubim and Seraphim.

A major evangelistic tour led by Abiodun was undertaken from Lagos in 1927, and by the end of that year, Cherubim and Seraphim branches had been established in many important Yoruba towns in the interior. These campaigns also popularized the society. Madam Christianah Olatunrinle, a wealthy merchant of royal lineage based in Ondo, joined Cherubim and Seraphim during a business visit to Lagos in 1927, and established a branch of the society in Ondo that same year.

In the early years, Cherubim and Seraphim largely based its activities on prayers, fasting, denouncing idolatry and traditional institutions that worshipped gods, and affirming the power of God to heal all sicknesses. Cherubim and Seraphim soon attracted opposition from the Anglican Church in Lagos, partly because many Anglicans were joining the society, and partly because an Anglican minister felt incensed that the society chose the Archangel Michael as its captain, and members were venerating Orimolade. Eventually, by 1928, most of the early members had severed their connection with the Anglican Church. Orimolade did not want to establish a church, but to help Christians understand the practical fruits of true Christian faith. Moreover, Cherubim and Seraphim did not arise from any anti-European sentiments, as was the case with the African

Churches in the late nineteenth century in Nigeria or with the Zionist Churches in South Africa.

Schisms and the Proliferation of Cherubim and Seraphim Churches

Schism and rifts have been characteristic of Cherubim and Seraphim from its early years, and these have produced a great variety of factions, a multitude of leaders, and much variation in religious practices. For example, fourteen different independent groups had been registered in Lagos by 1968. Conflict of personality between Orimolade, who was about fifty years old in 1929, and Abiodun, who was twenty-two then, and Abiodun's ambition to be recognized officially as the cofounder of the society, produced the first rift. While Abiodun's supporters were young men, Orimolade's supporters were elders. On a few occasions Abiodun and her supporters denounced and physically attacked Orimolade and his supporters. The final break came about March 1929, when Orimolade wrote to Abiodun conceding various disagreements, highlighting Abiodun's disobedience, and then encouraging her to form her own independent society with her supporters so that peace could reign. The letter formalized the rift. Orimolade named his faction the Eternal Sacred Order of the Cherubim and Seraphim, while Abiodun called hers Cherubim and Seraphim Society.

Within a short time, Orimolade disagreed with the leaders of the Praying Band. Added to this was Orimolade's fear that the educated elite in the Praying Band was trying to register a constitution without his knowledge, and thus remove him as the spiritual leader of the movement. Eventually, by 1930, the Praying Band broke away and named itself the Praying Band of the Cherubim and Seraphim under the leadership of Ezekiel Davies. In 1931, representatives of the seven important towns in the interior with Cherubim and Seraphim branches met to affirm their neutrality in the Lagos crises and to seek ways of reconciling the factions. Their efforts never yielded results, so they decided to go alone as a separate group called the Western Conference of the Cherubim and Seraphim. In 1932, a section of the Praying Band broke away and formed a new body, the Holy Flock of Christ, under the leadership of "Major" A. B. Lawrence, one of the early leaders of the Praying Band.

Orimolade died on 19 October 1933, but before his death, he had appointed Abraham Onanuga, a recent convert but a man with many spiritual and administrative qualities, as his successor. Within three months, a group opposed Onanuga's succession and argued that Peter Omojola, the senior brother of Orimolade who had been with him since the early years, ought to be Orimolade's successor. The groups eventually went their different ways.

Thus, by 1934 Cherubim and Seraphim had split into six independent churches.

Later, independent groups were either established through rifts and secessions or through the activities of prominent prophets. The most famous church with Cherubim and Seraphim background in the 1960s and 1970s was the Holy Apostles' Community of Aiyetoro, which had been disowned by the Cherubim and Seraphim in the 1940s. It distanced itself from the mainline Cherubim and Seraphim by insisting that the Bible is largely outmoded because the progress of humankind has been great, and hence old written words cannot meet all the expectations of humankind. Therefore, God now makes revelation to his Holy Apostles through the Holy Spirit. Persecution forced this group to migrate to an island (later called Aiyetoro, i.e., "the peaceful or settled world") in the coastal area of Southwestern Nigeria, where members renounced individual material possession and practiced a welfare state and communal living. Around 1980, this practice was abandoned and a capitalist economy adopted. While the communal living lasted, it was regarded as a fulfillment of the Kingdom of God on earth.

Doctrinal Emphasis and Practices

Cherubim and Seraphim affirms most doctrines central to mainline Christianity, such as beliefs in God, Jesus Christ, salvation, and the Trinity. However, a major emphasis of the church is the belief in angels, which has undergone elaborate developments. Referring to the Bible, members believe that Cherubim and Seraphim, that is, angels around the throne of God, are active in the lives of Christians and the church. The leaders of these hosts of angels are Michael, who is the captain of the society and who defends all godly people in the world; Gabriel, the vice captain of the society, who delivers joyous messages to the godly and gives children to the barren; Uriel, who helps the elects toward receiving God's grace; and Raphael, who is the "healer of the sick." In addition, individual members have guardian angels that provide them spiritual assistance.

Cherubim and Seraphim churches attach great importance to prophecy, speaking in tongues, and visions. They also regard the activities of prophets and visionaries as the visible signs of the activities of the Holy Spirit, and often see the Holy Spirit as almost a substitute for Jesus. Cherubim and Seraphim believes strongly in the existence of malignant spiritual powers, and often ascribes the causes of most diseases to witchcraft. It considers as idolatry the use of any means to effect healing other than prayers, faith in God, and the name of Jesus. In fact, the society's vehement attacks against witchcraft were very pleasing to many traditional rulers who sought ways of curbing this social menace in their domains. Some Cherubim and Seraphim churches have healing homes where patients are admitted for healing over a period. Cherubim and Seraphim believes that the sick must be assisted with certain tangibles, such as the use of water, oil, and traditional soap. The movement is not opposed to Western medical treatments, but believes strongly in divine healing, which has been one of the major means of recruitment for the church. In fact, most converts to Cherubim and Seraphim have been Christians from other churches.

Its unique pattern of worship, which incorporates many features from indigenous forms of worship—such as exuberant emotionalism, grassroots participation, ecstatic and noisy worship, and calling on the God of Moses Orimolade—is rather spectacular. Cherubim and Seraphim regards the premises of their churches or houses of prayer as sacred, believing that God reveals Himself there: hence, the wearing of shoes and women fresh from child delivery or who are menstruating are excluded from the premises. In addition, certain hilltops, seashores, or wilderness areas are also regarded as sacred, and the best places to receive spiritual power and revelation. Olorunkole Hill near Ibadan, consecrated by Orimolade's assistants, is the most important of such sacred hilltops.

Prophets are very prominent in Cherubim and Seraphim. It is believed that they have received spiritual power from God, and hence are capable of performing miracles. This preoccupation with power is not alien to traditional Yoruba religion, wherein a whole range of religious leaders are believed to have special spiritual powers. Cherubim and Seraphim prophets largely rely on charisma to lead their congregations, and the absence of a formally trained ministry for effective spiritual and administrative oversight constitutes a weakness resulting in many people claiming to be Cherubim and Seraphim prophets and visionaries.

In the mid-1970s attempts were again made to unify the various independent Cherubim and Seraphim churches. This resulted in the Cherubim and Seraphim Church (Unification), which has continued to grow but been unable to bring all Cherubim and Seraphim churches together. By the 1990s, some Cherubim and Seraphim churches in urban areas had adopted the practices and methods of Pentecostal churches by holding regular night vigil, holy ghost services, having television and radio programs, and organizing large city-wide crusades. However, while some mainline churches have moved closer to the Cherubim and Seraphim through a common membership in the Christian Association of Nigeria, a nationwide ecumenical body, the Pentecostal churches and charismatic ministries have continued to treat the Cherubim and Seraphim and other Aladura churches as pseudo-Christian churches.

Cherubim and Seraphim arose at a time when nationalist spirit was growing; hence, the society carried forward the aspirations of the earlier African churches of a church under African leadership responding to African aspirations. The evangelistic successes of Cherubim and Seraphim, its tremendous number of conversions, its indigenizing character, and its dynamism in providing solace for the underprivileged in the society are all proofs of its capacity to fulfil the aspirations of Africans.

Matthews A. Ojo

See also Aladura; Yoruba Religion

Bibliography

Ayandele, E. A. (1978) "The Aladura Among the Yoruba: A Challenge to the 'Orthodox' Churches." In *Christianity in West Africa: The Nigerian Story*, edited by O. U. Kalu. Ibadan: Daystar Press, 384–390.

Omoyajowo, J. A. (1970) "The Cherubim and Seraphim Movement." *Orita* 2, 4: 124–139.

——. (1978) "The Aladura Churches in Nigeria since Independence." In *Christianity in Independent Africa*, edited by E. Edward Fashole-Luke et al. London: Rex Collins Ltd., 96–110.

——. (1982) *Cherubim and Seraphim: The History of an African Independent Church*. New York: NOK Publishers International, Ltd.

Peel, J. D. Y. (1968) *Aladura: A Religious Movement Among the Yoruba*. London: Oxford University Press.

Turner, H. W. (1967) *History of An African Independent Church: The Church of the Lord (Aladura)*, 2 vols. Oxford: Clarendon Press.

Christ Apostolic Church

Christ Apostolic Church was the largest indigenous African church in Nigeria prior to the 1970s. Many of its doctrinal emphases and practices are distinctly Pentecostal, yet also African. These factors account for the church's considerable spread.

Development out of the Aladura Movement

Their background can be traced to a prayer group, known as the Precious Stone Society, formed in 1918 by a few members of St. Saviour's Anglican Church, Ijebu-Ode, for the purpose of seeking divine intervention in the influenza epidemic that affected Lagos and its environs in 1918. In response to a vision, the group devoted itself to prayer as the only cure against the epidemic. The rejection of infant baptism by the prayer group attracted opposition from the mainline Protestant churches and hastened a parting of ways. About 1919, a retired clerk, David Odubanjo, who had been acquainted with the literature of the Faith Tabernacle, joined the group. Because of the similarity in belief, in 1921 the Precious Stone Society affiliated with the Faith Tabernacle based in Philadelphia. Dismayed by a leadership problem at the American headquarters and the fact that Faith Tabernacle could not send missionaries to the aid of the Nigerian group as requested, the affiliation was broken off about 1926.

The beginning of the Christ Apostolic Church is also intertwined with the Aladura ("the praying people") revivals of the 1930s in Western Nigeria under the leadership of Joseph Ayo Babalola, now venerated by members as an apostle. Babalola was born of Yoruba parents at Ilofa, Nigeria on 25 April 1904. Having left elementary school, he was employed in the Public Works Department as a road roller operator. In October 1928, while on a road construction site repairing his steamroller, he claimed that Jesus Christ called him to abandon the job and preach the Gospel. He started to preach immediately in an itinerant manner in northeastern Yorubaland, and about 1929 he joined the Faith Tabernacle and was baptized in Lagos.

At a meeting of the leaders of Faith Tabernacle called in July 1930 at Ilesa to resolve some doctrinal issues and practices, Babalola prayed over a corpse, and it came back to life. The news spread rapidly and widely, and soon a revival ensued. The revival, which was steeped in prayer, prophecy, and healing, inspired widespread grassroots participation, and led to the emergence of many prophets and evangelists. Despite opposition from the Protestant churches, and restrictions by the British colonial authorities, the movement still spread very wide. With a bell and a Yoruba Bible in hand, Babalola toured Yorubaland and Eastern Nigeria, preaching repentance, renunciation of witchcraft and all forms of idolatry, the importance of prayer and fasting, and faith in God's power to heal all infirmities and sicknesses. In addition, he performed many healings with *omi iye* (the water of life — any water over which prayer has been said), while many people surrendered their traditional fetishes.

In 1931, through David Odubanjo's correspondence, Faith Tabernacle affiliated with the British Apostolic Church. The affiliation was formalized when three leaders of the British Apostolic Church visited Nigeria in September 1931, and ordained seven pastors and prophets.

Subsequently, most existing Faith Tabernacle groups became The Apostolic churches.

From 1937, crises began among the leaders of the Apostolic Church and also between some Nigerian leaders and the resident missionary in Lagos, George Perfect. The crises centered on some administrative, financial, and doctrinal matters. The most-emphasized was the accusation that the white missionaries were using medical preparations — a practice interpreted to mean that they did not accept divine healing, which hitherto had been the bedrock of the revival. While the missionaries defended themselves that quinine tablets were taken as a preventive measure because their constitution was not adapted to the climatic environment of West Africa, the Nigerian leaders viewed this as lack of faith. Eventually, the crises ruptured into a schism in the Lagos congregations. Those who supported the white missionaries remained as The Apostolic Church — thus continuing the affiliation in effect since 1931. On the other hand, Nigerians who disagreed with the white missionaries pulled out. They became Christ Apostolic Church, with Joseph Babalola as their spiritual leader.

Controversy and debate has surrounded the issue of whether CAC seceded from The Apostolic Church or vice versa. The Apostolic Church regards the establishment of CAC as arising from secession. On the other hand, CAC leaders maintained that they never affiliated with The Apostolic Church, but only cooperated. They also maintained that they had continuously carried on the traditions of the revival that ensued through Joseph Babalola, and that the Apostolic Church had in fact seceded from that tradition. The issue has gone beyond any historical explanation and has become an emotional one.

An epoch came to end in the Aladura revival with the death of Odubanjo and Joseph Babalola, both in 1959. Other leaders died in the 1960s. CAC regards Babalola's revival as the beginning of the church, and has marked this by building a retreat center where Babalola was first called in 1928.

Beliefs, Practices, and Problems in the Contemporary Church

Prayer, which is believed to solve all human problems, is the focal point of CAC doctrines and practices. In addition, dreams and visions require earnest fasting and praying. Believing in the absolute power of God to cure all diseases, CAC accepts divine healing without the use of any medicine, though this has not been strictly enforced since the 1970s. Evangelistic activities are important, and these are often carried out by evangelists and prophets, usually through evangelistic associations. The best known is the World Soul Evangelistic Association (WOSEM), established in 1974 by Timothy Obadare. Its evangelistic activities have resulted in the establishment of numerous CAC assemblies in Nigeria and in the Western world.

In the late 1980s, another crisis began when pastors in some assemblies in Ibadan attempted to bring administrative and constitutional reforms into the hierarchy of the church. Those who resisted the constitutional changes wanted charisma and prophetism to prevail as the main modality in the church, while the reformers wanted administrative standards and bureaucracy established. The reforms did not succeed and instead led to a split in the church. As of 1999, both factions claim the name Christ Apostolic Church, and can only be differentiated by their respective presidents.

Generally, most people reached by Christ Apostolic Church and other Aladura-inspired churches are among the underprivileged in the society—artisans, unemployed, subsistence farmers, and the like. CAC brought enthusiasm into worship, promoted grassroots participation in church activities, and popularized indigenous Christian choruses. The church also gave prominent roles to women. By the 1950s, the CAC has spread to several West African countries, and in the 1970s, branches were established in North America and Europe by Nigerians who have immigrated to those places.

The Aladura revivals and the resulting Christ Apostolic Church have engendered far-reaching social and religious changes in Southern Nigeria from the 1930s. The church created a deep-rooted indigenization of Christianity in Nigeria, provided a major thrust for the revitalization of the Christian faith, and created a spirituality that coped effectively with contemporary human needs. It also introduced and enhanced liturgical innovations such as indigenous music. Eventually CAC became a significant social institution in Western Nigeria and its therapeutic activities have spread the church far and wide.

Matthews A. Ojo

See also Aladura; Cherubim and Seraphim Movement; Faith Tabernacle Church

Bibliography

Adegboyega, S. G. (1978) *Short History of the Apostolic Church of Nigeria.* Ibadan: Rosprint Industrial Press, Ltd.

Alokan, Adeware. (1991) *The Christ Apostolic Church 1928–1988.* Lagos: Ibukunola Printers Nigeria, Ltd.

Ayandele, E. A. (1978) "The Aladura Among the Yoruba: A Challenge to the 'Orthodox' Churches." In *Christianity in West Africa: The Nigerian Story,* edited by O. U. Kalu. Ibadan: Daystar Press, 384–390.

Mala, Sam Babs. (1983) "The Christ Apostolic Church: Its Present Preoccupations." In *African Independent Churches in the 80s,* edited by Sam Babs Mala. Lagos: Gilbert, Grace and Gabriel Associates, 66–81.

Oshun, C. O. (1983) "The Pentecostal Perspective of Christ Apostolic Church." *Orita* 2, 15: 105–114.

Ojo, John O. (1988) *The Life and Ministry of Apostle Joseph Ayodele Babalola.* Lagos: The Prayer Band Publications.

Peel, J. D. Y. (1968) *Aladura: A Religious Movement Among the Yoruba.* London: Oxford University Press.

Vaughan, Idris. (1991) *NIGERIA: The Origins of Apostolic Church Pentecostalism 1931–52.* Ipswich: Ipswich Book Company.

Christian Evangelism in Africa

The word evangelism comes from the Greek noun, *euangelion*, and is translated as "glad tidings, good news, or gospel." The concept has been used by Christian missionaries since the Reformation to identify an assortment of Protestant beliefs, including the belief in the Bible as supreme authority and the inerrant word of God; the efficacy of Christ's life, death, and resurrection for the salvation of the human soul; the divinity of Christ; and the justification of grace through faith. While evangelists are individuals who preach the gospel of Jesus Christ, evangelizing is the task of entire churches in Africa. The noun "evangelist" and adjective "evangelistic" may also be applied to popular preachers on radio, television, and at missionary rallies, and the institutions that organize such events.

Missionaries, pastors, and preachers in Africa carry out evangelism: the promotion of the Christian faith among non-Christian people, or, the spreading of the "gospel" or the "news." The term should be distinguished from evangelicalism, which is a separate social movement with its own history (*see Evangelicalism*). Evangelism can be practiced by members of any Christian denomination and by Christians who are not affiliated with a particular denominational church. One primary theoretical assumption of evangelism is that there are people who are "evangelized," and consequently decide to become Christian, and those who are "unevangelized" or "unreached" and have not yet had the "opportunity" to have the gospel preached to them. In terms used by evangelists, they have not "heard the gospel." All Christian denominations have historically evangelized through missions and missionaries in Africa, including those of Anglican, Catholic, Lutheran, Methodist, and Pentecostal churches.

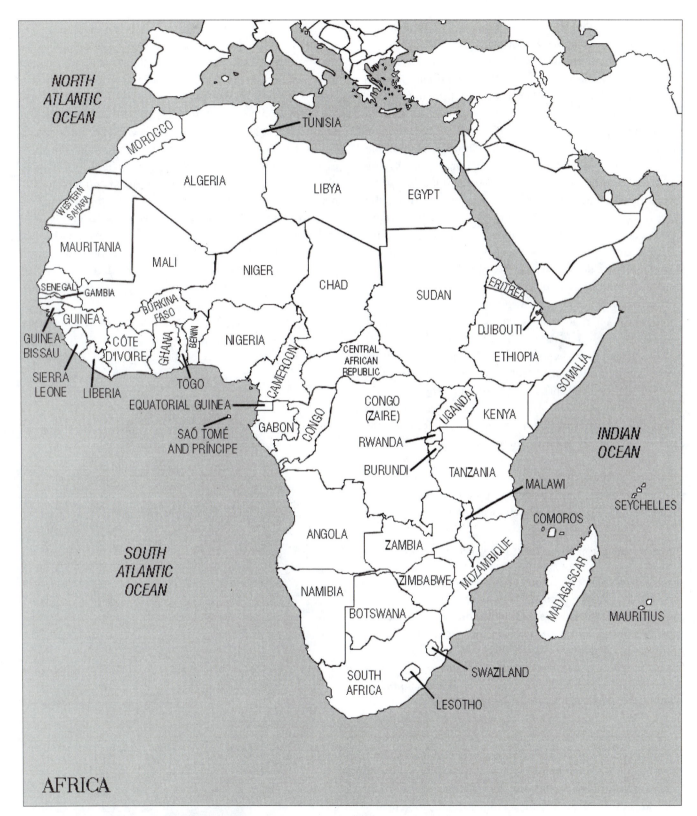

North Atlantic Ocean

MOROCCO
TUNISIA
WESTERN SAHARA
ALGERIA
LIBYA
EGYPT
MAURITANIA
MALI
NIGER
CHAD
SUDAN
ERITREA
SENEGAL
GAMBIA
BURKINA FASO
DJIBOUTI
GUINEA
GUINEA-BISSAU
CÔTE D'IVOIRE
GHANA
BENIN
NIGERIA
CAMEROON
CENTRAL AFRICAN REPUBLIC
ETHIOPIA
SOMALIA
SIERRA LEONE
LIBERIA
TOGO
EQUATORIAL GUINEA
GABON
CONGO
CONGO (ZAIRE)
UGANDA
KENYA
SAÓ TOMÉ AND PRÍNCIPE
RWANDA
BURUNDI
TANZANIA
INDIAN OCEAN
MALAWI
SEYCHELLES
COMOROS
ANGOLA
ZAMBIA
SOUTH ATLANTIC OCEAN
ZIMBABWE
MOZAMBIQUE
MADAGASCAR
NAMIBIA
BOTSWANA
MAURITIUS
SWAZILAND
SOUTH AFRICA
LESOTHO

AFRICA

From *Ethnic Groups Worldwide: A Ready Reference Handbook* by David Levinson published by Oryx Press, 1988. Used by permission.

Some of the largest concentrations of Christians in the world now live in Africa; it is estimated that there are more than 300 million Christians in contemporary Africa (Barrett 1992). The growing population of African Christians is a fairly recent development in the history of Christianity and is described by many scholars as a shift in gravity for Christianity, from the "first world" to the "third world." In fact, some theologians call the non-European Christian church the "third church" to emphasize the importance of growing numbers of Christians globally. Perhaps the most important components of the topic of evangelism in Africa are the issues of power and politics. Debates surrounding these issues have been central to the study of Christianity in Africa historically, and continue to stir controversy in the present. Central to these debates are questions of identity for evangelists. Embedded in issues of whether Christianity is spread by Africans or by Europeans are two questions: first, who holds the power in international churches and mission bodies that promote evangelism in Africa, and second, how is the gospel interpreted and lived by its converts. Changing structures of power within mission organizations have altered the way that Christianity has been spread and received on the continent. Christianity in Africa is also extremely diverse. The many cultures and languages existing on the African continent, as well as divergent historic experiences of Africans with Christian missionaries, have created multiple Christianities. Thus it is risky to speak of a unified "African Christianity." Evangelism as a social process has produced Christianities that take different forms in varied local contexts.

Colonial Evangelism: Missionaries and Native Catechists

Evangelism has been a feature of Christianity on the African continent since the introduction of the religion by Portuguese Catholic missionaries in the fifteenth century. In addition to an increasing number of people converting to Christianity, practices of evangelism and attitudes towards conversion have changed over time and in relation to the histories of colonialism in Africa. Evangelism is a social process described by some scholars as a dialectic in which both the evangelists and those who are evangelized are transformed.

Evangelism in Africa in its early stages was entwined with colonialism. The first Christian evangelists were missionaries sent by mission boards to "civilize" Africans and convert them to Christianity. For this reason, the primary debates surrounding evangelism in Africa emphasize the potentially coercive nature of Christian conversion. Historians, sociologists, and anthropologists of this era agree that the missionaries, although guided by what may have been in their minds the best intentions, carried colonial oppression along with Christian doctrine. Early missionaries saw African cultures

from the perspective of early European modernity and sought to transform African "savages" into "citizens." Anthropologists of the time documented what they perceived to be cultures in great transition. It was assumed that missionaries aimed to change Africans into model Europeans. For this reason, many anthropologists of the colonial era, and even today, argue that evangelism is coercive and changes cultures so radically as to be damaging to people. This was especially the stance of European social scientists who were trying to understand and document African cultures in colonial times. They viewed missionaries as protagonists of cultural innovation with a primary focus on undermining what anthropologists considered "traditional" ways of life. Much of the success of the colonial enterprise in Africa was due to strategies of modernization, and colonial conversion relied on such secular powers as access to medicine, material goods, and innovations in agricultural production.

What is usually forgotten is that many Africans were themselves evangelists from the late 1800s until the 1960s. Evangelism took place in local languages, and as missionar-

Emily Christmas Kinch, African Methodist Episcopal missionary to West Africa.
PHOTO COURTESY OF RANDALL BURKETT.

ies struggled to learn the vernacular and to translate the Bible into local dialects, local assistants, native catechists, and junior native pastors bore the brunt of most evangelistic work. While African catechists were at first the interpreters and companions of European missionaries, African evangelists subsequently spread Christianity as outreach from places where it had already "taken root," as in the coastal regions of West Africa and towns in South Africa.

Evangelism and Politics: African Independence Movements

As early as the 1920s, African Christians began requesting more power and control over missionary bodies. The initial intent of mission boards was to relinquish control to African clergy and to "plant" churches in Africa that were "of African soil" (Sundkler 1960). This intent was made urgent due to health problems that many European missionaries in Africa encountered at the turn of the century. With increased knowledge of medicine and the steady growth of mission churches, it soon became apparent that mission boards were reluctant to relinquish the power of the church to Africans. What resulted was the growth of church movements that proclaimed independence from the mission churches. Along with this rising anticolonial sentiment came real political resistance to colonial politics in the 1960s and beyond (some African states did not receive independence from settler rule until the 1980s and 1990s, as in the cases of Zimbabwe and South Africa). Many churches and evangelists in Africa took an active role in supporting anticolonial independence struggles, and continue to be active in such contemporary efforts for political justice as the international promotion of democracy. Colonial struggles for independent statehood were mirrored by, and in some cases intricately linked to, struggles for power over the church, as Africans took power and turned it against colonial regimes. In South Africa, for example, the apartheid regime of the colonial state promoted the growth of separate churches for black Africans. Ethiopian and/or Zionist churches synthesized "traditional" African and Christian cosmologies. While initially the birth of Independent churches in Africa was considered to be an effect of a breakaway movement from mainline mission churches, these churches are now considered to be separate socio-religious entities in their own right, with distinct philosophies, leaders, and doctrines for the conduct of Christianity.

What has emerged in postcolonial Africa is the phenomenon of African churches independent from mission bodies in Europe or America. Although the extent to which these churches today are self-supporting and self-governing varies greatly, this has meant a great deal for evangelism in Africa. In colonial times it may have been Africans who preached in local languages to other Africans, but they were neither church leaders nor ecclesiastical officials. Postcolonial Africa has been fueled by an African political elite educated in mission churches, and the new leaders in Christian Africa have all been touched by evangelism. If the missionaries of the colonial era intended to assimilate Africans through Christianity into a "European" style of life, they have been largely unsuccessful. Instead, the missionary movement changed the face of Christianity and transformed the cultural and demographic constitution of the Christian church globally.

Evangelism and Economic Development

Insofar as colonialism brought Africa into a global economic system, missionaries were its handmaidens (although this is debated, as scholar have noted that African empires and states were built on trade routes long before the arrival of European colonists). In addition to preaching the gospel, colonial missions built schools for Africans where the colonial government would not. They provided medicine. Gradually, Christian witness (the act of individuals proclaiming the gospel) replaced Christian missionaries and African churches and international nongovernmental agencies (NGOs) replaced Christian missions in providing social welfare for Africans. Many mission statements, for example, were model farms that encouraged innovations in agriculture. Paul Gifford (1990) has described this transformation as the "NGOization" of the churches of Africa. Linked to this is a specific evangelistic tenor called the Gospel of Prosperity (also called the Faith Gospel, or the Health and Wealth Gospel). These evangelistic approaches preach that believers will attain wealth and prosperity through their faith. They have been critiqued for their materialism, and for placing the burden of achievement upon individuals while masking the global political and economic structures that hinder possibilities of wealth and prosperity in contemporary Africa. Nonetheless, these theologies are increasingly popular in Africa today.

As African states have receded in their abilities to provide social welfare for their citizens (often at the behest of international structural adjustment programs instigated by the IMF and the World Bank) churches and NGOs have come to the rescue. Funded through international humanitarian organizations, churches build schools, provide clean water, and support such small-scale agricultural development programs as irrigation schemes and micro-enterprise development. Echoing projects of colonial mission churches, these schemes could at first glance be seen as neocolonial. Yet these parallels, even while treading upon well-worn missionary histories, exist in a contemporary global context.

A LETTER FROM FATHER LAWTON, THE SENIOR PRIEST AT THE DOMINICAN MISSION IN YABA, NIGERIA, NOVEMBER, 1951

To All Mission Supporters
This letter has been in the making since June 23ᵈ. It was on that day I boarded the eight-passenger Dove plane of the British West African Airways to go North to the Kaduna Province to give a series of retreats, before which I was to make a two-week tour of the Sokoto Province where one day, in perhaps the not too distant future, we are going to open some bush missions.... The Sokoto Province which we will visit on this tour is the largest and perhaps the most barren of the five provinces which go to make up the Kaduna Prefecture. Sokoto is some 36,000 miles of sagebrush land, which is very poor farming or cattle raising. There are over two million people living there, in many cases it might be better to say exist-ing. Among the two million, and this is the most disappointing figure of all the statistics of the area, there are only 957 Catholics, and you are not sure of that many.

Source: Salamone, Frank A. (1974) *Gods and Goods in Africa.* New Haven, CT: Human Relations Area Files, Inc., 161.

Much has changed in the theology of Christian evangelism in Africa since the times of colonial missionaries.

Contemporary Evangelism: Missiology and African Theology

Many contemporary theologians and missiologists (those who study Christian missions from a religious perspective) believe that evangelism in Africa transcends cultural bound-aries in search of universal truths. They assert that Christianity preached in Africa, by Africans, is uniquely African. Christian theologians also argue, in contrast to those who consider evangelism a form of cultural coercion, that bringing Christianity has liberatory potential. African theology is a type of evangelizing that involves translating Christianity into forms that can be understood by all Africans, even in the face of the vast cultural diversity of the continent. Evangelism requires more than literal transla-tion, as some concepts cannot easily be assigned words from one language to the next. Processes of making Christianity African have been called: Africanization, inculturation, indi-genization, and contextualization, among others. In the 1960s, in the early phase of African theology, the initiative was to reformulate the discourses of colonialization into methods for decolonization. These theologies attempted to make Christ and Christianity African. More contemporary theologies are concerned with showing Christ as inherently present in African culture. Those who study evangelism from a religious perspective (as in the disciplines of Missiology and Theology) no longer see Christianity in Africa as tied to the missionary enterprise. It has evolved into a new, African, entity with dynamics influenced by local cul-tures and contemporary global practices of technology and communication, as well as structures of economic and polit-ical inequality. Some theologians go as far to say that African religious thought has some basic affinity with Christian doc-trine and that the intersection of Christian faith and African heritage is no longer an encounter of European and African cultures. African Theology stands as a unique evangelistic, intellectual response to colonial evangelism, fueling the evangelistic enterprise that is uniquely African in the late 1990s, leading to the twenty-first century.

African Evangelism, Global Evangelism

Christian evangelism, and its reception in Africa by Africans, has changed significantly since its introduction in the fif-teenth century. It represents a set of social processes that have shaped the continent economically, politically, and his-torically, and will conceivably continue to do so. Previous scholarship on this topic has focused on the history of churches (both mission and independent) as the primary vehicles for evangelism in Africa. Further research might include a comparative study of African evangelism in differ-ent parts of Africa. As long as evangelists continue to convert non-Christians to Christianity, evangelism will intersect with politics, economics, and almost all other religions in Africa.

It is also a topic of transnational dimensions, as Africans begin evangelizing outside of Africa, and religious organizations in other parts of the world continue to send transnational capital to Africa with aims of fueling local evangelism. If Africa does indeed contain some of the largest numbers of Christians globally, and if the gravity of Christianity is shifting to places such as Africa, the future will unfold Africa's influence on Christian evangelism more globally.

Erica Bornstein

See also Cyberspace in African and African-Derived Religions; Christian Missionaries in Africa; Mission Schools; Pentecostalism in Africa

Bibliography

Barrett, David B., George Thomas Kurian, and Todd M. Johnson, eds. (1982) *World Christian Encyclopedia: A Comparative Study of Churches and Religions in the Modern World Ad 1900–2000.* Oxford: Oxford University Press.

Bediako, Kwame. (1995) *Christianity in Africa: The Renewal of a Non-Western Religion.* Edinburgh: Edinburgh University Press.

Beidelman, T. (1982) "Colonial Evangelism: A Socio-Historical Study of an East African Mission at the Grass-roots." Bloomington: Indiana University Press.

Comaroff, Jean, and John L. Comaroff. (1991) *Of Revelation and Revolution: Christianity, Colonialism and Consciousness in South Africa.* Chicago: University of Chicago Press.

Comaroff, John L., and Jean Comaroff. (1997) *Of Revelation and Revolution: The Dialectics of Modernity on a South African Frontier.* Chicago: University of Chicago Press.

Fields, Karen E. (1985) *Revival and Rebellion in Colonial Central Africa.* Princeton: Princeton University Press.

Gifford, Paul (1990) "Prosperity: A New and Foreign Element in African Christianity." *Religion* 20: 373–88.

——, ed. (1995) *The Christian Churches and the Democratisation of Africa.* New York: E. J. Brill.

Hastings, Adrian. (1976) *African Christianity.* New York: The Seabury Press.

ZION IN AFRICA

IN THE APRIL CRISIS we printed a letter criticizing severely the A. M. E. Zion Church for its failure in the West Africa Mission work. We have received from the missionary Secretary of the church certain printed matter in answer to the allegations of that letter.

The first criticism of this answer is one of bad bookkeeping. It would be difficult for an expert to find out just what has been received for missions and what has been expended. It is quite possible that there has been some extravagance and waste of funds, but there could be no proof of this without a better system of financial reports.

On the other hand, the real difficulty is absolutely clear. The A. M. E. Zion Church is trying to carry on missionary work in Liberia and on the Gold Coast of West Africa at the total expense of $11,000 per year, including the travels of Bishop and missionaries; but not including apparently the salary of the Bishop. From June, 1924, to December 31, 1925, the total expense was $21,496. Without further investigation it may be said flatly that no adequate mission work over a territory a thousand miles or more in length, embracing between five and ten millions of people and situated three thousand miles from home base, can be carried on for such a sum of money. It means inadequate supervision, small salaries, or none, and ineffective work. It is nonsense to think that ministers or other folk who happen to be good and self-sacrificing can be sent to Africa to live on prayer.

... What is needed in West Africa is first, a delimitation of the missionary field. The African Methodist, the Zion Church, and the Baptist ought to divide up the field; one of them working in Liberia, one on the Gold Coast; one in Nigeria. Each of them ought to spend at last $50,000 a year in small, well-organized African work, consisting of education, industry and social uplift, and carried on by educated people of good character who are paid salaries of at least $2,500 a year and traveling expenses; who are allowed six month's rest at home with salary every three years. Anything less than this program is nonsense and waste.

Source: *The Crisis: A Record of the Darker Races,* vol. 32 (June 1926): 63. New York: NAACP.

———. (1979) A History of African Christianity 1950–1975. Cambridge: Cambridge University Press.

———. (1994) The Church in Africa 1450–1950. Oxford: Clarendon Press.

McLean, S. D. (1996) "Evangelism." In Dictionary of Ethics: Theology and Society, ed. P. B. Clarke and A. Linzey. New York: Routledge, 342–345.

Mudimbe, V. (1988) The Invention of Africa. Bloomington: University of Indiana Press.

Pobee, John S. (1979) Toward an African Theology. Nashville, TN: Abingdon.

———. (1992) Skenosis: Christian Faith in an African Context. Gweru, Zimbabwe: Mambo Press.

Sanneh, Lamin O. (1989) Translating the Message: The Missionary Impact on Culture. Maryknoll, NY: Orbis.

Stewert, J. A., and E. G. Valdez, eds. (1997) Mission Handbook 1998–2000. 17th ed. Monrovia, CA: MARC Publications.

Sundkler, Bengt. (1960) The Christian Ministry in Africa. London: SCM Press Ltd.

———. (1961) Bantu Prophets. London: Oxford University Press.

Walls, Andrew F. (1996) The Missionary Movement in Christian History: Studies in the Transmission of Faith. Maryknoll, NY: Orbis Books.

Young, Josiah U. (1993) African Theology: A Critical Analysis and Annotated Bibliography. Westport, CT: Greenwood Press.

Christian Missionaries in Africa

Christian missionary work can be roughly defined as a Christian community introducing its beliefs to a non-Christian area, with the primary hope of convincing non-Christians to convert. The history of this sort of activity in Africa runs back to the early 300s CE, making it nearly as venerable as the history of Christianity itself. Starting from that time, the history has passed through three distinct phases: (1) Tyrene, Syrian, and Byzantine mission work in northeastern Africa starting in the 300s, (2) Portuguese-led Catholic missionary activity along the African coast from the 1500s to the early 1800s, and (3) the evangelical Protestant missionary expansion into the African interior that began around 1800 (an era slightly foreshadowed by initial Protestant mission work in southern Africa, and one that spurred a corresponding intensification of Catholic missionary efforts). The third phase is generally thought of as an era dominated by European, American, and African-American missionaries in Africa, but that impression masks the nearly simultaneous rise of converted Africans as local Christian evangelizers—in many locales, African converts became the de facto main missionaries.

European missionaries in the third phase preached a faith, rooted in Western religious thought, that was, in principle, exclusivist: Christian orthodoxy did not permit syncretic intertwinings of mission creeds with elements of indigenous religions. On the contrary, European missionaries in Africa devoted a great deal of time and energy to denouncing local beliefs and practices as false and/or immoral, to rooting out remnants of indigenous religious influences in the lives of converts, and to instilling the missionaries' (inescapably Western) version of a Christian outlook and consciousness into the new African Christians. Various denominations pursued this in slightly different ways and with differing degrees of rigor. Catholic missionaries, for instance, tended to take a far more relaxed approach to Africans' often ritualized consumption of home-brewed alcohol than did many of their Protestant counterparts. Virtually all the mainstream missionaries, however, maintained a basic abhorrence of religious syncretism.

African evangelizers of Christianity did not necessarily see things in quite the same light. Many were as strict as, or stricter than, their Western counterparts, but in other cases, as linguistic and cultural translators, they adopted a more flexible, intercommunicative, evangelical approach. African Christians tended to (and more fluidly could) translate Western ideas into local idioms and conceptual frameworks that allowed potential converts to appreciate Christianity's message. Indeed, it was through those acts of analogizing and cultural translation that most early African evangelists themselves understood the religion. Some European churches tacitly or even openly went along with the process, so long as "translation" did not slide into syncretism or heathenism. Consequently, variations on original mission creeds flourished throughout Africa. It was dangerous doctrinal territory for the missions, though: the history of Christianity in Africa contains myriad examples, scattered all across the continent, of African evangelizers breaking away from mission orthodoxy to preach heterodox ideas, and of Christian/indigenous hybrid faiths that mission authorities had never counted on and could not countenance.

Early Church Efforts in Northeastern Africa

The gradual spread of Christianity across northern Africa through the 300s CE arguably should be considered more a part of the early struggle over the character of the Church than an aspect of the mission enterprise per se. Many of the era's most noteworthy teachers and preachers, such as Origen of Alexandria (185–253 CE), sought confrontation with other groups and/or martyrdom at the hands of secular officials or rivals, at least as much as they desired to gain converts. It comes as no surprise that as Christian orthodoxy took shape in subsequent centuries, the methods and theologies of many of the early activists were retroactively denounced as heretical. The early activists' approach to preaching did not carry forward into the more conversion-oriented style of missionary enterprise that emerged in later centuries. Yet a tempered version of their zeal became an undercurrent of the ongoing missionary endeavor: the enthusiasts' positive desire for mutilation and martyrdom was reworked into a willingness to endure suffering, hardship, and, if necessary, martyrdom for the sake of spreading the Christian message.

The first acts of long-distance missionary outreach in Africa sprang from Eastern Christian churches, beginning with two Christian scholars from Tyre en route to India, who were waylaid by pirates in the early 300s. The pair washed ashore at Axum, a kingdom located between the Red Sea and the Nile valley. They gravitated to Axum's court circles and settled in, converting King Ezana to Christianity in 322. One of the pair, Frumentius, was then made Axum's first bishop, and Christianity began its association with the monarchs of what would come to be known as Ethiopia—a conjoining that endured until the final downfall of the monarchy in the 1970s. Other parts of Ethiopia were evangelized by Syrian missionaries in the later 400s, who translated the Bible into a local language, Ge'ez, and established evangelically oriented monasteries across the Tigre region within which Axum sat.

The Syrian missionaries sowed seeds of a version of Christianity under siege in the northern Mediterranean: they preached a Monophysite theology that stressed Christ's indivisible nature, repudiating the 451 CE agreement between the Roman and Byzantine Churches at the Council of Chalcedon, which ascribed both a human and a divine nature to Christ. The seed took: the Ethiopian Church became firmly Monophysite, and grew slowly but sturdily until an era of more rapid expansion in the 1300s. Its local missionaries reached out to non-Christians within and beyond the Ethiopian state's borders by gradually spreading their aggressively evangelical monasteries southward across the region's highlands, as far as Shoa. Byzantine royalty, sympathetic to Monophysite beliefs, also sent missionaries up the Nile to Nubia in the mid-500s. The missionaries rapidly made converts of Nubian royalty, giving rise to a Nubian Church that thrived in semi-isolation through the turn of the second millennium CE, but thereafter lost most of its adherents as Muslim rulers and immigrants gradually altered the region's religious culture. The eastern churches did little further missionizing in Africa after the 500s, for Byzantium lost power and influence below Anatolia with the rise of the Muslim Caliphate in the 600s.

Catholic Missionary Activity along the African Coast

Nearly a millennium passed before serious evangelical efforts began again in Africa, and then the renewed missionary work in Africa passed into the hands of Western Europe's Catholic Church. Their efforts began in the 1500s when missionaries shipped onto the Portuguese trade galleons reaching down the western African coast and around the Cape of Good Hope. The early lead that Portuguese missionaries took in spreading the faith prompted Pope Leo X to give Portugal effective control over African evangelization in 1514—a decision the Vatican would rue when Portuguese power went into decline later that century. Rome later looked to circumvent the authority it had given Portugal, by establishing its own missionary department, Propaganda Fide, in 1622.

In the 1500s, Portugal sent Catholic missionaries to proselytize territory that reached from Senegambia in the west to Swahili city-states in the east. However, Portugal's main interest in Africa soon crystallized around slave trading. No mainstream churches or Muslim denominations opposed slavery at the time, but it was a highly disruptive and violence-laden commerce that did not bode well for the establishing of native Christian churches. It can fairly be said that few of the early Portuguese evangelical efforts were wholehearted and even fewer successful: in some areas, local rulers complained that the few Portuguese priests present spent most of their time trading. In the Kongo region, missionaries got involved in slave trading and the local church was largely supported by its fees for baptizing newly enslaved captives.

A Roman Catholic missionary on his motorcycle outside a village in Nigeria in the early 1970s. PHOTO COURTESY OF FRANK SALAMONE.

Many of the clergy that Portugal sent to Africa were of less than unimpeachable character, and those more worthy of the calling were often loath to go, for Europeans tended to succumb quickly to deadly diseases along most of the sub-Saharan coast. The Portuguese who actually did undertake missionary labors usually tried to make quick converts of African royalty, which would enable the priests to then perform mass baptisms among the rulers' subjects. Most royals who converted in those circumstances understood their baptisms as little more than political and diplomatic gestures; similarly, the baptisms of their subjects had virtually no enduring impact on African beliefs and practices.

Two regions, however, saw missionaries achieve a degree of success in the 1500s through the 1700s: the Atlantic islands off the West African coast and the Kongo Kingdom in western central Africa. Sao Tomé and the Cabo Verde islands, deserted islands far enough offshore to be healthy for Europeans, were settled in 1483 as plantation colonies and well-situated bases for Portuguese operations between Africa and Brazil. The islands soon built up a substantial Luso (Portuguese)-African population that became mainly Christian, and, after the 1571 founding of a seminary on Sao Tomé, provided sub-Saharan west Africa with clergymen better able to withstand the rigors of living and preaching there. As late as the 1640s, Portugal's government considered even the dregs of its own clergy preferable to African clergy for evangelizing, but had to rely heavily on Luso-African and African converts despite its prejudices, especially along the Guinea coasts.

Portuguese missionary efforts had their greatest and most tragic success in the Kongo Kingdom. Kongo's king accepted baptism in 1491. The son who succeeded him as Afonso I in 1506 was a true believer, an active Christianizer of the kingdom, and a would-be ally of the Portuguese monarchy who requested a large missionary presence. But few priests or evangelizers were sent to Kongo; most immigrants were traders who spurred Kongo into a cycle of slave raiding and trading that made it the largest slave exporting region in Africa. The Portuguese immigrants did patronize and help maintain the Catholic Church in Kongo. They also intermixed with the local population, and some of their Luso-African offspring became clergymen. Overall, however, Kongo's shortage of Portuguese, Luso-African, or African priests was nearly as chronic as its surfeit of slavers; only the Kongolese kings' continued commitment to the Church kept the faith widespread.

The Vatican intervened in the 1640s, sending Italian Capuchin missionaries to Kongo to perform sacraments, offer basic teachings, and root out non-Christian practices. The last of these duties was performed with vigor by a European clergy stretched too thin to follow up their destruction of the old with thorough construction of the new. They alienated a great many people from the Church, even as the Kongolese state was sliding into disarray from the social and political violence associated with the slave trade. By 1700 Kongo's government had effectively disintegrated, and the Church collapsed with it. The Capuchins kept up a passable missionary presence in one part of the former Kongo, the coastal province of Soyo, until 1740; elsewhere they were reduced to virtually nil. Local catechists thereafter kept elements of Christianity alive in the Kongo, but had to do so in effective isolation from the Church that had carried the faith there.

Evangelical Protestant Missionaries in the African Interior

The third phase of missionary extension into Africa, stretching from the late 1700s to the present, drew on a far wider base of support in the West, and then, later, in Africa as well. The enterprise was much more intent and intensive, for its staffing came from dedicated organizations, backed by the sponsorship of mainstream churches and well-connected elites in England, France, the German territories, the United States, and other countries. Protestant groups effectively launched the third phase, guided by two strong inspirations: a general "warming" of Protestantism that had swept through the West in the eighteenth century, breathing new life into evangelical Christianity, and the growth of a religiously-grounded abolitionist spirit in several denominations. Early signs of both appeared in 1792, when William Carey founded the Baptist Missionary Society; and when the Sierra Leone colony was established by abolitionists and free blacks on the west African coast as a place to which African-Americans freed from slavery could "return" to Africa and, simultaneously, help plant Christianity there.

Numerous new mission societies appeared shortly afterwards, among them the London Missionary Society (1795), the Church Missionary Society (CMS, 1799), and the American Board of Commissioners for Foreign Missions (1810). Older groups, like the Moravians, were prompted into a resurgence of activity. In response, the Vatican, which had allowed Propaganda Fide to lapse into disuse, revived the organization in 1816 and established new orders like the White Fathers and the Holy Ghost Fathers for missionary work; chapters of these and other orders sprang up all across Catholic Europe. In both Protestant and Catholic circles, missionary efforts got the bulk of their financial support and most of their field staffs from the working and lower-middle classes.

Some of the earliest of the new activity took place in southern Africa, where mission stations were founded as early as 1793, both within the borders of the Cape Colony and beyond them, in African-ruled territories. Sierra Leone became the initial focus of successful missionary work in West Africa. Its prominence and significance grew after 1807, when Britain abolished the slave trade, then began interdicting slave ships and landing their freed captives at Sierra Leone. Ministering to this freed population became a primary activity of CMS activity after 1816. Other West African missions were founded in this era, and a start was made at developing an indigenous clergy. For example, Bishop Samuel Crowther was a Yoruba-speaking slave brought to Sierra Leone in 1822, were he was baptized and given a Christian education. He was ordained in 1843, put into missionary work shortly thereafter, and made a bishop in 1864. Formal efforts in East Africa took more time to launch, having little presence until 1844, when the CMS set up a missionary base near Mombasa, another settlement for freed slaves, called Freetown. The lead CMS missionary there, Johann Krapf, had a wider vision for the enterprise: he imagined a string of missions running across the continent, a bold goal, never nearly realized, that became the CMS's beautiful African chimera for the remainder of the nineteenth century. By the late 1870s, however, both Protestant and Catholic missions reached inland as far as Buganda.

The missionary movement got a tremendous boost from David Livingstone. His 1856 speaking tour combined descriptions of societies in the thrall of the slave trade but anxious for legitimate commerce and Christian enlightenment with his electrifying plea that more people become missionaries. He stirred a new group—elite, university-educated men—into mission work. Still, most nineteenth-century missionaries remained men of humbler backgrounds leading lonely, dangerous lives for the sake of their convictions, living or dying at the sufferance of local rulers and tropical diseases. The people to whom they preached often responded coldly or with skepticism; many Africans rightly saw in Christianity not just a religion, but a cosmology that undermined fundamental local structures of supernatural belief and worldly authority. They were interested in the Europeans ideas and trade goods, but not in wholesale abandonment of local ways.

The circumstances tried many a missionary's faith, and required many to sacrifice their lives; indeed, the Zambezi mission that Livingstone inspired collapsed under such difficulties by 1863. At first, a remarkably large proportion of missionaries handled these demands with patient, ongoing efforts. In the early nineteenth century, they learned local languages and prepared translations of bibles, catechisms, and other materials. They opened more missions, widening the net of preaching. They put real effort into the development of what was by then referred to as "native agency": an African staff of clergymen, evangelizers, and teachers.

Some African-Americans also saw themselves as potential go-betweens: men like Martin Delaney and Alexander Crummell encouraged free blacks to return to Africa as missionaries, arguing that they were the people best suited to bringing Christianity to the continent. By the later nineteenth century, however, many European missionaries were growing impatient with the difficulties thrown in their paths by African leaders defending their authority and beliefs, and frustrated by the reluctance of people to convert in large numbers. Missionaries began to long for a civil order that would aid their evangelical work, or at least limit the grosser obstructions to it. In short, many supported the European imperial takeover of the late nineteenth century.

Missionaries did gain converts more quickly under early twentieth century colonialism, partly through the greater receptiveness of people after local societies had been defeated by colonial forces, partly because missions controlled the native education system in many colonies, and partly because African evangelizers gradually spread Christianity farther, wider, and deeper into societies. Mainstream European missionaries occupied a peculiar, contradictory position in many colonies. They lived more in and among Africans than most Europeans, and understood and sympathized with some African concerns more than most colonizers. Yet virtually all missionaries supported colonialism as a Christianizing, civilizing project, and certainly opposed African confrontations with colonial authority. In many colonies missionaries became government-appointed spokesmen for "Native Interests"—because they went along with the official view that natives could not or should not speak for themselves in government. African opponents of colonial rule, themselves usually mission educated, tended not to trust missionaries; nor did most missionaries trust politicized colonial Africans. A few, fringe missionaries did, however, fuel anticolonial views, most notably the handful of Watchtower preachers whose millenarian visions were widely taken up in southern and central Africa as a promise of an imminent world without colonialism.

By the mid-twentieth century, the missionary movement in Africa was shrinking rapidly, though many missions continue to operate down to the present. Some thought the missionary project paternalistic and obsolete for independent Africa, but it faded largely because it had fulfilled its purpose by then. Vigorous, self-supporting local churches were firmly planted across sub-Saharan Africa by the 1960s, and continue to thrive today. African Catholic priests, in fact, are sometimes asked to help make up shortfalls of clergy in North America. Much Western-based evangelical work in Africa is now done through barnstorming tours, the circulation of audio and video cassettes,

QUOTE FROM CMS MISSIONARY J. ALFRED WRAY, POSTED IN THE TAITA HILLS OF KENYA FROM 1882 TO 1888.

The quote illustrates the growing late nineteenth century impatience of missionaries with African obstructions to their work, and their increasing desire to impose a European-based order on African societies. The quote is from 1887, and comes from two sequential letters.

If I were to start a new station [here] . . . I would build apart [from any village] and form a colony, whoever came to live with me would be under my control. The day he refused to be controlled by me he would simply leave my village; thus order would be preserved. I ought to preserve order in *this* village, [i.e., present the mission site], for it is ours by right.

Yesterday I called all the men together and asked for an explanation of the row the other day. I said, If such be your custom it is not ours and could not be allowed where I was, whoever wished to have rows let him go else-where and not bring them here. . . . Now in future anyone who wishes to come here must first ask *my* permission, and I will make him swear that he will *1st* bring no war here, *2* that he will sow no discord, *3rd* that he will con-form to the useages of the village.

Now here is the difficulty: how can [the state of affairs here] be remedied? The only way I can suggest is to make ourselves Masters of the village in lieu of all the goods they have eaten belonging to us. Besides this, they are all in debt to myself, debts contracted during the famine [of 1883-5]. . . . If I could get a dozen decent people to come up . . . here I should perhaps strike a little terror into them. Unless something of this sort is done, I don't see how we can make any progress here. . . . Mr Holmwood [the British consular officer in Mombasa with a detachment of soldiers under him] could do it, and he being so near, I have taken upon myself to write to him. . . . The only thing he would have to do would be to take two or three of the ringleaders to Zanzibar to chop sticks. . . . We might then bring them to their senses. . . . They owe their lives, their wives, and their little ones to the Society.

Source: CMS Archives, Birmingham, England. CMS Correspondence, G3 A5/04(b), J. Alfred Wray to Bishop Parker, 22/8/1887, and Wray to Downes-Shaw, 8/9/1887.

summer programs for young Western evangelicals, and multiyear Mormon missions of young people. But the speakers are generally now preaching to the converted.

Bill Bravman

See also African Charismatics; AIC; Christian Evangelism in Africa; Ethiopian Orthodox Church; Harrist Movement; Media Evangelism; Pentecostalism in Africa; Seventh-Day Adventist Church; Zionist Churches

Bibliography

Ajayi, J. F. A. (1969) *Christian Missions in Nigeria, 1841–1891: The Making of a New Elite.* Evanston, IL: Northwestern University Press.

Beidelman, T. O. (1982) *Colonial Evangelism: A Socio-Historical Study of an East African Mission at the Grassroots.* Bloomington: Indiana University Press.

Comaroff, Jean, and John Comaroff. (1991/1998) *Of Revelation and Revolution: Christianity, Colonialism, and Consciousness in South Africa,* vols. 1 & 2. Chicago: University of Chicago Press.

Elphick, Richard, and Rodney Davenport, eds. (1997) *Christianity in South Africa: A Political, Social and Cultural History.* Berkeley and Los Angles: University of California Press.

Gray, Richard. (1990) *Black Christians and White Missionaries.* New Haven: Yale University Press.

Hastings, Adrian. (1994) *The Church in Africa, 1450–1950.* Oxford: Clarendon Press.

Isichei, Elizabeth. (1995) *A History of Christianity in Africa.* Lawrenceville, NJ: Africa World Press.

Neill, Stephen. (1986) *A History of Christian Missions,* 2d ed., revised by Owen Chadwick. London: Penguin.

Oliver, Roland. (1952) *The Missionary Factor in East Africa.* London: Longmans.

Sanneh, Lamin. (1983) *West African Christianity.* London: Allen and Unwin.

Strayer, Robert. (1978) *The Making of Mission Communities in East Africa: Anglicans and Africans in Colonial Kenya, 1875–1935.* Albany, NY: State University of New York Press.

Church of Christ (Holiness) U.S.A.

The Church of Christ (Holiness) U.S.A. is a Black Holiness church founded by Charles Price Jones (1865–1949) in 1907. Jones was born in Arkansas and educated at Arkansas Baptist College. He was ordained and became a pastor in 1888. In 1893, he was attracted to the Holiness movement and experienced baptism of the spirit in 1894. He joined with Charles Harrison Mason in 1895, and the two actively preached the Holiness doctrine and began moving away from affiliation with the Baptist church. In 1900, he withdrew from the Baptist association and, in 1902, founded the Christ Temple Church and affiliated it with the Church of God in Christ. Jones served as its president. The Church attracted a large following of African-Americans who were disillusioned with the Methodist and Baptist churches, where they were placed in limited roles. In 1907, Mason was converted to Pentecostalism by William J. Seymour at the Azusa Street Mission and moved to take the Church in this new direction, precipitating a break with Jones and a schism in the Church. Jones ultimately withdrew from the organization and founded the Church of Christ (Holiness) U.S.A. in 1909, keeping the church in accord with its original Methodist Holiness orientation.

The Church is Methodist in its basic orientation but adheres to the Holiness doctrine of baptism of the Holy Spirit through which Christians are made perfect in love. At times, the Church has moved to affiliate with white Holiness churches, but the initiatives have been blocked by resistance on the part of some whites to mixed-race churches. Under Jones's leadership until his death in 1945, and the leadership of his successors, the Church has expanded to seven dioceses and nearly 200 churches. Estimates suggest a membership of over 10,000, with missions in Liberia and Nigeria.

David Levinson

See also Azusa Street Revival

Bibliography

Cobbins, Otho B. (1966) *History of the Church of Christ (Holiness) U.S.A., 1895–1965.* Chicago: National Publication Board of the Church of Christ (Holiness) U.S.A.

Jones, Charles P. (1901) *Jesus Only, Songs and Hymns.* Jackson, MS: Truth Publishing Co.

Mead, Frank. (1995) *Handbook of Denominations in the United States,* 10th ed. Nashville, TN: Abingdon Press.

Church of God and Saints of Christ

William Saunders Crowdy (1847–1908), a former slave and a cook on the Santa Fe Railroad, claimed that God had chosen him to lead African-Americans back to their historic religion and identity. After the Civil War, he purchased a 100-acre farm in Guthrie, Oklahoma, where he began to have visions in 1893. Shortly after, he began preaching in the streets of Guthrie (Wynia 1994: 21). As an itinerant preacher, he spread his message to Texas and on State Street in Chicago. In 1896, Crowdy arrived in Lawrence, Kansas— a city that had attracted an appreciable number of African-Americans. Indeed, 2,155 out of Lawrence's 9,994 residents in 1890 were black. Crowdy formed the Church of God and Saints of Christ in Lawrence on 5 November 1896. By 1898, the sect reportedly had 29 congregations in Kansas alone. Crowdy launched his church in Chicago and other sites in Illinois, and eventual moved its national headquarters to Philadelphia in 1900, where he reportedly was joined by some 5,000 members (Wynia 1994: 26).

Under Crowdy's leadership, the Church of God and Saints of Christ grew into a highly syncretic African-American Judaic-Christian sect with branches in several American cities and overseas. Crowdy argued that blacks are descendants of the ten tribes of Israel, whereas Caucasian Jews resulted from miscegenation with whites. His seven "keys" also emphasized repentance of sin, baptism by immersion, commemoration of the Last Supper, foot washing, observance of the Ten Commandments, the holy kiss, and prayer (Wynia 1994: 25). The Church of God and Saints of Christ observes the Jewish Sabbath and Passover and other Jewish holidays. It claims to be based upon the patriarchs, prophets, and apostles of the Old and New Testaments. The sect also has incorporated elements from Prince Hall Masonry, including the use of rosettes, sashes, crowns, belts and swords, bugles, mortar boards, certain greetings, handshakes, and marches (Wynia 1994: 47–48). Crowdy's written sermons are referred to as "epistles." In a sermon delivered in Lawrence in 1903, he "urged the congregation to wage an unrelenting war against oppression and discrimination" (Wynia 1994: 23). Crowdy performed miracles and received prophecies which served as the basis for the sect's beliefs, rituals, and organization.

The sect held four general assemblies in Lawrence, Emporia (Kansas), and Philadelphia during Crowdy's lifetime. At the first significant organizational meeting on 10 October 1899, the assembly of representatives from various states and Ontario created a presbytery consisting of northeastern, northwestern, southeastern, southwestern districts (Wynia 1994: 30–31). In addition to his ministry, Crowdy was an entrepreneur who came to own and operate a grocery store, a restaurant, a cafe, a furniture store, a printing office, and a barbershop. His followers worked in these business ventures (Wynia 1994: 26). Crowdy died on August 4, 1908, in Newark, New Jersey.

Prior to his death, he hand-picked Bishop H. Z. Plummer to serve as his successor. Plummer, who is considered to be a descendant of Abraham, stressed communalism and economic self-sufficiency. Under his jurisdiction, the Church of God and Saints of Christ relocated its headquarters to Belleville (an area within Portsmouth, Virginia) in 1917. The sect operated a 1,000-acre farm, several cottage industries, a school, and homes for orphans and the elderly at its Belleville headquarters, and a 110-acre youth camp for juvenile offenders in Galestown, Maryland. Most of these operations eventually closed, a reflection of the sect's decline in recent decades. The sect does provide low-rent housing at its Belleville headquarters and plans to construct residential units for the elderly there.

The Church of God and Saints of Christ reportedly has 53 tabernacles in the United States, seven in South Africa, and a few in the West Indies (Wynia 1994: 36–38). The majority of the congregations are located on the East Coast, including in Philadelphia, New Jersey, New York, Maryland, Massachusetts, Connecticut, Washington, D.C., and Virginia. The sect also has congregations in Chicago, Jacksonville (Florida), Gary, Cincinnati, Detroit, Greensboro, and Atlanta. At its zenith, the sect had at least 213 congregations. The sect split into two factions following Crowdy's death, one of which emerged in South Africa. At the present time the Church of God and Saints of Christ has an eastern and a western district in the United States.

The politico-religious organization of the sect includes bishops, boards of presbytery, evangelists at large, and ministers. Crowdy created the Daughters of Jerusalem in 1898 in Emporia for the purpose of catering to members in need. The Daughters also "were responsible for purchasing and/or making the uniforms (i.e., badges, ribbons, hairpieces), keeping records (i.e., births, deaths, weddings, etc.), and the rituals of the church services (i.e., funeral processes, mourning, footwashing, blessing of children, children's programs, junior quorums)" (Wynia 1994: 74). The Sons of Abraham is a men's association that takes care of the premises of the various congregations.

Hans A. Baer

See also Black Jewish Movements

Bibliography

Wynia, Elly M. (1994) *The Church of God and Saints of Christ: The Rise of Black Jews.* New York: Garland Publishing.

Church of God in Christ

Charles H. Mason and C. P. Jones served as the founders of a black Holiness sect that eventually evolved into the Church of God in Christ. Charles H. Mason joined C. P. Jones, J. A. Jeter, and W. S. Pleasant in conducting a Holiness-style revival in Jackson, Mississippi, in 1896. After being expelled from the Mount Olive Missionary Baptist Church for preaching "sanctification," Mason and Jones established a congregation in an old cotton gin in Lexington, Mississippi, which they eventually named the Church of God and shortly thereafter renamed it the Church of God in Christ to distinguish it from the white-controlled Church of God. Jones served as the general overseer, Mason as the overseer of Tennessee, and Jeter as the overseer of Arkansas in this new Holiness sect (Church of God in Christ 1973).

In early 1907, three COGIC leaders, C. H. Mason, J. A. Jeter, and D. J. Young, received the gift of tongues during their five-week stay at the Azusa Street Mission. Upon returning from the revival, Mason conducted revival meetings in Memphis. When the General Assembly of COGIC withdrew the "right hand" of fellowship from Mason as a result of his promotion of glossolalia, he convened his own General Assembly, which elected him the general overseer and chief apostle. Mason's incorporation of the name of the "Church of God in Christ" forced the original body headed by C. P. Jones to rename itself the Church of God (Holiness) U.S.A. (Cobbins 1966).

Since 1907, COGIC has held annual convocations in Memphis, avoiding the practice characteristic of many African-American mainstream denominations of rotating the convention site. During the 1910s and 1920s, COGIC evangelists began to establish congregations in Detroit, Dallas, Fort Worth, Houston, Los Angeles, and numerous other American cities. In the 1920s, COGIC began to expand its operations to the West Indies, Central America, and West Africa.

Shopshire categorizes COGIC's polity as an "episcopal-presbyterian system where bishops have preponderant power and authority, but assemblies, departments, and boards have enough leverage to decide and act on policy matters" (1975: 148). COGIC congregations within the United States are organized into 109 jurisdictions, each of which is presided over by a bishop. While COGIC, unlike most black Baptist bodies, allows women to preach in the role of evangelist, the offices of bishop and elder are restricted exclusively to males. To compensate for male dominance in the highest echelons of its politico-religious organization, COGIC has encouraged women to form strong women's departments. Presiding vice-bishops along with a National Board of Bishops and a National Board of Presbytery serve as the principal authorities of the group. State organizations function as abbreviated versions of the national association.

COGIC congregations range from modest rural churches and urban storefronts to substantial edifices. Despite the fact that Zion Holiness Church (pseudonym for a COGIC congregation in Pittsburgh) had been in existence for over fifty years, Williams (1974:48) found that the congregation still catered primarily to poor people. In contrast, Pentecostal Temple Institutional COGIC, located on the edge of downtown Memphis, is housed in an ornate modern structure, which was completed in 1981 at the cost of approximately $4,000,000 (Patterson 1984). James Oglethrope, COGIC's presiding bishop at the time, observed in his sermon during a Sunday morning service in April 1987 that many of his parishioners have been "blessed with nice homes, cars, and diamonds." Despite the presence of many professional people within the its ranks, the majority of Pentecostal Temple Institutional's members probably belong to the working class.

While COGIC still manifests many sectarian features, Pentecostal Temple Institutional and other large congregations exemplify the process of denominationalization within the group in recent decades. Another manifestation of denominationalization in COGIC is a growing interest on the part of some of its pastors, members, and congregations in social reform programs. COGIC provided the headquarters for the sanitation workers' strike, which was punctuated by the assassination of Dr. Martin Luther King, Jr., in Memphis in 1968. COGIC ministers have joined National Baptist and African Methodist ministers in campaigning for political candidates. COGIC members have won seats on city councils and in state legislatures and have been appoint-

ed to minor executive branch positions in the federal government (Tinny 1978: 265).

COGIC has grown into the largest black Pentecostal body in the world and claims to have some eight million members. While its membership count undoubtedly is greatly inflated, since it has never conducted a systematic census, COGIC, along with the three National Baptist denominations and the three major African Methodist denominations, constitutes one of the seven largest African-American religious organizations in the United States (Lincoln and Mamiya 1990).

Hans A. Baer

See also United States, African Religions in

Bibliography

Cobbins, Ortho B. (1966) *History of the Church of Christ (Holiness) U.S.A., 1895–1965*, New York: Vantage.

Church of God in Christ. (1973) *Official Manual with the Doctrine and Discipline of the Church of God in Christ.* Memphis: Church of God in Christ.

Lincoln, C. Eric, and Lawrence H. Mamiya. (1990) *The Black Church in the African American Experience.* Durham, NC: Duke University Press.

Patterson, James Oglethrope. (1984) "The Mother Church." Memphis: Pentecostal Temple Institutional Church of God in Christ.

Shopshire, James Maynard. (1975) "A Socio-Historical Characterization of the Black Pentecostal Movement in America." Ph.D. dissertation, Northwestern University.

Tinny, James S. (1978) "A Theoretical and Historical Comparison of a Black Political and Religious Movement." Ph.D. dissertation, Howard University.

Williams, Melvin. (1974) *Community in a Black Pentecostal Church: An Anthropological Study.* Pittsburgh: University of Pittsburgh Press.

Church of the Twelve Apostles

The Church of the Twelve Apostles is one of the earliest of the African-initiated churches that sought to express Christianity in an African context without its traditional Western trappings. The church is the product of the preaching tour of the Liberian Grebo prophet, William Wade Harris, in the Western Province of Ghana in 1914. Harris himself did not found a church, for he worked in collaboration with the Western missionaries. It was two of his earliest converts, Grace Tani and John Nackabar, who started the

Twelve Apostles Church, which is nicknamed "Nackabah" after its cofounder. The official name is derived from the practice of Harris of appointing twelve apostles in each station to cater to the needs of his converts. Grace Tani was one of Harris's wives, and functioned more as a charismatic figure who met the needs of the members through divination and healing, while Nackabar was responsible for the administration of the church.

Nackabar was succeeded by John Hackman who, in seeking to perpetuate his hegemony, appointed his nephew Samuel Kofi Ansah as his successor before his death in June 1957. Following the death of Bishop Ansah, the heads of the various districts started operating largely independently of the headquarters at Kadjabir, near Mpoho in the western Region of Ghana.

In recent times, women's and youth fellowships and other groups have emerged in most of the churches. This development is ostensibly borrowed from the mainline churches that have these fellowships. These fellowships have enhanced the church's characteristic of emphasizing communal living, thus serving as a surrogate family for its members as well as facilitating Christian education in the church.

In view of the fact that most of the prophets and prophetesses were illiterate and therefore could not undertake effective Biblical exposition, the office of the pastor has been instituted in the church. The pastors, who have received good basic education, conduct church services, especially on Sundays, and administer the financial and secretarial duties of the church.

In principle, the Church of the Twelve Apostles subscribes to the same articles of faith as the major Protestant denominations in Ghana, particularly the Methodist Church. However, in practice, doctrine is not as important as meeting felt needs of people, such as healing the sick, predicting future events, casting out evil spirits, and searching for security and prosperity.

The Bible and the dancing gourd-rattle (an African drum made from calabash netted with strings of beads) are two special sacred objects that are so central to the church that every regular member is expected to posses them. The Bible, for instance, is used for ritual purposes, such as placing it on a patient's head as part of the healing process rather that reading it. It is the belief of the church that the rattles are not only a potent means of chasing away demons but also an effective tool for healing. The church's belief in the use of these as sacred objects is based on the Bible, as found in Exodus 15:20: "And Miriam the prophetess, the sister of Aaron, took a timbrel in her hand; and all the woman went out after her with timbrels and with dances." Thus, it is not, as it were, an African traditional religious practice.

One striking thing about the regular place of worship is an adjoining "garden" where daily dawn prayer meetings, healing services, and other religious practices take place. In the center of the garden stands a tall white wooden cross. Adherents lift basins of water toward the cross for it to be consecrated and thus made potent to effect healing.

Neophytes are received into full membership by the marking of the sign of the cross on their foreheads, they are also given a hand of fellowship (a special handshake by leaders of the church) to mark a formal welcome into the church. The church has a code of conduct and offenders are given punishments such as suspension for some months followed by an act of penance and confession in public. Polygamous marriage and remarriage are allowed.

A common feature of the church is the use of "holy water," particularly for protection and the purpose of divine healing. Thus, they are often called "water carriers." Water is usually stored in a basin and kept under the white wooden cross in the church garden. With their top half naked and carrying a pitcher of "holy water" on their heads, patients dance, twist, and swirl until they become ecstatic enough for the Spirit to fall on the person in order for healing to take place. Violent outcries and shouts of joy and convulsions usually accompany healing. Fasting is emphasized as a means of enhancing one's chances of receiving God's grace for healing, reception of visions and revelations, and divine wisdom and discernment. Patients are usually given therapy on Fridays at the "Prophet's garden." Friday was chosen because Jesus Christ died on Friday and the potency of his healing power can best be experienced on that day. There are testimonies to the effect that healing does take place during such healing services.

The Twelve Apostles' Church is one of the religious movements that has over the years made efforts to blend elements from African culture with its Christian heritage. It has proved to be relevant to the Ghanaian context and has thus contributed in rooting Christianity on African soil.

Cephas N. Omenyo

See also AIC, Harrist Movement

Bibliography

Baeta, Christian G. (1962) *Prophetism in Ghana: A Study of some "Spiritual" Churches*. London: SCM Press.

Debrunner, Hans Wener. (1967) *A History of Christianity in Ghana*. Accra: Waterville.

Hollenweger, Walter J. (1972) *The Pentecostals*. London: SCM Press.

Civil Rights Movement *See* Abyssinian Baptist Church; Black Muslims; Black Theology; Peoples Temple; Progressive National Baptist Convention, Inc.; Rainbow Coalition; Social Activism; Southern Christian Leadership Conference; National Conference of Black Churchmen

Convince

Convince, also known as Bongo or Flenkee, is an Afro-Jamaican religion often grouped with Afro-Christian Revivalist forms such as Pukumina and Revival Zion though it is more African than either. Convince is essentially an ancestral cult—and is probably the oldest surviving form of Myalism—but Convince is organized around a core of shared common belief rather than kinship. The social and biological family is replaced by a religious family of archetypal spirits and spirits from the community of believers, practitioners, and initiates. Once much more widespread, Convince is now mainly found in Portland and St. Thomas parishes and even within this restricted geographical area has only a small and scattered following.

There are several theories about the origins of Convince but the most recent and comprehensive one is Mervyn Alleyne's. According to Alleyne, Convince was once much more widespread than it is now and is essentially a form of Myal that was introduced to the Native Baptists just before emancipation (see Alleyne 1988.)

While Convince is closely linked to Myal and Kumina, it is clear that at one time Convince formed a bridge between the preemancipation (1834) religious life of Africans enslaved in Jamaica and the Christian revival that later fed the black-led Native Baptist movement. The formerly secret African religion of Myal became public and some Myal leaders desired to legitimize their African practices by associating them with Christianity. The name Convince comes from the need of the candidate to present evidence to "convince" the Native Baptist minister of his readiness for baptism. The evidence regarded as qualification for Christian baptism was a religious experience involving dreams, swooning away, having visions while in that state, and finally, passing through a stage of intense excitement accompanied by violent physical contortions.

Congolese Africans arriving in Jamaica between 1841–1865 encountered this Afro-Christian form of Myal and re-Africanized it by introducing Kongo religious and linguistic elements. They called this new re-Africanized form Kumina. The Congolese involvement also kept Myal from getting any further away from its African roots and moving closer to Christianity than it already had. The form of Afro-Christian Myal thus created became called Convince and has remained essentially frozen in place ever since.

Convince has changed character several times since its formation in the nineteenth century. After its emergence out of Myal and Native Baptists, Convince became a nativistic cultural resistance movement expressing a great deal of bitterness and resentment towards whites. Convince has now degenerated almost into a form of entertainment.

The adepts of Convince call themselves Bongomen. Bongomen allow themselves to be mounted by the spirits or ghosts venerated in Convince in order to gain material benefits from the relationship. Because Obeah also involves use of ghosts, Bongomen may mix religion with magic and perform services apart from their occasional religious performances. Each Bongoman operates independently but also attends the meetings of other Bongomen.

Convince has a pantheon of beings and Christian names for beings that are African in their attributes and in the religious attitudes and behaviors devotees show toward them. Bongomen believe that spirits and humans live in a single unified world permeated with spiritual power. Spirits and humans interact with each other in that world and can influence each other's behavior, but spiritual power is morally neutral. God and Christ receive little attention from Bongomen because they are too remote and too consistently benevolent to merit it. Therefore Bongomen look to lesser spirits most of the time, including departed ancestors and people who were once members of Convince.

Convince ceremonies have some Christian elements such as readings from the Bible. Christian hymns alternate with special Bongo songs sung in a call and response format and accompanied by hand clapping. The ceremonies also feature dancing and spirit possession by the Bongomen. While possessed, Bongomen speak an English dialect peppered with African words, many of Congolese origin.

Bongomen feed their spirits with animal sacrifices once a year, and in return the spirits teach them the secrets of spiritual power, offer protection, bring good fortune, and assist them in performing magic (obeah.) Except for the annual sacrifice ceremony, Convince rituals only occur when there is a need for them. Memorial services for deceased members, rites to pacify spirits or to thank them for help, and ceremonies for recreation and to raise money are the main occasions. When asked to solve especially difficult problems Bongomen will hold special Obeah rituals.

Convince has been in a state of decline since the 1950s. The cultural isolation that helped Convince remain African has been broken by competition from better-organized and more orthodox Christian sects; these sects resent Convince intensely. Also, Convince's days as a widespread movement of cultural resistance are now long past; it has had to cede this role to a newer competitor, Rastafarianism. Most of the people attending the infrequent and sporadic public ceremonies are not believers. Many are Christians, who while understanding the reasons for the ceremonies and enjoying their participation in them, do not regard Convince as a religion at all.

George Brandon

See also Jamaica, African-Derived Religions in; Kumina

Bibliography

Alleyne, Mervyn. (1988) *Roots of Jamaican Culture*. Bridgetown, Barbados: Pluto Press.

Bastide, Roger. (1971) *African Civilizations in the New World*. New York: Harper and Row.

Curtin, Philip. (1968) *Two Jamaicas*. New York: Greenwood Press.

Hogg, Donald. (1960) "The Convince Cult in Jamaica." In *Papers in Caribbean Anthropology*, edited by Sidney Mintz. New Haven, CT: Yale University Publications in Anthropology, no. 58.

Schuler, Monica. (1979) "Myalism and the African Tradition." In *Africa and the Caribbean: The Legacies of a Link*, edited by Margaret Crahan and Franklin Knight. Baltimore: Johns Hopkins University Press, 65–79.

———. (1980) *Alas, Alas, Kongo: A Social History of Indentured African Immigration to Jamaica, 1841–1865*. Baltimore: Johns Hopkins University Press.

Simpson, George E. (1978) *Black Religions in the New World*. New York: Columbia University Press.

Costa Chica, Mexico

Recent research by Mexican historians is demonstrating that modern Mexican culture is not only a product of European colonization of the native population but also of elements from African cultures, and that Africans played a significant role in the formation of Mexican national identity. While Africans, originally imported as slaves, were found in every community occupied by the Spanish, the region of Mexico that continues to show the most African influence is the Costa Chica region on the Pacific coast. Africans brought to this part of Mexico found freedom by escaping into the rural mountains and forming hidden communities, and, as they built these communities, they adapted their religious traditions as a means of survival. They blended their own traditions with the beliefs of the native people with whom they had extensive contact. The Costa Chica is isolated, and the people there have maintained an African view of life through religion, dance, and oral traditions. Survival of African traditions in the Costa Chica was possibly due to this isolation from Europeans and the fact that the Africans who settled in this region shared similar religious traditions. In addition, the congruence of some African beliefs with those of their native neighbors served to reinforce beliefs and practices. Specific religious practices and a distinctively African philosophical view of the person have survived as part of the worldview of Afro-Mexicans (Aguirre Beltrán 1989: 279–289).

History

African people brought as slaves to the Americas were forced to accept life on the plantation. Plantation life was the major institutional force that shaped the breakdown of African culture, as slaves were forced to give up their culture and language in order to incorporate them into plantation society. Yet many people were able to retain much of their culture and they demonstrated a commitment to their cultural heritage. The first groups of Africans directly from Africa arrived after 1532, as before then slaves were sold only on the Iberian peninsula. In either case, the Crown and the Catholic Church believed that by quickly indoctrinating Africans into Catholic traditions they would be less likely to spread African paganism.

Africans and Europeans had been in contact many years before the Americas were explored and settled. The Sahara slave trade had taken Africans into Europe as slaves, and when the Muslims conquered Spain they brought with them Africans as military officials and as slaves. After Spain was reconquered, all Africans who converted to Catholicism were allowed to remain in Spain. These Africans were called Ladinos and they were the first group of Africans to arrive in the Americas. Most of the African women who arrived in the Americas in the sixteenth and seventeenth centuries were Ladinos and were brought from Spain as either free domestic servants or slaves from the city of Seville. These women, who despite acculturation often continued to practice a form of ancestor worship, were periodically likely to be accused of witchcraft because the Church considered the ancestral spirits to be devils (Mendoza Briones 1997: 89). The preeminence of women as communicators with the dead can be seen in the Afro-Mexican communities today as part of their Day of the Dead celebrations.

As the slave trade began to bring people directly from Africa, the West African cultural groups that made up the

Family gravesite with crosses made from flower petals in the community of Querrero, Costa Chica, Mexico. COURTESY OF BEATRIZ MORALES COZIER.

slave population, while speaking different languages, shared common institutions such as cultural practices, methods of agriculture, and similar belief systems. Later forced migrations brought people from the Caribbean who had previously originated among the Twi-speaking peoples, including the Akan, Fanti, and Gae. In the nineteenth century, European slave traders sold groups of Africans from the Niger Delta and from Old and New Calabar inhabited by the Ibo, Ibibo Ede, and Epie. These groups were brought first to Cuba and then sold into Mexico; they were known to escape and form "runaway" communities (Iliffe 1995: 129).

Many of the Africans who came to work in the Costa Chica as slaves were basically left alone by the Spanish owners who used them to manage their farms (*estancias* or *haciendas*). However, the escaped slaves who came to the Costa Chica were running from harsh treatment, including beatings to the point of death. When they escaped from the mines and plantations they often found a place on these *estancias* where they were hired as cattle ranchers by African overseers. Many would work as day laborers on the *estancias* until they found land near the water and became farmers and fishermen (Aguirre Beltrán 1989: 279–287).

Maria Mendoza Briones discusses the significant participation of Africans in the Mexican state of Michoacán in the middle of the eighteenth century. They used African culture to adapt to the new urban and rural milieu, with an approach that was unique and different from the Spanish and Amerindians. The personality of Africans in colonial Mexico is described as being frank, open, arrogant, and quite distinct from the more humble attitude of the Amerindians (Mendoza Briones 1997: 89). The energy and spirit of the Africans led them to rebel against the colonial system and to start struggling for freedom as soon as they arrived. As Perez notes, in Mexico the Africans constantly resisted slavery and refused to accept Christianity. While many obtained freedom, as Perez (1997: 76) points out, racism against people of African descent was present in all interpersonal relationships and even those who were free were classified as being of inferior status due to their darker skin.

In Mexico, African cultures merged with those of the Amerindians. African women escaped to the ranches in isolated areas where they could have their children born as free women and men. Wide social networks of Indians provided resources to Africans hiding from their owners and supported some of these women. Another form of assistance was the support of Indian women who acted as midwives to African women who wanted their children born outside of slavery. Many of these children were raised by Indian women in the Indian way of life. Often, the slave masters would attempt to make a claim of ownership on these children, but, as Guevara Sangines (1997: 48) states, the Indian women would fight in the courts to keep their foster children from being taken by the slave owners. Many children of African slaves were raised in native villages because of this practice. Thus, we see a situation where the people brought from Africa as slaves were influenced by the culture of the Indians but were also able to preserve significant portions of their own culture and beliefs (Palmer 1976: 166).

Beliefs and Practices

The various West African groups brought to the Americas shared similar religious beliefs, including cosmology, practices (especially ancestor worship), and a similar conception of self or personhood. In Mexico's Afro-Mestizo communities on the Pacific coast a person is defined in much the same way that a person is defined in communities in West Africa, in particular the Akan religious traditions (Aguirre 1948: 177). People of African descent in Mexico continue to believe that a person has placed in them a special divine power. They call this special power the Shadow or life force. The Shadow is that spiritual force that sets personality, attitudes, and the ability to assist or destroy others in human relationships. Among the Afro-Mexicans the Shadow, or spirit force, is what provides the person with a self-identity and personality. The Shadow is the most dynamic aspect of the persona and the idea of the Shadow in Afro-Mexican belief is more important than that of the soul. A person who is very negative is said to have a heavy Shadow. Alguirre Beltran states that Afro-Mexicans believe that most sickness and physical problems are caused by loss of the Shadow; consequently much of traditional healing is oriented towards restoring the Shadow, or life force. Afro-Mexicans have stories about the Shadow being stolen when it leaves the body when a person is sleeping; it is believed that a person can catch someone's Shadow in order to kill him or her. The Shadow at times is thought to stay around the living affecting their lives until it receives the attention it demands; the Shadow of a dead person can create problems between living family members if neglected. (Aguirre 1957: 177).

El Tono and the Crossroads

One major belief is that some people in the community may have a totem or animal double. They are called *naqual*, or *el tono*. When children are initiated into the *naqual* belief system, it is believed they will have an animal that shares their destiny. Whatever happens to the person will happen to the animal, and whatever happens to the animal will happen to the person. There are many stories about animals that had done much mischief or even killed someone, and when the animal was shot the human being whose *tono* it was also suffered and even died if the animal died. Those people who are *naqual* are feared for their spiritual powers (Aguirre Beltrán 1963). According to the stories, a member of the extended family may initiate children without their parents' permission. An uncle may take his sister's son and set the child down at a crossroads and begin the initiation process, calling his own *naqual* to initiate the boy and the small animal who will grow along with the boy. The uncle's *tono*, as the animal is called, will then take care of the boy's little *tono* until he is mature enough to go on his own. The uncle will take responsibility for passing on to the boy all of the necessary knowledge of a *naqual*. The native people in the area have very similar beliefs and practices, as do several groups in Africa. The element of the crossroads as the place of initiation, however, is different. It is significant because in several West African religious traditions the crossroads is sacred to Eleggua/ Legba/Exu, who is considered to be God's messenger and who makes any ritual possible. The crossroads is viewed as a place of enlightenment, where the messages are given and received, and destinies are met. Here the destiny is that of the child's spiritual partner, his *tono* (Añorve Zapata 1998).

The Day of the Dead

The Day of the Dead in Mexico is celebrated by all Mexicans as a national holiday. In the Costa Chica one may observe the preservation of African ideas about the dead in this context. When I observed a burial ground in an Afro-Mexican community, I saw that the mourners spread marigolds in the shape of a cross in front of the tomb, and also made a trail of flowers leading to their houses. Part of the intent of this practice was to provide a path for the dead to visit the living, a concept quite similar to African ancestor worship beliefs, where it is considered not at all unusual for the spirits of the deceased to have contact with the living. What is unique in Mexico is that for an entire month, from the middle of October to the middle of November, there is a pause in the life of the living to allow a space for the dead to enter into their lives. The Day of the Dead is a family activity, children and grandmothers getting on the bus with flowers, travelling to family gravesites with large bunches of yellow and red flowers. These would be shared among the family so that everyone could honor the dead. Women, more than men, seem to form this close bond with the dead person's spirit and they provide the leadership to honor their

The Diablos (the Devils) is a dance performed in Costa Chica, Mexico, by Afro-Mexican men dressed in rags and high boots with their faces covered by masks. The men dance through different villages on All Souls Day. Dancers ceremonially flog other dancers and children. Flogging is a common anti-witchcraft measure in many African cultures. COURTESY OF BEATRIZ MORALES COZIER.

FIELD NOTES FOR DAY OF THE DEAD

I arrived in the Costa Chica October 29 at five o'clock. Along the way I took the bus from Mexico City to Acapulco. When I arrived in Acapulco, I planned to take a *collectivo*, which is a shared car where the driver will take two or three travelers into Costa Chica. The price is about the same as the bus, but a trip that is five hours by bus is only two hours by car, because the bus makes all the local stops. For me as an anthropologist, the bus ride was not really an inconvenience because it gave me an opportunity to see all of the different ethnic groups that make up Costa Chica. Even in Acapulco there is a presence of black people, which becomes more obvious when you pass San Marco, which for some people is the beginning of black Mexican communities. The bus is an opportunity to enter for one day these communities, if only by looking through the window to see their mark or their style. My eyes were oriented toward looking at the stores that were set up to sell the items for the Day of the Dead.

When I went to my friend's burial ground in her community, I saw that she spread yellow flowers in the shape of a cross in front of the tomb. Part of the intent of this was to provide a path for the dead to visit the living.

The day of the angelitos was October 30. We went with my friend Jorges and his wife. On the 30th the bells ring a twelve o'clock to announce the arrival of the "little angels," children who died who were baptized. The parents set up shrines for the angelitos with their pictures and favorite foods, and lay a trail of flowers so that the dead can find their way to the house. There are earlier holidays for children who have died who were not baptized, and also for others who died in violent ways. The impression that I took with me was that the spirits of the dead are revered several times during the year through prayers, rosaries, and mass. This is similar to Chinese and African practices where the cult of the ancestors is maintained throughout the year.

Beatriz Morales Cozier

dead; they are generally the ones who decorate the graves, build the altars, and cook special foods for the dead. But everyone participates; schools and universities close as well as most businesses, so that families can gather together. In the Costa Chica the influence of African burial rituals can be seen in the choice of food and drink for the dead and in the fact that similar offerings to the dead are made throughout the year.

Secret Societies and the Dance of the Devils

In West Africa there are *egungun*, secret societies whose members masquerade and dance as a form of ancestor worship. The purpose of the dances is both to honor friendly and ancestral spirits and to cleanse the community of angry, harmful, or negative spirits. Groups that are more or less similar to these African societies may be found in the Americas as part of the heritage of the Diaspora. In Costa Chica *la Danza de los Diablos*, or the Dance of the Devils, is performed as part of the Day of the Dead celebration. The dancers wear masks and perform as a family tradition; their purpose is to honor the dead and to cleanse the community.

The idea and the word "devil" does not necessarily have the negative connotation among many African-descended communities as it might elsewhere. The term has picked up negative connotations because of the common accusation of "devil worship" levied against those who preserved their traditions of ancestor worship, and because of the identification of the African-derived Eleggua/Legba/Exu with the Christian Devil (i.e., the "crossroads devil" of the southern United States). To the Mexican participants "Dance of the Devils" means the dance of the ancestors, or the dance to drive away evil spirits.

The Dance of the Devils has been traced by some to medieval Europe and local Native American traditions. However, one may see in the dance the same elements visible in dances throughout the Diaspora—from the Abakua secret society in Cuba to the Gullah-speaking people who live on the Sea Islands off the coast of Georgia to dances done by fraternities in historically black universities. Most notable and widespread is the dance step in which the dancer stomps firmly on the ground, the original purpose of which was to drive away negative spirits. The dancers in Costa Chica have retained not only the form of this step but the meaning,

The Devil dancers use African-sounding drumbeats and even a drum which is very similar to the drum used by the Abakua in Cuba. In fact, both groups say that their drum sounds like a big cat—a leopard or tiger—and was once used for hunting such animals. Before the dance the masked "devils" parade through the community with whips, chasing children and adults. The flogging is believed to drive away evil spirits and sorcery, and to make men strong and women fertile.

The dance itself is a way to strengthen the community. It represents contact with the spirit world, the spirit of the Afro-Mexican community, and recalls the days when these communities were all isolated villages made up of runaway slaves who had to be prepared to defend themselves against outsiders. Through the ritual of the dance they created a strong community identity based on identification with the ancestors, and continue to create a similarly strong identity today.

Conclusion

The Costa Chica is unique in Mexico because in no other region can one see Mexicans who not only look black, but also whose religious beliefs and practices show a high degree of African influence. The Africans who came to the Pacific coast here laid a strong foundation from which their descendants can reclaim a sense of self and of African heritage. Mexicans in general are becoming aware of the role that African influences played in the formation of Mexican cultural identity. The descendants of the first Africans to arrive here are beginning to recognize that the uniqueness and richness of their culture is due to the contributions of their African ancestors.

Beatriz Morales Cozier

See also Akan Religion; Diabolism; Mexico, African-Derived Religions in

Bibliography

Adediji, J. A. (1983) "The Egungun in the Religious Concept of the Yoruba." In *Traditional Religion*. Ibadan, Nigeria: E.A.A. Adegbole West Daystar Press.

Aguirre Beltrán, Gonzalo (1992 [1963]) *Medicina y Magia. Estudio Ethnóhistorico.* Veracruz, Mexico: Universidad Veracruzada.

——. (1989 [1946]) *La Poblacion Negra de México.* Estudios Ethnóhistorico. Veracruz, Mexico: Universidad Veracruzada.

——. (1985 [1958]) *Cuijla, Esbozo ethnográfico de un pueblo negro.* Mexico, D.F.: Fondo de Cultura Economica. Lecturas Mexicana.

——. (1976) "Ethnohistory in the Stydy of the Black Population of Mexico." In *Contributions of the Latin American Anthropology Group, Vol. 1*, edited by Peter T. Furst. Washington, D.C.: Latin American Anthropology Group, 3–6.

Añorve Zapata, Eduardo. (1998) *Monographia*. Cuajinicuilapa: Ediciones Artesa.

Bastide, Roger. (1967) *African Civilizations in the New World*. London: C. Hurst & Company.

Carrasco, David. (1990) *Religions of Mesoamerica*. San Francisco: Harper and Row.

Chavez Carbaja, Maria Guadalupe. (1997) "Mestizaje y Reproducion en Valladolid Siglo XVII." In *El Rostro Collectivo de la Nacion Mexicana*, edited by Maria Guadalupe Chaves Carbaja. Morelia, Michoacan: Instituto de Investigaciones Historia de la Universidad de Michoaca de San Nicola de Higaldo, 36–42.

Flanet, Veronique. (1990 [1977]) *Vivire si Dios quiere*. Mexico D.F.: Instituto Nacional Indigenista.

Guevarra, Maria Sangines. (1997) "Relaciones Interetnicas en Guanajuato. Siglo XVIII." In *El Rostro Collectivo de la Nacion Mexicana*, edited by Maria Guadalupe Chaves Carbaja. Morelia, Michoacan: Instituto de Investigaciones Historia de la Universidad de Michoaca de San Nicola de Higaldo.

Gyekye, Kwame. (1987) *An Essay on African Philosophical Thought: The Akan Conceptual Scheme*. New York: Cambridge University Press.

Iliffe, John. (1995) *Africans, the History of a Continent*. Cambridge: Cambridge University Press.

Martinez Montiel, Luz Maria. (1993) "Mexico's Third Root." In *Africa's Legacy in Mexico*. Washington, D.C.: Smithsonian Institution, 24–30.

Mendoza Briones, Maria Ofelia. (1997) "Pertenencias Etnicas E Interlocucion al Sistema Colonial en Michocan: 1766–1767." In *El Rostro Collectivo de la Nacion Mexicana*, edited by Maria Guadalupe Chaves Carbaja. Morelia, Michoacon: Instituto de Investigaciones Historia de la Universidad de Michoaca de San Nicola de Higaldo, 82–106.

Mercier, D. (1963 [1955]) "The Fon of Dahomey." In *African Worlds Studies in the Cosmological Ideas and Social Values of African People*, edited by Daryll Ford. London: Oxford University Press.

Mintz Sidney M., and Richard Price. (1992 [1976]) *The Birth of African-American Culture: An Anthropological Perspective*. Boston: Beacon Press.

Morris, Brian. (1997) *Anthropology of the Self: The Individual in Cultural Perspective*. London: Pluto Press.

Palmer, Colin. (1976) *Slaves of the White God: Blacks in Mexico, 1570–1650*. Cambridge: Harvard University Press.

Pérez, Fernández, Rolando. (1990) *La Musica Afro-Mestiza Mexicana*. Veracruz, Mexico: Biblioteca Universidad Veracruzana.

Perez Munguia, J. Patricia. (1997) "De Libertad y Legislacion Para Negros." Siglo XVIII. In *El Rostro Collectivo de la Nacion Mexicana*, edited by Maria Guadelupe Chaves Carbaja. Morelia, Michoacon: Instituto de Investigaciones Historia de la Universidad de Michoaca de San Nicola de Higaldo.

Thompson, Robert Farris. (1983) *Flash of the Spirit: African and Afro-American Art and Philosophy*. New York: Random House.

Thornton, John. (1992) *Africa and Africans in the Makings of the Atlantic World, 1400–1680*. Cambridge, U.K.: Cambridge University Press.

Cuba, African-Derived Religions in

Since the triumph of the Cuban Revolution in 1959 the world has experienced increases in the number of practitioners who and communities which follow religious customs associated with Cuba's African-derived heritages. From Japan to Argentina, Canada to Germany, Mexico to Sweden and throughout the United States, peoples of all walks of life have been drawn to Afro-Cuban beliefs and practices and have amalgamated what they practice under the singular heading of "Santería." Although this admixture of practices is presumed to be synonymous with one of several antecedent religious traditions that originated in Cuba, until there is more comparative research between practices in the country and those outside it is important that we better understand the originating Cuban heritages. This article is designed to review the beginnings and principles of Cuba's African-derived religious traditions as a means of providing baseline understandings from which research on practices derived from Cuba but existing outside of that environment can be distinguished and compared.

Currently, there are four main religious traditions practiced throughout the island and clearly created from Cuba's African heritage: (1) Regla de Ocha, known as Lucumi or Santería, is derived principally from Yoruba cultures of western Africa (what we know as Nigeria); (2) Regla de Palo, known as Palo Monte or Mayombe, is derived from African cultures we associate with regions of Gabon, the Congo and Angola; (3) Regla de Arara, also known as GaGa and closely related to the Vodou of Haiti, is derived from Dogon cultures we associate with the Benin or Dahomey regions of West Africa; and (4) Nanigo or Abakuka, which is more accurately a closed fraternal association but has African-derived history, beliefs, and rituals.

Like much of Cuban culture, these sacred traditions are creole, i.e., they are new combinations created from two or more older forms. They are new human products, born from the distinctive contact of cultures in the African Atlantic

Diaspora (the cross-Atlantic, permanent disbursement of enslaved Africans into all of the Americas). The new religious creations include belief systems, ceremonies, rites, rituals, worship, and other practices that were created by colonial inhabitants of Cuba and passed on to their descendants using principles derived from the African continent. To comprehend present-day expressions of these Cuban creations we turn to the source of their origins: commonality of context and ontological perspective or worldview. These components are equally a foundation for many distinctions of the African Diaspora and distinguishable from core characteristics that undergird most Eurocentric heritages.

Context of Creation

Colonial Cuba's distinct system of African slavery contributed to the strengthening and continuation of the imported African traditions. The Cuban Catholic Church used a familiar system of religious guilds and societies to carry out doctrinal education of the enslaved population. The brotherhoods, small study groups intended to ensure education to Catholic teachings and the provision of services to the community, were permitted within the black populations, even among relatively ethnic-specific enslaved plantation groups. Although practice of African religious rituals was strictly forbidden, the shortage of priests and a disdain for mingling with Africans and their descendants meant that there was weak accountability for the Catholic content in the brotherhoods of the black population (Brandon 1995; Matibag 1996: 23).

The Afro-Cuban organizations were called *cabildos* or *cofradias* and they gave unintended but familiar structure to the lives of blacks in Cuba, both the enslaved and those who were free. Organized social groups with a variety of responsibilities that ensured a sense of cohesion or togetherness were well known to kingdoms throughout Western Africa; the Bakongo, the Yoruba, the Dahomey, etc. Descendants of these and others peoples transformed the *cabildos* and *cofradias* into ethnic membership groups and designated them as African *naciones* or nations. This transatlantic idea of nation was handed down through generations as it was continually adjusted to the Cuban situation (Yai 1995).

Within Cuban *naciones*, African descendants continued to practice many customs of their ancestors and reinforced an African sense of humanity. The social groupings were prevalent throughout colonial Cuba, were particularly visible and influential in urban areas, continued after Cuba outlawed slavery in 1886, and persist today by way of performing groups for carnival—an extravagant social celebration that pervades Latin America (Ortiz 1992; Brandon 1993;

Matibag 1996). The *cabildos* foster social belonging, sharing, and innovation, as well as the continuation of African-derived rituals, rites of passage traditions, languages, drum and dance rhythms, and the ever-important religious/sacred values and beliefs.

Cabildos and *naciones* also became locations of self-governance, the designated social organizations in which African-derived worship, liturgical calendars, devotional celebrations, ceremonies, and other religious events are under the control of descendants of the continent. The *cabildos* continue to exist today and have complex structures of social control that are intertwined with African religious traditions.

Worldview-Ontological Perspective and Shared Principles

Worldview is the unspoken, sometimes unconscious understanding people of a culture share about what it means to be or to exist; it defines the meaning of beingness. African-derived worldview contains ingredients that comprise the spiritual core of religious traditions that thrive in Cuba. These ingredients were brought by the populations of enslaved Africans and passed on to their blood descendants during periods of Cuban colonial history from the sixteenth through the eighteenth centuries. It was during the earlier centuries of Spanish rule that more than 850,000 enslaved Africans were imported as forced labor to the Caribbean island. Hundreds of thousands of additional enslaved Africans were brought across the Atlantic late in the eighteenth and early in the nineteenth centuries to supplement existing labor. The latter importations provided further cheap labor needed to harvest and process cane sugar as Cuba replaced Haiti in the multimillion-dollar international sugar economy.

Contrary to much misinformation, the voyage across the Atlantic Ocean did not strip the human cargo of all they knew—as horrific as that ship passage was. The minds, bodies, and spirits of the enslaved manifested comprehensions about how the world was ordered, even if that order was in turmoil. They retained beliefs and experiences as well as basic human values associated with their African religions. The enslaved brought their African worldview and these fragments of cultural knowledge to the new Cuban environment where they used them to appreciate and organize the new American circumstances.

Ethnic groups from the Bakongo family of peoples which we associate with regions of Angola and the Congo were the majority of those enslaved Africans brought to Cuba during the first centuries of the slave trade. After the middle of the eighteenth century through the end of Cuban slavery in 1886, ethnic groups from Yorubalands were the more prevalent enslaved Africans imported to labor in Cuba's sugar economy. The defeat of the Yoruba Empire put enslaved captives from this family of ethnic groups into exploitative labor relationships with the Americas. Consequently, it was the Bakongo who laid the first layers of African traditions in Cuba and the last nineteenth-century arrivals of Yoruba who gave the nation its final strata of distinct cultural beliefs and practices. Descendants from these two distinct cultural families, but families who share basic principles about natural phenomena, were also responsible for two major systems of current religious customs in Cuba: Regla de Palo of the Bakongo and Regla de Ocha of the Yoruba.

The Bakongo, Yoruba, Dogon, and other West African peoples, as well as their descendants in the Diaspora, share common understandings about how natural phenomena of the world function—common phenomenological principles. Most important of these is a common understanding about *beingness*, or comprehension of what it means to be part of and within the world. African-derived knowledge is based on the principle of Divine Creation: all things created are part of the state of being as these things contain some of the sacred spiritual essence or power bestowed by the Divine, Supreme, Creator. Different communities and societies have different names and practices with regard to the Supreme but most peoples reinforce a paramount respect for all that was created and understand that all creation has *beingness*; human and others. Similarly, African-derived knowledge understands that there are other-worlds, apart from the world of humans; the world of divine spirits/forces as well as the underworld of malevolent forces. This is not equal to Christian heaven and hell.

At the time of creation aspects of the sacred spiritual essence, known as *aché*, was distributed within everything created and extraordinary amounts of *aché* were bestowed in other divine things, spirits and forces. Humans can approach an appreciation of the creative power of *aché* through observing thunder, ocean, fire, wind, and earth, or the cycle of life, death, and life again. Divine spirits and beings acquired their extraordinary power and special status through revered actions carried out during their lives, which existed long before historical or contemporary humans. These divine spirits and beings can be available to assist humans to sustain right and righteous relations to all creation if they are properly revered and honored. It is from these understandings that contemporary African traditions of Cuba continue rituals that revere and invoke divine spirits.

Time too is a phenomenon that African-derived perspectives appreciate in a fashion that differs from that of Western or European thought. Present time is occupied by all material elements, human and others, as well as by spirits. Many spirits are those whose material selves have died but whose lives are still actively remembered by the materially living. If these familial and community spirits are correctly remembered by the living and are known to assist the quality of life for the living, and there is no living person who actually knew them, then these ancestral spirits are no longer part of the present but have moved on to other periods: the past and future time. Ancestral spirits, along with divine spirits, possess strong *aché* and are known for their ability to aide the living through proper reverence from the living.

Revelation is the process by which those who practice African traditions in Cuba receive ideas and images to affirm or amend their beliefs and customs. The existence of other-worlds from which humans receive revelations, as well as the revelations themselves, are a phenomenological principle shared among African peoples and their descendants of the Diaspora. The scholar John Thornton is correct in reminding us that it is through revelations that all religions are formed and changed, and the expectation of constant revelation from other-worlds is an important and commonly held African-derived understanding.

Divine spiritual forces called *oricha* are an additional phenomenon central to African sacred traditions of Cuba. Although all West African peoples do not specifically identify the spirits as *oricha*, most cultural groups of the region are and have been familiar with divine spirits who produce revelations to humans. It is Yoruba understandings—as the last African arrivals in Cuba, late in the nineteenth century—and their attentiveness to a pantheon of such *oricha* spirits that prevail, if not define, and distinguish Cuba's African-derived religious traditions.

Oricha are understood to have come into the world at its beginning and, within Cuban created religions, exemplify the linkage of monotheism and polytheism—the belief in a single Supreme Divine Being and the belief in multiple divine beings respectively. *Oricha* are genealogically linked with the Supreme Creator as they monotheistically share *ashe*, the divine essence that is the prerequisite of all creation. *Oricha* are personifications of *ashe* and can be activated to assist humans who honor them. *Oricha* may have drawn their name from Yoruba understandings of *ori*, "head," and *sha*, "source," whereby the head is the central source of one's connection with cosmic creation. As the origin of the older ancestral aspect of self that chooses one's destiny before birth, the *ori*, or head source, is considered the sacred origin of one's consciousness.

There are hundreds of *oricha* within the African context, but the Cuban historical experience blended and altered practices to retain some twenty *oricha* who are consistently known and nationally honored. *Oricha*, as personification of *ashe*, continue to be worshipped in all Afro-Cuban religions and are known to regularly possess practitioners who have completed a process of initiation.

Possession is intimately connected to revelation, as it represents the process of a state of amazing perceptive consciousness through which the other-world reveals ideas and images to humans. Possession occurs most regularly when the atmosphere of humans has been reordered to permit spirits to enter from the other-world time to present time. Such reordering is achieved through appropriate rituals that use spacial adornment, music, song, dance, drumming, and other offerings as liturgical and worship devices. In Afro-Cuban traditions, music and dance are not merely ambiance or a supplement but are a language of worship, a form of prayer, as well as a means of entering the perceptive consciousness of spirit possession. Drum rhythms, dance gestures, spacial adornment, and formulated chants are all coded to identities of the *oricha* and bring about the embodied experience of worship with the divine. When done correctly, this embodied worship is *oricha* possession and revelation, central to African-derived religions created in Cuba.

Catholic Appropriations

Many of the commonly understood African-derived phenomenological principles were also part of Cuban colonial Catholicism, blended by enslaved Africans as they built the foundations for new, Afro-Cuban sacred traditions. The contact between the two religious understandings was continuous. African and European traditions shared life, environment, people, and many principles about natural and supernatural phenomena. It is not surprising, therefore, that Afro-Cuban sacred traditions reflect this intimate relationship. Where colonial Catholic comprehensions about divine phenomena were associated with familiar understandings, those who were enslaved or descendants of enslaved blended the commonalties and centered them on an African core. Conversely, historical and contemporary governmental prohibitions against African practices facilitated a public presentation through the similar but Catholic forms. The result was a blending of those *oricha* and Catholic saints who were known to share related if not the same divine powers. These were, and continue to be, new religious combinations from different cultural origins that are together but not "mixed up": they are now *Oricha*-Saints, a new entity; distinct, with religious integrity that reflects African and Cuban Catholic components. The Cuban scholar, Miguel Barnet, described the blending process quite appropriately.

> In the natural and spontaneous ... process that began the instant the first African established paral-

lels between African divinities and the Catholic saints, Yoruba traits were decisive in fixing the conditions of such correlations. In the face of the repressive imposition of the Catholic Church, which acknowledged no other religion, African blacks set into motion a most complex sociological phenomena—a give-and-take of elements and attributes that nonetheless did not alter the basic concept transplanted from Africa. (Barnet 1997: 87)

Thunder was an *aché* associated with attributes of the *oricha* Shango and appropriately identified with the miraculous stories of the Catholic saint, Santa Barbara. Shango became understood as Santa Barbara and that Catholic saint *is* Shango. Yemeja is known as a dark-skinned *oricha* whose attributes and domain are large bodies of sea water. These characteristics became appropriately associated with the black-skinned Catholic saint whose statue was transported across the Atlantic and placed in the cathedral across the bay from Havana to become the Virgin of Regla. Yemeja became understood as the Virgin of Regla and that Catholic saint *is* Yemeja. Such new Afro-Cuban religious constructs have not lost their African identity even as they incorporate Cuban Catholic elements.

The Traditions Today

Despite accelerating and waning repressions against African-derived traditions in Cuba, these sacred ways of life are alive and thriving throughout the island. Regla de Ocha is the most practiced tradition, with Regla de Palo and Arara second and third in popularity. Nanigo, or Abakuka, the closed male association, draws practices and ritual from Regla de Ocha and Regla de Palo. During my participation in field research with Afro-Cuban practitioners, I have observed that the majority of male leaders of these two traditions are also Abakuka members.

Generally speaking, the African-derived traditions in western portions of Cuba—Havana, Matanza, Pinar del Rio, etc.—maintain practices that are somewhat separate and distinct, one tradition from the other. In the eastern portions of the island often referred to as "Oriente"—Santiago de Cuba, Las Tunas, Guantanamo—such demarcation is less obvious, as aspects or components of each tradition can be found in practices of all the others.

Jualynne E. Dodson

See also Orisha (Shango) Movement in Trinidad; Santeria; Santeria, Material Culture; Santeria, United States; Yoruba Religion

Bibliography

Abimbola, Wande, ed. (1975) *Yoruba Oral Tradition: Poetry in Music, Dance and Drama.* Ile-Ife, Nigeria: Department of African Languages and Literature, University of Ife.

——. (1976) *IFA: An Exposition of Ifa Literary Corpus.* Ibadan, Nigeria: Oxford University Press.

Andreu, Guillermo Alonso. (1992) *Los Araras en Cuba: Florentina, la Princesa Dahomeyana.* Havana, Cuba: Editorial de Ciencias Sociales.

Barnet, Miguel. (1968) *The Autobiography of a Runaway Slave, Esteban Montejo.* New York: Pantheon Books.

——. (1997) "La Regla de Ocha: The Religious System of Santeria." In *Sacred Possessions: Vodou, Santeria, Obeah, and the Caribbean,* edited by Margarite Fernandez Olmos and Lizabeth Paravisini-Gebert. New Brunswick, NJ: Rutgers University Press.

Brandon, George. (1993) *Santeria From Africa to the New World: The Dead Sell Memories.* Bloomington: Indiana University Press.

Brock, Lisa, and Digna Castaneda Fuertes, eds. (1998) *Between Race and Empire: African-Americans and Cubans before the Cuban Revolution.* Philadelphia: Temple University Press.

Bolivar, Natalia Arostegui. (1994) *Opolopo Owo.* Havana, Cuba: Instituto Cubano del Libro.

Cabrerra, Lydia. (1977) *La Regla Kimbisa del Santo Cristo del Buen Viaje.* Miami: Ediciones Universal.

Castellanos, Jorge, and Isabel Castellanos. (1988) *La Cultura AfroCubana,* vol. 1: *El Negro en Cuba, 1492–1844.* Miami: Ediciones Universal.

Diaz de Villegas, Carmen Gonzalez. (1998) *Ta Makuende Yaya y Las Reglas de Palo Monte.* Havana, Cuba: Union de Escritores y Artistas de Cuba.

Harris, Joseph E. (1993) *Global Dimensions of the African Diaspora, Second Edition.* Washington, D.C.: Howard University Press.

James, Joel, Jose Millet, and Alexis Alarcon. (1998) *El Vodu en Cuba.* Santiago de Cuba, Cuba: Editorial Oriente.

Lachatenere, Romulo. (1992) *El Sistema Religioso de Los Afrocubanos.* Havana, Cuba: Editorial de Ciencias Sociales.

Lopez Cepero, Mario. (1995) *Sincretismo Religioso?–Santa Chango Barbara.* Madrid.

Lopez, Rafael Valdes. (1985) *Componentes Africanos en El Etnos Cubano.* Havana, Cuba: Editorial de Ciencias Sociales.

Matibag, Eugenio. (1996) *Afro-Cuban Religious Experience: Cultural Reflections in Narrative.* Gainesville: University of Florida Press.

Mintz, Sidney W., and Richard Price, eds. (1992) *The Making of African-American Cultures.* Boston, MA: Beacon Press.

Mibiti, John. (1970) *African Religion and Philosophy.* Garden City, NY: Doubleday.

Ortiz, Fernando. (1992) *Los Cabildos y La Fiesta Afrocubanos del Dia de Reyes.* Havana, Cuba: Editorial de Ciencias Sociales.

Thornton, John. (1992) *Africa and Africans in the Making of the Atlantic World, 1400–1680.* Cambridge, U.K: Cambridge University Press.

Cyberspace, African and African-Derived Religions in

With the advent of cyberspace, the study and consideration of African "traditional" religion (ATR) and especially African-derived religions (ADR) in the African Diaspora has gained a new dimension—which might be called the "African digital diaspora religions" (ADDR). In many ways, revealing analogies can be made between these two different forms of the African Diaspora. Historically, diasporic circumstances have significantly transformed African religions and, now, the "African digital diaspora" is transforming the transformed in new ways.

Ongoing "cyber-transformations" of African and African-derived religions are leading to a number of fundamental changes. Many originally indigenous religious concepts and practices are now "leaving" their local setting and are becoming available to the contemporary world via modern communication technologies. In the process of becoming more international and global in scope and appeal, African-derived cosmological worldviews and ritual systems are now being transformed into new forms of world culture—with the whole world now being the potential public.

The Ontological Plane: From "Spiritual" Realms to Physical Computers

Witnessing this African "CyberCosmoGenesis" in its *status nascendi* allows some interesting observations to be made regarding the ontological relationship of certain aspects of African spirituality with the fundamental principles of cyberspace. The term "cyberspace" was popularized by the science-fiction author William Gibson in his "cyberspace-trilogy": *Neuromancer* (1984), *Count Zero* (1986), and *Mona Lisa Overdrive* (1988), in which he created a new mythology of virtual worlds, using concepts, metaphors, and personifications of the Vodou religion, correlating them with cyberspace terminology.

Important to the understanding of the affinity between *Ifá* divination and computer language is the binary code—the formal basis of both systems of communication. Therefore, *babaláwos* and scientists alike rightfully claim that the concept of cyberspace was anticipated by the *Ifá* numeric system as well as by African geomancy—although within the context of the "technology of the spirit." From this perspective, computer technology can be conceptualized as just another transformation of the same principles.

Another example of the link between African religions and cyberspace can be found in the *Orisha* religion. "Shangocentricity" is, most likely, the latest and most striking phenomenon in a long chain of transformations and cyber-transformations of African religious concepts: Shango was traditionally revered as the god of thunder and lightning in ancient Yoruba mythology and religious practice. As one of his most significant current metaphors in our postmodern digital age, Shango signifies electric current in the quality of the exponentially growing electronic lightning-thunderstorms within our computers, transforming present-day civilization into a radically new sphere of knowledge. It is, therefore, not surprising that dozens of African-American, even German and Dutch computer and software companies, have taken the names of Shango, Ifa, Orisha, or Voodoo for their respective trademarks.

The Sociocultural Level: From Physical to Virtual Religious Practice

On the sociocultural level it can be observed that the new cyber-worlds of ATR and ADR do not necessarily replace the old ways of practicing the religion, but rather tend to reinterpret old concepts according to new contexts, and add new dimensions to the forms through which religion is experienced. In this way, parallel worlds of religious practice are created. For example, many *babaláwos, santeros, mambos,* and religious specialists in other African-derived religions are now engaged simultaneously in three different social fields. First, in their role as priests within their traditional local "full-time-face-to-face-communities," with all the duties and obligations of their profession for their clients. Second, as teachers, religious specialists, and spiritual guides within modern international "part-time-face-to-face-communities," be it scientific conferences, practical workshops, Diaspora community meetings, or New Age circles. And, third, as webmasters, computer consultants, and religious entrepreneurs within the postmodern global "no-

RECOMMENDED WEB SITES

African Traditional Religion:
http://isizoh.net/afrel/index.html

Religions of the World – African & Derivatives:
http://members.aol.com/porchfour/religion/african.htm

African Traditional & Derived Religion – Research Guide:
http://www.holycross.edu/departments/library/website/africa nr.html

African Mythology:
http://www.angelfire.com/mi/myth/africa.html

OrishaNet:
http://www.seanet.com/~efunmoyiwa/

Ijo Orunmila:
http://www.artnet.net/~ifa/

Ifa Foundation:
http://www.ifafoundation.org/

Cultural Expressions:
http://www.cultural-expressions.com

Orisha Consciousness Movement:
http://www.geocities.com/RainForest/Andes/7587/

Organization for Lukumí Unity:
http://hom.ican.net/~vreznik/lukumi/

Ilé Axé Opô Afonjá – African Religion:
http://www.geocities.com/Athens/Acropolis/1322/ page9.html

Vodou Culture:
http://www.geocities.com/Athens/Delphi/5319/ tableofcontents.htm

Hightech and Macumba – religious shifts, politics and communication technologies today:
http://www.goethe.de/br/sap/macumba/endindex.htm

The logo from the Cultural Expressions website. USED WITH PERMISSION OF FA'LOFIN ELTON.

more-face-to-face-communities." The emerging "Digital Diaspora" has become the field of action for the latter group. They present themselves on the World Wide Web, network with their professional counterparts in Africa and in the African Diaspora, and recruit international clients for consultations and initiations.

More and more people involved in African and African-derived religions are becoming involved in more than one of these sociocultural fields. Their actions prepare the ground for ATR and ADR to open up vis-à-vis the wider public, sometimes also absorbing and "syncretizing" elements from other religious traditions, and finally becoming world religions in our postmodern cyber-age.

Information and Communication

The amount of information on ATR and ADR made available through the Internet within the last five years is quite impressive—and so is the variety of its quality. In the year 2000, an estimated 50,000 pages related to this topic might be visited on the Net, a number that doubles about every eighteen months. Some of the most popular pages, like *OrishaNet*, enjoy more than 100,000 hits a month.

These Web pages serve different purposes for different users, depending on their specific interests. First, many people use these sources to obtain general and specific information quickly and easily. High school, college, and university students are all doing their "field-work" on specific

aspects of ATR and ADR on the Net, be it merely by gathering information already there, or sometimes also through direct communication with their virtual hosts. Second, people use cyberspace to communicate with other members of their religious community, especially in typical diasporic situations, where they are sometimes separated by huge distances. Guest-books, news-groups, and chat-rooms serve to foster continued integration within these communities.

Third, priests, diviners, leaders of religious organizations, and cultural activists alike install homepages to present themselves. Whereas in the past the bulk of the information publicly available was compiled and written by academic researchers or journalists—who, in most cases, were not initiated members of the religious traditions that they tried to represent—some of the best information today comes from practitioners themselves. There are already countless Web sites maintained by representatives of their respective religions. The relation between self-representation and representation through the other on the Net is increasingly and speedily shifting toward promoting the insider view.

Fourth, institutions and individuals also use the Internet for organizing religious conferences, coordinating seminars and workshops, and for networking between professional individuals and groups throughout Africa and the Diaspora. Some *babaláwos* and *mambos* offer divinatory consultations and religious courses on the Net, conduct negotiations with their potential clients, announce *plantas*, and prepare the ground for new initiations.

Finally, the Net serves the commercial interests of a growing number of religious entrepreneurs, music stores and bookstores, and musicians and artists by creating a global marketplace for their religious products. Internet *Botanicas* (religious shops) offer an increasing amount of spiritual hard- and software.

Fighting for Religious Culture and Identity

Considering the historical fact that many African religions—especially in the Diaspora—had formerly been either family traditions, handed down orally from generation to generation, or were passed on in different kinship lines, which themselves had already undergone significant changes in past centuries, a number of conflicting issues arise in the process of their cyber-transformation.

One such issue is that of the authority or legitimacy of specific groups or organizations to represent certain traditions, guard ontological truth, and strive for unification (such as within the Orisha Movement, or the Organization for Lukumi Unity). Some of the more cosmopolitan representatives may be open for new influences. Others, often involved in African Consciousness Movements, may reject foreign influences within their religion and plead for re-Africanization of their religious heritage.

A great number of sometimes highly controversial discourses relating to ATR are taking place in several discussion forums. These touch on such sensitive questions as race, gender, and authority. Since more and more non-Africans, men and women alike, are joining African-derived religions, the issue of legitimization to represent the religion in public is frequently tackled by referring to genealogical lines of initiation—in some cases all the way back to African origins. Now, when ADDR and related cyber-anthropological research are both in their infancies, the outcome of these sociopolitical discussions is still open.

From a more theoretical point of view, one might also ask what changes might occur in the transformation process between first and second orality, that is, when a religious tradition, which so far has been handed down from generation to generation through personal initiation, seeks multimedia exposure in the Net? With regards to the enormous creative potential of the expressive components of ATR and ADR for multimedia applications, it can be predicted with some degree of confidence that we may look forward to experiencing another quantum leap of religious culture in cyberspace.

Manfred Kremser

See also Media Evengalism

Diabolism

The term does not designate African religious practices as such, but is a product of the encounter between Western missionaries and Africans. Especially in the nineteenth century, when Western missionary societies emerging in the framework of the European Awakening started to evangelize Africa on a large scale, missionaries depicted, albeit with varying emphasis, local religious beliefs and practices as "devil-worship." This view resonated with popular Christian diabology, which held—in contrast to enlightened Protestant theology—that, as a result of Lucifer's expulsion from Heaven, the Devil was a really-existing entity operating through his agents all over the world, especially among the "heathens." In this way, African religious beliefs and practices were recast as "heathendom" and local gods and spirits were integrated into the Christian universe of discourse. Rather than doing away with local gods and spirits, missionary Christianity thus reinvented them as Christian demons working under the auspices of Satan. In this sense, the image of Satan offered converts the possibility to keep on

dealing with all those matters Christians were supposed to leave behind.

Although there are strong indications that missionaries of a great number of denominations and nationalities active on the African continent preached that the Devil was the power behind African religions and that the impact of this view on African converts appears to have been considerable, this has hardly been a topic of research. This neglect reflects the compartmentalization of research on religion in Africa. While those researching African religion and matters such as spirit possession and witchcraft tended to neglect Christianity, scholars studying the spread of Christianity mainly focused on "African ideas about God." They provided no analysis of the meaning of the concept of the Devil or of converts' appropriation of diabolization. Yet, this omission cannot be taken as evidence that the image of Satan was meaningless to the people described in these publications (Meyer 1999). It may well indicate that students of African religions by and large have simply failed to investigate how indigenous and Christian concepts of evil blended together in historical processes.

Since the 1960s, African philosophers and theologians have criticized Western missionaries' negative, if not diabolizing, stance towards African cultures and religions and sought to formulate new theologies which integrated African elements in a positive, respectful way. Their attempts often resonate with cultural politics on the part of African states that seek to revalue African traditions. While Afro-American and critical Western audiences tend to favor the revaluation of an "African Heritage" and the formulation of new African theologies, many ordinary people are little-impressed with these attempts.

Especially in the Pentecostal and charismatic churches that have become increasingly popular all over Africa, the image of Satan reigns supreme. Basing themselves on the dualism of God and Satan, these churches (but also other denominations) exuberantly engage in the diabolization of new and old religious practices, and promise "deliverance" by breaking with these practices. Here Satan is depicted as being responsible for the lack of health and wealth and increasing moral decay—a powerful force whose operations believers are to know in detail in order to fight and overcome it. Interestingly, the image of Satan is not confined to churches; there is a host of popular articles, songs, pictures, plays, and films in which Satan figures prominently as God's evil counterpart, and serves as a means to distinguish good and evil. For the time being, the image of the Devil and the diabolization of the world, introduced in the course of the nineteenth century, thus appear to be very much alive all over Africa. While it may be concluded that, with their emphases on the image of the Devil, nineteenth-century missionaries and current Pentecostalists actively engage(d) in the reenchantment of the world, much remains to be researched in order to understand people's continuing fascination with this complex image at different times and places all over Africa.

Birgit Meyer

See also African Charismatics; Pentecostalism in Africa

Bibliography

Meyer, Birgit. (1999) *Translating the Devil: Religion and Modernity among the Ewe in Ghana.* IAL-Series. Edinburgh: Edinburgh University Press; and Trenton, NJ: Africa World Press.

Dinka Religion

The Dinka are a cattle-keeping people who live in the southern region of the Sudan, the largest country in Africa. There are some two million people who are ethnically identified as Dinka. The Dinka language is one of a number of African languages that linguists classify as Nilotic. Related languages include Anuak, Shilluk, Nuer, and Atuot. The late British anthropologist R. G. Lienhardt lived in various Dinka communities in the early 1950s and later wrote one of the most important and influential books on a traditional African theology and cosmology, titled *Divinity and Experience: The Religion of the Dinka.* Dinka religion is somewhat peculiar in relation to other indigenous African religions in that a creator being figures prominently in their explanations of well-being and misfortune; in many other African religions, notions of witchcraft or the sentiments of ancestors assume this role.

For the Dinka, life began when a spiritual being known as Nhialic, "the Creator," blew the breath of life into the first human being. According to legend, people of the time had no knowledge of life or death, of illness or misfortune. Then one day a newly married woman was pounding grain with a mortar and pestle for the evening meal and accidentally struck the Creator. In Dinka imagery, Nhialic became angry and decided that humans should know hunger, pain, and death from that moment forward. Soon a small bird flew by and severed a rope that connected Divinity with humanity. Since that time, Dinka religion has been concerned with ways to assure that people experience health and happiness and find ways to avoid and address despair and death.

One of the first human beings to gain this knowledge is known as Aweil Longar. Dinka assert that he was the first child of Divinity and was given the power over life and death, which Dinka call *ring.* A common theme in Dinka religious mythology is that Aweil stood by a riverside holding a thin spear used for fishing. As human beings "emerged from the river," as their idiom suggests, Aweil would grant life to some, but kill others with his spear. Important spiritual leaders in Dinka communities claim that they are descendants from Aweil Longar; they are known as "masters of the fishing spear," in reference to this primordial mythological image. Masters of the fishing spear carry with them the power of *ring,* which Dinka associate with knowledge, health, and well-being. Masters of the fishing spear live in all Dinka communities, and when a man or woman suffers from some physical, spiritual, or material misfortune, the masters of the fishing spear are consulted to find a means to deal with the issue at hand. Though masters of the fishing spear hold no political power, their religious authority is unquestioned.

Usually, Dinka reason, personal misfortune is caused by spirit possession: what Dinka conceive of as physical maladies are what we in the West would call diseases. Thus diseases endemic to this region of tropical Africa are known as spiritual agents, and Dinka express belief that an individual could spiritually inflict a disease on someone. Dinka have many different terms and means to deal with such illnesses. Masters of the fishing spear can be consulted in dire circumstances, but there are also individuals known as *tiet,* or "diviners," who are called upon to diagnose and treat disease and misfortune. Diviners lead séances that last hours into the early morning in order to exorcise malignant spirits from an individual. These rituals of exorcism always culminate in an act of sacrifice, where an ox, a goat, or a sheep is killed and dedicated to the malignant spirit as a mode of supplication. Ultimately, all sacrifices of this sort are dedicated to Nhialic, the supreme being, or divinity. Sacrifices of this sort have been a common and everyday experience for the Dinka early in this century, though these beliefs and practices were renounced by various Christian mission societies in Dinka country.

In addition to a variety of spiritual agents that Dinka refer to as a means to explain misfortune, ancestors and the ghosts of the recently deceased are thought to influence individual and collective experience. While asleep, the ghost of a close relative could possess a person and demand that upon awakening the person should sacrifice an animal for the ghost.

Today the Dinka live in the aftermath of the two most vicious and brutal civil wars recorded in this century. Many Dinka live as political refugees in the neighboring countries of the Congo, Uganda, Ethiopia, Chad, and Kenya. In consequence, some Dinka have given up their "traditional" religious practices because these practices seem unable to deal with the misery and privation of their present existence. Some Dinka, particularly in the western region of the southern Sudan, have adopted Islam as their faith. Still others, particularly those who attended Christian mission schools during the colonial era in Sudan (1898–1956), came to express Christian ideals.

But deep truths of their traditional faith continue to inspire religious beliefs for many Dinka today. Dinka continue to believe strongly that their only sense of immortality is through their posterity and thus they strive to produce large families to carry on their heredity, or, as they say, "so their names will be heard tomorrow."

John Burton

See also Nuer; Pastoralist Cosmoligies

Bibliography

Deng, F. M. (1970) *The Dinka of the Sudan.* New York: Holt, Rinehart and Winston.

Lienhardt, R. G. (1961) *Divinity and Experience: The Religion of the Dinka.* Oxford: Clarendon Press.

Diola Prophets

This article examines the history of an indigenous tradition of prophetic revelation within the West African religion of the Diola of Senegambia. Beginning in the precolonial era, oral traditions describe at least eleven men who claimed to be prophets, literally those "whom God (Emitai) has sent." Since the colonial conquest, in the late nineteenth century, over forty people, two thirds of whom are women, have claimed such revelations. Sixteen of these prophets have become active during the period of ecological, economic, and political uncertainty of the 1980s and 1990s. The most famous prophet was a woman named Alinesitoué Diatta, who introduced a series of spirit shrines (*ukine*) focused on the procurement of rain and who taught a religiously inspired critique of French colonial development schemes before being exiled in 1943. The history of Diola prophetism involves not only its growing intensity during the traumatic years of colonial rule and the postcolonial era; it involves the transformation of a long-standing prophetic tradition from an exclusively male phenomenon to a predominantly female one.

Presently, the Diola number over 500,000 people and include the largest number of adherents of a traditional religion within Senegambia. Until the twentieth century, when peanuts became a major cash crop, most Diola earned their livelihood from rice agriculture, supplemented by fishing, hunting, and various crafts. They are usually described as "stateless" peoples, who governed themselves through a system of shrine elders and village assemblies. Central to Diola religion is the idea of a supreme being who created a variety of lesser spirits, many of whom serve as intermediaries between humans and Emitai.

Precolonial Prophets Establish a Tradition

Within the precolonial era distinctions can be made between prophets whose activities are ascribed to the time of the "first ancestors," a period before the longest genealogies, and a more recent group in the eighteenth century. The first group is described as founders of their communities, both in a physical sense and in the sense that they introduced many of the spirit shrines that are central to Diola religious life. Representative of this group is Atta-Essou, the founder of Eloudia. Now considered a Diola township, Eloudia's first inhabitants and its founder were Bainounk. Atta-Essou was said to have come from Emitai, to have been the first person in the region, and to have received from the supreme being the necessary knowledge to be able to control many of the Bainounk spirit shrines, some of which were incorporated into what became Diola religion. Atta-Essou appeared to his descendants in dreams and provided instruction about creating new shrines as well as moral guidance. Descended from Atta-Essou are: Aberman Manga of Kadjinol and Djemelenkone Diatta of Kolobone. Aberman, son of Atta-Essou, was born at Eloudia and moved to Kadjinol, where he married and raised a family. During a time of famine, probably caused by drought, he prayed to Emitai to let him fly up to the heavens in order that his family would have one less person to feed. He fashioned a pair of wings from the fiber of a fan palm and rose up to the heavens. At his shrine, men performed rituals in which they directly invoked Emitai and asked for his assistance in obtaining rain. Traditions about Djemelenkone Diatta also stress his descent from Atta-Essou, his visions, and his ascent to the heavens. During a period of famine he introduced a spirit shrine that assisted people in obtaining rain and a bountiful harvest. The idea that these prophets ascended into the heavens suggests an overcoming of death and the bodily decay associated with burial. The present-day priest kings of the Diola are said not to have died, only to be lost. As creators of important spirit shrines for communication with Emitai and as ancestors of the priest-kings, these prophets can be seen as culture heroes, establishing patterns of ritual supplication to the supreme being for the Bainounk that were taken over by the Diola.

Beginning in the eighteenth century, traditions describe men whose souls were said to leave their bodies and travel up to Emitai, receive some instruction, and then return to the living. These traditions are no longer associated with Bainounk, but are considered Diola. The most important of these prophets is Kooliny Djabune, of Kadjinol, who had visions of Emitai during a regional war. In the midst of this crisis, Kooliny was told that he would fall into a sleep that resembled death. He told his wife that he was going to see Emitai and that she should not do anything to his body, which he was leaving behind. However, Kooliny's soul was away so long that his wife feared that he had died and she started the funeral rites. To protect his life, Kooliny hurried back to the living before his instruction was complete. However, in a dream he returned to Emitai and described the fears of the community. Emitai gave him a pipe and told him that he should look for a spear in his backyard. Kooliny found the spear and summoned his neighbors to perform a ritual at the new war shrine, Cabai, "the spear."

Colonial Prophets of Resistance

Shortly after the French occupation of the Huluf area, in 1901, three women claimed to have received direct revelations from Emitai. Traditions concerning Oueyah of Nyambalang, Djitabeh of Karounate, and Ayimpene of Siganar represent the earliest testimony concerning women whom "Emitai had commissioned." These women introduced a spirit shrine called *Emit*, or *Emitai*, which was used to pray directly to the supreme being, to obtain rain, and to heal the sick.

While there were other prophets who claimed direct revelations from Emitai during the colonial period, the most important, in terms of her lasting influence, was a woman named Alinesitoué who was active from 1941 until 1943. In the midst of a severe economic depression and the frequent droughts of the late 1930s, a teen-age girl named Alinesitoué, from Kabrousse, began to seek dry-season employment in Dakar, the capital of French West Africa. One day, in 1941, while walking in the market, she felt the presence of Emitai, who told her to return home and introduce a series of rain shrines. Early in 1942, Alinesitoué summoned the elders of Kabrousse and revealed the nature of her visions. She told them that Emitai had given her two spirit shrines that would help them to obtain rain and that Emitai was continuing to speak to her directly through dreams and visions. In the midst of a severe drought and increasing demands by the French for rice, labor, and soldiers, Alinesitoué was able to create a religious movement that drew support from both northern and southern Diola.

In direct response to Catholic claims of access to the supreme being, she emphasized Emitai's direct revelation. She revived a Diola sabbath every sixth day, which gave a day of rest, not to people, but to the rice paddies. Her visions revealed the causes of the drought: the extension of French agricultural programs stressing the use of alien rice varieties (Asiatic, rather than African varieties of rice); peanut cultivation, which lured men out of a rice-centered family mode of production, shifting the burden of rice farming onto women; and, finally, the expansion of a European religion, Christianity, which offered no rituals to ensure the fertility of the land. In her critiques of French agricultural policies, Alinesitoué reaffirmed a central Diola idea of rice farming as a sacred task that provided both grain for food and for trade and could not be neglected for more ephemeral types of agricultural production.

Rituals performed under her guidance at her shrine of Kasila included the sacrifice of a black bull, which was also an act of charity, since providing the bull did not offer the donor any ritual privileges. Only Diola forms of rice could be offered at the shrine or served in communal meals. Men, women, and children served as priests and were chosen by divination, without regard to age, gender, or wealth. For seven days, the entire neighborhood took all its meals together, sang songs of the ancestors, and performed dances that reaffirmed Diola tradition.

Alinesitoué's new shrines attracted pilgrims from throughout the Diola areas around the Casamance River and from neighboring peoples in the Senegambian region. Her rejection of French agriculture and religion indirectly encouraged Diola peasant resistance to French taxes, which occasionally escalated into violent confrontations. Vichy officials, isolated and understaffed, watched anxiously as her influence continued to grow. In 1943 they arrested Alinesitoué and tried her under the Indigènat, the Native Law Code, for "having incited the people of Oussouye to systematic disobedience" and for causing embarrassment to French authorities. According to the transcripts of her trial, Alinesitoué responded by: "affirming that she was an envoy of God, who had appeared to her several times and all she did was 'transmit the directives He had dictated.' She rejected in the same fashion any participation in the revolt and all responsibility for its instigation." She was sentenced to ten years imprisonment in the French Sudan, where she died of starvation in 1944. Her fate was kept a state secret until 1987. Since then she has been declared a national heroine, and Casamance separatists have described her as a Casamançais Joan of Arc.

After her arrest the drought returned; the harvest of 1943–1944 was as bad as the years before Alinesitoué began to teach. By 1944, other women claimed to speak with the authority of Emitai. Koulouga was active in Kadjinol and Mlomp. Alandisso, from Etama, had been arrested by the French in 1918, after leading resistance to French taxation and military conscription, but in 1944, she was claiming to be a successor to Alinesitoué. In the northern, predominantly Muslim area, a woman named Kooweetaw also introduced a charity to obtain rain. In the 1950s new women prophets emerged, the most influential of whom was Alinesilumpa, who was born at Eloudia. She tried to revive Alinesitoué's Kasila and had some success within Esulalu. Still others, including a man named Ahangalene Diatta, were active in the 1960s, but none of them had the influence of Alinesitoué.

Postcolonial Prophets Revive the Tradition

Beginning in 1984, however, a new prophet, Todjai Diatta, claimed to speak with the authority of Emitai. Todjai had a long history of epileptic seizures and had sought medical treatment for her illness for many years. After going to medical doctors and mental health professionals, she tried a Muslim healer who told her that Emitai was speaking through her and she would only be cured when she accepted her mission. When she began to teach, the seizures stopped. As evidence of her authority, she described a night journey that her soul took to the home township of Alinesitoué. Todjai's description of her soul leaving the body and traveling at night resembles descriptions of the soul traveling to Emitai. In her night journey Todjai met the family of Alinesitoué and received their blessing for her work. Todjai revived the observance of the Diola day of rest and introduced a new Kasila, which demanded not only the sacrifice of a black bull and Diola rice, but also offerings of other Diola crops, which were rarely cultivated. She developed an extensive following, but it declined as the drought persisted.

During the 1990s, sixteen different prophets claimed to be sent by Emitai. Like their predecessors, these contemporary prophets seek an answer to the frequent droughts in the Diola homeland. Beyond that, they seek a way of returning to a Diola religious path, a family mode of economic activity, and community-based governance in which women and men both speak with authority in local assemblies. By emphasizing the continuity of their tradition, Alinesitoué and her successors garnered support among community elders and introduced new mechanisms for self-evaluation and innovation within a Diola religious path that has successfully adapted to the challenges of postcolonial Senegal.

Robert M. Baum

Bibliography

Baum, Robert M. (1999) *Shrines of the Slave Trade: Diola Religion and Society in Precolonial Senegambia.* New York: Oxford University Press.

Girard, Jean. (1967) *Genèse du Pouvoir Charismatique en Basse Casamance (Sénégal).* Dakar, Senegal: Institut Fondamental d'Afrique Noire.

Waldman, Marilyn, and Robert M. Baum. (1992) "Innovation as Renovation: The 'Prophet' as an Agent of Change." In *Innovation in Religious Traditions*, edited by Michael A. Williams et al. Berlin: Mouton de Gruyter: 241–284.

Divination

Divination is a cultural universal in Africa. In virtually all African societies at least some people believe in and practice revelatory divination. That is, they look to the supernatural world for explanations of events of the past. And, in many African societies, predictive divination is used as well, in an effort to predict and control the future. Across sub-Saharan Africa, people practice a number of different types of divination. Each type relies on belief and ritual to find meaning in what might otherwise be considered meaningless. Interpretive divination, for example, reads portents, omens, and prodigies. It tries to provide meaning for arbitrary events. Manipulated events are an element of interpretive divination, but more frequently less active forms such as projection, introjection, and free association, all intuitive techniques, are employed. Pyromancy, or divination by fire, is a highly dramatic form of divination. In a séance, for example, in sub-Saharan Africa, fire may unexpectedly explode upon the unsuspecting "guilty" person. Sometimes the diviner will throw an object into the fire and read signs in the way it reacts to the fire. Hydromancy, in contrast, uses water. Here the diviner reads reflections in shallow water or the movement of floating objects, such as tea leaves, in the water.

Cleromancy encompasses a number of related practices. In sub-Saharan Africa cleromantic practices include attributing magical qualities to objects the diviner keeps in his bag. The diviner may throw an object such as an animal's tooth or a dried intestine from a murdered person at a suspect's feet. The diviner then interprets the meaning of the objects or, perhaps, only of the central object.

There are many other forms of divination in Africa, including the casting of lots, and geomancy, which involves the throwing of objects on either a map or a figure which the diviner draws in the dirt. The diviner usually keeps up a line of chatter with the client, thereby drawing him or her out and discovering the client's problems. Through such questioning, the diviner introjects ideas and attitudes. The lots form a type of projective test.

Geomancy in West Africa is much more elaborate than simple lot casting. Elegant equipment and impressive learning are combined to produce a séance. During the séance, the diviner uses select verses. The client finds his answers from these verses. This Ifa divination of the Yoruba is a highly elaborate practice. The number of verses the diviner memorizes is phenomenal and the combinations of the stones that he casts reach staggering proportions. Each combination is tied to different combinations of verses.

In addition to these types of divination, there are also various forms of intuitive divination. Typically, the shaman, a part-time religious specialist, or curer, will employ a trance. Some shamans used idiopathic trances, those that come spontaneously from the self. Others use drugs. Still others will use autokinetic, or self-energized, techniques. These techniques include various forms of movement that lead to trance. In Africa, dance is a favored means to induce trance. However induced, the shaman generally provides an oracular utterance often accompanied by spirit possession. Frequently people believe that the real voice of a god speaks through the shaman. This spirit gives them direct guidance through the shaman.

In common with people elsewhere, many Africans believe that evildoers are different from innocent people. Therefore, tests for witchcraft or to find evil forces or spirits disguised in human shape often take the shape of trial by ordeal. Malevolent forces are immune to harm. Thus, if what harms an innocent person does no harm to someone, people have found the evildoer. Ordeals may take many forms—walking on coals or retrieving an object from boiling liquid are quite common. In sub-Saharan Africa an ordeal by poison is quite common. In this case, survival proves innocence.

General Characteristics of Divination

Divination is not limited to learning the future. It is generally concerned with obtaining information on very practical problems of everyday life. These problems may be either public or private. Divination seeks to obtain information that will aid in the solution of these problems. Getting such information, however, is not mundane.

The Zande (Azande) of the Sudan provide a nice example. There is a great deal of divination among the Zande, and Zande techniques appear to be easy. However, great specialists have developed to solve the most sensitive issues. A

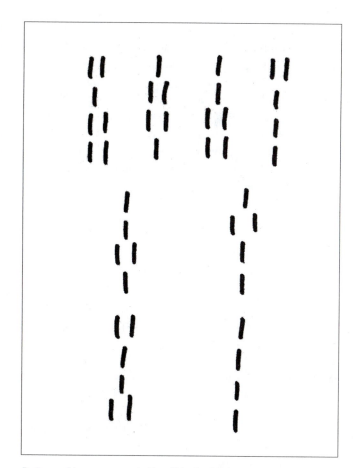

Design used by a geomancer in West Africa for developing a geomantic theme or reading. PHOTO COURTESY OF MANFRED KREMSER.

Zande oracle is one whose word can be believed without hesitation. The Zande rank oracles in a hierarchy. The king's oracle is the highest and the final authority on disputed issues. The Zande use divination to explore their own thoughts as well as to solve public and private disputes. They consult oracles before any serious endeavor.

Although there is truth to the assertion that divination functions to allay uncertainty, locate blame, or overcome misfortune, it is also true that the diviner must please his or her client. The diviner then must either be certain of the truth of his or her divination or else couch information in such a manner that it is a bit ambiguous and open to interpretation.

In sub-Saharan Africa, people often go from one diviner to another until finding a person whose words are convincing. Even the presence of obvious contradiction rarely leads to the questioning of the institution only, perhaps, to the credibility of a particular diviner.

Clients seek to find assurance on a course of action. The very practice of discussing their problems helps to clarify them and to set out alternative courses of action. Bringing serious problems to a diviner to solve—illness, drought, death, witchcraft, and so on—often forces a solution. Divination often sets limits on a problem. It defines a problem and locates areas of anxiety. A good, diviner orchestrates action, setting the stage and cuing performers to act in certain ways. By articulating secret fears the diviner can force a solution on the community. Divination often legitimates the making of problematic decisions. Divination is a dramatic means to solve problems. Its theatrical nature contributes to its efficacy.

Ifa Divination

Ifa divination falls within both categories of divination; that is, it seeks to foretell the future and to discover the hidden paths of one's destiny using occult or supernatural means. The Yoruba diviner, or *babalawo*, interprets messages that come from the spirits through the throw of his cowry shells. Yoruba consult their diviners for much the same reason other peoples of Africa consult theirs; namely, to find out why they are sick, cannot conceive, or to find out who is causing their problems.

The *babalawo* begins his session with a client by drawing lines in the sand on a tray. These lines intersect, representing the crossroads of life. These crossroads signify the various intersecting paths between this world and the intangible one. They allow spirits to communicate with the living. The diviner beats the sixteen palm nuts on his tray and taps his bell against the tray, calling the spirits to deliver their messages. The image of the Yoruba trickster god Eshu is on the divining tray and sits facing the diviner. Eshu's role is to carry the gifts that humans make to the gods during the Ifa process. All Ifa divination trays carry an image of the face of Eshu, generally portrayed with a small head and long hair. Other images are along the edges of the tray and portray the self-governing forces in the Yoruba cosmos. Generally they symbolize leadership, fertility, and sacrificial offering. Each diviner chooses which images, other than Eshu, will be on his tray.

Since divination is dramatic, a performance, the Yoruba *babalawo* has his ritual dress and other paraphernalia. He wears a beaded cap, carries a beaded fly whisk, a beaded walking staff, and beaded bags. There may also be a divining chain in his bag. These beaded goods serve no direct purpose in the divination, other than as stage setting. They are reminders of the regal nature of the art, for in the past they were reserved for Yoruba kings who extended their use to diviners. They have become symbolic of the regal nature of the diviner's art. Ifa is the highest ranked of all Yoruba cults, the king of them all.

The Ifa priest's ceremonial bag is in the shape of a triangle. Its stitching is with beads, translucent and opaque. Its straps are really lines of colored round beads. These beads are divided into segments by larger round beads. Various beads represent Ifa and others Eshu. The yellow beads are for Ifa and the black and white ones symbolize Eshu. The face on the beads represents one's personal destiny.

Other Examples of Divination

Diviners (*buor*) from the Lobi tribe in Burkina Faso use a statue called a *bateba*. These statues are decorated with images of the spirits (*thila*). These spirits aid the diviners in their work. They offer protection against evils, including witchcraft, hunger, sickness, and death. These *thila* belong not only to the diviners. Individuals may also own them. However, they are not also under the control of those people who are not diviners. If an individual feels that the *thila* are causing him problems, he will consult a diviner for aid. The diviner then seeks to find out what the spirits are demanding. About 10 percent of Lobi *buori* are women.

Lobi diviners sit next to their clients. The diviner spreads a cloth on a table in front of his client. The *bateba* faces them. The diviner and client hold hands, the client's left hand in the diviner's right. The diviner then questions the spirits. The diviner gets clues from the way the client's hands move in response to the questions placed to the spirits. Then the diviner selects his questions accordingly.

The variety of *bateba* is great, and each has a different type of power. Most have a pair of male and female figures who are standing. *Bateba* may protect against hexes and witchcraft. Other *bateba* may specialize in aiding fertility or protecting against sickness, or finding a marriage partner. The variety is limited only by the types of requests that people may have.

Diviners from the Sando secret society of the Senufo people of the Ivory Coast use statues that resemble those of the Lobi *bateba* figures. Senufo diviners also place them across from themselves and their cloths or mats. These statues observe the divination and aid in communicating with the bush spirits (*madebele*) or the ancestral spirits, either the primordial couple, or recently deceased elders. These statues speak to the Sando diviner and give her the power to interpret the objects she has cast. Among the Senufo almost all diviners are women. The diviner and the client hold hands. However, they sit on opposite sides of the table in contrast with Lobi divination.

The Sando statues, called *tyle*, are highly stylized male or female representations. The face of a *tyle* is heart-shaped and concave. It has almond-shaped eyes. The nose is an

SASSY WOOD

The magic of Africa often sounded like the stories about gypsy seers or the tarot card readers.

Everyone who visited Liberia heard about the sassy wood, the stick that tells the truth. And the local population swears by it!

When our survey crew was near Clay, tools went missing. Being told about the sassy wood, they figured they would like to witness a session. Though they did not really believe in it, they put up the money.

Their headman contacted the town chief and found out that the medicine man was prepared to "play the sassy wood." After negotiating with the medicine man, the price was established at $3 and it would be performed the next day.

Then the medicine man bought cane juice, a potent alcohol drink, for him and his friends on credit and they started drinking. Soon a drummer appeared and dancing started and the town party was in full swing a few hours later and lasting till deep in the night, and keeping the survey crew awake.

Early the next morning the medicine man disappeared in the bush and an hour later re-appeared with the sassy wood stick. It was daybreak. Everybody had come to the town square. A fire was prepared and a cutlass was placed in the fire with a bucket of water beside it. He sat himself in front of the fire with the sassy wood stick in his hands and started singing, the singing changed to crying and then yelling and after about half an hour he hardly knew what he was doing, he was sweating and his face was distorted. Then suddenly he sat down. There was a complete silence. He walked up to the fire, took out the cutlass, which was at one end red hot, took a wet cloth out of the bucket with water and walked up to the men, who stood in a group together. One by one he made their legs wet and then with the red hot cutlass came close to their legs so it sizzled, but not a man moved his leg, complete trust. He then came to a man who showed no confidence and was nervous. He made his leg wet and held the cutlass close. The man suddenly seemed to withdraw his leg, but the red hot cutlass was pressed against it, making a nasty burn. The man confessed to the stealing and the stolen tools were returned. Obviously, the sassy wood had judged right. The medicine man was paid.

The population was convinced of the power. My friends of the survey crew thought that the party the previous night had provided the medicine man with the information to identify the culprit. How else could he have selected the right man? Those disbelieving foreigners.

Source: Reilingh, Albert (1948–1949) Unpublished letters.

---

inverted V-shape. There is a small mouth over a thrusting chin. Male and female hairstyles resemble one another, but the female style is more elaborate. The statues are fully erect, with fully developed trunks. Their arms are bent at the elbows, and their hands are thrust forward. In sum, they depict human power at its height, reminding supplicants that the mandebele can either restore or take away this power.

Other people in the Ivory Coast present examples of a mouse oracle. The Guro, Baule, and Yaure employ mouse divination in consultations that cover a wide range of concerns—serious illness, establishing the time and scale of sacrifices, personal misfortune and public conflict. There are containers for these mice. Again there is a common pattern of geometric forms and the image of a face. There are chambers on two levels and a hole on the bottom so that the mouse can touch the earth.

The diviner places a mouse in a lower chamber. There is an inverted tortoise shell or small rectangular metal plate in the upper chamber. Rice is placed on the shell or plate. Additionally, there are ten narrow metal strips in a parallel pattern attached to the shell or plate. A lid is placed over the container. After a short time, the wunnzueyifwe (diviner) studies the new arrangement of the strips and interprets them. The people state that the mouse has listened to the problem and then descends to the earth for consultation. Finally, it arranges the strips in a meaningful manner. The diviner reads the pattern according to a preset frame of interpretation.

Of course, in this and in the spider divination of the Cameroons, it is necessary that there is a shared belief in the independence of the mouse or spider. The diviner shows his or her skill in reading the rearranged materials according to preconceived notions. A definite oral tradition governs the mode of interpretation.

There is also a parallel with Western or Chinese systems of prediction through the construction and reading of horoscopes. The Dagara tribe of West Central Africa successfully groups their people into five different categories—Earth, Water, Fire, Nature, and Mineral. Each of the five types of people plays a very specific role in Dagara culture. Every person fulfills different kinds of general social functions according to their category. It is, like the Chinese system, based on the year of a person's birth. Each person is also placed into a color category that is associated with a particular type of personality. There are yellow, red, green, blue, and white, signifying earth, water, fire, mineral, and nature respectively. Fire people, for example, link the village to the ancestral world. These people are the dreamers. They have intuition and perception. Other members of the community go to them to have their dreams interpreted.

Conclusion

West and Central African peoples have richly developed systems of divination. Divination rituals, ritual artifacts, and artistic ideas are shared, borrowed, and "stolen" from each other. Since all human societies seek to find meaning in their lives, this borrowing is not surprising. What works in one society will be fair game to another. As in most other aspects of African religion, there is a drive to restore harmony. Witches and other malevolent people and forces upset the harmony that is essential for the community and individual survival. Therefore, divination functions to find the source of evil and to find ways to restore harmony.

In most systems of divination consultation and discovery go together. There is a probing of the client's past by the diviner. The diviner is a catalyst or tool to explore the past and seek relationships that may have caused problems.

The Yoruba may have the most complex system of divination in Africa. It has not only a complex ritual process, but also a large body of oral literature. It has a long history with ties to kinship and an urban life style. Nevertheless, the Yoruba share a concern with other Africans about witchcraft and evil forces and seek to restore harmony to their universe. A paramount concern of those seeking the counsel of a diviner is a concern about witchcraft.

Although specific rituals vary among different groups, the rituals and their artifacts contain metaphors that help the client understand the messages contained in the process. No matter what the specific image: a dog, a werecreature, or whatever, the basic image is that of crossing a boundary. In a very real sense that boundary is between knowledge and uncertainty. The crossroads image is a strong one in African culture and it aptly symbolizes the need to make a decision and to end ambiguity.

Divination provides a means for resolving ambiguity. The skill of the diviner aids people in exploring their options and resolving issues. It forces them to make a choice and to be happy in that choice. Through seeking sources of community problems and aiding people to resolve those problems in a way that restores peace and harmony, divination is indeed a sacred and healing process.

Frank A. Salamone

See also African Geomancy; Ifa; Yoruba Religion; Zande Religion

Bibliography

Bascom, William. (1994) *Ifa Divination: Communication between Gods and Men in West Africa*. Bloomington: Indiana University Press.

———. (1994) *Sixteen Cowries: Yoruba Divination from Africa to the New World*. Bloomington: Indiana University Press.

Buckland. Raymond, with Kathleen Binger. (1992) *Book of African Divination: Interpreting the Forces of Destiny with Techniques from the Venda*. London: Inner Traditions International, Limited.

Cole, J. A. (1990) *Astrological Geomancy in Africa*. New York: North Scale Institute Publishing Company.

Drewal, Henry Jon, and Margaret Thompson. (1990) *Gelede: Art and Female Power Among the Yoruba (Traditional Arts of Africa)*. Bloomington: Indiana University Press.

Mason, Henry John. (1998) *Beads, Body, and Soul: Art and Light in the Yoruba Universe*. Los Angeles: University of California Press.

Ogbaa, Kalu. (1992) *Gods, Oracles and Divination: Folkways in Chinua Achebe's Novels*. Enugu: Africa World Press.

Peek, Philip M. (1991) *African Divination Systems: Ways of Knowing*. Bloomington: Indiana University Press.

Elder Solomon Michaux's Church of God

Elder "Lightfoot" Solomon Michaux (1884–1968) established one of the many Holiness-Pentecostal sects—black and white—that refer to themselves as the "Church of God." He was reared a Baptist, but began to attend St. Timothy Church of Christ after his wife, Mary, converted to the Holiness religion. In 1917 she persuaded her husband to establish Everybody's Mission—an interracial congregation in Hopewell, Virginia, in which "she could conduct services to her liking" (Webb 1981: 11). Michaux became an ordained minister and the Mission became affiliated with the Church of Christ (Holiness), U.S.A. With a small group of converts, who were for the most part "poor, propertyless, and without formal schooling" (Webb 1981: 15), he moved his congregation into a small storefront in late December 1919. Upon discovering that his bishop planned to transfer him to another mission, Michaux seceded from the Church of Christ (Holiness) and organized the Church of God in the spring of 1921.

His congregation purchased a three-story building in Newport News, Virginia. In keeping with his flamboyant style, Michaux led his congregation in a procession filled with exuberant singing through the streets of Newport News during the predawn of an October morning in 1922. Angry residents brought an end to subsequent marches by requesting police intervention. Michaux moved his headquarters to Washington, D.C. in 1928 and established new branches as many of his adherents migrated to the coal fields of northwestern Pennsylvania and northern cities such as Washington, D.C. and Baltimore. Michaux also formed new congregations following successful revivals in various cites throughout the South and the North. He "denounced jazz, dancing, and smoking, castigated the heathenism of communism, prophesied that the Second Coming of Christ was imminent" (Webb 1981: 26), rejected the theory of evolution, and defended prohibition. His message found appeal among some members of the Ku Klux Klan. Michaux even went so far, along with his wife and two other black female members, as to preach at an "all-white, KKK-infested congregation" in Essex, Maryland (Webb 1981: 28).

Michaux began a radio ministry in 1929 and adopted the theme song "Happy Am I" and a ministry that stressed repentance, salvation, and positive thinking. The ministry rapidly grew into a national and even international phenomenon.

When they released statistics on the program in 1934, CBS officials estimated that 25 million Americans tuned in on Saturday nights, a prime time, and that over 2 million listened to the "Happy Am I" program daily. Thousands rained fan mail on the evangelist.... Hundreds similarly showed appreciation for the program by going to Washington to observe a broadcasting session in the new Church of God edifice on Georgia Avenue. They made pilgrimages in heavily laden buses, on trains, and in automobiles. (Webb 1981: 43)

Michaux's followers dubbed him the "'Happy Am I' Preacher."

Into his theology and sermons Michaux incorporated a New Thought flavor, which viewed religion as an active effort to improve one's life in the present world. He also incorporated aspects of the Social Gospel by creating a social outreach program which provided shelter to homeless people, assistance in the search for employment, and support to orphanages. As early as the mid-1920s, he created a social welfare program called the Common Plan (Webb 1981: 26). Michaux supported Franklin D. Roosevelt in his presidential bid in 1932 and served as one of the forces that shifted the allegiance of most African-Americans from the Republican to the Democratic Party. Michaux created the Good Neighbor League in 1933 to assist victims of the Depression. He also established the Happy News Cafe, which fed thousands for a nominal charge. The Church of God also opened the Mayfair Project in 1946—a housing program that provided 594 apartments for African-Americans in Washington, D.C.

Michaux's ministry underwent a rapid decline after he was accused of mishandling fund-raising monies in 1937. He continued to broadcast weekly to a reduced audience until his death in 1968. Michaux encountered opposition from various black mainstream ministers who regarded him to be the leader of a "cult." The Interdenominational Ministers' Union of Washington threatened to take formal action against Michaux for allegedly hurting the "black church." Despite his own social outreach efforts, Michaux was critical of the civil rights movement and African-American nationalism. Although he claimed to have millions of followers, the actual membership of the Church of God probably never exceeded more than a few thousand (Webb 1981: 130). Michaux maintained a tight rein over his operations and the members of his organization. Following his death, the Church of God underwent a bitter legal battle with its founder's family over the remnants of the elder's financial empire.

Hans A. Baer

See also Social Activism

Bibliography

Webb, Lillian Ashcraft. (1981) *About My Father's Business: The Life of Elder Michaux.* Westport, CT: Greenwood Press.

Ethiopian Orthodox Church

The Ethiopian Orthodox Church is one of the five so-called Monophysite or Oriental Orthodox Churches. The other four are the Coptic Orthodox Church, the Syrian Orthodox Church, the Armenian Orthodox Church, and the Indian Orthodox Church. From the viewpoint of the Roman Catholic, Protestant, and (Eastern) Orthodox churches, the Monophysite churches are so-labeled because of their rejection of the Council of Chalcedon in 451 CE and the doctrine that Christ is of one person in two natures. The Monophysite churches believe that Christ's humanity and divinity are united and the Ethiopian Orthodox Church calls itself *tewahdo*, meaning "union." The Ethiopian Orthodox reject the label Monophysite and prefer non-Chalcedonian instead. Ethiopian Orthodoxy is the primary religion of Ethiopia and Eritrea with from 22 to 29 million adherents in Ethiopia and about 2 million in Eritrea. The Amhara and Tigray ethnic groups are the major followers of Ethiopian Orthodoxy, with other peoples in the region, such as the Oromo, being mainly Muslim. There are also churches in diaspora communities in the United States, Canada, Jamaica, and Trinidad.

History

It is unclear when Christianity first came to the Horn of Africa. Adherents believe that Christianity arrived in the first century CE, while most historians believe that Christianity was brought by the students Frumentius and Aededius from Tyre in the fourth century CE. With the support of King Ezana of Aksum in northern Ethiopia, they were allowed to seek converts and Frumentius was later appointed the first Bishop of Ethiopia by Athanasius the Great of Egypt. From then until 1951 the church was under the control of the Coptic Church in Egypt, with Coptic monks appointed as the bishops of the Ethiopian Church. In the fifth century, monks from Syria translated the Bible into Ge'ez, the regional language. The church was also in contact with Israel and Jews (although, again, the dates are unclear), and Ethiopian beliefs and practices reflect Jewish influence, including devotion to the Old Testament, circumcision, Saturday as the day of rest (along with Sunday), ritual fasting, and sanctification of the Ark of the Covenant, which the church claims to possess and replicas of which are in all churches.

In the seventh century the region was invaded by Muslim Arabs and, to a significant extent, the region and the church were cut off from the Christian world, although an Ethiopian presence was maintained in Jerusalem. During the following centuries there was a gradual merging of Orthodox beliefs and practices with indigenous ones, producing a distinct Ethiopian Orthodox Church. The church became a central institution among the Amhara as it owned much land. Men and women sought to become monks and nuns, children were educated at church schools, and church officials served as judges and political officials. In the sixteenth century, the Orthodox-Muslim rivalry became a civil war and many monasteries and churches were destroyed. In the following century the church suffered oppression at the hands of the Roman Catholic ruler of Ethiopia, who was aided by the Portuguese, and thousands of members died as martyrs.

In the twentieth century, the political situation improved. In 1929, the Coptic Church in Egypt allowed the Ethiopian Church to appoint four auxiliary bishops to assist the Coptic Bishop in charge of the Ethiopian Church. During the reign of Haile Selassie I (1930–1936, 1941–1974), the Amhara emerged as the dominant ethnic group and the church was designated the national church. In 1951, the Coptic Church allowed an Ethiopian to be appointed bishop for the first time, and in 1959 the autocephalic Ethiopian Orthodox Church was established. But in 1974, when Selassie was overthrown and a socialist government came to power, the Church was disestablished, its holdings (including some 900 monasteries) nationalized, and the bishop removed and perhaps executed by the government. The separation of Eritrea from Ethiopia in 1991 led to a breach in the church, with a separate Eritrean church with its own bishops and under Coptic Church control established in Eritrea. Church leaders in Ethiopia objected to the division, but their objections were rejected by the government.

Beliefs and Practices

Ethiopian Orthodoxy is a rigorous religion, with strict ritual requirements for members, although, as in all religions, various degrees of devotion are expressed by adherents. There are seven sacraments: baptism, confirmation, penance, holy communion, unction of the sick, holy orders, and matrimony, with the first four obligatory for all. Depending on the size and needs of the community, church services are held each morning or only on Sunday and holy days. Services last about three hours and worshipers are expected to stand the entire time. Fasting (eating only vegetable foods) is a major ritual activity, with Wednesday and Friday fast days, as also are many holy days throughout the year. The principal holy days are Easter, Christmas, Timqet (Epiphany, celebrated on 17 January), and Meskel, the day Saint Helena found the cross, celebrated on 27–28 September.

The primary clerical roles are bishop, priest, and deacon. Especially important at the local level are the *debtera*, a type of religious specialist, who may or may not be recognized by the church and who fill a wide range of roles including diviner, scribe, and healer. There are seminaries in Addis Ababa, where the Church is headquartered, and in Harer. The church is known to outsiders for its rich collection of iconography and its stone church buildings, some of which are carved from solid rock on site.

Current Situation

Since the overthrow of Haile Selassie in 1974, the church has experienced considerable difficulty in Ethiopia. Its wealth and influence has declined dramatically due to the nationalization of church property and government controls placed on the bishop. In addition, government financial support of the church was terminated, which has impacted both churches in Ethiopia and those in diaspora communities. Particularly difficult has been the appointment of Patriarch Abuna Paulos in 1993 by the government; he has not been accepted by most Ethiopian Orthodox and adherents continue to protest government interference in the leadership of the Church. At the same time, diaspora churches have been founded in the United States and Canada and they provide political support for their coreligionists in Ethiopia.

David Levinson

See also Oromo Religion; Zar

Bibliography

Ethiopian Orthodox Tewahdo Church Web site. www.students.uiuc.edu.

Haile, Getatchew. (1997) "Ethiopian Orthodox Church." In *Encyclopedia of Africa South of the Sahara*, vol. 2, edited by John Middleton. New York: Charles Scribner's Sons, 76–83.

Tamrat, l'Addesse. (1972) *Church and State in Ethiopia*. Oxford: Clarendon Press.

Ullendorff, Edward. (1968) *Ethiopia and the Bible*. London: Oxford University Press.

Faith Tabernacle Church

Faith Tabernacle Church was a very important source of support and healing for many people in Nigeria in the aftermath of World War I, which brought in its trail a worldwide influenza epidemic coupled with economic hardship. Postwar hardships had an adverse effect on the life of the church in Nigeria, as well as other parts of Africa. Churches were closed and most Western missionaries, helpless in the face of the crisis, had to go back home. Convinced that a solution could be found to the crisis in an African way, pockets of indigenous Christians emerged. Such like-minded people met in homes to pray for divine healing and for a breakthrough. One such prayer group, led by Mr. Sadare, a lay leader of the St. Savior's Anglican Church, adopted the name "Diamond Society." The group benefited from copies of *The Sword of the Spirit*, a magazine published by the Faith Tabernacle in Philadelphia, mainly because of its emphasis on gifts of the Holy Spirit—particularly healing—and established contacts with the publishers in 1923. Thereafter, they affiliated with the Faith Tabernacle and changed their name to "The Faith Tabernacle, Nigeria."

Group members disagreed with the Anglican church on the issue of infant baptism, which eventually culminated in their being expelled from their parent church and consequently forming the Faith Tabernacle Church (FTC) in 1922. Thus, the FTC in Nigeria emphasized adult baptism as a sequel to one's open confession of faith in Christ, as manifested in all the gifts of the Holy Spirit, particularly divine healing. The church spread fast in Nigeria and within a few years branches were opened in the northern and eastern parts of the country.

Having been pleased by reports about the tremendous growth of the church in Nigeria, the head of the Faith Tabernacle in the United States of America appointed some Nigerian leaders as pastors to take oversight of the branches in Nigeria. Meanwhile, after more than four years of establishing the distant relationship with the FTC in Nigeria, none of the American leadership had paid pastoral visits to the church in Nigeria. This led to discontent on the side of the Nigerians, erosion of American control of FTC in Nigeria, and, eventually, Nigerian succession from the American church.

Another issue that deepened the differences between the FTC in Nigeria and its American counterparts was the realization that the American partners did not uphold some of their basic tenets of faith. For instance, they disagreed on such beliefs as the practical outworking of the gifts of the Holy Spirit in the life of the believer and in the church, particularly speaking in tongues. The American FTC interpreted speaking in tongues as delusion and Satanic. What finally led to a definite break with the American FTC was an internal crisis in the Philadelphia headquarters in 1925. The FTC in Nigeria, already disenchanted with its American partners, decided not to take sides. Instead, it declared its autonomy in 1928.

Developments in the Nigerian FTC saw a remarkable turning point when the young Yoruba prophet Joseph Ayo Babalola, born in 1904, appeared on the scene. Around late

1928, Babalola had some spectacular experiences that he interpreted as a divine call to a prophetic and evangelistic ministry. He went around preaching, holding a Bible and a large bell. He organized prayer meetings in his local Anglican Church at Ilofa. Excommunicated by the church for manifesting the gifts of prophecy, healing, and for using water to heal, he nonetheless attracted an extremely large following. He encountered Pastor Adubanjo of the FTC who rebaptized him and brought him into the FTC.

Babalola was very instrumental in a major revival that broke out in the FTC in Ilesa. He was said to have raised a dead child and healed many that were sent to his revival meetings. Thus, he drew large crowds. In his preaching he appealed to his audience to renounce evil practices and witchcraft.

The FTC emphasizes intense prayer and fasting as means of solving problems. Prayers in the church are intermixed with shouts of "Hallelujah," "Glory," and "Amen." One dimension of the Church's prayer life is the practice of confinement to some sacred hills and "Prayer Mountains" for solitary prayers with guidance from pastors, prophets, and prophetesses. In their healing practices they apply water and sometimes anointing oil as aides. They completely reject traditional healing methods as well as Western orthodox medicine. As an aspect of holy living FTC encourages modest dressing. They insist on monogamous marriage that must be blessed by the church, and couples who divorce are not allowed to remarry.

Later developments caused FTC to affiliate with the British Apostolic Church in Bradford. However, the relationship did not last long, due to various differences coupled with division in the British church itself. In 1939, the Nigerian church broke away to form the Christ Apostolic Church Nigeria. The FTC is a clear example of African initiative in Christianity. At a time when mainline churches were providing answers to questions that believers were not asking, FTC and other African churches were addressing the concerns and needs of African believers.

Cephas N. Omenyo

Bibliography

Ayebgboyin, Deji and Ishola Ademola. (1997) *African Indigenous Churches: An Historical Perspective*. Lagos: Greater Heights Publications.

Clarke, Peter Bernard. (1986) *West Africa and Christianity*. London: Edward Arnold.

Walls, Andrew Finlay. (1977) "African Independent Churches" In Tim Dowley et.al. (eds.) *Eerdman's Handbook of the History of Christianity*. Grand Rapids: W B Eerdmans.

Fire Baptized Holiness Church of God of the Americas

The Fire Baptized Holiness Church of God of the Americas is a Holiness Pentecostal church which, like many other modern black churches, formed as an independent church when racial discrimination in the post-Civil War period limited African American participation in white churches. The church was founded in 1908 by the Rev. William E. Fuller (1875–1946). Fuller began preaching in 1893, experienced spirit baptism in 1895, and baptism by fire in 1897. In 1898 he was the only African American founding member of the Fire Baptized Holiness Association. The Association emerged as part of the fire-baptized movement in the American Southeast, which added a belief in baptism by fire to the existing Holiness beliefs of justification and sanctification. Initially, African Americans were admitted as equal members of the Association, and by 1908 Fuller had recruited about 900 African American members. However, discrimination by outsiders made mixed-race worship services difficult and in 1908 Fuller left the Association and founded the Colored Fire Baptized Holiness Church in Greer, South Carolina. By May of that year the church had one ruling elder, 16 ordained ministers, 50 local ministers, and 925 members in 27 churches. The development of the Church was aided by the decision of the Association to deed to the new Church $25,000 in property.

With a large and stable membership, the Church began publishing *The True Witness* in 1909, organized its first Sunday School Convention in 1910, founded the Fuller Normal Industrial Institute in Atlanta in 1912, and established the Sisters of Charity in 1916. In 1922 it changed its name to the Fire Baptized Holiness Church of God and in 1926 to the Fire Baptized Holiness Church of God of the Americas.

Church belief and practice are based on the Bible and supported by citation to biblical passages:

1. Jesus Christ shed His blood for the remission of sins that are past, for the regeneration of penitent sinners, and for the salvation from sin and from sinning.

2. We teach and firmly maintain the scriptural doctrine of justification by faith alone through the blood.

3. Jesus Christ shed His blood for the complete cleansing of the justified believer from all in dwelling sin and from its pollution subsequent to regeneration.

THE CHRISTIAN ALPHABET POEM

A lthough things are not perfect
B ecause of trial or pain
C ontinue in thanksgiving
D o not begin to blame
E ven when the times are hard
F ierce winds are bound to blow
G od is forever able
H old on to what you know
I magine life without His love
J oy would cease to be
K eep thanking Him for all the things
L ove imparts to thee
M ove out of "Camp Complaining"
N o weapon that is known
O n earth can yield the power

P raise can do alone
Q uit looking at the future
R edeem the time at hand
S tart every day with worship
T o "thank" is a command
U ntil we see Him coming
V ictorious in the sky
W e'll run the race with gratitude
X alting God most high
Y es, there will be good times and yes, some will be bad,
but . . .
Z ion waits in glory . . . where none are ever sad!

A Soldier of Christ
(Submitted by Sis. Melanie Conley)

Source: www.fbhchurch.org/jr7inform.html

---

4. That sanctification is the second definite instantaneous work of grace, obtainable by faith on the part of the fully justified believer.

5. That pentecostal baptism of the Holy Ghost and Fire is obtainable by a definite act of appropriating faith on the part of the wholly sanctified believer, and that the initial evidence of the reception of this experience is speaking with other tongues as the spirit gives utterance.

6. In divine healing as in the atonement.

7. In the eminent personal pre-millennial second coming of our Lord Jesus Christ, and we love and await for His appearing.

8. The Fire Baptized Holiness Church of God of the Americas is utterly opposed to the teachings of Christian Scientists, Mohammedism, Spiritualists, Unitarians, Universalists, and Mormons. We deny as false teachings of the Seventh Day Adventists, annihilation of the wicked, conditional immorality and anti-nomianism, absolute perfection, teaching against an organized church, the resurrection life, the redemption of glorification of the body in this life, the doctrine of restitution of all things set forth in millennial dawnism, Jehovah's Witness and the false teaching that we are not born of God until we are sanctified wholly, Roman Catholicism, and the teaching of Jesus only.

In the 1990s, the Church was divided into three episcopal dioceses and in 1990 had 1,050 churches and some 25,000 members, with the largest numbers in South Carolina, Georgia, and Ohio. The Church remains affiliated with the Fuller School located in Greenville, South Carolina and continues to support the Fuller Press and an active youth program.

David Levinson

Bibliography

Discipline, F. B. H. (1962) *Church of God of the Americas.* Atlanta, GA: Fuller Press.

Fire Baptized Holiness Church of God of the Americas. (2000) www.fbhchurch.org

Mead, Frank S. (1990) *Handbook of Denominations in the United States*, 9th ed. Nashville, TN: Abingdon Press.

Gaga (Rara cult) in the Dominican Republic

Gaga is the name Dominicans give serving the Rara spirits. The origin of the Rara spirits has been traced to the Arada region of the former Kingdom of Dahomey in West Africa. Gaga is a major African-derived religion in the Dominican Republic, a country which shares the Caribbean island of

Hispaniola with the Republic of Haiti. Gaga is a complex religion that consists of beliefs and practices and is found mainly in rural areas. It has been linked to the hacienda system of sugar production. The cult is widely practiced by Haitian contract laborers, but has also attracted followers among Dominicanos of Haitian descent. As noncitizens, Haitians in the Dominican Republic are poor and have few rights. Gaga is a highly adaptive social and political movement that serves the needs of these migrants. The religion provides its followers with a complex system of magical beliefs and practices through which they can address the problems and uncertainties of everyday life; in addition, it offers escape from persistent patterns of political oppression, degradation, and abuse.

Like other African-derived religions in the Caribbean, Gaga reflects the influence of both French and Spanish Catholicism. The religion recognizes a pantheon of spirits divided into distinct families. Depending on one's family affiliation, spirits may be seen as either malevolent or beneficial. Considerable scholarly attention has been given to the potential malevolence of Haitian Petro spirits like Ezurlie, Aux Rouge, Baculu, Mastia, Lessife, and Grand Brigitte, but less attention has been given to serving the Gaga (Rara) spirits. Dominican followers of Gaga maintain that proper ritual behavior mollifies all spirits (Gaga and Petro) and will prevent spirits from doing harm.

Dominican rituals for Gaga are similar to the rituals performed in Haitian Vodou. However, some practices in the Dominican Republic differ from those of Haiti. Such differences are most evident in the Dominican emphasis on Amerindian spirits and shamanic practices (Alegria-Pons 1993) as well as differing patterns of influence between Vodou practitioners in Haiti and the Roman Catholic Church (Deive 1988). Some of these differences can be explained historically. Shortly after the Haitian Revolution, the Roman Catholic Church withdrew all priests from Haiti for a period of about 50 years. This absence of Catholic clergy allowed Haitian Vodou to develop independently—quite apart from the church. By contrast, African-derived religions in the Dominican Republic developed under the constant and watchful eye of the church hierarchy.

An important public ceremony within Dominican Gaga is the annual rite celebrating the end of the sugarcane harvest and the beginning of spring. Harvest rituals begin with the washing of hands and feet. This is followed on Holy Thursday by a blessing of clothing and, on Friday, by a pilgrimage to other villages. The weeklong ceremony is marked by keeping a perpetual flame, performances of secular and religious music, and mock battles between villages. According to Alegria-Pons (1993: 61), harvest rites are simultane-

ously rituals of reconciliation and rituals of rebellion. They serve a variety of spiritual, social, and political functions.

David Levinson and Stephen Glazier
(from materials written by Jose Alegria-Pons
and provided by Ricardo Alegria).

See also Vodou

Bibliography

Alegria-Pons, Jose Francisco. (1993) *Gaga y Vudu en la Republica Dominicana*. San Juan, Puerto Rico: Editorial Chango-Prieto.

Deive, Carlos Esteban. (1988) *Vodu y Magie en Santo Domingo*. Santo Domingo: Museo del Hombre Dominicana.

Rosenberg, June. (1979) *El Gaga: Religion y Sociedad de un Culto Dominicana*. Santo Domingo: Editoria de la UASD.

Grenada, African-Derived Religions in

Initially claimed for the Spanish Crown by Columbus during his third voyage to the Americas in 1498, Grenada and its sister island Carriacou were successively colonized by the French from 1674 to 1763 and the English from 1763 to 1974. Following the systematic extermination of the indigenous Carib populace, European landholders instituted a plantation economy that eventually relied almost entirely on African slave labor. Although it is unclear how many Africans were brought to Grenada during the colonial era, the captive population grew exponentially in the eighteenth century. Tallied at only 525 individuals in the year 1700, the number of bonded servants burgeoned to 11,991 by 1753 and reached a high point of 35,000 in 1779. In 1808, the further importation of slaves was prohibited and in 1838 slavery itself was abolished. Today, peoples of African descent comprise more than 80 percent of the nation's approximately 100,000 inhabitants and numerous social customs based on African traditions continue to be observed.

Popular Devotional Rites

Among the most pervasive African-derived spiritual practices in Grenada and Carriacou are commemorative rites in which ancestors, both recently deceased and distantly removed, are feted with food, libations, and other ritual activities. These feasts are variously referred to, often interchangeably, as Saracas—derived from a series of Arabic-influenced West African terms connoting sacrifice, alms-giving, and ritual observances for the dead—Sacrifices, Ancestor's Plates, Parents' Plates, Maroons, and Thanks-givings. Organized either by the members of one or more extended families or the collective residents of a village, the celebrations are generally staged in conjunction with the changing of seasons (e.g., the onset of rains, the harvest), rites of passage (e.g., birth, marriage, death), and official church or national holidays (e.g., Ash Wednesday and Good Friday).

They may also be held for a variety of other reasons including the occurrence of a dream in which an ancestor asks for food, following a personal misfortune, or prior to a momentous undertaking such as the building of a new home or a business venture. On the occasion of a major community feast, often referred to as a Big Drum Dance or Nation Dance, participants traditionally formed cliques based on notions of shared African lineage (e.g., Ibo, Kongo, Mandingo) and, over the course of several days, performed countless songs and dances in honor of each ethnic group. At present, this practice occurs almost exclusively in Carriacou.

Shango-Based Religious Practices

In Grenada, Shango has replaced Nation Dance as the preeminent form of African-derived communal worship. A ritual system based primarily on Yoruba spiritual beliefs, the origin of Grenadian Shango can be traced back to the arrival in 1849 of 1,055 indentured African laborers, most of whom came from Ijesha, Nigeria. Although these immigrants initially formed closed communities at Munich, Concorde, and La Mode, their descendants eventually intermingled with other segments of the population and promulgated their unique religious traditions. In Shango ceremonies the Yoruba language is used, although not always understood, and devotees invoke Yoruba deities (orishas) such as Eshu, Shango, Ogun, Yemanja, and Oshun. Although permanent temples are not constructed, worshipers do maintain private altars, or "stools," for selected divinities. Under the direction of respected elders, normally females referred to as Queens, temporary shrines (palais) are periodically erected at pilgrimage sites (e.g., springs, lakes, streams) and at the homes of adherents. During the propitiatory rites and healing rituals performed in the palais, many of the participants experience an altered state of consciousness that is interpreted as psychic possession by orishas or lesser spirits (were). The emphasis on spirit possession, a behavior not normally associated with the saraca or Big Drum and Nation Dance traditions, is likely responsible for Shango's expansion in Grenada.

Few, if any, of the Grenadians who engage in Shango ceremonies worship African deities exclusively. Instead, they are usually affiliated with Catholic, Anglican, or Protestant denominations. As is the case elsewhere in the Americas, syncretic or hybrid traditions have emerged. The leaders of Afro-Christian faiths commonly referred to as Shango Baptists and Spiritual Baptists (also known as Shouters or Shakers) frequently sponsor Shango or Shango-inspired ceremonies under the rubric of "African dances" or "African work." Norman Paul, a charismatic religious leader who founded an influential independent Protestant congregation in 1948, routinely held three-day "African feasts" in honor of Ogun and other Orishas. Although Paul claimed that these were not Shango rites, the ceremonies were nevertheless rooted in the same cultural milieu and represented key segments of a ritual continuum. Rather than conceptualizing African and European spiritual traditions as mutually exclusive, the members of many independent churches in Grenada view them as complimentary sets of sacred principles that enable humans to act in accordance with the divine plan of God, the creator of the universe and the father of mankind.

Religion and Society

Typical of plural societies in the Caribbean, sharp distinctions between the elite and the folk, or peasant, class have long dominated Grenadian society. Participation in African-influenced religious traditions such as saraca, the Big Drum Dance, Shango, and, more recently, Rastafarianism, has frequently played a crucial role in social, cultural, and political discourses in Grenada. For much of the twentieth century, for example, laws proscribing Shango ceremonies were enacted, though not always enforced. Conversely, in the early 1950s, the former prime minister, Sir Eric Gairy, enlisted Shango leaders as campaign chaplains in an effort to garner popular support for his political party. Although hardly numerous, Grenadian Rastafarians were instrumental in the success of the 1979 Marxist revolution that removed Gairy from office. Subsequently, the leaders of the new regime persecuted the Rastas, labeling them as criminals and potential threats to the revolutionary consciousness. Over the course of the last several decades, however, African-derived religions in Grenada have become more widely regarded as vital features of the nation's cultural heritage.

Patrick Arthur Polk

See also Big Drum Dance of Carriacou; Ogun; Orisha (Shango) Movement in Trinidad; Rastafari; Spiritual Baptists

Bibliography

Bell, Hesketh, J. (1970 [1889]) *Obeah: Witchcraft in the West Indies*. Westport, CT: Negro Universities Press.

Brizan, George. (1984) *Grenada: Island of Conflict*. London: Zed Books Ltd.

Fichte, Hubert. (1980) *Petersilie: Die afroamerikanishen Religionen*. Frankfurt am Main: S. Fischer Verlag.

———. (1985) *Lazarus und die Waschmaschine: Kleine Einfurung in die Afroamerikanische Kultur*. Stuttgart: S. Fischer Verlag.

McDaniel, Lorna. (1998) *The Big Drum Dance of Carriacou: Praisesongs in Rememory of Flight*. Gainesville, Fla.: University of Florida Press.

Hill, Donald R. (1977) *The Impact of Migration on the Metropolitan and Folk Society of Carriacou, Grenada*. Anthropological Papers of the American Museum of Natural History, vol. 54, part 2. New York: American Museum of Natural History.

Pollak-Eltz, Angelina. (1993) "The Shango Cult and Other African Rituals in Trinidad, Grenada, and Carriacou and their Possible Influences on the Spiritual Baptist Faith." *Caribbean Quarterly* 39, 3–4: 12–25.

Polk, Patrick A. (1993) "African Religion and Christianity in Grenada." *Caribbean Quarterly* 39, 3–4: 74–81.

Simpson, George Eaton. (1978) *Black Religions in the New World*. New York: Columbia University Press.

Smith, M. G. (1963) *Dark Puritan: The Life and Work of Normal Paul*. Kingston: Department of Extra-Mural Studies, University of the West Indies.

———. (1965) *The Plural Society in the British West Indies*. Berkeley and Los Angeles: University of California Press.

Guadeloupe and Martinique, African-Derived Religions in

The main religion of the Caribbean islands of Guadeloupe and Martinique is Catholicism. About 90 percent of the population adheres to it. Hindu is followed by about 10 percent on Guadeloupe and 5 percent of the population on Martinique, and there many smaller Protestant movements and sects. In the Lesser Antilles, religion has been often been described as a popular European Catholic practice, but in reality, Guadeloupean and Martiniquan Catholicism has not much to do with its European counterpart. It is merely a reinterpretation of both Catholic and African traditions on American soil. Unlike in Haiti, Cuba, Trinidad, or Jamaica, where such "spectacular" religions as Vodou, Santeria, Shango, and Kumina have flourished, in Guadeloupe and Martinique no specific religion developed. Instead, Catholicism itself has been creolized and has become a particular worldview that can be described as a continuum of practice and belief.

Although Catholicism is the official religion, participation in the rituals of the Catholic church do not exclude recourse to "magical" practices, which do integrate witchcraft. These practices have been described in two ways. On the one hand, they are seen as folklore, as the dependency on France did not allow slaves to develop their own culture and Catholic ritual was substituted for traditional practice. On the other hand, these practices have been described as psychological disorders: in Guadeloupe, Creole healers, called *gadèdzafè* (derived from French *garder les affaires*, i.e., looking into someone's future with the help of saints and keeping it secret) are seen as highly fantastic personalities who work without proper initiation or training. In Martinique the situation is much the same, with healers called *kenbwazè* (from *kenbwa* [malefice] derived from the French *tiens bois*, i.e., please drink). In Guadeloupe and Martinique the boundaries of a person are considered to be permeable. The components of a person are the body, the breath, the soul (*bonanj*), the guardian angel, and the hidden first name; and for the *gadèdzafè or kenbwazè* also the guardian saint that protects against evil forces. The breath is attached to the body and is the vital element that disappears at the moment of dead. The soul holds the power of the word and is the spiritual element that maintains the bonds between the world of the living and the world of the dead. It manifests itself to the living by giving advice and transmitting the messages of the saints. Depending on the manner in which the person died, the spirit returns to earth as a good or bad one. Therefore, a magnificent night-watch is organized at the moment of death in order to help the dead person to become a good spirit. The guardian angel protects the soul. It is the intimate friend that, in exchange for regular prayers, protects every person. The hidden first name is a secret one that is only known by those who are close to its possessor, because it can be used and manipulated for witchcraft purposes.

The island worldview is characterized by a struggle between the forces of God and those of Evil. Both the Catholic priests and the *gadèdzafè or kenbwazè* have the power to intervene in this struggle and Catholic symbolism as religious imagery, pilgrimages, and prayers, as well as trances and sacrifices are all significant. Actually, Guadeloupean and Martiniquan Catholicism can be considered a kind of "Pagan Christianity." Participation in both Catholic rituals and magical practices is not conceived as a conflict between opposites, because both belong to one and the same worldview. Depending on one's life circumstances, for example when illness or misfortune strikes, individuals move along a continuum by taking several positions. At one pole they follow the prescriptions of the Catholic church by attending mass and reading the Bible. At the other, relations with the dead are acknowledged and the dead are worshiped for their specific powers.

Since the 1970s, many Protestant movements, including Adventism, Baptism, Evangelism, Pentecostalism, and sects including Mahikari (Japanese) and Jehovah's Witnesses, have attracted adherents on the islands. These religions and movements can be seen as manifestations counterhegemonic to the dominant Catholic worldview. Some of them reject a dichotomous worldview that divides all between good and evil. For them evil doesn't exist. Others simply declare that they are much stronger than evil. People are most attracted to these religions and movements when "Pagan Christianity" has proven itself not sufficiently powerful to solve their problems.

Since Guadeloupe and Martinique are integrated overseas departments of France, they are often seen as totally assimilated into French culture. Religion, though, is a domain that shows the cultural vitality of this society. Even if the dominant French culture prevented the development of distinct Guadeloupean and Martiniquan religions, its particular cosmogony remains a vital component of daily life.

Catherine Benoît

See also Caribbean, African-Derived Religions in

Bibliography

Annezer, J. C., D. Bégot, and J. Manlius. (1980) "L'univers magico-religieux: l'exemple de la Guadeloupe." In *L'historial antillais*, 1, edited by J.-C. Bonniol. Fort-de-France, Martinique: Dajani, 459–478.

Benoît, Catherine. (2000) *Corps, Jardins, Mémoires. Anthropologie du corps et de l'espace ^ la Guadeloupe.* Paris: Éditions de la Maison des Sciences de l'Homme/Éditions du CNRS.

Delawarde, Jean-Baptiste. (1983) *La sorcellerie à la Martinique et dans les "les voisines : ses positions et ses réactions dans ses rapports avec le culte chrétien ambiant.* Paris: P. T_qui.

Henry Valmore, S. (1988) *Dieux en exil.* Paris: Gallimard.

Massé, Raymond. (1966) "Fishing Rites and Recipes in a Martiniquan Village." *Caribbean Studies* 6, 1: 3–24.

———. (1978) *Les Adventistes du septiéme jour aux Antilles françaises.* Fonds St Jacques, Ste Marie—Martinique. Montreal: Presses de l'Université de Montreal.

Harrist Movement

The Liberian prophet William Wade Harris (c. 1850–1929) started the Harrist Movement in the second decade of the twentieth century along the western coast of Africa. Harris's evangelical work and the founding of the Harris Church were significant events in the history of African religion for three reasons. First, the Harris movement was the largest mass movement of conversion to Christianity in West African history. Second, many Africans in Ghana and the Ivory Coast who were attracted to Christianity later joined mainstream Christian churches. And, third, the Harris Church was a founding church that led to the establishment of other independent African churches in the region. In 1998, the World Council of Churches accepted the Harris Church as a new member.

William Wade Harris was born of Grebo parents in Liberia. Educated at an American mission school, he became an Episcopalian and worked as a teacher, seaman, and interpreter. He was also marginally involved in the movement to end American control over Liberia and was jailed for his participation in a plot to replace American control with British rule. According to one version of the story, while in prison in 1910, Harris experienced a religious conversion that included a visit and message delivered by the archangel Gabriel. Harris emerged from the experience as a prophet whose mission was to prepare the people of West Africa for the return of Jesus Christ.

Harris's message was straightforward. He preached the authority of the Bible, adherence to the Ten Commandments, and baptism, and he rejected traditional African religious practices, particularly the use of amulets and fetishes to ward off evil. He also condemned adultery, lying, and stealing. He was a striking figure as he set out on his conversion journey along the coast of West Africa in either 1912 or 1913. Accompanied by two women who sang, danced, and banged rattles, he wore a white turban and robe and carried a cane cross, a gourd filled with water for baptism, and a Bible. His journey took him from Liberia to the Ivory Coast and then to Ghana (then called the Gold Coast). He attracted perhaps as many as 120,000 Africans from a variety of ethnic groups to the movement. Immediate baptism marked entry into the church and converts were told to either attend mission churches already established in their villages or new churches that were established by the twelve apostles appointed by Harris. The movement was most effective in the Ivory Coast, with about 100,000 converts there alone. The French colonists at first supported Harris's effort because he advocated work and personal responsibility, but in 1914 the government recognized the movement's potential threat to French control and expelled Harris and destroyed the new churches. Harris continued to preach in Liberia, but his years of great success ended in 1915. Catholic and Protestant missionaries took advantage of Harris's success and converted many of his followers to their denominations. Many of Harris's followers, however, remained loyal to their new churches, many of which continued as independent Harris churches. At the close of the twentieth century these included the Church of the Twelve Apostles in Ghana and the Églises Harristes and the Deima movement in the Ivory Coast.

Harris insisted that women as well as men be converted to Christianity, a practice that distinguished him from other Christian missionaries. Because he was African, Harris understood the role of matrilineal descent in a person's spiritual life, and, therefore, the importance of women being active in the church. In contrast to many other independent churches, Harris accepted people of different faiths and ethnic groups into his church. However, Harris's criticism of some local customs and beliefs differentiated his movement from other indigenous movements that supported the continuation of African culture. His willingness to criticize African culture was a product of Harris's Liberian heritage, as American values were held to be superior to African ones in Liberia. The influence of the Harris Movement went far beyond converting a large number of Africans to Christianity. It did much to help prepare the people of the western coast of Africa for the modernizing innovations brought by missionaries and colonialists. The opposition of the French government to Harris's church, moreover, gave the movement an association with reform and African independence that Harris himself did not actively seek. Harris's cooperation with other Christian religions—Catholic and Protestant—encouraged among his followers an openness to new ideas that promoted an ecumenical spirit. The movement also attracted foreign support for African goals, including, eventually, independence. His stress on the importance of the Bible encouraged literacy among his followers. That Harris churches still exist is a testimony to their success as means to modernization and as bridges between traditional African beliefs and Christianity.

Frank A. Salamone

See also Christian Missionaries; Pentecostalism in Africa

Bibliography

Haliburton, Gordon M. (1971) *The Prophet Harris*. London: Longman.

Krabill, James R. (1995) *The Religious Revolution in the Ivory Coast: The Prophet Harris and the Harrist Church*. New York: Peter Lang Publishing.

Sanneh, Lamin. (1983) *West African Christianity: The Religious Impact*. Maryknoll, NY: Orbis Books.

Shank, David A. (1994) *Prophet Harris, the 'Black Elijah' of West Africa*. Studies of Religion in Africa, no. 10. Leiden: Brill Academic Publishers.

Walker, Sheila S. (1995) "Women in the Harrist Movement." In *The New Religions of Africa*, edited by Benetta Jules-Resette. Norwood, NJ: Ablex, 87–115.

Healing in African and African-Derived Religions

Traditional African religious, philosophical, and healing systems share a number of features in common despite their apparent formal and concrete diversity. Each of the African systems fall into clear regions or culture/ecological areas (the most important geographical ones for us being West and Central Africa) that have experienced the impact of the non-African religions of Islam and Christianity. In a like manner, the Afro-American religious and healing systems have entered into a variety of relationships with Christianity, Spiritualism, Hinduism, and the indigenous religions of what was to become the plantation Americas. Although typologies and classifications of religious phenomena in both African and the New World African religions have been attempted separately, there has not yet been an attempt to erect a classification that would include them both. Surely, one day it will be attempted; but certainly not now and not in the space of this article. In this article I illustrate selected examples of traditional African healing and healers, and their counterparts in the Caribbean and in Central and South America.

Africa

Egypt was clearly the pinnacle of the ancient African civilizations. The several extant Egyptian medical papyri reveal a considerable knowledge of anatomy, especially as attested to by the existence of hieroglyphic symbols denoting the major organs, parts of the circulatory system, the spinal cord and brain, as well as ideas concerning their normal physiological functioning, interrelationships, and pathology. From instructions contained in papyri dealing with surgery, of which the most important is the Edwin Smith papyrus, as well as from archaeological artifacts, it becomes clear that the ancient Egyptians had accumulated a great deal of knowledge about the nature and treatment of a variety of traumatic lesions and how to repair them. The papyri also contain a considerable body of magic and religious thought as well as prayers and incantations which locate some of the causes of disease and suffering in an invisible spiritual realm.

Egyptian physicians practiced several forms of physical diagnosis, including palpation, urine and feces examination, taking the pulse, abdominal and chest percussion and testing a number of muscular extensions and reflexes. They also possessed a large *materia medica*—animal, herbal, fungal, and mineral—which they dispensed in a variety of forms, including pills, suppositories, enemas, and infusions, to achieve antiseptic, antibacterial, sedative, dilatory, and stimulatory effects. Diet seems to have been given a fundamental role in the etiology of disease.

These physicians were priests, trained in temple schools in which religion was an assumed background. Although the medical practices of these physician/priests was sometimes quite specialized, probably because they possessed highly developed medical knowledge transmitted in hieroglyphic papyruses and secret oral teachings, the curriculum of the temple schools was dedicated to training a priesthood and profession in the fundamentals of a unified science that encompassed medicine, hieroglyphics, mathematics, astronomy, religion, music, and philosophy.

Egyptian medicine, and the whole of African traditional healing as well, is the product of persistent scientific—but not experimental—observation over a long period of time. These medical systems represent the codification of that experience, including the religious framework within which it occurred. Egypt and the Mediterranean Ocean became vital collection and dispersion points of Old World culture, collecting, melding, and dispersing cultural elements to southern Europe and North Africa. But Egypt was also the outgrowth of earlier traditions in the Nilotic region, with later relatives to the east in Ethiopia and west and south in the Yoruba and Kongo kingdoms. Still other civilizations, while not quite on a par with Egypt, nonetheless shared profound affinities with it. Within this range of civilizations and societies there are a wide array of medical traditions and healers which, nonetheless, can be categorized into a few broad types.

Among the remaining African hunter-gathers such as the !Kung and San of South Africa and the Mbuti and Ituri pygmies of the Congo region the major medical practitioner is the shaman. The shaman mediates directly between the visible world of everyday experience and an invisible world of spirits and extraordinary powers on behalf of the patient. Shamans use such means as rituals, trance states, and even sleight-of-hand in their efforts to cure patients. They often have a depth of knowledge of plant, animal, and mineral healing agents that most people in their cultures do not possess. They acquire knowledge in several ways: as revelations from spirits, through personal investigation guided by dreams, and by apprenticeship to a senior shaman. The shaman is a key figure in the history of medicine. The majority of the humans species' time on earth up to the present was spent as hunter-gathers, and since the shaman is the characteristic medical practitioner of this way of life—not only in Africa but worldwide—all other forms of medical practice must trace back to the shaman in some way. The African shaman can be seen as an archetypal healer whose various functions became separated out over time. As societies increase in technological and political complexity, these functions are found separately assigned to newer distinct healer types. However, just as the remaining hunter-gathers are marginal in the societies where they exist, so are contemporary shamans marginal healer types in those same societies. The traditional healers for the majority of African people fall into three different types of healers: the herbalist, the doctor/diviner, and the spirit medium. These three main healer types are distinct but not mutually exclusive, and, in Africa, their practices carve out distinctive but also overlapping sectors in the continuum of health-care resources.

In the rural areas of tropical Africa nearly everyone is a minor healer and herbalist in that they know a variety of herbs and can use some simple therapeutic procedures to treat common ills. In some societies or ethnic groups there are even medicinal recipes that are passed down family lines as home remedies, part of a larger body of knowledge considered to be "owned" by particular families. When complaints or situations arise that are beyond what this lay medicine can be expected to cope with or the family feels the need to contact someone whose knowledge is wider and more specialized, they may contact an herbalist. In the rural areas an herbalist may be just a few minutes walk away, but in the larger villages and the cities you will find them in the market or in their own home offices. In the rural areas, herbalists tend to be part-time, often working out of their home garden, where they cultivate the medicinal herbs they prescribe. Urban or market herbalists tend to be full-time in the vocation and function as herb traders and vendors as well as healers.

The position of doctor/diviner is a professional full-time status. This practitioner has usually experienced a call to the vocation in the form of a dream, vision, or traumatic illness, and has subsequently been compelled to undertake training as a diviner and/or herbalist. Their concern with discovering the underlying causes of suffering and disease leads them to study diagnostic techniques based on divination. Regardless of the mode of divination or the apparatus used, divination reveals a hidden causal structure in which the ultimate origins of disease and misfortune are found in disturbed or conflicting social relationships and in moral transgressions. The disturbed social world is expressed in and mediated through magical and religious concepts that determine the direction

RELIGIOUS AND SECULAR HEALERS
AMONG THE AMHARA OF ETHIOPIA

While the secular healer is indistinguishable from other peasants, the *debtera* is conspicuous by his ecclesiastical identity, with his distinctive dress, liturgical performances at the Mass, and conversational presence in the churchyard. The *memher* teacher of *kiyne* is most visible of all *debteras,* not so much by his appearance as through all the activities of his ubiquitous students. The services of these students are generally indispensible to establishing, and often maintaining, public recognition of the *debtera's* claims to the "*awakiy*" title.

Source: Young, Allan L. (1970) "Medical Beliefs and Practices of Begemder Amhara." Doctoral dissertation, University of Pennsylvania, 227.

treatment takes. Doctor/diviner therapy consists of finding out the witch, spirit, social conflict, or other cause of the sickness or misfortune and advising patients on how to propitiate the spiritual entities involved, and also prescribing herbal remedies to ameliorate and remedy the damage the sufferer has already endured.

Diviners and herbalists both give plant medicines, but the herbalist dispenses a single herb most of the time and behaves more like a pharmacist who gives the customer what they need while not having to be interested in the underlying origin or cause of the disease. The diviner gives more complex combinations of herbs and tends to treat more serious complaints than the herbalist and is able to access the cause of the disease and misfortune through his divination methods. The access to unknown causes (often sorcery or witchcraft) and the complexity of the prescriptions clothe the doctor/diviner in an aura of esotericism, secrecy, and power that offers protection. A further distinction is that the herbalist dispenses medicine and then the medical encounter is over. The doctor diviner, on the other hand, diagnoses and prescribes and, although the patient usually does not have to maintain a long-term relationship with the diviner, the patient may have to establish an ongoing relationship with a spiritual or ancestral agency of some kind.

Spirit mediums constitute a third type of healer. Spirit mediums seek the etiology of suffering in terms of the spirits recognized within the medium's own cult group. Spirit mediums tend to be female and therapy involves dealing with the spirits that cause or may cause ailments through collective rituals that are performed by the cult group and involve spirit possession, exorcism, and purification rites.

The spirit medium has direct access to spiritual power and understanding through the mystical experience of possession and, while not interested in the etiology of the dis-

ease, is guided to it, not by a divinatory apparatus, but either through becoming a divinatory apparatus herself during a diagnostic trance state or though being guided through the interventions of her guiding spirits or the traditions of the cult group to which she belongs. Over and beyond the collective rituals performed by the spirit medium to treat the patient, the patient may have to establish a long-term relationship with the medium and the cult group. A condition of the patient's continuing cure or ongoing recovery may be the requirement that they participate in the group's rite regularly or that they train as a spirit mediums and later assist in the treatment of others suffering from the same affliction as themselves.

The New World

The three types of traditional African practitioners—the herbalist, the doctor/diviner, and the spirit medium—all have their counterparts in communities of the African Diaspora and correspond quite closely to those described by Michel Laguerre in his survey of Afro-Caribbean folk medicine: the "root doctor" or "weed woman," the "magical doctor," and the "faith healer" (Laguerre 1988). The African herbalist described here corresponds to his "root doctor" or "weed woman"; his "magical doctor" corresponds to what I call the doctor/diviner even including their focus on conjuration and witchcraft; and his "faith healer", found within Haitian Vodun and Cuban Santeria as well as elsewhere, corresponds quite closely to the African-style spirit medium. With additional refinements and shifts of emphasis the same thing holds, in a general way, for the healer types found among blacks in the United States, as well as in some Afro-Latin populations of Central and South America.

Some Herbalists and Their Herbs

In the New World it is not uncommon for the herbalist also to be well versed in magical techniques and the New World herbalist is just as likely to practice within a religious framework as outside of one. This is particularly the case with the bush doctor, a term used throughout the English-speaking West Indies to refer to a black folk healer who also practices magic. The bush doctor combines magic with herbalism and dispenses both as forms of medicine. Much of the magic that bush doctors practice is of European rather than African origin and generally of a benign nature. The term bush doctor overlaps some with that of the *obeahman*, also widespread throughout the West Indies. The *obeahman*, while also expert in herbalism, magic, and medicine, will employ magic to harm as well as cure. The French West Indies also has figures similar to the bush doctor, though known under different names. An example from Guadeloupe and Martinique is the *guerisseur*, a folk healer specializing in herbal medicines and cures. Some *guerisseur* are secular and work outside of any religious framework and make no use of magical techniques; others combine both religion and magic with their herbal recipes. The *surusie*, a specialist in curing with plant medicines found among the mixed African and Amerindian Garifuna (or black Carib) populations of Belize, Honduras, Costa Rica, Guatemala, and Nicaragua, is another example of this kind of healer.

In colonial Brazil, enslaved Africans served as healers for both blacks and whites. One type of Afro-Brazilian healer was the *benzador*. The *benzador* was an herbalist who specialized in physical disorders. Some *benzador* were probably also religious practitioners; some were not. Historian Stanley Stein describes some of the herbal prescriptions used by *benzador* on the Brazilian coffee plantation of Vassouras during the late nineteenth century. These included, among many others, a treatment for tuberculosis using St. Mary's herb, drunk on an empty stomach first thing in the morning (Stein 1957).

Although the majority of the plants these healers use originate in the New World, a few were transplanted from Africa. The Portuguese imported the African medicinal plant called *ago* from their colony at Sao Tome during the slavery era. *Ago* found its way into the healing practices of enslaved Afro-Brazilians and remains part of folk and religious healing into the present day. *Bejuco de Angola*, a medicinal plant used to treat aching and broken bones throughout Afro-Latin America, was imported into the New World during the Atlantic slave trade as well, its name reflecting the memory of its African origin. Jamaican herbalists use the seeds of the *bichy* (also *bissy*) bush to treat malaria and high blood pressure and also use it as a poison antidote. The *bichy* was imported from Guinea in West Africa. Other medicinal plants were cultivated both in the New World and the Old. Custard apples (*Annona squamosa*), often thought to be native to tropical America, were also cultivated in the tropical regions of the Old World as well. Adepts of the Afro-Cuban religion of Santeria use the bark and roots of the custard apple to treat acidosis, cystitis, and bladder problems.

Doctor/Diviners

In the New World plant medicine is not the exclusive province of the herbalist; the doctor/diviner and the spirit medium often know it, too, but supplement it with a great variety of other techniques. Hence it is often necessary to distinguish between, for example, the bush doctor and the *obeahman* in terms of their magical practices rather than their herbalism. In the case of the Garifuna, one must be careful to distinguish between the *surusie* and the *buyai* who, while also involved in herbal medicine, is primarily a spirit medium. The same also holds for the distinction between the Haitian *docteur feuille* (leaf-doctor) and the *mambo* or *houngan* in Haitian Vodun. In both cases, despite their herbal knowledge, the Garifuna *buyai* and the Vodun *mambo* or *houngan* are primarily spirit mediums rather than herbalists and as a consequence tend to specialize more in magical/spiritual and religiously caused problems than purely physical ones.

While many Venezuelans view the *curioso* simply as a fortune teller who provides them personal predictions, others—rich and poor, black and white—go to these Afro-Venezuelan traditional healers and diviners for treatment of their physical ailments, spiritual afflictions, and emotional problems. The *curioso's* divinatory diagnosis often reveals humoral imbalances and sorcery as fundamental causes of human suffering. Therapy requires plant medicines and patent drugs to restore an adequate hot/cold balance within the body and a variety of antisorcery ritual techniques to counter the effects of malignant magic.

On Guadeloupe, the parents of a child whose illness seems to defy explanation may seek out the services of a *gade z'affair* (also called *mentimenteux*), a religious folk healer specializing in divination. The *gade z'affair* works primarily with children's ills and is supposed to be able to diagnose the problem without assistance from the patient. Their divinatory skills are supposed to enable them to see the disease and its symptoms even when they are not visible to ordinary sight.

The imagery of extended sight is also present in the Afro-Surinamese *lukuman*. *Lukuman* is a Sranan-Tongo term meaning "those who look." The *lukuman* is a diviner in the

Afro-Surinamese religion of Winti who represents the Winti spirits and deities. *Lukuman* may be male or female, may specialize in dealings with a particular type of spirit, and are usually compensated for their work. In their role as religious officials, *lukuman* supervise celebratory rituals; in their role as diviners they diagnose problems and conduct curing ceremonies. People go to the *lukuman* to find out what lies behind a relative's recent death or to understand a portentous event or omen. The *lukuman's* divinatory diagnosis traces illnesses back to violations of food taboos or other instructions from the Winti deities, agricultural problems, or the activities of sorcerers. Some of the illnesses are thought to result from the unfulfilled demands of one of a person's multiple souls or from conflict between one of these souls and a Winti spirit familiar. Because their most important tasks often involve intimate and specialized negotiations of the relationship among a person's own souls as well as between these souls and Winti spirits, the *lukuman* is often looked upon as a diviner who cures souls (Herskovits 1966).

Within Santeria the *santera* approximates the role of spirit medium while the *babalawo's* role resembles closely that of the doctor/diviner. Santeria devotees practice several forms of divination. While most priests and priestesses are spirit mediums, they can do at least the simpler forms of divination. Other priests, however, specialize as diviners, especially those who practice a complex oracle called Ifa and have the title *babalawo*, meaning "father who owns the secret." On the basis of divinatory outcomes the *babalawo* prescribes protective and curative rituals. *Babalawos* are often, but not always, herbalists as well, but they are not usually spirit mediums. The situation is essentially the same in the Candomblé of Brazil, where there is also a group of specialized doctor/diviners using the Ifa oracle, as well as a priesthood of spirit mediums who use a simpler divination method involving sixteen cowrie shells. Ifa and cowrie-shell divination are found in both Santeria and Afro-Brazilian Candomblé.

Spirit Mediums

One type of traditional healer found among the Garifuna of Belize, Honduras, Guatemala, and Nicaragua is the *buyai*. *Buyai* translates from the Garinagu "spirit woman" and this role has been filled predominantly by women since the 1960s. The *buyai* is a specialist in the use of medicinal plants but is distinguished from other Garifuna herbalists by being a trance medium. The *buyai* assumes her role through a sickness, which is interpreted as spirit possession. Initiation involves an obligatory period of seclusion and fasting during which the future *buyai* learns the techniques of mediumship. *Buyai* conduct diagnostic rites called *arairaguni*. *Arairaguni*, literally "a descension of the spirits," are diagnostic trance sessions during which spirit helpers communi-

cate through the medium to the suffering person the cause and cure of their affliction. *Buyai* also supervise the major Garifuna placatory rituals, the *cugu* and *dugu*. During these rituals they invoke ancestors and are expected to go into spirit possession and induce possession in other participants. An analogous kind of African-Amerindian mixture and a similar type of curing ceremony is the *chamada* of the Afro-Brazilian religions of Amazonas, especially in the city of Belem and its environs, which is in Para state, but which most geographers place in the Amazon region. In the *chamada*, the medium calls upon her principal spirit, or *encantado*, to come into the ceremony and give consultations to clients. Parallel to the *chamada* is the *passagem*. As in the *chamada*, the healer is a trance medium who calls their spirits to possess them and help cure patients. But in the *passagem* there are no patients actually present. Apparently the spirit medium is thought to be able to effect some parts of the therapy at a distance.

The *houngan*, or *mambo*, of Haitian Vodun is an initiated servant of one of the major deities of the Haitian Vodun pantheon, part of whose service includes ceremonial spirit possession. Most often the *houngan* or *mambo* is a farmer, as well as a priest or priestess, and often derives a considerable part of the meager income from work as a healer. The *houngan* and *mambo* use a variety of ritual and magical techniques to treat problems such as insanity, tuberculosis, epilepsy, and other illnesses and misfortunes when their causes lie within the complex, densely populated invisible world of Vodun. Where the medical doctor or the herbalist fails, the *houngan* and *mambo* expect to succeed because they understand the forces from which these problems originate when they are caused by malign magic, the ancestors, or the deities people serve. The *houngan* and *mambo* depend on the guidance of their deities, the *lwa*, who will assist them with any client's problems as long as the medium is honest. If they are dishonest with the client, their *lwa* will abandon them and take the knowledge through which the *mambo* and *houngan* heal. Priests and priestesses of the Cuban Santeria are also spirit mediums and are often called upon to act as healers for physical as well as spiritual and religious ills. Specific Santeria deities are said to rule different parts of the body and to be connected to the diseases affecting them. Sorcery, spirit intrusion, and soul loss are significant spiritual problems that sometimes manifest as physical ills or social and psychological problems. Diagnosis may be by divination or mediumship or both. Therapies include herbal, ritual, and quasi-psychotherapeutic techniques. Aside from their work in private consultations, *santeros* and *santeras* sometimes perform cleansing and purification rites during public ceremonies while they are in the possession/trance state.

Ritual Techniques

Doctor/diviners and spirit mediums employ a variety of ritual practices. I will give as examples two ritual therapeutic strategies from the Winti religion of the Coastal Creole population of Suriname. Many other ritual therapies from other Afro-Caribbean and Afro-Latin groups share some of their features. Invariably these ritual techniques are closely connected to both the etiological system of the practitioner and the specific religious ideology within which the healer works. Baths, incantations, music, sacrifices, dancing, and the negotiation of social, spiritual, and ancestral relationships are important in all of them. Even where concrete physical manifestations appear to be the target, the underlying causes in the social and spiritual worlds are the real foci of attention. The two examples that follow could just as easily have come from many other New World African-based healing systems.

Meki wan sweri is a ritual therapeutic strategy within the religion of the coastal Creoles of Suriname. *Meki wan sweri* means "making a contract with the *winti*." Making such a contract involves interrogating the *winti* to find out its nature and desires and then negotiating a deal or contract on which both the *winti* and the sufferer can agree. The most important situation for making a contract with the *winti* is in the case of a life-threatening illness when everyone thinks the patient will surely die. Since *winti* are inheritable and pass down family lines, the person dying from *winti*-caused illness will want to keep the *winti* from later striking their siblings or descendants. To do this they have to have a doctor/diviner, the *winti*-man (also called *lukuman* or *bonuman*), negotiate terms with the *winti*.

The *winti*-man, with the aid of an ensemble of drummers, brings the *winti* to the part of the body where its ill effects have been localized, then negotiates a set of conditions under which the *winti* will pass the moribund person's family by, releasing them from future harm. Finally, the *winti*-man asks the *winti* where it wants to be sent. Most often the *winti* wants to go to a silk cotton tree. There are plenty of these on the outskirts of Paramaribo and Para, the major Creole cities, and the *winti*-man sends the offending *winti* to one of them.

A second type of coastal Creole curing ritual is the *seti winti*. *Seti winti* means "pacifying the *winti*." Pacifying the *winti* involves manipulating several layers of relationships between humans, *winti* spirits, and the sick person's multiple souls. The extended family of the sufferer invariably is called upon to participate in relieving the affliction. The task of probing and delicately adjusting the social relationships involved to attain a balance in all the worlds affecting the sick person falls to the *winti*-man, who must use a number of divining methods. Curing techniques for *seti winti* include a bath in an herbal infusion to which white chalk and bluing

have been added. The *winti*-man employs a black or white cock as a purifying sponge in a cleansing ritual where the cock is wiped up and down the person's body. Sometimes the *winti*-man substitutes bread. If the *winti*-man uses a cock, it is sacrificed after the bath and its testicles examined for an omen of the success or failure of the cure. Dancing in worship of the offending *winti* comes next. The client may dance or the *winti*-man can dance on the client's behalf.

Psychotherapeutics

A number of folk syndromes clearly reflecting oppressive social structures, interpersonal conflicts, and psychological problems attendant to identity dilemmas and cultural change have come to light. These were within the medical domains of herbalists, doctor/diviners, and spirit mediums and have been treated by them. *Banzo*, for example, was a syndrome repeatedly described among African-born slaves in Brazil. The word probably derives from the Quimbundu word *mbanza*, meaning "village." In Brazil, *banzo* referred to a dire nostalgia or homesickness, though neither of these terms seems adequate to describe either the emotional state or its object. The enslaved African suffering from *banzo* went into a marked physical decline and deep depression, gradually wasting away until finally dying in a resigned and expectant state. Alcoholism, narcotic use, and geophagy (dirt-eating) were frequent accompanying symptoms. Evidently, this psychological syndrome was frequent enough and distinctive enough for it to be named and noted. *Banzo* was most prevalent among males slaves in Brazil; so was suicide, to which *banzo* seems closely allied. Some enslaved Africans also believed that one could return to Africa by means of suicide. If death from *banzo* was a way to get back to Africa, suicide was a way to get back much more quickly. The most frequent methods of suicide were hanging and taking any of a number of poisons cooked up from herbs and other substances that sorcerers would provide.

One of the basic tenets of African religion and healing is that disturbed social relationships and unresolved conflict between relatives, spouses, and other intimates can cause sickness. This belief survives in Haiti and takes form as the belief in a magical insect called *fiofio*. The *fiofio* is created by tension and discord in personal relationships. *Fiofio* enters the body when close friends, relatives, or spouses quarrel and are unable to resolve their differences and achieve a true reconciliation. Sickness is the result.

Madairitiya hungua is one of a number of illnesses that black Carib healers recognize and believe to be caused by spirit intervention. Often referred to by Garifuna spirit mediums as "listlessness" and described as a kind of malaise, the term translates literally as "they don't find themselves." It is generally, but not exclusively, women who become afflicted in this way, and the most dramatic symptom the sufferer presents is a dissociative state, which the spirit mediums interpret as possession by malevolent ancestral spirits called *gubida*. In modern times, this symptom often arises when a person undergoes Western medical treatment for an illness but the treatment proves unsuccessful and results in no cure. Since the moment of possession, which may even take place in the doctor's office, often signals the sufferer's willingness to resort to traditional methods of curing, it seems apt that black Carib spirit mediums should use this term to describe the mental state of the person who then seeks them out for a diagnostic seance.

In Santeria much of human suffering is seen to be rooted in interpersonal relations and relations with the Other World of ancestors, spirits, and deities. Devotees, priests, and diviners cultivate relationships with the spiritual world and have consistent obligations to particular beings there, but many people have never given anything to the spirits. The ancestors, *orisha*, and spirits, however, affect people whether they are aware of it or not. From the point of view of the *santero*, people who have no orderly relationship with the spiritual world lack control over important aspects of their own lives; this is because those aspects of their lives are affected by spiritual beings with whom they do not communicate. Initiation and the acquisition of media (objects, dolls, icons, etc.) through which one relates to the spiritual world play a role in healing and the alleviation of suffering and misfortune by giving the sufferer a measure of control over the situation.

The Santeria diviner sometimes prescribes the erection of a doll as "something to be done." The dolls differ according to the spiritual entities they represent and the purposes they serve. Frequently the doll represents a spirit whose personality and attributes the diviner perceives as compensatory for something the person lacks. In other instances the diviner notes a source of inner strength in the person they need to develop and enhance; erecting a doll is supposed to help do this. Only after ritual preparation does an ordinary doll become transformed into a charged center of power through which the *orisha* and the Dead become susceptible to offerings, honor, and command. The diviner describes who the doll is, how the doll should be dressed, the nature of the offerings to be presented to it, and how it ought to be treated. Relations between humans and spirits are never one-sided; they are reciprocal; people give to the spirits and expect to receive from them in turn. The promise is that through offerings to the spirit the doll represents, through speech and through veneration, the person can convert a disordered or disturbing influence into a cooling and beneficial one over which the person can exercise some control.

George Brandon

See also African-Derived Religions; Candomblé; Ifa; Obeah in the West Indies; Healing in Sub-Saharan Africa; Santeria; Santeria, Material Culture; Suriname, African-Derived Religions in; Vodou; Vodou, Material Culture

Bibliography

Ayensu, Edward. (1981) *Medicinal Plants of the West Indies.* Algonac, MI: Reference Publication.

Barrett, Leonard. (1979) *The Sun and the Drum.* London: Heinemann Press

Bastide, Roger. (1971) *African Civilizations of the New World.* New York: Harper and Row.

——. (1971) *African Religions of Brazil.* Baltimore: Johns Hopkins University Press.

Bermudez, Eduardo, and Maria Matilde Suarez. (1995) "Venezuela." In *No Longer Invisible*, edited by Minority Rights Group). London: Minority Rights Publications, 243–269.

Bougerol, Christiane. (1978) "Donnees de Medicine Populaire a la Guadeloupe." *Journal D'Agriculture Traditionelle et de Botanique Appliquee* 25, 3: 163–183.

Brandon, George. (1983) "The Dead Sell Memories: An Anthropological Study of Santeria in New York City." Ph.D. dissertation, Rutgers University.

Buckley, Anthony. *Yoruba Medicine.* Brooklyn, NY: Athelia Henrietta Press, Inc.

Cabrera, Lydia. (1971) *El Monte.* Miami: Coleccion del Chicereku.

Cassidy, Frederic. (1961) *Jamaica Talk.* New York: Macmillan and Co.

de Craemer, Willy, Jan Vansina, and Renee Fox. (1976) "Religious Movements in Central Africa." *Comparative Studies in Society and History* 18, 4 (October): 458–475.

Drake, St.Claire. (1979) *The Redemption of Africa and Black Religion.* Chicago: Third World Press.

Finch, Charles. (1983) "The African Background of Medical Science." In *Blacks in Science, Ancient and Modern*, edited by Ivan van Sertima. New Brunswick, NJ: Transaction Books, 140–156.

Foster, Byron. (1986) *Heart Drum: Spirit Possession in the Garifuna Communities of Belize.* Belize: Cubola Productions.

Ghalioungui, P. (1973) *The House of Life: Magic and Medicine in Ancient Egypt.* Amsterdam: BM Israel.

Guzman, Carlos. (n.d.) *Nueva Libreta Lucumi.* New York. Privately published in New York.

Herskovits, M. J. (1966) "The World View of an Urban Community: Paramaribo, Dutch Guiana." In *The New World Negro*, edited by Frances Herskovits. Bloomington: Indiana University Press, 267–320.

Horowitz, Michael. (1967) *Morne-Paysan: Peasant Village in Martinique.* New York: Holt, Rinehart and Winston.

Kerns, Virginia. (1989) *Women and Ancestors: Black Carib Kinship and Ritual.* Urbana: University of Illinois Press.

Labelle-Robilliard, Micheline. (1972) "L'Apprentissage du Monde dans un Village Guadeloupeen." In *L'Archipel Inacheve, Culture et Societe aux Antilles Francaises,* edited by Jean Benoist. Montreal: Presses de l'Universite de Montreal, 179–203.

Laguerre, M. (1988) *Afro-Caribbean Folk Medicine.* South Hadley, MA: Bergin Garvey.

Leacock, S., and R. Leacock. (1972) *Spirits of the Deep.* Garden City, NJ: Doubleday, Natural History Press.

MacGaffey, Wyatt. (1991) *Art and Healing of the Bakongo.* Stockholm: Folkens Museum-etnografiska.

Manniche, Lise. (1989) *An Ancient Egyptian Herbal.* Austin: University of Texas Press.

Mercier, Jaques. (1997) *Art that Heals: The Image as Medicine in Ethiopia.* New York: Prestel Museum for African Art.

Metraux, Alfred. (1959) *Voodoo in Haiti.* London: Andres Deutsch, Ltd.

Middleton, John, and John Beattie, eds. (1969) *Spirit Mediumship and Society in Africa.* London: Routledge and Kegan Paul.

Morris, Brian. (1996) *Chewa Medical Botany: A Study of Herbalism in Southern Malawi.* International African Institute Monograph, no.2, London. Hamburg: Lit Verlag.

Newsome, Frederick. (1983) "Black Contributions to the Early History of Western Medicine." In *Blacks in Science, Ancient and Modern,* edited by Ivan van Sertima. New Brunswick, NJ: Transaction Books, 127–139.

Nunez, B. (1980) *Dictionary of Afro-Latin Civilization.* Westport, CT: Greenwod Press.

Pierre-Noel, Arsene. (1971) *Nomenclature Polyglotte des Plantes Haitiennes et Tropicales.* Port-au-Prince: Presses Normales de Haiti.

Stein, Stanley J. (1957) *Vassouras, a Brazilian Coffee County 1850–1900.* Cambridge, MA: Harvard University Press.

Taylor, Douglas. (1951) *The Black Caribs of British Honduras.* Viking Fund Publications in Anthropology, no.17. New York: Wenner-Gren Foundation for Anthropological Research.

Young, Allan. (1975) "The Practical Logic of Amhara Traditional Medicine." *Rural Africana* 26: 79–89.

Healing in Sub-Saharan Africa

Religious beliefs and practices, which are universal features of every human society, constitute part of a people's culture and are felt in different ways at different periods within every society. Similarly, healing is a complex and integrated concept and practice found in most cultures of the world. Healing includes wholeness of a person, the restoration of the physical body to normalcy, mental vitality, and a general sense of well-being. Healing remedies ill health and brings back soundness into a person's life. Religion and healing are linked because both are aspects of, and are shaped by, a people's culture. Even in the industrialized Western societies, despite the fact that religion and healing have been separated into distinct institutions, they continue to interact regularly. For example, chapels and chaplains can still be found within many hospitals. Moreover, the mystery of certain illnesses and the quest for cures continue to make people depend on the supernatural.

In Africa, traditional religions have been the basis of medicine and healing. Africans conceive diseases and healing as religious experiences requiring religious approaches. Hence, priests in traditional religion also function as healers. In some societies, certain divinities are associated with healing and medicinal preparations.

There are three general dimensions of the etiology of diseases in Africa. First, Africans believe that diseases are biological or natural phenomenon that could be due to visible natural causes such as aging, accident, and overwork. Second, diseases could be caused by evil agencies such as the Devil, evil spirits, witches, or enemies. Third, illnesses could come from God or his ministers or ancestors as punishment for sins. Such illnesses can only be cured by the moral repentance of the sufferer. In correspondence with these beliefs, three medical systems can be distinguished. These are biomedicine, traditional healing, and spiritual healing of the Christian or Islamic type. In whatever healing system, the method of healing is definitely linked to the etiologies already identified. Quite often Africans make use of plurality of therapeutic systems whenever they are ill, because they believe that every system has its own benefit.

Healing in African Traditional Religions

Traditional medicine involves the use of indigenous knowledge and practices in the diagnosis, prevention, and elimination of physical, social, mental, and spiritual imbalances. Healing is achieved using herbs, vegetables, animals, and mineral substances that may be accompanied by certain rituals that invoke the power of the deity to activate the

Zomay, a Binza Avule (traditional Zande shamanic header) transforming himself into a leopard during an Avule seance in Zaire in 1974. PHOTO COURTESY OF MANFRED KREMSER.

healing effects in the prepared substances. It is the total worldview of the people that determines the specific herbal preparations and such religious elements as rituals, sacrifices, and incantations, to be used in the healing process. Healing is believed to come from the supreme deity through some lesser divinities and the ancestors, who first practiced the art of healing and transmitted it to specific priest-doctors.

The causal influence of rituals or incarnations on the herbal preparations is difficult to prove to one who is not an initiate in the art of traditional healing. It is primarily a matter of faith that healing comes from the deities who taught the knowledge of pharmacopoeias to certain divinely chosen individuals who must observe the order of ritual preparation of the herbs, vegetables, and animal substances for these to be efficacious. The rituals also function to assure the patient that the gods are listening to the supplications for healing, and favorably dispose the patients toward the efficacy of the preparation. Because Africans believe in a supreme deity who made the universe, they believe it is only the creator who knows all the secrets about the harmonious functioning of the human body and can restore soundness.

There are different categories of traditional healers. First, there are herbalists who possess advanced and esoteric knowledge about the use of herbs and plants. In contemporary Africa, those who have extensive knowledge of medicinal herbs do make them available to others by hawking or selling them in specific shops. Second are the medicine men or traditional practitioners who combine divination with healing techniques including herbal preparations. Divination is used as a diagnostic strategy that is combined with experience and observation to determine the nature of illnesses and the appropriate remedy required. Most diviners not only treat symptoms but also look for and eliminate the spiritual causes of diseases. Third, there are traditional priest-healers who associate rituals with certain divinities to achieve healing. Rainmakers are in this category. Their initiation as priests automatically qualifies them as healers as well. Among these different healers there are specialists as well. Some specialize in restoring fractured bones, other treat specific illnesses like madness, barrenness, tuberculosis, and so on.

Traditional healers become qualified to practice through various ways. Some are endowed or possessed by certain spirits, or called in dreams and visions; some inherit the healing art from their parents and families; some undergo formal and informal training, and most are initiated into guilds. Apart from curing the sick, African healers also deal with misfortunes of every kind. Traditional healers are aware of the social order, and often operate within the religious awareness of the people. The African healing system is holistic because it aims at restoring harmony of the body and mind, as well as achieving harmony between the metaphysical and human worlds.

Indigenous healers are widely patronized, especially in rural areas where western medical facilities are lacking or are expensive for the people to patronize. Africans believe that traditional healers have more success treating psychological disturbances than do Western-trained physicians. It is difficult to assess the level of patronage they receive in urban areas, because many people who patronize the healers do so secretly. What can be safely said, however, is that with increasing socioeconomic hardship, the readily available and cheap traditional medicine is receiving wide patronage.

More recognition has come to traditional healers since the 1960s, when many African countries gained political independence and embarked on indigenization. By the last decade of the twentieth century, many governments had given support to indigenous healing systems by integrating them into modern hospital systems and facilitating the formation of associations of traditional medical practitioners.

Healing in the Qur'an and Among African Muslims

In Islam, healing has a religious basis because there are many Hadiths, that is, traditions of Prophet Muhammad concerning illness and its treatment. From the Qur'an and Hadiths it is affirmed that Allah is the source of every human disease, and hence he has sent down remedy for each disease. Therefore, Muslims believe that all human problems and diseases are curable through the help of Allah. Islamic healing practice is not restricted to the recovery of health but also to the prevention of illness and preservation of health.

The Qur'an promotes healing in three different ways. First, through legislation that prohibits matters that are hazardous to health, and stipulates matters that maintain and promote health. Examples are the prohibition of the consumption of alcohol, excessive eating, sexual promiscuity, homosexual relations, and sexual intercourse during the menstrual period. Legislation that is health-promoting includes breast-feeding of babies, ablution, bathing, washing of hands, and fasting, which is believed to improve the immunity of the human body.

Second, Muslims believe the entire teaching of the Qur'an provides guidance that regulates the society and the conduct of individuals, and hence has indirect positive effect in maintaining health. Third, Muslims believe that verses of the Qur'an have direct healing effects on diseases. For example, Qur'an chapters 113 (Al-Falaq) and 114 (Al-Nas) are used in various ways to effect healing and guarantee protection. Other verses of the Qur'an are recited at specific times for healing purposes. The writing of some verses on a slate and washing off the written verses and then drinking the water is also practiced as a form of healing. The medicinal potency of the water is believed to derive from the Qur'an, which is believed to be the word of Allah. Related to this is the preparation of amulets, which are verses of the Qur'an written on pieces of paper, folded, and carried about as a form of security.

Generally, African Muslims employed different kinds of healing methods available from various religious traditions including Islam, traditional, and Western. Many Muslim healers, who frequently combine traditional and Islamic medicine, flourish in the urban areas. In addition, Muslim clerics often function as traditional healers but with new powers. For example, Qur'an verses have been used for magical purposes such as making protective charms. In fact, some Muslim clerics often prescribe and use herbal preparations associated with divination or the observance of non-Islamic rituals. Likewise, the production and use of amulets and charms have become common, and have taken on magicoreligious appearance similar to traditional soothsaying and divination. Certainly, African Muslims have shown compromising and accommodating attitudes to other healing systems that may be contrary to strict Qur'anic injunction.

Healing among African Christians

Healing in the context of Christianity is a complex phenomenon that goes back to its biblical roots. The Bible furnishes many examples of the linkage between religion and healing, both in the literal sense and in symbolic terms. The Bible clearly indicates that healing and wholeness are some of the blessings from God, and, likewise, diseases could be punishment from God. The history of he Christian Church is replete with instances of faith or divine healing, that is, healing without the use of any herbal or medical preparations. However, in the twentieth century, healing received much publicity when it became a proselytizing strategy used by many Christian denominations.

African Independent Churches

The African Independent Churches devote significant attention to healing as a focal issue in their religious activities. For example, a major factor for the rapid growth of the Aladura churches in Western Africa in the 1920s and 1930s was the concern to cure people of sicknesses. Consequently, healing is second only to the interest in revelation among members of the Church of the Lord (Aladura) in West Africa. Likewise, the healing miracles of the late Samuel Oschoffa, the founder of Celestial Church of Christ, were a significant factor in the church's expansion in Africa. In the Cherubim and Seraphim, there is a strong emphasis on prayers to cure illness and the use of some "healing tangibles" such as consecrated water, oil, candles, and soaps to effect healing. The Zionist churches in Zimbabwe and South Africa appealed to people because of their emphasis on healing. Other prophets and founders of African Independent churches such as Simon Kimbangu, John Maranke, and Isaiah Shembe all possessed healing powers, and the headquarters of their churches eventually became associated with many miraculous healing.

However, most African Independent Churches have an indecisive attitude toward traditional medicine. Some forbid

THE MEDICINE-MAN AND WITCH-DOCTOR COMPARED

The Zulu [of South Africa] medicine-man is a personage totally distinct from the Zulu diviner or so-called witch-doctor. Even so, the two professions do still considerably overlap, the medicine man dealing very largely in magic and charms, and conversely the witch-doctor possessing an extensive acquaintance with disease and curative herbs, although his office is rather to indicate than to actually administer. Both are commonly called an *i-nyanga* though the medicine-man is sometimes distinguished as the *i-nyanga yokwelpha* (the doctor for curing), and the witch-doctor as the *i-nyanga yokubhula* (the doctor for divining).

The latter has the further titles, solely confined to his own class, of *um-ngomo* (apparently originally meaning "the drumming-one" . . . and *isa-nusi* (the smeller-out—probably from a now obsolete Zulu word *nukisa*, abbrev. form *nusa* meaning to help "smell out"), and so-called from their practices respectively of drumming or beating a hide, or perhaps originally on a drum, during certain ceremonies, and of "smelling-out" all manner of secret evil and the workers thereof.

Source: Bryant, A. T. (1966) *Zulu Medicine and Medicine-Men.* Capt Town: C. Struik, 13–14.

---

its use, some prescribe caution, while some use it freely. The same attitude applies to Western medicine as well. The centrality of healing in the African prophet-healing churches is due to the traditional African concern for health and well-being, so that society as a whole can live in peace and harmony. Generally, African independent churches, being a product of the interface between Christianity and African cultures, have come to recognize the strong relationship between religion and healing.

Pentecostal and Charismatic Churches

This concern for healing has continued to attract much attention in the Pentecostal and charismatic churches in Africa. Since the emergence of the African charismatic movements in the 1970s, no doctrinal emphasis and religious practice has been so widespread and dominating as healing. In fact, most founders and leaders of charismatic organizations are claiming to be healers and "miracle workers." There are even cases of Western-trained medical personnel who have abandoned their medical practices and become founders and leaders of charismatic organizations.

Regarding the etiology of diseases, charismatics believe that Satan and its evil forces, such as demons and witches, can intrude into the lives of believers and cause diseases. Second, charismatics believe that sins may cause illness. The concept of sin is very comprehensive, including all personal moral mistakes or unchristian attitudes. Satan and sins are used as religious metaphors to depict the prevailing evils within society. Consequently, these etiologies of dis-

eases are supportive of their expectations that only spiritual power can effect healing.

Charismatic emphasis on healing is very wide in scope and application and can be classified into four main components. Physical healing is by far the most common. The open-air evangelistic meetings and healing services have popularized this kind of healing. Advertisements in the electronic and print media routinely announce these activities and invite the sick, the blind, the barren, and the lame to services. Physical healing can also be handled privately, either by individual believers or leaders or pastors.

There are different ways for a charismatic who is ill to deal with the illness. It could be by reading an inspirational book or by praying for oneself or going to seek assistance from fellow charismatics or attending a "faith clinic" or using testimonies for support. However, prayer is the most common method employed. Since Western medicine is viewed as a competing healing system, leaders of charismatic groups often play down its importance and try to portray their healing as more efficacious. Traditional medicine is condemned because charismatics believe that it is usually "contaminated" with divination, magic, and sacrifice: things that Christians should keep away from.

Second, charismatics have appropriated their traditional African backgrounds and have defined healing to include freedom from demonic attacks and oppression. Since these illnesses caused by demonic forces can best be comprehended within an African milieu, one can see a close resemblance between the position of charismatics and the traditional beliefs about attacks by spiritual forces. Charismatics often prescribe that anyone under demonic attack and oppression cannot pray for oneself, but ought to be delivered or set free. The process of effecting the remedy is called "deliverance."

A significant metaphorical application of healing is a preoccupation with the intervention of the supernatural in the socioeconomic and political structures of a nation. For example, Pentecostals and charismatics claim that presently Africa is ill because there are political instability and economic problems. Interethnic wars, increasing sickness and disease, and corruption are all cited to support this claim. The causes of a nation's ill health, in African nations particularly, are attributed to the activities of Satan and demons, and to the sins of her citizens. Prayer is the major means of effecting healing, and some groups that emphasize this aspect have coined the term "prayers for the nation" to describe this healing process. The charismatics' emphasis on healing of the political situation developed and became widely utilized in conditions of rapid social change in Africa in the last three decades of the twentieth century.

Last, the very modern orientation of the charismatic movements is significantly reflected in the metaphorical application of healing to enhance the quality of life and to empower the individual. This new emphasis, termed "success and prosperity," emerged as a distinct doctrinal emphasis in the mid-1980s. According to the prosperity preachers, failure, poverty, and all forms of difficulties should not be the lot of Christians, rather every Christian should enjoy abundant material prosperity, including enough money, beautiful houses and cars, jobs, and so on. Some leaders teach that some Christians do not prosper because they are unaware of the divine will for prosperity, while others are not taking advantage of God's promise of prosperity. Success and prosperity are perceived as a form of healing when the Christian overcomes failure, poverty, and backwardness, and lives a life of sufficiency and abundance. To be prosperous, one is expected to give liberally toward the cause of the gospel, or "plant seed-money" or "seeds of faith," as some charismatics say.

There is a relevance of this teaching to traditional African cultural values. For example, wealth is a means to recognition in the society, and the means toward political power in postcolonial Africa. People have used various means to acquire wealth, and ultimately to be recognized in the society. It is revealing how the hidden obsessions with wealth and power have provided powerful stimuli for metaphorical application of healing.

Charismatics have utilized healing not only within its literary meaning but also as a powerful metaphor in negotiating wider concerns within their sociocultural background and contemporary situation. Because of nonprofessionalization and lack of dependency on specialized healers, the charismatics' healing system has a flexibility that makes it possible to adjust to every situation and to respond both to social and personal needs. Although healing is hardly restricted to the African Pentecostals and charismatics, they have significantly invigorated the concept. Therefore, they are changing African religious concepts and are applying biblical premises to the social challenges confronting them in contemporary times.

Summary

The interaction between religion and healing is complex and in many respects ambivalent. Religious beliefs are products of a people's culture; likewise, cultures define what constitutes sickness and the meanings associated with specific illnesses. It is also within specific cultures that healing is sought, and appropriated.

The popularity of healing in religious movements in Africa is partly due to the fact that modern medicine reaches only a small portion of the African population. In addition, unlike the Western medical system, healing within religious traditions is readily available, and like the traditional healing system, it is carried out with family and community support. Another attraction of the African healing system is that people are familiar with its practitioners, generally men and women of reputable integrity, well trusted in the community. Religious healing systems contrast sharply with inefficient and inadequately funded government health services. Besides, their holistic concern with a patient's mind, spirit, soul, and body cannot be matched by Western medicine. Despite the influence of education and Western culture, the prevalence of traditional interpretations of diseases and healing will continue to have influence on any religiously constructed therapeutic system in Africa.

Matthews A. Ojo

See also African Charismatics; Aladura; Cherubim and Seraphim Society; Divination; Pentecostalism in Africa; Zar; Zionist Churches

Bibliography

Aderibigbe, Gbola, and Deji Ayegboyin, eds. (1995) *Religion, Medicine, and Healing.* Ikeja: Nigerian Association for the Study of Religions and Education.

Appiah-Kubi, Kofi. (1981) *Man Cures, God Heals: Religion and Medical Practices among the Akans of Ghana*. New York: Friendship Press.

Daneel, M. L. (1970) *Zionism and Faith-Healing in Rhodesia: Aspects of African Independent Churches*. The Hague: Mouton & Company.

Du Toit, Briam M., and Ismail M. Abdalla. (1985) *African Healing Strategies*. New York: Trado-Medic Books.

Haar, G. ter, and S. Ellis. (1988) "Spirit Possession and Healing in Modern Zambia" *African Affairs* 347, 87: 185–206.

Hetsen, Jac, and Raphael Wanjobi. (1982) *Anointing and Healing in Africa*. Eldoret, Kenya: GABA Publications.

Milingo, Emmanuel. (1984) *The World in Between: Christian Healing and the Struggle for Spiritual Survival*. London: C. Hurst & Company.

Omoyajowo, Joseph A. (1982) *Cherubim and Seraphim: The History of an African Independent Church*. New York: NOK Publishers.

Peel, John D. Y. (1968) *Aladura: A Religious Movement Among the Yoruba*. London: Oxford University Press for the International African Institute.

Simpson, George E. (1980) *Yoruba Religion and Medicine in Ibadan*. Ibadan: Ibadan University Press.

Sofowora, Abayomi. (1982) *Medicinal Plants and Traditional Medicine in Africa*. Chichester: John Wiley & Sons Ltd.

Turner, Harold W. (1967) *History of an African Independent Church: Church of the Lord (Aladura)*, 2 vols. Oxford: Clarendon Press.

Westerlund, David. (1989) "Pluralism and Change: A Comparative and Historical Approach to African Disease Etiologies." In *Culture, Experience and Pluralism: Essays on African Ideas of Illness and Healing*, edited by Anita Jacobson-Widding and D. Westerlund. Stockholm: Almqvist & Wiksell International, 177–218.

Yoder, P. S., ed. (1982) *African Health and Healing Systems*. Los Angeles: Crossroads Press.

Holiness-Pentecostal (Sanctified) Movement

Pentecostalism has its roots largely in the Holiness movement that emerged out of an effort to restore John Wesley's doctrine of "entire sanctification" within Methodism following the Civil War. Most of the major white Holiness sects developed during the Jim Crow era and often manifested racist tendencies. Nevertheless, some Holiness sects appeared on the periphery of the movement and allowed for interracial gatherings of poor whites and blacks. According to Shopshire (1975: 40), the first African-American Holiness sects emerged in rural areas of the South. While several black Holiness bodies arose out of the African Methodist Episcopal and African Methodist Episcopal Zion churches, most of them emerged as schisms from various Baptist associations and conventions (Shopshire 1975: 51). As many of the Holiness groups attained respectability and became more sedate, they spawned Pentecostal sects that viewed speaking-in-tongues as an additional indicator of sanctification. Founders of Pentecostal sects typically were charismatic men or women who were revered by their followers. As these founders died, they "were succeeded by their sons (or daughters), or by close associates according to charisma and seniority in the organizations" (Shopshire 1975: 144).

The Development of African-American Pentecostalism

Scholars have engaged in a considerable amount of debate on the origins of Pentecostalism in the United States. Many scholars, and many white Pentecostalists, trace modern Pentecostalism to Charles Fox Parham's Bible school in Topeka, Kansas, in 1901. Parham's teaching that speaking-in-tongues or glossolalia constitutes the only overt manifestation of a convert's reception of the Holy Ghost or Spirit played a vital role in the beginnings of Pentecostalism. But it was the Azusa Street revival of 1906–1909 in Los Angeles, under the leadership of William J. Seymour, an African-American Holiness preacher and a former student at Parham's Houston Bible school, that "acted as the catalytic agent that congealed tongue-speaking into a fully defined doctrine" (Synan 1971: 121). Due to Seymour's role in the Azusa Street revival, Tinny contends that he was the "father of modern-day Pentecostalism" (1978: 213).

In addition to an interracial audience consisting largely of poor working-class people, many seekers from all over the country attended the revival. Some of them went on to establish Pentecostal sects of their own. In early 1907, Charles H. Mason, J. A. Peter, and D. J. Young spoke-in-tongues during their five-week stay at the Azusa Street Mission. After he returned to his headquarters in Memphis, Mason asked an assembly of the Church of God in Christ (COGIC), a Holiness sect that he had cofounded with C. P. Jones, to become a Pentecostal group. This move forced his compatriot to form the Church of Christ (Holiness) U.S.A. Both before and after 1906, Mason ordained many white ministers of independent congregations because COGIC was one of the few legally incorporated Holiness-Pentecostal bodies in the Mid-South. The United Holy Church, established in 1886 in Method, North Carolina, also evolved from a Holiness sect into a full-fledged Pentecostal sect.

PENTECOSTALS AND RELATED FORMS OF CHRISTIAN FAITH

There is some confusion about the particular labels to use for Christians who are sometimes labeled Pentecostals, but all of whom share the same beliefs or practices. Harvey Cox, of the Harvard Divinity School, suggests five different categories:

Born-again: People whose faith is based on a personal experience with Christ.

Evangelical: People whose faith is based on a personal experience with Christ and also a belief in the sanctity of the Scriptures and who work to spread the message.

Fundamentalist: People whose faith is based on a belief in the inerrancy of the Bible and a life based on a literal reading of the Bible.

Pentecostals: People whose faith is based on expressive and ecstatic worship which creates an encounter with the Holy Spirit.

Charismatics: People who adhere to a Pentecostal form of worship but do so in their own Catholic or Protestant church.

Source: Cox, Harvey *The Atlantic Monthly*, Nov. 1995. www.theatlantic.com.issues.

While specific African-American religious groups refer to themselves as either "Holiness" or "Pentecostal," the distinction between the two terms is not always clear-cut. Indeed, within the African-American community there is a strong tendency to lump these two categories together by referring them to them as "Sanctified churches" (Hurston 1983). Many of the religious bodies that anthropologist George Eaton Simpson categorizes as "Pentecostal," because they exhibit "Fundamentalism, millennialism, baptism by total immersion, and the 'baptism of the Spirit' evidenced by talking in tongues" (1978: 255–256), employ the terms "Holiness" or "Holy" in their names.

The initial interracial character of the Pentecostal movement began to break down in the years following the Azusa Street revival. In 1914, COGIC-ordained white ministers formed the Assemblies of God in Hot Springs, Arkansas, at a gathering which reportedly was addressed by Bishop Mason. During the 1920s, Parham occasionally preached at gatherings of the Ku Klux Klan and wrote articles for a racist, anti-Semitic, anti-Catholic periodical. Conversely, many white Holiness and Pentecostal bodies instructed their members not to join the Klan, not because of its racial policies but on the grounds that it was a secret organization. The division along racial lines in 1924 of the Pentecostal Assemblies of the World, which initially had "roughly equal numbers of Negroes and whites as both officials and members," formally ended the interracial period in American Pentecostalism (Synan 1971: 221).

While the roots of the African-American Pentecostal movement in the rural South still await detailed examination, Goldsmith's (1985) research on the emergence of black Pentecostalism on the Georgia coast provide some clues. As elsewhere, the black Baptist and Methodist missionaries who arrived on the Georgia Coast following the Civil War disapproved of the exurban religion practiced by the ex-slaves. By the end of the nineteenth century, "the energetic 'shout' had disappeared from [St. Simons] island's religious worship, and the stately hymns sung by the Baptists nationally were adopted in its place" (Goldsmith 1985: 80). In their evolution from conversionist sects into mainstream denominations, many African-American churches emulated the somber style of white middle-class churches, even though most members of the former continued to be working class. In 1927 Pentecostal evangelists made their first converts on St. Simons Island. The initial converts did not renounce their membership in the Baptist churches, but their ministers and fellow congregants objected to their ecstatic outbursts and ultimately forced them out. For various working-class blacks, Pentecostalism substituted high religious status for low social status. As Goldsmith observes, "The appearance of Pentecostal 'sanctification' on the Georgia coast offered a means of disregarding the dominant socio-economic criteria for measuring success in life" (1985: 94).

Flourishing beyond its roots in the rural South, African-American Pentecostalism has functioned for some time as an urban phenomenon as well. Southern-based Pentecostal sects, such as COGIC, established new congregations in the wake of their members' migration to the North beginning around World War I. Sernett observes that "as a result of the Great Migration the Pentecostal and

Holiness movements, which spawned scores of groups other than COGIC and the Church of Christ (Holiness), U.S.A., became important alternatives to the near hegemony of the Baptist and Methodist denominations" (1997: 95). The "mission" that Mother Beck (pseudonym used to protect the privacy of the people studied), a COGIC evangelist, formed with the assistance of several other women in her home around 1918 served as the beginnings of Zion Holiness Church (pseudonym) in the Hill District of Pittsburgh (Williams 1974: 153). Complying with Mother Beck's request, in 1919 C. H. Mason sent Elder Baxter (pseudonym) to pastor the new congregation and serve as the overseer of Pennsylvania and Delaware. COGIC also branched out to numerous other Northern cities such as Chicago, Detroit, Philadelphia, and Brooklyn. In addition to the formation of the Church of God (Holiness), U.S.A., as a response to Mason's conversion to Pentecostalism, COGIC has spawned several other schisms.

In addition to the black Pentecostal evangelists who followed migrants to the North, numerous Pentecostal or "Sanctified" sects appeared in the "Promised Land" alongside a wide array of Judaic, Islamic, and Spiritual sects. These included the Church of Our Lord Jesus Christ of the Apostolic Faith, established by Bishop R. C. Lawson in Harlem in 1918, and the Church of All Nations established by Elder Lucy Smith in Chicago in 1916. Smith was born on a Georgia plantation in 1875, migrated to Chicago in 1910, came into contact with white Pentecostals, and established a prayer meeting in her home in 1916 (Sernett 1997: 195). In August 1927 Bishop S. E. Looper organized the First Unity of God Church in Cleveland as a schism from COGIC and eventually established branches of the sect in Cincinnati, Columbus, Akron, Chillicothe, and Barberton (all in Ohio, Blackwell 1949: 208). In 1932 Bishop J. Bowie of Hot Springs, Arkansas, established the Church of God in Christ, Congregational. Fourteen COGIC bishops formed the Church of God in Christ, International, in 1969 in Kansas City (Melton 1978: 1, 298).

A seemingly countless number of other African-American Holiness-Pentecostal or Sanctified sects emerged over the course of the twentieth century. Some of these included Elder "Lightfoot" Solomon Michaux's Church of God (est. 1921), Daddy Grace's United House of Prayer for All People on the Rock of the Apostolic Church (est. 1921 in Wareham, Massachusetts), the Mt. Sinai Holy Church (est. 1924), the Greater Mt. Zion Pentecostal Church of America (est. 1944), the Deliverance Evangelistic Centers (est. 1956 in Newark), and Fredrick K. C. Price's Crenshaw Christian Center (est. in 1973 in Los Angeles) (DuPree 1996).

Politico-Religious Organization of the Black Holiness-Pentecostal Movement

The Black Holiness-Pentecostal movement has no overarching organization to coordinate or define its structure, doctrines, and ritual activities. Many Sanctified congregations are affiliated with one of the many national or regional associations. The Black-Holiness movement encompasses many leaders, each of whom exerts some degree of influence over an association, an informal assemblage of congregations, or an independent congregation. Even at the ideological level, Sanctified groups exhibit considerable variation. Many African-American Pentecostal sects, for example, adhere to a Unitarian conception of the Godhead as opposed to the traditional Trinitarian view. In her compendium of Holiness-Pentecostal bodies, DuPree (1996) lists 73 "Trinitarian Pentecostal groups," 137 "Apostolic Pentecostal groups," and 106 "evangelical charismatic or neo-Pentecostal groups." Even more so than the Baptist and Methodist traditions, fission and fusion have characterized the Holiness-Pentecostal movement. Over the course of its history, the Pentecostal Assemblies of God the World spawned the Church of Our Lord Jesus Christ, the Church of the Lord Jesus Christ of the Apostolic Faith, the Living Witnesses of the Apostolic Faith, and the Bible Way Churches of Our Lord Jesus Christ World Wide. As Tinney observes, a specified Sanctified congregation "may be affiliated with several denominations at different times in its history, or with none at all" (1978: 250).

While, in theory, most Sanctified associations exhibit an episcopal polity in that they are overseen by a senior bishop or board of bishops, in reality, their politico-religious organization tends to combine aspects of the episcopal, presbyterian, and congregational forms. The larger Sanctified associations have created boards, assemblies, committees, and councils at the national, regional, and even local levels to administer affairs such as evangelism, Sunday schools, publications, and pensions. In this regard, their politico-religious organization has begun to resemble that of African-American mainstream denominations. For example, COGIC is governed by an executive body called the General Board of Twelve Bishops and the General Assembly, which elects the General Board. The presiding bishop is the chief executive officer and selects his first and second assistant presiding bishops from the members of the General Board, appoints the department heads and national officers, and appoints new bishops. The General Assembly meets during the Annual Convocation in November as well as in April. Delegates to the General Assembly include members of the General Board, jurisdictional supervisors of the women's auxiliaries, pastors and ordained elders, two district missionaries and one delegate from the over 100 juris-dictional assemblies, and foreign delegates (Robinson n.d: 46). Each bishop presides over an annual jurisdictional assembly and appoints new pastors and ordains elders.

Composition and Practices of Sanctified Congregations

Most Sanctified congregations are housed in modest facili-ties—storefronts, house churches, and apartments in cities and simple frame structures in small towns and the country-side—but some are situated in either substantial edifices for-merly occupied by white congregations or in modern struc-tures. The Boston congregations affiliated with Mt. Calvary Holy Church of America, Inc. are housed in a range of facil-ities fairly typical of Holiness-Pentecostal associations. Gamma church meets in "a commercial building, a frame structure about thirty feet deep and fifty feet wide . . . [which] comfortably holds no more than forty or fifty peo-ple. The Alpha church is somewhat larger" (Paris 1982: 39). The Beta church, which serves as the national headquarters of the association, has a sanctuary (seating 200–300) for reg-ular church services, and a facility (seating nearly 1,000) for convocations and revivals.

Historically, Sanctified congregations have held their greatest appeal for lower-class and working-class African Americans. Older members of the Holiness Church of Christ (pseudonym), a store-front in Washington, D.C., took jobs as domestics, cooks, seamstresses, night watchmen, jan-itors, and unskilled laborers after migrating to the city (Moore 1985: 81–82). While they clearly remained within the working class, many improved their material standard of living. The young women of the congregation hold positions as cooks in government buildings, charwomen, secretaries; young men are employed as janitors, store cashiers, electri-cians, painters, and musical performers.

In contrast to the relatively modest socioeconomic com-position of most Sanctified congregations, Lincoln and Mamiya argue that the class situation within the Church of God in Christ is changing rapidly. It is estimated that more than half of COGIC members are within the coping mid-dle-income strata (largely working-class and some middle-class members). Many of their churches are reflecting the socioeconomic change from storefront to regular church edifices (Lincoln and Mamiya 1990: 163).

While the politico-religious organization of most Sanctified congregations closely resembles that of African-American Baptist and Methodist ones, women in the former often occupy many of the offices monopolized by men in the latter. Williams (1974: 33–36) delineates four categories of members in Zion Holiness Church: (1) elite members, (2) core members, (3) supportive members, and (4) margin-al members. Elite members, including the pastor, the church secretary, the president of the pastor's aide group, the chairperson of the deacon board, and the church treas-urer (also a deacon), generally sit within or around the "sacred inner space" during services. Core members, who include the remainder of the deacons, the trustees, the pas-tor's aide group, the financial captains, the choir, choral members, the missionaries, the ministers, and other officers, pay tithes and participate on a regular basis in most church activities. Supportive members generally attend Sunday morning services, annual meetings, and special programs or activities. Marginal members include teenagers, "chronic backsliders," and individuals who exhibit physical, mental, and financial problems. While Sanctified churches empha-size puritanical moral standards, which include a taboo on the consumption of alcoholic beverages, dancing, and non-marital sex, they tend to welcome individuals who have led "sinful" lives but want to be "saved."

While COGIC and various other Sanctified churches maintain a relatively patriarchal politico-religious structure, many Sanctified groups have provided women with opportu-nities to achieve religious leadership. As Drake and Cayton observe, "The ban on women pastors in regular churches has increased the popularity of the Pentecostal, Holiness, and Spiritual churches, where ambitious women may rise to the top" (1945: 165). The women of the Mt. Sinai Holy Church of America, Inc. provide excellent examples of the heights that many women have attained in the Holiness-Pentecostal movement. Bishop Ida Robinson formed the sect in Philadelphia in 1923, later appointing Elmira Jeffries to serve as "vice-bishop" (Fauset 1971: 13–21). Although Mt. Sinai Holy Church also has many male officers, women make up a notable portion of its elders and ministers.

Sundays are extremely busy for Sanctified congrega-tions, beginning with Sunday school in the early morning and evolving into the Sunday worship service in the late morning and early afternoon. A musical performance may occur in the late afternoon. Finally, an evening service often brings the most sacred day of the week to a close. This round of religious activities may be punctuated by a midday meal or a picnic. Many Sanctified congregations conduct services and Bible classes during the week. Other than occasional instances of speaking-in-tongues and ritual healing, there is little that an African-American Baptist would find unfamil-iar in a Sanctified service. In general, the "Saints" are more inclined to clap their hands, stomp their feet, shout, and dance. When Gospel music made its advent in Chicago and other northern cities during the 1920s, it found a ready haven among Sanctified as well as Spiritual congregations at a time when most African-American churches eschewed

GLOSSOLALIA

Glossolalia is the technical term for speaking in tongues. Glossolalia is a form of religious behavior in which an individual in a state of religious ecstasy or trance speaks in words, phrases, or sentences which are not from a language which the individual speaks or comprehends. It is commonly assumed that people speaking in tongues are speaking in an actual language that is different from their own language and is a language that they do not know. For example, a speaker of English speaks in Hindi or a speaker of Spanish speaks in Inuit. Actually, research shows that people who are speaking in tongues do not speak in a language unknown to them or actually in any language at all. Rather the sounds or words they make are random utterances that are not part of any language nor do they form a language of their own. In addition to the words, speaking in tongues also involves other forms of linguistic expression including the use of repetitive sounds, rapid changes in pitch and intensity, and singing or chanting. Glossolalia occurs in many societies around the world, and is a widespread, though not especially common, form of religious expression. In all religious contexts, glossolalia is a form of emotional worship which indicates a close relationship with a supernatural force (a god or spirit) and in many cultures it is believed that the force is speaking through the individual. Glossolalia is most common and it has drawn the most attention in Pentecostal worship in the twentieth century. In Pentecostalism, speaking in tongues is seen as a holy gift; as a visible manifestation of baptism through the Holy Spirit. It was closely associated with the emergence of Pentecostalism in the United States from 1900 to 1906, with its spread around the world, and since the rise of the New Pentecostalism in the second half of the twentieth century has been component of worship in some mainstream Protestant and Catholic churches as well.

David Levinson

this important form of religious expression. In time, of course, many of the Baptist and Methodist churches came to adopt Gospel music. In addition to speaking in tongues, Sanctified churches recognize eight other gifts of the Holy Spirit, including interpretation-of-tongues, teaching, preaching, prophesy, and healing. The emphasis given to speaking-in-tongues and healing varies considerably from congregation to congregation.

Role of the African-American Holiness-Pentecostal Movement in African-American Society

Following the "culture shock" hypothesis, several social scientists have interpreted the African-American Holiness-Pentecostal movement as an attempted adjustment to the social disorganization and cultural conflict that many black migrants experienced in the cities. They view testimonies and various ecstatic rituals, including glossolalia, as providing members with an emotional release from the frustrations and anxieties that social dislocation created in their everyday lives. Sanctified congregations often substitute high religious status as "Saints" and God's elect for a relatively humble social status in the larger society. In William's view, Zion Holiness Church provides its members not only a "refuge from the world" but also a com-

munity that "allocates social status, differentiates roles, resolves conflicts, gives meaning, order, and style to its members' lives, and provides for social mobility and social rewards within its confines" (1974: 157).

Anderson (1979: 224) maintains that Pentecostalism in general emerged as a response to the transition from competitive to monopoly capitalism during roughly the same period (1890–1925) that populism, labor/capital labor conflict, and progressivism appeared in American society. While in theory Pentecostalism rejected "the world," in reality it encouraged its followers to adjust to processes of industrialization and urbanization. In a similar vein, Paris asserts that black Pentecostalism emphasizes "the mediation of an economy of salvation and not the secular political economy" (1982: 147).

While Pentecostalism historically has a strong accommodationist orientation in its eschewal of social action efforts, in recent decades some Sanctified ministers and congregations (particularly ones affiliated with COGIC) have become involved in protest activities that challenge racist and even classist features of American society. COGIC provided the headquarters for the sanitation workers' strike, which was punctuated by the assassination of Dr. Martin Luther King, Jr., in Memphis in 1968. An increasing number of black Pentecostals have won political offices in city councils and state legislatures and have obtained minor political appointments in the executive branch of the federal government. From a theological perspective, Sanders asserts that Sanctified people can be best characterized as "liberal literalists ... because the exilic experience of being black in racist society forbids them to follow uncritically conservative, fundamentalist readings fostered by descendants who used the Bible to justify slavery" (1996: 140).

Hans A. Baer

See also Black Holiness Churches; Church of God; Church of God and Saints of Christ; Elder Solomon Michaux's Church of God; Mt. Sinai Holy Church; United House of Prayer for All People

Bibliography

Anderson, Robert Mapes. (1979) *Vision of the Disinherited: The Making of American Pentecostalism.* New York: Oxford University Press.

Blackwell, James Edward. (1949) "A Comparative Study of Five Negro 'Store-Front Churches' in Cleveland." M.A. thesis, Western Reserve University.

Drake, St. Clair, and Horace R. Cayton. (1945) *Black Metropolis.* New York: Harcourt, Brace.

DuPree, Sherry Sherrod. (1995) *African-American Holiness-Pentecostal Movement: An Annotated Bibliography.* New York: Garland Publishing Company.

Fauset, Arthur H. (1971) *Black Gods of the Metropolis.* Philadelphia: University of Pennsylvania Press.

Goldsmith, Peter D. (1989) *When I Rise Cryin' Holy: African-American Denominationalism on the Georgia Coast.* New York: AMS Press.

Hurston, Zora Neale. (1983) *The Sanctified Church.* Berkeley, CA: Turtle Island.

Lincoln, C. Eric and Lawrence H. Mamiya. (1990) *The Black Church in African American Experience.* Durham, NC: Duke University Press.

Melton, J. Gordon, ed. (1978) *The Encyclopedia of American Religions.* Wilmington, NC: McGrath.

Moore, Sidney Harrison. (1975) "Family and Social Networks in an Urban Black Storefront Church." Ph.D. dissertation, American University.

Paris, Arthur E. (1982) *Black Pentecostalism: Southern Religion in an Urban World.* Amherst: University of Massachusetts Press.

Robinson, Robert. (n.d.) *An Introduction to Church of God in Christ: History, Theology, and Structure.* Little Rock, AR: Robert Robinson.

Sanders, Cheryl Jeanne. (1996) *Saints in Exile: The Holiness-Pentecostal Experience in African American Religion and Culture.* New York: Oxford University Press.

Sernett, Milton C. (1997) *Bound for the Promised Land: African American Religion and the Great Migration.* Durham, NC: Duke University Press.

Shopshire, James Maynard. (1975) "A Socio-Historical Characterization of the Black Pentecostal Movement in America." Ph.D. dissertation, Northwestern University.

Synan, Vinson. (1971) *The Holiness-Pentecostal Movement in the United States.* Grand Rapids, MI: W.B. Eerdmans.

Tinny, James S. (1978) "A Theoretical and Historical Comparison of Black Political and Religious Movements." Ph.D. dissertation, Howard University.

Williams, Melvin. (1974) *Community in a Black Pentecostal Church: An Anthropological Study.* Pittsburgh: University of Pittsburgh Press.

Ifá

Ifá is considered the most elaborate of all African divination systems. It is practiced by *babaláwos* ("Fathers of the Secrets"—Ifá high priests), both in traditional Yoruba religion in Nigeria as well as in Yoruba-derived religious traditions throughout the African Diaspora. Ifá divination is consulted for all major life changes—including births, marriages, and deaths—and also for determining the destiny of the person in a ritual (Mano de Orúnmila for men, Kofa for women). The term Ifá is also used colloquially to identify a specific *orisha*, namely Orúnmila, who speaks through divination.

Ifá originated among the Yoruba in southwestern Nigeria and parts of the neighboring Republics of Benin and Togo. During the Atlantic slave trade, Yoruba diviners were forcefully displaced to many parts of the Americas, where they kept the practice alive. Since the 1960s, Cuban *babaláwos* in exile have introduced Ifá to the United States. Many African-Americans are now going directly to Nigeria for training, since Ifá is considered the cornerstone of Yoruba culture.

Today, Ifá as a divination system is very active in the continental United States, Puerto Rico, Cuba, Brazil, Venezuela, and Trinidad. Since the early 1990s, an increasing number of non-African Americans have become involved in the practice of Ifá. Due to modern communication technologies, cyber-transformations of this ancient African divination system are currently taking place. Consequently, readings and consultations are also offered on the Internet at OrishaNet, Ifascope, Ijo Orunmila:

Early twentieth century divining tray "Opon Ifá" with the face of Ésu, intercessor, guardian, and messenger, at the top of the board. PHOTO COURTESY OF MANFRED KREMSER FROM THE L. FROBENIUS COLLECTION.

Spreading Ifa to all of Olodumare's Children, and comparable Web sites.

The actual divination can be performed using a variety of methods. The most important involves the sixteen *ikin*, or palm nuts, sacred to Ifá. After a preliminary ritual offering and invocation, one of the palm nuts may be put aside to honor the fundamental unity behind all existence. The *ikin* are then passed from hand to hand by the diviner, until one or two nuts are left in one hand. This procedure is repeated, until two tetragrams, geomantic figures known as *Odù* (containers of Ifá's wisdom) have been generated. In contrast to African Geomancy, in Ifá divination only two tetragrams are cast and the interpretation is based on the pairing of the *Odù*. The sixteen major *Odù* (doubled) are considered to be divine personalities, or energies, in their own right. When they are mixed and recombined, they produce 256 possible *Odù*, each with hundreds of verses, with which the *babaláwo* may diagnose a client's situation or problem. However, the system can become even more complicated if the two tetragrams in one *Odù* are different, one speaks of a minor *Odù*. All possible combinations of minor *Odù* equal 240 plus the sixteen major *Odù* result in 256 *Odù*.

Because an extensive oral literature is associated with each *Odù*, they can be considered as sacred "books" belonging to a "library" housed in the collective memory of Ifá priests. Each of these *Odù*, major or minor, is the center of a circle of myths, stories, and ritual actions. During the inter-

pretative phase of the consultation, metaphors of the chosen story-road of the *Odù* become transparent indications of specific difficulties in the client's attitude and environment.

Among the sacred artifacts used in the divination process is the wooden divining tray, or *Opon Ifá*. It is usually carved with the face of Ésu, the messenger, guardian of the crossroads, and the trickster or "uncertainty principle" inherent in the workings of fate. Serpentine markings represent the play of fortune. The *Opon Ifá* is used to record the divination, the *Odù* signs being marked on the board with the fingers in a powder made of pulverized wood infested with the sacred ant, the termite.

The divining chain, or *Opele*, is believed to be a recent innovation in Ifá. It is said to "chatter" faster and is, therefore, in practice, the more common vehicle of Ifá divination. It consists of eight seed pods or cowries linked on a chain weighted at each end. The chain is thrown, and the tetragram is determined on the basis of whether the convex "male" or the concave "female" side of the pod is uppermost. Because the *Opele* is a relatively quick and easy means of casting, it is not considered as reliable as the more traditional palm nuts.

Whichever method is used, the tetragram is always interpreted as the reverse of the one actually cast. For example, if the *babaláwo* is left with a single palm nut in one hand, it is recorded as two dots on the divining tray. This is because of the mischievous Ésu, the trickster who delights in doing the reverse of what Ifá tells him to do.

The palm nuts are normally only used by an initiated *babaláwo*. Novices practice by casting pieces of coconut shell set with a cowry. High priestesses, Iyalorisha, use sixteen cowry shells. A cowry-shell divination system called Dílógún, with cultural and metaphysical links to Ifá, has become the main method of divination in Cuba and Brazil.

Manfred Kremser

See also African Geomancy; Brazil, African-Derived Religions in; Cuba, African-Derived Religions in; Caribbean, African-Derived Religions in; Yoruba

Bibliography

Abímbólá, Wándé. (1977) *Ifá Divination Poetry*. New York: NOK Publishers.

Bascom, William. (1969) *Ifá Divination: Communication Between Gods and Men in West Africa*. Bloomington: Indiana University Press.

———. (1980) *Sixteen Cowries: Yoruba Divination from Africa to the New World*. Bloomington: Indiana University Press.

Epega, Afolabi A., and Philip John Neimark. (1995) *The Sacred IFA Oracle*. New York: HarperCollins.

Gleason, Judith. (1973) *A Recitation of Ifa, Oracle of the Yoruba.* New York: Grossman.

Ifascope [Web site]. http://www.ifafoundation.org/ifascope. html.

Ijo Orunmila: Spreading Ifa to all of Olodumare's Children [Web site]. http://www.anet.net/~ifa/.

OrishaNet [Web site]. http://www.seanet.com/~efunmoyiwa/ ochanet.html.

Islam *See* Ahmadiyya Movement; Black Muslims; Islam, East Africa; Islam, West Africa; Maitatsine Sect; Moorish Science Temple; Mouride Brotherhood; Pilgrimage; Sudanese Brotherhoods

Islam in East Africa

Islam on the East Coast of Africa owes its origins to Arabian peninsular Islam and, thus, tends to have a more Arabic texture than elsewhere. Arabian Peninsular Islam is culturally, ritually, legally, and doctrinally diverse. This variety is reflected on the East Coast, where there have developed a number of different schools of Islamic law, both the Sunni and Shi'a traditions and a number of variations of the latter including a Ithnashari or Twelver Islam and Ismaili or Sevener Islam, to which the influential Ismaili Khoja tradition, which owes allegiance to the Aga Khan, and Daudi Bohoras belong. The Ahmadiyya movement, present in West Africa since the early years of the twentieth century, is also established in East Africa.

The main Arab cultures to influence the development of Islam on the East African coast initially were the Shirazi, the Omani, and the Arab families from Hadramaut. A distinctive Muslim culture derived from Arab, Persian, Swahili, and Bantu elements was to emerge later along the coast of Kenya, from where it spread to the interior. Further diversity was triggered by contact with Sudanese Islam, itself a product of Egyptian and Arabian influences.

As in West Africa, Islam's early development on the East Coast was slow. It spread more easily and evenly among the nomadic and semi-nomadic populations of Somalia and the Horn, generally, while further south it remained confined to many of the island populations, including those of Lamu, Pate, Pemba, Comoros, Mombasa, and Zanzibar, and to a few settlements on the coast itself. The best documented of the early coastal settlements is Kilwa, founded, according to scholarly sources, by Shirazi immigrants in the tenth century or in the twelfth century (the latter is probably more accurate). Early Islam was not confined exclusively to the coast. In the late ninth century Arab immigrants had established a Muslim state far inland, in Shoa, Ethiopia, which was later absorbed by Ifat, one of seven Muslim kingdoms that were all tributaries of Christian Ethiopia.

By the first half of the fourteenth century there was a well-developed Muslim society on parts of the coast of East Africa. Ibn Battuta, the chronicler and traveler, who visited Mogadishu in Somalia in 1331, describes a deeply Islamized court around the ruler (and/or *shaykh*) who could speak Arabic and who was assisted by a Muslim judge, or *qadi*, from Egypt. By this time East African students were traveling to study in the Islamic university of Al-Azhar in Egypt.

Trade was a crucially important vehicle in the spread of Islam to East Africa. Trading contacts had existed between East Africa and southern Arabia long before the beginnings of Islam in the early seventh century, and these continued on into the Islamic era. Such trade links provided the main route for Islam's entry to East Africa via the Indian Ocean before or during the eighth century. The principal commodities provided by East Africa were incense and aromatics from the northern coast of the Horn; and ivory, leopard skins, and slaves from further south along the coast; while gold from Zimbabwean mines was obtained from the port of Sofala in Mozambique. The ninth century trade in slaves from the Kenya-Tanzania sector of the East African coast suggests a Muslim presence there by this time, and by the mid-twelfth century the majority of the inhabitants of Zanzibar and of Kilwa were more than likely Muslims, while a century later Zayla and Mogadishu were also Muslim towns.

East African Islam soon began to fuse with local coastal customs and traditions and this, as in West Africa, was to create the context for reformers to engage in *jihad*, or holy war. The reformer Ahmad B.Ibrahim (1506–43), better known as Ahmad Gran, waged several *jihads* from the Muslim state of Adal, situated in the interior and further east, into the Christian kingdom of Ethiopia. These campaigns involved not only the purification of Islam but also the conversion of Christians. Paradoxically, the indirect consequence of the jihads was the disintegration of the largely Muslim region of Adal, the main area of relatively settled Islamic life in the interior, although Harar, to the south of Adal, remained, for Somalis, a center of Muslim orthodoxy. In the second half of the sixteenth century the Galla, originally from south central Ethiopia, began to expand and by the nineteenth century a number of ethnic groups further north, including the Wallo, were largely Muslim.

Islam made little further progress in the East African interior until the nineteenth century, although Arab Muslim culture had begun to interact with the indigenous Bantu cultures through marriage and concubinage to produce the new and distinctive culture known as Swahili, an Arabized-Bantu lingua franca spoken in Kenya, Tanzania, and in the eastern sector of the Democratic Republic of the Congo. The Muslim presence on the coast, on the other hand, was strengthened by the arrival of the Ottomans, who occupied Masawa in 1557 and came into conflict with the Portuguese, who had burnt down Zayla' in 1517.

East African Islam Turns Inland

The focus of East African Islam prior to the 1830s was the Muslim world beyond Africa. From then on, an increasing economic expansion inland began to effect a profound reorientation in outlook, attitude, and priorities among the Muslims of the coastal settlements. Muslim traders and agriculturists began to move into the interior—to Tabora, Ujiji, Nyangwe, Buganda, Lake Nyasa, Katanga, and elsewhere—and while not actively proselytizing they were, nonetheless, spreading Islamic culture by imitation.

There were also examples of large-scale conversion to Islam. The Yao people, situated midway between Lake Nyasa and the Indian Ocean and part of a trading network that included slave trading stretching from the Indian Ocean west to Katanga, were the only major ethnic group south of Somalia to turn Muslim prior to colonization in the late nineteenth century. The first Muslims arrived in Buganda,

Old Mosque, Mombassa, Kenya. PHOTO COURTESY OF PETER B. CLARKE.

part of present day Uganda, from Zanzibar in the mid nineteenth century during the reign of Kabaka Suna. Arab influence increased in the 1860s under Suna's successor Mutesa, not a full Muslim himself—he was not, for example, circumcised—and this was manifest in Buganda's adoption of the Islamic calendar, the observance of Ramadan, and the wearing of Arab dress, which had become fashionable.

Tension created by the uneasy relationship between the demands of Islam and local custom and culture was never far below the surface and erupted in violence as protests by strict, orthodox Muslim visitors to Buganda against Mutesa's leading of the Friday prayers led to a backlash in which a hundred Muslims were massacred. The situation was further complicated by the arrival of Christian missionaries in Buganda in 1877. Though in 1888 Christians and Muslims united to expel Mutesa's successor Mwanga, too much a pagan for either, unity soon turned to hostility as the Muslims expelled the Christians and installed Kalema as Kabaka. A civil war followed and by 1890 the Christians had gained the upper hand and were to receive the backing of the colonial regime. By the treaties of 1890 and 1892, Captain, later Lord, Lugard, acting in the name of the Imperial British East African Company, allocated Bugandan landed chieftainships along religious lines in favor of Christians; this was confirmed by the Ugandan Agreement of 1900. Christianity's dominance in Uganda was now institutionalized.

Not everywhere was turning Christian. Islam was taking hold in some of the rural areas, including the Vanga-Shimoni area, situated near the present border between Kenya and Tanzania. Rural converts from this region were tending increasingly to remain in their villages rather than move to the towns, thus consolidating the slow process of rural Islamization.

Though always crucially important in the spread of Islam in East Africa, trade was not the only factor in the Islamization of the hinterland. Agriculture and intermarriage also were often crucial. With the increase in the external demand for grain and agricultural produce, Muslims from the coast turned in greater numbers to commercial farming and began searching in the interior for suitable land and labor. The interest in ivory and slaves continued. But trade remained the main attraction of the interior: for example, Muslim traders built residences in Giriama and other villages of the Mombasa hinterland and gained a monopoly on the gum copal trade in the surrounding forests.

The conversion of the Segeju people of the Vanga-Shimoni area, one of the first indigenous African peoples of the hinterland to become Muslim, is a good example of conversion through agricultural enterprise. Intermarriage with the Vumba Swahili also played a part. Agricultural settlement by the Tangana Swahili from Pemba island and intermarriage, as well as trade, led in the 1850s, 1860s, and 1870s to the conversion of the rural-based Digo people who lived south of Mombasa. Agricultural expansion also brought the Muslims from Bagamoyo into contact with the Zaramo of the hinterland and laid the foundations for the latter's conversion to Islam. On Muslim plantations such as those of Malindi, which became a prosperous plantation town, Islam became the religion of the workers, mostly slaves.

Among the obstacles to Islamic penetration of the interior of East Africa was the rivalry and competition for control of trade and of those trade routes that had been established by the indigenous inhabitants. African chiefs refused right of passage to Muslim traders in direct competition, while others denied protection to anyone who was unwilling to pay tribute and conform to local custom in such matters as dress and food. Often Muslim settlements in the interior were small, and of the relatively few indigenous people who came into contact with Islam only a minority of these converted.

As on the coast, the presence of Islam in the interior often remained confined to the urban or commercial centers: Tabora is a good example. By the 1870s, Tabora, situated in Unyanyembe, an Unyamwezi chiefdom in the central interior of Tanganyika, present day Tanzania, had grown into a large Muslim settlement with a Muslim population of around 5,000, according to Stanley. Initially the Muslim influence of such towns was often very limited. Tabora, inhabited mainly by Arabs and Swahili, had virtually no impact at first on the Nyamwezi people living in the surrounding areas.

Urban Islam continued to expand on the coast as new settlements, including Dar es Salaam, founded by the Sultan of Zanzibar and now the capital of Tanzania, were established during the nineteenth century. Other urban centers with relatively large Muslim populations, such as Bagamoyo and Pangani, both at the terminus of the caravan trade and close to rich reserves of good quality gum copal, underwent considerable expansion in the nineteenth century.

Islam and Christianity and Colonialism

Christianity entered East Africa in the middle years of the nineteenth century and, unlike Islam, steered clear of the coastal towns, with the exceptions of Zanzibar, Bagamoyo, and Mombasa, where it pursued the strategy of converting freed slaves whose freedom—in many instances—had been purchased by the missions themselves. This conversion strategy was also used in West Africa early on, but in both situations it proved unsuccessful. The absence or weakness of

Islam in the interior was a major reason for the concentration of Christian missionary endeavor among the indigenous peoples there. Where Islam had but a weak presence in the interior, as was the case in Kisumu, in Kenya, Christian mission work had the effect of diminishing this still further and, in some cases, removing it entirely.

The colonial factor was to turn everything upside down. As the Germans advanced along the coast in the second half of the 1880s, Muslim hostility deepened and in 1888, led by Abushiri b.Salim al-Harthi, some resorted to armed resistance. The resistance was crushed and Abushiri hanged in 1889. Further west, in the Congo Free State, Arab power based on trade, including the supplying of ivory and labor, had been destroyed by 1894. Islam was also assisted by colonialism, particularly in Tanzania where it penetrated more widely and deeply into the interior of Tanzania during the era of the German colonial administration. After completing their conquest of the coastal areas, the Germans hired Swahilis as their civil servants or administrators (akida), whom they brought with them into the interior. They also used Muslim soldiers who, along with the administrators, played a crucial role in the wider dissemination of Islam in the interior of Tanzania.

The clearest sign of indirect German support for Islam was the decision of 1891 to make Tabora the administrative and military headquarters of German East Africa. Later, with the arrival of the railway in Tabora in 1912, the rural Nyamwezi, who had for more than 50 years resisted Islam, began to fall under its influence as they migrated to the town in ever-increasing numbers. Some were to return to their villages and with them a process of Islamization also began in the rural areas, many of which by independence in 1964 were largely Muslim.

While colonial rule undoubtedly contributed in the early stages to Islam's progress in former German East Africa—though not all Muslims supported or collaborated with colonial rule—the employment of Muslims by the colonial administration also worked against its advance: such a policy had the effect of alienating the indigenous peoples opposed to foreign domination. Strong opposition to colonial rule came in the form of the Maji-Maji (maji in Swahili means water) rebellion (1905–1907), organized by Kinjikitile, a Sufi, or Muslim mystic.

British colonialism and its system of indirect rule, which replaced the German system after World War I, tended to slow the progress of Islam in Tanzania and elsewhere in East Africa. Indirect rule at the level of local government tended to protect the power of the local chiefs from being undermined by wealthy Muslim merchants from the coast. Moreover, with the building of Christian schools and the growth of literacy in English and numeracy, Christianity

Members of a Sudanese Sufi Brotherhood in Atbara, Sudan, take a communal meal. Sufi Brotherhoods constitute one of the forms through which Islam is expressed in East Africa. PHOTO COURTESY OF STEPHEN HOWARD.

began to supply the local administrators, teachers, police, and army personnel. It became the religion of modernization and progress, while Islam was gradually sidelined, its role in administration and politics greatly reduced.

The decline in Islamic influence and power and the rise of Christianity was to provoke a reaction from reformist Muslims, many of them from the Asian subcontinent, after World War II. Such reformers, while visiting Tanzania and elsewhere in East Africa to encourage renewal, also took up political issues and backed the struggle for independence, playing a leading role in the foundation in 1954 of the independence party TANU (Tanganyikan African National Union). Several Muslims came to occupy leading positions in TANU while many others held minor positions in the party.

Islam in East Africa since Independence

Since independence, Muslims in Tanzania have continued to exercise considerable political influence. While the late president of the country Julius Nyerere, a Catholic, was the principal architect of *Ujamaa*, or Tanzania socialism, this policy bears many of the features of what is referred to as Islamic socialism—although it is opposed by a number of Muslim groups, the majority of them of Asian origin, and in particular by the East African Muslim Welfare Society (EAMWS) founded in Mombasa in 1945 by the then Aga Khan. EAMWS moved its headquarters to Dar es Salaam in 1961 where, until its dissolution by the government in 1968, it concentrated on educational and religious activities, putting much of its energy into the construction of schools and mosques. One of its aspirations in the field of education was realized in 1993 with the founding of an Islamic university in Zanzibar.

Education has been the main concern of Muslims in Tanzania, as in Nigeria, since independence. It was generally felt that Muslims were at a disadvantage in a society where Christian schools had so much influence and appeal. The government's decision, thus, to nationalize schools in 1969, was supported by most Muslims. In more recent times Muslims have welcomed the greater opportunities allowed for the establishment of private schools and have opened a number of educational institutions on the mainland, including Kunduchi High School in Dar es Salaam.

Once again, as in Nigeria and elsewhere in West Africa, post-independence Tanzania has witnessed controversy over *shari'a*, Islamic law. Prior to 1971, Muslims, like Christians and Hindus in Tanzania, followed their own marriage laws, while traditionalists followed customary law. Civil marriage existed for those who wished to contract a monogamous marriage. Proposed government reform of the marriage laws in 1969, in particular the proposals that a Muslim should seek the permission of his first wife if he wished to marry a second wife, and that men should be forbidden to punish their wives corporally, gave rise to intense debate in Muslim circles. Many Muslims opposed any changes in the law that conflicted with the *shari'a*, and in particular family law, which is central to Muslim law. Although the government's proposals were passed into law in 1971 with only minor amendments, the issue was by no means settled in Muslim opinion and reemerged in 1987 with proposals to reinstate Islamic courts.

Though Tanzanian Islam has undergone a process of radicalization since independence, and though tension between Muslims and Christians has been a feature of educational, economic, political, and religious life, there has been cooperation on a number of sensitive issues including on conversion strategy, where both sides have agreed to respect the wishes of parents where minors are concerned.

Muslims on the rest of the East African coast never fully united in a concerted effort to achieve their goals. Unlike the Muslims of Tanzania, those of Kenya were unprepared for independence in 1963. Immediately prior to self-rule

Mosque, Nairobi, Kenya. PHOTO COURTESY OF PETER B. CLARKE.

they were of two minds as to how to respond to the new order. Some, mostly the members of the Mwambao movement, lulled by the fiction of separate status under colonialism, aspired to political autonomy in a separate coastal state, while others contemplated some form of special arrangement with Zanzibar.

Witnessing the progressive marginalization of Islam reform movements, including the National Union of Kenyan Muslims (1975), the Ansaar Muslim Youth organization (1976) and the Muslim Education and Welfare Association (1986) began to focus on the modernization of Islamic education and the expansion of Islam through *dawa*, or missionary activity, using the Christian approach to evangelization as a model. This includes not only education but the provision of basic medical care in the form of dispensaries and social welfare centers attached to the mosques. It is difficult to assess how effective this strategy has been. Certainly the number of mosques in the Kenyan interior has greatly increased, presumably in response to greater demand, but there are no reliable statistics on the overall size of the country's Muslim population. What is evident is the steady increase in Muslims in what were traditionally non-Muslim areas such as the Meru country in Central Kenya. The estimates by some observers that

Muslims make up more than 5 percent of the total population is too low, while that of 30 percent is too high. Somewhere between 15 and 20 percent seems a more realistic assessment of their number.

Though recently there has been progress both in improving the quality of Muslim education and the development of a more cohesive and unified community, Kenya's Muslims continue to lag behind educationally and to display considerable diversity. While the number of mosques is growing in the interior and on the coast, many of them paid for with financial assistance from the wider Muslim world, there are many obstacles to further expansion, not the least of which is the intense competition from the evangelical Christian churches, the fastest growing religious bodies in the country. The position of Islam in Kenya in overall terms remains, if not fragile, then less than that of a strong and powerful minority. Looking at East Africa more generally, during its 1,000 year or more presence there, Islam has made itself an integral part of the cultural, religious, economic, and political life of the region.

Peter B. Clarke

See also Religion and Healing; Sudanese Brotherhoods

155

Bibliography

Clarke, Peter B. (1990) "Islam in Tropical Africa in the Twentieth Century." In *Islam,* edited by Peter Clarke. London: Routledge, pp. 180–192.

Hunwick, John. O. (1990) "Islam in Tropical Africa to c. 1900." In *Islam,* edited by Peter Clarke. London: Routledge, pp. 164–179.

Lohdi, Abdulaziz Y., and David Westerlund. (1999) "Tanzania." In *Islam Outside the Arab World,* edited by David Westerlund and Ingvar Svanberg. Richmond, Surrey: Curzon Press, pp. 97–110.

Nimtz, August H. (1980) *Islam and Politics in East Africa: The Sufi Order in Tanzania.* Minneapolis: University of Minnesota Press.

Pouwels, Randall L. (1987) *Horn and Crescent: Cultural Change and Traditional Islam on the East African Coast.* Cambridge: Cambridge University Press.

Rasmussen, Lissi. (1993) *Christian-Muslim Relations in Africa: The Cases of Northern Nigeria and Tanzania Compared.* London: British Academic Press.

Trimingham, James Spencer. (1964) *Islam in East Africa.* Oxford: Oxford University Press.

Westerlund, David. (1980) *Ujamaa na Dini: A Study of Some Aspects of Society and Religion in Tanzania.* Stockholm: Almvqist and Wiksell International.

Islam in West Africa

It was through principally commerce that Islam spread initially to West Africa and, indeed, to most of sub-Saharan Africa, and was adopted at first by the rulers and the higher social strata. During the eighth century Muslim merchants of both Arab and Berber origin, many of whom appear to have been members of the Ibadite branch of the purist and fundamentalist Islamic movement, the Kharijites, began to work their way across the trans-Saharan trade routes to the Ancient kingdoms of Ghana and Kanem Borno, situated within the most northern frontiers of what is today western Africa. One of the principal trade routes that ran from North Africa across the Sahara to West Africa was established in the 770s and ran from Tahert in southern Algeria south through the Saharan towns of Wargla and Tadmakka before terminating at Goa, situated south of Tombouctou (Timbuktu) and below the bend of the River Niger in the modern day West African republic of Mali, which is predominantly Muslim.

The Sanhaja of the western Sahara, whose descendants are at present waging a war of independence against Morocco from their base in Mauretania, also made an important contribution to the early spread of Islam in West Africa. It was they who guided and provided protection for those North African Muslim merchants who risked crossing the Sahara to trade in slaves, food products, and, later, gold in return for cloth, salt, and horses. Influenced by their contact with these Muslim merchants, the Sanhaja gradually turned to Islam, as did many of those West African merchants from Ancient Ghana and Kanem Borno who came into contact with the same Muslim merchants of North African origin.

Islam was not only brought to West Africa by Muslim merchants who belonged to a highly exclusivist, zealous, and doctrinally rigorous sect, it was also influenced from the outset by radical Muslim reform movements, the most thoroughgoing of which was the Almoravid movement, launched among the Sanhaja in the first half of the eleventh century by Abdullah b.Yasin. West African Islam, though extremely varied and often highly syncretistic, has never lost this radical streak. For their part, the Almoravids, who were later to conquer Spain, forged close links with a number of West African kingdoms, including the Ancient Kingdom of Ghana and the Senegalese kingdom of Takrur, and left a legacy of reform that was to shape the course of Islam in West Africa throughout the following centuries.

The Almoravid movement stamped out a number of unorthodox beliefs and practices among West African Muslims—in particular what it considered to be the heretical beliefs of the Ibadites spread by the previously mentioned North African Muslim traders—and extended the frontiers of Islam. Commerce and trade, however, rather than radical Islamic reform movements, remained the principal means of expansion from the tenth to the seventeenth century. Muslim traders, among them the Mande, also known in the literature as Dyula, Marka, Yarse, and Wangara, established themselves in towns along the trade routes that crisscrossed West Africa. There was little by way of an active strategy of proselytizing. On the contrary. These merchants, like those from North Africa, generally lived mostly separate lives from the rest of the people residing in their own quarter of the town. What they established were pockets of Islam.

It is important, however, to note their indirect contributions to disseminating the Islamic way of life and to raising its profile among the non-Muslims with whom they traded. Others, groups of Muslim clerics, among them the Jakhanke and Torodbe from the Senegambia, who, while also involved in trade, were more directly concerned with education and missionary activity. The efforts of militant Islamic reform movements and the rise of kingdoms and empires governed by Muslim rulers notwithstanding, the first five hundred years of Islam's development in West Africa was slow, and the influence of traditional religion on

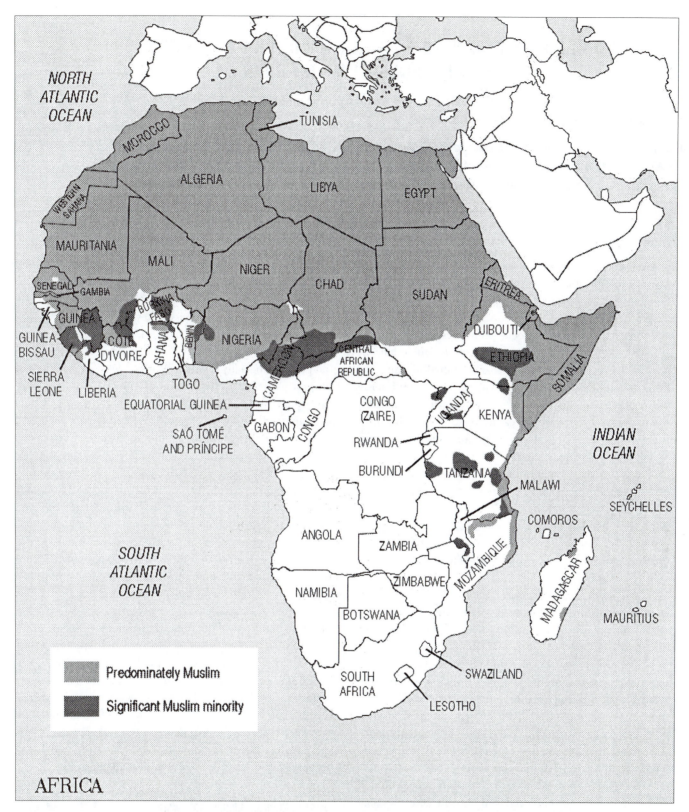

NORTH ATLANTIC OCEAN

MOROCCO
TUNISIA
ALGERIA
LIBYA
EGYPT
WESTERN SAHARA
MAURITANIA
MALI
NIGER
CHAD
SUDAN
ERITREA
SENEGAL
GAMBIA
GUINEA
BURKINA FASO
DJIBOUTI
GUINEA-BISSAU
CÔTE D'IVOIRE
GHANA
BENIN
NIGERIA
CENTRAL AFRICAN REPUBLIC
ETHIOPIA
SOMALIA
SIERRA LEONE
LIBERIA
TOGO
CAMEROON
EQUATORIAL GUINEA
CONGO (ZAIRE)
UGANDA
KENYA
SAÕ TOMÉ AND PRÍNCIPE
GABON
CONGO
RWANDA
BURUNDI
TANZANIA
INDIAN OCEAN
MALAWI
SEYCHELLES
COMOROS
ANGOLA
ZAMBIA
MOZAMBIQUE
MADAGASCAR
SOUTH ATLANTIC OCEAN
ZIMBABWE
NAMIBIA
MAURITIUS
BOTSWANA
SWAZILAND
SOUTH AFRICA
LESOTHO

Predominately Muslim

Significant Muslim minority

AFRICA

Distribution of Islam in Africa. Adapted from *Ethnic Groups Worldwide: A Ready Reference Handbook,* by David Levinson, published by the Oryx Press, 1998. Used by permission.

COMPETITION BETWEEN CHRISTIANS AND MUSLIMS IN NIGERIA

The priest said about his fellow Gungawa who converted:

Even those who became Muslims at the time of the Sarduana, before the British left, come to me, for I am stronger than the Muslims and they know it. Yes, there is Allah, but he is too far away to help men. He cannot be bothered with men. But my spirits will travel to me from even America in a twinkling of an eye and will help anyone I ask them to help.

Source: Salamone, Frank A. (1974) *Gods and Goods in Africa*. New Haven: Human Relations Area Files, Inc., p. 127.

government and society remained strong. Few, if any, Muslim rulers could ignore it, as the rulers of the kingdom Songhay, which covered much of the Niger region and a large area of the Sahel, were to discover in the late fifteenth and the early part of the sixteenth centuries.

With some notable exceptions, which included the Torodbe, many of whom were educationalists, and the Fulani pastoralists of northern Senegal who moved across the region in search of water and pasture for their cattle, the majority of those who became Muslims were from the ruling and merchant classes. The traveler Ibn Battuta (1304–1368) provides an account of the state of Islam in the capital of the Mali empire, which he visited during the reign of its most illustrious and best known ruler, Mansa Musa, who was emperor from 1307–1332. Ibn Battuta was impressed by the meticulous observance of the Friday prayers, the importance attached to the learning of the Qur'an by heart, and the fidelity with which *zakat*, or alms-giving, was practiced.

Ibn Battuta also pointed to what has been a feature of Islam in West Africa since its beginnings there: mixing. He noted the retention in Muslim circles of numerous traditional religious customs, several of which, including divination, prostration before a ruler, and the matrilineal system of inheritance, were considered to be contrary to Islam. Such mixing not only provided the pretext for the Almoravid movement but also for the many subsequent jihads, or holy wars, that came to influence the course and content of West African Islam from the seventeenth through to the nineteenth century and earn it a reputation for militancy.

Though its progress was slow and its scope limited, Islam, between the tenth and seventeenth centuries, had established a base in every major state in the western Sudan from Senegal in the west to the Upper Nile in the east. It had come to be perceived—as Christianity later came to be perceived—as a religion of progress: a modernizing faith that offered wider commercial, diplomatic, and military contacts; a useful and widely used trading and diplomatic language; and important skills such as numeracy and literacy. The latter were appreciated not only for the commercial advantages they gave but also for what were believed to be their magical properties. The instruments of writing in particular were invested with supernatural power, especially the ink and other coloring used in writing on paper, slate, papyrus, and skins. It became a widespread practice to wash such coloring off the writing surface containing the Qur'anic verses and drink it down as if it embodied the power of the divine words themselves.

Islam was also to bring a new form of spirituality and community in Sufism and the *turuq*, or Muslim brotherhoods, among them the Tijaniyya and Qadariyya Sufi orders, new forms of healing and counseling, new techniques and aids for understanding and fulfilling one's destiny and purpose in life, new methods of reform and renewal, new kinds of work, new attitudes to art, sculpture, leisure, and entertainment, and new laws governing commerce, education, inheritance, and personal and family matters. Renowned spiritual leaders and scholars emerged whose teachings and way of life drew to them large numbers of students. One of the most influential and prestigious was Shaykh Sidi al-Muhktar-al Kabir al-Kunti (1729–1812), who was born near Arawan to the north of Tombouctou. A pacifist, he is credited with having assisted the expansion of a deeply spiritual and intellectual form of Islam not only among his people the Kunta but over a vast area from Air in present day Niger to Senegal. Others, no less renowned, adopted, as we shall see, a more militant approach.

Islamic Reform: Jihads (Holy Wars)

Islam's growing influence in tropical Africa, leading to greater internationalization, did not spell the end for local cultures and religions, as we saw in the case of Mali above. There was much mixing, much backsliding, and at times

Islam went through a thorough process of domestication, all of which provided not only the reform-minded but also the oppressed, deprived, and marginalized with sound theological reasons for renewal through jihad, or holy war. An ideology of reform developed, as we have seen, with the Almoravid movement, while later scholars, notably Al-Maghili from Tlemcen in southern Algeria, would continually warn Muslim rulers in the late fifteenth and early decades of the sixteenth century of the duty incumbent on them to eradicate all forms of mixing.

In the 1490s al-Maghili (1425–1505) spent several years teaching Islam and counseling rulers in Hausaland (situated in present day northern Nigeria) and the central Sudanic kingdom of Songhay (present day Niger), and wrote a highly influential treatise, *The Crown of Religion Concerning the Obligation of Princes*, which laid out in detail how a good Muslim ruler should govern. This document was to have a deep impact on the subsequent history of Islam in West Africa, providing all future Muslim reformers with the essential elements of a manifesto for jihad. Al-Maghili's writings and teachings also made a significant contribution to the development of an Islamic millenarian tradition in West Africa, which was given expression by such leading Muslim scholars and reformers as Shaykh Uthman dan Fodio (1785–1882), who launched a full scale jihad in northern Nigeria in the late nineteenth century, the outcome of which was the establishment of the Sokoto Caliphate.

There was already a history of holy war in West Africa prior to the Sokoto jihad. Nasir al-Din, from southern Mauretania, possibly influenced by the radical tradition initiated by the Almoravids, attempted by militant means to bring about an Islamic revival in the Senegambia in the 1670s. As with other previous and later jihads, the motives for waging this one were mixed and included not only the reform of Islam but was also the ending of the domination of the southwestern Sahara by Arab overlords in the form of the Hassani aristocracy.

Though Nasir al-Din's jihad collapsed rather quickly, it inspired other Muslim scholars living in societies which, they felt, discriminated against them, and which were experiencing the tensions created by the trans-Saharan slave trade, a trade that created countless displaced persons and refugees. It also led to an increase in the importation of firearms and ammunition, and to growing competition from outsiders for control of trade and commerce. This was the context in which reformers took up arms with a view to creating Islamic states such as Bundu in the Senegambia and further afield in the late seventeenth century and later. Often, reforming Muslim clerics received most of their support from pastoralists such as those of the Fulani clan.

The most decisive holy war for the future of Islam in West Africa was the previously mentioned Sokoto jihad, which changed the cultural and religious landscape of the region during the first half of the nineteenth century. Launched for the reform of Islam, it was also greatly concerned with social reform. In formulating his reasons for the holy war in his manifesto, Shaykh Uthman dan Fodio relied heavily on the writings of Al-Maghili and, like him, condemned not only such idolatrous practices as the veneration of trees and rocks on which libations were poured and sacrifices performed, but also the evil practices of Muslim rulers.

The principal target of this jihad, one of the most complete in its consequences in the history of Islam, were the urban-based officials whom Shaykh Uthman accused of every kind of negligence, corruption, and oppression, including the imposition of unjust and illegal taxes, such as the *jangali*, or tax on cattle. Defense of the poor and oppressed by means of jihad should not be taken to imply that Shaykh Uthman dan Fodio was thinking along radical socialist lines. Such reforms, he reasoned, were inspired by religious principles for, he argued, to oppress a Muslim was to be guilty of infidelity on the grounds that a believer was duty-bound to befriend a believer. Shaykh Uthman was also, like William Wilberforce, an abolitionist, using his jihad to end the enslavement of the free Muslims of Hausaland by the Atlantic slave trade.

In the nineteenth century, jihads also developed an anti-colonial dimension, although this was not always their primary intention. Jihad was used as a means of resistance to colonial rule in the second half of the nineteenth century by the Senegalese Muslim leader Al-Hajj Umar Tall, although this was a war not only against French colonialism but also to extend the power and influence of its author over rival Muslim rulers in West Africa.

Islamic Millenarianism

The opinions of Al-Maghili and of the Egyptian Muslim jurist and one time Supreme Judge of the Muslim world, al-Suyuti (1445–1505), on the advent of the Mahdi, or God-guided one—who would come to destroy *dajjal*, or the anti-Christ, eradicate all evil, ensure the triumph of Islam, and inaugurate an era of universal peace and justice—were widely known in West Africa from the early years of the sixteenth century. They also taught that other similarly disturbing and unsettling doctrine of the *mujjadid*, or renewer. Al-Maghili, following a *hadith*, or tradition, recounted in the ninth century by Abu Dawud, wrote that God would send a scholar at the beginning of every century, a scholar who would regenerate Islam; while al-Suyuti listed those he believed would be the renewers for each century. The time predicted for the advent of the Mahdi was the thirteenth Muslim century (1785–1882).

By the nineteenth century these beliefs had become the most widely held beliefs in popular West African Islam. Prominent and respected Muslim leader Shaykh Uthman dan Fodio insisted in his preaching and teaching—prior to launching his jihad—that the nineteenth century would witness the advent of the Mahdi, who would ensure the triumph of Islam, and allowed others to speculate that he himself was in fact the Mahdi. The late nineteenth century also saw the rise of Muhammad al Madhi of the Sudan and the foundation of a Mahdist state. Like that in Sokoto, the Sudanese Mahdi's reform movement was also both rural-based and directed against the corrupt urban-based rural elites, mostly Turco-Egyptian officials.

Millenarianism continued on into the twentieth century as a powerfully persuasive belief, as *mahdis* from Nigeria, Niger, Senegal, and elsewhere in West Africa and beyond caused great alarm in colonial administrative circles as they proclaimed the end of evil and corrupt governments (colonial governments) and predicted the total triumph of Islam. In the early years of British Colonial rule in northern Nigeria, much to the great dismay and concern of government officials and producers, hundreds of thousands of ordinary people, mainly farmers, from northern Nigeria, were to abandon their fields and travel east to the Sudan, there to await the arrival of the God-guided one.

The Advance of Islam in the Twentieth Century

Generally, the pace of Islam's advance was to quicken markedly during the twentieth century with the coming of the railways; the construction of enlarged networks of roads; improved technology; more varied economies; increased trading outlets; and colonial regimes' dependency on, and, in northern Nigeria and elsewhere, development and expansion of existing Islamic legal, educational, administrative, and bureaucratic arrangements to non-Muslim—so-called pagan—areas. Some idea of the rapidity and extent of Islam's expansion in the urban areas of tropical Africa in the twentieth century can be had from a consideration of its development in towns such as Lagos, in Nigeria. By the 1960s Islam would be the majority religion of this town of several million inhabitants which, according to the traveler Richard Burton, had no than 700 Muslims when he visited the city in the mid 1860s.

The British colonial administration in northern Nigeria, as in the Sudan, undertook the reform and revitalization of the Islamic educational and legal system, which they regarded as essential to the maintenance of law and order, while Muslims further south in the towns of Ibadan and Lagos were faced with the newly implanted western, "Christian"-based legal and educational institutions. From the outset, schooling was a source of controversy; it led to the introduction of a school curriculum that provided for the teaching of Islamic subjects. Muslim societies such as the Nawair-ud-din and Ansar-ud-din societies, inspired by the progressive approach to education of the Ahmadiyya movement, attempted—with considerable success—to integrate the Western and Muslim education systems. Their main purposes were to remove the fundamental reason why Muslims rejected Western learning and to ensure that they were equipped with the skills to compete with Christians for work in the modern sector of the economy, then developing at a relatively rapid pace.

In more recent times a major concern of Islam in tropical Africa has been the conditions under which it cooperates with non-Muslims in government at the national and continental levels. In contemporary Nigeria, Muslims are no longer associated by the non-Muslim population of the country with Hausaland and Borno in the northern sector of the country. Since independence, in 1963, Muslims have created a nationwide network of Islamic institutions and have supported the territorial integrity of the federation when threatened by secessionist movements, the most serious of which, in recent times, came from the eastern region and resulted in the Biafran Civil War (1967–1970). On the other hand, in the middle years of the 1970s, as the country prepared to return to civilian rule after more than a decade of military government, Muslim members of the Constituent Assembly, appointed to approve the Constitution of the Second Republic, became embroiled in a serious controversy over the establishment of a Supreme Sharia (Islamic) Court at the federal level. This controversy threatened the unity of the nation, as Christians believed that Muslims were making excessive demands.

It is on such occasions as constitution-making that the strength, influence, and national objectives of Muslims are spelt out to the rest of the population. In Nigeria, where there is a delicate balance between Muslims and Christians, the response by the latter has been characterized mostly by fear and uncertainty, and occasionally by defiance and a determination to resist demands for a more Islamic ethos in government. There has also been resistance by non-Muslims to the call from radical Muslim elements since independence for successive administrations to participate in Muslim organizations such as the Arab League and the Islamic Conference Organization (ICO) and to withdraw from Western political organizations.

ETHNIC VARIATION IN MUSLIM NIGERIA

A striking example of the fact that the quiet behavior of the Hausa is not pan-Islamic was given in Yauri by the Chief-of-Police, a Kanuri. He was open in his likes and dislikes and would rush into situations that most Hausa would enter obliquely. He was himself very clear in pointing to this difference between himself and Hausa, Nupe, and Fulani Muslims. "To be a Muslim you do not have to be secretive like these people here. Look at us Kanuri. We were Muslims when the Fulani were still pagan savages. Yet they are haughty. You know, Sulieman, you cannot trust these Fulani and others like them. They brood on their injuries and then, unlike true men, they kill you secretly years later. We Kanuri are also a proud people, but we respect all men while bowing to no man. People know exactly where we stand on any issue. We are good Muslims, and that means being open and truthful. We have been Muslims since the time of Muhammad and practice the religion correctly, more correctly than the Fulani."

Source: Salamone, Frank A. (1974) *Gods and Goods in Africa.* New Haven: Human Relations Area Files, Inc., p. 151–152.

Also perplexing and felt to be danger to religious liberty by many Nigerians was the Muslim call for the removal from the preamble to the constitution of the term "secular state" on the grounds that it promoted secularism, atheism, and immorality. No less disturbing were the Muslim demands for the banning of alcohol and the ending of what was described as the "Christian structure" of the working week, suggesting that Friday rather than Sunday be the day of rest, at least in predominantly Muslim areas. What is new and threatening to the non-Muslim is the vigorous way in which Islam is asserting itself at the national level, beyond its more traditional objectives in Muslim-dominated areas such as Hausaland.

The nature and extent of Islam's influence on West African thought and culture has been a subject of much discussion in recent times. Its impact on traditional cosmology in particular has received much attention. Some have suggested that Islam has added little new to the central pillar of West African cosmology, which has always featured a Supreme Being. Rather, like Christianity, Islam simply acted as a catalyst by precipitating a greater concern for beliefs in a Supreme Being, which were already integral, if largely latent, in the cosmologies of West Africa. While much further research is needed before any definitive conclusion can be reached on this complex issue, it is worth noting that Islam in West Africa has often been considered, even by pioneering Christian evangelists such as the West Indian Edward Wilmot Blyden and the Nigerian Mojolo Agbebi, to be more African in the sense of displaying greater empathy for African culture and values, and more disposed to promote African leadership and initiative than mission Christianity.

The contemporary situation is complex and manifests a variety of tendencies from reformist to accommodationist to modernizing. There is also evidence of a secularizing trend, particularly among young urban-based Muslims. This latter development notwithstanding, Islam in West Africa, if judged both in terms of the force or the seriousness with which it is adhered to and its scope or the range of contexts in which it is considered relevant, remains an integral part of the mainstream of religious and cultural life of the region; and it is very difficult to predict how its situation might change in the future.

Peter B. Clarke

See also Maitatsine Sect; Religion and Healing

Bibliography

Clarke, Peter B. (1982) *West Africa and Islam.* London: Edward Arnold.

——. (1988) "Islamic Reform in Contemporary Nigeria: Methods and Aims." *Third World Quarterly* 10, 2 (April): 519–539.

Cruise O'Brien, Donal, and Christian Coulon, eds. (1989) *Charisma and Brotherhood in African Islam.* Oxford: Oxford University Press.

Hiskett, Mervyn. (1984) *The Development of Islam in West Africa.* London and New York: Longman.

Hopkins, John. F, and Nehemiah Levtzion. (1981) *Corpus of Early Arabic Sources for West African History.* Cambridge: Cambridge University Press.

Westerlund, David, and Ingvar Svanberg, eds. (1999) *Islam Outside the Arab World.* Richmond, Surrey: Curzon Press, especially: Part One: Africa, pp. 37–111.

Jamaa

Jamaa, "family-group" in Swahili, is the name of a religious movement in the Democratic Republic of the Congo (formerly Zaire). It appeared first in 1953 in a workers' settlement near the town of Kolwezi in the mining region of Katanga. At the height of its growth it may have counted as many as 200,000 followers. Among the striking features of the Jamaa is the fact that it goes back to an "encounter" (as they say) between a group of Africans and a European, the Belgian Franciscan missionary Placide Tempels. Research covering a period between the mid-sixties and the mid-eighties (no work seems to have been conducted more recently) has shown that "baba Placide" continued to guide the Jamaa long after he had left the Congo. His work and biography are crucial to an understanding of this movement. Conversely, in order to appreciate some of the ideas for which Tempels became world-famous, one should know how they were put into practice by the Jamaa.

Father Placide Tempels

Placide (Placied Frans) Tempels (1906–1976) was born in Berlaar (Province of Antwerp, Belgium). He grew up in surroundings that were deeply rooted in Flemish popular Catholicism. In 1924 he joined the Franciscan order and studied philosophy and theology. After being ordained, he was sent as a missionary to the Congo in 1933. He began his work in several up-country posts in Katanga among groups speaking Kiluba. Like many of his fellow missionaries, he was interested in the language and culture of the Luba and began to publish articles in journals and newspapers. As he learned more about the people he had been sent to convert, he tells us, he was more and more plagued by misgivings and doubts regarding the role his Christian religion was assigned to play in colonizing Africans. Tempels became interested, and participated, in local political debates about the sense and future of Belgium's *oeuvre civilisatrice*, its "civilizing mission." The public debate was occasioned by social unrest, popular uprisings, and mutinies in the colonial army that intensified toward the end of World War II. He experienced a deep personal crisis and became convinced that neither faith in his vocation nor his ethnographic studies helped him to overcome the barriers against mutual comprehension that separated missionaries from African Christians and, generally, colonizers from colonized. As he put it: "We eat (that is, destroy) each other metaphysically." Only an encounter on the level of deepest beliefs and ideas had a chance to bridge the gulf between Europeans and Africans.

In 1944, he began to write a series of essays in Dutch in which he explored what he called the "ontology," the basic principles of a worldview shared by the Luba and, he believed, by Africans in general. These writings first appeared as a small book in French with the title *Philosophie Bantoue* (Bantu philosophy, 1945, Elisabethville, Belgian Congo). Tempels described, always in contrast to what he referred to as European rationalism, a vitalist worldview, a philosophy of being centered around the concept of life-force (*force vitale*; *vigeur vitale* in the revised translation). His translator, A. Rubbens, a liberal colonial magistrate and later sympathizer of Patrice Lumumba, had seen to it that the book drew the attention of colonial circles in the Congo. Representatives of the colonial regime, administrators, company managers, and the higher clergy, decided that *Philosophie Bantoue* contained subversive ideas likely to encourage Africans in their claims for equal rights and, eventually, independence. As a result of their efforts (which included denunciation at the Vatican), Tempels, who had returned on his first leave to Belgium in 1946, was kept there in virtual exile until 1949.

Unforeseen was the book's spectacular success among African intellectuals (foremost among them Leopold Sedar-Senghor), among anthropologists, and later also philosophers. Many praised *Philosophie Bantoue* as a liberating manifesto, others denounced it as ethnographically questionable and philosophically weak (and the controversy continues unabated to this day).

Tempels enjoyed the praise and was not discouraged by the criticism and repressive measures against him; in Belgium he experienced a profound personal crisis, which left him even more convinced that he needed to work out practical applications of his ideas for the preaching of Christianity. He did this in an essay he called *Catéchèse Bantoue*, a text that contains the first signs of his transformation from missionary to charismatic leader. He also found some highly-placed supporters in the clergy, among them the later Cardinal J. Cardijn, the founder of the Belgian Catholic young workers' movement, and the later Cardinal L. J. Suenens, who in the seventies became a leader of the worldwide Catholic charismatic renewal.

In 1949, Tempels was allowed to return to the Congo. For a short time he resumed his work among the Luba up-country until he was assigned to a parish in a miners' town near Kolwezi. With a small group of workers and their wives he began to exchange and discuss what he called "our deepest human aspirations." Together they developed a vocabulary, a body of teaching, and a rudimentary ritual. By 1953, the group became known as Jamaa and soon other groups were started by the highly mobile founding

FROM A JAMAA *MAFUNDISHO* (INSTRUCTION IN THE DOCTRINE) RECORDED IN LUBUMBASHI IN JUNE 1966. TRANSLATED FROM KATANGA SWAHILI.

After the meal, we all moved to a group of chairs arranged around a low table in the adjoining living room. Microphone and tape recorder were ready and, for a second, everyone's attention seemed to be caught by these intrusive pieces of technology. Someone made a remark I did not catch, the group broke out in laughter, and then Baba Nkondo pronounced the Jamaa greeting, *yambo yetu*. We responded, and in his calm yet resonant voice, he asked us:

Fathers and mothers, what are we called? Let us state this first. What are we called here? Animals? We are bantu, people. Because we are people we must understand our *umuntu*, what it means to be human. *Muntu*, human being. Let us take just the name *muntu*. We can ask: What is man according to our teaching, the teaching in the holy Jamaa of God?

We answer that *muntu* is *mawazo*, thoughts. Yes, *muntu* is *mawazo*. What kind of *mawazo* is man? We will have to ask further and we answer: "Man is thoughts of searching." That is the point where man and God are different, because the thoughts of God are not thoughts of searching, as is the case with us people. But the thoughts of men are thoughts of searching.

The reason is this: When God has a desire in his thoughts, when he thinks and has a wish, it comes true immediately, just as he desires. Because he has all the power. But we people, when we think our thoughts the way God has given them to us, when we wish, we must search. This is how we get what is necessary and good. Without searching we are incapable of getting anything. This is where man and God are different. Clearly, God has all the power, all the might. And we people know we must search. It is necessary to search so that we get what is necessary and good.

Now let us get to the *mawazo* we spoke about: the fact that man is *mawazo* . . . From where did man get these *mawazo*? Every human being got these *mawazo* from God himself. He got them from God. And how did we get these *mawazo* from God? Each in a different way or all in the same way? We people, all of us, received these *mawazo* in one and the same way, without regard for tribe or color—no matter whether one is big and fat or short or tall, whether he is old or young, a man or a child. We got these thoughts from God in one and the same way.

And these thoughts we received from God, how many were there? All the thoughts we received from God were the three great *mawazo*. Name the three thoughts, *baba*. (Baba X answers:) We were given the thoughts of *ubaba*, fatherhood, of *umwana*, childhood, and of the Holy Spirit, love.

Source: Johannes Fabiano

members (who worked in the mines and on railway construction). He described and explained his movement to other Catholics in *Notre Rencontre* (Our encounter), in 1962. In the same year he left the Congo for reasons of health, never to return. The Jamaa had made him again a controversial figure and he spent the last fourteen years of his life under a gag rule from the church (that did not include his private correspondence with members of the Jamaa and others), confined to the Franciscan convent at Hasselt, near his birthplace.

Jamaa Movement

Three traits were characteristic for the Jamaa as a movement: (a) It was conceived as renewal and as an intensification of Christian life within the Catholic mission church. (b) As a rule, only married couples could be members (exceptions being made for widowed Catholics, priests, and a few nuns and female social workers). (c) The movement had no formal organization, no membership lists, no statutes, and none of the visible signs (special clothing, meeting places, and symbolic paraphernalia) typical of many African religious movements. Other distinctive characteristics of the Jamaa were that it lacked an ethnic basis (such as the *Legio Mariae* among the Luo in East Africa). It had no explicit social or political program and actively refrained from practices often associated with religious enthusiasm (such as trances, faith-healing, exorcism, and speaking in tongues observed, for instance, among the Bapostolo, the Apostles of John Maranke, a movement that came to the Congo from the former Rhodesia at the same time and roughly to the same place as the Jamaa). Less obvious was the fact that Tempels' teachings contained elements linking the Jamaa to global developments in Christianity. Especially his doctrine of encounter was connected to worldwide encounter movements inside and outside the church. In some ways, for instance, it anticipated the Catholic *cursillo* movement, a predecessor of the charismatic renewal that began to spread from the United States in the early seventies. Observers of neo-Pentecostalism have pointed to African and African-American roots and the Jamaa may well have been among them.

Jamaa followers, though they were exemplary Catholics who participated actively in the ritual of the church, identified with the Christian-humanist teachings of baba Placide. Candidates and members regularly followed instructions (*mafundisho*) in the common Swahili language of Katanga, later also in the languages of other regions of the Congo and neighboring countries. As a core concept, the "life-force" of *Philosophie Bantoue* had given way to *umuntu*, best translated as "what it means and takes to be human." *Umuntu* expressed itself in the "three great thoughts," *uzima* (life, conceived as wholeness), *uzazi* (fecundity), and *mapendo* (mutual love). In a manner reminiscent of Gnostic ideas, the movement as a whole and each of the member-couples were to realize these *mawazo* (thoughts, another central concept), in spirit and body. This was to be accomplished through gradual initiation into the *njia tatu* (three ways), each grade being preceded by instruction, *mashaurio* (counseling), and more intensive *mapatano* (encounter) between initiating and initiated couples and the "first Jamaa on earth," Bwana Yesu (Lord Jesus) and Bikira Maria (Virgin Mary).

Induction into the Jamaa was conceived as giving birth (*kuzaa*), and members always used *baba* (father) and *mama* (mother) when addressing each other. Local groups (*nkundi*) were constituted as lines of spiritual descent, (*kizazi*) generally led by the most "fertile" couples, i.e., by those who had initiated the largest number of couples. They derived their charismatic authority (in Max Weber's sociological sense of the term) from their ability to articu-

late the doctrine, give counsel, and often also as interpreters of dreams that had an important role in the spiritual ascent through the grades of initiation. Groups met for regular, usually weekly, instruction. Contacts between local groups were maintained by correspondence, visits, and an annual Easter meeting.

This simplified and somewhat idealized picture of the Jamaa is valid for the period of its emergence and consolidation in the sixties. But it is also true that, almost from the beginning, its structure contained the seeds of tension and serious conflict. Pursuit of fecundity led to competition between leaders for "children." Some of them tried to increase their role by multiplying stages of initiation. Tempels had left vague the boundaries between deep encounters in spirit and body, making Jamaa members subject to accusations of sexual practices and excesses. Early on, a heterodox branch (called *katete*) emerged, most probably as a result of leaders of the officially banned Congolese Kitawala, or Watchtower, movement using the Jamaa as a cover.

Jamaa teaching contained tenets and tendencies that were judged to deviate from Catholic theology. Members of the mostly expatriate clergy could join the movement, some even became leaders, but always on the terms of the movement. Most missionaries soon perceived the Jamaa as a threat to their authority. Preceded by local measures of control and suppression, this led, at the beginning of the seventies, to an open confrontation between the movement and the mission church. In 1973, a conference of bishops was convened in Lubumbashi and decided to resolve the problem by formulating an acceptable version of Jamaa teaching and forcing Jamaa members publicly to confess and abjure their "errors." Those who refused were excommunicated, denied participation in ritual (including communion, marriages, and funerals), and, in some instances, persecuted in the civil sphere.

This could have been the end of one of the most impressive attempts to Africanize Christianity. More recent field research (in 1985 and 1986, most of it as yet unpublished) has shown, however, that the movement has survived through diversification. Next to a Jamaa recognized by the church (Jamaa Takatifu Katolika), some of Tempels' oldest followers joined an independent church recognized by the civil authorities (Jamaa Takatifu mu Afrika). There were also an unknown number of groups who, though they refused to participate in the rite of abjuration, continued to practice Catholicism (tolerated by liberal members of the clergy). Finally, there were many individual followers of Tempels who were not organized in groups. Nevertheless, it appears that the Jamaa has been losing ground (and members) to the "prayer groups" of the charismatic renewal. Its basis among workers is being eroded by the decline of the mining industry and the rise of a new middle class; and its exclusive focus on adults and failure to establish a youth branch may further contribute to its demise.

Short references to the Jamaa may be found in most writing on African religious movements. De Craemer (1977) and Fabian (1971) remain the only book-length studies of the movement. Theoretical and methodological significance of research on the Jamaa are discussed in several essays in Fabian (1991). For developments up to the mid-eighties see Fabian (1994). Tempels' main work was translated into English (1959), a critical edition and new translation into French, with many references, was published by Smet (1979); his important transitional writings (n.d. [1948], n.d. [1962]) are not easily accessible. An introduction to the philosophical debate about Tempels, especially among African philosophers (such as A. K. Appiah and V. Y. Mudimbe), may be found in Masolo (1994). Texts representing Jamaa teaching (in Swahili and English) may be found in the sources cited above and on a web site devoted to language and popular culture in Africa (http:/www.pscw.uva.nl/lpca).

Johannes Fabian

Bibliography

De Craemer, Willy. (1977) *The Jamaa and the Church. A Bantu Catholic Movement in Zaire*. Oxford: Clarendon.

Fabian, Johannes. (1971) *Jamaa: A Charismatic Movement in Katanga*. Evanston, IL: Northwestern University Press.

——. (1991) *Time and the Work of Anthropology: Critical Essays 1971–1991*. London: Harwood Academic Publishers.

——. (1994) "Jamaa: A Charismatic Movement Revisited." In *Religion in Africa: Experience and Expression*, edited by Thomas D. Blakely, Walter E. A. van Beek, and Dennis L. Thomson. London: James Currey/Portsmouth, NH: Heinemann, 257–274.

Masolo, D. A. (1994) *African Philosophy in Search of Identity*. Bloomington: Indiana University Press.

Tempels, Placide. (1945) *La philosophie bantoue*. Elisabethville: Lovania.

——. (1959) *Bantu Philosophy*, translated by Colin King. Paris: Présence Africaine.

——. (1979) *Philosophie Bantu*, introduction and revised translation by A. J. Smet. Kinshasa: Faculté de Théologie Catholique.

——. (n.d. [1948]). *Catéchèse bantoue*. Bruges: Abbaye de Saint-André.

——. (n.d. [1962]). *Notre Rencontre*. Léopoldville: Centre d'Études Pastorales.

Jamaica, African-Derived Religions in

The practice of African-derived religions in Jamaica can be traced officially to the eighteenth century. However, legal codes against African cultural practices suggest that African-derived religions were operative in Jamaica well before the eighteenth century. In 1740 and 1774 Charles Leslie and Edward Long published respective histories of Jamaica. Both authors noted the presence of African religious practices in the island. The texts make references to the practices of Obeah and Myal within enslaved African communities. Missionary documents and tourist journals also describe these traditions up through the twentieth century.

Obeah and Myal in the Early Colonial Period

Obeah is a body of mystical practices, popularly known as magic. Although it is also widely known that clients seek the assistance of Obeah practitioners to counter illnesses and misfortunes, Caribbeans have come to associate it most often with evil magic or sorcery,. During the twentieth century, scholars have written about Obeah, not only in Jamaica, but also in the wider British and French Caribbean. Many Caribbean writers and artists also incorporate Obeah as a considerable theme or subtext in their works. For example, Derek Walcott, the Saint Lucian poet, introduces Obeah as a healing element in his epic poem *Omeros* (1990).

Fewer scholars have written about Myal, which, unlike Obeah, appears to be a distinct eighteenth-century Jamaican tradition of which most Jamaicans today are unaware. A number of documents offer similar descriptions of Myalists gatherings:

> Myalists meet in large companies, generally at night, and dance in rings, till they become excited and frenzied, singing Myal songs accusing others of being Myal-men, and pretending to discover enchantments which have been made by them.... These Myalmen also pretend to catch the shadow or spirit of persons who may have lost their lives by lightning or accident. When the spirit is caught, it is put into a small coffin and buried, by which the ghost, as the superstitious of this country would call it, is laid to rest. The Myalmen are resorted to in a great variety of cases, when disease is obstinate, or the nature of it not understood; if a man's wife has forsaken him; if he thinks there is danger of losing the favour of his employers; if he supposes his horse has been bewitched; in all such cases the Myalmen are consulted. (Blyth 1852, 172–175).

Myal is a dynamic religious expression that has been integrated into other African-derived traditions over time. Today, it is known as the highest form of ancestral spirit possession in the Kuminia religion, an African-derived religion with Central African (Bakongo) roots.

During the eighteenth and nineteenth centuries, Obeah and Myal were described as antagonistic, antithetical practices, the former representing "bad magic" and the latter representing "good magic." Today most scholarly treatments of Obeah and Myal continue to promote the moral dichotomy between the two traditions. In reality, the main distinction between Obeah and Myal, as practiced during the eighteenth and nineteenth centuries, was structural, not moral. Obeahists are solo practitioners who access mystical power to effect changes in the lives of their clients. Genuine Obeahists are skilled herbalists and diviners, or "readers," who utilize elements such as water or leaves and other instruments to assess the nature of their clients' problems and to prescribe the antidote to those problems, whether physical, emotional, or social. During a divination session, an experienced Obeahist will be able to reveal personal details about the client's past experiences, especially those experiences that have any bearing upon the client's problem. Apart from the rituals enacted to access power for divination, healing, and various other uses, Obeah does not involve a community that convenes to worship a divinity or perform rituals at regular intervals. The practice, which is also known in popular culture as "science," is passed down from one practitioner to another, at times within familial circles.

Myal religion of the eighteenth century consisted of groups of ecstatic worshipers featuring a charismatic religious leader possessing gifts of prophecy and healing. Like Obeahists, Myal leaders were skilled in the uses of herbs and were reputed to resuscitate dead persons by using specially prepared herbal concoctions. They were consistently described as wearing long white robes with sashes around their waists, and were constantly observed gathering for worship around silk cotton trees. One of the Myal legacies bequeathed to contemporary Jamaicans is a variety of taboos concerning the silk cotton tree, which is still regarded in popular culture as having tremendous religious significance.

As an African-derived religion, Myal stood in jeopardy before the law, colonial administrators, and the missionary establishment. Thus Myal underwent several phases of transition during the nineteenth and twentieth centuries, which led to the eventual disintegration of its more traditional eighteenth century practice. In the 1830s, just fourteen years after the London Baptist missionaries arrived in Jamaica with the specific aim of evangelizing the African population, Myalists either adopted aspects of the Baptist tradition or joined with other Africans who had been converted and launched their own practice of the faith. They became known as the "Native Baptists" and were actually associated with the earliest Baptist communities in Jamaica, established by George Liele. Liele, an African American missionary, had been enslaved in Georgia and won his freedom during the American Revolutionary War. He subsequently traveled to Jamaica as an evangelist in 1783. Liele's presence and ministry in Jamaica was controversial and provoked harsh responses, including beatings and jail sentences, from local authorities. The London Baptists traveled to Jamaica in response to Liele's request for assistance in his mission of carrying the gospel to enslaved Africans. Once in Jamaica, the London Baptists were sure to distinguish their mission and theology from those of the Native Baptists, which reflected a Myal spirituality and understanding of the world. Native Baptists continued to embrace communotheism (multiple divinities), ancestral veneration, and spirit possession as essential religious practices. Adherents were also expected to give personal and convincing testimonies about their prophetic dreams and visions before being fully initiated into the religion.

In 1760, Obeah was officially outlawed after it was discovered that the leader of the most brutal uprising (Tacky's Rebellion) to that date was a well-respected Obeahist who relied upon mystical powers to safeguard his plot and ensure victory over death. Obeah oath-rituals requiring conspirators to swear allegiance to antislavery military campaigns were commonplace among rebel Africans across the Caribbean. Obeah was repeatedly detected as an instrument of African resistance to slavery in the form of aggressive combat, sabotage, poison, and guerilla warfare tactics. Although it is safe to conclude that Myalists were active in resistance campaigns against slavery, there is no conclusive extant evidence noting specific Myal participation in slave revolts before the Native Baptist War of 1831–32. Properly viewed, the Native Baptist War was a Myal uprising, which eventually contributed to the official emancipation of Africans from slavery in 1834 and from indentured servitude in 1838 in the British West Indies. The Native Baptists, led by an inspiring charismatic preacher, Samuel Sharpe, recruited converts from the London Baptist congregations to participate in a slave labor strike planned for the day after Christmas, 1831. The strike quickly unfolded into a full-scale revolt involving 20,000 enslaved Africans who took control of the plantations for two weeks. Moreover, Sharpe's incorporation of the Obeah oath-ritual among his top officials points to the significant sociopolitical function of African-derived religions as an internally derived force for social transformation indigenous to the traditions of enslaved Africans.

Critical Developments in the Post-Emancipation Era (1841–1865)

In 1842, Myalists in the parishes of Trelawny and Saint James launched what has been described as an "anti-Obeah" campaign, claiming to literally unearth Obeah paraphernalia buried on various estates for the malicious purpose of causing economic decline and premature death. This post-emancipation protest reinforced the view that Obeah and Myal were innately antagonistic traditions and polarized along moral lines. Obeah had become a synonym for the illicit practice of sorcery and was identified as the source of a series of calamities, including unexpected deaths. Today, Obeah still suggests sordid antisocial behavior and is feared or considered suspect in the minds of most Jamaicans. In truth, Obeah is neutral mystical power that can be accessed for positive or negative purposes, depending on the context, moral intentions, and means utilized to achieve one's goals. The client and the Obeah specialist are morally responsible for how they access and utilize the neutral power that is called Obeah.

The period between 1841 and 1865 was a crucial time of cross-fertilization among practitioners of African-derived religion in Jamaica. During this time, the practice of Myal was modified and reinvented within novel religious expressions. Myal, in its Native Baptist form, had been suppressed after emancipation and was transformed into Revival/Zion religion after an extensive Christian revival in 1860–61. Some scholars note that another African-derived religion, Pocomania or Poco, also emerged after 1860. Pocomania is described as similar to Revival/Zion but more conspicuously African in ritual practices and spiritual beliefs. There is evidence to suggest that since the 1860s Pocomania groups have represented the strongest revitalization of Myal religion within Revival/Zionist circles, and that the term is externally derived and used primarily by Christian outsiders to derogate its Myal-based religious identity and practices.

Both Revival/Zionists and groups known as Pocomania venerate a community of supernatural beings, including the Christian Trinity, African ancestors, and supernatural beings, which they call "Spirit Messengers." Revival priests are also proficient diviners with expert knowledge of herbal medicine. In the past, many noted Revival healers were women who held their worship services and divination/healing sessions in primitive outdoor structures called "booths." Today Revival/Zion churches often feature male leaders and are constructed with special "reading" rooms adjacent to the sanctuaries where clients seek regular consultations.

Finally, between 1841 and 1865 some 8,000 West and Central Africans were transported to Jamaica after being res-

cued by the British navy from Spanish slave ships en route to Cuba. Many of the Central Africans were resettled in eastern Jamaica to work as indentured laborers on plantations abandoned by the formerly enslaved Creole (black) population after emancipation. They established themselves as worshippers of a Bakongo (Central African) supreme divinity, Nzambi, with entrenched customs, including birth, marriage, and burial rituals; an African language; and a religious practice called Kuminia involving drumming, dancing, ancestral possession trance (the highest form being Myal possession), animal sacrifice, divination, and herbalism. These traditions are still honored by Kuminia communities in eastern Jamaica today. However, specific marriage and birth rituals documented by Zora Neale Hurston during the 1930s have not been observed by scholars in recent times. One of the most striking characteristics of the Kuminia religion is the high status accorded to women. Kuminia

Altar used for divination practices and consultation from a reading room in a Revival Zion Church. Holy Mt. Zion Baptist Church, Yallas, St. Thomas, Jamaica, 1996. PHOTO COURTESY OF DIANNE M. STEWART.

UNWANTED GUESTS SHOULD BE SPAT ON

Mr. Marcus Garvey at Meeting of U.N.I.A. Convention Again Attacks "Ginger"

Meeting in connection with the Convention being held at Edelweiss Park continued this week. One day was given up to a discussion of Music. In previous meetings, Mr. Marcus Garvey said at Monday night's Court, they had covered the range of Art and Literature. What they decided during the Convention at Edelweiss, he told his audience, would be seriously considered by the Governments of the world. The only reason why the U.N.I.A. and the convention meetings were not regarded with greater seriousness by the people of Jamaica was that they were ignorant; they were two hundred years behind the times.

Mr. Garvey gave his audience to understand that the Negro was on the threshold of a new attitude towards other peoples. He spoke at length on the theme of the Negro's relations with other races and adjured his hearers not to thrust themselves into company where their presence might be unwanted and where they had not been invited. He stressed so hard and so long the point that to go without an express invitation to any place was a horrible offence; the TIMES reporter, who has solicited an invitation to the proceedings, became squeamish.

Mr. Garvey could not resist an attack on "Ginger" [an English columnist for the *Jamaica Times*] and launched out in much the same style he had adopted on a previous occasion. He challenged "Ginger" to appear at Edelweiss Park, saying that he hid behind a *nom de plume* and was afraid to show himself.

In his opening speech, Mr. Garvey also referred to the Ras Tafari cult, speaking of them with contempt.

Several of Mr Garvey's poems, which had been, he said, most admirably set to music by Mr. B. de C. Reid, were rendered by a choir.

Source: *Jamaica Times*, 25 August 1934.

"queens" or "mothers" wield tremendous power as central leaders and as the primary teachers of Kuminia history, rituals, and esoteric traditions.

African Roots of African-Derived Religions in Jamaica

Scholars offer varying opinions concerning the African ethnocultural roots of African-derived religions in Jamaica. Leonard Barrett posits an Akan origin for Obeah and links it etymologically to the Twi term *obiafo*, or *bayi*, which means "witch." Orlando Patterson, however, argues more convincingly that Obeah best corresponds with the Akan concept of Obeye, which conveys the idea of neutral mystical or medicinal power. While the etymological origin of the term Obeah situates it within the cultural context of the Asante and Fante Twi-speaking populations of Ghana, it is probable that Obeah has evolved to include beliefs and practices from other West African ethnic groups.

Scholars are even less certain about the African ethnocultural roots of Myal. Eighteenth-century Myalists might have combined beliefs and practices from various West African societies. Patterson suggests a Dahomean (modern-day Republic of Benin) origin, given similarities between Dahomean Mawu-Lisa and Jamaican Myal death and resurrection rituals. Although Monica Schuler posits a Central African origin, there is no conclusive evidence to support her thesis. It is especially tempting to conclude that Myal has strong African roots in the Bakongo cultures of Central Africa because it is currently known in Jamaica as the most potent form of possession trance in the Kuminia religion. It is likely that Myal was adopted by Kuminia practitioners after having been exposed to Myal practices from neighboring Native Baptist and Revivalist communities during the late nineteenth century.

Conclusion

Although credible statistics documenting the number of participants are lacking, African-derived religions have been practiced in Jamaica at least since the eighteenth century and remain a vital aspect of Jamaican culture today. Despite legal censorship and social condemnation, the oldest

African-derived traditions, Obeah and Myal, are still upheld, by solo practitioners in the case of the former, and by the descendants of Myal practitioners who today constitute the Revival/Zion and Kuminia religions. Although in most cases Revival/Zionists identify as Christians, their spirituality and religious practices are Myal in content and African-derived in character. Myal spirit possession is also found amongst Kuminia worshippers who pay homage to the divine creator, Nzambi, and a host of African ancestors in their rituals. Obeah, Revival/Zion, and Kuminia adherents continue to generate African-based practices, including drumming and dance, invocations and songs, divination, ancestral, and divine visitations in the form of possession trance, sacrifice, and offerings. Specialists usually organize ceremonies or hold divination sessions for the purpose of healing. They also practice their religious traditions with the aim of restoring harmony within creation, and honoring ancestors. During the period of African enslavement in Jamaica, slave revolts were organized and executed within the structure of African-derived religions. Although Africans began converting to the Christian religion in massive numbers during the late nineteenth century, African-derived religions continue to have tremendous influence over the cultural disposition, aesthetic proclivities, and spiritual outlook of Jamaican people.

Dianne M. Stewart

See also Kongo Religion; Kumina; Revival

Bibliography

Alleyne, Mervyn. (1988) *Roots of Jamaican Culture*. London: Pluto Press.

Banbury, R. Thomas. (1895) *Jamaica Superstitions, or the Obeah Book*. Kingston: de Souza.

Barrett, Leonard. (1974) *Soul-Force: African Heritage in Afro-American Religion*. New York: Anchor.

Bastide, Roger. (1971) *African Civilisations in the New World*. New York: Harper & Row.

Blyth, George. (1851) *Reminiscences of Missionary Life, With Suggestions to Churches and Missionaries*. Edinburgh: William Oliphant & Sons.

Brathwaite, Edward. (1978) "Kumina—The Spirit of Africa Survival." *Jamaica Journal* 42: 44–63.

———. (1981) *Folk Culture of the Slaves in Jamaica*. London: New Beacon Books.

Chevannes, Barry. (1993) "Some Notes on African Religious Survivals in the Caribbean." *Caribbean Journal of Religious Studies* 42/5 (September).

Cooper, Thomas. (1824) *Facts Illustrative of the Condition of the Negro Slaves in Jamaica*. London: J. Hatchard and Son.

Guano, Emanuela. (1994) "Revival Zion: An Afro-Christian Religion in Jamaica." *Anthropos* 89: 519–542.

Hogg, Donald. (1960) "The Convince Cult in Jamaica." *Yale University Publications in Anthology* 58: 3–24.

Hurston, Zora Neale. (1983) *Tell My Horse*. Berkeley, CA: Turtle Island for the Netzahualcoyotl Historical Society.

Kerr, Madeline. (1952) *Personality and Conflict in Jamaica*. Liverpool: University Press.

Lewis, Gordon. (1983) *Main Currents in Caribbean Thought: The Historical Evolution of Caribbean Society in its Ideological Aspects, 1492–1900*. Baltimore, MD: John Hopkins University Press.

Mbiti, John S. (1969) *African Religions and Philosophy*. London: Heinemann.

Mintz, Sidney W. (1960) *Papers in Caribbean Anthropology*. New Haven: Yale University Publications in Anthropology 57.

———. (1989) *Caribbean Transformations*. New York: Columbia University Press.

Murphy, Joseph. (1994) *Working the Spirit: Ceremonies of the African Diaspora*. Boston: Beacon Press.

Patterson, Orlando. (1967) *The Sociology of Slavery*. London: MacGibbon and Kee.

Seaga, Edward. (1969) "Revival Cults in Jamaica." *Jamaica Journal*. 3, 2: 1–12.

Schuler, Monica. (1979) "Myalism and the African Tradition." In *Africa and the Caribbean: The Legacies of a Link*, edited by Margaret Crahan and Franklin Knight. Baltimore, MD: John Hopkins University Press.

Simpson, George. (1978) *Black Religions in the New World*. New York: Columbia University Press.

Warner Lewis, Maureen. (1977) "The Nkuyu: Spirit Messengers of the Kumina." Pamphlet 3. Kingston: Savacou Publications.

Williams, Joseph J. (1932) *Voodoos and Obeahs: Phases of West India Witchcraft*. New York: Dial Press.

Kardecism (Kardecismo)

Spiritism is based on the belief that the spirits of the dead can get in touch with the living, mainly through mediums in trance, who are in contact with their control-spirits, working as intermediaries. It is also believed that the spirits may call the attention of the living through parapsychological phenomena, such as noises or by moving objects. In Europe, spiritism was further influenced by mesmerism. Kardecism is a more sophisticated and scientific version of spiritism that was invented by Hyppolyte Leon Denizard

THE SPIRITS' BOOK

containing
The Principles of Spiritist Doctrine
on
**The Immortality of the soul, nature of spirits
and their relations with men; the moral law;
the present life, the future life, and the destiny of the human race.
ACCORDING TO THE TEACHINGS OF SPIRITS OF HIGH DEGREE,
TRANSMITTED THROUGH VARIOUS MEDIUMS,
COLLECTED AND SET IN ORDER
BY
ALLAN KARDEC
Translated from the Hundred and Twentieth Thousand
by
ANNA BLACKWELL
BOOK SECOND: THE SPIRIT-WORLD, OR WORLD OF SPIRITS
Chapter 1
Spirits
Origin and Nature of Spirits**

76. What definition can be given of spirits?

"Spirits may be defined as the intelligent beings of the creation. They constitute the population of the universe, in contradistinction to the forms of the material world."

Note: The word spirit is here employed to designate the individuality of extra-corporeal beings, and not the universal intelligent element.

77. Are spirits beings distinct from the Deity, or are they only emanations from or portions of the Deity, and called, for that reason, "sons" or "children" of God?

"Spirits are the work of God, just as a machine is a work of the mechanician who made it; the machine is the man's work, but it is not the man. You know that when a man has made a fine or useful thing, he calls it his 'child' - his 'creation.' It is thus with us in relation to God. We are His children in this sense, because we are His work."

78. Have spirits had a beginning, or have they existed, like God, from all eternity?

"If spirits had not had a beginning, they would be equal with God; whereas they are His creation, and subject to His will. That God has existed from all eternity is incontestable; but as to when and how He created us, we know nothing. You may say that we have had no beginning in this sense, that, God, being eternal, He must have incessantly created. But as to when and how each of us made, this, I repeat, is known to no one. It is the great mystery."

Source: Allen Kardec's *"The Spirits' Book"* Homepage in Brazil. www.lsi.usp.br

Rivail, who called himself Allan Kardec, and lived between 1804 and 1867 in France. An intellectual who was originally influenced by the teachings of Pestalozzi, Kardec's best-known work, *Le Livre des Esprits,* was published in Paris in 1857. It is said that the teachings set forth in this volume were revelations of highly developed spirits, who dictated their wisdom to Kardec. The teachings of Kardec combined Christianity with spiritism, and concerned the relationship between the material world and the immaterial world. Kardec was also greatly influenced by the Hindu concepts of karma, reincarnation, and nirvana.

The most important concepts of Kardecism/spiritism are found in many different cultures and during different eras. In Europe, his ideas only found short-lived interest, but Kardecism soon spread to Latin America, where many intellectuals organized mediumistic séances around the turn of the century. Spiritistic organizations proliferated in Puerto Rico, Cuba, and especially in Brazil, where Kardecism became an important root of Umbanda and influenced other Afro-American religions. In Latin America, the original Kardecistic beliefs practices that were popular with intellectuals were mixed with other beliefs and practices, mainly of African origin, which made Kardesim more diverse and more widely appealing. In the late twentieth century, the forgotten teachings of Kardec were revived in Europe and new centers were opened in Germany and in former communist countries, where people were searching desperately for a new expression of their religious sentiments.

Beliefs and Practices

The teachings of Kardec embrace some fundamental concepts. The *soul* is considered to be an immaterial power or fluid that animates the human body. When a person dies, the soul separates from the body and becomes a *spirit* that may roam around for some time before it reincarnates in another human being, either in this or in other worlds. According to the law of *karma,* the spirit is purified in each existence by obeying universal moral laws, until, after many reincarnations, it turns into an *evolved spirit of light.* Kardec distinguished between three categories of spirits: the impure roaming spirits of the lowest level, the spirits that incarnate as souls in human beings and who are still struggling for improvement in each existence, and the pure and perfect higher spirits. These spirits manifest themselves in the mediums in order to teach their wisdom to mankind. The spirits, between incarnations, may inhabit other planets and return to earth from time to time. For Kardec, God is the immaterial, almighty creator of the universe and also of the spirits.

The Ten Commandments are accepted by the spiritists and the reading of the Bible is mandatory.

Kardec tried to interpret the Bible in spiritistic terms. He codified his theology, inspired by revelations he received through mediums. His teachings were more philosophical than religious. A summary of his principal beliefs follows:

1.) The communication of human beings with disincarnated spirits is possible.

2.) The spirit of human beings experiences multiple reincarnations after death.

3.) Karma, or the "law of cause and effect," guides the soul/spirit on its way to perfection.

4.) Humans cannot escape from the consequences of their actions.

5.) There are many worlds that are populated by beings; each world is a step on the path of progress. The earth is considered to be the third step on this path. The spirits of light are found in the seventh dimension, similar to nirvana.

6.) There is neither a distinction between the supernatural and the natural realm, nor between science and religion.

7.) The progress of an individual on the path to perfection depends entirely on himself and his acts, as he has a free will.

8.) God does not live close to humans, but He does exist.

9.) The spirits of light of the seventh dimension are closer to the human beings than God, they help us with love and with *dharma* on the path of perfection.

10.) The disincarnated spirits of those who died recently help the living to gain merits in order to improve their future existence.

11.) Jesus Christ was the spiritual entity of greatest power who ever lived on earth.

12.) The mediums in trance communicate with the spirits and receive messages that they transfer to those who attend the sessions.

True Kardecism lacks ceremonies and rituals as the spiritists do not venerate the spirits but only communicate with them. Dances or sacrifices are unknown. Usually the mediums are paid by those who organized the sessions.

Kardecism in Latin America

In the 1990s, Kardecism in various forms continued to be widely practiced in Brazil, where it had a long history of practice and many meeting places. Currently, the Federation of Kardecists has affiliated groups in all larger cities. Groups of only five to ten meet regularly in private homes. Meetings in temples may attract a few hundred. During the reunions the mediums sit around a table. The organizer starts the meeting with a Christian prayer while soft music is played in the background. Then the spirits of light are invoked to come to the session. Sometimes the organizer reads a short passage from the Bible. The lights are turned down. There is silence and the participants concentrate their minds on the spiritual world. One by one, the mediums fall in trance and receive their spirit-guides. They hyperventilate, close their eyes, and knock at the table, but remain calm while in trance. Then the spirit identifies himself and communicates messages or offers advice through the mouth of the medium. The mediums—through their spirit-guides—get in touch with the spirits of people who recently died or with other spirits of importance, in order to converse with them. The relatives of the recently departed are interested to obtain certain information from them. Other questions may be answered. Not all the spirits that manifest themselves in the mediums are of the highest dimension, they may come from lower *astral* dimensions. During the sessions, arms and legs are not supposed to be crossed. In some centers the mediums are dressed in white. They are not allowed to have sex the day and night before the reunion takes place. Sometimes candles are lit on the table and incense is burned. In special sessions, emphasis is placed on teaching, as the spirits of light offer advice concerning doctrines and cosmic theories. Many adherents take part in courses offered by the Kardecist Federation. In Brazil, most Kardecists belong to the urban middle class and the sessions are considered an exiting pastime.

In Brazil in the 1930s, Kardecism gradually incorporated beliefs in Amerindian nature spirits (*caboclos*), African divinities (*orishas*), and spirits of the departed slaves (*pretos velhos*), and later the spirits of famous medical doctors or other important personalities were incorporated too. Thus the Umbanda was born in Rio de Janeiro with roots in African religions and Kardecism. The Kardecist sessions turned into consulting sessions, whereby the spirits communicate with the clients through the mediums. The faithful flock to the temples, because they are sick or in despair. Sacrifices, drum beats, dances and other rituals are performed in order to please the spirits or to thank them for their attention. Kardecism turned into a utilitarian religion that expanded rapidly. Kardecist elements are found in most Afro-Brazilian religions, where not only African divinities are venerated but also disincarnated spirits are summoned to help the needed, where mediums play an important role in healing rituals, and where concepts such as reincarnation and karma are widely known.

A similar development occurred in Venezuela more or less at the same time, when Amerindian spirits and—after the Cuban Revolution—the Yoruba divinities were incorporated in what became the Cult of Maria Lionza. The spirits are invoked to cure diseases and to give advice to the faithful. Puerto Rican spiritism developed in a similar way, but was later absorbed into the Santeria. Kardecistic practices were absorbed into healing rituals by Mexican shamans already around at the turn of the century. In Argentina, Trincado, a disciple of Kardec, taught that the mediums are able to summon the soul/spirit of a living person in order to receive advice.

Angelina Pollak-Eltz

See also Brazil, African Derived Religions in; Cuba, African Derived Religions in; Venezuelan Cult of Maria Lionza; Mexico, African Derived Religions in; Puerto Rico, African Derived Religions in; Santeria; Yoruba

Bibliography

Hess, David J. (1991) *Spirits and Scientists: Ideology, Spiritism, and Brazilian Culture.* University Park: Pennsylvania State University Press.

Kardec, Allan. (1942 [1898]) *Spirits Book.* Kessinger Publishing Company.

———. (1994) *Book on Mediums; Or, Guide for Mediums and Invocators.* Samuel Weiser. Translated by Emma A. Wood.

Kongo Religion

Kongo religion is the body of traditional beliefs and ceremonies that bind the Kongo communities of Central Africa together and sustain them spiritually in daily life. It is the only Central African indigenous religion with an extensive written record, going back five centuries, and also the most studied for the ways in which spiritual beliefs determine the social organization and rhythm of life of the people.

Today the Kongolese are a sharply defined ethnic group numbering about five million and occupying the west coast of Africa from Angola on the south, through the Democratic Republic of Congo into the Republic of Congo on the north, and extending inland about two hundred miles. Their common language is Kikongo, one of the many Bantu languages of Central and Southern Africa. The Portuguese, visiting them in the 1490s, found a highly organized kingdom that could rival most European states in cultural sophistication, luxury, and political effectiveness. The slave trade and European conquest broke up the political unity of the Kongo Kingdom and introduced Christianity, though these developments did not appreciably change indigenous beliefs or diminish the sense of being a coherent nation whose identity rests on its own spiritual traditions.

Beliefs and Practices

In the Kongo belief system, the key mediators between God and human beings are the ancestors. These are the people who were the most unselfish and devoted to the good of their communities and who therefore have advanced and grown powerful in the spirit world until they have become beings of light without bodily form. Only special individuals can become ancestors, and then only after several generations have passed. Prayers are not offered to the ancestors. Worship is reserved for God alone, known as Nzambi Mpungu Tulendo, who is both unknowable and the source of life and unlimited power. Except in rare emergencies, God is never approached directly but rather through the ancestors, to whom people bring their daily problems and needs. Ancestors, as the link between God and humanity, provide everything needed for the well-being of the community. When misfortune occurs, offerings are made to the ancestors, who are believed to be angry or dissatisfied.

The Kongo community is therefore not limited to the living, but also includes the invisible world with the dead and the yet-to-be-born. Since the unborn are not yet here, the land must be protected for their future use. It cannot be sold or its fertility destroyed. It belongs to the ancestors; the living are only caretakers. Death is viewed as only a transition from one level of life to another. Life itself is continuous and unending, and the invisible world is an integral part of the visible one and very much like it. Death brings a change of awareness, not a change of place. Those who have lived in harmony with their ancestors are rewarded by going to Mpemba, the land of the ancestors, where they will carry on essentially the same life they had here except without pain and suffering. Those who have not lived according to their ancestors' expectations, who have done harm to others, will have no place in the spirit world but are forced to roam the earth restlessly. Pineapples are planted on their graves to discourage them from bothering the living.

In the Kongo universe, good and evil are not suprahuman forces competing for control of human souls. Good and bad are found in all people as part of human nature. No one is perfect or expected to strive for perfection. Good is that which contributes to the peaceful unity and well-being of the group; evil is anything that disrupts or destroys. The problem of human society is to negotiate a balance between these forces in the community rather than to work toward a more perfect social order. Life is seen as timeless, not evolving or progressing toward a final goal or a catastrophic end. The idea of the millennium is foreign to Kongo thinking.

The way in which the Kongo community works for such balance is to recognize certain individuals as imbued with special skills and knowledge in dealing with the invisible powers. Since all power comes from the spirit world, it can be channeled for good or evil according to human intentions. On the positive side are those people known as *nganga*, who are healers, diviners, or teachers, along with their apprentices. They devote themselves to furthering the well-being of the community. On the negative side are the harmful *ndoki*, whose objective is to use spirit power to sicken or kill others and disrupt the harmony of the group. Chiefs and heads of families serve as representatives of the ancestors. It is their responsibility to see that the people are fed, that everyone shares and does his or her part, and that conflicts and problems are resolved wisely and peaceably.

Simon Bockie

Bibliography

Andersson, Efraim. (1958) *Messianic Popular Movements in the Lower Congo*. Uppsala: Almqvist & Wiksells boktr. (agent).

——. (1991) *Art and Healing of the Bakongo, Commented by Themselves: Minkisi from the Laman Collection / Kikongo Texts Translated and Edited by Wyatt MacGaffey*. Stockholm: Folkens Museum-Etnografiska; distributed in North America, Bloomington: Indiana University Press.

Batsikama ba Mampuya ma Ndwala, Raphael. (1999) *Ancient Royaume du Congo et les BaKongo*. Paris: L'Harmattan.

Bockie, Simon. (1993) Death and the Invisible Powers: The World of Kongo Belief. Bloomington: Indiana University Press.

Janzen, John M. (1974) *An Anthology of Kongo Religion: Primary Texts from Lower Zaire*, by John M. Janzen and Wyatt MacGaffey. Lawrence: University of Kansas.

——. (1978) *The Quest for Therapy in Lower Zaire*, by John M. Janzen with the collaboration of William Arkinstall, foreword by Charles Lesli

——. (1982) *Lemba, 1650–1930: A Drum of Affliction in Africa and the New World. New York.* Garland. e. Berkeley: University of California Press.

Laman, Karl Edward. (1953–62) *The Kongo*. Studia ethnologica Upsaliensia, 4, 8, 12. Uppsala: [Stockholm, Victor Pettersons Bokindustri Aktiebolag].

MacGaffey, Wyatt. (1970) *Custom and Government in the Lower Congo*. Berkeley: University of California Press.

——. (1983) Modern Kongo Prophets: Religion in a Plural Society. Bloomington: Indiana University Press.

——. (1986) Religion and Society in Central Africa: The BaKongo of Lower Zaire. Chicago: University of Chicago Press.

Simbandumwe, Samuel S. (1992) *A Socio-Religious and Political Analysis of the Judeo-Christian Concept of*

Prophetism and Modern Bakongo and Zulu African Prophet Movements. Lewiston, NY: E. Mellen Press.

Thornton, John Kelly. (1998) *Africa and Africans in the Making of the Atlantic world, 1400–1800,* 2d ed. Cambridge and New York: Cambridge University Press.

——. (1998) *The Kongolese Saint Anthony: Dona Beatriz Kimpa Vita and the Antonian Movement, 1684–1706.* Cambridge and New York : Cambridge University Press.

Wing, Joseph van. (1959) *Etudes Bakongo; sociologie, religion et magie,* 2d ed. Bruges: Desclee, De Brouwer.

Kumina (Cuminia)

Kumina (Cuminia) is a form of ancestor worship found primarily in the extreme eastern region of Jamaica. It is generally considered to be a member of the family of various African-derived religions in the New World, e.g., Vodun, Santeria, and Candomblé, although the beliefs and practices of Kumina do not reflect the degree of African influence found in these other religions. The relative lack of African traits in Kumina can perhaps be attributed to the fact that, unlike, Vodun, Santeria, and so forth, its origins in Jamaica are not traced back to the early slave period, a period during which the misplaced Africans worked diligently to retain and perpetuate their native beliefs. Rather, it is generally agreed that the appearance of Kumina in Jamaica is almost certainly the result of the post-emancipation influx of Bantu-speaking peoples of central Africa. The significance of ancestor worship in central Africa was subsequently transferred to Jamaica, a factor that would explain the relative lack of traditional African gods in Kumina and the emphasis on the spirits of family ancestors.

Since the practice of Kumina is family-based, the homes of all families that affiliate themselves with this practice in Jamaica serve as the ceremonial compounds. There are, however, no large formal shrines or ritual compounds devoted to Kumina; rather, a room or a special area in or around a individual's home will be set aside for worship. Each family will associate their lineage with one of seven or eight different African "tribes" or "nations." The knowledge and lore required to direct Kumina rituals is extensive, and a particular family will generally bring in certain individuals to direct the ceremonies. A male will act as a "master of ceremonies," coordinating and directing all the various activities and the individuals who will carry them out. Also important are the "Queen," her assistants, and the "Mother," all of whom serve as mediums, the drummers and other musicians, and other individuals who tend to the more mundane tasks of worship.

Imogene Kennedy ("Miss Queenie") posing with her Kumina drums at her home in St. Catherine, Jamaica, 1996. The most popular and most recognized Kumina leader in Jamaica history, Miss Queenie died in 1998. PHOTO COURTESY OF DIANNE M. STEWART.

The largest and, perhaps, the most important Kumina ritual is the "memorial" dance that a particular family will hold in honor of their ancestors. Often, Kumina practitioners will travel long distances to attend these affairs. These memorials generally begin at dusk on Friday and will last approximately twenty-four hours. Other smaller family-based ceremonies are held as well, to celebrate a marriage or the birth of a child.

Three basic classes, or levels, of spirits are recognized, the sky gods, the earthbound gods, and family ancestors. The sky gods are thought to be the most powerful of all the spirits and will occasionally possess worshipers at the various ceremonies. Only one (Shango) is clearly an African god, although many of the other terms used for sky gods could possibly be associated with the various African tribal or nation affiliations presently recognized by Kumina practitioners. The earthbound gods, some of whom have Biblical names, are also considered to be powerful, although their domain is strictly terrestrial; many spirits in this category are thought to possess worshipers as well. Finally, there are the ancestors, sometimes referred to as "ancestral zombies." These spirits are former practitioners of Kumina in one capacity or another, and, while most are ancestors that are known to their family, some actually attain a status that transcends familial affiliation and become known by many Kumina practitioners. These latter spirits are often considered to be as powerful as many of the earthbound gods.

Perhaps the most salient and significant aspect of Kumina worship is possession. As in many other religions of this type, drumming and singing (some of which is done in utterances that have been identified as Kikongo, a central African language) act as a catalyst for possession. Again, as in many possessions of this type, the onset of possession is characterized by a lack of motor control and the gradual loss of consciousness. Later, once the spirit "settles" on the worshiper, the individual begins to dance and generally comport themselves in a manner characteristic to the particular spirit that is the possessing agent. These possessions can last anywhere from a few minutes to a few hours. Many Kumina rituals are closed with the sacrifice of an animal, generally a goat. In addition to goats' blood, rum and chicken blood are also used in ceremonies involving libations to feed the ancestors, a ritual that is sometimes carried out at the graves of the departed souls.

James Houk

See also Caribbean, African-Derived Religions in; Jamaica, African-Derived Religion in

Bibliography

Barrett, Leonard. (1976) *The Sun and the Drum: African Roots in Jamaican Folk Tradition.* London: Heinemann Books.

Crahan, M. E., and F. W. Knight, eds. (1979) *Africa and the Caribbean: The Legacies of a Link.* Baltimore: Johns Hopkins University Press.

Hogg, Donald W. (1964) "Jamaican Religions: A Study in Variations." Ph.D. dissertation: Yale University.

Simpson, George E. (1978) *Black Religions in the New World.* New York: Columbia University Press.

——. (1980) *Religious Cults of the Caribbean: Trinidad, Jamaica and Haiti.* Rio Piedras, Puerto Rico: Institute of Caribbean Studies.

Warner Lewis, Maureen. (1977) *The Nkuyu: Spirit Messengers of the Kumina.* Kingston, Jamaica: Savacou Publications.

Lumpa Church

One of the early prophetic movements in Africa was established by Alice Lenshina Mulenga (c. 1919–1978) in Zambia. She founded the Lumpa Church after recovering from a near-death experience. In a message reminiscent of all prophetic movements, she claimed a divine visitation and a spiritual injunction to preach the good news and build a church on "a rock." She studied in the same primary school at the Presbyterian Mission of Lubwa as Kenneth Kaunda, who later became the president of Zambia and whose father had been the mission's first African minister. "Lumpa" in Bemba language means the highest, the supreme, or to be superior. The Lumpa Church started within the Presbyterian Church of Zambia, but within two years, Lenshina's strong anti-witchcraft massage and robust millennial impulse led to a radical break with Presbyterianism.

Lenshina promised spiritual wholeness and a new life to those who abandoned traditional magic and witchcraft to follow her. She vehemently condemned polygynous marriage, sorcery, and divination. Like Isaiah Shembe (c. 1870–1935) in South Africa, she was an inspired composer of hymns and songs. In most of her hymns, she defined her role as analogous to that of John the Baptist. She believed she was sent back to the world to prepare the Second Coming of Christ. Her followers often called her *tondwe* (the woodpecker), who usually proclaims the arrival of a guest by pounding on a tree. Lenshina established a holy village, which she called the New Zion, at Kasomo. Many Africans believed that, because white missionaries had hidden the book that should have been given to them, God had given her a sacred book specifically meant for Africans. Her followers were opposed to government taxation and political authority. They believed that the end of all things was near, and, increasingly pulled away from a sinful world.

Lenshina's Christology is a remarkable achievement in theological creativity. She described Jesus as the ideal man and her younger brother, the suffering servant who had tremendous compassion for women. For her, Jesus understood the pain of women. She described Jesus Christ as the *mulongwe*, the perfect weaverbird or the ideal husband; the *shibwinga*, the bridegroom; *kanabesa*, provider of food; and *imfumu mulopwe*, the kind master. In essence, Lenshina portrayed Jesus as someone always ready to assist people, especially in their time of need. Her Christological construct was a reflection of the sociocultural reality in her country. She focussed on both the Jesus of history and Jesus who would soon return.

ONE OF ALICE LENSHINA'S HYMNS
(IN BEMBA AND ENGLISH)

Ring wesu natufwale
Chipangano ca Mafunde

Let us wear our Ring
It is a sign of our adherence to
wisdom of the clan.

Moneni kubanenu abashuka
Abaitwa na Tata.
Chupo cabo chabalika
Chabalika ngo lutanda
Sungeni amafunde ya Mfumu
Mwe bashuka lolesheni pantanshi

Look at your happy friends
called by the Lord.
Their marriage sparkles
sparkles like a star.
Keep the wisdom of the Lord
You happy ones, look forward.

Source: Hinfelaar, Hugo F. (1994) *Bemba-Speaking Women of Zambia in a Century of Religious Change, 1892–1992.* Leiden: E.J. Brill, 93.

The Lumpa Church emphasized the sanctity of the home, monogamy, and marital faithfulness. Lenshina gave the home of Jesus, Mary, and Joseph as the paradigm of a good home. Those who go against this command of conjugal fidelity and purity were told that their action would bring untold calamity and destruction to the community. The home must be the epitome of love, joy, purity, and divine virtues. Lenshina composed many hymns to convey the deeper meaning of love and marital dedication. Sanctity, purity, and wholesome living could only be achieved through an unadulterated union of husband and wife within a legal marriage.

The Lumpa Church was proscribed in 1964 after staging an armed insurrection against the government led by Kenneth Kaunda shortly before Zambia gained independence from Britain in October 1964. Alice Lenshina died in detention in 1978. Before her death, she complained that her political proclivities in the 1950s had obscured her original message of conversion and intense spirituality.

Akintunde E. Akinade

See also Woman and Religious Movements in Sub-Saharan Africa

Bibliography

Garvey, Brian. (1994) *Bembaland Church: Religious and Social Change in South Central Africa, 1891–1964.* Leiden: E.J. Brill.

Hastings, Adrian. (1994) *The Church in Africa 1450–1950.* Oxford: Clarendon Press.

Hinfelaar, Hugo F. (1994) *Bemba-Speaking Women of Zambia in a Century of Religious Change, 1892–1992.* Leiden: E.J. Brill.

Isichei, Elizabeth. (1995) *A History of Christianity in Africa.* Michigan: Wm. B. Eerdmans Publishing Co.

Macumba

The origin of Macumba can be traced back to the arrival of African slaves in Brazil in the sixteenth century. Macumba did not, however, become a full-fledged religion until the mid-nineteenth century. African slaves arrived in Brazil with their religious sensibilities thoroughly jolted, but not destroyed. The Afro-Brazilian religious later labeled as Macumba were led by leaders called *pais de santo* (fathers of the saints) and *maes de santo* (mothers of the saints). Macumba is an integral part of Afro-Brazilian spiritual genius. It is a system of worshiping the orishas, the Yoruba gods and goddesses responsible for the components and dynamics of natural and human reality. They are personifications of forces of nature and are sometimes associated with the earth and the atmosphere. At the core of Yoruba religious sensibility is a belief in the reality of superhuman agency. Yoruba people experience reality as greater than the empirical aspects of society, cosmos, and nature. Along with visible realities, there exists a motley of gods, goddesses, impersonal spirits, and forces. However, the common understanding among Yoruba people is that the social domain (human beings), the natural world, and the supernatural world are mutually dependent. These gods and goddesses are remembered through myths, songs, prayer, sacrifice, possession states, and other ritual activities. The orishas have preferences and aversions regarding colors and food. They are powerful and authoritative within certain spheres of influence and they can be either life affirming or life diminishing.

Yoruba slaves arrived in Brazil with these traditional religious ideas. They were determined and competent to maintain their culture and religion in a new situation in which the meaning and succor they provided were terribly needed. The crux of the issue was that the slave owners in Brazil did not allow Africans to freely practice their religion, but commanded them to convert to Catholicism. The description of Euro-Brazilian saints and their pictorial representations allowed Africans to establish parallels between the saints and the orishas. Jesus Christ became Oshala; Saint Lazarus was compared to Obaluaiye, the orisha of smallpox and pestilence. Yemanja Our Lady of the Immaculate Conception, the mother of Jesus. She rules the oceans, and if she is given a suitable ritual celebration and offerings at New Year's Eve, she brings prosperity and good fortune for the people. Orishas with maternal instincts like Osun and Oba were also compared with the Virgin Mary. Africans were able to celebrate the feast days of the saints because they perceived the divine beings they were venerating not as white saints, the spiritual beings of their oppressors, but as representations of their own orishas. This was an adept operation in religious accommodation and transformation. The slave owners intended to obliterate the indigenous spirituality of Africans by imposing the Catholic religion on them, but African people were able to devise an authentic way of preserving their own religion.

Yoruba religion dominated all other African religions in Brazil that preceded it, especially those of Central African origin. In the company of enslaved Yoruba people were priests and priestesses who had been sold into slavery partly as a result of internecine civil wars between Yoruba kingdoms and between Yoruba and their neighbors.

All over Brazil, Macumba defines all the details of daily existence, from the food the people eat to the colors and types of clothes they wear. The religious centers in Macumba are called the *terreiros*, *centros*, or *tendas*. The centers are designated for ritual worship and sacrifice. Religious groups are organized according to detailed hierarchies. The highest in rank is the *pai de santo*, who is also described as the overseer. The *pai de santo* controls the *filhos* (sons) and *filhas* (daughters) of the saints. One of the most important aspects of Macumba is the *consulta*—consultation in which a medium gives spiritual counsel to those who need help. This consultation operates with the triad of prediction, explanation, and control of people's problems and misfortunes. Most of these problems are associated with witchcraft. For instance, a devotee of Macumba that is childless will see his or her predicament as the product of witchcraft of someone, rather than being a medical problem.

Macumba is also a complex structure that provides religious and philosophical rationale for the vicissitudes of human life, both individual and corporate. People's spiritual passion is evidenced both in normal human behaviors and in public and private ritual practices, the goals of which are to establish and maintain the cosmic balance between the human and spiritual realms, the visible and the invisible. Macumba provides an enduring legacy in religious adaptation and innovation. The influence of Macumba in Brazil is very pervasive. It is part of the popular culture and the Brazilian way of life.

Akintunde Akinade

See also Brazil, African-Derived Religions in; Candomblé; Yoruba Religion

Bibliography

Bastide, Roger. (1978) *The African Religions of Brazil: Toward a Sociology of the Interpretation of Civilizations.* Baltimore: John Hopkins University Press.

Bramly, Serge. (1994) *Macumba: The Teachings of Marie-Jose, Mother of the Gods.* San Francisco: City Lights Books.

The Maitatsine Sect

The Maitatsine religious movement is one of the three major Islamic religious movements in modern northern Nigeria. The other two movements are the Izala movement and the so-called Shiite movement. Of the three, the Maitatsine movement is generally considered to be the most radical, the most antistate, and the one which relies heavily on a millennial-based belief system. The movement is named Maitatsine after Alhaji Marwa Maitatsine, the name given by the people of Kano in northern Nigeria to Muhammadu Marwa, the leader of an Islamic sect that started a riot in that city in December 1980. Marwa was killed in the fighting that took nearly 5,000 lives. The name is derived from a Hausa phrase he usually used against his critics, *Alla ya tsine maka albarka*, meaning, "May God deprive you of his blessing." Because the group was wary of outsiders, and because the riots in Kano gave rise to various charges against the group, little reliable information exists about the movement or its leader.

Muhammadu Marwa was reportedly from the region of Marwa, a city in northern Cameroon. He is said to have come to the city of Kano in 1945, but nothing is known of his activities in the city until the early 1960s. By this time, he had gained considerable reputation as an interpreter and commentator of the Qur'an and was given the honorific title of "Mallam Mai Tafsiri," meaning someone well versed and well respected in the interpretation of the Qur'an. The religious and political situation in Kano in the years after Nigeria's independence in 1960 was chaotic and Muhammadu Marwa took full advantage of this situation to build a movement that stood in opposition to the Nigerian state and to Islam. He told people to resist the message of orthodox Islam. In 1962, the ruler of Kano, Emir Muhammadu Sanusi, had Marwa brought before a Muslim judge on allegations of illegal preaching and an offense known in Arabic jurisprudence as *shatimati*, or abusive language. Marwa was sentenced to three months in prison and was later deported to Cameroon. In the late 1960s, Marwa returned to Kano. He lived in an area of Kano called Yan Awaki, where many of his followers lived. His radical message especially appealed to young people and many of his followers were Qur'anic students, known as *almajirai* or *gardawa*.

This movement clearly falls within the mahdist-millenarian tradition. The idea of a Madhi, one rightly guided by God, is well established in Sunni and Shi'a Islam. The idea rests on the belief that at a certain point in time a Deliverer or Savior will come to reestablish order, peace, justice, and true religion to a morally corrupt world torn by dissension. This Deliverer or Savior is the Madhi. In restoring justice and peace, the Madhi will also reshape Islam into its pristine form. The belief that a Madhi would come to destroy the infidel, get rid of injustice, ensure prosperity and well-being, and bring about the ascendancy of Islam has been well entrenched in the minds of many Muslims in West Africa since the latter half of the eighteenth century. Maitatsine was able to tap into this deep-seated religious belief. He saw himself as the forerunner of the Madhi.

In addition to rejecting both religious and political authorities, Maitatsine condemned all those who enjoyed modern Western consumer goods such as television sets, radios, watches, and automobiles. He rejected the Hadiths and preached against facing Mecca during the *salat*, the mandatory prayer requirement in Islam. He also condemned any Muslim who includes "Allah Akbar," meaning "God is Great" in his or her prayer. There were reports that after his death copies of the Qur'an found in his house had the name of the Prophet replaced by his own. His followers believed that Maitatsine was their true prophet. They called upon Muslims in northern Nigeria to stop mentioning the name of Prophet Muhammad, whom they referred to as an Arab. Marwa accepted the Qur'an as an authentic source of religious teaching and instruction, but as a prophet he also claimed the prerogative to promulgate new religious commandments, or new interpretations of the Qur'an.

Many people saw Marwa's message as a menace and orthodox Muslims consider the group heretical. There were persistent rumors that Marwa planned to take over the city's two mosques. On 26 November 1980, the governor of Kano State issued an ultimatum stipulating the breakup of the community Marwa had built in the Yan Awaki section in Kano. The governor did not, however, take any immediate action on the expiration of this ultimatum. In December 1980, there was a violent encounter between the followers of Maitatsine and the Nigerian police. Almost four thousand people were killed in this mayhem. The Nigerian army was finally called upon to control the bedlam and confusion. Marwa was shot in the leg, and died as a result of the wound. His followers buried his body, but it was later exhumed and cremated by the government, in the vain hope of permanently eliminating this movement. In October 1982, another violent occurrence connected to Maitatsine took place in the city of Maidiguri in northeastern Nigeria. Other disturbances occurred at Yola in March 1984 and in Gombe in April 1985. In the 1990s Maitatsine adherents continue to operate in secret in northern Nigeria, with much animosity displayed toward the government and its agents, the army and police.

Akintunde E. Akinade

See also Islam, West Africa

Bibliography

Best, Shedrack Gaya. (1999) "The Islamist Challenge: The Nigerian 'Shiite' Movement." www.oneworld.org.

Clarke, Peter B. (1972) *West Africa and Islam*. London: Edward Arnold Publishers.

Lubeck, Paul. (1987) *Islam and Urban Labor in Northern Nigeria: The Making of a Muslim Working Class*. Cambridge: Cambridge University Press.

Manjako of Guinea-Bissau

The Manjako of the northwestern coastal areas of Guinea-Bissau (West Africa) are divided into about twenty "lands" (*usaak*, sing.), which, though once united under a single king, are now quite diverse, with kinship, age group systems, language, and other cultural traits varying significantly, even over short distances. (The linguistic representations used here correspond to pronunciation in Caió, in the southwest corner of Manjakoland.) All Manjako, however, share strong beliefs in earth spirits, several species of bush spirits, and the ancestor spirits. And all Manjako believe that some humans have special links with the spirit world, either because they are born with "the sight" (including "witches"), or because they acquire it (diviners). Manjako also occasionally speak of a high god (*nasiin bati*), though it remains a very distant, abstract notion which rarely enters into everyday life.

Earth spirits (*usai*, sing.) have fixed places of residence, which can be marked by an uncut grove, a rock, a cotton-wood tree, or simply a hollowed out place in the soil. They perform services (protection from illness, a good job, vengeance, etc.) in exchange for offerings of palm-wine, livestock, and rice dishes. If the contract is broken, (i.e., if payment is not made for services rendered), the earth spirit reacts by sending illness, death (especially to children of the same clan), or some other catastrophe. At the more important and powerful earth-spirit shrines, initiated shrine priests (*amanyã*, sing.) perform the rites on behalf of the consultants, while at the lesser spirit shrines anyone can make a request or a payment, acting on his or her own. Spirits occasionally appear as humans—white-skinned and with long flowing hair—or as animals, especially pythons.

Each Manjako land has a master earth spirit, with whom all Manjako of that land identify. It is at the master earth-spirit shrine that community-wide rituals are held, and that all the men of the land are circumcised in a ceremony which traditionally takes place every twenty-five years or so. (The circumcision cycle is shared with the Diola, the Ehring, and other Bak peoples.) Anthropologist Eric Gable was told that the master earth spirit is a sort of policeman, making sure that contracts are respected and punishing those who do not make the promised offerings in return for services rendered.

Other types of spirits are also available to perform services for humans, though, as opposed to earth spirits, they

Earth-spirit hut of the Manjako. PHOTO COURTESY OF MARGARET BUCKNER.

Ancestor posts of the Manjako. PHOTO COURTESY OF MARGARET BUCKNER.

are quite mobile and usually enter into private partnerships. The *banjanguran* (pl.) are described as small, one-legged and impish; it is interesting that the term takes the human prefixes *na-* (sing.) and *ba-* (pl.). These bush spirits are sometimes born as children, especially as a twin, though they usually die very young. A second kind of bush spirit is the *pëwiti*, described by Gable as a sort of rogue *nanjanguran*, one who is incredibly helpful, yet whose price is very high. In fact, entering into a contract with any bush spirit is dangerous, in that, though they are quick to offer their services, they are also ruthless in demanding payment, and will feed on the souls of children of their "partner's" clan if the latter does not keep them satisfied.

Some Manjako (of both sexes) receive signs (such as recurrent illness or extraordinary happenings) that they are to become diviners (*napene*, sing.). Through a long series of rituals culminating in "death" and "rebirth" they develop "the sight," which allows them to see and communicate with the spirits. Diviners are said to tame bush spirits (*banjanguran*) which then become assistants in finding cures for illness and misfortune. Diviners also help to

unmask "witches" (*bakalam*, pl.), who are said to live off the souls of fellow kinsmen.

Every Manjako homestead has an ancestor shrine, which consists of a dozen or so ancestor posts (*isaap*, pl.) representing the souls of the ancestors (*balugum*, pl.). Years after a man has died, he lets it be known through signs (usually destructive events or illnesses) that it is time for him to be commemorated. A post is planted in his honor, and he joins the collectivity of ancestors, and, with them, continues to watch over the living. As opposed to the spirits, which are seen as opportunities to actively seek wealth and success, ancestors are viewed in a negative light; they must be appeased, for if they are not properly remembered and honored, they wreak destruction on a homestead.

Though neighboring groups adopted Islam long ago, and though Catholic missionaries have proselytized in the region for decades, traditional beliefs in earth spirits and ancestors remain vigorous. Paradoxically, though Manjako have emigrated to France and Portugal and lived for decades in Paris or Lisbon, their contact with the spirit shrines and the ancestors remains constant. If anything, the more successful an emigrant, the more he or she is tied to the home spirits.

Margaret Buckner

See also Islam, West Africa; West African Religion

Bibliography

Carreira, António. (1946) *A Vida Social dos Manjacos*, Centro de Estudos da Guiné Portuguesa, no. 1. Bissau.

Crowley, Eve L. (1990). "Contracts with the Spirits: Religion, Asylum, and Ethnic Identity in the Cacheu Region of Guinea-Bissau." Ph.D. dissertation, Yale University.

Gable, Eric (1990). "Modern Manjaco: The Ethos of Power in a West African Society." Ph.D. dissertation, University of Virginia.

Media Evangelism

Evangelism, traditionally and in theological circles, means the practice of spreading the Christian gospel. However, since the late twentieth century, methods and principles inherent in evangelism have been appropriated by other religions, particularly Islam. One of these methods is media evangelism. Media evangelism means the utilization of any social or technological device, such as radio, television, video, or literature for the selection, transmission, and reception of the Gospel.

Overview of Evangelism

The traditional method of proclaiming any religious message is by oral communication and by peripatetic missionaries. These methods were much suited to nonliterate populations. With the invention of the printing press in the fifteenth century, literature became an additional means of propagating the Gospel to millions who could not be reached personally. The Protestant Reformers particularly utilized the new printing invention to disseminate their teachings over wide geographical areas within a short time. Moreover, in the introduction of Christianity to Africa in the nineteenth century, Western missionaries utilized both oral communication and literature in carrying out their evangelistic activities.

A great boost came to evangelism from the mid-twentieth century with the development of mass media on a commercial scale. Media evangelism does not involve face-to-face interaction, but is impersonal and essentially a one-way flow of religious messages and images from the transmitting agent to a wider audience. It is usually a generalized diffusion of messages and images to an indeterminate audience principally for achieving conversion. Televangelism, a term coined in the United States, refers only to the dissemination of Christian messages through the television and cable network. It has become one of the main distinguishing features of the religious culture of the American Pentecostal and Fundamentalist movements.

Forms of Media Evangelism

Generally, there are two broad forms of media evangelism: print-media evangelism and electronic-media evangelism. Print-media evangelism involves the institutionalized production and generalized diffusion of Christian messages and images through any printed medium such as books, magazines, newspapers, tracts, and posters. This is the oldest form of media evangelism. With the introduction of the printing press, there was the gradual shift from oral proclamation of the Gospel to print-media evangelism.

Print-media evangelism uses available print technology to extend religious messages and images in great quantities in time and space to recipients who are generally not physically present at the place of production and transmission. Indeed, Christianity has been a literary religion; therefore, it is no surprise that the production and consumption of print media is widespread and basic to most Christian organizations.

Electronic-media evangelism uses those technological means of social communication that involve the conversion of oral and visual signals into electrical impulses, and the conversion at their points of destination back into audio and/or visual signals. Primary among the many forms of electronic media are the radio and television. Through these means religious messages have been disseminated and received over a wide geographical area and to a large heterogeneous population. Increasingly, since the 1970s, various Christian denominations have been buying airtime on radio and television to disseminate their messages.

Other forms of electronic-media evangelism include the use of audiocassettes and videocassettes in the transmission of religious messages, songs, images, and ideas. In fact, the Christian use of cassettes in Nigeria has developed rapidly since the 1970s, and has become very popular, and has given rise to the "cassettization" of modern religious culture. The Internet (World Wide Web) is also used to disseminate Christian messages, images, and values. However, because of poorly developed and inefficiently maintained public utilities, including telecommunications and electricity, accessibility to the Internet in many parts of Africa is limited and available only to a few.

Patterns of Media Production and Utilization

The mass media and media technology are increasingly shaping and reshaping contemporary culture. In fact, mass media are so ubiquitous in modern society that no aspect of life escapes from their influence. In modern Africa, never before has the role of the media been more central to the formation of religious consciousness and identity than as it is at present. Virtually all Christian groups in Africa are involved in media evangelism, but it is more characteristic of the Charismatic and Pentecostal groups.

A major development in media production and utilization in West Africa in recent years is the commercial production of home videos. Moving pictures are provided with narratives on video recorders and marketed on videocassettes of varying length and duration. Christian home videos with themes of drama, Gospel songs, and sermons, are increasingly becoming a stable and popular genre of media evangelism. As a contemporary African art form, home videos have displaced celluloid cinema films as the medium of choice, because nonprofessionals can make video films on a low budget. The video films relate the Christian message to the social and cultural milieu of the people. Through entertainment they offer hope and some kind of intelligibility to people in a rapidly changing and disruptive sociocultural and political milieu.

Video technology is becoming more attractive because video affords the opportunity to many Christian groups lacking technical expertise to combine production, dissemination, and consumption of religious experience and activity into one single media form. In addition, the accessibility and portability of home videos provide the opportunity for constant exchange and the shift of religious messages from the private to the public sphere. This dispersed and diverse system of dissemination makes the consumption of the religious message available to a wider audience.

Charismatic and Pentecostal movements in Africa have continued to increase in their visibility by their appropriation of other media forms such as publicity materials, cloth banners, billboards, handbills, and T-shirts. In recent years, these materials have grown in sophistication and complexity. Attention is paid both to their textual contents and their aesthetics. The material illustrations do not always stand on their own but are often used to reinforce the advertised miracle crusades, healing programs, retreats, or sermons in tracts and magazines. Thus, the expressive power of these material inscriptions makes them a potential tool for capturing the imagination of converts and the wider public. Certainly, a global cultural form—advertis-

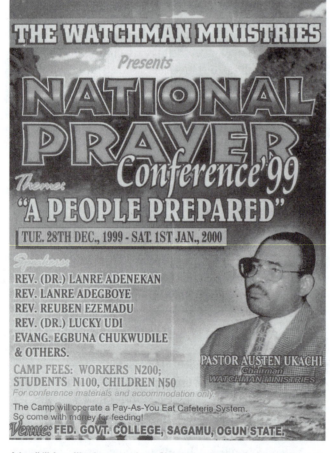

A handbill from Nigeria announcing a Christian conference. Such handbills are commonly used in West Africa to announce all sorts of public events, religious and otherwise. COURTESY OF MATTHEWS A. OJO.

ing—has provided room for religious self-expression in an African environment.

Pentecostal posters have evolved a unique linguistic characteristic. The images of conquest, destruction, "prayer missiles," firepower, wind, and the like on the posters are commingled with the worn-out but still popular images of the grandiose: miracle, success, health, and wealth. The military images of contemporary Pentecostalism constitute a specific religious ideology that is popularized through the mass media. Africans who are politically disenfranchised and socially and economically marginalized have embraced this imagery because religion has continued to empower them to face social crises.

With the pluralization of beliefs and the emergence of different religious groups all struggling for visibility and support in the public space, the battleground has shifted to the media. The media are often used to advertise options and generate "differences" (real or imagined). In this instance, the media are being used as instruments for reasserting religious power and influence, and the recruitment of new members. Besides, the myth of media power has given rise to paying close attention to the form, rather than the substance, to presentation and packaging, rather than issues and policies.

Televangelism has been used by religious conservatives to gain political power and social influence within the wider society. The American Fundamentalist and Pentecostal preachers with their own private television stations or slots on commercial channels are a good example. For example, Pat Robertson's 700 Club and similar religious programs have gained much social prominence, and their presenters comment boldly on American domestic and foreign policies. The more religious a society has been, the more likely that religion can be used to shape public values through the media.

Media evangelism can also be focused inwardly into the Christian fold as a tool for enhancing revival, enriching religious worship, and sustaining Christian growth. In fact, technical systems of symbolic production and transmission of culture are increasingly mediating personal experiences of individuals. Accounts abound of individuals who supposedly became converted to their new religions upon listening to religious messages in the electronic media.

Although Christian organizations have largely dominated the media, Muslim organizations in Africa since the 1980s have been utilizing services offered by the print and electronic media for Islamic broadcasts. Islamic resurgence in the Middle East and its international consequences, the need to educate Muslims about their faith, and the political manipulation of religious pluralism have continued to encourage the Muslim use of the media. A significant development in the 1990s was the establishment of the Muslim Media Practitioners of Nigeria to advance Islamic interests in the media. In increasing numbers, Islamic groups have been utilizing the press, video, radio, and television to advance Islam. Undoubtedly, the media have provided much visibility to Islamic groups in contemporary Africa.

In the religious marketplace, now opened by media, new patterns of consumption are generated through an unlimited variety of choice. For example, video productions have helped to commodify religious messages for commercial purpose. While the media make possible the circulation of symbolic religious forms over a wide geographical area, not everything is of a public dimension. Much of what is produced and disseminated through the media by religious organizations is usually consumed in private homes. Mediated religious experience is consequently a privatized religious experience. Therefore, the privatized nature of the consumption of media products presents a challenging paradox.

Modern Social and Religious Implications

The mass media are a dominant institution in contemporary society. Most media specialists and nonspecialists alike are increasingly appreciating the centrality of the media in urban life and in people's self-understanding. The media not only act as channels of information; they are increasingly becoming purveyors of ideology, taste, and consciousness. As mass communication brings about a complex recording of patterns of human interaction across space and time, so also media evangelism generates imagined quasi-communities.

Media evangelism has diverse social impacts. On the positive side, it creates a favorable climate whereby viewers or listeners and readers are predisposed to pay attention to the religious messages. It also provides programs of worship and inspiration for those Christians and others who do not attend worship services. Media evangelism as a specific form of Christian communication is also a source of interaction among Christian groups and individuals. Media technology has created the possibility of limitless influence over a wide space, and has enhanced the power of religious organizations in the contemporary world.

Conversely, media evangelism has a splintering effect on the fabric of Christian unity by the pluralization and privatization of Christian beliefs and values. There is a great deal of self-serving spirituality, distinct from institutionalized religion. At times, marketing techniques used by televangelists trivialize the Christian message and compromise the integrity of the gospel. These shortcomings notwithstanding,

media evangelism is clearly a tool of expansion, and a reflection of globalizing aspirations.

The media offer a much-needed switch from the private to the public sphere and vice versa. However, religious discourse is now carried out more often in the public sphere. Hence, what is available to most people is a media image of religion. There is also a corresponding switch from traditional Christian models of spiritual growth to mediated glamour, from experience to slogans, and from making followers to attracting fans. The media are dramatically altering the manner in which people are experiencing religion, the way they are experiencing themselves as religious persons, and the manner in which they are interpreting their religious experiences for others.

Although in Africa it was the print media that were first put into religious use, the globalization of the media from the mid-1980s has opened up more public space for religious organizations to expand their horizon. Although media technology is Western, the resulting media products have largely been indigenized.

Matthews A. Ojo

See also Christian Evangelism in Africa; Christian Missionaries in Africa; Cyberspace, African and African-Derived Religions in; Pentecostalism in Africa, Rastafari in Global Context

Bibliography

Akindele, Femi. (1989) "The Structural Organisation of the Electronic Media Church." *Orita: Ibadan Journal of Religious Studies* 1 & 2, 20 (December): 93–103.

Field, Martin. (1991) *Faith in the Media?* London: Hodder & Stoughton.

Hackett, Rosalind I. J. (1998) "Charismatic/Pentecostal Appropriation of Media Technologies in Nigeria and Ghana." *Journal of Religion in Africa* 3, 28: 258–277.

Hoover, Stewart M. (1998) *Religion in the News: Faith and Journalism in American Public Discourse.* London: SAGE Publications.

Hoover, Stewart M., and Knut Lundby. (1997) *Rethinking Media, Religion and Culture.* London; SAGE Publications.

Marshall-Fratani, Ruth. (1998) "Mediating The Global and Local in Nigerian Pentecostalism." *Journal of Religion in Africa* 3, 28: 278–315.

Nabofa, M. I. (1994) *Religious Communication: A Study in African Traditional Religion.* Ibadan: Daystar Press.

Silk, Mark. (1995) *Unsecular Media: Making News of Religion in America.* Urbana, IL and Chicago: University of Illinois Press.

Thompson, John B. (1995) *The Media and Modernity: A Social Theory of the Media*. Stanford: Stanford University Press.

———. (1990) *Ideology and Modern Culture: Critical Social Theory in the Era of Mass Communication*. Cambridge, U.K.: Polity Press.

Ukah, Franklin-Kennedy. (1997) "Religion and Mass Media: A Sociological Perspective." Masters thesis, University of Ibadan, Nigeria.

Methodists. *See* African Methodist Episcopal Church; African Methodist Episcopal Zion Church; African Zoar United Methodist Church

Metropolitan Spiritual Churches of Christ, Inc.

Of the numerous local, regional, and national associations within the African-American Spiritual movement, the Metropolitan Spiritual Churches of Christ (MSCC), Inc., is the largest and probably the only U.S.-based Spiritual body that has overseas congregations. Nevertheless, MSCC probably has never exceeded 100 congregations—a pattern in keeping with the decentralized nature of both white and African-American Spiritualism.

Bishop William F. Taylor and Elder Leviticus L. Boswell established the "mother church" of MSCC in September 1925 in Kansas City, Missouri (Tyms 1938: 12). Taylor and Boswell, as well as Clarence Cobbs, a longtime president of Metropolitan, reportedly were gay. While most members of Metropolitan are not gay, like many Spiritual groups, MSCC has historically provided a haven for gay African Americans. Furthermore, MSCC began to ordain women ministers in 1926 and thereby appealed to females who were denied access to the pulpit in most black mainstream churches as well as some Holiness-Pentecostal ones.

By 1937 Metropolitan had grown to thirteen congregations. These included the national headquarters in Kansas City, two congregations in Chicago, one in Gary, Indiana two in St. Louis, one in East St. Louis (Illinois), one in Detroit, one in Tulsa, one in Oklahoma City, one in Omaha, and two in Los Angeles. In 1942 MSCC merged with the Divine Spiritual Churches of the Southwest, based in New Orleans under the leadership of Bishop Thomas B. Watson, to form the United Metropolitan Spiritual Churches of Christ. About the same time, a succession crisis developed in the new organization following the death of

Bishop Taylor. Watson became the leader of the United group and Cobbs, the founder of the First Church of Deliverance on Chicago's South Side in 1929, emerged at the head of a reconstituted MSCC (Jacobs and Kaslow 1991: 46–47).

Metropolitan prospered under the astute leadership of Cobbs, affectionately called "Preacher" by his followers. The six-foot, slender Cobbs came to symbolize the gods of the black metropolis with his dapper mannerisms and love of the "good life." Metropolitan obviously underwent tremendous growth during Cobbs' tenure as its president. In 1987 Metropolitan had several congregations in Accra, Ghana, a congregation in Monrovia, Liberia, and a congregation in London, which consisted primarily of West Indians. Even more so than was the case following Bishop Taylor's death, Cobbs' death in 1979 precipitated a major succession crisis in Metropolitan. Various schisms, including the Christian Ministers' Council, the First Church of Love, and the United Evangelical Churches of Christ, emerged out of the crisis. Dr. Logan, the pastor of the Cornerstone Church of Christ in Baltimore and a heterosexual, emerged as the president of MSCC, and Indianapolis was selected as headquarters. While Metropolitan has congregations in many parts of the United States, most of them are concentrated in the Midwest, particularly in cities such as Chicago, Detroit, Gary, Indianapolis, and Kansas City.

Like other Spiritual churches, Metropolitan draws elements from American Spiritualism, African-American Protestantism, Roman Catholicism, and voodoo or *vodun* (Baer 1984). According to Melton (1978, vol. 2: 106), the association incorporates elements from Christian Science and Pentecostalism and emphasizes a "foursquare gospel" consisting of preaching, teaching, healing, and prophecy. In reality, ritual content and beliefs both vary somewhat from congregation to congregation in the association. In keeping with the process of institutionalization, Metropolitan has moved away, as have most other Spiritual groups, from the Spiritualist practice of conducting seances. Although pastors and other mediums belonging to MSCC continue to give messages in both public "bless" or "deliverance" services and private consultations, the Holy Spirit acts as their source much more than a deceased love one or even a Catholic saint. Like Spiritualism and the African-American Spiritual movement specifically, Metropolitan emphasizes individualized access to spiritual power.

In their shift toward the model of black mainstream denominations, many Metropolitan congregations have shed some of their Catholic paraphernalia. Some, if not many congregations in MSCC, eschew active contacts with

Spiritual churches in their local areas that do not belong to the association. In their search for respectability, these congregations have sought to establish ties with Baptist and Methodist congregations instead.

Institutionalization, however, has by no means transformed Metropolitan into a denomination (Baer 1988). While the larger congregations in the association have some relatively affluent members, most of the members of these congregations—and particularly the smaller congregations—continue to be working and lower-class African Americans. Like the larger Spiritual movement, MSCC appears to have passed its zenith. The factors contributing to this decline in popularity both within and outside of Metropolitan is not entirely clear, but in part it may be related to the generally apolitical and thaumaturgical orientation of most Spiritual groups.

Hans A. Baer

See also Kardecism; Spiritualism

Bibliography

Baer, Hans A. (1984) *The Black Spiritual Movement: A Religious Response to Racism.* Knoxville: University of Tennessee Press.

———. (1988) "The Metropolitan Spiritual Churches of Christ: The Socio-Religious Evolution of the Largest of the Black Spiritual Associations." *Review of Religious Research* 30: 140–150.

Jacobs, Claude F., and Andrew J. Kaslow. (1991) *The Spiritual Churches of New Orleans: Origins, Beliefs, an Rituals of an African-American Religion.* Knoxville: University of Tennessee Press.

Melton, J. Gordon. (1978) *The Encyclopedia of American Religions.* Wilmington, NC: McGrath.

Tyms, James Daniel. (1938) "A Study of Four Religious Cults Operating among Negroes." M.A. thesis, Howard University.

Mexico, African-Derived Religions in

African-Americans in Mexico did not preserve or reconstruct their original cultural traditions. Their original status as slaves, subjected to Christian masters, limited their religious expressions. Even in the cases of runaway slaves or freemen, contact with Indians and persons of Spanish ascendancy resulted in new cultural elaborations. While the Mexican indigenous ethnic groups retained and reconstructed their cultural traditions in Mexican society, African-Americans were only able to maintain some of their cultural characteristics and physical features. African cultural and physical features now exist in certain regions of Mexico. African-derived religions did not survive the colonial period (1507–1812), although African influence exists in certain religions present in Mexico.

Africans in Mexico

The first Africans to reach Mexico came from Mediterranean vessels that bought slaves in West Africa. From there they were shipped to the port of Seville in Spain and to the Canary Islands. Their arrival in the Americas was usually at Cuba and Santo Domingo (currently the Dominican Republic). From these islands many were later sent to Mexico, which, during the colonial period under Spain, was known as the "Nueva España," or the New Spain. Many of the Spanish elite brought with them their own African slaves, who often accompanied their owners in their explorations through the native Indian kingdoms.

Persons of African origin were forced to defend their Spanish masters during the conquest of Mexico. Yet runaway slaves also sought protection in Indian communities. Racial relations were and are complex in Mexico. Acceptance and discrimination were both present in the relations between Africans and Indians in colonial Mexico, although both groups were exploited under the imperial rule of the Spanish crown.

The majority of Mexico is of mixed ascendancy. The "mestizo" person has both Indian and Spanish ancestors. Persons of African ascendancy have always been a minority in Mexico. According to the noted Mexican anthropologist, Gonzalo Aguirre Beltran (1972), only 250,000 individuals came from Africa to Mexico during the three centuries of the colonial period, when the slave trade was legally accepted. Africans readily mixed with both Indians and Spanish-derived populations, thus contributing to the current "mestizo," or mixed, population of Mexico.

Terrible epidemics and exploitation by the Spanish minority greatly decreased the original Indian population of Mexico. Workers and laborers were needed for the maintenance of mines, sugarcane plantations, and great estates known as *haciendas*. European colonists considered the Africans as strong as beasts of burden in their racist ideology. So slaves were sent from Africa to replace the decreasing Indian populations. Indians were not enslaved after the conquest, due to the mercy of Pope Alexander the Fourth, who, at the beginning of the sixteenth century, forbid their enslavement in order to save their souls. The colonial authorities of the Catholic Church did not hold similar concerns for African people.

Due to the scarcity of laborers, the colonial economy required slave workers, and New Spain was an important market for slaves. Many Portuguese and Italian slave dealers sent their human cargo to Mexican ports via the Caribbean. For example, in 1542 the merchants Marin and Lomelin from the Italian city of Genoa brought 900 slaves to the Mexican port of Veracruz. Most of them were acquired by one man, Hernán Cortés, the Spanish conqueror of the Aztec Empire, in order to work in his extensive properties (Aguirre Beltrán 1972). African laborers were soon considered indispensable in order to maintain the Spanish colonial economy. Slaves were important merchandise to own and possess.

However, as in the rest of Latin America, sexual relations often crossed racial divisions. European women were not common in Mexico during the beginning of the colonial period. The Spanish elite frequently had African-American or Indian mistresses and had children with them. A large part of the population thus had mixed "blood." This population continued to grow and the Spanish empire created a complex social organization in order to regulate their relations and access to power. This system of classifications was according to castas, or castes. This form of stratification maintained a rigid color line that classified every person according to a social space due to the blood of his parents and grandparents.

Mexican anthropologist, Claudio Lomnitz has written on this subject; "The Spanish hierachial order was also used to create a caste society based on the notion of purity of blood (limpieza de sangre). The notion of purity of blood also led to a kind of nationalization of the church and faith. As the 'Old Christians' were the Spaniards and the converted Indians, Moslems and the Africans were supposed to be spiritually unreliable and were therefore legitimately subordinated to the Spaniards. Thus the Hispanicization of the church through an ideology of racial purity was a key antecedent to the construction racial hierarchy in Mexico" (Lomnitz 1992: 264).

Religious Repression in Colonial Mexico

Why is there not a strong presence of African-derived religions in Mexico? The African religious traditions survived during the colonial period, but were subject to fierce repression from the imperial state and the church. Catholicism was the only religion that was permitted by law in New Spain. The archives of the Spanish Inquisition in Mexico frequently mention the presence of Africans and African-Americans among the accused, identifying them as "negros, mulatos, o pardos" (blacks, mulattos, or browns). Their social practices clearly show the syncretization of beliefs and rites from Africa with Indian and Spanish elements. In many cases, the persons accused of witchcraft, or brujería, are persons with African traditions that clearly are not of Catholic origin. African and African-American female servants and mistresses, according to the records of the Inquisition, were often accused of placing magic spells on their Spanish masters in order to control them (Aguirre Beltrán 1994).

Another serious offense was that of blasphemy, or speaking with disrespect of Catholic dogma and the Christian God. On this subject, Lomnitz states, "Moreover, the Inquisition was especially punctilious in punishing any sign of renunciation of the Christian faith. Blasphemy was a serious offense for the slaves because the blasphemous slave was not deriving 'the correct moral' from slavery. (Ideally, violence was being used to bring the slave into the fold of Christianity, not out of it). The public punishment of blasphemy stressed the relationship between infidelity to the church and slavery: The slave was stripped naked, attached to a sign of submission (the rope), and gagged. The legitimacy of slavery was thus upheld at the same time that the blasphemer was punished. The public presentation of blaspheming slaves was a way of revitalizing the legitimization of black slavery; the slaves were new Christians that were not eligible for unsurveiled freedom. These public events also reinforced the idea that blacks lacked honor and were untrustworthy" (Lomnitz 1992: 268). The high courts, or "Tribunales," of the Spanish Inquisition were established in the American empire under Spain in the cities of Lima, Peru and Mexico City. The Christianization of slaves was more strongly enforced in regions under its direct surveillance, as occurred in these two important centers of the Spanish empire. It can be considered that the persecution of African religions by the Inquisition in Mexico was relatively successful in their repression.

The Spanish inquisition was terminated by Mexico's independence from Spain in 1812. Yet, even afterwards, African religions did not recover. The slave trade was also officially abolished in 1812 by the new Mexican government, which considered it inhuman and cruel. Trade with Africa ended completely. Strangely enough, an effect of the early abolition of slavery in Mexico (much earlier than in Cuba, the United States, and Brazil) was that cultural contacts with Africa were lost afterward.

African-derived religious institutions and organizations did not persist in Mexico, as they did (often secretly) in

Brazil and Cuba. There are communities of "afro-mestizos" (Mexican African-Americans of mixed blood) in the coastal states of Mexico such as Guerrero, Oaxaca, and Veracruz. The influence of Africa's cultural traditions remains very strong there. This is evident in many aspects of music, dance, oral traditions, and feasts such as the celebration of the Carnival. However, the religion that is accepted is folk Catholicism, which is characterized by devotion to the Virgin Mary and ceremonies honoring the patron saints of the localities. In the last twenty or thirty years, Pentecostal churches have appeared in many towns. However, African deities are not worshiped or recognized in these communities. The only elements of African religions that remain form part of syncretic beliefs that also combine aspects of Indian and Spanish cultures.

Religious Syncretism

A new religion will rarely be accepted completely. There will be a preference for those aspects which can gain a new meaning within traditional expressions of culture or that may imply modifications on the use of symbols which are accepted and integrated by people. The elaboration of religious elements by the members of a culture in a situation where different social systems or traditions come into contact is commonly known as syncretism. This is one of the forms by which social groups may appropriate foreign elements and integrate them to native beliefs and rituals.

The syncretism of African elements with Indian beliefs appears in many rural communities in Mexico. An important example is that of the concept of *sombra*, or shadow, studied by Aguirre Beltrán. The anthropologist considers that the notion of *sombra*, as found in many Mexican ethnic groups, is part of the African belief of a spiritual force that exists in all living creatures. This force has different strength, whether found in human or animal. The power of the shadow is related to the strength of the blood of living creatures. Sickness of the blood will affect the shadow. In many African-derived religions, the blood of living creatures may bestow spiritual power during ritual sacrifices. The loss of the shadow will cause sickness and even death. This concept is still common in Mexican folk medicine.

Other religions in Mexico have African influences. In witchcraft ceremonies carried out in the state of Veracruz, African systems of divination using conch shells are present. Mexican spiritualists receive diverse spirits, but they are not possessed by African spirits as in Brazil and Cuba. Mexican Pentecostalism is derived from the Asuza Street Mission in Los Angeles, California. Afro-American pastor, William Seymour, received many Mexican immigrants after found-

ing his church in 1907. Oral history of contemporary Mexican Pentecostals states that Seymour cured Romanita Valenzuela there in 1914. She later returned to her place of origin, Villa Aldama in the state of Chihuahua in Mexico, where she founded the first Pentecostal church in the country in the year of 1917. Pentecostalism has spread greatly in the Indian villages and in poor urban areas. Yet, few Pentecostal believers are now aware of its syncretic African-American origins.

Afro-Cuban Santeria has a limited distribution in Mexico. It is practiced mostly by musicians, singers, and other artists. Many, though not all, are of Caribbean origins. Cuban musicians and dancers are highly appreciated in Mexican cities, especially within the entertainment industry. These migrants also brought their religious beliefs to the country. Santeria is officially registered as a legal religious association by the Subsecretary of Religious Affairs under the Ministry of Government (Subsecretaría de Asuntos Religious de la Secretaría de Gobernación). This agency regulates church-state affairs. Believers in Santeria tend to be discrete about their religious practices, because Mexico is still predominantly a Catholic country.

Carlos Garma Navarro and Margarita Zarate

See also Costa Chica, Mexico; Pentecostalism; Santeria

Bibliography

Aguirre Beltrán, Gonzalo. (1972) *La Población Negra de México, 1519–1810.* Mexico City: Fondo de Cultura Económica.

———. (1974) *Cuijla, Esbozo Etnográfico de un Pueblo Negro.* Mexico City: Fondo de Cultura Económica.

———. (1994) *El Negro Esclavo en Nueva España.* Mexico City: Fondo de Cultura Económica.

Garma, Carlos. (1998) "The Socialization of the Gifts of Tongues and Healing in Mexican Pentecostalism." *Journal of Contemporary Religion* 13, 3: 353–363.

Lomnitz, Claudio. (1992) *Exits From the Labyrinth, Culture and Ideology in the Mexican National Space.* Berkeley: University of California Press.

Martinez Montiel, Luz Maria. (1993) "La Cultura Africana: La Tercera Raíz." In *Simbiosis de Culturas, Los Inmigrantes y su Cultura en México,* edited by Guillermo Bonfil. Mexico City: Fondo de Cultura Económica.

Palmer, Colin (1976) *Slaves of the White God. Blacks in Mexico, 1570–1650.* Cambridge, MA: Harvard University Press.

Mission Schools in Africa

Mission schools in Africa played a prominent role in the provision of education in the colonial era. They continue to do so today in the postcolonial period. Until recently, these schools have been given little sustained attention by social scientists such as anthropologists. This is curious, given the fact that schooling has a vital place in cultural production and reproduction and in identity formation. There have been few efforts to give detailed accounts of everyday life in such institutions and to evaluate the impact of mission schooling upon African students. Student voices have often remained muted, though there are some notable exceptions (see Berman 1975; Carmody 1992; Comaroff and Comaroff 1991, and forthcoming). Missions and mission schools, on the other hand, feature prominently in much African literature (Achebe 1958, 1964; Ngugi wa Thiongo 1964, 1965; Nzekwu 1962).

Historians, however, and other commentators on the region have regularly noted the part that missionaries played in the establishment of Western-style schooling by the main colonial powers—France, Great Britain, Belgium, and Portugal (see Reader 1997; Fage 1995; Mazrui 1993; Adu Boahen 1985; Oliver 1952; Davidson 1983; Clignet 1970). Missionaries from America and Europe were often at least partially funded by colonial powers, though the amount of funding dedicated for education in no way met the demand. In many African countries today, mission educators retain a strong presence, even where they do not enjoy the same degree of independence they once had, and they continue to offer much sought-after schooling.

Mission Education in Colonial Africa

Mission schooling has first to be understood within the context of the European colonizers' civilizing project during the scramble for Africa. There had been both Catholic and Protestant missionaries and mission schools prior to this period. Portuguese Catholic missionaries reached Ghana in the latter part of the fifteenth century and Jesuits penetrated into Mozambique in 1560. The Protestant missionary enterprise in Africa started early in the eighteenth century—first at the Cape and later in West Africa. Yet it was the evangelical revival toward the end of the eighteenth century in Europe and North America that set the stage for the outpouring of Protestant mission society work in Africa.

The nineteenth century missionary and doctor, David Livingstone, in an address at Cambridge University in 1857, expressed his vision for Africa in the "three Cs" of Christianity, Commerce, and Civilization. Schooling was seen as the primary means of effecting conversion to Christianity in Africa's fifty colonies. Establishing schools was also the primary means by which missionaries staked their claims to spheres of influence. Indeed, the school was placed before all else in order of importance. In 1928, for example, at a meeting of Catholic bishops and missionaries in Dar-es-Salaam, the Apostolic visitor suggested that, if necessary, missionaries should neglect their churches in order to perfect their schools (Oliver 1952: 271). Being "educated" and being a Christian became virtually synonymous. But what kind of education was on offer? And what were the expectations of the consequences of this schooling by missionaries, Africans, colonial powers, and white settlers? For the missionaries the school was primarily a means to win converts, to train African catechists and semi-skilled workers. Initially, postprimary education was not encouraged. Indeed it was thought to have dysfunctional potential—in that an educated African might well "get above himself." Where, as in Northern Rhodesia, white settlers were present in numbers, they concurred with the missionaries' "cautious" approach, as they saw the widespread provision of postprimary education as a threat to their own livelihoods (see Coombe 1967; 1968). The emphasis was on inculcating what were considered certain Christian virtues to counteract what missionaries and colonialists characterized as African degeneracy. Even as late as 1960, the Catholic patriarch of Lisbon, in his Christmas message to "Portuguese Africa," expressed himself thus:

> We need schools in Africa, but schools in which we show the native the way to the dignity of man and the glory of the nation (Portugal) which protects him. We want to teach the natives to write, to read, and to count, but not to make them learned men. (Quoted in Davidson 1983: 185)

Much—especially secondary—education was offered in single-sex boarding schools. A quasi-monastic regime that insisted upon the puerility of the pupils, despite the fact that the pupils were often in their late teens or early twenties, often obtained. Schooling was heavily weighted in favor of boys, an imbalance that persists to the present, when education continues to be seen in many parts of Africa as primarily a masculine enterprise. The usefulness of the claustration of the young in order to "educate" and "form" them had long been recognized in the European tradition of education (see Aries 1965: 213). There was clearly a missionary attempt to establish a *cordon sanitaire* to "protect" children and young people from local "corrupting" influences beyond the mission pale. Missionary condemnation of such practices as circumcision, especially female circumcision, in East Africa led, in part, to the establishment of Kikuyu schools in the 1930s in opposition to the mission schools (Anderson 1970; Reader 1997: 491). The Kikuyu insistence on the retention of female circumcision was only one aspect of their campaign, which included their demand to have access to a literary education with English as the medium of instruction.

There were marked differences of educational policy and in the conduct of education offered in the various colonies. Furthermore, missionaries of different nationalities and of different religious orders varied considerably in many ways and so it would be unwise to characterize mission educators and the schooling they offered as in any way identical (see Beidelman 1982). However, one persistent outcome was the formation of an African elite—a development in conflict, many would say, with Gospel values.

From the beginning there were struggles over the schools—over what was taught and, especially, over the language of instruction. Education for the African was portrayed from the colonial perspective as something bestowed as a favor rather than something given as a right, though the exploitation of Africa's natural resources and the construction of markets for Western goods dictated that some Africans at least should be given at least elementary instruction. The primary missionary aim was to secure conversions and so a great deal of time was spent on religious education and instruction—secular subjects were offered as bait. Where education was offered in local languages, schools were shunned by many young Africans conscious of the developing colonial world around them and thus of the capital acquired by proficiency in the language of the colonial power. Where teaching was offered in the language of the colonial power, many young people flocked to take advantage of it—thereby acquiring their passport onto the lower rungs of the colonial system of governance. It was perhaps more often less the promise of salvation than the provision of education that was the real attraction (see Taylor and Lehmann 1961).

In the French colonies there were, initially, few resources—a small number of missionaries and professional teachers and a larger force of Senegalese ex-soldiers. French was taught from the very first year of primary school and a policy of assimilation was adopted in all schools in a deliberate attempt to block aspirations towards independence and self-expression. By contrast, in British colonies, where schools were often modeled on the British public school, there was a greater degree of autonomy enjoyed by individual schools. Mission education was subsidized and it was in the early period expected to have a strong vocational element. The Belgian colonial power, like the British, ceded

the running of schools to missionaries, though the Belgians kept tight control over the curriculum and organization of the schools (see Clignet 1970).

The collusion of colonial administrations and mission agencies at times has contributed to tragic outcomes, as the recent example of Rwanda and Burundi demonstrates (Reader 1997: 672). Here both German and Belgium administrations supported the Catholic Church as the principal source of education. From the 1930s until well after World War Two, in the policy of advancing Tutsis to the detriment of Hutus, they were as one. The administration wanted a Tutsi bureaucracy and the Church education program supplied it. Hutus were schooled, but for work in the mines and industry. Ironically, virtually the only route to higher education for Hutus was through the Catholic seminaries. The seeds were sown for the violent ethnic conflict that was to come.

While initially assisting in attempts to limit African aspirations throughout Africa, a number of mission school students ironically became leading nationalists in the later struggle for independence. Notable among them are Julius Nyerere, Tom Mboya, Eduardo Mondlane, Leopold Senghor, Kwame Nkrumah, and Robert Mugabe. The Kenyan political leader, Tom Mboya, commented that he could not "recall a missionary fighting back and denouncing the colonial regime and social setup, or trying to create among Africans a new spirit of pride and confidence in themselves. Rather, they undermined this confidence by a negative attitude" (quoted in Berman 1975: 42–43).

About education in the colonial period, Julius Nyerere declared in 1967 that "colonial education induced attitudes of human inequality, and in practice, underpinned the domination of the weak by the strong, especially in the economic field" (quoted in Davidson 1983: 185). Nyerere's project of education for self-reliance expressed in his program of ujama was a flawed attempt to rectify the situation in Tanzania. Throughout Africa, the consequences of elite formation persist and are reproduced in much mission and other schooling in the twenty-first century, when so many children and young people are denied their right to even basic education.

Postcolonial Mission Schools

Mission schools in Africa in the twenty-first century remain rich sites of the many worlds of conversion, "modernity," "progress," and ambition. It is perhaps impossible to assess their power as instruments of conversion to Christianity as the term "conversion" itself is a highly complex notion. Christian identity need not necessarily imply a rejection of local cosmologies or the abandonment of local understandings of suffering and misfortune. However, it is certainly the case that being Christian implies being "modern" and "educated" in many parts of the region. Mission education has greatly added to the religious pluralism of Africa, especially in the multiplication of Independent Churches, many of whose founders attended, and reacted against, mission schools. Contests around various expressions of Christianity are widespread among young people in mission schools today. Older established denominations of mission educators are regularly challenged by their students' often Fundamentalist and Pentecostal expressions (see Simpson 1998; 1996). In addition, there has also been a shift in missionary understandings of what constitutes "conversion" and a consequent change in their endeavors, as many missionaries, among them the numerous Catholic orders and congregations still engaged in education throughout the region, have reexamined their mission and recognized their involvement in the creation of social inequalities at the expense of the poorest of the poor.

Many mission-educated Africans express gratitude and appreciation for the education that they received. The stereotypical representation of all-powerful mission educators dismantling indigenous culture and replacing it with a Christian and a European one is a very inadequate picture of the dynamics of the encounter. Students are in no way passive recipients of mission education and mission schools are not the only sites where identity formation takes place. The experience of teaching in Africa has also had a considerable impact on the missionaries themselves, leading many to have at least some misgivings about their contribution. Yet many mission-educated students also suspect that the education on offer, implicitly or explicitly formulated as a civilizing process, has had detrimental effects and disabling consequences. Christian mission education has led, and may continue to lead, many students and former students to a conviction of their own inferiority vis-a-vis whites and, as a consequence, to self-denigration and a rejection of their negritude.

The postcolonial Christian mission school, in all its complexities and contradictions, may simultaneously provide the "fortunate few" with the credentials to obtain employment in an unpredictable labor market and yet undermine the constructions of positive "African" identities, making students strangers to themselves.

Anthony Simpson

See also Christian Evangelism in Africa; Christian Missionaries in Africa

Bibliography

Achebe, Chinua. (1958) *Things Fall Apart*. London: Heinemann.

———. (1964) *Arrow of God*. London: Heinemann.

Adu Boahen, Albert, ed. (1985) *General History of Africa*, Volume 7: *Africa Under Colonial Domination 1880–1935*. Berkeley: University of California Press.

Anderson, John. (1970) The Struggle for the School: The Interaction of Missionary, Colonial Government and Nationalist Enterprise in the Development of Formal Education in Kenya. London: Longman.

Aries, Philippe. (1965) *Centuries of Childhood*, translated by Robert Baldick. London: Cape.

Beidelman, Thomas. (1982) *Colonial Evangelism: A Socio-Historical Study of an East African Mission at Grassroots*. Bloomington: Indiana University Press.

Berman, Edward (1975) *African Reactions to Missionary Education*. New York: Columbia University Teachers College Press.

Carmody, Brendan. (1992) *Conversion and Jesuit Schooling in Zambia*. Leiden: E.J. Brill.

Comaroff, John, and Jean Comaroff. (1991, 1997, and forthcoming) *Of Revelation and Revolution*, vols. 1, 2, and 3. Chicago: University of Chicago Press.

Clignet, Remi. (1970) "Education and Elite Formation." In *The African Experience* vol, 1, edited by John Paden and Edward Soja. London: Heinemann, 304–330.

Coombe, Trevor. (1967, 1968) "The Origins of Secondary Education in Zambia. Part 1. Policy Making in the Thirties; Part 2. Anatomy of Decision 1934–1936; Part 3. Anatomy of a Decision 1937–1939." *African Social Research*, 3: 173–205; 4: 283–315; and 5: 365–405.

Davidson, Basil. (1983) *Modern Africa: A Social and Political History*. London and New York: Longman.

Fage, John. (1995) *A History of Africa*. London and New York: Routledge.

Mazrui, Ali. (1993) *General History of Africa since 1935*. Berkeley: University of California Press.

Ngugi wa Thiongo. James (1964) *Weep Not Child*. London: Heinemann.

———. (1965) *The River Between*. London: Heinemann.

Nzekwu, O. (1962) *Blade Among the Boys*. London: Heinemann.

Reader, John. (1997) *Africa: A Biography of the Continent*. London: Hamish Hamilton.

Oliver, Roland. (1952) *The Missionary Factor in East Africa*. London: Longmans, Green and Company.

Simpson, Anthony. (1996) "Religious Formations in a Postcolony." Ph.D. dissertation, University of Manchester.

———. (1998) "Memory and Becoming Chosen Other: Fundamentalist Elite-Making in a Zambian Catholic Mission School." In *Memory and the Postcolony*, edited by Richard Werbner. London: Zed Books, 209–228.

Taylor, John, and Dorothy Lehmann. (1961) *Christians of the Copperbelt*. London: S.C.M. Press.

Missions and Missionaries
See Christian Evangelism in Africa; Christian Missionaries in Africa; Media Evangelism; Mission Schools; Pentecostalism in Africa; Seventh-Day Adventist Church; Unification Church; World Vision International

Moorish Science Temple

Timothy Drew, a migrant from North Carolina, established with the assistance of a Dr. Suliman the first African-American Islamic or Muslim sect called the Caaanite Temple in Newark in 1913. Little is known about Drew's past, other than that in his late twenties he began to preach a homespun version of Islam to fellow migrants. According to Moorish Science legend, Drew claimed that he visited North Africa, where he received a commission by the king of Morocco to teach Islam to African Americans. Upon his return, some followers assert, he met with the president of the United States to receive a "charter" for his work (Essien-Udom 1962).

Teachings of Noble Drew Ali

Noble Drew Ali taught his followers that they are "Asiatics," "Moors," or "Moorish Americans" rather than "Negroes," "colored people," or "Ethiopians." He asserted that this "is a new era of time now, and all men must proclaim their free national name to be recognized by the government in which they live and the nations of the earth, this is the reason why Allah the Great God of the Universe ordained Noble Drew Ali, the prophet, to redeem the people from their sinful ways" (Bontemps and Conroy 1966: 205–206). The prophet maintained that African Americans are "the descendants of the ancient Moabites who inhabited the North Western and South Western shores of Africa" (Bontemps and Conroy 1966: 206) before being brought to the New World as slaves. He taught that Morocco constitutes the homeland of Moorish Americans. Drew taught that Jesus was a black man who attempted to redeem the

Moabites and was executed by the white Romans. In spite of their suffering, the Moors or Asiatics are descendants of a proud nation with a royal history and a glorious future. Following the coming destruction of white people, the Moors will establish "a world in which love, truth, peace, freedom, and justice will flourish" (Fauset 1971: 48). They view themselves as a separate nationality within the United States and believe that they need to have their own territory to fulfill their identity.

Drew blended together elements from Islam, Christianity, Freemasonry, Theosophy, and pan-Africanism in his creation of a syncretic religious system (Turner 1997: 9–92). In 1927 he published a short book called the Holy Koran, also called Circle Seven Koran, which went through several versions and drew upon the Qur'an, the Aquarian Gospels of Jesus Christ, and Unto Thee I Grant, a Roscrucian tract. DeCaro (1996: 19) asserts that the Holy Koran also drew upon a Tibetan writing known as Infinite Wisdom. Drew bolstered the new Asiatic identity of his eager followers with a rich array of national symbols, including a national flag (a star within a crescent on a field of red), a distinctive garb (red fezzes and long beards), a sacred book (the self-composed " Holy Koran"), and membership cards (which identified holders as Muslims). He also established a number of small businesses where his followers could work (Essien-Udom 1962: 47). As Turner notes, "Drew Ali attempted to invert the religious values of American culture by presenting Christianity as an inferior European religion which had been surpassed by Islam, the 'true religion' of African Americans" (1997: 96).

Difficult Growth of the Movement

Throughout much of its history, the Moorish Science movement has been plagued by internal conflicts. The first of these resulted in the split of the Moorish Science Temple into two factions in 1916. One faction renamed itself the Holy Moabite Temple of the World and remained in Newark (McCloud 1995: 11). The other faction continued its allegiance to Drew and moved to Chicago in 1925, where it called itself the Moorish Holy Temple of Science, a name which was changed to the Moorish Science Temple of America in 1928. The sect spread to Pittsburgh, Detroit, Philadelphia, Charleston (West Virginia), Newark, Pine Bluff (Arkansas), Cleveland, Youngstown (Ohio), Richmond and Petersburg (Virginia), and Baltimore. In 1929 Drew Ali began to delegate more authority to his subordinates, who reportedly tried to "exploit the members by selling herbs, magic charms, and literature on the movement to the extent that some of them became wealthy" (Marsh 1984: 48).

McCloud provides the following account of Drew's demise:

> Noble Drew Ali was murdered in 1920, and buried in Burr Oak Cemetery in Chicago. The circumstances surrounding his death remain shrouded in mystery. The *Chicago Defender* reports his death and some of the circumstances surrounding it in a story of 20 July 1920. The story begins with a reference to the murder of Claude D. Greene, Ali's business manager, by other members of the Moorish community. At the time of this murder, the police moved in and arrested a number of community members, including Noble Drew Ali himself. Ali died soon after his release on bail, either from the complications of police beatings, or from a beating administered by community rivals. However he died, it was understood within the community that he would reincarnate. (McCloud 1995: 18)

After Drew's death, the Moorish Science Temple split into numerous factions, in large part because he did not designate a successor. The council of governors of the sect elected C. Kirkman Bey, Ali's former secretary, to the position of Grand Sheik. John Givens-El, Ali's former chauffeur, claimed that he was the reincarnation of Drew and assumed leadership over a contending faction. The FBI capitalized upon factionalism within the Moorish Science movement by infiltrating its temples during the 1940s, and continued a program of systematic harassment into the 1970s (Turner 1997: 107–108).

Modern Practices and Development

Grand sheiks serve as leaders of the temples. They are assisted by ministers, elders, and stewards. Members refer to each other as brother and sister. All Moors attach the term "El" or "Bey" to their names. Moorish American women are organized into the Sisters National Auxiliary. The two principal Moorish Science sects at the present time are the Moorish Science Temple of America and the Moorish Science Temple Divine and National Movement of North America. According to Murphy, Melton, and Ward, the former group seems to have peaked in the 1940s, at which time it had active centers across the Midwest and Northeast and into the South (Richmond, Virginia, and Chattanooga, Tennessee).

In more recent years, while continuing to exist, it has not shown a great deal of vitality. In 1981 headquarters were moved to Baltimore/Washington, D.C. area. There is also a small center in Chicago (Murphy, Melton, and Ward 1993: 507). Following the death of Sheik Timothy Givens-El, Sheik Richardson Dingle-El became the latter group's leader sometime in the 1930s (Murphy, Melton, and Ward 1993: 506). It has its headquarters in Baltimore.

Moorish American pray three times a day—at sunrise, noon, and sunset—facing Mecca. They observe Friday as their holy day. The Moorish Science temple visited by Fauset (1971: 51) conducted its services on Friday, Sunday, and Wednesday evenings and a Sunday School that met from 5 to 7 P.M. The Moors celebrate Noble Drew Ali's Birthday on 8 January, the New Year on 15 January, Flag Day in August, and Christmas. Only some Moors celebrate Ramadan. They abstain from meat, eggs, alcohol, and tobacco. Moors were also encouraged not to serve in the military. The Moorish community published several newspapers, including the *Moorish Guide National Edition* (est. 1928), the *Moorish Review* (est. sometime in the 1950s), the *Moorish Science Monitor*, *Moorish Voice*, and *Moorish American Voice* (McCloud 1995: 56). The community has been involved in various social outreach programs, including feeding the poor and operating drug and alcohol rehabilitation programs and the Moorish Uplifting Fund. By the 1980s, the Moorish Science Temple of America was operating in many federal prisons.

Hans A. Baer

See also Black Muslims

Bibliography

Bontemps, Arna, and Jack Conroy. (1966) *Any Place But Here.* New York: Hill and Wang.

DeCaro, Louis A. (1996) *On the Side of My People: A Religious Life of Malcolm X.* New York: New York University.

Essien-Udom, E. U. (1962) *Black Nationalism: A Search for Identity in America.* Chicago: University of Chicago Press.

Fauset, Arthur H. (1971) *Black Gods of the Metropolis.* Philadelphia: University of Pennsylvania Press.

Marsh, Clifton E. (1984) *From Black Muslim to Muslim: The Transition from Separation to Islam, 1930–1980.* Metuchen, NJ: Scarecrow.

McCloud, Amihah. (1995) *African American Islam.* New York: Routledge.

Murphy, Larry G., J. Gordon Melton, and Gary L. Ward. (1993) *Encyclopedia of African American Religions.* New York: Garland Publishing.

Turner, Richard Brent. (1997) *Islam in the African-American Experience.* Bloomington: Indiana University Press.

Mother Earth and the Earth People

Mother Earth (Jeanette Macdonald, 1934–1984) was the founder of the Earth People of Trinidad, a millennialist Africanist group who have certain affinities with the current "eco-feminism" of North America.

Early Life

Jeanette was born in the slum areas of the capital, Port-of-Spain, her maternal grandmother having come to the Caribbean from Africa after slavery ended. Her mother had arrived in Trinidad from Grenada to work as the domestic servant for a white family, and Jeanette was raised with the children of her employer. Her parents had not been married in a church and she only occasionally met her father. She spent part of her childhood with various relatives, including the African grandmother, who was a Shango Baptist (close to the Spiritual Baptists but with more African elements). At sixteen she left her grandmother to live with a boy, a relationship that broke up, and she returned to live with her grandmother and then one of her mother's former partners. She "scuffled," getting by with help from family and boyfriends: "a little job here, a next one there. I often planned to get married but something happen: I ai'nt fussed."

Her life in Laventille, Port-of-Spain, was like that of most working-class women, facing an endless round of bearing children and caring for them. Notable crises included quarrels over her providing school uniforms, credit agreements that she needed for a sewing machine to make the clothes, and more generally, over the treatment of poor black people by the new post-colonial government. One childbirth in the hospital occasioned particular anger when the midwife apparently pushed the baby back as it was being born. After the 1970 Black Power mutiny, Rupert, her partner at the time, took her to the north coast together with six of her twelve children. They squatted on an old cocoa estate growing a wide variety of foods and products, which they sold to a nearby village. Both Jeanette and Rupert had been Shouter Baptists and they continued to "pick along in the Bible" and interpret the visionary import of their dreams.

Her Visions

From 1975, after the birth of twins in their wooden hut, until 1976, Jeanette Macdonald experienced a series of revelations which became the foundation of the Earth People. She came to understand that the Christian teaching of God the Father as creator was false and that the world was the work of a primordial Mother, whom she identified with nature and with the Earth. Nature gave birth to a race of black people, but the rebellious Son (God) re-entered his mother's womb to gain her power of generation and succeeded by producing (or forcing her to create) white people. The whites, the Race of the Son, enslaved the blacks and have continued to exploit them. The Way of the Son is that of science—of cities, clothes, schools, factories, and wage labor. The Way of The Mother is the way of nature—a return to the simplicity of the Beginning, a simplicity of nakedness, cultivation of the land by hand and with respect, and of gentle and nonexploitive human relationships.

The Son, in a continued quest for the power of generation, has recently entered into a new phase. He has now succeeded in establishing himself in Trinidad's Africans and Indians and is also on the point of replacing humankind altogether with computers and robots. Nature, who has borne all this out of love for the whole of her creation, has finally lost patience. The current order of the Son will end in a catastrophic drought and famine, or a nuclear war, a destruction of the Son's work through his own agency, after which the original state of nature will once again prevail.

Jeanette herself is a partial manifestation of The Mother who will fully enter into her only at the End. Her task in 1980 was to facilitate the return to nature by organizing the community known as Hell Valley, the Valley of Decision, to prepare for the return to the Beginning and to "Put out the Life" to her people, the Black Nation, The Mother's Children. She has to combat the false doctrines of existing religions which place the Son over the Mother and to correct the distorted teaching of the Bible where she is represented as the Devil. She stands for life and nature, in opposition to the Christian God who is really the Son, the principle of science and death. As the Devil she is opposed to churches and prisons, education and money, contemporary morals and fashionable opinions. Because God is "right" Mother Earth teaches the left, and the Earth People interchange various conventional oppositions: left for right; evil or bad for good. Seeming obscenities are only natural words for She Herself is the Cunt, the origin of all Life.

The exact timing of the End is uncertain but it will come in Jeanette Macdonald's physical lifetime. Then time will end, sickness will be healed and the nation will speak one language. The Son will be exiled to his planet, the Sun, really the Planet of Ice which is currently hidden by Fire placed there by The Mother Fire —which will eventually return to where it belongs, back to the heart of the nurturant Earth.

Earth People

The Earth People are an Africanist community settled in a place they call Hell Valley (or the Valley of Decision) on the

Earth people at their commune/settlement. PHOTO COURTESY OF ROLAND LITTLEWOOD.

north coast of Trinidad. Earth People originated in the ideas of Mother Earth (Jeanette Macdonald, 1934–1984). She taught that the world was on the brink of a cataclysm which would result in widespread starvation.

Mother Earth's revelations ceased in 1975–76 after an episode called The Miracle in which she brought the sun closer to the earth. At this time her family were still living with her in a deserted village some fifteen miles from the nearest settlement, and they were joined by an assortment of young men, mostly old friends and neighbors of hers from Port-of-Spain, together with Rastafarians attracted by a newspaper article written about this family going naked in the bush. Her ideas were now consolidated in reflection and debate. By 1978 her title of Mother Earth was adopted, possibly after a recent Carnival masquerade, which had portrayed a large fecund Earth Mother.

Mother Earth continued to have visions in her dreams, but these were similar to those of other members: premonitions and answers to the immediate organizational problems on which her attention was now focused. A confirmation of her status as divine Mother occurred with the Coming of the Makers (a group of visiting Rastas).

While around sixty people have been active Earth People at different times, in October 1981 twenty-two were resident in the Valley, with perhaps twenty sympathizers and occasional members in town. There were annual marches into Port-of-Spain which sometimes ended in mass arrests and stays in the state psychiatric hospital for Mother Earth, together with raids on the settlement by social workers which resulted in confinement of the younger children to an orphanage: Mother Earth's youngest son escaped and trekked back to the commune across the mountains. There were, however, supportive articles in two local periodicals, *Ras Tafari Speaks* and *The Bomb*. Trinidad's first prime minister had recently died and the government was preoccupied with an election: the Hell Valley group were left to themselves.

Only one other member of the group was female, with sixteen young male followers between eighteen and thirty-three, most previously associated with Rastafari or Spiritual Baptism, besides Mother Earth and her immediate family. The reason they gave for joining (to a visiting anthropologist in 1981) was the corruption and spiritual decay associated with the post-independence government, and a wish to return to a simpler African lifestyle. In opposition to the *material* world, the group all went naked, sleeping out on the bare ground, and maintained themselves through fishing and cultivation of the land using only cutlasses.

The center of the community was the old wooden house of the deserted village into which Mother Earth had moved in 1972, together with some added African-style huts. For about half a mile in each direction, the secondary bush and scrub of the seasonal rain forest had been cleared and a variety of trees and perennial cultigens were grown: medicine bushes; trees and plants for cordage and wrapping and for basketry and calabashes; timber for building; plantain and banana; roots like cassava, sweet potatoes, dasheen, yam, tannia; aubergine, pineapple, tomato, pigeon peas, callaloo, okra; Indian corn, pumpkin, ginger, sugarcane, christophene; trees bearing oranges, grapefruit, guava, nuts, mango, avocado, pawpaw, pomerac, tamarind, and breadfruit; garlic and bushes with pepper, shodoberry, and other flavor herbs. Above the settlement, reaching into the lower reaches of the mountains of the northern range, were cocoa and coffee, cannabis and tobacco. In the nearby bush were cress and watermelon, mauby bark, mammy apple, passion fruit, star apple, nutmeg, and soursap, whilst along the coast grew coconut and almond. The variety of crops, virtually every Trinidad food plant, justified the boast of the Earth People that they were living in the original Eden.

Although all members accepted Mother Earth's role as the Original Mother, the group were very "this worldly" in their emphasis on present cultivation of the land and this focus on the preparation and consumption of food. Daily agricultural labor ended with a swim in the sea and Mother Earth ritually dealing out the cooked vegetable food to the group. The central "rite of synthesis" (as anthropologists would put it) was this daily meal. The evening was passed with the smoking of cigars and ganja spliffs, and communal drumming and dancing with singing of their favorite anthems "Beat them Drums of Africa," "The Nation It Have No Food," and "We Going Down Town to Free Up the Nation."

Each new member took a "fruit name"—like Breadfruit, Coconut, Cassava, or Pumpkin. Relations between members were fairly egalitarian, and not especially religious, recalling those of the average Trinidad working-class family. Supposedly, the group was living in the Beginning of the End, a run-up to the eventual, very physical, end of the world, but little time was spent on millennial speculation. Painted words on the main house proclaimed "Fock God"—a sentiment in accord with the group's opposition to Christianity and Islam (although there was a more sympathetic attitude to Rastafari and Shango as being "half-way there").

In 1982, with disputes in the group relating to differences in practical authority, and Mother Earth's continued illness, relations deteriorated, splits occurred and the settlement was burned. Mother Earth died of her illness in 1984, and by the late 1990s, the Earth People were split into four groups: (1) Her biological sons and daughters living in the slum areas of town who visited the original site occasionally and went naked then; (2) A few members with some new recruits, going naked on the original site; (3) Rupert, her ex-partner, going naked with some new companions near his original village twenty miles away; and (4) A more "Rasta-orientated" group in Port-of-Spain who were apparently clothed and who had repudiated Mother Earth's eschatological teaching. For all four, what has remained central is less her personal messianic vision than some sense of a more "natural" and "African" style which her own life had embodied.

Roland Littlewood

See also Rastafari in West Africa

Two children at their commune/settlement. PHOTO COURTESY OF ROLAND LITTLEWOOD.

Bibliography

Chevannes, Barry. (1995) *Rastafari and Other African-Caribbean Worldviews*. London: Macmillan.

Littlewood, Roland. (1993) *Pathology and Identity: The Work of Mother Earth in Trinidad*. Cambridge: Cambridge University Press.

"Earth People Split." (1983) *Trinidad Mirror*, Port-of-Spain, 4 February.

"Eddoes: Dasheen and Breadfruit in My Garden." (1985) *Trinidad Mirror*, Port-of-Spain, 6 August.

"Minister Meets the Earth People." (1982) *Trinidad Guardian*, Port-of-Spain, 22 January.

"Paradise Lost." (1983) *Trinidad Express*, Port-of-Spain, 26 March.

"Why We Don't Wear Clothes." (1982) *The Bomb*, Port-of-Spain, 22 January.

Mt. Zion Spiritual Temple

King Louis H. Narcisse was one of the most colorful, yet overlooked, of what Fauset (1971) termed the "black gods of the metropolis." He founded the Mt. Zion Spiritual Temple in 1943 and incorporated it in 1945. King Narcisse maintained an "international Headquarters" in Oakland, California, and an "East Coast Headquarters" in Detroit. In addition to these temples, in the early 1980s, the association had seven other congregations, including a second temple in Detroit and temples in Sacramento, Richmond (California), Houston, Orlando, New York City, and Washington, D.C.

I had the opportunity to meet King Narcisse, a tall stately man who appeared to be in his sixties, in 1979 upon my third visit to the King Narcisse Michigan State Memorial Temple in Detroit. He arrived midway during the Sunday morning service in a chauffeured shiny black Cadillac limousine with his title and name inscribed upon the door. As he entered the sanctuary, two attendants rolled out a white carpet and the congregants stood to greet their regal leader. His attire included a golden toga, a cape with a white surplice, a white crown with glitter and a golden tassel, eight rings on his hands, and a ring in his left ear. He preached a sermon and presided over various rituals (including a prophesy for a woman). Narcisse sat on a throne on the elevated inner sanctum of the temple, he occasionally sipped some sort of beverage from a golden goblet. On one occasion, he spit some of the liquid on a large plant situated near the pulpit. During the service, his assistant occasionally took the religious monarch's cape off or put it on him. Narcisse was also attended by a nurse who wore a blue cape. He also maintained phone contact with congregants in Oakland and possibly other cities. One member told me that Narcisse was a Masonic Grand Master and had two residences—one in Detroit and the other in the East Bay Area.

At the end of the service, he announced the "consecrated offering" and asked those who could give $10 to stand. Four women came to the front of the sanctuary and formed a short line. He told the congregation, "It is not wrong to be successful or rich. The harm is when it goes to your head." Other contributors came forward while the organ played. Following the service, Narcisse distributed bulletins to his royal subjects and asked his subjects to sit in the front pew while he quizzed me about the details of my research on the African-American Spiritual movement and whether I was affiliated with either the Communist Party or the CIA (Baer 1984).

A large picture depicting a much younger monarch, referred to as "His Grace," faced the congregation and had a sign below it that read:

GOD IS GREAT AND GREATLY PLEASED TO BE PRAISED IN THE SOVEREIGN STATE OF MICHIGAN IN THE KINGDOM OF "HIS GRACE KING" LOUIS H. NARCISSE, DD WHERE "ITS's [sic] NICE TO BE NICE AND REAL NICE TO LET OTHERS KNOW THAT WE ARE NICE."

The altar was adorned by statues of Jesus and Mary and large votive candles.

In contrast to the elaborate altar and chandeliers of the sanctuary, housed in a large auditorium erected in 1929, only some 20 congregants were in attendance, suggesting that Narcisse's kingdom has undergone a period of decline. He reportedly died at some time in the late 1980s.

The Mt. Zion Spiritual Temple is one of a variety of Spiritual associations that exhibit a kingdom-style politico-religious organization. It refers to its ministers by titles such as "Reverend Queen," "Reverend Princess," "Reverend Prince," "Reverend Father," "Reverend Mother," and "Reverend Lady." King Narcisse periodically anointed "others into the privileged circle in a ceremony resembling 'knighting' rituals" (Davis 1985: 1).

In his detailed analysis of African-American sermons, Davis refers to Narcisse's preaching style as the most eclectic of the three preachers discussed in his study.

It is entirely possible that Narciss . . . knowingly borrowed this philosophical stance from the Society of Friends (Quakers), whose literature is known to him.

This would not be unusual for Narciss's ministry, for in addition to the Lord's Prayer, he uses the Hail Mary, both chanted antiphonally, during the course of the sermon. The explanation offered by a follower was that the Hail Mary allowed Narciss to honor men and women, the Lord and His mother. (Davis 1985: 69–70)

In keeping with the highly syncretic nature of the Spiritual movement, he regularly modified the "conventional structures of the American-American sermon" (Davis 1985: 72). Davis (1985: 142–151) provides readers with the text of an untitled sermon delivered by Narcisse.

Hans A. Baer

Bibliography

Baer, Hans A. (1984) *The Black Spiritual Movement: A Religious Response to Racism.* Knoxville: University of Tennessee Press.

Davis, Gerald L. (1985) *"I Got the Word in Me and I Can Sing It, You Know": A Study of the Performed African-American Sermon.* Philadelphia: University of Pennsylvania Press.

Fauset, Arthur H. (1971) *Black Gods of the Metropolis.* Philadelphia: University of Pennsylvania Press.

Mouride Brotherhood

The Mouride brotherhood was established in Senegal in the late nineteenth century, not long after the French had started a campaign to conquer the Wolof states, a time when the traditional structures of Senegalese feudal society were crumbling. The Mouridiyya (the formal name for this *tariqa* (brotherhood, the name is from *murid*, a traveler on the path) is part of the Sufi tradition whereby a group of believers are organized around a charismatic leader or a holy man known to possess *baraka* (divine grace). In this instance the holy man is Cheikh Amadu Bamba Mbacke (1852–1927) and his *baraka* was so great that he promised paradise not only to his disciples, but to anyone who read or even repeated his *qasa'id* (religious poetry). Cheikh Amadu Bamba was initiated in the teachings of Senegal's two other main brotherhoods (the Qadiriyya, having its roots in the Middle East, and the Tijaniyya, coming from Morocco), but his message to his disciples heralded a novel and deceptively simple formula. He commanded the newly converted, "Go and work!"

The Mouridiyya attracted many converts, particularly from the disenfranchised members of Senegal's lower castes and slaves. By 1945 the brotherhood had entered Senegal's electoral politics and today has grown to roughly two million members, making it the second largest brotherhood in Senegal. Founded at the site of a vision by Cheikh Amadu Bamba, Touba, the Mouride holy city, lies in Senegal's barren interior and is the destination for annual pilgrimages (called *magals*). This rapidly expanding Mouride city retains its autonomy from the Senegalese government and is home to one of Africa's largest and most beautiful mosques.

In the Saloum region of Senegal, Amadu Bamba was born in 1852 into a religious family. His father, Mame Mor Anta Sali Mbacke (d.1880), was a *qadi* (Islamic judge) in the court of the king MaBa, while his mother, Mame Diarra Bousso (1830–1862), was from a family that claimed descent from the Prophet. In Senegal, great importance is attached to the status of daughters of important *shaykhs* (Islamic notables) and women inherit *baraka* from their mothers as well as fathers. Oral and written sources proclaim that Mame Diarra was an exceptional woman of noble blood and that through her purity and piousness she won Allah's favor. As a result, she gave birth to a saint and became known forever as the "mother of Mouridism" and attained the status of Diarratulahi (Allah's neighbor).

The young Bamba, schooled in Arabic and Islamic jurisprudence, turned to scholarship, and although he was summoned to the aid of the last colonial resistance leaders, he preferred the pen over the gun. His personal preference was for solitude; still disciples flocked to this new shaykh to perform their *jebblu* (gesture of allegiance). Colonial rulers feared an Islamic uprising and deemed Cheikh Amadu Bamba too powerful. On 21 September 1895 Amadu Bamba was sent to Gabon. When he returned to Senegal in 1902, he was accompanied by numerous legends of *karamat* (miracle working) that confirmed his invincibility to his followers and his dangerousness to the colonial authorities. Soon the Mouride leader was deported a second time, this time to Mauritania where he was confined for three years in the compound of Shaykh Sidia, a leader of the Qadiri. When Amadu Bamba returned to Senegal in 1907, the Mouridiyya became a distinct brotherhood based on the founder's unique prayer formula.

In Sufism *baraka* is inherited, and the brotherhood spawned a number of important families founded by the brothers, sons, and great *taalibes* (disciples) of Amadu Bamba. The most remarkable among them was Cheikh Ibra Fall (1858–1930), one of the founder's first disciples to whom he gave the title of *shaykh*. The ultra-devoted Ibra Fall took Mouride traditions to the extreme and was given dispensation from certain obligatory Islamic practices. Due to a covenant between Ibra Fall and the founder, the Bay Fall (disciples of Ibra Fall) are not required to pray nor fast during Ramadan. The Bay Fall minority are often criticized as un-Islamic but they consider themselves to be the "real" Mourides.

"Pray as if you will die tomorrow but work as if you will live forever." Like the earliest disciples, Bamba's modern-day followers have taken that counsel to heart. Mouride determination is manifest in *dahiras* (urban associations) springing up in cities worldwide. Originally established to provide organization to the masses of devotees forced to leave their rural communities in search of work in the city, these weekly gatherings teach members the art and advantages of associating with one another. Outsiders have suggested that the modern *dahira* overseas may provide much-needed respite from the challenge of negotiating life in a foreign country. But Mourides have always been pioneers, working hard and enduring hardships as they spread from the cities of West Africa to Europe, Scandinavia, Australia, and America, taking with them the insistently recalled memory of the brotherhood's founder.

Rose Lake

See also Islam, West Africa

Bibliography

Cruise O'Brien, Donal. (1971) *The Mourides of Senegal.* Oxford: Clarendon Press.

Villalon, Leonardo A. (1995) *Islamic Society and State Power in Senegal.* Oxford: Oxford University Press.

Movement for the Restoration of the Ten Commandments of God

This religious movement in Uganda is the best known of a number of small religious movements that emerged in East Africa in the 1990s. The movements have been led by charismatic leaders who warn of the coming end of the world and gather followers around them to prepare for a new social and spiritual order. Little is known about these movements and they are often repressed by national governments when they are believed to attract rebels who seek to overthrow the government. As with many millennial movements throughout history and across cultures, these movements are caused in part by serious social disruptions. In some East African nations these have most recently been caused by famine, political instability, and AIDS— and the failure of government and church organizations to deal with these problems.

The Movement for the Restoration of the Ten Commandments of God is the best known of these movements and probably the only one known by the public outside East Africa. On 17 March 2000 some 530 members of the movement died when their church in Kanungu, in southwest Uganda, was destroyed by fire. The mass death was initially classified as a mass suicide, but police in Uganda a few days later indicated that the deaths of the seventy-eight children were being treated as murders and that it was likely that some adults were murdered as well. The fire was evidently set by movement leaders, who used a mixture of gasoline and sulfuric acid to produce a fire and explosion that reduced many bodies to ash and bones. The remains were buried in a mass grave by authorities. In the days following the fire, the murder theory gained more acceptance as additional bodies of people who had been beaten or hacked to death or perhaps poisoned were found on the site, and at three other sites used by the movement or its leaders. One of these sites was at Buhunga, less than fifty miles from the church at Kanungu, and it yielded 153 bodies, some of which had been dead nearly four months. Another site at Rushojawa yielded eighty-one bodies and the fourth was at Rugazi, where 155 bodies were found. As of April 2000, Ugandan authorities believed that about 925 people had died, and perhaps all were murdered. They also believed that more bodies—perhaps hundreds more—would be found later. The 925 confirmed deaths are the most associated with a religious cult in modern times.

The movement evidently began in neighboring Rwanda in the 1970s and 1980s when school children reported visions of the Virgin Mary on play fields. The movement attracted some who were dissatisfied with the Catholic Church and its perceived failure to deal with emerging problems such as AIDS, and was brought to Uganda by Credonia Mwerinde, who claimed to have been in contact with the Virgin Mary since 1984. Mwerinde and several other women recruited Joseph Kibwetere of Kabumba, in southern Uganda, to lead the movement. Kibwetere was a Roman Catholic, an organizer and supervisor of church schools, and was involved in local politics. He was a relatively wealthy and respected member of the community, and with his wife, also a teacher, had sixteen children. The women members of the Virgin Mary cult told him that he had been selected to lead a religious movement to spread the word of God. Kibwetere accepted their offer and become the public spokesman for the movement, with the ultimate goal of creating a world based on the Ten Commandments. He also predicted that the world would end at the end of 1999 and required members to sell their possessions and turn the proceeds over to the movement. Although Kibwetere was the public leader of the movement, former members reported to authorities after the massacres were discovered that Mwerinde played a major role in establishing rules for the group, communicating with the Virgin Mary, and overseeing group communal activities. Prior to her involvement with the movement, Mwerinde ran a beer and liquor shop in Kanunga. The group was led by "twelve apostles," at least four of whom had close ties to Mwerinde.

Kibwetere's new role and activities created conflict with his family (the church was initially established at his farm) and with the Roman Catholic Church. He was excommunicated from the latter and in 1992 he and his followers moved to Kanunga, where they established the church. Church doctrine was set forth in the 163-page *A Timely Message from Heaven: The End of the Present Times*, which emphasized Kibwetere's and other leader's revelations and prophecies. At the compound, church members were required to live an ascetic life, with sexual relations prohibited and communication restricted to sign language. Fasting was regularly required and some members worked in the movement's fields growing cassava, bananas, beans, and other crops. As the number of people living in the compound grew, reports suggest that children were isolated from their mothers. Estimates suggest that between 1,000 and 4,000 people were members of the church, although not all lived in the compound and not all died on 17 March or in the other killings. In 1997, the group reported to the government that it had 5,000 members. Membership was evidently fluid, and much that was learned about the movement following the 17 March fire was from former cult members or relatives of deceased members. It is believed that dissension developed after the world failed to end on December 31, and some members sought to withdraw and demanded that their money be returned to them. Reports by relatives of victims suggest that those who were killed before 17 March were those who sought to withdraw and that the mass killing or suicide reflected Kibwetere's and Mwerinde's loss of control over their followers.

It is believed that one movement leader, Dominic Kataribabo, a former Catholic priest, died in the fire, but that Kibwetere and Mwerinde escaped and are being sought by Ugandan authorities. As of April 2000, the national government had arrested one local official for failing to report complaints about the group by other people in the region and had asked for international cooperation in finding the leaders who may have escaped.

David Levinson

Bibliography

Bamford, David. (2000) "Cults: Why East Africa?" *BBC News Online: World: Africa* (20 March). http://news.bbc.co.uk/low/english/world/africa/newsid_683000/683388.stm.

Cauvin, Henry. (2000) "Fateful Meeting Led to Founding of Cult in Uganda." *The New York Times* (27 March): 8.

Fisher, Ian. (2000) "Uganda Cult's Mystique Finally Turned Deadly." *The New York Times* (2 April): 12.

Music, Black Hymnody

By the late eighteenth century, free and enslaved Africans in America had embraced Christianity in large numbers. Methodism had claimed large numbers of African-Americans in urban areas because of its official antislavery stance. The celebrated religious leader (and founding member of the Free African Society) Richard Allen founded the African Methodist Episcopal (AME) church in 1794 after a break with the mostly white St. George's Methodist Church in Philadelphia. In 1816, he established the AME church as a body independent from the mother Methodist church. In 1801, Allen published a collection of religious songs (with the texts only) entitled *A Collection of Spiritual Songs and Hymns from Various Authors*. It appears to be the first hymnal geared toward black Christian worshippers. This work was a compilation which featured hymns by well-known hymn writers such as Isaac Watts, among others, but many were anonymous. It eventually became the most widely used religious songbook in African-American Protestant churches around the country. By 1897, *A Collection of Spiritual Songs* had reached its eleventh edition. This publication included the text and the notated music.

Another religious phenomenon of the early nineteenth century which involved African-Americans was the camp meetings. These were outdoor, continuous religious services inspired by the Second Great Awakening, a religious movement that spread around the country early in the century. Many African-Americans participants were known to do dances such as the "ring shout" and "shuffle step." Such religious behavior was criticized by some purists (like Richard Allen), but was clearly acceptable among a growing sector of African-American worshippers.

Spirituals

There is little question that spirituals have been the most enduring musical contribution of the enslaved African-

STEAL AWAY TO JESUS!

Refrain:
Steal away, steal away,
Steal away to Jesus!
Steal away, steal away home,
I ain't got long to stay here.

My Lord calls me;
He calls me by thunder;
The Trumpet sounds within my soul,
I ain't got long to stay here.
Refrain:

Green trees are bending;
Poor sinner stands atrembling;
The Trumpet sounds within my soul,
I ain't got long to stay here.
Refrain:

Tombstones are bursting;
Poor sinner stands atrembling;
The Trumpet sounds within my soul,
I ain't got long to stay her.
Refrain:

Source: http://ingeb.org

American population of the nineteenth century. After liberation, spirituals gained the attention of collectors, scholars, and those with a casual interest in the musical genre. They are an outgrowth of the African enslavement experience in America and Protestant Christianity. A similar tradition apparently did not develop on the African continent, nor anywhere else within the African Diaspora (where African enslavement was practiced) so to that degree, the spirituals are, from all existing evidence, uniquely American.

There are few absolute features that can be pointed to when trying to distinguish one spiritual from another. Up-tempo songs such as "A Great Camp Meetin'," might have been called "jubilees" while an equally spirited "I'm Gonna Lift Up a Standard for My King" might have been regarded as a "shout." The terms "plantation songs" and "slave songs" were also used. An apparent standard feature of the spiritual was its employment of African-American dialect. One of the earliest collection of spirituals was *Slave Songs of the United States* (1867). It was a collaborated work of William Allen, Charles Ware, and Lucy McKim Garrison, all of whom had abolitionist backgrounds. In the preface of the work, they commented on the uniqueness of African-American vocal styles and the inability of conventional Western musical notation to accurately transcribe the unique vocal effects such as the screams, yodels, falsetto, and glissandi that they heard when the songs were performed.

It was the apparent disregard of the above performance practices (among other things) which would lead some scholars like George Pullen Jackson, Neuman White, and Donald Wilgus to promote a "white" spiritual theory. They argued that because it was the Europeans who gave Christianity to the enslaved Africans, they also gave them the music with which to worship. This argument has been soundly refuted, however, because Jackson, who was the principal representative of this school of thought, had compared printed versions of spirituals (i.e., arranged spirituals in Western musical notation) to those of Western European folk songs and saw similarities in melodies and time signatures. This school of thought also neglected the fact that the majority of spirituals employ a call-and-response performance technique that was not a traditional feature of western European folk song.

A tradition related to spirituals, in addition to their religious capacity, were the "alert" and "map" songs. While the text of these songs were ostensibly religious, the alert songs encoded messages or signals about escape attempts for enslaved Africans or planned secret meetings. Examples of such songs were "Steal Away to Jesus," "Good News the Chariot's Comin'," "Wade in The Water," and "I'm Packin' Up." "Wade in The Water" was known to be a frequently used alert song of the celebrated Underground Railroad conductor, Harriet Tubman. In addition to the religious meaning of the song, there was a very practical use for "wading in the water." It could also throw off any body scent,

This advertisement from *The Crisis: A Record of the Darker Races* (August 1926) indicates the popularity of African-American religious music as a form of entertainment.

WPA GUIDE:
VIRGINIA'S FOLKLORE AND MUSIC

Customs retaining the flavor of ante-bellum days have survived among the Negroes in rural areas and small towns and even in the Negro districts of cities. Group participation in plantation labor meant social participation in play-party games, dances, molasses boilings, tobacco strippings, and corn huskings. A pseudo-spiritual of slavery days evidently refers to secret religious meetings in a secluded spot. The title, 'Lie Low, Lizzie, Lie Low,' implies, as much as the song, a message between the lines:

Lie low, Lizzie, lie low, Cause dey ain't gwine be no meeting here tonight. Meat selling nine pence a pound, And coan five dollars a barrel. So lie low, Lizzie, lie low. Cause dey ain't gwine be no meeting here tonight. Ain't gwine be no meeting here tonight. Don' you know, don' you know? Creek's all muddy, and de pond all dry. Warn't fo' de tadpole, de fish all die. So lie low, Lizzie, lie low. Cause dey ain't gwine be no meeting here tonight.

The natural musical talents of the Negro were noticed by Thomas Jefferson in his Notes on Virginia: 'In music they are more generally gifted than the whites with accurate ears for tune and time, and they have been found capable of imagining a small catch.' But general recognition of the artistic value of Negro songs and music and interest in their preservation are comparatively modern, and no successful attempt to collect them was made before 1830. William Francis Allen, Charles Pickard Ware, and Lucy McKim Garrison published their collection of Slave Songs of the United States in 1867. Cabin and Plantation Songs as Sung by the Hampton Students was compiled in 1874 by Thomas P. Fenner, and Religious FolkSongs of the Negroes as Sung on the Plantation was arranged from this work by the musical director of Hampton Institute in 1909. In 1918 Hampton Institute published Negro Folk Songs collected and edited by Natalie Curtis Burlin. Songs of the Negroes of some of the counties of Mississippi, Georgia, North Carolina, and Tennessee were gathered by Howard W. Odum and Guy B. Johnson of the University of North Carolina and compiled in their book The Negro and His Songs, published in 1925. Since many Negroes in these States spring from slaves originally bought in Virginia, their songs partly represent the Old Dominion. Dorothy Scarborough of Columbia University made a collection of songs from several Southern States, including Virginia, for her book, On the Trail of the Negro Folk-Songs, also published in 1925. Negro workers on the Federal Writers' Project have recorded many Negro songs, hymns, and spirituals that otherwise would have died with the last of the ex-slaves.

Negro singing, first made known to the general public by singers from Fisk University in Tennessee, was then popularized by singers from Hampton Institute, and later by those from other Virginia Negro schools. Thomas P. Fenner came from Providence, Rhode Island, to Hampton Institute in 1872 to establish a department of music. The Hampton singers at first numbered 17, and the first concert to raise money for Virginia Hall was given in Lincoln Hall, Washington, D.C., February 15, 1873. Hampton now has a regular choir that tours America. Each year the Virginia State College Choral Society from Petersburg gives a concert in honor of the governor of Virginia. Negro spirituals are strangely haunting. Those current among the Virginia Negroes today differ little from those sung several decades ago. 'Swing Low, Sweet Chariot' was noted in Fisk jubilee Songs, 1871. The Hampton version is a variant. This theme, or one similar to it, occurs in the first movement of Dvorak's New World Symphony, and the same theme also occurs in John Powell's 'Negro Rhapsody.' 'My Lord Delivered Daniel' was noted in Slave Songs of the United States, Jubilee Songs (1872), and Hampton Plantation Songs. 'The Old Ship of Zion,' a spiritual widely current in Virginia, has many variants. 'Go Down Moses,' a song of slavery, is an interpretation of Hebrew history. 'Deep River' is a spiritual highly prized in Virginia. 'Steal Away to Jesus' was first sung as a notice to the other slaves on the plantation that a secret religious meeting would be held that night.

Source: *Approaching Appalachia: Southern Hillfolk in the American Mind.* AS@UVA .

which made it more difficult for the search dogs to follow those who were escaping. Map songs were designed to give directions to fugitive or runaway Africans. In the song, "Sheep, Sheep, Don't You Know the Road?" the use of the word "road" could have encoded some message about a specific escape route. "Follow the Drinking Gourd" was another map song, a metaphoric allusion to the Big Dipper, which the escapees were to follow north to freedom.

It was clear that by the 1870s (i.e., the generation after the Civil War), the genre known alternately as spirituals, plantation songs, and jubilees (however loosely defined) was inextricably linked to the African-American enslavement experience, and was viewed by much of the American public as an acceptable form of religious expression: evidence resides in the large numbers of spiritual collections that appeared throughout the balance of the nineteenth century and well into the twentieth century. Volumes and collections such as *Hampton and Its Students* (1874), *The Story of the Jubilee Singers* (1877), *The Jubilee Singers* (1883), *Jubilee and Plantation Songs* (1884), *Old Plantation Melodies* (1899), and *Songs of the Confederacy and Plantation Songs* (1901), among many others, illustrate this point. This list of spiritual collections could easily extend into the 1920s and 1930s.

Attention was being drawn to spirituals not only through the collections, essays, books, and articles, but through live performances as well. By the 1870s, concerts of spirituals had become a fund-raising vehicle for several struggling African-American colleges, most notably Calhoun, Fisk, Hampton, and (to a lesser extent) Tuskegee. Several of these groups made highly successful overseas tours. By the 1890s, Europeans and Americans alike were exposed to a different kind of African-Americans musical talent than that which had been featured in the minstrel shows. When the celebrated Bohemian composer Antonin Dvorak recognized the uniqueness of the genre and encouraged his students, including Harry T. Burleigh and Will Marion Cook, to compose and arrange more spirituals, it was given a new level of acceptance and recognition.

Other arranged spirituals (in solo or choral versions) came from composers/arrangers like R. Nathaniel Dett. Dett was best known at Hampton Institute for starting a choir made up of students and community members and transforming the group into an internationally-renowned touring organization that specialized in African-American sacred music. Many of the songs that the choir performed were Dett's own compositions or arrangements of spirituals. The production of arranged spirituals and hymnals would continue in the skillful hands of other musical luminaries such as Hall Johnson, John W. Work, Florence Price, J. Rosamund Johnson, and W. C. Handy.

Twentieth-Century Sacred Musical Traditions

Although much scholarly and casual interest was directed to the spiritual, other African-American sacred music traditions emerged by the end of the nineteenth century as the African-American church movement itself gained momentum. By the 1890s, the Holiness and Sanctified Church movement had crystallized. The largest denomination within this tradition, the Church of God in Christ, was founded by the Memphis-based religious leader, Charles Henry Mason, formerly of Lexington, Mississippi. Collectively, the Holiness/Sanctified churches believed in spirit possession, speaking in tongues (a form of glossolalia), and improvisatory singing. "Holy" dancing was also seen as an acceptable form of religious behavior. Certain instruments like drums, tambourines, triangles, guitars, and cymbals were frequently used to accompany the singing. Initially, their performances were more spontaneous and performed collectively. A hymnal tradition did emerge during the 1920s.

A figure at the turn of the century who played a role in what would come to be called "gospel" music was Reverend Charles Albert Tindley. Tindley was a Maryland-born Methodist camp meeting preacher and singer who, in the 1870s, settled in Philadelphia. There he founded the East Calvary Methodist Episcopal Church in 1902. It was later re-named the Tindley Temple. Tindley established a practice of sponsoring periodic concerts of church songs and subsequently had many of his compositions published in 1916 in a collection entitled *The New Songs of Paradise*. Included in this collection were songs like "Leave it There," "What are They Doing in Heaven Tonight," "We'll Understand it Better By and By," and "I'll Overcome Someday," which was the melodic basis of the 1960s civil rights anthem, "We Shall Overcome." The collection was so popular that several subsequent editions of it would appear by the 1940s.

Although Tindley had the support of his congregation, other religious song writers received support from organizations like the National Baptist Convention (founded in the 1880s). It became a vehicle for groups to perform; for exposing congregations and individuals to religious music. In 1921, the National Baptist Convention produced a collection of 165 religious songs entitled, *Gospel Pearls*. This work was enormously popular in many African-American congregations, without regard for denomination.

By the 1920s, singing ministers or so-called "shout" preachers began recording brief three to five minute sermons and song performances. These recorded sermons might include a congregation, or a small choir. Celebrated names in this tradition were Reverends Ford Washington McGee of Memphis, J. C. Burnett of Kansas City, Theodore

Frye from Mississippi, E. H. Hall of Chicago, and A. W. Nix and J. M. Gates of Atlanta. Gates's style was captured in numerous recordings that are still extant. These include "The Need of Prayer," recorded in 1926, and "Down Here Lord, Waiting on You," recorded in 1929.

Gospel Hymnody

Although the term "gospel" music does not become standard when referring to a specific African-American sacred musical genre before the 1930s, as we have seen, its predecessors had long been in place. Chicago came to be known as the birthplace of gospel music because many of its churches produced pioneering singers and composers. The figure most closely associated with the rise of the so-called blues-based gospel was Thomas A. Dorsey (1899–1993), commonly known as the "Father of Gospel Music."

Born in rural Georgia, Dorsey was the eldest child of a Baptist minister whom he frequently accompanied on the keyboard during his father's evangelizing trips. Dorsey moved to Atlanta when he was a teenager and played keyboard in brothels and saloons. In 1916, Dorsey made a stop in Chicago and it became his home base for the rest of his life. Initially, as a blues musician, he was known at varying points in his career as "Georgia Tom," "Barrelhouse Tommy," and by a few other names. Several of his blues compositions were recorded by jazz greats like Joseph "King" Oliver, among others.

Although Dorsey had strong credentials as a bluesman, he continued to foster his religious music beginnings from his childhood. He attended the National Baptist Convention in 1920 and had one of his songs, "Some Day, Somewhere" published in the Convention's 1921 collection, *Gospel Pearls.*

Around 1927, he began "peddling" (i.e., Dorsey accompanying a singer at the keyboard) his religious songs in Chicago areas churches, but they were rejected by many ministers because of their stylistic affinity to the blues. In 1931 he composed "Take My Hand, Precious Lord," which has remained his most celebrated and most frequently performed work. Dorsey composed close to one thousand compositions, many of which were arranged for choral groups.

By the 1930s, Dorsey was more devoted to composing and promoting religious music. In 1931, he formed the world's first gospel choir at Ebenezer Baptist Church in Chicago and opened the first publishing company devoted to gospel music. With his colleague, Sallie Martin, he founded the National Convention of Gospel Choirs and Choruses as a vehicle for training gospel choirs and soloists. More than any single individual, Dorsey was responsible for elevating gospel music to its current professional status.

Gospel Traditions and Groups

By the end of 1930s, gospel music had established at least two generic performing groups. The first was the all-male "gospel quartet," which was made up of four or five singers dressed in business suits and singing in *a cappella* barber shop-style harmonies. There was also the "gospel chorus," which could be women and men (or all women) dressed in choir robes and accompanied by piano or organ. Groups in the first category included the Golden Gate Jubilee Quartet, the Famous Blue Jay Singers, the Jubilaires, the Mighty Clouds of Joy, the Fairfield Four, the Soul Stirrers, the Five Blind Boys of Mississippi, and many others. The second category included the Ford Family Quartet, the Roberta Martin Singers, the Clara Ward Singers (another group that Thomas Dorsey would discover and help to promote), and, later, the Barrett Sisters. By the end of the 1950s, gospel music had shaken itself free of its Pentecostal/ Holiness roots to reach widespread acceptance in many African-American Protestant Churches around the United States. Instrumentally, the organ also became the standard accompanying instrument for most church-based gospel ensembles.

During the 1960s, large community-based gospel choirs such as the Mississippi Mass Choir, the Abyssinian Choir (led by Alex Bradford), the Greater Metropolitan Church of Christ Choir (led by Isaac Whittmon), the Harold Smith Majestics, the Donal Vail Choraleers, the Charles Ford Singers, the Triboro Mass Choir (led by Albert Jamison), the Chicago Community Choir (led by Jessy Dixon), the Voices of Tabernacle (led by James Cleveland), and the Michigan State Community Choir (led by Mattie Moss Clark) made successful recordings and/or tours around the country.

Contemporary Gospel

From the 1970s, gospel music has reached a mainstream audience and become a commercially viable tradition. Musicians who have remained more or less within the tradition while reaching large crossover audiences include Andrae Couch, Tramaine Hawkins, Walter Hawkins, Lynette Hawkins, Jessy Dixon, and the Winan family. Coming from Detroit, the Winan family gospel group (comprised of Benjamin "BeBe", Cecelia "CeCe", Marvin, Carvin, Michael, and Ronald) was encouraged by Andrae Crouch, who helped them make their first recording. Since then, the careers of BeBe and CeCe have blossomed. The brothers won a Grammy Award in 1985 for "Let My People Go."

Gospel music has continued to flourish as a genre and business. Although the Grammy Awards introduced a category to recognize the importance of gospel music in the 1970s, among gospel music enthusiasts the Dove Award (gospel music's own counterpart to the Grammy) is just as prestigious. In 1999, among the winners were for Songwriter of the Year, Michael W. Smith; Male Vocalist of the Year, Steven Curtis Chapman; Female Vocalist of the Year, Jaci Velasquez; Group of the Year, Sixpence None the Richer; Artist of the Year, Steven Curtis Chapman; New Artist of the Year, Ginny Owens; and Producer of the Year, Brown Bannister.

Christopher Brooks

Bibliography

Brooks, Tilford. (1984) *America's Black Musical Heritage.* Englewood Cliffs, NJ: Prentice-Hall.

Southern, Eileen. (1998) *Music of Black Americans.* New York: Norton.

Music, Spiritual Baptist

While membership in Spiritual Baptist churches (primarily in Trinidad, St. Vincent, Grenada, Venezuela, United States, Canada) is predominantly black, the faith has also attracted sizeable numbers of East Indians, Chinese, and whites. As might be expected, all of the above ethnic groups have had a profound impact on Spiritual Baptist music; for example, Indian ragas have become increasingly popular within Spiritual Baptist services.

Most studies of Spiritual Baptist music have dealt with churches in Trinidad. Much of what can be said of Spiritual Baptist music in Trinidad also holds for Spiritual Baptist music in the United States, South America, and Canada, but holds to a lesser degree for music in Grenada and St. Vincent, where churches are much more conservative and make fewer provisions for musical innovation.

Kenneth Bilby, in his "The Caribbean as a Musical Region" (1988), characterizes Spiritual Baptist music as a product of large-scale Protestant missionization in the Anglophone Caribbean during the mid-nineteenth century. Spiritual Baptist music, Bilby argues, blends Protestant devotional songs (many of them taken from nineteenth-century British and American hymns) and polyrhythmic clapping, banging of pews, and forceful stomping (sometimes called "adoption" or "hocketing") to create a unique and constantly evolving musical format that has influenced and continues to influence other Caribbean musical forms. For example, calypsonian David Rudder grew up in the Belmont section of Port of Spain and was thrice-baptized (Anglican, Spiritual Baptist, and Roman Catholic), and also attended Orisha ceremonies (Rudder 1990). In 1986, Rudder won the Calypso Monarch competition with two songs "The Hammer" (with its obvious Baptist and Orisha rhythms) and "Bahia Gyal" (which features Spiritual Baptist "adoption" and trumpeting and mentions the Spiritual Baptists by name). The Spiritual Baptists were also the focus of calypsonian Austin Lyons's (a.k.a. Blue Boy's) winning "Soca Baptist" (1980), but while Lyons's treatment of the faith was clearly derisive ("What to them suppose to be spiritual, to me, it was just like bacchanal"), David Rudder's "Bahia Gyal" cites the Baptists as the embodiment of a Pan-African spirit, emphasizing similarities between Baptist trumpeting and Brazilian samba rhythms.

Role of Music in Worship

In the absence of a trained clergy and formal written creeds, Spiritual Baptist theology is embedded in ritual, sermons, dance, and—most notably—in its musical forms. Music has been one of the most persistent forces for the perpetuation and transmission of Afro-Caribbean culture (Behague 1994). Malm (1983) has suggested that over 90 percent of Spiritual Baptist ceremonies are taken up by music—most of it singing. This is a conservative estimate, since it fails to take into account the considerable overlap of sermons, rituals, and music. While segments of Baptist music might initially appear to be derived from nineteenth century Protestantism and African rhythms, Baptist ceremonies need to be analyzed in their own terms. They follow their own rules and aesthetic principles, which only the initiated can fully appreciate.

Baptist attitudes toward music and musical performance might best be described as pragmatic. Music has many uses. It can be used to dispel unwanted spirits, set a mood, and mark ritual phases (Williams 1985; 63–64). For example, "Lead Us Heavenly Father Lead Us" is common in processionals, "Nearer My God to Thee" is commonly sung while placing "bands" over the eyes of a "pilgrim," and "When the Saints Go Marching In" usually signifies a return from baptism. Different churches might use different hymns at different times, but once a hymn has been established it tends to be used regularly. While music serves to demonstrate and document patterns of authority within a church (Glazier 1991), it also serves to "guide" candidates for baptism, offer supplication, and invoke the presence of the Holy Spirit. Most hymns can be sung in a variety of ways (e.g., slow or fast; allowing or not allowing for improvisations). Inasmuch as hymns are regarded as "tools," certain hymns are selected because they are thought to work better than other hymns within a particular context. Aesthetics is always a secondary consideration. Sometimes—but not often—hymns provide veiled messages to congregants. Williams (1985: 109) cites an example of a pilgrim who had a reputation for moving from church to church. His spiritual mother admonished him by raising up the hymn "I Was a Wandering Sheep."

Musical Development and Composition

Williams (1985: 55) follows Herskovits and Herskovits (1947, Simpson (1961), and Glazier (1980) by classifying Spiritual Baptist music into four basic categories: 1) hymns, 2) "Sankeys" 3) trumpeting, and 4) intoned prayers. Hymns, Williams contends, are mostly taken from the Anglican Book of Common Prayer. Although the melodies of such hymns are often the same as those sung by Anglicans, the style of performance sometimes differs among Baptists. Sankeys are hymns found in the books published by Sankey (and sometimes by Moody). In the performance of Sankeys, there is much rhythmic accompaniment provided by hands and feet. "Trumpets" are short musical phrases which may or may not have texts. These may be introduced during a prayer, and may induce altered states of consciousness. Intoned prayers may include hymns, Sankeys, and trumpets and may assume the form of a chant.

According to Williams (58–61), hymns are performed in a simple meter such as 2/2, 3/2, or 4/4. Songs begin on one of the notes of the I (tonic triad) and end on the tonic. Antiphony is evident together with little ornamentation, and rendition of texts is mostly melismatic. Sankeys are performed in 4/4 meter with stress on the first and third beats. Harmony is sporadic. Trumpets are performed in 4/4 meter. Harmony is not evident, but voices perform different parts with constant repetition in a call-and-response pattern. There is much improvisation and each performance is dependent on the creativity and virtuosity of the members present. No trumpet performance is ever the same, but there are notable regularities that have yet to be adequately explored. In my research, for example, I have isolated four distinct trumpet tones which correspond to different sequences of worship as well as regional variations. An important characteristic of trumpeting is the production of inhaled and exhaled notes to induce hyperventilation. Intoned prayers are performed slowly with little evidence of set tempo or meter. A major characteristic are call-and-response, overlapping repetition of words, and harmony based on the I and V chords. Intoned prayers start with the supplicant's hymn and end with recitation of the Apostle's Creed or a selected psalm. Psalm 23 is the most common.

Opening hymns are subdued, and give forth a "heavy, doleful, dragging effect" (see also Pitts 1993: 103). Many Spiritual Baptist renditions would be barely recognizable to the American and British missionaries who originally brought these hymns to the Caribbean. The hymnals available to Baptists provided only the lyrics. This was of minor consequence to converts since most nineteenth-century Spiritual Baptists could not read music. Melodies had to be improvised and were borrowed from selected bits and pieces of music that they had heard elsewhere. Moreover, even the lyrics had to be improvised since many early Baptists were also illiterate. Hymns are learned by repetition in much the same way members learn to follow the general order of worship and to interpret cues used during ritual performance.

Richard Alan Waterman (1952: 209) points out that the musical traditions of Africa and Europe both emphasize the same basic concepts of scale and harmony, and that it was inevitable that European hymns would be seized upon by Africans and remodeled into their own musical forms. Waterman makes special note of overlapping call-and-response patterns in which a leader sings phrases that alternate with phrases sung by a chorus. This pattern is common throughout the world, but in African and Caribbean music "the chorus phrase regularly commences while the soloist is still singing and the leader begins his phrase before the chorus is finished" (Waterman 1952: 214). Such overlapping patterns are an especially striking characteristic of Spiritual Baptist music, and are most notable during opening hymns and intoned prayers.

Spiritual Baptist music appears eclectic because Spiritual Baptist participants are often simultaneously involved in a number of musical traditions. Of the ten musical forms of sacred music outlined by Jon Michael Spencer (1990), seven of them—spirituals, the blues, the ring shout, the tongue song, holiness-Pentecostal music, gospel music, and the chanted sermon—can be identified within Spiritual Baptist worship services. There is also ample evidence for what Kenneth Bilby has termed "polymusicality." Some prominent Baptists are themselves accomplished professional musicians; most notably, drummers who perform frequently at Orisha feasts and/or are members of steel orchestras. Two prominent Belmont Baptists are part of the Hilton Hotel's Friday night "folkloric" show. One Spiritual Baptist church in Tunapuna includes among its members two local calypsonians, members of a local reggae band, a jazz trio, and a concert violinist who has performed in Canada and the United States. The impact of popular music can never be overestimated. Music—all kinds of music—is everywhere in Trinidad, blaring from houses, cars, taxis, buses, stores, sidewalk vendors, and boom boxes in infinite variety. Whether from India, Jamaica, Brazil, or the United States, if it is a hit somewhere it can probably be heard in Trinidad and Tobago. Much popular music makes its way into Spiritual Baptist music, and in turn, Spiritual Baptist music has made its way into Caribbean musical consciousness. In 1976—long after Frankie Vallee and the Four Seasons were off the Billboard charts in the United States but were experiencing something of a revival in Trinidad—an unusually somber rendition of "I Heard the Voice of Jesus Say" was countered from the back of the church by a falsetto version of "I'll Be A Big Man in Town" and "Dawn, Go Away I'm No Good for You." I have since identified bits and pieces from the music of Johnny Cash, the Beatles, Michael Jackson's "Thriller" album, Sammy Davis Jr.'s rendition of "Mr. Bojangles," and Elton John.

Performance

The way in which Baptist music is structured allows each participant to act as his or her own conductor, chorus member, and innovator. In theory, any member—under the influence of the Holy Spirit—could "raise up" any hymn at any time. But hymns are far from random, and Spiritual Baptist services are extremely regular. While each church has a paramount leader who often owns the church building outright and is ultimately responsible for all aspects of worship, there is a great deal of turn-taking, and leadership shifts constantly throughout the two-to-three hour service. Baptists state that they value full participation by all congregants, and that any attempt to direct an entire service would detract from rather than enhance a paramount leader's authority and reputation. Nevertheless, such "battles of the spirit" do occur, especially among senior leaders and within established churches (Glazier 1991). After service is well underway, it is permissible—but not desirable—for individual participants to attempt to "spontaneously" lead the congregation in a particular hymn; often, two or more church members will lead different hymns at the same time. Whichever hymn predominates is believed to reflect the will of God the Holy Spirit; and thus, the individual who initiated that hymn is thought to be closer and more "in tune" with God's will. It is common for dissident church members to try to make the congregation stray from a paramount leader's hymn choice. This is taken as a challenge to that leader's authority. A series of successful challenges could indicate a paramount leader's weakening position and could result in the selection of a new pastor. Hymn selection, therefore, is serious in its consequences and provides a means of pitting one's spiritual powers against the spiritual powers of one's co-religionists.

Like much Caribbean music, there is no rigid division of audience into active performers and passive listeners.

Performers and audience blend into one. Baptists hope that each member has at least a brief opportunity to perform and that each member takes time to listen to others' performances. If a service is to be deemed a success, everyone must have participated (including guests and the visiting anthropologist). It is not simply a matter of virtuosity, but total involvement by all members that makes for a "sweet" (outstanding) ceremony. The quality of interaction between participants is a major concern and is often discussed for several weeks following a service.

Although Spiritual Baptists focus on group performance and cooperation, there is an equally strong emphasis on individual style. Like in jazz, one notes considerable turn-taking and each member in succession tries to "stand out" from the crowd. As in other Caribbean musical forms (most notably calypso), flamboyant innovation and technical virtuosity are greatly admired, and while innovation and technical skill are not the only measures of a "good" performance, these are nonetheless highly regarded.

Ideally, musical instruments (aside from the human voice) should not be part of Spiritual Baptist worship. Exceptions abound. I noted that a number of suburban churches (St. Joseph, Tunapuna, and Daberdie) featured electronic organ music just prior to service, but in most cases the organ was physically removed from the church prior to opening hymns and the arrival of the paramount leader. Baptist leaders are emphatic that drums are forbidden in Spiritual Baptist churches. However, I have noted trumpets, rhythm sticks, and chac-chacs (maracas) being incorporated into service, but such inclusions were always a matter of controversy. Spiritual Baptist music, it is contended, should be performed a cappella. All churches have several handbells, which are believed to be the "Voice of God." Bell ringing calls the service to order, indicates transitions in services, provides a mechanism to concentrate or diffuse spiritual power, or simply serves as a way to get congregants' attention.

In the absence of drums, other ritual objects have been modified to take their place. Shepherd's crooks can be rhythmically struck on the concrete or wooden floor to considerable effect. Such crooks are often selected for their tonal qualities. Benches in Spiritual Baptist churches are of varying woods, heights, widths, and lengths. These, too, can produce dramatically different tones, which roughly correspond to the tonal drumming in Orisha ceremonies (Waterman 1952; Simpson 1961). Indeed, as noted previously, a number of Spiritual Baptist participants are also professional Shango drummers. Some carryover is to be expected.

Spiritual Baptist music features the body itself as the ultimate musical instrument. Music is believed to be pleasing to both men and spirits, and is understood as an offering to

God. At the same time, music can be intensely political. It is a test which, over time, reveals whether one is "in tune" or "out of tune" with the Holy Spirit.

Stephen D. Glazier

See also Spiritual Baptists

Discography

Charlies Roots—The Hammer. (1987) Kingston, Jamaica: Dynamic Sounds Recording Co.

Glazier, Stephen D. (1980) *Spiritual Baptist Music from Trinidad; Recorded in Trinidad by Stephen D. Glazier.* Washington, DC: Smithsonian/Folkways (Ethnic Folkways 4234).

Malm, Krister. (1983) *"Jesus going to prepare a mansion for me" (St Teresa S. B. Church). An Island Carnival: Music of the West Indies. Recorded and edited by Krister Malm (1969–71).* Nonesuch Explorer Series 72091.

Simpson, George Eaton. (1961) *Cult Music of Trinidad: Recorded in Trinidad by George Eaton Simpson.* Washington, DC: Smithsonian/Folkways (Folkways Ethnic 4478).

Soca Baptist Sung By Blue Boy (A. Lyons). (1979) Bridgetown, Barbados: Romney's Disco 45 RPM.

Bibliography

Behague, Gerard H., ed. (1994) *Music and Black Ethnicity: The Caribbean and South America.* New Brunswick: Transaction Publishers.

Bilby, Kenneth. (1988) "The Caribbean as a Musical Area." In *Caribbean Contours,* edited by Sidney Mintz and Richard Price. Baltimore: The Johns Hopkins University Press, 181–218.

Glazier, Stephen D. (1991) *Marchin' the Pilgrims Home: A Study of the Spiritual Baptists of Trinidad,* rev. paper ed. Salem, WI: Sheffield Press.

Herskovits, Melville J., and Frances S. Herskovits. (1947) *Trinidad Village.* New York: Alfred A. Knopf.

Manuel, Peter, with Kenneth Bilby and Michael Largey. (1995) *Caribbean Currents: Caribbean Music from Rumba to Reggae.* Philadelphia: Temple University Press.

Pitts, Walter F., Jr. (1993) *Old Ship of Zion: The Afro-Baptist Ritual in the African Diaspora.* New York: Oxford.

Rudder, David. (1990) *Kaiso, Calypso Music: David Rudder in Conversation with John LaRose.* London: New Beacon Press.

Spencer, Jon Michael. (1990) *Protest and Praise: Sacred Music of Black Religion.* Minneapolis: Fortress Press.

Waterman, Richard Alan. (1952) "African Influence on the Music of the Americas." In *Acculturation in the Americas,* edited by Sol Tax. Chicago: International Congress of the Americanists, 207–218.

Williams, Mervyn R. (1985) "Songs from Valley to Mountain: Music and Ritual Among the Spiritual Baptists ("Shouters") of Trinidad." Master's Thesis. Indiana University.

National Baptist Convention of America

The National Baptist Convention of America (NBCA), originally and colloquially called the Nation Baptist Convention, Unincorporated, is a product of the 1915 split in the National Baptist Convention, U.S.A., which was founded in 1895. The factor of "incorporation" was the longtime distinguishing characteristic between both factions, although both conventions are now fully incorporated. The central issue in this conflict was the publishing house in Nashville, Tennessee. The dispute involved the "Boyd faction" led by the Rev. Ronald Boyd, secretary of the Publishing Board, and the "Morris faction," led by the Rev. Edmond Morris, president of the convention. Ultimately, the Boyd faction took the name "National Baptist Convention of America" and remained unincorporated until recently. The Morris faction retains the original name of the convention, but incorporated to become the National Baptist Convention, U.S.A., Inc. Both groups claim to be the original parent body. Both claim the founding date of 1880. In fact, no unified National Baptist Convention existed in 1880, which was the founding date of the oldest of the three entities that merged in 1895. In short, while three Baptist bodies went into the funnel in 1895, two emerged from the other end in 1915.

History

The conflict was set in motion shortly after the NBC, U.S.A., Inc., was created, when the American Baptist Publication Society, upon complaints from Southern Baptists, withdrew its invitation for black leaders to write articles for one of its publications. As a result of this impasse, the National Baptist Convention determined to establish its own publishing capabilities. The new Publishing Board was initially placed under the Home Mission Board, of which the Rev. Ronald Boyd, who introduced the resolution proposing the printing committee, served as corresponding secretary.

Under Boyd's leadership and on the basis of his own financial credit, the Publishing Board quickly became a successful business venture, since thousands of black Baptist churches began buying their Sunday School and church publication materials from the Board. New printing facili-

CHURCHES

The event of the month in religious circles has been of the great meeting of the Baptists. Some 3,000 delegates and visitors assembled at Luna Park, Pittsburgh, for the annual meeting of the national Baptist convention. The local arrangements were wretched, and to the casual visitor the meeting of the mass of men and women looks like a great unregulated assembly. Gradually, however, beneath the crudeness and lack of system, one sees the tremendous power and possibility of these men. They represent 2,411,701 members, they have 18,000 churches, worth $25,000,000, and they spend each year $2,371,176. Their schools enroll 18,450 students and are valued at $3,500,000. Much of their work has been organized, and more and more strong men like R. H. Boyd, who is at the head of the publishing house, reported gross receipts of $187,753 last year. He has mailed during the past twelve months 9,000,000 periodicals and articles. The women, under the presidency of Mrs. S. W. Layton, held an interesting series of meetings. Dr. E. C. Morris presided, and W. E. B. Du Bois was among the speakers.

Source: *The Crisis: A Record of the Darker Races*, vol. 2 (October 1911), p. 231. New York: NAACP.

ties were built on land owned by Boyd in Nashville, who had the agency incorporated in the state of Tennessee, and materials produced by the publishing house were copyrighted in his name. In 1905, when president Morris acted to separate the publishing house from the Home Mission Board, Boyd and other members of the board resisted, and a decade-long controversy ensued, centered around the question of ownership and control of the publishing interest. Ultimately the conflict was resolved in Boyd's favor by the courts of Tennessee. The convention itself was unincorporated and so unable to own property in its own name, and although it had created the Publishing Board, it had neglected to make proper provisions for a legal claim to it.

The National Baptist Publishing Board became the nucleus of a separate National Baptist body, the NBCA, which was organized in Chicago on 9 September 1915. As this convention moved to establish additional boards, an agreement was struck whereby all foreign mission work of the new group would be conducted through the Lott Carey Convention, an autonomous group affiliated with the NBC U.S.A. The latter thereby strengthened its hand in missions, while the NBCA gained an enlarged audience for its literature. Over the years, however, this working relationship declined and NBCA ultimately organized an independent Foreign Mission Board. In addition to the issues of prohibition, evangelism, and education, the NBCA gave early support to civil rights organizations, urban social service programs, and the anti-lynching campaign.

The Boyd family continues to be prominent in the NBCA publishing house. Henry Allen Boyd succeeded his father, Ronald Boyd, in 1922, and he in turn was succeeded by his nephew, Thomas Boyd, Jr., who led the publishing

house from 1959 to 1979. Since 1979 the Publishing Board has been headed by Thomas Boyd, III, in his capacity as executive director. Rev. Edward Jones was elected president of the NBCA at the time of its organizing. His successors were John Woods, 1923; James Hurse, 1930; Gary Prince, 1933; Charles Pettaway, 1957; John Sams, 1967; and Everett Jones, 1985.

In 1988 a new schism occurred in the NBCA over the question of the Boyd family's control of the publishing house. With an estimated 25 percent of the membership, the Boyd faction called itself the National Missionary Baptist Convention of America (NMBCA). It remains to be seen whether this group will emerge as the fourth major black Baptist denomination.

Organization

The National Baptist Convention of America is the second largest of the three black Baptist conventions having a national constituency, and the third largest of all the black denominations. In 1990 its estimated membership was 2.4 million members in 7,800 local churches. These churches are served by about 3,000 clergy, which suggests that a substantial number of them are small rural churches. Some four hundred associations, ranging from five to one hundred local churches, and thirty-five state conventions in twenty seven states, are affiliated with the convention.

The NBCA convenes every year on the Wednesday following the first Sunday in September. Convention delegates called "messengers" include lay and ministerial representatives from local churches, associations, and state conventions. Each church is assessed a minimum of $50, or $1 per member for the first messenger, and $10 for each additional messenger; each general association and state convention pays $100 for the first five messengers, and $10 for each additional messenger.

The officers of the convention are elected annually and include a president; first, second, and third vice presidents; recording secretary; first, second, third, and fourth assistant recording secretaries; corresponding secretary; statistical secretary; treasurer, auditor, and director of public relations; historian, and secretary of youth activities. The presidents of the state conventions and moderators of the general associations are associate vice presidents. The Executive Board, which conducts the business of the convention when it is not in sessions, consists of the elected convention officers and presidents of the state conventions. The constitution provides for five administrative committees: Registration, Budget, Finance, Bills and Accounts, and Credentials.

The NBCA has seven program boards: Home Mission, Foreign Mission, Baptist Training Union, National Baptist Publishing, Evangelical, Benevolent, and Educational. The membership of each board consists of one member from each state convention and general association. The auxiliaries of the convention include two Women's Missionary auxiliaries, Junior Women's Auxiliary, Brotherhood Union, Ushers, Nurses Corps, and Youth Convention. Each board and auxiliary elects its own officers, although the officers of the latter are subject to ratification by the convention. The constitution also specifies four commissions: Transportation, Christian Education, Social Justice, and Army and Navy Chaplains. The NBCA does not have a centralized national headquarters, though the publishing house has remained in Nashville. The principal officers do not ordinarily relinquish their offices as local pastors.

Lawrence H. Mamiya

See also National Baptist Convention, U.S.A.

Bibliography

Fisher, Miles Mark. (1927) "What Is A Negro Baptist?" *The Home Mission College Review* 1,1 (May).

Fitts, Leroy. (1978) *Lott Carey, First Black Missionary to Africa.* Valley Forge, PA: Judson Press.

———. (1985) *A History of Black Baptists.* Nashville: Broadman Publishing Co.

Hamilton, Charles. (1972) *The Black Preacher in America.* New York: William Morrow.

Jackson, Joseph. (1980) *A Story of Christian Activism: The History of the National Baptist Convention, U.S.A., Inc.* Nashville: Townsend Publishing.

Tinney, James. (1977) "Selected Directory of Afro-American Religious Organizations, Schools, and Periodicals." In *The Black Church: A Community Resource,* edited by Dionne Jones and William Matthews. Washington, D.C.: Howard University Institute for Urban Affairs and Research.

Washington, James Melvin. (1986) *Frustrated Fellowship: The Black Baptist Quest for Social Power.* Macon, GA: Mercer University Press.

The National Baptist Convention, U.S.A., Inc.

African-American Baptists constitute the largest sector of black Christians in the United States, numbering between 10 to 15 million members. They are currently divided into three conventions with the National Baptist Convention, U.S.A., Inc. as the largest group, claiming between 6 to 8 million adherents. The National Baptist Convention, U.S.A., Inc., is by far the largest of all the black denominations, and is considered the largest organization of African-Americans in existence. The NBC, USA, Inc., has estimated its membership between 6 to 8 million. This membership encompasses nearly one-fourth of the entire black population of the United States and at least one-third of the estimated number of black members of Christian churches. Over 29,000 clergy and 30,000 local churches are affiliated with the convention, as are 4,700 associations and 59 state conventions.

History and Beliefs

The cultural origins of African-American Baptists were in the South rather than the North, and this fact had implications for the development of national organizations among the Baptists. Although the Baptists had founded the earliest independent black churches in the Bluestone Church on William Byrd plantation in Mecklenberg, Virginia, and the Silverbluff Baptist Church, on the South Carolina bank of the Savannah River, between 1750 to 1772, it was the black Methodist groups in Philadelphia and New York City that succeeded in establishing the first independent black denominations, the African Methodist Episcopal Church (1816) and the African Methodist Episcopal Zion Church (1822). Black codes in the slave-holding Southern states prevented any organizing by black Baptist leaders until after the Civil War. The earliest all-black Baptist associations were organized not in the South but in the "West": Providence Association, in Ohio in 1834; Union Association, also in

Ohio in 1836; Wood River Association, in Illinois in 1839; and Amherstburg Association, in Canada and Michigan in 1841. The question of slavery was also divisive among white Baptists, splitting the American Baptist Convention (Northern) from the Southern Baptist Convention in 1844.

The majority of black and white Baptist churches adhere to the principle of congregational autonomy, of each church and its pastor making its own decisions. While this form of church governance provides for great independence, it can also give rise to schisms and splits in larger associations. Following the example of Jesus' baptism in the river by John the Baptist, most Baptists also believe in "complete immersion" in water during the ritual of baptism, hence the origin of their name. Black Baptists also have more emotional worship services and come largely from lower economic classes.

After several failed attempts at developing a national convention—including the Consolidated American Baptist Missionary Convention in 1866 and the American National Baptist Convention in 1886—the National Baptist Convention, U.S.A. was successfully established in Atlanta on 28 September 1895. The Rev. Edmond Morris was elected as the first president of the new convention. However, class tensions and ideological differences were often at the root of failures and schisms among the Baptists. For example, in 1897 the Lott Carey Foreign Mission Convention was established by the better-educated members from Virginia, North Carolina, and the District of Columbia. In 1905 the Lott Carey Convention and the National Baptists ostensibly reconciled but they have continued to function as independent bodies while maintaining loose affiliations.

In 1915 a major schism occurred in a dispute over the ownership of the convention's publishing house, and the National Baptist Convention of America emerged. As a result of the schism, the NBC, U.S.A., incorporated itself and the Rev. Morris continued as the president of the incorporated body until 1922. Following the loss of the publishing house in 1915, a new board was created, the Sunday School Publishing Board of the National Baptist Convention. Foreign missions and the education of missionaries to Africa also became a major concern during this period. The convention also involved itself in domestic issues, establishing nearly 100 elementary and secondary schools and colleges, protesting racial violence, and waging campaigns against segregation in public accommodations and discrimination in the armed services, education, and employment. Much of this activity was carried out within the prevailing ideological framework of Booker T. Washington's self-help program. The NBC, Inc. strongly supported the NAACP and was vocal on such matters as the right to vote and to serve on juries. At the time of the split in 1915, the National Baptist Convention, U.S.A. represented nearly three million black people in over 20,000 local Baptist churches. Spurred by the northern migration of African-Americans over the next several decades, both Baptist conventions experienced a shift from rural to urban churches and a rapid growth in membership.

Rev. Morris was succeeded as convention president by William Parks, who served only one year before L. K. Williams took office in 1924. Daniel Jemison was elected president in 1941 and served until 1952. In 1953 Joseph Herbert Jackson became president and held that office for a record twenty-nine years.

Under the Rev. Dr. Joseph H. Jackson's leadership, the NBC, USA, Inc. took a decidedly conservative turn. Jackson represented a strong vocal opposition to the Rev. Dr. Martin Luther King, Jr. and King's strategy of civil disobedience and nonviolent protest. Under his slogan of "from protest to production!" he located himself in the patriotic, law and order, anti-communist, procapitalist school of gradualism. Although his was a position out of favor with most younger African-Americans, Jackson succeeded in blocking the participation of the convention as an institution in the civil rights movement. King, for his part, left the NBC, USA, Inc. as one of the leaders of the Progressive National Baptist Convention, a splinter group founded in 1961.

In contrast, Jackson's successor, Rev. Dr. Theodore Jemison, son of former convention president Daniel Jemison, was a veteran of the civil rights movement, having organized a bus boycott in Baton Rouge, Louisiana in 1953 that served as a model for the Montgomery Bus Boycott led by King in 1956. Jemison also served as the first general secretary of the Southern Christian Leadership Conference. Upon his election in 1982 Jemison pledged his support for social action in pursuit of civil rights, and initiated a nationwide voter registration drive.

Organization and Activities

In order to prevent lifetime appointments as president of the convention, as occurred under Joseph Jackson's twenty-nine years, a limit of two four-year terms was established. In 1990 the Rev. Dr. Henry Lyons of Florida was elected as president. Although he was elected to a second term in 1994, his leadership unraveled when he was convicted and sentenced to prison for financial fraud and misusing the convention's funds. The Rev. William Shaw of Philadelphia was elected in 1999 under a campaign to reform the financial and reporting procedures of the convention.

The NBC, U.S.A., Inc. convenes once a year, on the Wednesday after the first Sunday in September, which is the same time that its rival convention, the NBCA, also meets. Local churches, associations, and state conventions are required to pay a fee ranging from $10 to $50 for representative delegates, depending on the size and type of the sponsoring group, except that state conventions pay $200 for the first two representatives. In Baptist polity, delegates are called "messengers." Individuals may join the convention by paying an annual membership fee of $10, but they are not entitled to vote. Life membership is awarded upon payment of $200. The officers of the convention are elected annually, their positions specified in the constitution. The convention is governed by a board of directors that consists of fifteen members-at-large elected by the convention, in addition to the named officers.

Traditionally, the purpose of the National Convention has been to carry on work in areas such as education, mission, and publishing that could not be done effectively by individual churches and would be done less efficiently by multiple regional bodies. More recently the national body has also assumed responsibility for matters such as ministerial pension plans. The scope of the convention's activity includes Foreign Mission, Home Mission, Sunday School Publishing, Baptist Training Union (B.T.U.), Education, Evangelistic and Benefit boards, and Usher's and Moderator's Auxiliaries. The Laymen's Movement Auxiliary, Women's Convention Auxiliary, and Congress of Christian Education are specifically provided for in the constitution. A Young People's Department, operated as a subsidiary of the Women's Convention, is subdivided into several units based on age and marital status of the girls and young women. The Laymen's Auxiliary has a department for boys. Various commissions are appointed from time to time to address such matters as social service, rural life, theological education, theology, church-supported schools, ecumenical Christianity, the United Nations, civil rights, and intercultural relations. According to the constitution, each board is to be made up of one member from each state and territory represented at the convention, plus an additional eight members from the state in which the board is located. Each board determines its own laws and regulations, nominates its own officers, and selects its own employees, who are then subject to ratification by the convention or its board of directors. Several of the boards have counterpart departments to implement the various programs. The auxiliary conventions generally meet in session at the same time as the National Convention. They have their own officers and committee structures, and in some instances a separate constitution and their own publications.

In the mid-1990s the convention built a $12 million National Baptist World Center in Nashville to serve as its national headquarters. However, the Center has yet to fulfill its functions as a national headquarters. The old tradition of Baptist autonomy prevails and the home church of the convention's president serves as an unofficial headquarters.

Lawrence H. Mamiya

See also National Baptist Convention of America; Progressive National Baptist Convention; Social Activism; Southern Christian Leadership Conference

Bibliography

Fisher, Miles Mark. (1927) "What Is A Negro Baptist?" *The Home Mission College Review* 1, 1 (May).

Fitts, Leroy. (1978) *Lott Carey, First Black Missionary to Africa*. Valley Forge, PA: Judson Press.

——. (1985) A *History of Black Baptists*. Nashville: Broadman Publishing Co.

Hamilton, Charles. (1972) *The Black Preacher in America*. New York: William Morrow.

Jackson, Joseph. (1980) A *Story of Christian Activism: The History of the National Baptist Convention, U.S.A., Inc.* Nashville: Townsend Publishing.

Tinney, James. (1977) "Selected Directory of Afro-American Religious Organizations, Schools, and Periodicals." In *The Black Church: A Community Resource*, edited by Dionne Jones and William Matthews. Washington, DC: Howard University Institute for Urban Affairs and Research.

Washington, James Melvin. (1986) *Frustrated Fellowship: The Black Baptist Quest for Social Power*. Macon, GA: Mercer University Press.

National Conference of Black Christians

In the eighteen-year history of this organization—1966 to 1984—it was known by four different names: National Committee of Negro Churchmen, National Committee of Black Churchmen, National Conference of Black Churchmen, and National Conference of Black Christians—NCBC for short. The final change was made only a year before it became inactive, to acknowledge the participation of women.

These name changes correspond to major social changes and social movements in these eighteen years. During the civil rights movement of the 1950s and early 1960s, most African-Americans were still referred to as Negroes. In the last years of the civil rights movement, especially from 1966 to 1968, many younger activists became disenchanted with the movement's philosophy and tactics, and initiated a new movement, the Black Power movement, which was more assertive and less religious. At that time the nomenclature changed from Negro to Black.

NCBC was a product of these tumultuous times. It was organized by black ministers from the urban, northeast region of the United States, half of whom belonged to predominantly white denominations, and many of whom worked for the National Council of Churches (NCC), an ecumenical organization that brought together many church denominations, both white and black, for cooperative efforts. The NCC had been supportive of the civil rights movement, and was uncomfortable with the Black Power Movement. White ministers in the NCC were concerned that the religious coalition was being rejected. They did not understand the meaning of Black Power—which was never a threat to whites, but rather was a call for the more equitable distribution of resources and influence in American life.

NCBC came into being with a three-fold purpose: to interpret Black Power to the white religious establishment, to establish and maintain relations with the younger activists of the day, and to encourage the more conservative representatives of black churches to be open to more progressive thinking. The language that NCBC members developed in seeking to dialogue with these three constituencies came to be known as "black liberation theology," the essence of which was that Jesus was the liberator, and Christians were mandated by the gospel to be engaged in seeking political and economic empowerment of the oppressed.

NCBC was introduced to the general public by way of a "Statement on Black Power" in a full-page ad in the *New York Times* signed by forty-eight prominent black church leaders on 31 July 1966. On 3 November 1966, nearly 150 ministers, clad in clerical robes, processed to the Statue of Liberty where a statement on "Racism and the Elections" was read. The same statement was published in the *New York Times* on 6 November over the signatures of 172 church officials.

Having carried out these activities as an ad hoc group led by the Rev. Benjamin Payton, executive director of NCC's Commission on Religion and Race, the organization was formalized in Dallas, Texas, in November 1967. NCBC's most active years were from 1967 to 1972. Because its purpose was to interpret the Black Power Movement in Christian theological terms, most of NCBC's effort was given more to reflection than to action. Of its four program commissions—the Commission on African Relations, the Commission on Urban Mission and Crisis, the Commission

on Education, and the Theological Commission—the latter was the most active and the most productive. The chair of the Theological Commission was the Rev. Gayraud S. Wilmore. Numerous well-known black theologians and scholars of religion became involved in its work, including James H. Cone, Major Jones, Henry Mitchell, Deotis Roberts, Joseph Washington, and Preston Williams.

At its peak, NCBC had some 1,200 members. The membership ratio of clergy to laity was approximately five to one. About 40 percent came from white denominations, and 60 percent from black denominations, with many of the latter being younger, seminary-trained ministers. The heaviest concentration of members came from the northeast region. Consequently, when NCBC moved from New York to Atlanta in 1972, many ministers from that region became involved in another organization, the Black Theology Project, based in the New York City area. Other members became involved in a new scholarly organization called the Society for the Study of Black Religion, and still others in a new ecumenical effort closely aligned with the NCC called Partners in Ecumenism.

With the change nationally to a more conservative and political climate, NCBC's primary activity from 1973 to 1982 became the holding of annual convocations, which served as forums for continuing to address concerns that had brought members together in the first place. Significantly, numerous members of the national group organized local ecumenical organizations—in Philadelphia, Atlanta, Oakland, and Massachusetts, for example—that were effective in imparting black theology and its activist mandates to local constituencies. NCBC's most enduring legacy, however, is the arena it provided for the very formulation of black liberation theology which is now a part of the curriculum of most liberal Protestant seminaries.

Mary R. Sawyer

See also Black Theology; Social Activism

Bibliography

Cone, James H., and Gayraud S. Wilmore, eds. (1993) *Black Theology: A Documentary History*, vol. 1: *1966–1979*, 2d ed. Maryknoll, NY: Orbis Books.

Sawyer, Mary R. (1994) *Black Ecumenism: Implementing the Demands of Justice*. Valley Forge, PA: Trinity Press, Intl., ch. 3.

Wilmore, Gayraud S. (1998) *Black Religion and Black Radicalism: An Interpretation of the Religious History of Afro-American People*, 3d ed. Maryknoll, NY: Orbis Books, ch. 9.

Ndembu Religion

The religious system of the Ndembu of northwestern Zambia is one of the best-known in Africa due to the systematic ethnographic work of Victor and Edith Turner. Ndembu rituals have remained part of their identity, even in regions of Zambia where considerable intermarriage with other ethnic groups has taken place since the nineteenth century.

At the time of Turner's work, in the 1950s there were eighteen thousand Ndembu in Mwinilunga District, scattered in villages of about a dozen huts each, and spread in a region of over seven thousand square miles. Today it is difficult to suggest an exact number for the Ndembu, as the Ndembu and the Kosa of the region tend to call themselves Lunda. At one point or another both groups shared a common chief, and they both claim to have come from the land of chief Mwantiyanvwa. Geographically, the Ndembu live to the west of the Lunga River, which runs north to south in the district, and the Kosa live to the east of the river.

Ndembu religion is performed through rituals of two main types: life-crisis rituals and rituals of affliction (Turner 1967: 6). Within the life-crisis rituals, the physical or social development of an individual is communally celebrated and socially marked, e.g., birth, puberty, or death. The rituals of affliction reflect the Ndembu association of misfortune in hunting, women's reproductive disorders, and sickness with the active life of the spirits of the dead, i.e., dead relatives (*makishi*, or plural, *akishi*). The spirits of dead relatives may return to interfere with the living because the spirits have either been forgotten or because they disapprove of certain actions of their living relatives.

Life-Crisis Rituals

The most important life-crisis rituals are the Ndembu initiation ceremonies for boys and girls. Such extended rituals express particular changes within a village community and a larger Ndembu network of kin. Boys are circumcised and are initiated collectively, while girls are initiated individually (and do not undergo clitoridectomy). Boys are initiated before girls, at the start of puberty, while girls are initiated later when they are ready for marriage.

The instruction within long rituals of initiation (circumcision) for boys (Mukanda) is based on obedience to the discipline of the elders and the endurance of hardship, through a communal time of learning together in the bush, away from the village. For girls, the emphasis is on learning about sex and reproduction. These lessons are taught to them within the village. Through Mukanda (boys initiation) men gain access to the hunting cults, and through Nkang'a (girls puberty ritual), women are prepared to take part in the Ndembu fertility cults.

Through the funeral rituals relatives mourn the deceased, and new social ties come into place during a period of time in which funeral rites are celebrated around the Ndembu mourning camp (Chipenji or Chimbimbi). It is during this period that the spirit of the diseased is more active, and it needs to be put to rest in its own graveyard. For example, a deceased husband who does not approve of his widow remarrying can inflict sickness on all kin. At funeral and initiation rituals, masked dancers (makishi) perform dances wearing different costumes and representing deceased Ndembu.

Rituals of Affliction

When the spirit of a dead relative returns, a person becomes ill, and the cause of such affliction needs to be identified. If successfully cured, this person can become a vehicle of communication with the world of the dead and, therefore, a healer who can diagnose the causes of illness in others. Afflictions can be caused by different spirits: (a) a male spirit can cause a man to miss his target in hunting, (b) a female spirit can cause women kin to have reproductive disorders and miscarriages, and (c) male and female spirits can cause illness in different relatives, who subsequently experience pains in the body, loss of weight, and undiagnosed sickness.

The rituals of affliction for these three causes involve the hunting cults (Wuminda and Wuyang'a for men), the fertility cults (Nkula, Wubwang'u, Isoma, and Chihamba for women), and the curative cults (Chihamba and Kalemba for men and women). Participation in the different rituals allows Ndembu to acquire supernatural powers, so that in the case of hunters, for example, successive degrees of initiation into a cult allows hunters to see animals quickly, to attract them to a particular place, and ultimately to become invisible to them (Turner 1967: 12, 289, 295).

Mario I. Aguilar

Bibliography

Turner, Victor W. (1957) *Schism and Continuity in an African Society.* Manchester: Manchester University Press for the Rhodes-Livingstone Institute.

——. (1967) *The Forest of Symbols.* Ithaca: Cornell University Press.

——. (1975) *Revelation and Divination in Ndembu Ritual.* Ithaca and London: Cornell University Press.

Nuer Religion

The Nuer are a Nilotic-speaking people who live in the southern Sudan. They are historically related to the Dinka, Atuot, Shilluk, and Anuak, also speakers of Nilotic languages. It is estimated that about 500,000 people speak the Nuer language. The Nuer are a cattle-keeping people and also grow a variety of crops to supplement their diet.

The Nuer of the southern Sudan were made famous in anthropology through the many writings of the late British anthropologist Sir Edward Evans-Pritchard. In addition to numerous articles in professional journals, Evans-Pritchard wrote three books on Nuer society and culture, focusing on their modes of livelihood and political system, their concepts and practices of kinship, marriage, and descent, and finally, their religious values and practices. First published in 1956, Evans-Pritchard's book titled *Nuer Religion* was among the first anthropological accounts of an African religion and theology that made direct comparisons with so-called world religions. In fact, he suggested early in the book that Nuer religion, as he interpreted it, had many strong affinities with concepts and practices described in the Old Testament. Some have suggested that Evans-Pritchard's personal religious beliefs colored or influenced his understanding and description of the Nuer religion, but any person with first-hand knowledge of the Nuer would regard this account as accurate, richly descriptive and authentic.

Indeed, his book on Nuer religion deeply influenced all anthropological writing on non-western religions, and the Nuer beliefs and practices he described set a standard for the understanding of the ritual and symbolism.

When he lived among the Nuer in the 1930s, Evans-Pritchard found that they expressed their religious devotions toward a divinity they called Kwoth, which Evans-Pritchard translated as "God" or "Supreme Spirit." In Nuer thought, Kwoth (which can also mean breath or moving air) is a distant being that animates all existence. Kwoth is the origin of all life and the source to which life returns upon death. Evans-Pritchard explained that to the Nuer, Kwoth was ubiquitous—at once in all places, but nowhere specifically, but somehow, symbolically, associated with the heavens. Though in some ways Kwoth is distant from human beings, Kwoth is ever present, and Kwoth manifests its power to human beings in unpredictable ways. In this way, unexplainable or unexpected events or phenomena are said to be manifestations of Kwoth. For example, if there is a prolonged drought and cattle and crops die, Nuer are resigned to say "ee Kwoth," meaning, only Divinity could make this happen. If during a severe rainstorm lightning should strike a homestead or a person, Nuer will likely say "ee Kwoth." Should a woman give birth to twins instead of the expected single birth, Nuer will say "ee Kwoth." Evans-Pritchard suggested, in fact, that to the Nuer, Kwoth is a mystery, indicating that for them, as most other people, circumstances

NUER RELIGIOUS SPECIALISTS

Kwaar Kwac (Leopard-Skin Chief): Arbitrates disputes, performs rituals to control the climate, rain, and crops, leads rituals associated with resolving serious crimes and insuring success in war.

Wut Ghok (Cattle Expert): Perform rituals to protect cattle from harm, ensure cattle fertility, and ensure the taking of many cattle from other groups.

Totemic Experts: Influence the behavior of ritually important animals such as lions and crocodiles for the benefit of the community.

Gwan Muot (War Expert): Makes an invocation against the enemy.

Kuaar Thoi (Water Expert): Performs rituals to ensure an abundance of water, to prevent poisoning by water, and to protect cattle from predators in rivers.

Gwan Buthini: Performs rituals for life-cycle events such as marriages and funerals.

Kuaar Juath: Performs rituals to prevent disease.

Diviners and Magicians: Control and sell fetishes to prevent misfortune.

Sources: Butt, Audrey. (1952) *The Nilotes of the Anglo-Egyptian Sudan and Uganda.* London: International African Institution. Howell, Paul P. (1954) *A Manual of Nuer Law.* New York: Oxford University Press.

inevitably transcend explanation. But he also stressed that Nuer were not "mystified" by Kwoth, that Nuer had a mental attitude as rational as any other human beings. In this light he intimated that to the extent any religion is true, all religions are true.

In different contexts the term *kwoth* refers to a series of "lesser" divinities that are associated with physical and psychic maladies that affect women, men, boys, and girls, throughout the life cycle. Diseases that we in the west would ascribe to biological processes Nuer speak of as manifestations of *kwoth*, or spirit, and thus diviners and healers are called upon in such circumstances to perform rituals of exorcism to extract malignant spirits to achieve health and well being.

Like other peoples in this region of Africa, Nuer also ascribe personal misfortune to the wills and intentions of the ghosts of the recently deceased. Nuer say that "ghostly visitation" may cause psychological problems, barrenness, and even death. At funeral ceremonies, therefore, close relatives and friends of the deceased are called upon to open their hearts and confess, or express, their feelings towards the deceased, pleading that the dead should leave the living along and cause no misfortune. They assume that even while a dead relative may no longer be physically among them, the ghost or memory of the deceased continues to have a very active influence on their daily lives. Thus, at all important social gatherings, such as births and marriages, the names of the recently deceased are invoked and praised so that they will not interfere with the living.

According to Evans-Pritchard, the central feature and attending sentiments of Nuer religious action are focused on sacrifice, an act that accompanies every significant social and individual occasion: birth, initiation, marriage, incest, the planting of crops, as well as death and burial. When unexpected events occur Nuer will also sacrifice animals to Kwoth or a lesser spirit. In these and many other situations Nuer will say it is necessary to "sacrifice a cow" (*nake yang*), though rarely is the sacrificial victim actually a cow. Typically, a goat or sheep is sacrificed to Kwoth or a lesser spirit. Nuer say that what matters most in such circumstances is not the actual victim that is sacrificed, but the sincerity of the intentions of the sacrifice. All sacrifices are ultimately dedicated to Kwoth, but lesser spirits may also be placated through invocation and sacrifice.

Throughout his account Evans-Pritchard argued that there really is, for the Nuer, no singular practice, sentiment, or inclination that is singularly "religious;" instead, religious ideals and values permeate all of Nuer social and religious experience. In this regard he depicted the Nuer as a deeply religious people, not because they were piously fixated, but because Nuer religion was a "total social phenomenon" that

touched upon all facets of life. There is, in fact, no single word in the Nuer language that can be translated as "religion." When Evans-Pritchard lived among the Nuer, the objective and active existence of Kwoth was as unquestionable as their own.

In recent years, however, as a consequence of endemic civil war and the introduction of capitalism, deeply significant changes have emerged in much of Nuer religious sentiment and practice. During the past twenty years many Nuer have adopted Christian values and practices; for them, sacrifice, once the most central religious act, is regarded as a meaningless waste of a precious resource. These and related changes have been described and interpreted in detail by the anthropologist Sharon Hutchinson in her book titled *Nuer Dilemmas*.

John Burton

See also Dinka Religion; Pastoral Cosmologies

Bibliography

Evans-Pritchard, E. E. (1956) *Nuer Religion*. Oxford: Clarendon Press.

Hutchinson, Sharon E. (1996) *Nuer Dilemmas: Coping with Money, War, and the State*. Berkeley: University of California Press.

Obeah in the West Indies

Throughout the West Indies, the term *obeah* (or *obia*) is generally synonymous with black magic, sorcery, and witchcraft. Perhaps the most familiar spiritual idiom of African origin employed within the Anglophone Caribbean, it is broadly used to describe arcane rites performed, or at least rumored to be enacted, by a wide variety of ritual specialists, folk healers, and occultists. The word itself is likely derived from *obayifo* (witch) or similar linguistic constructions found in the Akan language family of West Africa. Analogous to North American "conjure," "hoodoo," or "rootwork," obeah initially referred to cultural practices instituted by enslaved or indentured Africans, but now serves as a catchall metaphysical category that encompasses diverse African, European, East Indian, and Native American esoteric and pharmacopoeial traditions.

Innate psychic abilities and special training in the magical arts are said to give *obeah men* and *obeah women* superb mystical knowledge and unparalleled divinatory abilities. Additionally, supernatural control over the "shadow" world enables them to summon ghosts, *duppies*, *jumbies*, or revenants that are put to "work" either for the purpose of inflicting harm, misfortune, and madness or to bring luck, prosperity, and wellbeing. Obeah is frequently divided into two modalities: "science" and "bush magic" or "bush medicine." Individuals (scientists) who follow the first path place great value in cabalistic grimoires, such as *The Sixth and Seventh Books of Moses*, as well as mass-produced talismans, charms, and potions distributed by wholesalers of spiritual products and occult supplies. Those who adhere to the second, more traditional, mode of conjuration prefer to amass ritual paraphernalia such as animal products (e.g., bones, teeth, feathers), minerals, native plants, and household goods (e.g., cloth, coins, bottles) that are readily available within the local environment.

Obeah is generally conceptualized as a solitary, clandestine, and principally malevolent vocation. Orlando Patterson writes that during the slave era, obeah was "a type of sorcery which largely involved harming others at the request of clients, by the use of charms, poisons, and shadow catching. It was an individual practice, performed by a professional who was paid by his individual clients" (1967: 188). The malign and socially destructive behaviors associated with the practice of obeah, whether real or imaginary, have inspired numerous organized countermovements. From the colonial era up to the present day, antiobeah ordinances have been used as a means of suppressing ritual activities (African-derived almost by definition) that are construed as socially disruptive, superstitious, or seditious. Mishaps and misfortunes attributed to the influence of obeah have likewise played a prominent role in narratives of religious conversion and in the valorization of church-based spiritual movements. The development of Myalism in nineteenth-century Jamaica was, for example, propelled by zealous efforts on the part of ecclesiastical leaders to expose and eradicate the allegedly widespread practice of obeah.

Although much of the discourse on obeah—as enacted and imagined within contemporary West Indian society—leaves long-standing assumptions concerning the cultural significance of the related behaviors unquestioned, the constructive, therapeutic, and empowering aspects the belief system have been given increased consideration. Accordingly, obeah has been variously characterized as an explanatory model for alienation, suffering, and distress; a mechanism that diffuses social tensions that cannot be controlled through any other means; and as a "weapon of the weak" that counteracts the effects of cultural hegemony. At the same time, the xenophobic dimension of witchcraft accusation in the West Indies, which often causes members of specific racial or social classes to be singled out as malefactors, has also become more apparent.

Patrick Arthur Polk

See also Healing in African and African-Derived Religions; Jamaica, African-Derived Religions in

Bibliography

Abrahams, Roger D., and John Szwed. (1983) *After Africa*. New Haven and London: Yale University Press.

Alleyne Mervyn C. (1988) *Roots of Jamaican Culture*. London: Pluto Press.

Beckwith, Martha. (1929) *Black Roadways: A Study of Jamaican Folk Life*. Chapel Hill: The University of North Carolina Press.

Bell, Hesketh J. (1893) *Obeah: Witchcraft in the West Indies*. London: Sampson, Low-Marston & Co.

Hedrick, Basil C., and Jeanette E. Stephens. (1977) *It's a Natural Fact: Obeah in the Bahamas*. Museum of Anthropology Miscellaneous Series no. 39. Greeley: University of Northern Colorado Museum of Anthropology.

Herskovits, Melville J., and Frances S. Herskovits. (1947) *Trinidad Village*. New York: Alfred A. Knopf.

Hogg, Donald W. (1961) "Magic and 'Science' in Jamaica." *Caribbean Studies* 1, 2: 1–5.

Littlewood, Roland. (1993) *Pathology and Identity: The Work of Mother Earth in Trinidad*. Cambridge: Cambridge University Press.

McCartney, Timothy. (1976) *Ten, Ten The Bible Ten: Obeah in the Bahamas*. Nassau, Bahamas: Timpaul Publishing Company.

Newall, Venetia. (1978) "Some Examples of the Practice of Obeah by West Indian Immigrants in London." *Folk-Lore* 89: 29–51.

Patterson, Orlando. (1967) *The Sociology of Slavery*. London: Associated University Press.

Sereno, Renzo. (1948) "Obeah: Magic and Social Structure in the Lesser Antilles." *Psychiatry* 11, 1: 15–31.

Williams, Joseph J. (1932) *Voodoos and Obeahs: Phases of West Indian Witchcraft*. New York: Dial Press Inc.

——. 1934. *Psychic Phenomena of Jamaica*. New York: The Dial Press.

Ogun

Ogun is an ancient West African deity who is recognized today by millions of people in Africa and the Western hemisphere. He is known by different names, including Ogum in Brazil, Ogou in Haiti, and Gu in the Republic of Benin, yet everywhere he is recognized as one of many gods and goddesses who have occupied the pantheons of West African religious systems. The pantheons involving Ogun are found in communities stretching from ancient Dahomey, in today's Republic of Benin, to the Yoruba and Benin kingdoms and adjacent communities, in Nigeria, although Christianity and Islam have diminished their strength.

During the slave diaspora of the sixteenth to nineteenth centuries, Ogun and many other African deities were taken to the New World where they flourished in Brazil, Cuba, Haiti, Puerto Rico, Trinidad, and other Caribbean locales. Knowledge of the deity became even more widespread during the twentieth century when Ogun devotees migrated to places in South and North America. Historically, Ogun was considered the deity of hunting, iron-making, and warfare, but these occupational endeavors expanded in response to changing social and economic conditions. In Roman Catholic contexts, Ogun was often merged with saints, especially the warrior, Saint George. In the U.S. and Canada his sacred persona was extended into secular realms where he was transformed into a rugged environmentalist, instigator of violence, or brave hero of romance fiction.

Ogun in West African Religious Systems

The ancient religions of West Africa were as rich and complicated as any found in ancient Greece, Rome, or South Asia. Among the Yoruba-speaking peoples, of whom there are more than twenty million, Ogun was one of about ten major *orisha* (deities) In turn, these major deities presided over a hierarchy of lesser orisha, said to be between two hundred to four hundred in various locations.

The religions of West Africa were not centrally organized, and this led to marked differences in belief and practice. There was no centrally trained priesthood and no system of standardized worship or written liturgy, and therefore each community organized its religious life in different ways. A deity could be venerated in one community and not another. Some deities were worshiped separately, and some together with other gods and goddesses. Specialist priests and priestesses maintained a deity's shrine and sacred paraphernalia and performed ritual duties. Ceremonies were held by individuals or families wishing to pay homage to a patron deity, or by an entire town in huge civic gatherings lasting for days and forming part of an annual ritual cycle.

Despite variations in practice, Ogun and other deities retained their uniqueness and could be identified by followers throughout the world. This sameness arose out of the frequent movement and contact of people and their continuous retelling of myth and performance of ritual. Such reenactments were powerful tools in the production of collective memory.

The Distinctiveness of Ogun

The unique character and qualities of Ogun are revealed in song, myth, dance, liturgy, color, or sacrificial food. Almost universally, Ogun is known through his relationship to iron and vocations based on metal. He is associated with potentially dangerous technology (weapons, motor vehicles, trains, electricity) and professions (iron-making, hunting, and warfare in the past; transportation, construction, mechanics, and engineering in the present). An entire corpus of poetry, known as *ijala* (hunter's chants), is devoted to heroic myths and stories extolling Ogun's accomplishments. Symbols that signify Ogun include dogs, *mariwo* (young palm fronds), iron, anvils, miniature tools, swords, the color red, and certain trees. In Yorubaland, the deities have distinctive personalities that may even be mirrored by their devotees. Ogun's fierce temperament is exposed by his fiery red eyes and the abrupt movements of those who dance in his honor carrying swords or wearing miniature iron tools (Barnes 1980). Repeatedly he is portrayed as a fierce, angry, vengeful god who is linked to destruction and conflict, but because of his bravery, also is seen as a protector, innovator, or pathfinder.

Rituals emphasize many of these qualities. One of the ideal ritual contexts for Ogun was the forge or smithy, where special ceremonies were held in conjunction with smelting iron or preparing for warfare or hunting. Today sacrifices and prayers take place in motor parks, automobile repair shops, or at special shrines designated by pieces of iron or by ceremonial swords owned by chiefly families. Wherever they are held, the rituals appease Ogun's destructive side so that followers may avoid danger, especially accidents, and benefit from his protectiveness.

The History of Ogun

Linguistic evidence indicates that a concept of ogun possibly existed as long ago as 2,000 years and that its most basic sense referred to "killing." Among the Idoma people who are northern neighbors of the Yoruba, the concept ogun referred not to a deity, but to a ritual performed by blacksmiths to purify an individual who killed another human (Armstrong 1997: 34).

Archaeological remains from the sixteenth century show that Ogun's ritual objects—in the form of miniature iron tools—were present during a time when imported iron began to flow into eastern Yorubaland. These miniatures were depicted on a brass sculpture of the fifteenth or sixteenth century that once hung in the royal palace at Benin. Even earlier, in the thirteenth or fourteenth century, ritual battles and sacrifices that are now appropriate only for Ogun were performed annually in the Kingdom of Benin. Throughout eastern Yorubaland, the Kingdom of Benin, and westward into the ancient Kingdom of Dahomey, similar ritual reenactments of battle long figured in civic pageants dedicated to Ogun.

The first written evidence was a 1604 account by a surgeon aboard a Dutch trading ship who described a war ritual in southern Yoruba territory in which people sacrificed dogs to a deity who must have been Ogun, since dogs are sacred only to this deity (Jones 1983: 24). Missionary writings from the second half of the nineteenth century confirmed that Ogun was known throughout Yorubaland, especially eastern kingdoms, and that his ancient occupational characteristics of hunting, smithing, and soldiering had been expanded to include agriculture and snake handling, although these attributes were later lost (Peel 1997: 263–83).

By mid-twentieth century, Ogun in Nigeria had become a patron deity to sculptors and other artists, barbers, circumcisers, drivers, explorers, pilots, computer technicians, engineers, and a host of other occupations in which metallic tools and high-tech objects were significant. The history of Ogun reveals many additions and subtractions in the ways he was portrayed, the actions he was thought capable of carrying out, and the domains over which he had influence. This layering of knowledge and symbolic attributes made him a highly complex figure who represented different things in different periods of time.

The Philosophy of Ogun

Despite his complexity, in every way Ogun is portrayed, past and present, his every action is interpreted as good for some and bad for others. As a blacksmith, Ogun creates the tools and weapons that, when put to use by some people increase their productivity, but when used by others destroy innocent lives. As a hunter he depletes the natural world in order to nurture his own cultural world. As a social activist, he is a Robin Hood-like figure who steals from the powerful to help the powerless.

The Nobel Prize-winning Nigerian author Wole Soyinka counts Ogun as his patron deity and has made him famous in many plays, poems, and essays. Soyinka draws on Yoruba mythology in the same way authors for centuries have drawn on myths of Greek gods and goddesses to illustrate the predicaments of human existence. His poem, "Idanre" (1967), is about a warrior who, following a terrible battle, flies into a drunken rage and kills his own people. The warrior is Ogun and Idanre is his mythical homeland. In the poem Soyinka likens Nigeria's civil war of the 1960s to a return pilgrimage of Ogun, using Idanre as a symbolic

site where, during revolutionary crisis, neighbors turn on neighbors . He devotes the poem to exploring the contradiction that in his role of revolutionary warrior Ogun eliminates an old order only to establish a new one.

The double-edged sword is an image that metaphorically captures the meaning of Ogun. It serves as a visual representation of the existential paradox that destroying is an intrinsic aspect of creating. His followers are aware of the philosophical challenges posed by their deity. Through him they confront the reality that human actions, especially actions of leaders, warriors, and innovators, are as advantageous to some as they are harmful to others, and that this is an inevitable aspect of the human condition.

Ogun in the New World

Ogun has grown in importance in the Western hemisphere, as have many African-derived religious practices and beliefs. In Brazil, he is a symbol of that country's national identity. He is portrayed as an aggressive, violent defender in the fight for a just and balanced social order. The religions that include Ogun are Candomblé, Umbanda, and Macumba. They have more than 30 million adherents and are spreading rapidly into Uruguay, Argentina, and other nearby countries. They draw on an eclectic range of ideology from African, European (Roman Catholic), and indigenous

Mud sculpture of an Ogun shrine in the compound of Chief Ize-Iyamu in Benin City. PHOTO COURTESY OF DAN BEN-AMOS.

sources. A substantial middle-class intelligentsia plays a leading role in disseminating knowledge and doctrines of Ogun and other Africa-based religious ideologies to followers who come from all racial, vocational, and socioeconomic walks of life.

Large numbers of Caribbean migrants have moved northward and are spreading the knowledge with which to give rise to even more African-based religious expressions. The most visible Afro-Caribbean religious florescence grew out of the Cuban exodus beginning in the late 1950s that took hundreds of thousands of people to Puerto Rico, Venezuela, and North America. Dade County, Florida, which received 550,000 Cubans by 1980, is a flourishing center of Santeria, Lucumi, Santerismo (a faith based on Cuban Santeria and Puerto Rican Esperitismo), Espiritismo, and Orisha-Vodon groups, all of which make a place for Ogun.

Haitians migrated to the U.S. much earlier, as a result of their 1791–1804 slave rebellion against the French. They began an interracial Vodon group in Louisiana that was known to operate between 1822 and 1830. Much later, in the 1980s, at least 450,000 Haitians moved to the eastern U.S. bringing hundreds of Vodon priests and priestesses. In the 1980s and 90s entire ceremonies in Philadelphia and New York City have been devoted to Ogun, in search of his restorative powers.

Trinidadians also moved to urban centers throughout North America and brought with them a rich spectrum of religious groupings known as Spiritual Baptist, Orisha, and Shango. In every case, Ogun is included in the ritual practices and theology of the group. The extensive movement of peoples with knowledge of Old World traditions means North America is experiencing an African renaissance; many new groups include Ogun in their pantheons. Some are known as Orisha groups, but others prefer to keep a separate identity, such as the well-known Oyotunji Village in South Carolina or Yoruba Theological Archministry of Brooklyn. The divine role model in North America is still a social activist, pursuing justice and ethical behavior in the fight to end racism, hate, and oppression (Mason 1997: 366). Votive candles decorated with Ogun/St. George decals, and intended to protect devotees, are sold in supermarkets, and popular fiction casts Ogun as a brave, yet divine, hero. The media give Ogun a secular face which he displays as an anti-hero in the Hollywood film, *The Believers*, and a shady figure in *Miami Vice* (Cosentino 1997: 291).

Conclusion

Ogun is an ancient deity whose association with death and destruction is deeply embedded in history, yet whose concern with inequality makes him a protector and defender of human rights. These characteristics have not disappeared over the centuries; rather they remain as a basic theme on which new improvisations take place. The military governor of a Nigerian state recently took the oath of office on a cutlass symbolizing Ogun in his dual role of warrior and guardian of justice. Motorcyclists in the Republic of Benin protect themselves with fearsome iron images of Ogun attached to their fenders (Barnes 1997: xiv). The possibilities for symbolizing the contending tensions found in Ogun philosophy—destroying and creating, harming and protecting—are rich and enduring.

As with many aspects of West African tradition, Ogun is a global figure who has gained prominence. His survival is assisted by the flow of ideas in popular media and the intercontinental migrations that occur on a scale and speed unprecedented in world history. His significance rests on an ability to absorb newness—to incorporate new occupational specialties and new technologies into his repertoire, and to provide meaning in the lives of those who must adapt to the social transformations that fundamental change provokes.

Sandra T. Barnes

See also Yoruba Religion and various articles on African-derived religions in the Americas

Bibliography

Armstrong, Robert. (1997) "The Etymology of the Word Ogun." In *Africa's Ogun: Old World and New*, edited by Sandra T. Barnes. Bloomington: Indiana University Press, pp. 29–38.

Barnes, Sandra T. (1980) *Ogun: An Old God for a New Age.* Philadelphia: Institute for the Study of Human Issues.

Barnes, Sandra T., ed. (1997) *Africa's Ogun: Old World and New*, second expanded edition. Bloomington: Indiana University Press.

Cosentino, Donald. (1997) "Repossession: Ogunin Folklore and Literature." In *Africa's Ogun: Old World and New*, edited by Sandra T. Barnes. Bloomington: Indiana University Press, pp. 290–314.

Jones, Adam. (1983) German Sources for West African History, 1599–1669, Weisbaden: Franz Steiner Verlag.

Mason, John. (1997) "Ogun: Builder of the Lukumi's House." In *Africa's Ogun: Old World and New*, edited by Sandra T. Barnes. Bloomington: Indiana University Press, pp. 353–367.

Peel, J. D. Y. (1997) "A Comparative Analysis of Ogun in Precolonial Yorubaland." In *Africa's Ogun: Old World and New*, edited by Sandra T. Barnes. Bloomington: Indiana University Press, pp. 263–289.

Soyinka, Wole. (1967) *Idanre and Other Poems.* London: Methuen.

The Orisha (Shango) Movement in Trinidad

The Orisha Movement, as it is now called in Trinidad, is a Yoruba-derived religion that was brought by slaves who were sent to Trinidad in the early nineteenth century. Today, it is a dynamic, growing, and increasingly accepted form of religious behavior. Its strong connections to its African origin have made it particularly attractive to younger and more politicized people who seek in its worship an affirmation of their identity as Africans.

History and Background

Although very little is known about its early history in the island, most scholars think that it was not until the arrival of free people of color in the post-emancipation era of the 1830s and 40s that the religion really took hold. Orisha, or Shango as it was formerly known, is identified as a syncretic form since its practice involves the mixture of both African-derived and Roman Catholic elements. It is generally believed that the combination of the two forms came about because of the prohibition of African forms of worship that required its "disguise." The official religion, Roman Catholicism, was brought to the New World by Spanish colonizers; the African religion was merged into Roman Catholicism in order to disguise its origins. But at least one scholar has cast some doubt on the "disguise" theory (Trotman 1976). In this view, although Yoruban deities or Orisha are identified with Roman Catholic saints, the drumming, dancing, and possession experiences that accompany the Yoruban religious form could not possibly be confused with Roman Catholic practices. Moreover, only those Catholic saints who shared similar characteristics with their Orisha were carefully chosen to "represent" them. If they were merely used as disguises, any saint would have fit the bill. A more likely scenario is that the two religious forms gradually evolved together and, while Catholicism was useful to draw attention away from the African elements, the two gradually merged together and a comprehensive belief system evolved. While in the earlier period, St. Michael may have substituted for Ogun, gradually the two came to be understood as aspects of the same deity. Certainly, today most Orisha worshippers believe that to be the case.

The term "syncretic" to describe Orisha worship is now thought to be pejorative among some people for whom the question of authenticity has become paramount. These newer, younger, and more politicized worshippers seek to reaffirm their African identity through Orisha worship. In subscribing to the disguise theory of its origins, they believe that it is now necessary to liberate the religion of its colonial Catholic history. In some Orisha shrines, there is now a concerted drive to reassert the uniquely Yoruban elements of the worship.

Beliefs and Practices

The Orisha religion is based on that of the Yoruba of Nigeria. Along with other West African groups, their religion is characterized by a number of features. These include ancestor veneration, spirit possession, use of herbs, oils and other organic products, animal sacrifice, divination procedures, and the belief in the living reality of the deities. All of these elements have been retained in Orisha worship in Trinidad. The Orisha religion is pantheistic with a large number of deities who control various aspects of the world. At the head is Obatala, who is the supreme Orisha, and at his side are deities such as Ogun, the god of iron and war; Shango, who is identified with thunder and storms; Oya, goddess of the winds; Oshun, goddess of the waters; and many others. The Orisha manifest in the real world by taking over or possessing the "heads" of their devotees during ceremonies called feasts (now usually referred to with the Yoruban term *ebo*). This phenomenon of spirit possession is one of the strongest characteristics of the religion. During possession, devotees dance, act out stories, give counsel and advice to their followers, and dispense medicines. Possession is a learned behavior and is stimulated by darkness, candlelight, and the hypnotic and dramatic sound of the drums. Most Orisha devotees experience their first possession at an early age. The shrine leader where their first possession takes place is usually recognized as a spiritual mother or father and will identify the name of the possessing deity. One of the shrine leader's functions is to teach the young the doctrines and songs, as well as how to control and manage their possession. Orisha worship tends to run in families. Most devotees had a mother, grandmother, or aunt who headed or played a major role in a shrine. In some instances, living next to or near a practicing shrine provided the context in which the faith was experienced or learned early in life. Young children and even infants are brought to feasts and so begin to learn the faith and the ritual early in life.

Herbs, oils, flour, and other products are used in various parts of the ritual. The ceremony lasts for four days and nights and begins with a flag raising on a Tuesday evening. Most activity occurs at night. At daybreak, it is usual to sacrifice animals such as goats, chickens, and guinea fowls to the various deities. The meat is cooked during the day and is used to provide food for the participants. A portion without salt is prepared for the deities.

A typical ceremony begins with a series of Christian, primarily Catholic, prayers including sometimes the litany of the saints. Worshippers at times chant prayers while on their

An Orisha elder blesses an ancestral stone with the assistance of Badeo Panday, the Prime Minister of Trinidad. PHOTO COURTESY OF VINCENT GOLDBERG.

knees. A number of Christian hymns are sung. Even in those shrines that are attempting to Africanize, there is some praying to begin the ceremony. After the leader is satisfied that enough prayers have been chanted, the drummers are signaled and begin drumming. A circle of devotees is formed, and they dance in a clockwise fashion chanting Yoruban songs. The first set of songs is sung to Eshu, the Yoruban trickster, who must first be propitiated so that he does not interfere with the ceremony. After that, the participants sing and drum to Ogun. If all goes well, Ogun "arrives" in the head of a devotee, usually the shrine leader. Other deities are then sung to and will manifest on their favorite "horses," or devotees. There can be as many as eight to ten concurrent possessions. On the other hand, an entire night may pass without any Orisha appearing.

These ceremonies take place in the leader's yard that, in addition to the house, contains various ceremonial structures. The main one is the *palais*, in which the dancing and drumming takes place. The *chapelle*, or small church, contains an altar on which the ritual implements of the deities, as well as pictures of the saints, are kept. At the entrance or gateway to an Orisha shrine, a series of raised cement or hardened earth structures are placed. These "stools" are sacred areas dedicated to the major deities worshipped by the leader. Colored flags symbolizing the deities are also located there.

Divination by the throwing of obi seeds is regularly practiced by leaders in order to provide counsel, select propitious times and dates, and generally help make future decisions. All Orisha worshippers strongly venerate their ancestors and those who have gone before them. Past leaders in the faith, as well as more immediate deceased kin, are regularly prayed to and venerated. Younger members today strongly influenced by the "authentic" African elements of their worship are particularly keen to emphasize the role of the ancestors. Living older members of the community are usually referred to or addressed as "elder." In earlier times, the more colloquial "old head" was a term used to designate a knowledgeable person of some standing. A few shrine leaders of particular seniority, authority, and prestige are termed *iya* (women) and *mongba* (men).

Social Organization

The Orisha movement is a non-centralized, highly individualistic religion. Each individual shrine leader sets the tone for its ceremonies, decides which Orisha are to be honored on an evening, makes arrangements to bring drummers to the *palais*, and is in charge of all other arrangements. Each shrine has a following composed of people from the area, as well as those who live in the city but who are attached to the shrine whose leader they recognize as their spiritual parent. The ceremonies take place after Easter and run throughout the year. In the past, little attention was paid to scheduling and more than one feast took place in the same time period. Today, greater attention is paid to dates so that conflicts occur less frequently. The very active participants of this religion tend to travel and attend as many feasts, or *ebos*, as they can. Since Trinidad is relatively small, it is possible to drive to a ceremony and drive back home at its conclusion. Some very active participants travel from feast to feast following a particular itinerary based on their relationship to shrine leaders whom they especially respect. Unlike other religions that are centralized, there is no one central place of worship. Orisha religion does not have a written tradition, so all prayers, songs, chants, in fact, all of its practices must be learned orally, either by direct teaching or by attendance at ceremonies.

Anyone is free to attend an ebo as long as they behave with proper respect. A typical feast will, therefore, have a large number of onlookers who generally do not participate but simply watch. Another group of people identify themselves as members or participants, and a third, and much smaller group, is comprised of very active participants. The members of the latter group, which includes the shrine leaders, are the ones who most often get possessed and who enjoy the most status within the group.

Orisha Religion Today

The religion today is undergoing some dramatic changes. In addition to Africanizing its rituals and ceremonies, younger members are attempting to develop a centralized infrastructure and organization. There is now a nominated Council of Elders, which creates policy and attempts to bring Orisha worship into the public arena. The two main Orisha groups are now incorporated and Orisha has been recognized by the government as a legitimate religion whose elders can officiate at weddings, births, and deaths. Many more notable members of Trinidadian society, especially those from the artistic community, identify with it and have become participants. Even the public has become more accepting of this formerly despised religious organization. Its membership has expanded, and although numbers are difficult to estimate, a recent survey found 75 Orisha shrines varying in their level of activity. Estimates of membership range from about 8,000 (Houk 1995) to at least 50,000, but more accurate estimates probably would place membership at around 20,000.

Frances Henry

See also Caribbean, African-Derived Religions in; Yoruba

Bibliography

Henry, [Mischel] F. (1957) "African Powers in Trinidad: The Shango Cult." *Anthropological Quarterly*. Vol. 30, number 2, pp. 45–59

——. (1983) "Religion and Ideology in Trinidad: The Resurgence of the Shango Cult." *Caribbean Quarterly* 29: 63–69.

Houk, James T. (1995) *Spirits, Blood, and Drums*. Philadelphia: Temple University Press.

Mauge, C. E. (1996). *The Lost Orisha: House of Providence*. Mt. Vernon. NY: House of Providence.

Simpson, George Eaton. (1965) *The Shango Cult in Trinidad*. [Rio Pedras]: University of Puerto Rico, Institute of Caribbean Studies.

Trotman, D. (1976) "The Yoruba and Orisha Worship in Trinidad and British Guinea, 1838–1870." *African Studies Review* 19, 2.

Warner-Lewis, Maureen. (1990) *Guinea's Other Suns: The African Dynamic in Trinidad Culture*. Dover, MA: The Majority Press.

Oromo Religion

The Oromo-speaking peoples live within the national boundaries of southern Ethiopia and northern Kenya. Their large population, over twenty million, makes them one of the largest African groups, but one that in its own traditions has been systematically oppressed, particularly by the monarchical rule of Ethiopian kings within the nineteenth and twentieth centuries.

The historical origin of the Oromo has been traced to the tenth century. At that time the Oromo and the Somali lived in southern Ethiopia, however, by 1530 the Oromo expanded towards the province of Bali in southern Ethiopia, after campaigns against the Ethiopian kings. Nevertheless, the Oromo themselves consider Dirre and Liban in southern Ethiopia as their homelands. Until the nineteenth century and before the conquest of emperor Menelik of Shoa they were united by a social, religious and political system, the Gada system, that made them a unified and cohesive group of people.

The Gada system, documented by the monk Bahrey in the sixteenth century, has dominated all discussions of Oromo religion and, indeed, discussions of Oromo nationalism. The Gada system provides a unifying national and cultural identity and a social organization; its ideology remains a source of cultural cohesion for all Oromo.

Within Gada, all adult male Oromo are initiated into categories, where groups of neophytes are incorporated into a particular age-set that moves through a series of age-grades. Each age-set is given a particular name, and as the age-set moves through different age-grades they assume different social responsibilities. The first initiation takes places forty years after each person's father's initiation. A cycle of eight years marks the national festivals where all age-sets move one grade up. Within these complex systems, the last grades are known as *Gadamoji*, those who do not exercise political or active functions any longer, but are required to bless and to keep their communication with the God of the Oromo and its divine manifestations.

The supreme being of the Oromo is known as Waqqa (God/sky). He lives in the skies and is the source of all life. Everything that exists has been blessed by Waqqa, and as a result the world remains at peace and in harmony when Waqqa is properly acknowledged. The Boorana Oromo recall that a long time ago Waqqa sent the Kallu, their sacred priest and leader. One day there was a man that appeared on a hill. The Boorana greeted him by bringing coffee-beans (*buna*) that they had picked from their own trees. Later, they brought him a maid, so that he would stay with them. Thus, the Kallu became the ritual leader of all Oromo. In the past, Oromo made long pilgrimages to see the Kallu, to bring gifts, and to ask for his blessings on their families and their animals.

Under the reign of Menelik, in Ethiopia, the Oromo underwent enormous pressure to convert to Christianity. However, in many cases they converted to Islam instead, as Islam was used as a symbolic resource for cultural resistance. Within contemporary Ethiopia and Kenya the Oromo maintain their allegiance to the Gada system, and even those who have converted to Islam or Christianity perceive their new symbolic allegiances as an extension of the ever-present Waqqa.

In the case of the Boorana, who pride themselves as having pure Oromo descent, they continue exercising their link with Waqqa by keeping the *Nagaa Boorana* (the peace of the Boorana). Daily religious and social activity for all Boorana meant to keep the *Nagaa Boorana* include household prayers and the frying of coffee-beans (*buna qalla*).

Other ritual activities include namings and burials; and Oromo symbols such as grass are often used in Christian or Muslim burials.

In the 1990s, religious practices related to the Oromo have intensified, and their connection with nationalistic discourses has also been intensified. Within the Oromo diaspora in Europe and North America the importance of Oromo religion has been highlighted, and it has been pursued as a cultural and religious tradition that can coexist with Christianity and Islam, as manifested in *The Journal of Oromo Studies* and *The Oromo Commentary*, journals concerned with the Oromo and their religion.

Mario I. Aguilar

Bibliography

Aguilar, Mario I. (1998) *Being Oromo in Kenya.* Trenton, NJ: Africa World Press.

——. (1998) "Reinventing *Gada* : Generational Knowledge in Boorana." In *The Politics of Age and Gerontocracy in Africa,* edited by M. I. Aguilar. Trenton, NJ: Africa World Press.

Bartels, Lambert. (1983) *Oromo Religion: Myths and Rites of the Western Oromo of Ethiopia. An Attempt to Understand.* Berlin: Dietrich Reimer Verlag.

Bassi, Marco. (1996) *I Borana: Una Societá Assembleare del' Etiopia.* Milan: Franco Angeli.

Baxter, Paul T. W., and Uri Almagor, eds. (1978) *Age, Generation and Time: Some Features of East African Age Organisations.* London: C. Hurst and Co.

Baxter, Paul T. W., Jan Hultin, and Alessandro Triulzi, eds. (1996) *Being and Becoming Oromo: Historical and Anthropological Enquiries.* Uppsala: Nordiska Afrikainstitutet, Lawrenceville, NJ: The Red Sea Press.

Hassen, Mohammed. (1990) *The Oromo of Ethiopia: A History 1570–1860.* Cambridge: Cambridge University Press.

Holcomb, Bonnie K., and Sisai Ibssa. (1990) *The Invention of Ethiopia: The Making of a Dependent Colonial State in Northeast Africa.* Trenton, NJ: The Red Sea Press.

Jalata, Asafa. (1993) *Oromia & Ethiopia: State Formation and Ethnonational Conflict, 1868–1992.* Boulder and London: Lynne Rienner.

Knutsson, K. E. (1967) *Authority and Change: A Study of the Kallu Institution among the Macha Galla of Ethiopia.* Goteborg: Etnografiska Museet.

Legesse, Asmarom. (1973) *Gada: Three Approaches to the Study of African Society.* New York: Free Press.

Van de Loo, Joseph. (1991) *Guji Oromo Culture in Southern Ethiopia: Religious Capabilities in Rituals and Songs.* Berlin: Dietrich Reimer Verlag.

Oshun

Oshun is the Yoruba deity of cool water and female authority. She plays a prominent part in the Yoruba oral literature called Ifá, which describes her cosmological role and interactions with human beings. In one collection of Ifá verses it is told that when Olodumare—God Almighty—created the earth he sent seventeen deities (orisha) to organize and civilize it. Sixteen of the orisha were male; the seventeenth was the powerful woman, Oshun. The sixteen ignored Oshun in their world building and soon their efforts began to fail. The rains wouldn't fall and bitterness and strife overtook them. They turned to divination to discover that their misfortune was due to their neglect of the woman among them. Reluctantly they asked Oshun's aid and she agreed, provided they would offer her proper respect and compensation. Oshun brought the rains back but the sixteen orisha forgot their promise. Oshun then refused to stop the waters and their world was engulfed in spreading floods. At last the sixteen recognized the power of Oshun and that all temporal and spiritual work can only succeed with the aid of the orisha of water.

Yoruba oral literature records that the first human beings to encounter Oshun were migrants from the city of Ilesha, in present-day Nigeria. They were searching for a new place to settle and felled a tree across a river to mark a likely spot. As the tree crashed in the shallow water the voice of Oshun commanded them to recognize that the river was hers and that they might settle there only at her pleasure. They made appropriate sacrifices and the thriving town of Oshogbo grew around the area. The river is today named for Oshun, as is a state in the Nigerian nation. Every year the people of Oshogbo re-enact the pact between their sovereign and the river Oshun in a grand festival that has become an international tourist attraction.

Oshun's character is associated with coolness, wealth, and gestation. She is owner of brass, a radiant metal that is cool to the touch and speaks of wealth and power. Her shrines are decorated with brass ornaments and her devotees carry brass fans as their emblems, suggesting refinement, ease, and soft breezes. Oshun is the orisha who heals with cool water and her devotees see in her waters the ultimate medicine. Oshun's waters are the basis of the body fluids that bring new life and so she is seen as the creative force in the conception of children.

Oshun is also a woman of power and substance. She is a proud and wealthy market woman who can drive the hardest of bargains. She is alade, the wearer of the crown, a royal personage who permits kings to reign. And she is also the keeper of women's secrets, holding a hidden power of life and death that men ignore at their peril.

In the late eighteenth and early nineteenth centuries, Yoruba men and women were enslaved in great numbers and taken across the Atlantic. In many areas, particularly in Brazil, Cuba, and Trinidad, they were able to maintain their devotion to Oshun and look to her for ways of coping with the dreadful challenges that faced them. Oshun's character expanded to include a variety of images appropriate to the new worlds in which her devotees found themselves. Her regal character and readiness to aid petitioners suggested to her Brazilian and Cuban devotees parallels with the Catholic Virgin Mary. Her abode within the waters brought to mind her image as a beautiful mermaid. And her wealth and style allowed some to see her as a sensuous courtesan and even a holy prostitute whose frank eroticism brings healing and children.

Devotion to Oshun continues to spread throughout the African diaspora. With the arrival of Cuban devotees in the wake of the Cuban revolution of 1959, her veneration is growing in the United States. Latinos, African-Americans, and white Americans are finding in the "Crowned Woman" a source of spiritual beauty and empowerment at the dawn of the new millennium.

Oshun is a lovely and vivacious deity whose glimmering surface conceals strong currents and hard truths. She reveals the presence of strength in softness, guile in generosity, death in life. The dialectic of these qualities establish Oshun as one of the greatest images of divinity in Africa and the African diaspora.

Joseph M. Murphy

See also Yoruba Religion

Bibliography

Abiodun, Rowland. (1989) "Women in Yoruba Religious Images." *African Languages and Cultures* 2.

Badejo, Diedre L. (1996) *Osun Seegesi: The Elegant Deity of Wealth, Power and Femininity*. Trenton, NJ: Africa World Press.

Murphy, Joseph M., and Mei-Mei Sanford, eds. (2000) *Osun Across the Waters: A Yoruba Goddess in Africa and the Americas*. Bloomington: Indiana University Press.

Thompson, Robert Farris. (1983) *Flash of the Spirit: African and Afro-American Art and Philosophy*. New York: Random House.

Verger, Pierre. (1957) *Notes sur le Culte des Orisa et Vodun*. Dakar: L'Institut Français d'Afrique Noire.

Pagelança and Catimbo

Pagelança is a healing cult practiced mainly in the states of Para, Piau, and Maranhon in Northeastern Brazil, both in rural and urban areas. It is based on shamanistic practices of Amerindian origin, although the native spirits are inserted in a religious structure of African derivation. The influence of Kardecist spiritism is also apparent. Mediumistic trance is of outmost importance, and there are only a few traces of syncretism with Catholic folk religion (the rituals usually begin with a Catholic prayer or song, and statues of saints decorate the altars). It seems that Native American elements were first influenced by magic techniques of European origin and only later syncretized with Afro-American elements, when Indians and mestizos got in closer touch with black slaves and free peasants, who moved from Maranhon to Para. Kardecism was introduced in this area only after the turn of the last century.

Beliefs and Practices

In Pagelança the leading figure is the *pagé* (shaman), who is in charge of *mesas*, curing sessions called *table*. These rites usually take place during the night and may last until the following morning. There are no temples, and the *pagé* is invited by the clients—who bear all the expenses—to perform in their homes. There are no religious congregations or brotherhoods, but the *pagé* may have a few helpers, who are in training to become *pagés*. He works in his own fashion and organizes the healing rites in favor of his clients, who invite their friends and relatives who are in need of spiritual help, to the performances. In order to call the spirits, sometimes Afro-American-type drums are used. The *pagé* usually sits in front of an altar that is decorated with lithographs of Catholic saints, candles, flowers, bottles of rum, and cigars. Animals are never sacrificed and blood is not used for ritual purposes. The *pagé* gets in touch with his guardian spirits, who either take possession of his body or inspire his work, giving him advice through visions. The spirits come and go, while the *pagé* smokes one cigar after another and consumes a lot of *cachaça* (strong rum). The cigars are wrapped in *tauari* bark, which may have a narcotic effect on the smoker. Gifts for the spirits—beer, rum, feathers, and scarves—are offered by the clients.

The rites are very simple. After invoking God, the saints, and the spirits, the *pagé* falls in trance and is possessed by the *Mestres de Cura* (the guardian spirits). These supernatural beings are often conceived as animals, such as *Cobra grande* (the big serpent), but other have names such as *Principe encantado* (the enchanted prince), *Rei do Mar* (King of the

Sea), or *Rei nago* (King of Nago). Here we may observe African influence, as the Yoruba of Nigeria are known under the term *nago* in Brazil. In order to keep order in the large number of spiritual beings, who may manifest themselves in the shaman, they are considered to belong to different *linhas*, or lines. One of the lines is called "African." Other lines are lines of the jungle, of sweet water, of salt water, and of the air. When they take possession of the shaman, he starts dancing, imitating the movements of animals.

The *Mae d' Agua*, the Mother of Water, the guardian spirit of rivers and lakes, is an important Native South American mythological figure and was syncretized with African-derived deities in other Brazilian religions, such as Yemanya or Oshun. Rituals for these water divinities may take place near running streams. Many so-called *caboclo* spirits of Amerindian origin, such as Jurema or Sete Flexas, often appear in the sessions. Some used to be great warriors, chiefs, or beautiful Indian princesses. Many of these figures are also invoked in the Umbanda healing rituals. The *Encantos*, or nature spirits, guardians of sacred places in the jungle, are supposed to live in *Encantarias* (places that are haunted by spirits). They may be good or evil. As we can see, of all these supernatural beings belong to the Amerindian pantheon or the Brazilian folklore.

After falling in trance and being possessed by a spirit, the *pagé* is consulted by the sick clients. Each spirit is a specialist in curing a certain illness. The shamans have a wide knowledge of herbal and other natural remedies, but they are also well versed in magic rituals in order to heal psychosomatic ailments. In the healing rituals, they take the whole person in consideration and are well aware of the fact that body and mind form a unity. They also give advice to the clients when they have other problems, such as spirit possession or bewitchment.

The client is first purified with tobacco smoke. Then the *pagé* invokes the evil spirits that most likely provoked the illness or problem, so that they may leave his body. In Amerindian fashion, the spot where the ailment is supposed to be located is touched with a rattle. The shaman sucks on the body of the patient and sometimes produces a pebble or another object, pretending that he extracted it from there. Ritual baths in herbal concoctions are often prescribed. The plants are available in local markets. Baths are prescribed to get a job, to find a lover, to be protected against all evil. Any prescription of medicine is always accompanied by a list of *resguardos* (dietary restrictions) that the patients must observe.

The *pagé* may also be called to neutralize an evil spell that apparently was cast on the client by a sorcerer. The shamans of other villages may often be accused of evil, while no *pagé* would ever admit such a thing in public and always pretends that he only works in benefit of the client. Businessmen may call a *pagé* to "clean" their shop of all evil spells. The *Mestres de Curas*, when possessing the shaman, may also give advice or identify a thief or find a hidden object. The clients are usually members of the lower urban classes or peasants. Of course, it is necessary to pay the shaman for his services, otherwise they will be useless. His success depends on satisfying his clients and competing against competitors.

Catimbo

Catimbo is another, similar curing and magic cult based mainly on Native American traditions. It is also popular in Northeastern Brazil. The word *catimbo* is derived from the term *cachimbo*, meaning "pipe" in a Bantu language. The same expression is used by Afro-Venezuelans in the same sense. Although the term is African, the use of tobacco in magic and healing rituals is common in all Native South American cultures.

The *catimbozeiro* receives his clients in his own home and does not perform in the patient's house, as the *pagé*. He usually has a good knowledge of herbal and other natural remedies. In contrast to the *pagé*, the *catimbozeiro*, when performing in favor of his clients, drinks an infusion of Jurema (*Mimosa hostilis*), a narcotic and hallucinogenic substance that provokes visions. The drink is prepared with honey and rum. The bark and the roots of the plant are also used to prepare baths and are burned in some of the ritual fumigations. This plant is also widely used by Native Sourth American shamans in the Amazonas region, where it gained popularity among Europeans and Americans in search of visionary experiences. The faithful believe that Jurema is a sacred plant that gives power and happiness. When the *catimbozeiro* is drugged, he receives his guardian spirits, who are usually of Amerindian derivation, but sometimes an Afro-American divinity, an *orisha*, may appear. The guardian spirits are called *mestres*, although the same term may also refer to the shaman himself. They belong to many different *linhas*, as do the spirits of Pagelança.

The consulting sessions take place in front of all the clients waiting their turn. The *catimbozeiro* talks at length with the patient and then prescribes remedies, often including pills and injections from the drugstore. He is not only a healer, but he also prepares amulets to protect his clients against the attacks of evil forces, he solves problems among lovers, he prays over children afflicted by the "evil eye," he fixes aphrodisiacs, and he practices exorcisms. Some of these rituals may be of African origin, other magical acts he per-

forms are common all over the world. Blood is never used. It is said that the practitioners of Catimbo also work evil. As they are paid for their work, they are only the executioners of the rituals and the client, who ordered and paid for the spell, is responsible for its outcome.

The *catimbozeiros* communicate with or receive a number of spirits of different origin when in their narcotic trance. In recent years, the Amerindian *caboclos* frequently are invoked to cure the patients, but there are also Afro-American *orishas* who may appear in the sessions, especially those who in other Afro-Brazilian religions specialize in curing the sick. *Pombagiras* and *eshus*, who play a leading role in Umbanda, also appear in Catimbo sessions. They are considered to be evil spirits who have to be exorcised. When the problem of the client is diagnosed as due to harassment by an *eshu*, the patient has to prepare a gift for this evil spirit, consisting of a bottle of rum, a few yards of black ribbon, a certain number of candles, a bowl of food, and a box of matches. In the fashion of Umbanda rituals, these gifts are placed on a crossroads in the evening and candles are lit. Such *despachos* can be found in all parts of Brazil, left there by Afro-Brazilian cultists. Some shamans get in touch with the spirits of dead *catimbozeiros*, in the style of Kardecism.

It is interesting to note that the narcotic Jurema plant was already widely used in rituals in the *Terreiros Gege-Nago* in Bahia province around the turn of the century, proving that Amerindian influence had existed in Afro-Brazilian rituals long before Umbanda developed in Rio de Janeiro.

Religious Amalgamation

As we have seen, Pagelança and Catimbo are practices derived from the Native American shamanistic traditions, but were influenced by Afro-American elements, even as they penetrated the Afro-Brazilian religions. This is especially true in the case of Batuque, a Yoruba-derived cult that developed in Belem on the Amazon. The African elements of this religion came from Sao Luis (Maranhon) to Belem around the turn of the century, when black peasants migrated north. The rituals for African divinities were syncretized with the worship of the *caboclos*, also known in Pagelança and Catimbo. Healing and magic rituals of these two cults greatly influenced the practices of Batuque. In Brazil today, Umbanda, Candomblé, Batuque, and the healing cults of the Northeast are becoming ever more integrated with one another and it is a decision of the leader of a spiritual or healing center what kind of ritual he uses. Usually these leaders are pragmatic in their practices and often insert new practices taken from reports by anthropologists, television reports, and esoteric books when they believe that the additions or changes might be of use to their clients. The globalization of African-derived cults, Native American shamanism, and French Kardecism has proved to be very influential.

Angelina Pollak-Eltz

See also Batuque; Brazil, African-Derived Religions in; Catimbo; Kardecism; Orisha; Oshun; Venezuela, African-Derived Religions in; Venezuelan Cult of Maria Lionza; Yoruba Religion

Bibliography

Ferretti, Mundicarmo. (1985) *Terreiros de Sao Luis.* Sao Luis: Universidade de Maranhon.

Leacock, Seth. (1972) *Spirits of the Deep.* New York: Doubleday.

Pollak-Eltz, Angelina. (1994) *Las religiones afroamericana—hoy.* Caracas: Planeta.

Thaussig, Michael. (1997) *The Magic of the State.* New York: Routledge.

Pastoralist Cosmologies

Pastoral groups inhabit primarily arid lands within northeast Africa, but are also present in North and West Africa (e.g., the Fulani, Tuareg). Their way of life coexists together with other groups, though it has certainly been challenged by developments within African nations and the contemporary influence of more globalized rather than localized economies. Thus, African pastoralists are not "isolated, self-sufficient systems" (Fratkin et al. 1994: 8), and the idea of "pure pastoralism" has been a false reflection of relatively static traditions that nonetheless were able to change in the face of uncertainty (Spencer 1998: 1–2).

Pastoralist societies reflect the economic and symbolic centrality of cattle and animals both as a means of subsistence and as a key element of a ritualized cosmological understanding. Originally semi-nomadic societies, pastoral societies have constructed models of religion and of religious practices associated with the ecological systems that surround them, as well as with their own cultural and social organization.

Most pastoral societies in North and West Africa identify themselves with Islam, while pastoral societies in East Africa have experienced conversions to Islam and Christianity. In the face of these imported religions, pastoral societies are able to maintain a sense of cultural identity by emphasizing myths of origins in communal rituals, and by teaching those myths as part of an initiation into adulthood before marriage. As economic diversification has worked to their advantage, so pastoral societies have diversified their perceptions of the world to their own advantage, while keeping the centrality of their own ideal cosmological worlds. Within such a process of religious diversification, symbolic elements from Islam and Christianity have been incorporated within cultural systems expressed in ritual and religious terms. As suggested by Richard Waller and Neal W. Sobania, those religious changes have coincided with changes in the position of pastoralists and the perceptions of pastoralism within Africa since 1890 (Waller and Sobania 1994: 45). By the 1950s pastoralists in East Africa had been relegated to the economic periphery, however, they had also suffered a disruption in their cycles of ritual and religious festivals, due to the fact that they could not move across administrative borders as easily as in the past. The same situation continued within the postcolonial and independent nations of Africa (see for example, Baxter and Hogg 1990, and essays by Bassi and Schlee in the same volume).

The common characteristics of the pastoralist cosmologies point to a creator god who lives in the sky, and it is therefore represented by the material features of the sky. This supreme being "is appealed to in prayers for peace, rain, and fertility, but this creator is a distant force which is not directly concerned with affairs on earth" (Fratkin 1998: 52). A long time ago God gave animals and an orderly social system to pastoral societies. According to pastoralists today, God sends his blessings by the birth of young animals, the birth of children, and the presence of rain. The power of the older men to bless reflects the fact that human beings return to God when they die, and therefore children and particularly older men are perceived as close to God and therefore able to greet, to bless, and to keep society in peace within itself and with the natural landscape around it.

Examples of Pastoral Cosmological Systems

In describing three different pastoral cosmologies, it is possible to illustrate the unifying factors of pastoral cosmologies already mentioned, and at the same time to suggest that every pastoral society has its own creative way of describing social rites that actualize and symbolize the relation between pastoralists and their creator.

The Maasai Cosmology

The Maasai are the most well-known African pastoralists. They inhabit land in Tanzania and Kenya. Through the colonial and the postindependence periods, they have kept their own vision of the cosmos centered on their special relation to God, and through God to cattle, the symbol of life

AGE GRADES OF THE MAASAI OF KENYA

All the boys circumcised during a series of circumcision years belong to an age class (ol borór). Within them the boys form, since they are circumcised at yearly or somewhat longer intervals, annual courses by way of divisions.

The first annual course of an age class is the el ja (char) ng (char) en (char) ob (char) ir ; they are followed by the el bari (char) ngo-duallan ; the youngest annual course of the ones circumcised during the eircumcision years is the el ger-imbot. They are followed by a fourth one, the el oirogua. These are circumcised only after the circumcision years have officially ended by the celebration of the e (char) n geb (char) ata festival ordered by the ol oiboni. Anyone who wishes to be circumcised after this festival may not take part in celebrating the above-mentioned festival, otherwise his circumcision is not permitted.

Every two age classes together form an association (ol adji) in which the older is designated as the right circumcision (emorat' ertatenne), the younger one as the left circumcision (emorat' ekediënje). Each of them has definite rules forbidding for them the uttering of certain words or the enjoyment of certain foods. The emorat' ertatenne may eat neither head nor tail pieces of slaughtered livestock and do not say e(char)g a(char) en dare for goat-kraal, but rather e merata en dare; moreover, they say ol ogunja for head, and not ol uku (char) ngu, and for tail piece, not ol gorom, but rather en aisu-ba. The others may eat neither gourd nor cucumber, and for arrow poison they say en duerai, instead of e saj (char) et. It is an insult, which often leads to immediate violence, if the one does or says the things forbidden to the other, which are called en dorotj, in the latter's presence.

It is to be inserted here that the girls who have been circumcised in the period from the beginning of a series of circumcision years to the beginning of the next series are counted in the age class in which the boys circumcised within the same period up to the en geb (char) ata festival are reckoned.

Source: Merker, Meritz (1910) *The Masai: Ethnographic Monograph of an East African Semite People.* Berlin: Dietrich Reimer. HRAF English edition, 94–95.

---

itself. Even within a contemporary economy of souvenirs and tourism, Maasai have kept their cosmological paradigm and their central symbolic assertion, that "all cattle belong to the Maasai." Further, and as forcefully argued by Peter Rigby, "ritual activities and their associated verbal performances do not merely 'reflect' changes; they control and channel them" (Rigby 1992: 77).

There are different versions of the myth that explains how Maasai obtained cattle from Enkai (God). Maasai narrate how, long time ago, when sky and earth were one, God let cattle descend from the sky along a bark rope, or a leather strap or a fire stick. The Maasai received all the cattle, while the Dorobo (hunters and gatherers despised by Maasai) did not receive any. The Dorobo became envious and proceeded to cut the rope. As a result, the flow of cattle stopped and the sky and earth separated. The main cosmological features of this myth—God's gift of cattle to Maasai, and therefore the link between God and Maasai through cattle—and other symbolic features within Maasai, point to the close relation between God and Maasai. Kaj Århem has argued that "cattle symbolically link earth and sky, man and God. They, in a sense, materialise God on earth" (Århem 1985: 9).

The main ritual period in the life of a Maasai is the inauguration of a new age-set, the circumcision and creation of a state of murranhood. The Maasai murran or "warriors" are younger men, already circumcised, though unmarried. Within such group there are levels of murran seniority, however, "warriors" cannot marry till they become elders. It is through the "unifying ceremony" (olngesher) that a complete transition into elderhood and marriage is achieved. (Spencer 1993).

The Boorana Cosmology

The Boorana, who are part of a larger group of Oromo-speaking peoples within East Africa, live in northern Kenya and southern Ethiopia. At the end of the nineteenth century, the new colonial administrative boundaries prevented them from continuing their expansion, and prevented a possible military and cultural clash with Maasai.

The Boorana were originally central participants within the Gada system, the social and political system of the

Oromo. Within such systems all adult male Oromo are initiated into a system of age, where groups of neophytes are incorporated into a particular age-set that moves through a system of age-grades. Each age-set is given a particular name, and as the age-set moves through different age-grades they assume different social responsibilities. The first initiation takes places forty years after each person's father's initiation, and a cycle of eight years marks the national festivals where all age-sets move one grade up. Within such complex rituals, the last grades are assumed as Gadamoji, those who do not exercise political or active functions any longer, but are required to bless and to keep their communication with the God of the Oromo and its divine manifestations.

By the 1930s, most Boorana in Kenya had declared themselves Muslims, while the Boorana in southern Ethiopia had been discouraged to follow their cultural practices by the self-declared Christian monarchy in Addis Ababa. However, within all those changes the Boorana continue recognizing that whatever his name in other traditions, God (Waqqa) created everything and sent a king, a ritual specialist known as the Kallu, to the Boorana. In the past, the pilgrimage to the Kallu was undertaken by the Boorana in order to request his blessings on families and their animals. Therefore, the Boorana cosmology can be described as a circle that unites god and the Boorana. God, who lives in the skies, sends the rain, the rain makes grass grow, the Boorana herds eat grass and drink water, the Boorana survive by the products from cattle, and, in a process of age and maturation, new Boorana are born and die. Finally, when they die the Boorana return to Waqqa, to the sky and to god.

Within such a cycle of life, social and individual rituals take place in order to acknowledge different moments in the life of Boorana, within their constant acknowledgement of God and God's care for them. The main Boorana rituals are the communal celebration of arrival of a new person (ritual of naming, Waqlal), the circumcision, the wedding, and the burial ritual (Aguilar 1998a). Within daily life, every household remembers the arrival of the Kallu by the frying of coffee-beans (buna qalla), and their consumption immersed in milk and butter. Coffee-beans were offered to the Kallu by the Boorana in Ethiopia when he appeared for the first time, and therefore the ritual frying of coffee-beans reminds all Boorana of their myth of origin and their beginnings. If coffee-beans cannot be prepared more often, due to the fact that they are a cash crop in Kenya, prayers are said in the morning and in the evening in every household.

The Gabra Cosmology

If Maasai base their idea of the cosmos as a mediation between God—the giver of cattle—and themselves,

Boorana and Gabra understand nature as the place where God works. However, the Gabra do not have an intermediary such as the Boorana Kallu.

The Gabra live in the northern part of Kenya, where they constantly move with their camels. Waaqa is their "celestial Supreme Power who punishes evil and who is invoked in their prayers" (Tablino 1999: 256). In Gabra thought, "God is," and his presence is felt through all moments of Gabra life, moments that are all marked by some simple and some more complex rituals. It is through the right performance of those rituals that the Gabra feel the presence of God in a more evident manner. The presence of God is also assured by the keeping of the tradition, the right model of behavior (aada), and the constitutions of classes and age-grades (luba)—which take part in the ceremonies (Jila), when members of those classes pass through their own personal rites of passage. As a result, peace (nagaya), order, the absence of attacks from enemies, and harmony are achieved and perceived as the greatest gift from God. Rituals are used in order to ask for rain (rooba), which allows abundance for animals and the Gabra.

There are some elements within Gabra myths that describe a cosmological vision particular to them. One central element refers to the fact that once upon a time the Sky and the Earth were close to each other. When human beings erred in their ways, the Sky/God moved away from the earth. Other elements are connected with myths of origin of three different peoples in northern Kenya: the Boorana, the Gabra, and the Waata. A myth states that those three groups come from the same father. He was an old and tired man who one day tripped and fell. He was wearing a cloth around him and when he fell the cloth fell and left him uncovered. One of the sons laughed, the second turned his face away, the third took his own cloth and covered his father. The father blessed the last two sons and assured them of a future with plenty of camels and in peace. However, to the first he mentioned that he would live with dogs in the future and that he would only be able to eat by hunting. The myth states that the third son was the founder of the Boorana, the second son the founder of the Gabra, and the first son the founder of the Waata (myth narrated in Tablino 1999: 137).

The Centrality of Pastoral Cosmologies

Two elements are central to an understanding of the possibilities of change and continuity in the future of these pastoralist cosmologies. First, they are based on a myth of origin that is somehow easily connected with Christian and Muslim narratives of creation; thus the sky provides an encounter with religious narratives of a Creator who lives above human beings. Second, due to their pastoral mobility and their residence in dry areas of Africa, pastoralists perceive God in rain, water, and grass, considered as gifts from God, and central parts of a nurturing nature created and sustained by God. From those two characteristics it follows that the pastoral narrative of a myth of origin will remain central to the cultural identity of pastoralists, regardless of their practice of any other religious systems. For them religious systems are culturally located and are certainly markers of identity rather than universal systems of human philosophical understanding.

Mario I. Aguilar

See also Nuer Religion; Oromo; Secret Societies; Zulu Religion

Bibliography

Aguilar, Mario I. (1998a) *Being Oromo in Kenya*. Trenton, NJ: Africa World Press.

———., ed. (1998b) *The Politics of Age and Gerontocracy in Africa: Ethnographies of the Past and Memories of the Present*. Trenton, NJ: Africa World Press.

Århem, Kaj. (1985) "The Symbolic World of the Maasai Homestead." *Working Papers in African Studies* 10, African Studies Programme, Department of Cultural Anthropology, University of Uppsala, Sweden.

Bartels, Lambert. (1983) *Oromo Religion: Myths and Rites of the Western Oromo of Ethiopia—An Attempt to Understand*. Berlin: Dietrich Reimer.

Bassi, Marco. (1990) "The System of Cattle Redistribution among the Obbu Borana and Its Implications for Development Planning." In *Property, Poverty and People: Changing Rights in Property and Problems of Pastoral Development*, by Baxter and Hogg. Manchester: Department of Social Anthropology and International Development Centre, University of Manchester, 32–37.

Baxter, Paul T. W., and Uri Almagor, eds. (1978) *Age, Generation and Time: Some Features of East African Age Organisations*. London: C. Hurst.

Baxter, Paul T. W., and Richard Hogg, eds. (1990) *Property, Poverty and People: Changing Rights in Property and Problems of Pastoral Development*. Manchester: Department of Social Anthropology and International Development Centre, University of Manchester.

Evans-Pritchard, E. E. (1956) *Nuer Religion*. New York and Oxford: Oxford University Press.

Fratkin, Elliot. (1998) *Ariaal Pastoralists of Kenya: Surviving Drought and Development in Africa's Arid Lands*. Boston and London: Allyn and Bacon.

Fratkin, Elliot, Kathleen A. Galvin, and Eric Abella Roth, eds. (1994) *African Pastoralist Systems: An Integrated Approach*. Boulder and London: Lynne Rienner.

Rasmussen, Susan J. (1997) *The Poetics and Politics of Tuareg Aging: Life Course and Personal Destiny in Niger*. DeKalb: Northern Illinois University Press.

Rigby, Peter. (1992) *Cattle, Capitalism, and Class: Ilparakuyo Maasai Transformations*. Philadelphia: Temple University Press.

Saitoti, Tepilit Ole. (1986) *The Worlds of a Maasai Warrior: An Autobiography*. Berkeley and Los Angeles: University of California Press.

Schlee, Günther. (1990) "Holy Grounds." In *Property, Poverty and People: Changing Rights in Property and Problems of Pastoral Development*, by Baxter and Hogg. Manchester: Department of Social Anthropology and International Development Centre, University of Manchester, 45–54.

Spear, Thomas, and Richard Waller, eds. (1993) *Being Maasai: Ethnicity and Identity in East Africa*. London: James Currey; Athens, OH: Ohio University Press.

Spencer, Paul. (1965) *The Samburu: A Study of Gerontocracy in a Nomadic Tribe*. London: Routledge and Kegan Paul.

———. (1988) *The Maasai of Matapato: A Study of Rituals of Rebellion*. Manchester: Manchester University Press.

———. (1993) "Becoming Maasai, Being in Time." In *Being Maasai: Ethnicity and Identity in East Africa*, edited by Spear and Waller. London: James Currey; Athens, OH: Ohio University Press, 140–156.

———. (1998) *The Pastoral Continuum: The Marginalization of Tradition in East Africa*. Oxford: Clarendon Press.

Tablino, Paul. (1999) *The Gabra: Camel Nomads of Northern Kenya*. Nairobi: Paulines Publications Africa.

Waller, Richard, and Neal W. Sobania. (1994) "Pastoralism in Historical Perspective." In *African Pastoralist Systems: An Integrated Approach*, edited by Fratkin, Galvin, and Roth. Boulder and London: Lynne Rienner, 45–68.

Peace Mission

Father Divine's Peace Mission is one of most studied groups in the African-American religious experience (Hoshor 1936; Parker 1937; Harris 1971; Burnham 1979; Weisbrot 1983). Perhaps more than any other religious figure, Father Divine embodied the tradition of the "gods of the black metropolis" (Fauset 1971). The Peace Mission movement incorporated much of the complexity of African-American religion, including its juxtaposition of protest and accommodation to the larger society. This sect incorporated, to a greater or less extent, aspects of the mainstream churches with their commitment to social reform, messianic-nationalism with its emphasis on racial pride, the Holiness-Pentecostal sects with their emphasis on emotional exuberance and puritanism, and the Spiritual churches with their emphasis on miracles and salvation in this life.

Initial Development of the Peace Movement

While various writers have situated Baker's birthplace in Savannah, Georgia; Mineola, Long Island; and Providence, Rhode Island, Watts (1992) provides archival evidence that he was born in Rockville, Maryland, where his mother brought him up in the Jerusalem Methodist Church. After his arrival in Baltimore in 1889, he worked as an itinerant gardener and jack-leg preacher. Baker was a person with little formal education and no religious ordination. In the course of his new-found ministry, he met Samuel Morris, who referred to himself as Father Jehovia and St. John the Divine Hickerson in 1906. Both Morris and Hickerson taught that God dwells within the individual—a notion common to New Thought. New Thought emerged in the late nineteenth century as a movement that emphasized mind-body connections and positive thinking as a means for achieving health and prosperity. Baker viewed himself as a harbinger for Morris and referred to himself as "the Messenger." Whereas Morris was the incarnation of God the Father, Baker was the incarnation of God the Son. Hickerson had been involved in a series of Holiness-Pentecostal sects. While in Baltimore, Baker also became acquainted with New Thought and continued his investigations into this religious perspective while on a missionary trek in Los Angeles. He reportedly attended the Azusa Street revival—an event that resulted in the explosion of Pentecostalism on the American religious scene—in that city as well. His exposure to various religious traditions prompted him to develop a new syncretic religion that "blended New Thought with Methodism, a little Catholicism, Pentecostalism, and African-American storefront theology" (Watts 1992: 30). In 1912, both Hickerson and Baker broke with Morris and established their own ministries.

Baker left Baltimore, served a stint as an itinerant preacher in the southeastern United States, and established a following in Valdosta, Georgia in 1914. According to Watts, "the Messenger's teachings contained liberating potential for women. His earliest recorded comments indicate that he rejected gender distinctions.... He eschewed gender identification even for himself, often claiming that he was father and mother, sister and brother, to his children" (Watts 1992: 35).

In Valdosta, Baker simply referred to himself as God. After being arrested for his evangelical activities and being found guilty of insanity by a jury, the judge released him, despite opposition by members of the local African-American community, and instructed him to leave Valdosta. He established a base of operations in Americus, Georgia, but made his way in late 1914 to Harlem where he contacted a former colleague, Reverend Bishop Saint John the Vine, the founder of the Church of the Living God, the Pillar and Ground of Truth. After converting some of the sect's members to his flock, Baker continued his search for followers in other locations. In 1917, he established a congregation in Brooklyn where he began to conduct his famous communion banquets. Baker lived communally in one house with his followers, operated a job-placement service for his followers, and administered their earnings. He also began to advocate celibacy among his members on the grounds that sex was an act of depravity.

The First Established Congregation at Sayville, Long Island

In 1919, Baker, along with his first wife (Pinninnah), became the first African-American residents of Sayville, Long Island, and established a congregation there. Pinninnah, who was a few years older than the Messenger and considerably taller, became his devoted assistant. Baker signed the deed of sale with the name "Major J. Devine." He, his wife, and his followers lived in the same apartment and partook in communal meals. Devine placed many of his followers in domestic jobs in surrounding estates, stressed hard work, sobriety, and sexual abstinence, and declared himself to be the Second Coming of Christ. According to Burnham, at Sayville, Father Divine led a rather quiet life through the twenties. He ran weekly ads in the *Suffolk County News*, offering to supply workers for all sorts of household duties. Gradually more followers came to live with him. By 1934, according to one follower, the group had thirty or forty members. By 1926 it was an integrated group. In 1930 a busload of Holiness Church members of various complexions came to visit from West New York, New Jersey (Burnham 1979: 10).

During the Sayville years, Devine incorporated ideas from the writings of Robert Collier, Jiddu Krishnamurti, and other New Thought exponents (Weisbrot 1983: 28). According to Harris (1971: 128), the Peace Mission promoted "visualization of the positive." Although his followers had referred to him as Major Jealous Divine, he began to refer to himself as "Father Divine" in 1930. Indeed, during the 1930s and the 1940s, this charismatic and enigmatic prophet repeatedly stated: "My name is MR. MAJOR J. DEVINE as a civilian and citizen of the United States; but as a Minister of the Gospel, REVEREND MAJOR J. or M.J. DIVINE, better known as FATHER DIVINE." In addition to African Americans, Father Divine began to attract poor whites from Holiness and metaphysical sects to his group. He drew busloads of followers to his services, much to the annoyance of locals who unsuccessfully attempted to shut down his congregation by declaring him as a "public nuisance." As Weisbrot (1983: 28) observes, "Divine never surrendered his evangelical religious style; within his home he and his followers regularly held emotional, stirring services that recalled their rural southern roots." At any rate, the police raided his services at his home on 15 November 1931, and arrested some 80 members. Judge Lewis J. Smith found Father Divine guilty on 25 May 1932. Father Divine asserted that he was the victim of racial discrimination. African-American newspapers around the country covered the case closely. Father Divine's followers believed that God had punished the judge when he died suddenly of a heart attack three days after he pronounced sentence. Although Father Divine spent 33 days in jail, an appellate division of the Supreme Court in Brooklyn reversed the decision. As Burnham observes, from this time on, the followers proclaimed the divinity of their leader at meetings, at parades, at the various legal proceedings in which the movement became involved, and in their weekly newspaper. Accused of being evasive in court, Father Divine did not hesitate to declare himself God before his followers and visitors, nor did he avoid having his own remarks printed for all to read (Burnham 1979: 22).

Expansion on the East Coast and Beyond

Despite his victory, in 1933, Father Divine moved the headquarters to 20 West 115th Street in Harlem, where he was in great demand. He evangelized up and down the East Coast and established homes along the way. Father Divine generally dressed in a conservative blue or black suit coat, tie, and white shirt. He forbade sexual relations among his members, even between spouses. Divine remained single between 1937, when Pinninnah died, and 1946, when he married a white, blond follower called "Sweet Angel," the former Edna Rose Ritchings of Vancouver, Canada.

Between 1938 and 1941, the Peace Mission established the Crusaders and the Rosebuds, male and female auxiliaries, respectively, with rigid membership requirements and uniforms. The sect created a string of hotels and other businesses (including grocery stores, barber shops, restaurants, apartment buildings, and a coal business) in several states, thereby creating jobs for his followers. It became legally incorporated as the "Peace Mission" in 1941 and 1942. In 1942, the Peace Mission moved its headquarters to Philadelphia where it added to its property holdings, including two hotels—namely the Divine Lorraine on North Broad Street and the Divine Tracy adjacent to the University of Pennsylvania campus. It also operated an agricultural cooperative, called "Promised Land," in Ulster County, New York. The Peace Mission also engaged in the reform of inmates and delinquents by emphasizing a program of honesty and self-discipline.

Father Divine ran Peace Mission enterprises in such a way that they did not have to pay income taxes. Furthermore, the Mission purchased properties with cash. In reality, the "Father Divine organization was not a single economic unit but a series of independent cooperatives, owned and operated by the followers" (Kephart 1982: 170). Hotels formed the economic backbone of the movement and constituted the primary sites of the famous banquets that drew considerable publicity. Many of Father Divine's followers resided in these hotels, although others lived in other forms of housing, including apartments and rooming houses. As in Sayville, the Peace Mission continued to operate an elaborate job placement service during the 1930s and 1940s. In most cases, churches, or the "heavens," were situated in hotels. The kingdoms were sexually segregated, even in the case of married couples, and children were reared separately from their parents. Father Divine implemented an "International Modesty Code" which stipulated "no smoking, no drinking, no obscenity, no vulgarity, no profanity, no undue mixing of the sexes, no receiving of gifts, presents, tips, or bribes."

Membership During Peace Mission's Heyday

Unlike most other predominantly African-American religious groups, the Father Divine movement came in time to attract many white people, despite an ideology that portrayed a diminutive, black man as the incarnation of God. As Weisbrot (1983: 108) notes, "The boldness of the Peace Mission's stand on integration is further underscored by the absence of almost any other predominantly black church or cult that deliberately encouraged an interracial membership." The Peace Mission incorporated three movements in one: (1) an Eastern section, composed largely, but not exclusively, of poor African Americans; (2) a Western section, located primarily in California, that catered to a largely European-American membership (many of whom were middle class); and (3) a foreign section that appealed primarily to urban working-class people in Canada, Australia, and Western Europe.

The vast majority of Divine's early followers were African Americans and West Indian immigrants. Women constituted between 75 and 90 percent of the Peace Mission members (Weisbrot 1983: 60). They occupied a large number of the higher-echelon and middle-echelon positions in the movement. Father Divine tended to place whites into upper- and middle-echelon leadership positions. According to Weisbrot (1983: 77), "[N]early all Father Divine's secretaries during the thirties were white, as were the lawyers. Whites also contributed greatly to the quality of the Peace Mission publications. On the other hand, "Faithful Mary," a poor black woman with a police record, became Father Divine's closest disciple and served as personal envoy to the new California missions in 1934, where she received much credit for their rapid success." Arthur Madison, Father Divine's personal attorney and perhaps closest confidant, also was black. Father Divine also attracted a high percentage of elderly people.

While Father Divine claimed some two million followers, Weisbrot contends that Divine's strength in New York City was never much more than 1,000. Since over 10 percent of all Peace Mission centers were in New York City and since Father Divine focused his leadership there, one could place the number of his strongest supporters at about 10,000 as an upper limit (Weisbrot 1983: 69). Some 150 to 160 Peace Mission branches were in operation during the Depression and through the early 1940s. The stronghold of the movement, however, was situated in New York, New Jersey, and eastern Pennsylvania. Approximately one third of the Mission's branches in the United States were situated west of the Mississippi, the majority of which were in California, where roughly 70 percent of the membership was white. Although the sect had twelve branches in the South, Father Divine rarely visited these branches. The existence of branches in countries with predominantly white populations attested to the universal nature of his message.

The Social Reform Nature of the Peace Movement

The Peace Mission challenged the oppressive conditions encountered by African Americans. Father Divine was committed to a wide range of social reform efforts. He provided outreach services in the form of health care, food, clothing, shelter, classes, and jobs for his adherents. Father Divine encouraged his followers to register and vote in national and local elections. He supported the Harlem Political Union and in 1936 helped to form the All People's Party, a coalition of 89 Harlem-based organizations that endorsed a small slate of radical candidates, including Italian-American Vito Marcantonio and African-American Communist and labor organizer Angelo Herndon. Father Divine cooperated with the Communist Party in Harlem between 1934 and 1936 because he viewed it as much more progressive on racial issues than both the Democrats and the Republicans. During the mid-1930s, the Peace Mission created the

Righteous Government Platform with 14 planks, including three concerned with economics, education, and politics, and eight concerned with racial issues.

Despite Father Divine's sponsorship of cooperative ventures and brief flirtation with the Communist Party, he was a reformer committed to working within a capitalist political economy. He staunchly advocated the Protestant work ethic, self-help, savings, investments, and private property (Burnham 1979: 50). Father Divine regarded corporate titans such as Henry Ford and Andrew Carnegie as role models for his followers (Weisbrot 1983: 198) and sang praises to the U.S. Constitution and the Declaration of Independence.

Religious Beliefs

Although the Peace Mission resembled black mainstream churches in its emphasis on social reform, it also exhibited some dimensions, at least in subtle form, of messianic-nationalism. Father Divine taught that color is inconsequential, but he held himself up as living testimony of the notion that "black is beautiful." After all, had not God decided to take on the body of a black man? In this, Father Divine joined with black Judaic, Islamic, and Christian nationalist sects in their uniform rejection of a white God. Like the Garvey movement, Father Divine emphasized self-help and the establishment of business enterprises and cooperatives. Elijah Muhammad apparently recognized the inherent rivalry between the Nation of Islam and the Peace Mission and told Essien-Udom (1962: 101) that alienating followers from the Peace Mission was an official policy of the Nation. Conversely, because, unlike most messianic-nationalist sects, Father Divine promoted integration, he was severely criticized by militant nationalists.

Like Holiness-Pentecostal or Sanctified sects, the Peace Mission emphasized salvation through profound personal transformation. Father Divine rejected pie-in-the-sky religion and attempted to provide solutions in the here and now. Although ecstatic behavior per se was not a central focus of the Peace Mission, the elaborate banquets that Father Divine held for his followers were often characterized by dancing, shouting, clapping, testifying, and joyous singing (Harris 1971: xxi–xxii). He carefully orchestrated his famous banquets in such a way that beverages were served first, followed by starches and some fruits and vegetables, and finally, when his guests had largely filled up on these less expensive foods, climaxed with the arrival of elaborately prepared roasts, ducks, and chickens. Father Divine generally delivered electrifying sermons at his banquets and frequently spoke out against racism at these times. He denied personally curing people of their ailments, but many of his adherents believed that his touch or mere presence could cure them. His adherents were expected to abide by a strict code of conduct prohibiting alcoholic beverages, smoking, social dances, gambling, theatergoing, and most notably, all forms of sex. Despite the addition of New Thought and social activism to his religious repertoire after he arrived in New York, Father Divine never gave up the evangelical fervor associated with his early ministry. His members also refused to accept public welfare. Father Divine stressed the importance of education in the improvement of his follower's socioeconomic status. He also regarded education as essential to overcoming racial prejudice and instilling tolerance of cultural differences.

Declining Years

The Peace Mission evolved from a multiracial international movement into a more centralized organization that relied heavily upon the *New Age*, the group's primary publication, instead of several newspapers. In 1953, it acquired Woodmont, a palatial suburban Philadelphia estate, which became the residence of Father and Mother Divine. Father Divine received a visit in 1956 from Jim Jones, white minister of Disciples of Christ who went on to establish the ill-fated Peoples Temple.

Despite efforts to create a bureaucratic structure, the Peace Mission began to undergo a period of steady decline following its heyday in the 1930s for a variety of reasons, including various scandals that rocked the movement, general improvement in the socioeconomic position of African Americans during World War II, and the growing split between leaders and rank-and-file members emanating from the rigid hierarchy within the group. In his later years, Father Divine shifted his political stance from that of a liberal reformer to that of a reactionary as he engaged in an increasing number of anti-Communist and anti-union tirades. Father Divine spent most of his retirement at Woodmont. He became seriously ill by 1955, began to restrict his public appearances, made his last public appearance in 1963, and died in 1965. During his last years and following his death, Mother Divine became the official spokesperson of the Peace Mission movement. Father Divine's body rests in a $300,000 shrine at Woodmont.

The Peace Mission still conducts communion banquets, services, and anniversary celebrations, and even operates some businesses. It continues to publish the *New Day*, which includes messages that Father Divine delivered during the 1930s and 1940s. Under the leadership of Mother Divine, the sect has persisted with its stronghold in eastern

Pennsylvania, but with a scattering of members in California, Colorado, New York, and New Jersey. For the most part, however, the Peace Mission has evolved into an introversionist sect that emphasizes personal transformation rather than social transformation.

Hans A. Baer

See also Black Muslims; Holiness–Pentecostal Sanctified Movement; Social Activism

Bibliography

Burnham, Kenneth E. (1979) *God Comes to America: Father Divine and the Peace Mission Movement.* Boston: Lambeth Press.

Essien-Udom, E. U. (1962) *Black Nationalism: A Search for Identity in America.* Chicago: University of Chicago Press.

Fauset, Arthur H. (1971) *Black Gods of the Metropolis.* Philadelphia: University of Pennsylvania Press.

Harris, Sara. (1971) *Father Divine.* New York: Collier.

Hoshor, John. (1936) *God in a Rolls-Royce.* New York: Hillman-Carl.

Kephart, William M. (1982) *Extraordinary Groups: The Sociology of Unconventional Life-Styles.* New York: St. Martin's Press.

Parker, Robert A. (1937) *The Incredible Messiah.* Boston: Little, Brown.

Watts, Jill. (1992) *God, Harlem U.S.A.: The Father Divine Story.* Berkeley: University of California Press.

Weisbrot, Robert. (1983) *Father Divine and the Struggle for Racial Equality.* Urbana: University of Illinois Press.

Pentecostalism in Africa

Pentecostalism is usually defined as that branch of Christianity that traces its origins to the ministry of the Black American preacher Charles Parkham (1872–1929) and the Azusa Street Revival of 1906 in Los Angeles. This dynamic movement, which today claims over 300,000,000 followers worldwide, gets its name from the manifestation of "spiritual gifts" mentioned in the New Testament book of the Acts of the Apostles where on the Day of Pentecost the Holy Spirit descended on the followers of Christ, giving them spiritual gifts including the gifts of healing, prophecy, and speaking in tongues (Acts 2: 1–20).

Although such phenomenon appeared at various times in Church history, since the Protestant Reformation in the

NTSIKANA'S HYMN

He, the great God, high in Heaven,
Great "I am" of truth the Buckler,
Great "I am" of truth the Stronghold,
Great "I am" in whom truth shelters.
What art Thou in Highest Heaven,
Who created life around us,
Who created Heaven above us,
And the stars, the Pleiades.
We were blind until he taught us.
(Thou mad'st us blind, it was Thy purpose.)
With a trumpet gave the message,
As he hunted for our spirits.
Toiled to make our foes our brothers.
(Thou our leader who dost guide us.)
Then he cast His cloak about us,
Cloak of Him whose hands are wounded,
Cloak of Him whose feet are bleeding,
See the blood that streameth for us;
Flows it, though we have not asked it?
Is it paid without our praying?
Heaven our Home with no beseeching?

Source: Gerard, Albert S. (1971) *Four African Literatures.* Berkeley: University of California Press, 26.
Taken from Shephard, R.H.W. and B.G. Paver (1947) *African Contrasts.* Cape Town, 164–165.

sixteenth century a general belief was accepted that these miraculous gifts disappeared after the establishment of the early church. The claim made by Parkham and modern Pentecostalism was that God had restored these gifts to the church and that the gift of tongues, which includes ecstatic speech, is one of the main characteristics of true Christianity.

After the first awakening in Azusa Street, the Pentecostal movement rapidly spread throughout the world, creating many new Christian denominations such as the Assemblies of God and the Foursquare Gospel movement. In doing so, it attracted large numbers of followers from what were usually underprivileged groups such as American Blacks and the urban poor. In the 1960s the nature of Pentecostalism changed with the growth of charismatic movements, or neo-Pentecostalism, within historic denominations such as the Anglican, Methodist, and Roman Catholic Churches. It is

against this background of both traditional Pentecostalism and the charismatic movement that African Pentecostalism is usually understood.

Actually, Pentecostalism, or perhaps one should say charismatic Christianity, is as African as choral music and dance. Prayers for healing, speaking in tongues, and similar phenomena were a part of many traditional African religions long before the arrival of European missionaries. In fact, when they observed traditional practices many early missionaries thought that Africans were either a lost tribe of Israel or people whose ancestors had been Christians.

The African Origins of Pentecostal Movements

European and North American scholars usually trace the origins of Pentecostalism in Africa to the work of Daniel

Bryant (?), who was sent out from Zion City, Illinois by John Alexander Dowie (1847–1907) to evangelize Africa in 1903, and to the later influence of the Azusa Street Revival, which is linked with the names of Petrus L. le Roux (1865–1943), Johannes Bücher (?), and John G. Lake (1870–1935), who founded the Apostolic Faith Mission of South Africa (AFMSA) on 14 October 1913 in South Africa. Thus it is usually seen as a European import into Africa. A recent variation of the European origins thesis is presented by Paul Gifford in *The Religious Right in Southern Africa* (1978) and other books where he argues that many contemporary charismatic movements are the result of American dollars, capitalism, and even the CIA. Frankly, both types of argument are nonsense in the face of African realities.

A good case can be made that rather than Americans, or Europeans, influencing Africa, it was the other way around. David B. Coplan has shown in his *In Township Tonight* (1985) that American missionaries took a stream of African converts to America from the 1870s on and convincingly argues that these visits had a profound effect on African music in both Africa *and* America. No similar study has documented the effect of these visits on religion, but they must have had significant influence. Further, both Europeans and Americans were open to religious influences from Africa through the writings and preaching of Andrew Murray (1828–1917), whose popular works on healing prepared the way for American Pentecostalism.

The earliest recorded Pentecostal-type movement in Africa is that of the remarkable South African Xhosa prophet, the visionary Ntsikana (1780–1821). Very little is known about Ntsikana's origins except that he underwent a conversion experience without contact with missionaries, other Christians, or Europeans. This dramatic event changed his life and led to an itinerant ministry involving healing, preaching, prophecy and the writing of hymns. Traditionalists claim that Ntsikana never had contact with whites. But Janet Hodgeson has convincingly argued in her *Ntsikana's Great Hymn* (1980) that this view is wrong and that according to some oral traditions he did meet missionaries after his conversion. Whatever the truth of the matter, he developed a theistic theology that prepared his followers for the acceptance of Christianity.

Missionaries are often portrayed as ignorant individuals who destroyed indigenous cultures. No doubt some were like this caricature, but many more were not. Once again we must look to South Africa because this was the area of earliest sustained missionary contact with Africans. Here people like the former Quaker, Henry Callaway (1817–1890), the first missionary Bishop of the Anglican Diocese

of Kaffraria, in the Transkei, that later became St. John's Diocese, translated most of the Bible (1883) and the Anglican Book of Common Prayer (1882) into Zulu. More importantly, he published major collections of Zulu folk tales and history and encouraged indigenous expressions of religiosity. Influenced by Johann Gottfried Herder (1744–1803) and German Romanticism, Callaway believed that God works through all people at all times. Thus he argued that the Holy Spirit was already present in African culture long before the arrival of the missionary. As a result he accepted the validity of such African religious experiences as dreams and visions. He also compared the experiences of his converts with those of early church fathers like St. Antony and Hilarion, and other early saints. Most importantly, Callaway records that the initiation of traditional diviners involved sounds very similar to speaking in tongues, which he described as the composition of "songs," many of which were "without any meaning": in other words, ecstatic speech similar to speaking in tongues.

German missionaries, particularly those of the Berlin Mission, shared Callaway's enthusiasm for Romanticism. They systematically taught Africans stories about the early church fathers, Christian reformers, and saints throughout history and encouraged Africans to make these stories their own by drawing analogies between their own experiences and those of great Christians in the past. Thus Africans were encouraged to tell stories about themselves as "fathers" of local congregations and churches. Not unexpectedly, some of these congregations grew into what are today called African Independent/Indigenous Churches. The Germans also taught African converts that Christianity could be followed in a distinct ethnic manner acceptable to the customs of their ancestors.

African Independent/Indigenous Churches

Although there is considerable evidence that the first African Independent Churches in various parts of Africa were offshoots of German missions, usually the Methodist preacher Nehemiah Tile (?–1891) is credited with founding the first African Independent Church in 1883. Unfortunately, this brave experiment disintegrated soon after Tile's death. From the 1890s onwards, however, African-initiated religious movements, usually called "separatist" movements because they separated themselves from mission churches, are recorded throughout Africa. Usually these were small affairs that attracted few followers and soon failed. It was not until the turn of the century that African Independent Churches finally took root with the

Isaiah Shembe, founder of amaNazaretha. PHOTO FROM AN UNKNOWN SOURCE COURTESY OF IRVING HEXHAM.

establishment of Isaiah Shembe's (1867–1935) ama-Nazaretha in 1913 in South Africa. This was followed by the founding around 1915 in West Africa of William Wade Harris's (1860–1929) Harrist movement (although he had received his first vision in 1910); the Kimbanguist movement of Central Africa, founded by Simon Kimbangu (1889–1951) in 1921; and the South African Zion Christian Church of Ignatius Lekganyane (1885–1948), founded in 1924.

The growth of African Independent/Indigenous Churches (AICs), which are without exception Pentecostal/charismatic in their theology and practice, is truly amazing. As G. C. Ooshuisen has rightly pointed out, today AICs are rapidly becoming *the* Church of Africa. For example, in South Africa in 1913 there were thirty-two recognized AICs, by 1949 this number had risen to 800, in 1960 there were over 2,000, and by 1990 the number had grown to 6,000. Around two million people belonged to AICs in 1960. By 1990 the number had grown to a phenomenal eight million and their rapid growth shows no sign of abating. Thus, AIC membership grew from around 18 percent of South African blacks in 1960 to 35 percent in 1990. This means AIC membership is greater than either the Roman Catholic or Methodist Churches that are the largest mainline, or mission, churches, and this same pattern is repeated throughout Africa.

The proliferation of African independent churches or denominations is to be explained by the fact that they are essentially house-church movements with a strong emphasis on healing, prophetic gifts, and lay participation. Bengt Sundkler (1948), F. B. Welbourn (1961), Inus Daneel (1987), and others point out that AICs blend aspects of the traditional African with the ever-changing secular culture of modern society. Further, they are aggressive in their evangelism and devote a far larger proportion of their incomes to evangelistic efforts than mission-type churches.

Pentecostal Influences on Mainline or Mission Churches

Apart from creating independent churches, African Pentecostal/Charismatic theology has profoundly influenced mainline or mission churches and through them Christianity worldwide. One such development is the *Iviyo loFakazi bakaKristu* (Legion of Christ's witnesses), which is documented by Stephen Hayes (1990). *Iviyo*, as it is known, is a charismatic renewal movement within the Anglican church of the Province of Southern Africa that appeared in Natal and Zululand, South Africa, in the 1940s. Thus it existed twenty years before a similar charismatic movement in mainline churches originated at Van Nuys, California, in the early 1960's. Further, it was the white African David du Plessis (1905–1967), who—deeply affected by the spirituality of black South African Christians for whom healing, tongues, dreams, and visions were simultaneously and quintessentially African and Christian—helped bring American Roman Catholics into the charismatic revival of the 1960s, and spread the charismatic movement worldwide.

Another Africa-wide, mildly charismatic, but solidly Anglican evangelistic movement, is Africa Enterprise (AE), founded in 1962 by Michael Cassidy (1936–). Originally a South African movement, it soon spread through Africa with branch organizations in East, West, and Central Africa. In South Africa, AE worked closely with Bishops Desmond Tutu and Adolphus Zulu. In East Africa the gifted charismatic Anglican Bishop of Uganda Festo Kivengere (1919–1988) led the movement.

More successful in drawing monster crowds to explicitly Pentecostal meetings is the German Pentecostal evangelist Reinhard Bonkke (1944–) who was inspired by the black South African evangelist Nicolas B. H. Bengu (1909–1986). With great success, Bonkke, a missionary in Lesotho, followed Bengu's example in the organization of his crusades and preaching style. Bonkke also worked very closely with blacks, becoming a sensation in South Africa before extending his ministry to the whole of Africa. In the late 1990s he regularly drew crowds of over 200,000. Finally, Bishop

THE ACTS OF THE APOSTLES 2: 1-20.

1 And when the day of Pentecost was fully come, they were all with one accord in one place.

2 And suddenly there came a sound from heaven as of a rushing mighty wind, and it filled all the house where they were sitting.

3 And there appeared unto them cloven tongues like as of fire, and it sat upon each of them.

4 And they were all filled with the Holy Ghost, and began to speak with other tongues, as the Spirit gave them utterance.

5 And there were dwelling at Jerusalem Jews, devout men, out of every nation under heaven.

6 Now when this was noised abroad, the multitude came together, and were confounded, because that every man heard them speak in his own language.

7 And they were amazed and marvelled, saying one to another, Behold, are not all these which speak Gallilaeans?

8 And how hear we every man in our own tongue, wherein we were born?

9 Parthinians, and Medes and Elamites, and the dwellers in Mesopotamia, and in Judea, and Cappadocia, in Pontus, and Asia.

10 Phrygia, and Pamphylia, in Egypt, and in the parts of Libya about Cyrene, and strnagers of Rome, Jews and proselytes.

11 Cretes and Arabians, we do hear them speak in our tongues the wonderful words of God.

12 And they were all amazed, and were in doubt, saying one to another, What meaneth this?

13 Others mocking said, These men are full of new wine.

14 But Peter, standing up with the eleven, lifted up his voice, and said unto them, Ye men of Judaea, and all ye that dwell in Jerusalem, be this known unto you, and harken to my words:

15 For these are not drunken, as ye suppose, seeing it is but the third hour of the day.

16 But this is that which was spoken by the prophet Joel;

17 And it shall come to pass in the last days, saith God, I will pour out of my Spirit upon all flesh: and your sons and your daughters shall prophesy, and your young men shall see visions, and your old men shall dream dreams:

18 And on my servants and on my handmaidens I will pour out in those days of my Spirit; and they shall prophesy:

19 And I will shew wonders in heaven above, and signs in the earth beneath; blood, and fire, and vapour of smoke:

20 The sun shall be turned into darkness, and the moon into blood, before that great and notable day of the Lord come:

Idahosa (1936–) of Nigeria is one of the few black African evangelists to have made a significant impact in North America through his links with Chapel Hill Harvester Church in Atlanta.

In the 1990s African Pentecostal missionaries were at work in Europe and North America. Many Africans in these places belonged to the African Pentecostal Churches that were gradually taking root outside of Africa itself in big cities like Frankfurt-am-Main, London, and New York. These churches have not broken out of their original ethnic origins.

Conclusion: A Place to Feel at Home

Fred Welbourn (1961) suggested that the creation of a sense of community, or, as he put it, "a place to feel at home," was a key factor in the creation of African Independent Churches which, unlike traditional mission churches, cater to all aspects of their members' lives. More recently a similar conclusion was reached by Inus Daneel in his *Quest for Belonging* (1987). This simple yet profound fact explains the appeal of Pentecostal/Charismatic movements throughout African and their continual rapid growth. It also forces us to recognize that African Pentecostalism is truly African, even though few Americans, particularly white Americans, recognize the African roots of many aspects of contemporary charismatic spirituality. Nevertheless, as Karla Poewe (1994) argued, it is beyond dispute that African Pentecostal Christianity has profoundly influenced the charismatic movement and through it the church worldwide.

Irving Hexham

See also AIC; amaNazaretha; Azusa Street Revival; Harrist Movement; Holiness-Pentecostal (Sanctified) Movement

Bibliography

Anderson, Allan. (1991) *Moya: The Holy Spirit in an African Context.* Pretoria, South Africa: University of South Africa Press.

Coplan, David B. (1985) *In Township Tonight: South Africa's Black City Music and Theater.* Johannesburg, South Africa: Ravan Press.

Daneel, Inus. (1987) *Quest for Belonging.* Harare, Zimbabwe: Mambo Press.

Gifford, Paul. (1988) *The Religious Right in Southern Africa.* Harare, Zimbabwe: University of Zimbabwe.

Hodgson, Janet. (1980) *Ntsikana's Great Hymn: A Xhosa Expression of Christianity in the Early Nineteenth Century Eastern Cape.* Cape Town, South Africa: Centre for African Studies.

Hollenweger, Walter J. (1988 [1972]) *The Pentecostals.* Peabody, MA: Hendrickson.

Oosthuizen, G. C. (1992) *Healer-Prophet in Afro-Christian Churches.* Leiden: E.J. Brill.

Poewe, Karla, ed. (1994) *Charismatic Christianity as a Global Culture.* Columbia, SC: University of South Carolina Press.

Sundkler, Bengt. (1961 [1948]) *Bantu Prophets in South Africa.* London: Oxford University Press.

———. (1975) *Zulu Zion and some Swazi Zionists.* London: Oxford University Press.

Welbourn, F. B. (1961) *East African Rebels.* London: SCM Press.

Peoples Temple

Peoples Temple was a religious movement and a communal society that began in the 1950s and ended in November, 1978. It is perhaps the best-known American religious movement of the 1960s and 1970s primarily because the movement ended in a mass murder-suicide of 900 people in Jonestown, Guyana. Over twenty years later several basic questions about the movement remain unanswered: most importantly, was the mass suicide voluntary and what role the United States government had in pushing the movement leadership to murder-suicide?

Peoples Temple was not a traditional African-American church or movement, but the membership was composed of many African-Americans (mainly women and their children). Many of these women came to the Temple from black churches, and members believed strongly in racial equality and social justice. The leader, the Rev. Jim Jones (who was white), was motivated in part by apocalyptic visions of a fascist takeover of the United States that would climax in race wars and concentration camps. To save the group from this fate, Jones organized a communal society in the jungle of northwest Guyana. Former members and relatives of current members criticized the Temple, and in November 1978, U.S. Congressman Leo Ryan traveled to Jonestown to investigate charges that people were held against their will. Ryan's visit and the accompanying media attention evidently confirmed the apocalyptic fears of Jones and at least some members, and on 18 November, followers of Jones assassinated the Congressman and four others at an airstrip five miles from Jonestown. Shortly thereafter, members of the community apparently took the lives of their children, their elderly relatives, and themselves by drinking or injecting fruit punch laced with potassium cyanide and tranquilizers.

History

Jim Jones (1931–1978) was a charismatic preacher and faith healer who founded a series of churches that attracted interracial congregations in Indianapolis, Indiana in the 1950s. Jones was impressed by the social service work of Father Divine's Peace Mission. Jones was much interested in racial equality and cooperation and social justice, and his churches provided social services for the poor. Primary responsibility for these programs rested with Jones's wife Marceline Baldwin Jones (1927–1978), a registered nurse. In 1955, Jones named his church the Peoples Temple Full Gospel Church. In the same year, Jones and associates formed Wings of Deliverance as a nonprofit foundation of the Temple. The African-American community in Indianapolis lauded the work of the church in promoting racial harmony and social services, and in 1961 Jones was appointed director of the city's Human Rights Commission. The Temple was accepted as a congregation within the mainstream Disciples of Christ denomination and in 1964 Jones was ordained as a minister.

Jones took a leave of absence from 1963 to 1965 and worked in Brazil. A vision of nuclear holocaust persuaded him to take his congregation to Ukiah in the Redwood Valley region of northern California in 1965, and by 1969 the movement had settled in a complex called "Happy Acres." From there the movement, which was still predominantly white, expanded south to San Francisco and began to attract African-Americans. In 1970, it opened a large facility in the African-American Filmore district of San Francisco. While it continued to maintain social services and facilities in Redwood Valley, the Temple moved its program to San Francisco, and then expanded to Los Angeles. From the eighty members who had followed Jones to Ukiah, it had now expanded to some 3,000 members.

As in Indianapolis, Jones was praised in San Francisco for his community work and was appointed to the Housing Authority. In 1973 the Temple began experiencing difficulties, as eight of Jones's aides resigned and criticized his leadership style and the *San Francisco Examiner* ran a series critical of the Temple and Jones. In response, Jones looked to move the Temple and, in 1974, a small group began to clear forest land in Guyana to create a new community, based on an agreement with the government of Guyana. Guyana was especially desirable because the national leadership was Afro-Caribbean, English was the primary language, and the government followed a socialist ideology. In 1977, some 1,000 members emigrated from California to Guyana in the space of six months. About 900 people lived in Jonestown from 1977–1978, while another 80 to 100 lived in Georgetown, Guyana's capital. Another 50 to 100 remained in California for administrative purposes. About 75 percent of the members were African-American, 20 percent were white, and the remaining 5 percent were Asian, Latino, or Native American. The large and somewhat unexpected arrival of the 1,000 members placed much stress on the emerging community and the settlement experienced severe economic problems as only about one-third of the members were adults capable of working to support the community by farming, producing crafts for sale, and other activities. The remaining two-thirds were split about equally between senior citizens and children under the age of eighteen.

Jonestown experienced additional problems beginning in 1976 when a group calling itself the Concerned Relatives, comprised of former Temple members and relatives of current members, charged that Jones was a dictator and that members were forced to work long hours, and were subject to forced confessions, beatings, and other forms of physical or mental coercion. Jones was accused of being consumed with power and control and the group claimed that one member who had sought to leave had been murdered. The accusations led to local, state, and federal investigations by United States agencies into the Peoples Temple, although no evidence of wrongdoing on the part of the organization was ever produced.

In June 1978, the group drew increased scrutiny when Concerned Relatives publicly raised the possibility of mass suicide by the Temple members. The Relatives became more active and vocal and persuaded California Congressman Leo Ryan that people in Jonestown were being held against their will. As a result, Ryan and several reporters traveled to Guyana and visited the community on 17 November 1978 and Ryan praised the community and what it had accomplished. On 18 November when Ryan, his aides, the reporters, and a dozen residents who had chosen to leave the community, reached the airstrip at Port Kaituma, about five miles away, a Peoples Temple truck pulled up and gunmen killed Ryan, three reporters, and one Temple member.

After Ryan's party had left Jonestown, Jim Jones had gathered the community at its central pavilion. There nurses mixed a vat of fruit drink with potassium cyanide and tranquilizers. Parents killed their children by giving them poison to drink or by injecting them. Senior citizens were injected in their sleeping quarters. Most adults seemed to have taken the poison willingly, although questions remain about the extent to which they were coerced. Jim Jones and his nurse Annie Moore (1954–1978) evidently committed suicide by shooting themselves.

After the mass murder-suicide and the extensive coverage in the media, African-American political and religious leaders criticized the Temple, Jones and the effects of Jones, the movement, and Jonestown on the African-American community. A special two-day conference, "A Consultation on the Implications of Jonestown for the Black Church," concluded that Jones was a dishonest exploiter of African-Americans and that the Temple had harmed the African-American community. African-American organizations in San Francisco initiated programs to assist survivors of Temple members who died at Jonestown.

Beliefs

Peoples Temple ideology was a unique mix of Pentecostalism, apocalysticism, racial equality, social justice, socialism, and liberation theology. Rebecca Moore suggests that there were at least two belief systems operating in the Peoples Temple that can be combined under the rubric "apostolic socialism." The first was that of Jim Jones; the second was that of the majority of Christian members. Jones combined a Pentecostal style of preaching and worship with a socialist, anticapitalist model of the existing American social order and an apocalyptic vision of the future. While his preaching was revivalist, at the same time he emphasized the Gospel's message of liberation from poverty

MATTHEW 25: 31–46

31 When the Son of man shall come in his glory, and all the holy angels with him, then shall he sit upon the throne of his glory;

32 And before him shall be gathered all nations; and he shall separate them one from another, as a shepherd divideth his sheep from the goats:

33 And he shall set the sheep on his right hand, and the goats on the left.

34 Then shall the King say unto them on his right hand, Come, ye blessed of my Father, inherit the kingdom prepared for you from the foundation of the world:

35 For I was an hungred, and ye gave me meat: I was thirsty, and ye gave me drink: I was a stranger, and ye took me in:

36 Naked, and ye clothed me: I was sick, and ye visited me: I was in prison, and Ye came unto me.

37 Then shall the righteous answer him, saying, Lord, when saw we thee an hungred, and feed thee? Or thirsty, and gave thee drink?

38 When saw we thee a stranger, and took thee in? Or naked, and clothed thee?

39 Or when saw we thee sick, or in prison, and came unto thee?

40 And the King shall answer and say unto them, Verily I say unto you, Inasmuch as ye have done it unto one of the least of these my brethren, ye have done it unto me.

41 Then shall he say also unto them on the left hand, Depart from me, ye cursed, into everlasting fire, prepared for the devil and his angels:

42 For I was an hungred, and ye gave me not meat: I was thirsty, and ye gave me no drink:

43 I was a stranger, and ye took me not in; naked, and ye clothed me not: sick, and in prison, and ye visited me not.

44 Then shall they also answer him, saying, Lord, when saw we thee an hungred, or athirst, or a stranger, or naked, or sick, or in prison, and did not minister unto thee?

45 Then shall he answer them, saying, Verily I say unto you, Inasmuch as ye did it not to one of the least of these, ye did it not to me.

46 And these shall go away into everlasting punishment: but the righteous into life eternal.

---

and inequality. Jones claimed his ultimate goal was the establishment of a new social order free of racism, competition, poverty, and injustice and he viewed Christianity as a vehicle toward this end. At the same time, Jones had a pessimistic view of the future, in which he saw the emergence of a police state and a nuclear holocaust.

Almost all the members at Jonestown were Christians and the majority had been raised in, or had been members of, black churches. Their beliefs differed from Jones's in their sources, as many followers lived in the tradition of the social gospel, that is, the message of hope, liberation, and justice found in the Bible and in the teachings of Jesus. Acts 2: 44–45 and Matthew 25: 31–46 in the Bible were especially important and many members believed they were practicing Christianity by being part of Peoples Temple. To what extent followers knew of or supported Jones's socialist, anticapitalist agenda is not clear, although it seems likely

that the congruence between their faith and Jones's program is what made the Peoples Temple appealing.

One basic question that remains unanswered is why members agreed to Jones's program of "revolutionary suicide," which was presented as an act of protest against capitalism and against Jonestown's enemies. The extent to which suicide drills occurred, in which members drank punch and pretended to fall down dead is in dispute. Some say it occurred rarely, and only among a small leadership group. Others say the entire Jonestown community practiced them with regularity.

Conclusions

Jonestown, as a religious movement, communal society, and mass suicide has drawn much media and scholarly attention since 1978. Nonetheless, many gaps remain in the information and two basic questions remain unanswered. First, did all or most of the members die voluntarily or were they coerced or murdered? Conflicting information gathered immediately after the mass death and inadequate studies have failed to answer this question and it will likely remain a question for speculation in the future. Second, does the United States government bear some responsibility for the mass murder/suicide? There are several partial answers to this question. First, it is likely that governmental investigations did threaten the group and push it toward its final act of defiance. Second, there have long been claims that the CIA was monitoring the commune and may have done nothing to halt the murder/suicide or that it even ran the commune. Social scientists have been unable to address this question fully, as the twelve volumes of the official report on Leo Ryan's death prepared by the U.S. House of Representatives in 1979 remains under CIA control.

David Levinson

Bibliography

Hall, John R. (1987) *Gone From the Promised Land: Jonestown in American Cultural History*. New Brunswick, NJ: Transaction Books.

Maaga, Mary McCormick. (1998) *Hearing the Voices of Jonestown*. Syracuse, NY: Syracuse University Press.

Melton, J. Gordon. (1990) *The Peoples Temple and Jim Jones: Broadening Our Perspective*. New York: Garland.

Moore, Rebecca. (1985) *A Sympathetic History of Jonestown*. Lewiston, NY: The Edwin Mellen Press.

Reiterman, Tim, with John Jacobs. (1982) *Raven: The Untold Story of the Rev. Jim Jones and His People*. New York: E. P. Dutton.

Weightman, Judith M. (1987) *Making Sense of the Jonestown Suicides: A Sociological History of the Peoples Temple*. Lewiston, NY: The Edwin Mellen Press.

Pilgrimage

A pilgrimage is a journey to a holy or sacred site. Although both Muslims and Christians in Africa make pilgrimages, only Muslims are enjoined to do so as a religious duty, as making the *hajj* to Mecca is the fifth of the Five Pillars of Islam, the basic beliefs and practices required of all Muslims. Therefore, most pilgrimages made by Africans are to Mecca, the holiest of holy sites for Muslims. By so doing, they openly acknowledge their membership in a worldwide community. The more than three million pilgrims from Muslim communities around the world present convincing evidence of the ethnic, linguistic, and political diversity of Islam itself. In addition, the theoretical elimination of worldly distinctions when pilgrims are in a cognitive-emotional state that anthropologists label "liminal" expresses the unity of Muslims around the world.

With Muslims from other areas, African Muslims believe that creation began at Mecca, that Abraham built the first house of worship there, and that the Kabah, a stone sacred to the Arabs, is there. Muhammad, God's final messenger, has made Mecca holy and all Muslim prayers are offered facing this site.

Early African Pilgrimages to Mecca

Once Islam entered sub-Saharan Africa from the north and east, it soon became obvious to African rulers that Islam gave them an advantage in centralizing their domains as well as in trade relations with Arab and other Islamic traders across the trans-Saharan routes. The rulers of Mali (1200–1450) made it the first great African empire to embrace Islam, and used Islam to build Mali's material and political power.

Mali, on the upper Niger River in the west of Africa, had gained control over the salt and gold trade, previously monopolized by the Kingdom of Ghana. Added to its good farmland and skill at trading, this monopoly made it a powerful force in the Sudanic area. Slavery and control of its end of the slave trade further consolidated Mali's wealth. A group of Islamic hermits, the Almoravids, spread Islamic teachings throughout the Sudan, and Ghana's downfall had been triggered by an Islamic revolution brought about by the Almoravids. Many of the ruling families of the Sudan quickly learned that it would be best to become Muslims. Among the converted were the Keita family of the Mandingo people who forged the kingdom of Mali. Sundiata (1230–1255), a magician or sorcerer, was the direct founder of the kingdom. He had previously been a royal slave among the Soso people who had taken over the Ghanaian Empire.

Perhaps the most famous of its Mandinka rulers was Mansa (Lord) Musa (1312–1327). Musa's pilgrimage to Mecca is the stuff of legends. In 1324 he set out for Mecca with 500 slaves and 500 golden staffs. He traded gold along his route, devastating the economy of the Cairo region by causing a ruinous inflation. However he affected the economy, Musa achieved his goal of gaining an international reputation for both himself and his empire. That reputation brought further trade with Islamic areas and aided in his transformation of Mali into a fully centralized state.

Musa's piety, however, was genuine. He was a famous builder of mosques, and his university at Timbuktu was a worldwide cultural center. He built other universities and sponsored libraries throughout the empire. His fame, enhanced by the pilgrimage, enabled Musa to lure scholars from throughout the Muslim world to his realm. The Muslim traveler Ibn Battuta's account of his travels in 1352–1353 notes how Musa's fame helped spread Islamic influence in the western Sudan.

Ibn Battuta notes that Musa's retinue elicited superlatives from the Arab rulers in Cairo and Mecca who received him. Musa's journey took him and his party from his capital of Niani on the Upper Niger River to Walata (Oualâta, Mauritania) and on to Tuat before reaching Cairo. According to Battuta, Musa's entourage included "an impressive caravan consisting of 60,000 men including a personal retinue of 12,000 slaves, all clad in brocade and Persian silk. The emperor himself rode on horseback and was directly preceded by 500 slaves, each carrying a gold-adorned staff." Musa also had a baggage train of 80 camels. Each camel carried 300 pounds of gold. The historian 'al Umari noted that the residents of Cairo were still praising Musa's generosity twelve years after Musa had left Cairo. Musa's pilgrimage, it should be noted, was not the first by a West African ruler but it was the most spectacular and successful.

A Nigerian Example of the Importance of the Hajj (Pilgrimage)

In Nigeria access to the hajj is quite easy. The government has taken on the responsibility to provide free or cheap transportation to Mecca for those who cannot afford to take the pilgrimage privately. Wealthy Muslims have also been generous in their support of the trip. However, this opening of the pilgrimage to a wider audience than previously has also served to subvert the universalizing of Islamic belief and orthodoxy among the pilgrims. Some pilgrims have taken the pilgrimage as an opportunity to spread local versions of Islam more widely.

Traditionally, the hajj has served to put Nigerian Muslims in contact with Muslims in other areas. The transformative impact of these pilgrimage routes has been well studied. Reforms, brotherhoods, law, medicine, and other broad aspects of Muslim life have entered and changed the Hausa practice of Islam. At the same time Hausa practices have been exported along the pilgrimage route. Most prominent among these practices have been those associated with the *bori*. The *bori* practices stem from the pre-Islamic Hausa religion and deal with spirit possession. The *bori* priest controls the spirit-possession ceremony. Although forbidden by Islam, the practices continue in Nigeria. In addition, there are a number of other among the Hausa and other peoples in West Africa that also date to pre-Islamic times. These include the belief in and practices associated with magic and the regular use of amulets and spells.

This process of exchange, orthodox Muslim practices and beliefs on the one hand and *bori* and other traditional curing practices on the other, has been a longstanding one. It has been overlooked in many accounts of the hajj that treat it as a homogenizing factor in the Islamic world. Certainly, the hajj has served to standardize practices. However, it has also spread the knowledge of local beliefs, especially from African Islam, to a broader public. In fact, many of the symbols of the hajj, including the title Al Haji, are used to reinforce the power of the *bori* when they return to Nigeria.

AFRICAN PILGRIMS IN THE EARLY NINETEENTH CENTURY

The greater part of them are quite destitute, and find their way to Mecca, and back to their own country, by begging and by what they can earn by their manual labour on the road. The equipments of all these pilgrims are exactly alike and consist of a few rags tied around the waist, a white woolen bonnet, leather provision sack carried on a long stick over the shoulder, a leather pouch containing a book of prayer or a copy of a few chapters of the Koran, a wooden tablet, one foot in length by six inches in breadth, upon which they write charms, or prayers for themselves or others to learn by heart, an ink stand formed of a small gourd, a bowl to drink out of, or to collect victuals in from the charitable, a small earthen pot for ablution, and a long string of beads hanging in many turns around the neck.

Source: Burckhardt, John L., quoted in Irene M Franck and David M. Brownstone (1984) *To the Ends of the Earth*. New York: Facts on File, 264.

The hajj grew in importance from the nineteenth century onward. It was an understandable response to colonization. Hausa also began to migrate east; some suggest that the ideology of the pilgrimage helped pull them east. Certainly, the Hausa have taken care to distinguish themselves from the local communities in which they settle through stressing the pilgrimage as well as the other Pillars of Islam.

The pilgrimage has continued to be a vital means for economic and religious exchange since the days of Mansa Musa. Trade, information, and ideas have flowed over the pilgrim routes. That there have been political and economic issues associated with the hajj is not surprising. Also, the fact that the *bori*, who have been under attack from orthodox Muslims in Nigeria, have turned to the hajj to redefine themselves while capitalizing on the fame of the power in the Muslim world is also not surprising.

Nigerian pilgrims have suffered a good deal in their pilgrimages. The Nigerian government, which made the hajj easier, has begun to try to restrict it to certain types of Muslims. They hope to raise the reputation of their pilgrims in Arabia by doing so. However, the *bori* are adept at countering that move and presenting themselves as good Muslims. They know that their healing practices have a great reputation in Arabia and the Sudan. In turn, their trips to Mecca enhance their healing reputation in Nigeria through associating their healing with Islam.

Islam has provided an incentive to a great increase in intellectual culture of all types. Individual travelers have their own agendas that may differ from the official agendas of governments and *mullahs* (religious teachers). However, considerable intellectual activity of diverse types results from the mere fact of travel to Mecca. Africans have proven to be great adherents of travel and pilgrimage.

Rulers of West African states had made pilgrimages to Mecca before Mansa Musa, but the effect of his flamboyant journey was to advertise both Mali and Mansa Musa well beyond the African continent. He stimulated a desire among the Muslim kingdoms of North Africa, and among many European nations as well, to reach the source of this incredible wealth.

Other Pilgrim Traditions

There are other traditions of pilgrimage in Africa in addition to those of the Muslims. There is, for example, a tradition among the Cushites of Ethiopia and Somalia. There is a traditional custom of pilgrimage among the Somali, a people who have been Muslim for some time. There is a pilgrimage to Waqa, the god of sky and earth and the creator and sustainer of life. This god is the guardian of public morality. He is the dispenser of all good things. The lineage of priests provides his special earthly agents. Pilgrims come to these priests to receive their blessings. These blessings sanctified the entire social system of the people. Today there are spirit-possessed leaders among people in the Ethiopian highlands. People still come on pilgrimage to receive the blessings of these leaders.

In Nigeria, pilgrimages to famous *bori* priests, those who are masters of the *bori* cult of spirit possession, are recorded both in the writings of Muslim scholars and Europeans. People came from all over West Africa to consult with these traditional healers, who also controlled spirits who possessed adherents. The most famous of these healers resided in the emirate of Yauri, along the Niger River. The power of the *bori* priest was so great that he cloaked it behind a facade of clowning. He dressed simply, in an old green tunic, and made himself eminently approachable. Telling fortunes through his familiar spirits, who spoke through his pots or in trees, the *bori* controlled considerable power, even petitioning Ubangida, the high god of the skies. Those, including Muslims, who had failed to be cured or to have their other petitions met, came on a pilgrimage. Although the pilgrimage to the *bori* is decidedly not a Muslim pilgrimage, some Muslims secretly seek his assistance. They turn to the *bori* when other alternatives are exhausted.

Similarly, there is a tradition of Catholic pilgrimage. Somewhat in response to Muslim pilgrimages to Mecca, there have grown up Catholic-sponsored pilgrimages to Rome, Jerusalem, and sacred shrines, like Fatima. Originally, European and American missionaries began to offer free pilgrimages to their converts. In Nigeria, for example, a priest at a remote station in Yauri, along the Niger River near Sokoto, used the occasion of a Holy Year to prepare members of his congregation for a trip to Rome. His preparation included practical as well as spiritual matters. He gave lessons in using indoor toilet facilities, modern manners, and behavior, as well as what to do to get used to airline travel and eating with plastic and silverware. Such pilgrimages have more meaning than meeting the immediate spiritual needs of pilgrims, as they also have become a means for Catholic Nigerians to gain prestige to match that of Muslim pilgrims. Catholics, too, could be pilgrims—show off their holy trinkets and be well-traveled people of distinction.

Nigerian Catholic priests have organized more recent excursions to holy areas, competing with their Muslim brothers. The pilgrims' tourist art rivals that of Muslims and carries its own religious cachet. Catholics, through these trips, demonstrate that they, also, are part of a worldwide religious network. In turn, pilgrims are able to help inculcate Catholicism in Nigeria in much the same way that Muslim pilgrims have influenced Islamic practices.

Conclusion

Pilgrimage has a long history in Africa. There continue to be ancient pilgrimages that preceded both Islam and Christianity. Islamic pilgrimages have been part of African tradition since the earliest Muslims carried Islam to the continent. West African pilgrimages go back at least to the eleventh century, before the famous pilgrimage of Mansa Musa. Musa's spectacular pilgrimage has had an influence into the present, setting a pattern for two-way exchange in the Arabic-African world.

Similarly, Christian pilgrimages go back at least to the time of the Egyptian and Ethiopian churches; that is, to biblical times. They have continued into the present. Missionaries encouraged them in more recent periods to combat the influence of the Islamic hajj. African priests have continued and expanded the tradition, booking tours to sacred places with modern tourist agencies.

Each of these general pilgrimage types serves as an ethnic and religious boundary marker, setting off people of one type from another while forging ties among participants. As competition among various ethnic groups for power, prestige, and economic gain in Africa's multiethnic states continues, there will also be a continued use of religious practices to mark off boundaries. However, these religious practices serve economic and political purposes as well. They have done so from before Mansa Musa's day and they will continue to do so into the future.

Frank A. Salamone

See also Islam, East Africa; Islam, West Africa; Mouride Brotherhood

References

Abdalla, Ismail. (1985) "The Ulama of Sokoto in the Nineteenth Century: A Medical Review." In *African Healing Strategies*, edited by Brian du Toit and Ismail Abdalla. New York: Trado-Medic Books.

——. (1997) *Islam, Medicine, and Practitioners in Northern Nigeria*. Lewiston, New York: Edwin Mellen Press.

Adamu, Mahdi. (1978) *The Hausa Factor in West African History*. Zaria, Nigeria: Ahmadu Bello University Press.

Adler, Philip. (1996) *World Civilizations*. Minneapolis: West Publishing Company.

Al-Azmeh, Aziz. (1993) *Islams and Modernities*. London: Verso.

Al-Naqar, Umar. (1972) *The Pilgrimage Tradition in West Africa*. Khartoum, Sudan: Khartoum University Press.

Ashkanani, Zubaydah. (1991) "Zar in a Changing World: Kuwait." In *Women's Medicine: The Zar-bori Cult in Africa and Beyond*, edited by I. M. Lewis, Ahmed Al-Sa, and Sayyid Hurreiz. Edinburgh: Edinburgh University Press.

Brenner, Louis. (1993) "Constructing Muslim Identities in Mali." In *Muslim Identity and Social Change in Sub-Saharan Africa*, edited by Louis Brenner. Bloomington: Indiana University Press.

Davidson, Basil. (1991) *African Civilization Revisited*. Toronto: African World Press.

Eickelman, Dale F., and James Piscatori, eds. (1990) *Muslim Travellers: Pilgrimage, Migration, and the Religious Imagination*. New York: Routledge.

Ferme, Mariane. (1994) "What 'Alhaji Airplane' Saw in Mecca, and What Happened When He Came Home: Ritual Transformation in a Mende Community." In *Syncretism/Anti-Syncretism: The Politics of Religious Change*, edited by Charles Stewart and Rosalind Shaw. London: Routledge.

Greenberg, Joseph. (1946) *The Influence of Islam on a Sudanese Religion*. New York: J.J. Augustin.

Hiskett, Mervyn. (1984) *The Development of Islam in West Africa*. London: Longman Press.

Jackson, John. (1970) *Introduction to African Civilizations*. New Brunswick, NJ: The Citadel Press.

Lewis, I. M. (1966) "Spirit Possession and Deprivation Cults." *Man* 1: 307–329.

——. (1971) *Ecstatic Religion: An Anthropological Study of Spirit Possession and Shamanism*. Hammondsworth, England: Penguin Books.

——. (1983) "The Past and the Present in Islam: The Case of African 'Survivals'." *Temenos* 19: 55–67.

Lovejoy, Paul E. (1980) *Caravans of Kola: The Hausa Kola Trade (1700–1900)*. Zaria, Nigeria: Ahmadu Bello University Press.

O'Brien, Susan. (1997) "'Sumbuka Ya Shigo Gari': Schoolgirl Possession, Islamic Exorcism, and Hausa Constructions of Islam and Gender in Contemporary Kano." Paper presented at the African Studies Association Annual Meeting, Columbus, Ohio.

Paden, John. (1973) *Religion and Political Culture in Kano*. Berkeley: University of California Press.

Tangban, O. E. (1991) "The hajj and the Nigerian Economy, 1960–1981." *Journal of Religion in Africa* 3: 241–255.

Trimingham, J. S. (1949) *Islam in the Sudan*. London: Frank Cass.

——. (1959) *Islam in West Africa*. Oxford: Clarendon Press.

Wilks, Ivor. (1966) "The Position of Muslims in Metropolitan Ashanti in the Early Nineteenth Century." In *Islam in Tropical Africa*, edited by I. M. Lewis. Oxford: Oxford University Press.

Pocomania *See* Revival

Primitive Baptists

The Primitive Baptist movement emerged in the southern United States in the years before the Civil War, accelerated after the war, and gained general recognition in 1927. The primary cause of the movement was efforts by some in the Baptist movement to centralize and institutionalize missionary and publication programs. These efforts were opposed by other Baptists, who placed greater value on maintaining the independence of each Baptist church. African-American Baptists were involved in the movement before the Civil War and independent Black Primitive Baptist churches emerged after the war, with complete segregation of white and black churches taking place from the 1880s on.

In 1907, the Rev. Clarence F. Sams of the prominent Zion Primitive Baptist Church in Key West, Florida, formed the National Primitive Baptist Convention, U.S.A., which has remained the central administrative organization for Black Primitive Baptists and their churches. It supports a Sunday school program and publications. Some additional unity was created among these churches in the 1950s when Elder E. J. Barry founded the Primitive Baptist Publishing House in Elon, North Carolina and published the *Primitive Messenger* from 1953 to 1957. However, both white and black Primitive Baptist churches have tended to maintain their independence in religious belief and practice and are not well known to the general public.

For Primitive Baptists the label "primitive" means "original" and refers to the original teachings of the Baptist church. It has also come to mean simplicity, as church services involve only praying, preaching, and singing. Churches do not provide formal religious education, nor do they support youth groups, the use of musical instruments, or personal miracles. Preachers are selected from the membership rather than formally trained. Because of the absence of a central administrative authority, there are variations in belief and practice across churches, although most churches adhere to the following Doctrine of Salvation:

1. Total Depravity of Natural Man—All men are sinners by nature and are dead to spiritual things while in their natural state.

A CHILD OF JEHOVAH, A SUBJECT OF GRACE

A Child of Jehovah, A subject of grace,
I'm of the seed royal, a dignified race,
An heir of salvation, redeemed with blood,
I'll own my relation, my Father is God!

He loved me of old, and he loveth me still,
Before the creation, he gave me by will,
A portion worth more than the Indies of gold,
Which can not be wasted, nor mortgaged nor sold.

He gave me a Surety, a covenant Head,
To live in my name, and to die in my stead,
He gave me a righteousness wholly divine,
And viewed all the merits of Jesus as mine.

He gave a Perceptor infallibly wise,
And treasures of grace to be send in supplies;

Yea, all that I ask for my Father hath given.
To help me on earth, and to crown me in heav'n.

He gave me a will to accept what he gave,
Though I was averse to his purpose to save;
He wrote in his will my repentance and faith,
And all my enjoyments for life and for death.

My trails and sorrows, my comforts and cares,
The spirit of prayer and the answer of prayers,
The steps that I tread, and the station I fill,
My Father determined and wrote in his will.

My cross and my crown are both willed by my God,
He swore to his will, and then sealed it with blood.
"Tis proved by the Spirit, the witness within,
"Tis mine to inherit, I'll glory begin.

2. Personal and Unconditional Election—All who are to possess spiritual life were individually chosen by God to receive such life; moreover, this choice was not based upon any merit seen or foreseen in the elected; rather, this election was motivated by the sovereign love of God.

3. Special Atonement—The saving benefits of Christ's death were intended for the elect only; furthermore, His redemptive work was alone sufficient to secure their salvation.

4. Irresistible Grace—All of the elect will be quickened by the Spirit of God at some point in their natural lives.

5. Preservation of the Saints—The blood of Christ is sufficient both to procure and secure salvation of all for whom it is shed. Therefore, all of the elect will finally be saved.

6. Direct Operation of the Holy Spirit—The Holy Spirit accomplished the new birth by direct operation upon the heart, and therefore works independently of all agency of man, including the gospel as preached by man.

7. Revealing Gospel—The purpose of the gospel is to bring those quickened by the Spirit to the intelligible discovery of the Lord Jesus Christ, and transform them to the example of His life, in both truth and works, that God may be glorified thereby.

Primitive Baptist belief and practice is based solely on the Bible, which they view as the true word of God. The 1611 King James version is considered most reliable and scripture is cited to support all beliefs and practices such as restriction of eldership to males, the use of unleavened bread and wine in communion, washing of feet during communion, taking communion only with Primitive Baptists, baptism by immersion, rebaptizing, prohibitions on the display of crucifixes and pictures of Jesus, and rejection of individual spiritual gifts such as speaking in tongues.

Estimates from 1990 indicate that there are about 50,000 Primitive Baptists in the United States in about 1,200 churches, with an average membership of 41 people per church. Primitive Baptist churches are found in some twenty-three states, with the largest number in Georgia (13,559 in 273 churches), followed by Virginia (5,582 in 146 churches), Alabama (3,986 in 112 churches), and North Carolina (3,508 in 151 churches). As these numbers suggest, membership is mainly in the South, although there are several thousand Primitive Baptists in total in the northern states of Illinois, Washington, Pennsylvania, Oregon, Ohio, and Indiana. The number of Black Primitive Baptists is unknown, and estimates run from as low as 5,000 to as many

as over 250,000 and there may be 10,000 or more Primitive Baptists outside the United States.

David Levinson

See also National Baptist Convention of America; National Baptist Convention, USA; Progressive National Baptist Convention

Bibliography

Glenmary Research Center. *Churches and Church Membership in U.S., 1990.* Mars Hill, NC, 1990.
Primitive Baptist Homepage. www.pb.org.

Progressive National Baptist Convention, Inc.

Born out of the turmoil of the civil rights movement, this newest of the major black Baptist conventions adopted as its motto: "Unity, Service, Fellowship, Peace." Besides the civil rights movement, the Progressive National Baptist Convention (PNBC) was most supportive of the black power movement, and was one of the earliest Baptist groups to publicly oppose the war in Vietnam. The term "Progressive" in the convention's title is indicative of its stance on social and political issues. In more recent years, it has given emphasis to black political development, economic development, education and job training, and strengthening the black family. Around 1970 several white Baptist churches established dual affiliations with PNBC. Conversely, PNBC churches today maintain dual affiliations with one of the white conventions.

History

The Progressive National Baptist Convention, U.S.A., Inc., (PNBC) came into existence in 1961 as a result of conflict within the National Baptist Convention, U.S.A., Inc. The dissension began in 1957, when ten pastors were expelled from the NBC, Inc., for challenging the president, Joseph Jackson, in court, on his ruling that an amendment setting a four-year limit on tenure as president was invalid, inasmuch as it had been adopted in 1952 in a manner that was procedurally unconstitutional. Jackson's position was upheld by a federal court.

Jackson's opponents, reacting to the larger issue of what was perceived as autocratic rule, subsequently organized around the candidacy of Rev. Dr. Gardner Taylor. The "Taylor team," as it was called, included Martin Luther

King, Sr., Martin Luther King, Jr., Ralph David Abernathy, Benjamin Mays, and a number of other clergy committed to King's social change strategies, which Jackson condemned as inadvisable and injurious to the cause of racial advance and harmony. Jackson's extreme conservatism on civil rights and his law and order, anticommunist, pro-Vietnam war, and procapitalist positions alienated many of the politically progressive black Baptist clergy.

At the 1960 convention in Philadelphia, the nominating committee unanimously presented Jackson's name for term, whereupon he was declared reelected. When the Taylor team protested, demanding a roll-call vote by states, the convention was declared adjourned. The delegates remained, however, and conducted an election in which Taylor won. When the Jackson faction refused to acknowledge the vote results, the Taylor team proceeded to conduct a sit-in at the convention. The Taylor faction claimed throughout the following year to be the rightful officers of the convention, but the courts again ruled in Jackson's favor.

In 1961 in Kansas City, Missouri, the Taylor delegates, who had been sitting in separate session, were initially denied admission to the larger assembly. When they were admitted, physical confrontations erupted as they moved to take control of the platform. Ultimately, a court-supervised election was held, and Jackson emerged victorious. Taylor acknowledged the results, and he and Dr. Martin Luther King, Jr. both called for unity. Before the convention was ended, however, Martin Luther King, Sr., Martin Luther King, Jr., Dexter King, Marshall L. Shepard, Charles Adams, and others were removed from any offices they held, including membership on the board of directors.

Rev. L. Venhael Booth assumed leadership of the opposition and, as the chairman of the self-proclaimed Volunteer Committee for the Formation of a New National Baptist Convention, called for a meeting in November 1961 at his church, Zion Baptist Church in Cincinnati. The thirty-three people who attended from fourteen states voted to start a separate convention. The first annual meeting was held in Philadelphia the following year. Rev. Thomas Chambers was elected the first president; he was succeeded in 1967 by Gardner Taylor.

Organization

The Progressive National Baptist Convention, Inc., is the smallest of the three National Baptist Conventions. In 1990 the denomination claimed 1,000 clergy with 1.3 million members in 1,000 churches, giving it an average congregation size of 1,000 members. Its estimated budget was $1.2 million for that year. The unusually large size of the congregations is attributable to the fact that the convention's membership consists primarily of churches in major metropolitan areas, many of which have memberships from two to three thousand, while including relatively few rural churches. Unlike the other two Baptist conventions, PNBC is divided into regions. Within the four regions, a total of thirty-five state conventions are affiliated with the convention; the number of associations is not known.

The departments of PNBC include Women, Laymen, Youth, Ushers and Nurses, Moderators, and the Congress of Christian education. Other agencies include the Board of Christian education and Publication, Home Mission Board, Foreign Mission Bureau, Progressive Pension Plan Board, and Chaplaincy Endorsing Agency. Committees and commissions are Program, Convention, Arrangements, Internal Affairs, Cooperative Christianity, Civil Rights, and Community Economic Development.

For several years PNBC met in September at the same time as NBCA and NBC, U.S.A. Inc. In the mid-1970s the convention began convening during the first week following the first Sunday in August to accommodate school schedules and encourage the participation of families. The constitution calls for affiliated churches to pay membership fees equivalent to 1 percent of their previous year's operating budget, with the number of official messengers or delegates from each church determined by the size of the church. Each state convention upon payment of $200 is entitled to two messengers. Fellowships must pay $150 for two messengers, and associations $50 for one messenger. Any members of an affiliated church may attend the convention; however, only representative members so designated by the churches, associations, or state conventions may vote. Individuals may secure life memberships, with voting privileges, upon payment of $500.

In a departure from the other conventions, PNBC presidents since 1967 have been limited to two consecutive one-year terms. Thus, in its forty-year history, the convention has already had twenty different presidents. This tradition of severely limiting the term of the president reflects the turmoil of the earlier history of the NBC, U.S.A., Inc. and the controversy of the lifetime presidency of Joseph H. Jackson. Most of the other officers are subject to the same tenure rule. The objective is to prevent autocratic rule in the administration of the convention at all levels.

The sixty-member Executive Board, which is responsible for oversight of the convention when not in session, consists of the elected officers, the heads of the departments, chairpersons of all boards and officers, the heads of the departments, chairpersons of all boards and commissions, past presidents, the general secretary, and one representative chose by each state convention. An executive committee, consisting of the president, vice presidents, general secretary, recording secretary, treasurer, and five additional members, may be empowered to act on behalf of the Executive Board. Standing committees of the Executive Board are Personnel, Planning and Evaluation, and Finance and Property.

National headquarters with a permanent staff are located in Washington, D.C. In another departure from the other conventions, the general secretary of the PNBC is a full-time employee responsible for the day-to-day administration of the convention's program. Consequently, the role of the president aside from presiding at official sessions, is largely that of ambassador to the larger world. PNBC has no publishing house of its own.

Lawrence H. Mamiya

See also National Baptist Convention of America; National Baptist Convention, U.S.A.; Social Activism

Bibliography

Butler, Charles. (1982) "PNBC: A Fellowship of Partners." *The Crisis* 89,9 (November 1982): 44–45.

Fisher, Miles Mark. (1927) "What Is a Negro Baptist?" *The Home Mission College Review* 1, 1 (May).

Fitts, Leroy. (1978) *Lott Carey, First Black Missionary to Africa.* Valley Forge, PA: Judson Press.

——. (1985) *A History of Black Baptists.* Nashville, Broadman Publishing Co.

Hamilton, Charles. (1972) *The Black Preacher in America.* New York: William Morrow.

Jackson, Joseph. (1980) *A Story of Christian Activism: The History of the National Baptist Convention, U.S.A., Inc.* Nashville: Townsend Publishing.

Tinney, James. (1970) "Progressive Baptists." *Christianity Today* (9 October): 42–43.

——. (1977) "Selected Directory of Afro-American Religious Organizations, Schools, and Periodicals." In *The Black Church: A Community Resource*, edited by Dionne Jones and William Matthews. Washington, D.C.: Howard University Institute for Urban Affairs and Research.

Washington, James Melvin. (1986) *Frustrated Fellowship: The Black Baptist Quest for Social Power.* Macon, GA: Mercer University Press.

Puerto Rico, African-Derived Religions in

The cultural and religious composition of Puerto Rican society, as well as the actual sociodemographic composition of the Puerto Rican people, is a product of the colonial era.

As a consequence of colonialism, Puerto Ricans have a physical, cultural, and spiritual heritage that mingles distinct Native American, European, and African contributions. When Christopher Columbus first set foot on Puerto Rico on 19 November 1493, he encountered an indigenous tribal society (the Taino Indians, a group of South American Arawak origin) who possessed a belief in a pantheon of spiritual beings associated with various forces and structures in nature and a shamanistic tradition of spirit contact to achieve healing or redress misfortune. In the years after Columbus's arrival, the indigenous peoples of Puerto Rico were killed off, driven out (to other Caribbean islands), or (through intermarriage) physically absorbed into the colonial Spanish regime that displaced the island's original inhabitants. The Spanish colonialists brought with them the Catholic Church, as well as a strong tradition of folk Catholic belief and practice centered on the veneration of a rich array of saint heroes who were seen as accessible intermediaries between needy mortals and God. The Spanish also brought slaves from Africa to replenish the colonial work force once the indigenous peoples were decimated. While various African religious practices were introduced to the island, the dominant African tradition in colonial Puerto Rico was *orisha* worship as conducted by the Yoruba people of Nigeria. Ultimately, these diverse sociocultural elements merged and produced a set of syncretic religious folk traditions on the island, some of which have significant African components.

The Varied Roots of Puerto Rican Espiritismo

The most notable African religious elements in Puerto Rican religious practice are found within the folk tradition of Espiritismo (Puerto Rican spiritism). From the black spiritual churches of the American South to Candomblé, Batuque, Umbanda, and Macumba of Brazil, and from Mexican Espiritualismo to Vodun in Haiti, Shango in Trinidad and Grenada, Kele in St. Lucia, Santeria in Cuba, and Espiritismo in Puerto Rico, the circum-Caribbean region supports a rich diversity of spiritist cults, most of which of have strong African elements. These religio-therapeutic traditions share a common belief in communication with and possession by incorporeal spirits, including those of Native American, Catholic, and African origin. Generally found in these popular folk systems is a set of rituals designed to either protect participants from harm and misfortune or to heal them after they have been menaced by a wayward spirit or through an overt act of sorcery. According to González-Whippler (1984: 9), all of these traditions are characterized by a core "magical-religious system that has its roots in nature and natural forces."

Additionally, Espiritismo was shaped by two other influences. First, there was a set of ideas popularized by the Spiritualist Revival that swept across Europe and the United States in the mid-nineteenth century, especially through the writings of the Frenchman Leon Denizarith Hippolyte Rivail, better known by his nom-de-plume of Allan Kardec. This quasi-religious revival was focused on belief in and communication with the spiritual realm, conceived of as a plane of existence populated by the souls of deceased individuals. At first, spiritualism was embraced by the intellectual and social elite, who saw it as a scientific approach for studying the spiritual world, just as the natural sciences were seeking to comprehend the material world of nature. Members of the Spanish intelligentsia brought spiritualism to Puerto Rico, where it filtered down to the urban poor and rural peasants. During this process of cultural diffusion, European spiritualism combined with Taino and African curing practices and folk Catholicism to produce a full-blown religious healing system. As Macklin (1974: 393) notes, the folk sector "borrowed those pragmatic elements of the system which were useful in solving daily problems of life, illness, and death. These they transformed in the oral tradition as well as in family and neighborhood curing and cultic rituals." In its present form, Espiritismo functions as a "voluntary organization, a religion, a way of ordering social relationships, a vehicle for enhancing one's status through development as a medium, and an identity" (Harwood 1977: 69).

Second, Espiritismo has—to varying degrees—long been under the influence of the spiritualist tradition from the neighboring island of Cuba. In addition to a common language, the peoples of Cuba and Puerto Rico share deep historic and cultural roots, although given the larger size of Cuba and its success in winning independence from colonial domination, the pathway of cultural diffusion has tended to move from Cuba to Puerto Rico. Cuban Santeria traditionally has retained more explicit African elements than Puerto Rican Espiritismo, a consequence of the larger African population transported to Cuba during the colonial era. However, continual contact between Cuba and Puerto Rico, including the co-residence of Cuban and Puerto Rican migrants in places like Miami, Florida and New York City, and the ongoing Puerto Rican re-migration from the U.S. back to the island, have continued to nourish the African elements in Puerto Rican Espiritismo.

Consequently, understanding the development of Cuban Santeria is critical to understanding the historic place of African elements in Puerto Rican Espiritismo. Brandon (1997) has developed a history of the development of Santeria in the New World that is organized into five phases. Phase I is the African phase, the period of develop-

ment of the Yoruba people as a distinctive tribal ethnic identity in Western Africa, as well as the period of development of their particular religious system. In the regionally varied Yoruba religious tradition, there is belief in a supreme, yet remote spiritual being named Olodumare. Olodumare is never represented in pictures or sculptures, appears to lack human attributes, and has neither a priesthood nor temples. Below Olodumare are the orishas and the *egungun*, such as Obatala, Oduduwa, and Orunmila, spirit beings who are the objects of worship through temples, shrines, and secret societies. Belief in some of the orishas is widespread among the Yoruba, while others are only venerated locally. The egungun are ancestor spirits, founders of particular patrilineal family lines. This set of beliefs is bound together with an elaborate ceremonial system with a rich symbolic imagery and formal priesthood structure. Phase II (1760–1870) is the period of Santeria formation in the Caribbean. During this period, African slaves were exposed to Catholicism, resulting in the initial sycretizations that lead to the emergence of a folk Afro-Catholicism. On rural sugar plantations, which were only minimally under the sway of the Catholic Church, African cultural and religious traditions were able to flourish, despite the new environment and the oppressive social system encountered by the slaves. Among runaway slaves, who were able to hide in the mountains and to establish enduring maroon communities, African religious traditions had even freer expression. From the Catholic tradition, the slaves adopted the Spanish organization of the *cabildo* or *cofradia*, a brotherhood whose primary mission in Catholicism was to venerate certain saints, take part in church festivals like carnival processions with members dressed in the elaborate garb of their respective saint heroes, and provide aid and support to their members. Black slaves and freemen living in Spain had been admitted to these brotherhoods (variously in integrated, wholly African, and wholly mulatto fraternities) by the fifteenth century. In the New World, with some degree of tolerance from the diocesan priests, the *cabildo* became a gateway for the entrance of African religious practices into folk Catholic practice. For example, *cabildos* sponsored African religious music, drumming, and dancing, as well as spirit possession. Although the Catholic Church attempted to regulate these practices, for example by limiting dancing to Sundays and other holidays, the African elements remained strong.

Phase III (1870–1959) is the transformative phase in Santeria's evolution. Two important developments occurred during this period. First, Yoruban gods were syncretized with the Catholic spiritual realm. In this process of blending traditions, the Yoruba high god Olodumare was syncretized with God as known in Catholicism, Olofi was syncretized with Jesus, the orishas were syncretized with the Catholic saints, and the Egun with the souls of the deceased. For example, the Yoruban god of thunder, Shango, was merged with Saint Barbara, despite the gender differences in these two figures. In this way, pure Yoruba belief and practice became increasingly replaced by an emergent blended religion known as Santeria. Secondly, during this period, various local and regional-centered Nigerian religious traditions were merged into a single generalized religious pattern under the structure of Santeria. While this represented a second step away from actual African practice, it allowed a strengthening of specific African elements in New World Santeria.

Contemporary Espiritismo and Santerismo in Puerto Rico

In the subsequent years (Brandon's Phases IV and V), Santeria found expression in varied forms and experienced new intensification and popular interest. One important development was the emergence of Santerisimo, a blend of Santeria with Puerto Rican Espiritismo. Santerismo has been described by a number of researchers (Leutz 1976; Salgado 1974; Garrison 1977; Harwood 1977; González-Whippler 1973). Work by Garrison and Harwood, especially, distinguishes the Santeria and Espiritismo elements in the syncretized centros of Santerismo (spiritist worship and healing centers). The key Santeria elements that have diffused into Espiritismo include possession by Yoruban deities such as Shango, veneration of other Yoruban spirit deities, inclusion of some Santeria ritual items and statuary within Santerismo centros, use of various prayers and chants, and the ritual use of pictures, necklaces, candles, and statues signifying a unified septet of syncretized orishas/saints known as the Seven African Powers (consisting of Shango/Santa Barbara representing sensual pleasure, Eleggua/Holy Guardian Angel representing opportunity, Obatla/Our Lady of Mercy representing peace and harmony, Oshun/Our Lady of Caridad de Cobre presenting marriage, Oggun/Saint Peter representing war and work, Orunla/Saint Francis of Assisi representing power, and Yemaya/Our Virgin of Regla representing fertility and maternity).

Singer and Borrero (1984) have presented an ethnographic account of the African Santeria elements in a Puerto Rican Centro de Espiritismo/Santerismo, a one-room storefront "church" lead by a madrina (godmother). While leadership within this centro has adopted the Santeria concept of godparenthood, the relationships among the head medium, other mediums, participants, and clients are transitory rather than lifelong, as in pure Santeria. Similarly, the familial obligations that characterize a Santeria grouping as a religious family are limited in this centro. Rather, participants come

and go over time, and some people visit the centro only for specific healings rather than as enduring members. These patterns are typical of the structure of Puerto Rican spiritist centers (Brandon 1997). The focus of ritual within the centro described by Singer and Borrero (1984) is the mesa blanca (white table). On the table, there is a large bowl of water (fuente) symbolizing the Espiritismo notions of clarity and purity. The water is used to diagnose and ritually cleanse clients of the negative vibrations (given off by wayward spirits) that disrupt and unbalance their lives. When consulting with a client about the problems they are facing—such as bodily pains or depression, family or interpersonal conflicts, substance abuse problems, desire for love, or problems related to work—the madrina is able to see offending spirits in the water and she uses this identification to initiate spiritual efforts to make the spirit leave.

To the left and right of the bowl of water stand statues of St. Lazarus (patron saint of the centro) and St. Barbara, the madrina's primary spiritual guide. When the madrina is possessed by St. Barbara, she takes on the reported behaviors of Shango, including drinking rum, smoking cigars, and acting in a somewhat bellicose fashion, behaviors that contrast with the usual mild mannered personality of the madrina (Singer and Garcia 1989). Also found on the table are a collection basket for donations and a rosary. On a second table to the left of the mesa blanca and on shelves behind the main table are statues of various saints and orishas. These spirits, whether of Catholic or Yoruban origin, are venerated equally.

While it cannot be denied that there is some degree of discrimination among darker-skinned Puerto Ricans (Friedman et al. 1998; Wagenheim 1975), Puerto Ricans generally recognize and commonly admit and celebrate their African heritage. Thus, African religious elements are numerous, readily identifiable, and generally accepted in Puerto Rican folk Catholicism as it is practiced outside of the formal church institutions, in people's homes and in spiritist centers. From masks to dance, to drumming, to appeals for assistance from Yoruban deities, these African practices and religious items hold a central and cherished place in Puerto Rican folk religion.

Merrill Singer

See also Caribbean, African-Derived Religions in; Kardecism; Santeria; Spiritualism; Yoruba Religion

Bibliography

Brandon, George. (1997) *Santeria from Africa to the New World.* Bloomington: Indiana University Press.

Friedman, Samuel, Benny Jose, Bruce Stepherson, Alan Neaigus, Marjorie Goldstein, Pat Mota, Richard Curtis, and Gilbert Ildefonso. (1997) "Multiple Racial/Ethnic Subordination and HIV among Drug Injectors." In *The Political Economy of AIDS*, edited by Merrill Singer. Amityville, NY: Baywood Publishing Co., pp. 105–128.

Garrison, Vivian. (1977) "Doctor, Espiritista or Psychiatrist? Health-Seeking Behavior in a Puerto Rican Neighborhood of New York City." *Medical Anthropology* 1, 2: 65–180.

González-Whippler, Migene. (1973) *Santeria: African Magic in Latin America*. New York: Julian Press.

———. (1982) *The Santeria Experience*. Englewood Cliffs, NJ: Prentice Hall.

Harwood, Alan. (1977) *RX: Espiritist as Needed*. New York: John Wiley & Sons.

Leutz, W. (1976) "The Informal Community Caregiver: A Link Between the Health Care System and Local Residents." *American Journal of Orthopsychiatry* 46: 678–688.

Macklin, J. (1974) "Belief, Ritual and Healing: New England Spiritualism and Mexican Spiritualism Compared." In *Religious Movements in Contemporary America*, edited by I. Zaretsky and M. Leone. Princeton, NJ: Princeton University Press, pp. 383–417.

Perez y Mena, Andres. (1977) "Spiritualism as an Adaptive Mechanism among Puerto Ricans in the United States." *Cornell Journal of Social Relations* 12, 2: 125–136.

Salgado, Ramona Matos. (1974) "The Role of the Puerto Rican Spiritist in Helping Puerto Ricans with Problems of Family Relations." Ph.D. dissertation, Columbia University Teacher's College.

Singer, Merrill, and Maria Borrero. (1984) "Indigenous Treatment for Alcoholism: The Case for Puerto Rican Spiritism." *Medical Anthropology* 8, 4: 246–272.

Singer, Merrill, and Roberto Garcia. (1987) "Becoming A Puerto Rican Espiritista: Life History of a Female Healer." In *Women as Healers*, edited by Carol Shepherd McClain. New Brunswick, NJ: Rutgers University Press, pp. 157–185.

Wagenheim, Kal. (1975) *Puerto Rico: A Profile*. New York: Praeger Publishers.

Pygmy Religion

The cultural heterogeneity of the various Pygmy groups spread over the vast African equatorial belt complicates the task of providing a summary of the religion of these hunting-gathering peoples. Adding to the complication are some long-standing, fundamental disagreements between some of the researchers on the subject, in particular on the Pygmy conceptualization of god. To some, such as Paul Schebesta and other followers of the once-influential primal monotheism theory on the origin of religion proposed by Pater Wilhelm Schmidt in the 1930s, this supernatural agent, among the Mbuti is a well-delineated and personified "Forest God." In the opposing view, held by Colin Turnbull, the same god figure is a diffuse divinity, pantheistically embodied through the Forest, perceived by the Mbuti as a benevolent, paternal spiritual entity. This notion results in the sacralization of their forest environment and the consequent profaning of the deforested village environment, that is inhabited by the various non-Pygmy, black horticulturists to whom the Pygmies have been linked through somewhat precarious ties of dependency for centuries (and whose language they have come to adopt).

Looking beyond the Mbuti, the best known of the dozen or so Pygmy groups, we find some common elements of supernaturalism: the figures of a creator god, named Bembe by the Aka or Komba by the Baka (Biaka), who has become remote and removed from the affairs of humans and of a forest god (Ezengi), who is part of a divine family from mythic times. Another prominent member of this large ancestral family is a culture hero, called Waito by the Baka, who stole fire and brought carnal knowledge to humans, while among the Efe we come across Bale, a full-fledged trickster figure. Other supernatural figures are ghosts of the dead, who may become reborn as forest spirits who mediate between humans and the forest god.

The Pygmies have a rich ritual complex, which is more elaborate than that of most other African hunter-gatherers (for instance, the Bushmen). This applies especially to rituals of the hunt, the more important subsistence element in the hunting and gathering economy of these tropical foragers. The hunt, in the case of the net-hunting Pygmy groups, is a labor-intensive affair that involves the participation of virtually the entire community. This includes women—who in most other hunter-gatherer societies have little to do with the hunt—as beaters, driving the animals into the net where they are killed by the men. While the ritual surrounding the hunt, consisting of such acts as divination and propitiation and expiation of forest and game spirits, is primarily a male affair, women are involved in the most urgent of hunting rituals, the one held at the occasion of the failed hunt (such as the *bobanda* ritual of the Baka). At this most critical existential crisis in the lives of the hunters, women perform a vital ritual that confers to the hunters spiritual and magical powers, as well as recharged energy and a renewed sense of optimism. Moreover, the women participate, actively and vigorously, in the

PYGMY CREATION MYTHS

The Water and The Earth

Many, many moons ago the Water was down below, and the Earth was way up in the sky. When it rained it rained dirt, and the dirt ruined all the water vegetables and spoiled all the water food, so that it had to be thrown away. The Water said to the Earth: "You are spoiling my water gardens by raining dirt. You come down here and I'll go up there."

The earth agreed, so the Water moved up and the earth came down. When they had changed places, the Water said: "Now I'm going to rain on *you*, but *I'm* going to rain water." And the Water rained on the Earth. The earth vegetables flourished and the earth gardens grew. The Water said: "See, when I rain I don't spoil your food like you spoiled mine. It is good like this."

And from then onward the Water stayed up in the sky and the Earth stayed down below.

Basi

The Sun and The Moon

The Sun and the Moon, who were close friends, had a big discussion. The Sun said to the Moon: "Come on up, high, high up; you and I will be higher than anything else—but now we should part. I will be high up over there in the east, and you will be high up over there in the west."

The Moon said: "Yes, I would like that, and it is good that we should stay apart because you are bright and shine like I do."

And so they divided the heavens between them. When the Sun disappeared in the hours of the night, then the Moon passed by, all by itself. The Sun said: "This is very good. Your path is there, and mine is over here, but we must never cross at the same time; that would be very, very bad."

So they parted forever. That is why the Sun always shines in the daytime, and the Moon at night.

Basi

Source: Turnbull, Colin. (1965) *The Mbuti Pygmies: An Ethnographic Survey.* New York: American Museum of Natural History, 190–191.

actual hunt that is part of the rite. "It is the women," the Baka woman Makanda told Marion McCreedy, "who are responsible for the spirit of the *bobanda*" (1994: 34). Such instances of gender complementarity are found among the other Pygmy groups as well, for instance the Mbuti *begbe* and *musilo* ritual hunts.

The most significant crisis ritual of the Mbuti, which is performed both at the occasion of hunting failure and when people are afflicted with disease and death, is the *molemo*. At death it lasts for a month and involves the use of props that concretely symbolize the forest: objects such as vines, feather, leaf, and flower adornments, and a wooden trumpet are ritually treated with the forest environment's cardinal elements of water, earth, fire and air. The men sing plaintive

nocturnal songs into the Forest, to awaken him to the plight of "his children" so that he may restore continuity and unity to the community.

Among the Aka the death ritual will sometimes give rise also to the male initiation rite, which is performed with polyphonic song and ardent community participation and has the effect of cushioning the blow death has left on the community and helps to reaffirm its solidarity. Among the Mbuti, rather than the male rite, it is the female initiation rite, the *elima*, that receives the greater degree of ritual attention and also includes the less-formalized initiation of boys. At the occasion of the *elima* the lads may woo the now betrothable girls and, by killing a large game animal, demonstrate to them their skill as hunters and providers. A more formal male initiation ceremony is the *nkumbi*; however, as a ritual that is part of the religion of the Mbutis' village masters, it has little spiritual or social significance for the Pygmies.

Like the trance dance among the Bushmen, the death *molemo* of the Mbuti has the effect of instilling a sense of ethnic identity and political assertiveness vis-à-vis the villagers, signaling, perhaps more pointedly than at any other time, the social and cultural barriers the Pygmies have set up to distance themselves from the villagers. At its performance in the forest all paths leading from the village are closed off, no villagers are allowed to be present, and all village food and clothing are shunned. Participants are drawn from all the bands of a region, rather than from just the band of the deceased. According to Colin Turnbull, "it is undeniable that the *molemo* is now functioning as a political as well as religious institution" (1965: 312). The strong autonomy of each band acts as a countervailing force in this development of a religiously inspired sense of ethnic identity and political purpose.

Mathias Guenther

Bibliography

Bahuchet, Serge. (1985) *Les pygmees Aka et la forêt Centrafricaine*. Paris: Selaf, CNRS.

Bahuchet, Serge, and J. M. C. Thomas. (1987) "Pygmy Religions." In *Encyclopedia of Religion*, edited by Mircea Eliade. New York: Macmillan, 107–110.

Gusinde, Martin. (1956) *Die Twiden: Pygmäen und Pygmoide im tropischen Afrika*. Vienna: Wilhelm Braumüller.

Joiries, Daou V. (1996) "A Comparative Approach to Hunting Rituals among Baka Pygmies (southeastern Cameroons)." In *Cultural Diversity among Twentieth-Century Foragers: An African Perspective*, edited by Susan Kent. Cambridge: Cambridge University Press, 245–275.

McCreedy, Marion. (1994) "The Arms of the *Dibouka*." In *Key Issues in Hunter-Gatherer Research*, edited by Ernest S. Burch and Linda J. Ellanna. Oxford: Berg, 15–34.

Schebesta, Paul. (1952) *Die Bambuti-Pygmäen vom Ituri: Ethnographie der Ituri-Bambuti, Die Religion*. Brussels: Mémoires, Institut Royal Colonial Belge, collection 4, vol. 2, part 3.

Turnbull, Colin. (1957) "Initiation among the Bambuti Pygmies of the Central Ituri." *Journal of the Royal Anthropological Institute* 87: 191–216.

——. (1961) *The Forest People*. New York: Simon & Schuster.

——. (1965a) *The Mbuti Pygmies: An Ethnographic Survey*. New York: American Museum of Natural History.

——. (1965b) "The Mbuti Pygmies of the Congo." In *Peoples of Africa*, edited by James L. Gibbs. New York: Holt, Rinehart and Winston, 279–318.

Vorbichler, Anton. (1979) *Die Oralliteratur der Balese-Efe im Ituri Wald (Nordost-Zaire)*. Studia Instituti Anthropos 34. St. Augustin bei Bonn: Verlag des Anthropos-Instituts.

Rainbow Coalition

The Rainbow Coalition under the leadership of Rev. Jesse Jackson (1941–) constitutes a recent counter-hegemonic manifestation of African-American religion. Jackson, a minister affiliated with the Progressive National Baptist Convention, was a chief lieutenant for Martin Luther King, Jr. in the Southern Christian Leadership Conference's desegregation campaign in Chicago in 1966. He was placed in charge of the SCLC's Operation Breadbasket, which he utilized for his own political base after making a break with the organization several years following King's assassination in 1968. Operation PUSH emerged out of Operation Breadbasket in 1971 as a national religious reform-oriented movement.

On 3 November 1983, Jackson announced his decision to run as a Democratic candidate for the U.S. presidency. While Jackson's agenda has been largely reformist, many progressives, not only among African Americans but also among European-Americans, Hispanic-Americans, Asian-Americans, and Native Americans rallied around his agenda under the umbrella of the Rainbow Coalition. Jackson inspired millions of African-American voters in the 1984 and 1988 presidential campaigns. By utilizing the sermonic folk discourse of black political revivalism, as Washington observes, "Jesse has steered progressive black Christians into new, uncharted waters" (1985: 105). As in the civil rights movement, African-American congregations have provided the support base of the Rainbow Coalition. Jackson's political rallies were well attended by black ministers and were conducted in a style modeled upon black religious services. People affiliated with local branches of Operation PUSH, the majority of whom were ministers, served as the coordinators of about half of the viable state organizations of the Rainbow Coalition (Collins 1986).

The vast majority of the black churches responded to the campaign's appeal, and competed for a place on Jackson's itinerary. Well over 90 percent of the black clergy endorsed the campaign within two months of Jackson's announcement speech. They were helped by the endorsement of such nationally known figures as T. J. Jemison, president of the

National Baptist Convention. The support of the Pentecostal churches—especially the Church of God in Christ (the fastest-growing black denomination)—also marked this period as different from the civil rights era (Collins 1986: 134).

During the 1988 presidential campaign, Jackson considerably broadened his appeal outside the African-American community (Reynolds 1997). The Rainbow Coalition has regarded itself as the voice of the powerless—the poor, small farmers, women, gays and lesbians, and ethnic minorities. As a result of his coalition-building abilities, Jackson received 18.2 percent of all the votes in the 1984 Democratic primaries and 19.3 percent of all the votes in the 1988 Democratic primaries. Jackson called for a defense budget freeze, full employment, self-determination for Palestinians, and political empowerment of African Americans and other working-class people. He has criticized the exploitative practices of American-based multinational corporations. Despite his popular appeal and the fact that Jackson trailed only Michael Dukakis in delegate votes at the 1988 Democratic convention, the Democratic presidential nominee chose Lloyd Bentsen, a conservative senator from Texas, as his running mate. Such decisions lent poignant support to Noam Chomsky's assertion that the United States has a one party system—namely the Business Party—with two factions.

In 1989, Jackson moved the headquarters of the Rainbow Coalition from Chicago to Washington, D.C. Since that time, he has focused on addressing inner-city crime, violence, drug abuse, teenage pregnancy, voter registration, health-care reform, affirmative action policies, the anti-apartheid movement, and the struggle for democracy in Haiti. In 1996, the Rainbow Coalition and Operation PUSH coalesced into the Rainbow/PUSH Coalition. In its Web site, Rainbow/PUSH states:

> God has been with Rev. Jackson and Rainbow/PUSH through each and every struggle, campaign, and initiative. When we look back over the years of struggle and service we know that only a God could have delivered an organization with a vision which the founder received, continues to write, publish and make plain to the masses.

Since its high point in 1988, the Rainbow Coalition has undergone a decline due to serious organizational and financial problems. Some critics have argued that Jackson has functioned in a top-down mode that has shut the membership of the Coalition out of decision making, and that it has been difficult to distinguish him from the larger organization. As Marable (1992: 177) so astutely observes, "Jackson's frenetic, larger-than-life personality and his chaotic organizational style, consisting of a coterie of loyalists who rarely disagree with the boss, works against genuinely democratic decisionmaking."). In reality, this is a pattern not unique to Jackson but rather one inherent in the role of the black ministers and perhaps in ministers, priests, and religious leaders around the world.

Hans A. Baer

See also Social Activism

Bibliography

Collins, Daniel F. (1986) *The Rainbow Coalition: The Jackson Campaign and the Future of U.S. Politics.* New York: Monthly Review Press.

Marable, Manning. (1991) *The Crisis of Color and Democracy: Essays on Race, Class, and Power.* Monroe, ME: Common Courage Press.

Reynolds, David. (1997) *Democracy Unbound: Progressive Challenges to the Two Party System.* Boston: South End Press.

Washington, James Melvin. (1985) "Jesse Jackson and the Symbolic Politics of Black Christendom." *Annals of the American Academy of Political and Social Science* 480: 88–105.

Rastafari

The Living Testament of Jah! Rastafari is as complex as its many practitioners but as simple as its basic truths. Referring to the range of practices and principles in Rastafari, Rastafari say that *in my Father's house there are many mansions.* Because any individual can identify himself or herself as Rastafari it is appropriate to accept a self-definition as an individual measure of Rastafari. However, within the community of Rastafari there is ongoing discussion about how to distinguish between genuine and false Rastafari.

In 1983 the Rastafari International Theocratic Assembly adopted a resolution that one particular orientation in Rastafari, known as the House of Nyahbinghi, be accepted as the foundational Rastafari orthodoxy. Proclaiming the basic truths of Rastafari, the House of Nyahbinghi attests that, within this dispensation or era, His Imperial Majesty (H.I.M.) Emperor Haile Selassie I of Ethiopia is the Living God, Ethiopia is Zion, and, since all African people are one (Pan-Africanism), the descendants of those who were forcibly stolen from Africa to be enslaved in Babylon (the oppressive society of the West), have the right of repatriation to Zion or Africa. While the House of Nyahbinghi can be used as a frame of reference for Rastafari orthodoxy, nevertheless, both individuals and communities frequently define their orientation to the faith according to their experience of *coming up in the faith*, and the personal inner relationship they have with H.I.M.

Rastafari has been variously described as a religion, a culture, and a social movement, among other designations. Rastafari prefer the term *livity*, contending that Rastafari is a way of life informed by theocratic principles. A theocracy is a form of divine governance and those who organize themselves according to such principles claim a divinity as leader. Elder Sam Brown once said that if you see Rastafari as King, you get a King's reward; if you see H.I.M. as God, your reward is divine; but if you see Rastafari as God and King, then you are doubly blessed. Many Rastafari, even those who have the respected status of Elder, decline to be called a leader, because they say that Jah (a short form of Jehovah) is the head of us all, the only leader. In the theocratic worldview, sacred and profane, church and state, are inseparable, because one moral foundation informs all behavior. Still, within Rastafari as a whole there is a constant dialogue about the relative weighting of the *churchical* and the *statical*, orthodox and secular influences respectively.

While the core of the House of Nyahbinghi may be fixed, as a living testament, Rastafari is also socially and ideologically fluid, an organic testament in the process of becoming, something like the living documents to which policy writers occasionally refer. While Rastafari as we know it today emerged in Jamaica in the early decades of the twentieth century, many Rastafari claim that the first Rastafari was the first captured African forced into exile in the Diaspora, who struggled to maintain an African identity and to return home.

In the course of its recent seventy-year history in Jamaica, Rastafari has developed and changed in a dynamic relationship with the dominant society. And as Rastafari spreads internationally, it adapts to local circumstances, with feedback taking place constantly between the various Rastafari communities that are part of its global network. Since Rastafari can be seen as both timeless and seamless, it is extremely difficult to generalize about Rastafari without misrepresentation. For these and other reasons, Rastafari has confounded virtually every research methodology which has been summoned to interrogate it.

Social Organization

Sociologically speaking, Rastafari comprises several apparently contradictory social tendencies that coexist in a state of dynamic tension. Rastafari has not imposed a centralized organization structure on its adherents. It is basically a social network with nodal points and organized sectors. While most Rastafari do not belong to formal organizations, many belong to several duly constituted groups. In fact, throughout the course of Rastafari history, many organizations have waxed and waned in prominence.

A common theme in Rastafari discourse has been the admonition to organize and centralize in order to repatriate. There have been various attempts to form umbrella organizations consisting of many different Rastafari organizations, such as the short-lived Organization of Rastafari Unity in the 1980s, and the Rastafari Centralization Organization (R.C.O.) formed in the 1990s and still very active in 2000. The R.C.O., for example, consists of a coalition of such groups as: Rastafari Patriotic Unity, Rasses International Sistren, Rastafari International Theocracy Assembly, and the Peace Makers Association. Several Rastafari organizations in Jamaica also have international memberships. For example, the Twelve Tribes of Israel (founded 1968), various locals of the Ethiopian World Federation (founded 1938), the Ethiopian National Congress, otherwise known as Bobo Dreads (founded mid-1950s), and the House of Nyahbinghi (various loosely affiliated streams dating to the 1930s). Individual Rastafari may even belong to more than one organization.

In addition, the Ethiopian Orthodox Church has been active in Jamaica since 1970, and many Rastafari belong to its branches throughout the Caribbean, North America, and the United Kingdom. Finally, Rastafari groups such as Africa House in Barbados and Rastafari For Unity in Bermuda registered as nongovernmental organizations (NGOs) in the 1990s. Rastafari have a great deal of experience in forming organizations, to the extent that we may speak of social "heterarchy." That is, Rastafari form social groups in order to serve certain purposes, and when their usefulness is done, outdated organizations disappear and new ones arise.

There is a strong democratic principle in Rastafari that promotes egalitarianism, as expressed in the terms for each other, brother and sister. At the same time there is respect for elders, and many communities are organized in a hierarchical style, around a powerful and charismatic male elder. Moreover, there has been an ongoing discussion within Rastafari, particularly since its globalization from the 1980s on, about the relationship between Rastafari women and Rastafari men. The public face of Rastafari and its image in popular culture tends to be largely male.

In Nyahbinghi orthodoxy, women are excluded from key ritual activities in the place of worship and have other gender-specific rules to follow, particularly when they are having their menses, during which time they are regarded as unclean. On the other hand, sisters have had strong

Sister Ina, Bongo Qualla, Sister Daphney, and Ma-Ashanti in St. Thomas, Jamaica, 1987. PHOTO COURTESY OF JOHN HOMIAK.

presences in many Rastafari activities, especially in the international arena. For example, many played key roles in organizing international gatherings and other events. Among them are Sisters Masani Montague, I JahQueen, Liveth Ivory, Farika Birhan, Makeda Blake Hannah, Maureen Rowe, and Desta Tonga. It is the brothers, however, who do most of the international *trodding* (traveling) on a regular basis.

Gender relations in Rastafari is a clear example of an area of behavior where egalitarianism and hierarchy are in a state of dynamic tension and under review. While male-female separation is frequently supported with references to the Bible, it is also well known that Emperor Haile Selassie broke with tradition to have Empress Menen, his wife, crowned alongside himself. The icon of their coronation is increasingly a point of reference in this ongoing dialogue. Rastafari argue that the family is the strength of the nation: to build a strong African nation, African women and African men have to reconstitute their interpersonal and social relationships, which were destroyed during the time of enslavement and are undermined by the continuing impoverish-

ment of African people. Elder Mortimo Planno has frequently pointed out that Europeans melted the slave chains to make coins, and it is now for lack of money that African people are not free.

There is also a dynamic tension in Rastafari between the particular values associated with strengthening African identity in a racist and white-dominated world, and the more universal values of peace, love, truth, and justice that attract people from non-African backgrounds to the faith. Captured Africans struggling for freedom, striving against all odds to keep alive the memory of Africa until, through the guidance of H.I.M., they can return, embodies the essence of Rastafari Redemption. Yet there are vital Rastafari communities in Japan, among the New Zealand Maori and other indigenous peoples, and among people of European descent.

History

Taking the Bible as a guidebook and compass, Rastafari have developed a tradition of interpreting history in terms of cyclical *dispensations* of time. Hence, the same oppressions that the ancient Israelites faced during their exile in Egypt are repeated among modern-day Africans who were forcibly carried into captivity in the New World. And just as Christ was persecuted in his time, so Emperor Selassie I was attacked and opposed by European rulers who sought to conquer and divide his kingdom. However, while Christ came as a Lamb to be sacrificed during his dispensation, His Majesty comes as the Conquering Lion who will deliver the faithful and righteous. Informed by such perspectives, Rastafari brethren and sistren cultivate a knowledge of history as it relates to the struggle of African peoples both on the continent and in the Diaspora.

In terms of its specific development in Jamaica, there exists no codified history of Rastafari. This reflects the movement's decentralized structure and the multiple voices of its participants as much as it does the impossibility for any one researcher to canvass its complete scope. The history of the movement does, however, interweave a number of related themes. These include a determined ethic of resistance to colonialism and white domination, a creative ability to draw upon African cultural *roots* and other symbolic resources to fashion a basis for community, and the individual and collective willingness to stand as a *Living sacrifice* for their African culture and identity.

In Jamaica and throughout the Diaspora, then, Rastafari has flourished under conditions of oppression, creating a dynamic culture from a multitude of sources. Brethren and sistren emphasize *remembrance* as the key in using history as a source of collective strength. They draw upon the oral testimony of elders who emphasize their refusal to *bow to Babylon*, their unbroken *Covenant with Jah* and faith in the destiny of African people, and the internal creativity by which they culture, edify, and inspire others and themselves. Elders routinely council younger members and others that *without a tribulation there can be no testimony and without a cross there can be no crown.*

The following historical outline, punctuated by the testimony of various brethren and sistren, provides a very brief capsule history of the movement as it developed in Jamaica. These testimonies where recorded by Homiak between 1980 and 1999. Some are excerpts from communal reasonings and reflect the process by which the ethnographer is 'grounded' in the faith. Others were recorded as direct testimonies from Rastafari to the ethnographer and other Rastafari and non-Rastafari listeners. They serve as examples of how speakers publically witness to their faith and at the same time position themselves in relation to its historical development. All of these testimonies draw upon the understandings and experiences of individuals who have lived and created the history of Rastafari. They attest to the fact that the movement has developed *from stage-to-stage and from strength-to-strength.*

The Rastafari Movement emerged in Jamaica during the early 1930s. The first expounders of the faith, including Leonard Percival Howell, Archibald Dunkley, and Joseph Nathaniel Hibbert, were all immigrant laborers returning to the island around this time. It is generally recognized, however, that Leonard Howell was both the first and most successful preacher of Ratafari doctrine. In the contemporary Rastafari Movement, only a handful of Elders—now in their late seventies and older—can witness to having had direct contact with these early Rastafari prophets. One such patriarch is Ras Derminite (possibly the oldest living member of the Nyahbinghi Order), a dockworker who returned from Colon, Panama, to Kingston in 1938. In the early 1980s, Homiak frequently reasoned with Derminite as he moved between yards in West Kingston and a Rastafari camp in Bull Bay. At a gathering in his humble gates [dwelling] in Riverton City, West Kingston, the Elder regaled the ethnographer and several brethren and sistren with an account of the first time he heard Howell preach in West Kington, the same year that he [Derminte] returned from Panama:

> We never know Haile-I Selassie-I crown except from Leonard Howell. Is Howell leave from here [Jamaica] and go to Ghana—dat is the Gold Coast in Ethiopia [Africa]—and he come back here and he say to we on a preaching business outta Dog Park [West Kingston], he say, ABredrin and sistren, your King crowned in Ethiopia, ya know. We ask which king. De Black King, him say—Haile-I Selassie-I. And him give we a photograph—I give him a shilling feh it. So, from there—from [Robert] Hinds, [Joseph Nathaniel] Hibbert, and some next bredrin, and plenty more, we carry on. But Howell is de first.

Leonard Percival Howell is, in fact, the first person acknowledged to have preached the divinity of Haile Selassie. Like Marcus Garvey (the most important Jamaican of his time), and virtually all of the first generation Rastafari preachers, Howell was a well-traveled individual who had firsthand experience among black people and West Indian laborers in North and Central America. Upon his return to Jamaica in 1931, he formed the King of Kings Mission and began to preach about Haile Selassie and the repatriation of black people to Ethiopia, focusing his early preaching in the Eastern parishes of the island. Here he came into contact with the descendants of Central Africans who were carried to Jamaica as post-Emancipation immigrant laborers between 1845 and 1865. These were self-identified Kongo people who, of all Jamaicans, had the most recent memories of Africa. It is generally not appreciated that prior to the preachings of Marcus Garvey or Howell, many of these African-Jamaican people already aspired to repatriate themselves to the continent.

In 1933, Howell was tried and convicted of sedition for preaching allegiance to Haile Selassie. After serving two years in prison, he published *The Promised Key* (1935), a text which introduced a number of formative ideas into the Movement and its theology. These included the concepts of Black Supremacy, theocracy and the Solomonic dynasty, and the symbolic oppositions between Zion and Babylon—two mutually opposed domains ruled over by Emperor Haile Selassie I and the Pope of Rome, respectively. Howell was also instrumental in introducing the symbols and observances of African nationhood into the nascent movement.

In 1936, Howell and his followers inagurated the celebration of August 1 (the anniversary of slave emancipation in the British West Indies), as a Rastafari day of observance. These and other events continue to be vividly remembered and frequently recounted by the remnants of Howell's followers who now live scattered throughout the parish of St. Catherine and elsewhere. During one of Homiak's several visits to Tredeigar Park, St. Catherine, in 1995, he spoke at length with Brother Edgar Reid, an officer in Howell's organization and the manager of Howell's bakery on Princess Street in Kingston. For Brother Reid, the first Rastafari Emancipation marked their determination to assemble and preach their message. It was also indicative of the persecution which colonial authorities visited upon Rastafari during its formative years:

> Mr. Howell lead an "army" from St. Thomas to 108 Princess Street in Kingston and he gather us der to have a function that was on the first of August there. And when everybody was there ... he was going to hice [raise] the flag. And when de flag hice, the scepter was in the paws of de Lion, up there waiving, Mr. Howell said we must sing:
>
> We are the children of the red, yellow, purple, green,
>
> We are the children of the red, yellow, purple, green,
>
> We are the children of the red, yellow, purple, green,
>
> Ethiopia is calling us home ...
>
> And when dat [celebration] was carrying on, the police dem range up upon de place and they tear us down. They tear down the flag and mash up everything. They take away all the herb and they take some of our people—over a hundred men—to Central Police Station. Some pay 40 pounds, some

> pay 4 pounds according to how they try them and charge them. So you must see how wicked they down upon us!

In 1940, after being harassed and driven out of eastern Jamaica by the colonial authorities, Howell founded the now-legendary commune of Pinnacle, where he relocated nearly 1,000 of his followers. It was at this location above Spanish Town (on the site of the first Black Free Village founded after emancipation), that Howell formed the Ethiopian Salvation Society. At this site, Howell reworked a host of diasporic resources that infused Rastafari with both African and East Indian influences. These influences—including Ki-Kongo and Hindi language, the Congo-derived drumming tradition known as Kumina, and both African- and Christian-derived chants—formed part of the ritual and religious life at Pinnacle.

Although Pinnacle was a bounded and self-sufficient community (somewhat like a Maroon enclave), it was never isolated from the wider Rastafari Movement. Brethren and sistren from Kingston and elsewhere in Jamaica made regular visits to attend Howellite ceremonies and to obtain herbs. Elders such as Ras Sam Brown, Ras Boanerges, Bredda Louva, Brother Job, and Sister Merriam Lennox are among those who traveled to and from Pinnacle from the mid-1940s until 1954, when the commune was raided and destroyed by colonial authorities. Through these connections, the Howellite influences on the wider Rastafari movement remained strong.

Rastafari themselves trace a more-or-less direct influence from Howell (and the doctrine of Black Supremacy) to the formative years of the House of Nyahbinghi. An important linkage in this regard—but by no means the only one—came through a group known as the Youth Black Faith that formed in Trench Town in the late 1940s. Perhaps the most prominent member of this group, Ras Boanerges, has expounded widely on this connection. In 1988, while assembled in a yard in Central Kingston with several other Elders who were preparing to travel on a delegation to the United States, Ras Boanerges provided Homiak with the following biographical statement:

> I [Ras Boanerges] visited Pinnacle in 1945, '46, and '47 and had face-to-face [meetings] with Howell. Howell and him followers wasn't speaking of Nyabingi der but was playing kumina drums. After dat, I-n-I return to KingstonYcame to Trench Town and create this sound [the Nyahbinghi drums]. At dat time, we get communication from Sylvia Pankhurst through de book, The Black International which show forth dat de King's Order was de

Nyabinghi. So, from that, I create the Nyabinghi Order in 1947 and start dis tradition 'pon de street wid de bass drum and repeater.

From both additional oral and written testimony, we know that several important camps founded in the early 1950s were influenced by this connection. These include the Rastafari Repatriation Center of Samuel Livermore Brown on the Foreshore Road, the Church Triumphant of Ras Shadrack on Foreshore Road, the camp of Brother Louva in East Kingston near Mountain View Road, and into the Dungle and Salt Lane in West Kingston where master drummer Skipper Meeks resided.

Other influences from Rastafari in West Kingston were woven into this early Howellite-Nyahbinghi connection. Sister Merriam Lennox, a Rastafari woman who coordinated with Robert Hinds, Archibald Dunkley, Joseph Myers, and Raphael Downer in the late 1940s recalls part of this development during the street preaching era of Rastafari. One evening in April of 1987, Sister Merriam offered the following testimony to Homiak and a group of Rastafari who were reasoning at Church Street, a yard in Central Kingston:

> In 1947 I was living in Jones Town and it was between 1948–49 [that] I go and meet the [Rasta] service one night. I stood at Clocktower [in Trench Town] observing and I see it was a very sweet loving place. A spirit call to me and say, "Go and enter that place and see what it is." . . .
>
> It was January 1st, like it's Rasta Christmas and it go all up for a month it last. It was Brother [Joseph] Myers' group . . . he use to keep an Inity thing—every year he calls a feast. That happen before Bobo Emmanuel comes in existence. Dat said night I was enrolled. For the bredrin there say, "All de dawta who outside or bredrin who like to enroll there name can come to the altar . . . to the table." I tell you mon, it was Irie, sweet!
>
> Brother Myers had de biggest "church" we had . . . right in Clocktower. Bigger than even Brother Hinds'. Him play a nice role. I walk with dem first. I walk with Brother Myers until we had de Youth Black Faith. That come through Brother Arthur . . . who come after Brother Myers. He has a mission and we were all at Third Street [in Trench Town]. So at Third Street we all develop until de Youth Black Faith come out of his "church." Yes, it spring right outta Third Street outta Brother Arthur. And then Watto [Ras Boanerges] start to travel with it. So Youth Black Faith, when deh sprang up in the late '40s, deh was only young people, younger generation

who come up and see us as Rasta. So deh call dem the Youth Black Faith.

The connections between these developments and the Nyabinghi concept must actually be traced back to 1935, the same year Leonard Howell published *The Promised Key*. It was during this year that Mussolini's Italian troops invaded Ethiopia (3 October 1935), an event which highlighted all manner of Ethiopianist identifications throughout the African world. Shortly thereafter, the term "Nyabinghi" entered Jamaica through reportage about the Italian-Ethiopian conflict which stated that Emperor Selassie I was the head of the Nyabinghi Order, a secret anticolonial society. From that point forward, the term, interpreted as *death to black and white oppressors*, became a fixed part of the Rastafari and Jamaican vocabulary.

By the early 1950s, the Nyabinghi ethos was broadly associated with a growing and zealous practice within the movement of wearing dreadlocks. According to some oral accounts, this was inspired in part by the example of Mau-Mau leaders who adopted the practice of wearing locks in their struggle against colonialism. The growing of locks and *precepts* (beards) thus became a militant form of public witnessing to the faith and to a proud and uncompromising stance of the Rastafari in the face of persecution by the wider society. The ethos shared by many of those who entered the movement at this time involved a rejection of any formal criteria of membership.

The majority of contemporary elders in Jamaica emerged during this period. During the 1950s and 1960s they not only suffered persecution for their faith, they developed a principled Nazarene-like code of separation from the wider society that has become known as *livity*. Reprisals against Rastafari by the colonial government during these years were common and included well-remembered events like the Coronation Market Riot (7 May 1959), the Henry Affair (1960), and the Coral Gardens Massacre (11 April 1963). Once, while comparing accounts of this event with Bongo Pidow, an Elder from Mannings Hill (above Kingston), Pa-Ashanti, a master Nyahbinghi drummer who was also a member of the Youth Black Faith, recalled the Coronation Market incident. The riot, which destroyed Back 'o Wall, he remembers, began as a confrontation between members of the Kingston fire brigade and a brethren named Ras Amos:

> It was an argument, feh deh disrespect de Rastamon [Ras Amos] and de whole dispute turn right into Back 'o Wall . . . and Back 'o Wall turn into a battleground. The 7th of May, 1959, it was a day that the Rastas in Jamaica should never forget. It was fire ena

Back 'o Wall when de police burn every shack flat. Burning and beating, dem bring on some brigades of police dat mon haffa run feh get way. Dem lick one "belly-woman" [pregnant woman] round der, jus lick de baby outta her—and she haffa move said way else she dead. The younger Rastas known nothing about but I know dat de Elders feel it!

It was in Rastafari communities like Back 'o Wall, Trench Town, and the Dungle that Nyabinghi religious observances developed. The heart of these rituals centers around the Nyabinghi, or *akete*, drums, a three-part drumming ensemble composed of the bass drum, the *funde*, and the *repeater*. Rastafari regard these as *the harps of David*, the instruments upon which *praises* are composed to Jah. By the late 1950s, Ras Boanerges had developed much of the formal structure which would come to characterize Nyabinghi worship. This included a circular tabernacle within which brethren and sistren would chant *ises* (praises) to Jah Rastafari. The ever-present tri-colors of red, gold, and green, rods carried by male members, portraits of His Majesty, and a five- or seven-cornered altar at the base of circular tabernacle were all features of Nyabinghi ritual.

In such a specially prepared space, often referred to as *the Rainbow Circle Throne Room of Jah Rastafari*, brethren and sistren would chant throughout the night. During such worship, it is customary for one or more elders stationed around the altar to recite prayers and Psalms from the Bible and to hold forth in impassioned biblical verse. Throughout a Nyabinghi session, drummers will typically take turns with the range of chants on any given occasion being a reflection of the assembled group. During this dance-drumming worship, it also became customary for brethren to dance across the open space of a tabernacle, *trampling the Dragon*. Inasmuch as organic metaphors run throughout Nyabinghi worship—from *herbs* (cannabis) smoking to the power of the drums—the chanting of *ises* are seen as a ritual means for summoning the forces of nature (lightning, thunder, and earthquake) to *crash the wicked* and *move the oppressors*.

It was through Nyahbinghi that the various practices now known as livity have become central to Rastafari daily life. The origins of this code are, as pointed out, multiple. The testimony of Bongo Shephan, one of the Elders who grounded Homiak during his first years of fieldwork, attests to the collective spirit at work behind the creation of the livity complex:

Even though the Movement generated itself from Kingston City, de roots of de movement are really in de various country parishes. Ya see, bredrin come from various country parts all around and I-n-

I meet in the city—in places like Back 'o Wall, Ackee Walk, the Dungle, Foreshore Road, and Trench Town. Dat is where we come together to pool our views and get a stronger sense of generating de fullness of dis culture. Feh we reason one-to-another and graduate ourselves in dis faith.

While Nyabinghi has generally been regarded as having a *churchical* orientation with respect to Rastafari, it has never been exclusive of other social and political forms of organization. During the same period described above, other Rastafari brethren and sistren also organized under the banner of the Ethiopian World Federation, effectively orienting themselves to the realities of the Ethiopian theocratic state. These Rastafari were in continual communication with the settler community in Shashamane, and took practical steps to learn Amharic, the language of the Ethiopian nobility. These orientations coexisted (and continue to coexist), validated by shared understandings about *unity within diversity* and *freedom with principle*. Shashamane is a land grant given to the Black peoples of the West by Emperor Haile Selassie. It was granted to those Black people who helped Ethiopia in her time of need after the Italian invasion in 1936.

On 21 April 1966 the state visit of Emperor Haile Selassie I to Jamaica marked a watershed for the Rastafari and the relationship of the movement to his postcolonial state. While the Emperor's visit had been calculated to quell Rastafari demands for repatriation, it projected the Rastafari for the first time onto the stage of national events. Selassie awarded thirteen gold medals to Rastafari leaders, including Mortimo Planno, Ras Sam Brown, Prince Edward Emmanuel, Ras Timothy Hill, and others.

By the late 1960s and early 1970s, the movement was becoming increasingly diverse, beginning with the formation of the Rastafari Movement Association in 1969 and the Twelve Tribes of Israel from EWF Local 15 in 1972. Local 15 of the EWF had been founded in 1968. The latter marked the first significant crossover of middle-class Jamaicans into the Rasta movement. Buoyed by reggae, which was used in the political campaigns of 1972 and 1976, this unprecedented recognition also set the stage for its co-optation in the postcolonial era under Manley's Democratic Socialism.

It was in this social climate of supposed normalization (during the early 1970s) that the most traditional Rastafari associated with the House of Nyabinghi began to organize island-wide Nyabinghi celebrations. These ritual pilgrimages *out of Babylon*, lasting for three or seven days, marked a renewed effort among traditionalists to define the terms of their own reality as Africans sojourning in Babylonian exile.

The Nyabinghi *trods in yard* were a harbinger of things to come. (Yard can refer to a collective housing unit or to Jamaica itself as distinguished from *foreign*.)

Knowing and Practices

How does one *come up in the faith* of Rastafari? Rastafari is seen as an inborn conception, the fullness of which can only be comprehended through the direct experience of the *Living Wordsoundpower of Jah!Rastafari* from within. If one has been Rastafari from birth, then what triggers this realization? Most Rastafari can point to a moment when, as they say, the scales fell from their eyes, and Rastafari provided the meaning they needed to make sense of their life experiences as an oppressed African. Over the course of its seventy-year history Rastafari has witnessed many changes, as its predominantly oral culture of small-group teaching and street meetings has increasingly incorporated both electronic and cybernetic technology to manifest the *Living Testament of Jah!Rastafari*, especially in the international arena. The technologizing of the Word through recordings, books, and videos has expanded the parameters of coming up in the faith.

Rastafari assert that to know is to know, but to believe is to imply doubt. Therefore, Rastafari are encouraged to discover the truth of Rastafari for themselves, through reasoning, meditation, and the giving of thanks and praise in the form of chanting and drumming. Revealed knowledge is trusted more than mere belief. Correspondingly, the term Rastafarianism is not a popular one, because "ism" implies schisms and divisions. Traditionally, younger Rastafari studied with elders, those more experienced in the faith. Elders lived in yards (collective dwelling units which included families) or camps (generally all-male enclaves in more isolated settings). Face-to-face small group-reasoning sessions continue to be the classic way to know Rastafari.

Reasoning is a form of collective and visionary discourse in which individuals explore the implications of a particular insight, which could be based on subjects as diverse as a Bible passage or an event in the day's news. Everyone has the opportunity to speak for as long as necessary, and the reasoning is not completed until a general consensus has been achieved. Reasoning is a cooperative affair, not a competitive one. It is designed not to entertain but to elucidate. It gives ample room to the play of inspiration, while demanding a degree of disciplined concentration. During the course of a

Bongo Stevens, Bongo Shephan, Bongo Quallo and unidentified Rasta "reasoning" in St. Thomas, Jamaica, 1987. PHOTO COURTESY OF JOHN HOMIAK.

reasoning, Rastafari might also give witness to their experience in the faith. Thus reasoning may take a very long time, perhaps all night, in which case the session is called *bleaching*. The purpose of reasoning is to reach ever higher heights, accreting layer upon layer of meaning, until a satisfactory view of reality in the Light of Jah!Rastafari is reached. When reasoning is used to witness the faith by interpreting Bible passages, it is known as *citing* or *sighting up*.

The Sacramental Use of Cannabis

For Rastafari, cannabis, or *holy herbs*, commonly known in Jamaica as *ganja*, is a sacred God-given plant to be used for the *healing of the nation*. Its consumption is central to Rastafari spiritual practice. However, using cannabis in more secular contexts—as tea, in tonics, in the bath, in food and medicine—should not be interpreted as any less sacred.

In keeping with the practice of knowing Jah!Rastafari as God directly for oneself, the ingestion of herbs encourages inspiration and insight through the process of sudden illumination. Sociologists would call this a visionary state characterized by the experience of oneness or interconnectedness. Rastafari insist there is a *duty* incumbent upon them to praise the Creator in this way, and thus herbs is also known as *incense*. The use of herbs then is the sacrament known as *communion* that accompanies reasoning. Herbs may be consumed individually in a *spliff* or collectively in a water pipe, or *chalice*. For young aspirants, the term *baptism* is used to refer to initiation into the sacrament through the use of the chalice.

The growing, harvesting, and curing of the holy herbs is considered an art and science among Rastafari. The preparation of herbs for smoking in a water pipe or *chalice* follows a special procedure. The herb is carefully cleaned, kneaded, and cut on a special board. The chalice, usually made of an organic material such as horn or coconut, must be cleaned, filled with water and tested, or gauged, by drawing air through a hose that is attached to it. A small amount of water is poured on the ground as an offering. The herb is carefully packed into a clay bowl, known as a *cuchi* or *chillum*. This has a narrow opening in its bottom, in which a small object, known as a gritty stone, is placed to prevent the herb from falling into the water but to allow the air to circulate so that the chalice can be lit.

An elaborate protocol also surrounds the use of the chalice once it has been prepared. Male participants sit in a loose circle and remove their crowns or head coverings, displaying their dreadlocks. The chalice is blessed and then lit by the person who has prepared it or by the ranking elder present. It is an honor to bless and light the chalice, taking the first draw. The chalice then proceeds through the assembly, passed to the left, across the heart. When it is finished or burned, it might be filled a few more times, in which case it usually begins again with the last person who burned it, depending upon how much was still in it when they last had it. One draws the chalice energetically in such as way as to maximize the amount of smoke taken into the lungs, which is then released in a controlled manner, sometimes enveloping the participants.

The symbolism surrounding the sacrament invokes the original Creation. The elements of earth, water, fire, and air are present. The smoke itself is a form of incense. Indeed, it is considered a blessing which heals, so that young children or babies, whether ailing or not, may have smoke blown upon them. When there is a general consensus that the reasoning has been completed, the chalice is carefully emptied, cleaned, and stored until the next occasion. At Nyahbinghi celebrations, which extend for several days, the use of herbs, both individually or collectively, is combined with chanting, drumming, and dancing in the giving of praises, as described above.

Bonga Bigga with a steam chalice in St. Thomas, Jamaica, 1987. PHOTO COURTESY OF JOHN HOMIAK.

Rastafari Practice in Daily Life

Livity refers to the daily life practice of Rastafari. Some practices of livity are based upon the Code of the Nazarene and other Old Testament references, which prohibit the cutting of the hair, and proscribe the eating of certain foods, based on Leviticus. Rastafari use the term *ital*—in the sense of natural or organic—to embrace their livity practices. Within the Nyahbinghi context, *ital livity* then includes foodways that are as close to organic as possible, and avoid the use of flesh, dairy products, and artificial preparations.

Livity practices also include grooming and dress codes. In general, dreadlocks, sometimes referred to as the Covenant, are regarded as holy and powerful. Rastafari often say that one should not grow locks until a firm commitment to the faith has been made, because in the *putting on of the Covenant* one makes a holy vow to Jah. One also exposes oneself to possible persecution because of the stigma attached to the wearing of the locks by the dominant society. Therefore, the wearing of the locks is seen to strengthen one in the faith. Dreadlocks are also considered instruments of telepathic communication with Jah. In Nyahbinghi orthodoxy they are to be covered with *crowns* while in Babylon, although brothers must remove them for giving praises, while sisters are generally expected to keep their heads covered in public. Adherence to this practice varies considerably outside Nyahbinghi.

In addition to the dreadlocks as a powerful form of symbolism, Rastafari have also developed a distinctive style of communication based upon a form of parlance they call *I-ance*. This is based upon the concept that all life is connected, as in *I and I* or *InI*, an understanding that could be related to the unifying experience of the sacrament. *I* is also a reference to the role that *sight* and *sounds* play in coming up in the faith. Hence the phrase *wordsoundpower*. Metaphors for seeing to mean "comprehension" abound in Rastafari, as does the image of the mystical eye itself. Therefore, many syllables in words are replaced by the sound *I*. At the same time, because the sounds of words are considered to carry power, the meaning of syllables is often taken literally and then changed to convey a more appropriate *sound*. For example, *oppression* becomes *downpression*, and *understanding* becomes *overstanding*. Nor is this, strictly speaking, a formulaic exercise. Rastafari delight in word plays as a communication style in itself, and frequently in reasonings sessions individuals display their talents in this area.

The practice of Rastafari is also based on the charge that one has a *duty* to serve Jah. In this sense Rastafari is seen as a *mission* because it is said that *words without works is dead*. This means that individuals need to find the most appropriate way to *do the works*, based on their particular relationship with Rastafari. One's works then become a measure of how others see one's standing within the faith.

Rastafari at the Turn of the Century

Rastafari as a Living Testament has changed and evolved with time. Since it develops in a dynamic relationship with the wider society, it is necessarily affected by outside influences, which compel reasoning within the movement on some fairly fundamental issues. Gender relations within Rastafari are increasingly open to reevaluation. While Rastafari have always actively promoted repatriation, in the decades of the 1980s and 1990s some engaged themselves much more extensively in the international movement for reparations for African people. Even the relationship between Emperor Haile Selassie I and Jesus Christ is open to increasing scrutiny and debate. Some Rastafari have called to *burn Jesus* while others have urged a more careful reflection upon this issue. For example, Sister Makeda Blake Hannah has stated:

> I praise and worship the Son, Iyesos Krystos [Jesus] the Christ in his first Manifestation through the Ethiopian Orthodox Church, and I praise and worship the Father JAH in the Nyabinghi temple through the vision of His Imperial majesty [H.I.M.] as the Second Manifestation of Christ.

The relationship between oral and textual sources of authority are now also more complex. While in the earlier days of Rastafari there were few texts available to all, with the exception of the Bible, in the 1990s many more relevant writings became widely accessible, in particular, the collected speeches of Emperor Haile Selassie. Based on the themes of recent international Rastafari conferences as well as publications by Rastafari, reasonings upon and *sighting up* H.I.M.'s words will likely become a more common practice among Rastafari in the twenty-first century.

Indeed, Rastafari are more directly affected by events in Ethiopia itself and the politics of the diasporic Ethiopian community. Efforts by descendants of His Imperial Majesty to restore the monarchy in Ethiopia have generated much interest in the movement. The victory by the Ethiopians over the Italians at the battle of Adwa on 1 March 1896 is increasingly being celebrated by Rastafari and the Ethiopian community. This event was never observed before its 100th-anniversary celebration in 1996.

Along with the movement's traditional emphasis on repatriation and on practicing livity as an expression of African identity, all of these recent themes will continue to shape Rastafari ideology and practice. At the same time,

Rastafari is certain to continue its development as a dynamic cultural formation throughout the Caribbean, in North American and Europe, and on the African continent.

Carole D. Yawney and John P. Homiak

See also Jamaica, African-Derived Religions in; Rastafari in Global Context; Rastafari in West Africa; Rastafari in the U. S.

Bibliography

Campbell, Horace. (1985) *Rasta and Resistance: From Marcus Garvey to Walter Rodney.* London: Hansib Publishing.

Chevannes, Barry (1994) *Rastafari Roots and Ideology.* Syracuse, NY: Syracuse University Press.

Forsythe, Dennis. (1996) *Rastafari: For the Healing of the Nations.* New York: One Drop Books.

Hannah, Barbara Makeda Blake. (1997) *Rastafari: The New Creation.* Kingston, Jamaica: Headstart Publishers.

Howell, Leonard P. (1996 [1935]) *The Promised Key.* With Introduction by Miguel Lorne. Kingston, Jamaica: Headstart Publishers.

Pulis, John, ed. (1999) *Religion, Diaspora, and Cultural Identity: A Reader in the Anglophone Caribbean.* Amsterdam: Gordon and Breach.

Rastafari in Global Context

Many people throughout the world became familiar with Rastafari when reggae performers, most notably Bob Marley, started to bring its message to an international audience in the 1970s. Indeed, Rastafari is an exceptional example of a religious movement that has spread globally since that time through the medium of popular culture. However, although Rastafari as we know it today emerged locally in Jamaica in the 1930s, from its inception it has had an international orientation. And the most continuous influence in its dissemination throughout its history until today has been travel by Rastafari themselves. Today there are reports of Rastafari throughout the Caribbean, North America, Europe, Africa, Japan, the Pacific, Australia, and New Zealand.

Resonating with events in Africa, the originators of Rastafari in Jamaica took the Coronation of Emperor Haile Selassie I on 2 November 1930 to be a fulfillment of prophecy and proclaimed His Imperial Majesty (H.I.M.) to be Jah! Rastafari, the Living God. (Ras is a title for nobility in Ethiopia, and Tafari was the family name of H.I.M.) Furthermore, this Rastafari seed fell upon the fertile ground of the teachings of Marcus Garvey, Ethiopianism, and Pan-Africanism, with the result that Rastafari declared themselves to be not Jamaican, but Africans forced into a Babylonian exile in the Diaspora, and demanded the right of repatriation to Africa, from which they had been stolen.

The Italian invasion of Ethiopia in 1935 and the subsequent refusal of the League of Nations to honor its commitment to that country focused much attention by Africans in the Diaspora upon Ethiopia's plight. From the very beginning Rastafari were actively engaged in supporting African liberation struggles. All these influences situated Rastafari squarely in the arena of international politics.

Rastafari History in Global Perspective

The history of the global spread of Rastafari is not a linear one, although one can point to discrete events and phases. Nor is it an entirely translucent process. Even in the Rastafari world view as expounded by Elder Mortimo Planno, the concepts of invisible history and the invisible establishment are used in reasoning to analyze how the world really works. The local scene of Trench Town, from where Ras Planno launched his teachings, provides a metaphorical example. Legend since slavery days has it that Trench Town is honeycombed with subterranean tunnels, or "trenches," that reach beyond its borders to provide unseen ingress and egress. Similarly, the Caribbean is not an isolated region. Indeed, it has always been a kind of frontier, a crossroads for trade and travel, allowing for an exchange of ideas as well as labor. Caribbean people have been forced for economic reasons to move throughout the Diaspora in search of work, with the result that there are substantial Caribbean communities in North America and the United Kingdom. In these areas people from various islands and circum-Caribbean countries have had the opportunity to interact with each other, frequently across language and cultural barriers, and to engage in labor struggles together. As well, strong links between the Caribbean and its own cultural Diaspora—the metropoles of Europe, North America, and the African continent—have always been maintained, with people and ideas travelling back and forth regularly. Rastafari themselves continue to be an important part of this two-way flow.

There is ample evidence that the leaders who had a considerable influence on early Rastafari—such as Marcus Garvey, Leonard Howell, Claudius Henry, and others—spent substantial periods of time in the United States as well as in the circum-Caribbean region (Panama, Costa Rica, Cuba), which was under the influence of American economic expansionism. The Ethiopian World Federation (E.W.F.), founded at the instruction of Emperor Haile Selassie as an organization of repatriation, was launched in New York City in 1937. From its beginning, Jamaicans were involved. And after a recruitment drive by the E.W.F. in Jamaica in the mid-1950s, Rastafari there were increasingly drawn into repatriation politics based in New York City.

Contemporary Rastafari in Global Perspective.

Not only do we have to appreciate the interactional nature of the spread of Rastafari, as it moves back and forth throughout the African and Caribbean Diaspora, but we also need to acknowledge that Jamaica is just one node in this web of Rastafari communication patterns. In this regard, there are parallels between the historical development and geographic spread of Rastafari. Just as Rastafari has always encompassed a multitude of themes that may receive different levels of emphasis over time, so the various locations in which it has taken root may be foregrounded in importance at different moments of its spread. We therefore need a reticulate model that allows for both multiple centers and many channels of diffusion. Barbados, Trinidad, New York City, Washington, D.C., Toronto, London, Paris, Amsterdam—in addition to Jamaica and Shashamane, Ethiopia—all generate sustained relationships with Rastafari in other locales, particularly in Africa. Largely through the efforts of Rastafari in Barbados and Trinidad, Rastafari spread to the smaller islands of the eastern Caribbean. Rastafari in the United Kingdom have played a major role in repatriation missions and Elder's *trods* (visits) to Ethiopia, South Africa, Tanzania, and Zimbabwe. And Rastafari from Jamaica, such as the

Bobo Dreads, have directly involved themselves in furthering connections with Ghana.

The Rastafari message—assisted by the common rhythmic sensibilities in music shared among African-Caribbean peoples—has also crossed over from English-speaking communities into French- and Dutch-speaking communities. This presents a challenge for Rastafari of an entirely different kind, as most Rastafari materials are written in English. In the Caribbean, however, there are substantial Rastafari communities in Cuba, Costa Rica, Panama, Colombia, and Venezuela. Rastafari traveled frequently to Cuba during the time when Michael Manley was Jamaican prime minister. But there is also evidence that some key Rastafari in the Spanish-speaking Caribbean have also lived in the Spanish-speaking communities in New York City and Miami, where they were exposed to the message. In turn, some of them have visited Jamaica to learn more. There is also a large Rastafari population in Brazil, in the Bahia, where Portuguese is spoken. Rastafari move back and forth between Surinam and Holland as well. While Rastafari in Guadeloupe and Martinique have linkages with France, some have also repatriated to French-speaking Africa, to places like Benin. In Japan, a section of Tokyo has been designated Trench Town. Reggae performers frequently play in that country, and Japanese Rastafari are no strangers in Jamaica.

In addition to Rastafari, who as individuals travel and reside in communities other than Jamaica, and reggae musicians who move as a group taking up temporary residence

Nyahbinghi Drummers at the Steel Shed, Queens Park, Bridgetown, Barbados. Rastafari International Conference, August 1998. PHOTO COURTESY OF JOHN HOMIAK.

wherever they perform, there have also been directly purposeful and well-organized missions of Rastafari Elders and activists whose primary intention for *trodding* (travelling) is communication.

The Emergent Rastafari Ambassadorial Tradition

Elders' missions (trods) like the "Voice of Thunder" trod to Canada (1984) or "The Rainbow Circle Throne Room of Jah Rastafari" trod to the United States (1988) have had multiple goals. They have sought to missionize a version of Rastafari orthodoxy among Rastafari brethren and sistren who have not always "come up in the faith" through the traditional means of repeated face-to-face reasonings. At the same time, they have sought to strengthen local communities that must strive in the midst of a wider society that is variously hostile and racist and that criminalizes Rastafari; or, alternatively, that commodifies, trivializes, or romanticizes Rastafari. The international Rastafari trods and the international Rastafari conferences and gatherings, which have taken place since the early 1980s, have served as a means of community-building and greatly facilitated communication among brethren and sistren globally.

The 1992 Centenary of His Imperial Majesty's birthday (23 July 1892), which Rastafari celebrated in Ethiopia, served as an important catalyst that has spurred the pace of the movement's globalization. Preparations for this event produced an unprecedented level of networking and coordination among Rastafari in England, the United States, Jamaica, and the Eastern Caribbean, as well as on the continent. Among other things, the Centenary Trod served to focus renewed Rastafari attention on the land-grant settlement in Shashamane, Ethiopia, both as a development project requiring international coordination and as an annual pilgrimage site for the international Rastafari community. Emblematic of this focus was the subsequent launching of the Nyabinghi Tabernacle Project that same year.

The Centenary Trod to Ethiopia—and the associated international networking among Rastafari—set the stage for the international conferences that took place in 1994 and 1995 as well as the International Nyabinghi Mission to South Africa in 1996. And the active role played by Rastafari sistren in planning and coordinating many of these international events since the early 1980s can be seen as directly related to a new level of dialogue and debate among Rastafari themselves about the role of women within the culture.

Contrary to many recent superficial accounts that outline Rastafari globalization, the international spread of Rastafari culture cannot be equated simply to the diffusion of reggae and dancehall. Since the early 1980s, globalization has entailed a much more complex interplay between popular expressions of Rastafari (e.g., traveling reggae groups) and more orthodox or "rooted" practices. Together with an increasingly strong "ambassadorial" tradition of traveling elders, Rastafari continues to globalize itself via newspapers and newsletters, radio programs, publications by Rastafari themselves, and the circulation of other media. For example, it is now increasingly the case that elders travel with their own audiovisual resources in the form of videotapes that document Rastafari testimony, events, celebrations, and activities. These tapes—screened, dubbed, and circulated among community members—serve as a means of strengthening communication among Rastafari globally.

Most of this Rastafari trodding is inspired by the Movement's general mandate to "organize and centralize" and by the issues of reparations and repatriation that have been heightened politically in recent years. Here there is a strong intersection between the Rastafari vision of a return to the African continent and the reemergence of pan-African organizations and agendas in the twenty-first century. In the midst of this unprecedented global movement, the Shashamane Nyabinghi Tabernacle Project in Ethiopia serves as a symbolic focal point for brethren and sistren globally as they seek to realize their collective goal of repatriation.

Carole Yawney and John P. Homiak

See also Rastafari; Rastafari in the U.S.; Rastafari in West Africa

Bibliography

Bilby, Kenneth. (1990) "Puentes Composicionales en un Mundo Insular: Vinculos Espontaneos en la Tradicion Musicale Caribena." *Del Caribe* 6, 16 and 17: 112–119.

Homiak, John P. (1995) "From Yard to Nation: Rastafari and the Politics of Eldership at Home and Abroad." In *Ay Bobo: Afro-Karibische Religionen*, edited by Manfred Kremser. Vienna: WUV-Universitatsverlag.

Jah Bones. (1985) *One Love: History, Doctrine and Livity.* London: Voice of Rasta.

Mack, Douglas. (1999) *From Babylon to Rastafari: Origin and History of the Rastafarian Movement.* Chicago: Frontline Distribution.

Yawney, Carole D. (1994) "Rasta Mek a Trod: Symbolic Ambiguity in a Globalizing Religion." In *Arise, Ye Mightly People: Gender, Class, and Race in Popular Struggles*, edited by Teresa Turner. Trenton, NJ: Africa World Press, 65–83.

———. (1995) "Tell Out King Rasta Doctrine Around the Whole World: Rastafari in Global Perspective." In *The Reordering of Culture: Latin America, the Caribbean and Canada*, edited by A. Ruprecht and C. Taiana. Ottawa: Carleton University Press, 57–73.

IMPORTANT DATES IN RASTAFARI HISTORY

1834   Abolition of slavery in the British Caribbean, August 1.

1887   Birth of Marcus Garvey, St. Ann's Bay, Jamaica, August 17.

1892   Birth of Emperor Haile Selassie I, Ethiopia, July 23.

1896   Emperor Menelik II of Ethiopia defeats the Italians at the Battle of Adwa, March 1.

1898   Birth of Leonard P. Howell, Clarendon, Jamaica, June 16.

1900   The First Pan-African Conference is convened in London, England, July 23–25.

1914   Marcus Garvey founds the Universal Negro Improvement Association and the African Communities League in the Jamaica, August 1.

1924   Publication of *The Holy Piby* (otherwise known as *The Black Man's Bible*) by Shepard Athlyi Rogers in Newark, New Jersey.

1926   Publication of The Royal Parchment Scroll of Black Supremacy in Jamaica by Rev. Fitz Balintine Pettersburg.

1927   Marcus Garvey arrives in Jamaica December 10, after being deported from the United States.

1930   Ras Tafari Makonnen is crowned Emperor Haile Selassie I in Addis Ababa, Ethiopia, November 2.

1933   Leonard Howell, the first person to preach the divinity of Emperor Haile Selassie, is arrested for sedition in Jamaica, on January 1.

1934   The Ethiopian Research Council is founded in Washington, D.C., under the guidance of Dr. Malaku Bayen and Professor Leo Hansberry.

1935   The Italians under Mussolini invade Ethiopia, October 3.

1936   Emperor Haile Selassie I leaves Ethiopia on May 2 for a five year exile in England. In July 1936 he makes his historic address to the League of Nations on June 30.

1937   Dr. Malaku Bayen founds the Ethiopian World Federation in New York City, August 25.

1937   Local 17, the first Ethiopian World federation (E.W.F.) Local in Jamaica, is established with L. F. C. Mantle as president and Paul Erlington as vice-president. Joseph Nathaniel Hibbert, Archibald Dunkley, and others are foundational members of Local 17.

1939   Leonard Howell establishes the Ethiopian Salvation Society.

1940   Leonard Howell founds Pinnacle, a Rastafari settlement based on communal principles.

1941   Joseph Nathaniel Hibbert establishes a branch of the Ethiopian Mystic Mason, loosely affiliated with the Ethiopian Coptic Church.

1941   Jamaican authorities raid Pinnacle and arrest Howell, one in a series of colonial government interventions to destroy Howell's Rastafari community and organization, July 25.

1941   Emperor Haile Selassie I reenters Ethiopia on May 5 after the defeat of the Italians.

1947   Ras Boanerges, Bredda Arthur, Philip Panhandle, Kurukong, and others found the Youth Black Faith in Trench Town, West Kingston.

1954, 1955, 1956   Prince Edward Emmanuel, Ras Boanerges, and others hold annual conventions in Back 'o Wall, in West Kingston.

1954   The Jamaican state raids Pinnacle on May 22, finally destroying the community.

1955   Emperor Haile Selassie announces the Shashamane land grant administered under the Ethiopian World Federation.

1955   Mamie Richardson visits Jamaica to publicize the E.W.F. land grant and to promote the organization among Jamaicans and Rastafari.

1955   A number of Jamaican Rastafari, including Brother Raphael Downer, former head of the Afro-West Indian Brotherhood, immigrate to England.

1958   Prince Emmanuel Edwards and other Nyahbinghi Rastafari convene the first major national *groundation* (celebration) of Rastafari in Kingston, March 1 to March 21. The event leads to the formal founding of the Ethiopian African International Congress, Order of the Nyahbinghi.

1959   Police and Rastafari clash in the so-called *Coronation Market Riot*, on May 7, which leads to police destruction throughout much of the Rastafari community in Back-o-Wall, Kingston.

1960   The University of the West Indies conducts research on Rastafari at the invitation of members of the Rastafari movement. Its report includes a recommendation that the government of Jamaica send a mission to Africa to arrange for immigration of Jamaicans. This mission should include Rastafari.

1960   On April 7 the police arrest Rev. Claudius Henry, a Rastafari preacher, and several of his followers, charging them with treason.

(cont.)

1961   The government sends a mission to Africa which includes three Rastafari: Mortimo Planno, Douglas Mack, and Samuel Clayton. It visits five African countries. It tables two reports, a majority one, and a minority one, written by Rastafari.

1962   Police raid and dismantle the Wareika Hill Rastafari camp of the I-gelic House, a group of Italist Nyabinghi Rastafari.

1963   On April 11, in Coral Gardens, Montego Bay, killings blamed on Rastafari resulted in a nationwide persecution of Rastafari.

1964   Miriam Mkeba and Stokely Carmichael visit the Rastafari community in Back o' Wall, Kingston.

1966   Emperor Haile Selassie I makes a state visit to Jamaica, April 21 to April 24. The Emperor honors the Rastafari, awarding gold medals to 13 leading brethren.

1966   Police destroy the Back-o-Wall Rastafari community in West Kingston, July 12.

1967   Emperor Haile Selassie meets Rev. Winston Evans, the Director of the Ethiopian World Federation Inc. of Chicago, February 13 and February 14. On behalf of his organization Rev. Evans receives a land grant reported to be 10,000 acres.

1968   Vernon Carrington, also known as Prophet Gad, founds the Twelve Tribes of Israel, in Kingston, Jamaica. The Twelve Tribes becomes one of the most successful Rastafari organizations, with an extensive international membership.

1968   Walter Rodney, a black nationalist active among the Rastafari, is banned from Jamaica, October 15, triggering widespread student protests.

1969   Ras Solomon Wolfe departs Jamaica for Ethiopia, September 18. On October 1, 1970, Ras Wolfe receives the E.W.F. administrative responsibility for the Shashamane land grant from His Imperial Majesty.

1972   Michael Manley is elected Prime Minister of Jamaica after mounting a campaign organized around Rastafari slogans and symbols.

1973   Ras Mortimo Planno visits Canada.

1972   Count Ossie and the Mystic Revelation of Rastafari tour Trinidad.

1973   Release of *The Harder They Come*, a full length Jamaican motion picture, featuring a prominent role for Ras Daniel Heartman.

1974   Emperor Haile Selassie I is deposed on September 13.

1974   Council of Nyahbinghi Elders formally establish the Theocratic Government of His Imperial Majesty, Emperor Haile Selassie I.

1974   The Ethiopian African International Congress moves from Davis Lane, Kingston, to the community of Bull Bay.

1975   Ras Boanerges carries the Nyahbinghi Order to Barbados, in April.

1975   Ras Michael (Sons of Negus) travel to perform in Antigua.

1975   Emperor Haile Selassie I disappears on August 27.

1975   Ras Mortimo Planno and Ras Reginald Huntley visit Canada to participate in a forum on Rastafari and the press.

1976   Ras Ruggles, a Rastafari artist, visits Washington, D.C. as the only Rastafari representative at the Festival of American Folklife.

1976   Primer Minister Manley meets with a Council of Nyahbinghi Elders (Judah Coptic Issemble of Elders) at 11 Welcome Avenue, Waterhouse, Kingston.

1976   Publication of *Dread, The Rastafarians of Jamaica*, by Joseph Owens, which becomes a popular text on Rastafari. The book presents the theology and culture of Rastafari largely in the words of Rastafari themselves.

1978   Ras Samuel Livermore Brown travels to Rhodesia/Zimbabwe.

1978   Rastafari hold a Nyahbinghi in Heroes Park, Kingston, in August, with a focus on repatriation and the legalization of the herbs. The police forcibly evict the Rastafari when they overstay the time allowed by their permit to assemble, demanding instead to meet with the prime minister and the cabinet to discuss repatriation.

1978   Rastafari Universal Zion, a community-based organization is established in the Tottenham area of North London, January.

1978   *Jahugliman*, a Rastafari vernacular publication, is launched in Jamaica. It later moves to the United Kingdom, where it continues to be published by Rastafari, and is now known as *Jahug*.

1980   Rastafari celebrate the Golden Jubilee of Emperor Haile Selassie's coronation.

1980   Ras Mortimo Planno and Ras Arthur Kitchin visit Canada to participate in a workshop on Rastafari.

1980   In November, Rastafari celebrate the Golden Jubilee anniversary of H.I.M.'s Coronation, St. Catherine, Jamaica. Event is attended by many Rastafari from outside Jamaica.

1980   Rastafari Movement Association becomes International Rastafari Theocratic Assembly.

1980   Bob Marley performs at the Independence Day celebration in Zimbabwe, April 18.

1980	*Rastafari Speaks*, a Rastafari-produced newspaper, is launched in Trinidad, as a vehicle for news throughout the Caribbean Rastafari community.
1982	First International Rastafarian Conference, Toronto, Canada, July 23 to July 25.
1983	Second Annual International Rastafari Theocratic Assembly, July 18 to July 25.
1984	*Voice of Thunder: Dialogue With Nyahbinghi Elders*, Toronto, September 23 to October 21. First official Nyahbinghi Elders' mission outside the Caribbean.
1985	*A Sense of Rasta*, photographic exhibit by Omobowale Ayorinde at the National Center of Afro-American Artists, Boston, Mass.
1985	Universal Rastafari Improvement Association of Tanzania sends a mission to Jamaica, December 29, 1985 to January 28, 1986.
1986	Visit of Prince Dawitt to Jamaica and the United States, connecting with the House of Nyahbinghi and various Rastafari communities.
1986	*Rastafari Focus*, Commonwealth Institute, London, July 14 to July 27. First International Rastafari conference in the United Kingdom.
1987	*The Nyahbinghi Project*, a forum for Rastafari in Britain, based at the Yaa Asantewa Arts Centre in London, is launched.
1987	Centenary of Marcus Garvey's birthday, August 17, is celebrated in Jamaica with a month-long round-island Nyahbinghi celebration attracting international visitors.
1988	In February, for three consecutive Sundays, at the Yaa Asantewa Arts Centre in London, England, Ras Ikael Tafari, visiting spokesperson for the House of Nyahbinghi in Jamaica, moderates educational sessions on Nyahbinghi celebrations.
1988	"The Rainbow Circle Throne Room of Jah Rastafari Trod" (Mission) departs Jamaica May 23. The House of Nyahbinghi sends a seventeen-member delegation of Elders to New York, Baltimore, Philadelphia, and Washington, D.C., May-August.
1989	"2nd Trod of the Rainbow Circle Throne Room of Jah Rastafari" with visits to Washington, D.C., Chicago, Atlanta, Philadelphia, and New York, June-August.
1990	"3rd Trod of the Rainbow Circle Throne Room of Jah Rastafari." Elders participate in a public program at the American Museum of Natural History, New York, and later release an album entitled *Rastafari Elders*, a compilation of Nyahbinghi testimony and chants.
1991	Ras Sam Brown serves as the spokesman at *Nyabinghi: A Celebration of the Lion and the Lamb* co-sponsored by the Smithsonian's Anacostia Museum and the Rastafari Community of Washington, D.C., March 23.
1992	"Centenary Trod" to Ethiopia to commemorate the 100th celebration of the birth of Emperor Haile Selassie, June 28 to August 1992, and occasion of first international assembly of Rastafari in Ethiopia.
1993	The First Annual Rastafari-Ethiopian Cultural Celebration, Philadelphia, organized by Ras Al and Sister Kaya Selassie, November 13.
1994	First International Gathering of Rastafari, sponsored by ICOMRAS (International Communicators of Rastafari), in Honor of African Liberation Day and the Organization of African Unity, Miami, May 22 to May 26.
1995	Second International Gathering of Rastafari, sponsored by International Rastafari Gathering Committee (formerly ICOMRAS), Toronto, July 15 to July 24.
1996	International Nyahbinghi Mission to South Africa led by Ras Boanerges, October to November.
1997	Reggae Unites Africa Concert commemorating the 101st Victory of the Battle of Adwa, Addis Ababa, March 2.
1997	Ethiopian Crown Princes Ermias Sahle-Selassie and Bekere Fikre Selassie visit Jamaica, August 16 to August 23.
1998	First International Eastern Caribbean Conference on Rastafari, Barbados, August 17 to August 27. One of the conference resolutions is to observe the birth date of Leonard Howell (June 16, 1898) as a Rastafari day of celebration.
1998	Second Barbados International Conference, November 2 to November 16.
1998	"Emancipation 150: Trodding To Mount Zion," a Caribbean Rastafari Conference sponsored by Rastafari Livity Educational Forum, University of the Virgin Islands, St. Thomas, Virgin Islands, November 25 to November 29, and December 5 to December 6.
1999	The Official Opening of the Rastafari Tabernacle in Shashamane, Ethiopia, and occasion of two international gatherings, July 22 to August 5, and November 1 to November 14.
1999	"From the Cross to the Throne," Rastafari Conference convened by Ras Mortimo Planno at the University of the West Indies, August 16–17.

Rastafari in the United States

From its inception in the early 1930s until the mid-1960s, the Rastafari movement was primarily a Jamaican phenomenon or limited to a few Anglophone countries of the West Indies. However, in recent decades the movement has managed to transcend its island home and is presently enjoying vibrant growth and a process of worldwide diffusion. Perhaps nowhere has Rastafari found more fertile soil to lay down roots, outside of the Caribbean, than in the urban centers of North America. Although initially brought to the United States by Jamaican and other West Indian immigrants in the 1960s and 1970s, the popular appeal of reggae music has been an equally important source for the spread of Rastafari beliefs and practices to other ethnic groups. In the U.S. today there are growing numbers of African, African-American, white, Hispanic, Asian, and Native American Rastafarians. The influx of new groups and individuals into the movement has begun to have an impact on aspects of traditional Rastafari belief and practice, encouraging a more universalistic and gender-inclusive orientation.

The Jamaican Roots of Rastafari

The Rastafari movement was born in the squalid slums of colonial Jamaica during the height of the worldwide depression of the 1930s. Yet it reflected several centuries of popular opposition movements and indigenous religious practices from Myalism and Revivalism to Pan-Africanism and Ethiopianism. Its first preachers appeared in Kingston armed with a new doctrine that proclaimed the divinity or messianic character of the newly crowned emperor of Ethiopia, Ras Tafari Makonnen (1891–1975), who took as his official coronation name and title "His Imperial Majesty, Haile Selassie I ["Might of the Trinity"], King of Kings, Lord of Lords, Conquering Lion of the Tribe of Judah, Elect of God, and Light of this World." These titles, traditionally associated with Christ in the New Testament, were interpreted by early Rasta leaders such as Leonard Howell (1898–1981), Joseph Nathaniel Hibbert (1893–1985), Archibald Dunkley, and Robert Hinds (d. 1950) to mean that Selassie was the returned "Black Christ," that the end of days was at hand, and that Selassie would bring about the great redemption and restoration of the black race to its ancient glory. These same preachers announced that Ethiopia was Zion, the true promised land spoken of in the Bible; that black people in the diaspora were living in Babylon, a hopeless hell; and that the emancipation, liberation, and salvation of African peoples everywhere could only be achieved by a collective "exodus" from Babylon and repatriation to the motherland (Barrett 1977; Campbell 1987; Chevannes 1994; Owens 1976).

Consistent with the message they preached, early Rastafari leaders organized their urban followers into highly decentralized, polycephalous (multi-leader), and grassroots organizations with names such as the "King of Kings Mission," the "Ethiopian Coptic Faith," and the "Ethiopian Salvation Society." Membership was typically drawn from the poorest strata of Jamaican society, especially among those who had been inspired by the Back-to-Africa preaching and organizing of Marcus Garvey (1887–1940) and the Universal Negro Improvement Association (UNIA) during the 1920s. While sometimes mistaken as an early Rasta prophet, Garvey himself was critical of the movement and its namesake, Haile Selassie. This has not deterred Rastafarians, however, from incorporating Garvey and aspects of his philosophy and ideology into their movement. Indeed, Marcus Garvey is broadly perceived by present-day Rastafarians as John the Baptist preparing the way for the coming of Selassie.

Although Rastafari began as an urban movement, the colonial state's early surveillance and suppression forced the nascent Rastafarians into rural camps where, during the late 1930s and 1940s, a collective pattern of communal work and living evolved. It was here that many of today's distinctive Rasta practices and ideology, such as the cultivation of dreadlocks; the ritual smoking of "ganja," or the "holy weed of wisdom" (marijuana); Nyabinghi drumming and chanting; the proud display of the red, gold, and green colors of the Ethiopian flag; the reaffirmation of black pride and dignity; a close identification with nature; and an antipathy to Eurocentric values, capitalism, and modernity; first developed. By the 1960s and 1970s, Rastafarians emerged as a popular force throughout Jamaican society and culture. With the advent of reggae and the increasing out-migration of Jamaican laborers during the same period, Rastafari began its global expansion.

Rastafari in North America

At present, it is not possible to date the formal beginnings of Rastafari in the U.S., nor to accurately estimate the numbers of followers. Leading Rastafari researcher Leonard Barrett (1977, 197–201) dates the movement in North America to the early 1960s. However, both Hill (1983) and Hepner (1998a) explore evidence that suggests an earlier connection between North American urban centers like New York City and the rise of the movement in Kingston, Jamaica, in the early 1930s. Although Rastafari activists were moving between Jamaica and North America from the 1930s through the 1960s, the first formal Rastafari institutions and organizations were founded in New York City in the mid 1970s. Subsequently, the movement spread and Rastafarians, like other Jamaican immigrants, are now to be found in every state in the country. While the largest numbers are located in eastern seaboard cities, such as New York, Philadelphia, Boston, New Haven, Miami, and Washington, D.C., there are also sizable communities in Los Angeles, Oakland, San Francisco, Chicago, and Houston. While the exact population of Rastafarians in the U.S. is not known, in New York City the movement represents tens-of-thousands with an even larger periphery of sympathizers.

Like the movement in Jamaica, North American Rastafari remains loosely organized and polycephalous. A score of formally organized "mansions" (churches, political associations, and community centers) compete for the allegiance of a larger, institutionally unaffiliated sector of fellow enthusiasts. As in Jamaica, the majority of U.S. Rastafarians do not formally belong to any of the official Rastafari organizations. Nonetheless, these groups and organizations play a highly active role in proportion to their actual size. Among these, perhaps the most prominent are the Twelve Tribes of Israel, the Nyabinghi Order of Divine Theocracy, the Ethiopian Orthodox Church, and the Ethiopian World Federation. All are headquartered in New York City but have established branches in various other cities and states. There are several dozen smaller formations, including a new legally recognized Rastafari church, the Church of Haile Selassie I in Bedford-Stuyvesant, Brooklyn (see Hepner 1998b). In recent years there have been numerous attempts to bring the far-flung movement under the banner of a single leadership or coalition-like umbrella. So far these attempts have failed.

The lack of an authoritative leadership structure results in a decentralized movement characterized by heterogeneity in belief and practice. But it also affords its followers enormous freedom to interpret and practice their "faith" as their conscience dictates. Some North American Rastafarians do not even claim to be "religious." For some, the political and cultural aspects of the movement are sufficient to identify themselves as Rastafari. For others, the religious and theological affirmations are central, and Bible study and worship become important sources for grounding their faith. For both "kinds" of Rastas, greater institutionalization of the movement seems to be an increasing demand.

What all Rastafarians share is a rejection of western Eurocentric hegemony in the cultural, political, and religious spheres of modern society—what Rastas refer to as "Babylon"—and a profound attachment to Africa as "Zion," the promised land of black people everywhere and the ultimate motherland of all peoples. Around the mythopoetic symbols of Babylon and Zion Rastafarians have created an array of linguistic practices, cultural norms, a political the-

ology, and a worldview that assists in the maintenance of individual and group identity (Johnson-Hill 1995; Pollard 1994). In the absence of common organizational affiliation, Rastafarians rely upon a ritualized discursive practice known as "reasonings" (intensive small group discussions) to provide the context for socializing and educating new movement enthusiasts. Larger periodic gatherings of the faithful are referred to as "groundations" or "Nyabinghis" and are accompanied by traditional drumming, chanting, and fire rituals. In both settings, the sacramental smoking of ganja typically plays a prominent role, although it should be pointed out that the vast majority of Rastafarians militantly reject all other drug usage, including alcohol and tobacco. Most Rastafarians practice a vegetarian or "Ital" diet, employ herbal and alternative medicinal traditions, and attempt to live a life free of the contaminants of modern consumerist society. Most of all, Rastafarians reject all forms of white supremacist and racist ideology that denigrates, subjugates, or "downpresses" (oppresses) peoples of color.

The unconventional appearance of Rastafarians (especially dreadlocks) and their religious use of ganja, or marijuana, frequently brings them into conflict with law enforcement. Across the U.S. today thousands of Rastafarians languish in the nation's growing prison industrial complex. There are probably few religious movements, immigrant or otherwise, that suffer the incarceration rates that Rastas presently endure. Law enforcement agencies throughout the country have been a principal source for the negative stereotyping of Rastafari in print and electronic media, and Hollywood has contributed its own distorted images of Rastafarians as murderous drug-crazed cultists in films such as *Marked for Death*.

To counter such negative publicity, Rastafarians have reached out to friendly academic scholars who have presented Rastafarian beliefs and practices in a more neutral or objective light. More recently, Rastafarians have begun producing their own writers and journalists and have made increasing use of the Internet to network with others and to spread the positive "livity" (lifestyle and practice) of Rastafari. Most of all, Rastafarians have relied upon the message-laden lyricism of reggae music to tear down the walls of discrimination and prejudice and to win over new enthusiasts to the Rastafari vision of world justice and peace. In the highly politicized and spiritual lyrical content of reggae, prayer and protest are united in a way that makes for a compelling popular—and increasingly international—cultural medium, capable of articulating the needs and interests of struggling peoples in diverse contexts. The success of this medium is evident in the large numbers of new Rasta "manifests" (converts) from every ethnic and socioeconomic group across American society. Rastafarians have been especially successful at attracting urban youth. The popularity of reggae on U.S. college campuses has resulted in Rastafarian-oriented radio programs and concerts that have been important vehicles for introducing young people to the movement's history and teachings. Even more recently, Rastafarians have begun to attract a following among young people on some Native American reservations.

The influx of new groups and individuals into the movement has had a transforming impact on traditional aspects of Jamaican Rastafari. Whereas the movement was once cast as a narrow Afrocentric liberationist and "black supremacist" sect, today's North American Rastafarians embrace a broader, more universal conception of human liberation that includes people of all ethnic backgrounds. Similarly, many contemporary Rastafarians challenge the patriarchal and sometimes sexist norms of Jamaican Rastafari belief and practice (Yawney 1994). The emergence of Rasta women activists and new North American Rastafari communities that focus on the socialization of children within the Rasta family has contributed to a greater sense of gender-inclusivity within the movement.

Conclusion

Of all the African and Afro-Caribbean religions present in the U.S. today, few have had the widespread cultural impact of Rastafari. While there are forces that remain hostile to Rastafari in North America, receptive audiences abound. Given the current globalization of the movement, it would not be foolish to imagine Rastafari becoming a significant religious and cultural force in the new century. Especially as Rastafari gives voice and concrete expression to those who suffer under a new world (dis)order that seems disposed to reward a few at the expense of the many does its success as an emergent religious movement seem assured. Rastafari has established itself in the U.S. against great odds. It is a movement, a people, a political theology, and an African religious presence that has added a new and vital dimension to the religious landscape of North America.

Randal L. Hepner

See also Rastafari; Rastafari in Global Context; Rastafari in West Africa

Bibliography

Barrett, Leonard. (1977) *The Rastafarians: Sounds of Cultural Dissonance*. Boston: Beacon Press.

Campbell, Horace. (1987) *Rasta and Resistance: From Marcus Garvey to Walter Rodney*. Trenton, NJ: Africa World Press.

Chevannes, Barry. (1994) *Rastafari: Roots and Ideology*. Syracuse: Syracuse University Press.

Hepner, Randal L. (1998a). "'Chanting Down Babylon in the Belly of the Beast': The Rastafari Movement in the Metropolitan United States." In *Chanting Down Babylon: The Rastafari Reader*, edited by Nathaniel Samuel Murrell, et al. Philadelphia: Temple University Press, 199–216.

———. (1998b) "'The House That Rasta Built': Church-Building and Fundamentalism Among New York Rastafarians." In *Gatherings in Diaspora: Religious Communities and the New Immigration*, edited by R. Stephen Warner and Judith G. Wittner. Philadelphia: Temple University Press, 197–234.

Hill, Robert. (1983) "Leonard P. Howell and Millenarian Visions in Early Rastafari." *Jamaica Journal* 16, 1: 24–39.

Johnson-Hill, Jack A. (1995) *I-Sight: The World of Rastafari: An Interpretive Sociological Account of Rastafarian Ethics*. Metuchen, NJ: The American Theological Library Association.

Owens, Joseph. (1976) *Dread: The Rastafarians of Jamaica*. Kingston, Jamaica: Sangster Books.

Pollard, Velma. (1994) *Dread Talk: The Language of Rastafari*. Kingston, Jamaica: Canoe Press.

Yawney, Carol. (1994) "Moving With the Dawtas of Rastafari: From Myth to Reality." In *Arise Ye Mighty People: Gender, Race and Class in Popular Struggles*, edited by Terisa Turner. Trenton, NJ: Africa World Press, 65–73.

Rastafari in West Africa

Since the mid- to late-1970s the Jamaican Rastafarian movement has spread beyond its island homeland and taken root in a number of diverse geographical and cultural settings. But nowhere, apart from the Caribbean, has this socioreligious movement been so widely and readily accepted as in Sub-Saharan Africa. Parallel with and spurred on in part by the emergence of Jamaican reggae onto the international pop music scene in the mid-1970s, Rastafari has within the last two decades attracted a dedicated following among young, urban-based West Africans. Its attendant forms of cultural expression (i.e., reggae music, the religious and secular use of cannabis, or *ganja*; Dread Talk, or *iyaric*; and clothing and ornaments adorned in the "Rasta colors" of yellow, red, green and black) are everywhere in evidence.

Mediums of Dissemination

Although the total Rastafarian population in West Africa may by most standards be considered relatively small and

SPECIAL REGGAE FESTIVAL

As part of activities marking the Nation's independence anniversary, a Special Reggae festival for Rastafarians will be held at the Orion Cinema on March 6.
According to the organisers of the programme, the festival will feature two foreign reggae bands alongside ten loval bands.

Newspaper in Ghana listing a reggae festival as part of the independence day celebration.

insignificant, the impact of reggae music and Rastafarian culture on young people in many of the region's urban centers is definitely not. To cite one particularly revealing illustration, in 1989 a large reggae concert was organized at Labadi Beach as part of Ghana's Independence Day celebrations. Sponsored by the government-run Ghanaian Tourist Board and billed as a dawn to dusk *Reggae Sunsplash Beach Festival*, this afternoon event featured three local reggae groups as well as a massive sound system manned by local DJs. It drew a large and appreciative crowd numbering in the thousands, the vast majority of whom were not Rastas. Also, that very same evening another Independence Day event billed as a *Reggae Concert for Rastafarians* was organized by the local chapter of the Twelve Tribes of Israel at a large cinema complex in Accra.

The Music

That reggae music caught on fairly quickly in West Africa is not surprising, given the tremendous interest Caribbean music has generated throughout the continent over the course of the past fifty years. In the 1960s and 1970s, for example, Zaire represented one of the largest markets in the world for the sale of salsa and rumba records, and much of the African pop music heard today—that is, the ubiquitous Zairian *soukous* and its many offshoots—has been heavily influenced by Latin American (especially Afro-Cuban) rhythms and melodies. Since the late 1970s, Africa has also functioned as a major international market for reggae music. And, as is the case elsewhere across the globe, it was Bob Marley who served as the foremost apostle of reggae and the culture of Rastafari.

The impact of Bob Marley's music and Rasta-inspired philosophy on young West Africans should not be underestimated. Throughout much of the region his songs can be

heard blasting out of boom boxes and stereo systems in bars, discos, and taxicabs; a complete catalogue of his cassettes are available for sale in urban and even rural marketplaces; and his dreadlocked profile can be seen staring out from t-shirts and wall posters in market stalls, homes, and restaurants. Along with Muhammad Ali, James Brown, and Michael Jackson, Marley ranks among the most popular and influential pan-African heroes of all time—widely known, listened to, admired, and idolized by young Africans everywhere. And for many the name Bob Marley is synonymous with both reggae music and the religion and culture of Rastafari.

Reggae music continues to function as a major force in the urban pop music scenes of numerous, especially Anglophone, West African nations. And while the reasons for this are fairly complex and varied—ranging from the structural and functional affinities that exist between indigenous African musical forms and reggae, the potent appeal of the music's religiously inspired and socio-politically charged lyrics, and the eagerness on the part of young people to identify with a Black transnational pop music genre—there is little doubt that as foreign musical styles and influences go, reggae holds a prominent place in the hearts and minds of a large contingent of young West Africans. As one astute Nigerian reggae artist observed,

The images and tribulations portrayed through the records of reggae musicians make the music very attractive to the African people. The fact that the original roots of reggae music is Africa facilitates the swiftness in rekindling the flames of the music, especially after its refinement with scientific tools and instruments in the Western world, even though the messages remain very original and unadulterated. Just like cocoa seeds taken away raw and brought back fully refined as cocoa drinks, beverages, and body lotions, reggae will always find a place in the heart of our people at all times. (Steffens 1990: 64)

In Anglophone West Africa there is a profusion of cassettes by Jamaican, Anglo-Jamaican, and African reggae artists on sale in record shops and market stalls in all major cities and most large towns. Reggae is also frequently played on local radio stations, in taxis, at discos, and on street corners and other places where young people congregate. Furthermore, many West African pop musicians have either played reggae music at one time in their careers or utilized reggae rhythms and/or Rasta-inspired lyrics in their repertoires.

In Ghana, for example, nearly all the music outlets (from large record shops to tiny market stalls) in the capital Accra and other Ghanaian urban centers stock a wide assortment of cassettes by African, Jamaican, and Anglo-Jamaican reggae artists. Accra even boasts a number of music shops specifically devoted to reggae, one of which is owned and operated by an expatriate Jamaican. In a survey conducted in 1989 by the ethnomusicologist Andrew Kaye of some two hundred randomly chosen young people in Accra and Kumasi, Bob Marley ranked highest in popularity from among a list of a dozen well-known foreign and Ghanaian musicians. Reggae also receives a significant amount of airplay on Ghana Broadcasting Corporation's (GBC) Radio One, averaging 25 percent of all airtime devoted to music programming.

In Ghana and much of West Africa, reggae music functions as a *lingua* or *musica franca*—transcending ethnic, national, and regional boundaries through its perceived connections to Caribbean and transnational pop-music culture and its heavy reliance on the use of English, and in Francophone countries both English and French, lyrics. And while many West African musicians over the years have incorporated stylistic elements borrowed from reggae into their music, a few like Alpha Blondy of the Ivory Coast have taken things one step further by creating a totally new form of syncretic African reggae, singing for the most part in their own native languages and employing indigenous African instruments, melodies, and rhythms in their mixes.

The attraction reggae holds for West Africans may be attributed to the fact that the music functions simultaneously on two very important levels—first, as an entertaining and danceable form of consciousness raising, and second as a means of expressing pan-African solidarity with their brothers and sisters in the African Diaspora. Furthermore, reggae also serves as the principle medium for disseminating information about the religion and culture of Rastafari throughout the region.

Of the two hundred Rastas that I interviewed in Ghana in 1988–89 when I conducted fieldwork there, 80 percent admitted that their initial interest in Rastafari was inspired by their exposure to reggae. And in the vast majority of cases it was the music of Bob Marley in particular that made the greatest and most lasting impression on these individuals (although Jamaican reggae artists like Peter Tosh, Jimmy Cliff, and Burning Spear, and African reggae artists like Blondy, the Nigerians Evi-Edna Ogholi and Majek Fashek, and the South African Lucky Dube have also exercised considerable influence).

That reggae played such a crucial role in the spread of the Rastafarian movement in West Africa is not surprising in view of the special emphasis placed on music, and in a number of instances popular music, among many of the region's new urban-based religions. Strong links are known to exist, for example, between juju music and the Nigerian

Aladura churches, while many of the musicians and hymns used by independent Christian spiritual churches in Ghana are drawn from highlife music, these churches having in turn spawned a new and popular musical genre called "spiritual highlife."

Local Rasta musicians, who have been instrumental in promoting the spread of the religion and culture of Rastafari throughout West Africa, continue to function as outspoken critics of the divisive ethnic tendencies that work to impede national as well as regional unity and growth. With their apparent lack of ethnic chauvinism, their frequent use of English as a lingua franca in their song texts, and their intense commitment to pan-Africanism, these Rasta musicians provide a highly visible model for young West Africans seeking to establish wider, more inclusive networks of allegiance and belonging.

Cannabis

As is the case with reggae music, the use of and trade in cannabis in West Africa is closely associated with the culture of Rastafari. Like their Jamaican counterparts, most West African Rastas smoke cannabis on a regular basis and a substantial number are or have in the past been involved in either selling or smuggling this illicit substance. Interestingly enough, Ghanaians will commonly refer to any young man seen hanging out on the street smoking or peddling *wee* (a local Ghanaian term for cannabis) as "Rasta."

Among other things, the smoking of cannabis by Rastafarians serves to create well-defined social boundaries between those who belong or who may someday belong to the movement and the rest of society. And while few West African adherents would openly admit that their involvement with Rastafari was in any way influenced by their prior or parallel involvement with cannabis, my research shows that in a substantial number of cases initial entry into the local Rasta scene came about as a direct result of an adherent's fondness for smoking cannabis and/or his dealings with Anglo-Jamaican or West African Rasta cannabis dealers. And while an interest in reggae may have provided the initial attraction for many to the movement, the smoking of cannabis (often in the context of extended "reasoning sessions") continues to serve as the most prominent ritual activity engaged in by West African Rastas everywhere, an activity that helps to inspire in neophytes a serious commitment to Rastafari by providing the insights, visions, and transformative experiences that commonly lead to full-scale conversion to the faith.

From a review of the available archeological, historical, and ethnographic records, it would appear that the introduction of cannabis into West Africa was relatively recent. In his comprehensive survey of the diffusion of cannabis in

Africa, Brian Du Toit remarks upon the lack of evidence for the traditional use of cannabis among West African populations and claims it to have only been widely available in the region beginning around the time of the Second World War (when it may have been introduced into Nigeria and perhaps a handful of other West African countries by sailors and soldiers returning from the Far East, the Middle East, and North Africa).

A number of my informants (both Rastas and non-Rastas) claimed that the spread of reggae and the culture of Rastafari into West Africa was directly responsible for the upsurge in cannabis use that occurred here within the past two decades. In Ghana, for example, the cultivation and smoking of cannabis has, in a relatively brief amount of time, increased to the point where 1990 was officially declared the Year of War on Wee (*People's Daily Graphic*, 6 January 1990). Taking into account on the one hand the evidence outlined above that points to the fairly recent introduction of cannabis use into West Africa and on the other the strong links that exist everywhere throughout the region between cannabis and the culture of Rastafari, these claims may in fact be quite valid.

The Fashions

One of the most conspicuous aspects associated with the spread of the Rastafarian movement in West Africa is the fashion trends it has inspired here, trends engendered in large part by the widespread popularity and proliferation of reggae music. In a great many instances the appropriation of Rasta fashions represent the total extent to which young West Africans personally relate to Rastafari, especially those who maintain no connections with any of the organized Rasta communities currently functioning in the region and who as a result have no role models, overarching precepts, and/or standards of behavior to guide their actions and education in the faith.

Throughout West Africa, dreadlocks, Rasta colors, and Dread Talk are frequently adopted and utilized by young men wishing to identify with this global, pan-African movement or subculture, many of whom possess little or no insight into the historical, religious, and sociopolitical aspects of Rastafari. Among these individuals, the appropriation of Rasta-inspired hairstyles, clothing, ornaments, and speech represent little more than another Western or transnational pop-culture idiom that can be manipulated and employed to serve specific ends—like joining a reggae band and touring the U.S. and Europe, interacting with young American and European tourists, and gaining the respect of one's peers that comes with the appearance of being trendy.

Among more orthodox West African Rastas, on the other hand, these components serve merely as external symbols of their inner commitment to the fundamental precepts and practices of the faith, as well as the "higher consciousness" they have achieved as a result of their adherence to Rastafari, their alienation and estrangement from the wider society, and their solidarity with other young people of color the world over who, driven by deep religious convictions and/or ardent anticolonial fervor, have donned the mantle of Rastafari.

With young Nigerians in Kano performing break dancing routines at traditional durbar celebrations honoring the local Emir; with American rap and reggae music blaring out of discos, bars, and taxi cabs throughout the region; with movies, television shows, and music videos featuring African-Americans all the rage in places like Lagos, Banjul, and Accra; and with U.S. cosmetic companies hawking their products to an increasingly receptive African market—it is impossible to overlook or ignore the expanding role played by Caribbean and African-American pop music, fashions, and culture in urban, and to an increasing extent even rural, Sub-Saharan Africa. Viewed from this perspective, the spread of Rastafarian music and fashions in West Africa represents just one more chapter in the ongoing assimilation by urban-based African youth of the culture of the Diaspora (which in many instances includes elements derived in part from indigenous African sources).

Beliefs and Practices

The strong emphasis and reliance placed on Judeo-Christian teachings by Rastafarians—mainly the Hebrew Bible and the millenarian visions and prophesies found in the New Testament Book of Revelation—also accounts in part for the movement's initial as well as continued success in attracting adherents in West Africa. For individuals already familiar with the basic tenants of Christianity as a result of the missionary work carried out on the continent by Catholic and Protestant evangelical orders over the course of the past four centuries, the Biblical themes and imagery pervading Rastafarian belief, symbolism, and practice have a familiar ring and are readily understood and accepted. But perhaps more importantly, Rasta critique of the dogmatic, institutionalized "white" versions of Christianity promulgated by American and European Christian denominations finds a particularly receptive audience here, especially among those who find it difficult accepting in toto these alien and Eurocentric teachings and practices.

In Ghana, for example, close to 90 percent of all Rastas come from Christian families, and the prevailing Christian orientation of contemporary Ghanaian urban society appears to function as one of the major factors responsible for the relatively large number of orthodox Rastas found in this country today. Further confirmation of this hypothesis may be gleaned from the fact that the only other nation in West Africa that harbors a sizable Rastafarian population, Nigeria, also contains the largest total number of Christians in the region (approximately 25 million).

Similarly, the relatively small following the movement has garnered in Senegal and other Islamicized West African nations may be due in large part to the absence there of large Christian populations. With the exception of a handful of Rastas living on the island of Gorée off the coast of Dakar, few Senegalese or Gambian Dreads (the term "Dread" is often used by Rastas to refer to anyone who sports "dreadlocks") express any serious interest in or commitment to the more religiously based precepts of Rastafari. Few of these individuals actively read the Bible and most refuse to accept the divinity of Haile Selassie or to adhere to the biblically derived prescriptions and prohibitions that are part and parcel of the "authentic" Rastafarian experience. In most cases Senegalese and Gambian Dreads either continue to maintain a nominal affiliation with Islam or claim to identify with no organized religion whatsoever.

But it is in their commitment to and outspoken support of pan-Africanism and black solidarity where non-religiously oriented West African Dreads exhibit the greatest degree of concordance with their more orthodox brethren. Concerns centering around the political and economic unification of Africa and the global brotherhood of all peoples of African descent inform the thinking and rhetoric of nearly all West Africans who consider themselves "Rastas," and such thinking serves as one of the few areas in which all adherents (both the serious and the more fashion-minded) can agree.

And while many West African Rastas do little more than pay lip service to these principles, a number are actively working to bridge the gap dividing themselves from other Africans and peoples of African descent. Through their establishment of business partnerships with individuals from other ethnic groups and African countries, as well as with blacks from Europe, the Caribbean, and the U.S.; through their promotion of interethnic and interregional cooperation and understanding via the universal language of pop music; and perhaps most importantly, by serving as role models for others seeking an alternative to the ethnic rivalries and chauvinism that still feature so prominently in many contemporary African nations—West African Rastas view themselves (and the movement as a whole) as being vital contributors to positive social change and active participants in the centuries-long struggle to make the pan-African dream of ethnic, regional, and continental unity a reality.

Transnational Apostles from Jamaica

Due in large part to the Afrocentric nature of Jamaican Rastafarianism and the strong emphasis placed within the movement on African repatriation, various Jamaican and Anglo-Jamaican Rastas have, over the course of the 1980s and 1990s, either resettled in or traveled extensively throughout the African continent. A number of these individuals proved instrumental in spreading the gospel of Rastafari during their sojourns.

By far the most orthodox and committed Rastas are those affiliated with communities established by Jamaicans or Anglo-Jamaicans, many of whom have continued to remain in close contact with the groups they spawned. It was one such Jamaican apostle of Rastafari who founded a chapter of the Ethiopian World Federation (EWF) in Accra, Ghana during the mid-1970s. Similarly, it was an Anglo-Jamaican who in the early 1980s established the small Senegalese Rasta community on Gorée island. The largest group of Rastas in Ghana, the Twelve Tribes of Israel, was originally set up as an African branch of the Jamaican organization by its leader, the Prophet Gad, who made a trip to Ghana in the mid-1980s for this very purpose. To this day many Jamaicans and Anglo-Jamaicans associated with the Twelve Tribes continue to maintain close personal contacts with the Ghanaian chapter, spending long periods of time or just vacationing for a few weeks with the group at their headquarters compound in Labadi Beach, Accra.

It is the literature provided by these transnational apostles of Rastafari and, perhaps more importantly, the deeper personal knowledge and understanding of the movement that they bring to Africa (a much deeper knowledge and understanding than can be gleaned through just listening to reggae music) that accounts in large part for the more serious attitudes and commitment shown by West Africans affiliated with either the EWF, the Twelve Tribes, or the Gorée community.

West African and African Roots of Jamaican Rastafarian Religion

On the whole, West African Rastas refuse to view their adoption of Rastafarian religious beliefs and practices, music, and fashions as a "rip off" of Western culture. Rather, they believe that what they borrowed, they borrowed from their own people—that is, their "cousins" across the Atlantic in Jamaica. Being immediately recognizable and fairly easy to imitate and reproduce, Rastafarian religion and culture, according to many West African Rastas, has its origins in Africa and as such has legitimate meaning for all Africans and people of African descent who have shared in the suffering and humiliation brought upon their race through centuries of European exploitation and colonial/neocolonial domination.

The donning of dreadlocks provides an excellent example of African influence on the development of Rastafarian culture in Jamaica. According to the West Indian scholar and educator Horace Campbell, Jamaican Rastas first began wearing their hair in "locks" in the 1950s after seeing photos of dreadlocked Mau Mau in Kenya (matted locks served as a major symbol of this East African anticolonial movement, and the potent image of dreadlocked Kenyan freedom fighters took physical shape in Jamaicans' appropriation of the hairstyles of these "dread" African warriors).

Another more recent and equally compelling example of African influence on Jamaicans' adoption of dreadlocks has its origins in Ethiopia. According to Stephen Davis (1982), the photo of two dreadlocked Ethiopian Coptic Christian monks (bahatawis) that appeared in the December 1970 issue of National Geographic is the single most frequently cited piece of evidence used by Jamaican Rastas to support the claim that their adoption of matted locks is in fact rooted in ancient African practices.

Interestingly enough, the sporting of dreadlocks may represent a pan-African phenomenon. In Senegal the royal soldiers (tyeddo) of pre-Islamic Wolof society wore their hair in "long knotted tresses," as do present-day members of the heterodox, Islamic-based Baye Faal sect. Furthermore, throughout much of West Africa matted hair is frequently worn by traditional healers and religious practitioners—in Ghana, for example, many Akan fetish priests and priestesses (okomfo) have in the past worn and continue to wear their hair in such a manner.

West African Rastas, like their Jamaican counterparts, also hold that the Bible and European Christianity represent a corruption of original African sources (i.e., those rooted in ancient Judaism and Ethiopian Coptic Christianity), and as such justify their appropriation and use of specific aspects of European religion as a means (though admittedly imperfect) by which they can reconnect with ancient African religious traditions.

Rastafarianism and the Study of the African Diaspora

Ultimately, the African Diaspora experience must, as the Nigerian scholar Okon Edet Uya contends, be placed within the basic continuum of the African experience, both representing the "saga of African people and [of] culture challenged, modified and altered by the New World milieu" (1982: 79). The transplantation of Jamaican Rastafarian reli-

gion, music, and culture onto West African soil represents another important link in this centuries-old process wherein blacks and black culture in the Diaspora have had a substantial impact in Africa (one earlier example being the various African-American religious organizations like the A.M.E. Church that were active in establishing both religious and political ties between African-Americans and Africans from the late eighteenth century onward).

With the serious efforts being made by multinational corporations to find new markets for their products and the continuing inclusion of the developing world into the global capitalist economy, with the growing sophistication and reach of the electronic communications media and the rapidly expanding influence of transnational popular culture, with blacks in the Diaspora actively seeking to renew or recreate cultural links with their ancestral homeland, and with Africans looking to connect to the global system and forge closer ties with their "brothers" and "sisters" in the Diaspora, it is getting increasingly more difficult to untangle the many threads of influence and cross-influence currently stretching between and uniting Africa, Europe, and the Americas. By examining the various manifestations of the Jamaican Rastafarian movement functioning in West Africa today, and by isolating and describing a number of these individual threads, a more accurate and engaging picture of the complex processes, personal networks, and institutional linkages that have in the past bound and continue to bind Africans to the New World African Diaspora is revealed.

Neil J. Savishinsky

See also Jamaica, African-Derived Religions in; Rastafari; Rastafari in Global Context; Rastafari in the U.S.; West African Religions

Bibliography

Alleyne, Mervyn. (1988) *Roots of Jamaican Culture.* London: Pluto Press.

Bishton, Derek. (1986) *Black Heart Man: A Journey Into Rasta.* London: Chatto and Windus.

Campbell, Horace. (1987) *Rasta and Resistance.* New Jersey: African World Press.

Chevannes, Barry. (1994) *Rastafari: Roots and Ideology.* Syracuse, NY: Syracuse University Press.

Clarke, Peter B. (1986) *Black Paradise: The Rastafarian Movement.* Great Britain: The Aquarian Press.

Clarke, Sebastian. (1980) *Jah Music: The Evolution of the Popular Jamaican Song.* London: Heinemann Educational Books Ltd.

Crahan, Margaret E., and Franklin W. Knight, eds. (1979) *Africa and the Caribbean: The Legacies of a Link.* Baltimore: The John Hopkins University Press.

Davis, Stephen. (1982) *Reggae International.* New York: Rogner and Bernhard.

Du Toit, Brian M. (1980) *Cannabis in Africa.* Rotterdam: A. A. Balkema.

Jules-Rosette, Bennetta, ed. (1979) *The New Religions of Africa.* New Jersey: Ablex Publishing Corporation.

Martin, Tony. (1983) *The Pan-African Connection: From Slavery to Garvey and Beyond.* Dover, MA: The Majority Press.

Savishinsky, Neil J. (1994) "The Baye Faal of Senegambia: Muslim Rastas in the Promised Land?" *Africa* (The Journal of the International African Institute) 64, 2: 211–219.

———. (1994) "Rastafari in the Promised Land: The Spread of a Jamaican Socioreligious Movement Among the Youth of West Africa." *African Studies Review* 37, 3: 19–50.

———. (1998) "African Dimensions of the Jamaican Rastafarian Movement." In *Chanting Down Babylon: The Rastafarian Reader,* edited by Nathaniel S. Murell, William D. Spencer, and Adrian A. McFarlane. Philadelphia: Temple University Press, 125–144.

———. (1999) "Transnational Popular Culture and the Global Spread of the Jamaican Rastafarian Movement." In *Across the Boundaries of Belief,* edited by Mort Klass and Maxine Weisgrau. Boulder, CO: Westview Press, 347–366.

Stapleton, Chris, and Chris May. (1987) *African All-Stars: The Pop Music of a Continent.* London: Paladin Grafton Books.

Steffens, Roger. (1990) "Reggae Returns to the Motherland." *The Beat* 9, 2: 14–15.

Turner, Harold W. (1979) *Religious Innovation in Africa: Collected Essays on New Religious Movements.* Boston: G.K. Hall and Co.

Ullendorff, Edward. (1989) *Ethiopia and The Bible.* London: Oxford University Press.

Uya, Okon Edet. (1982) "Conceptualizing Afro-American/African Relations: Implications for African Diaspora Studies." In *Global Dimensions of the African Diaspora,* edited by Joseph E. Harris. Washington, DC: Howard University Press.

Religious Skepticism in Africa

Studies of skepticism in African religious practice have inevitably been framed in contrast to the European religious experience. It has long been argued that to understand religion in Western society, you have to study how religion responds to skepticism. Indeed, the history of religious change in the West is often imagined as a tense struggle between "science"—a form of knowledge which emerged out of an increasingly organized skeptical scrutiny of biblical dogma—and an ever-threatened congeries of religious "beliefs," which often articulate a certain skepticism for the truth claims of empiricism and rationality. The Western religious experience is generally conceived as a growing shift away from religion as a totalizing truth and toward religion as a contested belief—a faith a person clings to despite the evidence.

Because studies of African religion have tended to emphasize (if usually implicitly) the contrast between traditional religious experience and modern (and Western) experience there has not, until recently, been much in the way of sustained studies of indigenous forms of skepticism as constitutive of African religious practices. Skepticism has largely been invisible as a topic in its own right—as a glance at the index of any one of the vast number of monographs on African religious practices would reveal. This lack of attention to skepticism is because it has usually been assumed that so-called traditional African religions are very different from Western religions forged and tempered in a modern skeptical climate. Traditional African religions are, after all, religions without texts, and therefore they have no easily accessible body of dogma that can be critically scrutinized for internal contradictions and inconsistencies. Traditional religions have generally been conceived and analyzed as practices reflecting implicit and collective "representations" of the world rather than practices communicating explicit systems of thought that invite personal conscious reflection, revision, and critique. People, so the scholarly wisdom had it, did this ritual or participated in that ceremony out of habit, because everybody else did, because that was what always was done, rather than out of personal conviction or commitment. They knew rather than believed.

Nevertheless, arguably the best analysis of skepticism in traditional religion—Evans-Pritchard's *Witchcraft, Oracles and Magic Among the Azande*—was written about an African society. By focusing on the various ways that religious practices persist despite considerable skepticism about, for example, the efficacy of particular diviners, the accuracy of particular witchcraft accusations, and the efficacy of particular rites and charms, Evans-Pritchard's monograph explicitly blurred the boundaries between Western and African modes of thought. For Evans-Pritchard, Zande were just as suspicious of the truth claims of others, just as likely to test forms of curing and so forth empirically as were Westerners. The rationality of their skepticism was, however, piecemeal, and therefore the exposure of charlatans, or of medicines ineffectively administered had the unintended consequence of reinforcing their general belief that the world indeed contained witches and medicines useful for countering their deleterious effects. Evans-Pritchard's monograph, which was first published in 1937, continues to be crucial for appraisals of skepticism in the context of African religious practice.

Skepticism and Rationality

Among the many anthropologists who have followed Evans-Pritchard's lead, Horton (1973, 1993) stands out for a certain clarity of vision and serves as a convenient foil for those who disagree with what they deem as an overly intellectualist approach to religion. Horton has consistently posed two questions. He has asked why "beliefs" would change—why people would stop performing traditional rituals and accepting as obviously true the knowledge that underwrote such rituals. And he has asked why people in African villages would continue to practice, continue, seemingly, to believe, even when exposed to more rationally compelling alternatives. In general Horton has argued that West African religious systems generate considerable piecemeal skepticism. Horton argues, for example, that spirits in this region are local and "personalized" and human-beings relate to them in ways analogous to the ways they relate to one another. Spirits are more powerful and invisible, but otherwise they are like human beings. They can be construed as fallible, inefficient. As people doubt the efficacy of particular spirits, shrines can go out of fashion. However, like Evans-Pritchard before him, he assumes that such piecemeal skepticism will never amount to a paradigm shift. You doubt particular spirits, particular shrines, particular diviners, but not all diviners and shrines, and above all not the existence of spirits whose wills are being divined.

Initially, Horton made what others characterized as a too-sharp dichotomy between modern Europe and traditional Africa for why African traditional "thought" persisted despite skepticism. In Horton's scheme, African religious thought operated as a "closed system" because root paradigms—whether spirits existed or not—were not put to the test of "refractory experience." Yet, in explaining why such beliefs would not be so tested, Horton could not depend on experience alone—a "lack of awareness of alternatives" (1967: 156). He also had to posit an intrinsic psychologically motivated inertia to belief systems in general and to traditional belief systems in particular—to the "sacredness of beliefs" and to "anxiety about threats to them" (1967: 156). Consequently, according to Horton, Africans often

clung to "traditional" beliefs despite becoming aware of alternative explanations.

Later Horton moved away from a theory of persistence, which depends on individual psychology, and towards a more interactionist theory of social relations. In this newer version, which scholars such as Anthony Appiah find much more compelling, Horton stresses an atmosphere of social accommodation that he claims typifies discourse in villages. According to Appiah, cosmopolitan Africans visiting or returning to postcolonial villages persist in performing rituals, and continue to pay lip service to their efficacy, rather than openly doubt or criticize their more rustic peers because they wish to create and maintain this society of shared interest. Skepticism, as it were, takes a back seat to the desire to go on acting together as a community.

Skepticism and Performance or Embodiment

More recently, scholars of African religion have been much less interested in exploring local religious practices as manifestations of "thought"—as a logically coherent "system" of "beliefs"—than were Horton and Evans-Pritchard. Most scholars working in the field today (year 2000) believe that they have gotten "beyond belief" and are working on something at once much more essential about local religious practice and also less obviously ethnocentric—its embodied factuality. Such an argument against the intellectualization of traditional religion has several virtues that make it nearly unassailable. In the first place, it is easy for its proponents to play the ethnocentrism card. If the "West" is generally assumed by its faithful natives to be the seat of (an exaggerated and complacently arrogant) assertion of the power of reason, and if "belief" is itself a rather narrowly Christian (and late-modern at that) concern, then discussions of religious practice that begin with bodies and embodied experience seem not only universally more applicable, but less ethnocentric as well. Yet, an approach to African traditional religion as embodiment has, until recently, tended to finesse the problem of skepticism. If you do a ritual, say, if you bend your knee, or cut into yourself in an initiation, then you (as many scholars of religion put it) "inscribe" thought into your body. Belief has nothing to do with experiences so tangible, so sensible. Nor, it is often assumed, is this sensibility subject to a kind of endogenous challenge. Body trumps mind. Skepticism is not an issue.

However, it is precisely in new approaches to the topic of embodiment that skepticism is becoming a central theme, particularly in the emerging literature on that subset of embodiment most likely to reveal its limits—possession, masquerade, performance, parody. Mimicry and parodic imitation have long been assumed an essential component of "traditional" African religious practice. In Igbo, as elsewhere, youths learned religious activity by largely unsupervised, often overtly playful, imitation. If elders had their secret societies and rites, then juniors developed parallel institutions. Young people made offerings to shrines of their own invention; they initiated still younger people in cults they created and maintained. Yet, "play" has ambiguous connotations, as Margaret Drewel (1992) emphasizes for Yoruba religious practices where unmasking is as crucial to performative efficacy as is masking. Indeed, one of the most imaginative anthropologists writing on the performative in religion today, Michael Taussig, has argued that forms of embodied skepticism are nearly universal elements of religious practice, and that this is especially apparent when we look at the rapid juxtapositions of exposing, hiding, and revealing that are a central component of secret society legerdemain among such organizations as Poro and Sande in West Africa. The playful incorporation of skepticism can make belief as easily as it can unmake it.

Such insights have had a particularly powerful influence on current appraisals of possession cults and practices in Africa. Such performances have been of longstanding scholarly interest because mimetic performances such as masquerades have been seen as iconic of traditional religious practices—practices enacted, rather than thought. More recently, though, there has been a resurgence of interest in such practices as exemplifications of indigenous response to colonialism and its aftermath. In Africa (as in the Caribbean and the colonial world generally), colonized people often performed masquerades or possession rites in which they embodied or mimicked their colonial rulers. Although it is generally assumed that such forms of embodiment entailed the mimetic appropriation of foreign powers, it is also usually the case that such performances are also inevitably portrayed as parody founded in skepticism about foreign authority. As Graham Huggans notes, anthropologists have often evinced a romantic double standard in such analyses. On the one hand, scholars have stressed that mimesis is parody when they interpret such performances as allegorical critiques of the powers-that-be. On the other hand, scholars have tended to stress the power of mimesis to embody and make experientially real when analyzing mimetic enactments of indigenous authorities and spirits. But closer attention to the ways that skepticism can itself be integral to religious performance will lead to more subtle analyses of the knowing or witting qualities inherent in the mimetic embodiment. Skepticism, in short, can be as much a part of religious practice as it can be of religious belief. And a closer scrutiny of the embodiment of skepticism in collective religious practices such as secret society initiations, possession cults, and ceremonial masquerades will go a long way toward blurring the too-sharply drawn boundary between traditional religion characterized by habitual public acts and a modern religion characterized by private introspection.

Eric Gable

Bibliography

Appiah, K. Anthony. (1991) "Is the Post- in Postmodernism the Post- in Postcolonial?" *Critical Inquiry* 17: 336–357.

——. (1992) *In My Father's House: Africa in the Philosophy of Culture*. New York: Oxford University Press.

Drewal, Margaret Thompson. (1992) *Yoruba Ritual: Performers, Play, Agency*. Bloomington: University of Indiana Press.

Evans-Pritchard, E. E. (1937) *Witchcraft, Oracles and Magic among the Azande*. Oxford: Clarendon Press.

Horton, Robin. (1967) "African Traditional Thought and Western Science." *Africa* 37, 2: 155–187.

——. (1973) "Levy-Bruhl, Durkheim and the Scientific Revolution." In *Modes of Thought: Essays on Thinking in Western and Non-Western Societies*, edited by Robin Horton and Ruth Finnegan. London: Faber and Faber.

——. (1993) *Patterns of Thought in Africa and the West*. Cambridge: Cambridge University Press.

Huggan, Graham. (1998) "(Post) Colonialism, Anthropology, Mimesis." *Cultural Critique* 38.

Ottenberg, Simon. (1989) *Boyhood Rituals in an African Society: An Interpretation*. Seattle and London: University of Washington Press.

Stoller, Paul. (1995) *Embodying Colonial Memories: Spirit Possession, Power, and the Hauka in West Africa*. London: Routledge.

Taussig, Michael. (1993) *Mimesis and Alterity: A Particular History of the Senses*. New York: Routledge.

——. (1999) *Defacement: Public Secrecy and the Labor of the Negative*. Berkeley: University of California Press.

Revival

Revival is Jamaica's most widespread folk religion, with Zion and Pocomania its two major forms. The name, Pocomania, is a corruption of Pukumina or Pukkumina (Seaga 1969), and was used deliberately to deride African-Jamaican religious beliefs and rituals, with the explanation that it meant "a little madness," in Spanish. Pukumina first came to public attention in 1861. The Spanish had fled in 1655.

History

Revival had its origin in a religious movement known as Myal, which first came to public attention at the time of the slave rebellion led by Taki in 1760. Although Taki was Akan-speaking, he was able to mobilize Africans of other ethnic origins through the beliefs and rituals of Myal, in a manner identical to the ritual origins of Haitian Vodou in the Bois Caiman. Schuler (1979) quite correctly identifies Myal as a pan-African religious movement. Boukman, who presided over the Bois Caiman ritual, was described as having come from Jamaica (see Deren 1953). Not surprisingly, therefore, Myal beliefs, while acknowledging a Sky-God, the supreme creator, focused on an order of lesser spirits and powers, ritual interaction with whom empowered human beings in this world.

Myal incorporated into its belief systems certain important elements, following the encounter of the Africans with Protestant Christianity in the last quarter of the eighteenth century. Jesus, John the Baptist, Isaiah, Jeremiah, and other Old Testament prophets were some of the new powers incorporated, along with the Bible itself, as important sources of power. With these changes, an important trend in Myal became known as the Native Baptists, after the leading European nonconformist religion preached to the slaves. Despite the missionaries' attempt to keep their religions pure, many of those they relied upon as deacons and other officers were also leaders of Native Baptism. For example, the main organizer of the 1831–32 Slave Rebellion, Samuel Sharpe, was a Deacon in the Baptist Church but a leader among the Native Baptists as well. Myal not only unified the people with a common worldview and empowered them to resist the order of slavery, it also fortified them in their community life, where it developed rituals of healing and carried out campaigns against *obeah*, or sorcery.

In late 1860, a Christian revival that began in the anglophone north Atlantic spread through Jamaica, providing Myal with a new platform of evangelism under a new name, Revival. But as the religious revival deepened, early in the following year, a new variant, Pukumina, also appeared. Revivalists since distinguish the two trends as "the sixty" and "the sixty-one" people.

The principal difference between the two lay in the acknowledgment and worship of earth-bound powers by Pukumina, including the "fallen angels," such as Satan and Rutibel, who in the Christian cosmology were ejected from heaven, and ground spirits, including ancestors. To the Pukumina trend, spirits were defined by their power, not their morality, and in this sense they might be of service to mankind. For this reason, Pukumina was associated in the public mind with *obeah*. The Sixty trend, or the Zionists, on the other hand, worshipped the sky-bound spirits, the foremost being Jesus and some of the Old Testament prophets, though they acknowledged the existence of the earthbound and ground spirits. Their manner of spirit possession remains also different. In Zion the male turban leaves the crown of the head open, to receive the sky-bound spirits; in Pukumina the entire head is wrapped.

Under the charismatic preacher and healer, Alexander Bedward, and his Zion Apostolic Church, Revival Zion grew into a powerful religious force between the 1890s and 1920, with branches all over Jamaica and among the migrant communities in Central America. Bedward's potential as a political force, given his anticolonial rhetoric, was not lost on the colonial government, which succeeded in using the power of the state to crush him. The colonial government would have recalled, as did Bedward, the 1865 Morant Bay Rebellion led by Paul Bogle, and the 1831–32 Sam Sharpe Rebellion: both leaders were Native Baptists.

In the succeeding decades, particularly after the Second World War, Revival underwent a series of far-reaching changes, the most profound being its merging with North American Pentecostalism (Austin-Broos 1998). Many captains and shepherds, as Revival leaders are known, sought to overcome the social stigma attached to their churches by affiliating with these foreign groups. It brought them greater access to material resources, social prestige, and legitimacy in the eyes of the state; and allowed them to retain the central aspect of the folk religion, namely personal empowerment through spirit possession. In return, such Revival groups set aside their belief in any spirit but one, namely the Holy Spirit. The result has been a very sharp rise in the number of adherents of the various Pentecostal churches and sects. Between 1943 and 1960 Pentecostalism doubled its proportion of nominal membership, from 6 percent to 12 percent. Now they account for 30 percent of the population, including large and still-growing sections of the middle classes.

Second, Revival groups have undergone other forms of modernization. Churches and dioceses have replaced the bands and yards, Pastor or Bishop replaced Captain and Shepherd. Instead of the street corner and village square meetings, campaigns and regular Sunday worship are the norm.

Ritual Worship and Possession

Revival worship has a basic two-part structure. The first part is devoted to the singing of choruses to the rhythms of the bass and rattler drums, and to reading of the psalms. In the

Shrine for the River Maid, one of the spirit messengers venerated by Revival Zionists. Holy Mt. Zion Baptist Church, Yallas, St. Thomas, Jamaica, 1996. PHOTO COURTESY OF DIANNE M. STEWART.

second the spirits are invoked and possession takes place. In Zion, possession follows trumping, a form of hyperventilating, accompanied by forward and backward steps, while moving sideways, counterclockwise in a circle. In Pukumina, full possession, by earthbound spirits such as the Water Mother and the Indian Spirit, is sudden, without warning, and is followed by "labouring," as trumping is called.

Revivalists meet several times a week, as do most Christian churches. Sunday would be "divine worship," with specific liturgies, such as healing and prayer meeting, taking place at night during the week. Baptism takes place in the larger rivers and follows days, sometimes weeks, of seclusion and fasting.

By far the most important ritual is the Table, so called because of an actual table spread with fruits, bread, and other foods, and decorated with candles and flowers and other sacred objects, around which members dance counterclockwise, and possession occurs. Tables, which last three, sometimes four days, are held periodically for thanksgiving, petition, destruction, appeasement, or other reason. The ritual sacrifice of a goat is made on the final day.

Healing

Many Revival leaders build their churches on reputations for healing. This takes the form of first divining the nature of the ailment or problem, and its causes, and then prescribing prayers and charms, or administering ritual baths and other efficacious acts. Healing sites, once known as balm yards, are now churches, sometimes erected in the leader's yard. As adepts, Revival leaders are consulted for a range of problems—fate, bad luck, mental deterioration, or physical debility—and by clients spanning a range of social classes.

Seals

These are sacred objects, including certain herbs and shrubs, and sacred spaces associated with the spirits. The main exterior seal, located at the front of the church, is marked by a flag pole surrounded at its base by basil, mint, croton, leaf-of-life, or other plants sacred to named spirits, and marked off by whitewashed stones. Inside the church the main seal will be the altar. All seals, however composed, will also have a basin or a glass of water, and, at night or during ceremonies, a candle.

Leadership, Structure, and Gender

Revival leadership may be female as well as male, but the proportion is skewed in favor of males. A female leader is called Mother. Wedenoja (1979) notes that most Mothers are healers, and most *obeah* practitioners are male.

Generally, a Mother who is the founder of the church, although the main authority, will appoint a male as pastor, whose role is to preach. Beneath the pastor are the deacons, usually males but sometimes females, and next in hierarchy the evangelists, missionaries, and armor bearers. Evangelists are mandated to explain the sacred scriptures, missionaries to proselytize, and armor bearers to discern the spirits, "to cut and clear" evil and danger, and assist the leader when possessed.

Barry Chevannes

See also Jamaica, African-Derived Religions in; Obeah in the West Indies

Bibliography

Austin-Broos, Diane. (1997) *Jamaica Genesis: Religion and the Politics of Moral Orders.* Chicago & London: University of Chicago Press.

Deren, Maya. (1953) *Divine Horsemen: The Living Gods of Haiti.* New York: Thames and Hudson.

Schuler, Monica. (1979) Myalism and the African Religious Tradition in Jamaica. In *Africa and the Caribbean: The Legacies of a Link*, edited by Margaret E. Crahan and Franklin Knight. Baltimore: Johns Hopkins University Press.

Seaga, Edward. (1969) "Revival Cults in Jamaica: Notes towards a Sociology of Religion." *Jamaica Journal* 3, 2.

Wedenoja, William. (1978) "Religion and Adaptation in Rural Jamaica." Ph.D. dissertation, University of California.

Santeria

Santeria is a New World Neo-African religion that is a transatlantic extension of Yoruba religion into the African Diaspora. The religion of the Yoruba people, mainly found in the countries of Nigeria, Togo, and the Republic of Benin, is an ancient religious system with millions of adherents on the African continent as well as in the Americas. Just as there are regional and doctrinal variants within the Christian, Buddhist, and Islamic religions, there are Yoruba religion variants as well, and Santeria is simply a Cuban variant of this older, more extensive Yoruba religious tradition.

Placing Santeria in the context of New World African religions highlights its relationship to other kindred African-based religious forms as well as its hybrid heritage. Santeria is but one of a series of related, Yoruba-based religions that exist in the Caribbean, in Central and South America, and, now, in the United States. The Shango (or Orisha) religion of Trinidad and Grenada is an example, as are the Xango and Candomblé of Brazil and Kele on St. Lucia. Yoruba religion also entered prerevolutionary Haiti, where it united with the religions of people Central and Africa to create the religion of Vodou (Vodon). Since all of these religions have been influenced by Christianity to a greater or lesser extent, and some of them by other religions as well, all of them are places where mixtures of preexisting religions have given rise to new religious forms that are both hybrid and distinctive. In the case of Santeria, that hybrid heritage includes Christianity (in the form of Roman Catholicism), traditional African religion (i.e., *orisha* worship as practiced by the Yoruba people of Nigeria, Togo, and Benin), and Kardecan spiritism, a religion which originated in France in the mid-nineteenth century and later became fashionable throughout the Caribbean and South America.

History and Development

The history of Santeria begins with the formation of the Yoruba people and their entry into Nigeria at some point before 1000 CE. Yoruba religion and the Yoruba city-states evolved there and a network of interrelationships and mutual influences developed between the Yoruba and Benin kingdoms in Nigeria and also the kingdom of Dahomey. The large-scale involvement of these states in the Atlantic slave trade is a late phase of their precolonial development and overlaps with a prolonged period of warfare among the three kingdoms during the eighteenth and early nineteenth centuries.

In the 1760's Cuba's agricultural economy blossomed in response to the European and North American demand for sugar and tobacco, and centuries of stagnation gave way to a ravenous hunger for African slave labor. In earlier periods Yoruba were only a small segment of the enslaved Africans brought into Cuba, but, in the peak years of the trade (1840 to 1870), more than one-third of all the Africans imported into Cuba were Yoruba.

From about 1760 through the 1860s there evolved in Cuba a kind of Yoruban Afro-Catholicism that probably constituted the earliest form of Santeria. Just as the kingdom of Spain and the slave trade had appropriated the Africans' bodies and freedom; and the Cuban plantation system the slave's labor power; Cuba's Catholic church attempted to appropriate the Africans' spiritual and religious life. Catholic churchmen tried a number of strategies to convert the Africans to their religion and to guide religious change within both the free and the slave African populations. In the urban areas they established what were called *cabildos*. *Cabildos* were Catholic fraternities and mutual-aid societies whose membership was organized on the basis of belonging to particular African ethnic groups, among them the Yorubas, there called Lucumi. Their activities included catechism, devotion to a specific Catholic saint, participation in Carnival celebrations, and providing funeral expenses for members. In some cases these Afro-Catholic religious societies were able to buy their members out of slavery and, through the Catholic church, secure them literacy and the rudiments of an education. In Catholic Cuba, then, the *orisha*—the deities of the Yoruba pantheon—became identified with the saints of Roman Catholicism and began to be called *oricha* (Sp.) and *santo* interchangeably, hence the term Santeria, meaning worship of the saints. In the early phases of their development, the *cabildos* in which this took place were encouraged to exhibit the African cultural symbols distinctive to their groups in the public celebrations of Catholic feast days and even to inject an African flavor into their Catholic religious rites. But over the course of time, as it became clear that these African cultural and religious expressions were not about to disappear, both the church and the state began to suppress these influences and, late in the nineteenth century, they suppressed the *cabildos* themselves.

The spiritist literature of Hippolyte Rivail, also known as Allan Kardec, began to arrive in Cuba in the 1850s. Since Roman Catholicism was not only the state religion of colonial Cuba but also the only legal religion there, Kardec's books had to be smuggled in along with other banned texts. In the decade of the 1870s, adherence to the teachings of this French engineer who claimed his books were dictated to him by spirits became a veritable rage throughout the Spanish and French Caribbean, and Central and South America as well. Cuba was no exception. The middle-class

Creoles of the time embraced Kardecism as a scientific, egalitarian, and potentially liberating ideology that opposed the Catholic church and Spanish domination. When Kardecism seeped down to the lower classes and out into the rural areas, it blended with the prevalent forms of folk Catholicism and became more oriented towards healing than the middle-class version had been. Another change was that the during their trances both white and black spiritist mediums manifested spirit guides belonging to African ethnic groups. The spirit guides who spoke through them were Yoruba, Mandingo, Mina, and Kongolese people who had suffered and died during the slave trade.

Spirit mediumship was an element shared by both Kardecism and Santeria and allowed them to be integrated with relative ease. Some Santeria priests and priestesses came to view an apprenticeship in Kardecism as a valid and even necessary preparation for Santeria and became adepts in both groups. Although these dual adepts began by keeping the two practices apart (performing them at different locations, separating their orisha and spiritist altars), some intermixture developed anyway and elements of Kardecism's ideology and healing methods were incorporated into Santeria.

After winning independence from Spain, the middle and ruling classes of Cuba took a variety of stands in relation to the Afro-Cuban religions. Policies of racial and cultural "whitening" and assimilation alternated with religious persecution. Criminalization of the religion preceded an era of cultural appropriation by Cuba's artistic avant-garde as the society grappled with the place of Santeria in the island's national culture and identity in the 1930s and 1940s. This social ambivalence was not altered by the Communist revolution of 1959.

Because of this complex process of development there is a great deal of diversity in the details of ideology and ritual practice among Santeria groups in Cuba. At one end of a continuum of belief and practice are Santeria communities whose rites closely imitate Catholic ceremonies. These ceremonies contain "Our Fathers," "Hail Marys," candles, incense, and the appropriate Catholic ritual gestures and material symbols. At the other end are groups in which these Catholic elements never appear. In these groups neither chromolithographs nor statues of the saints adorn the altars. Symbolic colors and stones represent the santos/orisha and the emphasis is on ceremonial spirit possession.

Despite the correspondences set up between the Catholic saints and the African deities, and the influences derived from Kardecism, the ritual system and cosmology of Santeria remain essentially African in character, with a strong fidelity to Yoruba practices. Among the faithfully preserved aspects of Yoruba religion in Santeria are the names and personalities of the Yoruba deities, divination procedures, ceremonial spirit possession and trance, Yoruba liturgical music and musical instruments, dance as a medium of worship, Yoruba language prayers and incantations, beliefs in ancestor veneration and reincarnation, and sacrificial practices. Santeria also contains a vast compendium of herbal medicine and healing ritual, much of which also has African analogues.

Organization and Leadership

The basic unit of social organization in Cuban Santeria is the *casa* (Spanish) or *ile* (Yoruba). This is a personal network which may, or may not, overlap with a specific residence or physical location. The *casa*, or "house," is the sum of the individual relationships linking each devotee to a specific Santeria priest or priestess (called a *santero* or *santera* respectively) who is seen as its head. Each devotee acquires this link through an initiation ceremony that is performed by the head priest and culminates in the presentation of a set of bead necklaces to the devotee. This is the lowest level of initiation and membership in the *casa*. The *casa*, then, is focused on a single *santero* or *santera* who has initiated one or more devotees at this level and is entitled to advise and assist them, and guide their development up to and beyond initiation into the priesthood.

An idiom of ritual kinship links the *santero/a* and the devotee in a relationship of godparent to godchild to create a kind of religious family. The ritual kinship idiom extends outward to include other godchildren of the same godparent, and also extends vertically, going back in time via the godparent through a series of godparent-godchild relationships that link previous generations of priests and priestess into a extended family of priestly ancestors. This ritual genealogy is recited frequently since these past *santeros* must be invoked during libations, initiations, and all the major ceremonies the *santero/a* performs.

The devotees will secure whatever religious services they need from the godparent or through referrals by the godparent, and within the Santeria community identify themselves as belonging to that person's *casa*. The godparent-godchild relationship is expected to be lifelong and if, for whatever reason, the relationship is definitively broken, the devotee may affiliate with another *casa*, but, especially if the new house is not ritually related to their old one, they will be asked to go through the entrance ritual again and receive another set of necklaces to replace the previous ones.

Although most *casas* function as autonomous units, in some instances the *casa* extends beyond the direct links between devotees and their godparents to include other *casas* established by priests or priestesses initiated by the godparents. The existence of *casas* like this depends on the ability of the focal priests to exercise control and authority over the priests they have initiated, and, through them, over those priests' godchildren. Some of these large *casas* are named, have long histories, and include several living generations of priests. These *casas* approximate the older institution of the Afro-Catholic *cabildo* and probably descend from them. For a few Cubans, Santeria practice is essentially a family tradition, passed down family lines without any real connection to *cabildos* or *casas*. This is a tradition in which people provide rituals and services primarily for themselves and their biological families rather than for nonfamily members. Santeria is not congregational and so does not depend upon the existence of a temple or church building. Most worship takes place outside in natural settings or in front of the altars devotees keep in their homes.

Beliefs

Santeria has an intensely hierarchical, human-centered and this-worldly cosmology that does not draw a line between either the human and the divine or the living and the dead.

The Pantheon

Its theology recognizes a Supreme Being called variously Dios, Olodumare, Olorun, or Olofi. The Supreme Being created the universe and all things in it including the *orisha* who are the main focus of worship. The *orisha* are powerful spiritual beings—at once forces of nature, guardians of particular facets of human life, and magnified human personality types—sent by Olodumare to populate the earth and order its life. The number of *orishas* known to Yorubas in Nigeria is very large, but only a few of these are prominent in Santeria. Also important are the spirits of people who have died.

The ancestral Dead are closer to human beings than they are to Olodumare or the *orisha*, and deceased family members continue to have an intimate connection with their descendants. The ancestral Dead are capable of intervening in the affairs of their living relatives and can be called upon to intercede with the *orisha*. Though they are less powerful than the *orisha* and less attention is given to them, they still receive respect and veneration, and every devotee has a small shrine devoted to them.

An encompassing energy, *ache*, flows through and envelopes the entire hierarchy of beings from Olodumare, through the *orisha*, the ancestral dead and other spirits, plants, animals, and the entire natural world. This energy can be manipulated through rituals and can be made to manifest itself in different forms. Each *orisha* has its own divine power, or *ache*, through which it is sustained and through which it acts on the aspects of the world over which

Olodumare gave it dominion. When the *orisha* first formed human beings they also taught them how to access each *orisha's* power. This knowledge is the basis of the rituals and doctrines of the different priesthoods. Through these rituals devotees expect to achieve an active harmony with the supreme being, a closer relationship with the *orisha* and the natural world, and increased control over the forces affecting their lives and personal fortunes.

Fate, Personal Destiny, and Reincarnation

According to Santeria belief, every human being bows at the feet of Olodumare to receive a personal destiny before being born into the world. Unfortunately, the memory of their contract with God is erased from people's minds once they are born. Human beings would go on and live their lives in complete ignorance of their fates if it were not for Santeria's two major divination systems: the *dilloggun*, sixteen cowries whose backs have been filed off and which all priests and priestesses can utilize; and the Ifa oracle, a more complex and elaborate system involving a divining chain and a number of auxiliary objects, which is practiced by a specialized male priesthood whose members bear the title *babalawo*, meaning "father who owns the secret." The outcomes of both divination systems direct people to a large body of myths, proverbs, and poetry, which diviners are supposed to have memorized. This divination literature chronicles events from the lives of the *orisha* as well as ancient people from the distant past. It also describes the problems and situations they faced, how these problems are related to the *orisha* or the ancestral Dead, and how the person can resolve the problem through offerings, sacrifices, and other sorts of rituals, prayers, specific social actions, and the development of personal character.

While Santeria has much to say about fate and the path through this life via its divination systems, it has little to say about death or the afterlife. Generally, devotees and priests believe in a kind of progressive reincarnation in which a person evolves to become better, wiser, and more elevated over the course of several lifetimes.

Ceremonies

Spirit mediumship is at the core of the *bembe*, the most characteristic form of communal ceremonial life in Santeria. *Bembes* are great feasts and celebrations often correlated with the feast days of those Catholic saints who have *orisha* associated with them or coincident with the initiation of a priest or priestess, the anniversary of priest's initiation, or the fulfillment of some other religious obligation of the priest to the *orisha*.

These ceremonies fall into two main parts: the invocation of the ancestral Dead and the *orisha*, and, then, the presence of the *orisha* among their devotees. The invocations are libations and prayers performed before an altar in Lucumi, the Cuban variant of the Yoruba language, which is the liturgical tongue for all religious observances in Santeria. These are followed by music directed at the altar by an ensemble of drummers who accompany call and response chants sung in Lucumi by a motionless group of standing devotees. In the second part of the ceremony, devotees perform dances imitating the personalities, attributes, and attitudes of the each of the *orisha* as their chants are sung in an attempt to attract the *orisha*, to compel them to come and take over the bodies of their priests and priestesses, thereby manifesting themselves in a visible human form. When this event occurs, the possessed priests and priestesses are garbed in the colors and clothing appropriate to the *orisha* who has mounted them and they interact with the community of believers: talking to them, confronting them, consoling them, healing them, making prophecies, or recommending that they carry out certain rituals. Eventually the *orisha* return to their invisible realm, leaving behind a group of exhausted priests who have no memory of what their bodies did while they were possessed. A purification rite ends the second part of the ceremony; a communal meal follows; and, finally, there is a general distribution of a portion of the fruits and desserts which have surrounded the altar throughout the events.

Healing

For Santeria, much of human suffering is rooted in disturbed relationships among human beings, and in faulty relationships between human beings and the ancestors, spirits, and *orisha*. The most prominent *orisha* are associated with specific parts of the body which they can afflict as well as cure. The ancestral Dead intervene in offenses against family morality; sometimes this results in sickness. Malicious people do not necessarily cease to be so once they have died and may seek out victims, on their own or at the bidding of a sorcerer. Since people are ignorant of their fates—and the ancestors, *orisha*, and spirits affect people whether they are aware of them or not—the first resort is to divination. Divination diagnoses the problem, describing its spiritual and psychological components in terms of the influence of the *orisha*, the ancestral Dead or malign spirits, and suggests solutions based on the traditional precedents found in its oral literature.

Diviners often prescribe offerings or animals sacrifices for the *orisha* or the Dead, as well as a number of purification procedures called *despojos* (Sp., cleansings). The Santeria healers' arsenal also includes other ritual procedures dealing with the spiritual aspects of the problem. The person's head—considered to be the seat of their personality, the conduit for their fate, and point of intimate contact with the *orisha*—is a major focus of ritual attention. Sometimes the solution requires the person to deepen their involvement in Santeria by undertaking a number of initiations, up to and including initiation into the priesthood. This can be a long-term process monitored by divination at each step of the way. Initiation and acquiring the consecrated material media through which one relates to the spiritual world help alleviate suffering and misfortune by giving people a measure of control over the forces affecting their lives.

Santeros also use herbal infusions, decoctions, and baths to treat the physical and spiritual bases of a broad range of problems. These range from bad luck to spirit intrusion, from discolored hair to venereal disease, tuberculosis, and skin inflammations; and include respiratory infections, difficult childbirth, and abortion. In some of the more spiritist oriented groups, *santeras* employ a kind of psychodrama, and also use other techniques aimed at their clients' internal conflicts, that may have psychotherapeutic value.

Current State

Santeros fought on both sides during the 1959 Cuban Revolution and, although some *santeros* fled the island and the revolution and went into exile, many could not and many did not. Early on, the Cuban government declared that there is no contradiction between the aims of religion and the aims of socialism, but relations between all religious groups and the Cuban Communist Party have vacillated.

In the early years of the Revolution, there were times when groups of Santeria devotees came into violent conflict with the Revolution, only to be equally violently suppressed. Sometimes ceremonies were interfered with or broken up, and sacrificial animals seized. On the one hand, the Castro government has given the Afro-Cuban religions public recognition as an element of the national cultural heritage and as "people's folklore." In this guise Santeria is represented in an important anthropological museum and by government-sponsored dance and theatre companies that travel throughout Cuba and to foreign countries. From the 1960s through the 1980s, though, government pressure kept prominent Santeria singers from performing sacred music on the radio or in public outside of the government-sponsored groups. A famous 1987 interview in which Castro used the Catholic-based Latin American Liberation Theology Movement as an example of how religion and revolutionary struggle could be complementary forces ushered in a new period of tolerance for Santeria practitioners, who were—at once—ardent supporters of the revolution, openly religious, and also considered themselves Catholic.

The spread of Santeria outside of Cuba owes its origins mainly to Cuban exiles who left in 1959 and also those who were part of the exodus from the port of Mariel in 1980. They brought Santeria to the United States, where it spread to other Latino communities, and to African-American, white, and Asian communities as well. From these contacts in the United States Santeria has made its way back into the Caribbean to Puerto Rico and the Dominican Republic. Cubans transplanted the religion to Mexico, and also to Venezuela where the *santos/orishas* have already begun to win new devotees and exert an influence on the Venezuelan popular religions. A small number of exiled *santeras* have made their way to Europe and, through them, Santeria became established in Spain, spreading from there to other European countries.

In the year 2000 a Santeria revival was occurring in Cuba, fueled by increased tolerance from the government and increased contacts within the Santeria diaspora created by the Revolution. And, aided by high speed travel and the Internet, there was greater intercommunication between a growing number of people on four continents who saw themselves as devotees of the *orisha* and as participants in the wider Yoruba religious diaspora of which Santeria formed a part.

George Brandon

See also Cuba, African-Derived Religions in; Ifá; Healing in African and African-Derived Religions; Kardecism; Yoruba Religion

Bibliography

Abimbola, Wande. (1973) *Ifa Divination Poetry*. Bloomington: Indiana University Press.

Akinjobin, I. A. (1972) "Dahomey and Yoruba in the 19th Century." In *Africa in the Nineteenth and Twentieth Centuries*, edited by Joseph C. Anene and Godfrey Brown. New York: Humanities Press, 255–269.

———. (1966) "The Oyo Empire in the Eighteenth Century: reassessment." *Journal of the Historical Society of Nigeria* 3, 3: 449–460.

Bascom, William. (1980) *Sixteen Cowries: Yoruba Divination from Africa to the New World*. Bloomington and London: Indiana University Press

———. (1972) "Shango in the New World." Occasional Publication of the African and Afro-American Institute University of Texas, Austin, no. 4.

———. (1969) *Ifa Divination: Communication between Gods and Men in West Africa*. Bloomington: Indiana University Press.

———. (1952) "Two Forms of Afro-Cuban Divination." *Proceedings of the Twenty-fourth Conference of Americanists*, 196–199.

———. (1950) "The Focus of Cuban Santeria." Southwestern Journal of Anthropology 6, 1: 64–68.

Bermudez, Armando Andre. (1967) "Notas para la Historia del Espiritismo in Cuba." *Etnologia y Folklore* 4: 5–22.

Brandon, George. (1991) *Light from the Forest: How Santeria Cures through Plants*. New York: Blue Unity Press.

———. (1993) *Santeria from Africa to the New World: The Dead Sell Memories*. Bloomington: Indiana University Press.

Brown, David H. (1996) "Toward an Ethnoaesthetics of Santería Ritual Arts: The Practice of Altar-Making and Gift Exchange." In *Santería Aesthetics in Contemporary Latin American Art*, edited by A. Lindsay. Washington, DC: Smithsonian Institution Press.

Cabrera, Lydia. (1975) *El Monte*. Miami: Ediciones Universal.

Cancio, Felix. (1981) "Cuba and Venezuela: Religious Communities in the Americas." *Caribe* 5, 4 (Fall/Winter): 9–10.

Castro, Fidel. (1987) *Fidel and Religion: Castro Talks on Revolution and Religion with Frei Betto*. New York: Simon and Schuster.

Crahan, Margaret (1979) "Salvation through Christ or Marx: Religion in Revolutionary Cuba." *Journal of Inter-American Studies and World Affairs* 21, 1 (February): 156–184.

Edwards, Gary, and John Mason. (1985) *Black Gods—Orisha Studies in the New World*. Brooklyn, New York: Yoruba Theological Archministry, 488 Putnam Avenue, Brooklyn, NY 11221.

Harber, Francis. (1980) *The Gospel According to Allan Kardec*. Brooklyn, NY: Theo Gaus, Ltd.

Herskovitz, Melville J. (1937) "African Gods and Catholic Saints." *American Anthropologist* 39: 639–643.

Kardec, Allan. (1963a) *El Libro de Los Espiritus*, 9th edition. Tlacoquemecatl, Mexico: Editorial Diana, S.A. .

———. (1963b) *El Libro de Los Mediums*, 9th edition. Tlacoquemecatl, Mexico: Editorial Diana, S.A. .

Miller, Ivor. (1999) "The Singer as Priestess: Interviews with Celina Gonzalez and Merceditas Valdes." In *Sounding Off!, Music as Subversion/Resistance/Revolution*, edited by Ron Sakolsky and Fred Wei-Han Ho. Brooklyn, NY: Autonomedia, 287–306.

Murphy, Joseph M. (1993) *Santería: African Spirits in America*. Boston: Beacon Press.

Ortiz, Fernando. (1921) "Los Cabildos Afro-Cubana." *Revista Bimestre Cubana* 16: 5–39.

———. (1959) *Los Bailes y el Teatro de los Negros en el Folklore de Cuba, La Habana*. Havana: Editorial Letras Cubanas.

———. (1973 [1906]) *Hampa Afro-Cubana: Los Negros Brujos*. Miami: Ediciones Universal.

Pollak-Eltz, Angelina. (1994) *Religiones Afroamericanas Hoy.* Caracas: Editorial Planeta Venezolano.

Rogers, Andres R. (1973) *Los Caracoles: Historia de Sus Letras.* Washington, DC: RICO Publishing.

Sandoval, Mercedes Cros. (1979) "Santeria as a Mental Health Care System: An Historical Overview." *Social Science and Medicine* 13B: 137–151.

———. (1975) *La Religion Afrocubana.* Madrid: Colleccion Libre Plaza Mayor.

Thompson, Robert Farris. (1984) *Flash of the Spirit: African and Afro-American Art and Philosophy.* New York: Vintage Books.

Trotman, David V. (1976) "The Yoruba and Orisha Worship in Trinidad and British Guyana: 1838–1870." *African Studies Review* 19, 2 (September): 1–17.

Santeria, Material Culture

The world of Santeria practitioners is imbued with the *ashé*, the energy, of the *orisha*, spirit beings. Every natural and manufactured object is associated with an *orisha* and understood to contain the *ashé* of that *orisha* to a greater or lesser extent. In practical terms this means that a *santero* or a *santera* (Sp. initiated priest) does not need to go to a church, synagogue, or mosque to communicate with his or her gods. They are everywhere, at the crossroads, in the river and at the ocean, in the thunder and lightning, in plants and animals, in the color of flowers or clothing, and even in the persona of the policeman or physician. In many cases the relationship between the object and the deity is so strong that the object is considered to contain the living presence of the *orisha* itself.

Although they can be found everywhere, in a very special way the *orisha* live in the homes of their priests. As part of the initiation ceremony a set of objects are especially imbued with the *ashé* of different *orisha*. These objects called *fundamentos* (Sp. foundation) are placed in ceramic or wooden containers and given to the new priest to care for. All initiated priests have a set of these *orisha fundamentos* in their homes. Santeros consider these *fundamentos* to be the actual living presence of the *orisha* whom they worship and propitiate. Each priest builds a chapel for her *orisha* somewhere in her home. Often a spare bedroom, dining area, or perhaps only a closet is given over to the *orisha*; sometimes one or more *orisha* altars are constructed in the living room or another public area of the home. In these spaces the priest places the colorful pots containing the *orisha fundamentos* and surrounds them with objects representing aspects of the *orisha*. The *orisha fundamentos* are so sacred

that only initiated priests can look at them. However with the permission of the priest, anyone can visit the *orisha* chapel, observe the containers holding the *fundamentos* and the objects surrounding them and pay tribute to the *orisha* inside the containers.

The study of material culture is the study of the things people use in their everyday lives. When we study the material culture of religion we study the things people use in their spiritual and religious lives to learn more about them and more about their religion. A fruitful area for such study within Santeria is the consideration of the altars, often called *tronos* (Sp.), or thrones, which practitioners build for special occasions. When a new priest is initiated, an area is demarcated to house him or her and the new *orisha fundamentos* created during the one-week initiation period. This is called the *trono del asiento*, (Sp. throne of the "crowning" ceremony). Whenever an *orisha* is honored with a drum dance an altar called a *trono del tambor* (Sp. throne of the drumming) is constructed for that *orisha*. But the most common of these special altars are those constructed to celebrate a priest's initiation into the religion, the *trono del cumpleaños*, (Sp. birthday throne).

Birthday Thrones

Once a year, on the anniversary of their initiation, *santeros* build a special type of altar for their *orisha*. These so-called birthday thrones are elaborate displays meant to beatify, honor, and entertain the *orisha*. It is in front of these thrones that many people are first introduced to the *orisha*. Because these thrones are created from a cluster of objects that can be used to tell stories of the *orisha*, they provide a marvelous site of material culture analysis. Every throne is different. Even two thrones built by the same priest at two different times are different. At the same time every throne follows certain rules that makes it possible for us to "read" a throne as if it were a sacred text.

When first seeing a throne a visitor may be struck by the vibrant colors and the expanses of cloth. Unless they are enshrouded in cloth, the various ceramic vessels that hold the *orisha fundamentos* will be visible. But also noticeable are the panoply of objects—including fruit, flowers, candles and an array of consumer goods—that surround the *orisha* containers. The throne is constructed by forming a "room" within a room. Cloth is hung to form the walls and ceiling and a straw mat covers the floor. Once the cloths are hung and the mat is in place the throne area becomes sacred space. Only initiated priests may stand under the cloth ceiling or on the mat below. The principle *orisha* of the priest, that is the *orisha* of her head, is generally in the highest or most prominent position. The containers for the other

SANTERIA BIRTHDAY THRONE OF CHANGO LADÉ.

Houston, Texas 1999. © Mary Ann Clark, 1999.

Santeria birthday throne

A priest of Shango built this altar for the eleventh anniversary of his initiation. Panels of red and white cloth delimit the space, while hanging raffia mark the front boundary of the throne. The vessels of each Orisha are elevated on cloth-covered pedestals of various heights. The Orisha can be identified by their colors, their positions, and the objects surrounding them. Shango, the primary Orisha of this priest, assumes the highest spot in the center of the display while Yemaya, who is the second Orisha or "mother" of this priest, has the next highest position directly in front of him.

Arrayed in front of Shango are the goddesses associated with this most manly of Orisha. To the left sits Oshun in a bright orange pumpkin-shaped pot. Just to the right, slightly elevated, is the blue and white pot of Yemaya, the mother of the Orisha. Continuing to the right is Oya and in front of her pot is the pot of Obba. In the mythology, Obba, Oya and Oshun are wives or consorts of Shango while Yemaya is said to be his mother. Obba, Shango's first or legitimate wife, has the position of honor directly in front of Yemaya, while the other two wives are arrayed beside and behind her. The two small pots and dolls of the Ibeji, the sacred twins, sit in front of their purported mother, Oshun.

Obatala, the father of all the Orisha, occupies a position nearly as high as Shango, but on the far left of the display. His white sopera sits on a pedestal draped with white and silver cloth. In front of him, sitting on a pedestal in the shape of an elephant, is Oshanla, another of the white Orisha who is said to be especially peaceful and calm. To their right hidden behind cloth and raffia are the mysterious Orisha Babalu-Aiye and his mother Nana Buruku.

Santeria birthday throne

The dark wooden container to the right of the female Orisha belongs to Aganyu, another fiery Orisha who is often considered to be the father of Shango. At his feet sit the pots of Inle the hunter-physician with his wife Abata.

Objects on and around the Orisha tell a portion of their stories. For example, the cascade of beads enveloping Shango's betea reminds us that as the king of Oyo he was entitled to wear a beaded crown with a veil of beads. It also alludes to the priest's sacred name *Chango Ladé,* crown of Shango. The leopard cloth under the betea of Aganyu is another sign of kingship among West Africans. The merry-go-round-style horse with a fireman's hat topping the pole barely visible on the far right are both New World additions to Shango's material culture. The horse, painted red and white—Shango's colors—reminds us of the role of mounted troops in the formation of the Oyo Empire, while firemen and their equipment are extensions of his association with lightning and fire.

We recognize Inle's pot not only by its color but also by the stethoscope balanced on its lid. Obba's tools are positioned on a wooden anvil in front of her pot while Oya's hang from a chain draped on the lid of her pot. Along the bottom of the photo we see machetes, sugarcane and arrows. These are associated with The Warriors Eleggua, Ogun, and Ochosi who sit on the floor, outside the frame of the photo, guarding the display.

WARRIORS OF MARY ANN CLARK.

Houston, Texas 1995. © Mary Ann Clark, 1995.

Warriors of Mary Ann Clark

Like many followers of Santería, one of my first initiations was to receive the group of Orisha called *Los Guerreros* (Sp. the warriors). The warrior Orisha included in this ceremony are Eleggua, Ogun, Ochosi, and Osun. As part of this initiation I received a set of objects (called *fundamentos*) consecrated with the *ashé* (power) of these Orisha. After the ritual I brought them home and put Eleggua, Ogun, and Ochosi on the floor near the door of my home and Osun on the top shelf of a bookcase. All of these Orisha are protectors who will fight for the well-being of their devotees, but each has a special role based on his place in the larger pantheon.

As the messenger of the gods and the Orisha who is believed to open and close both spiritual and material doors, the figure of Eleggua can be found not only in Santería homes but also in the homes and temples of Orisha-worshippers around the world. The *fundamento* of this Orisha can take many forms. The most common in the United States is a six-inch stylized head fashioned of cement with eyes and mouth of cowry shells embedded in the surface. My Eleggua, however, is in an alternate form made from a small conch shell with the cowries in a single line. When properly propitiated, followers believe that Eleggua "opens the door" to opportunities, love, wealth, and all the good things in life while shutting out all illness, bad fortune, and the like.

Ogun and Ochosi live together in an iron caldron. The railroad spikes and other metal objects recall Ogun's association with blacksmithing, metal work, and all forms of technology. In addition to his role as a fierce fighter, Ogun can use his trademark machete to clear my path of obstacles on both the visible and invisible plane. Ochosi, the hunter deity, not only fights for his devotees but also with his clear eye and flawless aim helps me determine the goals to aim for and the best

Warriors of Mary Ann Clark

path to reach them. As the true warrior Orisha Ogun and Ochosi provide the tools and manpower required to protect me from my enemies and to "wage war" on them when necessary.

The *fundamento* of Osun, a silver cup mounted on a six-inch pole and decorated with tiny bells, is not placed on the floor near the other warriors but on a shelf high above my head. From his high perch Osun watches my life. He warns only of the most serious dangers. If he falls over, I know that my life is in jeopardy. Divination will determine the source of the problem and the remedy for escaping death.

Once a week I give Eleggua, Ogun, and Ochosi special ritual attention in the form of candles, water, rum, tobacco, red palm oil, and other materials. During this short ritual I tell them what is happening in my life, thank them for past favors, and ask for their blessings, help, and protection. As I have performed these simple ritual acts over the years, my relationship with these deities has grown and deepened. I see their actions in my life and I recognize the blessings they have brought through my door.

orisha are arranged around the primary orisha. Often the priest may use stories from Santeria mythology to decide where to place each individual container. For example, a priest of Shango might cluster the pots of Obba, Oya, and Oshun, the wives and consorts of Shango, around his *betea* (Sp. the wooden container used for the *fundamentos* of Shango and Aganyu). Another might separate Obatala, who is the father of the *orisha* and is associated with the sky, from Olokun, who is considered by many to be the king of the ocean depths, because of Olokun's challenge to Obatala's supremacy.

Since each *orisha* is associated with a particular color or combination of colors, it is easy to determine which *orisha* live in which containers. A pure white pot generally belongs to Obatala, a golden yellow to Oshun, blue belongs to Yemaya and Olokun (who share the ocean), maroon is the color of Oya, while her rival Obba generally lives in shades of pink. Shango and Aganyu, who are both fiery deities, live in wooden containers because they are considered too strong for delicate porcelain. The warrior orisha Eleggua, Ogun, and Ochosi live in open containers. Eleggua is often placed in unglazed pottery while Ogun and Ochosi live together in an iron pot.

Position is also important. The pot of Obatala, who is the oldest and wisest of the *orisha*, is usually one of the highest in the display. Often it is put above and behind the primary *orisha* where it might watch over and guard from above. The warriors generally sit on or close to the floor, toward the front of the display where they may guard from below. *Orisha* who are rivals in the mythology may be separated while those who are companions or lovers are kept together. The two *orisha* who are the spiritual mother and father of the priest generally are given higher positions.

Although a throne may be constructed solely of bolts of cloth and the *orisha* containers, often santeros include other objects that they associate with the individual *orisha*. Obatala, who is associated with everything white, may have birds or elephants, silver bells, or swords surrounding his pot. Shango, who was the fourth king of the city of Oyo before he was an *orisha*, might have a small horse, or a beaded crown, both symbols of royalty among the Yoruba people of Africa. Yemaya, the queen of the ocean, may have a boat or seashells, a ship's wheel or anchor. Oshun is associated with sweet water, the river. All things yellow belong to her including honey, sunflowers, champagne, and golden bracelets. Ochosi, the hunter, may have a bow and arrow or a statue of a deer. Inle, the fisherman, may have a fishing rod or small fish. Since he is also associated with the healing arts, many *santeros* put a physician's stethoscope with his pot. Each priest is free to include as many or as few objects as she wants on her throne. What she includes tells us about her understanding of each *orisha* and its place in the pantheon.

Food of the Gods

Food, both raw and processed, is also used on the birthday throne. Fruit is spread out in front of the altar space as a gift to the deities. Along with the fruit the display also includes a variety of deserts and cakes. All of this food is also representative of the *orisha*. Pears, milk, meringue, and eggs are offered to Obatala, while Shango is represented by bananas, and okra, both phallic symbols, and his trademark corn pudding. Along with bananas, okra and corn are especially potent phallic symbols. Not only are both the appropriate shape and teeming with seeds, but both are noted for their milky semen-like juice.

Female fertility is noted in Yemaya's watermelons and Oshun's pumpkins. In both of these cases the shape of the fruit is reminiscent of the pregnant belly while the plethora of seeds inside speak of fertility. And while the pumpkin reminds us of Oshun's trademark color, the watermelon by its very name reminds us of Yemaya's association with the ocean. All this fruit is purchased from the market and placed in front of the throne in an area called the *plaza* (Sp. market). At the end of the birthday celebration, the fruit is distributed to all those who attended the party. Imbued with the *ashé* of the *orisha*, it is taken home and eaten or used in other rituals.

Along with the fruit and other offering to the orisha, the priest makes a set of desserts for them. Designed to soothe and "cool" the *orisha*, these desserts also are representative of them. Obatala may be presented rice pudding, a white coconut custard called *tembleque* (Sp. shaking, trembling, quaking), or mountains of meringue. While Oshun, the queen of gold, love and sensuality, may be given *flan*, a lush egg pudding with a caramel sauce, Yemaya favors the harsher flavors of brown sugar and molasses. Yemaya's dessert is a dish called *Coco Dulce*, which is coconut cooked in brown sugar and molasses. These desserts tell us more about these *orisha*. Yemaya is often seen as the harsh and stern older woman. She is the mother who is both loving and strict. She is often identified as African by her dark completion. In Cuba, Oshun is often portrayed as the softer, sweeter, younger woman with the honey complexion. But the relationship between these foods and the *orisha* are multifaceted. Obatala, whose name means "the king of the white cloth," is more than a shaky old man. His food reminds us that old age is the time of wisdom, serenity, and calm judgment. Yemaya and Oshun both represent all facets of women's lives. Just as it is important to remember that honey can sour and a firm hand can be hidden within a soft exterior, we are reminded that both of these *orisha* are forces to be respected, not to be trifled with or trivialized.

Sugar in all its forms is an essential ingredient in the *orisha* desserts. Sugar has many connotations: it sweetens the road of life and enhances feelings of joy and well-being. In the form of rum and other alcoholic drinks it enlivens the spirit and lubricates conversation. Sugared desserts presented to the *orisha* carry all of these significations, but in this context they also serve as a reminder that it was the cultivation of this white gold that brought most Africans to the Caribbean and to Cuba. The proliferation of sweet desserts serves to remind devotees of the many ancestors who brought their religious culture with them on the Middle Passage and of those who reconstructed that religious culture in an alien world.

Human Figures

It is interesting to note that there are few if any human figures found on Santeria altars, neither birthday thrones nor other types of altars. Figures are not entirely absent. During their development of the religion in Catholic Cuba, *santeros* associated each *orisha* with a Catholic saint. Obatala became associated with the Virgin of Mercy (*Virgen de Merced*), who is clothed in white, and Shango with St. Barbara (*Santa Barbara*), who wears his colors of red and white. Yemaya was seen in the face of the Virgin of Regla (*Virgen de Regla*), while Oshun was associated with the Virgin of Charity of Cobre (*Virgen de Caridad de Cobre*), who is the patron saint of Cuba. Many santeros associated the *orisha* with other figures as well. Obatala has many characteristics of the Buddha. Native American figures grace Ochosi altars while mermaids can be found near Yemaya and Olokun. Some *santeros* collect dolls dressed in the clothing associated with the *orisha* and you may find these dolls included on some *tronos*. But these dolls and other figures, even the Catholic saints, are not understood to be the *orisha*. The *orisha* themselves are embedded in the *fundamentos* hidden inside the pots and other containers. Like the fruit, the colored cloth and the other objects found on *orisha* altars, these figures are not understood to represent the *orisha*. Rather they represent some aspect of the *orisha*, or, as is often the case with the dolls, they may represent the priests and followers of the *orisha* placed on the altar.

This scarcity of human figures occurs because *santeros* don't need human representations of their *orisha*. In other religions where the deities are invisible and distant it may be necessary to create representations to draw the human mind in worship. In Santeria, however, the deities are always present in the *fundamentos*, the living presence of the *orisha*. It is these sacred objects that enable the *santeros* to pay homage to their deities directly. In addition to the *fundamentos*, the *orisha* are represented by a wide-ranging array of natural and manufactured goods. All of these objects point to particular aspects or characteristics of the *orisha* so as to draw their worshipper into a relationship with the *orisha* themselves, but they are not the *orisha* in the minds of devotees.

Mary Ann Clark

See also Ogun; Orisha; Oshun; Santeria; Yoruba Religion

Bibliography

Brandon, George. (1993) *Santeria from Africa to the New World: The Dead Sell Memories.* Bloomington: Indiana University Press.

Brown, David H. (1993) "Thrones of the Orichas: Afro-Cuban Altars in New Jersey, New York, and Havana." African Arts 26, 4: 44–59, 85–87.

———. (1996) "Toward an Ethnoaesthetics of Santería Ritual Arts: The Practice of Altar-Making and Gift Exchange." In *Santería Aesthetics in Contemporary Latin American Art,* edited by A. Lindsay. Washington, D.C.: Smithsonian Institution Press.

———. (1999) "Altared Spaces: Afro-Cuban Religions and the Urban Landscape in Cuba and the United States." In *Gods of the City: Religion and the American Urban Landscape,* edited by R. A. Orsi. Bloomington: Indiana University Press.

Clark, Mary Ann. (1998) "Santería." In *Sects, Cults, and Spiritual Communities: A Sociological Analysis,* edited by W. W. Zellner and M. Petrowski. Westport, CT: Praeger Publishers.

———. (forthcoming). "Asho Orisha: Material Culture as Religious Expression." In *African American Religion,* edited by A. B. Pinn. Gainesville: University Press of Florida.

Curry, Mary Cuthell. (1997) *Making the Gods in New York: The Yoruba Religion in the African American Community.* New York: Garland Publishing, Inc.

Flores-Peña, Ysamur, and Roberta J. Evanchuk. (1994) *Santería Garments and Altars: Speaking Without a Voice.* Jackson: University Press of Mississippi.

Mason, John, and Gary Edwards. (1981) *Onje Fún Òrisa (Food for the Gods).* Brooklyn: Yoruba Theological Archministry.

Murphy, Joseph M. (1993) *Santería: African Spirits in America.* Boston: Beacon Press.

———. (1994) *Working the Spirit: Ceremonies of the Africa Diaspora.* Boston: Beacon Press.

Thompson, Robert Ferris. (1993) *Face of the Gods: Art and Altars of Africa and the Africa Americas.* New York: The Museum for African Art.

Santería, United States

Santería is a popular name for a religious tradition that has developed in Cuba from roots among the Yoruba people of present-day Nigeria. In the late eighteenth and early nineteenth centuries hundreds of thousands of Yoruba men and women were enslaved and transported to Cuba to labor in the island's burgeoning sugar industry. The Yoruba were called Lucumi in Cuba, and in several cities and towns they were able to form *Lucumi cabildos*, assemblies of people from their regions of origin in Yorubaland. At the meetings of the *cabildos*, they spoke their own language, sang old songs, and worshiped the *orishas*, the Lucumi deities.

Santería Beliefs and Practices

Lucumi theology recognizes one Supreme Being, called variously Olodumare, Olorun, or Olofi. The Supreme Being created the *orishas* to populate and civilize the earth and endow it with the essential powers necessary for the harmonious existence of all living things. Each *orisha* was given a particular form of divine power, called *aché*, which sustains the *orisha* and all the realms of creation in its purview. While there are innumerable *orishas* throughout the world, a few have special prominence in Santería. Eleggua is the restless *orisha* of beginnings who stands at life's crossroads. Ogun is the *orisha* of iron and technology. Ochossi is *orisha* of the hunt, weaponry and the forest. Obatala is the white-clad senior king of the center of the world. Yemaya is the maternal *orisha* of the ocean waves. Chango splits the skies with thundering power and lightning justice. Oya is a warrior woman with hurricane force. Ochún is a beautiful, gentle river with hidden depths. Babaluayé is the *orisha* of the tranformative power of disease.

When human beings were formed by the *orishas* they were taught how to access each *orisha's aché* in order to achieve harmony with the Supreme Being, nature, and themselves. Before each individual is born into this life he or she kneels before the Supreme Being and receives a personal destiny that can be met with knowledge or ignorance; and so each life can be a rewarding challenge or a frustrating struggle. The key to the liberating knowledge of one's destiny lies in two great systems of divination: Ifá and *dilogun*. These oracles are collections of verse which outline the stories of the *orishas* at the time of the earth's formation, their struggles to bring it to order, and the solutions they found to achieve success. When individuals encounter problems in life they come to a Santería priest or priestess and ask him or her to consult Ifá or *dilogun* on their behalf. Special nuts or shells are thrown and the pattern revealed by their random fall corresponds to the verses appropriate to the seeker's problem.

Practitioners of Santería testify to the extraordinary accuracy with which their problems are diagnosed by the oracles and the remarkably effective solutions that they prescribe.

The Ifá and *dilogun* oracles usually prescribe offerings to a particular *orisha* that allows the devotee to gain access to its *aché* and to develop a mutual bond of respect and devotion between the *orisha* and the human devotee. The offerings take many forms depending on the advice of the oracle. A devotee may be instructed to construct a display of the *orisha's* favorite foods and drinks or perform the *orisha's* special prayers and songs. These may be offered at a home altar, or at sites in the natural world associated with the *orisha* such as rivers or woods, or occasionally at large feasts when the entire community is welcomed to take part.

As the exchange of *aché* with the *orishas* becomes a natural part of a devotee's life, one particular *orisha* will usually begin to reveal itself as the devotee's special patron or patroness. When divination confirms this special relationship, preparations are made to initiate the devotee as a priest or priestess of the tradition, properly called a *santero* or *santera* in Spanish, and *babalocha* or *iyalocha* in Lucumi. Initiation forms an irrevocable bond between the devotee and his or her *orisha*, actually placing the *aché* of the *orisha* inside the head of the devotee, making him or her a vehicle for the *orisha's* power.

The initiation ceremony (*kariocha*) is an elaborate rite of passage that takes place over several days and involves the entire community. Under the direction of a senior *santero* or *santera* the initiate is prepared as a "bride" (*iyawo*) for his or her new relationship with the *orisha*. He or she is isolated from all ordinary contact with the world for several days. He or she is fed special foods, wears special clothes, and is surrounded by a host of restrictions that emphasize his or her extraordinary state. The initiate's head receives particular attention as it will become the seat of the patron *orisha*. It is shaved and repeatedly bathed in herbal and sacrificial preparations. The most dramatic moment of the rite occurs when the fundamental symbols of the *orishas*, their sacred stones, are placed on the head of the initiate. At this moment the *orisha* may choose to "descend" (*bajar*) on the initiate and cause him or her to fall into trance. In trance, the personality of the human being becomes transparent to that of the *orisha*, who takes control of the initiate's body to speak, move, dance and heal amid the assembled community.

The rite of initiation into the Santería priesthood closes with a special divination on behalf of the initiate called *itá*. Here a highly skilled diviner (*italero*) consults the *dilogun* oracle to determine the life path of the new initiate. Through the *itá* the initiate learns his or her strengths and weaknesses, and the paths to follow to avoid misfortune and consolidate success. The initiate is shown the deep path of his or her *orisha*: how to know its ways and how to develop himself or herself in harmony with them.

Spirit mediumship is at the heart of the great Santería feasts called *bembés* or *guemilerés*. These are drum dances usually held on the annual feast day of an *orisha* or a devotee's anniversary of initiation. All the community is invited, drummers are hired, the most costly foods and sweets are prepared for the *orishas*. The drums call the *orishas* in intricate rhythms and the members of the community dance their *orisha's* favorite steps. As the ceremony heats up, the *orishas* may choose to descend on the heads of their initiated mediums and join the feasting. Chango may arrive in the body of a young woman, who will radiate the masculine energy of the king of thunder; or Ochún may descend upon an elderly man, transforming his demeanor into that of a lovely lady. The community flocks to the incarnated *orishas*, for their presence brings healing and their speech is prophesy and wisdom. *Bembés* may last all night as each of the *orishas* are called to join the community's feasting.

The Spread of Santería in the Americas

Santería is one of many African-derived religious traditions that have been developed in the Americas. It shares important beliefs and practices with Haitian *vodou*, Brazilian *candomblé*, and dimensions of African-American Christianity. The extraordinary growth of Santería in the United States at the end of the twentieth century owes its impetus to Cuban exiles from the revolution of 1959 and the great Cuban exodus from the port of Mariel in 1980. Many senior *santeros* and *santeras* have established thriving Santería communities, particularly in Miami and New York. The religion has become an inspiration for thousands of African Americans who have found in the *orishas* a liberating spiritual expression of black identity. The most famous African-American development of the worship of the *orishas* is the village of Oyotunji in Sheldon, South Carolina. In Oyotunji, African-American initiates work to model all aspects of their lives on traditional Yoruba culture in an ongoing attempt to create a wholly African lifestyle in the midst of plantation America.

Santería today is practiced by thousands of Americans of all racial and ethnic backgrounds. It has spread from the Cuban diaspora to other Latino communities, and to African-American, white, and Asian communities as well. The Internet has provided unprecedented opportunities for the exchange of information about the religion and there are scores of sites maintained by devotees.

Santería came to national attention in 1992 when a Santería community called the Church of Lukumi Babaluaye brought an appeal before the Supreme Court to exercise the free expression of the religion in the face of an ordinance passed by the city council of Hialeah, Florida. The ordinance forbade "animal sacrifice," and was aimed at prohibiting the Santería practice of the ritual slaughter of farm animals as offerings to the *orishas*. While the city expressed concerns about sanitation and the humane slaughter of the animals, the Supreme Court recognized that the prohibition of "sacrifice" was an infringement on the rights of the Santería community and unanimously voted to overturn the ordinance.

The name Santería says a good deal about the future of the tradition. It means "the way of the saints" and refers to the correspondences that the Lucumi made between their *orishas* and the Roman Catholic saints. Forced by Spanish law to be baptized as Catholics, the Lucumi constructed an elaborate system of codes to represent the *orishas* through the iconography of the saints. Thus an image of the Virgin Mary could be publicly displayed to represent Yemaya or an image of St. Lazarus could stand for Babaluayé. In recent times many devotees no longer find utility in the Catholic correspondences, and see the name "*santería*" as a remnant of a colonial society where African traditions had to be concealed in the face of persecution and discrimination. Often the name chosen in the place of "*santería*" indicates different communities of devotees. Many of those with ties to Cuba often look to "Lucumi" or "Lukumi," while many African Americans prefer "Yoruba religion" or "New World Yoruba" to emphasize the African roots of the tradition. The anglophone term "Orisha Religion" or Spanish-based variants like Oricha or Ocha are popular. Whatever the name, there is a growing consciousness that devotions to the *orishas* is a World Religion with millions of practitioners in both hemispheres.

Joseph M. Murphy

See also Condomble; Brazil, African-Dervied Religions in; Caribbean, African-Derived Religions in; Cuba, African-Derived Religions in; Santeria; Santeria, Material Culture; Yoruba Religion

Bibliography

Brandon, George. (1993) *Santeria from Africa to the New World: The Dead Sell Memories*. Bloomington: Indiana University Press.

Cabrera, Lydia. (1975) *El Monte*. Miami: Ediciones Universal.

——. (1980) *Koeko Iyawo: Aprende Novicia*. Miami: Ediciones Universal.

Flores, Ysamur, and Roberta J. Evanchuk. (1994) *Santería Garments and Altars: Speaking Without a Voice*. Jackson: University Press of Mississippi.

Lindsay, Arturo, ed. (1996) *Santeria Aesthetics in Contemporary Latin American Art*. Washington, D.C.: The Smithsonian Institution.

Murphy, Joseph M. (1988) *Santeria: An African Religion in America*. Boston: Beacon Press.

Thompson, Robert Farris. (1984) *Flash of the Spirit: African and Afro-American Art and Philosophy*. New York: Vintage Books.

Secret Societies

A secret society is a type of social association whose members share knowledge that is not known by outsider. Contrary to popular belief, it is the knowledge that is secret, not membership that is secret, as in many societies in Africa all adult men of a certain age or all adult women of a certain age are members. Typically, it is control of this secret knowledge—whether it be about religious, political, social, or other matters—that is an important source of power in the community and society. Secret societies usually admit only persons from certain social categories as members (for example, men or women, wealthy persons, or members of a particular community), create members through formal initiation rituals, and have grades or levels so that some members may rise in rank within the society over time. Secret societies are found around the world (college fraternities and sororities are one example), but those in Africa, and especially in West Africa, have throughout the twentieth century drawn considerable attention from anthropologists, political scientists, and historians. One reason social scientists have studied secret societies in Africa is that many of these societies were sources of political power during the colonial era and some have reemerged since independence in the 1960s to become an element of the new power structure.

West Africa

West Africa has been the major center of secret societies. What is secret is some activity or some religious insight of the group. In regions where power was largely decentralized and there was no central ruler, or only a weak central ruler, these secret societies had major significance as they functioned across kinship lines and united people from different families, political groups, and villages or settlements. Thus, they were an important mechanism of social cohesion.

Membership in these West African secret societies was frequently graded. When European or other trade influence reached these decentralized societies, some members were able to use this new source of wealth to purchase higher membership status, thus attaining positions that were previously closed to them. Newly rich men could therefore achieve political influence, which had also been previously closed to them. These associations functioned as a type of centralizing government.

In two nations, Sierra Leone and Liberia, and in the area east of the Niger delta, for example, secret societies achieved vast power and were crucial to the preservation of law and order. The Sande, a women's society, was essential for preserving peace in Liberia and Sierra Leone. The male Poro society, however, was mainly responsible for punishing such serious offenses as incest and homicide. Members of the highest rank in the Poro formed councils to settle disputes and chiefs frequently relied on their Poro grade to support their power. There were local Poro councils composed of members of the highest grade, and a chief's authority often rested on his Poro rank. So effective were the Poro that the organization spread among a number of ethnic groups in the area, including the Gola, Kpelle, and Mano of Liberia and the Mende of Sierra Leone. The Poro occasionally united self-ruling chiefdoms and helped create a united political alliance to resist colonialism. In 1898 the Mende Poro, for example, organized the opposition to British expansion into Sierra Leone.

These secret societies continue to emphasize traditional ties between their religious and political aspects. Such ties are not unusual in Africa, where the distinction between secular and sacred has never carried the weight that it has in post-Enlightenment Europe. In Guinea, Sierra Leone, and Liberia, all boys in Poro areas generally join their local Poro at the age of puberty. The boys are separated from the rest of the group for a period ranging from a few weeks to several months. They inhabit a secluded forest area. There they learn the secrets of the society, their expected behavior, and their responsibilities, forging with their age-mates ties that last throughout their lives. When they leave the forest initiation site, they emerge as men. The Sande society conducts similar ceremonies for women, asserting the harmony of creation and life.

It is important to emphasize that these secret societies are secret in that members may not reveal their rituals to nonmembers. These rituals are essential to their function of maintaining control and serving political and religious ends. Dancers control these ritual ceremonies. Dancers wear costumes made of raffia and wooden masks, which symbolize the spirit of the forest.

Poro elders once appointed and dismissed chiefs. As part of enforcing rules and appropriate behavior, they punished lawbreakers. When the offense was serious enough, incest or murder, for example, they could order the offender to be poisoned. Alternately, they could have the offender killed with a three-bladed knife, making it appear that a leopard had done the deed. (Secret societies, such as the Leopard society or the Crocodile society, often have ties with particular animals.) Senior Poro priests even met with priests from other villages and coordinated political and religious actions over a large region.

The Ekpe secret society in what is now Nigeria provides an intriguing example of a politically dominant secret society. In the nineteenth century, the Ekpe secret society was influential in Calabar, the Efik capital at the mouth of the Cross River in southeastern Nigeria. The Ekpe society was the main mechanism keeping the illegal and dangerous activities of the oligarchy of wealthy traders in check. Since there was no government force strong enough to control these men, it was vital that the threat of Ekpe action usually ensured compliance with the rules of society. The Ekpe was able to control Calabar society and make it a highly stratified one. Membership consisted of free members of society; slaves were not members. The traders were rich members of the community, not foreigners.

In addition to controlling traders, Ekpe also subordinated Calabar's large number of slaves. Unlike its neighbors, Calabar kept its slave population from being incorporated into its population. The Efik kept their unexported slaves on agricultural land as serfs. Generally, they did not follow their neighbors' custom of intermarrying with them. Some former slaves did manage to become wealthy, and then, in turn, they became slave owners. However, Ekpe members did not allow former slaves to join the society. They rigidly maintained the free/slave dichotomy. Consequently, Calabar was marked by slave uprisings and bitter battles.

The Ekpe demonstrate a basic social outcome of secret societies. Such societies often establish socially stratified societies, with an individual's or a family's social status based on amounts of wealth relative to others in the community. In this way, the more successful elders became distinguished from their less successful junior kin. It is a romantic fantasy that depicts small-scale societies as egalitarian. Research indicates that there were always differences in social status among members and that secret societies helped to institutionalize these differences. Even among those societies of the Cross River that seemed to be most egalitarian, the Yako and the Mbembe, one of their foremost secret societies was the one which used to punish young men who did not work appropriately for their fathers.

East Africa

In East Africa, age grades tend to function in the same manner as West African secret societies. These groups, based on

age, were, like West African secret societies, nonresidential groups that cut across kinship ties and thus promoted broader social solidarity. These young men form ties that last a lifetime. Members of the group perform secret rituals together. They, like members of West African secret societies, help maintain law and order and uphold religious traditions. These age groups go through a series of rank age grades. Members of junior grades generally defer to their elders. Each grade has a specific function to perform, such as warriors, or elders who advise. The Masai, for example, provide a well-known example of an age-graded society.

The Mau Mau of Kenya provided an example of the use of a modern secret society based on traditional premises. The Mau Mau was a Kikuyu guerilla organization that emerged during postwar turmoil in colonial Kenya. In 1951 and 1952, the Mau Mau carried out a terrorist campaign. The British blamed Jomo Kenyatta, future president of Kenya, for running the Mau Mau. The arrest did not stop the Mau Mau, who retaliated with increased violence. The violence continued until 1956.

The Mau Mau punished many of the Kikuyu who were cooperating with the British. They used traditional religious symbols to strike terror into the hearts of their fellow ethnic members. Although the military campaign failed, it served to bring the issue of the evils of colonialism to the fore. It served to reassert traditional respect while challenging colonialism and British right to rule. Within a few years Kenya was independent and Jomo Kenyatta was its president.

Masks and Rituals

Secret societies typically use masks, and many people outside Africa have come to know of secret societies through their interest in masks. Masks have a basic connection with secret societies and are part of a vast network of African values. Masks, for example, are part of a clan legacy with ties to spiritual power. The person entrusted with the mask is responsible for keeping it spiritually active. He or she does so through maintaining its aesthetic purity, specifically by painting and redecorating in such a manner as to keep its symbolism and form. The masks are constructed from many materials including tapa (bark cloth), raffia, wood, and the pith of certain reeds. Typically, these materials are painted in brilliant colors, including brick red and acid green.

Secret societies wore masks when disciplining their members. Many Africans say that the wearer of the mask becomes the spirit represented and that the spirit works through the masquerade. These masquerades are essential in strengthening the power of secret societies. Masks enable their wearers to act anonymously while punishing offenders.

Certainly, some masks represent aggressive supernatural spirits of a terrifying nature. Secret societies often perform their rituals at night, wearing ancestor masks that remind people of the ancient origin and approval for their conduct. These ceremonies seek to prevent wrongdoers from upsetting the balance of society while maintaining the tribe's appropriate activities and values.

Along the Guinea coast of West Africa, for instance, many masks represent ancestors. These ancestors are quite specific and the mask represents cultural roles. The masks are donned by chosen members of the secret society and represent sanction and control. The Dan and Ngere tribes of Liberia and Ivory Coast, for example, use ancestor masks having generic features. These masks are go-betweens with the gods. People channel their requests and offerings of respect by means of these masquerades. The performance of these activities enables the mask wearers to exert a strong control over the community. These masked rituals help link past, present, and future, not only providing a sense of continuity but demonstrating that the community consists of the living, dead, and those not yet born.

Masks are important in the coming-of-age initiations of tribal members. These initiations typically are the prerogative of secret societies. They instruct future members in their responsibilities as adults and the basic rules that aid tribal stability. Elders wear masks that represent ancestral and other spirits. Often there are masks that are set aside only for initiation. Around Kinshasa in the Congo, for example, there are strikingly impressive masks with exquisitely carved human faces. These masks are helmet-like. When a young man emerges from his initiation site, he wears a mask during his introduction to the community. An initiate of the Pende tribe in the Congo puts this mask aside upon completion of his initiation and replaces it with a miniature ivory duplicate. This charm guards against misfortune. It also symbolizes the youth's manhood.

Senufo men and women, in common with other groups, each have their own secret societies. These societies impart the sacred knowledge of male or female to young initiates. Elders symbolically kill these initiates, signifying their death to their old identity. Upon completion of their initiation, these youth are brought back to their villages. Here they celebrate their return. An essential aspect of their celebration is the ritual symbolizing the interdependence of males and females. As is traditional, these new adults wear masks and dress in costumes of raffia and cloth. They show their gratitude for women through their dance. They perform acrobatic moves and cavort gracefully.

Masks, then, play vital roles in initiation and funeral rites. They are used as a means to mark movement from one stage of life to another. During these sacred liminal periods, ties between the worlds of the sacred and the everyday are particularly strong. Rituals assert social order and help make these sacred, dangerous periods less threatening. Masks have the appropriate sacred gravity to aid in these transitions. Only those with sufficient authority, typically male elders, can wear masks. Masks themselves can be male or female but they are considered by men to be too powerful for women. In most cases, women do not view masks, at least not close up.

Senufo of the northern Ivory Coast continue to use masks in their Poro rituals, especially initiations and funerals. These rituals continue to assert the connection between past, present, and future, as well as providing a means for social control. The *kponyugu*, for example, is among the most powerful masks. It is a full body mask, worn over the head of a dancer. The dancer can only see through the mask's jaws. The mask has the interesting name of "fire spitter" because the concealed dancer performs with sparks shooting from the mask's jaws. Additionally, the mask pulls together some powerful elements from animals. It combines warthog tusks, crocodile jaws, antelope horns, birds (often hornbills), and chameleons. This aggressive image, the opposite of the Poro ideal, helps reinforce the need for the Poro society to control the destructive forces that threaten the community.

Secret Societies in Light of Current Developments

As Sierra Leone and Liberia, among other areas of Africa, have seen a decline in the power of the central government, traditional secret societies have reappeared and begun to exert political power again. Their higher-ranked elders have again started to appear in public in their masks. The old dances are no longer mainly for tourist consumption or cultural activities. These so-called bush devils have acquired real power in the political vacuum that has developed in West Africa. The Poro society has begun to assert its authority in rural areas of Liberia and Guinea, while the Poro in Sierra Leone have picked hunters for a South African security company to train. These young Poro soldiers are working to establish a stable government in Sierra Leone.

War and anarchy are leading to a revival of the Poro's powers in Sierra Leone and Liberia. Elders, as is common everywhere, bewail the lack of respect found in young people. Since the central government is conspicuous by its absence, they have begun to revive the Poro in all its power to reassert the rules of society for the sake of stability and security. Once again, masked dancers have begun to appear in the villages. They inflict beatings on those who have broken the rules.

So powerful are these societies becoming that politicians have begun to use them in West and Central Africa. In Liberia, for example, Charles Taylor, a Poro member, has used his membership as a means for enlisting Poro aid to advance his cause. However, this use of the Poro is mainly confined to the cities. In the villages, the Poro control the government and not the other way around.

Conclusion

Secret societies have served to help unite societies that otherwise are decentralized. They have cut across residential and kinship ties, united groups and people who often reside at some distance from each other, enabled groups to coordinate joint action, and enforced common rules for order. Secret societies have organized resistance to colonial authority, aided or opposed modern politicians, initiated youth, enforced laws, administered justice to offenders, and kept religious ritual alive.

These societies have forged and maintained ties between living, dead, and those not born. They have provided a means for new talent to rise to leadership positions. They have also helped forge stratified societies in which inequality flourished. Power of elders over young men and women, or of slaveholders over their slaves, has been aided by secret societies. Often using masks, which represented sacred powers, elders of the societies used ancestral and divine authority to keep law and order.

In the current chaotic situation of much of West Africa, societies have reassumed some of their earlier power to restore balance to society. In Liberia and Sierra Leone, especially, the old Poro and Sande societies have reemerged as potent forces. Their reemergence lends weight to those who view them as a type of centralizing government and a force for stability in society.

Frank A. Salamone

See also Pastoralist Cosmologies; West African Religion

Bibliography

Achebe, Chinua. (1958) *Things Fall Apart*. London: Heinemann International.

Butt-Thompson, Frederick W. (1970) *West African Secret Societies*. Westport, CT: Greenwood.

Gittins, Anthony J. (1987) *Mende Religion: Aspects of Belief and Thought in Sierra Leone*. Netteretal: Steyler Verlag.

Hackett, Rosalind I. J. (1989) *Religion in Calabar: The Religious Life and History of a Nigerian Town*. Berlin: Mouton.

Imperato, Pascal James. (1983) *Buffoons, Queens, and Wooden Horsemen: The Dyo and Gouan Societies of the Bambara of Mali*. Ibadan: Kilma House Publishers.

Mair, Lucy. (1974) *African Societies*. Cambridge: Cambridge University Press.

———. (1977) *Primitive Government*. Bloomington and London: Indiana University Press.

Schapera, Issac. (1967) *Government and Politics in Tribal Societies*. New York: Schocken Books.

Seventh-Day Adventist Church

The Seventh-Day Adventist Church is an American-based Christian church founded in 1863. It was established by former followers of William Miller, the central figure in the Millerite movement, which disintegrated after Miller's predictions of the end of the world failed to prove true. The founders of the Seventh-Day Adventist Church retained some of Miller's end-of-the-world eschatology, but over time it developed into a church with a much broader and deeper set of basic beliefs and a diverse membership. Seventh-Day Adventists adhere to twenty-seven fundamental beliefs which emphasize the Holy Scriptures, the Trinity, the divine-human relationship, the struggle between Christ and Satan, the Second Coming of Christ, salvation, the role of the Church, and the required behavior of members. To outsiders, the Church is best known for the celebration of the Sabbath on Saturday (the seventh day of the week), the conservative lifestyle of it members, and its active missionary work around the world.

In 2000, the Seventh-Day Adventist Church had about 45,000 churches and over 10 million members in 205 nations, with over 90 percent of members in nations other than the United States. About 18 percent of the United States membership is African-American and about five million people in Africa and two million people in the Caribbean and bordering nations in South and Central America are members. The Seventh-Day Adventist Church is divided into twelve administrative divisions, with the churches in Africa administered by the Africa-Indian Ocean, Eastern Africa, South Africa, Trans-European, and Euro-Africa divisions and those in the Caribbean region by the Inter-American division. The large membership in the Caribbean and Africa reflects the Seventh-Day Adventist Church's aggressive missionary program in less-developed nations and the involvement of African Americans in the church since the late nineteenth century. In addition to the local churches, the Seventh-Day Adventist Church also supports an extensive network of schools and colleges, hospitals, nursing homes, retirement centers, children's homes, publications, and the Adventist Development and Relief Agency International.

In Africa and the Caribbean, Africans and Afro-Caribbeans play a major role in the church hierarchy and in church activities. In the United States, the founders of the movement were strong opponents of slavery, which made the missionary effort to whites and blacks in the South difficult. It was not until 1898 when James Edson White, son of church founders James and Ellen White, founded the Southern Missionary Society that blacks in the South were brought into the Seventh-Day Adventist Church in significant numbers. In the North, work among African-Americans did not begin until the early twentieth century and was initially led by J. H. Carrol, a former Roman Catholic and his student, former Baptist minister James K. Humphrey, in New York City.

Despite the anti-slavery position of the leadership, both in the North and South, segregation was the policy and black organizations and churches existed separate from white, although under control of the white church leadership. Blacks leaders lived with this situation until 1943 when overt discrimination against a black Adventist at an Adventist hospital led to the formation of the National Association for the Advancement of Worldwide Work among Colored Seventh-day Adventists. In 1944, the General Conference agreed to new rules that allowed regional groups to form new black conferences and several were soon formed across the United States. The conferences played the primary role in increasing African-American membership in Seventh-day Adventist Churches over the next several decades. In 1965, the General Conference voted to end segregation in church institutions and since the 1970s several African Americans have attained senior positions in the church.

David Levinson

Bibliography

Butler, Jonathan. (1974) "Adventism and the American Experience." In *The Rise of Adventism: Religion and Society in Mid-Nineteenth-Century America*, edited by Edwin S. Gaustad. New York: Harper and Row, 173–206.

Cleveland, E. E. (1970) *Free at Last*. Washington D.C.: Revue and Herald Publishing Association.

General Conference of Seventh-day Adventists. (1996) *Seventh-day Adventist Encyclopedia*, two volumes. Hagerstown, MD: Review and Herald.

Graybill, Ronald D. (1971) *Mission to Black America*. Mountain View, CA: Pacific Press Publishing Association.

Reynolds, Louis B. (1984) *We Have Tomorrow: The Story of Seventh-Day Adventists with an African Heritage*. Washington D.C.: Revue and Herald Publishing Association.

Seventh-Day Adventist Church. www.adventist.org.

The Shrine of the Black Madonna, Detroit

The Shrine of the Black Madonna in Detroit, the home of the Black Nationalist Christian Movement, traces its origins to 1953 when the Reverend Albert Buford Cleage, Jr. (b. 13 June 1911, Indianapolis, Indiana, d. 20 February 2000, Beulah Land, South Carolina) and 300 parishioners withdrew from Saint Mark's Presbyterian Church to form a new congregation that eventually became known as Central Congregational Church (United Church of Christ). Throughout the 1950s and early 1960s, Central Congregational Church developed a strong youth program, supported the civil rights movement, and provided leadership for a wide range of political issues that affected Detroit's black population. In 1962, Reverend Cleage was the Freedom Now party candidate for governor of Michigan.

With the rise of the black power movement and emergence of liberation theology, Revered Cleage began to formulate a new black theology and vision of the black church. On 22 March 1967, Easter Sunday, he preached a sermon that became the basis for the Black Christian Nationalist Movement and unveiled a fifteen foot Black Madonna and Child painted by Glanton Dowdell. The painting, hung over the altar at the front of the sanctuary, replaced a stained-glass window showing the pilgrims landing at Plymouth Rock. Central Congregation Church became known as the Shrine of the Black Madonna, and in 1970 Reverend Cleage changed his name to Jaramogi Abebe Agyeman, Swahili for "Defender/Holy Man/Liberator of the People."

As the movement grew, it opened nine additional shrines, and in 1975 established a Southern regional headquarters in Atlanta and in 1977 a Southwest regional headquarters in Houston. At a 1978 meeting in Houston, the group proclaimed itself a new denomination, the Pan African Orthodox Christian Church, with Jaramogi Abebe Agyeman as its founder and Holy Patriarch. Below him, there is a hierarchy that includes cardinals, bishops, and other officials. Although independent, the domination maintains a weak affiliation with the United Church of Christ.

The Pan African Orthodox Christian Church is in many ways a continuation of the African Orthodox Church, which had a black Madonna and Christ and was associated with the Marcus Garvey Movement. PAOCC beliefs begin with God as the cosmic energy and creative intelligence from which everything was created. Humans, as a part of God's creation, have a spark of divinity; and the PAOCC, as a sacred circle where the power of God is concentrated, is an instrument of radical social change. Central to PAOCC teachings is that Jesus was the revolutionary black Messiah who came to liberate the black nation of Israel from oppression and exploitation by the white gentile world. Jesus, therefore, is Messiah not because of his death on Calvary, but because of his dedication to the struggle for his people. Today, the revolutionary spirit of God that Jesus embodied is still at work in the liberation of black people from a world system that dominates and exploits them and that perpetuates the myth of their inferiority, all of which is in opposition to the will of God and the divine system.

The PAOCC emphasizes that survival of black people and salvation are dependent on working for the good of the community and rejecting individualism. To this end, the church seeks to build a nation within a nation, where black people can create institutions to promote and sustain their economic, political, social, and psychological well-being. Therefore, the church has established centers that focus on community service, day care, youth, education, technology, and culture. Lay ministries promote social action, wellness, benevolence, creative arts, and fellowship. The church's purchase of 2,600 acres of land in Abbeville, South Carolina, along with plans to expand to 5,000 acres, is an effort to rebuild black civilization. The Beulah Land Farm Project is designed not only to grow, process, and distribute food to black people elsewhere, but to promote the communalism that the church sees as an essential part of its teachings.

PAOCC worship consists of elements found in all denominations: meditation, hymns, prayers, responsive readings, choir selections, scripture, offerings, announcements, and preaching. Everything that occurs in worship reinforces the theology of the church. The Lord's Prayer is reworded as the Prayer of the Black Messiah. Holy Communion is the Sacrament of Commitment. In addition to Christianity, PAOCC beliefs and rituals reflect other sources, including African, in the offering of libations to the ancestors, and Asian, in meditation techniques that emphasize breathing and opening the body's chakras. The church supports gender equality by ordaining women as ministers and consecrating them as bishops.

The Shrine of the Black Madonna has played a major role in Detroit politics. As supporters of the Black Slate, members worked for the election of Coleman Young to mayor of Detroit, and Barbara Rose Collins and Carolyn Cheeks Kilpatrick to the U.S. House of Representatives.

While the Shrine's membership is not in the thousands as it was when the movement began in the late 1960s, the church attracts several hundred people to its Sunday service and sizable numbers to its cultural programs.

Claude F. Jacobs

See also African Orthodox Church

Bibliography

Cleage, Albert B., Jr. (1972) *Black Christian Nationalism: New Directions for the Black Church*. Detroit: Luxor Publishers.
——. (1989) *The Black Messiah*. Trenton, NJ: Africa World Press.
Ward, Hiley H. (1969) *Prophet of the Black Nation*. Philadelphia: Pilgrim Press.

Slave Religion

Slave Religion in North America was a product of the cultural interaction between acquired Christianity and inherited African religious traditions. Africans in a new land found in Christian ritual a way to renew the wholeness lost in their separation from their culture. Slaves embraced Christianity selectively, fusing it with African traditions and an emphasis on justice and liberation to create their own religion.

Seized and transported from Africa into a new and hostile world, enslaved Africans shared a "deep and poignant sense of loss—of deities, tribe, family, prophets, priests, diviners, and medicine men" (Sobel 1979: 224). In Brazil and the Caribbean, concentrations of Africans created religions—Candomble, Vodun, Santeria, and Shango—which retained African deities and practices. However, specific deities and religious practices were lost in the sea change to North America, where smaller concentrations of Africans and slaveowners' deliberate separation of tribal and language groups made shared practices difficult to duplicate. What had been a unified religious outlook in Africa, in which virtually all experience was religious, had become fragmented and diversified in the new environment.

Slaves, however, were able to use characteristics of their African perspective—adaptability, courage, openness to change, and practicality—to synthesize their fragmented knowledge of both African and European religious practices. As they learned the languages and theology of Christianity, they "selected, squeezed, and shaped" its teachings to serve their needs (Sobel 1979: 45).

The First Colored Baptist Church in North America was founded by Andrew Bryan, a freed slave, in Savannah, Georgia. From Simms, James (1888) The First Colored Baptist Church in North America. Philadelphia: J. P. Lippincott.

According to Charles Joyner (1984: 142), African religious beliefs and practices continued to flourish among bondspeople in three streams. One merged with Christianity, as demonstrated in the use of biblical imagery and language in prayer, preaching, music, and spirit possession. The second, the belief in hags and witches as well as other spirits, continued to exist among slave Christians as a sort of parallel consciousness, neither part of their Christianity nor completely outside it. Underground alternative non-Christian religious systems, including conjure and sorcery, also survived in the third stream.

Biblical Imagery and Language

Africans enslaved in the late 1600s and 1700s were determined to learn the English language and found that missionaries of the English SPG (Society for the Propagation of the Gospel in Foreign Parts) were their most available and systematic teachers. Therefore, standard biblical English

became the language of the black church. Africans in America did not share a single oral history, so they appropriated the Christian one for their won. Bible history became African bondspeople's own sacred past: they identified with the lost and wandering children of Israel and made Abraham, the father, and Moses, the liberator, uniquely their own heroes. The Old Testament became common black sacred history, and the New Testament promise of redemption became the core vision of the future.

In order to increase their effective use of biblical English, religious leaders also gained skills in reading and writing. The first published narratives by former slaves told of their astonishment at seeing Europeans reading aloud and of their conviction that there was a voice in the book being read. The popularity of the "voice in the text" account, which appears in several early narratives by former slaves, shows the special value they placed on the skill of reading. Also, some Africans were practicing Muslims before enslavement and had learned from the daily reading of the Koran to respect the reader of the printed page as an authority. Therefore, those slaves who aimed to become religious leaders went to heroic lengths to learn to read the Bible.

Preaching

From their African heritage as well as from European Christianity, black preachers used language, rhythm, and movement in ways that moved their audiences. Some preachers became renowned for their ability to infuse ordinary existence with profound spiritual meaning. They used physical gestures and activity to great effect and used modes of expression similar to those in West Africa. These techniques included repetition of the last word of an utterance as the first word of the next, chanted prayers that brought a "sung speech" response from the audience, and falsetto shrieks and high, forced tones. The preacher used all these techniques to shape his sermon aesthetically, with an underlying sense of beauty and order that may be traceable to West Africa. Early black preachers were famed for their dramatic techniques and their ability to relate biblical symbolism to everyday occurrences while remaining true to the Gospel.

Whether or not they could read the Bible, slave preachers demonstrated skill and power with language. The preacher based his sermon on biblical phrases, verses, and whole passages he knew by heart, and delivered it with a whole range of oratorical devices: repetition, parallelisms, and dramatic use of voice and gesture. The sermon would begin with normal prose and build to a rhythmic cadence, regularly marked by exclamations of the congregation, and climax in a tonal chant accompanied by shouting, singing, and ecstatic behavior.

Prayer

Enslaved Africans' portrayals of God in prayer exemplified the intermeshing of African and Christian symbolism and demonstrated their creative use of biblical English. Slaves found parallels between African conceptions of God and descriptions of the biblical God. For example, the psalm verse "He is a rock in a weary land" is close to the Yoruba description of the supreme God as "the Mighty, Immovable Rock that never dies." Blacks paraphrased Bible verses to make them their own; for example, two lines often heard in prayers by black speakers, "my soul have rest" and "there the wicked will cease from troubling and the weary will be at rest" are derived from Job 3:17: "There the wicked cease from troubling; and there the weary be at rest." These prayer lines, couched in the English of the King James Bible, developed in the nineteenth century and recorded in the twentieth, were relatively resistant to change over time (Pitts 1993: 69).

Prayers demonstrated one of the major characteristics of African-American religion: its emotional urgency. The cadence and intensity of slaves' prayers made them unique and meaningful. An observer noted that slaves' "prayers are full of fire, and often exceedingly vivid and impressive" (Raboteau 1978: 265). The following prayer by a South Carolina slave known only as Jemmy (as recorded by an English visitor) shows the powerful images and majestic cadences of this slave prayer, which also echoes in Christian ritual the African concept of God as all-powerful, just, and compassionate:

> O Lord,
> in whose palm of his hand be the waters of the
>   ocean—
> who can remove mountains—
> who weighs the earth in a balance—
> who can still the waves of the storm—
> who can break the pines of the forest—
> who gives us a land of rivers of waters—
> O Jesus!
> Who died on the cross for us—
> O forgive us our sins;
> help us in this time of trial and need. . . .

(Joyner 1984: 169)

Music

From their earliest contacts with Europeans, slaves readily embraced and adopted European hymns and harmonies, while Europeans were deeply moved by the intensity of black music shaped by the slaves' African heritage. In Africa, the elements of music—rhythm, tone, and dance—were the essence of spirituality, paths to reaching gods and spirits. The drum, the medium to induce rhythm in African ritual, was almost completely forbidden in North American slavery, but rhythm survived through substitutes: spoons, tin buckets, "axe blades, blades of hoes, oars, sticks, dry seed pods," or "bodily rhythms of hand-clapping, foot-stomping, body-slapping" (Epstein 1981: 25–27).

Along with unique rhythms and motion, slaves added their own "sperchuls" to their repertoire of European American hymns and harmonies. The spirituals were composed in the act of singing, on the plantation, or at all-night camp meetings. Even when slaves patterned spirituals after European tunes, they selected or altered tunes to conform to West African music patterns. Black spirituals kept evolving throughout slavery and afterward and had a profound impact on white church music as well. The classic gospel song's two most common features, a repeated chorus or

A SLAVE NARRATIVE: MANY BELIEVE IN WHAT THEY CALL CONJURATION

There is much superstition among the slaves. Many of them believe in what they call "conjuration," tricking, and witchcraft; and some of them pretend to understand the art, and say that by it they can prevent their masters from exercising their will over their slaves. Such are often applied to by others, to give them power to prevent their masters from flogging them. The remedy is most generally some kind of bitter root; they are directed to chew it and spit towards their masters when they are angry with the slaves. At other times they prepare certain kinds of powders, to sprinkle about their masters dwellings. This is all done for the purpose of defending themselves in some peaceable manner, although I am satisfied that there is no virtue at all in it. . . .

[A conjurer] said if I would pay him a small sum, he would prevent my being flogged. After I had paid him, he mixed up some alum, salt, and other stuff into a powder, and said I must sprinkle it about my master, if he should offer to strike me; this would prevent him. He also gave me some kind of bitter root to chew, and spit towards him, which would certainly prevent my being flogged. According to order I used his remedy, and for some cause I was let pass without being flogged that time.

I had then great faith in conjuration and witchcraft. I was led to believe that I could do almost as I pleased, without being flogged. So on the next Sabbath my conjuration was fully tested by my going off, and staying away until Monday morning, without permission. When I returned home, my master declared that he would punish me for going off; but I did not believe that he could do it, while I had this root and dust; and as he approached me, I commenced talking saucy to him. But he soon convinced me that there was no virtue in them. He became so enraged at me for saucing him that he grasped a handful of switches and punished me severely, in spite of all my roots and powders. . . .

I wanted to be well thought of by [young women], and would go to great lengths to gain their affection. I had been taught by the old superstitious slaves, to believe in conjuration, and it was hard for me to give up the notion, for all I had been deceived by them. One of these conjurers, for a small sum, agreed to teach me to make any girl love me that I wished. After I had paid him, he told me to get a bull frog, and take a certain bone out of the frog, dry it, and when I got a chance I must step up to any girl whom I wished to make love me, and scratch her somewhere on her naked skin with this bone, and she would be certain to love me, and would follow me in spite of herself; no matter who she might be engaged to, nor who she might be walking with.

So I got me a bone for a certain girl, whom I knew to be under the influence of another young man. I happened to meet her in the company of her lover, one Sunday evening, walking out; so when I got a chance, I fetched her a tremendous rasp across her neck with this bone, which made her jump. But in place of making her love me, it only made her angry with me. She felt more like running after me to retaliate on me for thus abusing her, than she felt like loving me.

Source: Bibb, Henry (1849) Narrative of the Life and Adventures of Henry Bibb, An American Slave. New York.

---

refrain and verse written in rhyming pairs, or a pattern of call and response, reflected African antecedents.

Blacks and whites differed in the topics emphasized in their music. For whites the promised land was a heavenly hereafter; for blacks it was an eschatological new order—with Jesus directing the Judgment—that could make everything right. Spirituals also reflected the emphasis on freedom that characterizes black theology: the double emphasis on believing that God and Jesus wanted freedom on this earth for the oppressed and the proclamation of the liberating freedom in salvation.

Conversion and Spirit Possession

Conversion was linked to spirit possession, and thus marked the continuation among enslaved Africans of one of the most persistent features of African religion in the new world. Evangelical churches required prospective members to experience a meeting with God, a conversion experience, in order to become church members. Sometimes, conversion was a more private affair than spirit possession had been in Africa. Individual slaves heard their own drummers and shouts, often alone in the woods or in their cabins. Their God didn't mount them, as in Africa, but they met and talked with God, who then came to be and remained in their hearts. More often, as in Africa, conversion was a communal experience. Methodists, for example, called the process of moving towards conversion "seekin'." Candidates would go "on trial" and would use spiritual guides: these guides advised the candidate, prayed for her, and led her on until she "came through the Spirit," that is, experienced the presence of God. The seeker's prolonged praying and meditating during a spiritual journey induced an ecstatic trance without which conversion was not considered authentic.

A trance could also be produced during extended services, often at camp meetings or revivals. The "ring-shout," or simply the "shout," a repetitive and formally structured hitching dance movement and chant, was widely practiced and designed to lead to trance and to spirit possession.

The slave journey to conversion signified more than the traditional European Christian one. Blacks spoke of having "come though" on their journey, of having been made "free at last." Those slaves being saved almost always underwent a kind of spiritual danger and then a rescue as the Lord led them to safety from the devil or his minions. Conversion was a liberating force to the slave: "Christian liberation—affirmed in a setting that also affirmed a black Christian community—made liberation a communal experience and community a liberating experience" (Calhoon 1988: 135).

Sacred Spaces

Slave religious worship took place in "hush harbors," "pray's [or praise] houses," plantation chapels, small town or country churches, and city churches. Hush harbors were meeting places that slaves created outside the plantation quarters. The term "hush harbor" parallels "brush arbor," the name whites gave the camp-meeting revivals, and places of worship they created in barns or groves. However, as the name implies, the site and occurrence of these slave meetings were often secret. Even when slaves were allowed to attend religious meetings on plantations, they wanted to hold secret meetings as well, in order to share what they remembered of African lore and cultural wisdom and to preserve control of their own practices. Hush harbors were

usually built in or near the slave quarters, typically in forests, in dugouts and hollows, or by riverbanks. Wooded areas were so identified as sites for slave religion that after being granted their freedom many African Americans began their churches in the same sites. Slaves made hush harbors of poles and brush and sawed rough planks from small logs for seats; they turned a big pot upside down for noise control.

A Hush Harbor Meeting

Typically, a hush harbor meeting began when slaves decided on a time and a place to meet, with the directions sometimes masked in a spiritual sung at a regular service. The first ones to arrive would frequently break boughs from the trees and bend them in the direction of the selected spot.

When others arrived, they would ask after each other's health and the state of their minds. A regular hymn began the service as a slow initiation to more intense uses of music and rhythm later in the service, or a more joyous or prayerful "sperchul" which mentioned members of the community might be used to start the service. After the first hymn or spiritual came a lengthy prayer. The prayer would often give group solace to those who were in pain or trouble, or call upon God to help the troubles. Any man or woman could lead prayer, but a preacher, chosen by the community for ability to interpret the scared word, conducted the lesson and sermon. While the prayer and the lesson were framed in the Elizabethan English of the King James Bible, the folk preacher used vernacular English and concrete examples related to ordinary life for his sermon. Black folk preachers, in their use of everyday words and symbols beyond time, gradually increased the cadence and active delivery of their message, and built up the excitement that would lead, through more spirituals and the ring shout, to trance possession.

After the sermon came the shout. The selected dancers moved in counterclockwise circle, shuffling to the dirgelike music created by singers and instrumentalists. The shout could go on for hours as its performance became louder and more energetic. The percussive rhythm from the swaying, stamping, singing, and dancing resulted in some of the worshippers "getting the power" or being "filled with the spirit." The excitement of the hush harbor transported them "out of the valley of oppression up to a spiritual summit" and helped them endure the trials of their lives, as they slogged home through the woods (Pitts 1993: 93–94).

Praise Houses, Chapels, and Churches

In addition to hush harbors, slaves worshipped in plantation structures designed as religious buildings. Praise, or "pray's," houses were usually small buildings on plantations that

A SLAVE NARRATIVE:
THE SLAVES ASSEMBLE IN THE SWAMPS

Not being allowed to hold meetings on the plantation, the slaves assemble in the swamps, out of reach of the patrols. They have an understanding among themselves as to the time and place of getting together. This is often done by the first one arriving breaking boughs from the trees, and bending them in the direction of the selected spot. Arrangements are then made for conducting the exercises. They first ask each other how they feel, the state of their minds, etc. The male members then select a certain space, in separate groups, for their division of the meeting. Preaching is in order, by the brethren; then praying and singing all round, until they generally feel quite happy. The speaker usually commences by calling himself unworthy, and talks very slowly, until, feeling the spirit, he grows excited, and in a short time, there fall to the ground twenty or thirty men and women under its influence. Enlightened people call it excitement; but I wish the same was felt by everybody, so far as they are sincere.

The slave forgets all his sufferings, except to remind others of the trials during the past week, exclaiming: "Thank God, I shall not live here always!" Then they pass from one to another, shaking hands, and bidding each other farewell, promising, should they meet no more on earth, to strive and meet in heaven, where all is joy, happiness, and liberty. As they separate, they sing a parting hymn of praise.

Sometimes the slaves meet in an old log cabin, when they find it necessary to keep a watch. If discovered, they escape, if possible; but those who are caught often get whipped. Some are willing to be punished thus for Jesus' sake. Most of the songs used in worship are composed by the slaves themselves, and describe their own sufferings. Thus:

"Oh, that I had a bosom friend, To tell my secrets to, One always to depend upon In everything I do!" "How do I wander, up and down! I seem a stranger, quite undone; None to lend an ear to my complaint, No one to cheer me, though I faint."

> Some of the slaves sing- -
> "No more rain, no more snow,
> No more cowskin on my back!"
> Then they change it by singing- -
> "Glory be to God that rules on high."

In some places, if the slaves are caught praying to God, they are whipped more than if they had committed a great crime. The slaveholders will allow the slaves to dance, but do not want them to pray to God. Sometimes, when a slave, on being whipped, calls upon God, he is forbidden to do so, under threat of having his throat cut, or brains blown out. Oh, reader! this seems very hard- - that slaves cannot call on their Maker, when the case most needs it. Sometimes the poor slave takes courage to ask his master to let him pray, and is driven away, with the answer, that if discovered praying, his back will pay the bill.

Source: Randolph, Peter (1893) *Slave Cabin to the Pulpit.* Boston.

served for worship on Sundays and for prayer services and other gatherings during the week, often led by slaves themselves. Praise houses were so identified by slaves as their own places of worship that they were replicated after freedom; a few are still in existence. Chapels were built by slaveowners and slaves identified less with them. Some were showplaces built to show the slaveowners' wealth or commitment to religion, but the majority were simple wooden buildings, often windowless, resembling toolsheds or slave houses. Religious services on plantations also took place in barns, carriage houses, the piazzas or interiors of plantation houses, or cotton-gin houses.

Slaves also worshipped in regular churches: denominational churches at rural crossroads and in small towns, and city churches, both biracial and separate black churches. The major southern denominations—Catholic, Methodist, Baptist, Presbyterian—included slave members in their congregations. However, in biracial churches, slaves attended separate services and Sunday schools. In mixed congregations, they were usually segregated to galleries or the back of churches, and were admitted to church membership and communion separately after the white members. Though intended to retain white exclusiveness and control, this segregation allowed slaves to develop their own religious practices, solidarity, and leadership.

Leadership

African spirituality, in its theological view, aims to create group solidarity, beginning with God and proceeding through ancestors to the community and the immediate family. Connected with this communal perspective was the sense of the importance of leadership. The discipline exerted by the leader or leaders and followed by the community was an aspect of African life, and efforts were made by enslaved Africans to replicate it in their religious practices.

During the first generations of slavery, spiritual leaders and diviners provided a direct link with and a representation of the African past. From African diviners may have emerged the practice of "spiritual parents"—men and women whose position was unauthorized by whites, but central to slaves' spiritual and religious orientation (Washington 1988: 57). Some of these leaders incorporated their influence into the Christian religion; others remained outside of it. These doctors or conjurors were highly regarded by enslaved Africans for their efforts to combat witches or hags who brought evil via magical actions. Spiritual parents, root doctors, and conjurers were bridges between old and new traditions.

Christian denominations offered new opportunities for leadership. In the late 1700s and early 1800s, during the Great Awakening and the Second Great Awakening, enslaved and free blacks responded eagerly to the popular appeal of Methodism, with its opportunities for the lowly and uneducated to participate in preaching, prayer, and love-feast testimonials. Baptist independent structure allowed African bondspeople to form their own worship groups, some completely independent from whites and some in communion with them. Blacks, slave and free, joined whites in organizing churches in the frontier and were accepted equally into membership. Slave and free black women and men appear as church founders alongside whites, as in Alabama's Cane Baptist Church, whose founders in 1818 included a "slave

girl, Jane." David George, a slave, was one of the first preachers for the Silver Bluff Church in coastal South Carolina. Another Baptist pioneer, George Lelile, freed from his owner, ministered to whites and plantation slaves from his church near Savannah before leaving for Jamaica. Andrew Bryan founded the First African Baptist Church in Savannah while he was still enslaved. He was succeeded by his nephew, Andre Marshall, also a freed slave. Alexander Campbell, another former slave, took the name of his church's founder when he organized a Disciples of Christ congregation in Midway, Kentucky.

Religious Leaders on Plantations

In the 1820s and the 1830s, Methodists, Baptists, Presbyterians, and Episcopalians paid missionaries to travel to plantations to mission to slaves. The slave missions continued until the end of slavery, with the greatest number of missionaries and slave converts recorded by Methodists, Baptists, Presbyterians, and Episcopalians. To make their missions effective and long-lasting, Episcopal missionaries appointed plantation slaves as prayer leaders. Methodist local preachers, often slaves, held love feasts and encouraged prayer and testimony. In the Baptist churches, watchmen and deacons conducted special services on Sunday afternoons, held prayer meetings during the week, and presided at discipline meetings where blacks voted to admit new members or release those having to move and discussed each other's behavior. Despite their need to cooperate with whites, these leaders were considered "pillars of strength in the slave quarters" and "used their position of power with measure, fairness, and to the benefit of the slave community" (Washington 1988: 58, 284).

Slave Revolts

Some slave congregations, however, refused to assimilate into the white structure. The South Carolina and Georgia Sea Islands counted many Baptist "societies," with black leaders and rituals little-connected to the white-led Baptist denominations. These groups insisted on retaining their own traditions.

Slave religion's liberation theology and the circumstances of bondage inspired some religious leaders to revolt. Gabriel Prosser, Denmark Vesey, and Nat Turner are only the best known of those who used the language and beliefs of Christianity and African tradition to rebel against slavery.

Black Religion in Antebellum Southern Cities

Even though black preaching and assembly were outlawed in most southern states, independent black city churches, attended by both free and enslaved blacks, operated with little interference from the law or white society. African Americans owned these churches and hired their own black preachers. Henry Adams, Loudon Ferrill, and William Harris also founded large all-black Baptist congregations in Louisville and Lexington, Kentucky, and in Huntsville and Mobile, Alabama. Slaves and free blacks who were members of these large independent congregations cast a considerable net of influence over slave religion through training black Baptist leaders. In cities of the border south, such as St. Louis and Baltimore, churches of the national black denominations, AME and AME Zion, had slave as well as free black members.

In the 1840s and the 1850s many black congregations in the South separated from white congregations, either because of space or as a matter of preference. Methodists, for example, encouraged black members to separate and establish their own churches in southern cities in the 1850s as a way to increase black independence, remove responsibility from whites, and increase the count of missions. Many city churches listed as biracial were actually quasi-independent black churches. In Charleston, for example, thousands of black members of biracial churches overwhelmed the numbers of whites. They conducted their own prayer service, Sunday schools, and catechism classes, all after the biracial service on Sunday mornings.

The Black Church at the End of Slavery

During and after the Civil War, the secret church of the hush harbor combined with the institutional church in which many black leaders were trained. What Randy Sparks has termed a "dramatic and significant merger" (1994: 187) set black churches apart from white churches of the same denominations. Black men and women, many of them former slaves, also established their own churches, associations, colleges, and schools. The phenomenal growth of African-American churches in the post-Civil War years did not represent a complete break with the past. Expansion was made possible by reliance upon a corps of ex-slaves and prewar free blacks who had gained acceptance as religious leaders in hush harbors and churches during the antebellum years.

Janet Duitsman Cornelius

See also African Methodist Episcopal Church; African Methodist Episcopal Zion Church; Music, Black Hymnody; National Baptist Convention, USA; United States, African-Derived Religions in

Bibliography

Boles, John, ed. (1988) *Masters and Slaves in the House of the Lord: Race and Religion in the American South*. Lexington: University Press Kentucky

Calhoon, Robert M. (1988) *Evangelicals and Conservatives in the Early South, 1840–1861*. Columbia: University of South Carolina Press.

Cornelius, Janet Duitsman. (1999) *Slave Missions and the Black Church in the Antebellum South*. Columbia: University of South Carolina Press.

—— (1991) *When I Can Read My Title Clear: Literacy, Slavery, and Religion in the Antebellum South*. Columbia: University of South Carolina Press.

Epstein, Dena. (1981) *Sinful Tunes and Spirituals: Black Folk Music to the Civil War*. Urbana: University of Illinois Press.

Hopkins, Dwight N., and George C. L. Cummings, eds. (1994) *Cut Loose your Stammering Tongue: Black Theology in the Slave Narratives*. Maryknoll, NY: Orbis Books.

Johnson, Clifton H., ed. (1945) *God Struck Me Dead: Religious Conversion Experiences and Autobiographies of Ex-slaves*. Philadelphia and Boston: Pilgrim Press.

Johnson, Paul E. (1994) *African-American Christianity: Essays in History*. Berkley: University of California Press.

Joyner, Charles. (1984) *Down by the Riverside: A South Carolina Community*. Urbana: University of Illinois Press.

Pitts, Walter F., Jr. (1993) *Old Ship of Zion: The Afro-Baptist Ritual in the African Diaspora*. Oxford and New York: Oxford University Press.

Raboteau, Albert. (1978) *Slave Religion: The "Invisible Institution" in the Antebellum South*. Oxford and New York: Oxford university Press.

Sobel, Mechal. (1979) *Trabelin' On: the Slave Journey to an Afro-Baptist Faith*. Westport, CT: Greenwood Press.

Sparks, Randy. (1994) *On Jordan's Stormy Banks: Evangelicalism in Missississippi, 1773–1876*. Athens: University of Georgia Press.

Spencer, Jon Michael. (1990) *Protest and Praise: Sacred Music of Black Religion*. Minneapolis: Fortress Press.

Washington, Margaret. (1988) *A "Peculiar People": Slave Religion and Community-Culture among the Gullahs*. New York: New York University Press.

Social Activism

From its very beginnings, African-American religion has exhibited a contradictory nature. On the one hand, slave masters employed Christianity as a mechanism of social control and encouraged their slaves to seek their salvation in an ill-defined afterlife. On the other hand, people of African ancestry shaped European-American Christianity in its various forms, as well as in some cases Judaism and Islam, to meet their own needs and into the single social institution that they have been able to call their own. Like other subordinate groups in complex societies, African Americans have used religion as a response to their social status within the context of the American society. As Genovese so aptly observes, the "moral content of black religion emerged to justify accommodation and compromise as a properly Christian response and simultaneously drew the teeth of political messianism and revolutionary millennialism" (1979: 7).

Social Activism in Slave Religion and the Independent Church Movement during the Nineteenth Century

Although slaves were often depicted as a rather submissive and docile lot, many of them came to view Jesus as an eschatological king and deliverer. Certain slaves, such as Gabriel Prosser, Denmark Vesey, and Nat Turner, found biblical justifications in assuming the leadership of slave insurrections. Viewing himself as the new Samson, Prosser believed that he could lead the slaves in the establishment of a black kingdom in Virginia and led them in an insurrection outside of Richmond in 1800. Vesey, an ex-slave who belonged to the Hampstead African Methodist Episcopal church of Charleston, found a following among both free blacks and slaves in a rebellion in 1822. He was assisted by Gullah Jack, a conjurer, who directed his occult powers in the revolt. In the slave rebellion of 1830 in Southampton, Virginia, Nat Turner drew inspiration for his mission from the prophetic tradition of the Old Testament.

Wilmore refers to the independent black church movement as "the first Black freedom movement" and as a "form of Black insurrection against the most vulnerable and accessible form of institutionalized racism and oppression in the nation: the Black churches" (1983: 78). Representatives of black churches, particularly in the North, were involved in antislavery, abolitionist, and proto-black nationalist movements. The Convention movement began as a secular adjunct of Northern black churches and opposed slavery, black emigration to Africa as advocated by the American Colonization Society, and racial discrimination. All of the black Baptist and Methodist associations based in the North voiced some degree of opposition to slavery, not only in the form of resolutions but also by helping slaves to escape. Yet, the abolitionism of African-American churches tended to be moderate rather than radical. As Sernett observes, in their stance toward slavery, Absalom Jones (the founder of the African Episcopal Church of St. Thomas) and Richard Allen (the founder of the Bethel African Methodist Episcopal Church in Philadelphia), were "gradual emancipationists" who "looked forward to that day when all men

would be free and urged the slaves to take comfort in the Gospel promises until that time" (1975: 150).

During Reconstruction, Southern black ministers served as federal and state officials, state legislators, and members of the U.S. Congress. Indeed, many white Southerners disparagingly referred to independent black churches as "political churches" (Dvork 1991: 157). Black clergymen, such as Henry McNeal Turner (a bishop in the African Methodist Episcopal church), became advocates of black separatism and the belief that God is black. For the most part, however, the routine activities of the church and the struggle for survival in the face of meager resources and white hostility prevented greater attention to the vital social issues of the day. With the reinstitution of restrictive black codes throughout the South in the late nineteenth century, political activities increasingly became relegated to the confines of the church itself.

Social Activism in Mainstream Denominations

Individual ministers belonging to the black mainstream denominations (namely, the National Baptists, African Methodists, and black congregations in white-controlled denominations) historically have varied widely in the extent of their social activism, ranging from those who were ultra-accommodationists to those who were militant reformers and even occasionally socialists or radicals of one stripe or another. Reverdy Ransom, an AME bishop, was an outspoken Christian Socialist and proponent of the Social Gospel (Morris 1990). He established Institutional Church and Settlement in Chicago in 1900—a congregation devoted to a wide variety of social outreach programs, including a nursery, kindergarten, cooking and sewing classes, manual training classes, an employment agency, and social clubs. W. E. B. Du Bois referred to Ranson's experiment as the "most advanced step in the direction of making the church exist for the people rather than the people for the church" (quoted in Sernett 1997: 131). George Washington Woodbey, a black Baptist preacher, served as a delegate to the Socialist Party conventions of 1904 and 1908 (Foner 1983). George Frazier Miller, the rector of the St. Augustine Protestant Episcopal Church in Brooklyn, regarded Jesus as a revolutionary messiah and ran for Congress on the Socialist ticket in 1918 (Taylor 1994: 122). J. C. Austin, the pastor of the Pilgrim Baptist Church in Chicago, transformed his congregation into a welfare, education, health care, job training and placement center and viewed capitalism as a flawed system (Burkett 1994: 138–139). His critical posture, however, probably served as an impediment in his repeated bids for the presidency of the National Baptist Convention, USA.

Some black mainstream ministers, such as Adam Clayton Power, Jr., worked for social reform in the ghetto alongside Communist-sponsored organizations during the 1930s and 1940s. Despite the involvement of some black mainstream ministers and congregations in social activism, most of them tended to invoke the Bible as the solution to social problems. Various mainstream ministers discouraged blacks from joining labor unions and argued that capitalism would serve as an important source of employment for black workers. Indeed, various black mainstream ministers along with the Urban League, urged black workers to function as punctual and industrious workers. Most black mainstream ministers remained silent when African-American radicals such as W. E. B. Du Bois and Paul Robeson fell victim to anti-Communist political purges.

African-American religious congregations with activist leaders historically have often served and continue to serve as local organizational and resource bases for supporting a larger protest movement. At the denominational level, however, political involvement on the part of black mainstream churches, particularly the National Baptists and African Methodists, tends to focus more on ecclesiastical politics than on the politics of liberation. The organizational structure of mainstream denominations, especially that of the National Baptists, however, does allow ministers, lay members, and constituent congregations considerable flexibility in choosing whether to participate in social activism.

Although most black congregations stood on the sidelines of the events following the Supreme Court's Brown vs. Topeka Board of Education desegregation decision of 1954, many black ministers, particularly ones affiliated with the mainstream denominations, and their congregations joined the civil rights movement. The minister's status as the formal leader of his congregation has received far more consideration than the role of the mainstream congregation as a whole in supporting or restricting the scope of his activities. Morris contends that African-American congregations are "not ideal as the decision-making center of a mass movement in that they are too numerous and preoccupied with too many functions not related to protest" (1984: 21–22). Nevertheless, in situations where a clerical activist and a nucleus of activist members are present, a congregation may function as a local organizational and resource base which supports a larger protest effort. As McAdam argues in his analysis of the civil rights movement, "in the case of most church-related campaigns, it was not so much that movement participants were recruited from among the ranks of active churchgoers as it was a case of church membership itself being redefined to include the movement participation as a primary requisite to the role" (1982: 129).

Martin Luther King, Jr., a young middle-class Baptist minister with an affinity for the Social Gospel, and particularly for Gandhian nonviolence, served as the pivotal figure in the civil rights movement, starting with his involvement in the Montgomery bus boycott in 1955 and ending with his assassination in 1968. King's Southern Christian Leadership Conference (SCLC) served as a political arm of the black church. He called his view of the Christian social ideal the "Beloved Community"—a term that he learned while a doctoral student at the Boston University School of Theology during 1951–1955. Cartwright asserts that King believed that the "Beloved Community would gradually emerge as the by-product of the practice of nonviolence and the realization of wider and wider degrees of social cooperation" (1993: xli). King drew inspiration for his social activist posture from his father, Martin Luther King, Sr., who served for many years as the pastor of the Ebeneezer Baptist Church in Atlanta, as well as Howard Thurman, a black Southern-born minister who had met Gandhi while traveling in India. Moses (1997) contends that King gained an understanding of the intricate structural relationship between race and class in American society by drawing upon the work of both A. Philip Randolph, an African-American socialist and labor organizer, and Ralph J. Bunche. Bunche instilled in him an awareness of the global nature of the color line—one rooted in imperialism as an international expression of capitalism. Although King rejected the manner in which Marxist theory had been applied in Communist regimes, he admitted to having found inspiration in the writings of Marx in late 1949 and admired his passion for social justice. In his last years, King became an outspoken critic of American foreign policy in Southeast Asia and expressed concern for the economic plight of black working-class people. He encouraged African Americans to build alliances with the labor movement and the poor in general. Indeed, on the eve of his assassination, King was supporting the efforts of sanitation workers in their strike against the city of Memphis.

Toward the end of his life, King's increasingly strident positions created a rift between himself and many of his colleagues in the SCLC (Garrow 1986: 527–574). Nevertheless, in time this organization came to adopt stances akin to those advocated by its foremost member. According to Sawyer,

> While SCLC has never explicitly predicated its program on class analysis nor engaged in the more radical forms of civil disobedience entertained by SCLC shortly before King's death ... SCLC has addressed human rights concerns in Central America, South Africa, the Middle East, Haiti, and Ethiopia. Throughout the Reagan and Bush

administrations, SCLC was a persistent advocate for affirmative action, voting rights, black colleges, and housing and employment programs. The organization has addressed issues ranging from black land loss, to discrimination in the criminal justice system, to the resurgence of white supremacist groups, to the disposal of toxic wastes in black impoverished communities. (1994: 62–63)

In the wake of the Black Power movement of the late 1960s, progressive African-American clergy created the National Conference of Black Churchmen (NCBC) and black caucuses in the National Council of Churches and many white-controlled denominations, such as the United Methodist and Catholic churches. Chapman (1996: 82) asserts that the NCBC served as a bridge between pre- and post-Black Power religious thought. This organization included within its ranks social activists such as James Cone, Henry Mitchell, Gayraud Wilmore, J. Deotis Roberts, and Preston Williams. Although the NCBC continued to convene into the 1980s, by 1972 it had lost much of its momentum. Many black clergy affiliated with white-controlled denominations have served as outspoken critics of racism and sometimes class relations in the larger American society. For example, Gayraud S. Wilmore, author of the now classic *Black Religion and Black Radicalism* (1983), has served for many years as a minister in the United Presbyterian Church. Nathan Wright, Jr., an Episcopal priest, chaired the National Conference on Black Power, which convened on 20–23 July 1967. Paul Washington, the rector of the Episcopal Church of the Advocate in North Philadelphia, provided a meeting place for Black Power advocates, the Black Panther Party, the Black Economic Development Conference, and numerous other groups that challenged racial and social inequality in the larger society (Washington 1994).

The Rainbow Coalition under the leadership of the Reverend Jesse Jackson, a minister affiliated with the Progressive National Baptist Convention, emerged in the 1980s as yet another activist manifestation of African-American religion. Although Jackson's agenda was largely reformist in a social democratic vein rather than a revolutionary one, many progressives among European-Americans, Hispanic-Americans, Asian-Americans, and Native Americans rallied around his bids for the Democratic Party's presidential candidacy in 1984 and 1988. As they did in the civil rights movement, black churches served as a vital support base. Jackson's political rallies were well attended by black ministers and were conducted in a style modeled after African-American religious services. Although Jackson espoused a variant of

black capitalism during the early 1970s, the federal government's minimal efforts to promote black entrepreneurial activities prompted him to adopt consumers' rights tactics.

Social Activism in Other African-American Religious Groups

Changes in the political economy of the United States coupled with the onset of World War I resulted in the massive migration of African Americans from the rural South to the cities of the North and South. In the midst of the social crisis faced by the migrants from the rural South, African-American religion underwent a process of diversification that resulted in the emergence of messianic-nationalist sects (e.g., black Judaic and Islamic groups), conversionist sects (e.g., Holiness-Pentecostal groups), and thaumaturgical sects (e.g., Spiritual groups)(Baer and Singer 1992). Just like the mainstream churches, these sects juxtapose elements of protest and accommodation to the larger society.

Messianic-Nationalist Sects

Messianic-nationalism is a variant of African-American nationalism that combines religious belief with the ultimate aim of achieving some degree of political, social, and cultural autonomy. The best-known messianic-nationalist sects are those that subscribe to Islam. W. D. Fard, an itinerant peddler, possibly of Middle Eastern origin, established the Nation of Islam in Detroit in the early 1930s. In the wake of a succession crisis resulting from Fard's mysterious disappearance in 1933, Elijah Muhammad assumed leadership of the main faction of the Nation and moved its headquarters to Detroit. The Nation grew due to the charismatic preaching of Malcolm X, the minister of the Harlem Temple, during the late 1950s and 1960s. Toward the end of his life, Malcolm X came to downplay his anti-white rhetoric and became an outspoken critic of American foreign policy and capitalism, a posture that had contributed to a rift between him and Elijah Muhammad.

Over time, messianic-nationalist sects generally have mollified their radical theological and political stances. This process manifested itself further in the original Nation of Islam's transformation into the American Muslim Mission under the leadership of Wallace D. Muhammad, one of Elijah's sons. Conversely, Louis Farrakhan formed a reconstituted Nation of Islam and has served as perhaps the most visible critic of institutional racism in the United States during the 1980s and 1990s. He teaches that W. D. Fard was Allah incarnate, blacks are the original human beings, and whites are devils. Farrakhan's program includes the same demands of all black people found in every issue of the original Nation's *Muhammad Speaks*. The reconstituted Nation of Islam created the Muslim Political Action Committee in Washington, D.C., in the 1980s (Turner 1997: 230). Farrakhan served as the key organizer of the 1995 Million Man March—the "greatest black manifestation thus far in U.S. history" (Gardell 1996: 5). He has created much controversy with his anti-Semitic statements, favors a corporate economy backed up by an authoritarian state, espouses traditional gender relations, and opposes abortion and homosexuality.

Conversionist Sects

Although conversionist sects often manifest a posture of political fatalism by stressing salvation in the afterlife, some Holiness-Pentecostal or Sanctified congregations, particularly those affiliated with the Church of God in Christ, have become increasingly involved in social activism since the 1960s. That church provided the headquarters for the sanitation workers' strike, which was punctuated by the tragic assassination of Martin Luther King, Jr., in 1968. Black Pentecostals have won seats on city councils and in state legislatures, and they have been appointed to minor cabinet positions in the executive branch of the federal government. Al Sharpton, a controversial and flamboyant COGIC minister based in Brooklyn, made an unsuccessful bid for the U.S. Senate in 1992 (Taylor 1994: 229). He has had links with the New Alliance Party, has blamed "capitalist Zionists" for the socioeconomic problems faced by African Americans, and has embraced Louis Farrakhan.

Thaumaturgical Sects

Thaumaturgical sects, such as a wide array of groups belonging to the Spiritual movement (Baer 1984; Kaslow and Jacobs 1991) and Reverend Ike's United Church, appear to be accommodative in terms of their strong tendency to substitute individualistic magico-religious rituals for social activism in an effort to solve the problems of their adherents. Nevertheless, Spiritual churches often protest existing social relations in a variety of subtle ways, including their rejection of the Protestant work ethic as a sufficient means for obtaining material prosperity and their criticism of "pie-in-the-sky" religion. Certain Spiritual groups have even incorporated elements of messianic-nationalism, and some Spiritual pastors occasionally comment critically upon business practices, politics, and racism in American society.

Conclusion

Many African-American theologians have become proponents of Black Theology—an effort that views Jesus Christ as a liberator against racial oppression. Some black theologians, such as James Cone and Cornel West, have been engaged in a Marxist-Christian dialogue with liberation theologians in the Third World and have called for an African-American revolutionary Christianity. Female black theologians have developed a Womanist Theology that challenges sexism not only in the larger society but also in black churches (Grant 1993). Despite the fact that Black and Womanist Theology continue to remain phenomena primarily situated in seminaries, their influence has gradually come to filter down to various African-American congregations. While black religion in its variegated forms will continue to manifest accommodative qualities, its more progressive expressions can be expected to be part of any vanguard for radical social-structural change emanating from the African-American community.

Hans Baer

See also National Council of Black Christians; Rainbow Coalition; Southern Christian Leadership Conference

Bibliography

Baer, Hans A. (1984) *The Black Spiritual Movement: A Religious Response to Racism.* Knoxville; University of Tennessee Press.

Baer, Hans A., and Merrill Singer. (1992) *African-American Religion in the Twentieth Century: Varieties of Protest and Accommodation.* Knoxville: University of Tennessee Press.

Burkett, Randall L. (1994) "The Baptist Church in the Years of Crisis." In *African-American Christianity: Essays in History,* edited by Paul E. Johnson. Berkeley: University of California Press, 134–158.

Cartwright, John Henderson. (1993) "Martin Luther King, Jr. and Modern African American Religion." In *Encyclopedia of African American Religions,* edited by Larry G. Murphy, J. Gordon Melton, and Gary L. Ward. New York: Garland, xxxvii–xlvi.

Chapman, Mark L. (1996) *Christianity on Trial: African-American Religious Thought Before and After Black Power.* Maryknoll, NY: Orbis Books.

Dvork, Katherine L. (1991) *An African-American Exodus: The Segregation of the Southern Churches.* Brooklyn: Carlson Publishing.

Foner, Philip S., ed. (1983) *Black Socialist Preacher: The Teachings of Reverend George Washington Woodbey and His Disciple, Reverend G. W. Slater, Jr.* San Francisco: Synthesis.

Gardell, Mattias. (1996) *In the Name of Elijah Muhammad: Louis Farrakhan and the Nation of Islam.* Durham, NC: Duke University Press.

Garrow, David. (1986) *Bearing the Cross: Martin Luther King, Jr., and the Southern Christian Leadership Conference.* New York: W. Morrow.

Genovese, Eugene D. (1979) *From Rebellion to Revolution: Afro-American Revolts in the Making of the Modern World.* Baton Rouge: Louisiana State University.

Grant, Jacquelyn. (1993) "Womanist Theology: Black Women's Experience as a Source for Doing Theology." In *Encyclopedia of African American Religions*, edited by Larry G. Murphy, J. Gordon Melton, and Gary L. Ward. New York: Garland, xlvii–lviii.

Jacobs, Claude F., and Andrew J. Kaslow. (1991) *The Spiritual Churches of New Orleans: Origins, Beliefs, and Rituals of an African-American Religion.* Knoxville: University of Tennessee Press.

MacAdam, Doug. (1982) *Political Process and the Development of Black Insurgency, 1930–1970.* Chicago: University of Chicago Press.

Morris, Aldon D. (1984) *The Origins of the Civil Rights Movement: Black Communities Organizing for Change.* New York: Free Press.

Morris, Calvin S. (1990) *Reverdy C. Ranson: Black Advocate of the Social Gospel.* Lanham, MD: University Press of America.

Moses, Greg. (1997) *Revolution of Conscience: Martin Luther King, Jr., and the Philosophy of Nonviolence.* New York: Guilford Press.

Sawyer, Mary R. (1994) *Black Ecumenism: Implementing the Demands of Justice.* Valley Forge, PA: Trinity Press International.

Sernett, Milton C. (1975) *Black Religion and American Evangelicalism.* Metuchen, NJ: Scarecrow.

———. (1997) *Bound for the Promised Land: African American Religion and the Great Migration.* Durham, NC: Duke University Press.

Taylor, Clarence. (1994) *The Black Churches of Brooklyn.* New York: Columbia University Press.

Turner, Richard Brent. (1997) *Islam in the African-American Experience.* Bloomington: Indiana University Press.

Washington, Paul M., with David M. Gracie. (1994) *Other Sheep I Have: The Autobiography of Father Paul M. Washington.* Philadelphia: Temple University Press.

Wilmore, Gayraud S. (1983) *Black Religion and Black Radicalism.* Maryknoll, NY: Orbis Books.

Southern Christian Leadership Conference

The Southern Christian Leadership Conference (SCLC) was formed in 1957 to coordinate local civil rights protests that were emerging at that time in various communities of the South. The Rev. Dr. Martin Luther King, Jr. (1929–1968) was named as the first president of SCLC. SCLC in turn served as the organizational vehicle through which King exercised his leadership of the national civil rights movement until his assassination in 1968.

In their own words, the agenda of SCLC was to secure "full citizenship rights, equality, and the integration of the Negro in all aspects of American life." Furthermore, the organization sought to "foster and create the 'beloved community' in America where brotherhood is a reality," and to achieve "genuine intergroup and interpersonal living—integration" ("This is SCLC" brochure). In pursuit of this vision, SCLC identified two primary goals: abolishing the existing system of racial segregation and securing the vote for southern African Americans who had been effectively disenfranchised since the turn of the century. In seeking the exercise of full citizenship rights, SCLC saw itself as also pursuing the good of the nation as a whole. SCLC's moral mission was expressed in the motto it adopted, "To Save the Soul of America." The philosophy of SCLC, as well as its method for seeking change, was that of nonviolence, and specifically Christian nonviolence. The inclusion of the word "Christian" in the organization's title was to denote that its support base was the black church, and its theology that of "redemptive love."

Most of the members of SCLC's board of directors and staff were black ministers, and the majority of them Baptist ministers. Most local SCLC affiliate organizations were church-based, although some were civic leagues, lodges, labor organizations, and voter-registration projects. In 1963, SCLC had eighty-five southern affiliates and thirty northern affiliates, with the primary function of most northern affiliates being fundraising.

The purpose of southern affiliates was to respond to community grievances, which commonly involved segregation issues related to public schools, public transportation, eating establishments, voting rights, and police conduct. Protests typically took the form of economic boycotts, sit-ins, marches, and other forms of direct action. On occasion, local affiliates requested the assistance of the parent SCLC organization in conducting sustained, city-wide campaigns. Among the more famous campaigns are those conducted in Albany, Georgia (1961–62); Birmingham, Alabama (1963); St. Augustine, Florida (1964); and Selma, Alabama (1965).

Civil disobedience was the tactical extension of the philosophy of nonviolence. Members of SCLC were committed to the idea that one had a moral obligation to defy unjust civil laws that violated a higher moral law. Through acts of civil disobedience, protesters were able to generate "creative tension" which exposed the evil nature of local customs and policies. Media coverage of these protests and the violence directed at protesters, especially in the Birmingham and Selma campaigns, served to engender national and international condemnation of racial injustice and, conversely, sympathy for the passage of federal legislation outlawing racist practices. The Civil Rights Act of 1964 outlawed racial segregation in public facilities and institutions and the Voting Rights Act of 1965 prohibited discrimination in voting practices and established federal oversight of elections in the South.

With the passage of these laws, the focus of the civil rights movement shifted to black political development. From 1966 to 1968, King's emphasis changed significantly as well, from individual attitudes and racial integration to systemic change and societal transformation. Under his leadership, SCLC gave increased attention to economic equity and to building a multicultural coalition of poor people to challenge the economic and political power structure. Most of King's colleagues disagreed with his stance on opposing the Viet Nam conflict, however, and sought to confine SCLC to more traditional civil rights concerns.

At his death, King was succeeded as president of SCLC by his closest aide, the Rev. Ralph David Abernathy. Financial support for SCLC dwindled and the organization's program was correspondingly reduced. Stability was regained in the twenty-year tenure of the Rev. Joseph E. Lowery, who served as president from 1977 to 1997. During his administration, SCLC continued to address such issues as voter education and registration, workers' rights, and economic development, but added to its agenda the concerns of drug abuse, community violence, the status of the black family, and the impact of the AIDS epidemic. In 1998, Martin Luther King III became the fourth president of SCLC, which continued to maintain its headquarters in Atlanta, Georgia.

The Southern Christian Leadership Conference was one of the most significant civil rights organizations of the 1950s and 1960s. Together with the NAACP and the Congress of Racial Equality (CORE), it was at the forefront of securing civil and electoral rights not only for African Americans but other disenfranchised and underrepresented peoples as well. Democracy was thereby significantly enlarged, and the common good of America well served.

Mary R. Sawyer

See also Social Activism

Bibliography

Branch, Taylor. (1988) *Parting the Waters: America in the King Years, 1954–63.* New York: Simon and Schuster.

Fairclough, Adam. (1987) *To Save the Soul of America: The Southern Christian Leadership Conference and Martin Luther King, Jr.* Athens, GA: University of Georgia Press.

Garrow, David J. (1986) *Bearing the Cross: Martin Luther King, Jr., and the Southern Christian Leadership Conference.* New York: William Morrow.

Spiritual Baptists

Spiritual Baptists are a rapidly expanding international religious movement with congregations in St. Vincent (where many Trinidadian Baptists claim their faith originated), Trinidad and Tobago, Grenada, Guyana, Venezuela, London, Toronto, Los Angeles, and New York City. In addition, there are a number of similar religious movements on other Caribbean islands whose rituals parallel those of the Baptists (the "Tieheads" of Barbados, Jordanites of Guyana, and the "Spirit Baptists" of Jamaica). A major consideration is that many Spiritual Baptists do not consider these others to be a part of their religion and seldom participate in joint worship services, pilgrimages, missions, and other activities with members of these other groups. They do, however, maintain close and active ties with brethren in St. Vincent, Trinidad and Tobago, Grenada, Venezuela, the United States, Europe, and Canada.

Spiritual Baptist membership is predominantly black, and—like many other Afro-Caribbean groups—the Baptists seem to have started out as a "religion of the oppressed." In recent years, however, congregations in Trinidad have attracted membership among middle-class blacks as well as a sizeable number of wealthier East Indians, Chinese, whites, and individuals of mixed heritage. While some Baptist leaders take great pride in their multiethnic congregations, the Spiritual Baptist faith is still overwhelmingly a black religion, with Asians and Whites comprising less than 5 percent of total adherents. Membership in Trinidad and Tobago has fluctuated between 10,000 and 12,500 over the past ten years.

The greatest growth has been in churches outside the Caribbean; notably among West Indian migrants to Canada, Europe, and the United States. For example, St. Peter's Spiritual Baptist Church (SBC) in Brooklyn is said to have over 2,000 members and two Spiritual Baptist churches in Toronto claim over 1,000 members each. The "New Jerusalem" SBC outside of London claims over 200 members.

Relationship to African-Derived Religions

Many Trinidadians confuse Spiritual Baptists and followers of the African-derived Orisha movement (Houk 1995; Lum 2000). They assume that Spiritual Baptist and Orisha rites are identical. Members of these two faiths. however, do not share this confusion. A large percentage of Spiritual Baptists condemn Orisha rites as "heathen worship." Orisha devotees, for their part, assert that the Spiritual Baptists copy their ideas and try to "steal their power." On occasion, Spiritual Baptist leaders have picketed Orisha centers prior to their ceremonies.

In examining the relationships between Spiritual Baptist churches and Orisha centers, four distinct types of organiza-

The line drawing shows ritual objects and their placement in a typical Spiritual Baptist church. In the front of the church is a raised platform. To the rear of the platform on a table sits a multi-tiered Spiritual Baptist altar. On top of the altar is the Christian cross. Lighted white candles represent purity and light. These are placed at all church entrances as well as at the altar and the center pole. Cut flowers are offerings to the Holy Spirit. Hand bells are the "voice of God." The Chariot Wheel symbolizes the Prophet Elijah's vision. The center pole (also resting on a tiered altar) is the axis mundi by which the Holy Spirit enters the church. DRAWING COURTESY OF STEPHEN GLAZIER.

tions may be discerned: 1) Spiritual Baptist churches with Orisha connections, 2) Spiritual Baptist churches without Orisha connections, 3) Orisha centers with Spiritual Baptist connections, and 4) Orisha centers without Spiritual Baptist connections. These distinctions reflect ways in which members of these religions think of themselves. Are they, for example, Spiritual Baptists who also "do" Orisha work or followers of the Orisha who also "do" Baptist work?

Both the Spiritual Baptists and Orisha devotees combine beliefs and practices from a wide variety of religious traditions. A major difference is that Baptist rituals are directed to their version of the Holy Trinity while Orisha rites are directed toward and incorporate African-derived deities. Spiritual Baptists profess that they are Christians and "do not worship them others." This is not to imply that Spiritual Baptists do not acknowledge the power of the Orisha. They believe strongly in the power of African deities, but do not believe that these deities should be venerated. A frequent assertion is that Spiritual Baptists do not fear the Orisha because "Christ gives us power over Orisha."

Although the Spiritual Baptists and Orisha are clearly separate traditions, they are interrelated on a number of levels. Their memberships overlap. I would estimate that about 90 percent of all Orisha devotees in Trinidad and Tobago also participate in Spiritual Baptist services and that about 40 percent of all Baptists also participate in African-derived religions. Of course, there are degrees of participation. Not all leaders in the former religion are necessarily officials in the latter and vice versa.

Close associations between Spiritual Baptist churches and Orisha are unique within the Caribbean. Participants in other African-derived faiths—like Cuban Santeria and Haitian Vodun—maintain ties with the Catholic Church; for example, the first step in serving the Haitian *lwa* (spirits) is a Catholic baptism. Spiritual Baptists, however, are the only Protestant group in the region that serves as an institutional base for an African-derived religion. The relationship between Orisha devotees and Baptist churches could be described as symbiotic. Spiritual Baptists maintain permanent buildings, while most Orisha devotees do not. Spiritual Baptists meet twice a week, while Orisha feasts are held only once or twice a year. Thus, Spiritual Baptist churches provide a convenient location for Orisha devotees to organize feasts and plan their activities as well as a setting for opening prayers for Orisha ceremonies.

Beliefs and Practices

For the Spiritual Baptists, their central and most controversial rite is the ritual known as mourning. The Spiritual Baptist concept of mourning has a very different connotations than it has in many other religious traditions. Among Baptists, it does not relate directly to physical death and bereavement, but is an elaborate ceremony involving fasting, lying on a dirt floor, and other so-called deprivations (Glazier 1985; 1991), although contemporary rites give greater emphasis to symbolic deprivation than actual physical deprivation. Death symbolism is apparent in mourning rites, but the ritual's central role has always been to remind mourners of human frailty and imperfection in the midst of life. Baptists participate in mourning ceremonies for a variety of reasons: to cure cancer, to see the future, or to communicate with the deceased. On a more mundane level, mourning enables Baptists temporary escape from family obligations, provides an opportunity for fellowship, and even allows the possibility of weight loss (while fasting is no longer encouraged, some mourners find it easy to diet within the context of the ceremony). For many, it is a vision quest; an attempt to discover the "true" self in relation to God the Father and God the Holy Ghost. The major stated goal of mourners, however, is to discover one's "true" rank within a twenty-two-step church hierarchy. Every Baptist is expected to mourn often, and every Baptist desires to advance within the church hierarchy.

Many Baptists complain that the mourning ceremony has been radically misinterpreted by outsiders. Rather than emphasize deprivations (visual, sleep, dietary), these Baptists see the rite as a time of meditation, similar to a Catholic retreat. As noted above, Baptist leaders frequently take it upon themselves to make mourning rites less demanding. Over the past twenty years, most ceremonies in most churches have been abbreviated from three weeks, to one week, to three days. Mourning rites are no longer uniform for all participants. Older mourners may be assigned a full-time nurse (this is a spiritual rank, but very often nurses have had some medical training) for the entire duration of the rite. Leaders are expected to assess the health of each potential participant and adjust the rite accordingly. Greater care is taken in terms of diet (only the prohibition on salt remains; all other food restrictions are left to the discretion of the individual leader). Those who want to observe a strict "fast" are encouraged to do so at home.

Lastly, mourners are no longer anonymous. In the past, mourners in the chamber were given numbers and referred to as "Mourner #1," "Mourner #2," and so on, throughout the rite. This underscored the loss of individuality associated with death. Now, senior mourners—especially those of higher rank—are referred to by name during the ceremony. This represents an abrupt departure from prior practices.

As noted, mourning is believed to have curative powers, and because so many individuals enter the rite in an unhealthy condition, occasionally participants die during the ceremony. Deaths may result in a routine government inquiry or a legal suit. This has happened seven times since I began fieldwork in 1976. In government inquiries, the government attempts to determine whether poor diet and damp conditions in the mourning room could have been contributing factors to mourners' deaths. Government officials assert that Baptist leaders should refuse to mourn participants believed to be too weak to withstand the rigors of the ceremony. Leaders defend themselves by claiming that they took every possible precaution to insure the mourner's physical survival, but point out that their primary responsibility is for the "spiritual" survival of the mourner. According to Baptist ideology, mourning rituals are believed to have been "spiritually" effective even when the mourner dies. Religious interpretations seem to have prevailed. Thus far, no Spiritual Baptist leader has been indicted as a result of a government inquiry. Most legal suits have been settled out of court. One case that did make it to court was later dismissed because it could not be shown that the mourner had died as a result of the ceremony (she died almost two years later in a traffic accident). All cases were brought by members of mourners' immediate families and were unsuccessful because other mourners (the only witnesses) refused to testify against the spiritual leaders who had directed their ceremonies.

Without exception, Spiritual Baptist leaders interpret attempts to scrutinize the mourning ceremonies as an assault on religious freedom. Those leaders who claim religious persecution make much of a 1917 ordinance introduced in the Trinidad and Tobago Legislative Council banning "shouting," bell ringing, and other components of Spiritual Baptist worship. The ban on shouting remained in effect from 1917 to 1953 (Jacobs 1996). Similar ordinances were introduced and passed on other islands of the British West Indies; most notably on Jamaica, Grenada, St. Kitts, and St. Vincent. A number of my informants stressed that the Trinidad ban lasted longer and was more rigorously enforced than on other islands. On the other hand, leaders who do not believe that the Spiritual Baptist faith has been subject to persecution point out that the ban was sporadically enforced and that it did little to slow the spread of the Baptist religion. For example, the Belmont church, alleged to have been the target of the original ordinance, continued to conduct weekly services throughout the period of the ban. A persistent theme in Baptist sermons is that the faith has made great "progress" in the face of adversity, and the period of the ban is likened to the Ancient Israelites' "forty years in the wilderness."

A number of dramatic changes have taken place among the Spiritual Baptists since 1976. Most dramatic of these changes are those that relate to the roles of women within the faith. In the past, Spiritual Baptist women were not permitted to occupy the same ritual space as men. In 1976, about 26 percent of the churches observed separate seating for males and females (males on the right; females on the left). Today, this practice has been abandoned. In the past, Spiritual Baptist women were expected to direct their attentions toward a raised platform at the center of the church (often called "the center pole"), while men conducted church services from a raised platform ("the altar") near the front of the church. Women never spoke from the altar platform, but addressed their concerns to the congregation in the form of a prayer, while kneeling at the center pole. While many churches still do not allow women to preach from the front altar, some larger suburban churches encourage low-ranking males to make their comments from the center pole and higher-ranking females to preach from the front of the church. Women have become much more prominent in denominational affairs. There are now two female bishops. In addition, two females serve as faculty members at the Spiritual Baptist theological seminary.

Social Advances in the 1990s

The 1990s ushered in a period of increasing respectability and visibility for the faith. In 1996, a general conference of Spiritual Baptist bishops and leaders was held at the Central Bank Auditorium in Port of Spain, one of the nicest, best-equipped conference facilities in the Caribbean. Not coincidentally, the Central Bank Auditorium was selected by the bishops because it was seen as a center of political and economic power. Several speakers (Baptist and non-Baptist) began their talks by remarking "Who would think that the Baptists be here?" Sen. Michael Ramsharam and other dignitaries were invited to address the conference. Future Prime Minister Basdeo Panday was also said to have been in the audience. Panday was instrumental in establishing a national holiday in Trinidad honoring the Spiritual Baptists.

The proceedings of this conference has been published under the title *Call Him By His Name, Jesus: Spiritual Baptists: Christians Moving into the 21st Century*, and has been widely distributed by the World Council of Churches in local bookstores and throughout the Caribbean. The proceedings contains the full texts of all bishops' remarks as well as questions and comments from the floor. It is a remarkable document! Most notable is Archbishop Murrain's address calling for 1) a new cathedral with a library for researchers who want to "make a history" of the Spiritual Baptist faith, 2) the establishment of a trade school to help Spiritual Baptists get better jobs, and 3) the building of a "Spiritual Baptist Park "that will serve as a pilgrimage site for Spiritual Baptists in the Caribbean and throughout the world.

The day of the repeal of the Shouters Prohibition Ordinance in 1953 has been designated as a national holiday in Trinidad and Tobago, and Baptists have been granted land to establish an "open space"—a national memorial park—and to build a cathedral and a trade school. They chose to locate their "open space" and cathedral at the confluence of two major highways: the Uriah Butler Highway (the main road to San Fernando and the South) and the Priority Bus Route (which parallels Eastern Main Road to Arima). The church has also established a governing body, the Council of Elders, with headquarters on Saddle Road in Maraval.

The comprehensive *Spiritual Baptist Minister's Manual* was published in 1993. Its 238 pages include precise, detailed instructions for conducting dedication of infants, baptisms, and mournings as well as a suggested "Order of Worship" and a list of appropriate hymns and scripture passages for each juncture of the service.

It is extremely difficult to gauge the impact of these proposed changes on rank-and-file believers. Thus far, the impact has been minuscule. Southland School of Theology in La Brea has no fulltime students, the *Spiritual Baptist Ministers' Manual* is rarely consulted, and construction has yet to begin on the park, the trade school, and the cathedral. The majority of Spiritual Baptist churches remain small and lack a solid financial base. And, I suspect that for the average church member things continue "pretty much as before."

Stephen D. Glazier

See also Orisha (Shango) Movement in Trinidad; Trinidad, African-Derived Religions in

Bibliography

Glazier, Stephen D. (1985) "Mourning in the Afro-Baptist tradition: a comparative study of religion in the American South and in Trinidad." *Southern Quarterly* 23 (3): 141–156. 1991.

———. (1991) *Marchin' the Pilgrims Home: A Study of the Spiritual Baptists of Trinidad*. Salem, WI: Sheffield.

———. (1993) Funerals and mourning in the Spiritual Baptist and Shango traditions. *Caribbean Quarterly* 39: 1–11.

Houk, James T. (1995) Spirits, Blood, and Drums. Philadelphia: Temple University Press.

Jacobs, C. M. 1996. *Joy Comes in the Mourning: Elton George Griffith and the Shouter Baptists*. Port of Spain: Caribbean Historical Society.

Lum, Kenneth. (2000) *Praising His Name in the Dance: Spirit Possession in the Spiritual Baptist Faith and Orisha Work in Trinidad, West Indies*. Amsterdam: Harwood Academic Publishers.

Pollack-Eltz, Angelina. (1970) "Shango Kult und Shouter Kirche auf Trinidad und Grenada." *Anthropos* 65: 814–832.

Simpson, George Eaton. (1966) "'Baptismal,' 'Mourning,' and 'Building' Ceremonies among the Shouters in Trinidad" *Journal of American Folklore* 79: 537–550:

Thomas, Eudora. (1987) *A History of the Shouter Baptists in Trinidad and Tobago.* Tacarigua: Calaloux.

Zane, Wallace W. (1999) *Journeys to the Spiritual Lands: The Natural History of a West Indian Religion.* New York: Oxford.

Spiritualism

Spiritualism, as a distinct religious movement based on the belief in communication with departed spirits, emerged in the United States in the middle of the nineteenth century. Spiritism, a similar movement with the additional belief in reincarnation, arose in Europe during the same period. Spiritualism became associated with North America and Britain while Spiritism spread from continental Europe to Latin America and the Caribbean. Although Spiritualism and Spiritism are currently only minor religions, features of both have persisted as a consequence of syncretism, or mixing, especially with African-American Christianity in North America and African beliefs and rituals in the Caribbean and Brazil.

Although Spiritualism and Spiritism, grew up on different sides of the Atlantic and developed distinctively, they share many of the same intellectual antecedents: the tradition of spirit possession in medieval Christianity, astrological theories of Paracelsus, ideas concerning disease and cures formulated by Mesmer and other eighteenth- and nineteenth-century animal magnetists, and doctrines of radical religious groups such as the French Comisards, English Quakers, and Shakers in America.

Among the European writers who attempted to codify these strains of thought was Leon Denizarth Hippolyte Rivail (1804–1869), a Frenchman, who wrote under the name Allan Kardec. His revelations concerning reincarnation became a fundamental doctrine of the Spiritist circles on the Continent and in the southern hemisphere of the New World. Kardec's ideas initially attracted European and Latin American intellectuals and urban elites who saw them as a revolutionary ideology suited to their anticlericalism and disaffection for traditional religion, interest in the writings of Saint Simon and August Comte, and efforts to reformulate the concept of the human spirit in scientific and rational terms. As elements of Kardec's philosophy filtered into other sectors of Latin American society, they combined with a variety of folk-healing techniques, as well as Catholic and African beliefs and rituals.

Spiritualism and Spiritism share many basic beliefs: the existence of an eternal and good God; an emphasis on spiritual over material in the universe; the Golden Rule as the highest ethical teaching; and the progressivist and democratic concepts of the perfectibility and equality of spirits. In this worldview, the universe is composed of a visible, material plane inhabited by incarnated spirits, and an invisible, spiritual plane where disembodied spirits dwell. Both types of spirits are ranked in pyramid fashion from lowest to highest, culminating in God, the all-good universal Spirit. The relationship between one's own spirit and other spirits in the universe is crucial, since some spirits can bring harm and danger, or if they are spirit guides, saints, or guardian angels, offer help and protection.

Mediums, who have highly developed capacities to communicate with the spirit world, can assist people in need by exorcising evil spirits and contacting enlightened ones. During services or seances, mediums may also use their powers to contact spirits and convey messages that include practical advice regarding diet, regimen, and interpersonal relationships. While a medium may reveal that a person's problems are due to the influence of low, undeveloped, or restless spirits, messages sometimes indicate that the fault is the individual's attitude or spiritual development. The message in these cases is that while some help may come from the spirit world, proper thoughts and emotions are also important, since people make their own problems and can shape their own destinies.

Spiritualism in the United States

The origins of Spiritualism in the United States can be traced to 1846, the year that Andrew Jackson Davis published *The Principle of Nature: Her Divine Revelation* describing his experiences with the spirit realm. Two years later, in 1848, Margaret and Kate Fox began to report strange raps and messages from spirits in their Hydesville, New York home. Following these events, Spiritualism spread rapidly, initially as parlor entertainment among family and friends, afterwards as a loosely organized religious movement with services often patterned on Protestant worship, and later on in several institutionalized forms.

Spiritualism's growth in the United States was due in part to its ability to satisfy the needs of people who lived amidst increasing sociocultural change and geographical mobility. The second half of the nineteenth century saw waves of European immigrants settle in American cities and advances in science and technology transform patterns of work and family life. Conflict and epidemic diseases made death a common occurrence. While the Civil War claimed the lives of thousands of young men, yellow fever, cholera, and a variety of ill-defined fevers carried off people of all ages. A preoccupation with death coupled with a fear of dying pervaded the country, and traditional religious groups seemed unable to console the bereaved. In this context, Spiritualism offered proof of a future life. Although Spiritualists claim that the movement attracted some of the best-known individuals in American history, including Daniel Webster, James Fenimore Cooper, William Cullen Bryant, Abraham Lincoln, and George Washington Carver, the leading figures were lesser-known persons, such as Andrew Jackson Davis and the Fox sisters, who attained fame entirely from their participation in Spiritualist activities.

An accurate count of American Spiritualists during the nineteenth century is not available. Estimates range from one to eleven million. In addition to the opponents to orthodox Christianity and other traditional religions, many people who joined the Spiritualist movement in the 1800s were social reformers who supported abolition, temperance, health reform, prison reform, women's equality, Native American rights, and labor unions, and objected to capital punishment. By the end of the nineteenth century, however, this reformist tendency in the movement had largely disappeared.

Although Spiritualism may be described generally, the composition of the movement was quite diverse. There were both atheists and those who claimed to be Christians. Among the latter, Jesus was thought to be divine in a special way, yet his existence only pointed to human divinity in general. In comparison, non-Christian Spiritualists tended to look upon Jesus as a skilled medium, who because of his uniqueness might never be a model for others. Even Christian Spiritualists generally denied two of the central beliefs of orthodox Christianity: the Trinity and the Atonement. Meetings of the different types of Spiritualists varied considerably. Some had a church atmosphere and included prayers, lectures, and music from a Spiritualist hymnal that modified well-known hymns to suit the group's belief system. Others dispensed with such practices entirely. Regardless of the type of meeting, the most important part of the service involved communion with the dead and receiving spirit messages.

As Spiritualism emerged in the middle of the nineteenth century, people associated with the movement formed local societies, circles, and regional associations. In the 1850s, a group of elite Creoles of color in New Orleans formed a Spiritualist circle and were in contact with similar groups in Europe and elsewhere in North America. The membership included notable local persons such as J. B. Valmour, Nelson Desbrosses, Henriette Delille, and Henry Rey. During their

meetings, the group kept seance registers that recorded poetry and revelations from a variety of spirits, such as Voltaire, Robespierre, Baudelaire, and St. Vincent de Paul.

It was not until the late 1800s, when Spiritualism began to decline, that there was any successful organization on a national level. The National Spiritualist Association, the first of a series of organizations, was formed in 1893. From this association, the Progressive Spiritual Church was founded in 1907, and the National Spiritual Alliance in 1913. As racial problems flared up at the close of World War I, white members of the National Spiritualist Association moved to exclude blacks from that group by segregating them in a separate organization. Not without some dissension among blacks over these events and the subsequent proceedings, the National Colored Spiritualist Association formed in 1925. The group took as its model the National Spiritualist Association and in 1926 adopted a constitution and bylaws.

It is not known how many African Americans were attracted to Spiritualism. Nevertheless, African Americans were organizing Spiritualist churches in Chicago, New Orleans, and elsewhere by the second decade of the twentieth century, and they were being recognized as talented leaders and mediums. In New Orleans, the best-known Spiritualist leader in the early part of the twentieth century was a woman named Leafy Anderson (d. 1927). While Spiritualist circles had existed in New Orleans prior to Leafy Anderson's arrival to the city, they appear to have involved primarily French-speaking Creoles. What she did was to introduce Spiritualism to the city's non-Creole blacks. It is unclear to what extent, if any, the racial policies of the National Spiritualist Association were a factor, but by the 1940s almost all of the churches that Leafy Anderson and her followers established had shortened the name to Spiritual and incorporated more mainstream Christian theology into their belief system.

Although members of the Spiritual churches deny any connection between their religion and Spiritualism, there is evidence from several sources of such links. A Spiritualist minister from Lily Dale, New York, one of the oldest and most important centers for American Spiritualism, spoke to members of Leafy Anderson's church in New Orleans in 1927. Further, statements of the Spiritual churches are strikingly similar to those of the Spiritualists in terms of comprehensiveness of purpose and emphasis on combining science and religion. For example, the National Spiritualist Association's objectives in part are "to teach and proclaim the science, philosophy, and religion of modern Spiritualism." The Israel Universal Divine Spiritual Churches of Christ, headquartered in New Orleans, describes its objectives as being of a "religious, scientific, literary, and charitable nature." Another indication that the Spiritual churches and Spiritualists share a common heritage comes from an old undated printed program of the First Church of Divine Fellowship of New Orleans, which was chartered through the National Spiritualist Association. On the cover of the program there appears a New Testament quotation: "God is a spirit and they that worship him must worship him in spirit and in truth" (John 4:24). No other Bible verse is heard more often than this one in the Spiritual churches. In addition, the program mentions the twelfth chapter of First Corinthians, which Spiritual ministers repeatedly cite as justification of their faith. This passage, "Concerning Spiritual Gifts," spells out the importance of healing, prophecy, the ability to distinguish between spirits, and the practice of speaking in tongues. All are central features of Spiritual belief and ritual.

Spiritism in Latin America and the Caribbean

The origins of organized Spiritism in Brazil can be traced back to 1873, when a society for Spiritist studies formed in Rio de Janeiro. While it is not certain how many Brazilians joined in the new movement in the nineteenth century, sizable numbers became associated with it in the early decades of the twentieth century and later on, especially after World War II.

Over the years, Spiritism in Brazil has become extremely diverse. There are intellectuals who see themselves as strictly following the teachings of Kardec as well as people who have snycretized Spiritism with African beliefs and rituals. Between these two extremes are Christian Spiritists, similar to the Spiritual churches in the United States. Syncretism has produced a new religion, Umbanda, that combines Spiritism with Macumba, another Brazilian religion that was in part a product of the introduction of Yoruba deities into an earlier Central African religion known as Cabula. Macumba's retention of the Central African belief in possession by the dead fit especially well with the Spiritist ideas about the departed. Although there is no accurate count, the number of Umbanda adherents has increased steadily. While some white Brazilians who have become Umbandists have attempted to eliminate animal sacrifices, drinking, and drumming and dancing from the ritual, black practitioners have criticized de-Africanization of the religion.

In places such as New York, Latin Americans from a variety of countries now live together. Spiritism, largely associated with Puerto Ricans, has come into contact with Santeria, the Afro-Catholic religion of Cuba. People's reaction to this complex situation has been varied. While some practitioners maintain that Spiritism's work with the dead should be kept separate from Santeria's work with the saints

and orishas (African deities), others do not. There are Spiritists who have borrowed rituals, music, and symbols from Santeria. Similarly, there are some santeros (priests and priestesses) who believe that they have to work with the dead in Spiritism before they can do the more powerful work with the saints and orishas in Santeria.

While Spiritualism in North America seems to have reached its limits, Spiritism in Latin America and now among Latin Americans settling in the United States has continued to be a dynamic cultural influence as a result of syncretism with other systems of belief and ritual. Umbanda, for example, has become a significant religious movement in Brazil, compared to the less well-known and presently declining Spiritual churches in the United States. The difference may be that while the membership in the Spiritual churches has remained overwhelmingly black, Umbanda is embraced by a wide spectrum of Brazilians representing different races and social classes, and in places such as New York the continual arrival of Latin American immigrants is keeping older syncretisms alive and creating new ones.

Claude F. Jacobs

See also Black Spiritual Churches; Brazil, African-Derived Religions in; Caribbean, African-Derived Religions in; Macumba; Kardecism; Puerto Rico, African-Derived Religions in; Santeria

Bibliography

Bell, Caryn Cossé. (1997) *Revolution and Romanticism and the Afro-Catholic Protest Tradition in Louisiana: 1718–1868.* Baton Rouge: Louisiana State University Press.

Garrison, Vivian. (1977) "Doctor, Espiritista or Psychiatrist?: Health-Seeking Behavior in a Puerto Rican Neighborhood of New York City." *Medical Anthropology* 1: 65–191.

Hess, David. (1991) *Spirits and Scientists: Ideology, Spiritism, and Brazilian Culture.* University Park: Pennsylvania State University Press.

Jacobs Claude F., and Andrew J. Kaslow. (1991) *The Spiritual Churches of New Orleans: Origins, Beliefs, and Rituals of an African-American Religion.* Knoxville: The University of Tennessee Press.

St. Kitts and Nevis, African-Derived Religions in

The Federation of St. Kitts (formerly St. Christopher) and Nevis is an independent nation formed in 1983 by two small islands in the Lesser Antilles. Its population is estimated to

UNA MAN PAISA (*PASS DOWN THE MONEY*)

by H. Hendrickson

The poem describes the origin, meaning and rituals of the Nevisian Masquerade.

Adorned with peacock feathered headdress,
Masked, trousers and long sleeve shirts,
An apron or mantel for the captain;
Decorated with mirrors, ribbons,
Handkerchiefs, tassels and bells.
Masquerade,
Indigenous of our African ancestors
From Yoruba, West Africa
They came —
Culturally rich.
The Big Drum keeps the beat,
The Kettle Drum the rhythm,
from the Bamboo Fife notes flow.
The music and dance attract —
'Shango' God of Thunder.
Mirrors capture the viewer's image
And connect with the spirit world,
Shango's visual power the Thunder-axe.
To religious rituals
Of their ancestors —
They dance.
Quadrille, Fine, Waltz
Jig, Bollolia and Wild Dance
Each movement precisioned.
Distinctive is Wild Dance
When they shout "Una Man Paisa."

be about 45,000. All but 3 percent of Kittitians and Nevisians are of African descent. Around 50 percent are Anglicans, with the rest adhering to the Catholic, Church of God, Methodist, and Baptist faiths.

While the massive disruption of enslavement and the intermingling of Africans from very different cultures prevented religious systems from remaining wholly intact, many Kittitians and Nevisians retained some African folk beliefs and practices in conjunction with their Christian faith. By far the most notorious of these folk beliefs is the sys-

tem of *obeah*, a West Indian form of sorcery. Although not as formalized as other African-derived West Indian religions, obeah influences the way most citizens of the two islands construct and conduct their lives. *Obeahmen* and *obeah-women* typically employ a bag of charms, which may include rusty nails, feathers, broken glass, and pieces of clay to work their magic, which can be for good or evil purposes.

Obeah potions are credited with the ability to make one succeed in one's endeavors and give one control over others. Not a few men are alleged to have been tricked into marriage after unwittingly consuming "come-to-me-sauce," which makes its victim irresistibly attracted to the woman who slipped it into his food. Wives are also known to have given their husbands "stay-at-home sauce" to curtail extramarital philandering. These potent substances are administered in cocoa, tea, or in *cou-cou*, a traditional cornmeal dish.

Other folk-religious concepts and traditions persist in diluted form in present-day St. Kitts and Nevis. *Soucouyan* is a live evil person who is capable of adopting different animal forms; it flies at night and sucks the blood of its victims. *Jumbies* appear as live people and are believed to be the spirits of the deceased that have returned to play pranks on the living. Jack o'Lantern is another phenomenon of the Kittitian psychic world, and appears as a huge ball of light in open stretches of canefields.

In contrast to these less-visible ways of folk cultural beliefs, one can see and feel the vibration of African-derived expressive religious culture at different traditional festivities, including Masquerades and Big Drum Bands. Masquerade is the old way of celebrating Christmas in St. Kitts. The origin can be traced back to the times of slavery. At the end of the harvesting of the sugar crop, certain "Crop-over" festivities were permitted. Christmas time was another occasion on which the people were given license to enjoy themselves.

The masquerade bands can be divided into various categories: Christmas Morning bands, Big Drum bands, the Cakewalk band, Maypole, Moko Jumbie Stilt Dancer, and Nagur Business bands. The first bands to go out after midnight on Christmas morning were generally known as *Shambololo* bands, often considered to be of African origin.

Today, the most visible expression of African religious performance can be experienced during the popular international cultural festivals, the St. Kitts Music Festival, and the Culturama in Nevis. By including *Soca* and Gospel music into its program, the St. Kitts Music Festival is a place to enjoy rhythms for the body as well as rhythms for the soul. The Masquerade during Culturama is a true depiction of Nevisian art, which is strongly influenced by its rich African heritage as well.

Manfred Kremser

See also Big Drum Dance of Carriacou; Caribbean, African-Derived Religion in; Obeah in the West Indies

Bibliography

Hamilton, Charles Annette. (1985) *Some Belief Systems and Practices in St. Kitts*. Cave Hill: University of the West Indies.

Matheson, Lloyd. (1985) *The Folklore of St. Christopher's Island*. Basseterre: Creole Graphics.

Nevis Culturama (Web site). http://nevisculturama.com/nevis-culturama/index.htm

St. Kitts Music Festival (Web site). http://www.geographia.com/stkitts-nevis/musicfestival.htm

St. Lucia, African-Derived Religions in

The population of the Caribbean island of St. Lucia is estimated at 150,000, with people of African descent constituting more than 90 percent of the population. Although English is the official language, St. Lucian Kwéyòl (Creole) is widely spoken. Because of the legacy of French influence, 85 percent of St. Lucians are Roman Catholics. Four ceremonial events with strong reference to African expressive and religious culture are unique to St. Lucia: the pageantry of Flower Societies, and the rituals and performances associated with A-Bwè, Koutoumba, and Kélé. Of these, Kélé has, in many regards, always held a special position in the cultural life of St. Lucia. The Flower Societies hold an annual round of revels that effectively divide Saint Lucian society into the Roses (Lawòz) and the Marguerites (Lamagwit). Beginning with Mass at dawn, each group, on its respective feast day (30 August for the Roses and 17 October for the Marguerites) stages a parade, complete with a court of kings and queens. The day and evening are spent feasting, dancing, and play-acting. A-Bwè was a singing ceremony with drinking songs performed in a competitive call-and-response manner. It took place in villages south of La Sorcière mountain during the Christmas season. It is rarely heard nowadays. Koutoumba, a particular funeral song-dance in several villages of the southwest (including La Grace, Laborie, and Piaye), was always performed at the death of a member of a particular group of people who, like some residents of the Babonneau region, call themselves Djiné. Djiné means persons born in Africa; that is, real Africans. It is the new St. Lucian Kwéyòl spelling for what was formerly spelled Guinée, a term which was frequently used synonymously for Africa. Koutoumba disappeared in 1986 with the death of the last drummer who could play the music.

Kélé is a religious ritual in which homage is paid to the African ancestors and powers. It is limited to only a few communities on the island, namely to the Djiné families in Babonneau district. Since the deaths of the last high priests, Noah (also Noe) Delaire in 1984, and Etienne Wells Joseph in 1993, this principal ritual of African Traditional Religion (ATR) in St. Lucia seems to have fallen into oblivion.

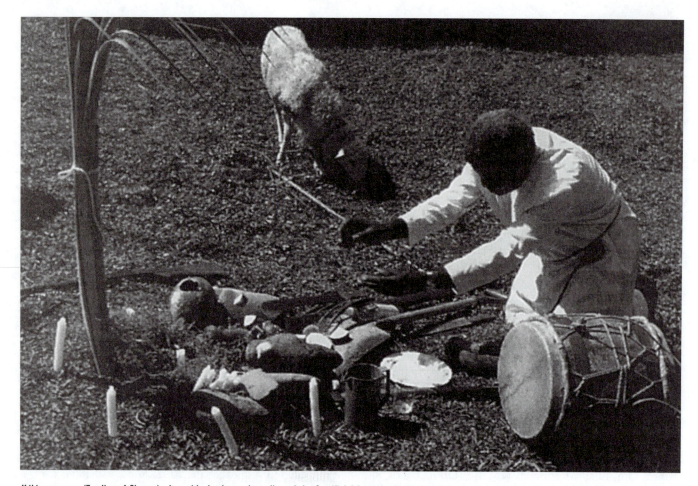

Kélé ceremony (Feeding of Shango) altar with ritual paraphernalia and the Sacrificial Lamb in the background. PHOTOS COURTESY OF MANFRED KREMSER.

Until the 1960s, this minority cult of the Djiné families had been the least known, but at the same time the most disputed of all the religious practices on the island. Repressed by the Roman Catholic Church, it had been practiced underground since it first appeared on St. Lucia in about 1867, shortly after the arrival of families from Western Nigeria (of the Ekiti-speaking Yoruba) about thirty years after the abolition of slavery (1834–1838).

Among these newly immigrated Djiné, or Afwitchen, (persons born in Africa, or "real" Africans) were leading members of Yoruba *orisha* traditions, specifically Shango and Ogun. They soon merged in St. Lucia to form a new cult, the Kélé. Whereas most other African-derived religions in the Caribbean have undergone some sort of syncretistic merger with Roman Catholicism, the development which brought Kélé into existence could rather be termed as a syncretism among different African religious traditions. Up until the present, no Christian influence has been found in Kélé ceremonies, even though some of the last high priests were prominent members of local Catholic Holy Name Societies, actively involved in many parish functions.

Kélé ceremonies are "given" several times a year: at about the time of the New Year, following Easter, at the anniversary of the death of a recent ancestor, for thanksgiving, or to ask African powers and ancestors for protection in all matters of importance, including a rich harvest, good health, and good fortune in general. Three African powers are addressed in the ritual and each is represented with specific paraphernalia:

Shango-stones symbolize the divine powers of African ancestors and enable the living to get in touch with them. Even though some of them are shaped like (Amerindian) stone-axes, Djiné claim to have brought them along from Africa. Therefore, Shango-stones are at the heart of their religious practices, and reportedly contain powerful protective and healing properties. As such, they are used for curing certain illnesses, for protecting one's house from fire, and for safeguarding one's journey.

In Djiné religious theory, Shango-stones link man with God—they are regarded as a physical representation of divine power. In using them in a ritual context, Djiné can bridge the distance between man and God, since "Shango comes from God." Almost all Djiné families keep Shango-stones in their homes, oil them regularly, use them in candlelit prayers in an African language resembling the Ekiti dialect of the Yoruba, and feed them during the Kélé ceremony. The African deity addressed in most of Djiné prayers is Ogun. He is represented on the altar with different agricultural tools made of iron: garden forks, spades, cutlasses, steel axes, saws, rifles, and an iron pole, to which a shoot of a coconut is tied (representing Ogun's clothes) and a ram is tethered. Medicinal fern and numerous yam roots are spread next to these ritual objects for Ogun. A comparison with West African religious practices indicates that, in many respects, St. Lucian Kélé resembles the Yoruba Ogun festival as it is celebrated in Nigeria.

A calabash representing Esu (locally called Akeshew) is placed nearby, containing secret "magical" substances (Djinéfication) mixed with ashes, as well as small pieces of sacrificial offerings: some of the ram's wool, pieces of raw yams, olive oil, white rum, water, bits of candles, and so on. Also, some of the blood of the sacrificial ram is poured into this calabash before it is sprinkled over all the other paraphernalia and personal objects that participating devotees place on the altar in order to have them blessed by the African powers.

The Kélé ritual requires economic and logistic preparations which may involve several months of planning. The actual ceremony involves the following: (1) setting-up a temporary altar with Shango-stones and other paraphernalia; (2) a purification rite such as the washing of the sacrificial ram; (3) drumming, singing, praying, and incantations; (4) the first feeding of Shango; (5) slaying of the ram; (6) cooking of the ritual offerings and meals; (7) the second feeding of Shango; (8) smashing of the oracular calabash; (9) taking food-offerings to the graves of recently deceased family members; (10) a communal meal; and (11) feasting and dancing among the Djiné community.

In the 1980s and 1990s the local Folk Research Center and its founder, Msgr. Patrick A. B. Anthony (director of the Pastoral Center, St. Lucia, editor of *Theology in the Caribbean*, and current president for the Caribbean region of the World Association for Christian Communication) worked to promote a better understanding and a more positive attitude towards the Kélé and other African-derived cultural traditions of the island. The award of the Nobel prize for Literature to the St. Lucian writer Derek Walcott in 1992 has given local artists and intellectuals an additional stimulus and inspiration for re-orienting their cultural awareness towards their own rich African and Creole heritage so frequently touched upon in Walcott's writings.

Manfred Kremser

See also Obeah in the West Indies; Ogun; Yoruba Religion

Bibliography

Anthony, Patrick A. B. (1986) "The Encounter between Christianity and Culture: The Case of the 'Kele' Ceremony in St. Lucia." In *Research in Ethnography and Ethnohistory of St. Lucia*, edited by Manfred Kremser and Karl R. Wernhart. Vienna: Ferdinand Berger & Söhne, 103–120.

——. (1996) "Changing Attitudes towards African Traditional Religion and the Implications for Afro-Caribbean Tradition in St. Lucia." In *AyBoBo—African-Caribbean Religions*, Part 1, *Kulte/Cults*, edited by Manfred Kremser. Vienna: WUV-Universitätsverlag, 69–84.

Guilbault, Jocelyne. (1993) *Musical Traditions of St. Lucia, West Indies: Dances and Songs from a Caribbean Island.* Smithsonian/Folkways Recordings SF 40416.

Kremser, Manfred. (1986) "The African Heritage in the Kélé-Tradition of the Djiné in St. Lucia." In *Research in Ethnography and Ethnohistory of St. Lucia*, edited by Manfred Kremser and Karl R. Wernhart. Vienna: Ferdinand Berger & Söhne, 77–101.

——. (1993). "Visiting Ancestors: St. Lucian Djiné in Communion with their African Kin." *Caribbean Quarterly* 39, 3 and 4: 82–99.

Simpson, George E. (1973) "The Kele (Chango) Cult in St. Lucia: Research Commentaries 3." *Caribbean Studies* 13, 3: 110–116.

Storefront Churches

Storefront churches were established in urban American settlements in the late 1800s with the first wave of black migration from the South. Storefront churches flowered with the expansion of the black population and persist in black working-class and poverty-stricken neighborhoods in the urban North. In the early 1900s storefront church leaders and members were frequently propertyless, unskilled, poorly educated, and dependent on the city's blue-collar labor market. By the late 1920s, there were countless storefront churches in black urban settlements. In Chicago, for example, there were 500 black churches by

1930, approximately 300 of them were in storefronts. Storefront congregations vary in membership from groups of approximately 20 to 400. It is the hope of storefront missions that they will reach a base from which to expand their buildings and their ministries. Storefront churches often have their beginnings in private homes and small prayer bands. The full range of black denominations is represented in the urban storefront landscape; however, the vast majority of these churches identify themselves as Missionary Baptist or Church of God in Christ.

Storefront churches are independent and supported by resources and volunteer work provided by church members. These churches arise from and depend on the spiritual interests and talents of the persons invested in them. Within the structure of these congregations members freely elect church leaders and determine the order of worship, church organization, and activities. They create routine events that frame a system of meaning and purpose. In storefronts they develop leaders who can speak about their issues in a way that make sense to them. They look to the teachings of the church to build lasting relationships among family members and to guide them in daily life as they deal with financial uncertainty, limited work opportunities, intractable health problems, random violent crime in their neighborhood, race discrimination, inadequate neighborhood institutions, and opportunities for social mobility. Storefront churches are often surrounded by boarded-up factories, condemned apartment buildings, and vacant commercial premises. They are surrounded by buildings, streets, and residential quarters in need of repair. Broken windows covered with plastic, gang graffiti, wrecked pavements, and litter abound near storefront churches. The buildings are makeshift quarters. Every congregation has members that share in the stories of finding building materials and labor.

Storefront congregations are structured by the congregation's symbolic rendering of the life, teachings, death, and resurrection of Jesus, who in their collective thought is the son of God and the savior of humanity. Within the context of church routines, congregations articulate narratives based on their interpretation of Scripture to give meaning to their lives and to create moral and social solidarity in the midst of the meaningless hardships of the ghetto. Within the routines and narratives they enact in their congregations, they resist and reverse degrading images of blacks that are the consequence of uneven economic distribution and race discrimination. The moral and social teachings of these churches posit a vision of black spiritual qualities and identity that opposes white contempt and demeaning dispositions towards impoverished inner-city blacks. Individual and group activity in this church is informed by the congregation's vision of God's distribution of spiritual gifts among them.

Theoretical Considerations

Early sociological and anthropological accounts viewed storefront churches as ephemeral. Some accounts argued that within them poor blacks articulated otherworldly and compensatory beliefs and practices that accommodated social and economic hardship and injustice. Early interpreters assumed, in advance of systematic empirical investigation, that religious thought and practices resulted from a culture of poverty and pathology. In these accounts, religion functioned to ease anxiety and frustration. This literature overlooked the history of the black church and black theology and thus missed the potential that working-class black religion embodies for constructing a usable past, social values, and collective purpose. Contrary to early studies that viewed storefront churches as black accommodation and capitulation to white power, I argue that within them blacks define a worldview that challenges the self-interested principles of the American mainstream. In my interpretation, storefront churches are examined within the framework of the three-hundred-year legacy of black struggle against white oppression and racism in America.

My interpretation has drawn from Emile Durkheim's conception of religion as sacred collective conscious, Max Weber's study of charismatic authority in religious movements among the urban poor, and anthropologists who have studied religious representations among oppressed evangelical Protestants in the Third World. Durkheim argues that the study of religion is concerned with sacred conceptual categories and the relationship between the principles encoded in them to the construction of collective moral and social order and solidarity. In his schema, a church is constituted by a group that is united by a shared system of sacred beliefs and practice. He argued that the system of beliefs and practices embodied in a church are also a source of moral and social solidarity.

Max Weber provided a model for interpreting the religious vocations of storefront ministers in his discussion of prophets, salvation, and charisma. According to Weber, prophets are legitimized by their personal calling and charismatic endowment, unlike priests who hold office by virtue of their training in a sacred tradition. In Weber's schema, prophets are instructed by God. They have the ability to directly receive God's word, which reveals his plan for humanity's salvation. For Weber, the prophet's divine revelations embody a system of moral and ethical knowledge. Weber also suggests that the prophet's words and deeds articulate a view of the cosmos, which meaningfully orders natural and social calamities, and encourages human beings in times of crises and affliction. Storefront ministers and lay leaders were poorly educated, from the rural South, and lacked formal theological training. Thus, they relied on their God-given gifts to guide their ministry. My approach has also been influenced by social anthropologists who have shown that poor and oppressed Christians create, in their collective religious imagination, discourse, and practice, spiritual symbols and principles that displace the oppressive symbols of powerful groups and critique an economic system that provides wealth for a few while leaving the masses in poverty.

Cosmology, Organization, and Routines

Storefront churches in black neighborhoods in the urban North have been shaped by black evangelical thought, white race discrimination, and black response to unjust white social and economic privilege. According to black evangelical thought, social institutions that stand between God and humanity must be supplanted by ones that allow human

beings to live according to divine rule. In this cosmos, charisma—a divine call manifested in extraordinary individual and group spiritual conviction and ability—inspired and justified the work of black men and women who established independent black churches against formidable white hostility and opposition.

Black churches expanded rapidly in the urban North in the context of race discrimination, de facto segregation, economic exploitation of the black masses, and social class stratification. Although middle-class blacks developed secular institutions to challenge racism and segregation, the black church remained a significant locus in the struggle against racism and oppression among low-income and poverty-stricken blacks. Blacks who accepted Christianity believed that they were obligated to challenge institutions and practices that violate the will of a merciful and loving God. Blacks became Christians in massive numbers when they saw in evangelical Protestantism a cosmological order that gave meaning to their suffering and delivered them from bondage. In biblical Scripture, blacks saw a powerful God who intervened in human and worldly affairs to vindicate the poor and to liberate oppressed people. In the

A storefront church in the Brixton section of London, England, in the late 1990s. Brixton has a large Afro-Caribbean population, and storefront churches in London suggest the ubiquity of the institution in African-ancestry communities around the world. PHOTO COURTESY OF KAREN CHRISTENSEN.

conception of black Christians, God was an eternal ruler in heaven, where faith in Jesus would deliver them. Black Christians believed that God knew about their suffering and would deliver mercy, justice, and liberation as he had to other enslaved biblical people. In Christianity, blacks found a God they could talk to personally at all times, without the mediation of the clergy. In Christianity, all human beings are created equal before the eyes of God; and blacks were drawn by the egalitarian principles embedded in this line of evangelical thought.

Within the context of worship services, Bible study, prayer meetings, and social gatherings in independent black churches, blacks gave voice to their collective interests and affirmed their humanity. According to black Christians, God is an omnipotent supreme being. For them, God has the power to deliver humanity from social injustice, suffering, and death. In black evangelical thought, religious authority is contingent on God's grace, which includes the gifts of faith, wisdom, knowledge, healing, and prophecy in the life of individuals and Christian communities. In the stories of the liberation of biblical peoples, blacks saw their own freedom.

For church members, God is an all-powerful being, a personal friend, and a savior. In their conception, God conquers evil, uncertainty, and death. According to their understanding of the enactment of God's relationship to humanity they seek to rectify the conflicts between anger and mercy, greed and generosity, love and hate, selfishness and sacrifice that in their view define human relationships. To know God and have eternal life involves a personal and collective struggle to overcome anger, greed, hate, and frustration over unfortunate setbacks and social injustice. In their spiritual quest they seek moral character development based on the principles of love, mercy, and faith represented in their rendering of Christ's teachings and passion.

Everyone who joins the church is blessed to work in the mission. In this congregation, having the capacity to work and having a job are considered divine gifts that lose their value if they are not returned to God through church stewardship. Church members share the hope that they will escape perdition through God's gift of everlasting life in his kingdom in heaven. They conceive of God as omnipresent, omniscient, and omnipotent. God created the world and all things in the world including humanity. They conceive of God as a triune being; he is the Father, the son Jesus, and the Holy Ghost. God the Father is the creator of all things in heaven and earth. God came to earth and lived and walked among humanity as Jesus Christ, the Son of God. Christ came to show humanity that he has power to conquer evil and death and to teach humanity the word of God, which embodies his plan for salvation. When Jesus completed his

work on earth God brought him back to heaven and returned as the Holy Ghost, also called the Spirit. The Holy Ghost is an active agent in day-to-day human affairs. The Holy Ghost imbues God's chosen people with spiritual gifts to serve God and humanity for their salvation. Church members invoke the Holy Ghost in daily prayer to give them strength to endure and make sense of everyday life. They petition God the Father through the Holy Ghost in their private prayers and church prayer meetings for protection against evil and suffering.

According to church members, God created every human being with the potential to do evil and he put humankind on earth where evil and temptation abound. God creates and dispenses adversity in human life for divine purpose. In their schema, the devil, also called Satan, is the agent of evildoing and death. In their cosmology, the devil is controlled and dispatched by God for divine purpose. When faced with tragedy, the congregation recalls Christ's suffering and death and the principles of forgiveness, patience, mercy, and faith embodied in his passion. In their eyes calamity and ruin are an opportunity for human beings to overcome fear, anger, and frustration.

In this cosmos God is in charge of individual social and economic welfare. God dispenses spiritual and material resources among human beings for divine purpose. God gives and takes away material comforts to strengthen individual commitment to the principles of Christian living. God expects individuals to show love for God and for humanity by giving a portion of their God-given labor, money, and talents back to God through the church. Church members believe that God answers the prayers of individuals who pray with a heart that has been converted and is filled with desire to praise and please God. However, in their vision, doubt and disobedience closes the channel from the mind to the heart and prevents human beings from receiving God's power and abundance. In this cosmos the privileges of money are subverted by the certainty of death and the hope for eternal life, which is possible through the will of God and service to him and humanity through the church.

The church organization is divided into committees, boards, and offices. With guidance and support of the pastor and church members an individual negotiates a church vocation. Among active members there is considerable competition for church positions that confer greater status and power. Mobility in the organization depends on gender, age, service, and financial resources.

The pastor is the top position in the church organization. The pastor is considered an authority on the Bible and the church looks for his judgment on interpretation of Scripture. In the eyes of his church, God chose him and blessed him to pastor the church. A pastor must bring God's word to the congregation through Bible study and worship. Delivering inspiring sermons is one of his/her principal duties. Through the pastor's voice individuals seek a message from God about their troubles, hoping that God will acknowledge their misfortunes and lift their burden. Storefront ministers have first-hand knowledge of the day-to-day troubles of church members. They understand the indignity church members suffer because they are poor and black. They understand what it feels like to do hard labor and not earn enough for basic provisions. They are concerned about the hungry and homeless. With parents, they share concern for losing a child to drugs, crime, and gangs. They know what it means to be hungry, jobless, and in a place where nobody knows your name.

Sunday is the most active day of the week in storefront congregations. God set Sunday apart from other days of the week to give good and faithful Christians a day to praise God, to learn about him, and to work for the salvation of humanity. Sunday is not a day of rest. Sunday school and mid-week prayer and Bible study are significant church routines. The Bible is considered the infallible word of God. In Bible study, individuals discuss their personal shortcomings, fears, and doubts. In class they seek spiritual enrichment and affirmation. Bible study for them is essential for developing spiritual strength and knowledge to endure life's hardships. They believe that every human experience is prefigured in the lives of biblical people whose stories provide models for their own lives. Through Bible study, individuals seek spiritual knowledge, which for them is the source of supreme power in the universe.

Conclusion

Durkheim's conception of the church as an embodiment of collective sacred beliefs and practices set forth in his *Elementary Forms of Religious Life* provided a model for my analysis of conceptions and precepts uniting the members of First Corinthians. Weber's analysis of the charismatic prophet and charismatic religious authority in building religious institutions guided my analysis of church leadership, vocations, and organizational structure. Following symbolic anthropologists who have worked among oppressed evangelical Christians in the Third World, we considered the counterhegemonic potential in the congregation's ideas and practices.

Previous sociological and anthropological accounts failed to provide an indigenous explanation of black evangelical storefront church beliefs and practices. These studies overlooked the place of evangelical Protestant thought in the black quest for liberation, social justice, and black moral and social solidarity and thus erroneously concluded that black

storefront missions are invariably ephemeral and a capitulation to white authority. An adequate account of evangelical storefront churches must include analysis of the historical and social context of which these institutions are a part. Storefront churches constitute a coherent and stable institution for people whose life chances are severely undermined by a declining inner-city manufacturing base, the rise to national political office of conservatives who argue that ghetto conditions are indicative of laziness and immorality created by welfare dependence, and a public that is reluctant to spend tax dollars on social programs for the poor.

Frances Kostarelos

Bibliography

Baer, Hans A. (1984) *The Black Spiritual Movement: A Religious Response to Racism*. Knoxville: The University of Tennessee Press.

Baer, Hans A., and Merrill Singer. (1992) *African-American Religion in the Twentieth Century*. Knoxville: The University of Tennessee Press.

Cone, James H. (1984) *For My People: Black Theology and the Black Church*. New York: Orbis Books.

Daniel, Vattel, E. (1940) "Ritual in Chicago's South Side Churches for Negroes." Ph.D. dissertation, The University of Chicago.

———. (1942) "Ritual Stratification in Chicago Negro Churches." *American Sociological Review*: 352–361.

Drake, St. Clair. (1940) *Churches and Voluntary Association in the Chicago Negro Churches*. W.P.A. Project Official Report 465-54-3-386.

Du Bois, W. E. B. (1903) *The Negro Church: A Social Study*. Atlanta: Atlanta University Press.

Durkheim, Emile. (1965) *The Elementary Forms of Religious Life*. New York: The Free Press.

Eddy, Norman. (1958) *Storefront Church Religion. Religion In Life* 27: 68–85.

Fauset, Arthur H. (1971) *Black Gods of the Metropolis*. Philadelphia: University of Pennsylvania Press.

Franklin, John Hope. (1974) *Reconstruction After the Civil War*. Chicago: The University of Chicago Press

Genovese, Eugene. (1974) *Roll Jordan Roll: The World the Slaves Made*. New York: Vintage Books.

Hamilton, Rev. Charles Larson. (1972) *The Black Preacher in America*. New York: William Morrow & Co.

Harrison, Ira. (1966) "The Storefront Church as a Revitalization Movement." *Review of Religious Research*: 160–163.

Hicks, Beecher H. (1977) *Images of the Black Preacher: the Man Nobody Knows*. Valley Forge, PA: Judson Press.

Johnson, Joseph A. (1971) *The Soul of the Black Preacher.* Philadelphia: The Pilgrim Press Book.

Johnston, Ruby. (1956) *The Religion of Negro Protestants.* New York: Philosophical Library.

Kostarelos, Frances. (1995) *Feeling the Spirit: Faith and Hope in an Evangelical Black Storefront Church.* Columbia: University of South Carolina Press.

Lincoln, Eric, and Lawrence H. Mamiya. (1990) *The Black Church in the African-American Experience.* Durham, NC: Duke University Press.

Love, Emanuel King. (1888) *History of the First African Baptist Church.* Savannah, GA: The Morning News Print.

Marable, Manning. (1983) *How Capitalism Underdeveloped Black America.* Boston: South End Press.

Mays, Benjamin, and Joseph W. Nicholson. (1969) *The Negro's Church.* New York: Russell and Russell.

Meier, August, and Elliot Rudwick. (1968) *From Plantation to Ghetto: An Interpretive History of American Negroes.* New York: Hill and Wang.

Morris, Aldon D. (1984) *The Origins of the Civil Rights Movement: Black Communities Organizing for Change.* New York: The Free Press.

Mukenge, Ida R. (1983) *The Black Church in America: A Case in Political Economy.* New York: University Press of America.

Paris, Arthur. (1982) *Black Pentecostalism: Southern Religion in an Urban World.* Amherst: The University of Massachusetts Press.

———. (1985) *The Social Teachings of the Black Churches.* Philadelphia: Fortress Press.

Raboteau, Albert. (1978) *Slave Religion.* New York: Oxford University Press.

Reid, Ira de A. (1926) "Let Us Prey." *Opportunity:* 274–278.

Sernett, Milton. (1975) *Black Religion and American Evangelicalism: White Protestants, Plantation Missions, and the Flowering of Negro Christianity, 1787–1865.* Metuchen, NJ: The Scarecrow Press.

———. (1985) *Afro-American Religious History: A Documentary History.* Durham, NC: Duke University Press.

Simms, Rev. James M. (1907) *The First Colored Baptist Church in America.* Philadelphia: J.B. Lipncott.

Simpson, George. (1978) *Black Religion the New World.* New York: Columbia University Press.

Simpson, Robert B. (1970) "A Black Church: Ecstasy in a World of Trouble." Ph.D. dissertation, Washington University.

Smith, Wallace C. (1985) *The Church in the Life of the Black Family.* Valley Forge, PA: Judson Press.

Spear, Allen. (1967) *The Making of a Negro Ghetto 1890–1920.* Chicago: The University of Chicago Press.

Sutherland, Robert. (1928) "Analysis of Negro Churches." Ph.D. dissertation, University of Chicago.

Washington, Joseph. (1964) *Black Religion: The Negro and Christianity in the United States.* Boston: Beacon.

———. (1972) *Black Sects and Cults.* New York: Doubleday and Co.

Weber, Max. (1978) *Economy and Society.* Berkeley: The University of California Press.

West, Cornel. (1982) *Prophesy Deliverance: An Afro-American Revolutionary Christianity.* Philadelphia: The Westminster Press.

Williams, Melvin. (1974) *Community in a Black Pentecostal Church.* Pittsburgh, PA: University of Pittsburgh Press.

Wilmore, Gayraud. (1983) *Black Religion and Black Radicalism: An Interpretation of the Religious History of Afro-American People.* New York: Orbis Books.

Wilson, William. (1987) *The Truly Disadvantaged: The Inner City, the Underclass, and Public Policy.* Chicago: The University of Chicago Press.

Woodson, Carter. (1921) *The History of the Negro Church.* Washington, D.C.: The Associated Publishers.

Sudanese Brotherhoods

Religion is central to the cultural heritage and social fabric of Sudan, Africa's largest country in area. The dominant geographic feature of the country, the Nile, has attracted lovers of God to its banks for millennia. The far North of Sudan is Nubia, home to the ancestors of Egypt's pharaohs. From the third century CE this was an early site of Christianity. African religions dominate the far South, bordering and influenced by today's Ethiopia, Kenya, Uganda, Congo, and Central African Republic.

Islam is the majority religion in Sudan today, overwhelmingly practiced in the northern two-thirds of the country, and scattered among the Christian and African religions in the South. From the sixteenth century CE, itinerant Muslim teachers and traders were attracted from the Hejaz region of the Arabian peninsula and Egypt to the central Nile valley, home, until the early nineteenth century, to the powerful Kingdom of the Funj (Spaulding 1985). These teachers were students themselves of important Islamic scholars of earlier centuries—representing schools of thought in Cairo, Damascus, Baghdad, and the Arab far-west, Morocco. The Moroccan Sufi Ahmad ibn Idris (1749–1837) influenced many of the Sudanese schools of the nineteenth century (Karrar 1992: 1). This article describes the brotherhoods, or spiritual organizations, that emerged from these schools and helped to spread Islam in Sudan, contributing to the character of Islam in Sudan today.

Sufi mission—public-speaking campaign in Atbara, Sudan. PHOTO COURTESY OF STEPHEN HOWARD.

Islamic Sufism

Sufism has been described as the "eye of the heart," an approach to Islam that is at once highly aware of God's presence, and constantly striving to remain in that presence. Tracing its origins to the Prophet Muhammad (570?–632 CE) and his *ansar*, or followers, Sufism is an aspect of the Islamic faith that is primarily a set of methodologies used to approach God as closely as possible. While Muslims would argue that this is the goal of all the religion's faithful, Sufis place a special value on ritual and association with like-minded individuals to strive to obtain perfect knowledge of God. In some cases, these associations, or "brotherhoods," in turn, have played a significant role in the political, agricultural, and commercial networks of Sudan. Sufism is often described as "mysticism," but it is not magic. It is both an internal and external experience of God reached through intense prayer, scripture, music, and some esoteric rituals. Other Muslims have borrowed poetry, song, or approaches to the Qur'an from the Sufi canon, but the Sufi is marked by the *intensity* of his or her experience of God.

Sudan's vastness inspired a highly decentralized form of religion. The fifteenth through the nineteenth centuries saw religious teachers traversing the country, some establishing schools (*khalwa, zowiya,* or *maseed*) in small towns that would then become minor sites of pilgrimage as word of a particular teacher (*shaykh*) spread. Later these towns would acquire a more spiritual cast as the teachers died and were buried in elaborate tombs. Sufis and their friends would visit such tombs, seeking the inspiring path of the great teachers that had walked before them, a practice that continues today. Because traditional Islam holds that the worship of anyone or thing other than God is a great sin—called *shirk*—the veneration of these "holymen" was always controversial. A good Sufi, however, would be careful to make the distinction between worship of God and admiration for his great teachers. *Karamat*, or divinely-inspired miracles, are thought by some to be influenced through and by the holymen. Central Sudan—the Gezira region—is dotted with the tombs of holymen—called *kubab*—and some of the towns such as Shikaniba, Tundub, Abu Haraz, Wad Medani, Taiba, Dongola, and Rufa'a are important sites of old religious schools as well as Sufi brotherhood activity.

Sudan and Africa were significant sites of the political and social changes that took place across the world in the nineteenth century. Islam and the Sudanese Sufi brotherhoods responded to change with an intensification of the link between Islam and politics. In the West of the country rose Muhammad Ahmad, who proclaimed himself the Mahdi or "divinely guided one," who would restore Islam in the world and unify its believers. He began his life's mission as a Sufi *shaykh*, or leader, and defeated the British at the Battle of Omdurman in 1885. His soldiers were known as dervishes, Sufi devotees with the sense of continual preparation for the after-life. Followers of the Mahdi continue to be organized for Sufi and political activities in Sudan today.

Opposing the forces of the Mahdi on both spiritual and military/political grounds was the Sufi-based religious movement in Eastern Sudan, the Khatmiya. The Sudanese branch of this sect was founded by Muhammad al-Hasan al-Mirghani in the mid-nineteenth century and attracted adherents from all over eastern, central and northern Sudan. Politically, the Khatmiya was close to the Turco-Egyptian rule in the country at the time, a cause of the Mahdi's opposition (Karrar 1992: 73–102). Khatmiya Sufis are well known for their *qasaid* or *medeh*, religious poetry sung in tribute to God and/or the Prophet Muhammad.

Contemporary Brotherhoods

An important twentieth-century development in Sudanese Sufism was the application of the spiritual methodologies described above to contemporary social and political problems. European colonialism and accompanying westernization throughout Africa and the Middle East had encroached upon the religion and culture of the region and its leaders. As Muslims viewed their religion as a frame for human life and society, there were some who taught that a return to Islam's roots would revive society's strength and set it upon a just path to human development. The foremost exponents of this modernist approach in Sudan were teacher/philosopher Mahmoud Mohammed Taha and his followers, collectively known as the Republican Brotherhood. The central principle of the movement was the continuation of the Sufi *longing* for perfect union with God, while adopting a more practical or "modern" guise. This meant that humanity would not be able to properly communicate with God unless the ever-increasing turmoil of modern life was addressed. *Hudur*, or perfect concentration in prayer, a presence *inside prayer*—a Sufi notion—would be achieved only when the distractions of the everyday were resolved.

Sufi "Dervish" at dhikir (ceremony) dedicated to praising God in Omburman, Sudan. PHOTO COURTESY OF STEPHEN HOWARD.

The Republican Brotherhood movement had its origins in the late pre-independence era in Sudan. Mahmoud Mohammed Taha (1909–1985) was a civil engineer who had been raised and taught in the deeply Sufi culture of the central Gezira, on the banks of the Blue Nile. He had attended Gordon Memorial College—later the University of Khartoum—while students and graduates were beginning to agitate against British-Egyptian colonialism in Sudan. Most Sudanese politicians at the time advocated either independence under the banner of a religious state ruled by descendants of the Mahdi—the Umma Party—or union with Egypt as advocated by the Khatimiya-dominated Democratic Unionist Party. Hence Sudanese politics continued to be heavily influenced by the country's Sufi heritage.

Taha believed that Sudan's special character and spiritual history should lead it to become independent as a republic, so he called his political movement the Republican Party. He went on speaking tours all over the country and collected a small band of devoted followers, many of whom were willing to join him in confronting the British colonial authorities. A prison sentence and a period of self-imposed isolation (*khalwa*) led Taha to emerge in 1951 with a new spiritual conception of his political movement. By the late 1940s it had also become clear that one of the political strains—the *Umma* Party or Democratic Unionist Party—would come to rule an independent Sudan. The Republican Party became the Republican Brotherhood, or officially, the New Islamic Mission, based on Taha's reading of the Qur'an. He published this approach as a book, *The Second Message of Islam*, in 1966.

The *Second Message* started with the common scriptural knowledge that some of the verses of the Qur'an were revealed to the Prophet Muhammad during his initial mission in Mecca, and some were revealed during the period after the *hijira* (migration) to Medina (622 CE): the Meccan texts consisted of universal and timeless messages from God to humanity, while the Medinan texts generally spoke to the specific historical circumstances faced by the new community of Muslims in Medina, a community under attack both physically and ideologically, and requiring strict discipline to hold it together. Hence the Medinan verses of the Qur'an detailed aspects of war and capital punishment, and tend to justify sexual inequality and other forms of social control. The earlier Meccan texts, which continued to be the Prophet Muhammad's *sunna* even after the migration to Medina, focused on believers coming to Islam through personal, heart-felt conviction rather than compulsion. The *sunna*, or personal conduct or custom of the Prophet, as guided by the Qur'an, was the source teaching of all Sufi practices and sects, and hence, Taha advocated that the sole correct path in Islam was *tariq Muhammad* or the path of the Prophet.

In Taha's view, Muslims in general and Sufi brotherhoods in particular had strayed from the path in modern times, a perspective that attracted much controversy to his organization. In 1971 he published *Tariq Mohammed*, which explained his sense that the Prophet Muhammad was the first and greatest Sufi, and that it was his behavior that humanity should imitate until the time of divine transformation. Taha was referred to by his followers as *ustadh* (teacher), and from that position he offered an entire methodology on how to reform human behavior in the light of the Qur'an and the practice of the Prophet. To follow any other path, in his view, was to engage in *dhikir bidun fikr* (remembering God without intensely thinking about it).

The Republicans formed a learning community, reminiscent of their Sufi heritage. Indeed, many were members of Sufi families; and others were disenchanted with radical politics or radical Islam in the form of groups like the Muslim Brothers. Many were well educated and attuned to Taha's intellectual message, which required deep study of the Qur'an. Young bachelors in the group lived communally in a few towns. These groups served both the modern social purpose of sharing urban living expenses, and the spiritual purpose of intensifying the knowledge of Islam and prayer through constant religious activity, reminiscent of the *khalwa* activity of the Prophet Muhammad and Sufis, where isolation was sought for spiritual renewal. Republican families living near each other would gather for frequent prayer and discussion meetings, particularly those who lived near Ustadh Mahmoud in Sudan's capital.

Several of the hallmarks of the Republican movement had either significant roots in Sufi tradition or were reactions to it, updating tradition or bringing what had "strayed" more in line with the practice of the Prophet Muhammad. For example, the Republicans eschewed the practice of the *tarawiah* prayer common to the fasting month of Ramadan, in favor of the "night prayer" of the Prophet, a daily occasion of prayer taking place in the middle of the night. *Tarawiah*, and the use of *sibha* (prayer beads) were seen as *bida'*, or post-Prophetic, innovation. The group also engaged in *dhikir* (remembrance), from the Qur'anic injunction to "always remember God," which involved forming a circle to chant "Allah"—the name of God. The Republicans were well known for their religious poetry (*inshad erfani*) and Qur'anic recitations, frequently performed in public. Women were included in all of the activities of the movement, which raised much controversy in the wider society. But Taha's point was that women would never develop spiritually and intellectually if they were assigned strictly to practice "popular Islam" and not given an opportunity to be good, orthodox Muslims alongside men. The daily life of the Republican Brotherhood was filled with aspects of prayer, hearkening back to the early purpose of Sufi brotherhoods. By referring to the methodology of prayer as the *path* of the Prophet, Taha and his followers restored the Sufi principle that Islam required progressive change to be a true adherent—moving along the path to become a better Muslim—and not just accepting the status of being Muslim from birth as an end in itself.

It is important to contrast the Republican Brotherhood movement with an organization with which it is frequently confused, the Muslim Brotherhood. The latter is a conservative religious/political organization originating as an Islamic reform movement in Egypt in the 1920s and extending in influence to Sudan and Jordan and elsewhere. In Sudan the Muslim Brotherhood became the political organization of the National Islamic Front, and at century's end was the dominant political power. Holding close to the theological and political views of governments on the Arabian peninsula, the Muslim Brothers viewed the neo-Sufi tendencies of groups like the Republicans as heresy and *shirk* (seeking intercession with God through means such as ritual, saints, etc.), as well as a threat to their political hegemony. Through the influence of the Muslim Brotherhood, a crackdown on the public activities of the Republican movement began in the early 1980s. Seventy members of the group, including four women, were placed in prison for campaigning against the imposition of Islamic law (*sharia*) in Sudan, and finally the movement was destroyed with the execution of the seventy-six-year-old Mahmoud Mohammed Taha on trumped-up charges of "apostasy" in January 1985. Sudan's Supreme Court posthumously overturned the decree in 1987, following the April 1985 overthrow of the government that executed Taha.

Conclusion

Sufi brotherhoods and their teacher-leaders were principle agents of the spread of Islam in Sudan. Serving as social and trade networks in addition to their obvious and primary role as religious fraternities, the Sufi brotherhoods laid the foundation for much of Sudan's economic and political history up to the present. The different brotherhoods were devoted to particular teachings of an early Islamic Sufi thinker, and the followers placed their religious education in the hands of a leader who was supposed to be learned in those teachings. But it is important to note that all of the Sufi brotherhoods generally agreed on the most fundamental theology and teachings of Islam—that is, that there "is no God but God and Muhammad is His Prophet." They differed in loyalty to particular holymen or saints, and the creation of a religious atmosphere around the act of prayer. Sufi brotherhoods

remain an important source of Islamic teaching and social organization in Sudan today; and many sons and daughters follow their fathers into the traditional organizations. There are also Sufi reform or revival movements, organized to use traditional Sufi practices to address the needs of the modern world. Thus, the culture of Sufism is a pervasive feature of Sudanese life today, no matter how deeply or loosely its religious principles are practiced.

W. Stephen Howard

See also Dinka Religion; Islam, East Africa; Islam, West Africa; Nuer Religion; Pilgrimage

Bibliography

Daly, Martin W., ed. (1985) *Al Majdhubiya and al Mikashfiya: Two Sufi Tariqas in the Sudan.* Khartoum: University of Khartoum (Graduate College Publications #13).

Karar, Ali Salih. (1992) *The Sufi Brotherhoods in the Sudan.* Evanston, IL: Northwestern University Press.

McHugh, Neil. (1994) *Holymen of the Blue Nile.* Evanston, IL: Northwestern University Press.

Spaulding, Jay (1985) *The Heroic Age in Sinnar.* East Lansing: Michigan State University Press.

Taha, Mahmoud Mohammed. (1987) *The Second Message of Islam,* translated by Abdullahi A. An-Na'im. Syracuse, NY: Syracuse University Press.

Trimingham, J. Spencer. (1965) *Islam in the Sudan.* London: F. Cass.

Suriname, African-Derived Religions in

The Republic of Suriname, independent from Dutch rule since 1975, lies on the northeast shoulder of South America, bounded by French Guiana to the east, Guyana to the West, Brazil to the south, and the Atlantic to the north. One of the most ethnically diverse nations in the Americas, Suriname's population of roughly 430,000 people (plus another 300,000 now living in the Netherlands) divides into 38 percent "Hindustani" (descendants of indentured laborers from India who arrived during the late nineteenth century), 31 percent "Creoles" (descendants of enslaved Africans), 15 percent "Javanese" (descendants of indentured laborers from Indonesia who arrived in the early twentieth century), 10 percent "Maroons" (descendants of enslaved Africans who escaped from plantations and formed their own societies in the forested interior of the country), and lesser numbers of Sephardic Jews, Chinese, and Lebanese/Syrians—

plus the several thousand remaining Amerindians (Galibi, Arawaks, Trios, and others). With the exception of most Maroons and some Amerindians, nearly the entire population lives along the coastal strip, with about half the population residing in Paramaribo, the capital.

The first lasting settlement dates from 1651, when one hundred Englishmen from Barbados brought over their slaves to found a plantation colony. In 1667, the Dutch took over and during the next century and a half imported about 250,000 Africans as slaves. The African origins of these enslaved men and women displayed remarkable diversity—scores of cultural and linguistic groups ranging from Angola to Upper Guinea. Suriname witnessed relatively early and rapid creolization, with the slaves creating new institutions (from new creole languages to new religions) largely by a process of inter-African syncretism—combining and elaborating their various African heritages with very little reference to European models.

Slave Religion

During the earliest decades of settlement, plantation slaves created a new Afro-Surinamese religion that already contained the main features of its two major twentieth-century variants—the religion of the coastal Creoles (usually called Winti) and the religions of the several Maroon groups that live in the interior of the country. The newly created religion of these Suriname slaves included spirit possession (by ancestors, snake gods, forest and river spirits, and others); specialized drumming, dancing, and singing for each of a number of deities; various kinds of divination performed to uncover the causes of a particular illness or misfortune; beliefs about multiple souls; ideas about the ways that social conflict can cause illness and misfortune; rituals for twins and their families; warrior cults; specialized healing cults; and a focus on large public funerals as the most important of all ritual and social occasions. White colonists depended on slave healers and diviners for many of their medical and spiritual needs. One eighteenth-century writer describes how, despite the presence of eight white physicians in the colony, the slaves "play the greatest role with their herbs and their pretended cures, both among Christians and among Jews" (Cohen Nassy 1974: 156). And the most famous eighteenth-century slave curer-diviner, Kwasi, became accustomed near the end of his life to receiving letters from abroad addressed to "The Most Honorable Gentleman, Master Phillipus van Quassie, Professor of Herbology in Suriname" (Price 1983: 153–159).

The religion of Afro-Surinamese slaves, with its multiplicity of interlocking rituals and beliefs, provided the focus of slave culture, tying individuals ritually to their ancestors,

descendants, and collateral kin. At the same time, it bound the slave community together in the face of a crushingly oppressive colonial regime. And in many cases, it served as the inspiration and catalyst for revolt. One European who knew the colony well noted the "subversive" aspects of slave religion—particularly spirit possession—in his description of a 1770s "Winty-play" on a plantation:

> Sage Matrons Dancing And Whirling Round in the Middle of an Audience, till Absolutely they froath at the mouth And drop down in the middle of them; Whatever She says to be done during this fit of Madness is Sacredly Performed by the Surrounding Multitude, which makes these meetings Exceedingly dangerous Amongst the Slaves, who are often told to murder their Masters or Desert to the Woods. (Stedman 1988: 521)

A large number of colonial laws prohibiting public drumming and Winti-plays stand as testimony to the planters' belief that slave religion formed the basis for the many rebellions experienced by the colony.

Coastal Creole Winti

The widely practiced folk religion of Suriname Creoles (that majority of the Afro-Surinamese population who are not Maroons) is usually referred to by outsiders as Winti (said to derive from the English "wind") or Afkodré (from Dutch *afgoderij*, idolatry). But like many folk religions (such as Haitian Vodun) it has—at least until recently—not had a special name used by its adherents. For them, it is simply the core of a way of life. Since general emancipation in Suriname in 1863, most Creoles have been nominal Christians, with most belonging to Protestant churches (in particular the Moravian church, though evangelical groups have been gaining ground of late) and the remainder to the Roman Catholic Church. Afro-Surinamers contrast with most diasporic Africans to the extent to which their Christianity and folk religion are compartmentalized. Compared, for example, to Haitian Vodun, Bahian Candomblé, or the cult of María Lionza in Venezuela, Winti evidences remarkably little syncretism between Christian and Afro-American beliefs and rites. Despite the participation of Creoles in modern, Western-style Caribbean life (and for the many migrants in the Netherlands, European life), Winti continues to flourish in contexts that are largely separate from Christianity. Wherever Creoles now live—whether in Paramaribo, Rotterdam, or New York—Winti continues to constitute a focus of their lives.

Winti provides a comprehensive design for living. The everyday visible world is complemented by a normally unseen world peopled by a multitude of gods and spirits who constantly interact with humans. Many scholars, and some Winti adherents, have tried to impose an order on this spiritual domain by grouping the gods into four pantheons of the air, the earth, the water, and the forest—all ranged below an otiose, distant, West African-type sky god. But such classification may well impose an inappropriate rigidity on a shifting set of beliefs and rites that are called into play to deal with diverse and practical everyday human needs—sickness, misfortune, life crises, social conflict, and so forth. The most important gods and spirits include a variety of *kromanti* (fierce healing spirits), *apuku* (often-malevolent forest spirits), *aisa* (localized earth spirits), *vodu* (boa constrictor spirits), and *aboma* (anaconda spirits), but there are many others. Like the spirits of the dead, who play an active role in the lives of the living and are a frequent focus of ritual activity, these non-human gods or spirits can speak through possessed mediums. Specialized rituals, involving unique drumming, dance, and song, are used to honor each type of spirit, and the spirits materialize on such occasions, through possession, to communicate directly with participants. Ritual specialists known as *bonuman* or *lukuman* (who may be men or women) preside over these rites. Many such practitioners specialize in rites for particular kinds of gods or spirits. Overall, however, Winti is a highly participatory religion in which every individual plays an ongoing role and in which special knowledge and roles are widely distributed among the population.

Winti is a practical religion, mainly concerned with everyday problems. In the event, for example, of an illness, bad dream, or minor misfortune, people seek the cause by divination, carried out by a *lukuman*. Using any of several techniques, he may find that a particular ancestor feels neglected, a jealous neighbor has attempted sorcery, a relative's snake spirit disapproves of a proposed marriage, or the person's "soul" requires a special ritual—and then prescribes an appropriate rite. During the course of a single case of illness or misfortune, large numbers of kin and friends may need to be mobilized and substantial financial resources expended—*bonuman* and *lukuman* are always compensated. Coastal Afro-Surinamers, practitioners of Winti, occasionally call on Maroon religious specialists from the interior for particular problems. Among Creoles, Maroons are reputed to have the "strongest" medicines.

Maroon Religions

There are six politically distinct Maroon peoples living along rivers in the interior of Suriname and neighboring French Guiana: The Saramaka and the Ndyuka each have a population of about 24,000, the Matawai, Aluku (Boni),

and Paramaka are each closer to 2,000, and the Kwinti number fewer than 500. Since the colonial government of Suriname signed treaties with the Ndyuka, Saramaka, and Matawai in the 1760s and later recognized the Aluku, Paramaka, and Kwinti, a loose framework of indirect rule has obtained. Although formed under broadly similar historical and ecological conditions, these societies display significant variation in everything from language, diet, and dress to patterns of marriage, residence, and migratory wage labor. From a cultural point of view, the greatest differences are between the Maroons of central Suriname (Saramaka, Matawai, and Kwinti), on the one hand, and those of eastern Suriname and western French Guiana (Ndyuka, Aluku, and Paramaka) on the other. Today, increasing numbers of Maroons live outside of their traditional territories, mainly in Paramaribo and the coastal towns of French Guiana. During the 1980s and 1990s, the national government of Suriname and the French regional government in Cayenne have intervened increasingly in Maroon internal affairs—the government of Suriname as part of ongoing development schemes, a devastating civil war that began in 1986, and subsequent mining and forestry projects; and the French government through its assimilationist program of francisation and its handling of Maroon refugees from Suriname's civil war.

Maroons have always enjoyed an extremely elaborate ritual life that is totally integrated into their matrilineally-based social organization. Such decisions as where to clear a garden or build a house, whether to make a trip, or how to deal with theft or adultery are made in consultation with village deities, ancestors, snake gods, and other powers. The means of communicating with these entities vary, from spirit possession and the consultation of oracle bundles to the interpretation of dreams. Both men and women participate in spirit possession, though mediums for some kinds of spirits, for example *vodu* snake gods, tend to be women, and those for others, such as *komanti* warrior gods, are almost always men. Gods and spirits, who are a constant presence in daily life, are also honored through frequent prayers, libations, feasts, and dances. Human misfortune is directly linked to other people's antisocial acts, through complex chains of causation involving witchcraft or sorcery, gods, spirits, or ancestors. Any illness or other misfortune requires immediate divination and ritual action in collaboration with these spirits and others, such as warrior gods. Pregnancy—the key to lineage continuity—is a period of heightened ritual danger and is managed in consultation with various spiritual powers. Birth, death, and other life crises are handled through extensive ritual, and much the same could be said of more mundane activities such as hunting a tapir or planting a rice field. Formal political life is also rife with ritual.

Village officials rule and adjudicate with the help of various oracles and shrines. For brief periods in Maroon history, particularly among the Ndyuka, authoritarian power has been exercised through religious means, as witch-finding cults or messianic movements have, for a time, taken root, before fading away.

Maroon religions incorporate a plethora of expressive forms, from esoteric ritual languages (Púmbu, Luángo, Komantí, Papá) to formal prayer and oratory. Special drum languages, known for the most part only by ritual specialists, mark particular rites. And libations to ancestors and gods, with proverbial speech forming the core of invocations, are an everyday occurrence in every village.

Funerals constitute the single most complex ritual event. Spanning a period of many months and involving hundreds, or even thousands, of people, they unite the world of the living with that of the dead through specialized ritual practices. These practices include carrying the coffin on two men's heads in a rite of divination, numerous other esoteric rites, and extensive singing, dancing, and drumming in many distinctive modes. Specialized cults, some dating back to the eighteenth-century wars of liberation, include those devoted to the birth of twins, to finding someone lost in the forest, to making rain, to "dangerous" or "evil" deaths, to bone setting, and to curing gunshot wounds; these remain the possessions of particular matrilineal clans. Individual Maroons may specialize in the treatment of particular types of spiritual problems or in particular ritual activities, such as drumming for snake-god rites. But most Maroon ritual knowledge is broadly spread; these are highly participatory religions.

Christian missions have had differing impacts on the Maroon groups. Moravians from Germany arrived in Saramaka right after the mid-eighteenth-century peace treaty and stayed for five frustrating decades, leaving a fascinating record of the brash encounter between Maroon religion and Christianity (R. Price 1990). During the mid-nineteenth century, missionaries returned and found a more receptive audience—today, several thousand Saramakas, and all Matawais, are nominally Moravians. Roman Catholic mission work, largely during the twentieth century, was most successful among the eastern Maroons. And during the 1980s and 1990s, newer evangelical churches have had some impact among all Maroon groups. Nevertheless, today the great majority of Maroons continue to practice the non-Christian Maroon religions forged by their runaway slave ancestors. From many different African traditions, those earliest generations of Suriname Maroons created a vibrant new synthesis. Resembling Winti in terms of many of the particular gods and spirits invoked, the Maroon religions stand apart in their more absolute integration of belief

and ritual into all aspects of everyday life. New World creations drawing on Old World ideas, these Maroon religions (which never cease to develop and change) remain today the most "African" of all religions in the Americas.

Richard Price

See also Slave Religion

Bibliography

Cohen Nassy, David de Isaac. ([1788] 1974) *Historical Essay on the Colony of Surinam*. Cincinnati: American Jewish Archives.

Herskovits, Melville J., and Frances S. Herskovits. (1936) *Suriname Folk-Lore*. New York: Columbia University Press.

Lier, R. A. J. van. (1971) *Frontier Society*. The Hague: Martinus Nijhoff.

Price, Richard. (1983) *First-Time: The Historical Vision of an Afro-American People*. Baltimore: Johns Hopkins University Press.

———. (1990) *Alabi's World*. Baltimore: Johns Hopkins University Press.

Price, Sally. (1993) *Co-wives and Calabashes*, 2d ed. Ann Arbor: University of Michigan Press.

Price, Sally, and Richard Price. (1999) *Maroon Arts*. Boston: Beacon Press.

Stedman, John Gabriel. ([1797] 1988) *Narrative of a Five Years Expedition against the Revolted Negroes of Surinam*. Baltimore: Johns Hopkins University Press.

Thoden van Velzen, H. U. E., and W. van Wetering. (1988) *The Great Father and the Danger: Religious Cults, Material Forces, and Collective Fantasies in the World of Surinamese Maroons*. Dordrecht, Netherlands and Providence, RI: Foris Publications.

Wooding, Charles J. (1981) *Evolving Culture: A Cross-Cultural Study of Suriname, West Africa, and the Caribbean*. Washington DC: University Press of America.

Tambor De Mina En Maranhon

Mina is the term used for the Afro-Brazilian religion practiced in Maranhon. As Xango and Candomblé in other parts of the country, this religion is ecstatic and initiatory, which means that its believers are in contact with or possessed by supernatural beings when in trance and that its practices are learned during a prolonged period of initiation, culminating in a solemn ritual of acceptance into the congregation. The *tambor de mina* is a characteristic celebration of adherents to this tradition.

There are many Casas das Minas in Sao Luis and other cities of northeastern Brazil. Although their beliefs and rituals do not always coincide, they follow the same pattern. A few of these temples were founded during the nineteenth century or even earlier. The most traditional congregation venerates the divinities of the Ewe-Fon pantheon of Dahomey (*vodouns*) but is now in decline, as the leaders have died and some of the rituals are forgotten. In the temples of more recent foundations the divinities of the Yoruba pantheon (*orishas*) are invoked. The believers also summon the *caboclos*, spirits of Native American origin, and disincarnated spirits of all kind. Other spirits belong to the Turkish nation that—according to their lore—inhabited Africa. Bantu spirits of Cambinda and Angola origin (*boiadeiros*) are also known. African divinities are called *senhor, senhora, patrao, patroa, or santo. The caboclos* are often called *guias.* The initiated members of a *casa* may receive a number of different spirits while in an altered state of consciousness. Usually immediately after initiation the believer receives a *caboclo* and only later in life an African *patrao*. The temples are headed by a *pai o mae de santo*, a term meaning male (*pai*) or female (*mae*) ritual leaders. The incorporation of Native American spirits (*caboclos*) and of figures of Brazilian folklore may have occurred during the nineteenth century.

Most of the members of these congregations are blacks belonging to the lower strata of society. They cannot afford to celebrate lavish feasts, as the Candomblés of Bahia (province), and animal sacrifices are therefore infrequent. The *festas* for the different entities are usually celebrated on the days of Catholic saints, who are connected with the African entities. They are animated with drum beats and songs and the dancers wear expensive costumes that are carefully preserved between *festas*.

The initiation ritual is secret but much shorter than in Candomblé or Xango. The new members only receive a short introduction and never learn all the secrets, so that upon the death of a leader, rituals are no longer practiced or his house is closed. Some leaders also practice *cura*, or healing rituals, but keep them separate from the *Mina* cult. The trance behavior of the dancers varies in intensity, but usually they keep silent and only show that they are possessed by wrapping a towel around their body. The temples have close contacts with each other and participate in one another's rituals.

Several times during the year each temple organizes a public feast called *Tambor de Mina* to venerate the African spirits. It takes place on the terrace in front of the temple or inside the house, and the initiated dance and sing, accom-

panied by drums and bells. Usually three songs are dedicated to each entity. The participants dance in a circle. Until recently, only women danced and received spirits; today some gay initiates take part in the ceremony and may also receive spirits. On other occasions, animals are sacrificed and food is distributed; other rituals have purifying purposes. The entertainment of guests depends on the financial contributions of the believers. In most temples a feast in honor of the Holy Spirit is celebrated once a year, which is an example of the syncretism with Catholic elements. The temples are usually decorated with images of saints, considered to be adorned by the spiritual entities that are venerated there. *Ladaihnas*, or Catholic prayers (some in Latin), are recited before a ritual takes place.

Tambor de Mina contains elements of the northeastern Brazilian Pagelança (curing rituals), of Kardecism (the invocation of disincarnated spirits), of Catholicism (worship of the Holy Spirit and of saints), and in recent years has also been influenced by Umbanda practices.

Angelina Pollak-Eltz

See also Brazil, African-Derived Religions in; Kardicism; Pagelanca, Xango

Bibliography

Bastide, Roger. (1971) *As religoes africanas no Brasil.* Sao Paolo: Ed. Pioneira

Ferretti, Mundicarmo. (1985) *Mina, una religao de origem africana.* Sao Luis, Brazil: SECMA.

———. (1995) *Tambor de Crioula.* Sao Luis, Brazil: SECMA.

Ferretti, Sergio. (1985) *Querebentan de Zomadonu, etnografia da Casa das Minas.* Sao Luis, Brazil: Ed. UFMA (Universidade federal de Maranhon).

Trinidad, African-Derived Religions in

As a result of the transatlantic slave trade, various derivations and innovations of African traditional religions were introduced to the Caribbean and the Americas. Often surviving under severe conditions of repression and persecution, the historical presence of African-derived religions in these regions attests to the flexibility of African religious orientations, the elasticity of African ritual practices, and the resiliency of New World African practitioners.

Located in the southern-most region of the Caribbean, the island of Trinidad lends much to the discussion of African-derived religions in the Western Hemisphere. Its two central religions of African derivation are Orisha (historically referred to as Shango) and Rada. Some scholars also include the Spiritual and Shouter Baptists among Trinidad's African-derived religions. Both the Orisha and Rada religions find their origins within the West African traditions of Nigeria and ancient Dahomey (now Benin Republic). The name "Orisha" is derived from the Yoruba word for deity and "Rada" is derived from the Dahomean city called Arada or Allada.

Colonization and Slavery in Trinidad

Known by indigenous people as *Kairi*, the island was later renamed by Columbus, who made the European discovery of the island on his third voyage in 1498. Trinidad received its first European settlers in 1592 under the governance of the Spanish Crown. After three-hundred years of Spanish rule, Trinidad became a British possession in 1797. Prior to the arrival of Columbus, the island was home to a diverse indigenous population of some 20,000–30,000 inhabitants consisting primarily of Caribs and Ienian Arawaks. Two centuries later, this indigenous population had dwindled to a mere 1,000 due to the conditions of forced labor and disease.

Trinidad was unlike most Caribbean colonies which had developed a dependence on Africans for plantation labor as early as the sixteenth century. Instead, Spanish settlers in Trinidad relied almost exclusively on the indigenous labor of the Arawaks up until the last two decades of the eighteenth century. It was not until 1610 that enslaved Africans were first introduced to Trinidad by the Dutch, who later became the major suppliers of African labor throughout the Caribbean and Americas under the auspices of the Dutch West India Company (1621). Following the initial importation of 500 Africans in the seventeenth century, the next considerable wave of Africans entering Trinidad was in 1783, after a significant resettlement plan of European planters. Census data taken prior to 1783 estimated the African population at 310. In 1797, this number had increased to some 10,009 and by 1800, the African population had risen to approximately 15,000. At the time of the emancipation of slavery in Trinidad in 1838, close to 24,000 Africans were manumitted.

Throughout much of the eighteenth and nineteenth centuries, Trinidad experienced massive increases in its population of African descent. According to historian Bridget Brereton, Trinidad's enslaved African community was overwhelmingly African-born in the early nineteenth century. By 1813, Brereton estimates that there were approximately 14,000 African-born slaves on Trinidad. About 39 percent of the African population originated from the Bight of Biafra in West Africa. The next largest areas from which enslaved Africans in Trinidad originated were the Central African and Senegambia regions.

Aside from direct importation, Trinidad's black population throughout the eighteenth and nineteenth centuries increased for four major reasons. First, in an effort to encourage permanent residents, the Spanish Crown in 1783 issued the *Cedula de Polbacion* (Decree for the population), offering tracts of land to those willing to migrate from neighboring Caribbean colonies. The decree stipulated that all foreign settlers must be Catholic and that their nation of origin must be in allegiance with Spain. It also stipulated that white planters be given tracts of land in accord with the number of slaves they brought with them to Trinidad: the more slaves, the more land. Many white planters of French origin came from the islands of Martinique and Hispaniola and brought thousands of African slaves with them. Second, Trinidad's black population increased following the war of 1812, when hundreds of black North Americans who fought on the side of British were relocated to Trinidad, forming six settlements known as "company villages." By 1838, there were 838 inhabitants residing within these black North American settlements. Company villagers were mainly from the Sea Islands off the Carolinas and were overwhelmingly Christian (Baptist). They had a greater influence on Spiritual Baptists in Trinidad than on the development of Orisha (though in the year 2000, Orisha ceremonies are conducted in most former company villages). Third, African migrants from the British territories of Sierra Leone and St. Helena came seeking employment in post-Emancipation Trinidad in 1841. Between 1841 and 1861, approximately 3,383 Africans migrated from Sierra Leone and 3,198 arrived from St. Helena. Finally, from 1834–1867, the British Naval Preventative Squadron rescued a total of 8,854 captives from slave ships bound for Cuba and Brazil. As a result, "liberated Africans" became an integral part of the Trinidadian black population, representing an array of diverse ethnic groups such as Yoruba, Fon, Ibo, Temne, Wolof, Ashanti, Fulani, and Mandingo.

The Development of Rada and Orisha in Trinidad

Among the multiple ethnic groups represented in Trinidad, the Yoruba and Dahomean-based traditions were the most influential in shaping the style and content of African-derived religions on the island. The development of Trinidad's African-derived religions offers a unique historical perspective, distinct from most Caribbean islands where the development of African-derived religions is directly

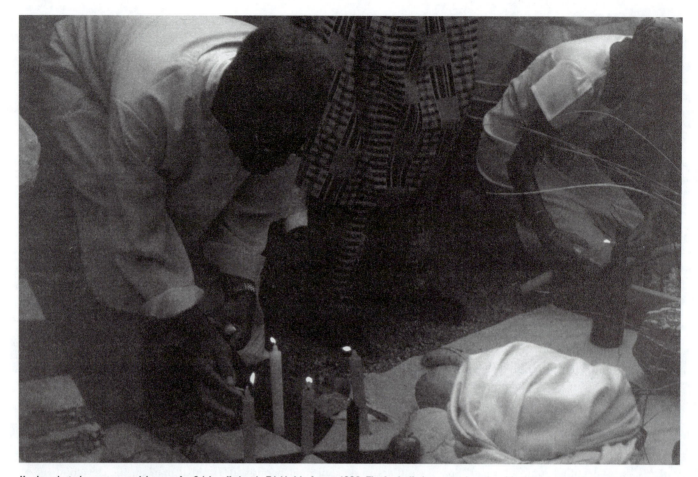

Yoruba priest gives a ceremonial prayer for Orisha offering, in Trinidad in August 1998. The food offerings were then placed in the water in order to pay homage to Oshun. PHOTO COURTESY OF DIANNE M. STEWART.

associated with slavery. Rada and Orisha religious traditions emerged for the most part from communities of Africans arriving in Trinidad in the post- rather than pre-Emancipation era.

The origins and geographical locations of the first Yoruba religious community in Trinidad are obscure. What is known is that a large influx of Yoruba arrived in Trinidad between the 1830s and the 1850s as "liberated Africans." It is also known that they settled as a free community in the northeastern section of Trinidad, that they greatly outnumbered the Rada, and that they became one of the dominant African ethnic groups in nineteenth-century Trinidad.

The history of Rada in Trinidad is very well documented. In the 1860s, a free Rada population from Dahomey settled in the Belmont section of Trinidad. At that time, efforts to reproduce Dahomean-based traditions were commenced by Abojevi Zahwenu, known as Papa Nanee in Trinidad (also known as Robert Antoine). Papa Nanee was born around 1800 in Dahomey. He arrived in Trinidad about

1855 and became a laborer on an estate in St. Joseph. According to Andrew Carr's 1956 study of Rada, Papa Nanee came to Trinidad as a trained diviner and skilled herbalist within Dahomean traditional religion. During the 1860s, Papa Nanee purchased a three-fifths of an acre of land in Belmont and created a residential compound on Belmont Valley Road that eventually became the center of Rada religious life in Trinidad. Until the death of Papa Nanee in 1899, this Belmont compound served as the fundamental resource for Rada rites and ceremonial activity. Structurally, the residential compound complemented Rada religious life and contained a *vodunkwe,* or "house of the gods," where public ceremonies took place and Dahomean deities were honored with numerous shrines. Although it is difficult to ascertain the precise amount and nature of African practices maintained in Papa Nanee's Rada ceremonies, it is recorded that ritual life was carried out according to a calendrical cycle and that the religious community was consistently regenerated through initiations of new *vodunsi.* The compound survived following Antoine's death and the group still existed in 2000, although it had been overshadowed by the growing Orisha movement.

As was the case for many African-derived traditions throughout the Americas and the Caribbean, practitioners were often subjected to repressive legal responses. Religious traditions affiliated with Africa were consistently denigrated and constantly met with much scorn and castigation. Within colonial territories throughout the New World, African rites and practices were pejoratively referred to as *obeah*, a misnomer of the Ashanti term *obayifo* and the Twi word *obeye*, both meaning spiritual energy. For colonists, *obeah* became an inclusive category for all African religious practices perceived as witchcraft, sorcery, and harmful magic. According to Brereton, "*obeah* was used in this period to include any religious or magical practices, including healing and conjuring of all types, that were believed to be African-derived." Brereton (1981: 134). In 1868, Trinidad instituted a series of laws against the practice of *obeah* making it a criminal offense with severe legal consequences. By 1872, fourteen persons had been convicted of *obeah* prac-

tice. The Rada community in Belmont was not exempt from these legal constraints, and in 1886 Papa Nanee was arrested for the alleged crime of *obeah* and was sentenced to six months hard labor and thirty-six lashes. Although his sentence was eventually commuted by the Court of Appeals, it nonetheless reveals the degree of legal repression against African-derived traditions in Trinidad. This repression lasted well into the twentieth century, when a preponderance of laws were passed in 1921 prohibiting public dance processions, singing, and dancing in public or private yards, and the beating of drums.

Rada and Orisha Beliefs and Practices

Like many African-derived religions in the African Diaspora, Rada and Orisha share similar theological features and ritual characteristics. Both Rada and Orisha (and its Shango precursor) traditions emphasize service to *vodu* or *orisha* (spiritual deities); engage in ancestral veneration; appease the spirits with food offerings and animal sacrifice; perform

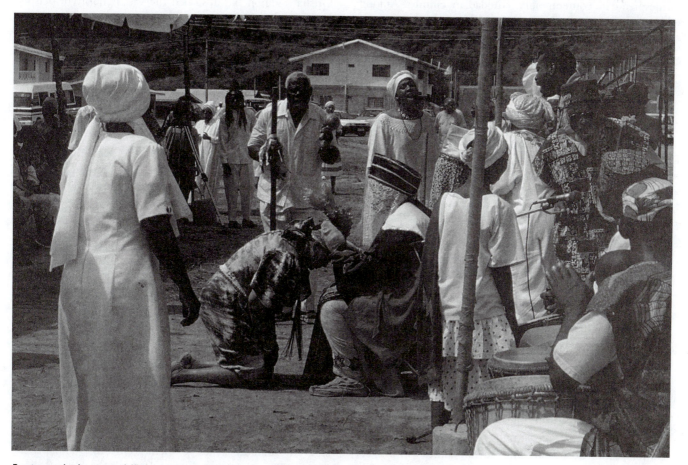

Devotees paying homage to deified ancestors at the ancestral veneration ceremony at Orisha family day celebration in Trinidad in March 1999. PHOTO COURTESY OF DIANNE M. STEWART.

divination readings; ritualize with song, chant, and dance; and embody the *vodu* or *orisha* through manifestation and possession.

Each tradition has its own distinct pantheon of spirits, with several deities overlapping in both traditions. Within the Rada pantheon, the spirits most readily celebrated include Dada Segbo (Creator), Dangbwe (Serpent deity), Elegba (God of the crossroads), Sakpata (Earth deity), and Ogu (God of iron). Carr's study indicates that *vodunu*, or religious celebrations to Rada spirits, occurred throughout the year. These celebrations, also called sacrifices because they often involved offerings of pigeons, guinea fowls, goats, and turtles, were given for various purposes that include commemorating the anniversary of Rada spirits, the blessing of one's household, the honoring of children, expressing thanksgiving, warding off illness, and the honoring of departed ancestors. Since the death of Papa Nanee in 1899, the frequency of these celebrations has declined significantly and, compared with Orisha, the Rada tradition retains merely a shadow of its former prominence.

Of the two traditions, Orisha practice is much more widespread in contemporary Trinidadian culture. Among the island's African-derived traditions, it possesses the greatest number of practitioners. Central to Orisha ceremonial life is the two to four day observance of an annual *ebo*, or feast. Within the Orisha tradition, feasts serve multiple purposes. Most importantly, feasts are a time when the bond between *orisha* and devotees is replenished through offerings of food and sacrifices of animals. Also, feasts serve as healing rites where supplications are made on behalf of health and other personal issues. Finally, feasts are a ritual forum in which the *orisha* are made manifest in human bodily form, bringing advice as well as admonishment to the community of devotees.

In Trinidad, Orisha feasts or *ebo* ceremonies are carried out in structured ritual environments. Worship life for devotees is centered around a *palais*, or public ritual space, with an earthen floor; a *chapelle*, or small altar room, where ritual paraphernalia and sacred items for the *orisha* are kept; and consecrated concrete mounds, or *stools*, where individual *orisha* are enshrined. The historical interplay and influence of Catholicism upon Orisha is often evident in the use of Catholic iconography and Catholic prayers in *orisha* shrines and ceremonies. As with many African-derived traditions in the New World, Catholic images and symbols were integrated into African religious systems primarily during slavery. As a result, associations of Catholic saints were made with African deities with respect to public representation. Though visible, the integration of these Catholic practices and imagery did not thwart African meaning and interpretation.

Finally, although its influence is fairly recent, Hindu practices have slowly been incorporated into the Orisha tradition. East Indian communities in Trinidad date back to 1845 with the arrival of 212 indentured servants following the abolition of slavery. By the late nineteenth century this immigrant labor force had increased to 27,425. According to Houk, by the 1950s, influences of Hinduism were apparent within the Orisha religion. This influence is most evident in the appearance of certain Hindu deities at Orisha ceremonies, the use of Hindu imagery in Orisha shrines, and in the rise of spiritual consultations held between Hindu *pundits* (priests) and Orisha practitioners. Although the presence of Hinduism is not very extensive within Orisha worship, it nonetheless speaks to the fluid nature of the religion.

Rada and Orisha at the End of the Twentieth Century

Since the rise of Black Power movements in the 1970s, the practice of African-derived religions in Trinidad has increased exponentially. Over the past thirty years, the Orisha tradition has absorbed the vast majority of persons interested in African-based religions on the island. Presently, there are over 150 Orisha shrines dispersed throughout the northern and southern tips of Trinidad.

Among this group of approximately 10,000 practitioners, two major trends have developed. First, as a means of gaining public legitimacy, Orisha practitioners have sought to be included in Trinidad's official grouping of religious bodies. In 1992, organizational efforts to collectively unify various shrines resulted in the formation of two governmentally recognized Orisha groups—Opa Orisha (Shango) of Trinidad and Tobago and the Orisha Movement. More recently, in 1999, practitioners were successful in petitioning the Trinidadian Parliament for the legalization of marriages performed by members of the Orisha priesthood. Finally, by conducting public celebrations such as the annual Oshun Festival and Orisha Family Day and by participating in Emancipation Day celebrations, the religion's public exposure has been increased. Trinidad was host to the Sixth World Orisha Congress in 1999.

The second major trend within Trinidad's Orisha community involves a recent internal movement among several practitioners to "re-Africanize" religious rites and practices. Concerned primarily with issues of authenticity and ritual purity, these practitioners seek to "purify" the tradition of all non-African elements. One of the central aims in this new movement is to re-orient religious standards in Trinidad in order to reflect that of Nigerian Yoruba. Conversely, dissenting practitioners contend that Trinidad's local interpretation of the Orisha tradition is in fact legitimate and valid. These practitioners, therefore, seek to privilege innovation and variation over purity. Adherents to both positions are helping to give shape and form to the religious identity of Trinidad's African-derived traditions in the twenty-first century.

Tracey E. Hucks

See also Music, Spiritual Baptist; Obeah in the West Indies; Orisha (Shango) Movement in Trinidad; Spiritual Baptists; Yoruba Religion

Bibliography

Anthony, Michael. (1997) *Historical Dictionary of Trinidad and Tobago.* London: The Scarecrow Press.

Bisnauth, Dale. (1989) *History of Religions in the Caribbean.* Kingston: Kingston Publishers Limited.

Black, Jan Knippers. (1975) *Area Handbook for Trinidad and Tobago.* Washington, D.C.: Foreign Area Studies.

Brereton, Bridget. (1981) *A History of Modern Trinidad 1783–1962.* London: Heinemann International.

Brereton, Bridget, and Gerard Besson. (1992) *The Book of Trinidad.* Trinidad and Tobago: Paria Publishing Company Limited.

Burton, Richard D. E. (1997) *Afro-Creole: Power, Opposition, and Play in the Caribbean.* Ithaca, NY: Cornell University Press.

Carr, Andrew T. (1989) *A Rada Community in Trinidad.* Trinidad and Tobago: Paria Publishing Company Limited.

Glazier, Stephen D. (1991) *Marchin' the Pilgrims Home: A Study of the Spiritual Baptists in Trinidad.* Salem, WI: Sheffield.

Herskovits, Melville and Frances. (1947) *Trinidad Village.* New York: Alfred A. Knopf.

Houk, James. (1995) *Spirits, Blood, and Drums: The Orisha Religion in Trinidad.* Philadelphia: Temple University Press.

Mintz, Sidney, and Richard Price. (1976) *The Birth of African-American Culture: An Anthropological Perspective.* Boston: Beacon Press.

Pollak-Eltz, Angelina. (1977) *Cultos AfroAmericanos: Vudu y Hechiceria in las Americas.* Caracas: Universidad Catolica Andres Bello.

Raboteau, Albert. (1978) *Slave Religion: The "Invisible Institution" in the Antebellum South.* New York: Oxford University Press.

Sankeralli, Burton, ed. (1995) *At the Crossroads: African Caribbean Religion and Christianity.* Trinidad and Tobago: Caribbean Conference of Churches.

Simpson, George Eaton. (1978) *Black Religions in the New World.* New York: Columbia University Press.

——. (1970) *Religious Cults of the Caribbean: Trinidad, Jamaica, and Haiti.* Puerto Rico: Institute of Caribbean Studies.

——. (1965) *The Shango Cult in Trinidad.* Puerto Rico: Institute of Caribbean Studies.

Warner-Lewis, Maureen. (1996) *Trinidad Yoruba: From Mother Tongue to Memory.* Tuscaloosa: The University of Alabama Press.

——. (1991) *Guinea's Other Suns: The African Dynamic in Trinidad Culture.* Dover, MA: The Majority Press.

Wood, Donald. (1986) *Trinidad in Transition: The Years After Slavery.* London: Oxford University Press.

Unification Church

The Unification Church is a new religious movement that developed during the latter half of the twentieth century. It was founded in 1954 by the Rev. Sun Myung Moon (1920–) in Korea as the Holy Spirit Association for the Unification of World Christianity. It moved to the United States in the 1970s after being persecuted by the Korean government. From the United States, Unification members, known derisively as Moonies, spread the religion to other Western nations and then, on a smaller scale, to Asia and Africa.

Claims that Rev. and Mrs. Moon are "the True Parents of all humanity ... the Savior, the Lord of the Second Advent, the Messiah" are at the core of Unification theology. As such, they are understood to have reversed the course of the human fall, subjugated Satan, restored the positions of Adam and Eve, established the first True Family, and ushered in what they termed the Completed Testament Age. Unification followers believe they can be engrafted into the new humanity through participating in the International Marriage Ceremonies, or "Blessings," presided over by Rev. and Mrs. Moon. Critical to their understanding is the belief that children born of unions blessed by the True Parents are free from the taint of original sin. Rev. Moon claims to have been commissioned at age fifteen (1935) by the risen Christ to complete the task of world salvation.

Rev. Moon and the Unification Church have been the subject of investigations and legal action by the government, religious watch organizations, and the media in the United States and Britain. The church has been attacked for its beliefs, its aggressive methods of recruiting members, its mass wedding ceremonies, the vast wealth of its founder (real estate, hotels, and newspapers), and its conservative political ideology. In 1984, Rev. Moon was jailed for income tax evasion in the United States. Although they do not agree with the church's teachings, civil rights and religious leaders have criticized government attacks as a violation of religious freedom.

Involvement of African-Americans and Africans

Involvement of African-Americans and Africans with the Unification Church began in the 1970s when the church established ties with black ministers in the United States and began seeking converts in sub-Saharan Africa, enjoying some initial success in Zaire. These efforts were opposed both by some people within the church and black ministers and community leaders. In the 1980s, as the missionary effort in Africa increased, converts were also gained in Zimbabwe, Zambia, the Central African Republic, and the Ivory Coast.

In the United States in the 1980s, perhaps the leading avenue for black involvement was through the Coalition for Religious Freedom, which was financially supported by the Unification Church. The coalition appealed to black clergy as fellow victims of discrimination and drew the interest, if not the allegiance, of several thousand black clergy. Prominent black clergy who showed public interest included former Black Panther and newly Evangelical Christian Eldridge Cleaver, Wyatt Walker, Ralph D. Abernathy, Joseph Lowery, and James Bevel, all members of the Southern Christian Leadership Conference and leaders of the civil rights movement. The presence of black clergy at church-sponsored events was widely criticized by other African-American leaders as an embracing of a conservative agenda. Also widely criticized were the interracial marriages promoted by the church, which were seen as an attack on the African-American community by some critics and even supporters of black clergy involvement in the church.

The major development during the 1990s in terms of the Unification Church's relationship with African and African-American Churches emerged in connection with the massive International Wedding Ceremonies presided over by Rev. and Mrs. Moon. The church, under the auspices of its affiliated Family Federation for World Peace and Unification (FFWPU), sponsored massive International Wedding Ceremonies in 1995, 1997, 1998, and 1999. These weddings, or "Blessings," featured large joint weddings in major venues with simultaneous ceremonies conducted around the world through satellite technology. Blessings '95 and '99 were held at Seoul Olympic Stadium, Blessing '97 was held at RFK Stadium, Washington, D.C., and Blessing '98 was held at New York's Madison Square Garden.

Only a small percentage of the participants in these gatherings were Unification Church members. The majority were previously married couples who were rededicating their marriages and a large number of these were members of African or African-American churches. In 1995, there were breakthrough encounters with leaders of the Nigerian Celestial Church of Christ and the Cherubim and Seraphim movement, also Nigerian-based. In 1996, the church conducted a six-month series of weekly True Family Values seminars in Washington, D.C. for 4,500 Christian clergy, the majority of whom were pastors of independent black churches. The church developed especially close ties with clergy in Chicago. Rev. T. L. Barrett, pastor of New Life Church of God In Christ, a large Chicago church, became the first clergyman in America to fly the Family Federation for World Peace flag over his church. Rev. Barrett opened his church to Mrs. Sun Myung Moon on several occasions, and some 120 black clergy from Chicago, many with their congregations, rededicated their marriages and bussed in to RFK Stadium for Blessing '97. In New York City, the Rev. Al Sharpton and his wife rededicated their marriage in a pre-Blessing ceremony and then officiated at several more. In a memorable response to press exposure of his association with Rev. Moon and the True Family Values Ministry, Sharpton stated, "[T]he world needs the message of true families. I don't care if it comes from Rev. Moon, Rev. Sun, or Rev. [M]idnight. This is the message God is sending us today." That the Rev. Sharpton, a high-profile and respected public figure and Democratic mayoral and senate hopeful, was unapologetic about his participation in Blessing activities inspired other prominent clergy and elders to rededicate their marriages.

After 1995, through its Chicago clergy contacts, the Unification Church also developed close ties with the Nation of Islam and its controversial leader, Lewis Farrakhan. Minister Farrakhan delivered a benediction on couples at Blessing '97. He and fellow Nation of Islam ministers participated in a number of church-sponsored functions and there were respectful references to Rev. and Mrs. Moon in the Nation's *Final Call* newspaper. In 2000, the church continued its efforts to attract followers in the African and African-American religious communities, but has yet to make deep or enduring inroads there and remains controversial everywhere.

Michael L. Mickler

Bibliography

Chryssides, George D. (1991) *The Advent of Sun Myung Moon.* New York: St. Martin's Press.

Craney, Glen. "CAUSA and the Black Clergy." *Christianity and Crisis* 47 (6 April 1987): 115–120.

Inglis, Michael, ed. (2000) *Forty Years in America: An Intimate History of the Unification Movement, 1959–99.* New York: HSA-UWC.

Sontag, Fredrick. (1977) *Sun Myung Moon and the Unification Church.* Nashville, TN: Abingdon.

United Church and Science of Living Institute

Frederick K. Eikenrenkoetter II, better known as "Rev. Ike," established the United Church and Science Living Institute, which is headquartered in the former Loew's United Palace Theater at Broadway and 175th Street in Manhattan. He was born around 1935 in Ridgeland, South Carolina, and reared in the Holiness-Pentecostal (Sanctified) tradition. After earning a bachelor's degree from the American Bible College in Chicago and completing a tour of duty in the U.S. Air Force, Rev. Ike opened the United Church of Jesus Christ for All People in the late 1950s in his hometown. He created the United Christian Evangelistic Association in 1962. In the mid-1960s, he moved his church to Boston and later to the Sunset Theater in Harlem, and purchased the five-thousand-seat theater in Washington Heights as his base of operations. Rev. Ike later returned the administrative arm of his organization to Boston and operates a church there as well.

Gallatin (1979) delineates four phases in Rev. Ike's ministry: (1) the conversionist period from 1958 to 1968, (2) the transitional period from 1969 to 1972, during which he began to adopt a New Thought perspective, (3) the gnostic period from 1972 to 1976, during which New Thought became the institutionalized dimension of the group, and (4) the consolidation of the group after 1976, during which he rediscovered Jesus but essentially continued to operate with a strong New Thought orientation.

In his early ministry, Rev. Ike preached a literal interpretation of the Bible, the importance of speaking-in-tongues, the imminence of the Second Coming of Jesus Christ, the traditional concepts of heaven and hell, and an ascetic morality. During the second and third phases, he adopted the following premises: (1) the belief that salvation must be achieved in the here-and-now, (2) positive thinking, (3) the belief that God dwells in everyone, (4) the belief that thoughts shape behavior, (5) the notion that individual desire leads to healing, (6) a rejection of the Devil as a concrete entity, (7) an approval of monetary and material acquisitiveness, and (8) a rejection of the traditional Christian doctrine of sin (Gallatin 1979: 194–209).

Beginning in the late 1960s, Rev. Ike began to instruct his followers to abandon "pie-in-sky" religion and seek prosperity and health in this life. He regards the Bible to be a "psychology book" that will help his followers to learn that God dwells inside of them. Rev. Ike maintains that the "lack of money is the root of all evil" (quoted in Gallatin 1979: 109), and often refers to successful individuals in his sermons and literature. Rev. Ike asserts that donations to his church are an integral part of his "Blessing Plan," which will ensure health, property, and success to his followers. In addition, he encourages his followers to visualize, affirm, and meditate upon the attainment of these goals. Snook provides the following description of Rev. Ike's style in the early 1970s:

> Ike . . . expects to applaud the success of his people and to see them rejoice in his prosperity. He laughs and jokes with the congregation, and the "testifying" he encourages is a series of recitations of how following his leadership paid off in material success and attendant happiness. . . . It is a nonpolitical message; Ike's advertising states that "people of all races, religions and those with no religion are welcome." . . . In his talk to the congregation, the preacher emphasizes that they have no black power among them, only green power. (Snook 1973: 86)

Unlike most African-American ministers, he does not provide pastoral counseling, messages, or healing. As a consequence, Gallatin (1979: 245) regards Rev. Ike's ministry as a "supplementary religion" for most of his followers, who often attend other churches. Rev. Ike operates a nationwide TV and radio ministry and makes frequent public appearances. His services "are broadcast over eighty-nine radio and twenty-two television stations primarily in the eastern United States and Hawaii" (Payne 1991: 124). In May 1973, he lectured in the psychiatry department at Harvard Medical School, in January 1975 at the University of Alabama, in November 1975 at the Atlanta University Center, and in 1977 at Rice University (Murphy, Melton, and Ward 1993: 247). He claimed in 1982 that more than seven million received his quarterly magazine and that more than seventy million had ordered the red prayer clothes that he distributed at no cost. In more recent years, Rev. Ike has toned down his more flamboyant mannerisms. In keeping with his ideological shift to Mind Science, Rev. Ike ceased wearing pink suits and other loud outfits, sometimes including a cape, and began wearing more reserved clothing, including three-piece business suits, as obvious symbols of his philosophy of world success and prosperity. The United Church publishes a periodical called *Action*.

Hans A. Baer

Bibliography

Gallatin, Martin V. (1979) "Rev Ike's Ministry: A Sociological Investigation of Religious Innovation." Ph.D. dissertation, New York University.

Murphy, Larry G., J. Gordon Melton, and Gary L. Ward, eds. (1993) *Encyclopedia of African American Religions.* New York: Garland Publishing.

Payne, Ward J. ed. (1991) *Directory of African American Religious Bodies.* Washington, DC: Howard University Press.

Snook, John B. (1973) *Going Further: Life-and-Death Religion in America.* Englewood Cliffs, NJ; Prentice-Hall.

United House of Prayer for All People

Although not as well known as Father Divine and his Peace Mission, "Sweet Daddy" Grace, the founder of the United House of Prayer for All People, served as one of most flamboyant "gods of the black metropolis." Bishop Charles Emmanuel Grace was born Marcelino Manoel da Graca on 25 January 1891, in Brava, Cape Verde Islands, a Portuguese territory in the Atlantic Ocean. Around 1900 he moved to New Bedford, Massachusetts. In 1921, Daddy Grace established the United House of Prayer for All People on the Rock of the Apostolic Faith in Wareham, a suburb of New Bedford (Alland 1981: 347).

Due to the slow growth of the sect in Massachusetts, Grace evangelized in the South, where he attracted a substantial following in cities such as Charlotte, North Carolina, and Norfolk and Newport News, Virginia. He established a congregation in Brooklyn in 1930 and one in Manhattan in 1938 as well as congregations in Stamford, Hartford, Bridgeport (all in Connecticut), Detroit, Los Angeles, Maryland, Delaware, New Jersey, South Carolina, and Georgia (Whiting 1952; Robinson 1974). Grace located the headquarters of the United House of Prayer for All People in an elegant seventeen-room mansion in Washington, D.C. The sect had its greatest concentration of members in the southeastern states of North Carolina, South Carolina, and Georgia.

In contrast to Father Divine's conservative business attire, Sweet Daddy Grace attracted attention with "his one-to-three inch fingernails, his shoulder-length hair, his colorful cutaways, and his flashy jewelry" (Robinson 1974:

213). His sect assumed many of the characteristics associated with Holiness-Pentecostal groups, including speaking in tongues and eschewing smoking, drinking, dancing, gambling, and sex outside of marriage. Daddy Grace presented himself as a messianic figure who manifested the spirit of God. While he did not claim that he was God, he reportedly told his followers, "Never mind about God. Salvation is by Grace only. . . . Grace has given God vacation, and since God is on His vacation, don't worry him. . . . If you sin against God, God cannot save you" (quoted in Fauset 1971: 26). Indeed, his followers genuflected before him and prayed before his image. In contrast to the founders of messianic-nationalist sects, Grace's assertion that he was white may have reinforced feelings of racial inferiority in his members. He promoted the utilization of various magico-religious articles, which could be purchased at each House of Prayer, to bring his followers good luck. These included healing-power products, soap, cookies, facial creams, hair dressing, toothpaste, coffee, tea, stationary, and the *Grace Magazine*.

Grace's followers showered their messiah with money by building money trees and houses. These were models of trees and houses with money attached to them. After his death on 12 January 1960, the Internal Revenue Service assessed the net worth of his estate at the end of 1956 to have been $4,081,511.62 (Robinson 1974:217). His estate reportedly included 111 churches and missions, as well as apartment houses, stores, an eighty-four-room mansion in Los Angeles, a twenty-two-acre property near Havana, and large houses in several cities. Despite the fact the United House of Prayer had a General Council, the sect functioned essentially as Grace's theocratic kingdom during his lifetime.

Over the course of his career, Daddy Grace encountered a series of lawsuits. In 1934, he was charged in Brooklyn of having violated the Mann Act (an antiprostitution law) for allegedly having cohabited with a pianist in the United House of Prayer. He initially was found guilty but later was acquitted, following his appeal. Grace also had charges brought against him in 1957 by female members but was cleared of charges in both cases.

Walter ("Sweet Daddy Grace") McCullough succeeded Bishop Charles Emmanuel Grace as the leader of the sect following a series of contested elections and court actions (Robinson 1974: 226–228). McCullough, who died in 1991, established a ministerial school in Richmond, Virginia, and gave the United House of Prayer a more traditional Pentecostal cast. According to Hodges, "The House of Prayer for All People, as its name implies, is open to all, regardless of race, color, or creed. Many of the first members of the organization were from lower-economic backgrounds. And though this particular group still accounts for the majority of the organization's membership, there is an ever increasing number of well-educated middle-class blacks" (Hodges 1989: 173).

Despite McCullough's efforts to preserve the theocratic kingdom of Sweet Daddy Grace, he was not able to prevent the formation of a rival sect called True Grace Memorial House of Prayer. In contrast to Father Divine and other messianic figures, such as Elijah Muhammad, Malcolm X, and Louis Farrakhan, Daddy Grace and his sect have not received much scholarly attention.

Hans A. Baer

Bibliography

Alland, Alexander. (1981) *To Be Human: An Introduction to Cultural Anthropology.* New York: John Wiley.

Fauset, Arthur H. (1971) *Black Gods of the Metropolis.* Philadelphia: University of Pennsylvania Press.

Hodges, John O. (1989) "Charles Manuel 'Sweet Daddy' Grace." In *Twentieth-Century Shapers of American Religion,* edited by Charles H. Lippy. New York: Greenwood Press, 170–179.

Robinson, David M. (1974) "A Song, a Shout, and a Prayer." In *The Black Experience in Religion,* edited by C. Eric Lincoln. New York: Doubleday, 212–234.

Whiting, Albert N. (1952) "The United House of Prayer of All People: A Case Study of a Charismatic Sect." Ph.D. dissertation, American University.

United States, African-Derived Religions in

Scholars from a variety of disciplines have recognized the central significance of religion in African-American culture. Scholarly studies on African-American religion in the United States can be traced back to W. E. B. Du Bois's *The Negro Church* (1903). Just as African-American culture is characterized by a considerable amount of diversity, the same applies to its religious expressions. African-American religion developed within the larger contexts of slavery in the antebellum South, the caste-like system of race relations in the South during the Jim Crow era, and the Great Migration to the cities of the North beginning around World War I. It has served as a significant form of cultural identity and both a refuge from and challenge to racism and social inequality in the larger society (Baer and Singer 1992). The development of African-American religion has taken variegated forms, particularly during the twentieth century.

The Development of African-American Religion Under Slavery

African religious concepts and rituals, such as ancestor worship, initiation rites, spirit possession, healing and funeral rituals, magical rituals for obtaining spiritual power, and ecstatic ceremonies enlivened by rhythmic dancing, drumming, and singing came to permeate the slave religion in the United States and other parts of the Americas (Raboteau 1978). Initially, a shortage of missionaries resulted in only a small number of slaves being instructed in Christian doctrine prior to the American Revolution. Most planters initially were reluctant to proselytize their slaves because they suspected that Christianity would provide their subjects with an egalitarian ideology and a thirst for freedom. With assurance from missionaries, most slaveholders recognized that a selective interpretation could be instrumental in fostering docility and subservience among their slaves. Nevertheless, many slaves came to adapt Christianity to their own needs and viewed it as an instrument of liberation that portrayed Jesus as a messianic deliverer from their bondage rather than as a meek and humble figure.

Some blacks joined the evangelical churches, particularly the Methodist, Baptist, and Presbyterian, during the First Awakening (1720–1740). Many slaves and free blacks converted to Christianity at revivalistic camp meetings during the Second Awakening (1790–1815). The Methodists initially opposed slavery but began to downplay this posture after their General Conference of 1784. The Baptists never opposed slavery with the fervor of the Methodists and came to accept it as they developed into a mainstream southern denomination. They, in particular, may have been able to make inroads among the slaves because baptism by immersion resembled the initiation rites associated with West African religions.

The slaves worshipped in a wide variety of settings, including with whites and free blacks, or exclusively with fellow slaves. Whites often found the numerical predominance and emotional exuberance of blacks in many congregations disturbing and encouraged the creation of separate black churches. Conversely, blacks welcomed the opportunity to worship in their own way. Slaves often held semisecret or secret religious meetings in their quarters, "praise houses," or "hush arbors" deep in the woods, swamps, and caverns. Sometimes slave religious gatherings provided a cover for slave rebellions and plans for escape to freedom.

The Black Church Independence Movement

Many relatively autonomous African-American congregations and religious associations emerged during the antebellum period in both the South and the North. Various early

COLORED PREACHERS

Some discussion has arisen over the standing of the Negro as a preacher. The Literary Digest quotes several opinions of this subject. The discussion begins with an article in the Southwestern Christian Advocate (colored), written by the Rev. Robert E. Jones, who asserted that the race had produced no preacher of real eminence. In other walks there have been colored men of much distinction, but not in the pulpit, he claimed, they have not shone, in spite of their religious temperament.

"In spite of the fact that there are approximately 10,000 Negroes who are ministers of the Gospel," he says, "we have no man among us who has made outstanding and unquestioned success as a preacher. In making this statement we are not unmindful of the fact that here and there are preachers who have local reputations and who are somewhat known in the nation, but there is no towering, masterful, persuasive preacher of the Gospel. There is certainly no man among us who is to the nation what Talmage or Moody or Beecher was. Nor is there any man among us who is the undisputed Talmage or Moody or Beecher of the race.

"True enough, we have the spiritual temperament. Our preachers are particularly apt at giving the Gospel narrative and expounding the truth. These are men of piety, and, in some instances, there are men of scholarly attainment, but the preacher has not yet arrived. We are not attempting to assign a reason for this, we are simply stating a fact."

Mr. John Edward Bruce writes to the New York Sun, joining in the discussion and taking the opposite view. He gives a list of distinguished Negro preachers:

"The Rev. John C. Penington, born a slave, was a great preacher and highly esteemed by all who knew him. He was a member of the Hartford Central Association of Congregational Ministers ... In 1841 he published a book, 'The History and Origin of the Colored Race.' ... He was elected by the State of Connecticut in 1843 as a delegate to the world's anti-slavery convention and to represent it in the world's peace convention held the same year in London. . . .

"Henry Highland Garnet, of New York, is another Negro clergyman who may be said to have been pre-eminent as a preacher. He was the first Negro Chaplain of the National House of Representatives by special invitation. President Arthur made him United States Minister to Liberia in 1881. . . .

"Dr. Alexander Crummell, the late pastor of St. Luke's Protestant Episcopal Church, Washington ... was a preacher of great force and power. His books, 'The Greatness of Christ' and 'Africa and America' are masterpieces of good English. . . .

"The Rev. John Chavis, of Wake County, N.C., had the remarkable distinction of being not only a great preacher, who preached to white congregations only, up to 1833 ... The accomplishments of such men as I have mentioned entitle them, I think, to be called pre-eminent."

Source: *The Crisis: A Record of the Darker Races*, vol. 1 (January 1911), p. 12. New York: NAACP.

---

slave congregations included one established in 1758 on the plantation of William Byrd III near Mecklenberg, Virginia, and the Silver Bluff Church, established sometime between 1773 and 1775, in South Carolina. Early northern Baptist congregations included the Joy Street Baptist Church (est. 1805) in Boston and the Abyssinian Baptist Church (est. 1808) in New York City. Black Baptists in the Midwest were the first to create separate regional associations. In 1835, six black Baptist congregations formed the Providence Baptist Association, which merged in 1853 with the Wood River Association to become the Western Colored Baptist Association. Membership in independent black Baptist churches increased dramatically after the Civil War. The National Baptist Convention, USA, finally emerged as the first African-American nationwide Baptist association in 1895.

African-American Baptists also established independent congregations and associations during the antebellum, although primarily in the North. Various free blacks belonging to the Free African Society, a mutual-aid group within St. George's Methodist Episcopal Church in Philadelphia, broke their ties with the parent body sometime between 1787 and 1792 in response to racial discrimination (George 1973). Most of the schismatics established St. Thomas's African Episcopal Church, but a minority contingent, under the leadership of Richard Allen, formed Bethel African Methodist Episcopal Church—the "mother church" of what became the African Methodist Episcopal (AME) Church. The racially mixed St. John's Street Church in New York City served as the focal point of what eventually developed into the second major black Methodist denomination, the African Methodist Episcopal Zion Church. Other black Methodist bodies that developed during the antebellum period included the African Union Methodist Protestant Church and the Union American Methodist Episcopal Church. Although the AME and AME Zion churches made substantial inroads into the South following the Civil War, the white-controlled Methodist Episcopal Church, South, implemented the structure for the Colored (later Christian) Methodist Episcopal Church. Especially in the North, representatives of independent black churches were involved in antislavery, abolitionist, and proto-nationalist movements. For the most part, however, the routine activities of the church, along with attempts to ensure its survival in the face of meager funds and hostility, prevented greater attention to the vital social issues of the day.

Religious Diversification During the Twentieth Century

African-American religion underwent a process of diversification in the early twentieth century as an increasing number of blacks migrated from the rural South to the cities of both the North and the South. By this time, the National Baptist and the black Methodist denominations had become the "mainstream" churches of African-American communities throughout the country. Congregations affiliated with these denominations catered to a diversity of blacks both in rural and urban areas, but tended to aspire to middle-class standards of respectability and decorum. In contrast, black congregations affiliated with white-controlled Episcopalian, Presbyterian, and Congregational churches tended to cater primarily to the "black bourgeoisie."

Despite the concerted efforts on the part of many mainstream congregations to meet the social, economic, and emotional needs of the migrants, many of them chose to meet these needs by creating storefront and house churches, many of which eventually affiliated themselves with one of the black-controlled mainstream denominations. Conversely, the migrants often were attracted to the new "gods of the

black metropolis" (Fauset 1971), namely the charismatic prophets and messiahs who established a wide array of Judaic, Islamic, Holiness-Pentecostal (Sanctified), and Spiritual sects as well as groups such as the African Orthodox Church and Father Divine's Peace Mission movement. The Depression accelerated the process of religious diversification. As Gayraud Wilmore asserts, "the black community, by the end of the 1930s, was literally glutted with churches of every variety" (1983: 163). Regardless of their religious orientation, storefront churches represented an effort on the part of migrants to re-create the communal ethos of the black rural church. Many storefronts evolved into the foundations of a diversity of unconventional African-American sects. Many others were relegated to the dustbin of history as their founders died or moved to other cities.

Mainstream Denominations

The mainstream denominations are committed, at least in theory, to a reformist strategy of social action that will enable African Americans to become better integrated into American society (Lincoln and Mamiya 1990). Although many of their congregations exhibit expressive religious services, which include testifying, exuberant sermons, and "shouting" or ecstatic dancing, many ministers and congregations affiliated with mainstream denominations have a strong commitment to social activism and outreach. Their members generally believe in the American Dream, but often oppose the racist barriers that block the ability of African Americans to share in the benefits of the larger society. Most contemporary mainstream congregations are affiliated with one of the following historic black-controlled denominations: the National Baptist Convention, USA; the National Baptist Convention of America; the Progressive National Baptist Convention; the African Methodist Episcopal Church; the African Methodist Episcopal Zion Church; and the Christian Methodist Episcopal Church. A fair number of African Americans, particularly middle-class ones, belong to white-controlled denominations, such as the Episcopal, United Methodist, Roman Catholic, Presbyterian, Congregational, Disciples of Christ, and even the Southern Baptist Convention.

Although most black mainstream congregations stood on the sidelines of the events that followed the Supreme Court school desegregation decision of 1954, many black mainstream ministers and congregations joined the civil rights movement. Needless to say, Dr. Martin Luther King, Jr., a young, middle-class Baptist minister with an affinity for the Social Gospel and Gandhian non-violence, became a pivotal figure in that movement—and with his assassination, its most poignant symbol. As Morris observes, King's

W.E.B. DU BOIS ON THE
AFRICAN-AMERICAN CHURCH

The Negro church of to-day is the social centre of Negro life in the United States, and the most characteristic expression of African character. Take a typical church in a small Virginia town: it is the "First Baptist" – a roomy brick edifice seating five hundred or more persons, tastefully finished in Georgia pine, with a carpet, a small organ, and stained-glass windows. Underneath is a large assembly room with benches. This building is the central club-house of a community of a thousand or more Negroes. Various organizations meet here – the church proper, the Sunday-school, two or three insurance societies, women's societies, secret societies, and mass meetings of various kinds. Entertainments, suppers, and lectures are held beside the five or six regular weekly religious services. Considerable sums of money are collected and expended here, employment is found for the idle, strangers are introduced, news is disseminated, and charity distributed. At the same time this social, intellectual, and economic centre is a religious centre of great power. Depravity, Sin, Redemption, Heaven, Hell, and Damnation are preached twice a Sunday after the crops are laid by; and few indeed of the community have the hardihood to withstand conversion. Back of this more formal religion, the Church often stands as a real conserver of morals, a strengthener of family life, and the final authority on what is Good and Right.

Source: Du Bois, W. E. B. (1903) *The Souls of Black Folk.* Electronic Text Center, University of Virginia Library, 136.

Southern Christian Leadership Conference served as the "decentralized political arm of the black church" in the struggle for civil rights (1984: 79–99).

In the wake of the civil rights movement, various progressive clergy affiliated with mainstream denominations created the National Conference of Black Churches. Certain mainstream ministers also became involved in the Black Theology movement that began to emerge in the late 1960s. Despite their various differences, black theologians view Jesus Christ as a liberator against human oppression and racism. While most black theologians remain uncritical of the class structure of American society, some adopt a democratic socialist stance as being an essential component of developing an African-American revolutionary Christianity (West 1982; Cone 1984). As was the case for the civil rights movement, black mainstream churches served as the main supporters of Reverend Jesse Jackson's presidential bids in 1984 and 1988 under the banner of the Rainbow Coalition.

Messianic-Nationalist Sects

These sects generally are established by charismatic figures who are regarded by their followers as messiahs who will deliver black people from white oppression. Messianic-nationalist sects often repudiate "Negro identity" and insist that African Americans are "Moors," "Hebrews," "Asiatics," "Muslims," or some other type of ethnic identity. They often regard blacks to have been the original human beings and view whites as some kind of biologically degenerate form. Messianic-nationalist sects often create alternative schools, businesses, and schools that will enable them to rise above the vicissitudes of poverty and racism.

African-American religion has exhibited Judaic, Islamic, and Christian forms or even has syncretized elements from two or all three of these religious traditions. Black Jewish congregations began to appear around 1915 in Washington, D.C., and other cities, although there is some evidence of earlier groups, including in the South. Messianic-nationalist sects drawing upon Judaism include the Church of the Living God, the Pillar Ground of Truth for all Nations, the Church of God and Saints of Christ, and the Original Hebrew Israelite Nation.

Black Islamic sects have been the most prominent manifestation of messianic-nationalism. The earliest of these was the Moorish Science Temple established by Noble Drew Ali in Newark, New Jersey, around 1913 (Turner 1997). Although remnants of the Temple still exist, its main thrust was picked up by the Nation of Islam, a sect that was initially established by W. D. Fard in Detroit in the early 1930s (Lincoln 1973). Upon Fard's mysterious disappearance in 1933, the group underwent a succession crisis which resulted in several factions. Elijah Muhammad emerged as the leader of the largest of these, but he removed the headquarters of the Nation to Chicago where it underwent a slow process of growth until the 1960s. At that time, Malcolm X, the charismatic minister of the Harlem Temple, brought the Nation to national prominence and recruited many young blacks to it. Nevertheless, other black Islamic sects, including the Ahmadiyya Moslem movement in Chicago, the Hannafis of Washington, D.C., and the Asaru Allah community of Brooklyn, competed for membership with the Nation. Shortly prior to his assassination in 1965, Malcolm X broke with Elijah Muhammad, embraced a more universal form of Islam, and established the Muslim Mosque, Inc. Following the death of Elijah Muhammad in 1975, Wallace D. Muhammad, one of his sons, led the transformation of the Nation into the World Community of Islam in the West and still later the American Muslim Mission, which adopted orthodox Islamic practices and even admitted whites into its ranks. Louis Farrakhan established in 1978 a reconstituted Nation of Islam that he claimed would preserve the original teachings of Fard and Elijah Muhammad (Gardell 1996). Despite his anti-Semitic remarks, he eventually emerged as one of the leading black spokespersons in the nation and in particular has found great appeal among young disenfranchised blacks.

The most prominent Christian messianic-nationalist sect was the African Orthodox Church under the leadership of George Alexander McGuire, a former Episcopalian priest from Jamaica (Burkett 1978). This body emerged in the 1920s out of Marcus Garvey's Universal Negro Improvement Association, the largest mass organization in African-American history, and promoted the veneration of the Black Madonna and the Black Christ. Albert B. Cleage, a former United Church of Christ minister, established the Shrine of the Black Madonna in Detroit in the 1960s and became a pivotal figure in the Black Theology movement that portrayed Jesus as a black revolutionary messiah who came to free peoples of color from white oppression.

Conversionist Sects

Conversionist sects exemplify a desire by many African Americans to return to "that old-time religion." They encompass Holiness-Pentecostal (or Sanctified) groups and various smaller Baptist groups, such as the Primitive Baptists. Conversionist sects emphasize a profound conversion experience and various expressive ritual activities, such as shouting, testifying, and speaking-in-tongues as outward signs of "holiness" or "sanctification." They also stress a puritanical morality and tend to be other-worldly and apolitical. Conversely, some conversionist ministers and congregations have become involved in social activism.

The Church of God in Christ, headquartered in Memphis, Tennessee, has grown into the largest black Pentecostal body in both the nation and the world and

Marcus Garvey (1887–1940), Black nationalist and founder of the Universal Negro Improvement Association. PHOTO COURTESY OF RANDALL BURKETT.

claimed to have had some 3.7 million members in the early 1990s, although this figure is probably somewhat inflated. Although it still preserves many conversionist features, COGIC began a process of mainstreaming in the middle of the twentieth century. Many congregations within COGIC have substantial numbers of middle-class and prosperous working-class members, and various COGIC ministers, including the flamboyant Al Sharpton of Brooklyn, have become involved in various forms of social activism (Taylor 1994). COGIC provided the headquarters for the sanitation workers' strike, which was punctuated by the assassination of Dr. Martin Luther King, Jr., in Memphis in 1968. Other conversionist sects include the Church of Christ (Holiness) U.S.A., Christ's Sanctified Holy Church, the Pentecostal Assemblies of the World, and the Primitive National Baptist Convention.

Thaumaturgical Sects

These sects maintain that the most direct means to achieve socially desired goals, such as economic security, prestige,

APPROXIMATE MEMBERSHIP OF MAJOR BLACK-CONTROLLED CHRISTIAN DENOMINATIONS IN THE UNITED STATES

African Methodist Episcopal Church	3,500,000
National Baptist Convention of America	3,500,000
Progressive National Baptist Convention	2,500,000
African Methodist Episcopal Zion Church	1,230,000
National Baptist Convention, USA	1,000,000
Christian Methodist Episcopal Church	718,000

The African Methodist Episcopal Church and the National Baptist Convention of America are the eighth and ninth largest religious bodies in the United States.

Source: www.adherents.com

love, and health, is to conduct various magico-religious rituals. They also encourage their adherents to adopt a positive attitude and to overcome negative thoughts. Thaumaturgical sects generally accept the cultural patterns of the larger society but tend to eschew social activism as a strategy for achieving these goals. Spiritual churches constitute the foremost example of the thaumaturgical sect (Baer and Singer 1992; Jacobs and Kaslow 1991). They began to appear in various large cities, such as Chicago, New Orleans, and Detroit, in the 1910s.

Spiritual churches syncretize elements from American Spiritualism, Roman Catholicism, African-American Protestantism, and Voodoo, or *vodun*. Depending upon the association or congregation, they may incorporate elements of other religious traditions, such as Judaism or New Thought. In large part, African Americans in these groups adapted Spiritualism to their own experience and began to refer to their churches as "Spiritual" rather than "Spiritualist" by the 1930s and 1940s. Spiritual churches generally urge their members to seek salvation in the here and now by burning candles before the images of Jesus, the Blessed Virgin, or the Catholic saints, obtaining messages from prophets and mediums in bless services or private consultations, and taking ritual baths.

Most Spiritual churches are small, cater primarily to working-class people, and often are situated in storefronts or houses, but some are located in substantial edifices and also include middle-class people in their ranks. While some Spiritual congregations are independent, most belong to an association consisting from as few as three or four congregations to over eighty congregations. The largest of the Spiritual associations is the Metropolitan Spiritual Churches of Christ, Incorporated (est. 1925 in Kansas City). Other Spiritual associations include the Universal Hagar's Spiritual Church (est. in 1923 in Detroit), the Mt. Zion Spiritual Temple, the Universal Ancient Ethiopian Spiritual Church, and Spiritual Israel and its Army.

Although not a part of the Spiritual movement per se, the United Church and Science of Living Institute (est. 1966) probably is the best known of the African-American thaumaturgical sects. Its founder Frederik Eikenrenkoetter II, better known as Reverend Ike, teaches that the absence of money is the root of all evil and urges his followers to obtain "green power" through visualization and the performance of various magico-religious rituals.

Conclusion

As in other parts of the Americas, African-American religion in the United States takes a multiplicity of forms and exemplifies the rich texture of African-American culture as a whole. To a greater or less extent, all African-American religious movements and groups form complex syncretic ensembles. As Bourguignon points out, "Afro-American religions, in their many different forms, represent a mixing and merging of African and European traditions and often the formation of new growth of belief and ritual, quite different from the courses for which they started" (1970: 190). The study of African-American religion also provides us with significant insights into the social condition of people of African ancestry. African-American religion has been characterized by a dual consciousness in that it has fostered both accommodation and protest to institutional racism and social stratification in American society. The "pragmatic spirituality" of African-American religion has roots in the African-American response to the harsh, yet always changing, realities of life in the United States. As in the past, the more progressive expressions of African-American religion hold the potential of being a part of efforts for radical social transformation emanating from the black community.

Hans A. Baer

See also African Methodist Episcopal Church; African Orthodox Church; Ahmadiyya Movement; African Methodist Episcopal Zion Church; African Orthodox Church; Black Catholics in the U.S.; Black Jewish Movements; Black Muslims; Black Theology; Christ's Sanctified Holy Church; Church of Christ (Holiness) U.S.A; Fire Baptized Holiness Church; Moorish Science Temple; National Baptist Convention of America; National Baptist Convention, USA; Rainbow Coalition; Shrine of the Black Madonna, Detroit; Spiritual Baptists; Universal Hagar's Spiritual Church; Universal Negro Improvement Association

Bibliography

Baer, Hans A. (1984) *The Black Spiritual Movement: A Religious Response to Racism.* Knoxville: University of Tennessee Press.

Baer, Hans A. and Merrill Singer. (1992) *African-American Religion in the Twentieth Century: Varieties of Protest and Accommodation.* Knoxville: University of Tennessee Press.

Bourguignon, Erika. (1970) "Afro-American Religions." In *Black America*, edited by John Szwed. New York: Basic Books, 190–201.

Burkett, Randall K. (1978) *Garveyism as a Religious Movement: The Institutionalization of Black Civil Religion.* Metuchen, NJ: Scarecrow.

Du Bois, W. E. B. (1903) *The Negro Church in America.* Atlanta: Atlanta University Press.

Fauset, Arthur H. (1971) *Black Gods of the Metropolis.* Philadelphia: University of Pennsylvania Press.

Gardell, Mattias. (1996) *In the Name of Elijah Muhammad: Louis Farrakhan and the Nation of Islam.* Durham, NC: Duke University Press.

George, Carol V. (1973) *Segregated Sabbaths: Richard Allen and the Emergence of the Independent Black Churches.* New York: Oxford University Press.

Jacobs, Claude F., and Andrew J. Kaslow. (1991) *The Spiritual Churches of New Orleans: Origins, Beliefs, and Rituals of an African-American Religion.* Knoxville: University of Tennessee Press.

Lincoln, C. Eric. (1973) *The Black Muslims in America*, rev. ed. Boston: Beacon Press.

Lincoln, C. Eric, and Lawrence H. Mamiya. (1990) *The Black Church in the African American Experience.* Durham, NC: Duke University Press.

Morris, Aldon D. (1984) *The Origins of the Civil Rights Movement: Black Communities Organizing for Change.* New York: Free Press.

Raboteau, Albert J. (1978) *Slave Religion: The "Invisible Institution" in the Antebellum South.* New York: Oxford University Press.

Taylor, Clarence. (1994) *The Black Churches of Brooklyn.* New York: Columbia University Press.

Turner, Richard Brent. (1997) *Islam in the African-American Experience.* Philadelphia: Temple University Press.

Wilmore, Gayraud S. (1983) *Black Religion and Black Radicalism.* Maryknoll, NY: Orbis Books.

Universal Hagar's Spiritual Church

Although Father Divine and his Peace Mission have received relatively extensive treatment, the Universal Hagar's Spiritual Church (UHSC) established in 1923 by Father George Willie Hurley, a contemporary of Father Divine and also a self-proclaimed god, has been largely neglected in the literature on African-American religion. Father Hurley was the founder of one of the earliest African-American Spiritual sects in the United States (Baer 1984).

Father Hurley was born on 17 February 1884 in Reynolds, Georgia. Upon completion of high school, he underwent ministerial training at Tuskegee Institute in Alabama and also taught in public schools in the South. After moving to Detroit in 1919, he joined the Triumph the Church and Kingdom of God in Christ. Hurley was quickly elevated to the position of elder in the church and became its "Presiding Prince of Michigan." In the early 1920s, he joined the International Spiritual Church but started his own UHSC shortly thereafter. By the time of Hurley's death in 1943, UHSC had grown into an association consisting of at least of thirty-seven congregations (eight in Michigan, eight in Ohio, six in Pennsylvania, seven in New Jersey, five in New York City, and single congregations in West Virginia, Delaware, and Illinois).

Father Hurley created an intricate cosmology and an elaborate politico-religious organization. Like other Spiritual groups, the Universal Hagar's Spiritual Church contains elements of American Spiritualism, Roman Catholicism, African-American Protestantism, and, possibly, Vodun. Father Hurley also incorporated concepts from the *Aquarian Gospel of Jesus Christ*, astrology, New Thought, Ethiopianism, and other belief systems. Sometime around 1933, if not earlier, he began to teach his followers that his body had taken on the Christ Spirit. Just as Adam had been the God of the Taurian Age, Abraham the God of the Arian Age, and Jesus the God of the Piscean Age; Father Hurley maintained that he was the God of the Aquarian Age—a period of peace and social harmony. He also asserted that while minor prophets would carry on his mission after his death, his would be the last gospel to be preached on the earth. Father Hurley taught his followers that the Spirit of God is embedded in each person. He also maintained that Ethiopians, or blacks, were the first people in the world, the original Hebrew nation, and the creators of civilization and hieroglyphics. The first religion was the Coptic Ethiopian religion. Conversely, whites were the offspring of Cain, who had been cursed with pale skin because of leprosy. Father Hurley argued that whites organized the Roman Catholic church, which in turn spawned our white-controlled religious bodies. He taught that the whites had enslaved the Ethiopian people and forced them to join an array of white churches. In some of his writings, many of which were published in a newsletter entitled *The Aquarian Age*, Father Hurley suggested that the Aquarian Age would be a period of black dominance. In 1924, he created the School of Mediumship and Psychology and also later established the Knights of the All Seeing Eye, a Masonic-like auxiliary open to both men and women.

In marked contrast to most Spiritual leaders, Father Hurley opposed racism and the exploitation of African Americans in the larger society. He urged his followers to vote for Franklin D. Roosevelt. As opposed to Father Divine and various African-American messianic-nationalist leaders such as Elijah Muhammad, Father Hurley did not provide his followers with an extensive system of cooperative and communal institutions designed as programs of social uplift. Instead, he provided his followers with thaumaturgical solutions, including prayer, meditation, and positive thinking, to their problems in a racist and class society.

Father Hurley's successors as head of the Universal Hagar's Spiritual Church have included Prince Thomas Surbadger, Mother Mary Hatchett, Prince Alfred Baily, and Reverend G. Latimer, one of Hurley's daughters. The Wiseman Board serves as the association's governing body and has consisted primarily of women in recent decades. The heaviest concentration of Hagar's congregations have been in southeastern Michigan, particularly around Detroit—the site of the sect's headquarters—and the New York-New Jersey megalopolis. Whereas in 1965 UHSC had forty-one congregations in eight states, in 1980 it had thirty-five congregations in eleven states. While Father Hurley's association appears to have passed its zenith, it continues to thrive in various parts of the United States. Ironically, current UHSC leaders do not strike out against institutional racism with nearly the vengeance that Father Hurley did at a time when it was much more dangerous to do so.

Hans A. Baer

See also Social Activism

Bibliography

Baer, Hans A. (1984) *The Black Spiritual Movement: A Religious Response to Racism.* Knoxville: University of Tennessee Press.

Universal Negro Improvement Association

The Universal Negro Improvement Association and African Communities League (UNIA), founded in Jamaica in 1914 by Marcus Moziah Garvey (1887–1940), became an international movement after Garvey moved his headquarters to New York City in 1917. To understand the movement's extraordinary mass appeal throughout the United States in the late teens and 1920s, it must be analyzed and appreciated as a religious movement. The sociologist of religion, Joachim Wach, identifies three distinctive components of any organization properly described as a religious movement, and these provide a convenient frame to analyze Garveyism. They are 1) a religious ethos, established through rituals and symbols specific to the organization; 2) a belief system with respect to the transcendent; and 3) rules of membership by which followers are organized into a collectivity.

Rituals and Symbols

The Garvey movement was replete with religious ritual and suffused with a religious ethos. The UNIA constitution required that every local chapter elect a chaplain, usually an ordained minister of any denomination. Meetings began with the missionary hymn, "From Greenland's Icy Mountains," and closed with "Onward, Christian Soldiers." The Ur-text of black religious nationalism in the United States from the early nineteenth century to the present, Psalms 68:31 (King James version)—"Princes shall come out of Egypt; Ethiopia shall soon stretch out her hands unto God"—was regularly invoked by Garveyites and was incorporated in the "Universal Ethiopian Anthem." This anthem, printed in the *Universal Negro Hymnal* compiled by the black Jewish Garveyite Arnold Josiah Ford (d. 1935), was sung at the conclusion of each UNIA gathering. The structure for each meeting was prescribed in the *Universal Negro Ritual*, written in 1921 by George Alexander McGuire (1886–1934), who also prepared the *Universal Negro Catechism* (1921). McGuire, an Anglican clergyman who was principally responsible for formalizing the religious ritual of the UNIA, soon founded the African Orthodox Church (effectively, a racial branch of the Protestant Episcopal Church) as a consequence of having "caught the

Garvey vision." McGuire's *Ritual* prescribed baptismal and burial services for UNIA members. In the baptismal service, the colors of the UNIA were laid on the infant being baptized, and parents promised to inculcate the Lord's Prayer, the Ten Commandments, and the *Universal Negro Catechism.*

Belief System

There are two principal sources for Garveyite theology: the hundreds of speeches by Marcus Garvey and other UNIA leaders who spoke from the platform of Liberty Hall in New York City (many published in the weekly *Negro World*); and Garvey's own confidential "Lesson Guides" for the School of African Philosophy (a training school for future UNIA leaders). His speeches and writings provide ample documentation for his theology, a coherent and internally consistent effort to interpret the world in an ultimately meaningful way. This went far beyond his much-publicized declaration that God must not be conceived as white. He did

This cut, from Garvey's weekly paper, the *Negro World*, illustrates the extent to which a religious ethos and religious rhetoric permeated the Garvey Movement. Chaplain General George Alexander McGuire preached on the resurrection of the Negro in relation to the resurrection of Jesus; National Baptist missionary J. Francis Robinson spoke on behalf of the UNIA; former AME minister Richard H. Tobitt, "leader of the Eastern Province of the West Indies" was ordained in McGuire's new denomination; and former Congregational clergyman and *Negro World* editor William M. Ferris (a graduate of both Harvard and Yale) likened Garvey to St. Patrick.

COURTESY OF RANDALL BURKETT.

CALL OF ETHIOPIA

Langston Hughes

Ethiopia,
Lift your night-dark face,
Abyssinian
Son of Sheba's race!
Your palm trees tall
And your mountains high
Are shade and shelter
To men who die
For freedom's sake–
But in the wake of your sacrifice
May all Africa arise
With blazing eyes and night-dark face
In answer to the call of Sheba's race:
Ethiopia's free!
Be like me,
All of Africa,
Arise and be free!
All you black peoples,
Be free! Be free!

Source: Hughes, Langston, (1935) "Call of Ethiopia." *Opportunity, Journal of Negro Life*, 13, 276.

firmly declare it idolatrous for people of color to worship a white god: "Whilst our God has no color, yet it is human to see everything through one's own spectacles, and since white people have seen their God through white spectacles, we . . . shall worship Him through the spectacles of Ethiopia" (*Philosophy and Opinions*, I, p. 44). Garvey also described God as absolute intelligence and absolute power, and then resolved the classic question of theodicy by insisting, "God is no respecter of persons." This allowed him the assurance that God never intended his race to be enslaved, while knowing that God would assist in his people's liberation, as promised in Psalms 68:31.

Garvey's Christology was relatively "low," in classic theological terms: Jesus was famously described as "The Black Man of Sorrows," the suffering servant whose cross was borne by the black Simon of Cyrenia. With the "blood of all races in his veins," Jesus was capable of redeeming all of humanity: he was perceived as the "greatest reformer" or "the greatest radical the world ever saw." Garvey placed less

emphasis on Jesus' salvific role, in accord with his strong anthropology. His doctrine of humanity emphasized its responsibility for its own destiny: "After the creation and after *man* was given possession of the world, the Creator relinquished all authority to his lord, except that which was spiritual . . . and man, therefore, became master of his own destiny and architect of his own fate" ("Dissertation on Man," *Negro World*, 29 April 1922, p. 1). Salvation was dependent on one's own work: it was both social and this-worldly. Finally, Garvey's eschatology was centered on the notion of the "Redemption of Africa" (about which he spoke much more often than the "back-to-Africa" caricature universally used by his opponents). The great anthropologist, St. Clair Drake, rightly identified the image of the redemption of Africa, from the nineteenth century forward, as "one important focus of meaningful activity among New World Negroes" and as "an energizing myth . . . for those pre-political movements that arose while the powerless were gathering their strength for realistic and rewarding political activity." It was this mythos of the Redemption of Africa that Garvey revitalized among people of African descent in the United States and throughout the African Diaspora in the early twentieth century. It functioned for him as both a legitimate political goal and as the eschatological goal toward which all of history was leading.

Organization

The organizational structure of Garveyism as a religious movement took shape after considerable internal debate between Garvey and his chief religious lieutenant, George Alexander McGuire, who was the UNIA Chaplain-General from 1920 to 1922. Deeply immersed in a High Church Anglican tradition, McGuire saw no problem in predicating much of Garveyism on the *Book of Common Prayer*, source of so much of the *Catechism* and *Ritual* he had compiled. Garvey could ill afford, however, to force all members to convert to Anglicanism in order to be members in good standing of the UNIA. He needed rituals, symbols, and a belief system at a sufficiently high level of generality so that no one would have to give up his or her specific religious beliefs, be they Muslim, Jewish, Orthodox, or any variety of Christian sect or denomination. Garvey forced McGuire to resign as Chaplain-General and made it clear that the African Orthodox Church had no official place with the UNIA. Garveyism, as a religious movement, could function only as a civil religion of the African Diaspora, open to all men and women of African descent.

Garvey's largest vision was to bring all men and women of African descent—the 400,000,000 people of color about whom he spoke so much—into a prideful peoplehood, a nation that would command the respect of all peoples of the world. To build this transnational nation, he created elaborate political rituals and civil institutions (a flag, a national anthem, a military corps, a steamship line, a civil service, and others); and he also created religious rituals whose transcendent goal was the redemption of Africa. The idea of the redemption of Africa struck a deep chord, especially among North American blacks who, over three centuries and more of their sojourn in an alien and hostile land, had increasingly come to view themselves as God's chosen people and as the bearers of true Christianity, for which they had a unique responsibility to redeem Africa, and through Africa, all of the world.

By tapping into this potent understanding of the meaning of the African's suffering and sojourn in the wilderness of America, Garvey was able to secure hundreds of thousands of followers, not only in the urban centers of the North, but also in Seattle, Portland, San Francisco, and Los Angeles; in Phoenix, Denver, Dallas, and Houston; in St. Louis, Minneapolis, Chicago, and Memphis; and in rural and urban places throughout the southern United States.

Randall K. Burkett

See also African Orthodox Church; Jamaica, African-Derived Religions in

Bibliography

Burkett, Randall K. (1978) *Black Redemption: Churchmen Speak for the Garvey Movement.* Philadelphia: Temple University Press.

——. (1978) *Garveyism as a Religious Movement: The Institutionalization of a Black Civil Religion.* Metuchen, NJ: Scarecrow Press.

Drake, St. Clair. (1970) *The Redemption of Africa and Black Religion.* Chicago: Third World Press.

Garvey, Amy Jacques, ed. (1991) *Philosophy and Opinions of Marcus Garvey.* New York: Atheneum.

Hill, Robert A., ed. (1983–1995) *The Marcus Garvey and Universal Negro Improvement Association Papers*, 9 vols. Berkeley: University of California Press.

Wach, Joachim. (1947). *Sociology of Religion.* London: Kegan Paul.

The Venezuelan Cult of Maria Lionza

The Venezuelan Cult of Maria Lionza is a syncretistic and utilitarian religion that has its roots in the Spiritism of Allan Kardec, Amerindian mythology and shamanistic practices, and the popular Afro-Cuban Catholicism. Concepts and practices are continuously changing, as the cult lacks a uniform structure and ritual rules accepted by all adherents. The leaders often invent new ceremonies and invoke a different set of spirits in order to attract the attention of the practitioners. The beliefs are based on concepts concerning witches and magic, as well as of good and evil spirits, which are common in all strata of the Venezuelan society. The cult is utilitarian, which means that the believers expect that their problems may be solved with the aid of spirits that manifest themselves in mediums. When they need help they attend rituals in different centers until they are satisfied with the results. They are willing to pay for the services. The practices are alternative forms of religious behavior, yet most adherents consider themselves to be Catholic and attend Sunday mass.

Belief Foundations of the Cult of Maria Lionza

The cult started in the 1920s as an outgrowth of spiritistic sessions that took place in the State of Yaracuy, where the holy mountain of Sorte is still considered to be the most important sanctuary. Around the turn of the century, many Venezuelan intellectuals practiced Kardecism as sort of a pastime, in order to contact the souls of the departed. Later, Spiritism as a philosophy was vulgarized. The disincarnated spirits were summoned now by common people in order to solve their problems. The mediums also began to incorporate Amerindian nature spirits. Soon the spiritistic séances turned into spiritual consultations.

One of these native Amerindian spirits was called Maria de la Onza, or Maria Lionza, and she soon gained importance. A legend sprang up about a beautiful Indian princess who was raped by an Anaconda snake, the guardian of a lake, which as a consequence was punished by God and exploded, while the spirit of the princess became the guardian of flora and fauna in the region around Sorte, in Yaracuy. To obtain her favors, worshipers met at the foot of this mountain—a spot that during colonial times was an indigenous sanctuary where the shamans used to get in touch with their guardian spirits.

Soon a number of other spirits of nature, the so-called Don Juanes or San Juanes, were also invoked. The spiritual helpers of native and mestizo shamans and spiritual healers of the region had always been called by these names and were figures of the local Amerindian mythology.

For a long time Maria Lionza was the most important and powerful figure in this pantheon. In the 1940s, however, when the cult gradually spread to the cities in the central valley, more spirits were added, such as the Indian Chiefs (Guaicaipuro, Tamanaco, and others). Some say that their inclusion was due to the fact that a private bank issued a series of gold coins with the images of these chiefs. Later, the spirit of the national hero Simon Bolivar and some of his famous generals were added. They are summoned to settle quarrels in the family and may also advise the faithful for whom to vote in the elections.

At this time it also became customary to invoke the spirits of deceased medical doctors, among them Dr. José Gregorio Hernandez, who died in 1918 in a car accident, when only five cars were registered in Caracas. For the Catholics he is a real saint, the most popular saint in Venezuela, although so far he has not been canonized. His spirit manifested itself in mediums to diagnose illnesses and prescribe remedies, but since the process of his beatification has further advanced, and since the Marialionzists make a distinction between saints and spirits, he no longer appears in the ritual but sends advice in visions and dreams.

In the 1960s the gods of the Yoruba pantheon, who are worshiped by Cuban Santeros, became popular and practically replaced the Don Juanes. Santería came to Venezuela with refugees from Cuba and by way of Miami and soon influenced the native cult.

In recent years, with the globalization of esotericism, national and international spiritual entities were incorporated into the cult. The statue of Buddha is frequently found on an altar. Sometimes the spirits of famous historical personalities or philosophers are invoked. In one of the centers the spirits of evildoers, Robin Hood types, and executed *guerrilleros*, are summoned for curing and problem solving. In other centers, "folk saints" (*anima milagrosas*) are invoked. These are the spirits of the dead, who were either considered by the common people to have lived a saintly life or their death occurred in accidents or under strange circumstances. Catholics pray to them, while the Marialionzists invoke their spirits.

For the purpose of making order in the pantheon, the ritualists invented the terms *cortes* or *lineas* of spirits. They distinguish between the Celestial Court (Maria Lionza and saints), Court of Patriots (Simon Bolivar and his generals), Court of Indians (Indian Chiefs), Court of Medical Doctors (Dr. Hernandez and the spirits of famous healers), Court of Evildoers (*malandros*, Robin Hood-type bandits), and the African Court (the *orichas* of the Santería, the most important ones are known as the Siete Potencias Africanas, the Seven Powers of Africa). In recent years the Court of the Vikings was added. These spirits are depicted on images as European savages, but they are considered to be Africans. Usually the Tres Potencias Venezulanas—Maria Lionza, the *indio* Guaicaipuro, and Negro Primero, the black general of Bolivar—are considered to be the main spirits of the cult. For some interpreters of the religion, these three powers represent the three races that have amalgamated freely in Venezuela. In this case Maria Lionza stands for the white race, as her image is that of a white woman, although the legend tells a different story. The spirits are represented on altars in images, small prints, as statues or with their emblems, such as wooden pieces or stones. Many believers have such altars in their home and pray to the spirits and to saints at the same time.

Spread and Dissemination of the Cult

The cult originated in Yaracuy, in the 1920s, but we lack precise data concerning its expansion. In the 1930s we know that one of the lovers of the dictator General Gómez was a priestess in Maracay and propagated the religion among the followers of the president. It is said that her picture was used to represent Maria Lionza on printed images. Others say, however, that these prints were inspired by a portrait of the Empress of France, Eugenia Maria de Montejo, that somebody brought from France.

In 1940 the Culto Orionico Atlantico was mentioned frequently in newspapers and it is believed that this was the original name of the Kardecist movement, which eventually turned into the Cult of Maria Lionza. During the dictatorship of Pérez Jiménez this religion came out into the open, mainly due to a statue that was erected on a freeway next to the new campus of the University of Caracas. Maria Lionza, pictured as a naked Indian woman, sits on a tapir holding a pelvis over her head. It is said that Pérez Jiménez was a sincere believer in the power of Maria Lionza.

Since the 1950s the cult has spread over the whole national territory, and many centers were founded in the poorer sections of the cities. Traditional rural healers also turned to Maria Lionza and her rituals. In the cities, Amerindian and African healing practices and Santería brought new elements into this multifaceted religion. With the proliferation of spirits, Maria Lionza gradually lost her central position and today she no longer appears in all sessions. It is said that the new inexperienced mediums do not have the power to support such a potent spirit.

Practices, Beliefs, and the People of Maria Lionza

Today centers of Maria Lionza are found in villages and towns. The adherents try to take a pilgrimage to Sorte at least once or twice a year, and the cult leaders organize these trips for the faithful. They always go in groups, pitch up camp along the Yaracuy River in Sorte and Quibayo (another site next to Sorte on the Yaracuy River), and perform rituals that are supposed to be stronger than ceremonies taking place at home. On weekends sometimes a hundred *caravanas* arrive from all parts of the country and the rites last all night. On 12 October, Columbus Day, and during the Holy Week of Easter, a few thousand pilgrims may be present in Sorte. On 12 October the mediums perform a ritual dance in burning ashes without hurting their feet.

The cult consists mainly of sessions during which the spirit manifested in the mediums can be consulted. The *bancos* (cult leaders) watch over the mediums, who fall in trance after breathing very heavily and rotating their head very vigorously many times. They also drink rum and smoke heavy cigars. Then they announce the name of the spirit, who is manifested in his/her body. After making some announcements or giving general advice, the faithful may now consult the spirit, for a fee or free of charge. Usually they are told to undergo an exorcism ritual in order to get rid of evil spirits that provoke misfortune and unhappiness and are the causes of illnesses. These rituals take place after the consultations

are over or on a special day during the week. During the consultation session, the medium may be possessed by a succession of different spirits that are recognized by a stereotyped behavior. Some foreign spirits barely speak Spanish, the Indian spirits may use a peculiar idiom, the *malandro* spirits (evildoers) may curse and shout, and some "folk saints" behave well. When Maria Lionza arrives, candles are burned and an Ave Maria is sung or prayed. The medium is dressed in a special robe and sometimes crowned. Only women incorporate Maria Lionza, but women may also incorporate male spirits, while gay men often incorporate female spirits. Some mediums smoke cigars and then make predictions or prophecies according to how the tobacco burns. Others drink a lot of rum or blow the liquid into the faces of the believers. The consultation sessions usually take place in the home of the *banco*, rarely in a real temple.

The working sessions sometimes are held during the night or in the wilderness, often near rivers or in caves. The faithful are exorcised with the help of tobacco smoke, perfumed sprays, water, alcohol, and incense. At the end of an exorcism ritual, the space is cleaned by burning gunpowder. Cars may be cleansed after accidents in the same fashion.

The most important ceremonies are called *velaciones* and are performed in a great variety of ways for any purpose. Usually the believer is put on the ground and candles of different colors are placed around his or her body and burned. Then the believer is sprinkled with rum, water, or the blood of a sacrificed animal. Dirt or flowers are placed on his body. Such *velaciones* were unknown until about twenty-five years ago but became very popular. Their origin is unknown. They may also take place to initiate mediums after they have learned the proper behavior of the spirits. Such rituals are supposed to be of special efficacy when performed in Sorte or in the caves of Agua Blanca. In these places, the faithful must take a ritual bath in a river and are carefully cleansed with the help of tobacco smoke before the *velacion* takes place. With the introduction of Santería animal sacrifices became popular, although they are forbidden in Sorte. The use of drums to call the spirits is another trait that derived from Santería. Since the 1960s, the most important spirits are identified with a certain color: blue for Maria Lionza, red for the African spirits, and so on.

Magic operations became popular when news spread of such interventions in the Philippines. The healers pretend to penetrate with their hands into the body of the patient in order to tear out the evil. They may be successful because people have faith. Healing rituals of all kinds are important in the Cult of Maria Lionza and many *bancos* have a fair knowledge of folk remedies and herbs.

The faithful meet during regular sessions that take place in centers that are founded by *bancos*, who are responsible for the training of mediums. Indeed, their success depends precisely on these mediums. Some permanent adherents may be responsible for certain ritual duties. Consultations are usually free of charge but *trabajos* (magic work) have to be paid for, as many objects are employed. These objects may be obtained in stores specializing in such things. A room is set aside for the practices and the mediums perform in front of an altar. Incense is burning and the statues and images of the spirits are illuminated with candles. The faithful sit on benches. Before the mediums fall in trance, the believers pray or meditate. The sessions end when the *banco* awakes the medium or mediums, who then take a shower or rest on a cot. They pretend that they know nothing about their behavior during trance and therefore are not responsible for their deeds.

The self-styled priests are often competing and accuse each other of being magicians and charlatans. For a while Beatriz Veit Tan, the self-styled Great Shamana, tried to unify the cult and create a superstructure, in part through a failed run for parliament on a religious ticket. Today, some of the more educated priests read ethnographic books from which they copy new rituals.

It is difficult to estimate the number of believers, as they often only attend ceremonies when they are in need of a miracle. Others join one cult group after another. Some better-educated people hide their belief from the public. The majority of the adherents, however, belong to the lower urban classes. There is no initiation necessary to become a Marialionzist. Probably about 30 percent of the population have experienced a ritual at least once or twice and about 5 percent regularly frequent ceremonies. Everybody in the country knows about Maria Lionza. The cult spread mostly in urban areas among marginalized groups but is also propagated by Venezuelan TV stations with films and in soap operas. I have found a center of Maria Lionza in Curaçao and on the Atlantic coast of Colombia, and the statue or picture of Maria Lionza on altars of spiritistic cultists in Puerto Rico, the Dominican Republic, Miami, and even in Buenos Aires. Statues of Guaicaipuro were sold in Panama and Ecuador.

The Syncretic Nature of the Cult of Maria Lionza

Altered states of consciousness are of special importance in all the rituals and also in healing ceremonies and are important features of African religious behavior. The introduction of African spirits into the cult occurred after 1960, but the Siete Potencias Africanas have obtained great significance.

Drums, animal sacrifices, and color symbolism are other African or African-American elements.

Syncretism with the Catholic cult of the Virgin is proved by the very name of the main divinity Maria and also by the fact that in Nirgua, a city in Yaracuy not far from Sorte, the original name of the parish during colonial times was Maria de la Onza del Prado de la Talavera de Nirgua. Catholic prayers and songs are frequently used and the mediums and *bancos* always wear big metal crosses around their neck. During Holy Week, a procession with the statue of the Nazarno, the suffering Christ, takes place in Sorte. Those who participate wear violet cloth and head covers in the fashion of the Spanish *penitentes*.

Amerindian traits are shamanistic rituals, performed mainly with the help of tobacco. The tobacco oracle of the Marialionzistas resembles a ritual described in a chronicle from the sixteenth century. The San Juanes, who originally were Amerindian bush spirits, are summoned by mediums specializing in healing. The legend of Maria Lionza contains native mythological elements: the guardian spirit of a lake, the protective spirit of the flora and fauna. New elements of various origins are the Viking spirits, the Buddha statues, and the *velaciones*.

It is easily observed that the cult is firmly rooted in Kardecism. Reincarnation and Karma are beliefs shared by all the adherents. Some believe that the spirits prepare themselves for reincarnation on other planets. The Cult of Maria Lionza may be seen as a variant of popular spiritism that absorbed religious elements and magic practices from different cultures in order to help the faithful cope with evil and adverse social and economic situations. The cult is supposed to satisfy the universal desire for happiness, wellbeing, health, success, love, longevity, and money.

Angelina Pollak-Eltz

See also Cuba, African-Derived Religions in; Santeria; Yoruba Religion

Bibliography

Clarac de Briceno, Jacqueline. (1992) *La enfermedad como lenguaje en Venezula*. Merida, Venezuela: Universidad de los Andes.

Garcia Gavidia, Nelly. (1987) *Posesion y ambivalencia en el Culto de Maria Lionza*. Maracaibo, Venezuela: Universidad de Zulia.

Manara, Bruno. (1995) *Maria Lionza, su entidad, su culto y la cosmovision anexa*. Caracas, Venezuela: Universidad Central de Venezuela.

Pollak-Eltz, Angelina. (1985) *Maria Lionza, mito y culto venezolano.* Caracas, Venezuela: Universidad Catolica Andres Bello.

———. (1994) *Las religiones afroamericanas hoy.* Caracas, Venezuela: Planeta.

———. (1995) *La religiosidad popular en Venezuela.* Caracas, Venezuela: San Pablo.

Taussig, Michael. (1997) *The Magic of the State.* New York: Routledge.

Vodou

Vodou designates the religion indigenous to Haiti. A largely mountainous country in the Caribbean, Haiti (from *aiti*, an indigenous Native American word meaning "mountainous country") has a land area of 10,700 square miles (comparable to Maine). Haiti shares a common border with the Dominican Republic and occupies the Western third of the Caribbean island of Hispaniola. No statistics show how many Vodou practitioners there are, but informal estimates suggest approximately 8 million.

Popular novels, films, and spurious travel accounts have often misconstrued Vodou by identifying it (or its derivatives, "hoodoo" and "voodoo") erroneously with cannibalism, zombification, witchcraft, and sorcery. More recently, "voodoo" has become synonymous with what is baseless and irrational. Thus, a program of economic recovery that has no sound basis and is sure to lead to disastrous ends has been referred to as "voodoo economics."

No portrayal of Vodou could be more inaccurate, as a scholarly examination of its rituals quickly reveals. It is a complex religion with a rich history, whose teachings have shaped the lives of millions of people. The name "Vodou" derives from the Dahomean word *vodu* or *vodun*, meaning deity or spirit. Hence, it is a religion that, through a system of myths and rituals, relates the life of the devotee to thousands of incommensurable spirits called *lwas* (from a Yoruba word for spirit), who govern life as well as the entire cosmos. These *lwas* (pronounced "loas") are believed to manifest themselves not only in nature but also through their devotee's bodies in spirit or trance possessions, a nonmaterial achievement in which they embody certain divine powers who they believe reveal themselves to the community of believers. Moreover, Vodou gives meaning to life: it instills in its devotees a need for solace and self-examination and provides an explanation for death that is treated as a spiritual transformation, a portal to the sacred world beyond, where morally upright individuals, perceived by devotees to be powerful ancestral spirits, can exercise significant influence on their progeny. In short, it is an expression of a people's longing for meaning and purpose in their lives.

The focus of Vodou's theology is the spirits whom Vodouists revere and whom they believe are active in their lives. Vodouists think of their reverence of the spirits as their "service" to the *lwas* and, hence, regard themselves as "servants" of the *lwas*. The significance of that statement bears testimony to the nature of belief in Haiti, for Vodouists think of their religion in practical terms. For their devotees the *lwas* are expected to reveal wisdom, guard against disease and danger, and assist in practical matters of life in general. In short, Vodouists think of belief as a way of life.

In actual practice, Vodou consists of different sects whose divergent theologies reflect the local communities that they serve. Despite this diversity, however, there are many similarities among them. Vodou is generally practiced in the home, but also maintains a religious calendar with special feast days that require its devotees' attendance at ceremonies in the temples, or *ounfos* (pronounced "unfo"), and at pilgrimages in sacred places throughout Haiti. These ceremonies are officiated by priests, or *oungans* (pronounced *unga*), and priestesses, or *mambos*, who constitute loosely organized, but powerful, local religious hierarchies. Vodou maintains neither theological nor ecumenical centers; hence, its religious specialists are trained informally by other practitioners, either through inheritance or through social contacts.

African Influence

Vodou was born in the slave communities on the sugar plantations of Saint-Domingue, as Haiti was called during the French colonial period (1697–1804). Although little has survived of the slaves' religious traditions, colonial writings note that the slaves were not allowed to practice their African religions openly but held their religious ceremonies in secret at night to avoid the officious interference of local authorities. The colonial masters feared the slaves' religious meetings, for many incited slave insurrections that threatened the political and social stability of the colony.

If African religious traditions flourished in Haiti, it was due to *marronnage*. It is a term that dates back to the colonial history of the region and refers to Africans' practice of running away from the plantations. The term "maroon" derives from the Spanish *cimarron*, a word used to designate a domesticated animal that had reverted to its original state of wildness. In the context of the colony it referred to runaway slaves who escaped the brutal treatment from their masters, and gathered deep in the hills in the interior of the island. There they organized communities, de facto republics actually, whose people derived from various parts of Africa. Today marronnage is considered as having had a far-reaching effect on Haitian history. It was instrumental not only in preserving whole enclaves of African religious traditions that shape Vodou's theology, but facilitated the blending of religious traditions from various African cultures represented in the colony. No one knows how many of these communities existed in Saint-Domingue, but one can assume that they multiplied to several hundreds by the eve of the Haitian Revolution at the end of the eighteenth century. They probably varied widely theologically, and their organizational forms probably depended on the demographic distribution of the different African ethnic nations (or tribes) represented in each of them. Hence, the degree to which each maroon community incorporated particular ethnic traditions in its theology depended upon the demographic composition of these republics. This religious diversity in these communities has contributed to the geographical diversity in Vodou beliefs and practices mentioned earlier in this essay.

Although much of African religious traditions survived in Haiti, the economic history of slavery and oppression altered African religious traditions on Haitian soil permanently, making Vodou a New World religion. Many of the African spirits were adapted to the new cultural milieu in the New World. Ogun for instance, the Nigerian patron of metal workers, took a new persona in colonial Saint-Domingue; he became Ogou, the military leader who fought against slavery. Thus, it can be said that Vodou is not an African religion but an African-derived religion that has successfully adapted itself to the New World's cultural situation.

Catholic Influence

The Europeans who came to Saint-Domingue were largely Roman Catholics. They regarded Vodou as an aberration, and sought to extricate it from colonial society. They enacted many edicts that regulated the religious lives of the inhabitants of the colony. One such edict, the Code Noir of 1685, made it illegal for the slaves to practice their African religions openly and, under stiff penalties to the contrary, ordered all masters to have their slaves converted to Christianity within eight days after their arrival to the colony.

The severity of such laws drove African rituals underground. The slaves soon learned to overlay their African practices with the veneer of Roman Catholic symbols and rituals. They used the Catholic symbols in their rituals as veils behind which they concealed their African practices. Soon they succeeded in achieving a blending of African and European religious traditions. This blending in Vodou's the-ology can be seen in the use of Catholic prayers and symbols in Vodou rituals and in the correspondences between the African gods and the Roman Catholic saints. These correspondences consist of a system of reinterpretations by which symbols associated with the African spirits were made to correspond to similar symbols associated with the saints in Catholic hagiology. Thus, for example, the Dahomean snake spirit Damballah was made to correspond with Saint Patrick because of the Catholic legend about Saint Patrick and the snakes of Ireland.

The encroachment of Vodou practices on Catholic theology has been embarrassing to the Haitian clergy, which has campaigned vehemently against "fetishism" in Haiti's history. Using the arm of the military, it has sought and burned Vodou temples and ritual paraphernalia throughout the country. These events had little effect on the eradication of Vodou, for Haitians continue to practice two religions simultaneously, and maintain their allegiance to them in parallel ways. An often quoted Haitian proverb is that one must be Catholic to serve the Vodou *lwas*. The truth of that statement illustrates the distinct roles that both religions play in Haitians' lives, and portrays what seems logical to Vodouists—that the world is governed by the Godhead and the *lwas* (and by extension the Catholic saints) who can be represented in two ways: by the Catholic priests who functions as the conduit to an impersonal Godhead who rules the universe, and by the *oungans* and *mambos* who establish contact with personal, yet mysterious spirits that reveal themselves to their servants in trance possession.

The Spirit World

The *lwas* (and by extension the Catholic saints) are grouped into families, or nations, called *nanchons* (pronounced "nansho"). The *nanchons'* names correspond to the geographical locations from which they originated in Africa. Vodouists believe that each *lwa* not only has its own persona by which it can be distinguished from another, but that each *nanchon* also possesses its own characteristic ethos that requires of its devotees certain corresponding attitudes. There are about seventeen *nanchons* of *loas*, but most Voduists are familiar with the Rada (from Arada, the name of a prominent kingdom in ancient Dahomey); the Ibo, whose name originates from Nigeria; the Kongo from the Bakongo region of West Africa; and the Petro, which derives from Dom Pedro, a legendary black leader in Haiti who reportedly led many slave insurrections against slavery. Today, the *nanchons* no longer designate geographical locations, but characterize "categories" or pantheons of *lwas*.

Many of the Rada *lwas* have Petro, Ibo, and Kongo counterparts. As if their images were inverted to reflect each other in a mirror, the personae of the Rada *lwas* either complement or are reversed in the other *nanchons*. For instance, a beneficent and creative *lwa* in the Rada *nanchon* manifests itself as malevolent and destructive in the Petro. Despite the notable differences in the *lwas'* personae and functions in the various *nanchons*, Vodouists do not understand these differences to represent several distinct divine entities. Rather, they believe that both personalities and functions are attributes of the same being. This belief corresponds to what may be described as a *coincidentia oppositorum*. On the one hand, a *lwa* expresses the diametric opposition of two divine personae—one beneficent and the other malevolent. Both spring from the same Cosmic Principle, Bondye (from the French *Bon Dieu*, meaning "The Good Lord") who is the Godhead or Grand Master who fashioned the cosmos. On the other hand is the nature of these personae, in the bodies of devotees who become spirit-possessed by them during ritual ceremonies. In these manifestations, the *lwas* present themselves by turns, or even sometimes simultaneously, as beneficent and terrible, as creative and destructive. But the different personae of each *lwa* as represented through the *nanchons* are merely different "faces" of Bondye, who is envisaged in West African and not in Christian terms. As in much of West Africa, the Godhead is considered much too impersonal to be approached directly; he can merely be invoked in rituals through less-hallowed spirit media.

Spirit Mediumship and Spirit Possession

The study of spirit possession and its apparent dissociative behavior has been the subject of much scholarly writing. Seen through the lenses of popular literature, it has been described as demonic manifestations in the bodies of host victims, resulting in alterations of mental faculties and behavioral disorders. Exorcisms were thus means of extricating these demons from the bodies of possessed individuals. In psychological literature, possession has been depicted as a product of psychopathology that included psychotic episodes involving "flights" from reality and amnesia. The exchange of one's personal identity for another also was construed as the result of multiple personality disorders that required clinical attention.

More recent studies of possession have disputed such claims. It is thought to be an altered state of consciousness—an experience that can be defined as a temporary alteration of one's identity, consciousness, memory, or behavior, resulting from the belief that one's body is "mounted" and "ridden" like a horse by *lwas* whose envisaged mythological personae replace the identity of the possessed. The possessed embody the mythology of the community by enacting the events in the lives of the *lwas*. Possessed individuals believe that they are anointed by the spirits during possession, that the *lwas* empower them spiritually and protect them from existential crises.

Hence, possession is a quintessential spiritual achievement in a believer's religious life that serves two main purposes (among others): first, because it is a public commitment to the religion it serves both as a testimony to one's religious fervor and as an experience that heightens one's exercise of religious authority in the community; second, it serves as a means of achieving communal bonding by reinforcing a community's mythology as observed in the behavior of the possessed. For these reasons, Vodouists would wish to have it conferred on them, not once, but several times in their lives. In short, one of the most important functions of the Vodou rituals is the opportunity for the spirits to use the bodies of their devotees to reveal themselves to the community.

Concepts of the Self

Vodouists believe that the human body is a manifestation of Bondye, who has fashioned it and has infused into it his divine energy. One's body is thus a vessel containing a divine essence that is shared by all members of the community. In Vodou, as in West African beliefs, the individual self is rooted in this divine essence and has no independent existence; it is conceived as a member of an extended family that not only includes the living but also the invisible community of ancestors. The self is thus conceived as a single-branching organism in which one is the centripetal force that draws to itself all those who are part of the visible and invisible worlds.

The self is also constituted of several compartments characterized by various psychic functions. In some ways, the Vodou notion of the compartmentalized self is analogous to Sigmund Freud's description of the theoretical divisions of the human psyche. The first compartment of the human spirit is the *gwo bon anj* (literally, "the big good angel"), a life-force, the sacred source of the energy of life itself that is implanted within the body that serves as its shell. The second compartment is the *ti bon anj* (literally, "the little good angel") the ego-spirit that is identified with personality, manifested in one's deportment and facial expressions. The third is the *met tet* (literally, "the master of the head"), the part of the spirit that is the manifestation of a guardian *lwa* who has protected a person from danger throughout his or her life. It is also the *lwa* that a devotee has "served" and who has possessed him or her most frequently during his or her life.

At death, a special ritual called *desounen* (literally, "the uprooting of life") is performed near the body shortly after death by the *oungan* or *mambo*. It extracts these compartments of the spirits from the body and dispatches them to their respective abodes: the *gwo bon anj* and the *met tet* to Ginen, the underworld, the *ti bon anj* to heaven (because of the Catholic influence), and the body to the navel of the earth where it will disintegrate.

As in Africa, ancestral spirits exercise authority over the living. In Ginen, they join the community of the "living-dead," ruled by Gede, the sovereign of the underworld. In time, they are thought to acquire sacred wisdom that allows them to see far into the future and into the past and to guide the living in their daily round of life. Their intelligence, past experiences, and creativity are reborn and preserved as a valuable legacy for the future prosperity of the living's progeny.

Vodou in the Diaspora

Unfavorable political and economic circumstances in Haiti since the 1970s have resulted in the emigration of substantial numbers of Haitians. Living in many of the world's largest cities, they have not only maintained their religious traditions but have often established communities that approximate those of the African and Haitian rural courtyards, or *lakou* (pronounced "laku"). In Haiti, a *lakou* is an area in which are gathered five to six extended families who live in separate dwellings, sometimes with one dwelling that serves as temple. The members of the *lakou* gather around the home of a patriarch (*chef lakou*), whom they regard as the link between the secular and sacred worlds.

The *lakou* has waned considerably in Haiti since the 1950s. Lucrative jobs and educational opportunities in urban centers have caused many young people to leave the *lakou*, resulting in the gradual disintegration of the rural *lakou* infrastructure. But it has reemerged in the diaspora. The "house systems" one finds in the United States are analogous to the *lakous*; they consist of an entire building in which several families live in individual apartments but share domestic and financial resources. They gather around a priest or priestess whose apartment serves as living quarters and temple. Perhaps one of the significant aspects of the houses that distinguishes them from the *lakou* is their multiethnic character. Membership in these houses is open to representatives of cultural groups from other parts of the world. These groups will eventually incorporate into Vodou's theology their own religious traditions, which will undoubtedly change the face of Vodou in the diaspora in the future—a characteristic that will distinguish it from Vodou in Haiti. For the second time in Vodou's history, its traditions will diversify theologically and, like the religion of the maroon republics during the Haitian colonial period, the

ethos of the theology of each house in the diaspora will depend upon its demographic composition.

In short, in the diaspora Vodou has become an urban phenomenon that has adapted itself readily to its new cultural milieu. Most of the ritual paraphernalia are readily available in the cities abroad. Even the pilgrimages are reproduced. For instance, July 16, the day devoted to the Virgin Mary in the Catholic liturgical calendar, is reserved for Ezili, the Vodou goddess of love. Many Vodouists in the diaspora make a pilgrimage to her at the Lady of Mount Carmel Church in New York, at St Anne de Beaupré near Québec City in Canada, or at other sacred Catholic sites in many other parts of the world.

Leslie G. Desmangles

See also Ogun; Vodou, Material Culture

Bibliography

Bourguignon, Erika. (1976) *Possession*. Columbus: Ohio State University Press.

Brown, Karen McCarthy. (1991) *Mama Lola: A Vodou Priestess in Brooklyn*. Berkeley: University of California Press.

Desmangles, Leslie. G. (1993) *The Faces of the Gods: Vodou and Roman Catholicism in Haiti*. Chapel Hill: University of North Carolina Press.

Hurbon, Laennec, and Lori Frankel. (1995) *Voodoo: Search for the Spirit*. Bergenfield, NJ: Harry N. Abrams Press.

Laguerre, Michel. (1982) *Urban Life in the Caribbean: A Study of a Haitian Urban Community*. Cambridge, MA: Harvard University Press.

The Legacy of the Spirits. Produced by Karen Kramer, 1982. A documentary presentation about the practice of Vodou in New York.

Métraux, Alfred. (1978) *Voodoo in Haiti*. New York: Shocken Press.

Vodou, Material Culture

Vodou so permeates Haitian culture that it is difficult to draw perimeters around what constitutes its material culture. The oil paintings of Hector Hypolite and the oil-drum sculptures of Georges Liautaud, masters of the "Haitian Renaissance" that began after World War II, are directly inspired by those spirits of the Vodou pantheon called the *lwa*. And now their modern successors, painters such as André Pierre and sculptors such as Pierrot Barra, give contemporary and even postmodern expression to the same spirits. However, while their art manifests the *lwa*, it was not made to serve them; and so is not part of the material culture of Vodou.

Nature of Material Culture of Vodou

But even if we limit the definition of Vodou material culture to objects actually used for religious ritual, problems of definition still remain. As they practice what might be called a "low-budget" religion, Vodouists manage to recycle many objects which pass their way, pressing them into divine service. Almost anything can be dedicated to a *lwa* and then set upon an altar or incorporated into some larger religious work. All objects thus possess magical potential, which the Yoruba define as *ashe*. They are all capable of being transformed from the natural into the supernatural. As André Pierre observed, "the world is made by magic, and all of us, in general, are magicians."

So it is that a rubber baby doll in a shiny Mattel box which arrives on a plane from Miami may be destined for the nursery of an elite family in Petionville. Or three hours later that same doll may have been redressed in a red scarf and saluted as the earth mother Ezili Danto; fitted into a whiskey bottle to contain the spirit of the luxury-loving Ezili Freda; turned upside down and bound in ropes to direct the energies of the violent Ezili Mapiange; or tied to a tree in the cemetery with a message for the Mother of the Dead, Gran Brigitte. About the only fate that doll would not meet is to be stuck with pins. Those kinds of "voodoo dolls" are a Hollywood fantasy and a staple of the tourist trade in New Orleans. Haitians find much more imaginative ways to transform imported toys.

Material Objects of Vodou

When we discuss Vodou material culture, context is everything. Any object used to summon, salute, signify, contain or direct the *lwa* is sacred. Some, such as drums, flags, and packets, are made expressly for that purpose. Others, like that hypothetical imported doll, may be pressed into various divine services. Following is a description of some of the most celebrated of those sacred objects. The list is necessarily provisional, since the *lwa* are notoriously fickle in taste and desire, and the Haitian people have little control over their import/export markets.

Drum and other Summoning Objects

The drum is the most sacred of all Vodou objects, for it speaks with a divine voice. Without it there would be no dance and no religion. Drums shape the ceremony, chan-

neling the *lwa* with their special rhythmic signatures. Representing the main cults of the religion, drums may be divided into two main types: (1) the Rada trio of peg-tuned, goblet-shaped drums, usually arranged along a continuum, small to large: *pitit*, *segon*, and *manman*, which summon the ancient spirits of Dahomey; and (2) the Kongo-derived,

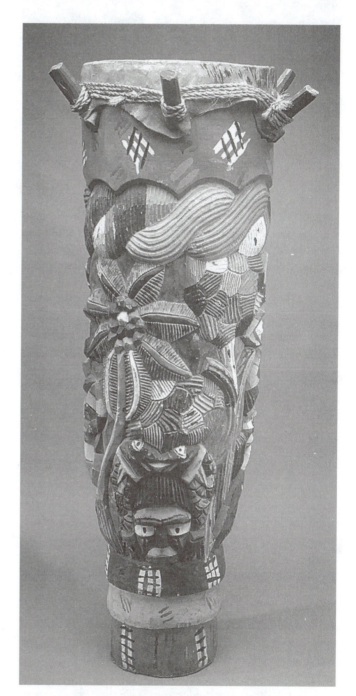

Rada drum with anthropomorphic heads, snakes, and plants carved in relief c. 1975 by a carver named Fleurissant. PHOTO BY DENIS NERVIG, COURTESY OF THE UCLA FOWLER MUSEUM.

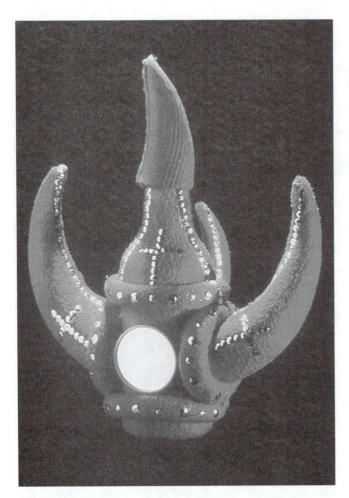

Reliquary made for Bosou Twa Kon from glass, fabric, sequins, mirror. PHOTO BY DENIS NERVIG, COURTESY OF THE UCLA FOWLER MUSEUM.

string-tuned Petwo drums, usually a pair, which play the sharper rhythms of the Petwo/Kongo rites, in which the crack of a whip can also bring down the *lwa*.

Other objects used to summon the *lwa* include the gourd rattle (*ason*) used by the priest/priestess at key points in a ceremony. *Ason* strung with beads or bones are used for Rada rites, plain ones (*tcha-tcha* or *maraca*) for Petwo/Kongo rites. Bells are also used to awaken the *lwa* in all kinds of private ceremonies.

Bottles and Other Spirit Repositories

Sequin and bead-covered bottles are often used on Vodou altars as offertories. Through patterned and appliqued imagery they are coded to honor particular *lwa*. Materials covering the glass include fabric, sequins, beads, and synthetic pearls. Bottles with doll's heads, used much less commonly, can be protective amulets (to ward off evildoing) or mediums for divination (e.g., lying sideways, the

doll's eyes close; upright, the eyes open and the doll can "see").

Other kinds of objects which may be spirit-infused or act as spirit repositories include packets called *pakèt kongo*. These are used on altars and in healing ceremonies, and are filled with leaves, herbs, earth, and other ingredients. Functionally and stylistically derived from the Kongo *nkisi*, *pakèt kongo* are wrapped with cloth, bound with ribbons, and often topped with feathers, or cruciforms in metal or wood. Jars called *govi*, containing the spirit essence of deceased members of the Vodou family, are kept upon an altar. Pots known as *po tèt* (head pots) are repositories for the nail and hair clippings of the initiates in a Vodou society. They too are kept on an altar and draped with the necklaces of the devotees. Calabashes (*kwi*) are commonly used for food offerings and may be painted with the *vèvè* of the designated *lwa*.

Flags

Probably inspired by the use of military flags during the Haitian Revolution, the *drapo* (flag) has evolved during recent decades into a unique art form of sequined tapestries comparable in design and function to stained-glass church windows. Traditional drapo are about 91.4 by 91.4 centimeters, the common size of a yard of fabric. The design is usually based upon the cosmogram (*veve*) that symbolizes the *lwa* being honored, and is not unlike a chromolithograph of a Catholic saint that serves the same purpose. A decorative geometric border surrounds the central image. As flags have become commodities in the international art market, designers now commonly stitch their own names into their compositions.

Altars

All of Vodou material and spiritual culture comes together in the altar. Altars are arranged to honor and invoke the *lwa*. They may be located in temple sanctuaries or in private bedrooms. Wherever they are found, they mark a sacred space where natural and supernatural worlds meet. On the altars, worshipers assemble divine images, together with offerings known to please divine tastes. In return, the *lwa* are expected to answer prayers for health, love, or good fortune.

To look at an altar cluttered with customized whiskey bottles, satin pomanders, clay pots dressed in lace, plaster statues of the saints or the laughing Buddha, holy cards, political kitsch, Dresden clocks, bottles of Moët et Chandon, rosaries, crucifixes, Masonic insignia, eyeshadowed Kewpie dolls, atomizers of Anais-Anais and

Rada Altar and Petwo/Kongo Altar from the "Sacred Arts of Haitian Vodou" exhibit, Fowler Museum of Cultural History, UCLA, 1995. PHOTOS BY GARY GARNICK COURTESY OF THE UCLA FOWLER MUSEUM.

Florida Water, wooden phalli, goat skulls, top hats, Christmas tree ornaments, and Arawak celts (inter alia) is to gauge the achievement of a religious community that has imagined a myth broad enough, and fabricated a ritual complex enough, to encompass all this disparate stuff. It is also to appreciate anew the ancient observation of Heraclitus, "a heap of rubble, piled up at random, is the fairest universe."

Haitians have reassembled all these found objects according to an aesthetic they carry in their heads, their hearts, their entire bodies. From material fragments of a terrible and glorious history, they have made working models of heaven. Theirs is the work of artists. "Frozen waterfalls" and "dances for the eyes" is how David Byrne, musician and impresario, has described their altar assemblages. He compares sacralized Afro-Caribbean detritus to "visual jazz, constantly reworked and reactivated." Altars are played like a musical instrument, augmented through constant use. Their aesthetic is improvisational. They are never "finished."

Each altar has a particular identity: *lwa* and objects are grouped according to spiritual "nation" and "family." The three most popular altar types are Rada, Petwo/Kongo, and Bizango.

Rada

Rada altars are set up to serve the *lwa* of the Rada nation, the spirits identified with Ginen (mythic Africa), whose roots may be traced back to the ancient Kingdom of Dahomey. The *lwa* of Ginen include Legba, Ezili Freda, Danbala, and Ayida Wedo (the Serpent and the Rainbow), Azaka (the Minister of Agriculture), Ogou (the General), Agwe (the Admiral), and Gede, the trickster lord of the dead. Catholic icons predominate on the Rada altar because "pure" African spirits have all found correlates among the Catholic saints. Thus St. Peter with his keys to heaven signals Legba, lord of the crossroads; or St. Patrick with his snakes underfoot signals the serpent patriarch Danbala.

Customary offerings of liquor, perfume, powder, soap, jewelry, and money are left on the altar to please the spirits. The altar is also the repository for the "head pots" of the initiates, draped with their ritual necklaces; the *govi*, containing the spiritual essence of ancestors and the *lwa*; and pots for the *marasa*, the divine twins of the pantheon.

Petwo/Kongo

Petwo rites are born jointly out of maroon resistance to slavery, and Kongo traditional religion. Found on such altars are the bound medicine packets known as *pakèt kongo*, consecrated to such spirits as Simbi Makaya and Rèn Kongo. Generally, fewer chromolithographs appear in Petwo sanctuaries, while pictures of popular politicians, such as former President Aristide, may rest near representations of such hardworking *lwa* as Ezili Danto or Ogou Balendjo, who are also expected to work hard for their devotees.

Bizango Altar from the "Sacred Arts of Haitian Vodou" exhibit, Fowler Museum of Cultural History, UCLA, 1995. PHOTOS BY GARY GARNICK COURTESY OF THE UCLA FOWLER MUSEUM.

Standing like tribunes at the side of the altar may be feathered standards (*moyoyo*), hung with carnival ribbons and fancy feathers. *Moyoyo* do double duty as homage to the Indian *caciques* and to the royalty of Central Africa, Wa Wangol (King of Angola) and Rèn Kongo (Queen of Kongo), for whom they are named.

Bizango

Bizango altars impart a fearful respect for the entwined mysteries of life and death, reflected in phallic and funeral imagery. The judgment at the crossroads and the powers of the Baron Samedi, the dread *lwa* of death, are strongly evoked in this sanctuary; bottles and other objects decorated with three horns evoke Bosou Twa Kon, the triple-horned bull enforcer of the hot *lwa*. The Baron and Bosou together broadcast warnings of danger and moral intimidation. Objects in this altar are tied down, or bound with string, rope, or chain; indicating powerful spirits being forcefully restrained. Often they are hung from the ceiling and/or seated on little chairs. These are working charms (*wanga*) infused with powerful spirits and restrained under what might be called "house arrest."

Justice is a chief concern for Bizango and related "societies of the night." Like the Freemasons, from whom much iconography and ritual behavior is borrowed, the Bizango are bound by oath and they protect their secrets well.

Summary

It is the temple (*ounfo*), with its peristyle, its shrine rooms, and the material accoutrements of its rituals that determines the material boundaries of the sacred. Many of the altar objects are found, haptic, bricolage. But they are not all generic. Votive objects often bear the idiosyncratic mark of their makers. Careful observers do not confuse a flag by Oleyant with one by Edgar, a cross by Liautaud with one by Bien-Aime, or a pre-fab altar by Pierrot Barra with the work of other copycat artists. Just like the secular art of the post-World War II "Haitian Renaissance" artists, Vodou religious art now finds itself hawked on the world market. Flags and bottles and packets and sequined dolls are now found in boutiques from SoHo in New York to Melrose in L.A., and in all sorts of fashionable emporia in-between. The attraction is apparent enough. For what Andrè Malraux observed a half-century ago is no less true today, "Haiti produces the finest popular art in the world."

Donald Cosentino

See also Vodou

Bibliography

Cosentino, Donald. (1998) *Volou Things.* Jackson: University Press of Mississippi.

———. (1996) "Arts of Vodou." *African Arts* 29: 66–71.

———. (1995) "Imagine Heaven." *Sacred Arts of Haitian Vodou*: 25–55. Los Angeles: Fowler Museum.

Polk, Patrick. (1997) *Haitian Vodou Flags.* Jackson: University Press of Mississippi.

Thompson, Robert F. (1995) "From the Isle Beneath the Sea: Haiti's Africanizing Vodou Art." *Sacred Arts of Haitian Vodou*, edited by Donald Cosentino. Los Angeles: Fowler Museum: 91–119.

———. (1983). *Flash of the Spirit: African and Afro-American Art and Philosophy.* New York: Random House.

Watchtower

The Watchtower or Kitawala is the most persistent millenarian movement in sub-Saharan African. The movement traces its roots to the American Jehovah's Witness religion, which began its missionary effort in Africa in the early twentieth century. Evidently, the founders of the movement relied on Witness texts that were provided to them by missionaries. However, the movement is rejected by the Jehovah's Witnesses who accuse them of engaging in devil worship, witchcraft, and indecent sexual behavior. Beginning in 1910, several Watchtower movements sprang up across eastern, central, and southern Africa. The Watchtower movement in Africa is unique because it does not consider itself a church, or even a sect, but an organization. It teaches that it is the religious responsibility of every member to try to convert nonbelievers, especially the lost followers of other religions. It neither seeks any accommodation with the world nor expects affirmation by the state. The best known Watchtower group was established by Elliot Kamwana of Nyasaland (in present-day Malawi) in 1908. This group hoped for the coming of a spiritual glorious age. The group was also was an opponent of the European colonial ideological hegemony.

The basic belief of the Watchtower movement is the imminent expectation of the end of all things, when the Kingdom of God will be established on earth, to be ruled over by Christ and the witnesses of his truth. Earthly principalities and powers represent the power of the Devil, who is the invisible ruler of the earth. These powers will eventually be defeated by Jesus Christ and all his hosts in the battle of Armageddon (this is an ever-present reality represented by political chaos in the world). This is the absolute truth. Members are encouraged to await the Kingdom. World War I was a ringing suggestion that Armageddon was, indeed, at hand. Members believed that Jesus Christ would soon return (the precise date has been moved forward several times). In this new spiritual world, sickness, death, and war will disappear. This promise of an imminent golden age was very appealing in many nations during the colonial period in Africa and the Watchtower movement was a vehicle of resistance to colonial authoritarian rule. It was particularly critical of the blatant racism of colonial authorities in southern and central Africa.

The millennial agenda set forth by the Watchtower movement in many parts of Africa is the expectation that social and economic problems would be obliterated by a supernatural intervention. Members of this movement defined the state as basically evil and they avoided all commitments to it other than the basic civic duty of paying taxes and keeping the peace.

The Watchtower movement is still prominent in Zambia, Zaire, Tanzania, and Angola. It is organized in village groups under the control of a charismatic prophet and it continues to give credible expression to the hopes and aspirations of common people. The relationships between African political elites and the Watchtower movement has to be seen against the background of a protracted and continuing involvement of this movement in Africa. Many African nations do not see the movement as foreign and exotic but as a local means of addressing the yearnings of the people.

Akintunde E. Akinade

See also Faith Tabernacle Church

Bibliography

Barrett, David B. (1968) *Schism and Renewal in Africa: An Analysis of Six Thousand Contemporary Religious Movements.* London and Nairobi: Oxford University Press.
Coker, S. A. (1917) *The Rights of Africans to Organize and Establish Indigenous Churches Unattached to and Uncontrolled by Foreign Church Organizations.* Lagos: Tika-Tore Printing Works.
"Devil Commission: Why Jehovah's Witnesses?" http://witnesses.about.com.
Welbourn, F. (1962) *East African Rebels.* London: SCM Press.

West African Religions

Islam has been a major religious influence in the Sudanic region since the ninth century, gradually increasing until by, the late nineteenth century, it was the major religious tradition of the region. Islam began to influence the regions of Upper and Lower Guinea by the fifteenth century, but has not become the dominant religious tradition of either region. The first West African contacts with Christianity probably occurred during the early Portuguese voyages of exploration and trade, rapidly intensifying in both Upper and Lower Guinea in the nineteenth and twentieth centuries, but Christianity has exerted relatively minor influence in the Sudanic region except in coastal areas of Senegal and Gambia and in Burkina Faso. Indigenous religions remain important in several areas of the Sudanic region and exert a pervasive influence in Upper and Lower Guinea. This article will focus on those religions that are indigenous to West Africa.

Historical and Geographical Context

West Africa can be regarded as a peninsula extending westward into the Atlantic Ocean between the Gulf of Guinea on the south and the Sahara Desert on the north, roughly from 5 to 20 degrees north latitude and from 12 degrees east longitude to 12 degrees west. On the west it is bordered by the Atlantic Ocean; on the north by the Sahara Desert, which itself was perceived as a "sea of sand" traversed by ships of the desert, camels; on the east by Lake Chad and the mountain ranges along the Nigeria-Cameroon frontier. It is an extremely diverse region, ranging from the southern Sahara, which receives less than five inches of rain per year, to the heart of the Guinean forest areas of Liberia and Sierra Leone, which receive over one hundred inches of rain per year. With close to two hundred million inhabitants, this region is the most populous area south of the Sahara. It also was the primary source of African people sold into slavery and transported to the Americas and to the Maghreb of northwest Africa. Thus, it is of critical importance both for understanding the diversity of African religions and for understanding the dominant influence in the development of African Diaspora religions.

Culturally, one can divide the region into three zones: (1) the Sudanic area, stretching along the Atlantic coast between the Gambia River and the Sahara and extending east to Lake Chad; (2) Upper Guinea, extending from the Cavally River along the Liberia/Ivory Coast border to the Gambia; and (3) Lower Guinea, the area extending from the Ivory Coast in the west to the Cross Rivers area along the Nigeria/Cameroon border. Though the southern portion of the Sahara and the Sahel borderlands supported primarily herding populations, major cities also developed in this area by the tenth century, based on their roles as trading centers at the southern end of the trans-Saharan trade. Precolonial urban communities were also important in Lower Guinea, from the Yoruba city-states of southwestern Nigeria to the major administrative and commercial centers of the Ashanti Empire in the sixteenth century. Most of the Sudanic region has depended on agriculture and animal husbandry for its primary economic activities, but it has been supplemented by important fishing industries, gold mining, cotton-cloth production, blacksmithing, and both long-distance and local trade. Peanuts and cotton became increasingly important during the colonial era. Further south, in Upper Guinea, wet-rice agriculture, supplemented by other grains, has predominated along the coast, while animal husbandry and the cultivation of millets and sorghums have predominated in the interior. Coastal salt production and a vigorous trade focused on dried fish, as well as important cloth, iron-working, and pottery-making activities have been important to the economies. In Lower Guinea, root crops like yams, sweet potatoes, and more recently, cassava, have been the staple crops, but in the nineteenth century, palm oil, and in the twentieth, cocoa and coffee, became increasingly important.

West African peoples have created hundreds of different religions, and while some of them are no longer practiced in ways that can be fully separated from Islam or Christianity, they continue to exert important influences within these relatively newer religious traditions, and continue to be important religious traditions for many African ethnic groups. Approximately half of West Africa's population would identify itself as Muslim and the remainder is split relatively evenly between Christianity and religious traditions that developed in West African communities. Categorized as a form of "unbelief" (*kaffir*) by Muslim travelers beginning in the ninth century, and in similar fashion by European travelers beginning in the fifteenth, it is fair to say that West African indigenous religions have been subjected to the most negative stereotyping of any of the world's religious traditions. As foreign administrators, missionaries, traders, and anthropologists spent longer periods of time in West Africa they became more aware of the existence of West African religions, though they continued to describe them in ways that emphasized their divergence from Western religious experience. Still, when missionaries sought to preach in African communities and to translate the liturgy and scriptures into West African languages, they had little trouble finding African terms for the supreme being. They insisted, however, that West African supreme beings were different from their god; they were *deus otiotus*, remote gods, rarely invoked in West Africa and standing in sharp contrast to adherents of Western religious traditions. Much of the debate about the intrinsic value of West African religions, has focused on the role of West African supreme beings, lesser spirits, and the systems of thought that are sustained by West African religions.

Supreme Beings and Lesser Spirits

While every West African religion has an idea of a supreme being who began the process of creating the universe and who created lesser spirits, they have different views of the roles of these supreme beings in their daily lives and in regard to the ways in which supreme beings should be worshipped. In many West African creation myths, the supreme being began the process of creation, but delegated the completion of the process to lesser spirits. Furthermore, this supreme being is the source of life-enhancing power that circulates throughout the universe. The Dogon of Mali call this power *nyama* and it is seen as originating with the supreme being, Amma. The Yoruba of southwestern Nigeria and Benin refer to this power as *ashe* and it is originating with the supreme being, Olorun or Olodumare. In other creation myths, the supreme being is seen as in close communication, or even in close physical proximity, to human beings until there is some kind of disruption, a dispute that leads the supreme being to distance itself from human society. Yet, the supreme being remains accessible for matters of major importance. A proverb told by the Igbo of southeastern Nigeria illustrates this view of the supreme being: "God is like a rich man. You approach him through his servants." The servants are lesser spirits who were created as intermediaries between the supreme being and humans, each with its own areas of expertise.

These images of a remote supreme being do not reveal the full range of West African views on the subject, however. In Ashanti and Fanti religious practice, the head of a family offers prayers and libations of water to the supreme being, Nyame, before starting the work of the day. Among the Igbo, the supreme being is able to speak to humans through spiritual mediums, usually women, who become possessed and speak in the voice of Chukwu or Chineke. Among the Diola, over fifty men and women have claimed to be prophets of the supreme being, Emitai. These prophets spread their teachings about rain rituals, warfare, and community social obligations throughout the coastal areas of southern Senegal, coastal Gambia, and northwestern Guinea-Bissau. In most West African religions, the supreme being both bestows life and judges human conduct after death. Among the Yoruba, Olorun breathes life into a newborn and assigns it a destiny, and when that person dies it is Olorun again who decides whether the deceased will become an ancestor and eventually be reborn, or whether it will go to the "heaven of potsherds," where those whose actions diminished the quality of life rest for all eternity. It is described as a hot place; but its hotness is that of West African peppers, not of the fires associated with Christian or Muslim views of eternal damnation. To give life and to act as a judge after death are not the actions of a remote deity, but of one who is central to West African views of the cycle of life and death.

While supreme beings generally play a more important role in West African religions than is generally acknowledged, a variety of lesser spirits are also important. These lesser spirits may be associated with natural forces like rain, thunder, the earth, the ocean, rivers; a variety of economic activities ranging from iron-working to palm wine tapping; or major community concerns like warfare and disease. According to Yoruba traditions, there are 401 different *orisha*, each with special powers and distinct characteristics. These *orisha* include Obatala, who Olorun gave the task of creating the universe, began the process, but got drunk on palm wine as he was beginning to create human beings.

Traditional Bambara geomancer from Sonongo, Mali. PHOTO COURTESY OF MANFRED KREMSER.

Another *orisha*, Oduduwa, completed the creation of human beings and became the first king of Ife, the place of creation. Shango is a widely worshipped god of thunder who once was an earthly ruler. Oshun was a female *orisha* associated with rivers, with feminine ideals of beauty and with birth. Ogun, initially a god of iron, has had his role expanded to offer protection to drivers and industrial workers, all those who work with iron products. Perhaps the two most important deities are Eshu, a messenger god invoked in most Yoruba rituals; and Ifa, the god of divination. All of these deities, however, derive their power from Olorun. Many of the *orisha* are worshiped in African-inspired traditions of Santeria, Vodun, and Candomblé that are practiced in the Americas.

Along the lower Guinea coast, especially among the Fon of Benin and the Yoruba, spirits make their presence known through an experience described as possession, in which the spirit fills the body of a devotee and is said to ride him or her like a person rides a horse. In a state of possession, the individual speaks and moves in the style of a particular spirit and communicates the wishes of the spirit to the community. In upper Guinea and the Sudanic region, there is a greater emphasis on lesser spirits communicating through dreams and visions rather than possession.

One distinct category of lesser spirits are the spirits of ancestors, which are important throughout West Africa. Among the Yoruba and the Diola, only people who led benevolent lives become ancestors. They remain linked to their living descendants, offering them advice and assistance, by appearing to them in dreams and visions. Eventually, they are reborn within their own lineages. There are also powers associated with an individual's fate or destiny, which originate with the supreme being and establish broad tendencies of every individual's life course. Among the Igbo, this force is known as *chi* and is explicitly linked to the supreme being, Chukwu or Chineke. Among the Yoruba, it is known as *ori* and is associated with a spirit that remains in the heavens, but can be worshipped in personal shrines in the family compound.

Religious Practices

It is in the category of lesser spirits that one can observe the greatest changes in West African religions. The growing importance of various types of spirit cults is influenced by environmental changes, epidemics, changes in economic activity, and the experience of conquest. These changes are often documented in oral traditions. For example, a Yoruba creation myth that centers on the city of Ife not only supports that city's claims to seniority among the Yoruba city-states, but in the account of Obatala becoming drunk on palm wine, historians see a symbolic representation of the substitution of Ife's patron god, Oduduwa, and Ife's triumph over the indigenous population that worshiped Obatala. The agricultural revolution that began 8,000 years ago probably increased the importance of a variety of earth-goddess cults like Ala among the Igbo and Asase Ya among the Ashanti. Increasing availability of iron, during the era of the Atlantic slave trade, helped to increase the influence of the Yoruba cult of Ogun and the Diola cult of Gilaite, both closely associated with blacksmithing. Among the Yoruba and the Diola certain types of spirit cults added new functions involving these religious institutions in the regulation of the slave trade. During the colonial era, among the Djukwa immigrants to the Ivory Coast and Ghana and in the Yoruba Gelede rituals, some spirits were represented as Europeans. Along the West African coast, from Sierra Leone to Nigeria, a new pan-African spirit cult developed, that of Mami Wata, whose images were derived from the increas-

ingly important coastal trade, borrowing female images of mastheads and South Asian portrayals of goddesses, to portray a goddess associated with the growing importance of commerce.

West African religious thought is often expressed in the recitation of oral traditions, through informal discussions between elders and young people, and through formal rituals of initiation. Throughout the Sudanic region and in parts of Upper Guinea, a specialized caste of oral historians learn the oral traditions and myths of a particular community and recite them, often accompanied by music. These specialists, who combine the roles of historian, philosopher, and musician, are often known as *griots*. They often accompany their public recitations with a stringed instrument known as the *kora*. *Griots* tend to limit their recitations to public knowledge; esoteric knowledge is taught in more private ways during rites of passage from childhood to adulthood, at the time of the birth of one's first child, or when taking on new ritual responsibilities. This knowledge is often limited to those who are seen as responsible enough to handle the power that comes from knowledge in a way that will benefit the community. Boys often endure an initiation school just before or after puberty, during which they are taught about their religious and social responsibilities. Such initiations may or may not be accompanied by circumcision, though some sort of physical ordeal is usually involved. Among the Bamana and Senufo of Mali, this initiation is extended other many years and focuses on the teaching of a complex system of symbols that must be learned by all the men of the community. Among the Diola, the knowledge imparted at the time of male circumcision is carefully separated from a second initiation involving the teaching of knowledge of death and of the cults associated with the priest-kings. Girls are often initiated just before puberty. Among a majority of West African communities, this involves female circumcision, though many West African communities now explicitly reject this practice. In most cases, religious instruction for women is continued during the seclusion that follows the birth of a woman's first child.

West African rituals often involve offerings in order to attract a spirit's presence and as a gift to receive its assistance. Such rituals focus primarily on lesser spirits rather than the supreme being, both because one should only make requests of the supreme being on matters of great magnitude or as a last resort, and because the supreme being already owns everything in the world. There is nothing to offer and only the intensity of one's need seems to succeed in enlisting the support of the supreme being. Offerings are often accompanied by libations of palm wine, millet beer, water, or, more recently, rum or gin. These liquids are all seen as having a life-enchancing power within them, which increas-

THE CULT OF THE ANCESTORS AMONG THE DOGON OF WEST AFRICA

In general, sacrifices and offerings on family altars are made both to honor the departed and to conciliate them. That is the cult of ancestors who have undergone death.

The cults of the Binou constitute what may be called, more out of convenience, Dogon totemism. It concerns worship rendered by small groups, scattered or not, to a forebear whose existence went on in the mythical period or to a genie. Usually the ancestor has manifested his desire to be the object of the cult by sending, either directly or by animal intermediary, to the heads of the group a stone, duge, which the latter will carry himself at first and which the priests succeeding him will carry next. This stone is the temporary support of the soul (kikinu say) and of the nyama of the Binou.

The word "Binou" means literally "he who came back" and "Babinou," the name given to the totemic power, has the sense of "father who came back." The definition is explained by the fact that the ancestor in question was living in the time when men were immortal. Having transformed himself according to the rule into a large snake, then into a Yeban genie, he finally belonged to a world separated from humans. Contact taken up again by this ancestor thus constitutes, for men, a veritable return of the departed, a return which is interpreted as a beneficent sign, like a substantial aid brought to the descendants on condition that they respect a certain number of prohibitions and institute a cult.

Source: Griaule, Marcel. (1938) *Dogon Masks*. Paris: Universite de Paris, Travaux et Memoirs de l'Institut d'Ethnologie, 33. HRAF English translation, p. 43.

---

es the power of the spoken word in prayer. Similarly, animal sacrifice releases the life force of the sacrificial animal, which combines with the power of the prayer and of the libations, thus increasing the effectiveness of the ritual. The congregation's common consumption of the meat of the sacrifice and the libations binds all those in attendance to work toward the goal of the ritual.

West African masking traditions and sculpture also serve important ritual functions. Among the Yoruba, Igbo, Fon, and Ewe of lower Guinea, wearing a mask and costume invites the presence of a god into one's body. Throughout West Africa, masking traditions are used to provide a tangible experience of a lesser spirit or an ancestor in the ritual community. Similarly, statuary is used in much of West Africa to represent lesser spirits. It is important to keep in mind that such images are not equated with the spirit. Medicines or rituals of consecration may attract the power of the spirit to the shrine, but they never contain the spirit. Neither masks nor statuary are used to represent the supreme being.

Religious Philosophy

West African explanations of the spiritual significance of suffering and the persistence of evil focus on disruptive spirits, on human wrong-doing, and on witchcraft. In West Africa there are a variety of spiritual beings, often referred to as tricksters, who are not agents of evil, but they enjoy chaos and uncertainty. Examples of trickster figures include Legba of the Fon and Eshu of the Yoruba, messenger gods who often garble messages in order to see what happens. Among the Dogon, Ogo is a solitary spiritual being who introduces various types of disruption into the world in a vain attempt to find a mate. These trickster figures often play important roles in divination in the Sudanic region and serve as more accessible messenger gods in Lower Guinea. Other spiritual beings will give someone great skill at such occupations as hunting or blacksmithing, but only at the price of something in exchange, such as the ability to have children. Only among the Igbo, and partially as a result of Christian influence, does one encounter a wholly evil form of spiritual being, Ekwensu, a deity who works for evil, who appears to have become important in Igbo religion in the late nineteenth century.

Other explanations of suffering focus on human neglect of religious and community obligations. Failure to take on ritual offices, or to greet the spirits important to one's family on a regular basis, or to meet communal work obligations all can result in spiritual chastisement in the form of illness or misfortune. Violations of community mores, such as committing acts of theft or incest are punished in similar ways. Still others, motivated by greed or a desire for power, practice acts of sorcery involving the manipulation of various types of medicines and speech for personal advancement at the expense of others.

Finally, some humans are said to engage in witchcraft. West African witches are people who are said to be able to separate their souls, or one of multiple souls, from their bodies and send them out in the night to attack other people or other people's property. These attacks are often seen as the underlying cause of many illnesses, deaths, and misfortunes. When a community has been stricken with a series of disasters, this has often led to elaborate witch-finding rituals, often relying on various forms of divination or poison ordeals. Such accusations are difficult to prove in other ways since, in sharp contrast to sorcery, there is no material evidence for witchcraft. Its activities are entirely confined to the spiritual realm. Among the Yoruba, witches are always female. They can kill people, cause infertility, and even consume the power (ashe) of a portion of a person's body. In upper Guinea and Senegambia, witches can be either male or female and often attack close relatives toward whom they harbor resentments they are unable to express in more public ways. People who hoard wealth or who engage in other forms of antisocial behavior are often accused of witchcraft. In many coastal areas of West Africa, accused witches were often sold as slaves. The number and frequency of witchcraft accusations greatly increased throughout West Africa in the wake of the European occupation of West Africa in the late nineteenth century and was a common explanation for the scourge of colonial rule. One cannot leave this subject, however, without mentioning that, at least in the Upper Guinea region, there are people who have the same powers as witches, but use these powers to combat such powers.

Most West African religions stress the importance of judgment after death and different fates for those who worked to enhance the life of their communities and their families and those who sought to weaken it. In most West African religions, it is the supreme being who decides one's fate. Those who worked to enhance life become ancestors who are venerated and who continue to communicate with their living descendants. Those whose actions diminished the quality of life in their communities are punished, excluded from their familial ancestry and isolated from their descendants. For the Diola, evil-doers become phantoms, unable to speak, and consigned to suffer a variety of torments in the forest outside their home communities. However, in most cases their punishment is not eternal, since everyone is eventually reincarnated and provided with another chance.

While a majority of West Africans at the end of the twentieth century primarily identify themselves as Muslims or Christians, African religions command a substantial number of adherents in most West African countries. Despite

---

WHO IS AN ANCESTOR IN AFRICAN TRADITIONAL RELIGION?

It is not possible to speak of traditional religion without touching on the subject of ancestors. Because they are nowhere and yet everywhere, it is difficult to speak of them comprehensively.

However, an ancestor is a person:

- who died a good death after having faithfully practised and transmitted to his descendants the laws left to him by the ancestors.

- who contributed to the continuation of the line by leaving many descendants.

- who was a peacemaker, a *link*, that fostered communion between the living and the dead, through sacrifices and prayers.

- A person who is the first-born is a candidate 'par excellence' to become an ancestor because he is able to maintain the chain of the generation in a long genealogy. The right of the first-born is an inalienable right.

Source: ATR Special Topics. Http://isizoh.net/afrel.

over a thousand years of contact with Islam in the Sudanic region, and over five hundred years of contact in Upper and Lower Guinea, as well as over five hundred years of contact with Christianity in coastal areas and over a century in the interior, African religions continue to meet the spiritual needs of many West Africans. Furthermore, they influence the practice of Islam and Christianity in the region, bringing religious concerns about community, healing, and fertility into their new religions, and contributing to the development of distinct West African forms of these religions. There is overwhelming evidence that African religions will continue to be an important force in West Africa cultures in the twenty-first century as well.

Robert M. Baum

See also Candomblé; Diola Prophets; Islam, West Africa; Santeria; Vodoun; Yoruba

Bibliography

Awolalu, J. (1979) *Yoruba Beliefs and Sacrificial Rites*. London: Longman.

Baum, Robert M. (1999) *Shrines of the Slave Trade: Diola Religion and Society in Precolonial Senegambia*. New York: Oxford University Press.

Dieterlen, Germaine. (1987) *Essai sur la Religion Bambara*. Brussels: Editions del'Université de Bruxelles.

Drewal, Henry, and Margaret Drewal. (1983) *Gelede: Art and Female Power among the Yoruba*. Bloomington: Indiana University Press.

Griaule, Marcel. (1965) *Conversations with Ogotemmeli*. London: Oxford University Press.

Hiskett, Mervyn. (1984) *The Development of Islam in West Africa*. London: Longman.

Ilogu, Edmund. (1974) *Christianity and Igbo Culture*. New York: Nok Publishers.

Parrinder, Geoffrey. (1969 [1949]) *West African Religion*. New York: Barnes and Noble.

Pelton, Robert D. (1980) *The Trickster in West Africa*. Berkeley: University of California Press.

Sanneh, Lamin. (1983) *West African Christianity*. Maryknoll, N.Y.: Orbis.

Women and Religious Movements in Sub-Saharan Africa

Women have long been involved in religious movements in sub-Saharan Africa. This participation has traversed the precolonial, colonial, and postcolonial periods. Movements have occurred amongst a wide variety of ethnic groups in all regions of the subcontinent. Participants have included rural and urban women, young and old and those of diverse socioeconomic statuses. These movements have been small-scale, spontaneous, and short-lived, as well as deeply embedded in wider religious, economic, and political structures over time. For our purposes "religious movement" will refer to "widespread and grassroots adherence to religious ideas, symbols and rituals, sometimes brief in duration, sometimes long-lasting; sometimes lacking and sometimes acquiring formal organizational structures" (Ranger 1986: 1).

Religion in sub-Saharan Africa has been a source of women's power and a source of their diminishment; indeed, in some contexts it has empowered and subordinated them in different ways at the same time. In the case of empowerment, African women have occupied a plethora of statuses in religious movements. In some, they are accorded exceptional respect as prophetesses, healers, and spirit mediums. Among the Shona of Zimbabwe in the precolonial period, spirit mediums installed chiefs and were said to have the power of ensuring perpetual fertility. In the latter years of the nationalist movement, Shona female mediums built alliances with guerilla forces and provided them with ritual and symbolic power. The significance of these contributions was evident at the time of the 1980 independence celebrations when cloth was printed to commemorate majority rule. It pictured both Robert Mugabe, the country's first prime minister, and a female spirit medium who was hanged in 1895 by the colonial state (Lan 1985). Such inspirational female figures have contributed to the success of many populist movements and become part of collective memory.

However, religious movements could also subordinate women. This was sometimes accomplished through their ideological devaluation as sexually polluting and in need of control. In some movements women were prohibited from participating in the ritual and political hierarchy monopolized by men. Ambivalent attitudes toward women are clearly evident in the Bapostolo (or Vapostori) independent church movement that has a wide distribution in East and Central Africa. Though women serve as healers, prophets, and judges, they are generally excluded from political leadership. At the same time, in a related church in Zimbabwe, women are highly celebrated as the symbolic bearers of tradition. Thus, in the same movement women may be at times excluded from ritual activities and/or engaged in parallel and complementary roles with men. These examples highlight a certain "double standard" in the status and treatment of women in ceremonial life.

Clarifying Conceptual Ambiguities

The extent of female participation in religious movements in Africa has been largely underestimated and undervalued. A case can be made that many women's movements that are viewed by Western observers as political movements are also religious in nature. The issue, as Jean Comaroff (1985) has argued, is not to be reductionist or rigid in our definition of social phenomena like religious movements, which are inherently multidimensional. The merits of taking this perspective to heart can be seen if we look at Audrey Wipper's (1985) study of the 1922 "Thuku disturbances" in Kenya, the 1929 "Aba riots" in Nigeria, and the 1958–59 "Anlu uprising" in the British Cameroons. These movements occurred in very diverse places and historical moments, yet they each deeply implicated both political and religious themes. Women walking naked and exposing their sexual organs, defecating in public areas, wearing medicinal leaves, and so on, are all indicative of profound spiritual and mystical power. If we only look at such movements as acts of political protest, we are unable to explain why it is that women engage in such actions that are "disgusting" from the viewpoint of each of these societies.

In fact these acts are deeply conventional in their own contexts. Wipper notes that women's mobilizations in the Cameroon Grassfields, referred to as the "Anlu uprising," have long been described as protests against British agricultural policy and/or manifestations of nationalist party politics. This is, however, a misreading of events that can only be understood fully in light of precolonial Grassfields morality, religiosity, and conceptions of well-being. The symbolism and discourse surrounding this movement—and similar mobilizations that occur today in Cameroon—explicitly invoke the bases of women's spiritual power in fertility and reproduction.

Many observers of social movements across Africa have noted that women intentionally remove clothing to expose their sexual organs; but with few exceptions (e.g., Ardener 1975) they rarely emphasize how this is a spiritual act and jural right conveying extraordinary power. When women mobilize by the hundreds, as they have done at different times in Sierra Leone, Nigeria, Kenya, Cameroon, and in many other countries of sub-Saharan Africa, the movements are at once political and religious. Neither are these movements simply resisting structures of authority or protesting the supposedly marginal position of women. Rather, they also may affirm existing political and religious institutions, celebrate women's spiritual authority, and assert their moral obligation to act on behalf of community welfare. Theirs is a history of acting within the system, as guardians of the system, not necessarily protesting outside of it, nor being sub-ordinate to it. Western observers have too frequently assumed that women in sub-Saharan Africa act only or primarily as subalterns, resorting to various forms of protest because they have no or few jural and ritual voices. Recent scholarship suggests this simply is not true in many societies.

Where early studies of female movements could overlook their religious dimension, the opposite can also be true. That is, scholars may focus primarily on the religious aspect of some movements, while downplaying or ignoring their political consequences. Or, scholars may recognize that movements have political implications, but view them nonetheless solely as a defense of old indigenous political structures attacked under colonialism and the missions. For example, the myriad antiwitchcraft movements that occurred across Africa in the early years of colonialism were frequently interpreted as attempts to reassert indigenous values. In other words, these movements tried to restore the balance or harmony of precolonial institutions. Viewing movements in this way is consistent with early theoretical assumptions surrounding the role of religion among these peoples. For some early scholars, religion may be expressive of personal or communal spirituality but lead to "false consciousness" about the political realities of the world. Or, religion is not politically instrumental; it simply provides emotional solace and/or communal solidarity. We can thank scholars like the historian Terence Ranger (1986) for pointing out that religion generally, and religious movements certainly contain important political insights about matters of social injustice. In a word, faith itself is political.

Religious Movements in the Nineteenth Century: A Historiographical Issue

There is a paucity of data on female religious movements in the nineteenth century and before. In part, this is the result of an incomplete historical record. It also reflects the biases of early European commentators who assumed that women played insignificant roles in religious institutions and practice. Historian Edward Alpers (1984) provides one of the few detailed descriptions of an early woman's religious movement for a spirit possession cult called Kitimiri in Zanzibar of the 1860s. His account draws on an unusually rich report by an Alsatian Catholic missionary who was the first vice-prefect apostolic of Zanzibar and head of the mission of the Holy Ghost Fathers in East Africa between 1863–1880. Alpers argues for a positive correlation between increasing rates of spirit possession among Swahili women in Zanzibar and their growing economic and political subordination. Greater demand for male labor on plantations also meant an increase in the social valuation of male activities generally. Together these contributed to an increase in and devaluation of the workload for women. The result was widespread spirit-possession movements amongst Swahili women, which "dramatized" the profound changes occurring in the social relations of production.

A second reason for the lack of attention paid to early movements may be due to conceptual prejudices. Indigenous African religion in the precolonial era has rarely been conceived of in terms of movements. Rather, religion was said only to buttress the major political, economic, and other institutions of society. Many studies of sacred kingship illustrate this bias: they suggest that it was not until colonialism, with its new institutional structures and cultural beliefs, that a violent wedge was driven between religion and the wider political order, and, moved to the margins, religion became a mechanism for protesting these profound and wrenching transformations.

This assumption—that religious movements only occurred in the wake of colonialism—has proven false in many cases. For example, Luo elders of the Roho independent churches of Kenya say that an indigenous charismatic movement came into existence prior to the arrival of European missionaries. These movements drew heavily from the practice of spirit possession, which was primarily a female preserve in Luo society. As a second example, the emergence of female movements during the expansion of Islam over vast areas of sub-Saharan Africa certainly would have predated European colonialism as well.

As Ranger (1986) has argued, religiosity always has the potential to both support and oppose other institutions: one must be careful to avoid treating religious movements as solely "movements" or solely "religious." As with any dimension of human behavior and belief, African women's actions are often religious, political, or economic, all at the same time. They may affirm some aspects of the social order, while at the same time critiquing other dimensions.

Religious Movements in the Twentieth Century

Much more is known of the involvement of women in religious movements in the twentieth century than in previous eras; and there exists in particular a fascinating body of research on female spirit-possession cults. One of the earliest analyses of spirit possession is the work of I. M. Lewis (1989). He argued that spirit possession was an instrumental means of gaining power in societies where women and dispossessed men are otherwise marginalized. He viewed it as an expression of women's subordinate status vis-à-vis the dominant culture of elite men.

The debate that Lewis's early research provoked has led to creative re-evaluations in the understanding of female spirit possession. It is increasingly conceptualized within a wider social and cultural context and viewed as both the cause and consequence of those influences. Other scholars question whether it is accurate to assume that possession cults were the only avenues by which women could gain a measure of power. Still others suggest that spirit possession represents a form of cultural resistance; for example, songs performed in the context of exorcism rites that aim to free the initiate from illness may offer discerning commentaries on relations of inequality. From this perspective, trance rituals of the Zar cult in Sudan are a therapeutic intervention intended to cure a range of spirit-related ailments. They also play an important role in defining women's identity on multiple levels, as women, independent of men, and as part of a distinct village identity (Boddy 1989). Women's own accounts of spirit possession point to meanings and symbols associated with pride and self-esteem.

Still other research on spirit possession focuses on the multiple motivations and/or consequences of such religious movements. For example, in Islamic northern Sudan and among the Luo of Kenya, women join these cults for a range of reasons that include greater autonomy, economic mobility, and leadership possibilities. Moreover, when we listen to women themselves, both here and elsewhere in Africa, it is clear that they experience important emotional well-being and psychological comfort through their participation in spirit-possession cults. Boddy (1989) has shown that these groups provide women with social networks, information sharing, health care, and practical advice and support, which are especially useful in urban areas where there may be few or no close kin.

Religion, Ideology, and Resistance

These perspectives raise interesting questions about the degree to which women are accepting and/or reinforcing their subordinate status as they participate in religious movements. Could it be that women may be doing both? For example, they may accept their domestic role in society yet alter the social value system. In the case of possession cults, materialist arguments consider the lavish gifts that are required to placate spirits, given by husbands on behalf of wives. These may have the consequence of actually redistributing commodities and redefining conjugal relationships. To be sure, spirit-possession cults may not effect revolutionary structural changes in gender relations, but this should not obscure the fact that men are affirming their responsibilities as men and husbands as they make significant financial expenditures and show concern for the health and well-being of their wives.

During and after the colonial period, women's religious movements also emerged in the form of African

ALICE LENSHINA NAMED
WOMAN OF THE CENTURY

In December 1999, *Zamzine: The Magazine of the Future* selected Alice Lenshina, founder of the Lumpa Church, as the Zamzine woman of the century. The magazine noted that: "It is difficult to agree with the strange doctrines that Alice Lenshina preached to her followers all over the country, but it is also difficult to ignore her influence. Alice Lenshina was the controversial founder of the Lumpa religion in the sixties. She claimed that she had died and risen again, and that God had chosen her to preach a message of Salvation to the people. She was so bold in her message that all kinds of people in Zambia believed her. This was at a time when tribalism was at its highest point of expression in Zambia, and yet she managed to have followers from all kinds of tribes. And it was strange to have a woman with so many male followers at a time when women were certainly considered to have a lower place in life, traditionally. And this is why Lenshina is our woman leader of the century."

Source: *Zamzine*, December 1999. www. zambia.co.zm/zamzine.

independent churches. Christianity had a particularly significant consequence for the lives of African women. Once colonialism and Christianity were well established in many areas of the subcontinent, Africans turned increasingly to starting churches of their own. These African independent churches emerged, in part, as a response to the denigration of indigenous religious practices by European missions. The "new churches" expressed Christian faith in African symbols, and established an African ethos in both the structure and practice of religion, portraying a different world than a white world. In short, these churches met spiritual needs on African terms.

African independent churches continue to draw on indigenous religious traditions as well as the Christian churches from whom they originally distanced themselves. A process of acceptance, rejection, and reinterpretation were endemic to this process of syncretism; and changes were sometimes counterintuitive. In some cases movements responded ambivalently toward indigenous tradition rather than in defense of it. In sum, African independent churches were not simply reactions against or escapes from the hegemonic rule of the colonial state, and they continue to synthesize a variety of traditions drawn from multiple historical periods in eclipsed, attenuated, and reinvented forms. New symbols, meanings, and practices are constructed out of changing interests, hopes, and what is and is not possible. Particularly in urban settings, for example, religious movements have taken on new functions. As with urban spirit-possession cults, movements may become important sources of mutual economic and social aid for members who have

often migrated to the cities, where they are otherwise bereft of many of their kin and friends.

A copious literature explores why women join these religious movements. As noted above, explanations given by members for their involvement vary widely and may shift over time. In South Africa in the 1920s, Christian women's prayer groups mobilized against state policies that promoted male out-migration, and unfair taxation and land registration. In Kenya, by contrast, Luo women joined the Roho religious movement, gaining the right to say mass and to administer sacraments, though they were barred from these roles when men came to monopolize them by the 1960s. Likewise, as a consequence of being excluded from holding office in early Christian churches in Nigeria, Ibo women helped to establish indigenous independent churches (Mba 1982). This suggests that women's status and power in the evolution of religious movements is fluid, influencing when and why women become adherents, as well as the degree of their participation.

To understand these shifts in the motivation and status of female adherents, scholars have begun to focus more on the "stories" or biographies of participants, as well as changing symbolism, metaphors, dress, songs, and other indicators. The growing numbers of ethnographic biographies and narratives about church members emphasize a new epistemological willingness to explore the expressive life of religious experience and emphasize the active agency of women. Emphasizing female agency can continue the tradition of viewing religious movements in instrumental and "rationalist" ways. Yet, the focus on biography also underscores the spiritual and expressive importance of these movements in the lives of their members (e.g., Jules-Rosette 1975).

Studies of the role of women in such movements are also coming to recognize that not all women in the group necessarily share the same status. For example, despite a sharply gendered division of labor and privilege system in many religious communities, it is not a foregone conclusion that women will necessarily be the staunchest supporters of female church leaders. Cases in point are Alice Lenshina's Lumpa Church of Zambia and the Legio Maria movement, also in East Africa. In both, charismatic women became leaders with the support of large numbers of men. It is not simply other women who guarantee women more freedom, economic independence, or political power.

The reality is that sub-Saharan African independent churches grant some women greater freedom and economic independence, yet they undercut and constrain it as well. There is no direct correlation between African women's emancipation and their participation in African independent churches (Jules-Rosette 1979). Still, the symbolic spheres of men and women may be clearly demarcated in these settings. This can work to increase the power and independence of women because they are able to make ritual and political decisions in their own right.

This implies a second point. Women involved in religious movements do not necessarily act on the basis of a so-called "feminist" identity. Although many movements may be primarily or even exclusively female, they are not feminist in the usual Western sense of that term. Scholars writing about "local" or "non-Western" feminism remind us that women in such movements may act out of a gendered view of their community or the world, but their female identity is embedded in other identities like farmer, petty commodity trader, or ethnic group membership (e.g., Mikell 1997). For example, Cameroonian women assert their right to be moral custodians of the community, and to mobilize on its behalf, for multiple reasons beyond the fact that they are women. To be sure, their role in giving birth and caring for children is formative of their moral vision of the world, but so is their identity as "farmers" responsible for household survival. It is no accident that they march repeatedly over many issues, including when cattle invade their farms or when political elites usurp community land (Diduk 1989).

Reconceptualizing the Study of Women and Religious Movements

More recent writings on women and religious movements reiterate that they need to be located within a wider sphere of human activity rather than as an autonomous subject of inquiry. Social constructionist approaches, in particular, see the emergence and development of social movements as a dynamic process involving thoughtful, creative agents. For example, Boddy's exploration of spirit possession in the Zar cult of Sudan captures the experiential, performance, and aesthetic dimensions of female possession. She also explores its inseparability from spirituality in the wider culture. This echoes a number of scholars—notably Iris Berger, Janice Boddy, and Jean Comaroff—who have called for a reappraisal and reconceptualization of religious movements in Africa. Women's roles in religious movements need to be viewed in the context of cultural, political, and other movements on the subcontinent generally.

In the future, it is to be hoped that the study of religious movements in sub-Saharan Africa will become more regionally comparative and international in focus. Scholars are increasingly interested in the African Diaspora, as well as the syncretism, or creative emergence, of new African religions based on both indigenous religions and those, like Islam or Christianity, imported from elsewhere.

For Christianity, this "internationalization" of religious movements will probably be most influenced by the enormous expansion of transnational evangelical and Pentecostal missions (Hackett 1995). They have large followings, great wealth, and highly organized bureaucracies with the power to promote new religious ideologies. Scholars have been examining the effects of these churches, especially in West Africa. Given the heavy involvement of women in these new Pentecostal and evangelical churches, we need to look more at the consequences of membership for women, particularly in terms of ethnicity, class, age, and educational level.

Finally and apropos of my comments above on non-Western feminism, to what degree is women's identity changing because of their involvement in new movements? A number of writers suggest that since the economic crises of the mid-1980s, and the resulting austerity measures and structural readjustment, African women are more aware of themselves as women in a sense more akin to Western feminism. Given that the "crisis" has placed a disproportionate burden on women, we might expect to see a new awareness among women of their role in economic survival and strategies for change. Both churches and more indigenously-based women's associations across sub-Saharan Africa are very active in addressing economic and political issues. Indeed, they provide an excellent example of grassroots involvement by elements of civil society as they contend for survival vis-à-vis African states and larger forces of change. The extent to which religious movements will be vehicles for growing "feminist" awareness and activism remains to be seen, but certainly deserves attention. Whether this emerges or not, the involvement of women in grassroots movements

WOMEN AS ZAR DOCTORS IN ETHIOPIA

The zar doctor, often a matriarch, differs only in degree from her flock; for she, too, must be possessed, must be forever afflicted by spirits. But she has managed to learn to control them, call upon her more powerful protective spirits to aid her against evil spirits more tricky but less powerful than hers. This enables her to relieve the sufferings of her clients; without, however, curing them. For a possessive spirit can be turned into an asset—into a protective spirit—once the spirit's demands are known and regularly fulfilled. Why should anyone wish to reject such as a protective spirit who helps solve the problems of life and even "beautifies the face" with an inner glow? Only a few hopelessly evil demons, mostly female, need to be exorcised.

Women, otherwise limited in cultural participation among the Amhara, particularly in the church institution where their expressive behavior and opportunity for service are almost entirely rejected, constitute a considerable majority in the zar societies, even in the top leadership; so that many men think of the zar cult as predominately feminine, and consult zar doctors by stealth only, at night. Men have ambivalent feelings about their wives attendance; they are often jealous of the "possessive" spirit; object to the financial outlays demanded by the "zar" spirits on pain of relapse into the patient's catatonic, schizoid or hysterical state; object to their wives being at the doctor's hut all night during worship-sessions; but admit that their wives are thereafter easier to live with, indeed, more beautiful when the "*neqabi*" (inspiration) "is on their face."

Thus the "zar" institution affects many other Amhara institutions: Marriage and the Family; Religion; Economics; Ethnic Relations; and even linguistics.

Source: Messing, Simon. (1957) *The Highland-plateau Amhara of Ethiopia.* Doctoral Dissertation, University of Pennsylvania, pp. 597-598.

If we focus on what women do, rather than what they cannot, we find them working in the spiritual realm on behalf of themselves, their families, households, or communities, channeling spirits' assistance or heading off their wrath, protecting future generations, even protesting injustice.

Source: Boddy, Janice. (1989) *Wombs and Alien Spirits: Women, Men, and the Zar Cult in Northern Sudan.* Madison: University of Wisconsin Press, p. 416.

---

almost always has deep religious roots. That this long history of religious activism by African women, especially rural women, may provide templates for a new civil society in Africa, is perfectly consistent with the dynamic and transformative power wielded by both women and religious movements.

Susan Diduk

See also Lumpa Church; Religion and Healing

Bibliography

Alpers, Edward. (1984) "'Ordinary Household Chores': Ritual and Power in a Nineteenth-Century Swahili Women's Spirit Possession Cult." *International Journal of African Historical Studies* 17, 4: 677–702.

Amadiume, Ife. (1997) *Reinventing Africa: Matriarchy, Religion and Culture.* London: Zed Books.

Ardener, Shirley, ed. (1975) *Perceiving Women.* London: Malaby Press.

Berger, Iris. (1981) *Religion and Resistance.* Tervuren: Musee Royale de l'Afrique Centrale.

Berger, Iris, and Francis White. (1999) *Women in Sub-Saharan Africa*. Bloomington: Indiana University Press.

Boddy, Janice. (1989) *Wombs and Alien Spirits: Women, Men, and the Zar Cult in Northern Sudan*. Madison: University of Wisconsin Press.

Comaroff, Jean. (1985) *Body of Power, Spirit of Resistance: The Culture and History of a South African People*. Chicago: University of Chicago Press.

Diduk, Susan. (1989) "Women's Agricultural Production and Political Action in the Cameroon Grassfields." *Africa* 59, 3: 338–355.

Fields, Karen. (1985) *Revival and Rebellion in Colonial Central Africa*. Princeton: Princeton University Press.

Hackett, Rosalind. (1995) "Women and New Religious Movements in Africa." In *Religion and Gender*, edited by Ursula King. Oxford: Basil Blackwell Publishers.

Hoehler-Fatton, Cynthia. (1996) *Women of Fire and Spirit: History, Faith, and Gender in Roho Religion in Western Kenya*. Oxford: Oxford University Press.

Jules-Rosette, Bennetta, ed. (1979) *The New Religions of Africa*. Norwood, NJ: Ablex Publishing.

Lan, David. (1985) *Guns and Rain: Guerrillas and Spirit Mediums in Zimbabwe*. London: James Currey.

Lewis, I. M. (1989) *Ecstatic Religion: A Study of Shamanism and Spirit Possession*. London: Routledge.

Mba, Nina Emma. *Nigerian Women Mobilized: Women's Political Activity in Southern Nigeria, 1900–1965*. Berkeley: Institute of International Studies.

Mikell, Gwendolyn, ed. (1997) *African Feminism: The Politics of Survival in Sub-Saharan Africa*. Philadelphia: University of Pennsylvania Press.

Ranger, Terence. (1986) "Religious Movements and Politics in Sub-Saharan Africa." *African Studies Review* 29, 2 (June): 1–69.

Wipper, Audrey. (1985) *Riot and Rebellion Among African Women: Three Examples of Women's Political Clout*. East Lansing, MI: Michigan State University, Working Paper # 108.

World Vision International

World Vision International is the largest Christian, non-governmental organization (NGO) involved in emergency humanitarian aid (relief) and economic development in the world. In 1995, with an annual budget of US$339 million, World Vision worked in 101 countries around the world, 25 of which were in Africa. Africa receives the largest amount of humanitarian assistance from World Vision of any world region (over US$163 million; World Vision Annual Report 1995).

The organization was founded in the late 1940s by an American evangelist and journalist stationed in Korea named Bob Pierce. Pierce's concern about the plight of a young child in an orphanage inspired him to commit to sending monthly remittances toward her support. This commenced what has become a global process of "child sponsorship" in which individuals in donor countries send monthly payments toward the sponsorship of children in need. Once monies by sponsors are received by World Vision support offices, they are pooled together to fund economic development projects such as improvements in health and sanitation, agricultural production, and the building of schools. Child sponsorship remittances are channeled through offices in donor countries toward offices in recipient countries— usually in what is considered to be the "less-developed world." The organization manifests an extensive administrative and bureaucratic apparatus to monitor and track both its sponsored children, and the development projects in communities where they live. Child sponsorship is the core of World Vision'ss fundraising success, and much of its project funds are garnered through child sponsorship.

Today, the organization is a complex transnational corporation. World Vision defines itself as a "global partnership," and is structured as a network of interdependent national offices (for example: World Vision Tanzania, World Vision Zimbabwe, World Vision South Africa, etc.). World Vision International, through an international council and board of directors, governs the World Vision Partnership and is the registered legal entity that coordinates its structure. The organization supports 5,049 projects in the 74 countries where there are World Vision offices (not all countries where World Vision works have World Vision offices). Over one million children are sponsored through World Vision (numbers as of 1995, see Irvine 1996: 270). In practice, national-level World Vision offices work with local governments and local populations to provide assistance with economic development. At some of World Vision's larger development projects, World Vision project officers live and work with members of rural communities to facilitate economic development projects. World Vision also employs community members from local project sites for this purpose.

World Vision in sub-Saharan Africa follows in the long tradition of missionaries in the region, focusing upon what it calls the "holistic" synthesis of material and spiritual "human development." World Vision proclaims that its organizational mission is to follow Jesus Christ in working with the poor and oppressed, "to promote human transformation, seek justice, and bear witness to the good news of the Kingdom of God" (Irvine 1996: 277). Although World Vision is a Christian organization, it generates some of the same types of development and relief projects as so-called "secular" NGOs. Despite its apparent similarity with nonreligious NGOs, Christianity is a motivational force behind the "core values" of the corporation. Within World Vision, all staff must sign statements of faith proclaiming their adherence to Christianity. While its Christian orientation serves as a solid corporate philosophy, the ways in which religious beliefs are interpreted in local contexts varies greatly. World Vision, like other transnational humanitarian NGOs, is synchronized with contemporary trends in international development such as gender and development, and participatory rural appraisal. The degree to which these programs achieve the goals of World Vision is largely a variable of local contexts and local leadership at national and field project offices.

Erica Bornstein

Bibliography

Gehman, Richard. (1960) *Let My Heart Be Broken With the Things That Break The Heart of God.* New York: McGraw-Hill.

Irvine, Graeme. (1996) *Best of Things in the Worst of Times: An Insiders View of World Vision.* Wilsonville, OR: Book Partners, Inc. & World Vision International.

Seiple, Bob. (1990) *One Life at a Time.* Dallas: World Vision.

World Vision International. (1996) *1995 Annual Report.* Monrovia, CA: World Vision International.

Yamamori, Tetsunao, Bryant L. Myers, Kwame Bediako, and Larry Reed. (1996) *Serving with the Poor in Africa.* Monrovia, CA: MARC Publications, a division of World Vision International.

Xango in Recife (Pernambuco)

Xango in Recife is, along with Bahian Candomblé and Batuque of Rio Grande do Sul, one of the traditional Afro-Brazilian religions. It is based on the belief system of the Yoruba of Nigeria, who were the last slaves to be imported in large numbers and whose arrival in Brazil lasted until almost the close of the nineteenth century. The Yoruba religion was maintained by contacts between Brazilian cult-leaders and their counterparts in Nigeria during the 1930s, when Pai Adao and others traveled to Lagos, where they learned the divination practices of the *babalaos.* For a long time, ritual objects, such as a special black soap and cowrie shells were brought from Africa. More recently, Xangoists established new contacts with Nigeria through students and professors from that country, who study in Brazil and now teach the Yoruba language and offer courses on African culture, although many of them no longer practice the ancestral rituals at home.

During the colonial era, Recife was an important port of entry for slaves, who worked on the sugar plantations of Pernambuco (region, now a state). A large portion of the population is still of African origin, although today the majority of Xangoists belong to other ethnic groups. Before the second World War, at least 16 *terreiros* (temples) existed in the city and were registered as charitable associations under the name of Catholic saints (*Associaçao benefica de Sao Bento*). Others were registered as carnival societies (*ranchos, maracatus*). During this period the practice of Afro-Brazilian religions was carefully supervised and often forbidden. This was the main reason for identifying the divinities with Catholic saints. Today at least 6,000 *terreiros* are found in the city and surrounding communities.

Beliefs and Practices

Xango is an ecstatic and initiatory religion: divinities possess believers in a state of trance, and in order to become a member of a *terreiro* it is necessary to be initiated. The candidate has to learn the secrets of the faith and must undergo a series of ordeals, whereby his hair is shaved and the skin receives a number of cuts. Bloody sacrifices are offered to the divinities and the new member of the congregation has to wear ritual cloth and remain in the temple for a certain period of time. During initiation he/she receives a guardian spirit, who will give lifelong protection. Initiation rituals are expensive but absolutely necessary. In this religion *axe*, or spiritual power, is transferred with blood and therefore sacrifices are of great importance. The divinities are fed with blood, while blood is used in rituals to give power to the believers.

In Recife, as in Salvador, the Yoruba divinities dominate the pantheon, although some Ewe-Fon deities (*vodouns*) and Bantu spirits from Central Africa are worshiped as well. The most important deities are Xango, Ogum, Yemanya, and Oxun. According to Yoruba mythology, the deities are related by birth or by marriage to each other. In Recife some of these stories were preserved, others are forgotten. One African concept that has been preserved is *ori*, which signifies a guardian angel or protective force. It may be identified as the soul that gives man his vital power. Each believer possesses a bowl made of white porcelain and covered with a white plate, which contains an object representing *ori*. Food is offered to this emblem from time to time (*obori*).

The Yoruba divinities invoked are superficially identified with Catholic saints, whose images are found on the altars. The heads, *babaloricha* or *yaloricha*, of a temple organize the rituals that take place on the name day of the associated saint. The *filhas do santo* take part in the ritual dances and often receive their guardian spirits in an altered state of consciousness. In order to fall in trance they sometimes drink rum or smoke marijuana. The dances may last a whole night and are accompanied by drum beats and songs, sometimes sung in a mixture of Yoruba and Portuguese. The animals, which are sacrificed a day or two before the feast takes place, are used to prepare traditional dishes, which are distributed to the faithful and their guests.

The divinities are associated with symbols, such as Xango with a double axe, Ogun with a piece of iron, and Ochun with pebbles from a river. At the entrance to the temple one finds a little hut belonging to Exu, the trickster figure and the youngest member of the Yoruba pantheon, who guards the doors and may do mischief, unless he is propitiated in advance. In the orthodox temples Exu does not take possession of the faithful, in newer temples influenced by Umbanda, he might.

In the traditional *terreiros* a ceremony starts with Catholic prayers. Sometimes a Catholic chapel is found next to the building where the divinities have their abode. During the month of May, in some temples, rituals in honor of the Holy Virgin take place. The syncretism of African and Catholic elements go back to the days when the temples were founded. Some priests practice divination with the help of *buzios* (shells) or playing cards, prophesize, and cure illnesses. They also prepare *despachos* (*ebo*), magic packages, that are placed on crossroads during the night and are dedicated mainly to Exu. They contain a bottle of rum, red and white pieces of cloth, cigars, and candles. It is said that the priests are also able to transfer a bewitchment or a disease from a living person to an object that later will be eliminated. The *eguns*, spirits of the dead, are honored. After a person dies, all the necessary rituals have to be performed, so that the *egun* is satisfied. In each *terreiro* we find a little structure called the *casa dos eguns* or *igbale*. The cult for the ancestral spirits is secret and completely separated from Christian rituals.

Modern Varieties of Xango

Xango of Recife was influenced by the worship of *caboclos* (Amerindian spirits) and later by Umbanda, and a variety of combinations of these different cults are found in the reli-

gious continuum of the city, from Pagelança (shamanic practices) to Mesa Branca (Kardecist sessions). There occurred a proliferation of spirits and divinities that were inserted in the original structure. We may distinguish among (1) the traditional Xango of African derivation as practiced by the descendants of the original founders of this religion; (2) Jurema- and Catimbo-style Xango, with emphasis on healing and no concern for structure; and (3) "Umbandized" Xango, which includes the organization of divinities in *linhas* and *falanges*, the invocation of disincarnated spirits, and the importance of *exus and pombagiras* (the female counterpart of the Yoruba trickster, invented in Brazil).

The so-called *gomeia* model of Xango and Candomblé is a recent development, in which new musical and choreographic styles were invented and the Yoruba mythology was altered under the influence of academia. The silent trance of the traditional groups was replaced by violent possessions. The divinities that speak from the mouth of the mediums are consulted by the clients. This new style can be observed not only in Xango but also in the other Afro-Brazilian religions that in recent years have mutually influenced each other and at the same time absorbed foreign traits not only from Africa but from many parts of the world.

Xango today is no longer the religion of a black proletariat, but especially in its Umbandized form, attracts artisans, small businessmen, and government employees, as well as students in search of their roots. The new rituals may take place in apartment buildings and no longer need wide open spaces. The media are responsible for the globalization of these religious practices and concepts, and freedom of religion is assured by law.

A version of the traditional Xango was also practiced in Laranjeras, a colonial city near Acarajú in the state of Sergipe. The Yoruba traditions were preserved in the *Terreiro de Santa Barbara*. In the same state, Afro-Brazilian practices under the name of *tore* have syncretized with curing rituals and the *caboclo* cults of Amerindian origin. Today Umbanda has also influenced these older rituals.

Angelina Pollak-Eltz

See also Brazil; African-Derived Religions in; Kardecism; Pagelança; Tambor De Mina En Maranhon

Bibliography

Carvalho, José Jorge, and Rita Laura Segato. (1987) *El Culto Shango en Recife, Brasil.* Caracas: CCPYT.

Motta, Roberto. (1980) *Cidade e devoçao.* Recife: Ed. Pirata.

Yoruba Religion

The Yoruba belief system is one of several continental African traditional religious systems that recognize several loose components including the belief in a Supreme Being, belief in lesser deities, belief in the departed ancestors and their ability to influence the living, belief in spiritual intermediaries, and recognition of certain practices such as medicine and magic to affect the experience of the living. The specific religious practices among the Yoruba vary widely from one area to another within the southwestern region of Nigeria and the western region of the Republic of Benin, where the ethnic group is largely concentrated. Although most Yorubas in Nigeria or Benin would identify themselves as Christians or Muslims, many still recognize, in some regard, the significance of the traditional religious practices. As a result of African enslavement in the Americas, many New World manifestations of Yoruba religions developed and continued to be practiced.

Yoruba Belief System

The Yoruba traditional belief system recognizes a Supreme Being, or god, who is known by many honorific titles, but the most universally accepted names are Olorun (owner of the sky) or, Olodumare (the almighty). He rules over the entire universe with the assistance of lesser deities known as *orishas*. Olorun, or Olodumare, is never directly worshipped. Instead, there is a tiered system within Yoruba religious practice. At the top of the tier is the Supreme Being (Olorun). Falling below him are the interim deities (orisha), and below them are humans (men and women). There is no direct relation between humans and the Supreme Being. It is the role of the orishas to intervene in behalf of humanity to the Supreme Being.

The practice of the religion in day to day life centers around priests and priestesses, known variously as *babalawos*, *babalorisha* (men), *iyawo*, and *iyalorisha* (women). They are the chief interpreters of the specific deities within the group of worshippers. They resolve conflicts within the group and may be the principal vehicle for "mounting," which is when deities may make themselves present among humans as in a ceremonial trance. There are literally hundreds of orishas. The numbers vary between four and six hundred. All the deities are believed to have once been human, but through some act or accident became immortalized. Each deity has a specific area of rule (such as thunder, clouds, plants, wildlife, certain diseases and afflictions, geographical locations, bodies of waters, destinies, etc.), and human aspect which they control (such as peace, purity, passion, war, employment, illness, marriage, death, love, etc.). Through consultation with the oracle (Ifa, god of destiny), a believer's orisha is determined. It then becomes the responsibility of the believer to identify himself or herself with that specific deity. For example, they must learn what the deity's likes and dislikes are (e.g., foods, various colors, or certain practices) and must adjust their behavior accordingly. In many instances the proper instruction on how to worship one's orisha is done through a period of initiation. This rite of passage may last over several months, or may be as brief as a few weeks. During this period, the initiate might be required to have their hair shaven, wear special clothing, adorn certain decorative jewelry, or receive certain marks (such as scarification) that identify them as belonging to a given orisha. After successfully completing this process the initiate is welcomed into the body of believers of the deity.

The Major Yoruba Orisha

Although there are literally hundreds of orishas, the majority of them are not well known outside of the specific worship circle. There are, however, several which have become well known off of the African continent, mostly through enslaved Africans in the Americas.

Shango

This is the well-known deity of thunder and lighting. According to myth, Shango was a former ruler of Old Oyo during the fourteenth century. After being disgraced by his generals and abandoned by his wife, he was said to have hanged himself, the ultimate disgrace for a king. His believers argued that the king did not hang himself, but was simply made into a god. Another version of the myth contends that Shango experimented with dangerous devices and caused lightening bolts to strike his palace and kill many people including his family. This calamity caused the ruler to abandon his throne and wander off. His followers believed thereafter that any subsequent storm was the work of the deified former ruler. Shango's symbol of authority was the double-edged ax, and statues dedicated to him reflect this.

Obatala or Orisha nla

Known variously by either name, Obatala, the god of the white cloth, is believed to be one of the creators of human beings. Because of that he is important to Olorun. People with physical deformities are considered precious to the deity because they remind those without such handicaps what this god is capable of. Obatala has several annual festivals held in his honor in Nigeria. Major observances are in March and August. His followers almost always adorn themselves in

WOLE SOYINKA ON YORUBA RELIGION: A CONVERSATION WITH ULLI BEIER

Beier: I wanted to talk to you about Yoruba religion, because you seem to be the only writer who has seriously tried to come to terms with it. Even many of the Yoruba scholars, who do research into language, literature, history of the Yoruba shy away from the subject—as if they were embarrassed about it.

Now in your own case, given the type of upbringing you had, I have asked myself how you became interested in Yoruba religion. There is an image, "Ake", that has made a very strong impression on me. You were living in the Christian school compound, that was surrounded by a high wall and when the Egungun masqueraders were passing by outside, you had to ask somebody to lift you onto the ladder, so that you could watch the procession going on outside.

Your upbringing was designed to shield you from the realities of Yoruba life ... and later on your education in the Grammar school, the University in England—they all were designed to take you further away from the core of your culture. How then did you find your way back into it? How did you manage to break the wall that had been built up around you?

Soyinka: Curiosity mostly, and the annual visits to Isara—which was a very different situation from Abeokuta! There is no question at all that there was something, an immediacy that was more attractive, more intriguing about something from which you were obviously being shielded. If you hear all the time "Oh, you mustn't play with those kids because their father is an Egungun man ... " you become curious: and then you discover that there is nothing really "evil" about it ... that it is not the way they preach about it. Even my great great uncle, the Reverend J.J. Ransome Kuti, whom I never met, composed a song whose refrain was: "Dead men can't talk ... " One was surrounded by such refutations of that other world, of that other part of one's heritage, so of course you asked questions about it. Yes, and even if I realized quite early on, that there was a man in the Egungun mask, that did not mean that a great act of evil was being committed—any more than saying that Father Christmas was evil.

I had this rather comparative sense and I wrote in "Ake" that I used to look at the images on the stained-glass windows of the church: Henry Townsend, the Rev. Hinderer, and then the image that was supposed to be St. Peter. In my very imaginative mind, it didn't seem to me that they were very different from the Egungun.

So one was surrounded by all these different images which easily flowed into one another. I was never frightened of the Egungun. I was fascinated by them. Of course, I talked to some of my colleagues, like Osiki, who donned the masquerade himself, from time to time.

The Igbale was nothing sinister to me: it signified to me a mystery, a place of transformation. You went into Igbale to put on your masquerade. Then when the Egungun came out, it seemed that all they did was bless the community and beg a little bit for alms here and there. Occasionally there were disciplinary outings: they terrorized everybody and we ran away from them but then, some distance away you stopped and regathered ... maybe my dramatic bent saw this right from the beginning as part of the drama of life.

I never went through a phase, when I believed that traditional religion or ceremonies were evil. I believed that there were witches—I was convinced of that—but at the same time there were good apparitions. And of course I found the songs and the drumming very exciting.

Source: *Isokan Yoruba Magazine*, Summer 1997, Vol. III, 3. Washington, D.C.

white, and dogs are considered inappropriate for the worship of this deity. Thus, followers do not own dogs and keep them away from sacred spots.

Shopona

Known as the god of smallpox or contagious disease, Shopona is one of the more feared orisha in the Yoruba pantheon. If not worshipped properly, the deity has the ability to bring on smallpox and was known, in the past, to devastate entire villages when angered. This deity is so feared that if someone even utters his name, they are expected to give themselves pain (such as biting or slapping themselves) to appease this god. Smallpox, according to Bascom is not seen as a disease, but as punishment from Shopona. In his incarnated form, the performer of this deity imitates the deity by appearing to be physically deformed, such as by moving with a severe limp.

Ogun

Also a very powerful deity is the god of iron and other heavy metals. This deity is the patron of steel smelters and blacksmiths, and the craftspeople who manipulate such metals. Other manifestations of Ogun's power would be automobiles, airplanes, ships, tractors, and other machines which require massive amounts of metal to function. Because warriors and hunters use spears and other weapons made of iron and steel, he is revered within those professions among others.

Eshu

This deity is known by several names including Elegba, Legba, or some variation of these. Although he is often known as the trickster god, that is, able to bring about good or bad fortune depending on his disposition, his formal role in the Yoruba pantheon is as the messenger of Olorun, the supreme god. Because Eshu can bring about both good and evil, he is revered by most traditional Yoruba believers. It is his ability to bring about evil that has caused him to be likened to the devil by Yoruba Christians. He is believed to be the protector of the crossroads, where two roads intersect, or symbolically where peoples lives and experiences may cross. Outdoor markets are also considered to be under the protection of this deity.

Oya

There are numerous female gods within traditional Yoruba belief as well. The goddess Oya is one of many female river deities. She was also believed to have been one of the loyal wives of Shango who later became deified and worshipped in her own right. The river Niger is her domain. She symbolizes the dual capability of water (and women in general) to be a

life-sustaining force such as for the growth of plants, food, and for drinking, but can also turn destructive and deadly, for example, when the river banks overflow and cause flooding. Oya is also believed to control the winds for the purpose of stirring up the waves of water when she deems it necessary. Another river deity is Yemonja, the protector of the Ogun River. Her powers are comparable to those of goddess Oya.

Moremi

Moremi was a highly regarded market woman who almost single-handedly saved the town of Ile-Ife from foreign invaders by appealing to the river goddess Esinmirin. In return, Moremi had to sacrifice her only son, Oluorogbo. Hailed as the "mother of mothers," she is honored in Ile-Ife every October with a major festival that honors her heroic sacrifice.

Yoruba Religious Traditions in the African Diaspora

By way of the African slave trade, Yoruba religious traditions survived in the Americas where they are found most prominently in several Latin American colonial enclaves. The Yoruba-derived religious practices are known by various names in different localities. In Brazil, for example, the practices are known as Condomble and Macumba, among other names. In Cuba they are known as Lucumi, (derived from *akumi*) and in Puerto Rico as Santeria. Many of the names of deities were altered: Shango became known as Chango, Ogun as Oggun, Eshu as Eleggua, and Shopona as Chankpana—more commonly referred to by his praise name, Babaluaiye.

Yoruba-based Religions in Catholic Settings

The unifying connection (although small in some instances) within these New World Yoruba religious practices seems to be their relationship to Christianity. As many of these traditional African religious practices were viewed as pagan by the Catholic colonizers, they were forced underground and, as a result, were syncretized within Catholicism. In that the Catholic Church recognizes God as the Supreme Being, the saints as intermediaries, and humans at the bottom of the tiered system, it was possible for traditional Yoruba belief practitioners to mask their orishas as European Catholic saints.

This syncretization manifested itself in various ways. For example, in Santeria (literally "Saints"), Shango is likened to Saint Barbara; Obatala is masked as Our Lady of Mercy (Las Mercedes); Ogun is masked as Saint Peter; and Shopona is masked as Saint Lazarus, or Saint Roderick. As there are hundreds of orisha, there are hundreds of saints, so it was simple for such masking to take place.

As deities within the Nigerian and Beninois Yoruba pantheon had specific likes and dislikes with regard to food, colors, and practices, so also do the deities in the New World Diaspora. In Santeria, for example, Obatala is uniformly associated with the color white, both in Africa and the New World. The same observation could be made of Shango (Chango), whose believers wear red and white in his honor.

De-Catholicization of New World Yoruba Tradition

Although the association with Catholicism is the most common in modern day New World Yoruba observances, there are communities in the Americas that have pursued the tradition practices without the Catholic influence. Such a community exists in Sheldon, South Carolina. The village is known as Oyotunji (to rise up, or be reborn). This community was established in South Carolina in 1970, although the genesis of the village began in New York City in the late 1950s, where it was first set up as a Yoruba temple known as the Shango Temple. The temple was made up mostly of African-Americans who had an interest in adopting a traditional Yoruba lifestyle in terms of names and practices. The village observes many traditional festivals throughout the year, including those of the gods Oshun, Shango, Obatala, and Babaluaiye, among others. Its leader, His Royal Highness Oseijeman Adefumni I, received his title through self-acclamation, but was subsequently made an *oba* (traditional Yoruba ruler) in a coronation ceremony in Ile-Ife, Nigeria.

Having learned several traditional Yoruba practices from the Cuban Lucumi tradition in the late 1950s and early 1960s, Oyotunji has since attempted to define its practices along the lines of Yorubas in Nigeria. The Cuban influence continues to manifest itself within certain festival observations (like the Babaluaiye festival) and in the song repertory at the village. Oyotunji is one of many efforts in the Americas, however reinterpreted, to bridge a gap between Yorubas in the New World and those on the African continent. There continue to be many practices that are derived from Yoruba religious observances, but are not formally acknowledged in the Americas. There has been a sustained scholarly interest in these traditions since the 1960s.

Christopher Brooks

See also Aladura; Candomblé; Macumba; Ogun; Orisha; Oshun; Santeria

Bibliography

Barnes, Sandra T., ed. (1997) *Africa's Ogun: Old World and New.* Bloomington: Indiana University Press.

Bascom, William. (1969) *The Yoruba of Southwestern Nigeria.* New York: Holt, Rinehart and Winston.

Brooks, Christopher. (1989) "Duro ladipo and the Moremi Legend." Doctoral thesis, University of Texas at Austin.

Buckley, Anthony D. (1985) *Yoruba Medicine.* Oxford: Clarendon Press.

Forde, Cyril Daryll. (1951) *The Yoruba-Speaking Peoples of South-Western Nigeria.* London: International African Institute.

Zande Religion

The Zande people (often called Azande, plural) live in the very center of Africa, along the Nile-Congo (ex-Zaire) watershed, straddling the intersecting borders of the modern-day nations of the Central African Republic, the Democratic Republic of the Congo (ex-Zaire), and Sudan. Up until this century, the Zande were organized into kingdoms, in which kings and princes of noble clans (Vungara and Bandia) ruled over commoners. Families lived in scattered homesteads grouped loosely around the prince's court. Over the last few centuries, the Zande kingdoms had been in full eastward expansion, slowly assimilating villages of neighboring non-Zande groups, which then adopted Zande language and customs. Zande kings maintained standing armies and received Arab traders and European explorers and, later, ambassadors at their royal courts, which were social and political centers of a blossoming Zande civilization, complete with bodyguards, courtiers, and harp-playing minstrels. The more or less simultaneous arrival of Belgian, French, and British colonizers at the end of the nineteenth century disrupted Zande expansion. As treaties were signed (and at least one Zande king forcefully deposed), European military officers, administrators, and traders penetrated Zandeland, and were soon followed by Christian missionaries.

Over the past eighty years or so, as a result of Protestant and Catholic evangelization efforts, traditional Zande beliefs have undergone radical change, making the task of describing "Zande religion," already complex, even more problematic. Still, it is possible to describe traditional, pre-Western Zande religion, thanks to the ample writings of British social anthropologist E.E. Evans-Pritchard, as well as other authors who lived in or visited Zandeland in the early twentieth century. Those accounts are generally supported by oral traditions of elderly Zande interviewed in the early 1980s who grew up in areas of Zandeland where traditional beliefs held sway until just a few decades ago. Furthermore, in spite of the influx of Christian dogma, traditional beliefs are still firmly anchored in Zande thought and behavior, justifying a description of those beliefs in the present tense.

Traditional Zande Beliefs

One of the first things to remark about the Zande is that they are a relatively secular people. Several of the hallmarks of "religion" are absent, or nearly so: prayer, sacrifice, a sense of awe during rituals, organized "church," things sacred, beings divine. Rather, the Zande seek explanations and remedies for illness and misfortune, sanctions for wrongdoing, means of controlling their world, and a feeling of *communitas* in witchcraft, magic, and—at least in the past— witch doctors' seances, all of which involve fellow humans. Some people have special (usually malevolent) powers, but they are nonetheless flesh and blood men and women. Accordingly, beliefs in a Supreme Being or in supernatural spirits (one of the primary criteria in definitions of religion) only infrequently intrude into daily life.

Witchcraft and Magic

For the Zande, virtually all misfortune is the result of the ill will of a fellow human being, either a witch (*mbe-mangu*) or a magician/sorcerer (*mbe-ngua*). Witches are born with a witchcraft organ (*mangu*) in their abdomen, which gives them the power to cause harm to others, from crop failures and unsuccessful hunting expeditions to serious illness and death. The witchcraft organ is activated by feelings of jealousy, spite, anger, greed, and other such emotions. In the past, autopsies were performed on deceased who were suspected of being witches, underscoring the belief in a physical witchcraft organ.

Magicians, on the other hand, are made, not born. They have no innate powers, but rather, during long apprenticeships, learn how to use plants (*ngua*) and other objects to work spells to cause harm or to do good, such as bring about cures of illness or good crop harvests. The Zande word *ngua* literally means "plant," but, because of the various powers of plants (curative, toxic, and "magical"), it is also used to refer variously to remedies, drugs, poison, and magic or sorcery. Evans-Pritchard categorized users of *ngua* into two groups: (good) magicians and (bad) sorcerers, in order to show the very wide range the term *mbe-ngua* (users of plants) can cover.

Witchcraft and magic are considered to be invisible "mystical causes" which set off the visible "sensitive cause" of events. For example, to use Evans-Pritchard's classic example, if a granary collapses, killing the people resting beneath it, the sensitive cause would be the termites that have obviously eaten away the wood of the posts. But only a mystical cause—witchcraft or magic—would account for the granary falling down at that particular moment while those particular people were resting in its shade, causing their deaths. The two causes are needed conjointly to result

in injury or harm: witchcraft or magic is what triggers accidents and illness, eventually causing death.

If someone has experienced a series of misfortunes or is seriously ill, he or she, or a family member, consults an oracle (*ka soroka*) to find out who is causing the misfortune or illness. An oracle is an object which has an inherent power (which, according to Evans-Pritchard's informants, is referred to as its *mbisimo*, "soul") to answer yes/no questions about the workings of invisible, mystical forces. There are many types of oracles and they range greatly in prestige and reliability. The Princes' poison oracle consisted of dropping a small amount of *benge* (*Strychnos icaja*) into the mouth of a chick; if the chick lived, the answer was yes, if it died, the answer was no (or vice versa, depending on the phrasing of the question). Oracles can also be simple devices that anyone can use, such as inserting two leafy twigs into a termite mound; if the one on the right is eaten first, the answer is "yes," the one on the left, "no" (or vice versa).

Once the witch (or magician) is designated, he or she is approached and asked to withdraw the harmful influence. If negotiations are successful (often involving uncovering hidden feelings of jealousy, or bringing hard feelings into the open to then resolve them), the run of failure ends, or the person gets well. A person accused of witchcraft can blow out water to prove his or her innocence, proclaiming aloud that if his/her witchcraft organ had caused harm, it would from then on cool off and remain cold, and the situation would return to normal. If the misfortune or illness continues, however, it means that the search must continue to find the witch responsible. When a person dies in spite of very energetic searches to find the person responsible and have him/her withdraw his/her evil influence, vengeance is enacted with the aid of special vengeance magic to hunt down and kill the witch or magician responsible.

An important public figure in Zande villages was the *binza*, translated by Evans-Pritchard as "witch-doctor." These men underwent years of training to learn to use the plants that would enable them to cure illness and relieve misfortune by locating and combating witchcraft; they ate certain plants to increase their power and to protect themselves from witches. A homestead which felt itself under a mystical threat would engage a witch doctor to conduct a seance to clear the air of witchcraft. The witch doctor, dressed in skins and feathers and armed with amulets, magic whistles, and pouches of special potions, danced a characteristic dance (*avure*), which involved wild and spectacular movements, and which revealed the mystical source of the misfortune. A witch doctor's dance was also required before collective undertakings to avert possible mystical mishaps. These popular seances were very important social events and public affirmations of the belief in witchcraft.

A *Binza Avule* (traditional shamanic healer) dancing an an *Avule* seance in Zaire in 1972. PHOTO COURTESY OF MANFRED KREMSER.

Mbori

The word *mbori* is customarily translated as "God," and many authors claim that belief in God has always been a crucial part of the Zande belief system, among them missionaries Reverend Gore and Monsignor Lagae, and administrator Captain Philipps, all of whom lived in Zandeland early in the twentieth century. However, though the subject is controversial, it can be argued that the Zande have never—traditionally—had much to do with an all-powerful Supreme Being.

Evans-Pritchard, for one, questioned claims that a godlike Supreme Being played an important role in Zande life. Although the frequent use of the word *mbori* was interpreted by some as evidence of prayer and worship, the term could just as easily be translated by "luck" or "fate": "The utterance of the man whose hens had disappeared, 'Oh, Mbori, you have not done well with me', ought, I consider, to be translated in our own idiom, 'Oh, I never have any luck', and we ought not to suppose that he was attributing to

the Supreme Being guardianship of his fowls or believed that if there had been divine intervention he would not have lost them" (Evans-Pritchard 1936: 172–3).

Rather than a pervasive, awe-inspiring, revered god, *mbori* was a somewhat distant, hazy, vague notion called upon from time to time when other means of explanation or control were useless or unavailable. Evans-Pritchard observed that the Zande called upon *mbori* only when anxious or fearful, and that "he" was seen as a sort of last resort. He further suggests that "*Mbori* furnishes a remote cause for anything and everything in the world. It is the horizon of Zande thought, an ambient haze into which every chain of causation ultimately fades" (201).

Though now associated with the Christian God of the heavens, *mbori* used to inhabit the heads of streams. According to some accounts, once a year, but especially in times of drought, people carried out the *maziga* ceremony at the heads of streams where *mbori* lived, making offerings of fruits, sweet potatoes, manioc, eggs, and other foodstuffs. Even today, elderly Zande concur, stating that before the missionaries arrived, *mbori* lived at the heads of streams and not in the sky. But heads of streams are also the favorite haunts of ghosts; in folktales, they are spooky places where spirits of the dead abound and serve as an entry to the underworld. In fact, Evans-Pritchard and others have noted that *mbori* was identified with the ghosts of the ancestors, and may in fact have been considered to be "a vague generalized unity of the ghosts departed" (199), or "a sort of generalized ghost" (200).

It might even be possible to suggest that the very word *mbori* is relatively new. Supporting evidence for this is found among the neighboring and closely related Nzakara people. (The Nzakara and Zande could actually be considered a single society, as their languages have only separated in the past five hundred years or so, and they share so many cultural traits.) In the Nzakara language, the ideas of "outside," "world," and "fate" are represented by a single term, *zagi*. Christian converts among the Nzakara now also use the same term to refer to "God," as there is no other Nzakara word for Supreme Being. In the Zande language, the word *zagi* also means "outside" and "world"; but the Zande, somewhere along the line, seem to have acquired a different term, *mbori*, to refer to "fate," and, nowadays, to "God."

The occurrences of the word *mbori* in age-old Zande trickster tales also lead to questions about its original meaning. It appears in the plural form, takes the third-person animal pronoun, and occurs with both kinds of possessive (*gi mbori* and *mbori-re*). It is only relatively recently, with the arrival of Christianity (and, in eastern-most areas, Islam), that *mbori* became singularized, masculinized, and capitalized into *Mbori*, or God.

ZANDE ON THEIR RELIGION

An elderly Zande man in Ngouyo (100 km north of Zemio) offered this account in the mid 1980s:

A long time ago, there was no religion (*pa mbori*, "matters of 'God'"). There was no religion here, here in Ikpiro's territory. We consulted our rubbing-board oracle, and danced our diviner's dance (*avure*), to see what was causing illness. When you were very sick, they danced *avure* for a long time, and they said what it was, and whatever the witch-doctor (*binza*) said, that's what they did so you would be saved. If the rubbing-board [oracle] was consulted, whatever it said they would do, and you would be saved. If the thing was still very serious, they went to seek *benge*, to consult (*soroka*) it about your condition, they took many chicks to drip *benge* into their mouths and then [the chicks] revealed the affair that was causing your death. Whether it was somebody, whether it was in your very own homestead, they would see it, they would know it. These are things of the past, that our forefathers used to do, when there was no religion. (Labanga)

A Zande man from Kitessa (45 km east of Zemio) gave the following account of the new role of the Nagidi:

Here among us, in Africa, the thing that was most common in the past among our forefathers was *benge*, consulted by putting it into the mouths of chickens. But nowadays, that no longer exists. What we use today is this: we cut the neck of a chicken, while addressing it [*sima ru*], so that if the answer to the question is 'yes', the [dying] chicken falls with its left wing topmost. Also, we go to the Nagidi. One goes there and explains the matter, and she sees a dream [*masuma*] about it. If you are not the guilty party, she says, no, it's not you. And if it is you who are responsible, the dream tells her that as well. (Gbaya)

A *Binza Avule* in trance during a *Avule* seance in Zaire in 1972. PHOTO COURTESY OF MANFRED KREMSER.

Ancestors and Ghosts

The Zande believe that the soul continues to live on after death. As long as the souls of the departed are remembered, they remain individualized and continue to play a role in the lives of the living. They are offered libations at a special shrine (*tuka*), though this custom is rapidly disappearing. But after a few generations, when no one is alive who remembers them, they fade into a sort of collective mass of ancestors' spirits or ghosts (*atoro*) that is sometimes associated with *mbori*. "[Zande] ideas about the ghost of a father are comparatively sharp and definite but ghosts genealogically further removed tail off into the notion of Mbori. Their individuality is lost and only the notion of Mbori remains to account for them" (Evans-Pritchard 1936: 199).

Like *mbori*, the ghosts are associated with calamities and misfortune that befall the entire community rather than individuals, events for which witchcraft cannot be responsible, such as drought. They remain placated and harmless if treated with respect, and if the proper offerings are made to them regularly. But they tend to be feared and viewed as malevolent, for they only come to the fore at times of misfortune.

Ghosts (used to) communicate with the living through "ghost-diviners [*aboro-atoro*, or *aira-atoro*]." These "are people who are able to communicate with the ghosts of the dead, usually through dreams, and are generally women" (177). It is the ghost-diviners, for example, who revealed when and where the yearly *maziga* ceremony should be conducted. However, opinions vary as to whether they communicate with ghosts or with *mbori*, for, as we have seen, "Azande make no clear conceptual distinction between the Supreme Being and the ghosts and these notions overlap one another" (198). Furthermore, Father Giorgetti cites Zande as saying that the ghost-diviner "is capable of knowing the evil acts committed by living persons, because he has been to where the ghosts of the ancestors live with God" (Giorgetti 1966: 251, my translation of the original Zande text).

"Modern" Zande Religion

After nearly a century of the progressive infiltration of Christian missions (and, in the Sudan, Islam), many Zande—most, according to some sources—have converted to Christianity, whether Catholicism or a Protestant sect. But beyond conversion to foreign religions, the traditional belief system itself is being adapted to include an omnipotent, omniscient, omnipresent, and moral Supreme Being who can see into the soul of an individual.

Perhaps the most striking development is a new Zande "church," founded in the 1950s by a woman named Marie Awa. She began to preach a new religion called Nzapa Zande (*Nzapa* is "God" in Sango, the national language of the Central African Republic) after dying when rocks rained down upon her and then coming back to life. The new religion spread as other "prophetesses" (so-called in the local French), or Nagidi, started their own congregations and followed Awa's teachings. Bagidi, or male prophets, also exist, but they are few and far between. The new church composed of these congregations is called Mission ti Afrika, and is headquartered just outside of Zemio, in the Central African Republic.

This new religion is a sort of hybrid that incorporates on one hand, the new concept of *Mbori* and the rituals and doctrine of Christianity, and, on the other, traditional Zande etiology. Grootaers describes the Mission ti Afrika as being elaborately organized, both spatially and with regards to hierarchy. In the larger towns churches similar to those of Christian denominations have been built, with areas marked off for certain officials and rituals. Regular and lengthy services are held, complete with sermons, hymns, prayers, processions, and consultations about individual problems.

But besides being religious leaders, the Nagidi (and Bagidi) fulfill the function of oracles. People who have experienced misfortune come forward at the appropriate time during the service to explain their problems, such as a bad harvest, infertility, failure at school, or repeated unsuccessful hunting expeditions. The Nagidi, after solitary reflection, "reads" the answer in the palm of her hand (whence the title

Nagidi, which means, literally, "she who reads") and advises the people concerned how to correct their ills. However, whereas oracles have an inherent power to discern witches and sorcerers, the Nagidi insist that they are merely the spokeswomen for *Mbori*, who alone can see into the hearts of men and women. Parenthetically, it is interesting to view these "new" prophetesses as continuing the tradition of (female) ghost diviners, the difference being that the former communicate with *Mbori*, while the latter communicated with the ghosts of the dead.

A second phenomenon that has become rampant in at least certain parts of Zandeland over the past few decades is that of the *kpiri*, said to be men who turn into crocodiles to kill their victims by drowning. In the past, death by drowning, as any death, was commonly attributed to witchcraft, but nowadays, a drowning would likely result in accusations of *kpiri*. Grootaers suggests that "kpirism" is replacing both witchcraft and magic as cause for misfortune in general, and has documented several recent *kpiri* trials in eastern Central African Republic.

Conclusion

As the power of the Zande royal clans diminished under colonial rule, and Western religions and economic practices were introduced, the Zande belief system evolved accordingly. Witch doctors were patronized by, and yet counterpoint to, the ruling noble clans, whose poison oracles also kept a lid on witchcraft; they maintained a politico-spiritual balance of power, so to speak, hinging on the belief in organic, psychic witchcraft. The demise of the Zande royal courts, and the social structure they supported, was accompanied by that of the witch doctors. At the same time, as new political, juridical, and economic orders took hold, the private use of individual magic to achieve personal goals and to exact vengeance soared, all the more so as unequal economic and educational opportunities led to the success of some and the failure of others.

The Nagidi of the new Mission ti Afrika have come to fill at least two traditional roles, even for Catholic and Protestant converts, who officially have nothing to do with Nzapa Zande. First, these prophetesses function as traditional oracles; they reveal the mystical causes for personal misfortune. However, they do so in a new way: through revelation from an omniscient Supreme Being. Second, they are public affirmations of beliefs in "mystical causes," as witch doctors' seances once were.

Finally, though specific beliefs have shifted, there still lives a deep-seated conviction that fellow humans, rather than the devil or other supernatural beings, are responsible for evil, and more effort is made to unmask evil human culprits than placating supernatural beings. The growing number of *kpiri* accusations reinforces the idea that people—rather than supernatural beings—are responsible for misfortune.

Margaret Buckner

Bibliography

Buckner, Margaret. (1995) "Modern Zande Prophetesses." In *Revealing Prophets: Prophecy in Eastern African History*, edited by David Anderson and Douglas Johnson. London: James Currey, 102–121.

Evans-Pritchard, E. E. (1937) *Witchcraft, Oracles and Magic among the Azande*. Oxford: Clarendon Press.

Evans-Pritchard, E. E. (1936) "Zande Theology." *Sudan Notes and Records* 19, 1: 5–46 (reprinted in 1962, *Essays in Social Anthropology*. London: Faber and Faber).

Giorgetti (Gero), Fr. Filiberto. (1966) *La Superstizione Zande*. Bologna: Editrice Nigrizia.

Grootaers, Jan-Lodewijk. (1996) "A History and Ethnography of Modernity among the Zande (Central African Republic)." Ph.D. dissertation, University of Chicago.

Lagae, Rev. C. R. (1920) "Les Azande sont ils animistes?" *Sudan Notes and Records* 3, 3: 143–156.

Zar

The term *zar* refers both to a type of spirit and to various practices associated with those spirits, which are common in much of northern Africa and the Middle East. Multifaceted phenomena, *zar* rituals combine music, drama, and political and social resistance, with ideas about sickness and healing and a particular understanding of the human body in relation to its wider social and religious world. *Zar* is clearly related to neighboring beliefs and practices in western and eastern Africa, particularly *bori* and *pepo*. While there are important similarities in *zar* practice and belief over a very wide area, significant ceremonial and cosmological differences are found, as well as variations in the sort of people attracted to *zar*. Most frequently found in Muslim societies, *zar* is also found among Christians, Falashas, and indigenous religions. Although frequently characterized as attracting poor, illiterate women, *zar* is practiced in wealthy, educated circles (such as the salons of contemporary Kuwait) and among predominantly male adherents (such as in Iran or the delta region of Egypt). As a set of beliefs, *zar* is generally shared by men and women, but ritual practices are most commonly dominated by women. While there is some debate about its origins, it is striking how *zar* persists in vig-

orous and dynamic form throughout this area, showing no sign of disappearing in the face of formal literacy, biomedicine, and other forms of Western capitalism.

The etymology of the term *zar* is obscure. Many writers, following Cerulli (1936), suggest it was an Amharic word, probably derived from the Cushitic supreme god, *djar* in Agau, which in Christianized Abyssinia became a malevolent spirit. It has also been suggested that the word is Persian (Modarressi 1968: 150; also Frobenius 1913), while Zwemer (1920: 228) and others associate the term with the Arabic *ziyara*, to visit. It also appears in various Arabic forms, reflecting local usage: *zaar, sar, tsar, dar, uzr*.

It seems increasingly evident that *zar* activities and beliefs are part of a highly complex and elaborate system of knowledge that is both widespread and probably very old in Africa (Ranger 1993). However, no description of it as *zar* is found in the written record before the early nineteenth century. That was probably when, in the armies of the Ottoman empire, specific *zar* practices spread through much of the Middle East and began to assume many of the distinctive traits that persist till today.

Historical Evidence

The earliest known mention of the term "zar" is from Gondar, Ethiopia, at the beginning of the nineteenth century, when the term was used to designate a category of spirits in an Ethiopian translation of Isaiah 34:14 (Natvig 1987: 676; after Rodinson 1967: 239). The earliest recorded accounts of *zar* also come from Ethiopia, in 1838: in April from Adowa, by the French traveler Antoine d'Abbadie (cited in Tubiana 1991: 20); and in October from Ankober, Shewa, when missionaries John L. Krapf and Charles W. Isenberg actually observed a *zar* ceremony in the house where they were staying. A woman suddenly broke into song and apparently entered a state of trance, which they were told was caused by *sar* (pl., *sarotsh*) spirits. A few years later (1843–7) W. Plowden described a procession of *zar* drummers from near Lake Tana, while another traveler, Mansfield Parkyns (1868), compared such practices to what he had observed in Sinnar, Sudan (cited in Constantinides 1991).

The earliest account from Egypt and Sudan was left in the 1860s by Dr. C. B. Klunzinger (1878), quarantine officer for the Egyptian government. He traveled widely in Upper Egypt, where by this period, *zar/sar* was widespread. Indeed, he noted that the Egyptian government had attempted, unsuccessfully, to ban *zar*.

By the 1880s, *zar* was also common in Arabia. Snouck Hurgronje (1931: 100–3) included a detailed description of *zar* ritual in his account of the diverse society in Mecca. Stimulated by his view that it spread from an Abyssinian/

Ethiopian origin, much of the early academic discussion about *zar* focused on its source of origin. Other writers felt that the complexity of *zar* beliefs and practices suggested a more syncretic derivation.

In the twentieth century *zar* was clearly widespread in the Middle East, having been described from Iran (Marsden 1972: Modarressi 1968), Iraq (Ilyas 1977), Bahrain (Dykstra 1918), Yemen (Ingrams 1949, Muammar 1988, Myers 1947, Stone 1985), Kuwait (Ashkenani 1991, Kline 1963, Rashida 1988), Muscat (Lutton, cited in Zwemer 1920: 234), Oman (Thomas 1931: 261), and Qatar (El-Islam 1974). It has been even more richly described from northeast Africa: Egypt (notably Fakhouri 1968, Kahle 1912, Kennedy 1967, Littman 1950, Morsy 1991, Natvig 1988, 1991, Nelson 1971, Saunders 1977), Sudan (Barclay 1964, Boddy 1988, 1989, Constantinides 1978, 1991, Kenyon 1991, 1991b, 1995, 1999, Makris 1996, Makris and al-Safi 1991, al-Nagar 1975, 1987, Seligman 1913, Trimingham 1949, Zenkowsky 1950), Ethiopia and Eritrea (Leiris 1958, Lewis 1983, Messing 1958, Morton 1977, Rodinson 1967, Trimingham 1952, Young 1975), and Somalia (Lewis 1969, 1986, Luling 1991). The close relationship of *zar* to west African *bori* is clearly elaborated in accounts by Abdalla (1991), Kramer (1993), and Last (1991).

Zar as Spirit

Zar spirits are often referred to as "wind" (Arabic. *rih*, cf. Hausa *iskoki* and Swahili *pepo*), usually distinguished as "red wind," *al-rih al-ahmar*, a term preferred by orthodox Muslims who denounce *zar* activities as anti-Islamic. Such winds are generally benign although they can bring disorder to the lives of people they actively possess and have been known to cause fatal problems. *Zar* spirits may be appeased through ritual means but are never exorcised. They remain with their host and often coexist with other distinct *zar* guests. *Zar* have distinctly human (rather than divine or spirit) origins. Several authors record the origin of *zar* spirits as grounded in holy texts, reinforcing their close relationships to human ancestors. For example, according to Abyssinian myth (which closely parallels a Hausa myth accounting for the origin of *bori* spirits), Eve gave birth to thirty children in the Garden of Eden. When God entered the garden to count them, Eve hid the fifteen most intelligent and beautiful. By way of punishment these remain forever hidden as "creatures of the night," the *zar* spirits. These envy their human brothers and sisters, the "children of the light," for their visibility, even though the latter are weaker and uglier (Messing 1958: 1122).

A Sudanese myth grounds the origin of *zar* in Islamic theology. *Zar*, along with other spirits like *djinn* (which may

or may not be conceptually distinct), are believed to be under the sway of the prophet Sulayman. He ordered them to descend to earth, but they refused. They said that they would only come down to the smell of incense and the sound of drums (al-Nagar 1987: 95). This tale underscores the capricious and disobedient nature of *zar* but also shows their love of beauty and cleanliness. Invisible and incorporeal, *zar* spirits recognize no physical boundaries (cf. Boddy 1989: 273). Yet each spirit has a name and/or social identity, and is associated with distinctive dress, food, perfume, incense, musical preferences, origin and history, and even individual habits and temperament. They are also social beings. *Zar* spirits represent both collective (tribal or ethnic groups) and individual entities. Like *pepo* spirits, *zar* are seen as having distinct foreign origins, reflecting the historic consciousness and social experiences of local communities. Through ritual enactment, *zar* spirits are characterized as strangers who are both dangerous and fascinating, outsiders and yet familiar, nonhuman and yet human. Some *zar* communicate verbally through the host they possess. Others make their wishes known only indirectly, through the medium of the *zar* leader.

Zar spirits are believed to dwell under the earth or water, until one of their manifestations takes up residence in a human body. This occurs for a variety of reasons. Possession may be inherited; and most commonly this is through the matriline, often (though not exclusively) from mother to daughter. Spirits may also be contagious; a guest at a *zar* ceremony recognizes they may be particularly vulnerable to possession.

Zar as Organized Ritual

Until recently there has been no overriding cult organization in *zar*. Rather it has been organized into local ritual groups around a leader (most commonly in Arabic, *shaykh*, fem., *shaykha*, though also often referred to as the mother or father) who partly inherits, partly earns her/his position. Usually middle-aged, she spends several years apprenticed to an older leader, after her special powers have been revealed. In turn she is helped by trainees, others with revealed spiritual powers who are responsible for drumming, serving refreshments, and administering fumigation, and who themselves are acquiring *zar* powers to be leaders. Each *zar* group is different, drawing its profile from both the heritage of the leader and from individual experiences in *zar* within the group. In recent years, efforts have been made to collectivize *zar* practice. In Sudan, for example, an association of *zar* Shaykhs was formed in the late 1980s (Hurreiz 1991: 152), and, more recently, leaders are required by law to seek a license for their ritual activities.

In some areas more than one form of *zar* is distinguished. In the early twentieth century, people in Sudan believed in several types of *zar*; in contemporary Sudan, people distinguish between *bore zar* and *tumbura zar*. They share a belief in the same type of spirit, but the identities of the spirits differ and the ritual and organization of the two types are also different. In particular, all *tumbura zar* groups share a belief that they are all related to the *tumbura* group of Khartoum North, while *bore* groups are all autonomous. They also have a hierarchy of male and female leaders not found in other types of *zar*. They claim that *tumbura zar* is harsher, more difficult, than *bore zar*, and this is commonly explained as "*bore* is feminine, *tumbura* is masculine." It has been suggested (Kenyon 1991, Makris 1996) that *tumbura* is rooted in Central African (particularly Zande) practices, whereas *bore* is more closely related to practices in Egypt. Today in Sudan, women possessed by *bore* spirits occasionally socialize with those in *tumbura*, and in this way strengthen their own spiritual powers. In Eritrea, by contrast, two forms of possession, *buda* and *zar*, are clearly related, but are in a state of total hostility so that the former attack and eat the latter (Tubiana 1991: 19).

Zar ritual operates on several different levels. Informally, when a person is troubled by a problem thought to be *zar*-related, she may have a variety of symptoms, which do not respond to diagnosis and treatment by medical practitioners.

> They forced me to marry my husband. . . . After two months of marriage, I was sleeping one night and in the middle of the night I found in my dress a bunch of cats and mice. . . . I ran out of the house. . . . My husband . . . came and sat beside me on the bed. We both stayed in the bed for forty days. . . . I felt pressure on my throat and I hallucinated. Sometimes I was happy and sometimes I used to scream and yell. I felt that my whole body was aching, I felt in a daze. I used to drink water and sugar and I don't know what else I used to eat. My husband took me to the doctor. The doctor told him that I only had a slight fever. But I knew that it was not a fever at all, I had *uzr* . . . [that came] from Sidi Ibrahim and from the Sayed il Badawi. (Morsy 1991: 199)

Instead, she seeks help from a leader in *zar*, often in an ongoing fashion. Depending on the region, and partly on local custom, this may be in the patient's home, in the leader's home, or in a special house of *zar* kept by some leaders to separate their spiritual activities from their domestic life. On a more complex level, regular meetings (weekly or sometimes more frequently) are held to summon spirits, through burning the appropriate incense, through drum-ming and song, and/or preparing suitable refreshments, particularly coffee and cigarettes. Human guests attend to ask the summoned spirit questions about matters of concern to them and their families.

The formal level of ritual is always elaborate and less frequent. One form is associated with a healing ceremony, sponsored by a patient and her family and lasting for several (typically seven) days. They include animal sacrifice and extensive feasting, the summoning of several (often all) *zar* spirits, and varied dramatic and musical performances that have clear historic, political, and aesthetic dimensions:

> The rhythm intensifies; the *ayana* [patient] rises to dance. Now visible over her *tob* is a red sash attached to a reddish waist cloth in the style of a Sam Browne belt. She is possessed, my companions say, by *Khawaja* (Westerner) spirits: a doctor, lawyer, military officer—all of these at once. Yet it is the latter-most she appears to manifest in dance. Her *tob* is folded cowl-like over her head, obscuring her face; she flourishes a cane—hooked, as in vaudevillian burlesque. Her dance is a slow rhythmic walk criss-crossing a chimeric square, feet first moving side to side, then forward and back. With a leap of the imagination she is an officer of the desert corps conducting drill. Every so often she bends rigidly at the hip and, cane pressed to forehead, bobs her torso up and down. I am told that her spirits have requested the white *tob*, cane cigarettes, "European" belt, and, yet to be purchased, a radio. (Boddy 1989: 126)

The focus of the ritual is on the well-being of the patient, on appeasing the spirits who are troubling her, and on seeking a solution to specific problems. The other major form of ritual is linked to important religious calendar events, including the Christian new year and the Islamic month of *Rajab*. These occasions are sponsored by the *zar* leader, supported by all those she has previously helped. They also commonly last up to seven days, and include sacrifice and theatrical forms, but the focus is on participants' relationships with the whole panoply of *zar* spirits.

Conclusion

In the face of various attempts to ban them, popularize them, professionalize them, diminish them, and control them by state and government authorities, *zar* beliefs and practices show great resilience and relevance over a very wide area for the many people who continue to draw support from them. It is striking how, in the face of serious opposition, *zar* beliefs are actually spreading into geographic areas where they were previously not reported, while *zar* practices are being reinterpreted and enjoyed as forms of traditional folk-culture, sometimes alongside the more serious rituals which continue to treat the sick and pay homage to the spirits. *Zar* continues to generate various academic theories purporting to explain its origins, its persistence, its dynamism, its creativity, and its effectiveness, even as it continues to provide meaning and power for large numbers of people in the face of rapidly changing surroundings.

Susan M. Kenyon

See also Religion and Healing in Sub-Saharan Africa

Bibliography

Abdalla, Ismail H. (1991). Neither Friend nor Foe: The *Malam* Practitioner—*yan bori* Relationship in Hausaland. In *Women's Medicine: The zar-bori Cult in Africa and Beyond*, edited by I. M. Lewis, A. al-Safi, and Sayyid Hurreiz. Edinburgh: Edinburgh University Press, 37–48.

Ashkenani, Zubaydah. (1991) "Zar in a Changing World." In *Women's Medicine: The zar-bori Cult in Africa and Beyond*, edited by I. M. Lewis, A. al-Safi, and Sayyid Hurreiz. Edinburgh: Edinburgh University Press, 219–229.

Barclay, Harold. (1964) *Burri al-Lamaab: a Suburban Village in Sudan*. Ithaca, NY: Cornell University Press.

Boddy, Janice. (1988) Spirits and Selves in Northern Sudan: The Cultural Therapeutics of Possession and Trance. *American Ethnologist* 15, 1: 4–27.

———. (1989) *Wombs and Alien Spirits*. Madison: University of Wisconsin Press.

Cerulli, Enrico. (1936). "Zar." *Encyclopaedia of Islam*. London.

Constantinides, Pamela M. (1977) "Ill at Ease and Sick at Heart": Symbolic Behavior in a Sudanese Healing Cult. In *Symbols and Sentiments*, edited by I. M. Lewis. New York: Academic Press, 61–83.

Constantinides, Pamela M. (1991) "The History of *Zar* in the Sudan: Theories of Origin, Recorded Observation and Oral Tradition." In *Women's Medicine: The zar-bori Cult in Africa and Beyond*, edited by I. M. Lewis, A. al-Safi, and Sayyid Hurreiz. Edinburgh: Edinburgh University Press, 83–99.

Dykstra, Mrs Dirk. (1918) "Zeeran." In *Neglected Arabia* 107: 17–23.

Fakhouri, Hani. (1968) "The Zar Cult in an Egyptian Village." *Anthropological Quarterly* 41, 1: 49–56.

Frobenius, Leo. (1913) *The Voice of Africa*. London: Hutchinson.

Gordon, D. H. (1929) "The Zar and the Bhut: A Comparison." *Man* 110: 153–155.

Hurgronje, C. Snouck. (1931) *Mekka in the latter part of the Nineteenth Century*. Leiden: Brill.

Hurreiz, Sayyid. (1991) "Zar as a Ritual Psychodrama: From Cult to Club." In *Women's Medicine: The zar-bori Cult in Africa and Beyond*, edited by I. M. Lewis, A. al-Safi, and Sayyid Hurreiz. Edinburgh: Edinburgh University Press, 147–155.

Ilyas, muti Yusif. (1977) "al-Zar baina 'l-raks a-sha bi wa'l-khurafa" [Zar between popular dance and fiction]. In *al-Turath al-sha bi majalla filkluriyya* [Baghdad] 11: 51–54.

Ingrams, Doreen. (1949) *A Survey of Social and Economic Conditions in the Aden Protectorate*. Asmara.

El-Islam, M. Fakr. (1974) "Culture Bound Neurosis in Qatari Women." *Social Psychiatry* 10: 25–29.

Kahle, Paul. (1912) "Zar-Beschworungen in Egypten." In *Der Islam* 3: 1–41, 189–90.

Kennedy, J. G. (1967) "Nubian Zar Ceremonies as Psychotherapy." *Human Organization* 26, 4: 186–194.

Kenyon, Susan M. (1991) *Five Women of Sennar: Culture and Change in Central Sudan*. Oxford: Clarendon Press.

———. (1991b) "The Story of a Tin Box: *zar* in the Sudanese town of Sennar." In *Women's Medicine: The zar-bori Cult in Africa and Beyond*, edited by I. M. Lewis, A. al-Safi, and Sayyid Hurreiz. Edinburgh: Edinburgh University Press, 118–136.

———. (1995) "Zar as Modernization in Contemporary Sudan." *Anthropological Quarterly* 68, 2: 107–120.

———. (1999) "The Case of the Butcher's Wife: Illness, Possession, and Power in Central Sudan." In *Spirit Possession, Modernity and Power in Africa*, edited by Heike Behrend and Ute Luig. Madison: University of Wisconsin Press, 89–109.

Kline, Nathan S. (1963) "Psychiatry in Kuwait." *British Journal of Psychiatry* 109: 766–774.

Klunzinger, C. B. (1878) *Upper Egypt: Its People and its Products*. London.

Kramer, Fritz. (1993) *The Red Fez: Art and Spirit Possession in Africa*, translated from the German by Malcolm Green. London and New York: Verso.

Last, Murray. (1991) "Spirit Possession as Therapy: *bori* among non-Muslims in Nigeria." In *Women's Medicine: The zar-bori Cult in Africa and Beyond*, edited by I. M. Lewis, A. al-Safi, and Sayyid Hurreiz. Edinburgh: Edinburgh University Press, 49–63.

Leiris, Michel. (1958) *La Possession et ses Aspects theatraux chez les Ethiopiens de Gondar*. L'Homme: Cahiers d'ethnologie, de geographie et de linguistique. Paris: Plon.

Lewis, Ioan M. (1969) "Spirit possession in Northern Somaliland." In *Spirit Mediumship and Society in Africa*, edited by J. Beattie and J. Middleton. London: Routledge and Kegan Paul.

———. (1971) *Ecstatic Religion*. Harmondsworth, Eng.: Penguin Books.

———. (1986) *Religion in Context: Cults and Charisma*. Cambridge: Cambridge University Press.

Lewis, I. M., A. al-Safi, and Sayyid Hurreiz, eds. (1991) *Women's Medicine: the zar-bori Cult in Africa and Beyond*. Edinburgh: Edinburgh University Press.

Lewis, Herbert S. (1983) "Spirit Possession in Ethiopia: An Essay in Interpretation." In *Ethiopian Studies dedicated to Wolf Leslau*, edited by S. Segart. Wiesbaden: Harrassowitx.

Littman, Ernst. (1950) *Arabische Geisterbeschworungen aus Agypten*. Leipzig.

Luling, Virginia. (1991) "Some Possession Cults in Southern Somalia." In *Women's Medicine: The zar-bori Cult in Africa and Beyond*, edited by I. M. Lewis, A. al-Safi, and Sayyid Hurreiz. Edinburgh: Edinburgh University Press, 167–77.

Makris, G. P. (1996) "Slavery, Possession and History: The Construction of the Self among Slave descendents in the Sudan." *Africa* 66, 2: 159–182.

Makris, G. P., and A. al-Safi. (1991) "The *tumbura* Spirit Possession Cult of the Sudan." In *Women's Medicine: The zar-bori Cult in Africa and Beyond*, edited by I. M. Lewis, A. al-Safi, and Sayyid Hurreiz. Edinburgh: Edinburgh University Press, 118–136.

Marsden, D. J. (1972) "Spirit Possession on the Persian Gulf." *Journal of Durham Anthropological Society* 2: 23–42.

Messing, Simon D. (1958) "Group Therapy and Social Status in the Zar Cult of Ethiopia." *American Anthropologist* 60, 6: 1120–1126.

Modarressi, T. (1968) "The Zar Cult in South Iran." In *Trance and Possession States*, edited by R. Price. Montreal: R.M. Bucke Memorial Society, 149–155.

Morsy, Soheir A. (1991) "Spirit Possession in Egyptian Ethnomedicine: Origins, Comparison and Historical Specificity." In *Women's Medicine: The zar-bori Cult in Africa and Beyond*, edited by I. M. Lewis, A. al-Safi, and Sayyid Hurreiz. Edinburgh: Edinburgh University Press, 189–218.

Morton, Alice. (1977) "Dawit: Competition and Integration in an Ethiopian Wugabi Cult Group." In *Case Studies in Spirit Possession*, edited by V. Crapanzano and V. Garrison. New York: John Wiley, 193–233.

Muammar, Abdullah. (1988) "Zar in the Yemeni Tihama." Paper presented at the Workshop on the Spiritual Dimension in Healing: The Contribution of the Zar Cult in African Traditional Medicine. Khartoum.

Myers, Oliver H. (1947) "Little Aden Folklore." *Bulletin de l'Institut Francais d'Archeologie Orientale* 44: 177–233.

al-Nagar, Samia al-Hadi. (1975) "Spirit Possession and Social Change in Omdurman." M.Sc. thesis, University of Khartoum.

———. (1987) "Women and Spirit Possession in Omdurman." In *The Sudanese Woman*, edited by Susan Kenyon. Khartoum: Graduate College, University of Khartoum and London [Ithaca Press], 92–115.

Natvig, Richard. (1988) "Liminal Rites and Female Symbolism in the Egyptian *Zar* Possession Cult." *Numen* 35, 1: 57–68.

———. (1991) "Some Notes on the History of the Zar Cult in Egypt." In *Women's Medicine: The zar-bori Cult in Africa and Beyond*, edited by I. M. Lewis, A. al-Safi, and Sayyid Hurreiz. Edinburgh: Edinburgh University Press, 178–188.

Nelson, Cynthia. (1971) "Self, Spirit Possession and World View: An Illustration from Egypt." *International Journal of Social Psychiatry* 17.

Ranger, Terence. (1993) "The Local and the Global in Southern African Religious History." In *Conversion to Christianity*, edited by Robert Hefner. Berkeley: University of California Press, 65–98

Rashida, Maryam. (1988) "Zar in Kuwait: Types of Zar and Traditional Folk Medicine in Kuwait." Paper presented at the Workshop on the Spiritual Dimension in Healing: The Contribution of the Zar Cult in African Traditional Medicine. Khartoum.

Rodinson, Maxime. (1967) *Magie, Medecine et Possession a Gondar*. Paris: Mouton & Co.

Saunders, Lucy W. (1977) "Variants in Zar Experience in an Egyptian Village." In *Case Studies in Spirit Possession*, edited by V. Crapanzano and V. Garrison. New York: John Wiley, 177–191.

Seligman, Brenda Z. (1914) "On the Origin of the Egyptian Zar." *Folklore* 25: 300–323.

Stone, Francine, ed. (1985) *Studies on the Tihama Expedition 1982 and Related Papers*. Burnt Mill.

Thomas, Bertram. (1931) *Alarms and Excursions in Arabia*. London.

Trimingham, J. S. (1949). *Islam in the Sudan*. London: Frank Cass.

———. (1952) *Islam in Ethiopia*. London: Oxford University Press.

Tubiana, Joseph. (1991) "*Zar* and *Buda* in Northern Ethiopia." In *Women's Medicine: The zar-bori Cult in Africa and Beyond*, edited by I. M. Lewis, A. al-Safi, and Sayyid Hurreiz. Edinburgh: Edinburgh University Press, 19–33.

Young, Allan. (1975) "Why Amhara get Kureynya: Sickness and Possession in an Ethiopian Zar Cult." *American Ethnologist* 2, 3: 567–584.

Zenkowsky, Sophie. (1950) "Zar and Tambura as Practiced by the Women of Omdurman." *Sudan Notes and Records* 31, 1: 65–81.

Zwemer, Samuel M. (1920) *The Influence of Animism on Islam*. London: Central Board of Missions and Society for Promoting Christian Knowledge.

Zimbabwe Assemblies of God Africa

Zimbabwe Assemblies of God Africa (ZAOGA) is one of Africa's most significant Pentecostal movements. It numbers 300,000–400,000 members in Zimbabwe and has branches in at least a dozen other African countries. Its social sources derived from the artisans and casual workers who lived in Harare and Highfields townships in Zimbabwe's capital during the late 1950s. The movement itself emerged from the South African-derived Pentecostal church, the Apostolic Faith Mission (AFM). A collection of young Pentecostal zealots—Joseph Choto, Raphael Kupara, Lazurus Mamvura, James Muhwati, Priscilla Ngoma, Caleb Ngorima, and Abel Sande—formed a prayer band and choir around the charismatic evangelist, Ezekiel Guti. This semi-autonomous group was expelled from the AFM in 1959 following a struggle with missionaries and an older male faction of the black leadership. The group subsequently joined the South African Assemblies of God of Nicholas Bhengu in association with the Pentecostal Assemblies of Canada. Once again they were expelled, and in 1967 they formed their own organization, Assemblies of God, Africa (AOGA).

The movement expanded along migrant labor networks into other Zimbabwean towns and cities as well as into Mozambique, Malawi, and Zambia. In the 1970s, Guti began to cultivate links within the American Bible Belt after studying at Christ for the Nations Institute (CFNI) in Dallas in 1971. After Zimbabwean independence in 1980 the movement mushroomed on a transnational scale, renaming itself Zimbabwe Assemblies of God Africa. Under the guise of the Forward in Faith Ministries International, it established itself in Botswana, South Africa, Rwanda, Zaire, Tanzania, and other African countries, and founded assemblies in the former colonial power, Britain.

Over its three decades and more of existence ZAOGA has undergone a profound transformation. The movement, which had begun like most sects as a collection of young zealots rebelling against what they perceived to be corrupt and spiritually dead religious establishments, has changed into a respectable, disciplined denomination with a rich associational life with youth, womens, and mens organizations, backed by a complex but personalized bureaucracy. Its formerly egalitarian structures of government have been replaced by an authoritarian hierarchy and personality cult centered on Guti, who, today, is formally addressed as Archbishop but popularly referred to as the "Prophet and Servant of God" or the "Apostle." The movement's desire to articulate popular sentiments is now matched by a search for respectability. ZAOGA leaders have begun in the 1990s to explore ways of making political capital out of their enormous membership. Politicians from the ruling party,

ZANU/PF, are invited to church functions, and ZAOGA sporadically adds its voice to government proclamations on moral issues. Thus, what was once a world-retreating township-based sect with strong links to rural Zionist-type independency, has transformed itself into a modern electronic church, part of the global born-again movement. The leadership's former aversion to jewelry, make-up, and fancy clothes, which marked their sectarian status, has given way to an embrace of the opportunities of the material world, and an espousal of an Africanized prosperity gospel.

These transformations are products of a variety of processes. First, ZAOGA has modernized by drawing upon external ideas and resources, even if this aid has remained unacknowledged, even suppressed, in the church's official history. From the outset the movement's founders had the support of influential white patrons as well as Pentecostal missionaries. More significant was Guti's period of study at CNFI in Dallas. The Institute became a dynamo for charismatic and Pentecostal advance, not just in America but also Africa, Asia, and Latin America. Guti's stay there gave him a clearer perception of the global born-again movement and its dynamics. It provided him with a pool of resources and a huge range of international contacts that he used to modernize the movement.

ZAOGA has also evolved by virtue of its own doctrines. Its teaching of sobriety and industry, its emphasis on clean-cut appearance and respectability, and its promotion of self-help and penny capitalism have enhanced the social mobility of its members and attracted aspirant Christians from the historic mission churches.

ZAOGA's phenomenal growth has not been without conflict. Guti's access to foreign resources provided him with a source of patronage with which to consolidate his control over the movement. In the 1980s and 1990s he edged out his cofounders and replaced them with his kin, his Ndau ethnic group, and businessmen. Moreover, as the movement has expanded across social classes and categories, it has become a microcosm of wider society and shares many of its tensions. Conflict between rich and poor is often expressed in theological terms as a clash between the prosperity gospel and an older populist Pentecostalism that values the socially humble person as more receptive to the gospel. More sophisticated members of the movement have become increasingly outspoken about the personality cult surrounding Guti.

David J. Maxwell

Bibliography

Maxwell, David. (1998) "'Delivered from the Spirit of Poverty'?: Pentecostalism, Prosperity and Modernity." *Journal of Religion in Africa* 28: 350–373.

———. (1999) "Historizing Christian Independency: The Southern African Pentecostal Movement 1908–1950." *Journal of African History* 40: 234–264.

———. (2000) "'Catch the Cockerel Before Dawn': Pentecostalism and Politics in Post-Colonial Zimbabwe." *Africa* 70.

Zionist Churches

"Ethiopianism" denotes a type of religious movement found among sub-Saharan Africans. It is associated with the first movement for religious and political freedom during the colonial era. Its origins are found in the 1880s in South Africa. African mission workers began to found independent all-African churches. Some of these early churches were the Tembu tribal church founded in 1884 and the Church of Africa in 1889. An African former Wesleyan minister, Mangena Mokone, first used the term when he founded the Ethiopian Church in 1892. There were a number of causes for the emergence of Ethiopian Churches. Primary among these was the frustration of Africans at being denied advancement in the mission churches and the color bar in general in South Africa. Additionally, Africans understand-

ably wanted a version of Christianity that was relevant to their beliefs and practices. In sum, Africans desired a more African church, one that would help restore tribal life and aid in bringing about political and cultural autonomy. The slogan "Africa for the Africans" and the word "Ethiopianism" perfectly express these desires.

Missionary opposition to African leadership and their raising of the color bar upset many Africans who turned to the new independent churches. Although they originated in the countryside, these churches spread rapidly to more highly settled areas.

The millenarian nature of these African independent churches disturbed missionaries, settlers, and administrators. Thus, there were efforts to curb them. Independent churches, in fact, subverted the norms of the colonial ethos and helped lead to its overthrow

The power of the term Ethiopianism came from the fact that the Bible mentions Ethiopia and an Ethiopian Church. The most significant Biblical passage is Psalms 68: 31: "princes shall come out of Egypt; Ethiopia shall soon stretch out her hands unto God." Moreover, when Christian Ethiopia defeated the Italian army at Adwa in 1896, Ethiopianism took on even more power. It came to symbolize the ancient dignity of Africa, as well as the place Africa should have in the modern world. God's choosing of ancient

---

EXTRACTS OF A SPEECH BY NELSON MANDELA AT THE ZIONIST CHRISTIAN CHURCH EASTER CONFERENCE

Moria, 20 April 1992

Your Grace Bishop Barnabas Lekganyane, head of the great Zionist Christian Church;

Reverend Gentlemen, Members of the ministers' council and Elders of the ZCC;

President F W de Klerk;

Chief Mangosuthu Buthelezi;

Congregants, Fellow worshippers and friends;

Permit me, Your Grace, to thank you for your kind invitation to attend your Easter Conference here at the holy city of Moria. Moria, a tabernacle erected by the Zionist Christian Church as a site of annual pilgrimage and renewal! I am honoured that you have invited me on this occasion to pay my respects to the leadership and the members of this mighty church on the sub-continent. Since my release from prison, I have attempted to find a time suitable to both myself and His Grace, Bishop Lekganyane, so that we could confer about our common aspirations and the challenges facing our nation in these trying times.

My coming here today is a long-awaited moment. I come to the Holy City of Moria as a pilgrim, with other pilgrims, senior members of the African National Congress, as a mark of respect and as an act of communion.

We have joined you this Easter in an act of solidarity, and in an act of worship. We have come, like all the other pilgrims, to join in an act of renewal and rededication.

We pray with you for the blessings of peace! We pray with you for the blessings of love! We pray with you for the blessings of freedom! We pray with you for the blessings of reconciliation among all the people of South Africa!

Khotso e be le lena! May peace be with you!

When Bishop Engenas Lekganyane founded this church in 1910, that occasion represented an important act of the oppressed to resist the theology of submission. It was an act of self-assertion on the part of a people who were expected to remain unheard and unseen while they ministered to the needs of others.

In its own way, the Zionist Christian Church was expressing what we of the ANC, two years later, tried to assert and have fought to entrench, as the basis of the politics of our country. That principle, so eloquently simple but yet so profound, has moved thousands through the ages to strive for a better world. We restate it today for emphasis: The brother and sisterhood of all human beings, and the common fatherhood of God Almighty!

The ZCC is part of that rich tapestry of experience, culture, and life style that make up all our people today. Both as a church and as individual members, you have lent your efforts to bring justice to our land. We applaud in particular your role in the trade union movement in pursuance of workers' rights. The struggles of our people for land and against apartheid-inspired land robbery—the forced removals—would be poorer were it not for the contribution of congregants of this church. We acclaim also the role played by ZCC businesspeople, who in the teeth of the discriminatory policies of the Pretoria government ran successful enterprises providing jobs and trade in far-flung villages.

The bond between you and the ANC is even clearer, when we consider that many members of our organisation belong to the Zionist Christian Church. Among them, Peter Mokaba and Ngoako Ramatlhodi, who are with us today, grew up and have become what they are in the struggle in great measure inspired by your teachings. Many others have fallen in struggle. Many have been subjected to terms in jail. But their spirit remains with the people.

Khotsong Masione! Peace be with you!

Those who are denied their just claims to the land of their birth come to you for solace!

Those condemned to the low wages and denied their rights as the creators of wealth look to you for spiritual leadership.

Those cast out into the darkness and bitter loneliness of poverty and depravation lean on you for sustenance.

Those whose homes and families have been destroyed so that the ugly designs of racial oppression may be realised, have come to you for comfort.

Those who are denied a voice in governing of their country because they are black turn to you for inspiration.

You have engendered high standards of morality and discipline in an era characterised by racism, poverty, and imposed powerlessness. It is because of these qualities, embodied in this mighty church, that year after year millions gather at Moria for this act of spiritual renewal.

On behalf of the African National Congress, we have come here in all humility to break bread and worship with you. To join you in this sacrament of spiritual rejuvenation.

Khotso e be le lena! May peace be with you!

The role your church can play is more crucial in these difficult times. The violence that is wrecking our country, tearing our communities apart from places far and wide, is a scourge that must be ended now! On the Witwatersrand, in Natal, in the eastern Transvaal we have been driven from our homes.

Uxolo Mazayoni! Khotsong Masione! May peace be with you!

Source: www.anc.org.zr/andocs.

I FOUND JESUS OVER IN ZION

I found Jesus over in Ziyun,
An' He's mine, mine, mine, mine, mine;
I found Jesus over in Ziyun,
An' He's mine, mine, mine, mine, mine.

I found the Holy Ghost over in Ziyun,
An' He's mine, mine, mine, mine, mine;
I found the Holy Ghost over in Ziyun,
An He's mine, mine, mine, mine, mine.

I got sanctified over in Ziyun,
An' it's mine, mine, mine, mine, mine;
I got sanctified over in Ziyun,
An it's mine, mine, mine, mine, mine.

I got baptized over in Ziyun,
An' I'm saved, saved, saved, saved, saved;
I got baptized over in Ziyun,
An' I'm saved, saved, saved, saved, saved.

He's mah Savior, He's mah Savior—
Of, He's mine, mine, mine, mine, mine.
He's mah Savior, He's mah Savior—
Yes, He's mine, mine, mine, mine, mine.

Source: Grissom, Mary Allen. (1969[1930]) *The Negro Sings a New Heaven: A Coleftion of Songs by Mary Allen Grissom.* New York: Dover Publications, 89.

Ethiopia, or Kush, became tied to a promise to redeem modern Africa and free it from its oppressors.

African churches materialized in many other African areas. They did so for the same general reasons, adapted, of course, to local conditions. In Nigeria there was an explosion of independent churches. The Native Baptist Church (1888), the formerly Anglican United Native African Church (1891) and its later divisions, and the United African Methodist Church (1917) were only a few important independent churches. In Cameroon there was the Cameroon Native Baptist Church (1887). Ghana had the Native Baptist Church (1898). In Rhodesia there was a branch of the African-American denomination, the African Methodist Episcopal Church, as well as the African Methodist Church (1947). Kenya had the Kenyan Church of Christ in Africa (1957).

These early Ethiopian or Zionist Churches amalgamated a number of elements, including tribalism, nationalist, and Pan-African movements and sympathies. Their close ties with independent African-American churches combined with their association with "back to Africa" advocates in America provided further ideas. Edward Wilmot Blyden and Joseph Ephraim Casely-Hayford of Ghana, who were leaders of the Pan African Union movement, provided further fuel for the Ethiopian movements.

Independent churches, in fact, were involved in the Zulu rebellion of 1906 and in the Nyasaland rising of 1915. John Chilembwe, founder of the independent Providence Industrial Mission, took a leadership role in the latter movement. Beginning in about 1920, Ethiopian churches came to be identified as Zionist churches. Christianity and African popular religion began to form a syncretistic union.

Current Beliefs and Practices

The Zionist Church is the largest denomination in South Africa. It has about seven million members. It is a powerful force within South Africa. Combining Christian belief with traditional beliefs and practices involving ancestral veneration and witchcraft has enabled it to become a societal organization more powerful even than labor unions or, indeed, any other civil organization.

Zionist Churches practice exorcism as part of a healing ritual. Belief in the devil has always been part of traditional Christianity as well as African spirituality and experience. In Africa, illness is generally taken to result from a lack of harmony involving people and spiritual forces. Healing results from the restoration of equilibrium through rituals, ceremonies, sacrifices, medicine, and other means. Africans, therefore, place a great deal of emphasis on maintaining equilibrium in all aspects of life—social relationships included.

Many practices of African Zionist Churches can be traced to the Christian Catholic Church in Zion, founded by John Alexander Dowie in Illinois in 1896; and the Apostolic Faith Mission, brought to South Africa by John

Lake, Thomas Hezmalhalch, and others. These movements supported faith-healing and presented Christ as a type of medicine man or healer. Additionally, they did not seek to hide Biblical references to possession by evil spirits or the presence of evil sorcerers. Their African converts adapted these practices for African needs. F. S. Edwards (1989: 210) notes that:

> The face-value similarities with the New Testament accounts may be an added incentive to prophet healers of the Zionist-type independent churches to make a specialty of healing, or attempting to heal, cases of *amafufunyana* spirit possession by exorcism in the name of Jesus, along with other supportive forms of treatment. The challenge is particularly attractive because the phenomenon of spirit possession "straddles their traditional religious world-view and their Christian experience."

An essential part of the healing service of the Zionist is confessing one's sins publicly and declaring ill health. This ritual is called *ukuhlambuluka* (*hlamba* = to clean or to clear). It creates a feeling of trust and mutual dependence. It creates an atmosphere in which members feel safe in supporting each other. People feel cleansed, and they express their joy in being cleansed through singing and dancing. Confession is an integral part of the curing process. Those who fail to confess everything and acknowledge their guilt fail to be cured.

African beliefs adapted to the Zionist system encourage a belief in spirit possession. This belief system holds that *ukufa kwabantu*, that is, ubiquitous evil forces and evil spirits, cause diseases. The Zionist Church has become a haven of harmony, and, therefore, it is a place to hide from evil spirits. The church protects people from these unruly forces.

An example of the function and roles played by Zionist churches in South Africa is provided by the more than twenty KwaMushu Zionist congregations (called bands) near Durban in the KwaMushu area. Most member of these bands are Zulu and a major function of the bands is to provide healing powers and rituals to cure spirit-induced illness. And, they serve other functions as well, including providing economic assistance to members and enhancing social cohesion by providing a framework for adult interaction within the bounds of the church's teaching.

Because Zionist men often perceive themselves as social loners, they tend to be ineffective recruiters in the "missionary outreach" efforts of the church. However, women are less socially isolated and mingle more freely with non-Zionists and this makes them better recruiters but also makes them more vulnerable to mystical experiences and to harm caused by evil spirits. This means that the churches must then organize and manage healing rituals to cure the women. These rituals are more than healing rituals, as they attract non-Zionists and thus serve also as recruitment events. In addition, the healing rituals strengthen the churches, as interaction is increased between the minister and congregation and the ceremony also gives the minister public authority, which serves to limit the influence of the prophets, who maintain their status by revealing visions and through their charismatic personalities.

The Zionist churches also perform an economic role in the KwaMushu area and tend to attract the poor, as the Zionist themselves are poor. Despite their poverty, the bands organize their resources to assist the membership and in some sense form a social welfare system of their own. For example, they maintain a form of insurance to take care of births, marriages, and deaths.

Thus, the KwaMushu bands are part of a modern world religion but they also help their members in dealing with traditional problems as well as working to maintain harmony in the community and encouraging all to work toward common goals.

Meaning of Zion

There are a number of different views regarding who or what Zion may be. In one view, the congregation is the New Jerusalem and the ministers are Zion. In another view, both the congregation and the ministry form Zion. And there are other interpretations as well, with opinions differing from group to group.

It is certain that there are four hills in Jerusalem, and Zion is one of these hills. It was the site of King David's palace. The Bible, which Zionists follow avidly, calls this palace the City of David and Zion. Sometimes, Jerusalem was mentioned as Zion. At times, the faithful were termed children of Zion. Early Christians adopted this perspective and called the early Church the New Jerusalem. Thus, since the Bible often uses the terms Zion and Jerusalem interchangeably, the term became used by Zionists for their church.

Zionists tend to follow this train of thought and then note that the Holy Spirit on Pentecost breathed life into the apostles and their associates and established Zion on Earth. Thus, the gifts of the Spirit, especially speaking in tongues and other spectacular manifestations, have become important to the Zionists. Zionists believe that this true church of the early Christians was lost in succeeding generations. A false way of worship came into being. It is their task to restore pure Zionist Christianity.

Restoration of the church, however, is inextricably tied in with the end of the world. When that church is established, the Lord will return so that all can see his power. He will return in His resurrected glory and gather his followers to him.

This millenarian belief fuels much of the power of Zionism as it forges close ties among the members who are awaiting the end of the world. During the colonial and apartheid eras there were many attempts to control and even end the Zionist Churches. Their power and ties with American Churches made them a formidable social force. Their African roots and nationalistic ideals aided the African nationalist movement and subverted the ideology of colonialism and apartheid. Their syncretistic melding of African and Christian beliefs has found a powerful response in African religious sentiment.

The power of the Ethiopian and Zionist movement has spread beyond South Africa. Similar churches have made great advances in Nigeria, for example, and Ghana. A search for a more African style of Christianity has even found a welcoming response in more mainstream versions of Christianity. Catholic charismatics, for instance, share many of the same beliefs as Zionists. Rather than lose members of their congregations, the more traditional churches have welcomed many aspects of Zionist Churches, seeking to harness them in their own cause.

Conclusion

The Ethiopian Churches and their Zionist offspring have been a powerful force in emancipating African Christianity from its European dominance. Directly, the independent churches have enabled Africans to assume leadership positions in their own religious denominations. They have provided a link to early forms of Christianity in which Africans played prominent parts. These movements, moreover, have given Africans a means to gain self-respect in periods when their contributions were being systematically denied by racists.

Using their religious base, moreover, Ethiopian and Zionist Churches have exerted powerful political influence. They were involved in a number of anticolonial and antiapartheid movements and riots. Their members, moreover, numbering in the millions, bring their values and directives into play in all aspects of civil life. Thus, both directly and indirectly, Zionist Churches exert an enormous influence on African religious and civil life today, carrying on a tradition that goes back into the late nineteenth century.

Frank A. Salamone

See also AIC; Aladura; Pentecostalism in Africa

Bibliography

Anderson, Allan. (1992) *Bazalwane—African Pentecostals in South Africa.* Pretoria: University of South Africa.

Anderson, Neil T. (1990) *The Bondage Breaker.* Portland: Oregon Harvest House.

———. (1991) *Released from Bondage.* San Bernardino, CA: Here's Life Publishers.

Andersson, Efraim. (1968) *Churches at the Grassroots.* London: Butterworth.

Beattie, John, and John Middleton. (1969) *Spirit Mediumship and Society in Africa.* London: Routledge and Kegan Paul.

Burger, Isak. (1987 [1960]) *Die Geskiedenis van die Apostoliese Geloof Sending van Suid-Afrika (1908–1958).* Braamfontein: Evangeliese Uitgewers Collectio Rituum.

Daneel, M. L. (1971, 1974) *Old and New in Southern Shona Independent Churches,* 2 vols. The Hague: Mouton.

Dickason, C. Fred. (1987) *Demon Possession and the Christian.* Chicago: Moody Press.

Fisher, J. D. C. (1970) *Christian Initiation: The Reformation Period.* London: Alcuin Club for the Society for Promoting Christian Knowledge.

Josephus Flavius. (1960) *Complete Works,* translated by William Whiston. Grand Rapids: Kregel Publications.

Kerkbode, Die. (1993) "Kan 'n Christen deur 'n bose gees beset word?" (29 October).

Kiernan, J. P. (1996) *The Production and Management of Therapeutic Power in Zionist Churches within a Zulu City.* Lewiston: Edwin Mellen Press.

Koch, Kurt. (1970) *Occult Bondage and Deliverance.* Berghausen: Evangelization Publishers.

Lagerwerf, Leny. (1987) *Witchcraft, Sorcery and Spirit Possession.* Gweru: Mambo Press.

Mostert, J. P. (1987) "Men of 'The Spirit'—or of 'Spirit'?" In *Religion Alive,* edited by C. G. Oosthuizen. Johannesburg: Hodder and Stoughton.

Oosthuizen, G. C. (1988) "The Interpretation of and Reaction to Demonic Powers in Indigenous Churches in South Africa." *Missionalia* 16, 1.

———, ed. (1989) *Afro-Christian Religion and Healing in Southern Africa.* Lewiston: Edwin Mellen Press.

———. (1992) *The Healer-Prophet in Afro-Christian Churches.* Leiden: Brill.

Storm, Rachel. (1993) *Exorcists—The Terrifying Truth.* London: Fount.

Sundkler, B. G. M. (1961) *Bantu Prophets in South Africa.* London: Oxford University Press.

Subritzky, Bill. (1985) *Demons Defeated.* Chichester: Sovereign World.

Whyte, H. A. Maxwell. (1974) *A Manual on Exorcism.* Monroeville: Whitaker House.

Zulu Religion

The Zulu are a nation of Nguni-speaking people whose area is now known as the province of KwaZulu-Natal, South Africa. The region is conventionally called Zululand. The Zulu are culturally related to the Swazi and Xhosa peoples. There are about nine million Zulu, making them the largest African ethnic group in South Africa. They are grain farmers who also raise herds of cattle. Shaka, the leader of the Zulu clan of the Nguni and later known as the "Black Napoleon," united them into a new nation in the early nineteenth century. They were a powerful force in the region and were feared by their neighbors whom they raided for cattle. However, they lost much of their power and wealth in the nineteenth century wars with the Boers and then the British, who defeated them in the Zulu War of 1879–1880.

Zulu religion reflects their patrilineal kinship organization and belief system and also the importance of cattle in Zulu culture. Much ritual activity centers on cattle—protecting cattle and producing sufficient rainfall—and important sacrifices require the sacrifice of cattle. The belief system centers on ancestor worship and a creator god and witches and sorcerers are the primary forms of religious specialists. Mirroring Shaka Zulu's political centralization, the king is in charge of all magic, rainmaking and other rites that have national significance, making him a priestly ruler. Rituals at important times, such as planting season, famine, drought, or war, again reflect the central importance of the royals. These rituals focus on the royal patriline.

Christianity entered Zululand with the first missionaries who arrived in 1835, with Roman Catholicism, the Anglican Church and other denominations now represented. Christianity in Zululand is notable for the large number of African Independent Churches, and about 50 percent of the Zulu are classified in 2000 as Christians, although for many Christianity is practiced alongside the traditional religion. Prophets predominate in the area and many are known for their great influence and wealth.

Izangoma, or healers, still maintain an honored role in Zulu society, and Christians, as well as traditionalists, frequent them, seeking their services. These healers treat both individual illnesses, such as headaches or fevers, and communal diseases, such as the drifting away of the community from its ancestors and losing of their guidance and protection. Izangoma prescribe treatments according to the nature of the illness. Thus, they may advise ritual treatments of song, dance, and prayer, or herbal recourse.

Zulu believe that izangoma are essential to maintaining a community's health, performing rituals, communicating messages from ancestors to a community, and bringing together visible and invisible realms. They, in sum, reinforce the unity of the community, reminding people that it consists of past, present, and future members. It is the izangoma who use the repetition of familiar songs and dances to preserve shared memories. Their songs, moreover, promote harmony, a harmony that is expressed in the complex harmonies of their songs.

Interestingly, the vast majority of izangoma are women; estimates range to about 95 percent. Moreover, this aspect of Zulu religion is one that helps empower women. Women have been in the forefront of those who bewail the ancestor neglect that they see as leading to the problems of Zulu society. These problems, furthermore, are considered a form of social disease. Health is not, for the Zulu, simply a physical ailment. It results from lack of harmony, whether social or physical. Zulu believe that evil results when supernatural spirits desert some aspect of a community because of that community's neglect. The gods are not malicious, but they will cease to protect a people who have forgotten them.

This belief is central to Zulu cosmology. Zulu, like many Africans, believe in a balanced world system. Their

A Zulu boy participates in a community ritual as adult men clap to the music in front of their beehive dwelling in Kwazulu, South Africa. PHOTO COURTESY OF FRANK A. SALAMONE.

ZULU MEDICAL PRACTICE

The method of the native doctor, then, in fighting disease is to deliver a fierce frontal attack against each symptom individually, which, as we may readily imagine, to one so innocent of the nature, strength, and position of the enemy, must often result disastrously. A patient down with severe dysentery that will tolerate no checking, he will proceed to drench at once from above and below with a combination of the most drastic astringents varied with a dose of the most drastic purgatives.

In spite of such blind empiricism it cannot be denied that the native doctor does sometimes work a cure, sometimes quite a startling cure, where the efforts of European physicians have proved utterly unavailing. Remedies he has, as we shall see, without number, and some of them truly helpful, suited to every ill—physical, mental, moral and social—that man is heir to. Frequently it is to these we may attribute his success; but not so in those phenomenal cases above referred to.

In the opinion of the writer the secret of many Kafir cures, and, it may be added, of many Kafir ailments, is not in the action of matter on matter, of drug on flesh, but in those occult regions where mind works on mind and mind on flesh.

It is not the quack's innocent mixture of tap-water and burnt sugar that drives out the malady, but that powerful battery of mental forces—confidence, imagination and will—hitherto inert within the patient's own self, and which the quack has so cunningly, and in the case of Kafir doctors, perhaps quite unconsciously, excited to activity by his convincing volubility and inspiring methods. We often say the native is favoured with remarkably recuperative powers. Are these attributable solely to a more robust physical system, and not rather, in a very large degree, to his possession of a mind working in more perfect harmony with the requirements of the body?

Source: Bryant, Alfred T. (1966) *Zulu Medicine and Medicine-Men.* Cape Town: C. Struik, 16.

---

origin myth, for example, has two (or three) great spirits who remain to this day. There is one male and one or, some say, two female gods. There is a balance of male and female energies. Both energies are required for creation. The male spirit, Mvelingqangi, is appropriately, austere, fierce when necessary, and, of course, virile. The Zulu depict him as striding in the heavens. His glory streams from him and thunder accompanies his movements. He takes any lesser female spirits that he desires as consorts.

Although his daughter, Nomkhubulwane, is more accessible, the Zulu believe that their gods must be approached through ancestral spirits. Nomkhubulwane's symbol is the rainbow, and the snake, especially a two-headed one, is her envoy. Light, rain, and fertility are her domains. She is perpetually a virgin who considers all Zulu female children as her daughters. Zulu believe that when neglected she walks away and causes droughts, storms, terrible winds, and exhausted, barren soil.

Frank A Salamone

See also Pentecostalism in Africa; Zionist Churches

Bibliography

Bryant, Alfred T. (1970 [1909]) *Zulu Medicine and Medicine Men.* Cape Town: Struik.

Gluckman, Max. (1935) "Zulu Women in Hoecultural Ritual." *Bantu Studies* 9: 255–271.

Kalweit, Holger. (1992) *Shamans, Healers, and Medicine Men,* translated by Michael H. Kohn. Boston: Shambhala.

Krige, Eileen Jensen. (1950) *The Social System of the Zulus.* Pietermaritzburg, South Africa: Shuter and Shooter.

Ngubane, Harriet. (1977) *Body and Mind in Zulu Medicine.* London: Academic Press.

Pettersson, Olof. (1973 [1953]) *Chiefs and Gods: Religious and Social Elements in the South Eastern Bantu Kingship.* Praetoria: University of South Africa Press.

Thorpe, S. A. (1991) *African Traditional Religions: An Introduction.* Pretoria: University of South Africa.

Appendix A.
The Anthropology of Religion in Africa: A Critique of Concepts and a Model

According to Dan Sperber, anthropology wastes time by mistaking local phenomena for universal concepts and then inconclusively wrestling with such questions as, "What is totemism? Sacred kinship? Do all cultures have myths? A form of science? What is the function of witchcraft? What are the differences between religion and magic? Possession and shamanism?" All these questions, he says, are ill posed because they are framed in interpretive terms. "There is no a priori reason to assume that these terms correspond to homogenous and distinct classes of phenomena, i.e., to potential objects of scientific inquiry" (Sperber 1987: 29). This is a disturbing critique.

Let us consider a particular field of such pseudoconcepts and pseudoquestions. It has become conventional in anthropology dealing with Africa to distinguish between witchcraft and sorcery. People writing new monographs feel that they have to observe this convention, even if they are writing in French, which lacks corresponding words. The distinction is borrowed from the Azande (Zande) of the Sudan, described for us by Evans-Pritchard, who thinks that a witch has an innate, mystical power to harm others; this power may operate without his knowledge, although the witch is able to cool his witchcraft by a prescribed ritual, when his attention is

drawn to the fact. On the other hand, a sorcerer is one who deliberately uses a quasi-technical device, external to himself. This distinction I shall call the distinction of means, mystical versus technical. It is important to the Azande because it differentiates two kinds of accusations and two likely outcomes for the accused: witches, after performing the cooling exercise, are let off, but sorcerers are punished (Evans-Pritchard, 1937). The distinction is regularly attributed to Evans-Pritchard himself, although he is merely reporting one made by the Azande. (See for example Middleton and Winter 1963: 2; Arens 1980: 169.)

Now in fact the anthropologist is unable to tell whether anyone is a witch or a sorcerer. To determine the presence of the phenomenon one must observe that the concept exists, distinct from other concepts, and that it is applied as a label to some apt individual by an approved social process. If the people in question do not distinguish witchcraft from sorcery it makes no sense for the anthropologist to do so by attempting to sort into Azande categories diverse and conflicting statements about how witches are supposed to operate.

The same kind of criticism is applicable to other contrasted terms such as spirit possession and spirit mediumship, ancestors and shades, spirit possession and soul loss

(Lewis 1971: 46, 51). None of these pairs is related to any of the available bodies of theory in social science by which we might be able to comprehend its nature and occurrence. As Augé says about "sorcery," monograhs that deal with it are based on an implicit scheme taken for granted; their descriptions and analyses illustrate an absent theory. A contradiction emerges between the supposed unity of the phenomenon described and the variety of functions attributed to it (Augé 1975: 85).

An alternative approach rests on the recognition that the ethnographer's primary material is social action, including verbal utterances in which are implicit on the one hand the philosophical and cosmological assumptions of the actors and, on the other, the political and economic constraints under which they act.

Social action is cooperative, and presupposes clues between the actors that identify the play to be performed. The decision as to which play is performed involves choice and is essentially political. For that reason, the conceptual distinction between one standardized behavior sequence, or play, and another is likely to be much clearer than the conceptual consensus about the content and meaning of any particular play or its performance. Herein lies the usefulness to the anthropologist of the distinction the Azande make between witchcraft and sorcery; it is question of which script they are to follow, rather than whether X in fact did what sorcerers are supposed to do, or even whether all are agreed what it is that sorcerers do, or whether witchcraft is hereditary, and so on.

Looking again to the Azande, we find that the set of choices that includes witch and sorcerer is incomplete without witchdoctor and magician, who are also distinguished from each other by the criterion of means. Like the witch, the witchdoctor is endowed with *magnu*, or witchcraft, substance, whereas sorcerer and magician rely on external devices. The difference between witch and sorcerer, on the one hand, and witchdoctor and magician, on the other, is a function of another criterion, that of legitimacy, a difference between approved and disapproved.

The four roles in the Azande set are thus differentiated by two intersecting criteria, the distinctions of means and legitimacy. This is the structure of the set of roles, a set of normative prescriptions for social action. This abstract set of relationships, of differences, is the proper object of anthropological study, rather than "witchcraft" or sorcery" conceived as single, universally identifiable, empirical realities.

The set of dealers in the occult recognized by the BaKongo of western Zaire is entirely different. Occult power is called *kindoki*, and four kinds are recognized, belonging to the chief, diviner, magician, and witch (these terms are convenient substitutes for, rather than translations of, the Kongo terms) (Buakasa 1968; MacGaffey 1970a). The structure of the set becomes evident to the anthropologist in the discriminatory comments people make to influence his judgment, or the similar remarks that healers make in order to define themselves in the eyes of their clients. The BaKongo distinguish private from public ends, and destructive and productive effects, that is, powers of life or death. Chiefs and witches kill, diviners supposedly use their powers in the public interest, whereas witches and magicians are egotistical. It is important to note that these definitions are functions of normative judgments, not descriptions of real behavior.

An example of the kind of verbal discrimination one encounters in the field was provided in an interview with a magician, published in the Kinshasa press in 1997. The man said, "In principle, a good healer does not kill. He should think of healing. Hence the longstanding discord between *nganga-buka*, 'sorciers guérosseurs,' and *ndoke*, 'sorciers maléfiques.'" He went on to say, "I am sometimes accused of asking excessively high prices," thus acknowledging the selfish component in the definition of the role to which he aspired. Most of what is known as healing in contemporary Kongo consists of little besides the claim by one wishing to be known as a healer that healing has taken place, and acceptance of that claim by others in accordance with the distinctions of ends and effects.

It follows from what has been said that BaKongo make no distinction between "witchcraft" and "sorcery." They are aware of both kinds of means as components of *kindoki*, but attach no significance to the difference. It also follows, in a formal sense, that whereas the minimal definition of Zande "witchcraft" is "a mystical power used illegitimately," the minimal definition of Kongo witchcraft is, "destructive power used for personal ends." The use of English expressions such as "witchcraft" and "magic" tends to conceal the fact that the Zande and Kongo concepts to which they are applied have nothing in common. Cross-cultural searchs for social and psychological correlates to these expressions is absurd, since their application has to do with English-speaking cultures.

It may be objected that what any two different peoples say about antisocial occultists is similar enough that we can use the word witchcraft with reasonable assurance that we will understand each other (Needham 1978: 42). In both instances, let us suppose, witches fly about at night, have red eyes, and appear upside-down in photographs. The trouble is that any two phenomena can be shown to have attributes in common, if the lists of attributes are made long enough. Proceeding on the basis of haphazardly selected attributes, we group heterogeneous phenomena in the same class, and perhaps exclude others that belong there. The total description of any single element is impossible, since different informants give somewhat different accounts of it.

The principle of comparative work, that only sets of elements can be compared and not elements in isolation, has long been accepted in kinship studies; nobody now studies the avunculate with reference to the kinship system to which the mother's brother belongs. It is not generally accepted in the anthropological study of religion. Arguing in favor of such an approach, Malcolm Crick points out that "witchcraft," like "totemism," is a term and a concept rooted in a specifically European conceptual field; where the conceptual field is radically different, as between the English in the seventeenth century and the Azande in the twentieth, "we could not reasonably expect to find the same phenomenon and so the one term should not be used twice" (Crick 1976: 112).

Typology of African Spiritual Practice

Identification of the Kongo set of religious commissions permits various interesting departures, of which I will mention only the fact that it brings order to the other world as well, the land of the dead. Verbal labels for descriptions of the several classes of the dead are largely interchangeable; attempts to classify the spirits according to purely verbal statements by informants lead to no clearly defined concepts. The various spiritual beings are most clearly distinguished by their roles, that is, by the activity pattern imposed on people by their perceived relationship to one or another class; so, an ancestor is an ancestor because he is addressed by his descendants. As Weber said, "[The] abstract conceptions becomes really secure only through the continuing activity of the 'cult' dedicated to one and the same god — through the god's connection with a continuing association of men, a community for which he has special significance as the enduring god" (Weber 1963: 10). Vansina, who is very skeptical about the notion of religious "systems," writes of the Tio, who are neighbors of the BaKongo:

What then had informants in common? Basic notions as to who the sorts of spirits were and what they were responsible for in terms of situations and rituals held in common; ritual action presupposed some common acceptance of the presence of other worldly spirits and they were named in it. Therefore all held this too in common. But once they went beyond this, everyone was free to believe what he wanted to. The Tio had no sacred books, no dogma, no catechism, no compulsion to believe the same things as long as they participated fully in the same rituals. (Vansina 1973a: 227)

This comment refers simultaneously to the impossibility of defining a nonliterate religion as a system of ideas, and the possibility of defining it as a system of behavior. In Kongo, as among the Tio, the four classes of the dead, corresponding to the ritual congregations of the living, are ancestors, ghosts, local or "nature" spirits, and charms. Ritual thus produced order in the domain of myth.

The perception of structures of difference provides us with endogenous categories in which to discuss historical change and variation within and between particular societies. For synchronic comparison, an example of a similar structure is provided by the Bolia group of western Mongo in Zaire, who recognize four types of living agents of the power called *iloki*, obtained from spirits through the mediation of ancestors. These agents are the political chief, the earth chief, the witch, and the magician. The cultural content of the set is very similar to Kongo, as is Bolia social structure (Van Everbroeck 1961).

Much further afield, among the Tonga of Zambia, described by Colson (1962), the cultural similarities are not quite so marked, but the role set is the same. From Colson's work we also learn the important lesson that the terms used for rainmaker, for example, are not constant from one part of the country to another. Linguistic analysis, that is to say, is no substitute for sociological analysis. Colson also shows how in recent times the functions of local priest have been partly taken over by prophets, whose local affiliations are less marked, although they too, like the priests, speak for communal spirits called *basangu*. In other words, the persistence of the category and function does not mean that the cultic content is fixed.

Tonga "local," "rain," or "earth" shrines are associated with the *basangu*, spirits originating from first settlers and believed to have power only in their own localities. Prophets were not so confined, though they too spoke for and were possessed by *basangu*, and were themselves called *basangu* and sometimes "lords of the rain." Tonga identify *basangu* with the *mhondoro* spirits of the MaShona, but in some areas *basangu* means "evil spirits" (Colson 1977; 1962: 216 note). *Basangu*, as rain spirits, "cannot be invoked as agents of individual ends. [They] concern themselves only about public matters" (1977: 124).

Tonga elders are thought to owe their survival to protective witchcraft, and are described as *basikulowanyina*, "those who bewitch one another." Colson translates *mulozi* as "sorcerer," because a *muloze* used medicines and therefore seems closer to Zande "sorcerer" than Zande "witch." "The line between having powerful medicines for protection and using these medicines against others is believed to be exceedingly thin," however. Divination performed by *munganga* is "a private consultation on behalf of an individual," whereas witch finding is a public service for which the client is the community (see also Colson, 1966). *Basangu* are supposed to be different from *mizimu*, "ancestors," but the essential difference lies in cult practice: those of the dead who might be *basangu* in another context are "ancestors" when they are addressed by kin groups (1962: 92–93).

The religious roles do not include modern "chiefs," who are government appointees. The complete Tonga set is:

	PUBLIC	PRIVATE
DEATH	elder (basikulowanyina)	"sorcerer" (mulozi)
LIFE	a. rain priest (musangu)	herbalist-diviner (munganga)
	b. prophet	
	c. witchfinder (musondo)	

On the basis of specified criteria, I have grouped the religions of the Kongo, Bolia, and Tonga as exhibiting the same structure. Another and radically different structure characterizes the religion of the Yakö of southeastern Nigeria. When Forde wrote of the "supernatural economy" of the Yakö, he referred to the choices available in a limited inventory or set, such as I have been describing:

> In the formulation and the selection of ritual action, the Yakö of Umor appear to be guided less by a sense of the logical implication of particular dogmas or of need to establish intellectually coherent relations among them, and more by the opportunities that they severally afford to allocate among specific supernatural agencies means for the achievement of particular ends of groups and persons. In other words: the various supernatural entities which have come to be established as objects of Yakö thought and ritual action are handled as a series of alternative and complementary, but at the same time largely dissociable, means for obtaining material and social benefits and for averting threats to these. Thus ritual activities seen as a whole take on something of the character of an economic system. (1964: 213)

The choices available include one between "witch" and "sorcerer" founded on a distinction of means like that employed by the Azande. As is often the case, however, it is necessary to distinguish between available roles and those that are in fact filled in the course of social action. Though the Yakö believe that sorcerers exist, and react to certain deaths in terms of that belief, no one is accused of sorcery,

so in fact the role is vacant. As a matter of social practice the religious activities of the Yakö center on matriclan shrines and diviners, both associated with life-giving powers. Sorcery is misuse of fetishes. In addition to the criterion of effects, a criterion of means is operative: witches and diviners both employ an internal, mystical capacity, whereas fetishes and shrines are external, "technical" devices.

There were two main classes of fetish objects serving as a means of access to spiritual forces. The *ase*, guardian spirits owned by the matriclans, were regarded as sentient and sympathetic beings capable of conferring benefits on the matriclans and the whole village, promoting fertility, harmony, protection, and the destruction of witches and sorcerers. Thus in the *ase* "generalized productive capacities had been mystically segregated," whereas *ndet* (punitive spirit) cults involved negative sanctions against any who threatened the social order (1964: 267). Adepts of the main *ndet* cults were recruited from local or patrilineal groups, but other *ndet* cults were owned by individuals. Anyone wishing to protect himself against theft could evoke a *ndet* to inflict on the thief a disease it controlled. The custodians of the corporate *ndet* had to swear they would not misuse them (sorcery). "*Ndet* were not thought of as primarily beneficent, for any benefit individually obtained from an *ndet* was usually that of withdrawal of the disability it was believed to control. To this extent *ndet* were completely antithetical to the *ase*, which were believed to confer health, fertility, prosperity, and peace" (1964: 278).

Witchcraft was generally believed to be inherited in the matriline, but it could also be acquired, either unwittingly or as an unintended effect of *edet* medicine. Diviners partook of the omniscience of Obasi (God), and could "see": they were initiated after a possession attack into a guide whose head was associated with the *ase* priests in the council of leaders (Yabot). The spirit world toward which cult activity was oriented is populated by Obasi, the creator; the ghosts of the recently dead; a multitude of punitive spirits (*ndet*); and the tutelary spirits of the matriclans (*ase*).

The set of cults described by Forde can be summarized in terms of contrasted values, as follows:

	MYSTICAL	TECHNICAL
DEATH	witches (yatana)	fetishes (ndet)
		a. public
		b. private
		i. legitimate
		ii. illegitimate (sorcery)
LIFE	diviners (yabunga)	matriclan spirits (ase)

This system is relatively complex, as befits the greater complexity of Yakö social organization, which includes more kinds of corporation than does Kongo. It also shows, below the level of primary categorization, two additional principles articulating hierarchically rather than orthogonally with the others. One of the primary distinctions is shared with the Zande set, the other with the Kongo:

Zande: distinctions of means and legitimacy
Kongo: distinctions of ends and effects
Yakö: distinctions of means and effects

To these we may add the Nyakyusa and related Safwa of Tanzania, who employ distinctions of means and ends (Wilson 1936; Harwood, 1970; MacGaffey 1972: 21).

Generalizations

With respect to the sets outlined above, the most conservative view would hold that each was unique, thereby denying the possibility of analytical comparison. In a less conservative perspective, culturally and structurally similar sets such as Nyakyusa and Safwa (neighbors) or Kongo and Tonga (distant but culturally related) could be regarded as being alike. We could speak of them as having "the same religion," but as having "religions of the same type" if, like the Azande of Sudan and the Kuranko of Sierra Leone (see below), they showed structural similarity with cultural difference. In the assessment of cultural similarity, language, myth, visual symbolism, historical connection, and the like will be essential factors.

Classification permits systematic rather than random comparison. If we can identify, shall we say, the Bolia and the Tonga as having the same religion, we can begin to discuss the historical origins of their beliefs and practices and compare the development of local trends. Since the Kongo set, or type, contrasts sharply with others such as the Yakö or Azande, yet is found through most of Central and much of Eastern Bantu-speaking Africa, it is presumably not a simple response to local social, political, or economic factors nor a product of any short-term history (Vansina 1990: 95). The Nguni peoples generally exhibit a different set of powers. The orthogonally related variables of Bantu systems do not appear in Nilotic religions (Nuer, Dinka, Atuot), for which hierarchical, tree-structure diagrams are appropriate (MacGaffey 1986: 180–87). Since the Nyakyusa are also Bantu-speaking, but make different distinctions among the holders of occult powers, the set is not merely a product of language; indeed we have already noticed that linguistic analysis alone is not a good guide to conceptual systems. The Kongo or Bantu set also occurs among the Alladian

lagoon peoples of the lower Ivory Coast (Augé 1975) and may be general in the forest zone of West Africa.

In the sets mentioned in this paper, the distinction of means (technical/mystical), effects (death/life), ends (public/private), and legitimacy (good/bad) are distributed as follows (other variables may appear in other sets):

DISTINCTION	MEANS	EFFECTS	ENDS	LEGITIMACY
1.	Kongo		+	+
	Bolia	+	+	
	Tonga	+	+	
	Alladian	+	+	
2.	Zande	+		+
	Lugbara	+		+
	Kuranko	+		+
3.	Nyakyusa	+		+
	Safwa	+		+
4.	Yakö	+	+	

Besides the comparison of whole sets, a still less-conservative position would assume the cross-cultural identity of constituent variable, such as the distinction of means, and seek sociological or other correlates. This relatively rash undertaking has in fact been standard procedure among anthropologists who have seen no difficulty in the assumption that the distinction of means (mystical witchcraft versus technical sorcery) is "the same" wherever it is encountered, even to the point of identifying it among peoples who themselves do not recognize it. Middleton and Winter find that "most . . . reports of African societies mention beliefs in both witchcraft and sorcery" (1963: 8), but this generalization is highly unreliable. When Gray says, for example, "The Wambugwe distinguish linguistically between 'witchcraft' and 'sorcery,'" he really means that they distinguish between *kindoki* and *kinganga*, and not "witchcraft" and "sorcery" as defined by the editors of the collection to which he is contributing (Middleton and Winger 1963: 143; Crick 1976: 117).

Religion and Social Structure

Where do these sets of values come from? Durkheim, in a critique of the materialist conception of history, agreed with the materialists that collective representations do not float in a vacuum; in order for them to become intelligible, "they must truly spring from something and, since they cannot constitute a circle closed in upon itself, the source from which they derive must be found outside them" (Durkheim

1982 [1897]: 171). For Durkheim, this source had to be the combination of the members of society in groups.

Exploring the sociological conditions of the distinction of means, Middleton and Winter (1963: 12–13) suggested that congruence exists between the use of witchcraft beliefs and ascriptive social relationships, on the one hand, and on the other, between achieved or voluntary relationships and reliance on sorcery beliefs for accusations.

Since not only witches and sorcerers but, among the Azande, witchdoctors and magicians are distinguished by the means they supposedly employ, the question becomes a broader one, and we must admit the conjugating of a criterion of legitimacy on equal terms with the distinction of means. With some adjustment, the hypothesis holds in systems that in fact include both these distinctions.

The distinction of means is really a question of claimed or disclaimed responsibility. The witch is allowed to disclaim responsibility by cooling his witchcraft, which takes the blame, so to speak. The witchdoctor, on the other hand, seeks in the name of his means, or *mangu*, an authority that the society does not routinely allot to him. The sorcerer, according to the theory of technical means, is not allowed to disclaim responsibility. Magic, on the other hand, is an external means, a sort of legitimate sorcery, employed as a right by the occupants of ascribed, categorical statuses: "Owners of medicines are usually old or middle-aged men.... Youths, like women, ought not to practice magic, which is the privilege and concern of their elders." Nevertheless, youths acquire medicines for youthful pursuits, and women for feminine pursuits (Evans-Pritchard, 1937: 428). Access to oracles, and the relative authority of oracles, follows the same hierarchy.

In other words, approved "technical" means (oracles, magic) characterize and are intended to maintain ascribed status distinctions; disapproved "mystical" (intrinsic) means (*mangu*) characterize the misuse of these same social responsibilities. Approved mystical means characterize certain marginal "achieved" statuses; sorcery accusations are a way to pin inescapable blame on similarly nonincorporated or "voluntary" figures.

This analysis also works for the Safwa (Harwood 1970), the Kuranko (Jackson 1975), the Yakö, and the Lugbara. For the Kuranko of Sierra Leone (no cultural continuity with any other society mentioned here), Jackson says "Turner challenges the analytical usefulness of the Zande distinction but for Kuranko society the distinction is apposite and the nature terminology supports it" (1975: 407, note 7). Witches are supposed to possess *suwa'ye*, "witchcraft," as are the masters of witch-finding cults. Medicines (*besekoli*), quite different from witchcraft, are private or collective. The set of functions is:

MEANS		GOOD	BAD
TECHNICAL		medicines	sorcery
		a.collective	
		b.private	
MYSTICAL		witchfinder	witch

Witch and witchfinder have it in common that they are associated with "wild" or intrusive bush spirits and animals. Medicines, on the other hand, especially the men's medical associations, are explicitly devoted to maintaining male prerogatives against women: "The Master of the Kome cult said, 'The work of the cults is to maintain the distance between men and women'" (Jackson 1977: 220). Jackson says, "The exclusiveness of the cults confirms the major social category distinctions" (221), and in this sense they are functionally similar to Zande oracles; both are hierarchically arranged as a set of powers attributed to corporate categories. As with the Azande, the cult system and the secular system of chiefship are thought of as being entirely separate.

The Azande, Lugbara, and Kuranko, though geographically separated and culturally contrasted, appear to share the same set of religious values, integrated with the political structure in the same way. In all instances, the political control exercised by chiefs or elders is linked with the highest order of cultic procedure: princes' oracles, in the case of the Azande, which alone can sanction military decisions and the equivalents of capital accusations; for the Kuranko, the medicine associations, especially the Kome cult, which provides ritual defenses for the boundaries of chiefdoms and other local units against enemies, witches, and dangerous bush spirits; for the Lugbara, the complex of shrines and oracles through which male elders contact their ancestors. In all instances, with or without the presence of "chiefs," political and local units are conceptually fused; their populations are largely recruited by clientage in a context of warfare, land shortage, poverty, and other hardships; and the presence of a difference between "insiders" and "outsiders" is associated explicitly with a distinction of means. All of these societies lack the bilateral descent features and the alliance strategies characteristic of most Bantu systems.

Though the hypothesis in its modified form applies satisfactorily to a certain range of data, its terms require closer examination. "Ascription" and "achievement" are value-laden expressions difficult to apply in practice. What Middleton and Winter have in mind as the principal empirical example of their generalization is the so-called harmonic social regime, in which "unilineal kinship principles [ascriptive] are employed in the formation of local residential groups larger than the domestic household" (1963: 12). In this situation, witchcraft accusations are to be expected. Sorcery accusations are to be expected in the negatively defined category of societies in which unilineal principles are not used to organize local groups, and a person's rights and obligations to his neighbors result from his choosing to live with them (achievement). Thus what is at issue is the relationship between locality and descent, which in turn expresses the relationship between the spatial extension of society as a productive system and its reproduction from generation to generation. As Jackson says, with respect to the Kuranko,

> The lineal (or vertical) dimension of Kuranko social structure is a reflection of growth and change through time.... The complementary principles of social organization which are variously called lineage/locality, kinship/residence, ancestors/Earth, descent/territoriality, can be abstractly and heuristically polarized as a distinction between temporal and spatial modes of structuring. Descent essentially defines modes of relationship between predecessors and successors; by contrast, the sociospatial dimension can be viewed in terms of modes of relationship between consociates and contemporaries. (1977: 24)

Since both locality and succession are socially determined and never "given," it is necessary to look beneath these modes of structuring for the processes that maintain them.

Religion and Economy

Though he was not prepared to accept the idealist position that concepts floated in independent abstraction, Durkheim also rejected the materialist contention that, as he put it, social phenomena could be reduced to the state of technology; he said, "we know of no means of reducing religion to economics" (1982: 172, 173). Nevertheless, both the local and lineal groups we have been led to consider exhibit an economic character.

In any society, people live together in groups of some kind that work to produce their means of subsistence. Such local groups are recruited and perpetuated by some rule or rules that offer individuals a more or less limited set of opportunities as to where they may reside and with whom they may enter into productive relations. Such rules govern the succession of generations replacing one another in the work force, and make possible the continued existence of local groups in time. This is Jackson's "vertical dimension." The possibilities of social reproduction in given African soci-

eties may include patrifiliation, matrifiliation, succession to office, inheritance of property, distinctions of class and estate, slavery and voluntary association, for example.

The rules need not be consistent, and they invariably offer alternative possibilities that individuals will exploit to their best advantage. In some chiefdoms, such as occur among the Kuranko and the Azande, the reproduction of local units is a matter of patronage relations and is obviously political. In others, the social placement of members of succeeding generations may appear to be a matter of genealogical prescription, but anthropologists are now aware how open genealogy is to manipulation. The availability of marriage goods, accusations of witchcraft, imposition of fines for ritual and other offenses, the cost of medical care, and the extent of support available from relatives and neighbors must be included among the political factors affecting the social prospects of individuals and groups. Though all lineages, as represented in the anthropologist's diagram, may seem to be equal, in practice some are more equal than others.

The economic aspect of all this is not simply the pursuit of profit but competition for access to the basic resources necessary for production and social reproduction. Usually, in Africa—until recently—land itself was not scarce; access to land was a matter of membership in some sort of productive group: a village, village section, or extended household. The principal object of competition was to increase the number of one's dependents, both as a source of productive labor and as a measure of one's social importance. Chiefship in noncapitalist Africa was and is above all a matter of sovereignty over people, rather than over land (Goody 1971). Dependents can be acquired by kinship, marriage, pawnship, slavery, clientage, and a variety of other allocations and transfers. Women as well as men may participate in such competition, though societies differed considerably in the opportunities they afforded to women to acquire wives, slaves, and dependents, or to become chiefs. Let us look at an example.

In nineteenth-century Kongo, production and exchange of subsistence goods were carried on in lineally heterogeneous local groups. Membership in such groups was governed by marriage, matrilineal descent, and their variations, including several degrees of slavery, which limited the choice of places of residence and work open to individuals. Women were expected to live with their husbands. Freeborn male members of a matrilineal clan lived on its land or on the land of another clan to which they were related as a result of marriages contracted in previous generations. For slaves, male and female, the range of possibilities was much narrower than for the freeborn.

The ascription of free or slave status was not automatic, and the term "ascriptive," as applied to descent, can be misleading. Slavery in Kongo meant not forced labor but interrupted pedigree, brought about by such means as capture, slave trading, transfers attendant on, for example, the acquisition of titles, and on judicial awards related to accusations of witchcraft. These activities were generally reserved to men. Exchanged in this sphere, including ritual fees and fines, local transfers of slaves between descent groups, and access to chiefly and other titles, were closely linked to the continental and Atlantic trade, the source of the prestige goods that mediated them. Competitive success was measured by accession to titles, which in turn provided the holder with opportunities to acquire more wealth and more dependents; although most titles were held by men, and the rituals associated with them employed predominantly virile imagery, women past the menopause were also able to become magicians and minor chiefs. Whole lineages, losers in competition, were reduced to clientage and slavery (MacGaffey 1986: 34–39).

The segregation of functions—routine production of subsistence goods in local groups and politically controlled circulations of dependents and prestige goods between descent groups—is ritually celebrated in the distinction of effects, production versus destruction. In the Bantu-speaking societies of the Central African rainforests, in many other societies of the southern savanna, and, I think, rather generally in the forest zone of West Africa, chiefs and witches are identified, in principle, by the power to kill. Conversely, priests and magicians are healers, although the concerns of priests in particular are more extensive than healing. Those who exercise the power of life in the public interest commonly attract a cluster of English labels, none of them entirely satisfactory, such as earth priest, priest of nature spirits, rainmaker, public diviner, and prophet. It is clear that they represent the concerns of local communities occupying land as productive units. Their business includes rain and the management of fertility and epidemic disease. This is the business primarily of women. It includes ironworking, a male occupation, because smiths produce tools. The power of death, on the other hand, exercised by chiefs and elders, primarily corresponds to the concerns of men and their activities in criminal justice, war, hunting, and trade, including trade in slaves. The segregation of these spheres is clearly indicated by the BaTonga, among whom prophets wear dark colors associated with rain clouds. Colson says, "Red beads or anything red in color is taboo during consultation because red symbolizes blood. An appropriate gift is a hoe blade, symbol of cultivation (and of femaleness). Spears and axes, symbols of maleness and the hunt and war, do not appear to be used as gifts to either prophets or local shrines" (1977: 126).

Competition for basic resources is explicit among both the BaKongo and the Yakö and is related in both instances to the distinction of effects, between destructive powers associated with masculine interests and benevolent powers associated with feminine interests. In Kongo theory, chiefs and ritual experts defended the people against witches, thieves, wrongdoers, and members of hostile clans. This segmentary model partly concealed a form of stratification in which the wealthy and powerful, using the beliefs and devices of ritual, extracted a continuous flow of wealth from the relatively poor (Rey 1975). Yakö ideology likewise emphasized the solidarity of clansmen in competition with members of other clans, and the common interests of men in politico-jural affairs. So doing, it tended to disguise the marked stratification of rich and poor within descent groups.

The economic interests of Yakö cult groups are patent. Of *ndet* fetishes, Forde says that some were held by associations of elders. The Leopard Spirit, Ekpe Edet, of the Korta association "was as negative as those of [the matrilineal shrines] were positive, for its powers were essentially punitive" (1964: 267). It sanctioned mainly "settlements appertaining to hotly disputed claims to land and inheritance of goods, as well as restrictions on external trading and other movements following inter-village quarrels." Another Leopard Spirit cult, Okengka, drew its members from the leaders of all the wards and settled disputes: "The rights of property of members and others were protected by such judgments" (1964: 268). Younger men also owned a Leopard Spirit, Ngkpe; membership in this cult was much sought after because it regulated disputes over debts and marital rights over women (1964: 277). Whereas the punitive and patrilineal *ndet* expressed the distinctive function of men in controlling resources in land and people, the matrilineal spirits were primarily responsible for the well-being of the village as a whole, for the fertility of crops and women, and for protection against fire and witchcraft.

In the Yakö instance, the opposition between death-dealing forces associated with male control of social reproduction and the life-giving forces associated with women and cultivation is combined with a distinction of means between the technical resources of dominant, "insider" men and the mystical resources of "stranger" women and marginal diviners. In Kuranko, Lugbara, and Azande, too, the insider occupants of "ascribed" statuses are male, perpetuation of their control over women, or at least the illusion of such control, is a major preoccupation, and the occult resources available to them are "technical." The local group is thought of as consisting of an autonomous corporation owning a discrete territory, and the religious expression of locality is in terms of "mystical" powers.

The gender contrast is not characteristic of Kongo thinking about the occult. Kongo social structure took the form of a nonterritorial network of patrifilial links between matrilineal nodes, so organized that no clan head could so much as pray to his ancestors or bury his predecessor without the participation of classificatory children and grandchildren from other clans, whether they lived locally or not (MacGaffrey 1970b: 212–14, 229–36). In such a system only slaves could be categorized as strangers. This, defined more positively, is the system referred to by Middleton and Winter as one in which unilineal principles are not used in the formation of local groups and in which "sorcery" accusations are to be expected—except that the type example they give of "sorcery" is the Nyoro *burogi*, formally and linguistically cognate with Kongo *kindoli*. Kongo "witchcraft" accusations have no local dimension and are not restricted to women. The similarity between northern BaKongo (BaKunyi) and certain peoples of the southern Ivory Coast has been remarked by Augé (1975: 195–233), who has independently analyzed the connection between the ideology of powers and the economic structure.

Conclusion

By nonintuitive and replicable procedures, I have shown how certain African religions, some of them widely separated in space, belong to the same or to different types. Four types have been identified, those of Kongo, Zande, Nyakyusa, and Yakö. The classification is not an end in itself: it prepares the way for an analytical exploration of sociological conditions and historical evolution. It is gratifying rather than surprising to find that such classifications as emerge from the use of this approach confirm, on the whole, both intuitive evaluations and the known distributions of language and culture (McCall 1982).

Durkheim thought that a demonstration of connections between religion and social structure or economy would be "scientific" because it would show causal relations. But, as Bateson put it, "Our categories 'religious,' 'economic,' etc., are not real subdivisions which are present in the cultures we study, but are merely abstractions which we make for our convenience when we set out to describe cultures in words. They are not phenomena present in culture, but are labels for various points of view in our studies" (Bateson 1972: 64). It follows that the vexed questions of causal relations among these abstractions are theoretical, a function of the way we conceive of them. Instead of laboring to discover causal or other relations between religion, society, and economy, we should assume that in "real" cultures they necessarily reveal the same structure. In focusing on the specificity of given

forms, we will be forced to abandon not only "witchcraft" and "sorcery" but "ancestor-worship," "spirit possession," "sacrifice," and many other traditional but misleading and ultimately nonproductive categories.

Wyatt MacGaffey

Bibliography

Arens, William. (1980) "Taxonomy versus Dynamics Revisited." In *Explorations in African Systems of Thought*, edited by I. Karp and C. C. Bird. Washington, D.C.: Smithsonian Institution.

Augé, Marc. (1975) *Théorie des Pouvoirs et Idéologie: étude de cas en Côte d'Ivoire*. Paris: Hermann.

Bateson, Gregory. (1972). *Steps to an Ecology of Mind*. New York: Ballantine.

Buakasa, G. (1968) "Notes sure le kindoki chez les Kongo." In *Cahiers des Religions Africaines* [Kinshasa] 3, 2: 153–170.

Colson, Elizabeth. (1962) *The Plateau Tonga of Northern Rhodesia*. Manchester: Manchester University Press.

——. (1966) "The Alien Diviner and Local Politics among the Tonga of Zambia." In *Political Anthropology*, edited by M. J. Swartz et al. Chicago: Aldine.

——. (1977) "A Continuing Dialogue: Prophets and Local Shrines among the Tonga of Zambia." In *Regional Cults*, edited by R. Werbner. London: Academic Press.

Crick, M. (1976) *Explorations in Language and Meaning*. New York: John Wiley.

Durkheim, Emile. (1982 [1897]) *The Rules of Sociological Method*, edited with an introduction by S. Lukes, translated by W. D. Halls. New York: Free Press.

Evans-Pritchard, E. E. (1937) *Witchcraft, Oracles and Magic among the Azande*. London: Oxford University Press.

Forde, Daryll. (1964) *Yako Studies*. London: Oxford University Press.

Goody, Jack. (1971) *Technology, Tradition and the State In Africa*. London: Oxford University Press.

Hardwood, A. (1970) *Witchcraft, Sorcery and Social Categories among the Safwa*. London: Oxford University Press.

Jackson, M. D. (1975) "Structure and Event: Witchcraft Confessions among the Juranko." In *Man* 10, 3: 387–403.

——. (1977) *The Kuranko*. New York: St. Martin's Press.

Johnson, D. H. (1994) *Nuer Prophets*. London: Oxford University Press.

Lewis, I. M. (1971) *Ecstatic Religion*. Baltimore: Penguin.

MacGaffey, Wyatt. (1970a) "The Religious Commissions of the BaKongo." In *Man* 5: 27–38.

——. (1970b) *Custom and Government in the Lower Congo*. Los Angeles: University of California Press.

———. (1972) "Comparative Analysis of Central African Religions." In *Africa* 42: 21–31.

———. (1980) "African Religions: Types and Generalizations." In *Explorations in African Systems of Thought*, edited by I. Karp and C. C. Bird. Washington, D.C.: Smithsonian Institution.

———. (1986) *Religion and Society in Central America*. Chicago: Chicago University Press.

McCall, D. (1982) "E-P and History." In *International Journal of African Historical Studies* 15: 467–474.

Middleton, John. and E. H. Winter, eds. (1963) *Witchcraft and Sorcery in East Africa*. London: Routledge and Kegan Paul.

Rey, P. P. (1975) "L'esclavage lignager chez les Tsangui, les Punu et les Juni du Congo-Brazzaville." In *L'Esclavage en Afrique precoloniale*, edited by C. Meillassoux. Paris: Maspero.

Sperber, Dan. (1987) *On Anthropological Knowledge*. Cambridge: Cambridge University Press.

Van Everbroeck, N. (1961) *Mbomb'Ipoku, le seigneur à l'abîme*. (Archives d'ethnographie 3.) Tervuren: Musée Royal de l'Afrique Centrale.

Vansina, Jan. (1973) *The Tio Kingdom of the Middle Congo, 1880–1892*. London: Oxford University Press.

——— (1990) *Paths in the Rainforests*. Madison: University of Wisconsin Press.

Weber, Max. (1963) *Sociology of Religion*. Boston: Beacon.

Wilson, G. (1936) "An Africa Morality." *Africa* 9: 75–99.

Appendix B.
Select Bibliography

The bibliography is provided as a supplement to the bibliographies that accompany the articles in this volume. It provides citations to a selection of books which the editor believes provide knowledge and interpretation central to the study and understanding of African and African-American religion. Some of the books listed here were written or edited by contributors to this volume and some are also cited in the article bibliographies. The emphasis is on recent publications, but several classical studies of African or African-American religion are included as well. Similarly, there is much from anthropology, but history, religious studies, sociology, political science, and other scholarly perspectives are covered. Readers who want either a general overview of African or African-American religion or a book-length introduction to any of the many topics that fall within the purview of this volume, will likely find those books listed here.

Akinade, Akintunde, and Dale T. Irwin, eds. (1996) *The Agitated Mind of God: The Theology of Kosuke Koyama*. Maryknoll. NY: Orbis Books.

Anderson, David M., and Douglas H. Johnson, eds. (1995) *Revealing Prophets: Prophets in East African History*. London: James Currey.

Angell, Stephen Ward. (1992) *Bishop Henry McNeal Turner and African American Religion in the South*. Knoxville: University of Tennessee Press.

Angell, Stephen Ward. (2000) *Social Protest Thought in the African Methodist Episcopal Church, 1862–1939*. Knoxville: University of Tennessee Press.

Aguilar, Mario I. (1998) *Being Oromo in Kenya*. Trenton, NJ: Africa World Press.

Baer, Hans A. (1984) *The Black Spiritual Movement: A Religious Response to Racism*. Knoxville: University of Tennessee Press.

Baer, Hans A., and Merrill Singer. (1992) *African-American Religion in the Twentieth Century: Varieties of Protest and Accommodation*. Knoxville: University of Tennessee Press.

Barnes, Sandra T. (1997) *Africa's Ogun: Old World and New*, new and expanded edition. Bloomington: University of Indiana Press.

Barrett, Leonard E. (1974) *Soul Force*. Garden City, NY: Anchor Books.

——. (1987) *The Rastafarians*, twentieth anniversary edition. Boston: Beacon Press.

Baum, Robert Martin. (1999) *Shrines of the Slave Trade: Diola Religion and Society in Pre-colonial Senegambia*. New York: Oxford University Press.

Bastide, Roger. (1971) *African Civilizations in the New World*. New York: Harper and Row.

——. (1978) *The African Religions of Brazil: Toward a Sociology of the Interpenetrations of Civilizations*. Baltimore: The Johns Hopkins University Press.

Besmer, Fremont E. (1983) *Horses, Musicians, and Gods: The Hausa Cult of Possession-Trance*. South Hadley, MA: Bergin and Garvey.

Blakeley, Thomas D., Walter E. A. van Beek, and Dennis L. Thomson, eds. (1994) *Religion in Africa: Experience and Expression*. Portsmouth, NH: Heinemann.

Blier, Suzanne P. (1995) *African Vodun: Art, Psychology, Power*. Berkeley: University of California Press.

Binsbergen, Wim van, and Matthew Schoffeleers, eds. (1965) *Theoretical Explorations in African Religion*. Boston: KPI.

Bockie, Simon. (1993) *Death and the Invisible Powers: The World of Kongo Belief*. Bloomington: Indiana University Press.

Boddy, Janice. (1989) *Wombs and Alien Spirits: Women, Men, and the Zar Cult in Northern Sudan*. Madison: University of Wisconsin Press.

Bond, George C., Walton Johnson, and Sheila S. Walker, eds. (1979) *African Christianity: Patterns of Religious Continuity*. New York: Academic Press.

Bravman, Bill. (1998) *Making Ethnic Ways: Communities and Their Transformations in Taita, Kenya*. Portsmouth, NH: Heinemann.

Brandon, George. (1993) *Santeria from Africa to the New World: The Dead Sell Memories*. Bloomington: Indiana University Press.

Bringhurst, Newell G. (1981) *Saints, Slaves and Blacks: The changing place of black people within Mormonism*. Westport, CT: Greenwood.

Brown, Diana. (1986) *Umbanda: Religion and Politics in Urban Brazil*. Ann Arbor, MI: UMI Research Press.

Brown, Karen McCarthy. (1991) *Mama Lola: A Vodou Priestess in Brooklyn*. Berkeley: University of California Press.

Burkett, Randall K. (1978) *Garveyism as a Religious Movement*. Metuchen, NJ: Scarecrow Press.

Burkett, Randall K., and Richard Newman, eds. (1978) *Black Apostles: Afro-American Clergy Confront the Twentieth Century*. Boston: G. K. Hall and Company.

Burrowes Stewart, Diane Marie. (1997) "The Evolution of African-Derived Religions in Jamaica." Ph.D. diss., Union Theological Seminary.

Burton, Richard D. E. (1997) *Afro-Creole : Power, Opposition, and Play in the Caribbean*. Ithaca, NY: Cornell University Press.

Campbell, Horace. (1992) *Rasta and Resistance: From Marcus Garvey to Walter Rodney*. Trenton, NJ: African World Press.

Carneiro, Eduardo. (1961) *Candomble da Bahia*. Sao Paulo: Companhia Editora Nacional.

Chapman, Mark L. (1996) *Christianity on Trial: African American Religious Thought Before and After Black Power*. Maryknoll, NY: Orbis Books.

Chevannes, Barry. (1994) *Rastafari: Roots and Ideology*. New York: Syracuse University Press.

Chevannes, Barry, ed. (1998) *Rastafari and Other African Caribbean Worldviews*. New Brunswick, NJ: Rutgers University Press.

Chidester, David. (1997) *African Traditional Religion in South Africa: An Annotated Bibliography*. Westport, CT: Greenwood.

Chireau, Yvonne and Nathaniel Deutsch, eds. (2000) *Black Zion: African American Religious Encounters with Judaism*. New York: Oxford University Press.

Chukwunyere, Kamalu. (1998) *Person, Divinity and Nature: A Modern View of the Person and Cosmos in African Thought*. London: Karnak House.

Clarke, Peter B. (1995) *Mahdism in West Africa: The Case of the Ijebu Prophet*. London: Luze Oriental.

Clarke, Peter B., ed. (1998) *New Trends and Developments in African Religions*. Westport, CT: Greenwood Press.

Comaroff, Jean. (1985) *Body of Power, Spirit of Resistance*. Chicago: University of Chicago Press.

Cone, James H. (1969) *Black Theology and Black Power*. New York: Seabury Press.

Consentino, Donald. (1998) *Voodoo Things: The Art of Pierrot Barra and Marie Cassaisee*. Jackson, MS: University of Mississippi Press.

Cornelius, Janet. (1999) *Slave Missions and the Black Church in the Antebellum South*. Columbia: University of South Carolina Press.

Deive, Carlos Esteban. (1979) *Vodu y magia en Santo Domingo*. Santo Domingo, Dominican Republic: Museo del Hombre Domincano.

Deren, Maya. (1970) *Divine Horsemen: Voodoo Gods of Haiti*. New York: Chelsea House.

Desmangles, Leslie G. (1992) *The Faces of the Gods: Vodou and Roman Catholicism in Haiti*. Chapel Hill: University of North Carolina Press.

Drake, St. Clair, and Horace Clayton. (1945) *Black Metropolis*. New York: Harcourt Brace.

Drewal, Henry John. (1983) *Gelede: Art and Female Power among the Yoruba*. Bloomington: Indiana University Press.

Drewal, Margaret Thompson. (1992) *Yoruba Ritual: Performance, Play, Agency*. Bloomington: Indiana University Press.

Du Bois, W. E. B. (1968) *The Negro Church*. Atlanta: Atlanta University Publications.

——. (1969 [1903]) *The Souls of Black Folk*. New York: New American Library.

Evans-Pritchard, Edward Evan. (1962) *Nuer Religion*. Oxford, U.K.: Clarendon Press.

Fabian, Johannes. (1971) *Jamaa: A Charismatic Movement in Katanga*. Evanston, IL: Northwestern University Press.

——. (2000) *Out of Our Minds: Reason and Madness in the Exploration of Central Africa*. Berkeley: University of California Press.

Fargher, Brian L. (1996) *The Origins of the New Churches Movement in Southern Ethiopia*. Leiden: E. J. Brill.

Fauset, Arthur Huff. (1944) *Black Gods of the Metropolis*. Philadelphia: University of Pennsylvania Press.

Fernandez, James W. (1985). *Bwiti: An Ethnography of the*

Religious Imagination in Africa. Princeton, NJ: Princeton University Press.

Fields, Karen E. (1985) *Revival and Rebellion in Colonial Central Africa*. Princeton, NJ: Princeton University Press.

Fortes, Meyer. (1959) *Oedipus and Job in West African Religion*. New York: Cambridge University Press.

——. (1987) *Religion, Morality and the Person: Essays on Tallensi Religion*. New York: Cambridge University Press.

Frazier, E. Franklin. (1964) *The Negro Church in America*. New York: Shocken Books.

Fulop, Timothy E., and Albert J. Raboteau, eds. (1997) *African American Religion: Interpretative Essays in History and Culture*. New York: Routledge.

Gardell, Mattias. (1996) *In the Name of Elijah Muhammad: Louis Farrakhan and the Nation of Islam*. Durham, NC: Duke University Press.

Galembo, Phyllis. (1993) *Divine Inspiration: From Benin to Bahia*. Albuquerque: University of New Mexico Press.

Gilford, Paul. (1998) *African Christianity: Its Public Role*. Bloomington: Indiana University Press.

Glazier, Stephen D. (1991) *Marchin' the Pilgrims Home*. Salem, WI: Sheffield.

Glazier, Stephen D., ed. (1980) *Perspectives on Pentecostalism: Case Studies from the Caribbean and Latin America*. Lanham, MD: University Press of America.

Gleason, Judith. (1992) *Oya: In Praise of an African Goddess*. San Francisco: Harper.

Goldsmith, Peter David. (1989) *When I Rise Up Cryin' Holy: African American Denominationalism on the Georgia Coast*. New York: AMS Press.

Gray, John. (1989) *Ashe, Traditional Religion and Healing in Sub-Saharan Africa and the Diaspora: A Classified International Biography*. Westport, CT: Greenwood.

Guenther, Mathias G. (1999) *Tricksters and Trancers: Bushman Religion and Society*. Bloomington: Indiana University Press.

Harris, Frederick C. (1999) *Something Within: Religion in African American Political Activism*. New York: Oxford University Press.

Harris, Sara. (1971) *Father Divine*. New York: Colliers.

Haynes, Jeffrey. (1996) *Religion and Politics in Africa*. London: ZED Books.

Herskovits, Melville J. (1941) *The Myth of the Negro Past*. New York: Harper and Brothers.

——. (1971) *Life in a Haitian Valley*. Garden City, NY: Anchor Books.

Hess, David. (1991) *Spirits and Scientists: Ideology, Spiritism, and Brazilian Culture*. University Park: Pennsylvania State University Press.

——. (1994) *Samba in the Night: Spiritism in Brazil*. New York: Columbia University Press.

Hoehler-Fatton, Cynthia. (1996) *Women of Fire and Spirit: History, Faith and Gender in Roho religion in Western Kenya*. New York: Oxford University Press.

Horton, Robin. (1993) *Patterns of Thought in Africa and the West: Essays on Magic, Religion, and Science*. New York: Cambridge University Press.

Houk, James T. 1995. *Spirits, Blood, and Drums: The Orisha Religion in Trinidad*. Philadelphia: Temple University Press.

Hurbon, Laennec. (1972) *Dieu Dans Le Vaudau*. Paris: Payot.

——. (1995) *Voodoo: Search for the Spirit*. New York: Henry Abrams.

Hurston, Zora Neale. (1981) *The Sanctified Church*. Berkeley, CA: Turtle Island.

——. (1990) *Tell My Horse: Voodoo and Life in Haiti*. New York: Perennial Library.

Hexham, Irving. (1987) *Texts on Zulu Religion*. Lewiston, NY: Edwin Mellen.

Hinson, Glen. (2000) *Fire in My Bones: Transcendence and the Holy Spirit in African American Gospel*. Philadelphia: University of Pennsylvania Press.

Hollenweger, Walter J. (1970) *Black Pentecostal Concept: Interpretations and Variations*. Geneva, Switz.: World Council of Churches.

Idowu, E. Bolaji. *African Traditional Religion: A Definition*. Maryknoll, NY: Orbis Books.

Jacobs, Claude F., and Andrew J. Kaslow. (1991) *The Spiritual Churches of New Orleans: Origins, Beliefs, and Rituals of an African American Religion*. Knoxville: University of Tennessee Press.

James, Wendy. (1988) *The Listening Ebony: Moral Knowledge, Religion, and Power among the Uduk of Sudan*. Oxford, U.K.: Clarendon.

Jedrej, M. Charles. (1995) *Ingessana: The Religious Institutions of a People of the Sudan—Ethiopia Borderland*. New York: E. J. Brill.

Johnson, Paul E., ed. (1990) *African American Christianity*. Berkeley: University of California Press.

Johnson, Walton R. (1977) *Worship and Freedom: A Black American Church in Zambia*. New York: Africana Publishing Company.

Johnson-Hill, Jack A. (1995) *I-Sight: The World of Rastafari: An Interpretive Sociological Account of Rastafarian Ethics*. Metuchen, NJ: Scarecrow.

Jules-Rossette, Bennetta. (1979) *The New Religions of Africa*. Norwood, NJ: Ablex Publishing Corporation.

Katz, Richard. (1982) *Boiling Energy: Community Healing Among the Kalahari Kung*. Cambridge, MA: Harvard University Press.

Kenyon, Susan M. (1991) *Five Women of Sennai: Culture and*

Change in Central Sudan. New York: Oxford University Press.

Kiernan, James Patrick. (1990). *Production and Management of Therapeutic Power in Zionist Churches within a Zulu City*. Lewiston, NY: Edwin Mellen.

King, Noel Q. (1986) *African Cosmos: An Introduction to Religion in Africa*. Belmont, CA: Wadsworth.

Kostarelos, Frances. (1995) *Feeling the Spirit: Faith and Hope in an Evangelical Black Storefront Church*. Columbia: University of South Carolina Press.

Kraay, Hendrick, ed. (1998) *Afro-Brazilian Culture and Politics*. Armonk, NY: M. E. Sharpe.

Kremser, Manfred, ed. (1990) *Ay Bo Bo: African Caribbean Religions*. Second International Conference of the Society for Caribbean Research, Vienna: WUV Universitat: verlag.

——. and Karl R. Wernhart, eds. (1986) *Research in Ethnography and Ethnohistory of St. Lucia: A Preliminary Report*. Horn: F. Berger and Shone.

Laguerre, Michel. (1980) *Voodoo Heritage*. Thousand Oaks, CA: Sage.

——. (1989) *Voodoo and Politics in Haiti*. New York: St. Martin's Press.

Lake, Obiagele. (1998) *Rastafari Women: Subordination in the Midst of Liberation Theology*. Durham, NC: Carolina Academic Press.

Landes, Ruth. (1994 [1947]) *The City of Women*, introduced by Sally Cole. Albuquerque: University of New Mexico Press.

Lanternari, Vittorio. (1963) *The Religions of the Oppressed*. New York: New American Library.

Lawson, E. Thomas. (1986) *Religions of Africa: Traditions in Transformation*. New York: Harper and Row.

Leacock, Seth, and Ruth Leacock. (1975) *Spirits of the Deep*. New York: Doubleday.

Lewis, David Levering. (1995) *W. E. B. Du Bois: A Reader*. New York: Henry Holt.

Lewis, William F. (1993) *Soul Rebels: The Rastafari*. Prospect Heights, IL: Waveland Press.

Lincoln, C. Eric. (1974) *The Black Experience in Religion*. Garden City, NJ: Anchor Books.

——. and Lawrence Mamiya. (1990) *The Black Church in the African American Experience*. Durham, NC: Duke University Press.

Littlewood, Roland. (1993) *Pathology and Identity: The Work of Mother Earth in Trinidad*. New York: Cambridge University Press.

Lum, Kenneth A. (1999) *Praising His Name in the Dance: Spirit-Possession in the Spiritual Baptist Faith and Orisha Work in Trinidad, West Indies*. Amsterdam: Harwood.

MacGaffey, Wyatt. (1986) *Religion and Society in Central Africa*. Chicago: University of Chicago Press.

MacRobert, Iain. (1988) *The Black Roots and White Racism of Early Pentecostalism in the USA*. New York: St. Martin's Press.

Martin, Sandy Dwayne. (1989) *Black Baptists and African Missions*. Macon, GA: Mercer University Press.

——. (1999) *For God and Race: The Religious and Political Leadership of AMEZ Bishop James Walker Hood*. Columbia: University of South Carolina Press.

Matory, James Lorand. (1994) *Sex and the Empire that Is No More: Gender and Politics of Metaphor in Oyo Yoruba Religion*. Minneapolis: University of Minnesota Press.

Maxwell, David. (1999) *Christians and Chiefs in Zimbabwe: A social history of the Hwesa people*. Westport, CT: Praeger.

Mays, Benjamin E., and Joseph R. Nicholson. (1933) *The Negro Church*. New York: Institute for Social and Religious Research.

Mbuti, John. (1969) *African Religion and Philosophy*. London: Heinemann.

McCloud, Aminah Beverley. (1995) *African American Islam*. New York: Routledge.

McDaniel, Lorna. (1998) *The Big Drum Ritual of Carriacou: Praisesongs in Rememory of Flight*. Gainesville: University Press of Florida.

Meeker, Michael. (1989) *The Pastoral Son and the Spirit of Patriarchy: Religion, Society and Person among East African Stock Keepers*. Madison: University of Wisconsin Press.

Metraux, Alfred. (1972) *Voodoo in Haiti*. New York: Schoken Books.

Meyer, Birgit. (1999) *Translating the Devil: Religion and Modernity among the Ewe in Ghana*. Trenton, NJ: Africa World Press.

Mintz, Sidney, and Richard Price. (1992) *An Anthropological Approach to the Afro-American Past: The Birth of African American Culture—An Anthropological Perspective*. Boston: Beacon Press.

Mitchell, Henry H. (1976) *Black Belief*. New York: Harper and Row.

Mitchell, Robert C., and Harold W. Turner, eds. (1966) *A Comprehensive Bibliography of Modern African Religious Movements*. Evanston, IL: Northwestern University Press.

Mulvaney, Rebekah Michele. (1990) *Rastafari and Reggae: A Dictionary and Sourcebook*. New York: Greenwood Press.

Murphy, Larry G., J. Gordon Melton, and Gary I. Ward., eds. (1993) *Encyclopedia of African American Religions*. New York: Garland.

Murphy, Joseph M. (1993) *Santeria: African Spirits in America*. Boston: Beacon Press.

——. (1994) *Working the Spirit: Ceremonies of the African Diaspora*. Boston: Beacon Press.

Murrell, Nathaniel Samuel, William David Spencer, and Adrian Anthony McFarlane, eds. (1998) *Chanting Down Babylon: The Rastafari Reader*. Philadelphia: Temple University Press.

Nelsen, Hart M., Raytha L. Yokley, and Anne K. Nelsen. (1971) *The Black Church in America*. New York: Basic Books.

Obene, J. Pashington. (1996) *Asante Catholicism: Religion and Cultural Reproduction among the Akan of Ghana*. Leiden: E. J. Brill.

Olmos, Margarite Fernandez, and Lizabeth Paravisini-Gebert, eds. (1997) *Sacred Possessions: Vodou, Santeria, Obeah, and the Caribbean*. New Brunswick, NJ: Rutgers University Press.

Olupona, J. K. (1991) *African Religions in Contemporary Society*. New York: Paragon House.

Oosthuizen, G. C., and Irving Hexham, eds. (1992) *Empirical Studies of African Independent/Indigenous Churches*. Lewiston, NY: Edwin Mellen Press.

Owens, Joseph. (1976) *Dread: The Rastafarians of Jamaica*. Jamaica: Montrose Printery.

Paris, Arthur E. (1982) *Black Pentecostalism: Southern Religion in an Urban World*. Amherst: University of Massachusetts Press.

Paris, Peter J. (1985) *The Social Teachings of the Black Churches*. Philadelphia: Fortress Press.

———. (1995) *The Spirituality of African Peoples: The Search for a Common Moral Discourse*. Minneapolis: Fortress Press.

Payne, Wardell J., ed. (1995) *Directory of African American Religious Bodies: A Compendium by the Howard University School of Divinity*. Washington, DC: Howard University Press.

Peek, Philip M., ed. (1991) *African Divination Systems: Ways of Knowing*. Bloomington: Indiana University Press.

Peel, J. D. Y. (1968) *The Aladura: A Religious Movement Among the Yoruba*. New York: Oxford University Press.

Perez y Mena, Andres Isiodoro. (1991) *Speaking with the Dead: Development of Afro-Latin Religion among Puerto Ricans in the United States*. New York: AMS Press.

Pinn, Anthony B. (1998) *Varieties of African American Religious Experience*. Minneapolis: Fortress Press.

Pitts, Walter F., Jr. (1993) *Old Ship of Zion: The Afro-Baptist Ritual in the African Diaspora*. New York: Oxford University Press.

Pollak-Eltz, Angelina. (1985) *Maria Lionza, mito y culto venezolano*. Caracas: Universidad Catolica Andres Bello.

———. (1994) *Religiones afroamericanas hoy*. Caracas: Planeta.

Polk, Patrick Arthur. (1997) *Haitian Vodou Flags*. Jackson: University Press of Mississippi.

Price, Richard, and Sally Price. (1991) *Two Evenings in Saramaka*. Chicago: University of Chicago Press.

Pulis, John W., ed. (1999) *Religion, Diaspora, and Cultural Identity: A Reader in the Anglophone Caribbean*. Amsterdam: Gordon and Breach.

Raboteau, Albert J. (1978) *Slave Religion: The "Invisible Institution" in the Antebellum South*. New York: Oxford University Press.

———. (1995) *A Fire in the Bones: Reflections on African American Religious History*. Boston: Beacon Press.

Ranger, Terrence O., and I. Kimmambo, eds. (1971) *The Historical Study of African Religions*. Berkeley: University of California Press.

Ray, Benjamin. (1976) *African Religions: Symbols, Rituals, and Community*. Englewood Cliffs, NJ: Prentice-Hall.

Rasmussen, Susan J. (1995) *Spirit Possession and Personhood among the Kel Eweg Tuareg*. New York: Cambridge University Press.

Roberts, J. Deotis. (1987) *Black Theology in Dialogue*. Philadelphia: Westminster Press.

Rodrigues, Nina. (1977) *Os Negros No Brasil*. Sao Paulo: Companhia Editora Nacional.

Rosenberg, June C. (1979) *El Gaga—religion y sociedad de un culto de Santo Domingo*. Santo Domingo, Dominican Republic: Universidad Autonoma de Santo Domingo.

Rosenthal, Judy. (1998) *Possession, Ecstasy, and Law in Ewe Voodoo*. Charlottesville: University of Virginia.

Ruel, Malcolm. (1997) *Belief, Ritual, and the Securing of Life: Essays on Bantu Religion*. Leiden: E. J. Brill.

Salamone, Frank A. (1970) *Anthropologists and Missionaries: Studies in Third World Societies No. 29*. Williamsburg, VA: College of William and Mary.

Salamone, Frank A., ed. (1999) *Anthropology and Theology: Gods, Icons, and God-Talk*. Lanham, MD: University Press of America.

Sawyer, Mary. R. (1994) *Black Ecumenism: Implementing the Demands of Justice*. Valley Forge, PA: Trinity Press International.

Sernett, Milton C. ed. (1985) *Afro-American Religious History*. Durham, NC: Duke University Press.

Shambaugh, Cynthia, and Irving I. Zaretsky. (1978) *Spirit Possession and Spirit Mediumship in Africa and Afro-America*. New York: Garland.

Shank, David A. (1994) *Prophet Harris: The Black "Elijah" of West Africa*. Leiden: E. J. Brill.

Simpson, George Eaton. (1978) *Black Religions in the New World*. New York: Columbia University Press.

Sobel, Mechel. (1988) *Trabelin' On: The Slave Journey to an Afro-Baptist Faith*, rev. ed. Princeton, NJ: Princeton University Press.

Spencer, Jon Michael. (1992) *Black Hymnody: A Hymnological*

History of the African American Church. Knoxville: University of Tennessee Press.

———. (1992) *Blues and Evil.* Knoxville: University of Tennessee Press.

Staewen, Christoph. (1996) *Ifa, African Gods Speak: The Oracle of the Yoruba in Nigeria.* Hamburg: Lit Verlag.

Stewart, Dianne. (1996) *Gift of the Sun: A Tale from South Africa.* New York: Farrar, Straus and Giroux.

Stoller, Paul. (1995) *Embodying Colonial Memories: Spirit Possession, Power, and the Hauka in West Africa.* New York: Routledge.

Swift, David E. (1985) *Black Prophets of Justice.* Baton Rouge: Louisiana State University Press.

Taylor, Clarence. (1994) *The Black Churches of Brooklyn,* New York: Columbia University Press.

Thomas, Linda E. (1999) *Under the Canopy: Ritual Process and Spiritual Resilience in South Africa.* Columbia: University of South Carolina Press.

Thompson, Robert Faris. (1984) *Flash of the Spirit.* New York: Vintage Books.

Turner, Edith E. B., William Blodgett, Singleton Kahona, and Fideli Benwa. (1992) *Experiencing Ritual: A New Interpretation of African Healing.* Philadelphia: University of Pennsylvania Press.

Turner, Harold W. (1977) *Bibliography of New Religious Movements in Primal Societies.* Boston: G. K. Hall.

Turner, Harold W., ed. (1979) *Religious Innovation in Africa: Collected Essays on New Religious Movements.* Boston: G. K. Hall.

Turner, Richard Brent. (1997) *Islam in the African American Experience.* Bloomington: Indiana University Press.

Turner, Victor W. (1968) *The Drums of Affliction: A Study of Religious Processes among the Ndembu of Zambia.* Oxford, U.K.: Clarendon.

Van Dijk, Rijk, Ria Reis, and Marja Spierenburg, eds. (2000) *The Quest for Fruition through Ngoma: The Political Aspects of Healing in South Africa.* Athens: Ohio University Press.

Verger, Pierre. (1968) *Flux et Reflux de la Traite des Negres entre le Golfe de Benin et Bahia de Todos los Santos, du XVIIe au XIXe Siecle.* The Hague: Mouton.

Voeks, Robert A. (1997) *Sacred Leaves of Candomble: African Magic, Medicine, and Religion in Brazil.* Austin: University of Texas Press.

Wafer, James William. (1991) *The Taste of Blood: Spirit Possession in Brazilian Candomble.* Philadelphia: University of Pennsylvania Press.

Walker, Sheila S. (1972) *Ceremonial Spirit Possession in Africa and Afro-America.* Leiden: E. J. Brill

———. (1983) *The Religious Revolution in the Ivory coast.* Chapel Hill: University of North Carolina Press.

Walsh, Thomas G., and Frank Kaufman, eds. (1999) *Religion and Social Transformation in Southern Africa.* St. Paul, MN: Paragon House.

Washington, James Melvin. (1986) *Frustrated Fellowship: The Black Baptist Quest for Social Power.* Macon, GA: Mercer University Press.

Washington, Joseph R., Jr. (1972) *Black Sects and Cults.* New York: Doubleday and Company.

———. (1984) *Black Religion: The Negro and Christianity in the United States.* Lanham, MD: University Press of America.

Waters, Anita M. (1985) *Race, Class, and Political Symbols: Rastafari and Reggae in Jamaican Politics.* New Brunswick, NJ: Rutgers University Press.

Weisbrot, Robert. (1983) *Father Divine and the Struggle for Racial Equality.* Urbana: University of Illinois Press.

Weisenfeld, Judith, and Richard Newman, eds. (1996) *This Far by Faith: Readings in African American Women's Religious Biography.* New York: Routledge.

Werbner, Richard P. (1998) *Memory and Postcolony: African Anthropology and the Critique of Power.* New York: St. Martin's Press.

Werbner, Richard P., ed. (1977) *Regional Cults.* New York: Academic Press.

Williams, Melvin D. (1974) *Community in a Black Pentecostal Church: An Anthropological Study.* Pittsburgh, PA: University of Pittsburgh Press.

Wills, David W., and Richard Newman, eds. (1982) *Black Apostles at Home and Abroad.* Boston: G. K. Hall.

Wilmore, Gayraud S. (1998) *Black Religion and Black Radicalism,* 3d ed. Maryknoll, NY: Orbis Books.

Woodson, Carter G. (1921) *The History of the Negro Church.* Washington, D.C.: Associated Publishers.

Wynia, Elly M. (1994) *The Church of God and Saints of Christ: The Rise of Black Jews.* New York: Garland.

Zahn, Dominique. (1979) *The Religion, Spirituality and Thought of Traditional Africa.* Chicago: University of Chicago Press.

Zane, Wallace W. (1999) *Journeys to the Spiritual Lands: A Natural History of a West Indian Religion.* New York: Oxford University Press.

List of Contributors

Aguilar, Mario
University of St. Andrews
Ndembu Religion
Oromo Religion
Pastoralist Cosmologies

Akinade, Akintunde
High Point University
Apostolic Church of Johane Masowe
Lumpa Church
Macumba
Maitatsine Sect
Watchtower

Angell, Stephen
Florida A & M University
African Methodist Episcopal Church

Baer, Hans
University of Arkansas
Black Catholics in the U.S.
Church of God and Saints of Christ
Church of God in Christ (Memphis)
Elder Solomon Michaux's Church of God
Holiness-Pentecostal (Sanctified) Movement
Metropolitan Spiritual Churches of Christ
Moorish Science Temple
Mount Zion Spiritual Temple
Peace Mission
Rainbow Coalition
Social Activism
United Church & Science of Living Institute

United House of Prayer for all People
United States, African Religions in
Universal Hagar's Spiritual Church

Barnes, Sandra
University of Pennsylvania
Ogun

Baum, Robert
Iowa State University
Diola Prophets
West African Religions

Benoit, Catherine
Ecole des Hautes Etudes en Sciences Sociales
Guadeloupe and Martinique, African-Derived
Religions in

Bockie, Simon
University of California, Berkeley
Kongo Religion

Bornstein, Erica
University of California, Irvine
Christian Evangelism in Africa
World Vision International

Brandon, George
City University of New York Medical School
Convince
Healing in African and African-Derived Religions
Santeria

Bravman, Bill
Marlborough School
Christian Missionaries in Africa

Brooks, Christopher
Virginia Commonwealth University
Aladura
Music, Black Hymnody
Yoruba Religion

Buckner, Margaret
Southwest Missouri State University
Manjako of Guinea-Bissau
Zande Religion

Burkett, Randall
Emory University
Universal Negro Improvement Association

Burton, John
Connecticut College
Dinka Religion
Nuer Religion

Chapman, Mark
Fordham University
Black Theology

Chevannes, Barry
University of West Indies, Mona
Revival

Clark, Mary Ann
Houston, Texas
Santeria, Material Culture

Clarke, Peter
King's College, London
Ahmadiyya Movement
Brazil, African-Derived Religions in
Islam, East Africa
Islam, West Africa

Clements, William
Arkansas State University
Azusa Street Revival

Copeland, M. Shawn
Marquette University
Black Catholics in the U.S.

Cornelius, Janet Duitsman
Danville Area Community College
Slave Religion

Cosentino, Donald
University of California, Los Angeles
Vodou, Material Culture

Desmangles, Leslie
Trinity College
Caribbean, African-Derived Religions in
Vodou

Diduk, Susan
Denison University
Women and Religious Movements in
Sub-Saharan Africa

Dodson, Jualynne
University of Colorado, Boulder
Cuba, African-Derived Religions in

Fabian, Johannes
Free University of Amsterdam
Jamaa

Gable, Eric
Mary Washington College
Religious Skepticism

Garma Navarro, Carlos
*Universidad Autonoma Metropolitana—Iztapalapa,
Mexico*
Mexico, African-Derived Religions in

Glazier, Stephen
University of Nebraska
Gaga
Music, Spiritual Baptists
Spiritual Baptists

Guenther, Mathias
Wilfrid Laurier University
Bushman Religion
Pygmy Religion

Henry, Frances
York University
Orisha (Shango) Movement in Trinidad

Hepner, Randal
Loyola University Chicago
Rastafari in the U.S.

Hexham, Irving
University of Calgary
amaNazaretha
Pentecostalism in Africa

Homiak, John P.
Smithsonian Institution
Rastafari
Rastafari in Global Context

Houk, James
Our Lady of the Lake College
Batuque
Candomblé
Kumina (Cuminia)

Howard, W. Stephen
Ohio University
Sudanese Brotherhoods

Hucks, Tracey
Haverford College
Trinidad, African-Derived Religions in

Jacobs, Claude
University of Michigan, Dearborn
Black Spiritual Churches
Shrine of the Black Madonna, Detroit
Spiritualism

Jules-Rosette, Bennetta
University of California, San Diego
Apostolic Church of John Maranke

Kenyon, Susan
Butler University
Zar

Kostarelos, Frances
Governers State University
Storefront Churches

Kremser, Manfred
University of Vienna
African Geomancy
Barbados, African-Derived Religions in

Cyberspace, African and African-Derived
Religions in
Ifá
St. Kitts and Nevis, African-Derived Religions in
St. Lucia, African-Derived Religions in

Lake, Rose
Cheikh Anta Diop University, Dakar, Senegal
Mouride Brotherhood

Levinson, David
Berkshire Reference Works
African Orthodox Church
AIC
Church of Christ (Holiness)
Fire Baptized Holiness Church of God
Gaga
Peoples Temple
Primitive Baptists
Seventh-Day Adventist Church

Littlewood, Roland
University of London
Mother Earth and Earth People

MacGaffey, Wyatt
Haverford College
Appendix A: Anthropology of Religion in Africa:
A Critique of Concepts and a Model

Mamiya, Lawrence
Vassar College
Black Muslims
National Baptist Convention of America
National Baptist Convention, USA
Progressive National Baptist Convention

Martin, Sandy Dwayne
The University of Georgia
African Methodist Episcopal Zion Church

Maxwell, David
Keele University
Zimbabwe Assemblies of God

McDaniel, Lorna
University of Michigan
Big Drum Dance of Carriacou

List of Contributors

Meyer, Birgit
University of Amsterdam
Diabolism

Mickler, Michael
Unification Theological Seminary
Unification Church

Morales, Beatriz
Morris Brown College
Costa Chica, Mexico

Murphy, Joseph
Georgetown University
Oshun
Santeria, United States

Ojo, Matthews
Obafemi Awolowo University, Ile-Ife, Nigeria
African Charismatics
Cherubim and Seraphim Society
Christ Apostolic Church
Healing in Sub-Saharan Africa `
Media Evangelism

Omenyo, Cephas
University of Ghana
Akan Religion
Church of the Twelve Apostles
Faith Tabernacle Church

Polk, Patrick Arthur
UCLA Folklore and Mythology Archives
Grenada, African-Derived Religions in
Obeah in the West Indies

Pollak-Eltz, Angelina
Univeridad Catolica Andres Bello, Caracas, Venezuela
Kardecism (Kardecismo)
Pagelanca and Catimbo
Tambor de Mina (Maranhao)
Venezuelan Cult of Maria Lionza
Xango (Pernambuco)

Price, Richard
College of William and Mary
Suriname, African-Derived Religions in

Salamone, Frank
Iona College
Divination, African

Harrist Movement
Pilgrimages
Secret Societies
Zionist Churches
Zulu Religion

Savishinsky, Neil
Columbia University
Rastafari in West Africa

Sawyer, Mary
Iowa State University
National Conference of Black Christians
Southern Christian Leadership Conference

Shannon, Janet
Davidson College
African Zoar United Methodist Church

Simpson, Anthony
University of Manchester
Mission Schools

Singer, Merrill
Hispanic Health Council, Hartford, Connecticut
Black Jewish Movements
Puerto Rico, African-Derived Religions in

Stewart, Dianne
College of the Holy Cross
Jamaica, African-Derived Religions in

van Dijk, Rijk
Leiden University
African Pentecostalism in the Netherlands

Warnock, Raphael
Union Theological Seminary
Abyssinian Baptist Church

Yawney, Carole
York University
Rastafari
Rastafari in Global Context

Zarate, Margarita
Universidad Autonoma Metropolitana—Iztapalapa, Mexico
Mexico, African-Derived Religions in

Index

*Number in **boldface** refer to extended treatment of a topic*

A

Abakuka, 107, 110

Abernathy, Ralph D., 249, 315, 344

Abiodun Akinsowon, Christianah Abiodun (Mrs. Captain), 32–34, 82–83

abolitionists, 14, 53, 159

abosom (deities), 28

Abushiri b.Salim al-Harthi, 153

Abyssinian Baptist Church, **1–2**, 348

Abyssinian Development Corporation, 2

aché (energy), 109–110, 290, 295, 365

Action Faith Ministries, 18

Acts Revival Church, 17

Adams, Charles, 249

Adams, Henry, 309

adoptions, 43

affliction, rituals of, 214

Africa House (Barbados), 257

African Charismatics, **2–6**
  beginnings and growth of, 2–3
  divine healing, 5, 142–143, 145
  doctrinal emphasis and practices, 5
  dynamics of movements, 3–4
  evangelism, 5
  foreign influence and, 3
  in French-speaking Africa, 3
  globalization of, 17
  leadership of, 3
  media evangelism of, 182
  militarization of popular speech, 5
  power, concern for, 4–5

sociopolitical relevance of, 5–6
  typology of, 4–5
    deliverance churches, 5
    faith-builders, 4
    faith-seekers, 4
    faith-transformers, 4
    modernists, 5
    reformists, 4
  urban communities and, 4
  women and, 3

African Church Movement, 32

African-derived religions (ADR), **21–22**
  in Barbados, 41–43
  in Brazil, 66–72
  in the Caribbean, 77–81
  in Cuba, 21, 107–110
  in Grenada, 128–130
  in Guadeloupe and Martinique, 130–131
  Internet and, 111–114
  in Jamaica, 1, 165–169
  major features of, 21
  in Mexico, 185–187
  in Puerto Rico, 250–252
  Spiritual Baptists and, 316
  in Suriname, 21, 135, 334–337
  in Trinidad, 338–343
  in the United States, 347–353

African digital diaspora religions (ADDR), Internet and, 111, 114

African Enterprise (AE), 238

African Episcopal Church of St. Thomas, 310

African geomancy, **6–8**, 118
  binary oppositions of markings, 7, 112
  mirror theme, 7
African independence movements, 89
African Independent/Indigenous Churches, 26, 237–239, 378
  healing arts and, 141, 238
Africanization, 90
African Methodist Episcopal Church (AME), **8–12**, 13–14, 144, 199, 210, 309, 349, 400
  Allen's establishment of, 8–10
  characteristic religious and social principles, 8–10
  educational efforts of, 11
  expansion of, 10
  General Conference of, 8, 11
  national and international expansion and evangelism, 10–11
  ordination of women, 10
  relationship with African Methodist Episcopal Zion Church, 13-14
  Service and Development Agency, 10
  social and cultural activism, 11–12
African Methodist Episcopal Zion Church (AMEZ), xi-xiii, **13–15**, 91, 144, 210, 309, 349
  antislavery movement and, 14
  ordination of women, 14–15
  relationship with African Methodist Episcopal Church, 13-14
African Orthodox Church, **15–16**, 351, 357
African Pentecostalism in the Netherlands, **17–19**
  cosmology and appeal of deliverance, 18–19
  social role of, 19
African traditional religion (ATR), **19**
  Internet and, 111–114
African Union Methodist Protestant Church, 349
African Zoar United Methodist Church, **20–21**
Afro-American Council, 14
Afro-Jamaican religion; *see* Convince
Afro-mestizos communities, 187
Aga Khan, 24, 151, 154
Agbebi, Mojolo, 161
Aguirre Beltran, Gonzalo, 185
Agyeman, Jaramogi Abebe, 301
Ahmad Gran, 151
Ahmadiyya Association for the Propagation of Islam, 25
Ahmadiyya movement, **22–25**, 151, 351
  Lahoris, emergence of, 24–25
  missionary outreach of, 23–24
  origins, beliefs, and claims, 23
  separatism of, 23
  succession dispute, 24–25

Ahmad, Mirza Ghulam, 22–25
Ahmad, Muhammad (Mahdi), 332
Ahrars, 23
AIC (African Independent Churches), **26**
Akala, Iyanasso, 66
Akan religion, **26–32**, 104
  ancestral spirits, 27–38
  belief about God, 27
  divinities (deities), 28
  human person concept, 29
  libation prayers, 29–30
  life cycle, 29–31
  lower spirit powers, 28
  morality, 31
  oral tradition of, 27
  present day, 31
  priesthood of, 28
  reincarnation beliefs, 30–31
  religious beliefs of, 26–26
  religious practices, 28
  salvation, 31
Aladura (owners of prayer), 5, **32–34**, 82, 85
  denominations of, 33
  emergence of movement, 32–34
  hymnal tradition, 33
  musical traditions, 33
  spread of movement, 34
Alegria-Pons, Jose Francisco, 128
Al-Hajj Umar Tall, 159
Ali, Muhammad, 25, 275
Alinesitoué, 116–117
Allen A.M.E. Church, 12
Allen College, 11
Allen, Rev. Richard, 8–9, 20, 199, 310, 349
Allen, William Francis, 200, 202
Alleyne, Mervyn, 101
Al-Maghili, Muhammad al-Hassan, 159, 332
Almoravid movement, 156, 243
Alpers, Edward, 376
Alpha Church, 147
al-Suyuti, 159
altars, 366–367
amaNazaretha (Nazareth Baptist Church), **34–37**, 238
  oral history of, 34–35
  Shembe and his church, 34–35
  spiritual experiences, 37
  theological controversies, 36–37
  twentieth century theological and leadership arguments, 35–35
A.M.E. Church Review, 12

AME Zion Community College University, 15
AME Zion Quarterly Review, 15
American Baptist Publication Society, 208
American Board of Commissioners for Foreign Missions (1810), 94
The American Catholic Tribune, 48
American Church Institute for Negroes, 16
American Independent Orthodox Church, 51
American Muslim Mission, 312, 351
American Pentecostal movement, 181
Amhara healers, 134
Ami, Ben, 55
amulets, 28
ancestor worship, 173–174
ancestral curses, 5
ancestral spirits, 27–28, 373–374, 390–391
ancestral zombies, 175
Anderson, Leafy, 60, 320
Anderson, Robert Mapes, 148
Anglican United Native African Church, 400
animal sacrifice, 21, 175, 296
Anlu uprising, 376
Ansaar Muslim Youth Organization, 155
Ansah, Samuel Kofi, 100
Anthony, Msgr. Patrick A. B., 325
Antoine, Robert, 340
apartheid, 89
Apostles of the Congo (RDC), 40
Apostolic Church, 33
Apostolic Church of Johane Masowe, xvii, 37–38, 164
Apostolic Church of John Maranke (Vapostori or Bapostolo), xvii, 38–40
Apostolic Faith Mission of South Africa (AFMSA), 237, 397
Apostolic Faith movement, 41
Apostolic Overcoming Holy Church of God, 41
Appiah, A. K., 165, 281
Aquarian Age, 354
Arab geomancy, 7
Arabian peninsular Islam, 151
Arab League, 160
arairaguni (decension of spirits), 136
Arkansas Baptist College, 97
Armenian Orthodox Church, 124
Arrabablahhubab, 33–34
Arya Samaj movement, 23
Asante, Molefe, xviii
Asbury, Francis, 10
Ashanti, 26–27
Assemblies of God, 18, 397
astrology, 59, 319, 354

asuman (lower spirit powers), 28
Austin, J. C., 310
Awa, Marie, 391
Aztec Empire, 186
Azusa Street Mission, 97, 144
Azusa Street Revival, 40–41, 144–145, 232
    African pentecostalism and, 235-237
    William J. Seymour and, 144

B
babaláwos ("Fathers of the Secrets"), 120, 136, 149–150, 287, 382
Babalola, Joseph ("Baba Aladura"), 33, 85, 125–126
Back-to-Africa preaching, 272
Baer, Hans A., xvii, 53–54
Bahia
    Candomblé terreios in, 66–68
Baily, Prince Alfred, 354
Baker (Father Divine), 232–235, 346–347, 353
Baker, Pinninnah, 232–233
BaKongo culture, 47, 109, 167
Bamana, geomancy and, 7
bancos (cult leaders), 359–360
Bannister, Brown, 205
banzo, 137
Bapostolo, xvii, 38–40
Baptist Missionary Society, 94
Baptist Church, 41
    Abyssinian, 1–2, 348
    Arkansas Baptist College, 97
    Bethel African, 10, 20
    Cameroon Native, 400
    Cane, 308
    Concord, 1
    Ebenezer, 204, 311
    Macedonia, xii
    Missionary, 326
    National Baptist Convention of America, 203–204,208–210, 256, 324,   349
    National Baptist Convention, U.S.A., Inc., 210–211, 248, 310, 348–349
    Native, 32, 166–167, 400
    Nazareth, 34
    Pilgrim, 310
    Progressive National Baptist Convention, 211, 248–250, 255, 312, 349
    Shouter, 339
    Silverbluff, 210, 308, 348
    Spiritual, 60, 129, 205–208, 316–318
    Zion Primitive, 247
Barahini-i Ahmadiyyah (Proofs of Ahmadiyya), 23

baraka (divine grace), 197
Barbados, African-derived religions in, **41–43**
Barnet, Miguel, 110
Barra, Pierrot, 364, 368
Barrett, Leonard, 168, 272
Barrett, Rev. T. L., 344
Barry, Elder E. J., 247
Bartleman, Frank, 41
basketmakers, 38
Bastide, Roger, xix
bateba (statue) for divination, 120
Bates, Daisy, 12
Batuque, **43–44**, 66, 75, 250
Becken, Hans Jürgen, 35
Bedward, Alexander, 283
Beltran, Alguirre, 104
bembe (communal ceremonies), 287, 296
Bengu, Nicholas B. H., 238
Bentsen, Lloyd, 256
benzador (Afro-Brazilian healer), 135
Berger, Iris, 379
Berlin Mission, 237
Beta Church, 147
Bethel African Church, 32
Bethel African Methodist Church, 10, 20
Bethel African Methodist Episcopal Church, 310, 349
Bethel Prayer Ministries, 17
Beulah Land Farm Project, 302
Bevel, James, 344
Bey, C. Kirkman, 192
Biafran Civil War, 160
Bible study, 329
Bible Way Churches of Our Lord Jesus Christ World Wide, 146
Big Drum Dance of Carriacou, **44–47**, 78, 129, 323
    Creole Dances, 45
    Frivolous Dances, 45
    history and language, 46
    Nation Dances, 45
    song/dance classification, 45
Bilby, Kenneth, 205–206
Bintana, 7
binza (witch-doctor), 388
Birhan, Farika, 258
birthday thrones, 290–293
Bishop, Rev. Josiah, 1
Bizango altars, 368
Black Catholic Lay Congresses, 48
Black Catholics in the United States, **47–51**
    contemporary status and institutions, 50–51
    history of, 47–48

twentieth century, 48–50
Black Christ, 15, 351
The Black Church in the African-American Experience
        (Lincoln and Mamiya), xviii
Black Churches in the United States, **51**
Black Church Independence Movement, 347–349
Black Divinity, 42
Black Economic Development Conference, 312
Black Hebrew Israelite Nation, 55
Black Holiness Churches, **51**
Black Holiness-Pentecostal movement; *see* Holiness-
        Pentecostal (sanctified) movement
Black hymnody, **199–208**
Black Jewish movements, **51–55**
    early congregations, 53–54
    Ford's ideology, 54
    major groups after 1900s, 54–55
    messianic-nationalist elements, 52–53
    roots in slave experience, 52–53
    shared central traits of, 54
black liberation, 80
Black Madonna, 15, 48, 351
    Shrine of the Black Madonna, 301–302
Black Muslims, **55–59**
    economic ethic of, 56–57
    Elijah Muhammad, 56–57
    Louis Farrakhan and Warith Deen Mohammed, 58–58
    Malcolm X, 57–58
    Master Fard, 56
    see also Moorish Science Temple
The Black Muslims in America (Lincoln), 55
Black Nationalism, 50, 56, **59**, 63
Black Nationalist Christian movement, 301
Black Panther Party, 312
Black Power movement, 12, 58, 213, 248, 312, 342
    African-American churches and, 62–64
    Cone's Black liberation theology, 64–65
Black Puritanism, 56
Black Slate, 302
Black Spiritual churches, **59–62**, 232, 352
    beliefs and practices of, 60–62
    criticism of, 61–62
    development in U.S., 60, 184–185
    healing and prophecy ceremonies, 61
    syncretism of elements of, 59–60
    women and, 59, 61
Black Supremacy, 260
Black theology, 12, **62–65**, 350–351
    Black Power movement and, 63–65
    Christianity and, 63–64
    Cone's Black Liberation theology, 64–65

current/recent status, 65
womanist theology, 65
Black Theology and Black Power (Cone), 64–65
A Black Theology of Liberation (Cone), 65
Black Theology Project, 213
Bluestone Church, 210
Blyden, Edward Wilmot, xviii, 161, 400
B'nai Zaken, 55
Boanerges, Ras, 260, 262
Bobo Dreads, 257, 267
Boddy, Janice, 377, 379
Body of Power, Spirit of Resistance (Comaroff), xviii
Bogle, Paul, 283
Bolivar, Simon, 358
Bongo; *see* Convince
Bongomen, 101
Bonkke, Reinhard, 238
Boorana cosmology, 229–230
Booth, Rev. L. Venhael, 249
bori practices, 244–245
born-again, 18, 145
Borrero, Maria, 252
Boswell, Leviticus L., 184
bottles and other spirit repositories, 366
Bourguignon, Erika, 352
Bowie, J., 146
Boyd, Henry Allen, 209
Boyd, Rev. Ronald, 208–209
Boyd, Thomas, III, 209
Boyd, Thomas, Jr., 209
Bradford, Alex, 204
Brahma Samaj, 22–23
Brandon, George, 251–252
Brazil, African-derived religions in, **66–72**
African gods and Catholic saints in, 69
beliefs and practices, 69–71
benzador herbalist, 135
Candomblé terreios in Bahia, 66–68
convergence of religions, 72
drums as sacred, 70
initiation rites, 70
Macumba, 176–177
orixas, nature and purpose of, 68–69
pagelança and catimbo healing cult, 226–228
possession, 70–71
Tambor de Mina en Maranhon, 337–338
Umbanda, 71–72
women and, 66, 68
see also Batuque; Candomblé
Brereton, Bridget, 339, 341
Bright, John D., 12

Briones, Maria Mendoza, 103
British Apostolic Church, 85
British Israel theory, 41
British Methodist Church (B.M.E.), 10
Broadway Tabernacle, 1
Brown Chapel A.M.E. Church, 12
Brown, Elder Sam, 257
Brown, James, 275
Brown, Morris, 10
Brown, Oliver, 12
Brown, Ras Sam, 260, 262
Brown v. Board of Education, 12, 311
Bryan, Andrew, 308
Bryant, Daniel, 237
Bryant, William Cullen, 312
Bücher, Johannes, 237
Bunche, Ralph J., 311
Burleigh, Harry T., 203
Burlin, Natalie Curtis, 202
Burnett, J. C., 203
Burning Spear, 276
Burton, Richard, 160
Burundi, 189
bush doctor, 135
Bushman Religion, **72–74**, 253, 255
puberty initiation rites, 74
rituals of, 74
trance curing dance, 74, 255
bush spirit, 180
Butts, Dr. Calvin O., III, 2
buyai, 136
Byrd, William, 210, 348
Byrne, David, 367

C
Caanite Temple, 191
cabildos, 108, 251, 285
caboclos, 338, 383
Cabo Verde island, 94
Cain, Richard, 10
California Gold Rush, 10
Callaway, Henry, 237
Cameroon Grassfields (Anlu uprising), 376
Cameroon Native Baptist Church, 400
Campbell, Alexander, 308
Campbell, Horace, 279
camp meetings, 4
Candomblé, 21, 60, **75–76**, 77, 79, 81, 219, 250, 285, 302, 337–338
in Bahia, 43–44
Catholicism and, 66-68, 75-76

Candomblé (*cont.*)
  healing and, 136
  terreiros, 44, 75-76
Cane Baptist Church, 308
cannabis, sacramental use by Rastfari, 264, 272, 274,
    276–277
Cardijn, Cardinal J., 162
Cardinal Gibbons Institute, 49
Carey, William, 94
Caribbean, African-derived religions in, **77–81**
  amalgam of traditions, 78–79
  the Caribbean diaspora and, 81
  Christian traditions in, 79
  divination and folk healing, 78
  Kumina (Cuminia), 174–175
  misconceptions of, 77–78
  music in worship, 205–206
  neo-African religions, 78
  Rastafari and Dread, 80–81
  religio-political movements, 78
  revivalist religions, 78
  St. Kitts and Nevis, 321–323
  St. Lucia, 323–325
  spiritism in, 320
  spiritualism in, 321
  spirit world, 79–80
  see also Spiritual Baptists
Carmichael, Stokely, 64
Carnegie, Andrew, 234
Carr, Andrew, 340, 342
Carriacou; *see* Big Drum Dance of Carriacou
Carroll, J. H., 301
Carter, Ben, 55
Cartwright, John Henderson, 311
Carver, George Washington, 320
Casas das Minas, 338
Casey-Hayford, Joseph Ephraim, xviii, 400
Cassidy, Michael, 238
casting of lots, 118–119
Castro, Fidel, 288
Catholicism, 15–16, 21, 130, 354, 362
  in Afro-Cuban religion, 110
  Candomblé and, 66-68, 75-76
  Christian Catholic Church in Zion, 400
  Creolized, 130
  de-Catholicization of new world Yoruba tradition, 387
  Federated Colored Catholics, 49
  missionaries and, 93–94
  North American Old Roman Catholic Church, 16
  Vodou and, 362
  Yoruba-based religions in, 386–387

  see also Black Catholics in the United States
Catimbo, 75, 226–228
catimbozeiro (shaman), 227
Cayton, Horace R., 147
Celestial Church of Christ ("Cele" or CCC), 33, 141
Cèn, 7
Central Congregational Church (United Church of
    Christ), 301
Central State University, 11
centros (worship and healing centers), 252
ceremonies, Santería beliefs, 287–288
Cerulli, Enrico, 392
Chambers, Rev. Thomas, 249
Chapel Hill Harvester Church (Atlanta), 239
Chapman, Mark L., 312
Chapman, Steven Curtis, 205
charismatic movements; *see* African charismatics
Cheikh Amadu Bamba Mbacke, 197
Cherry, F. S., 53
Cherubim and Seraphim movement, **82–84**, 141, 344
  doctrinal emphasis and practices, 83–84
  growth and development of, 82–83
  pattern of worship, 84
  Praying Band, 82–83
  schisms and proliferation of churches, 83
Cherubim and Seraphim Society, 32–33, 82
Chilembwe, John, 400
Chiluba, Pres. Frederick, 5
Choto, Joseph, 397
Christ Apostolic Church (CAC), 33, **84–86**
  contemporary practices and problems, 85–86
  development out of Aladura movement, 84–85
  women's role in, 86
  World Soul Evangelistic Association, 85
Christian alphabet poem, 127
Christian Catholic Church in Zion, 400
Christian denominations, 349–350; *see also* Baptist
    Church; Catholic Church; Episcopal Church;
    Methodist Church; *see also individual churches
    and movements*
Christian evangelism in Africa, **86–91**
  African theology and, 90
  contemporary evangelism, 90
  economic development, 89–90
  global evangelism, 90–91
  missionaries and native catechists, 88–89
  politics and African independence movements, 89
  see also African charismatics
Christianity
  Black theology and, 62–64
  colonialism and Islam and, 153–154

fundamentalism and, 145, 181–182
see also African charismatics; evangelism;
   Pentecostalism; Christian denominations
Christian Methodist Episcopal Church, 14
Christian missionaries in Africa, **92–96**
   Catholic missionaries along coast, 93–94
   early efforts in northeast, 92–93
   evangelical Protestants in interior, 94–96
   historical perspective on, 92
   Livingstone's influence, 95
   Portuguese missionaries, 93–94
Christian Missionary Society (CMS), 33
Christian Recorder, 12
Christian Science, 59
Christian Union (Nigeria), 2
Christ for the Nations Institute (CFNI), 397
Christ Temple Church, 97
Church of All Nations, 146
Church of Christ on Earth by the Prophet Simon
   Kimbangu, 26
Church of Christ (Holiness) U.S.A., **97**, 123, 144, 146, 351
Church of Christ's People, 33
Church of God in Christ (COGIC), 41, 97, **98–99**, 203,
   256, 313, 326, 351
   composition and practices of, 147
   Holiness movement and, 144–146
   women evangelists in, 99, 147
Church of God in Christ, Congregational, 146
Church of God in Christ, International, 146
Church of God in David, 53
Church of God and Saints of Christ, 53, **97–98**, 350
   politico-religious activities, 98
   seven "keys" of, 97
   syncretism of, 97
Church of Haile Selassie I, 273
Church of the Living God, the Pillar Ground of Truth
   for All Nations, 53, 232, 350
Church of the Lord (Aladura), 33–34, 141
Church of Lord (Nigeria), 26
Church of Lukumi Babaluaye, 296
Church Missionary Society (CMS), 94–96
Church of Our Lord Jesus Christ of the Apostolic Faith,
   146
Church of Pentecost, 17
Church of St. John Coltrane, 16
Church of the Twelve Apostles, **99–100**
   Bible and dancing gourd-rattle, 100
   fellowship groups of, 100
   use of holy water, 100
circumcision, 189, 214, 229
civil disobedience, 315

Civil Rights Act of 1964, 315
Civil Rights Movement, xi, 1, 12, 14, 49–50, 58, **101**,
   211–212, 248
   Black theology and Black Power, 62–63
   social activism churches and, 311
Clark, Mattie Moss, 204
Cleage, Albert B., 301, 351
Cleaver, Eldridge, 344
cleromancy, 118
Cleveland, James, 204
Cliff, Jimmy, 276
Clinton A.M.E. Zion Church, xii-xii
Clinton Junior College, 15
Coalition for Religious Freedom, 344
Cobbs, Clarence, 60, 62, 184
cofradias, 108
Cohortes, 78
Coker, Daniel, 10
Collier, Robert, 232
Collins, Barbara Rose, 302
colonial evangelism, 88–89
colonialism, xi, 95, 250, 339
Coltrane, John, 16
Columbus, Christopher, 78, 128, 250, 339
Comaroff, Jean, xviii, 376, 379
Combats Spirituelles, 17
Commandment Keepers, Holy Church of the Living
   God, Pillar and Ground of Truth, 55
Committee for the Advancement of Colored Catholics,
   49
Common Plan, 123
Communist Party, 234, 311
Community House, 1
communotheism, 21
Comte, August, 319
Conceicao, Escolastica Maria de, 68
Conceicao Nazare, Julia María, 68
Concord Baptist Church, 1
Cone, James H., 12, 62, 64–65, 213, 312–13
Congregation of the Aethiopian Hebrews, 55
Congress of Racial Equality (CORE), 315
conjuration, 305
Convention movement, 310
conversion, xi, 4–5
   slave religion and, 305–306
conversionist sects, 351
   social activism and, 313
Convince, 60, 78, **101–102**
   Alleyne's theory of origin, 101
   as ancestral cult, 101
   Bongomen and, 101

Cook, Will Marion, 203
Cooper, James Fenimore, 320
Coplan, David B., 237
Coptic Orthodox Church, 124
Coral Gardens Massacre, 261
Coronation Market Riot, 261
Cortés, Hernán, 186
cosmology
  aché and, 108–109
  Boorana, 229–230
  Gabra, 230
  Maasai, 228–229
  Pastoralist, 228–231
  Pygmy, 254
Costa Chica, Mexico, **102–106**
  African traditions in, 102, 104
  beliefs and practices of, 104
  Day of the Dead celebrations, 102, 104–106
  El Tono and the crossroads, 104
  history of slave trade, 102–103
  secret societies and dance of the devils, 106
  Shadow (or life force), 104
  totem (or animal double), 104
Couch, Andrae, 204
Council of Chalcedon, 124
Coupe Cou (moribund rituals), 45
Cox, Harvey, 145
creation; see cosmology
Creoles, 334–335
  coastal Winti, 335–337
  dances, 45
  healers, 130
Crowdy, William Saunders, 53, 97–98
Crowther, Samuel, 95
Crummell, Alexander, xviii, 95
Cuba, African-derived religions in, 21, **107–110**
  brotherhoods, 108
  cabildos and naciones, 108
  Catholic appropriations in, 110
  context of creation, 108
  divine creation and aché, 109
  espiritismo and, 251
  Nanigo (or Abakuka), 107
  oricha (divine spiritual forces), 109
  Regla de Arara, 107, 110
  Regla de Ocha of the Yoruba, 107, 110
  Regla de Palo of the Bakongo, 107, 110
  shared principles of, 108–110
  traditions today, 110
  worldview-ontological perspective, 108–110
  see also Santería

Cuban Revolution (1959), 107, 288
cults, xvi-xvii, 357–360
Cumina, 60, 78
curses, ancestral, 5
cursillo movement, 164
Cyberspace, African and African-derived religions in, **111–114**
  as binary geomancy, 112
  Ifá readings and consultations, 149
  information and communication, 113
  religious culture and identity, 113–114
  sociocultural level and new religious practice, 112–113
  web sites for, 112

D
d'Abbadie, Antoine, 392
Daddy Grace's United House of Prayer for All People on the Rock of the Apostolic Church, 146
Dale, Lily, 320
Danadana, Iyalusso, 66
dance, 45, 74, 100, 304
  see also Big Drum Dance of Carriacou
Dance of the Devils (la Danza de los Diablos), 106
Daneel, Inus, 238–239
Daughters of Jerusalem, 98
Davies, Ezekiel, 83
Davis, Andrew Jackson, 319–320
Davis, Cyprian, 48–49
Davis, Gerald L., 196
Davis, Stephen, 279
dawa (mission), 23
Day of the Dead celebrations, 102, 104–106
debtera, 134
decension of spirits, 136
De Craemer, Willy, 165
deities, 28
Delaine, J. A., 12
Delaire, Noah, 323
Delaney, Martin, 95
Delaware Conference, 20
Delille, Henriette, 320
Deliverance Evangelistic Centers, 146
deliverance rituals, 5, 18, 143
  appeal of, 18–19
Democratic Republic of the Congo, 172
  Jamaa and, 162–165
demonic healing, 5
Derminite, Ras, 259
Desbrosses, Nelson, 320
desegregation, 12
Desmangles, Leslie G., xix

destiny, 29
Dett, R. Nathaniel, 203
Dhlomo, Petros Musawenkosi, 35
Diabolism, 106, **114–115**
Diatta, Alinesitoué, 116–118
Dickson, W. D., 53
digital diaspora, 111, 113, 114
Dingle-El, Richardson, 192
Dinka religion, **115–116**
    power of *ring*, 115
Diola prophets, **116–118**
    Alinesitoué, 116–118
    colonial prophets of resistance, 117–118
    postcolonial prophets revive tradition, 118
    precolonial prophets establish tradition, 116–117
Diop, Cheikh Anta, xviii
divination, 7, 21, 70, **118–122**
    bateba (statue) for divination, 120
    different forms of, 118
    general characteristics of, 119–120
    horoscopes, 122
    mouse oracle, 121
    by obi seeds, 222
    other examples of, 120–122
    sassy wood, 121
    Zande (Azande) technique, 119
    see also African geomancy; Ifá
divine creation and aché, 109
divine grace, 197
divine healers, 5, 61, 133–136, 166, 180
Divine Spiritual Churches of the Southwest, 184
Divine Word Fathers, 49
Divinity and Experience: The Religion of the Dinka
    (Lienhardt), 115
Dixon, Jessy, 204
Djiné (persons born in Africa), 323–325
doctrine of salvation, 247–248
Dogon cultures, 7, 107, 109
Dominican Republic, Gaga (Rara cult) in, 127–128
door-to-door witnessing, 4
Dorsey, Thomas A., 204
Douglas, Frederick, 14
Dowdell, Glanton, 301
Dowie, John Alexander, 237, 400
Downer, Raphael, 261
Dozier, Rev. Esther, xii-xii, 13
Drake, St. Clair, 147, 356
dreadlocks (the Covenant), 261, 265, 277, 279
Dread movement, 78, 80–81, 257, 278–279
Drew Ali, Noble, 56, 191–192, 350
Drewel, Margaret, 282

Drew, Timothy, 191
Drew, Bernard A., xii
Drexel, Katherine, 49
drums and other summoning objects, 365–366
Dube, John, 35
Dube, Lucky, 276
Du Bois, W. E. B., xi-xii, xv, xvii-xviii, 12–13, 20,
    310–311, 347, 350
Dukakis, Michael, 256
Dunkley, Archibald, 259, 261, 272
du Pleiss, David, 238
DuPree, Sherry Sherrod, 146
Durkheim, Emile, 326, 329
Dutch West India Company, 339
Du Toit, Brian, 277
Dvorak, Antonin, 203

E
Earth People, xvi, 193–195
earth spirits, 179–180
East Africa
    Ahmadiyya movement in, 24
    charismatic movements in, 3
    geomancy, 7
    Islam in, 151–155
        Christianity and colonialism, 153–154
        reform and educational movement, 154–155
        since independence, 154–155
    Movement for the Restoration of the Ten
        Commandments of God, 198–199
    secret societies in, 298
East African Muslim Welfare Society (EAMWS), 154
East Calvary Methodist Episcopal Church, 203
Eastern Orthodox Church, 15
Eastern Star, 62
Ebenezer Baptist Church (Atlanta), 311
Ebenezer Baptist Church (Chicago), 204
Ebuhleni (holy city), 35
eco-feminism, 193
Edwards, F. S., 401
Edward Waters College, 11
effigies, 294
Eglash, Ron, 7
egungun (secret societies), 106
Egyptian medical papyri, 132–133
Eikenrenkoetter, Frederick K., II (Rev. Ike), 345–346, 352
Ekpe secret society, 298
Ekuphakameni (holy city), 34–35
Elder Solomon Michaux's Church of God, **122–123**, 146
    radio ministry of, 123
    social gospel of, 123

electronic-media evangelism, 181
Elementary Forms of Religious Life (Durkheim), 329
Emancipation, 10, 101
Empress Menen, 258
encantado (spirits), 44, 226
Encyclopedia Africana (Du Bois), xv
Endich Theological Seminary, 16
England, John, 47
Episcopal Church, 8, 14, 16, 349
   African Episcopal Church of St. Thomas, 310
   African Methodist Episcopal Church, 8–14, 144, 199, 210, 309, 349, 400
   African Methodist Episcopal Zion Church, xi–xiii, 13–15, 91, 144, 210, 309, 349
   Bethel African Methodist, 310, 349
   Christian Methodist, 14
   Good Shepherd Independent, 16
   Incorporated Methodist, 20
   Macedonia African Methodist, 64
   St. Thomas's African, 349
   Union American Methodist, 349
Episcopal Church of the Advocate (Philadelphia), 312
Eshu, 386
Espiritismo (Puerto Rican spiritism), 78, 250–251
Essien-Udom, E. U., 234
Eternal Life Spiritualist Association, 60
Ethiopia
   charismatic movements in, 3
   Rastafari and Selassie, 256, 262, 265–266, 268, 272
   religious and secular healers, 134
Ethiopianism, 398
Ethiopian National Congress (Bobo Dreads), 257
Ethiopian Orthodox Church, **123–125**, 257, 273
   beliefs and practices of, 124–125
   current situation of, 125
   history of, 124
Ethiopian Salvation Society, 260
Ethiopian World Federation (E.W.F.), 257, 262, 266–267, 273, 278
evangelism, 86, 145
   charismatics, 5–6
   Christian evangelism in Africa, 86–91
   contemporary movement, 90
   global evangelism, 90–91
   media evangelism, 180–183
   Muslim, 182–183
   overview of, 181
   see also African Charismatics; Christian evangelism in Africa
Evans-Pritchard, Edward, 215–215, 280–281, 387–389

Ewe-Fon pantheon of Dahomey (vodouns), 338
exorcisms, 28, 363

F
F*a*, 7
Fabian, Johannes, xix, 165
faith clinic, 142
faith healer, 134
Faith Tabernacle Church (FTC), 33, 85, **125–126**
Family Federation for World Peace and Unification (FFWPU), 344
Fanti, 25
Fard, W. D. (Master), 56, 312, 350–351
Farrad, Wali, 56
Farrakhan, Louis Abdul Haleem, 58–59, 312–313, 344, 347, 351
Farrakhan's Nation of Islam, 59
Farrow, Lucy, 40–41
Fashek, Majek, 276
fate, Santería belief, 287
Father Divine, 232–235, 346–347, 353
Father Divine's Peace Mission; *see* Peace Mission
Fathers of the Secrets, 120, 136, 149–150, 287, 382
fatwa (declaration), 23
Fauset, Arthur H., 53, 192, 196
Federal Colored Catholics, 49
Federation of Kardecists, 171–172
Fellowship of Christian Unions (FOCUS), 3
fellowships, 2
female circumcision, 189
feminism, 193
feng shui, 6–7
Fenner, Thomas P., 202
Ferrill, Loudon, 309
Field, Bishop Derks, 53
Fields, Karen E., xviii
Fire Baptized Holiness Association, 126
Fire Baptized Holiness Church of God of the Americas, **126–127**
Fire in the Bones (Raboteau), xviii
First Awakening, 308, 347
First Baptist Church of Gold Street, 1
First Church of Deliverance, 184
First Church of Divine Fellowship of New Orleans, 320
First Unity of God Church, 146
flags, 366
Flake, Floyd, 12
Flenkee; *see* Convince
flogging, as anti-witchcraft ritual, 105–105
folk medicine, 77, 134
Folk Research Center, 325

food offerings, 293–294
Foote, Julia, 15
Ford, Arnold Joshua, 52, 54, 355
Ford, Henry, 234
Forte, Joseph, xii
Fox, Kate, 319–320
Fox, Margaret, 319–320
Frazier, E. Franklin, xviii
Frederick K. C. Price's Crenshaw Christian Center, 146
Free African Society, 8, 199, 349
Freedom Church, 14
Freud, Sigmund, 363
Frivolous Dances, 45
Fruit of Islam, 56
Fry, Theodore, 204
Fuller, Rev. William E., 126
Fundamentalist movement, 145
    televangelism, 181–182

G
Gabra cosmology, 230
Gada system, 224, 229
gadèdzafè (Creole healers), 130
Gaga (Rara cult) in the Dominican Republic, 107, 127–128
    as socio-political migrant movement, 128
    sugarcane rite, 128
Gairy, Eric, 129
Gallatin, Martin V., 345
Gamma Church, 147
Gandhi, 311
Garifuna herbalists, 136
Garrett Seminary-Northwestern University, 64
Garrison, Lucy McKim, 200, 202
Garrison, Vivian, 252
Garvey, Marcus Moziah, 56, 259–260, 266, 351
    Rastafarianism and, 80–81, 272
    United Negro Improvement Association and, 16, 54, 81, 168, 272, 354–357
Gates, J. M., 204
gays and lesbians, 184, 256
Genovese, Eugene D., 52, 310
geomancy; see African geomancy
George, David, 308
Georgetown University, 48
Germany, African Pentecostalism in, 17
Ghana
    African Pentecostalism in, 17–18
    Aladura movement, 34
    AME missionary work in, 11

charismatic churches, 6
    Rastafari and reggae music in, 274–279
Gibson, William, 111
Gifford, Paul, 89, 237
The Gift of Black Folk (Du Bois), xv
Givens-El, John, 192
Givens-El, Timothy, 192
Glazier, Stephen D., 206
global evangelism, 90–91
glossolalia, 2, 33, 40–41, 98, 144, 148, 203
Glover, Rebecca, 10
Golden Rule, 319
Goldsmith, Peter D., 145
González-Whippler, Migene, 250
Good Neighbor League, 123
Good Shepherd Independent Episcopal Church, 16
gospel music, 203–204
    contemporary gospel, 204–205
    traditions and groups, 20
Gospel of Prosperity, 89
Grace, Charles Emmanuel "Sweet Daddy," 346–347
Gracia Real de Santa Teresa de Mose, 47
Grand sheiks, 192
Grant, Jacquelyn, 65
Great Awakening, 308
Great Barrington (MA), ethnographic profile of, xi-xiii
Great Barrington: Great Town, Great History (Drew), xii
Great Depression, 1, 123
Greater Mt. Zion Pentecostal Church of America, 146
Great Migration, 1, 12, 52, 56, 145, 347
Greene, Claude D., 192
Greening, Bruce, 51
green movement, 40
green power, 352
Grenada, African-derived religions in, **128–130**
    commemorative rites, 128–129
    popular devotional rites, 128–128
    religion and society, 129
    Shango-based religious practices, 129
Guadeloupe and Martinique, African-derived religions in, **130–131**
    creolized Catholicism in, 130
    healers in, 130
    Protestant movements in, 131
guerisseur (folk healer), 135
Guinea, charismatic movement, 3
Guinea-Bissau, Manjako of, 179–180
Guti, Ezekiel, 397
Guyana, Peoples Temple, 240–243

H
Hackman, John, 100
Haiti
  African-derived religions, 21
  AME missionary work in, 10
  see also Vodou
Haitian Renaissance, 364
Haitian Revolution (of 1791), 21, 128
hajj (pilgrimage to Mecca), 25, 58, 243–245
Hall, E. H., 204
Hall, Stuart, xix
Hampton Institute, 203
Handy, W. C., 203
Hannah, Makeda Blake, 258, 265
Happy News Cafe, 123
Harrist movement, xvii, **131–132**, 238
  importance of, 131
Harris, William Wade, 99–100, 131, 238, 309
Harwood, Alan, 252
Hatchett, Mother Mary, 354
Hausa practice of Islam, 244–245
Hawkins, Lynette, 204
Hawkins, Tramaine, 204
Hawkins, Walter, 204
Hayborn, Rev. James, 1
Haynes, Stephen, 238
healing arts, 5, 28, 84, **132–143**
  African Independent churches, 141–142
  among Christians, 141–143
  buyai and the arairaguni, 136
  in centros, 252
  Creole, 130
  divination and folk, 78
  divine healers, 5, 61, 133–136, 142–143, 145, 166, 180
  doctor/diviners, 133–136
  Egyptian medical papyri, 132–133
  herbalists and their herbs, 133–135, 140
  kenbwazè, 130
  of life failures, 5
  medicine men, 140
  the new world and, 134
  Pentecostal and charismatic churches, 142–143
  prayers for the nation, 143
  priest/healers, 140
  psychotherapeutics, 137–138
  in the Qur'an and among Muslims, 141
  revival and, 284
  ritual techniques, 137
  Santería, 288
  satanic oppression/attacks, 5
  shaman, history of medicine and, 133
  socioeconomic/political problems, 5
  spirit mediums, 133–134, 136
  in sub-saharan region, **139–143**
  in traditional African religions, 139–141
  water of life (omi iye), 85
healing cult; see Pagelança
Healy, James Augustine, 48
Healy, Patrick, 48
Henderson, Rev. Thomas, 1
Henry Affair, 261
Henry, Claudius, 266
Hepner, Randal L., 272
herbalists, 21, 28, 133–135, 140, 166
Herder, Johann Gottfried, 237
Herkovits, Melville J., 206
Hernandez, Dr. José Gregorio, 358
Herskovits, Frances S., 206
Herskovits, Melville J., xviii-xix
heterodoxy, 44
Hezmalhalch, Thomas, 401
Hibbert, Joseph Nathaniel, 259, 272
Hickerson, St. John the Divine, 232
Hickey, James Cardinal, 51
Hill, Ras Timothy, 262
Hill, Robert, 272
Hinds, Robert, 261, 272
Hinduism, 130, 334
Hindu reform movements, 22–23, 25
Hodges, John O., 346
Hodgeson, Janet, 237
Holiness church, 51, 97, 122, 126
Holiness doctrine, 97
Holiness-Pentecostal (Sanctified) movement, 15, **144–149**, 203, 232, 351
  composition and practices of sanctified congregations, 147–148
  politico-religious organizations, 146–147
  role in African-American society, 148–149
  social activism of, 313
  in the United States, 144–146
holiness sect, 53, 98
Holy African Church, 16
Holy Apostles' Community of Aiyetoro, 83
Holy Mountain of Nhlangakazi, 34
Hood, James Walker, 14
hoodoo, 59, 61
Hood-Speaks Theological Seminary, 15
Hood Theological Seminary, 15
horoscopes, 122
Horton, Robin, 281
hosannas, 38

houngan, 136
House of Nyahbinghi, 256–257, 260–262
Howard University, 49
Howell, Leonard Percival, 259–261, 266, 272
How to Eat to Live (Muhammad), 57
Huggans, Graham, 282
Hughes, Sarah Ann, 10
human figures (effigies), 294
Humphrey, James K., 301
"A Hungry God" (Powell, Sr.), 1
Hunt, Janet G., 50
Hunt, Larry L., 50
Hurgronje, C. S., 392
Hurley, Fr. George Willie, 353–354
Hurse, James, 209
Hurston, Zora Neale, 167
hush harbors, 306, 347
Hutchinson, Sharon, 216
hydromancy, 118
hymns; *see* music, Black hymnody
Hypolite, Hector, 364

I
iBandla amaNazaretha, 34
Ibn Battuta, 151, 158, 244
Ibra Fall, Cheikh, 197
Idahosa, Bishop, 239
Ifá, 7, 111, 119–120, 122, **149–150**, 295
    Oshun (Yoruba female deity), 225
I JahQueen, 258
'ilm al-raml (science of sand), 7
Imani Temple, 51
Incorporated Methodist Episcopal Church, 20
inculturation, 90
independence movements
    African, 89
    Black Church, 347–349
Indian Orthodox Church, 124
indigenization, 86
influenza epidemic (1918), 85, 125
initiation rites, 70, 74
Institutional Church and Settlement (Chicago), 310
Interdenominational Ministers' Union of Washington,
    123
Interdenominational Theological Center, 11
International Central Gospel Church, 17–18
International Spiritual Church, 353
Internet; *see* Cyberspace, African and African-derived reli-
    gions in
intoned prayers, 206
In Township Tonight (Coplan), 237

intuitive divination, 119
Isaiah Shembe, 141
Isenberg, Charles W., 392
Islam, 7, 23–24, 59, **151**
    Ahmadiyya Association for the Propagation of Islam,
        25
    Arabian peninsular influences, 151
    Christianity and colonialism, 153–154
    in East Africa, 24, **151–156**
    Farrakhan's Nation of, 59
    Hausa practice of, 244–245
    healing arts and, 141
    Maitatsine sect, 177–178
    media evangelism of, 182–183
    messianic-nationalism, 350
    Shi'a, 151, 178
    Shiite, 177
    social activism of messianic-nationalist sects, 312
    Sudenese Brotherhoods, 330–334
    Sufism, 331–332
    Sunni, 23, 25, 56, 58–59, 151, 178
    in twentieth century advance, 160–161
    in West Africa, 24, **156–161**, 177–178, 369
    see also Moorish Science Temple; pilgrimage
Islamic Conference Organization (ICO), 160
Islamic Review, 25
Islamic Sufism, 331–332
Israel Universal Divine Spiritual Churches of Christ,
    320
Israel Universal Spiritual Churches of Christ (New
    Orleans), 61
Iviyo loFakazi bakaKristu (Legion of Christ's witnesses),
    238
Ivory Coast
    Aladura movement, 34
    AME missionary work in, 11
    charismatic movement, 3
Ivory, Liveth, 258
Izala movement, 177

J
Jack, Gullah, 310
Jackson, George Pullen, 200
Jackson, Joseph H., 211, 248–249
Jackson, Michael, 275
Jackson, Rev. Jesse, 2, 255–256, 312, 350
Jalsal (annual meeting), 25
Jamaa, **162–165**
    characteristics of, 163–164
    Father Tempels and, 162–163, 165
    as a movement, 163–165

Jamaica, African-derived religions in, 1, **165–169**
    ethnocultural roots of, xix, 168
    herbalists, 135
    Kumina (Cuminia), 174–175
    Native Baptist War (1831-32), 166
    Obeah and Myral in early colonial period, 165–166
    post-Emancipation era (1841-1865), 167–168
    Rastafari movement in, 81, 257, 259–261, 272,
        278–279
    revival folk religion, 282–284
James, Thomas, 14
Jamison, Albert, 204
Jasper, John, 52
Jefferson, Thomas, 202
Jeffries, Elmira, 147
Jehovah's Witnesses, 369
Jehova Shalom, 32
Jemison, Daniel, 211
Jemison, Rev. Dr. Theodore, 211
Jemison, T. J., 255
Jeter, J. A., 98
jihad (holy war), 23, 66, 151, 158–159
Jim Crow era, 144, 347
Jiménez, Pérez, 359
Johnson, Guy B., 202
Johnson, Hall, 203
Johnson, J. Rosamund, 203
John Wesley Chapel, 20
Jones, Absalom, 9, 20
Jones, Charles Price, 97–98, 144
Jones, Edward, 209
Jones, Everett, 209
Jones, Jim, 235, 240–243
Jones, Le Roi, 52
Jones, Major, 213
Jones, Marceline Baldwin, 240
Jones, Robert E., 310, 348
Jonestown mass murder-suicide, 240
Joseph, Etienne Wells, 323
Joyner, Charles, 303
Joy Street Baptist Church, 348
jubilees, 203
Judaism; *see* Black Jewish movements

K
Kamwana, Elliot, 369
Kardec, Allan, 171, 251, 285, 319, 321, 357
Kardecism (Kardecismo), 44, **169–172**, 226, 338,
        358–360
    beliefs and practices, 171
    in Latin America, 171–172

karma, 171
Kataribabo, Dominic, 199
Kaunda, Kenneth, 175–176
Kaye, Andrew, 276
Kélé, 323–325
kenbwazè (healers), 130
Kennedy, Imogene (Miss Queenie), 174
Kenya
    charismatic movements in, 3
    Maasai cosmology, 229
Kenyan Church of Christ in Africa, 400
Kenyatta, Jomo, 298
Kibwetere, Joseph, 198–199
Kilpatrick, Carolyn Cheeks, 302
Kimbanguist movement, 238
Kimbangu, Simon, 238
Kinch, Emily Christmas, 88
King, B. B., xviii
King, Dexter, 249
King, Franzo, 16
King, Martin Luther, Jr., xv, 50, 59, 255, 349–351
    assassination of, 59, 99, 148
    Black Theology and, 62–64
    Malcolm X and, 58
    National Baptist Convention and, 211, 249
    social activism and, 311, 349
    Southern Christian Leadership Conference and,
        314–315
King, Martin Luther, III, 315
King, Martin Luther, Sr., 249, 311
Kitawala millenarian movement (Watchtower), 369
Kivengere, Bishop Festo, 238
Klunzinger, C. B., 392
Knight, Rev. Joel, 14
Knights of the All Seeing Eye, 354
Knights of Peter Claver, 47, 49
Kongo religion, **172–173**, 362
Kooliny Djabune, 117
Krapf, Johann, 95, 392
Krishnamurti, Jiddu, 232
Ku Klux Klan, 123, 145
Kumina (Cuminia), 21, 101, 167, **174–175**
Kupara, Raphael, 397
Kwame (God), 27
Kwasi (Phillipus van Quassie), 335

L
LaFarge, John, 49
Laguerre, Michel, 134
Lahoris movement, 25
Lake, John G., 237, 401

lakou (family dwelling), 364
Latimer, Rev. G., 354
Latin America
    Kardecism in, 171–172
    spiritism in, 320–321
    see also specific countries
Latin American Liberation Theology Movement, 288
Lawrence, "Major" A. B., 83
Lawson, R. C., 146
Lee, Jarena, 10
Legio Maria Movement, 379
Lekganyane, Ignatius, 238
Lelile, George, 308
Lennox, Sister Merriam, 260–261
Lenshina, Alice, 378–379
le Roux, Petrus L., 237
Leslie, Charles, 165
Lewis, David Levering, xi, xv
Lewis, I. M., 377
Liataud, Georges, 364
liberation theology, 64–65, 288
Liberia
    Aladura movement, 34
    AME missionary work in, 10–11
    Harrist movement, 131
    secret societies in, 297, 299
Liele, George, 166
Lienhardt, R. G., 115
life-crisis rituals, Ndembu ceremonies, 214
life cycle, Akan view of, 29–30
life-force, concept of, 162, 164
Lincoln, Abraham, 320
Lincoln, Charles Eric, xviii, 50, 55, 147
Little, Malcolm; *see* Malcolm X
Livingstone College, 15
Livingstone, David, 95, 188
Living Witnesses of the Apostolic Faith, 146
livty of Rastafari code, 257, 261–262, 265
locational geomancy, 6
Logan, Dr., 184
Loguen, Jermain, 14
Lomax-Hannon Junior College, 15
Lomnitz, Claudio, 186
London Missionary Society (1795), 94
Long, Edward, 165
Long Search Series, 35
Looper, S. E., 146
Louva, Bredda, 260
Lowery, Rev. Joseph E., 315, 344
Luba culture, 162
Lucumi, 21, 107

Lukuman (diviner), 135–136, 336
Lumpa Church, **175–176**, 378–379
Lumumba, Patrice, 162
lwas (spirits), 361–363, 365
Lyons, Austin, 205
Lyons, Rev. Dr. Henry, 211

M
Maasai cosmology, 228–229
Maasai secret society, 298
McAdam, Doug, 311
McClaskey, John, 9
McCloud, Amihah, 192
McCullough, Walter ("Sweet Daddy Grace"), 346–347
Macdonald, Jeanette (Mother Earth), 193–195
McDonnough, Gary Wray, 49–50
Macedonia African Methodist Episcopal Church, 64
Macedonia Baptist Church, xii-xii
MacGaffey, Wyatt, xix
McGee, Ford Washington, 203
McGuire, George Alexander, 15, 351, 355, 357
Macklin, J., 251
Macumba, 60, 75, **176–177**, 219, 250, 321
Madagascar, geomancy in, 7
Madison, Arthur, 234
magic, Zande beliefs and, 388
Mahdi (God-guided one), 23, 159–160, 178, 332
Maitatsine, Alhaji Marwa, 177
Maitatsine Sect, **177–178**
Maji-Maji rebellion, 153
Makonnen, Ras Tafari; *see* Selassie, Haile
Malawi, charismatic movements in, 3
Malay, geomancy, 7
Malcolm X, 57–58, 63, 312, 347, 351
    Martin Luther King, Jr. and, 58
Mali, 7, 156
Malm, Krister, 205
Malraux, Andrè, 368
mambo, 136, 361
Mamiya, Lawrence H., xviii, 50, 147
Mamvura, Lazurus, 397
Mandela, Nelson, 398
Manjako of Guinea-Bissau, **179–180**
    ancestor shrine, 180
    bush spirit, 180
    diviners, 180
    earth spirits of, 179
Manley, Michael, 262, 267
Marabale, Manning, 256
Maranke, Abel, 40
Maranke, John, 38–40, 141

Maranke, Makebo, 40

Marcus Garvey Movement, 302

Maria Lionza, 78, 172
    Venezuelan cult of, 357–360

Markoe, William, 49

Marley, Bob, 266, 275–276

maronnage, 79

Maroon religions, 334, 336–337

maroon republics, 79

marriage, polygamous, 33, 100, 175

marriage rites, Akan religion, 30

marronnage, 361–362

Marshall, Andre, 308

Marshall (Thurgood) Academy for Learning and Social
        Change, 2

Martinique, African-derived religions in, **130–131**

Martin, Sallie, 204

martyrdom, 93

Marwa, Muhammadu, 177–178

masks, secret societies and, 298–299

Masolo, D. A., 165

Mason, Charles H., 97–98, 144–146, 203

Masons, 62

Masowe, Johane, 37

Matthew, Wentworth Arthur, 54–55

Mau Mau, 298

mawazo (thoughts), 164

Mayfair Project, 123

Mayombe, 107

Mays, Benjamin, 63, 249

Mbori (God), 389–390

Mbuti, John, xix

media evangelism, **180–183**
    electronic-media evangelism, 181
    forms of, 181
    modern social and religious implications, 183
    overview of purpose, 181
    patterns of production and utilization, 181–183
    print-media evangelism, 181
    televangelism, 181–182
    video technology, 181–182

medicine man, 140, 142

medium (mandwa), 22

Melton, J. Gordon, 184, 192

Menininha, Mae, 68

mesmerism, 169

Message to the Black Man (Muhammad), 57

messianic-nationalism, 52, 232
    social activism and, 312–313
    in United States, 350–351

mestizo person, 185

Methodist Episcopal Church, 8, 14, 349

Methodist Church, **184**
    British, 10
    Mother African Zoar United, 21
    United African, 400
    United, 8, 14
    see also Episcopal Church

Metropolitan Spiritual Churches of Christ (MSCC),
        Inc., 61, **184–185**, 352
    gay members and, 184

Mexico, African-derived religions in, **185–187**
    historical background of, 185–186
    Pentecostalism and, 187
    religious repression in colonial era, 186–187
    religious syncretism, 187
    sombra (shadow) concept, 187
    Spanish Inquisition and, 186
    see also Costa Chica, Mexico

Michaux, Elder "Lightfoot" Solomon, 122–123, 146

millenarianism, 159–160, 193, 369, 402

Miller, George Frazier, 310

Millerite movement, 300

Miller, William, 13, 300

Mill Hill Fathers (Josephites), 47–48

Million Man March, 59, 313

Mina cult, 337–338

miracle workers, 142

Mirzais, 23

missionaries, xi, 88–89, 237
    in Africa, 11, 92–96
    German Romanticism, 237
    Pentecostal, 18

Missionary Baptists, 326

mission schools in Africa, **188–190**
    in colonial era, 188–189
    postcolonial schools, 189–190

missions and missionaries, **191**

Mitchell, Henry, 64, 213, 312

Mix, A. W., 204

Mmboya, Tom, 189

Modernists, African charismatics, 5

Mohammed, Farrad, 56

Mokone, M. M., 11, 398

Mondlane, Eduardo, 189

Monophysite churches, 123–124

monotheism theory, 253

Montague, Masani, 258

Montgomery Bus Boycott, xv, 211

Moon, Rev. Sun Myung, 343

Moore, Annie, 241

Moore, Rebecca, 241

Moorish Science Temple, xii, 56, **191–192**, 350
    modern practices and development, 192
    movement's growth and internal conflicts, 191–192
    teachings of Noble Drew Ali, 191–192
Moorish Science Temple Divine and National
        Movement of North America, 192
morality, Akan religion, 31
Moremi, 386
moribund rituals, 45
Morris, Aldon D., 349
Morris Brown College, 11
Morris, Calvin S., 311
Morris, Charles Satchell, 1
Morris, Edmond, 208–209, 211
Morris, Samuel, 232
Mosaic tradition, 52–53
Moses, Greg, 311
The Moslem Sunrise, 24
Mossell, Charles W., 10
Mother African Zoar United Methodist Church, 21
Mother Earth and the Earth People, xvi, **193–195**
    beliefs and practices, 193–195
    life and visions of Mother Earth, 193
Mother Earth (Jeanette Macdonald), 193–195
Mount Zion A.M.E. Church, 12
Mouride Brotherhood, **197–198**
Mourning Ground rituals, 43
mouse oracle (divination), 121
Movement for the Restoration of the Ten
        Commandments of God, **198–199**
Mt. Calvary Holy Church of America, Inc., 147
Mt. Sinai Holy Church, 146–147
Mt. Zion Spiritual Temple, **196–197**, 352
Mudimbe, V. Y., 165
Mugabe, Robert, 189, 375
Muhammad al Madhi, 160
Muhammad, Elijah, 56–59, 63–64, 234, 312, 347,
        350–351, 354
Muhammad Speaks, 58
Muhammad, Wallace Deen (Imam Warith), 59, 312,
        351
Muhwati, James, 397
mujjahid (renewer/reformer), 25, 159
Mulenga, Alice Lenshina, 175
mullahs (religious teachers), 245
Mupako, Peter, 38
Murphy, Joseph M., xviii
Murphy, Larry G., 192
Murrain, Archbishop, 318
Musa, Mansa (Lord), 243–246
music, Aladura, 33

music, Black hymnody, **199–208**
    contemporary gospel, 204–205
    gospel hymnody, 204
    slave religion and, 304–305
    spirituals, 199–203
    twentieth century sacred musical traditions, 203–205
music, gospel, 20, 203–205
music, reggae, 275
music, slave songs, 200, 202, 203
music, Spiritual Baptist, 60, 129, 205–208
    classifications and types of, 206
    musical development and composition, 206–207
    performance, 207–208
    role of music in worship, 205–206
Muslim Education and Welfare Association, 155
Muslim Girls Training, 56
Muslim Media Practitioners of Nigeria, 183
Muslim Mosque, Inc., 58, 351
Muslim Political Action Committee, 313
Muslims
    American Muslim Mission, 312, 351
    in East Africa, 154
    healing arts and, 141
    media evangelism of, 182–183
    see also Black Muslims
Muslim World League, 25
mutual aid societies, 47
Mwerinde, Credonia, 198–199
Myal religion, 101, 165–169, 217, 283
Myers, Joseph, 261
mysticism, 42

N
nabi, 23
naciones, 108
Nackabah; *see* Church of the Twelve Apostles
Nackabar, John, 99–100
Nago, 66
Naming Day, 70
Nananom Nsamanfo (spirits of ancestors), 27
Nanigo, 107, 110
naqual (*el tono*) belief system, 104
Narcisse, King Louis H., 60, 196
Nasir al-Din, 159
National Association for the Advancement of Colored
        People (NAACP), 12, 14, 62, 301, 315
National Baptist Convention of America (NBCA),
        203–204, **208–210**, 256, 324, 349
    churches, 209
    history and conflict, 208–209
    organization, 209–210

National Baptist Convention, U.S.A., Inc., **210–211**, 248, 310, 348–349
  history and beliefs, 210–211
  organization and activities, 211–212
National Baptist Publishing Board, 209
National Baptist World Center, 212
National Black Catholic Clergy Caucus (NBCCC), 50
National Black Catholic Seminarians Association (NBCSA), 50
National Black Lay Catholic Caucus (NBLCC), 50
National Black Sisters' Conference (NBSC), 50
National Catholic Conference for Interracial Justice, 49
National Colored Spiritualist Association, 320
National Committee of Black Churchmen, 212
National Committee of Negro Churchmen, 12, 212
National Conference of Black Christians (NCBC), **212–213**
  purpose of, 213
National Conference of Black Churches, 350
National Conference of Black Churchmen (NCBC), 62–64, 212, 312
National Conference on Black Power, 312
National Convention of Gospel Choirs and Choruses, 204
National Council of Black Churchmen, 12
National Council of Churches (NCC), 213, 312
National Islamic Front, 334
nationalism
  Black, 50, 56, 59, 63, 301
  messianic, 52, 232, 312–313, 350–351
National Missionary Baptist Convention of America (NMBCA), 209
National Office for Black Catholic (NOBC), 50
National Primitive Baptist Convention, U.S.A., 247
National Spiritual Alliance, 320
National Spiritualist Association, 320–321
National Union of Kenyan Muslims, 155
Nation Dance, 45, 129; see also Big Drum Dance of Carriacou
Nation of Islam, 56–59, 62, 234, 312–313, 350–351; see also Black Muslims
Native Baptist Church, 32, 400
Native Baptists, 166–167
Native Baptist War (1831-32), 166
Nazareth Baptist Church, 34
Nazarite movement, 36–37
Ndembu religion, **214**
  life-crisis rituals, 214
  rituals of affliction, 214
The Negro Church (Du Bois), 347
neocolonialism, 78

Netherlands
  African Pentecostalism in, 17–19
  Ghanaian Pentecostalism in, 17
New Alliance Party, 313
New Jewel Revolution, 46
New Life Church of God in Christ, 344
New Thought, 59, 232, 235, 345, 354
New Zion, 175
Ngoma, Priscilla, 397
Ngorima, Caleb, 397
Nigeria
  African Pentecostalism in, 17
  Ahmadiyya movement in, 24
  Aladura movement, 34
  AME missionary work in, 11
  charismatic movements in, 2–3, 6
  Christ Apostolic Church, 84–86
  Ekpe secret society, 298
  ethnic variation and Islam, 161
  hajj (pilgrimage), example of importance, 244
  importance of Faith Tabernacle Church in, 125–126
  Islamic Maitatsine movement, 177–178
Nigerian Celestial Church of Christ, 344
Nilotic language, 115, 215
nirvana, 171
Nkabinde, 34
nkrabea (destiny), 29
Nkrumah, Kwame, 189
nongovernmental agencies (NGOs), 89, 257, 381–382
North American Old Roman Catholic Church, 16
Ntsikana, 237
Nuer religion, **215–216**
Nur-ud-Din, Hakim, 24
Nyabinghi Order of Divine Theocracy, 273
Nyerere, Julius, 154, 189
Nzapa Zande, 391

O
Obadare, Timothy, 86
Obatala, 384–385
Obeah, 21, 101, 165–169
  in the West Indies, **216–217**
obeahman, 135, 322
obi seeds, 222
Odubanjo, David, 85
Odum, Howard W., 202
Ogholi, Evi-Edna, 276
Oglethorpe, James, 99
Ogun, **217–220**, 386
  distinctiveness of, 218
  history of, 218–219

philosophy and social activism of, 219–220
in West African religious systems, 218
in Western hemisphere, 219–220
okra (soul from God), 29
Olatunrinle, Christianah, 82
Oliver, Joseph "King," 204
Olodumare, 251, 287, 371, 384
Omojola, Peter, 83
Onanuga, Abraham, 83
One Mind Temple Evolutionary Transitional Body of
  Christ, 16
Onyame (Supreme Being), 27
Oosthuizen, G. C., 36–37, 238
Operation PUSH, 255–256
oracular system, 6
oral traditions, 116
Organization for Afro-American Unity, 58
Organization of Rastafari Unity, 257
oricha (divine spiritual forces), 109–110
Oriental Orthodox churches, 123
Origen of Alexandria, 92
Original Hebrew Israelite Nation, 350
Orimolade, Moses, 82–83
Orisha, 75, 149, 205, 218, 285
  Macumba and, 177
  Santería and, 287–288, 295
  Spiritual Baptists and, 316
  West African religions and, 371
orisha fundamentos, 290
Orisha (Shango) Movement in Trinidad, **221–223**,
  339–343
  beliefs and practices, 221–222
  current status of, 223
  divination by obi seeds, 222
  history and background, 221
  pantheistic elements of, 221
  social organization, 223
orixas
  African gods and Catholic saints, 69
  as archetype, 69
  nature and purpose of, 69–69
Oromo religion, **223–224**
  Gada system and, 224, 229–230
Oschoffa, Samuel, 141
Oshitelu, Josiah ("Arrabablahhubab"), 33–34
Oshun, 225
Oshunmi, Senhora, 68
Otabil, Dr. Mensa, 18
Owens, Ginny, 205
owners of prayer; *see* Aladura
Oya, 386

P
Pagelança and Catimbo, 75, 226–228, 338
  beliefs and practices, 226–227
  pagé (shaman), 226
  religious amalgamation, 227–228
pagé (shaman), 226
Palo Monte, 107
Pan African Orthodox Christian Church (PAOCC),
  301–302
Panday, Basdeo, 318
Pantheon, 287
Parham, Charles Fox, 40–41, 144–145
Paris, Arthur E., 148
Parkham, Charles, 235–36
Parks, William, 211
Parkyns, Mansfield, 392
Partners in Ecumenism, 213
Passover celebration, 39
Pastoralist cosmologies, **228–231**
  Boorana cosmology, 229–230
  centrality of, 230–231
  common characteristics of, 228
  examples of, 228–230
  Gabra cosmology, 230
  Maasai cosmology, 228–229
  myth of origin, 230–231
Patois, 44–46
Patterson, Orlando, 168, 217
Paul, Norman, 129
Paulos, Patriach Abuna, 125
Paul Quinn College, 11
Paul, Rev. Thomas, 1
Payne, Daniel A., 11–12
Payton, Rev. Benjamin, 213
Peace Makers Association, 257
Peace Mission, **231–235**, 240, 345, 353
  declining years, 235
  expansion on East coast and beyond, 233
  first congregation, Sayville, Long Island, 232–233
  initial development of, 232
  membership, 233–234
  religious beliefs, 235
  social reform nature of, 234
Pearse, Andrew, 45
Pedro, Dom, 362
Pentecostal Assemblies of God the World, 145–146, 351
Pentecostalism, xvii, 2, 5, 145
  African-American Pentecostalism, 144–146
  American movement, 181
  Azusa Street revival, 40–41
  healing arts in, 142–143

Pentecostalism (*cont.*)
  media evangelism of, 182
  Mexican Pentecostalism, 187
  mission-based form of, 18
  modern culture and, 4
  in the Netherlands, 17–19
  related forms of, 145
  role in African-American society, 148–149
  televangelism, 182
  in the United Kingdom, 17
  see also Holiness-Pentecostal (Sanctified) movement
Pentecostalism in Africa, **235–240**
  community and belonging, 239–240
  independent/indigenous churches, 237–238
  influences on mainline/mission churches, 238–239
  origins of movement, 235–237
  Zimbabwe Assemblies of God Africa, 397
Pentecostal Temple Institutional Church of God in
     Christ, 99
Peoples Temple, 235, **240–243**
  beliefs, 241–242
  history of, 240–241
  mass murder-suicide, 242–243
Perez Munguia, J. Patricia, 103
Perfect, George, 85
Pernambuco, 43, 75, 285, 337–338, 382–383
personal destiny, Santería belief, 287
personality soul (*sunsum*), 29
Peter, J. A., 144
Petro, 362–363
Pettaway, Charles, 209
Pettey, Charles Calvin, 14
Pettey, Sarah, 15
Petwo rites, 367
Philosophie Bantoue (Tempels), 162
Pierce, Bob, 381
Pierre, André, 364
pilgrimage, **243–246**
  Catholic traditions, 245
  early African pilgrimages to Mecca, 25, 58, 243–244
  Nigerian example of hajji's importance, 244–245
  other pilgrim traditions, 245–246
Pilgrim Baptist Church, 310
Pinnacle commune, 260
Planno, Mortimo, 258, 262, 266
plantation society, 102
plantation songs, 200–203
Pleasant, W. S., 98
Plowden, W., 392
Plummer, Bishop H. Z., 98
Pocomania (Poco), 167, **247**, 282; *see also* Revival

Poewe, Karla, 240
polygamous marriage, 33, 100, 175
Poole, Robert (Elijah), 56
Pope Alexander IV, 185
Pope Leo X, 93
Poro secret society, 297, 299
possession, 22, 45, 80, 110, 283–284
possession trance, 21–22, 44, 70–72
Powell, Adam Clayton, Jr., 1–2
Powell, Adam Clayton, Sr., 1, 311
praise houses, 306–307, 347
prayers for the nation, 143
praying bands, 32, 82–83
preaching, slave religion and, 304
Precious Stone Society, 84–85
Price, Florence, 203
priest/healers, 140
Primitive Baptists, **247–248**, 351
  doctrine of salvation, 247–248
Primitive National Baptist Convention, 351
Prince, Gary, 209
Prince Hill Masonry, 97
print-media evangelism, 181
Proctor, Dr. Samuel, 2
Progressive National Baptist Convention, Inc. (PNBC),
     211, **248–250**, 255, 312, 349
  history, 248–249
  organization, 249–250
Progressive Spiritual Church, 320
Proofs of Ahmadiyya, 23
The Promised Key (Howell), 260–261
prophecy, 28; *see also* Diola prophets; divination
Prophet Muhammad, 23, 25, 141, 178, 331–332
Prosser, Gabriel, 53, 308, 310
Providence Baptist Association, 348
psychotherapeutics, 137–138
Public Enemy (rap group), 59
Puerto Rico, African-derived religions in, **250–252**
  contemporary espiritismo, 252
  Santerismo, 252
  varied roots of espiritismo, 250–252
Pukumina, 101, 283–284
Pygmy religion, **253–255**
  conceptualization of God, 253
  creation myths, 254
pyromancy, 118

Q
Qadianis, 23
quilombos (secret settlements), 66
Quinn, William Paul, 10

Qur'an, 23–25, 56, 178, 191, 331, 333
   healing among Muslims, 141

R
Raboteau, Albert J., xviii, 52
racism, xv, xvii, 50, 64, 144
Rada, 339–343, 362–363
Rada altars, 367
Rainbow Coalition, **255–256**, 312, 350
Rainbow/PUSH Coalition, 256
rainmakers, 140
Raml (Arab geomancy), 7
Ramsharam, Michael, 318
Randolph, A. Philip, 311
Randolph, Florence, 15
Ranger, Terence, 376–377
Ransom, Reverdy, 12, 310
Rara spirits, 127
Rasses International Sistren, 257
Rastafari, xvii, 78, 102, 129, 194, **256–266**
   current developments, 265–266
   daily life practice of, 265
   history of, 258–263, 269–271
   in Jamaica, 259–260
   knowing and practices, 263–264
   livty code, 257, 261–262, 265
   Marcus Garvey and, 80–81, 272
   Nyahbinghi orthodoxy, 257
   Pinnacle commune, 260
   sacramental use of cannabis, 264, 272
   self-definitions of, 256
   social organization of, 257–258
   women and gender relations, 257–258, 265, 274
Rastafari Centralization Organization (R.C.O.), 257
Rastafari in global context, **266–268**
   contemporary perspective, 267–268
   emergent ambassadorial tradition, 268
   global perspective of history, 266–267
Rastafari International Theocratic Assembly, 256–257
Rastafari Movement Association, 262
Rastafari Patriotic Unity, 257
Rastafari in the United States, **272–274**
   decentralized nature of, 273
   Jamaican roots of, 272
   in North America, 272–274
Rastafari for Unity (Bermuda), 257
Rastafari in West Africa, **274–279**
   African Diaspora and, 279
   beliefs and practices, 277–278
   cannabis use, 276–277
   fashion trends of, 277

Jamaican transnational apostles, 278
   mediums of dissemination, 274–275
   reggae music, 274–276
   roots of beliefs, 278–279
Rawlings, Pres. Jerry, 6
Raymond, Rev. John T., 1
reading room, 167
Reconstruction, 14
Reformists, African charismatics, 4
reggae performers, 262, 266–267, 274–276
regional cults, xvi–xvii
Regla de Arara, 107, 110
Regla de Ocha of the Yoruba, 107, 109–110
Regla de Palo of the Bakongo, 107, 109–110
reincarnation, 30–31, 171
   Santería belief, 287
religion, as sacred collective conscious, 326
religio-political movement, 81
The Religious Right in Southern Africa (Gifford), 237
religious skepticism in Africa, **280–282**
   performance or embodiment and, 281–282
   rationality and, 281
Resurrection Power Evangelical Ministries, 17
retreats, 4
Reverend Ike, 313, 345–346, 352
Review of Religions, 25
Revival, 2, 18, 60, **282–284**
   Azuza Street, 40–41
   Great Awakening, 308
   healing, 284
   history of, 283
   leadership, structure, and gender, 284
   ritual worship and possession, 283–284
   seals, 284
   Second Great Awakening, 199, 308
   women and, 284
Revival and Rebellion in Colonial Africa (Fields), xviii
revivalist religions, 78
Revival Zion, 78, 101, 167, 169, 283
Rey, Henry, 320
Rigby, Peter, 229
ring, power of, 115
ring-shout, 306
Ritchings, Edna Rose, 233
rituals of affliction, 214
ritual worship, 283–284
   food offerings, 21
   secret societies and, 298–299
Rivail, Hyppolyte Leon Denizard, 171, 251, 285, 319
Roberts, J. Deotis, 64, 213, 312
Robertson's (Pat) 700 Club, 182

Robeson, Paul, 311
Robinson, Ida, 147
Robinson, Richard, 10
Roman Catholicism; *see* Black Catholics in the United
    States; Catholicism
Roosevelt, Franklin D., 123, 354
root doctor, 134
Rowe, Maureen, 248
Royal Order of the Essenes, 55
Rubbens, A., 162
Rudd, David, 48, 205
runaway communities, 103
Russell, Louis, xii
Russian Orthodox Church, 16
Rwanda, 189, 198
Ryan, Leo, 240–241, 243

S
Sabbath ceremony, 39–40
sacred spaces, slave religion and, 306
Sadiq, Muhammad, 24
Sadr Anujman-i Ahmadiyya, 25
St. Augustine Protestant Episcopal Church, 310
St. George's Church (Philadelphia), 8–10, 20, 199, 349
St. John's African Orthodox Church (St. John Coltrane),
    16
St. John's Street Church, 349
St. Kitts and Nevis, African-derived religions in, **321–323**
St. Lucia, African-derived religions in, **323–325**
St. Peter's Spiritual Baptist Church (SBC), 315
saints, 44, 60, 69
Saint Simon, 319
St. Thomas's African Episcopal Church, 349
salvation
    Akan religion, 31
    doctrine of, 247–248
samantwentwen (evil spirits), 28
Sams, John, 209
Sams, Rev. Clarence F., 247
Sanctified Church movement, 145, 203
    composition and practices of, 147–148
Sande, Abel, 397
Sanders, Cheryl Jeanne, 149
Sande secret society, 297
San Francisco earthquake (1906), 41
Sangines, Guevara, 104
Sankeys, 206
Santería (also Santeria), xvi-xvii, 21, 60, 69, 75, 77–81,
    134–136, 174, **285–289**, 302
    beliefs, 287–288
    ceremonies, 287–288

current state, 288–289
development in New World, 251
fate, personal destiny, and reincarnation, 287
healing, 288
history and development, 285–286
in Mexico, 187
organization and leadership, 286–287
the Pantheon, 287
psychotherapeutics, 137–138
see also Cuba, African-derived religions in
Santería, material culture, 290–294
    birthday thrones, 290–293
    food of the Gods, 293–294
    human figures, 294
    orisha fundamentos, 290
Santería, United States, 295–296
    beliefs and practices, 295–296
    spread of traditions, 296
Santerisimo, 252
Santos, Eugenia Ana, 68
Santos, Maria Estella de Azevedo, 68
Sao Tomé island, 94
saraca, 128–129
Saravati, Dayanand, 23
sassy wood (for divination), 121
Sawyer, Mary R., 311
Scarborough, Dorothy, 202
Schebesta, Paul, 253
Schmidt, Pater Wilhelm, 253
school desegregation, 12
School of Mediumship and Psychology, 354
Schuler, Monica, 168, 283
science of sand ('ilm al-raml), 7
Scripture Union (Nigeria), 2
seals, 284
Seals, Mother Catherine, 60, 62
séance, 118–119
Second Great Awakening, 199, 308
Second Vatican Council, 50
The Secret Ritual of the Nation of Islam (Fard), 56
secret societies, 106, **297–300**
    current developments, 299–300
    in East Africa, 298
    masks and rituals, 298–299
    in West Africa, 297–298
Sedar-Senghor, Leopold, 162
Selassie, Haile I, 81, 256, 258–262, 265–266, 278
    collected speeches, 265
    Ethiopian Orthodox Church and, 124–125
    Leonard Percival Howell and, 259–260, 272
    visit to Jamaica, 262

Senegal, Mouride Brotherhood, 197–198

Senegambia, 116

Senghor, Leopold, 189

separatist church movement, 23, 32

Seraphim Society, 33, 82

Sernett, Milton C., 145

Service and Development Agency, Inc. (SADA), 10

Seventh-Day Adventist Church, **300–301**

Seymour, William Joseph, 40–41, 97, 144, 187

Shadow (or life force), 104

shaman, 119, 133, 226, 227

Shango, 33, 60, 66, 77–78, 110, 129, 302, 384

    Orisha (Shango) movement in Trinidad, 221–223, 250, 285

Shango-stones, 324

Shannon, Mother Maud, 62

Shapiro, Deanne Ruth, 53

shari'a, 154

Sharpe, Samuel, 166, 283

Sharpton, Al, 313, 344, 351

Shashamane Nyabinghi Tabernacle Project, 268

Shaw, Rev. William, 211

Shaykh Sidi al-Muhktar-al Kabir al-Kunti, 158

Shaykh Uthman dan Fodio, 159–160

Shembe: The Revitalization of African Society (Vilakazi), 36

Shembe, Amos, 35–37

Shembe, Isaiah Mdliwamafa, 34–37, 175, 238

Shembe, Johannes Galilee, 35

Shembe, Londaukosi Insikayakho (Londa), 35–37

Shembe, Vimbemi, 36

Shepard, Marshall L., 249

Shi'a Islam, 151, 178

Shiite movement, 177

Shona area, 39–40

Shoniwa, Peter, 38

Shopona, 386

Shopshire, James Maynard, 99, 144

Shouter Baptists, 339

Shouters, 78, 129, 193, 306

Shouters Prohibition Ordinance, 318

shout preachers, 203

Shrine of the Black Madonna, Detroit, **301–302**, 351

Sierra Leone

    Aladura movement, 34

    AME missionary work in, 10–11

    Christian missionaries in, 94–95

    secret societies in, 297, 299

Sigle, Rev., 1

Sikidy (geomancy), 7

Silverbluff Baptist Church, 210, 308, 348

Simon Kimbangu, 141

Simpson, George Eaton, 145, 206

Singer, Merrill, xvii, 252

Sisters of the Blessed Sacrament, 49

skepticism, studies of, 280–282

slave rebellion leaders, 53

slave religion, *302–309*, 335

    in antebellum southern cities, 308–308

    at the end of slavery, 309

    biblical imagery and language, 303–305

    conversion and spirit possession, 305–306

    hush harbor meeting, 306

    leadership, 308

    music, 304–305

    plantation religious leaders, 308

    praise houses, chapels, and churches, 306–308

    prayer, 304

    preaching, 304

    sacred spaces, 306

    slave revolts and, 308

    social activism in, 310

slave revolts, 10, 66, 308

slavery, xviii, 47, 57, 75, 78, 347

    antislavery movement and, 14

    Judaism and, 52–53

    in Trinidad, 339

    Underground Railroad and, 14, 20, 200

Slave Songs of the United States, 200, 202, 203

slave trade, 93, 95

    in Americas, 102–103, 185

    in Cuba, 108–109

Small, Mary, 14

Smart, Ninian, 35

Smith (Edwin) papyrus, 132

Smith, Lucy, 146

Smith, Michael W., 205

Sobania, Neal W., 228

social activism, xv, xvii-xviii, 4, 232, **309–313**

    in conversionist sects, 313, 351

    during nineteenth century, 310

    in mainstream denominations, 310–312

    in messianic-nationalist sects, 312–313, 350–351

    Peace Mission and, 234

    in slave religion, 310

    in thaumaturgical sects, 313, 351–352

social gospel, 1, 12, 123, 310

Socialist Party, 310

Society of the Holy Family, 47

Society for the Propagation of the Gospel in Foreign Parts (SPG), 303

Society for the Study of Black Religion, 213

Sokoto jihad, 159
sombra (shadow), 187
Sons of Abraham, 98
Sons of God Apostolic Spiritual Baptist Church, 42–43
The Souls of Black Folks (Du Bois), xvii
South African Zion Christian Church, 238
Southern Christian Leadership Conference (SCLC), 211, **314–315**, 350
    Jesse Jackson and, 255
    Martin Luther King, Jr. and, 314–315
    social activism and, 311–312, 314
    Unification Church and, 344
Southern Missionary Society, 301
Soyinka, Wole, 219, 385
Spanish conquistadors, 78
Spanish Inquisition in Mexico, 186
Sparks, Randy, 309
speaking in tongues, 2, 33, 40–41, 144, 148, 203
Spellman, Fr. William, 1
Spencer, Jon Michael, 206
spiritism, 319; *see also* Espiritismo; Kardecism (Kardecismo)
spirit mediums, 133–134, 136, 363
spirit messengers, 167
spirit possession, 363
    slave religion and, 305–306
spirit powers, lower, 28
spirit repositories, 366
spirits, earth, 179–180
Spiritual Baptist Church, 42–43
Spiritual Baptist music, 60, 129, 205–208
    classifications and types of, 206
    musical development and composition, 206–207
    performance, 207–208
    role in worship, 205–206
Spiritual Baptists, **315–318**
    beliefs and practices, 316–318
    relationship to African-derived religions, 316
    social advances in 1990s, 318
spiritual churches; *see* Black Spiritual churches
spiritualism, **319–321**
    diversity of movement, 320
    in Latin America and Caribbean, 321
    in the United States, 319–321
Spiritual Israel Church and its Army, 53–54
Spiritual Israel and its Army, 61, 352
spiritual movement, 184
spiritual parents, 308
spirituals (hymns), 199–203; *see also* music, Black hymnody

spirit world, 362–363
Stallings, George Augustus, Jr., 51
Star of David, 54
The Star of Zion, 15
Stein, Stanley, 135
Stono rebellion, 47
storefront churches, **325–329**
    cosmology, organization, and routines, 327–329
    theoretical considerations, 326–327
The Story of Isaiah Shembe, 35
Streams of Power, 78
Student Christian Movement (Nigeria), 2
sub-saharan Africa
    healing arts in, 139–143
    women and religious movements in, 375–380
success and prosperity healing, 5
Sudan
    Nuer religion of, 215–216
    Sudanese Brotherhood in, 330–334
Sudanese Brotherhoods, **330–334**
    contemporary brotherhoods, 332–334
    Islamic Sufism, 331–332
    Republican Brotherhood movement, 333
Suenens, Cardinal L. J., 162
Sufi Ahmad ibn Idris, 330
Sufism, 331–334
Sufi tradition, 197
Suliman, Dr., 191
Sundiata, 243
Sundkler, Bengt, 35–37, 238
Sunni Islam, 23, 25, 56, 58–59, 151, 178
sunsum (personality soul), 29
Surbadger, Thomas, 354
Suriname, African-derived religions in, 21, 135, **334–337**
    coastal Creole Winti, 335–336
    Maroon religions, 336–337
    slave religion, 335
surusie (folk healer), 135
Swahili, 152
syncretism (mixed elements), 59–60
    Afro-Mexican religion, 187
    Christian missionaries and, 92
    Church of the Twelve Apostles, 99–100
    cult of Maria Lionza, 357–360
    Orisha (Shango) and Roman Catholic elements, 221
    Santeria, 285–286, 296
    Santerismo, 252
    spiritualism and, 319
Syrian Orthodox Church, 124

T
taboos, 28
Tacky's Rebellion, 166
Taha, Mahmoud Mohammed, 332–334
talismans, 28
Tambor de Mina en Maranhon, 66, 75, **337–338**
Tani, Grace, 99–100
TANU (Tanganyikan African National Union), 154
Tanzania, 153–154, 189
    charismatic movements in, 3
tariqa (brotherhood), 197
Taussig, Michael, 282
Taylor, Charles, xii, 300
Taylor, Rev. Dr. Gardner, 248–249
Taylor, William F., 184
*Teaching for the Lost-Found Nation of Islam in a
        Mathematical Way* (Fard), 56
televangelism, 181–182
Tempels, Placide, 162–163, 165
Temple of Islam, 56
terreiro (compounds), 44, 75, 177
testimonies, 4, 142
thaumaturigical sects, social activism of, 313, 351–352
theology, 326
    Black, 12, 62–65, 350–351
    Black Theology Project, 213
    liberation, 64–65, 288
    monotheism, 253
    Pygmy, 253–255
    reincarnation and, 30–31, 171, 287
    womanist, 65, 313
    see also cosmology; specific religions
The Theology of a South African Messiah (Oosthuizen),
        36–37
third church, 88
Thornton, John, 109
Thurman, Howard, 63, 311
Tie-Heads, 42–43
Tile, Nehemiah, 237
Tilghman, Perry, 20
Tindley, Charles Albert, 203
Tindley Temple, 203
Tinney, James S., 144, 146
Tiyen, 7
Todjai Diatta, 118
Tonga, Desta, 258
Tosh, Peter, 276
totem (or animal double), 104
trance curing dance, 74
trance state, 33, 71

Trinidad, African-derived religions in, **338–343**
    colonization and slavery in, 339
    company villages, 339
    Earth People, 193–195
    Orisha (Shango) movement in, 221–223
    Rada and Orisha in, 339–341
        at end of twentieth century, 342–343
        beliefs and practices, 341–342
    Spiritual Baptists and, 315–318
    music of, 205–208
Triumph the Church and Kingdom of God in Christ, 41,
        353
True Family Values seminars, 344
trumpeting, 206
Truth, Sojourner, 14
Tubman, Harriet, 14, 200
Tunolase, Moses Orimolade, 33, 82
Turnbull, Colin, 253, 255
Turner, Edith, 214
Turner, Henry McNeal, 10, 12, 310
Turner, Nat, 53, 308, 310
Turner, Thomas Wyatt, 49
Turner, Victor, 214
turuq (Muslim botherhoods), 158
Tuskegee Institute, 353
Tutu, Bishop Desmond, 238
Twelve Tribes of Israel, 257, 273
Twi (Ghanian language), 17
Tyen', 7

U
Uganda
    charismatic movements in, 3
    Movement for the Restoration of the Ten
        Commandments of God, 198–199
Ujamaa (Tanzania socialism), 154
Umbanda, xvii, 44, 60, 66, 71–72, 75, 78, 80, 171–172,
        219, 250, 321
umuntu (being human), 164
Underground Railroad, 14, 20, 200
un-Din, Kamal, 25
Unification Church, **343–344**
Union American Methodist Episcopal Church, 349
Union Theological Seminary, 12, 65
United African Methodist Church, 400
United Church of Christ, 301
United Church of Jesus Christ for All People, 345
United Church and Science of Living Institute, **345–346**,
        352
United House of Prayer for All People, **346–347**

United Kingdom, African Pentecostalism in, 17
United Methodist Church, 8, 14
United Metropolitan Spiritual Churches of Christ, 184
United Native African Church, 32
United Negro Improvement Association (UNIA), 81
United States, African-derived religions in, **347–353**
    Black Church Independence Movement, **347–349**
    conversionist sects, 351
    development under slavery, 347
    mainstream denominations, 349–350
    messianic-nationalist sects, 350–351
    religious diversification during twentieth century, 349
    thaumaturgical sects, 351–352
Universal Ancient Ethiopian Spiritual Church, 352
Universal Hagar's Spiritual Church, 54, 61, 352, **353–354**
Universal Negro Improvement Association (UNIA), 16, 54, 56, 272, 351, **354–357**
    belief system, 355–357
    Garveyism and, 354–357
    organization, 357
    rituals and symbols, 354–355
University of Ibadan (Nigeria), 2
University of Islam, 56
urban communities, African charismatics and, 4
Urban League, 311
Uya, Okon Edet, 52, 279

V

vahosanna (the hosannas), 38
Valle, Lincoln C., 48
Valmour, J. B., 320
Vapostori, xvii, 38–40
Varick, James, 13
Veit Tan, Beatriz, 360
Velasquez, Jaci, 205
Venezuelan Cult of Maria Lionza, **357–360**
    belief foundations of, 358
    practices, beliefs, and people of, 359–360
    spread and dissemination of, 358–358
    syncretic nature of, 357–358
Verger, Pierre Fatumbi, xviii, 69
Vesey, Denmark, 10, 53, 308, 310
Vessler, Rev. Van, 1
Vigilant (Fugitive Aid) Association and Committee, 20
Vilakazi, Absolom, 36–37
Vilatte, Rene, 16
Vintana (Malagasy geomancy), 7
Vodou, xvi–xvii, 21, 59–61, 69, 75, 77–78, 107, 128, **361–364**
    African influence and marronnage, 361–362
    Catholic influence, 362

    concepts of self, 363–364
    derivation of term, 361
    in the diaspora, 364
    practice of, 361
    spirit mediumship and spirit possession, 363
    spirit world, 362–363
Vodou, material culture, **364–368**
    altars, 366–367
    Bizanto altars, 368
    bottles and other repositories, 366
    drum and other summoning objects, 365–366
    flags, 366
    nature of, 365
    objects of, 365–366
    Petwo/Kongo, 367–368
    rada, 367
Vodun, 134–136, 174, 250, 302
voodoo dolls, 365
voting rights, 12, 315

W

Wach, Joachim, 354
Walcott, Derek, 165, 325
Walker, Wyatt, 344
Waller, Richard, 228
Walters, Alexander, 14
Ward, Gary L., 192
Ward, Thomas M. D., 10
Ware, Charles P., 200, 202
Warren, J. A., 40–41
washing of the soul, 29
Washington, Booker T., 12, 211
Washington, Joseph, 213
Washington, Paul, 312
Watchtower, **369**
Waterman, Richard Allen, 206
Watson, Thomas B., 184
Watts, Jill, 232
Weber, Max, 164, 326–327, 329
Web sites, 112, 149–150
    media evangelism and, 181
Webster, Daniel, 320
Wedenoja, William, 284
weed woman, 134
Weisbrot, Robert, 233–234
Welbourn, F. B., 238, 239
Werbner, Richard P., xvi–xvii
Wesley, John, 144
West Africa
    Ahmadiyya movement, 24
    geomancy in, 7

Manjako of Guinea-Bissau, 179–180
Ogun (deity), 217–220
secret societies and, 297–298
West African religions, **369–375**
historical and geographical context, 370
Islam in, 24, 156–161, 369
historical perspective of, 156–158
Maitatsine sect, 177–178
millenarianism, 159–160
reforms and jihads, 158–159
twentieth century advance, 160–161
Rastafari in, 274–279
religious philosophy, 373–375
religious practices, 372–373
supreme beings and lesser spirits, 370–372
West, Cornel, 313
Western Colored Baptist Association, 348
West Indies, Obeah in, 216–217
White, Ellen, 301
White, James Edson, 301
White, Neuman, 200
White, Rev. Sampson, 1
White, William, 9
Whittmon, Isaac, 204
Wilberforce University, 11
Wilberforce, William, 159
Wilgus, Donald, 200
Wilkins, Roy, 12
Williams, Delores, 65
Williams, Duncan, 18
Williams, George Washington, 12
Williams, Granville, 42
Williams, L. K., 211
Williams, Melvin, 99, 148
Williams, Mervyn R., 206
Williams, Preston, 213, 312
Wilmore, Gayraud S., xvii, 64, 213, 310, 312, 349
Winan family gospel group, 204
Winti-plays, 335
Winti religion, 21, 136–137, 335–336
Wipper, Audrey, 376
Wiseman Board, 354
witchcraft, 26, 83, 119, 186, 374
Zande beliefs and, 388
Witchcraft, Oracles and Magic Among the Azande (Evans-Pritchard), 280
witch-doctor, 142, 388
Womanist theology, 65, 313
women and religion
AME ordination of, 10
Candomblé and, 66

charismatic movement and, 3
Christ Apostolic Church, 86
Church of God in Christ, 99
Diola prophets and, 116–118
Lumpa Church, 175–176
ordination of by AME Zion Church, 14
Rastafari orthodoxy and gender relations, 257–258, 265, 274
revival and, 284
spiritual churches and, 59, 61, 184, 317–318
Women and religious movements in sub-Saharan Africa, **375–380**
conceptual ambiguities, 376
historiographical issue, 376–377
reconceptualizing study of, 379–380
religion, ideology, and resistance, 377–379
religious movements in twentieth century, 377
Woodbey, George Washington, 310
Wood River Association, 348
Woods, John, 209
Work, John W., 203
World Community of Islam, 351
World Council of Churches, 26, 131
World Muslim League, 23
World Soul Evangelistic Association (WOSEM), 85
World Vision International, **381–382**
Wray, J. Alfred, 96
Wright, Nathan, Jr., 312
Wynn, Rev. Robert D., 1

X
Xango in Recife (Pernambuco), 43, 75, 285, 337–338, **382–383**
beliefs and practices, 382–383
modern varieties of, 383
Xavier University, 47, 49

Y
Yemeja, 110
Yoruba, 46, 66, 69, 75, 79, 107, 109, **384–387**
in African Diaspora, 386–387
belief system, 384
in Catholic settings, 386–387
de-catholicization of new world tradition, 387
Eshu, 386
Ifá divination, 119–120, 122, 149–150
indigenous religious movement, 32
Macumba and, 176–177
major orisha, 384–386
Moremmi, 386
Obatala or Orisha nla, 384–385

Yoruba (*cont.*)
  Ogun, 386
  Oshun (female deity), 225
  Oya, 386
  Shango and, 384
  Shopona, 386
  see also Santería
Young, Coleman, 302
Young, D. J., 144
Yurugu (the Pale Fox) geomancy, 7

Z
Zahwenu, Abojevi (Papa Nanee), 340, 342
Zaire
  Jamaa and, 162
  Pentecostalism in, 17
Zambia, 5, 175–176
  charismatic movements in, 3
  Ndembu religion, 214
Zande religion, **387–392**
  ancestors and ghosts, 390–391
  divination, 119
  Mbori, 389
  modern religion, 391
  traditional beliefs, 388
  witchcraft and magic, 388
Zar, 380, **392–395**

historical evidence, 392–393
  as organized ritual, 393–394
  as spirit, 393
Zimbabwe
  Apostolic Church of Johane Masowe, 38
  Apostolic Church of John Maranke, 38–40
  charismatic movements in, 3
Zimbabwe Assemblies of God Africa (ZAOGA), **397**
Zion, 282, 284
  meaning of, 401–402
Zion Apostolic Church, 283
Zion Christian Church, 34
Zion Holiness Church, 99, 147–148
Zionist churches, 5, 141, **398–402**
  current beliefs and practices, 400–401
  meaning of Zion, 401–402
Zion Primitive Baptist Church (Key West), 247
zombies, 175
Zulu, Bishop Adolphus, 238
Zulu religion, 34, 36, **403–404**
  izangoma (healers), 403
  medical practice, 403–404
  medicine-man compared to witch-doctor, 142
  see also amaNazaretha
Zulu Zion (BBC film), 35
Zulu Zion and Some Swazi Zionists (Sundkler), 36
Zwemer, Samuel M., 392